EUROPEAN CASE LAW ON THE JUDGMENTS CONVENTION

EUROPEAN CASE LAW ON THE JUDGMENTS CONVENTION

Edited by

Peter Kaye
of Gray's Inn, Barrister
Professor of Private International and European Law at the
University of Wales Swansea, UK and Gastprofessor für
Common Law an der Universität Trier, Germany (1994–7)

JOHN WILEY & SONS
Chichester • New York • Weinheim • Brisbane • Singapore • Toronto

Published 1998 by John Wiley & Sons Ltd,
Baffins Lane, Chichester,
West Sussex PO19 1UD, England

National   01243 779777
International   (+44) 1243 779777
e-mail (for orders and customer service enquiries):
cs-books@wiley.co.uk
Visit our Home Page on http://www.wiley.co.uk
or http://www.wiley.com

Other Wiley Editorial Offices

John Wiley & Sons, Inc., 605 Third Avenue,
New York, NY 10158-0012, USA

WILEY-VCH Verlag GmbH, Pappelallee 3,
D-69469 Weinheim, Germany

Jacaranda Wiley Ltd, 33 Park Road, Milton,
Queensland 4064, Australia

John Wiley & Sons (Asia) Pte Ltd, 2 Clementi Loop #02-01,
Jin Xing Distripark, Singapore 129809

John Wiley & Sons (Canada) Ltd, 22 Worcester Road,
Rexdale, Ontario M9W 1L1, Canada

Library of Congress Cataloging-in-Publication Data

European case law on the judgements convention / edited by Peter Kaye.
     p.   cm.
    Includes bibliographical references.
    ISBN 0-471-94089-5 (cloth : acid-free paper)
     1. Judicial assistance—Europe.   2. Judicial assistance—Europe—Cases.
 I. Kaye, Peter, LL. M.
  KJC3795.E93 1988
  341.7′8—dc21   97-34189
                                                           CIP

British Library Cataloguing in Publication Data

A catalogue record for this book is available from the British Library

ISBN 0-471-94089-5

Typeset in 10/12pt Sabon by Poole Typesetting (Wessex) Ltd, Bournemouth, Dorset
Printed and bound in Great Britain by Bookcraft (Bath) Ltd, Midsomer Norton,
Somerset
This book is printed on acid-free paper responsibly manufactured from sustainable
forestry, in which at least two trees are planted for each one used for paper
production.

This work is dedicated to the memory of the late Professor R.H. Graveson CBE, Q.C., of King's College London, who introduced the editor to the conflict of laws as an undergraduate subject and subsequently supervised his doctoral thesis on the 1964 Hague Uniform Law on the International Sale of Goods, together with the late F.J. Cohn and A.G. Chloros. The most accomplished British private international lawyer of his generation and an inspiring teacher of his subject, Ronald Graveson was also revealed as a kind and benevolent man, who cared for his students, however humble their backgrounds.

CONTENTS

CONTENTS

X

CONTRIBUTORS

Alegría Borrás *(Spain)* Professor of Law, University of Barcelona, Spain

Julio D. González Campos *(Spain)* Professor at the Autonomous University of Madrid, Spain; Judge of the Spanish Constitutional Court

Brice Dickson *(Northern Ireland)* Professor of Law, University of Ulster, Northern Ireland

Thor Falkanger *(Norway)* Professor of Law, University of Oslo, Norway

Angus Glennie *(Scotland)* Advocate (QC, England and Wales)

Peter Kaye *(England and Wales, Ireland)* Professor of Law at the University of Wales Swansea, United Kingdom

Risto Koulu *(Finland)* Professor of Law, University of Helsinki, Finland

Rui Manuel Moura Ramos *(Portugal)* Member of the Institute of International Law; Professor of Law, University of Coimbra, Portugal; Judge of the Court of First Instance of the European Communities

Elina Moustaira *(Greece)* Advocate; Hellenic Institute of International and Foreign Law, Greece

Lennart Pålsson *(Sweden)* Professor of Law, University of Lund, Sweden

Marta Pertegás Sender *(Belgium)* Member of the Institute of International Trade Law, K.U. Leuven, Belgium

Maurice V. Polak *(The Netherlands)* Professor of Private International and Comparative Law, Leiden University, The Netherlands

Thomas Rauscher *(Germany)* Professor of Private International Law, Comparative Law, and Civil Law, University of Leipzig, Germany

Bruno N. Sassani *(Italy)* Professor of Civil Procedure, University of Perugia, Italy

Torben Svenné Schmidt *(Denmark)* Professor of Law, Denmark

Norbert A. Schoibl *(Austria)* Professor of Law, Institute of Civil Procedure, University of Salzburg, Austria

Kurt Siehr *(Switzerland)* Professor of Law, Centre of Private International Law, University of Zurich, Switzerland

Lilian F. A. Steffens *(The Netherlands)* Attorney-at-Law at Loeff Claeys Verbeke, Amsterdam, The Netherlands

Yves Tassel *(France)* Professor of Law, University of Nantes, France

Eiríkur Tómasson *(Iceland)* Professor of Law, University of Iceland, Iceland

Patrick Wautelet *(Belgium)* Member of the Institute of International Trade Law, K.U. Leuven, Belgium

Jean-Claude Wiwinius *(Luxembourg)* Avocat Général à la Cour Superieure de Justice de Luxembourg

PREFACE

Article 1 of Protocol No. 2 to the Lugano Convention on Jurisdiction and the Enforcement of Judgments in Civil and Commercial Matters of 1988 requires Contracting States' courts, when applying and interpreting the Convention's provisions, to pay due account to the decisions of courts of other Contracting States. Article 2(1) called for a system for exchange of information on judgments on Lugano and 1968 Brussels Conventions. Article 4(2) presaged the possibility of Lugano Convention revisions in the light of exchanges of views as to the functioning of the Convention — and it might reasonably have been predicted that such exchanges and revisions would likewise extend to the Brussels Convention itself.

Amendment is now in the air. Committees have met and discussed.

Yet, it has to be said, most legal practitioners and scholars remain excluded and unaware of the large amount of national case law which exists on these Conventions. Even where the cases are known, complex judgments will frequently pose difficult problems for lawyers seeking to understand and to apply the law.

It was in order to make information on cases accessible and comprehensible to the European legal professions and academia in general, therefore, that the present work was conceived.

The mission was seen as being to inform rather than to comment. Contributors were requested to explain and to clarify the reasoning of national Convention judgments and to confine their commentary to where this was essential in order to reveal the relative status of a particular judgment within a legal system, or its strength or unreliability and prospects of future reversal.

In this way, it was envisaged that the national judgments included in the work would be capable of citation in Convention proceedings throughout Europe. To be sure, the foreign decisions are unlikely to be treated as binding. Arguably, they will not even be of persuasive authority — although, that said, it will be no small thing for, say, an English court lightly to dismiss the judgments of German, Dutch or Italian Supreme Courts. What is virtually certain, however, is that the rulings of prestigious foreign courts will at least be *influential* and their reasoning employable. Thus, if there exists a foreign decision on a particular Convention issue and its treatment by a foreign court is believed to be attractive or compelling, the courts of other Contracting States will then be able to adopt that solution and to point to its source in the foreign legal system at the same time. If there is a line of similar cases in the foreign system or, of even greater effect, similarity of treatment in a number of different Contracting States' legal systems, this will amount to a correspondingly more powerful source of influence and employable Convention case material. For all of which reasons, efforts were deliberately made to present the case law so as to facilitate its easy citation. Mere skeletal accounts of facts and judgments would have been useless; too much detail would have led to a massive and unwieldy end-product. What was chosen instead, therefore, was a middle route between these two extremes. Contributors from amongst the leading experts in their respective countries were approached and invited to select important relevant case law from their systems, to extract its essential reasoning and to present it succinctly and coherently for use and reliability. This, it is hoped, has on the whole been achieved, although inevitably there will be disagreements over aspects of selection and as to the interpretation of judgments.

Readers who require a more detailed commentary upon the progress of Convention law over the past ten years may wish to acquire the editor's sequel to *Civil Jurisdiction and Enforcement of Foreign Judgments* (1987), entitled 'Development of the European Judgments Convention. A Personal Commentary', published in September 1998 by Barry Rose Publishing Ltd., Little London, Chichester, West Sussex, PO19 1PG, England.

The editor's thanks are due to the publishers of the present work for their indulgence concerning the amount of time which has elapsed since the inception of this project. One of the less attractive features of the British higher education system is that law professors do not generally have assistants — at least not at Swansea. This means inevitable delays.

Equally, apologies are extended to Irish readers for any inaccuracies which may have crept into the Irish account. Unfortunately, the Irish contributor withdrew at the last moment and the editor saw little alternative other than to prepare the Irish chapter himself. In this respect, his heartfelt thanks are due to Swansea's law librarian, Mr Seán Barr LL.B. (Queen's, Belfast), PG Dip.Inf.Manag., A.L.A., and to local practitioner, Mr Simon Hoffman LL.B. (Wales), Barrister, both of whom made it possible for the editor to acquire essential Irish materials at very short notice.

A number of other individuals deserve to be mentioned here. First and foremost, the contributors are owed a debt of gratitude by the editor for their generosity in agreeing to devote time and expertise to the production of this work.

Secondly, the editor wishes to thank his splendid senior publishing editor, Susie Hamblin, as well as Sue, Graham, Suzanne and Louise of the publishers for their essential administrations, in addition to which, special mention is reserved for Jane Belford and Andrew Prideaux, with whom the idea for this project was originally discussed and conceived.

Thirdly, gratitude goes to Janette Thomas, who expertly typed the manuscript of the English and Irish chapters.

Fourthly, it is believed to be entirely appropriate to thank all the editor's colleagues in the law department for combining to make such a pleasant working environment as that which exists at Swansea, in spite of — maybe because of — the impossible lack of staff, equipment and materials, and, for too long, proper accommodation.

It remains to be revealed that contributors to this work were requested to include case law up to 1 January 1997, although, in certain instances, it proved possible to record some later developments. Case presentations represent the personal selection and interpretation of the authors.

Worms Head,
Off Rhossili Bay,
Gower Peninsular.   P.K.
31 July 1997

HOW TO USE THIS BOOK

Each country's chapter consists of some or all of Sections A, B, C, D and E. Respectively, these latter comprise 'Courts and Legal System', 'Convention Implementation', 'Overview of Convention Case Law', 'Convention Cases' and 'Recent Cases'.

Section A describes the national courts which deal with Convention disputes and their relative status within the national legal hierarchy.

Section B is concerned with dates of implementation of the 1968 Brussels Convention on Jurisdiction and the Enforcement of Judgments in Civil and Commercial Matters, the Lugano Convention of 1988 of the same name, and with the various Accession Conventions.

Section C is a brief summary of the Convention experience within each legal system.

Section D consists of the actual accounts of national cases themselves. Whilst it may be indicated in the 'Case principles' or 'Comments' to cases that a decision of the European Court has been followed and applied by the national courts or that a national judgment is inconsistent with the European Court's ruling, the latter's decisions as such are not included in this work.

The structure of the treatment of national cases is as follows:

(1) Names of the particular Convention provisions are listed in numerical sequence, from Art. 1 onwards, and are broken down into parts of Articles, beginning with Art. 1, para. 1.

Articles are those of the Brussels Convention unless otherwise indicated by preceding words such as 'Lugano', '1978 Accession', and so forth.

Only those provisions in respect of which there has been some case law are included.

(2) There follows, in a box, the relevant wording of the Article or part thereof, normally in the order in which it appears in the English text of the provision. For example, for Art. 21, para. 1, 'same cause of action' is dealt with before 'same parties', corresponding with its sequence in the provision itself.

At the front of this book, there is a *Table* depicting every place in every chapter in the work in which particular wording has been dealt with in a national case.

Each of the cases is numbered consecutively in the margin from the beginning to the end of the book (to be distinguished from the usual European Court case references "——/—").

(3) Following the boxed wording, there are one or more 'Case principles' in bold type concerning the wording and numbered in respect of the latter.

(4) Underneath the Case principle(s), there is the case or cases from which the Case principle or principles were extracted, under the heading 'Case'.

Each case is divided into 'Facts' and 'Judgment' and some have an additional section entitled 'Comment(s)'.

(5) Following the case, there will either be one or more further numbered 'Case principles' in bold, relating to the particular wording and arising from different cases to those previously listed — or, if none, the account will proceed to the next boxed wording taken from the same or from a subsequent Convention Article or part thereof.

(6) Generally, facts of a particular case will only appear in the main place in which a case is dealt with. Further principles arising from the same case but relating to different Convention provisions, or parts thereof, are likely simply to refer to the main case account for a recitation of the facts, as well as to every other place in which the case is listed.

Section E 'Recent Cases' adopts the same structure as Section D. It consists of case law appearing too late for inclusion in Section D or in respect of which a full report was unavailable on the relevant date.

At the end of the book, certain materials previously referred to are appended, mainly the full English text of the Brussels Convention's provisions and Lugano variations, together with a Selected Bibliography of contributors' and other main writings in Convention and related fields.

There is also a Table of Abbreviations at the end of the book, explaining abbreviated forms used in case references and the like.

TABLE OF CASES

Belgium

Denmark

England and Wales

EUROPEAN COURT OF JUSTICE

Finland

France

Germany

Greece

Ireland

Italy

Luxembourg

Netherlands

Northern Ireland

Norway

Portugal

Scotland

Spain

Sweden

Switzerland

CONVENTIONS

Brussels Convention 1968

1971 Interpretation Protocol

1978 Accession Convention

Greek Accession Convention 1982

Lugano Convention 1988

Spain–Portugal Accession Convention 1989

LEGISLATION

Civil Jurisdiction and Judgments Act 1982

Rules of the Supreme Court 1965

1

AUSTRIA

Norbert A. Schoibl

A. LEGAL SYSTEM

The Republic of Austria is a Federal State consisting of nine (independent) States (*Bundesländer*).

Pursuant to Austria's Federal Constitution, jurisdiction is exclusively the responsibility of the Federal State, and consequently, only Federal courts decide in civil (and criminal) cases. The Bundesländer have no judicial authority.

According to Art. 83, para. 1 of the Austrian Federal Constitution Act, as amended in 1929, the civil (and criminal) courts system is laid down by Federal legislation only, and under the Constitution, civil law and civil procedure are exclusively Federal Law. Thus, the Civil Jurisdiction Act 1895 (*Jurisdiktionsnorm* — JN) governs civil litigation all over Austria. Proceedings are primarily regulated in the Austrian Code of Civil Procedure 1895 (*Zivilprozeßordnung* — ZPO) on litigation; in the Code of Non-litigious Procedure 1854 (*Außerstreitgesetz* 1854 — AußStrG) for non-contentious proceedings; and in the Code of Execution 1895 (*Exekutionsordnung* — EO) for the enforcement and execution of judgments, together with the respective introductory and other ancillary statutes.

Austria is a civil law country and Austrian law is, at least for the most part, codified statutory law. Austrian courts are only bound by the law as expressed in statutory provisions ('usage' may be a source of law as well). The ruling of a court does not amount to a source of law and consequently there are no binding precedents in Austria. Nevertheless, judges will observe published court cases in rendering their decisions and, therefore, although these decisions are formally not a source of law, precedents are of significance for the courts' decision-making, as are legal treatises and commentaries. Judges tend to hold in accordance with previous cases in point or with the majority view among scholars.

The Constitutional Court (*Verfassungsgerichtshof*) and the Administrative Court (*Verwaltungsgerichtshof*) both in Vienna, and a Regional Administrative Court (*Unabhängiger Verwaltungssenat*) in every Bundesland, safeguard the Constitution and the Administration under the Austrian Federal Constitutional Act itself (which also provides detailed rules for these judicial authorities). These courts are called courts of public law. They have no competence and no appellate jurisdiction in civil cases.

Under the rules concerning the organization of Austrian courts, the latter are divided:

(1) according to their field of activity, into courts of public law, civil courts and criminal courts; and

(2) according to the delimitation of their competences, into ordinary courts and other (extraordinary) courts.

Ordinary courts are the courts competent under Art. 1 of the Civil Jurisdiction Act to exercise civil jurisdiction in civil cases. They include:

(1) Local Courts (*Bezirksgerichte* — BG), 188 all over Austria;

(2) Regional Courts (*Landesgerichte* — LG), 18 are established in the main towns of the Bundesländer and at Feldkirch in the Bundesland Vorarlberg;

(3) Courts of Appeal (*Oberlandesgerichte* — OLG), established in Vienna, Graz, Linz and Innsbruck; and

(4) the Austrian Supreme Court (*Oberster Gerichtshof* — OGH) in Vienna.

Local Courts and Regional Courts, as a rule, exercise jurisdiction in (all) civil matters. However, there are exceptions to this rule. For the administration of jurisdiction in commercial matters a special Local Court for Business matters (*Bezirksgericht für Handelssachen* — BGHS) and a Commercial Court serving as a Regional Court (*Handelsgericht* — HG) have been established in Vienna, as has a special Labour and Social Court as a Regional Court (*Arbeits- und Sozialgericht* — ASG) for the administration of jurisdiction in labour and social matters.

Ordinary civil jurisdiction is, as a rule, exercised in three instances:

(1) in the first instance, by Local Courts or Regional Courts;

(2) in the second instance, by Regional Courts or by the Courts of Appeal; and

(3) in the third instance, by the Austrian Supreme Court.

In actions involving financial disputes, the competence of the courts of first instance is determined, as a rule, by the value of the matter in dispute, the so-called 'disputed value' (*Streitwert*). But there are certain cases in civil law, in which the Local Court or the Regional Court is the court of first instance, regardless of the disputed value.

Local Courts are currently competent, in principle, for financial disputes involving a disputed value not exceeding 100.000 Austrian Shillings (*Wertzuständigkeit des* BG), as well as for certain disputes irrespective of the value in litigation, such as disputes in family and paternity matters, proceedings regarding property bequeathed, matters involving rent, etc. (*Eigenzuständigkeit des* BG).

The Local Courts are also competent in the first instance in matters of non-litigious jurisdiction, including hereditary procedure, procedures concerning family matters (like adoption, uncontested divorce, declaration of death, etc.), matters of guardianship, matters concerning residential law, land register (*Grundbuch*), register of commercial enterprises (*Firmenbuch*), and in execution matters.

Regional Courts, as courts of first instance, are competent in some commercial matters (as in unfair competition, patent and trade mark suits and in procedures concerning copyrights in design, etc) and in all labour and social matters (*Eigenzuständigkeit des* LG). They are always competent for financial disputes over 100.000 Austrian Shillings, as far as they do not fall within the automatic jurisdiction of Local Courts (*Wertzuständigkeit des* LG).

The Regional Courts act through appellate chambers as second instance courts for judgments of the Local Courts. The Courts of Appeal act as second instance courts through chambers for judgments of the Regional Courts as courts of first instance. The Supreme Court acts through chambers as a third and final instance court for judgments of the Regional Courts as second instance courts and for judgments of the Courts of Appeal, and for cases of general importance with values in dispute exceeding 50.000 Austrian Shillings.

Remedies available in civil matters against all decisions rendered by the courts of first instance consist especially of the *Berufung* (appeal against a judgment) and the *Rekurs* (appeal against orders and decisions which are not judgments); against decisions of the second instance, there are the 'Revision' (appeal against a judgment of the second instance) and the (Revisions-)*Rekurs* (appeal against orders and decisions of the second instance which are not judgments), which latter are greatly limited by value-limits as well as by the fundamental importance of the legal problem in question.

B. IMPLEMENTATION OF THE CONVENTIONS

Lugano Convention 1988

Austria is party to the 1988 Lugano Convention on Jurisdiction and the Enforcement of Judgments in Civil and Commercial Matters (AB1 EG (1988)

L319/9), which came into force according to the Federal Law (BGBl.) (1996) 448 on 1 September 1996, and which is almost identical to the Brussels Convention amended according to the Spanish/Portuguese Accession Convention of 1989.

A special internal implementing law was not enacted in Austria: scholars and courts qualify it as a self-executing State Treaty.

In its legal rules on international procedure (Art. 79, ss EO), the national Austrian Law on Execution had already largely been adapted to the procedure of recognition and execution of Title III (Recognition and Enforcement) of the Lugano Convention by an amendment of 1995.

Brussels Convention 1968

In fulfilment of its obligation as a member of the European Union according to Art. 220 of the E.C. Treaty, Austria will also become party to the Brussels Convention on Jurisdiction and the Enforcement of Judgments in Civil and Commercial Matters of 1968 in accordance with the Austria/Finland/Sweden Accession Convention of 1996 (AB1 EG (1997) C15/1 ss).

The internal ratification will be prepared for winter 1997–98. Thus, it is most likely that the Brussels Convention will enter into force in Austria in the year 1998.

2

BELGIUM

Marta Pertegás Sender and Patrick Wautelet*

A. LEGAL SYSTEM

Courts

The judicial system is organized according to the law of 10 October 1967, enacting the new Code of Civil Procedure. Within the judicial system, there are four levels of ordinary Courts.

Belgium is divided into over 200 cantons, 26 judicial districts and 10 provinces. In each canton there is a Justice of the Peace and a Police Court. These are the so-called 'inferior Courts'. The Justice of the Peace has *general* jurisdiction for small civil and commercial claims not exceeding 75000 Belgian francs. This general jurisdiction is residuary, in that it does not encompass the specific grounds of jurisdiction granted to higher courts. The Justice of the Peace also has *exclusive* jurisdiction over a variety of specific cases regardless of the amounts involved, for example, disputes concerning real property and maintenance.

The 'intermediate Courts' are to be found in each of the 26 judicial districts: the Court of First Instance, the Commercial Court, the Labour Court and the District Court. The Court of First Instance has *general* jurisdiction. This court may hear all claims which have not been specifically reserved to other courts. In addition, the Court of First Instance has *exclusive* jurisdiction in several specific areas, for example, *enforcement of foreign court decisions and awards*. In case of urgency, the president of the court can grant *provisional measures*

*Both authors are members of the Institute for International Trade Law, K. U. Leuven, under the leadership of Prof. H. Van Houtte.

in summary proceedings. Finally, the Court of First Instance may hear cases which are brought to it on appeal from a Justice of the Peace. A decision of the Court of First Instance in first resort can be challenged before the Court of Appeal.

The Commercial Court has *general* jurisdiction in matters relating to commercial litigation. When the dispute concerns the so-called 'acts of trades' between merchants (defined as individuals or companies who earn a living through acts of trade), this court can exercise jurisdiction. The Commercial Court has *exclusive* jurisdiction in some cases, irrespective of whether the above mentioned conditions are fulfilled (maritime disputes, bankruptcy proceedings, claims relating to bills of exchange and promissory notes). The Commercial Court may also hear appeals against decisions by the Justice of the Peace when both claimant and defendant are merchants.

The president of the court has the same power as the president of the Court of First Instance, to grant provisional measures in cases deemed to be urgent.

The Labour Court has jurisdiction for matters relating to individual labour law and to disputes on social security legislation. The president of the court also has jurisdiction in summary proceedings. One may appeal against the decisions of the Labour Court to the Labour Court of Appeal.

The District Court adjudicates jurisdiction conflicts between the intermediate courts.

At a higher level one finds the appellate courts: the Court of Appeal and the Labour Court of Appeal. Appeals against decisions by the Court of First Instance or the Commercial Court may be brought before the (general) Court of Appeal. Appeals against decisions by the Labour Courts must be brought before the Labour Court of Appeal.

At the top of the hierarchy there is one supreme Court, the Court of Cassation. This court reviews decisions rendered in last instance. The Court of Cassation only deals with the correct application of the law. It does not reconsider the facts that have been established in earlier proceedings. The court may reject the request for review, or it may quash the lower court decision if it finds that the court improperly applied the law. In this case, the Court of Cassation will refer the case back to another court of the same level as the court which rendered the decision on appeal. The lower court is free not to follow the Court of Cassation, but its decision can then be brought again before the Court of Cassation. After a second review, the decision of the Court of Cassation is binding.

As a general rule, Belgian courts are not bound by decisions rendered by other, even superior, courts. Even the judgments of the Court of Cassation do not possess legal binding power. However, because of the prestige and expertise of the Court of Cassation, judges in practice most often apply the law as it is stated by that court. Appellate decisions are equally often taken into consideration.

B. IMPLEMENTATION OF THE CONVENTIONS

The Belgian legal order is a monist system. Once an international treaty has been approved by Parliament, it becomes part of Belgian law, without there being any need to implement it. The treaty's provisions will be directly applicable in the Belgian legal order. Since 1971, treaties even prevail over national legislation, the Constitution included. Therefore, in the event of a conflict between national statutory provisions and a treaty, the provisions of the treaty will prevail and the courts will have to apply the treaty provisions.

The European Judgments Convention was first approved by the Act of 16 February 1971, which entered into force on 1 February 1973. Subsequent changes to the Judgments Convention were only gradually approved in Belgium. The text, as amended by the Convention of 9 October 1978 on the accession of the United Kingdom and by the Convention of 25 October 1982 on the accession of Greece, was ratified by the Act of 21 August 1986. The latest version, resulting from the accession of Spain and Portugal (Convention of 26 May 1989) was finally accepted by the Parliament in January 1997 and entered into force on 1 October 1997. At the same time, Belgium ratified the Lugano Convention. These two treaties entered into force on 1 October 1997. Belgium has a particularly bad record of implementing international treaties. The Ministry of Foreign Affairs should realize the importance of keeping up with the obligations deriving from being a member of the international legal community.

C. OVERVIEW OF CONVENTION CASE LAW

Belgian Courts apply the Convention almost on a daily basis. More than 300 decisions have been published, and this probably represents only the tip of the iceberg. Most of these decisions were rendered by lower courts or courts at the appellate level. The Court of Cassation has only been called on in a limited way to control the application of the Convention by the lower courts. This does not mean, however, that all these decisions are equally important. In many cases, they only apply the Convention's basic principles as interpreted by the European Court of Justice. Arts 5(1) and 17 are among the provisions the courts most frequently apply. One striking conclusion from the compiling of the case law is that Belgian courts are generally eager to assert their jurisdiction over cases. To that end, they will eventually stretch the meaning of some of the Convention's rules, or even disregard a valid foreign jurisdiction clause.

Reports on Belgian case law based on the Convention are regularly published. The most important one is written by M. Fallon and H. Born.

D.   CASES

ARTICLE 1

"1.   . . . rights in property arising out of a matrimonial relationship . . . "

Case principle

Maintenance is not excluded.

Case

1   Court of Appeal of Brussels, 19 September 1995, Actualités Divorce (1996) 57

Facts

Both parties, husband and wife, were French nationals domiciled in Belgium. The husband brought divorce proceedings before the 'Tribunal de Grande Instance' of Paris. Some months later, while the divorce proceedings were still pending in France, his wife made a request to the Belgian judge for a provisional sum from her husband for her maintenance and that of their son. The judge of first instance declared that he had jurisdiction to grant provisional measures. On appeal, the husband claimed that the Belgian judge had no jurisdiction.

Judgment

The Court of Appeal, referring to the judgment of the Court of Justice in *De Cavel II*, reminded that maintenance obligations fell within the scope of 'civil matters' as understood under Art. 1 of the Convention. More specifically, the Convention was applicable to provisional measures with respect to maintenance, even when those were requested in the framework of divorce proceedings which were themselves excluded from the material scope of the Convention. In short, the applicability of the Convention had to be determined with respect to the specific action introduced before the judge, even when it was accessory to an action excluded from the Convention under Art. 1, para. 2(1).

Comment

Another judgment of the Court of Liège (23 March 1981, Revue Trimestrielle Droit Familial (1982) 450) wrongly stated that provisional measures relating to maintenance claims in the framework of divorce proceedings did not fall within the scope of the Convention.

Owing to the limited scope of the Convention, a problem will arise when the measures requested by the plaintiff have a mixed nature: some of them relate to property rights and others are closely linked to the status of the persons (for example, custody of children). This occurred before the Court of First Instance of Verviers (7 May 1986, Revue Trimestrielle Droit Familial (1988) 467), where the judge stated that the Convention was not applicable at all.

ARTICLE 1, PARAGRAPH 2(2)

" . . . proceedings relating to the winding-up of insolvent companies . . . "

Case principle

A debt claimed following bankruptcy, solely for the purpose of claiming against the bankrupt's estate, held to derive directly from the bankruptcy.

Case

Court of Cassation, 5 October 1982, Pasicrisie Belge (1982) I 183   **2**

Facts

The Court of Cassation upheld the judgment appealed from the Labour Court of Antwerp, on 19 February 1980. One party worked as commercial manager for the Belgian subsidiary of a Dutch company, which was declared bankrupt by the judge of Arnhem (The Netherlands), where the corporate seat of the company was located. The ex-worker then sued the trustee in bankruptcy before the Belgian judge to claim payment of arrears and compensation for termination of contract.

Judgment

The judge considered that the action as formulated by the plaintiff derived directly from the bankruptcy proceedings. The action had been introduced after the bankruptcy had been declared and the bankruptcy trustee appointed, for the sole purpose of having it accepted as a claim against the company's assets. The action was therefore considered a direct result of the declaration of bankruptcy and accordingly excluded from the scope of application of the Convention. On the basis of the bilateral Convention between The Netherlands and Belgium, the Dutch judge had exclusive jurisdiction to deal with the case.

> ## ARTICLE 1, PARAGRAPH 2(3)
>
> *"Social security . . ."*

Case principle

Convention inapplicable to social security authorities' actions to recover.

Case

3   Court of Cassation, 30 December 1985, Pasicrisie Belge (1985) 76

Facts

In a conflict between the Belgian Social Security authorities and two ex-workers, the legal problem at hand was whether the service abroad of the appealed judgment had been effected correctly in relation to the workers residing in The Netherlands. According to the writ, the judgment was served in accordance with Art. IV of the Protocol annexed to the Convention.

Judgment

The court recalled that the Convention was not applicable to social security matters. Applying Art. 10 of the Hague Convention of 15 November 1965 on the service abroad of judicial and extra-judicial documents in civil or commercial matters, the court concluded that service by registered letter to the foreign residence of the person was a valid way of serving abroad, as The Netherlands had not made a reservation to this method of service abroad.

> ## ARTICLE 5(1)
>
> *" . . . obligation in question . . . "*

Case principle

1.   For determination of place of performance, the court must first determine whether the obligation of compensation sued on is independent or replaces a broken contractual promise.

Case

4   Court of Cassation, 19 January 1984, Journal des Tribunaux (1984) 637

Facts

The dispute concerned the alleged wrongful termination of a contract whereby a German manufacturer granted an exclusive concession to a Belgian distributor. On the basis of the Belgian 1961 Act on the unilateral termination of contracts of distribution, the plaintiff claimed fair compensation in the absence of reasonable notice of termination, and additional compensation on the basis of Art. 3 of the Act. The German manufacturer contested the jurisdiction of the Belgian court.

Judgment

The Court of Cassation explicitly referred to the European Court's ruling in the case *de Bloos v Bouyer*. The court held that the two compensations were separate claims and that jurisdiction therefore had to be decided distinctly for the two. The first compensation was not an autonomous obligation, but under Belgian law an obligation replacing the unperformed contractual obligation. This compensation claim, which only arose if the requisite notice was not given, was intended to make good the loss arising from the *omission to give sufficient notice*. Since the obligation to give a period of notice was a manifestation of the defendant's fundamental obligation to respect the plaintiff's right in the area of the exclusive distributorship, the obligation must be located at the place where the unperformed obligation had to be performed. The Court of Cassation held further that the second obligation *was* an independent contractual obligation. While Belgian law classified the first of those two obligations as merely replacing the unperformed contractual obligation, the second obligation was seen as an independent contractual obligation. The place of performance of this independent obligation determined jurisdiction.

Comment

The Court of Cassation followed exactly the reasoning prescribed by the Court of Justice (for a similar ruling: *Knauer & Co. Machinenfabrik v Callens*, Court of Cassation, 6 April 1978, Pasicrisie Belge (1978) I 871). As a consequence, the place of performance of the two obligations can be located in two different places, giving rise to two different jurisdictions. To avoid this problem, one Court of Appeal (Appeal Court of Mons, 3 May 1977, Pasicrisie Belge (1978) II 8, dealing with the aftermath of the *de Bloos v Bouyer* case after the European Court gave its ruling) advocated that Art. 22 should be used to grant Belgian courts' jurisdiction over the two kinds of compensation. The Court of Appeal held that the court which has jurisdiction to decide on the first compensation also had jurisdiction to decide on the second, independent compensation because the two were related actions within the meaning of Art. 22 of the Convention. This course of action cannot be followed, however, because Art. 22 does not *confer* jurisdiction over related actions.

See, for other instances where the multiplicity of obligations led to a multiplicity of jurisdictions and hence to a division of the claims: Court of Appeal of Mons, 3 May 1977, Pasicrisie Belge (1978) II 8; Court of Appeal of Brussels, 21 June 1978, Journal des Tribunaux (1978) 685; Court of Appeal of Brussels, 25 June 1982, Tijdschrift voor Belgisch Handelsrecht (1982) 66; Commercial Court of Liège, 22 November 1984, Jurisprudence de Liège (1985) 111; and Commercial Court of Liège, 6 January 1986, Annales de Droit de Liège (1986) 275. This problem does not occur when the different obligations must be performed in the same country: Labour Court of Appeal, 5 January 1982, Jurisprudence de Liège (1983) 241.

Case

5 Court of Appeal of Brussels, 30 April 1987, Annales de Droit de Liège (1988) 90

Facts

A Belgian contractor which had been chosen to build a dam, ordered four turbines from a German manufacturer. One of the turbines delivered appeared to be defective. The contractor claimed damages for the repair works he had to carry out on the fourth turbine.

Judgment

The court held that it had jurisdiction on the basis of Art. 5(1) of the Convention. The contractual obligation on which the proceedings were based was not the obligation to pay damages, but the obligation it replaced, *i.e.* the duty to deliver goods conforming to the contract. The place of performance of this obligation was determined pursuant to the law governing the obligation at issue and in accordance with the rules on the conflict of laws of the court seised. The court applied the Hague Convention of 1955, which led to the application of the Uniform Sales Law of 1964, as the law of Germany, the country of the seller. As the parties had not presented any arguments on the Uniform Sales Law, the court stayed the proceedings to give them that possibility.

Comment

This judgment is part of a long line of case law where Belgian Courts use the provisions of other international instruments (the 1955 Hague Convention and the 1964 Uniform Sales Law, or, alternatively, the 1980 UN Convention on the International Sale of Goods) to interpret Art. 5(1) of the Convention. See Court of Appeal of Mons, 9 March 1983, Tijdschrift voor Belgisch Handelsrecht (1985) 386; Court of Appeal of Mons, 14 May 1987, Tijdschrift voor Belgisch Handelsrecht (1988) 303; Court of Appeal of Mons, 2 March 1994, Tijdschrift voor Belgisch Burgerlijk Recht (1996) 134; Commercial Court of Brussels, 2 September 1981, Belgisch Rechtspraak in Handelszaken (1982) 546; Commercial Court of Gent, 22 November 1985, Tijdschrift voor

Gentse Rechtspraak (1986) 10; Commercial Court of Liège, 17 April 1986, Tijdschrift voor Belgisch Handelsrecht (1988) 311; Commercial Court of Hasselt, 21 December 1993, Rechtskundig Weekblad (1995–96) 1350. Sometimes, the Convention is applied together with the Rome Convention on the law applicable to contractual obligations: Commercial Court of Antwerpen, 29 June 1994, Tijdschrift voor Belgisch Handelsrecht (1995) 429 (documentary credit).

Case principle

2. If more than one obligation is in issue, the principal obligation is the one to be taken for place of performance (*Shenavai* Case 266/85 applied).

Case

Court of Appeal of Brussels, 16 October 1987, Jurisprudence de Liège, Mons, **6** Bruxelles (1988) 50

Facts

The plaintiff (defendant in appeal) brought an action concerning the unilateral termination of a contract whereby the defendant had appointed the plaintiff to be exclusive distributor of his products in Belgium. The plaintiff claimed damages for the alleged wrongful breach of the contract by the defendant. Further the plaintiff asked for payment of sales commission which he claimed the defendant owed him.

Judgment

Faced with two different obligations (payment of damages and of commission), each performable in different states, the court decided that the obligation forming the subject matter of the dispute was the obligation to pay the commission. The other obligation, *i.e.* to pay damages for wrongful breach of contract, was only 'the logical consequence of the main obligation arising out of the contract', being the obligation concerning the payment of commission.

Comment

When multiple obligations form the subject matter of the plaintiff's claim, the place of performance of each separate obligation may differ. To concentrate and rationalize jurisdiction, the national court should, according to the *Shenavai v Kreischer* ruling, be guided by the maxim *accessorium sequitur principale* (see for an application of this doctrine: Commercial Court of Brussels, 29 March 1988, Tijdschrift voor Belgisch Handelsrecht (1990) 800). It is sometimes difficult to appraise which obligation is to be considered as the main obligation. The Court of Appeal held that the obligation to pay commission was the main obligation. This can be criticized, for the obligation to pay damages is, as such, *independent* of the obligation concerning the payment of commission. See for similar problems: Court of Appeal of Brussels, 30 June 1987, Tijdschrift voor Belgisch Burgerlijk Recht (1988) 557.

It can also be regretted that the court did not bother to inquire upon the applicable law, and assumed that the main obligation was to be performed in Brussels. See, for other instances where courts neglected to establish which national law was applicable to determine the place of performance of the obligation: Commercial Court of Antwerpen, 30 June 1987, Rechtspraak van Haven van Antwerpen (1987) 57; Court of First Instance of Brussels, 28 January 1993, Revue Régionale de Droit (1995) 79; Court of Appeal of Antwerpen, 3 January 1995, Tijdschrift voor Belgisch Handelsrecht (1995) 391 (application of the Convention's rules while the defendant was a Monaco-based company, Monaco not being a Contracting State!).

> " . . . the place of performance . . . "

Case principle

1. Agreed place of performance is sufficient and is not subject to Art. 17 formalities.

Case

7 Court of Cassation, 13 November 1981, Arresten Van Het Hof Van Cassatie (1981–82) I 336

Facts

A German had bought, on many occasions, products from a Belgian company. The German buyer had always paid the price into the Belgian bank account of the seller, as required in the seller's invoice. A problem occurred with one of the transactions. The buyer refused to pay. The seller sued him before a Belgian court. The German buyer contested the jurisdiction of the court.

Judgment

The lower court held that it had jurisdiction. The Court of Cassation saw no reason not to uphold this judgment. The court stated that the parties had agreed that the buyer would pay the price directly into the seller's bank account. Referring to the ruling of the European Court in the case *Zelger v Salinitri*, the Court of Cassation held that where parties agreed on the place of performance of a contractual obligation, that agreement would give rise to jurisdiction under Art. 5(1) of the Convention if it was valid according to the national law applicable to the contract by virtue of private international law rules. The court added that such an agreement did not have to fulfil the formal requirements laid down in Art. 17.

Comment

The same reasoning has been followed in a great number of Belgian judgments. See, *inter alia*: Court of Appeal of Liège, 6 November 1982, Tijdschrift voor Belgisch Handelsrecht (1984) 25; Court of Appeal of Gent, 9 June 1988, Tijdschrift voor Gentse Rechtspraak (1988) 105; Court of Appeal of Brussels, 26 March 1991, Jurisprudence de Liège, Mons et Bruxelles (1992) 1389; Court of Appeal of Antwerp, 3 January 1995, Tijdschrift voor Belgisch Handelsrecht (1995) 387; Commercial Court of Liège, 22 November 1984, Jurisprudence de Liège (1985) 111; Commercial Court of Brussels, 22 February 1985, Journal des Tribunaux (1985) 491; Commercial Court of Brussels, 13 April 1989, Tijdschrift voor Belgisch Handelsrecht (1991) 430.

However, if the performance agreement is purely for jurisdiction, Article 17 must be satisfied: *MSG v Les Gravières*, Case C–106/95 (ECJ).

ARTICLE 5(3)

" . . . *the place where the harmful event occurred.*"

Case principle

1. Harmful event occurs in place of causative event or damage.

Case

Court of First Instance of Brussels, 14 April 1978, Rechtspraak Van Haven **8** Van Antwerpen (1979–80) 276

Facts

A Russian ship was sailing on the Escaut with a Belgian pilot on board, as prescribed by Belgian law, when it collided with a Liberian ship, which was also guided by a Belgian pilot. The collision occurred in the Dutch part of the Escaut. The Liberian company claimed damages from the Belgian state, arguing that the collision was the fault of the pilots.

Judgment

The court held that it had jurisdiction on the basis of Art. 5(3) of the Convention, even though it acknowledged that the harmful event occurred in the territory of The Netherlands. The court argued that both parties had not objected to the jurisdiction of the court.

Case principle

2. Harmful event, in purchase of goods in breach of copyright, occurs where the buyer is subsequently prevented from marketing the goods.

Case

9   Commercial Court of Liège, 4 January 1983, Journal des Tribunaux (1983)
557

Facts

The plaintiff, a Belgian company, bought a large quantity of toys from the
defendant, a Dutch company. The toys proved to be illegal copies of a trade
mark-protected toy. The rightful owner of the trade mark, a German company,
asked the plaintiff to stop selling the counterfeited toys in Belgium. The plaintiff sued the defendant, claiming that the latter had failed to fulfil its contractual duty to provide merchantable goods, and had breached its duty of care
towards the plaintiff.

Judgment

The court examined the two claims separately. Concerning the tortious breach
of duty of care, the court decided that the place of occurrence of the causal
event was located in Belgium, since it was there that the plaintiff was prevented from selling the products.

Comment

It would have been more simple to locate the place where the damage occurred
than arbitrarily to pinpoint Belgium as the place of the causal event. The
decision to sell the goods had, after all, been taken in The Netherlands.
Further, an action based on tort cannot be related to a contract between the
same parties.

Case principle

3.   **Wrongful interference with contract held to occur both where interference
took place as causative act and where effects occurred as damage.**

Case

10   Commercial Court of Brussels, 4 June 1985, Tijdschrift Voor Belgisch
Handelsrecht (1986) 393

Facts

A German company had appointed a Belgian company by contract to be its
exclusive distributor in Belgium. When the contract was terminated, the parties
agreed that the claims of the Belgian distributor against its customers would be
transferred to the German manufacturer. The latter omitted to notify the
customers that it had become their creditor. A year later, the Belgian
distributor concluded another agreement with a Belgian factoring company,
whereby the distributor assigned once again all its rights against the

customers. When the factoring company started collecting money from the Belgian customers, the German company notified the customers that they were to pay it and not the Belgian factor. The customers stopped all payments pending the trial. The Belgian factor sued the German company.

Judgment

The court decided that the problem was one of tortious liability, and that both the causal event (the notification by the German company to the customers) and the damage (the fact that the customers refused to pay the factor) took place in Belgium.

Comment

The court located the harmful event in Belgium where the notification was sent from Germany. In respect of damage, this is too wide an interpretation of the concept of 'harmful event' *i.e.* the non-payment by the customers, occurred in Belgium, but it can be questioned whether the damage could be located at the central office of the Belgian company? Should the damage not be located at the place where the customers refused to pay, *i.e.* at their offices?

ARTICLE 5(5)

" . . . *branch, agency or other establishment* . . . "

Case principle

A mere contact point for negotiating parties for a short duration is not a branch, agency or other establishment within the meaning of Art. 5(5).

Case

Court of Appeal of Mons, 21 February 1995, Revue Régionale de Droit **11** (1995) 556

Facts

C.M.I., a Belgian undertaking, had asked a French company to clean-up an industrial plant in Belgium. The French company, which had an office in Belgium, sub-contracted part of the work to the plaintiff, a company based in Belgium. The subcontract was concluded after an exchange of telexes between the plaintiff, the Belgian office of the French company and the French company. The plaintiff billed the Belgian office for the works it performed, but the French company refused to pay.

Judgment

The court held that it had no jurisdiction to decide the case. It based its reasoning on Art. 5(1) and (5) of the Convention. Concerning Art. 5(5), the court proceeded to a detailed analysis of the factual situation. Referring to the definition given by the Court of Justice in the case of *Somafer v Saar-Ferngas*, the court indicated first of all that the French company had rented an office in Belgium for a very short period of time (three months), that during this time it used office equipment of the owner of the building, that the Belgian 'place of business' was at most a contact point for possible commercial partners and that third parties could in no way confuse the outlet with a branch, agency or establishment. Furthermore, the court held that the dispute was in no way related to the exploitation of the alleged 'branch'. No commitments had been undertaken by the Belgian office on behalf of the French parent body since the French company had directly accepted the offer of the Belgian plaintiff.

ARTICLE 6(1)

" *. . . one of a number of defendants . . .* "

Case principle

There must be required connection between claims.

Case

12 Court of First Instance, 11 October 1991, Tijdschrift Voor Belgisch Burgerlijk Recht (1992) 531

Facts

The plaintiff travel agency sued three defendants. Two of them, domiciled in Belgium, had booked a cruise through the travel agency and paid an advance of approximately one sixth of the total price. The third defendant was the shipping company which had organized the cruise and whose corporate seat was in France.

As a result of a fire during the cruise, many activities were cancelled. The two passengers refused to pay the total amount of the cruise price. This resulted in losses for the travel agency which had already paid the whole amount invoiced by the shipping company for the two passengers.

Judgment

The French company questioned the jurisdiction of the Belgian judge, arguing that Art. 6(1) could only be applied when there was a connection between the co-defendants. The judge considered that each judge must determine on the basis of his national law whether this connection existed. The actions against the different defendants were based on the same legal fact, that is, the cruise booked by the two customers. Furthermore, there was a contractual link between the three defendant parties because the travel agency had booked the cruise on behalf of its customers and the latter refused to pay due to faults which could be attributed in the first place to the shipping company. Art. 6(1) was therefore applicable.

Comment

Although the judge wrongly stated that the notion of co-defendant had to be interpreted in accordance with the *lex fori*, the requirements he applied seem to correspond to those defined by the Court of Justice in the *Kalfelis* case.

ARTICLE 6(2)

" . . . *unless these were instituted solely with the object of removing him from the jurisdiction of the court which would be competent in his case.*"

Case principle

1. Article 6(2) governs third party international jurisdiction even where the main action is non-international and the Convention consequently inapplicable thereto.

Case

Commercial Court of Antwerpen, 17 January 1995, Tijdschrift Voor Belgisch   **13**
Handelsrecht (1995) 521

Facts

A Dutch company (A) had ordered a fork-lift truck from an English company. The fork-lift truck did not fulfil the expectations of A, who decided to sell it to a Belgian company with its corporate seat in Genk (B). Although the contract provided the possibility for A to revoke the sale, B had in the meantime sold the truck to C, which was negotiating the truck's sale to a company located in Brussels. A repossessed the truck and C sued B for compensation for loss through non-delivery of the truck. B then brought an action on a guarantee against A, as an attempt to join the Dutch company in the proceedings.

Judgment

The judge examined the forum clause contained in the general conditions to which the agreement between A and B vaguely referred. The conditions of Art. 17 were not met. The judge considered whether he could accept jurisdiction on the basis of Art. 6(2). Having found that the proceedings in Antwerpen against B had not been instituted solely with the object of removing the third party A from the jurisdiction of the court which would be competent in this case (the action of C against B had no international element and was therefore submitted to the Belgian rules of territorial jurisdiction), the judge held that Art. 6(2) was applicable to attract A to the Belgian courts.

Case principle

2.   Article 17 agreements between *plaintiff* and third party held to prevail over Art. 6(2).

Case

14   Commercial Court of Liège, 10 March 1993, Tijdschrift Voor Belgisch Burgerlijk Recht (1995) 216

Facts

The defendant Belgian company had signed a contract with a French company (the contractor) with its corporate seat in Mulhouse. The contractor had to build an automatic installation to feed two high ovens with coal. Some works were subcontracted to another French company (the subcontractor).

A dispute arose between the defendant and the French companies as to payment and proper performance of the work. In a claim by the French subcontractor against the defendant Belgian company for payment for work carried out and compensation for delay, the defendant sought to bring in the French contractor as a third party under Art. 6(2). The French contractor resisted Belgian Art. 6(2) jurisdiction on the ground of a French jurisdiction agreement between it and the plaintiff French subcontractor.

Judgment

The judge investigated the formal conditions of validity of the forum clause. He held that the clause was valid and therefore declared that he had no jurisdiction over the claim between the two French companies. On the other hand, the judge accepted jurisdiction in the action between the subcontractor and the Belgian company and, before deciding on merits, waited for the report of the expert who had already been designated in interlocutory proceedings.

Comment

The judge confirmed that Art. 17 prevailed over Art. 6(2) whenever the formal conditions for the existence of a valid forum clause were fulfilled. In his observations on the judgment, Wauters observes that this solution might lead to undesirable results in some circumstances. For instance, in the present case, it was evident that the judge of the place where the works had been conducted was the best located to decide on the several actions. There was, furthermore, connexity between the action between the subcontractor and the Belgian company (which was decided by the judge in Liège) and the action between the subcontractor and the contractor (which had to be brought before the judge in Mulhouse).

ARTICLE 8, PARAGRAPH 2

" . . . *arising out of the operations of the branch, agency or establishment* . . . "

Case principle

'Operations' means something more than mere handling of claims.

Case

District Court of Tournai, 18 February 1980, Journal des Tribunaux (1980) **15**
391

Facts

A car accident had occurred in France between a French citizen, insured by the defendant, a French insurance company, and a Belgian driver. The Belgian driver sued the insurer before the Court of First Instance of Tournai. The French company operated in Belgium through a branch. The French driver had been insured directly by the French company. This company argued that the Court of First Instance had no jurisdiction. The matter was submitted to the District Court.

Judgment

The District Court held that the Court of First Instance had no jurisdiction as the defendant's branch was located in Brussels and not in Tournai. The court applied Art. 8, para. 2 of the Convention and held that the insurer had a branch in Belgium. The decisive element according to the court was that the plaintiff's claim had been handled directly by the Brussels branch, without any intervention of the French insurer.

Comment

This judgment is clearly defective in a number of respects. Article 8, para. 2 is only meant for insurers who are not established in any Contracting State, which was clearly not the case. It is true that Art. 7 refers to Art. 5(5). The injured party can therefore sue the insurer before the court of the place where the branch, agency or establishment is situated, provided the dispute arises out of the operation of the branch. This will only be the case when the insurance was directly bought from the branch. The fact that the branch was responsible for the processing of the injured party's claim does not mean that the dispute concerns the operation of that branch.

ARTICLE 16(1)(a)

" . . . have as their object . . . "

Case principle

1. Action for authorization to sell an interest in foreign land on behalf of a minor held to fall within exclusive jurisdiction.

Case

16   Court of First Instance of Kortrijk, 20 March 1983, Tijdschrift Voor Notarissen (1983) 174

Facts

A group of Belgian citizens had bought a piece of land in France. One of them died. His part of the property went to his children, who were at that time minors. They all agreed to sell the land. Since minors were involved, parties had to ask a court for authorization to sell without having recourse to a public auction.

Judgment

The court held that it had no jurisdiction since the matter concerned immovable property located in France.

Comment

It can be questioned whether Art. 16 was properly applicable to the dispute. Indeed, the subject matter concerned the specific authorization which was required and not the sale as such. That authorization formed part of the rules protecting minors, something which actually fell outside the Convention's scope.

Case principle

2. Claims for compensation for damage under a lease are included in Art. 16(1).

Case

Court of First Instance of Marche-en-Famenne, 26 February 1987, Tijdschrift   **17**
Voor Belgisch Burgerlijk Recht (1989) 387

Facts

A Dutch citizen, owner of a vacation home in Belgium, had rented it to two
Dutch persons. During the vacation the house burnt down. The owner was
reimbursed by his insurer, who claimed the amount back from the negligent
holidaymakers.

Judgment

The court, referring to the European Court's ruling in *Sanders v Van der Putte*,
held that disputes between lessors and tenants as to compensation for damage
caused by the tenant, were covered by Art. 16. The court saw no reason to
make an exception to the rule of Art. 16 on the sole ground that the dispute
concerned a lease concluded for a short letting, as had been advocated by the
Schlosser Report (but now see Art. 16(1)(b)).

Case principle

3.   Contractual aspects of sale of immovables fall outside Art. 16(1).

Case

Court of First Instance of Charleroi, 8 November 1991, Revue Régionale de   **18**
Droit (1992) 146

Facts

The plaintiff, a businessman living in Belgium, had sold an office located in
Brussels to a Luxembourg company. Following a series of unsuccessful transactions, the buyer was unable to pay the price. In the course of negotiations,
the parties agreed to terminate the sale. The plaintiff sued the defendant and
claimed damages for the aborted transaction.

Judgment

The court held Art. 16 to be inapplicable. The action was not, as such, concerned with a right *in rem*, but with the termination of a sales contract.

ARTICLE 17, PARAGRAPH 1

" If the parties . . . have agreed that . . . "

Case principle

1. A jurisdiction clause in general conditions is not binding if written in a language which the other party does not understand.

Case

19 Commercial Court of Kortrijk, 26 November 1985, Tijdschrift Voor Belgisch Handelsrecht (1986) 716

Facts

The parties had concluded many contracts of sale in English. Two of those contracts referred to general conditions of sale which were written in Dutch. A dispute arose concerning those two contracts. The general conditions contained a jurisdiction clause.

Judgment

The court decided that a jurisdiction clause appearing in the general purchase conditions of the buyer was not valid if it was written in a language which the seller did not understand. The court underlined that the two contracts had been written in a different language to the conditions.

Comment

The Commercial Court of Verviers followed the same reasoning (Commercial Court of Verviers, 8 March 1984, Jurisprudence de Liège (1984) 310), which is also to be found in the writings of Gothot et Holleaux (*La Convention de Bruxelles*, p. 105, no. 177). The validity of the agreement must be examined exclusively under the conditions of Art. 17. These strict requirements guarantee that parties have agreed on the clause. A court should therefore only disregard a jurisdiction clause when it is sufficiently proven that no agreement was possible due to the language barrier.

Case principle

2. A third party transferee of the business of a party to a jurisdiction agreement is bound by the jurisdiction agreement (extending *Tilly Russ* contracts assignment to transfer of business).

Case

20 Commercial Court of Brussels, 23 January 1986, Tijdschrift Voor Belgisch Handelsrecht (1988) 779

Facts

A Belgian company had ordered some goods from another Belgian company. The order form contained an express reference to the general conditions of sale of the buyer, printed on the back of the order form. One of those conditions was a jurisdiction clause in favour of Belgian courts. The seller signed and returned the order form. During the performance of the contract, the seller was bought by a French company, which undertook to deliver the goods. During a dispute, the question arose whether the French company was bound by the jurisdiction clause. The defendant argued that since it had not signed the jurisdiction clause, it could not be said to have agreed to it.

Judgment

The court held that according to Belgian law, the defendant French company had succeeded to the rights and obligations of the original seller. The jurisdiction clause was valid between the two original parties, and therefore the third party to the jurisdiction agreement was bound by the jurisdiction clause.

Comment

See also Court of Appeal of Mons, 16 May 1989, Tijdschrift voor Belgisch Handelsrecht (1990) 783. Compare with Commercial Court of Liège, 10 March 1993, Tijdschrift voor Belgisch Handelsrecht (1995) 395—a jurisdiction clause in a contract between the subcontractor and the contractor is a *res inter alios acta* for the prime contractor and this party cannot therefore rely on the clause.

Case principle

3. Application of jurisdiction agreement to transferee is subject to applicable national law on succession of rights and obligations (*Tilly Russ*).

Case

Court of Cassation, 18 September 1987, Tijdschrift Voor Belgisch **21** Handelsrecht (1988) 377

Facts

A Belgian plaintiff was the holder of a bill of lading issued by the defendant German carrier to a shipper, from whom the plaintiff had purchased goods. Those goods arrived at their destination in a damaged condition. The plaintiff claimed damages before a lower Belgian court. That court, and the appeal Court (Court of Appeal of Gent, 24 June 1985, Tijdschrift voor Belgisch Handelsrecht (1986) 444) declared that they had no jurisdiction on the ground of the jurisdiction clause in favour of German courts contained in the bill of lading. The plaintiff lodged an appeal in Cassation.

Judgment

The Court of Cassation referred to the ruling of the European Court in the case *Tilly Russ* and held that the succession to the shipper's rights and obligations under the bill of lading was governed by Belgian law. Article 91 of the

Zee- en Binnenvaartwet (Law of Maritime and Inland Transport) provides that the rights and obligations of the holder of the bill of lading are not those of the shipper, but are exclusively determined by the actual content of the bill of lading. Since there was no real succession, the defendant could not rely on the jurisdiction clause against the holder.

Comment

This is one of the numerous cases where the question arose whether a jurisdiction clause appearing in the bill of lading can be relied on against the holder of the bill of lading. (See also: Court of Cassation, 15 June 1988, Rechtskundig Weekblad (1988–89) 302; Court of Appeal of Antwerpen, 21 November 1979, Rechtskundig Weekblad (1980–81) 1674; 302; Court of Appeal of Antwerpen, 14 March 1990, Rechtspraak Haven Antwerpen (1991) 120; Court of Appeal of Antwerpen, 28 March 1990, Rechtspraak Haven Antwerpen (1994) 160; Court of Appeal of Antwerpen, 26 September 1995, Rechtspraak Haven Antwerpen (1996) 3; Commercial Court of Antwerpen, 24 June 1980, Rechtspraak Haven Antwerpen (1980–81) 475; Commercial Court of Antwerpen, 16 May 1983, European Transport Law (1985) 82; Commercial Court of Antwerpen, 7 May 1984, European Transport Law (1984) 397; Commercial Court of Antwerpen, 26 February 1985, European Transport Law (1987) 40; Commercial Court of Antwerpen, 30 June 1987, Rechtspraak Haven Antwerpen (1987) 57; Commercial Court of Antwerpen, 23 February 1993, Rechtspraak Haven Antwerpen (1995) 165; Commercial Court of Antwerpen, 16 February 1994, Rechtspraak Haven Antwerpen (1994) 367.) Before the ruling of the European Court in the case *Tilly Russ*, Belgian courts had refused to acknowledge that a jurisdiction clause appearing in a bill of lading could be valid in the relationship between the carrier and the holder of the bill (Commercial Court of Antwerpen, 29 May 1973, Rechtspraak Haven Antwerpen (1973) 250; Commercial Court of Antwerpen, 15 April 1975, Rechtspraak Haven Antwerpen (1975–76) 84). Those courts refused to recognize the supremacy of Art. 17 and held that jurisdiction clauses in favour of foreign courts were not valid. To put an end to this heresy, the Court of Cassation referred the matter to the European Court. This court held that reliance on the jurisdiction clause against the holder is possible under two conditions: first, the jurisdiction clause must be valid as between the carrier and the shipper; and secondly, by virtue of the applicable law, the third party, upon acquiring the bill of lading, must have succeeded to the shipper's rights and obligations. The question of the law applicable to this succession falls outside the scope of the Convention and must therefore be determined by the court seised in accordance with its conflict of law rules. Belgian courts invariably hold that the problem must be solved according to Belgian law. Generally they invoke the public policy character of Art. 91 of the above mentioned Maritime Transport law, which is applicable as soon as the ship sailed from or to Belgium. This provision is meant to give the holder of the bill autonomous rights, in order to protect him against agreements between the shipper and the carrier. It can be questioned, however, whether Art. 91 excludes the application of any other law with respect to the problem of the succession. Belgian courts do not even bother to examine whether foreign law, the application of which is excluded by the public policy exception, offers the same protection to the holder of the bill of lading. Accordingly, it is submitted that Belgian courts should preferably qualify this provision as being a mandatory provision rather than invoke its public policy character.

> " . . . *a court or the courts of a Contracting State* . . . "

Case principle

It must be clear from the contract that a particular Contracting State's courts have been chosen if Art. 17 is to apply.

Case

Commercial Court of Antwerpen, 12 June 1984, European Transport Law **22** (1986) 238

Facts

The Belgian plaintiff was the holder of a bill of lading issued by the defendant, an Indian carrier. The ship had been temporarily chartered by the owner to another company. A conflict arose between the owner and the time charterer. The owner ordered the captain to leave the goods at Sharjah instead of Damman, where they should have been delivered. The plaintiff claimed damages because he had to pay another carrier to deliver the goods to Damman. The defendant objected to the court's jurisdiction on the basis of the jurisdiction clause contained in the bill of lading.

Judgment

The court held that the jurisdiction clause could not be upheld on a number of grounds, one of which was that the clause was too vague. The clause read that jurisdiction was given to the court of the 'principal place of business' of the carrier. The court found that it was not clear who was the carrier (the owner or the charterer) and that it was even less clear where the carrier had its principal place of business.

Comment

This illustrates how Belgian courts will assert jurisdiction whenever a dispute involves a ship sailing from or to a Belgian port, even if it means disregarding a valid jurisdiction clause. The principal place of business can indeed easily be located in most cases. This argument should not be used to torpedo a jurisdiction agreement.

> " . . . *shall have exclusive jurisdiction* . . . "

Case principle

Article 17 excludes national laws on effects of jurisdiction agreements.

Case

23   Commercial Court of Brussels, 20 July 1984, Tijdschrift Voor Belgisch Handelsrecht (1985) 415

Facts

The parties had agreed to submit all litigation to the Courts of Hamburg, Germany. The dispute concerned the alleged wrongful termination of a contract of exclusive distributorship. The defendant argued that Art. 4 of the 1961 Act, which provided that Belgian courts would have exclusive jurisdiction over all litigation concerning the unilateral termination of distribution agreements when the exclusivity covered at least partly the Belgian territory, must yield to a jurisdiction clause.

Judgment

The court decided that the jurisdiction clause prevailed over the Act of 1961: the Act could not prevail over the Convention, which was part of European law and as such enjoyed supremacy.

> **ARTICLE 17, PARAGRAPH 1(a)**
>
> " . . . *in writing* . . . "

Case principle

1.   There is no agreement in writing where both parties contract on their own general conditions containing conflicting jurisdiction clauses.

Case

24   Court of Appeal of Liège, 30 April 1987, Annales de Droit de Liège (1988) 90

Facts

A German seller had sent an offer to the Belgian plaintiff. The latter accepted the offer and referred to his general conditions of sale in his acceptance. The seller replied and confirmed the sale. The confirmation referred to his own general conditions. The plaintiff finally confirmed his order and referred once again to his conditions. Both sets of conditions contained a jurisdiction clause, one for the German, the other for Belgian courts.

Judgment

The court held that neither of the two jurisdiction clauses were valid. Neither the seller nor the buyer had accepted the other party's general conditions in writing. There was no possibility of tacit acceptance as this was the first time the parties had done business together.

Comment

See also Commercial Court of Liège, 22 November 1988, Tijdschrift voor Belgisch Handelsrecht (1991) 424. In another instance, the Commercial Court of Brussels decided that two jurisdiction clauses eliminated each other. This may be true according to the general *Battle of forms* doctrine of Belgian commercial law. But under the Convention, one has to examine whether one of the two jurisdiction clauses has been the object of an agreement, and this *can* be the case even though both parties work with general conditions of their own (Commercial Court of Brussels, 20 December 1991, Tijdschrift voor Belgisch Handelsrecht (1992) 919).

Case principle

2. Express reference in the contract to general conditions containing a jurisdiction clause on the back satisfies the 'in writing' formalities in Art. 17 (*Salotti* Case 24/76 applied).

Case

Court of Appeal of Liège, 3 December 1990, Pasicrisie Belge (1990) II 84   **25**

Facts

A Belgian citizen had bought a car in Belgium from the local distributor of a French company. The car was defective. The buyer claimed damages from the seller, which lodged an 'action in guarantee' against the French company. The defendant in guarantee invoked a jurisdiction clause in favour of French courts, appearing on the back of the order form used by the buyer.

Judgment

The court held that the jurisdiction clause was valid. The buyer had signed the order form which contained an express reference to the general conditions appearing on the back. The court held that when a jurisdiction clause is contained in general conditions of sale, the clause will be regarded as being part of the contract when the document signed by both parties contains an express reference to the general conditions including a clause conferring jurisdiction.

Comment

An express reference to the jurisdiction clause contained in the general conditions need not appear in the document signed by the parties. A general, but explicit, reference to the conditions will suffice. This has been clearly stated by the European Court in *Estasis Salotti*, but some commentators still require an express reference to the jurisdiction clause as such.

In one case, the Commercial Court of Liège held that a *general* reference to the sales conditions appearing on the back of the order form did not establish that parties had agreed upon the jurisdiction clause contained in these conditions: Commercial Court of Liège, 12 February 1987, Jurisprudence de Liège, Mons et Bruxelles (1987) 933; see for a similar view: Commercial Court of Kortrijk, 26 November 1985, Tijdschrift voor Belgisch Handelsrecht (1986) 717.

In other instances Belgian courts have held that no *specific* reference to the jurisdiction clause is needed: Court of Appeal of Antwerpen, 21 February 1994, Pasicrisie Belge (1993) II 62; Court of Appeal of Gent, 14 September 1994, Tijdschrift voor Belgisch Handelsrecht (1995) 382 (applied the Convention's rules to an arbitration clause); Commercial Court of Brussels, 23 January 1986, Tijdschrift voor Belgisch Handelsrecht (1988) 779; Commercial Court of Liège, 10 February 1994, Tijdschrift voor Belgisch Handelsrecht (1995) 402.

See also cases where the general conditions containing the jurisdiction clause were not communicated to the other party: Commercial Court of Brussels, 13 April 1989, Tijdschrift voor Belgisch Handelsrecht (1991) 431; Commercial Court of Liège, 10 February 1994, Tijdschrift voor Belgisch Handelsrecht (1995) 402.

> " . . . *evidenced in writing* . . . "

Case principle

Failure to object to a jurisdiction clause in general conditions sent subsequent to oral conclusion of contract is not evidence in writing unless so as part of a continuing business relationship.

Case

26 Commercial Court of Antwerpen, 10 November 1993, Rechtskundig Weekblad (1994–95) 442

Facts

A Dutch company had sold goods to a Belgian company. The seller had billed the buyer after the goods had been shipped and received. The invoice referred to the general conditions of sale which appeared on the back of the document. Those conditions contained a jurisdiction clause in favour of Dutch courts. The buyer sued the seller before a Belgian court. The defendant claimed that the court seised had no jurisdiction.

Judgment

The court decided that the jurisdiction clause was not valid. The contract had been concluded orally, without any reference to general conditions. The buyer had not agreed in writing to the invoice. The mere fact that he had not objected to the general conditions appearing on the back of the invoice was not such as to establish a jurisdiction agreement, since there existed no continuing business relationship between the parties.

Comment

Under Art. 25 of the Belgian Commercial Code, an invoice can be tacitly accepted between merchants if one of them does not object to it. Belgian courts, however, hold that tacit consent to documents containing jurisdiction clauses is not allowed, unless the absence of objection to the document containing the jurisdiction clause is part of a continuous business relationship: Court of Appeal of Antwerpen, 21 February 1994, Pasicrisie Belge (1993) II 62; Court of Appeal of Antwerpen, 3 January 1995, Tijdschrift voor Belgisch Handelsrecht (1995) 387; Commercial Court of Liège, 6 January 1986, Annales de Droit de Liège (1986) 275 (express objection lacking against the invoice); Commercial Court of Liège, 17 April 1986, Tijdschrift voor Belgisch Handelsrecht (1988) 310 (no continuing business relationship); Commercial Court of Liège, 2 December 1988, Tijdschrift voor Belgisch Handelsrecht (1990) 179 (no continuous business relationship); Commercial Court of Hasselt, 3 February 1993, Limburgs Rechtsleven (1993) 234.

In the absence of a current business relationship, one court has tried to save a jurisdiction clause appearing in an invoice by using the other possibility offered in Art. 17(1)(c), *i.e.* that of the jurisdiction agreement in a form which accords with a usage of international commerce: Commercial Court of Gent, 26 April 1995, Tijdschrift voor Gentse Rechtspraak (1995) 178. The court held that general conditions appearing on the back of invoices bind merchants if they have not objected to them within a reasonable time. The court considered in fact that the rule of Art. 25 of the Commercial Code itself had the status of a usage. This is very questionable because Art. 25 is a Belgian legal provision, which is not necessarily observed by parties in international contracts.

Some courts have held that a jurisdiction clause appearing in an invoice cannot be valid, since invoices are generally sent after the contract has been concluded. The invoice would then, they argue, amount to a unilateral change of the contract provisions by one party. This neglects the fact, however, that a jurisdiction clause can be added to an existing contract, provided parties agree on the clause. Such an agreement can then take the form of absence of objection to a document containing such a clause, when parties have in the past contracted under the same clause. See Kaye, *Civil Jurisdiction* pp. 1045 *et seq.*

> ### ARTICLE 17, PARAGRAPH 1(b)
>
> *" . . . practices which the parties have established between*
> *themselves . . . "*

Case principle

Agreement may be according to a practice between parties whereby general conditions containing a jurisdiction clause are sent by a party following contract and not objected to by the recipient.

Case

27   Court of Appeal of Gent, 30 June 1995, Algemeen Juridisch Tijdschrift (1995–96) 262

Facts

A lower court had decided to hear a case, notwithstanding the existence of a jurisdiction clause in favour of Dutch courts, which appeared in the general conditions of one party. This party appealed against the decision, arguing that the lower court had neglected the jurisdiction clause.

Judgment

The Court of Appeal held that the jurisdiction clause was valid between the parties. The jurisdiction clause appeared on the back of the order form, amongst other general conditions of purchase and sale. Although the order form had not been explicitly accepted in writing by the other party, the court decided, however, that since the order form was part of a continuing business relationship between the parties, and since all preceding contracts had been concluded in the same way, *i.e.* with the mere sending of an order form, the parties had created between themselves a practice, according to which written confirmation of an oral agreement need not be accepted explicitly or in writing. The absence of objection to the general conditions was enough to incorporate them into the contract.

Comment

The Court of Appeal apparently referred in its ruling to the latest version of Art. 17, which mentions explicitly practices which the parties have established between themselves. At the time of the judgment, however, the 1982-version was still applicable in Belgium. In this version, no mention is made of 'individual' practices.

Nonetheless the outcome of the case would not have been different under the previous version. Since the ruling of the European Court in the case of *Segoura v Bonakdarian*, it was common knowledge that if the two parties were in a continuing business relationship governed by general conditions containing a jurisdiction clause, the mere written confirmation of the agreement by one party was enough to establish a jurisdiction agreement, provided that the other party did not object to that written confirmation.

See, for other cases where the existence of a continuing business relationship was at stake (application of the *Segoura v Bonakdarian* principles): Court of Appeal of Gent, 14 September 1994, Tijdschrift voor Belgisch Handelsrecht (1995) 382 (the court applied the Convention's rules to an arbitration clause); Court of Appeal of Antwerpen, 11 October 1994, Tijdschrift voor Belgisch Handelsrecht (1995) 385 (business relationship insufficiently long); Commercial Court of Brussels, 12 December 1985, Tijdschrift voor Belgisch Handelsrecht (1987) 381; Commercial Court of Gent, 26 April 1995, Tijdschrift voor Gentse Rechtspraak (1995) 178.

ARTICLE 18

" . . . *solely to contest* . . . "

Case principle

Bringing a counterclaim is as much of a submission as a defence on the merits.

Case

Commercial Court of Antwerpen, 28 January 1986, Tijdschrift Voor Belgisch **28**
Handelsrecht (1987) 124

Facts

The defendant had bought a machine from the plaintiff in 1978. In 1980, it ordered several parts which needed to be replaced. After delivery, those parts were never paid for. The plaintiff was declared bankrupt and the trustee sought payment for the parts delivered. The defendant appeared and contested the jurisdiction of the court. It also introduced a claim of its own.

Judgment

The court held that it had jurisdiction. The defendant did not simply formally acknowledge the substance of the action launched by the plaintiff. It also sought to have the plaintiff's action declared unfounded and it claimed damages from the plaintiff. The court held that the defendant had gone further than mere contestation of jurisdiction over the claim of the plaintiff and had therefore accepted the court's jurisdiction.

Comment

The court followed Droz (*Compétence judiciaire et effets des jugements dans le Marché Commun*, Paris, Dalloz, 1972, no. 222–B–139). Gothot and Holleaux, on the other hand, argued that the launching by the defendant of its own action does not necessarily imply that he has accepted the court's jurisdiction (*La Convention de Bruxelles du 27 Septembre 1968*, Paris, Jupiter, 1985, no. 195). See also Gaudemet-Tallon, *Les Conventions de Bruxelles et de Lugano*, Paris, L.G.D.J., 1996, no. 148. A final answer to this question can only be given by the European Court.

ARTICLE 21

" . . . same cause of action . . . "

Case principle

1. Actions for contractual enforcement and annulment involve the same cause of action (*Gubisch*).

Case

29 Commercial Court of Brussels, 31 March 1994, Tijdschrift Voor Belgisch Handelsrecht (1995) 418

Facts

An Italian supplier granted exclusive distribution rights for Belgium and Luxembourg to a Belgian company. The distribution agreement was terminated by the Italian supplier and its French subsidiary which had taken over the contract. The Belgian distributor sued both companies before the Brussels court. A month earlier, the Italian supplier and its French subsidiary had requested a judge in Udine (Italy) to declare that the agreement had been terminated as a result of unsatisfactory performances by the distributor and that no damages were due.

Judgment

The Belgian judge considered that there was the same cause of action in the Italian and Belgian proceedings. Both claims were based on the same distribution contract and, although they were not worded identically, they both concerned the validity of the agreement. The judge also took into consideration that, if he did not stay the proceedings, his judgment would never be recognized in Italy, on the basis of Art. 27(3).

As the jurisdiction of the Italian judge had been contested by the Belgian distributor, the judge stayed its proceedings until the jurisdiction of the Italian judge was established.

Case principle

2. Copyright actions relating to different territories do not involve the same cause of action.

Case

Court of First Instance of Brussels, 20 March 1992, Journal des Tribunaux **30**
(1992) 48

Facts

The plaintiff, the copyright owner of a record, sued an alleged copyright infringer, requesting an injunction prohibiting the reproduction of the record by the defendant in Belgium and compensation from the alleged infringer. The same claims had previously been introduced in France, where the injunction was to cover the French territory. The defendant questioned the jurisdiction of the Belgian judge and asked him to stay the proceedings on the basis of Art. 21.

Judgment

The judge considered that there was not the same 'cause of action' between the two proceedings. He stated that, because of the principle of territoriality in copyright law, a judge is not allowed to issue a judgment with cross-border effects. Furthermore, the amount of money claimed in each country differed considerably (750000 French francs in France and 1000000 Belgian francs in Belgium).

Comment

Although the conditions of *lis pendens* seemed to have been fulfilled, the judge decided not to stay the proceedings, on the basis of a substantive issue: the inability of Belgian judges to adjudicate on foreign copyrights (but see Case 397 *infra*).

> " . . . *shall of its own motion stay its proceedings* . . . "

Case principle

Article 21 held inapplicable to ancillary, provisional measures.

Case

31   Court of First Instance of Brussels, 28 December 1994, Actualités Divorce (1995) 76

Facts

A Greek woman requested provisional maintenance from her husband, also of Greek nationality. Prior to the Belgian proceedings, the husband had started divorce proceedings and had requested provisional measures before the Court of Grand Instance of Athens, both of which were still pending.

Judgment

Before considering whether the *lis pendens* exception applied, the judge examined his own jurisdiction to hear the case. Although the status, legal capacity and rights in property arising out of a matrimonial relationship are excluded from the Convention, ancillary provisional measures requested in the framework of proceedings dealing principally with those issues (*i.e.* divorce proceedings) may fall within the scope of application of the Convention (see *supra, Comment* on Art. 1(2), para. 1). Indeed, the judge considered that he had jurisdiction to decide upon urgent provisional measures with respect to the provisional maintenance and other claims on status matters and matrimonial property. It has to be stressed that the Belgian judge could adjudicate on the basis of the Convention only with respect to the maintenance claim. The judge did not apply Art. 21 to the ancillary provisional measures.

Comment

The Belgian judge should have applied the *lis pendens* rule contained in the Convention to proceedings which were ancillary, not merely provisional. As the Greek court had been seised prior to his Belgian colleague, the latter had to decline jurisdiction in favour of the Greek court.

> **ARTICLE 22, PARAGRAPH 2**
>
> " . . . *court first seised has jurisdiction over both actions.*"

Case principle

Article 22, para. 2 does not *confer* jurisdiction.

Case

32   Commercial Court of Antwerpen, 29 June 1994, Tijdschrift Voor Belgisch Handelsrecht (1995) 429

Facts

The plaintiff sued two defendants for an amount of money, corresponding to the price which had to be paid for the shipping of goods from Antwerp to Damman and Dubai. The shipping order was given by one of the defendants, acting as maritime agent of an English company. The agent, whose domicile was located in Germany, paid only part of the agreed price and issued a documentary credit to guarantee the payment of the rest. This amount was never paid and the issuing bank (the second defendant), whose corporate seat was also in Germany, refused to pay it because, according to the bank, the conditions agreed upon in the documentary credit had not been met.

Judgment

The defendants challenged the jurisdiction of the Belgian courts. With respect to the first defendant, the Belgian judge had jurisdiction on the basis of Art. 5(1), because the parties had agreed that the shipping price would be paid in Antwerp.

With respect to the bank, it was difficult to determine the place of performance of the obligation arising out of the documentary credit. The bank's decision to grant a documentary credit was a unilateral act. This did not imply that Art. 5(1) was inapplicable, because, according to the judge, one had to locate the unilateral act within the framework of the different contractual relationships. Thus, it was the court in Germany, where the corporate seat of the bank was located, which would be competent on the basis of Art. 5(1).

Incidentally, the judge also investigated whether he might have jurisdiction with respect to the bank on the basis of Art. 22. Unlike the equivalent head of jurisdiction in Belgian law, Art. 22 did not *grant* jurisdiction, as the European Court of Justice stated in *Elefanten Schuh*, and only applied to cases where the judge had jurisdiction on other grounds with respect to both claims. The judge concluded, therefore, that he lacked jurisdiction with respect to the bank.

ARTICLE 22, PARAGRAPH 3

" . . . so closely connected . . . "

Case principle

Article 6a limitation proceedings are related to a liability action.

Case

Commercial Court of Antwerpen, 9 March 1989, Rechtspraak Van de Haven **33** Van Antwerpen (1989) 285

Facts

After a ship collision in the port of Antwerp, one shipowner brought a liability claim before the German judge against the other shipowner. The latter applied for limitation of liability in the courts of Antwerp.

Judgment

The Belgian judge, seised under Art. 6a, decided to stay the proceedings on the basis of Art. 22 until the jurisdiction of the German judge was established. He considered that the mere existence of Art. 6a as a head of jurisdiction was sufficient to prove that there was a close connection between the two proceedings and that there was a risk of irreconcilable judgments if the actions were not brought before the same judge.

ARTICLE 24

" . . . *as may be available under the law of that State* . . . "

Case principle

Requirements of grant, such as urgency, are for applicable law of the forum.

Case

34 Commercial Court of Hasselt, 20 September 1996, Tijdschrift Voor Belgisch Handelsrecht (1997) 323

Facts

The plaintiff, a Belgium company, applied under Art. 24 for appointment of an expert. The expert had to evaluate the quality of the wall mounting systems for radiators. Those systems were supplied by the defendant, a German company, to the plaintiff, who claimed that the wall mounting system was defective and caused the radiators to fall off the walls.

Judgment

The judge considered that the plaintiff had sufficiently proven the urgent nature of the request and therefore based his jurisdiction on Art. 24. He designated an expert who had to accomplish the above mentioned tasks and to help the parties to reach an agreement on due compensation.

Comment

Belgian judges frequently require urgency in order to admit jurisdiction on the basis of Art. 24 (see, for another example, Court of Appeal of Mons,

2 February 1988, Tijdschrift voor Belgisch Handelsrecht (1989) 198). Although Art. 24 does not impose an 'urgency condition', Belgian judges seem to understand that such condition, which would apply in an internal situation on the basis of Art. 584 of the Belgian Code of Civil Procedure, is also necessary in the framework of the Convention.

Case

Court of Appeal of Gent, 8 December 1994, Algemeen Juridisch Tijdschrift **35** (1995–96) 151

Facts

Parties were bound by an agreement which referred to the 'General Conditions of the Metal and Electromechanical Industry'. An arbitration clause was contained in these General Conditions.

A dispute arose between the parties and the plaintiff, at first instance, asked the Belgian judge to designate an expert on the basis of Art. 24 of the Convention. The judge decided that he had no jurisdiction to hear the case.

Judgment

On appeal, the court confirmed the first judge's opinion. According to the court, the designation of an expert generally falls within the scope of application of Art. 24, even when the merits of the case are submitted to arbitration. Nevertheless, two essential elements were missing in the present case: the urgency requirement (see previous judgment) and the territoriality principle. The judge declared that he had no jurisdiction to designate an expert whose functions would be performed exclusively outside Belgian territory.

Comment

In the light of the judgment of the European Court of Justice in *Denilauler*, the Belgian judge might have applied the principle of territoriality too strictly. In *Denilauler*, the French judge was allowed to issue an order authorizing the creditor to freeze the account of the debtor in German territory. By way of analogy, the Belgian judge could have designated an expert whose work was to be performed in other countries.

ARTICLE 26

" . . . shall be recognized . . . "

Case principle

Judgment-State effects must be implemented in the recognition-State.

Case

36 Commercial Court of Liège, 8 March 1984, Jurisprudence de Liège (1984) 289

Facts

A French company, A, had sold an industrial machine to a Belgian company, C. The seller had bought the machine from another French company, B, which it represented in Belgium. The machine appeared not to work as had been promised. C refused to pay the remainder of the price and asked a French court to declare the contract void and to award him damages for breach of contract. A asked the same court to order payment. It also sued B on a guarantee. The French court found that A was responsible for the breach of contract. It declared the contract void, awarded C damages and held B liable as guarantor for the damages owed by A to C. However, B had contractually limited his liability to 5 per cent of any damages. A lodged an appeal in Cassation against this judgment. B brought a new action in Belgium, claiming the price it had charged A, minus what it owed him, *i.e.* 5 per cent of the damages awarded to C.

Judgment

The court held that B was prevented from suing A in Belgium. The French decision was to be automatically recognized in Belgium. This meant that the foreign judgment must in principle have the same effects in the state in which enforcement was sought as it did in the state in which judgment was given. The Court decided that the actual effects of this recognition lay outside the Convention's sphere and within that of the applicable national law. As it was impossible to give an autonomous definition of these effects on a European level, the court held that the national law of the country of origin had to be applied in order to determine those effects. Applying the national law of the state in which recognition was sought could lead to giving more effects to a foreign judgment than the judgment-State's law would.

Comment

Note *Hoffmann v Krieg*, Case 145/86 in the European Court. See too: Court of First Instance of Brussels, 31 October 1973, Rechtskundig Weekblad (1973–74) 881; Court of First Instance of Brussels, 28 April 1987, Pasicrisie Belge (1987) III 80; Court of First Instance of Brussels, 3 April 1995, Actualités du Droit (1996) 173.

ARTICLE 27

"A judgment shall not be recognized . . . "

Case principle

The onus of proof is upon the opponent of enforcement to establish one of the refusal grounds, not upon the applicant for enforcement to disprove these once raised.

Case

Court of Cassation, 16 June 1988, Journal des Tribunaux (1989) 277   **37**

Facts

One party sought enforcement of a foreign judgment in Belgium. A lower court granted leave to enforce. The other party appealed its decision. Before the Court of Appeal this party simply argued that the foreign decision did not meet the test of Art. 27(4), without specifying why. The party seeking enforcement did not bother to prove that this allegation was wrong. The Court of Appeal held that enforcement could not be granted because the party seeking enforcement had not shown that the decision of the State of origin did not conflict with a rule of Belgian private international law. This party lodged an appeal in Cassation.

Judgment

The Court of Cassation quashed the appeal judgment. The court held that the grounds of refusal of the Convention were to operate in a negative way: enforcement was the Convention rule and refusal thereof the exception, to be established against the applicant. The Court of Appeal had in fact done the contrary and rejected the appeal because the party seeking enforcement had not established that the conditions for enforcement were fulfilled.

Comment

For a similar statement as to the onus of proof that conditions for enforcement are met, see Court of First Instance, 12 April 1988, Tijdschrift voor Belgisch Burgerlijk Recht (1989) 422.

ARTICLE 27(1)

" . . . *contrary to public policy* . . . "

Case principle

1. Attachment of maintenance amount to variations in minimum wage scale held not contrary to Belgian public policy.

Case

38   Court of Appeal of Liège, 17 May 1984, Jurisprudence de Liège (1984) 381

Facts

A French court had divorced two people and granted maintenance to one of them in 1969. In 1977, another French court changed the maintenance order. The maintenance-creditor sought enforcement of those two decisions in Belgium. The debtor argued that the revised order was contrary to Belgian public policy in that the amount granted could vary according to the legal minimum wage.

Judgment

The court held that the maintenance order was in no way contrary to Belgian public policy. The first court had decided that the debtor owed maintenance. The only variable element was the amount, and no arbitrary increases were to be feared, as an objective point of reference had been established.

Case principle

2.   Stay of an enforcement action pending criminal proceedings on same facts held to be limited to domestic Belgian proceedings, and not to extend to foreign civil proceedings.

Case

39   Court of Cassation, 14 June 1985, Pasicrisie Belge (1985) I 1323

Facts

The applicant had been ordered by the Landgericht of Duisburg in Germany to pay the German state damages in the sum of 240000 German DM. The acts at the basis of the action were also a criminal offence according to Belgian law. The criminal case was still pending before a Belgian criminal court. The German government asked the Court of First Instance of Antwerp to grant leave of enforcement, which the court did. The plaintiff applied to Cassation to set aside the order of the lower court. He argued that the German decision was contrary to Belgian public policy in that it violated the principle *le criminel tient le civil en état*, whereby civil trials concerning facts that were at the same time criminal offences, are to be stayed until the criminal court decides on the criminal case.

Judgment

The Court of Cassation held that this particular aspect of public policy was limited to the Belgian legal order. The judgment did not violate public policy interpreted in this way.

Case principle

3. Awards of lawyers' costs is not against Belgian public policy, even though Belgian courts would be unable to make such an order.

Case

Court of Appeal of Gent, 22 December 1988, Pasicrisie Belge (1989) II 162 **40**

Facts

A German party successfully sued a Belgian citizen in Germany. As is customary in Germany, the German court awarded the German plaintiff the right to recover the lawyers' costs from the defendant. The German party sought enforcement of this decision in Belgium. The Belgian defendant claimed that it would be contrary to Belgian public policy to grant a plaintiff this relief, since Belgian courts cannot order reimbursement of lawyers' fees and costs, according to Art. 1018 Code of Civil Procedure.

Judgment

The court held that enforcement would not violate Belgian public policy. This would not even discriminate between Belgian and German citizens since all parties, including Belgian nationals, who instituted proceedings in Germany, could recover their costs.

Case principle

4. *Effects* of foreign judgment, not mere *content*, must be against public policy in the recognition-State for recognition to be refused.

Case

Court of First Instance of Liège, 9 October 1995, Actualités du Droit (1996) 80 **41**

Facts

The parties concluded a contract in 1970 whereby a German manufacturer granted exclusive distribution rights to a Belgian company. In 1989, the German manufacturer decided to rescind the contract. The Belgian distributor refused to pay for goods which had already been delivered. The German party sued in Germany. The defendant claimed that the Belgian Act of 1961 was applicable and asked to be compensated for the insufficient notice of termination. The German court gave judgment in favour of the German company, upheld on appeal. The German company applied for enforcement in Belgium.

Judgment

The court held that there was nothing contrary to public policy in enforcing the German judgment. The concept of public policy should, according to the court, be a matter for the national legal order of the state where recognition or enforcement was sought. The court added that the concept of public policy must, under the Convention, be interpreted very strictly in the light of the mutual trust between the different Member states. This was reinforced by the fact that the Convention was only applicable in civil and commercial matters, where the Member States were linked by common fundamental legal conceptions. According to the judges, the public policy ground ought only to operate 'in the most exceptional cases'. The court held finally that the fact that the German court did not apply the Belgian Act of 1961 was not as such a violation of Belgian public policy. This was because the serious inconsistency with public policy must result, not from the *content* of the decision and the rules applied therein, but from the *effects* which it would have in Belgian territory as a result of its enforcement there.

Comment

See, for other cases on the public policy exception: Court of First Instance of Brussels, 28 April 1987, Pasicrisie Belge (1987) III 80; Court of First Instance of Brussels, 2 June 1988, Jurisprudence de Liège, Mons et Bruxelles (1988) 1365. The due process requirement is sometimes held to be part of the public policy test: Commercial Court of Liège, 8 March 1984, Jurisprudence de Liège (1984) 289.

ARTICLE 27(3)

" . . . *irreconcilable* . . . "

Case principle

Irreconcilability for Art. 27(3) entails mutually exclusive legal consequences.

Case

42   Court of First Instance of Brussels, 12 April 1988, Tijdschrift Voor Belgisch Burgerlijk Recht (1989) 422

Facts

An Italian company sought enforcement of two Italian judgments, dating from 1978 and 1984, whereby a Belgian company had been ordered to pay damages for failure to perform a contract. Litigation between the parties had started in 1967. Belgian courts had rendered judgments in 1967, 1971 and 1972. Those decisions declared that the contract between the parties was invalid and awarded the Belgian party damages.

Judgment

The court held that the Belgian and the Italian decisions were irreconcilable. In order to ascertain whether the two judgments were irreconcilable, it should be examined whether they entailed legal consequences which were mutually exclusive. This was the case, as the Italian courts had awarded damages for breach of a contract which had been declared invalid by the Belgian courts. The court observed that Art. 27 did not require that the judgment given in the State in which recognition was sought should be earlier in time than the decision of which recognition was sought.

Comment

It has never explicitly been required for the application of this refusal ground that the national decision be rendered earlier than the foreign judgment. Nonetheless, in the case of *Hoffmann v Krieg*, Case 145/86, the European Court noted that the national decision had already acquired force of *res judicata* at the time the order for enforcement of the foreign decision was issued. This shows that national courts should at least pay attention to the time factor when deciding whether or not decisions are irreconcilable.

ARTICLE 28, PARAGRAPH 3

" . . . *jurisdiction of the court of the State of origin may not be reviewed* . . . "

Case principle

Jurisdiction review is not permitted even where the foreign ruling itself was as to jurisdiction.

Case

Commercial Court of Brussels, 29 March 1988, Tijdschrift Voor Belgisch **43** Handelsrecht (1990) 800

Facts

This case involved unilateral termination of a contract of exclusive distributorship. The German manufacturer had taken the precaution of requesting the German Landgericht to rule that it did not owe any compensation to the Belgian distributor. This was meant to prevent Belgian courts from asserting jurisdiction in the case. The German court decided that it had no jurisdiction to rule on the case, since the contract was to be performed in Belgium (Art. 5(1)). The distributor then sued its German counterpart before a Belgian court. This court examined whether or not it should recognize the German decision. The manufacturer claimed that the Landgericht had wrongly decided that it had no jurisdiction. The object of the dispute was not only fair compensation in the absence of a reasonable notice of termination, but also the additional compensation provided by Art. 3 of the Belgian Act of 1961. This last compensation was an autonomous obligation to be performed in Germany. The first compensation was not an autonomous obligation but, under Belgian law, an obligation replacing the unperformed contractual obligation. Therefore, this obligation had to be located at the place where the unperformed obligation had to be performed, *i.e.* Belgium. The German court could have declared that it had jurisdiction in respect of the second claim of the Belgian plaintiff, but the Landgericht had declined to do so.

Judgment

The court decided that the decision whereby the Landgericht declared that it had no jurisdiction, should be recognized without any special procedure being required (Art. 26). Further, it held that it had no power whatsoever to review the jurisdiction of the court of the state of origin. The court decided that it could not inquire upon this matter, because Art. 5(1) was not part of the exceptions foreseen in Art. 28. In an *obiter dictum*, the court added that the Landgericht was not wrong when it held that all claims had to be brought before the court where the main obligation had to be performed, *i.e.* in Belgium. The Landgericht had actually applied the ruling in *Shenavai v Kreischer* without mentioning it.

Comment

The duty to recognize judgments given in other Member States also covers decisions whereby a court declares that it has no jurisdiction, even though only an incorrect application of the Convention's rules leads to this conclusion—provided that the matter does not fall under s.3, 4 or 5 of Title II.

ARTICLE 29

"Under no circumstances . . . "

Case principle

1. Review of factors taken into account in granting an amount of maintenance is prohibited.

Case

44 Court of Appeal of Liège, 17 May 1984, Jurisprudence de Liège (1984) 381

Facts

A French court had divorced two people and granted maintenance to one of them in 1969. In 1977, another French court changed the maintenance order.

The maintenance-creditor sought enforcement of those two decisions in Belgium. The debtor argued that the maintenance was unreasonable in view of his income. He also claimed that the original judge had been influenced, when calculating the maintenance, by the fact that the debtor had since then remarried. The debtor claimed that the maintenance was granted in part as a penalty for his second marriage and, as such, violated the freedom of marriage.

Judgment

The court held that to adjudicate upon the debtor's allegations would amount to a prohibited review of the substance of the case.

Comment

The fact that a judge does not take the debtor's income into account when calculating the maintenance could, in some exceptional cases, be held to be contrary to public policy. The line between the (forbidden) review of the substance of the case and the (permitted) examination of such contravention of public policy is a thin one.

Case principle

2.   Review is even prohibited where the allegation is that the judgment-court decided in contravention of the EC Treaty.

Case

Court of First Instance of Liège, 9 October 1995, Actualités du Droit (1996) 80   **45**

Facts

See supra, Art. 27(1), Case 41.

Judgment

Besides the public policy exception, the Belgian plaintiff claimed that the German court had applied a legal provision (s.92 of the German Handelsgesetzbuch) which was contrary to the prohibition of discrimination on the ground of nationality (Art. 6 of the EC Treaty). The Belgian court held that it had no power to review the substance of the case in order to assess whether the provision was, as alleged, contrary to European rules.

Comment

On the lack of power to review the substance of the original decision, see also Commercial Court of Antwerp, 19 October 1978, Rechtspraak van Haven van Antwerpen (1979–80) 184; Court of First Instance of Brussels, 12 April 1988, Tijdschrift voor Belgisch Burgerlijk Recht (1989) 422; Court of First Instance of Brussels, 3 April 1995, Actualités du Droit (1996) 173.

ARTICLE 30

" . . . *may stay* . . . "

Case principle

Stay of enforcement is discretionary, not mandatory.

Case

46   Commercial Court of Liège, 8 March 1984, Jurisprudence de Liège (1984) 289

Facts

See supra, Art. 26, Case 36.

Judgment

The court held that the appeal in Cassation constituted an '*ordinary appeal*' in the sense of Art. 30. It noted that a stay of proceedings was not a duty but a mere possibility for the national court. None of the parties had asked the court to stay the proceedings, because they wanted to speed up the litigation. In order to decide whether or not to stay the proceedings, the court examined the different claims so as to see whether the appeal in Cassation could have any influence on these claims. The court came to the conclusion that there was no reason to stay the proceedings.

Comment

Belgian courts sometimes forget the possibilities offered by Arts 30 and 38 of the Convention! In one judgment, the Court of Appeal of Liège held that if an appeal had been lodged against the foreign judgment, of which enforcement was sought, this would in no way be an obstacle to granting leave to enforce (Court of Appeal of Liège, 25 January 1984, Jurisprudence de Liège (1984) 113). In another instance, the Court of First Instance of Brussels neglected altogether to consider the effects of an appeal pending against the French judgment it declared enforceable (Court of First Instance of Brussels, 3 April 1995, Actualités du Droit (1996) 173). In one case, a court refused to stay the proceedings because the original judgment appeared to have been well-founded, so that it was highly unlikely that it would be overturned on appeal: Court of First Instance of Nivelles, 23 June 1993, Revue Trimestrielle de Droit Familial (1995) 70. The nature of the proceedings (enforcement of maintenance orders, where any delay can be catastrophic for the plaintiff) also explains why some courts do not use the possibility offered by the Convention.

ARTICLE 39

" . . . *no measures of enforcement may be taken other than protective . . .* "

Case principle

Article 39 provisional powers held also to extend to judgment-court measures pending the enforcement-appeal.

Case

Court of First Instance of Brussels, 23 November 1987, Revue Régionale de Droit (1988) 96   **47**

Facts

A company with its corporate seat in France had been ordered by the Court of Appeal of Brussels to pay a considerable amount of money to a Belgian company as compensation for the lack of notice on termination of an exclusive distribution contract between them. The defendant did not pay and the plaintiff started enforcement proceedings in France and also attempted to execute his judgment in Belgium. The defendant opposed French enforcement, under Arts 36 and 37 of the Convention. A seizure on some properties of the defendant was authorized by the French judge on the basis of Art. 39. The Belgian company, nevertheless, considering that this seizure only guaranteed part of the debt, asked the *Belgian* judge to order a seizure on other properties located on Belgian territory. The debtor considered that this was not possible on the basis of Art. 39 which only allowed the plaintiff to take measures guaranteeing the enforcement in the country where the enforcement was requested.

Judgment

The judge considered that the drafters of Arts 38 and 39 could not have meant that protective measures were excluded in the country where the judgment was rendered. The fact that a seizure was authorized in France covering part of a debt did not affect the jurisdiction of the Belgian judge to order a new seizure.

Comment

In the majority of cases, Art. 39 is used to order seizures in the country where enforcement is sought (see, for instance, Court of First Instance of Brussels, 29 July 1993, Journal des Tribunaux (1994) 251). In this particular case, however, the judge provided an extensive interpretation of Art. 39. In his observations on the judgment, H. Born underlines the necessity of bringing a similar case to the Court of Justice so that the scope of application of this provision is clearly determined.

ARTICLE 47(1)

" . . . *documents which establish that . . . the judgment . . . has been served;"*

Case principle

The very fact of the debtor's appeal against enforcement held to amount to proof that the foreign judgment was served, in the absence of required documentary evidence.

Case

48   Court of First Instance of Tournai, 21 February 1991, Jurisprudence de Liège, Mons et Bruxelles (1991) 691

Facts

The Belgian company Promac was ordered by French courts to pay a sum of money to the French company Sogeservice. The latter had filed an application for enforcement before the Belgian judge. This application had been served upon the corporate seat of Promac. Under Art. 36, Promac opposed enforcement on the ground that Sogeservice had not produced the documents required under Art. 47(1).

Judgment

Copies of three documents had been annexed to the application for enforcement: the judgment of the French judge, the appeal introduced before the French judge and the order for seizure granted by the French judge. Although Sogeservice had not presented a document establishing that the judgment had been served, the fact that Promac had lodged an appeal against this judgment was considered to be sufficient proof that the judgment had been correctly served upon Promac.

Comment

This decision appears to indicate that the essence of this part of the requirements under Art. 47(1) is service of the judgment rather than the production of documentary proof thereof.

" . . . *according to the law of the State of origin* . . . "

Case principle

Service must have complied with one or more methods of service of the judg-ment-State's law.

Case

Court of Cassation, 23 September 1994, Arresten Van Het Hof Van Cassatie   **49**
(1994) 779

Facts

The representative (*vertegenwoordiger*) of a Belgian company was served with a German judgment against the company. The judgment had to be executed in Belgium. At first and second instance, the judges considered that the conditions of Art. 47(1) had been fulfilled. The Belgian company appealed further to the Court of Cassation, as it considered that serving the company through its representative was not in conformity with the law of the State in which the judgment was given, that is, Germany.

Judgment

According to the court, the judgment in the State of origin had not been prop-erly served upon the defendant. The Court of Cassation examined several German mechanisms to serve a judgment upon a foreign defendant and con-cluded that service on a representative was not a valid method of service abroad. Therefore, the conditions imposed in Art. 47(1) were not fulfilled. (Nevertheless, the Court of Cassation did not revoke the authorization of enforcement of the judgment, because it considered that the Belgian party had failed to state which specific provision of German law was infringed and there-fore, the appeal in Cassation was inadmissible.)

Comment

From the viewpoint of the Convention, it is noteworthy to stress that serving a representative of the company is not sufficient to fulfil the requirements of Art. 47(1) when the judgment-State is Germany.
  (As for the inadmissibility of the appeal in Cassation, the Belgian company had mentioned in its appeal several provisions in the bilateral treaty between Germany and Belgium, as well as Art. IV of the Protocol annexed to the Convention, neither of which mentioned the possibility of serving the compa-ny's representative. As those provisions are part of German law, one wonders whether the Court of Cassation was not too strict on the assessment of the Cassation grounds?)

> ## ARTICLE 52, PARAGRAPH 1
>
> *" . . . the Court shall apply its internal law."*

Case principle

1.   Internal law chooses between different rules on domicile.

Case

50   Justice of Peace of Brussels, 27 July 1990, Journal Des Juges De Paix (1990) 396

Facts

In 1978, a French court had divorced two French nationals. The woman claimed before a Belgian Justice of the Peace the payment of maintenance for her son. The defendant, a European civil servant, argued that he had a residence in Belgium, but that he was domiciled in France, where all claims therefore had to be brought.

Judgment

The Justice of the Peace referred to Art. 36 of the Code of Civil Procedure, according to which a person is domiciled where he is registered with the local authorities. As the defendant was not subject to the obligation to register, being employed by the European Community, the judge used the subsidiary definition of domicile (Art. 102 of the Civil Code) and found that the defendant had his principal establishment in Brussels. Jurisdiction was therefore established.

Case principle

2.   Effect of election of domicile for jurisdiction is for *lex fori*.

Case

51   Commercial Court of Antwerp, 30 June 1987, Rechtspraak Van Haven Van Antwerpen (1987) 57

Facts

The defendant, a German company, had carried goods for a third party from Antwerp to Greece. The goods were damaged during the trip. The buyer, holder of a bill of lading, claimed damages. The defendant argued that German courts had jurisdiction, as agreed in the bill of lading.

Judgment

The court set aside the jurisdiction clause appearing in the bill of lading because under Belgian law the holder of the bill of lading did not succeed to the rights and obligations of the shipper (see *supra*, Art. 17). More interestingly, it decided that its jurisdiction was also based on the domicile of the defendant. The defendant had given an address for service of process in Belgium. The court considered that this circumstance showed that the defendant had, as far as the proceedings were concerned, its domicile in Belgium.

Comment

The court should have applied its rules of private international law under Art. 53, para. 1 in order to determine where the defendant company had its seat. It would probably have found that the seat was located in Germany.

ARTICLE 54, PARAGRAPH 2

" . . . or in a convention concluded between the State of origin and the State addressed which was in force when the proceedings were instituted."

Case

Court of First Instance of Brussels, 12 April 1988, Tijdschrift Voor Belgisch **52** Burgerlijk Recht (1989) 422

Facts

An Italian company sought enforcement of two Italian judgments whereby a Belgian company had been ordered to pay damages. The defendant argued that the Convention's rules were not applicable, since the litigation was started in 1969, *i.e.* before the entry into force of the Convention.

Judgment

The court held that Convention Title III was applicable. The judgments were given in Italy after the entry into force of the Convention, *i.e.* in 1978 and 1984. Further, the judgment-court based its jurisdiction on Art. 2(5) of the Belgian-Italian Convention of 6 April 1962. Accordingly, jurisdiction had been based on a convention in force between the two States concerned when the proceedings were instituted. The court also noted incidentally that the jurisdiction ground of this bilateral convention, on the basis of which the original court heard the action, was similar to Art. 5(1) of the Convention.

**ANNEXED PROTOCOL/LUGANO PROTOCOL NO. 1
ARTICLE I, PARAGRAPH 2**

" . . . expressly and specifically so agreed."

Case principle

The jurisdiction clause with the Luxembourg party need not be contained in a separate document for it to be effective in accordance with Art. I, para. 2 and *Porta-Leasing.*

Case

53 Court of Appeal of Liège, 16 June 1992, Jurisprudence de Liège, Mons, Bruxelles (1992) 1397

Facts

A Luxembourg company had agreed to a jurisdiction clause in favour of Belgian courts. At the trial, it submitted that the clause did not fulfil the special conditions of Art. I.

Judgment

The court held that a jurisdiction clause has to be the object of a specific agreement which is expressly and specifically concerned with jurisdiction and specifically signed by the Luxembourg party. The mere signing of the contract is not sufficient, even if the jurisdiction clause has been specifically identified (underlined or printed in heavy type). The court decided, however, that it was not necessary that the specific agreement should be contained in a separate document from the one which constituted the written instrument of the contract. An express agreement, a specific provision of the contract specifically devoted to the clause, was sufficient.

Comment

See also Court of Appeal of Gent, 17 March 1988, Tijdschrift voor Gentse Rechtspraak (1988) 60; Commercial Court of Hasselt, 13 November 1991, Tijdschrift voor Belgisch Handelsrecht (1992) 897; Court of First Instance of Arlon, 10 April 1992, Tijdschrift voor Belgisch Burgerlijk Recht (1993) 281; Justice of the Peace of Brussels, 28 February 1991, Tijdschrift van de vrede- en politierechters (1992) 154.

3

DENMARK

Torben Svenné Schmidt

A.   LEGAL SYSTEM

Courts

The ordinary courts in Denmark are divided into three instances. At the bottom are the 82 towncourts (*byretter*). In most of these there is a single legally qualified judge, but the Towncourt of Copenhagen consists of a president and 41 judges. The four next biggest towns also have a president and various numbers of judges and other bigger towns have four, three or two judges. However, in civil cases, only a single judge sits on the bench.

Appeals from the towncourts go to one of the two High Courts for the eastern and western part of Denmark (*Østre Landsret* and *Vestre Landsret*). These courts consist of a president and 45 and 22 judges, respectively. In each civil case, the court is staffed by three judges. The High Courts may also be courts of first instance under certain circumstances—for instance, when a case is of a fundamental character or has a special far-reaching importance for one of the parties, the towncourt may refer the case to the High Court. Furthermore, and this is more important, if a civil case concerns a claim having a value of over 500000 Danish crowns (approximately £50000) each of the parties may demand that it is referred to the High Court as first instance.

The Supreme Court (*Højesteret*) consists of a president and 15 judges. In most cases, the court is staffed by five judges but a higher number of judges may be prescribed by the president. This court is an appellate court from the High Courts, but, contrary to the arrangement in many other countries, the Supreme Court may, in civil cases, consider both the facts and the law applied by the High Court. If a case is started at a towncourt, it may only be brought before the Supreme Court as third instance if a special authority (*Procesbevillingsnævnet*) permits it on application by one of the parties.

Besides the ordinary courts, Denmark has a special Maritime and Commercial Court (*Sø- og Handelsretten*) in Copenhagen in which the judge is assisted by two or four experts in maritime or commercial matters. Appeals from this court go directly to the Supreme Court.

In each towncourt there is a Sheriff's Court (*Fogedret*) which handles the enforcement of judgments. The sheriff is the towncourt judge or, usually, one of his legally educated deputies. In connection with the Judgments Convention, the Sheriff's Court is of importance, as the application under Art. 31 for obtaining a Danish enforcement order in respect of a foreign judgment must be made to the Sheriff's Court for the place where the judgment debtor lives or resides or, if he does not live or reside in Denmark, where he has assets.

Danish judgments are published in *Ugeskrift for Retsvæsen*. This weekly periodical publishes most Supreme Court judgments (together with the judgments of the lower court or courts in the case), and a selected number of judgments from the High Courts and the Maritime and Commercial Court.

B. IMPLEMENTATION OF THE CONVENTIONS

The Judgments Convention, as amended by the Accession Conventions of 1978 and 1982, has been in force in Denmark (with the exception of the Faroe Islands and Greenland) since 1 November 1986. In connection with Denmark's ratification of the Convention, a Danish statute, No. 325 of 4 June 1986, was passed. According to s.1 of this statute, the Convention and the 1971 Protocol on the interpretation of the Convention are in force in Denmark. The following paragraphs of the statute give detailed rules for the implementation of the Convention, especially for the enforcement of decisions from the other Contracting States. These rules are in accordance with the Convention.

Denmark has from 1 March 1996, ratified the San Sebastian Convention of 1989 and the Lugano Convention of 1988 between the EU and the European Free Trade Association.

C. ABBREVIATIONS

In this chapter, the following abbreviations are used:

CISG: United Nations Convention on Contracts for the International Sale of Goods
E.C.R.: European Court reports
H: Judgment of the Danish Supreme Court (Højesteret)

SH: Judgment of the Maritime and Commercial Court of Copenhagen (Só- og Handelsretten)
UfR: Ugeskrift for Retsvæsen (the Danish Law Reports)
VL: Judgment of the Danish Western High Court (Vestre Landsret)
ØL: Judgment of the Danish Eastern High Court (Østre Landsret)

D.   CASES

ARTICLE 1(1)

" . . . *civil and commercial matters* . . . "

Case principle

Litigation must have commenced for the Convention to apply.

Case

UfR (1991) 594 VL   **54a**

Facts and judgment

An application to a court for expert appraisal before a lawsuit cannot be characterized or compared with proceedings in civil or commercial matters. Accordingly, the jurisdiction rules of the Convention do not apply to such an application.

ARTICLE 1(2)(1)

" . . . *wills and succession* . . . "

Case principle

Partition agreement between heirs not an excluded matter of succession.

Case

UfR (1995) 647 H   **54b**

Facts

In 1979, in connection with the partition of the considerable estate of a Danish man who died in 1978, his wife A and their son B entered into an agreement according to which B placed an amount of 12 million Dkr. at the disposal of A and further promised to pay her for life a monthly amount of 50000 Dkr. (falling later to 25000 Dkr.). A, who now lived in Monaco, asserted that B, who was domiciled in Italy, had failed to fulfil the agreement and sued B in

Denmark. A was of the opinion that as the case concerned a matter of succession it was according to Art. 1(2)(1) not covered by the Judgments Convention and that the Danish court had jurisdiction according to s.246(3) in the Danish Code of Procedure (mentioned in Art. 3(2) of the Judgments Convention as an exorbitant ground of jurisdiction) because B had property in Denmark.

Judgment

The Eastern High Court held that although the cause of the agreement was a death and the partition of the estate, the agreement's content went far wider than a usual partition of an estate. The case was a civil case covered by the Convention and not a case of succession. Accordingly, as the defendant was domiciled in another Contracting State, the Danish court had no jurisdiction. The Supreme Court affirmed the High Court's decision and found it unnecessary to ask for an interpretation from the European Court.

ARTICLE 1, PARAGRAPH 2(2)

"Bankruptcy . . . "

Case principle

1. Proceedings to set aside transactions in fraud of creditors held excluded matter of bankruptcy.

Case

55   UfR (1990) 124 VL

Facts

A Danish estate in bankruptcy had sued a German company in order to have the debtor's transaction with the company set aside. The plaintiff claimed that the court had jurisdiction because the German company had property in Denmark. The defendant pleaded that the court should decline jurisdiction as it was not in accordance with the Convention.

Judgment

The court found that it had jurisdiction as the case, according to Art. 1(2)(2), was excluded from the Convention. In this connection the court referred to the European Court's decision in *Gourdain v Nadler*, Case 133/78.

Case principle

2. Bankrupt's claim to set-off against creditor held excluded matter of bankruptcy.

Case

UfR (1991) 348 VL   **56**

Facts

A Danish company was in bankruptcy. During the examination by a Danish bankruptcy court of a claim raised by a German creditor, the estate acknowledged the claim, but put forward a claim for set-off. The German creditor denied the jurisdiction of the bankruptcy court to handle the claim for set-off.

Judgment

Both the bankruptcy court and, on appeal, the High Court held that according to Art. 1(2)(2) the claim for set-off was not covered by the Convention and that the claim could be handled by the bankruptcy court according to Danish international jurisdiction rules.

ARTICLE 5(1)

" . . . *obligation in question* . . . "

Case principle

1. Obligation to give reasonable notice is the obligation in question in action for wrongful termination of exclusive distribution agreement.

Case

UfR (1991) 244 SH   **57**

Facts

A Danish exclusive distributor of the goods of a German firm brought an action against the firm for damages due to the firm's cancellation of the contract without notice. The defendant denied that the parties had made a contract regarding exclusive distribution, but it was shown that the plaintiff for a period of 15 years had sold the defendant's goods in Denmark.

Judgment

The court held that the action concerned the obligation to give due notice and that this obligation should be performed in Denmark so that the court had jurisdiction under Art. 5(1).

Comment

Unfortunately, the court did not discuss which law governed the contract, as it ought to have done according to the European Court's decision in *Tessili v*

Dunlop Case 12/76. Indirectly, the Danish court followed the European Court's decision in *Effer v Kantner* Case 38/81, as the court held that there was a contract between the parties although the defendant denied this.

Case principle

2. Obligation in question remains the defendant's, notwithstanding that he makes a counterclaim.

Case

58   UfR (1992) 886 VL

Facts

A Danish seller S sued a German buyer B for the payment of goods delivered. B did not deny owing the money, but denied the jurisdiction of the Danish court as he claimed to have a larger counterclaim, since S, without notice, had cancelled a contract for exclusive distribution. B was of the opinion that it was the place of performance of this counterclaim which was decisive for the application of Art. 5(1).

Judgment

The High Court refused to request the European Court of Justice for an interpretation, as it found that, considering the European Court's former decisions, the case did not raise special questions of interpretation. The court held that the obligation which was the basis of the case was B's obligation to pay the purchase price. To find the place of performance for this obligation, the court held that the contract of sale, according to Danish choice-of-law rules (*i.e.* the Hague Convention of 15 June 1955 on the law applicable to sale of goods) was governed by Danish law as the law of the domicile of the seller, and that the purchase price according to Danish law should be paid at S's place of business so that the case was within the court's jurisdiction. That B had put forward a counterclaim, the existence of which was denied by S, could not lead to another result.

Case

59   UfR (1992) 920 SH

Facts

The parties, a Danish seller S and a German buyer B, had traded with each other for several years. Regarding goods delivered in 1988–89, B asserted that the goods had defects, for which he claimed damages in the action brought before the Danish court in May 1990. After the legal proceedings had started, the parties continued to trade with each other and B had, until October 1991, in accordance with S's standard conditions, paid immediately on every delivery. In January 1992, S again sent an invoice for goods delivered, but in February 1992 B's German lawyer sent a declaration of set-off of this claim against B's claim for damages raised in the still pending lawsuit. During B's lawsuit, S asked for an independent judgment for the invoice claim and for damages for the loss he had suffered by not being punctually paid for the goods. B principally denied that the court had jurisdiction to try S's claims and as a subsidiary plea, B asked for dismissal as he asserted that he was entitled to set-off the invoice claim in his original claim for damages.

Judgment

The court held that it had jurisdiction to try S's invoice claim because the contractual relation between the parties had its closest connection with S's place of business so that the relation was governed by Danish law; and the court had jurisdiction according to Art. 5(1), because, under Danish law, a debt had to be paid at the creditor's place of business. Furthermore, the court held that Art. 5(3) gave it jurisdiction to try S's claim for damages. As the parties had, to a great extent, continued their trade after the dispute in 1989 and as B had, in the period until January 1992, paid for each delivery without asking for a set-off, the court held that B was not entitled without notice to claim set-off. Accordingly, the court gave an independent judgment for S's invoice claim, the amount of which B had not disputed. The treatment of S's claim for damages was postponed until the hearing of the lawsuit raised by B.

Comment

The decision has been criticized not because of its result, but because the court, in order to find out what law governed the contract, did not use the rules of the Hague Convention of 1955 on the applicable law regarding the sale of goods or—as one author presumably rightly has suggested—the rules of United Nations Convention on Contracts for the International Sale of Goods of 1980 (CISG) which, according to its Art. 1(1)(a), was applicable. Regarding the court's application of the Judgments Convention's Art. 5(3) to S's claim for damages for non-payment, it has further been suggested that this claim was not based on tort, but was a contractual claim for damages and accordingly covered by Art. 5(1).

Case principle

3.   Obligation in question is that on which claim is based (*de Bloos*).

Case

UfR (1993) 802 ØL   **60**

Facts

A Danish firm brought an action against an English firm for the payment of software installed in England. The plaintiff asserted that the case concerned a claim for money based on a contract which, according to Danish law, should be paid at the creditor's place of business. The defendant pleaded that the case concerned the plaintiff's duty to deliver faultless goods and this obligation should be performed in England.

Judgment

The towncourt held that the case concerned the latter duty of the plaintiff, for which reason the court denied its jurisdiction, and this decision was upheld by the High Court.

Comment

The decision is not in line with the decision of the European Court in *de Bloos v Bouyer* Case 14/76, according to which the obligation to which Art. 5(1) refers is the obligation 'which corresponds to the contractual right on which the plaintiff's action is based': see too *Custom Made Commercial v Stawa Metallbau* Case C–288/92, which, however, was decided after the Danish decision.

Case principle

4. Defendant's obligation continues to form basis of claim, even though plaintiff is transferee of original creditor.

Case

61   UfR (1996) 616 ØL

Facts

A Danish company P sued a German firm D in a Danish towncourt to pay for a number of invoices which had been transferred to P from another Danish firm F which had delivered goods to D.

Judgment

The towncourt held that P's claim was based on a transfer of F's contractual claims against D, so that P had entered into the contractual relation between D and F. The obligation to pay was covered by Art. 5(1) and according to CISG Art. 57 (both Denmark and Germany has ratified CISG) the place of performance was in Denmark so that the court had jurisdiction. The decision was upheld by the High Court.

Case principle

5. Main obligation in question to repurchase securities, even though to be arranged to be carried out by a third party.

Case

UfR (1996) 786 H

62

Facts

In a rather complicated case, a Danish stockbroker firm D sued an English stockbroker firm E regarding an asserted agreement according to which E was obliged to repurchase some securities.

Judgment

The Supreme Court held that it was not proved that an agreement which obliged E to repurchase the securities directly from D had been made, but it was found that E was contractually obliged towards D to ensure that another Danish stockbroker firm would be able to fulfil its obligation towards D to repurchase the securities. In relation to Art. 5(1), it was further held that as the performance of this obligation had taken place in Denmark, the case was rightly brought before the Danish courts.

> " . . . place of performance . . . "

Case principle

Place of performance is determined by conflicts rules of the forum (*Tessili*).

Case

UfR (1996) 937 HK

63

Facts

A Danish contractor P made a contract with a German firm D regarding the painting of some new houses which D was building in Germany. P sued D in Denmark for the payment of the amount due to him. D acknowledged that the Danish court had jurisdiction under Art. 5(1) if the agreement was governed by Danish law.

Judgment

The Supreme Court held that this question should be solved by the application of the EEC's Rome Convention of 19 June 1980. As the parties had not themselves chosen the applicable law, the Supreme Court used this Convention's Art. 4 and concluded that even if the houses were built in Germany by a German firm, there was no basis for departing from the presumption rule in Art. 4(2), so that the contract was governed by Danish law as that of the plaintiff characteristic performer and the Danish court thus had jurisdiction.

> ### ARTICLE 5(3)
>
> *"In matters relating to tort . . . "*

Case principle

Product liability claim held tortious, not contractual.

Case

64   UfR (1994) 342 ØL

Facts

A Danish insurance company A had, as liability insurer for the Danish owner of a merry-go-round, paid damages to a person who had been badly hurt during a ride on a merry-go-round. This machinery was produced by a Belgian company B and sold to the owner by a Dutch middleman D. A was of the opinion that the merry-go-round had defects and that, according to the rules on product liability, B and D were jointly responsible for the injury. Accordingly, A sued them both in Denmark to indemnify it for the amount it had paid to the injured person.

Judgment

The High Court held that A's claim was based on product liability and, although there was a contractual basis for the owner's acquisition of the merry-go-round, the claim could not be considered as contractual in the sense of Art. 5(1) but as a claim falling under Art. 5(3). Accordingly, the Danish court had jurisdiction to hear the case. The High Court found it unnecessary to ask the European Court of Justice for an interpretation.

> ### ARTICLE 5(5)
>
> *" . . . branch, agency or other establishment . . . "*

Case principle

To be a branch, agency or other establishment, there has to be an appearance of permanency.

Case

65   UfR (1991) 52 ØL

Facts

A Danish company D had engaged a Danish lawyer and later a German lawyer G to assist in the purchase of real estate in Germany. D wanted to claim damages from the two lawyers jointly and sued them in Denmark. D asserted that according to Art. 5(5) the Danish court had jurisdiction over G because G had rented a room in Copenhagen which he used when he visited the city.

Judgment

As G had no staff in Copenhagen and as the connection between D and G was established in Germany and the contact between them almost always took place at G's office in Germany, the court held that Art. 5(5) did not give it jurisdiction over G.

Comment

D also referred to Art. 6(1), but the court found that the two lawyers were not engaged jointly to take care of all aspects of the purchase and that at the present stage of the lawsuit it was not possible to decide whether the lawyers were jointly responsible. Accordingly, there was not a sufficient connection between the claims so that G could be sued in Denmark according to Art. 6(1).

ARTICLE 6(3)

" . . . *counter-claim* . . . "

Case principle

Article 6(3) covers claims for independent judgment, not mere defences.

Case

UfR (1996) 13 VL   **66**

Facts

A German firm O had, in 1979, made a Danish company D its sole agent in Denmark. The contract was agreed to be governed by German law and German courts were chosen for jurisdiction. In 1990, on the pretext that D had committed a serious breach of confidence, O cancelled the contract without notice. Later, O sued D before a Danish towncourt to pay for goods delivered at the beginning of 1990. D did not deny the debt, but put forward a counterclaim mainly for damages for the cancellation of the contract, which D claimed was unjustified. O referred to the jurisdiction clause in the contract and asserted that the Danish court had no jurisdiction to entertain D's (counter)claim.

Judgment

The town court held that there was not the required relation between the parties' claims to found Article 6(3) jurisdiction over D's claim. In this connection, it should be mentioned that the Danish version of Art. 6(3) uses the word 'modfordring' which covers not only counterclaims where the defendant asks for an independent judgment but also where his claim is meant only as a set-off against the plaintiff's claim. According to the Danish Code of Procedure s.249(2), a defendant's counterclaim with a demand for an independent judgment requires a certain relationship between the main claim and the counterclaim. Before the High Court, D altered his pleadings so as only to make his claim by way of defence against O's claim. The High Court asked the European Court for an interpretation of Art. 6(3) and in its judgment in *Danværn Production v Otterbeck* Case C–341/93, the Court ruled that Art. 6(3) only covered claims which the defendant put forward for an *independent* judgment and not claims as a *defence* and objection to the plaintiff's claim. The Court added that the kind of defences which a defendant could raise and the conditions for these were a matter for the national law. The High Court followed the European Court's decision and referred the case back to the towncourt as it found that this court, according to the Danish procedural rules, had jurisdiction to handle D's claim for set-off.

ARTICLE 16(1)(a)

" . . . *tenancies* . . . "

Case principle

Short holiday lettings included.

Case

67   UfR (1996) 709 VL

Facts

A German letting office S had let a summer cottage in Denmark for a week to a person domiciled in Germany. Although the written contract contained a clause giving jurisdiction to a court in Germany, S sued the tenant before the Danish towncourt at the place where the cottage was situated as S asserted that the cottage had been seriously damaged by the tenant.

Judgment

With reference to the European Court's decision in *Rösler v Rottwinkel* Case 241/83, the towncourt held that it had jurisdiction according to Art. 16(1), and this decision was upheld by the High Court.

```
ARTICLE 17(1)

          " . . . agreed . . . "
```

Case principle

Effects of jurisdiction agreement initially a matter of construction.

Case

UfR (1991) 245 SH   **68**

Facts

In a bill of lading issued in Rotterdam, a Dutch shipping company undertook to carry goods from Rotterdam to Luanda in a vessel belonging to a Danish shipping company. On arrival it appeared that the goods were destroyed and the persons interested in the cargo sued both the Dutch and the Danish shipping companies before the Danish courts. The bill of lading contained a clause according to which any dispute regarding the bill of lading should be decided 'in the country where the carrier has his principal place of business'.

Judgment

The court held that the Dutch company had not acted merely as agent of the Danish company and consequently, because of the jurisdiction clause, the Dutch company could only be sued in The Netherlands, its principal place of business.

Case

UfR (1992) 886 VL   **69**

Facts

See supra, Art. 5(1), Case 58.

Judgment

In a contract of sale there was no agreement on jurisdiction in Germany, as the plaintiff, a Danish seller, was unaware of the jurisdiction clause in the German buyer's *Verkaufs- und Lieferungsbedingungen* to which there was a reference in the buyer's order confirmation (see *supra*, Art. 5(1)).

ARTICLE 17, PARAGRAPH 5 (LUGANO 4)

" . . . *for the benefit of only one of the parties* . . . "

Case principle

A clause conferring jurisdiction upon courts of one party's domicile is not without more to be treated as only for the benefit of that party.

Case

70   UfR (1990) 597 H

Facts and judgment

An English jurisdiction clause in a container terminal contract between the English plaintiff, the owner of the container terminal, and some Danish shipping companies, was not concluded for the benefit of the plaintiff only. The lawsuit in Denmark against the Danish companies was, therefore, dismissed.

ARTICLE 18

" . . . *solely to contest* . . . "

Case principle

An unrepresented defendant pleading to merits without also challenging jurisdiction held not to have submitted to the jurisdiction, where the court failed to advise him of his right of challenge and he subsequently wishes to do so.

Case

71   UfR (1993) 792 VL

Facts

A Danish firm sued a French firm before a Danish towncourt. Usually, cases before the towncourts are not prepared by exchange of documents (except for original writ), but, according to a special rule in the Danish Code of Civil Procedure, the court may order that a case should be prepared in writing, which was ordered in the present case. In the first answer to the writ, the defendant, who at that time did not have the assistance of a Danish lawyer, did not contest the jurisdiction of the court, but pleaded for judgment in his favour. In a case before a towncourt the court has, according to Danish procedural law, an obligation to guide a defendant who pleads without a lawyer, over what he should do in his best interests and this obligation also includes guidance regarding the question of the court's jurisdiction. However, owing to the written preparation, the French defendant did not receive such guidance. The defendant then engaged a Danish lawyer who, in the second written answer for the defendant, claimed that the court lacked jurisdiction. The plaintiff asserted that this challenge to jurisdiction was too late, so that the court had jurisdiction according to Art. 18 (see the European Court's decision in *Elefanten Schuh v Jacqmain* Case 150/80).

Judgment

The towncourt held that as the defendant had not been represented by a lawyer and had not had the above mentioned guidance, the challenge to jurisdiction was not introduced too late, and the court lacked jurisdiction. On appeal, this decision was upheld by two to one judges in the High Court.

ARTICLE 21, PARAGRAPH 1

" . . . *first seised* . . . "

Case principle

Even where courts of different Contracting States are seised on the same day, one may be first seised in time.

Case

UfR (1992) 403 H

72

Facts

The case concerned a collision between a Polish and a Danish ship in Dutch territorial waters. The owner of the Polish ship sued the owner of the Danish ship before the Danish Maritime and Commercial Court in Copenhagen, but the defendant pleaded that the court should decline its jurisdiction because it had already sued the Polish shipowner before a court in Rotterdam.

Judgment

The Danish court found that the two cases were related in the sense of Art. 22, and as the cases concerned a collision in Dutch territorial waters and witnesses living in The Netherlands should give evidence, the court stayed its proceedings until a final decision was made in the case before the Dutch courts. This decision was upheld by the Supreme Court.

Comment

Clearly, the same principle of seisin may be assumed for Art. 21.

ARTICLE 24

" . . . *provisional, including protective, measures . . .* "

Case principle

Article 24 does not cover appointment of experts prior to litigation.

Case

73 UfR (1991) 594 VL

Facts

See supra, Art. 1, Case 53 bis.

Judgment

The court held that the application for expert appraisal before a lawsuit was not covered by Art. 24 on provisional, including protective, measures.

ARTICLE 27(2)

" . . . *sufficient time to enable him to arrange for his defence.*"

Case principle

Ex parte proceedings not served on a defendant do not comply with Title III nor Art. 27(2) specifically.

Case

74 UfR (1994) 991 ØL

Facts and judgment

A decree of seizure of property which was pronounced *ex parte* by a German labour court was refused enforcement in Denmark, as the defendant had not been given the possibility to defend himself before the German court, notwithstanding that the decree could be enforced in Germany. The Danish court thus followed—but did not cite—the European Court's decision in *Denilauler v Couchet Frères* Case 125/79.

> " . . . *duly served* . . . "

Case principle

No due service if required translation not served.

Case

UfR (1995) 816 ØL   **75**

Facts and judgment

A Belgian judgment by default could not be enforced in Denmark according to Art. 27(2), as the writ, which was written in French, was not duly served on the defendant who had not received a Danish translation of the writ (see Art. 5(3) of the Hague Convention of 15 November 1965, on the service abroad of judicial and extrajudicial documents in civil or commercial matters).

Case

UfR (1996) 1086 VL   **76**

Facts and judgment

See infra, Art. 47(1), Case 80.

> **ARTICLE 28, PARAGRAPH 3**
>
> " . . . *may not be reviewed* . . . "

Case principle

Review is prohibited even if the judgment-court failed to apply the Convention to jurisdiction.

Case

77 UfR (1990) 479 VL

Facts and judgment

An order of a Danish Sheriff's Court for the enforcement of a judgment of a German court over a Danish firm which had not appeared before the German court was upheld by the High Court. Although it was obvious that the German court by a mistake had based its jurisdiction on national German jurisdiction rules, the Danish courts could not, according to Art. 28(3), review the jurisdiction of the German court.

ARTICLE 38 PARAGRAPH 1

" . . . *may . . . stay . . .* "

Case principle

Stay granted where judgment creditor's interests are safeguarded by provisional enforcement measures.

Case

78 UfR (1990) 83 VL

Facts

Under a French judgment a Danish company, C, was ordered to pay an amount to a man, A, living in France. According to the judgment it was enforceable notwithstanding an appeal. C appealed but the French Cour d'Appel refused to order that enforcement be stayed pending the appeal decision. A obtained an order of enforcement from a Danish Sheriff's Court, but when A tried to distrain upon C's property, C offered a banker's guarantee for the payment of the amount and the Sheriff's Court stayed the proceedings until the French appeal court had made its decision. A appealed to the Western High Court against this stay and, at the same time, C appealed against the enforcement order to the High Court and asked for a stay of the proceedings under Art. 38(1) until the French Cour d'Appel had made its decision.

Judgment

The High Court stayed the proceedings, as A had not given any grounds why he should be allowed to take wider enforcement measures than protective against C's property. As the banker's guarantee was found to give A sufficient protection, the High Court also upheld the Sherrif's Court's staying order, but amended it so that the stay should last until the High Court had made a decision regarding C's appeal against the enforcement order.

Case

UfR (1989) 877 ØL   **79**

Facts and judgment

See infra, Art. 54(2), Case 81, as to operation of Article 38, para. 3.

ARTICLE 47(1)

" . . . *judgment . . . has been served . . .* "

Case principle

The judgment must have been served according to the law of the judgment-State, including any international service conventions which are applicable therein.

Case

UfR (1996) 1086 VL   **80**

Facts

A *Mahnbescheid* (a German document which institutes proceedings in a summary procedure) from a German court was served by a Danish bailiff on the defendant D living in Denmark. The service was carried out in accordance with Art. 5(2) of the Hague Convention on service abroad of judicial documents. The service was acknowledged by D in a letter to the German court in which he also asked for a Danish translation of the document. He did not get an answer and as he did not enter a formal objection to the *Mahnbescheid* the German court issued a *Vollstreckungsbescheid* which, according to German law, is a provisional judgment against which the defendant, within a certain time, may file an objection. If he does not do so, the *Vollstreckungsbescheid* is the final judgment. The *Vollstreckungsbescheid* was served on D by the bailiff, and D did not file an objection within the time prescribed. The German plaintiff now asked for the enforcement of the judgment in Denmark. The Sheriff's Court authorized the enforcement order and D appealed to the High Court.

Judgment

The High Court held that the service of the *Mahnbescheid* was voluntarily accepted by D (see Art. 5(2) of the Hague Convention) and that he could not demand a translation of the document, so that the enforcement condition in *Art. 46(2)* was complied with. On the other hand, the High Court held that the condition in *Art. 47(1)* was not fulfilled as it was not shown that D had voluntarily accepted the service *of the judgment* (*Vollstreckungsbescheid*) (see the Hague Convention Art. 5(3)). The enforcement of the German judgment was accordingly denied.

ARTICLE 54, PARAGRAPH 2

" . . . *accorded with those . . . in Title II . . .* "

Case principle

A national ground based upon a defendant's submission accords with Title II, Art. 18.

Case

81   UfR (1989) 877 ØL

Facts

In May 1984, a French firm F sued a Danish firm D before the Commercial Court of Bordeaux. D appeared and contested the court's jurisdiction on account of an arbitration clause in the parties' contract. The court held that it had jurisdiction as the dispute was not covered by the arbitration clause. D appealed to the Cour d'Appel in Bordeaux but, in a judgment in January 1988 (*i.e.* after Denmark's accession to the Judgments Convention), the appeal court upheld the lower court's decision and ordered D to pay approximately 300000 French francs. F obtained an enforcement order from a Danish Sheriff's Court and D appealed against this order to the High Court.

Judgment

The High Court held that according to the Accession Treaty of 1978, Art. 34(3), which corresponds to the Judgments Convention Art. 54(2), the Judgments Convention was only applicable if the French court's jurisdiction was based upon rules which accorded with the rules in Title II of the Convention (or bilateral convention). The High Court held that this was the case because, by appearing before the court in France, D had, with the exception of the arbitration objection, impliedly recognized the court's jurisdiction, so that the jurisdiction was based upon a principle corresponding to Art. 18. The High Court upheld the enforcement order, but as D had appealed against the French judgment to the Cour de Cassation, the High Court, in accordance with Art. 38(3), made the enforcement conditional on F's provision of security.

Comment

It may be added that a month after the High Court's judgment, the French Cour de Cassation quashed the judgment of the Cour d'Appel, as it held that the dispute was covered by the arbitration clause.

In any event, it is questionable whether D, with the exception of the arbitration objection, may be said tacitly to have accepted the jurisdiction of the French courts, since by virtue of the French jurisdiction rule in Civil Code, Art. 14, which was in force at that time, any other objections from D would have been futile.

4

ENGLAND AND WALES

Professor Peter Kaye

A.   LEGAL SYSTEM

The United Kingdom contains three separate legal systems: England and
Wales; Northern Ireland; and Scotland.

This chapter is concerned with one of these—that of England and Wales.

Courts

The overwhelming number of Convention cases in England and Wales will be
heard by the 'superior' courts: the High Court at first instance; on appeal, by
the Court of Appeal; and on final appeal, by the judges of the House of Lords.
(There also exists the Judicial Committee of the Privy Council, which sits as a
final appeal court from certain Commonwealth countries and is staffed by the
judges of the House of Lords.)

The superior courts sit in London with centralized jurisdiction, although for
some years the High Court has also sat in certain provincial centres.

Beneath the superior courts, there are about 400 county courts with local
jurisdiction over claims below £50,000 in civil matters. For the most part,
their judgments do not appear in the mainstream law reports. There are also
local magistrates' courts with divided criminal and civil jurisdiction, including,
notably, in the latter case, some matrimonial maintenance claims. Again,
reporting of judgments is left to more specialist series.

The fundamental feature of the common law system which gives it its distinguishing characteristics is that of *binding case precedent*: courts which are
higher in the legal hierarchy bind those lower down the scale; the High Court
does not bind itself, but the Court of Appeal generally does so, and only since

a Practice Direction of 1966 has the House of Lords itself, at the top of the hierarchy, been prepared to depart from its previous decisions, but it has very rarely exercised that power in the last 30 years. The binding part of judgments is the *ratio decidendi*; *obiter dicta* are merely persuasive.

Within the High Court, which delivers most Convention judgments, there are divisions, largely based upon history, but with allocated subject matter of cases: these are the Queen's Bench Division, the Chancery Division and the Family Division.

The majority of Convention cases will be heard in the Queen's Bench Division. The latter contains two so-called 'specialist courts' called the 'Admiralty Court' and the 'Commercial Court' (just as the Chancery Division contains the 'Patents Court'), which hear cases concerning the appropriate subject matter.

The Court of Appeal will in fact be the final appeal court in the majority of cases. When a case does go all the way to the House of Lords, the Lords decide the entire case, not just points of law for subsequent remission to lower courts whence they came in the manner of the Continental courts of cassation.

Lawyers and Judges

The legal profession is divided into barristers and solicitors. Barristers deal with points of law, complex drafting and litigation procedures; solicitors are mainly concerned with initial advice to the public and with pre-litigation procedures. Senior barristers are known as 'Q.C.s'—Queen's Counsel.

Judges in the English legal system are appointed mainly from amongst the most experienced members of the English bar—barristers—although there is now a route for some solicitors to become judges.

Judges of the High Court, Court of Appeal and House of Lords are known, respectively, as Mr/Mrs Justice Smith (Smith J.), Lord/Lady Justice Smith (Smith L.J.) and Lord/Lady Smith. High Court judges sit on their own; in the Court of Appeal, there will be a bench of three Lords Justices, reaching decisions which are either unanimous or by a two to one majority, with the dissenting opinion published; and in the House of Lords, a bench of five Law Lords, either delivering unanimous judgments or decisions by a majority of four to one or three to two with dissenting judgments published.

Procedural judges attached to the High Court are known as 'Masters', who may deal with questions of jurisdiction and who are responsible for initial registration for enforcement of foreign Contracting States' judgments (see Kaye, *Civil Jurisdiction* p. 1593).

In a case law system, the intrinsic nature of the law is to be found in court decisions, by no means all of which are published in the main series of law reports. Judges are *personalities*, in the sense that their personal and intellectual qualities, leanings and approaches are apt to become known and are intricately bound up with and of significance to the development of the law—so much so that even their dissenting judgments and *obiter dicta* are of importance and have led to major extensions of the law.

Traditionally, the best judgments have been finely focused upon the specific point of law involved in the proceedings. (A recent tendency towards more comprehensive and discursive Convention judgments, which stray from the central question at issue, is not altogether to be welcomed in this writer's humble opinion.)

It remains largely the position under the adversarial system of court procedure followed in England and Wales that it is for the barristers to plead the relevant legal arguments in Convention cases, as in others, and it is then for the judge or judges to deliver their judgments on the basis of those arguments. It is not wholly pleasing—as an academic—to report here that the overwhelming proportion of talent and ability within the English legal system has for some years now lain not in legal academia but within the English bar and judiciary. So far as the Brussels Convention is concerned, it has been largely the awesome skills of counsel and the judiciary—mainly of the commercial bar, but of Chancery too wherever called upon—which have led to virtually all of the major developments. Given the continuing, escalating calibre of the English bar and judiciary, and a most regrettable corresponding decline in academic standards, this situation is likely to persist for the foreseeable future.

B. IMPLEMENTATION OF THE CONVENTIONS

The Brussels Convention entered into force in the UK on 1 January 1987, given effect to by the Civil Jurisdiction and Judgments Act 1982. The form in which the Convention applies at the present time is in accordance with the amendments made by the 1989 San Sebastian Convention providing for Spanish/Portuguese Accession, under Statutory Instrument (S.I.) 1990 No. 2591, which came into force for the UK on 1 December 1991. (Previously, S.I. 1989 No. 1346 had given effect to the Greek Accession Convention on 1 October 1989.) The UK has not yet ratified the 1996 Austria/Finland/Sweden Accession Convention.

The Lugano Convention of 1988 entered into force in the UK on 1 May 1992, by virtue of the Civil Jurisdiction and Judgments Act 1991, amending the 1982 Act so as to incorporate references to the Lugano Convention.

In addition to the aforementioned legislation, procedural effect is given to certain Convention rules, whether on jurisdiction or recognition and enforcement of judgments, by the Rules of the Supreme Court (RSC) (or, as the case may be, County Court Rules (CCR)).

The Conventions are set out for convenience of reference in the Schedules to the 1982 and 1991 Acts.

The 1982 Act contains some implementational provisions as an essential supplement to Convention rules, for example, details for registration of judgments for enforcement under Art. 31 and for appeals under Arts 37(2) and 41 and on provision of Arts 46 and 47 documentation, as well as on the allocation of jurisdiction as between the separate legal systems of England and

Wales, Scotland and Northern Ireland within the UK (by virtue of the *famous* Sched. 4). The statute also confers power on the English High Court—otherwise lacking—to grant Art. 24 provisional, including protective, relief in aid of foreign Contracting (and now extended to non-Contracting) States' proceedings on substance and incorporates a special UK definition of domicile and seat for Convention purposes. The RSC (and CCR equivalents) contain provisions for authentication of Convention jurisdiction on issue for and service of writs outside England and Wales and for application for registration for enforcement of foreign Contracting States' judgments under the Convention.

C. OVERVIEW OF CONVENTION CASE LAW

Not surprisingly, the main areas of case law activity have been:

(1)   the Convention's scope—the relation between the Convention and shipping conventions under Art. 57, the Convention's application or not to certain arbitration issues, its effects upon the traditional non-justiciability of foreign intellectual property rights, the scope left to national English discretionary stays for *forum non conveniens*, including *lis alibi pendens*, and restraint of foreign Contracting States' proceedings in alleged contravention of arbitration or jurisdiction agreements;

(2)   the nature of Art. 5(1) matters relating to a contract;

(3)   place of harmful event in tort;

(4)   scope and operation of Art. 17; and

(5)   meaning of same cause of action, same parties and seisin under Arts 21 and 22.

Very little of the development has been at the highest House of Lords level, so that, in theory at any rate—although highly unlikely in practice—much of the case law could be overturned!

There have been some unsatisfactory areas. In the writer's view, the question of the date of seisin under English law for Art. 21 purposes had a false start with *The Freccia del Nord* in the High Court and was subsequently swept along; again, the superiority given to Art. 17 over Art. 21 is controversial, and the position over effects of non-exclusive jurisdiction clauses and Art. 17 remains obscure as a result of the esoteric judgment of Hoffmann J., as he then was, in *Kurz v Stella Musical Veranstaltungs GmbH*. All of the unsatisfactory aspects are at least balanced to some extent by the admirable outward-looking attitude and restraint of the Court of Appeal in permitting *forum non conveniens* to continue to operate against Convention jurisdiction in relation to non-Contracting State competing claims in *Re Harrods (Buenos Aires) Ltd*.

The following are some of the main elements of English case law on the Convention reported upon in this chapter.

(1) Generally, Convention jurisdiction should be proved on a good arguable case, meaning that there is a serious issue to be determined at trial where disputed substantive legal relations are actually a pre-requisite for Convention jurisdiction, for example, on the ground of contracts existence or place of performance under Art. 5(1) or tortious liability in Art. 5(3).

(2) National rules implementing or at least corresponding with those in Art. 57 conventions on particular matters receive Art. 57 priority over the Convention.

(3) There remained a sharp distinction between the power of the English courts to grant s.25(1) of the 1982 Act interim relief in aid of foreign Contracting State main proceedings on substance under Art. 24 and the absence of such powers in relation to non-Contracting State main actions, at least where service was required to be carried out upon a defendant outside England and Wales: now, Statutory Instrument S.I. 1997 No. 302 has removed this anomaly as from 1 April 1997, by extending s.25(1) (under s.25(3)(a)–(b)) to non-Contracting State proceedings and to those whose subject matter falls outside the civil and commercial scope of the Convention in Art. 1. Similar powers are conferred in support of foreign arbitrations by Arbitration Act 1996 ss. 2(3), 44, 107(2) and Sched. 4, as from 31 January 1997.

With regard to the test of 'inexpediency' of discretionary grant of relief under s.25(2), there has been some dissent and criticism of its own previous decisions at Court of Appeal level!

(4) *Forum non conveniens* is excluded as between Contracting States in relation to Convention grounds; but it still applies as between courts of different parts of the UK and in relation to non-Contracting States. It has further been held to apply—(controversially) including in circumstances of *lis alibi pendens*—as between Contracting States in relation to non-Contracting state defendants subjected to national jurisdiction grounds under Art. 4.

(5) Courts retain a national law discretion to grant injunctions restraining parties from continuing foreign Contracting State proceedings conducted in breach of a jurisdiction or arbitration agreement.

(6) Proceedings only fall outside the scope of the Convention's subject matter when their principal subject matter is excluded therefrom.

There are conflicting (*obiter*) decisions at High Court level over whether mandatory Convention jurisdiction prevails over the English courts' traditional rule of non-justiciability in respect of claims for infringement of foreign intellectual property rights. The weight of the developing authority favours the view that Convention jurisdiction overrides the previous obstacles and must be exercised (see *infra*, Art. 1, para. 1).

(7) Questions of excluded or other status of principal arbitral existence or validity proceedings continue to vex, with most courts successfully managing to avoid a full-on confrontation with the problem,

yet with at least one High Court decision in favour of the Convention's application.

(8)   Plaintiffs who wish to rely upon Art. 5(1) in the face of disputed contractual or obligations existence or validity or location of place of performance as matters of substance must establish a serious issue of such existence or place of performance for determination at trial of the merits.

(9)   There is a conflict, at High Court level, over whether actions for avoidance of insurance contracts for misrepresentation and breach of fiduciary duty of disclosure fall within Art. 5(1) as matters relating to a contract.

(10)   The Court of Appeal, after being refused assistance held to be beyond its jurisdiction by the European Court, decided by a two to one majority upon a contractual classification of an action for restitution of money paid under a contract void *ab initio*. Subsequently, the House of Lords, by a majority of three to two, reversed the Court of Appeal and held Article 5(1) to be inapplicable (and unanimously confirmed Article 5(3) also to be inapplicable).

(11)   English courts have been active in deciding, in accordance with *de Bloos* Case 14/76 and *Shenavai* Case 266/85, what is the contractual obligation in question and the principal obligation amongst several in relation to different types of contract under Art. 5(1), and the same in respect of *Tessili* Case 12/76 determination of place of performance of the relevant obligation, encountering particular problems with exclusive distribution agreements.

(12)   The standard of proof held to apply to disputed Art. 5(3) tortious liability and location of harmful event is akin to that of Art. 5(1) contracts existence.

(13)   High Court and Court of Appeal have shown a preference for place of substance of causal event or damage in tort as harmful event under Art. 5(3), where either of these is split between separate Contracting States.

(14)   The courts have engaged themselves generally in determining location of harmful event in tort for Art. 5(3) in a number of situations, especially in the light of European Court rulings in *Dumez* Case 220/88; *Marinari* Case C–354/93; and *Shevill* Case C–68/93.

(15)   Noticeably, English courts have been concerned to confine Art. 6 joined jurisdiction to circumstances in which this is proper and appropriate, although they have shown a clear sympathy towards claims to Art. 6a liability limitation fund jurisdiction.

(16)   The English courts have had to make careful calculations as to the scope of special protective provisions on insurance and consumer contracts.

(17)   They have applied the European Court's rulings in *Sanders* Case 73/77, *Reichert* Case 115/88 and *Webb* Case C–294/92 to determination of rights *in rem* in and tenancies of immovable property under Art. 16(1) and have extended these to timeshare transactions.

(18)   There have been difficulties over the meaning and scope of Art. 16(2) exclusive corporate jurisdiction and as to precisely which types of company activities fall within it.

(19) Jurisdiction agreements have predictably generated a large volume of case law:

- standard of proof;
- who can benefit;
- who is bound;
- whether parties have in fact reached an agreement upon jurisdiction for the purposes of Art. 17 and, if so, what the scope of that agreement is, in particular, as to whether it included claims in tort connected with the agreement;
- effects of jurisdiction agreements under Art. 17, in particular, upon exclusivity of chosen jurisdiction, including where non-exclusive jurisdiction is agreed to by the parties;
- the relationship between Arts 17 and 21 on *lis pendens* and whether the former is subject to the latter; and
- requirements to satisfy written formalities in Art. 17.

(20) Not surprisingly, the courts have had to define defendant's 'entry of appearance' within the meaning of Art. 18 in the context of English procedure, and thereafter to determine when such is merely solely in order to contest the jurisdiction.

(21) The English courts have been more active in the sphere of *lis pendens* under Art. 21 than in any other Convention area, applying leading European Court rulings in *Gubisch* Case 144/86 and *Maciej Rataj* Case C–406/92. The main fields of activity have been as to the following Art. 21 requirements:

- same cause of action, especially where actions *in rem* and *in personam* are involved;
- same parties, again, a difficult area with actions *in rem* and *in personam* and where some but not all the parties in two actions are the same, as well as introducing special problems concerning liability limitation proceedings; and
- meaning of definitive seisin in the English courts, applying the European Court's ruling in *Zelger* Case 56/79.

There has also been case law on the relationship between Art. 21 and Art. 57 conventions on particular matters.

(22) Decisions have been reached, including at House of Lords level, on the meaning of related actions and circumstances of exercise of discretion to stay under Art. 22.

(23) Extraterritorial *Mareva* asset-freezing injunctions and ancillary disclosure orders, pre- or post-judgment, have been held not to be in breach of Art. 16(5) exclusive enforcement jurisdiction, by virtue of Art. 24 provisional, including protective, jurisdiction.

(24)   Costs orders have been held to fall within the Convention's Art. 25
       definition of judgments, which has led to case law concerning
       whether orders for security for costs against plaintiffs who are res-
       ident in foreign Contracting States of the EU are justified or even
       in breach of EC Treaty law.

(25)   English courts dealing with effects of Convention recognition
       under Art. 26 and, in particular, estoppel arising therefrom, have
       had to navigate their way through the difficult waters of the
       European Court's decision in *Hoffmann v Krieg* Case 145/86, in
       order to provide rational solutions.

(26)   In refusal of recognition of judgments on public policy grounds
       under Art. 27(1), English courts have been able to take a more
       principled approach to the question of the examination of alleged
       fraud in the foreign judgment in the Convention context than has
       proved practicable through precedent at national law.

(27)   On the main rule of enforcement in Art. 31, there have been
       interesting case refinements of the scope of that provision and of
       relevant European Court jurisprudence.

(28)   Stays of enforcement-appeal proceedings under Art. 38 have pre-
       dictably generated some challenging case law.

(29)   Art. 57, dealing with conventions on particular matters, linked to
       the 1982 Act, s.9(1) on the internal United Kingdom level, has
       given rise to much case law on the Convention's scope where the
       national implementing legislation has gone beyond that of the Art.
       57 convention itself or was not in fact enacted specifically in order
       to implement the Art. 57 convention.

England and Wales is a common law, case system in which judges' words
are law-creative in the most complete sense. It is not at all surprising, therefore, that English courts have generated such a large volume of significant
case law in the 10 years or so since the Convention entered into force in the
UK. Moreover, there is no sign whatsoever that the flow of decisions is
slowing down!

D.   CASES

RULES OF THE SUPREME COURT, ORDER 6

" . . . *writ is indorsed . . . with a statement that the Court has power*
      . . . to hear and determine the claim . . . "

Case principle

Writs required to be indorsed with the statement that the English courts have jurisdiction to hear and determine the claim under the Convention may be assessed for compliance according to their spirit and contextual meaning, rather than strictly according to the letter.

Case

Nistri & Co. SRL v Tibbett plc (unreported) Court of Appeal, 22 July 1994   **82**

Facts

English rules of procedure (Rules of the Supreme Court (R.S.C.) Ord. 6, r.7(1)) require a writ which is to be served out of England and Wales without leave (permission) of the court, to be indorsed with a statement that the English courts have jurisdiction under the Convention (specifically, under the implementing legislation) to hear the claims made in the writ.

In these proceedings, the plaintiff's writ mistakenly claimed 'damages' as payment for goods sold and delivered to the Italian defendant. It should have asked for the 'price' of the goods. The defendant challenged English Art. 5(1) jurisdiction on the ground that since the writ disclosed no proper cause of action, there was no *contract* for Art. 5(1) to be founded upon, nor was any fact pleaded in any event which tended to show that England was the place of performance.

Judgment

The Court of Appeal rejected the defendant's challenge to the form of the writ.

First, the court could look at the meaning of the claim in context and not slavishly follow the letter. It was quite clear from this perspective that the plaintiff was claiming payment of the price from the defendant and this was how the defendant ought to have understood the writ.

Secondly, it was not a requirement of the procedural rules that the statement indorsed on the writ should disclose all facts substantiating Convention jurisdiction. At the issue stage, mere certification of jurisdiction was sufficient.

Comments

It seems reasonable that on a challenge to English jurisdiction, English courts should so refer to the nature of the claim as disclosed in the writ and indorsement therein (albeit not exclusively, for example, of the statement of claim).

In *Johnson v Ministry of Justice, Vienna, Austria* (unreported), 26 October 1994, Hale J., in the Court of Appeal, pointed out that if Convention jurisdiction was lacking because the defendant was domiciled and the harmful event had occurred abroad for purposes of Arts 2 and 5(3) respectively, there was no mechanism under the Convention (nor in the absence of jurisdiction at common law) for the court to adjudicate on the ground that the plaintiff might be at risk of deportation and further danger if he were to sue in the courts of the natural foreign forum.

See too, *infra*, Case 83, *Ritchie v Knusten* (unreported) Court of Appeal, 22 June 1995, concerning the effects of technical defects in a writ for service out of England and Wales in a Lugano Convention case under RSC Ord. 11, r.1. The result there would have been subject to similar considerations had the case been fought under RSC Ord. 6, r.7 (issue) rather than Ord. 11 (service).

ORDER 11, RULE 1(2)

"Service of a writ out of the jurisdiction is permissible without the leave of the Court . . . "

General

In Brussels or Lugano cases, under RSC Ord. 11, r. 1(2), a writ can be served outside England and Wales without the court's leave if the English courts possess jurisdiction under the Convention and, *inter alia*, the writ is indorsed before issue (without leave) with a statement under RSC Ord. 6, r.7(1)(b) that the court has power to hear and determine the claim and that no *lis pendens* exists in other Convention territories. In non-Convention cases where the defendant is not present for service within England and Wales, the plaintiff must apply *ex parte* for leave of the court to serve the writ upon the defendant abroad under Ord. 11, *r.1(1)*.

Case principle

If a writ is served out with leave under Ord. 11, r.1(1) when it could have been so served without leave under r.1(2), the writ need not be struck out as a consequence of the defect, which may instead be regarded as merely a technical irregularity capable of being cured by amendment, provided that the plaintiff is able to show: (i) that it would be unjust to him if the writ were to be struck out forcing him to start fresh proceedings; and (ii) that the defendant would suffer no injustice through such amendment.

Case

83   Ritchie v Knusten (unreported) Court of Appeal, 22 June 1995

Facts

The plaintiff sought an extension of time and leave to appeal against dismissal of his appeal from the Master's order setting aside the writ. Previously, the plaintiff had obtained leave to serve the writ upon the defendants outside England and Wales under RSC Ord. 11, r.1(1) and did so in Norway. The

Master set aside the writ on the ground that since Norway was a Lugano Contracting State at the time, r.1(1) was inapplicable: rule 1(2) should have been applied, enabling service out without leave in Convention cases. The plaintiff argued on appeal that the defect was merely a technical irregularity which could be cured under RSC Ord. 2, r.1.

Judgment

In the Court of Appeal, Ward L.J. agreed with by Auld L.J., granted the plaintiff an extension of time and leave to appeal on the ground that there was an arguable case to the effect that the defect was merely a technical irregularity which could be cured under Ord. 2, r.1.

Ward L.J. noted that in *Agrafax Public Relations Ltd v United Scottish Society Incorporated* [1995] I.L.Pr. 753 (see *infra*, Case 216), the Court of Appeal, whilst allowing an appeal on grounds that County Court equivalents of Ord. 11, r.1(2) should have been used rather than r.1(1), nevertheless directed amendment rather than fresh proceedings, given the perceived insignificance of the error.

Ward L.J. indicated two further factors to which the court would have regard in deciding whether to view the defect as technical and curable under Ord. 2, r.1 rather than striking out and requiring the plaintiff to start fresh proceedings.

First, it should be considered whether striking out would be unjust to the plaintiff. Here he viewed it as being arguable that it would have been so, since one of the defendants had already issued proceedings in Norway, which would have meant that a fresh English action would have had to have been declined in favour of first-sciscd Norwegian under Lugano Article 21.

Secondly, mere amendment must not unfairly prejudice the defendants. For example, injustice might arise from the fact that writs for service out without leave would have been endorsed with statements as to Convention jurisdiction and absence of *lis pendens*. A defendant to an action for which leave to serve out was sought *ex parte* would not have had notice of such matters at that stage and consequently could thereby have been placed at a comparative disadvantage. Evidently, however, in *Ritchie* itself, Ward L.J. considered it arguable that the defendants were not so prejudiced.

Comments

The test implicit in *Ritchie* of showing: (i) injustice to the plaintiff from striking out; and (ii) no injustice to the defendant from amendment rather than striking out, is reminiscent of the old method of obtaining stays of action for *forum non conveniens*—vexation or oppression of the defendant from English proceedings and no injustice to the plaintiff from a stay thereof (see *St. Pierre v South American Stores (Gath and Chaves) Ltd* [1936] 1 KB 382).

However, it seems unlikely that the former too will be relaxed so as to require the plaintiff principally to show injustice to himself through striking out rather than amendment, notwithstanding loss of legitimate advantages to the defendant from the reverse!

Ward L.J. also regarded it as arguable that the analogy with applications to extend a writ beyond the limitation period was false. To be sure, in this respect, it is believed that the task of persuading the court in the amendment situation ought not to be quite as difficult as in the case of limitation.

ORDER 11, RULE 4(1)(b)

" . . . *plaintiff has a good cause of action* . . . "

General

Under national English discretionary jurisdiction rules, there are three requirements, with various standards of proof, for exercise of the discretion to grant leave to serve a writ upon a defendant who is outside England and Wales as a proper case for such service under Ord. 11 r. 4(2).

(1)   In accordance with Ord. 11, r.4(1)(a), the case must fall within one of the heads of jurisdictional connection under RSC Ord. 11, r.1(1) —to be shown on a *good arguable case* (*Vitkovice Horni a Hutni Tezirstvo v Korner* [1951] AC 869);

(2)   In accordance with Ord. 11, r.4(1)(b), the plaintiff must have a good cause of action on the merits of the claim—the standard here is that there must be a *serious issue to be determined at trial*; and

(3)   England must be shown to be *forum conveniens*, in accordance with the decision in *The Spiliada* [1987] AC 460 (and RSC Ord. 11 r. 4(2).

Case principle

A particular standard of proof is required to be satisfied by the applicant for discretionary leave to serve a writ outside England and Wales under national English procedural rules.

Case

84   Seaconsar Far East Limited v Bank Markazi Jomhouri Islami Iran [1994] I AC 438 House of Lords, 14 October 1993

General

This judgment principally established the second of the preceding three requirements and confirmed the others.

Facts

The plaintiff, a Hong Kong arms dealing company, made a contract to sell artillery shells to the Iranian Ministry of Defence, payment to be made by letter of credit opened by the defendant Iranian bank in favour of the plaintiff, on presentation of specified documents to the Bank Melli Iran, London Branch. Two arms shipments were made, but the defendant refused to pay, on the ground that the documents presented were not in total conformity with the letters of credit. The plaintiff sued the defendant for damages for breach of contract and sought leave to serve the writ upon the defendant out of the jurisdiction under RSC Ord. 11, r.1(1)(d)(i) and (ii) (contract made in, or by or through an agent in the jurisdiction respectively), and under r.1(1)(e) (alleged breach of contract within the jurisdiction).

Judgment

At first instance, leave was granted in respect of the first presentation of documents, but not the second. A majority of the Court of Appeal then dismissed the plaintiff's appeal against refusal to grant leave in the case of the second presentation, on the ground that the plaintiff had failed to discharge the burden of proving that it had a good arguable case on the merits. The dissenting appellate judge disagreed with the application of this test, which was said to be too strict: a plaintiff should only have to show that he had a claim to a cause of action on the merits which was *worthy of consideration*.

The House of Lords unanimously reversed the majority decision of the Court of Appeal and held that leave should be granted to the plaintiff to serve out in respect of the second presentation of documents, not solely the first. After reviewing the history of the relevant rules of court, the Lords held that whereas the availability of one of the heads of jurisdiction in Ord. 11, r.1(1), required by r.4(1)(a) and (2), had to be established as on a good arguable case, the distinct requirement to show a good cause of action under r.4(1)(b), as an element of the court's discretion, alongside *forum conveniens*, would be satisfied if the plaintiff proved that there was a *serious issue to be tried*, so that the discretion to serve out *could* then be exercised—after which he should have to show that England was *forum conveniens* (not in issue in the case), so that the discretion to serve out *would* be exercised.

On the facts, the Lords concluded that the plaintiff had succeeded in proving that there were at least two serious issues to be tried which were relevant to the cause of action and accordingly leave would be granted.

Further findings of interest in the proceedings were that:

(1)   the merits cause of action condition and that of *forum conveniens* were separate and distinct, so that strength in one would not compensate for weakness of evidence in the other; and

(2)   certain jurisdiction heads in Ord. 11, r.1(1), including those relating to conclusion and breach of contracts within the jurisdiction, would require the plaintiff to prove (on a good arguable case) not only *location* of such conclusion or breach within England and Wales, but also contractual existence and, as the case may be, breach, itself in the first place, according to the higher standard of proof of good arguable case—and consequently, if the plaintiff's cause of action on

the merits in fact related to such contractual existence or breach, the lower standard of proof of this for purposes of Ord. 11 leave, as a serious issue to be tried on the merits, would *inevitably* be satisfied if the jurisdiction head itself were first established.

The preceding interpretation of *Seaconsar* has subsequently been confirmed by the Court of Appeal in *Canada Trust Co. v Stolzenberg (No. 2)* [1998] 1 All ER 318, on 29 October 1997.

1982 ACT SECTION 9(1)

" . . . *as they have effect in relation to that other convention itself.*"

Case principle

Section 9(1) extends Art. 57 priority to English statutory provisions and rules of law *to the extent that* these implement a convention on particular matters to which the UK is party. If the English jurisdiction *goes beyond that* in the Art. 57 convention, the additional national jurisdiction does *not* enjoy Art. 57 priority over the Convention.

Case

85   The Deichland [1990] 1 QB 361 Court of Appeal, 20 April 1989

Facts

See too infra, Art. 57.

The plaintiff cargo owners brought English *in rem* proceedings under national English law, laid down in the Supreme Court Act 1981, for damage to the cargo. The defendant German charterers challenged English jurisdiction, on the ground that the action should have been brought in the courts of their German domicile under Art. 2 of the Convention. The plaintiffs responded that in accordance with s.9(1), the English statutory provisions enacted to implement the 1952 Brussels Arrest Convention had the same priority over the 1968 Convention under Art. 57 as that of the 1952 Convention itself to which the UK and Germany were parties.

Judgment

The Court of Appeal held for the defendants. Whereas the 1952 Arrest Convention awarded *in rem* jurisdiction solely on the ground of arrest of a ship, ss.20 and 21 of the Supreme Court Act 1981 implementing that Convention went further and also conferred *in rem* jurisdiction upon English courts when the ship *could have been* arrested in England but for provision of, or undertaking for, security to prevent arrest. Thus, the latter was the basis of English jurisdiction in the present case, since *The Deichland* had not actually been arrested. Consequently, the Court of Appeal held, s.9(1) only had the effect of giving Art. 57-priority to ss.20 and 21 *in so far as* they implemented the 1952 Convention: this was limited to actual arrest thereunder, and mere ability to arrest was not covered in this case. National English jurisdiction was therefore excluded by 1968 Convention Art. 3, and German Art. 2 jurisdiction governed instead.

Comment

In the subsequent case of *The Po, infra*, Case 86, the Court of Appeal noted that the 1952 *Collision* Convention involved in that case was wider than the Arrest Convention, in that the former also included jurisdiction based on *ability to arrest*, as well as from arrest itself. Further, the court decided that s.9(1) even applied where national jurisdiction, which corresponded with the Collision Convention, had not in fact been enacted specifically in order to implement the particular aspect of the latter (see *infra*).

> " . . . *statutory provision . . . implementing any such other convention . . .* "

Case principle

National laws which confer corresponding jurisdiction to that in a convention on particular matters to which the Contracting State is party, have priority over the 1968 Convention under Art. 57, even if they were not specifically introduced in order to implement the particular convention.

Case

The Po [1991] 2 Lloyd's Rep. 206 Court of Appeal, 17 April 1991   **86**

Facts

See infra, Art. 57 Case 372.

The defendant Italian shipowners contested national English jurisdiction *in rem* based on provision of security to prevent arrest of their ship in proceedings over damage from a collision in Brazilian waters alleged to have been caused by their ship, the Po. Although the UK and Italy were parties to the 1952 Brussels Collision Convention which provided for such jurisdiction based on the fact that the ship *could have been* arrested as an alternative to arrest itself, the defendants said that s.9(1) meant that the English rules would not have Art. 57 priority unless they were introduced specifically in order to implement that 1952 Convention. Since they had not in fact been so introduced for this purpose and the 1952 Collision Convention had never in fact been given the force of law as such in the UK, English *in rem* jurisdiction based upon service upon a ship which merely *could have been* arrested was excluded from application by 1968 Convention, Art. 3 and Italian courts had jurisdiction instead under Art. 2.

Judgment

The Court of Appeal unanimously rejected this line of argument. The effect of s.9(1) was not to exclude from Art. 57-priority any national English jurisdiction which had not been introduced specifically in order to implement an Art. 57 convention. Mere correspondence with the latter was sufficient, if the UK was a party thereto. Section 9(1) had merely been included in order to avoid any doubt, not to place restrictions.

The case was expressly distinguished from *The Deichland* because in the latter, the 1952 Brussels *Arrest* Convention applied which, unlike the Collision Convention, did not have the alternative jurisdiction ground of *could have been arrested* rather than arrest itself. Therefore, in The Deichland the English jurisdiction rule allowing the former could not enjoy Art. 57 priority over 1968 Convention German Art. 2-domicile jurisdiction.

SECTION 25(1)

" . . . *shall have power to grant interim relief* . . . "

General

The Civil Jurisdiction and Judgments Act 1982 (Interim Relief) Order 1997 (S.I. 1997 No. 302) entered into force on 1 April 1997. It extended the existing power of the High Court in England and Wales and Northern Ireland under s.25(1) to grant interim relief in aid of main *Convention* proceedings in the courts of other *Contracting* States or of other parts of the UK, to:

(1) proceedings commenced or to be commenced in *non-Contracting* States; and

(2) proceedings whose subject matter is *not within the civil and commercial scope* of the Convention under Art. 1

pursuant to powers of extension in s.25(3)(a) and (b).

This reverses the effect of the House of Lords' decision in *The Siskina (infra)* in relation to such proceedings.

With regard to arbitrations under s. 25(3)(c), S. 107(2) of and Sched. 4 to the Arbitration Act 1996 in fact repealed this (and subsection (5)) as from 31 January 1997). *However*, s. 44 of the 1996 Act confers upon the courts powers to make various interim and protective orders in support of arbitration proceedings; and S. 2(3) also extends these to where the seat of arbitration is outside England and Wales or Northern Ireland (althoug this is expressly a factor which may make an order inappropriate).

The case law preceding these statutory changes (see *infra*, Cases 97–100) remains relevant for the wider legal reasoning enunciated therein *inter alia* as to the doctrinal nature of a cause of action, which may continue to have implications for broader areas of development and for the exercise of procedural powers of service.

Case principle

1. In cases where the English High Court has the power to grant interim relief in aid of foreign (*at that time*, Contracting State) proceedings on substance under the 1982 Act, s.25(1), RSC Ord. 11, r.1(2) applies to permit the service abroad of the writ without leave (*Haiti*).

Case

Republic of Haiti v Duvalier [1989] 2 WLR 261 Court of Appeal, 22 July 1988   **87**

Facts

The plaintiff, the Republic of Haiti, applied to the English courts for worldwide *Mareva* relief (injunction freezing assets) and disclosure by the defendants of their assets. The defendants, domiciled in France, were members of the Duvalier family, former rulers of Haiti, whom the plaintiff was suing in France for 120 million US dollars allegedly embezzled by the defendants during the presidency of Haiti.

The plaintiff sought to found English courts' statutory and procedural powers to grant the interim relief in aid of the French main proceedings on substance on:

- 1982 Act s.25(1) (power); and
- RSC Ord. 11, r.1(2) service abroad upon the defendants without leave, in Convention and 1982 Act 'claims' (procedure).

Although the defendants satisfied the alternative requirement in Ord. 11, r.1(2)(a)(ii) that they were domiciled in a Contracting State, they nonetheless argued that, according to the House of Lords in *The Siskina, infra*, a mere claim for an interim injunction was not one in respect of a 'cause of action' for purposes of discretionary Ord. 11, r.1(1)(b) (injunction ordering or restraining act within jurisdiction). Consequently, since a 'claim' referred to in Ord. 11, r.1(2) was to be equated with such 'cause of action' in Ord. 11, r.1(1), the s.25(1) application for a *Mareva* injunction fell outside Ord. 11, r.1(2), as not being a 'claim' for the purposes thereof.

Judgment

In the first place, the Court of Appeal held that RSC Ord. 11, r.1(2) *applied*. As a result of enactment of s.25, *either* an application for an interim injunction *was now* a cause of action and consequently also a claim for purposes of Ord. 11, r.1(2); *or*, it was possible for there to be a 'claim' without also being a cause of action—it did not matter which, since the issue was one of semantics.

Secondly, even if Ord. 11, r.1(2) had been unavailable, the Court of Appeal considered *obiter* that Ord. 11, r.1(1)(b) itself might in any event have been available in respect of s.25(1) interim relief where r.1(2) was not (see *X v Y, infra*, Case 89—now confirmed and superseded by RSC Ord. 11. R.8A).

Comment

In *Union Bank of Finland Ltd v Lelakis* [1996] 4 All ER 305, 13 May 1996, the question was whether an order for examination of a judgment debtor under RSC Ord. 48 had properly been served out of the jurisdiction of England and Wales without leave under RSC Ord. 11, r.9(4), which allowed this where the writ in the proceedings which had led to judgment 'may' have been served out without leave? The Court of Appeal held r.9(4) to be satisfied, because the writ in the proceedings could have been served out without leave under r.1(2)(a)(ii) (although it was in fact served within England and Wales) by virtue of a jurisdiction clause in the contract valid according to Convention Art. 17 (see *infra*, Article 17 ' . . . agreed . . . court . . . to have jurisdiction . . . ').

Case principle

2.   Section 25(1) applications for English interim relief in aid of foreign (*at that time*, Contracting State or other UK) proceedings on substance do not concern the same cause of action as the foreign main proceedings on substance.

Case

88   Republic of Haiti v Duvalier [1989] 2 WLR 261 Court of Appeal, 22 July 1988

Facts

The plaintiff brought proceedings in France for alleged misappropriation of funds by the defendants, domiciled in France, and subsequently applied for *Mareva* relief in England. RSC Ord. 11, r.1(2) permits service of the writ out of the jurisdiction without leave (court permission) in Convention cases against a defendant domiciled in a Contracting State, as there, provided that there are no proceedings between the parties concerning the same cause of action pending in the courts of another Contracting State, in accordance with Ord. 11, r.1(2)(a)(i). Thus, the defendants argued against such service out without leave in respect of the *Mareva* application, on the ground that the same cause of action was pending before the French courts.

Judgment

The Court of Appeal rejected the defendants' argument.

Either the statutory right to English interim relief in aid of foreign Contracting State proceedings on substance in s.25(1) did not involve any cause of action at all; *or*, if it did, it was novel and distinct and not the same as the French substantive cause of action.

RSC Ord. 11, r.1(2) gave procedural effect inter alia to the S. 25(1) power, equivalent to Art. 24 on international jurisdiction; and the relationship between Arts 21 and 24 correspond to the position as held in respect of Ord. 11, r.1(2)(a)(i)—English Art. 24 provisional and French substantive causes of action were not the same (see *infra*, Arts 21 and 24).

Case principle

3. If the conditions of application of RSC Ord. 11, r.1(2) were not satisfied, as, for example, where the defendant to the foreign Contracting State proceedings on substance was not domiciled in any Contracting State as required thereunder, Ord. 11, r.1(2) could not apply; but Ord. 11, r.1(1)(b) requiring leave (application to serve out for injunction within the jurisdiction) could apply instead (confined to its statutory basis in s.25 in relation to, at the time, Contracting States and other UK main substance proceedings. This is now superseded, as from 1 April 1997, by Ord 11 r.8A, specifically permitting service out with leave in aid of Contracting or non-Contracting State main proceedings (where r.1(2) is not satisfied) (see S.I. 1997 No. 415).

Case

X v Y [1989] 3 All ER 689 High Court, 10 April 1989   **89**

Facts

The plaintiff French bank made agreements for provision of finance to the defendant Saudi Arabian businessman in 1983 and brought an action against the defendant in the French courts in April 1988 for default in payments due, claiming nearly 31 million French francs. In December 1988, the plaintiff obtained a *Mareva* injunction from the English courts restraining the defendant from disposing of his English assets and obtained leave to serve English process upon the defendant out of the jurisdiction in Saudi Arabia.

The defendant challenged English service under RSC Ord. 11, r.1(1)(b) (as well as grant of the *Mareva* itself, even if service had been proper) as being contrary to *The Siskina*, excluding RSC Ord. 11, r.1(1)(b) from applying to an application for an interim injunction in aid of foreign main proceedings on substance at common law (see *infra*).

The plaintiff argued that service was not defective on three alternative bases: (1) where s.25 applied, RSC Ord. 11 service out was not required at all; (2) s.25 itself impliedly authorized service out, so that Ord. 11 was not required; (3) Ord. 11, r.1(1)(b) could apply to a *s.25* application for an interim, *Mareva* injunction, notwithstanding *The Siskina*.

Judgment

Deputy High Court Judge Diamond Q.C. held as follows.

First, s.25 contemplated service outside the jurisdiction on a defendant—but was not *itself* intended to deal with it. Consequently, procedure for service out was for the rules of court and s.25 did not dispense with the need for this. *Mareva* jurisdiction was *in personam* and this required service, in or out of the jurisdiction.

Secondly, for the same reasons, s.25 itself did not authorize such service.

Thirdly, on the facts, RSC Ord. 11, r.1(2), permitting service abroad without leave, was not available because the defendant was not domiciled in a Contracting State, as required, *inter alia*, by r.1(2)(a)(ii). However, the purpose of s.25 was to reverse the effects of *The Siskina* in cases to which the former would apply; and if the s.25 power were to be unavailable through procedural incapacity to serve in cases where defendants were not domiciled in a Contracting State, this would be inconsistent with its purpose.

Accordingly, in such cases of inapplicability of Ord. 11, r.1(2), Ord. 11, r.1(1)(b) should nevertheless be construed as being available with leave for purposes of s.25 and *The Siskina* held to be overridden to that extent in the circumstances.

Thus, power to grant leave to serve process out of the jurisdiction under RSC Ord. 11, r.1(1)(b) (as well as grant of the *Mareva* itself) was upheld by the deputy judge.

The defendant sought to argue that the court should still have exercised its discretion against grant of interim relief under s.25(1), by reference to s.25(2). However, the conditions for operation of s.25(2) (the fact that the English courts have no jurisdiction over substance makes it inexpedient for the court to grant interim relief) were not satisfied because: (i) the defendant actually had previously agreed to English non-exclusive jurisdiction; (ii) he had unconditionally submitted to French courts' jurisdiction over the plaintiff's French action; and (iii) the evidence was that any French judgment on substance would not be enforceable in Saudi Arabia.

Case principle

4.   Section 25 interim relief applications are 'actions' for the purpose of domestic procedural rules in RSC Ord. 28, r.7(1) permitting a counterclaim to an 'action' begun by originating summons.

Case

90   Balkanbank v Taher [1995] 2 All ER 917 Court of Appeal, 18 November 1994

Facts

The plaintiff brought substantive proceedings for fraud against the defendant in Ireland in 1990 and obtained Irish and English *Mareva* injunctions. The Irish action was unsuccessful and Irish and English *Marevas* were lifted. The defendant wished to counterclaim in England for breach of contract and breach of fiduciary duty, under domestic procedural rules permitting this in the case of actions brought against the defendant. However, the plaintiff argued that a s.25 application for mere interim/ancillary relief was not an 'action' for these purposes, which was limited to substantive merits claims.

Judgment

The Court of Appeal unanimously held that s.25 applications were 'actions' for such procedural counterclaim purposes. Textually, there were no such restrictions as suggested by the plaintiff as would exclude s.25 claims; and avoidance of multiple actions and irreconcilable judgments and achievement of full and final settlement of all disputes between the parties were both procedural-counterclaim and international-Convention objectives.

There was, furthermore, no displacement of Convention counterclaim jurisdiction, because the plaintiff was a non-Contracting State domiciliary and consequently, national English rules applied by virtue of Art. 4.

Case principle

5. Section 25(1) power in relation to foreign (at the time, Contracting State) proceedings on substance is also exercisable in relation to extraterritorial, not merely local, interim relief.

Case

Crédit Suisse Fides Trust S.A. v Cuoghi (unreported) Court of Appeal, 14   **91**
December 1995

Facts

The plaintiffs claimed s.25(1) worldwide *Mareva* relief in aid of Swiss civil proceedings against the defendant to recover monies involved in an alleged investment fraud. At first instance, the plaintiffs were successful before Mance J., whereby it was incidentally confirmed, therefore, that the s.25(1) power in relation to foreign (at that time, Contracting State) proceedings on substance was also exercisable in relation to extraterritorial, not merely local territorial, interim relief—as if ever doubted.

The defendant made a request to the Court of Appeal for leave to appeal to that court against the first instance order.

Judgment

Hirst L.J. reminded that the appellate court could only interfere with the lower court if either the judge had misdirected himself in law, or did not take account of material matters, or the decision was manifestly wrong.

Thus, seemingly, according to Hirst L.J., since Mance J. may have misapplied the European Court's *Denilauler* decision and appeared to have failed to appreciate that extraterritorial orders should be *very exceptional* in the light of *Rosseel* (see *infra*), it was arguable, though by no means certain, that the challenge would succeed on these grounds, and accordingly, leave to appeal against the worldwide aspect of the *Mareva* would be granted by Hirst L.J. (before moving on to further aspects of the application).

The Court of Appeal eventually came to decide the matter in:

Case

Crédit Suisse Fides Trust SA v Cuoghi, [1997] 3 All ER 724 Court of Appeal,   **92**
11 June 1997

Facts

See supra, Case 91.

Since the defendant, resident and domiciled in England, was not resident in Switzerland, the Swiss courts were said to have no power to order him to disclose assets wherever they might be.

Judgment

The Court of Appeal upheld Mance J.'s decision to exercise jurisdiction in favour of interim relief under s.25 as being unassailable and the defendant's appeal was dismissed.

Millett L.J. concluded from the structure of s.25(1) and (2) that the English courts should in principle be willing to grant the interim relief, notwithstanding their merely ancillary role in support of foreign main proceedings, unless the circumstances of the particular case were such as to make the grant inexpedient. There was no reason in principle why a s.25 *in personam* order should not also extend to assets outside England and Wales where the defendant was domiciled in the latter; and it would be contrary to the policy of s.25 and Art. 24 for it not to do so.

On the other hand, if the defendant was domiciled outside England and Wales, it would be most appropriate for courts of the *situs* of assets and of the defendant's domicile to grant orders operating, respectively, directly against assets and against the defendant personally (including disclosure).

Conceding that great caution was necessary in such matters, Millett L.J. nonetheless refused to accept that the English courts were limited to granting types of interim relief available in main Swiss courts and in circumstances there prevailing, such as that the defendant must be resident in Switzerland. In this way, the effect of s.25 was to supplement the powers of the Swiss courts, not to breach comity by remedying perceived deficiencies in Swiss law!

He went on to express regret that in *S. & T. Bautrading v Nordling* (*infra*, Case 93), the Court of Appeal had appeared to ask whether extraterritorial grant would be even more exceptional when in aid of foreign proceedings—rather than merely *inexpedient*, as would have been proper under s.25(2).

Millett L.J. concluded his treatment by listing what he described as two highly material considerations for s.25(2) discretion:

(1)   situation of the defendant's domicile, and
(2)   likely reaction of the foreign main court of substance—if the latter itself had refused a similar order, it would generally be wrong to interfere, whereas if that court simply lacked power to make an order against a non-resident defendant, it did not follow at all that the court would find the English court's order objectionable.

Lord Bingham L.C.J. followed up on the latter theme, at the same time agreeing to a cautious approach. He considered it unwise to try to list all considerations which might make it inexpedient to grant s.25 relief, whether confined to England and Wales or worldwide. But he nonetheless proposed the following:

(1)   it would weigh heavily, probably conclusively, against the grant, if the latter would obstruct or hamper the management of the case by the main court or would give rise to a risk of conflicting, inconsistent or overlapping orders in other courts;

(2)   similarly, if the primary court could have granted the relief but had not done so, particularly if it had declined an application for it; but

(3)   it could weigh in favour of the grant that the defendant was present in England and Wales, which would make it likely to be effective, provided that by the grant of relief the English court did not tread on the toes of the primary court nor of any other involved in the case.

Thus, the role of the English courts in a s.25 application was essentially to be subordinate to and supportive of the foreign court of substance.

Comments

Given that s.25(2)—although inelegantly drafted and not very susceptible to close textual analysis, as Millett L.J. put it—expressly presupposes that the English court has no jurisdiction over the defendant apart from that under s.25, it seems rather strange that Millett L.J. should thus have attempted to draw a distinction, for purposes of *inexpediency* of grant thereunder, according to whether the defendant was domiciled and resident in England and Wales or not, since the former would itself ensure such jurisdiction under Art. 2 and consequential inapplicability of s.25(2).

His comments, therefore, are probably best limited to where the defendant is not in any event domiciled in England and Wales, but may or may not be resident there, and to the extended s.25(3) non-Contracting or non-Convention cases. Noticeably, in contrast, Bingham L.C.J. preferred to refer to the defendant's 'presence' in England and Wales or not.

Generally then, the courts should, according to s.25(2), look at the circumstances behind the absence of English jurisdiction: whether, say, lack of English domicile is also accompanied by absence of residence or presence of the defendant which would threaten to make an interim order ineffective and consequently inexpedient.

The other factors mentioned by the court, mainly concerning likely reactions of the foreign courts of substance and *situs* of assets sought to be affected extraterritorially, are only indirectly the result of the English court's lack of substantive jurisdiction. Yet, they remain perfectly material nonetheless: s.25(2) is not the *only* factor affecting the English court's discretion, which is still completely generalized under s.25(1), whether the English court would otherwise have possessed jurisdiction over the defendant or not.

The Court of Appeal's criticism of *S. & T. Bautrading* for seeming to have viewed s.25(2) as imposing *increased* exceptionality (beyond the degree usually required for extraterritorial orders) rather than mere expediency as condition of grant of (extraterritorial) relief, is generally logical and acceptable—yet not in fact in relation to *S. & T. Bautrading* itself, where s.25(1), but not s.25(2), was applicable according to their terms since the English courts *would have* possessed jurisdiction over substance apart from the section (under Art. 2) by reason of the defendant's English domicile (see *infra*).

Case principles

6. Where *extraterritorial Mareva* relief is required in aid of foreign, as opposed to English, main proceedings, it should only be granted in even more exceptional circumstances than in the latter case (following *Rosseel NV v Oriental Commercial and Shipping (UK) Ltd*, see *infra*, Case 95).
7. This applies even if the foreign action was *initiated* by the defendant, not by the plaintiff/applicant, and where the plaintiff/applicant *could* have brought English proceedings in the first place.
8. If a plaintiff brings an English action to enforce a foreign authentic instrument in the course of which extraterritorial *Mareva* relief is sought, the English action is classified as enforcement proceedings in aid of *foreign* main proceedings on substance, not as the original main action itself, for present *discretionary* purposes.

Case

93 S & T Bautrading v Nordling [1998] I.L.Pr. 151 Court of Appeal 29 July 1996

Facts

The defendant signed a formal acknowledgement of a debt of 17.5 million DM owed to the German plaintiff, in 1991, enforceable without further court proceedings under German law (*Schuldanerkenntnis*). However, the plaintiff subsequently agreed to discharge the debt and, in 1994, the defendant brought an action in the German courts to have the discharge declared valid. This was challenged, however, by the plaintiff on grounds of alleged fraud. In 1996, the plaintiff sought an extraterritorial *Mareva* injunction over the defendant's assets from the English courts, in support of the plaintiff's counterclaim for payment of the debt in the German action. The first instance deputy High Court judge confined the *Mareva* to the English assets of the defendant, on the ground that extraterritoriality should be even more exceptional when the *Mareva* was required in aid of foreign (here, German) main proceedings as opposed to those in England. The plaintiff appealed against this limitation upon the *Mareva* discretion.

Judgment

The Court of Appeal upheld the restriction upon the *Mareva* to the English assets of the defendant. *Rosseel, infra*, Case 95, was cited by Saville L.J. in support of the principle that discretion to order worldwide *Marevas* was all the more exceptional when this was in aid of foreign, as opposed to English, main proceedings on substance, as binding precedent, notwithstanding the plaintiff's willingness to provide undertakings in respect of extraterritorial scope. This limitation would not fetter the courts' discretion but was merely a guideline— and, on the facts, the very exceptional circumstances did not exist, despite the plaintiff's allegation of fraud.

Nor did it make any difference to the discretion that the foreign main action had been initiated by the defendant as opposed to the plaintiff applicant itself and that the latter could have brought an action on validity of the discharge agreement before the English courts against the defendant under Art. 2. What mattered was that the main action had not been brought in England by the plaintiff applicant on the facts.

The plaintiff further attempted to discount the German main action from the additional discretionary restriction by asserting that its application for *Mareva* relief could be viewed as being in aid of *English main proceedings* to enforce the German acknowledgement.

However, the Court of Appeal, noting the first instance court's finding— against which there had been no appeal—that the acknowledgement amount- ed to an 'authentic instrument' within Art. 50 (see *infra*, Case 365), drew the conclusion from this that any such English proceedings would merely be for enforcement of a *foreign main* instrument analogous to an Art. 25 judgment and consequently the *Mareva* would still be in aid of *foreign*, not English, pro- ceedings for purposes of the extraterritorial discretion.

Comment

In the further Court of Appeal proceedings in the *Crédit Suisse* case *supra*, Case 92—*Crédit Suisse Fides Trust SA v Cuoghi*—Millett L.J. criticized the Court of Appeal in *S. & T. Bautrading* for not having considered s.25(2) *inex- pediency* and for introducing an *increased* 'exceptional' criterion into the s.25(2) process instead (see Comments to Case 92, *supra*).

> ### SECTION 25(1)(a)
>
> " . . . *commenced in a Contracting State* . . . "

Case principle

Section 25(1) applies retrospectively so as to confer power on English and Northern Irish High Courts to grant provisional, including protective, inter- im relief in aid of main proceedings on substance in foreign Contracting States, where the Convention had not yet entered into force as between the UK and the foreign Contracting State at the date of institution of the foreign main proceedings.

Case

94 Alltrans Inc. v Interdom Holdings Ltd [1993] I.L.Pr. 109 Court of Appeal, 30 January 1991

Facts

The plaintiff shipping company, Alltrans, appointed an English company, JSA, to be its port agent in 1977, and the defendant, Interdom, associated to JSA, agreed with the plaintiff to guarantee payment by JSA of monies JSA held to the plaintiff's account.

In 1985 the agency with JSA was terminated, but JSA failed to pay the plaintiffs approximately £600,000 held for them, because JSA had begun proceedings against the plaintiffs in February 1986 in the Dutch courts and wished to ensure that the plaintiffs did not make these funds disappear when they might otherwise be used to satisfy any Dutch judgment against them in JSA's favour. The plaintiffs therefore sued the defendants in England under the guarantee, for which they eventually obtained judgment in January 1990 in the sum of the £600,000. However, in December 1989 the English courts granted a *Mareva* injunction against the plaintiffs in order to prevent them from dissipating the amount recovered prior to any judgment against them in the Dutch proceedings.

The plaintiffs sought to have the *Mareva* discharged on the ground that the English courts lacked power and jurisdiction to grant it.

- Because both s.25(1) of the 1982 Act, giving English courts *power* to grant interim relief in relation to foreign Contracting State main proceedings on substance, and Art. 24, providing *jurisdiction* to do so, had only entered into force in the UK on 1 January 1987 (under 1982 Act, Sched. 13, Pt I).
- Whereas the Dutch main proceedings were instituted before that date (and even before 1 November 1986 when the 1978 Accession Convention entered into force in The Netherlands) in February 1986.

Art. 34(1) of the 1978 Accession Convention provided that the Convention only applied to proceedings instituted *after* its entry into force in the State of origin. Consequently, s.25(1) and Art. 24 were inapplicable.

Judgment

The court, conceding Art. 24's transitional inapplicability, nonetheless held s.25(1) to confer the power of interim relief upon the English courts in the circumstances:

(1) Section 25(1)'s purpose was not exclusively linked to giving internal effect to Art. 24, as indications of its actual or potential broader scope in s.25(1)(b) and (3) clearly showed, so that inapplicability of Art. 24 did not automatically import the same for s.25(1); and

(2)   as a rule of procedure, s.25(1) could operate retrospectively in rela-
       tion to Dutch proceedings instituted before its entry into force,
       unless Parliament had indicated otherwise in the legislation, which
       it had not.

Consequently, English courts' powers of interim relief (otherwise non-
existent in relation to foreign proceedings on substance at common law, see
The Siskina [1979] AC 210) were applicable in relation to the prior Dutch
action, unaffected by Art. 34(1) transitional constraints.

Comment

Presumably, the same conclusions may be drawn as to the applicability
of s.25(3)(a) and (b) powers in relation to non-Contracting State/non-
Convention proceedings instituted before 1 April 1997, as well as afterwards.
   The inapplicability of Article 24 is now subject to some doubt—see *infra*,
Case 381.

SECTION 25(2)

" . . . *no jurisdiction apart from this section* . . . "

Case principle

1.   Section 25(2) says that an English court can refuse interim relief in aid of
     foreign (Contracting State) proceedings on substance under s.25(1), if the
     fact that the English court would itself lack such jurisdiction makes it
     inexpedient for the court to grant the interim relief.

Case

Rosseel NV v Oriental Commercial and Shipping (UK) Ltd [1990] 3 All ER   **95**
545 Court of Appeal, 31 July 1990

Facts

The plaintiffs sought to enforce a New York arbitration award in England
under s.3 of the Arbitration Act 1975 and requested a worldwide *Mareva*
order in aid of enforcement.

Judgment

The Court of Appeal upheld the first instance judge's refusal to exercise his
discretion to extend the *Mareva* to cover extraterritorial assets, where the
final enforcement would need to take place in a foreign jurisdiction. Lord
Donaldson M.R. referred to s.25(2) as confirming power to refuse relief where
absence of jurisdiction over substance made such measures inexpedient.

See too supra, Republic of Haiti, Case 87 and Crédit Suisse Fides Trust SA v Cuoghi, Case 92.

Comment

In *Crédit Suisse Fides Trust SA, supra,* both Millett L.J. and Lord Bingham M.R. in the Court of Appeal voiced a certain surprise, if not criticism, over the Court of Appeal's earlier refusal to grant relief in *Rosseel,* which was ascribed to the Court of Appeal's failure there to take account of the fact of the defendant's English residence. Similar, indeed stronger, remarks were made about the Court of Appeal's *S. & T. Bautrading* decision (*supra,* Case 93), where it was said that no consideration at all had been given to s.25(2) and 'inexpediency' thereunder.

Thus, under s.25(2), the criterion against discretionary relief was 'inexpediency', and, in the absence thereof, the relief should have been granted, and not prevented by any principle based upon a requirement of 'even more than usual exceptional circumstances', see *Crédit Suisse, supra.*

Case principle

2. Hypothetical English substantive jurisdiction may be assessed for existence under the Convention or, if Convention jurisdiction grounds are inapplicable, under national English jurisdiction rules.

Case

96   The Xing Su Hai [1995] 2 Lloyd's Rep. 15 High Court, 22 February 1995

Facts

The plaintiff shipowners of the Xing Su Hai wished to sue the Liechtenstein charterers, together with the charterers' German agent and its German controlling shareholder, for contractual misrepresentation and inducement of breach of contract, in the English courts. When it became clear that substantive English jurisdiction was lacking over the German defendants through the operation of Convention Art. 2 (see too *infra,* Arts 6(1) and 18), the plaintiffs sought interim *Mareva* relief over the defendants' assets, should they now be compelled to bring their proceedings on substance in the German courts. The English courts' power to grant such relief in relation to, *inter alia,* foreign Contracting State proceedings on substance was conferred by s.25(1)—but s.25(2) provided that the court might refuse relief, if the fact that the English court had no jurisdiction apart from under s.25 itself made it inexpedient for the court to grant it.

Having determined that English courts *did not* possess jurisdiction over the German defendants *under the Convention* (and that the latter applied and was not excluded under Art. 1, para. 2(4) simply because the plaintiffs might also wish to pursue arbitration), the question arose whether s.25(2) would have permitted the English court to examine whether substantive jurisdiction existed under *national English rules,* had the Convention been held not to apply to the case?

Judgment

Rix J., in a judgment regrettably suffering from a certain lack of clarity and presentational finesse, held that the operation of s.25(2) was not limited to where jurisdiction would otherwise exist *under the Convention's grounds* in relation to defendants domiciled in Contracting States.

The important trigger for the operation of the interim powers in s.25(1) was, *inter alia*, foreign (at that time) Contracting State *proceedings*, irrespective of defendant's Contracting or non-Contracting State domicile.

Accordingly, it was quite permissible to determine for s.25(2) purposes whether substantive jurisdiction would exist in the English courts, where the action on substance was in fact intended to be brought in a foreign Contracting State, even if the defendant was not domiciled in a Contracting State, so that national English jurisdiction grounds would have applied to the substantive claim had it been brought before the English courts, by virtue of Convention Art. 4.

Rix J. went on to find that it was inappropriate generally on the facts in any event to exercise the discretion to grant *Mareva* relief over the German defendants' assets. The proper place for the plaintiffs to apply for such interim protection was in the German courts themselves, where the plaintiffs ought to bring their main proceedings on substance.

SECTION 25(3)(a)

" . . . *otherwise than in a Contracting State* . . . "

General

The inability of the English courts to grant interim relief in aid of non-Contracting State main proceedings on substance, from *The Siskina infra*, is now reversed by the Civil Jurisdiction and Judgments Act 1982 (Interim Relief) Order 1997 (S.I. 1997 No. 302), which extends s.25(1) powers to non-Contracting State main proceedings and to those outside the Convention's civil and commercial scope in Art. 1, pursuant to s.25(3)(a) and (b) respectively, as from 1 April 1997.

As previously see, s.44 of the Arbitration Act 1996 conferred interim and protective powers upon the courts in respect of arbitrations (referred to in S.25(3) (c) and (5), repealed by 1996 Act S.107(2) and Sched. 4) as from 31 January 1997—and these powers also extend to arbitrations with their seat outside England and Wales and Northern Ireland under 1996 Act s.2(3).

However, certain of the principles pronounced upon in the now superseded case law below (see Cases 97–100) still retain some wider doctrinal significance, for example, in respect of the nature of a cause of action and procedural powers of service.

Case principle

1. English procedural powers for discretionary leave to serve originating process on a defendant outside England and Wales were unavailable where the only relief sought was an interim *Mareva* injunction and the main proceedings on substance were being or to be conducted in courts of a non-Contracting State. An interim injunction was not itself based upon a legal or equitable right and was merely ancillary relief to a substantive cause of action pending or to be brought before the English courts. An anticipatory breech of contract was not an existing cause of action.

Case

97 The Siskina, Siskina (cargo owners) v Distos Cia Naviera S.A. [1979] AC 210
House of Lords, 26 October 1977

Facts

The plaintiff cargo owners claimed against the defendant Panamanian owners of the sunken ship, Siskina, in the English courts for a *Mareva* injunction preventing disposal of assets including 750,000 US dollars insurance monies likely to be paid by London insurers, where Italian courts possessed exclusive jurisdiction over the cargo owners' substantive claim for damages for loss of the cargo, under a jurisdiction clause in the bill of lading. The plaintiffs wished to rely, for national English jurisdiction over the *Mareva* application, on RSC Ord. 11, r.1(1)(b) (an order to the defendant to do or to refrain from doing anything within the jurisdiction).

Judgment

The House of Lords unanimously held RSC Ord. 11, r.1(1)(b) to be unavailable in relation to an interlocutory injunction such as a *Mareva*, because the latter *presupposed* existence of a cause of action before the English courts and was not itself a cause of action which could stand alone. It was said to be dependent upon an invasion, actual or threatened, of a legal or equitable right of the plaintiff, for the enforcement of which the defendant was amenable to the English courts' jurisdiction. The right to obtain an interlocutory injunction was merely ancillary and incidental to the pre-existing cause of action.

Comment

The precise scope of the House of Lords' judgment in *The Siskina* was defined and refined in a number of further English judgments over the years (see *infra*, and Kaye, *Civil Jurisdiction* pp. 1157–60, and see ow Ord. 11 r.8A).

In *James North & Sons Ltd v North Cape Textiles Ltd* [1984] 1 WLR 1428, the Court of Appeal held that RSC Ord. 11, r.1(1)(b) was still available for grant of a final and permanent injunction in order to prevent a merely *threatened* breach of contract and tort within the jurisdiction of England and Wales through passing off and trade mark infringement. *The Siskina* had not excluded this possibility, and in the circumstances, England was *forum conveniens* and the discretion would be exercised in favour of the grant of leave to serve the writ out of the jurisdiction.

Case

Zucker v Tyndall Holdings plc [1992] 1 WLR 1127 Court of Appeal, 7 May 1992   **98**

Facts

The plaintiff was allotted shares in a Swiss company on terms that he could exercise a 'put option' to have his shares repurchased at a formula price if the defendant controlling shareholder lost its control through selling or otherwise disposing of its interest, subject to Swiss law and courts. When the defendant was taken over, the plaintiff, advised by his Swiss lawyer that this was a circumstance in which the put option could be exercised, sought to do so and duly brought proceedings in the Swiss courts for payment of the sums owed in March 1992. One week later, he obtained a *Mareva* injunction from the English courts, which the defendant thereafter successfully applied to have discharged. The plaintiff appealed.

Judgment

The Court of Appeal unanimously confirmed the discharge of the *Mareva* order.

An interlocutory injunction such as a *Mareva* could not stand alone under national English law; it had to be ancillary to an existing cause of action.

Consequently, the English courts had no power to grant a *Mareva* in aid of a main cause of action carried on before a foreign, non-Contracting State's court (1982 Act s.25(1), conferring the power in relation to foreign *Contracting* States or other UK proceedings, did not apply because the date of the application for the *Mareva* was prior to May 1992 when the UK became party to the Lugano Convention with Switzerland—although see *supra*, Case 94). Thus, the decision of the House of Lords to this effect in *The Siskina* was expressly followed.

In addition, it was held that there could be no cause of action, in any event, if there was merely an 'anticipatory' breach of contract (as here, since, although the defendants denied the plaintiff's right to exercise the put option in the circumstances, payment did not fall due for another six weeks). What was needed was an 'actual' breach of contract, or at least a threatened breach of an 'existing' obligation.

Case principles

2. *Obiter*, English courts lacked the procedural power to proceed under RSC Ord. 11, r.1(1)(b) (injunction sought ordering the defendant to act or not to act within the jurisdiction) so as to grant *Mareva* relief in aid of proceedings on substance in a non-Contracting State, because, under r.1(1), a *Mareva* had to be ancillary to a main cause of action (the House of Lords in *The Siskina* [1979] AC 210, followed).

3. Position reserved on whether power existed in principle when the defendant was subject to the English courts' personal jurisdiction (or to other heads of jurisdiction in Ord. 11, r.1(1), aside from (b)).

Case

99 Mercedes-Benz AG v Leiduck [1995] 3 All ER 929 Judicial Committee of the Privy Council, 24 July 1995

Facts

The plaintiff engaged the German defendant to sell its vehicles in Russia and provided substantial expenses for the defendant, which the defendant then allegedly misappropriated through a Hong Kong company in which he owned almost all the shares. The defendant was arrested in Monaco and the plaintiff began civil proceedings against him there. However, the Monaco court lacked the power to affect the defendant's shares in Hong Kong, and consequently the plaintiff applied for a *Mareva* injunction in Hong Kong in 1994 in aid of its Monaco proceedings against the defendant. The Hong Kong courts followed the House of Lords' judgment in *The Siskina* [1979] AC 210 that English (for which, read Hong Kong) courts could not proceed to grant a *Mareva* interim injunction under RSC Ord. 11, r.1(1)(b), because an interim injunction was not itself a cause of action and consequently had to be ancillary to a substantive cause of action *before the English courts* for it to fall within Ord. 11, r.1(1)(b).

The plaintiff appealed to the Judicial Committee of the Privy Council.

Judgment

The Judicial Committee held that even if it possessed the *Mareva* power, the discretion could not be exercised in favour of grant of a *Mareva* on the facts in any event because as it happened there were deficiencies in the required documentation: no writ was extant in which *Mareva* or any other relief was claimed.

However, a majority of four to one members of the Judicial Committee went on to uphold *The Siskina*, to the extent of denying that it was procedurally possible to proceed under Ord. 11, r.1(1)(b) in aid of foreign proceedings, because a *Mareva* had to be ancillary to a substantive cause of action in the English courts.

As to whether the power existed in principle, aside from procedural difficulties, so that its exercise would be possible if the defendant were personally subject to the English court's jurisdiction (or under another ground in Ord. 11, r.1(1)), the Judicial Committee reserved its judgment.

The fifth judge, Lord Nicholls, in a very powerful dissenting judgment, criticized the House of Lords' earlier ruling in The Siskina (and Zucker following it) on the grounds that it had been given at an early stage in the development of Mareva powers, times had moved on since then and it made no commercial sense to deny the Mareva power to come to the aid of enforcement of a foreign judgment on substance. Therefore, Ord. 11, r.1(1)(b) should be available and the power held to exist in all events in principle.

Comment

The limitation on the English courts' powers to grant *Mareva* relief over foreign substance proceedings was restricted at the time to those in *non-*Contracting States: s.25(1) of the 1982 Act conferred the statutory power in the case of foreign Contracting States' (and other UK) proceedings on substance and RSC Ord. 11, r.1(2) provided the procedural complement for service (see *supra, Haiti* and *X v Y*, CAses 87 and 89).

The power in relation to Contracting States' proceedings under s.25(1) could be extended *inter alia* to non-Contracting States by Order in Council under s.25(3)(a), and *The Siskina* would thereby be reversed, which, as seen, has now been carried out. Together with complementary procedural service out with leave under Ord. 11 r.8A where Ord. 11 r.1(2) is not satisfied, obviating the need to resort to r.1(1)(b) in such cases.

In the earlier *Channel Tunnel* case in the House of Lords (see *infra*, s.25(3)(c), Case 100), the Lords held *obiter*, in relation to interlocutory injunctions generally, in aid of foreign proceedings or arbitration, rather than in respect of *Marevas* specifically, that English courts *did* possess the power in aid of foreign substantive proceedings, provided that:

- they *would have* possessed jurisdiction on substance over the action, had it been or were it to be brought before the English courts; and
- on the basis of either: (i) personal jurisdiction over the defendant; or (ii) heads of RSC Ord. 11, r.1(1) other than (b) itself.

" *. . . (c) arbitration proceedings.* "

Case principles

1. At national English common law, English courts did not possess the power to grant interim injunctive relief generally in respect of proceedings on substance conducted or to be conducted in a foreign, non-Contracting State (see *supra, The Siskina* , Case 97).

2. *However,* if the English court would nevertheless *possess personal or RSC Ord. 11, r.1(1) substance jurisdiction* over the defendant, it could exercise its inherent discretion or general statutory discretion under s.37(1) of the Supreme Court Act 1981 to grant interim injunctive relief in aid of foreign non-Contracting State court proceedings on substance or of arbitration in the foreign State (*obiter, Channel Tunnel*).

Interim and protective relief in support of English or foreign arbitration proceedings is now conferred by ss.2(3) and 44 of the Arbitration Act 1996 as from 31 January 1997 (and 1982 Act s.25(3)(c) and (5) is repealed by 1996 s.107(2) and Sched. 4).

Case

100 Channel Tunnel Group Ltd v Balfour Beatty Construction Ltd [1993] 1 All ER 664 House of Lords, 21 January 1993

Facts

The plaintiff channel tunnel concessionaire made a contract in 1986 with the defendant whereby the defendant was to carry out construction work on the tunnel. A dispute arose over the price to be paid to the defendant for the building of a cooling system. When the defendant threatened to stop work on the system until the matter was settled, the plaintiff issued an English writ claiming an interim injunction restraining the defendant from stopping work on the tunnel while the price was being settled. The defendant asserted the Brussels arbitration clause in the contract and sought a stay of the English action.

The Court of Appeal granted the mandatory stay in favour of the non-domestic arbitration under s.1 of the Arbitration Act 1975. The plaintiff appealed to the House of Lords. The question for the Lords was whether an English court had the power to grant an interim injunction in respect of arbitration conducted abroad?

Judgment

The House of Lords held that English courts did possess the general power to grant an interim injunction in aid of foreign (non-Contracting-State) court proceedings or foreign arbitration under s.37(1) of the Supreme Court Act 1981, conferring the general power of injunctive relief.

The earlier decision of the House of Lords in *The Siskina* [1979] AC 210, in which it was held that the courts could not grant such relief, was stated to be limited to where the English courts *would not possess jurisdiction over the substantive claim* if it had been brought before the English courts, or otherwise allowed to be so in the case of a stay of English substance proceedings in favour of agreed foreign jurisdiction or arbitration. Here, on the facts, the English courts would possess such jurisdiction over the defendant and consequently had the power to grant interim relief in aid of agreed Belgian arbitration.

Comments

The preceding judgment was in fact *obiter*, since the actual *ratio decidendi* on which the House of Lords' judgment was based was that the case was not an appropriate one for interim relief in any event, because if the interim injunction were to be granted ordering the defendant not to stop work on the cooling system pending arbitration, the work would probably be completed by the time the matter came to be dealt with by the arbitrators and the plaintiffs would have got what they wanted!

The House of Lords incidentally also decided that the power to grant interim injunctions in aid of arbitration *under s.12(6)(h) of the Arbitration Act 1950* was limited to arbitrations held within the English jurisdiction and not in a foreign country.

This *obiter* judgment of the House of Lords in favour of interim powers in aid of foreign (non-Contracting State) proceedings was not wholly consistent with the subsequent *obiter* findings of a four to one majority of the Judicial Committee of the Privy Council on Appeal from the Court of Appeal of Hong Kong in *Mercedes-Benz AG v Leiduck* [1995] 3 All ER 929, PC (see *supra*, s.25(3)(a), Case 99), in respect of *Mareva* powers in particular, where the *absence of an English substantive action* meant that English courts at least lacked the procedural power to proceed under Ord. 11, r.1(1)(b)—judgment being reserved on whether in principle the power existed and was exercisable in respect of foreign proceedings where the defendant was personally within the jurisdiction or otherwise within one of the other grounds of Ord. 11, r.1(1).

Channel Tunnel was followed and applied to new facts by Evans-Lombe J. in *Phonogram Limited v Def American, The Times*, 7 October 1994 High Court, 30 August 1994. The defendant American record company, which had begun breach of contract proceedings in Californian courts against the plaintiffs sought a stay of the latters' subsequent English contract action, in favour of Californian *forum conveniens*, together with an interlocutory injunction to prevent the plaintiffs from obstructing the defendants' music business in the UK in the meantime. The plaintiffs consented to the stay, but challenged the injunction, on the grounds that *The Siskina* excluded such power where the applicant had no cause of action on substance before the English courts, and that *Channel Tunnel* would not help the defendants, because that decision concerned where there was *arbitration*, not foreign court proceedings, for dealing with substance. As for s.25(1), this only conferred the power in relation to foreign *Contracting* State proceedings on substance (at that time).

Evans-Lombe J. made two important findings (the first of which was of immediate relevance to the *Channel Tunnel* case): (i) the latter had restricted *The Siskina* to where the English courts would *not otherwise possess jurisdiction over* the claim, such jurisdiction otherwise being sufficient for the interlocutory injunction even if the English courts were not actually seised of substance—and this applied as much to foreign non-Contracting State court proceedings as to arbitration; but (ii) the general requirement for an interlocutory injunction in *The Veracruz* [1992] 1 Lloyd, Rep.353, namely, that the applicant should have an existing cause of action to support, was not satisfied here by the defendant on the evidence—and even if it had been, the court would not have exercised its discretion to grant it where the same powers were available to Californian *forum conveniens* on substance: so, in the end, no injunctive relief for the defendant applicant.

The *Channel* case was relied upon by the Court of Appeal in rather different circumstances in *Department of Social Security v Butler* [1995] 4 All ER 193, decided on 21 July 1995, after *Channel* and shortly before *Mercedes-Benz*. In *Butler*, a government department, the Department of Social Security, claimed alleged arrears of maintenance of about £4,000 from the defendant under an assessment made by the Child Support Agency. The Secretary of State possessed such enforcement powers to apply to the magistrates' courts for a liability order under the Child Support Act 1991, but the 1991 Act made no provision for the grant of a *Mareva*-style interlocutory (interim) injunction in aid of the proceedings. Therefore, the question arose as to whether such an order could be made *by the High Court* under s.37(1) of the Supreme Court Act 1981, conferring the general power to grant injunctions where this appeared to be just and convenient, in aid of substantive proceedings before the magistrates? This in turn raised the issue of the difference of approach between *The Siskina* (narrower) and *Channel* (wider). *Channel* had favoured the free-standing nature of provisional relief, at least in relation to foreign arbitrations and probably also foreign court proceedings, alongside the express provision in s.25(1) itself, notwithstanding absence of English proceedings on substance. Consequently, the plaintiff argued that this could be extended so as to allow the High Court to grant *Mareva*-style relief in aid of proceedings in the magistrates' courts.

In the event, the Court of Appeal held against the existence of such power on the facts.

In the first place, although there was no objection in principle to the extension of *Channel* in order to permit the High Court to grant *Mareva*-type relief in aid of magistrates' proceedings, nonetheless, as a matter of statutory construction of the 1991 Act, the latter was comprehensive as to powers of enforcement and did not include such *Mareva* relief in the High Court, even where the defendant was otherwise subject to its personal and territorial jurisdiction.

Secondly, the 1991 Act simply conferred powers of enforcement upon the plaintiff government department—it did not also create a cause of action in this respect to support the *Mareva*-style relief as required by *The Siskina* and *Veracruz Transportation Inc v VC Shipping Co Inc, The Veracruz* [1992] 1 Lloyd's Rep. 353.

(As it happened, even if the power had been held to exist, the court would not have exercised the discretion to grant the relief, because it was said that enforcement should be left to the magistrates under the 1991 Act and not duplicated nor supplemented in the High Court.)

Again, *Channel Tunnel* was referred to by Evans L.J. in the Court of Appeal on 15 February 1996 in *Desert Sun Loan v Hill* [1996] 2 All ER 847, at 856, in the different context of operation of issue estoppel to procedural matters decided upon in foreign interlocutory proceedings, required to be final and 'on the merits'—in which latter connection, such interlocutory, procedural issues were considered to have independent existence in appropriate circumstances, notwithstanding absence of a 'cause of action' in its strict sense.

SECTION 26(1)(a)

" . . . *order that the property arrested be retained as security . . .* "

Case principles

1.   Section 26 retention is not subject to Art. 21 on *lis pendens*.

2.   Section 26 powers of retention and security are not available where
     English courts lacked international jurisdiction over the main merits
     action *in rem* declined.

Case

The Nordglimt [1988] 1 QB 183 High Court, 31 July 1987   **101**

Facts

A cargo carried on board the ship Nordkap from Antwerp to Jedda, Saudi
Arabia, arrived in a damaged condition. The plaintiffs brought *in personam*
proceedings for damages in Belgium and, subsequently thereto, an action *in
rem* in the English courts against the Nordkap's sister ship, Nordglimt, arrested and released on payment of security. The owners challenged both main
English *in rem* jurisdiction (unsuccessfully—see *infra*, Art. 21) and, in the
event that they had won on this, the English courts' powers to make s.26
orders for retention of security pending Belgian *in personam* proceedings.

Judgment

Hobhouse J. held against the defendants on both of these grounds (see *infra*,
Art. 21, on the challenge to main merits jurisdiction).

   (1)   With regard to s.26, although not identical, this was based largely
         upon Art. 7 of the 1952 Brussels Arrest Convention, and since the
         latter had priority over the Judgments Convention by virtue of Art.
         57 of the latter, it would be a contravention of this system for Art.
         21 to be applied to s.26 powers so as to require these to be stayed
         in favour of the Belgian proceedings.
   (2)   However, Hobhouse J. did go on to find that if the reason for declin-
         ing main English merits *in rem* jurisdiction were to have been not a
         decision to stay and to give preference to foreign courts, but absence
         of English merits jurisdiction *ab initio*—for example, as falling
         outside the 1952 Convention or corresponding English Admiralty
         jurisdiction—then it would have been improper for orders to be
         made and retained under s.26.

Comments

With regard to point 1 preceding: (i) on the one hand, Hobhouse J. was incorrect to regard Art. 21 as inconsistent with and consequently excluded by the
1952 Convention (see *infra*, Art. 21, *The Linda*, Case 259); but (ii) on the
other hand, it has also been held that Art. 21 does not operate to require stay
and decline of executory or provisional security proceedings in favour of foreign Contracting State proceedings on substance because the causes of action
are not the same (see *infra*, Art. 21, *Gamlestaden* and *Boss*).

As an addition to point 2 preceding, in *The 'Sylt'* [1991] 1 Lloyd's Rep. 240, Sheen J., in the High Court, in fact refused to grant a stay of their own English action to the plaintiffs in favour of their other proceedings in Sierra Leone. However, Sheen J. noted *obiter* that if the stay *had* been granted, s.26(1)(a)(ii) made it a condition for retention of security thereunder that the judgment of the Sierra Leone court should be *enforceable* in England.

It should be noted finally that by virtue of s.107(2) of and Sched. 4 to the Arbitration Act 1996, the references to stays or dismissals in favour of *arbitration* have been removed from s.26 and are now contained in the specially dedicated s.11 of the 1996 Act substantially reproducing 1982 Act s.26 in relation to arbitration—and s.2(2) of the 1996 Act expressly provides that *inter alia* s.11 also applies to arbitrations having their seats outside England and Wales or Northern Ireland

---

SECTION 30(1)

" . . . *proceedings are principally concerned with* . . . "

General

Section 30(1) of the Civil Jurisdiction and Judgments Act 1982 provides that English (and Northern Irish) courts have jurisdiction over actions for trespass and other torts to immovable property situated outside the UK, unless the proceedings are principally concerned with a question of title to or the right to possession of such property.

This reverses the position at common law, whereby English courts lacked jurisdiction in tort in relation to foreign immovable property (see *British South Africa Co. v Companhia de Moçambique* [1893] AC 602 and *Hesperides Hotels Ltd v Aegean Turkish Holidays Ltd* [1979] AC 508). Such lack of jurisdiction is now limited to actions principally involving title to or possession of the immovable property.

Case principle

An action for the tort of trespass to foreign immovable property, dependent upon the plaintiff being able to establish a right to possession of the property in the first place, is not *principally* concerned with the right to possession so as to prevent the exercise of English jurisdiction under national English private international law applicable to defendants who are not domiciled in any Contracting State, by virtue of Art. 4.

Case

102 Re Polly Peck International plc, The Times, 27 December 1996 High Court, 29 November 1996

Facts

The applicants owned property in the northern part of the Republic of Cyprus when the Turks invaded in 1974 and established the Turkish Federated State of Cyprus (TFSC) in Northern Cyprus which was not recognised internationally. They alleged that the subsidiaries of the defendant, PPI, now in administration, had illegally taken up occupation of the properties under TFSC laws and that in 1995 the administrators of PPI, in realising its assets, had sold PPI's shares in the subsidiaries to a third party.

In their English action, the applicants sought leave of court to bring proceedings, without the consent of PPI's administrators, against PPI and its administrators, claiming an account of profits made from the sale of the shares, on the ground that the subsidiaries had occupied the properties as trespassers.

For such leave to be granted, the applicants had to prove that they had a seriously arguable case on the draft statement of claim against the defendants. The defendants denied that the applicants possessed such a claim on two grounds: (i) lack of English jurisdiction over the immovables in Cyprus because the claim *principally* involved a question of the applicants' right to possession of the properties, which meant that s.30(1) was not satisfied; and (ii) even if this was not so and s.30(1) provided jurisdiction, the action was still bound to fail on the merits because there was no seriously arguable cause of action against PPI.

Judgment

Rattee J. held that the claim did not *principally* concern the right to possession of the Cyprus properties.

'Principally' in s.30(1) was to be construed in its ordinary sense as meaning 'for the most part' or 'chiefly' as in the Concise Oxford English Dictionary; and whilst existence of a right to possession was always a *sine qua non* of trespass, the former was not the chief *purpose of* and *issue in* the present proceedings to establish trespass as the prerequisite to an account of the profits by the defendants as constructive trustees.

Thus, English jurisdiction existed. The court went on to conclude that there was a seriously arguable case for a cause of action on the merits and, accordingly, that the applicants should be granted leave to make their claim (see too *infra*, Comment 4 to Case III).

SECTION 34

"No proceedings may be brought . . . "

Case principle

The s.34 defence against further proceedings being brought in England upon a cause of action in respect of which judgment has previously been granted in the plaintiff's favour abroad, is subject to waiver by, or estoppel against, a defendant who otherwise wishes to use the defence.

Case

103   Republic of India v India Steamship Co. Ltd [1993] AC 410 House of Lords, 18 February 1993

Facts

The plaintiff, the Republic of India, issued English proceedings *in rem* against the defendant, India Steamship Co., in August 1989, served on the defendant's ship, the Indian Endurance, in the English port of Middlesbrough, in May 1990, claiming damages of £2.6 million for defective delivery of a cargo of munitions carried on the defendant's ship, the Indian Grace, in June to September 1987, from Sweden to India. En route, there was a fire. About 51 artillery shells were jettisoned, and the remaining munitions were ruined by water and crushing.

The defendants raised s.34 as a defence to the plaintiff's English action: the plaintiffs had previously sued them in the Indian courts for non-delivery of the 51 shells which were jettisoned and had obtained an Indian judgment *in personam* in the sum of £6,000 as damages in December 1989.

The defence succeeded before Sheen J. at first instance and on appeal to the Court of Appeal. The plaintiff appealed to the House of Lords, on the ground that, through their conduct, the defendants had waived, or were estopped-by-representation from, reliance upon s.34 (and that even if s.34 did apply, its conditions of same cause of action and same parties were not satisfied—see *infra*). The defendants responded that s.34 was mandatory and could not be so waived or subjected to estoppel.

Judgment

Lord Goff, agreed with by the other Law Lords, held that s.34 was merely a defence and that such estoppel *per rem judicatam could* be neutralized by waiver or by estoppel-by-representation.

This was possible from the wording of s.34; and, as a matter of policy, it would enable justice to be done in cases like the present, in which the plaintiffs otherwise stood to lose a large sum of money through operation of s.34.

Consequently, the House of Lords sent the case back to the High Court's Admiralty Division to determine whether, on the facts, the defendants had waived, or were estopped from relying upon, s.34.

Comments

The Admiralty Court would also deal with the plaintiff's new argument that Indian *in personam* and English *in rem* proceedings were not the *same cause of action* (see *infra*, s.34 and Art. 21).

The House of Lords itself also commented, generally, upon whether Indian and English proceedings involved the same cause of action for s.34 (see *infra*).

A summary of the sequence of these proceedings, involving four reported cases, is as follows:

(1) s.34 was held by the House of Lords to be subject to waiver and estoppel by the defendant, in the present case;

(2) the case was then remitted by the House of Lords to Clarke J. in the Admiralty Court, who decided

- the question asked by the House of Lords as to whether, on the facts, the defendants were estopped from using s.34, which he held that they were, *and*

- in case he were wrong on this, he also dealt with the newly-raised issue of whether *in personam* and *in rem* were the same cause of action (see *infra*, s.34, Comment to Case 104), which he held to be so, but *not* also to involve the same parties;

(3) on appeal from Clarke J.'s finding against same parties in (2) preceding, the Court of Appeal held that *in rem* and *in personam* did involve the same parties (see *infra*, s.34, Case 106 and Art. 21—it was accepted on the appeal that the cause of action was the same, *ibid*);

(4) on appeal to the House of Lords, the Court of Appeal's decision on sames parties and absence of estoppel on the facts was upheld (see *infra*, Comment to Case 106) in *The Indian Endurance (No. 2)* [1997] 4 All ER 380 on 16 October 1997. Lord Steyn, with whom the other Lords unanimously agreed, also made the point that, even though at the date upon which the English *in rem* action had initially been commenced, the Indian *in personam* judgment had not yet been delivered, *continuation* of the former on the latter's delivery was included within the concept of being "brought," on a sensible and purposive construction of s.34.

> " . . . *cause of action in respect of which a judgment has been given in his favour* . . . "

Case principles

1. A cause of action in this context means facts, remedies and heads of damage which the plaintiff must prove in order to obtain judgment.

2. English and foreign causes of action may still be the same in this sense, even if brought in a different form.

3. Minors' interests are overriding as a matter of public policy in the construction of s.34. Consequently, s.34 is not a defence if the foreign proceedings were not in a plaintiff minor's best interests.

Case

104 Black v Yates [1992] 1 QB 526 High Court, 5 May 1989

Facts

The plaintiff's husband was killed as a result of the defendant's negligent driving in Spain. She sued the defendant in England in November 1984 as administratrix of her deceased husband's estate claiming: (i) compensation for herself and for their two children aged 11 and 12, as dependants, under the Fatal Accidents Act 1976; and (ii) damages for the deceased's estate, under the Law Reform (Miscellaneous Provisions) Act 1934.

The defendant claimed that the plaintiff's action was barred under s.34, because in May 1984 a Spanish court had already made an award of compensation for the plaintiff and children, although for an amount less than that which would have been ordered in England. The Spanish proceedings had originally been brought as a criminal prosecution by the public prosecutor, but, under Spanish procedure, civil claimants were permitted to participate, leading to a combined criminal-civil judgment, unless the civil parties expressly reserved their right to proceed separately. The plaintiff in this case was represented in the criminal proceedings by a Spanish lawyer who had been engaged by her English solicitor and in this way she took part in the Spanish process.

The plaintiff argued against operation of s.34, on the ground, *inter alia*, that the Spanish civil remedy in criminal proceedings was not the same cause of action as that based upon dependancy ('loss of breadwinner') under the English Fatal Accidents Act 1976.

Judgment

Potter J. held as follows.

(1) 'Cause of action' meant the facts, remedies and heads of loss which a plaintiff had to prove in order to obtain judgment, and a certain latitude in assessing equivalence was required in the international context: in particular, it was not the same as 'form of action'. Thus, since both English and Spanish actions involved death, negligence, dependancy and loss, they were essentially the same, even though some of these aspects had been dealt with as part of the criminal process and Spain had no exact equivalent of the Fatal Accidents Act 1976.

   The defendant, therefore, had a defence against the plaintiff under s.34 in respect of this aspect of the claim (see *infra*, 'same parties', Case 105, as to the decision under the 1934 Act claim).

(2) With regard to the Spanish claim *on behalf of the children* as dependants, however, Potter J. considered that s.34, as a matter of public policy protection of minors, ought not to be construed as having been intended to provide a defence where the foreign proceedings

were not brought in the children's best interests. This was held to be the position in the present case, where far higher damages would have been made available in the English courts but the plaintiff's English lawyer allegedly had not taken the advice of counsel as to the possible effects of the 1982 Act and therefore should have reserved the right of the plaintiff not to participate civilly in Spain.

Comments

Potter J.'s findings as to the meaning of 'cause of action', for s.34, bear a close similarity to the European Court's test of same cause of action for purposes of Art. 21 in *The Maciej Rataj* Case C–406/92 (para. 39), as essentially the same facts and the rule of law relied on as the basis of the action (see *infra*, Art. 21).

However, his constructional gloss on s.34 in relation to minors seems highly questionable.

The further condition in s.34, that the Spanish judgment was entitled to recognition and enforcement in England, was held to be satisfied according to pre-Convention English private international law rules applicable at the time: the judgment was final and conclusive and the Spanish court had international jurisdiction.

In the proceedings before the House of Lords in *Republic of India v India Steamship Co. Ltd.* [1993] AC 410 (HL(E)), the plaintiffs, as shown (see *supra*, s.34 Case 103), argued that the defendant was estopped from relying upon s.34 as a defence—a plea with which the House of Lords agreed in principle, but sent back to the Admiralty Court to decide on the facts. In the alternative before the House of Lords, the plaintiffs argued that even if s.34 was available as a defence, Indian and English causes of action were not the same, as they were required to be thereunder, because the Indian action and judgment were for *short* delivery, whereas the English action was for delivery of *defective* products.

The House of Lords rejected this approach and held causes of action to be the same for purposes of s.34, in terms wholly consistent with *Black v Yates*: both actions were in relation to the same facts and legal relationship in the form of the carriage contract ('cause of action') and both sought a remedy in damages for breach of contract ('subject matter')—even though the breach in Indian and English proceedings was in relation to a different term of that contract (full and correct performance, respectively). Lord Goff contrasted the situation with that in a negligence case in which different damage—to person and property—arose from the same accident, which would be a situation in which the causes of action were different.

As seen, the House of Lords, having held that s.34 *could* be waived or denied through estoppel (see *supra*), then sent the case back to the Admiralty Court for it to decide whether the defendants *were* so estopped on the facts (as well as the new question of whether *in rem* and *in personam* actions were the same cause of action).

Thus, in *The Indian Grace (No. 2)* [1994] 2 Lloyd's Rep. 331, on 9 February 1994, Clarke J. held that, on the facts, the defendants were estopped (by convention or acquiescence) from relying upon s.34 as a defence.

However, in case he were wrong (at 346 col. 2), he went on to consider, *inter alia,* whether the condition of same cause of action in s.34 was satisfied. His conclusions were:

(1)   actions *in personam* and *in rem* involved the same cause of action for s.34—a finding for which he expressly drew support from Convention case law on Art. 21 (at 349, 350, 352 and 354—see *infra,* Art. 21); but

(2)   *such actions did not also involve the same parties, which meant that s.34 could not apply as a defence in this case.*

Subsequently, on appeal by the defendants from Clarke J. to the Court of Appeal in *The Indian Endurance (No. 2)* [1996] 3 All ER 641, on 23 April 1996, it was accepted that Indian and English proceedings involved the same cause of action (at 654)—but the Court of Appeal, borrowing from the European Court's ruling in relation to Art. 21 in *The Maciej Rataj* Case C–406/92, overturned Clarke J. as to the absence of same parties (see *infra,* s.34 'in proceedings between the same parties', Case 106, and Art. 21 'same parties', holding instead that the parties were the same). Subsequently, the House of Lords upheld the Court of Appeal's judgment, on 16 October 1997, in *The Indian Endurance (No. 2)* [1997] 4 All ER 380.

"*. . . in proceedings between the same parties . . .*"

Case principles

1.   Parties are the same even if in one set of proceedings a party merely intervened as a civil party in what were originally criminal proceedings.

2.   The rule of estoppel, that parties must have acted in the same capacity in both sets of proceedings, does not apply with the same rigour in the operation of s.34.

Case

105   Black v Yates [1992] 1 QB 526 High Court, 5 May 1989

Facts

See supra, s.34 'cause of action in respect of which a judgment has been given', Case 104.

Judgment

(1)   The defendant was held to be entitled to use s.34 as a defence in the case of the plaintiff's claim (but not also in respect of her claim on behalf of the children—see *supra*) under the Fatal Accidents Act 1976, because both cause of action and parties in England and Spain were the same, notwithstanding that the plaintiff was not an original party to the criminal prosecution and that in the English action she brought the claim as administratrix of her deceased husband's estate in accordance with the Fatal Accidents Act 1976 procedures, rather than in her personal capacity as in Spain. Potter J. explained that in the context of s.34, forms and procedures of actions were likely to vary in different states and that, in essence, the dependants were still the real parties and beneficiaries in the English action, hardly divergent from the Spanish.

(2)   However, in the case of the plaintiff's claim on behalf of the deceased's estate under the Law Reform (Miscellaneous Provisions) Act 1934, the parties were held by Potter J. not to be the same. Spain did have a similar procedure to that of the 1934 Act, whereby one of the deceased's heirs was nominated to bring an action on behalf of the 'community of heirs'. But the plaintiff had not in fact acted according to this procedure in Spain. She had pursued the claim personally on her own and the children's behalf. Section 34 was therefore unavailable to be pleaded by the defendant as a defence to the plaintiff's English action under the 1934 Act.

Comment

Section 34 says that the foreign proceedings must have been between the same parties 'or their privies'.

It is uncertain when exactly a party will be held to have been so *privy*. However, in the non-s.34 case of *House of Spring Gardens Ltd v Waite* [1991] 1 QB 241 of 11 April 1990 (see *infra*, Art. 27(1), *Interdesco*, Case ●●●), the English Court of Appeal—in the context of estoppel through an Irish judgment which had found against fraud in a previous Irish judgment against three defendants, where the first-mentioned judgment was reached in proceedings brought by only two of those defendants who had alleged fraud—held that there was sufficient 'privity of interest' of the third defendant for him to be estopped from making further allegations of fraud of the original Irish judgment, in the course of (pre-Convention) enforcement proceedings before the English courts (' . . . he was content to sit back and leave others to fight his battle, at no expense to himself . . . that is sufficient to make him privy to the estoppel . . . ').

Case principle

3.   A hybrid action both *in rem* and *in personam* is between the same parties (and on the same cause of action) as an action *in personam*

leading to judgment in a foreign State so as to be barred from being brought or continued with under s.34.

Case

106   The Indian Endurance (No. 2), Republic of India v India Steamship Co. Ltd [1996] 3 All ER 641 Court of Appeal, 23 April 1996

Facts

See supra, s.34, 'no proceedings may be brought', Case 103, and 'same cause of action' (Comments to Black v Yates, Case 104), and infra, Art. 21, 'same cause of action' and 'same parties'.

Judgment

The Court of Appeal applied Art. 21 case authorities to provide a purposive construction of s.34. The word 'brought' in s.34 and Art. 21 (proceedings *brought*) was not to be taken to indicate that solely the initial character of English proceedings *in rem* was to be referred to for the purposes of deciding whether parties were the same as in the previous Indian *in personam* action. Since the defendant shipowner subsequently acknowledged English *in rem* service personally so as to convert the English action into hybrid *in rem-in personam*, the latter should be treated as its real nature, held to involve same parties (applying European Court in *Maciej Rataj*, see *infra*, Art. 21).

Comments

The Court of Appeal's judgment in *The Indian Endurance (No. 2)* was unanimously upheld by the House of Lords on 16 October 1997, [1997] 4 All ER 380:

1.   Hobhouse J. had been incorrect to find hybrid *in rem-in personam* to involve different parties from *in personam* for Article 21 in *The Nordglimt*, on the ground that date of commencement as *in rem* was the pertinent date to assess parties, notwithstanding subsequent change to hybrid, and same parties thereafter, *infra* Case 299, and the same was true for s.34, especially in the light of the European Court's *Maciej Rataj* Case C–406/92 decision; and

2.   on the facts, the defendants were not estopped by convention or by acquiescence from relying upon s.34.

In *'The Sylt'* [1991] 1 Lloyd's Rep. 240, Sheen J. in the High Court suggested *obiter* that parties were the same for s.34 even *at the inception* of the English *in rem* action (followed by Saville J. in *The Havhelt* [1993] 1 Lloyd's Rep. 523 in the national *forum non conveniens* context). However, Sheen J. appeared to base his conclusion on a generalization of the Court of Appeal's finding in *The Deichland, supra*, Case 85, that charterers were in substance 'defendants' for purposes of identification of relevant domicile under Art. 2: if they were thus defendants, so too were they 'parties' for purposes of s.34 and doubtless also Art. 21. However, that is a big leap to make and lacks explicit confirmation at appellate level.

SECTION 41

" . . . *resident in the United Kingdom* . . . "

General

Article 52, para. 1 assigns domicile of individuals to the internal *lex fori*. In the United Kingdom, this is laid down for Convention purposes in s.41 of the Civil Jurisdiction and Judgments Act 1982.

For such domicile in the UK, or in a part thereof (England and Wales, Scotland and Northern Ireland), to exist under s.41, two things are required: *residence* and a *substantial connection*. There is a rebuttable presumption of the latter from the former's existence for the last three months or more.

Case principle

Residence in s.41 means *settled or usual place of abode*, connoting some degree of permanence or continuity in accordance with the normal English meaning.

Case

Bank of Dubai Limited v Fouad Haji Abbas [1997] I.L.Pr. 308 Court of Appeal, 17 July 1996   **107**

Facts

The plaintiff Dubai bank wished to sue the defendant Mr Abbas in the English courts in 1994 for money alleged to be owing on accounts. The defendant challenged English jurisdiction under RSC Ord. 12, r.8. The plaintiff sought to base jurisdiction upon the national English discretionary ground for leave to serve the writ out of England and Wales under RSC Ord. 11, r.1(1)(a), requiring it to be shown on a good arguable case that the defendant was domiciled in England and Wales. (Since the subject matter of the case appeared to fall within the Convention's civil and commercial scope, it is inexplicable why jurisdiction was not sought to be founded upon Art. 2 of the Convention itself, in which event leave to serve out would not have been required.) Under Ord. 11, r.1(4), s.41 also applied to the meaning of domicile in Ord. 11, r.1(1)(a).

Judgment

The Court of Appeal held that the defendant was not resident in England and Wales nor consequently domiciled there for jurisdiction.

In the first place, the court did not dissent from the view that s.41 should be construed for discretionary national English jurisdiction as it would be for Convention purposes—although since the normal English meaning applied to the latter in any event, such finding was of reduced moment.

Secondly, as to the normal English meaning of residence, the Court of Appeal adopted the definition of the House of Lords in *Levene v Commissioners of Inland Revenue* [1928] AC 217 for taxation purposes, namely, a settled or usual place of abode, connoting some degree of permanence or continuity. The Court of Appeal rejected the idea that the threshold was necessarily quite low in view of the mere three month presumption of substantial connection in s.41, because this said nothing about the residence element itself. The latter had to be ascertained according to all relevant facts and circumstances of a particular case, and duration of connections with a jurisdiction could be of greater or lesser significance when balanced against those with other territories: for example, a person who came to England in order to retire and who had terminated all previous foreign connections might acquire an English residence *immediately*.

Thirdly, on the facts, it was not proved on a good arguable case that the defendant had established a settled or usual place of abode in England and Wales. His company had taken a lease on a flat in London, where his wife—from whom he was allegedly separated—and family had their home; but the evidence was that he himself only occasionally paid visits there, never overnight, preferring to stay in hotels. Nor was it true, as Potter J. at first instance had been led to believe in finding in favour of English residence, that the defendant was registered for community charge as occupier of the London flat, a matter treated as otherwise being of some significance by the Court of Appeal.

Thus, the defendant was neither resident nor consequently domiciled within in England and Wales (and in view of the fact that the first instance judge had been seriously mistaken about the poll tax registration, the Court of Appeal did not believe that it was carrying out a review of fact at the appellate stage contrary to established jurisdictional principles, but was merely instead considering the matter afresh).

Comment

The Court of Appeal's treatment of the meaning of 'residence' in s.41 is quite consistent with the discussion in Kaye, *Civil Jurisdiction* pp. 350–76 and 384–400.

SECTION 42(6), (7)

> " . . . *seat in a state [/Contracting State] other than the United Kingdom* . . . "

Case principle

A company has its seat as domicile in a foreign State under the UK's meaning of seat for Convention purposes, if it is *either* incorporated there with registered office (s.42(6)(a)) *or* its central management and control is exercised there (s.42(6)(b)), and, in either case, the foreign Contracting State's courts regard it as having its seat in that State (s.42(7)).

Case

The Deichland [1990] 1 QB 361 Court of Appeal, 20 April 1989   **108**

Facts

The plaintiff cargo owners sued the defendant charterers for damage to the cargo in the English courts on national English jurisdiction grounds which the plaintiffs argued applied under Art. 4, para. 1 on the basis that the defendant company was incorporated with its seat in Panama, a non-Contracting State, under s.42(6)(a). They argued that this was not affected by the fact that central management and control of the company was exercised in Germany, a Contracting State, for purposes of s.42(6)(b), nor that German courts would recognize the German seat under s.42(7), because s.42(6)(a) took precedence over s.42(6)(b)—the latter only applied if there was no state in respect of which both incorporation and registered office were satisfied. The defendants asserted German jurisdiction as that of their domicile under Convention Art. 2.

Judgment

The Court of Appeal unanimously rejected the plaintiffs' argument and held for German Art. 2 domicile jurisdiction. It would be unnatural to interpret s.42(6)(a) and (b)—state of incorporation and registered office and state of central management and control, respectively—as anything other than equal, alternative bases of seat. If Germany satisfied s.42(6)(b) and (7), the defendant was domiciled in Germany for Art. 2 and it was immaterial that Panama would also satisfy s.42(6)(a). Any problems of multiple jurisdiction of Contracting States would be dealt with by Arts 21 and 22.

SECTION 49

" . . . *not inconsistent with the 1968 Convention.*"

Case principle

1. Section 49 preserves stays for *forum non conveniens* where not inconsistent with the Convention. As between Contracting States, Convention jurisdiction grounds are not subject to stays on the ground of *forum non conveniens*, which would be inconsistent with the Convention.

Case

109 Aiglon Ltd and L'Aiglon S.A. v Gau Shan Co. Ltd [1993] 1 Lloyd's Rep. 164
High Court, 23 June 1992

Facts

English and Swiss plaintiffs in the overall proceedings were in dispute with
the defendant concerning a contract made in 1981 for the sale of cotton. The
matter went to English arbitration where the defendant was successful in
February 1992. The defendant wished to enforce the arbitration award in the
English courts and added further claims of fraudulent preference in alleging
that the first plaintiff was transferring its assets to the second in order to
avoid enforcement.

Jurisdiction over the second plaintiff was based upon Art. 6(1) of the
Lugano Convention applicable in the UK and Switzerland—as joint 'defendant' to the defendant's claim against it and the first plaintiff, domiciled in
England. In this application, the second plaintiff requested a stay of English
proceedings in favour of Swiss jurisdiction as *forum conveniens*.

Judgment

Hirst J. held that *forum non conveniens* did not apply to Convention jurisdiction between Contracting States and would be inconsistent therewith for purposes of s.49. This was in order to achieve certainty as to jurisdiction under
the Convention and was in accord with statements in the Jenard and Schlosser
Reports and in the Court of Appeal in *Re Harrods (Buenos Aires) Ltd* (*infra*,
Case 111).

On the facts, however, Hirst J. considered that even if *forum conveniens* had
been applicable, a stay would not have been granted: English courts were most
appropriate to deal with allegations of asset-stripping of an English company
in the position of the first plaintiff.

See too Arts 1, para. 2(2), 5(3), 6 and 54; and Fox v Taher Case 313.

Case principle

2. It is not inconsistent with the Convention for the English court to apply
    its discretionary national principles of stay for *forum non conveniens* and
    lis alibi pendens in relation to national jurisdiction over non-Contracting
    State defendants under Art. 4, even in respect of competing foreign
    Contracting State jurisdiction.

Case

110 Sarrio S.A. v Kuwait Investment Authority [1996] 1 Lloyd's Rep. 650 High
Court, 12 October 1995; [1997] 1 Lloyd's Rep. 113 Court of Appeal, 12
August 1996

See infra, Arts 4 and 21.

Case principle

3. *Forum non conveniens* continues to operate in relation to Convention (or non-Convention Art. 4) jurisdiction, in favour of non-Contracting States' jurisdiction.

Case

Re Harrods (Buenos Aires) Ltd [1991] 3 WLR 397 Court of Appeal, 19 **111** December 1990

Facts

A 49 per cent Swiss shareowner in the English company, Harrods (Buenos Aires) Ltd, applied to the English courts for an order that a different Swiss company owning 51 per cent of the shares in Harrods should purchase the former's 49 per cent shareholding, on the ground that the Harrods company's affairs were being run in an unfairly prejudicial manner. The defendant Harrods' registered office was in England, although its business to run a department store was factually carried on from Argentina. The 51 per cent Swiss company requested the English court to stay its proceedings in favour of Argentina as *forum conveniens*. Since the English courts possessed jurisdiction over Harrods under Art. 2, on the grounds of its English seat as domicile, the 49 per cent Swiss company objected that the English court was not permitted to stay or decline its Convention jurisdiction on the ground of England as *forum non conveniens*—even in favour of a non-Contracting State's courts such as those of Argentina.

Judgment

The Court of Appeal unanimously held that the English courts possessed the power to stay (and, in further proceedings, Argentina was considered to be *forum conveniens*).

Whereas *forum non conveniens* would be inconsistent with the Convention as between Contracting States for whom Convention jurisdiction was mandatory and exclusive under Art. 3, this was not also the case in relation to non-Contracting State competing jurisdiction, and s.49 consequently was not contravened. The Convention, in accordance with Art. 220 of the EC Treaty, was intended to introduce a mandatory system of international jurisdiction as between Contracting States and had no interest in regulating relations with non-Contracting States.

The Court of Appeal also unanimously agreed that earlier High Court decisions in *S. & W. Berisford plc v New Hampshire Insurance* [1990] 2 All ER 321, 27 November 1989 and *Arkwright Mutual Insurance Co. v Bryanston Insurance Co. Ltd* [1990] 2 All ER 335, 24 January 1990, to the effect that English courts lacked the ability to stay their Convention proceedings in favour of non-Contracting State *forum conveniens* and *lis pendens* respectively, were—*respectfully*—not to be followed and, naturally, were not binding at appellate level.

Comments

1. Although *Re Harrods* itself concerned *forum non conveniens*, the preceding reference to the High Court decision in *Arkwright* (*lis pendens*), not just *Berisford* (*forum conveniens*), indicates that *lis pendens* is also within the scope of the Court of Appeal's decision in favour of its continuation in relation to non-Contracting State jurisdiction. Furthermore, *forum conveniens* and *lis pendens* are now regarded, in any event, in England as forming part of a single overall doctrine of most appropriate forum (see Kaye, *Private International Law of Tort and Product Liability* Chap. 4, and *Sarrio v Kuwait Investment Authority* [1996] 1 Lloyd's Rep. 650, Mance J.).

   Eventually, the House of Lords, aided by the European Court of Justice, will reach a definitive decision between opposing High Court and Court of Appeal positions, although, until that time, the Court of Appeal naturally takes precedence (and rightly so, in the writer's view—see 'The EEC Judgments Convention and the Outer World: Goodbye to *Forum Non Conveniens*?' (1992) *Journal of Business Law* 47, pp. 74–6). Stays in favour of non-Contracting (Antiguan) State *forum conveniens* in *Re Harrods* (and the mirror-image refusal to injunct continuation of the foreign proceedings claimed to be in 'contravention' of Contracting State Convention jurisdiction—see *infra*, *Société Commerciale de Réassurance*, Case 112) were reaffirmed by the Court of Appeal (Steyn L.J.) in *Nike v Parker* (unreported), 31 October 1994.

2. In both *Berisford* and *Arkwright*, the High Court judges considered that, if they were wrong about inapplicability of s.49 stays of Convention jurisdiction in favour of non-Contracting States' courts, there would nonetheless have to be very strong connections with the foreign country for the discretion to stay to be exercised on the facts.

Berisford

Facts

The two plaintiffs were English and New York companies, parent and subsidiary respectively, carrying on the business of selling jewellery in New York. They were insured with the defendant New Hampshire insurance company, which carried on business in New York and London. The plaintiffs sued the defendant in England for payment under the policy in respect of losses of jewellery worth 54 million US dollars, allegedly stolen in New York, but which the defendants said was due to poor auditing. The defendants sought a stay of the English proceedings, on the ground that New York was *forum conveniens* to hear the action. The plaintiffs responded that this was not possible because

English jurisdiction was based upon the Convention ground, under Art. 8, paras 1(1) and 2, of deemed English domicile of the defendant American insurer through English branch or agency.

Judgment

As seen, Hobhouse J. regarded *forum non conveniens* as inapplicable to Convention jurisdiction, even in relation to non-Contracting State—here, American—competing jurisdiction.

However, if this were wrong, he nevertheless declined to stay in favour of New York courts as clearly more appropriate to hear the case, because: (i) in Convention cases, there would have to be very weighty factors in favour of the non-Contracting State jurisdiction—on the facts, this was not the case, since the connections with England and New York were fairly evenly balanced; and (ii) the existence of a non-exclusive English jurisdiction agreement created a strong presumption that England was most suitable.

Arkwright

Facts

The plaintiff Massachusetts insurance company sought to recover sums paid to an American insured from the defendant reinsurers. The reinsurers denied liability on grounds, *inter alia*, that the plaintiff had overpaid the insured and failed to take all businesslike steps to settle and quantify the claim. In May 1989, the defendants brought proceedings in the New York courts for a negative declaration of non-liability and the plaintiffs commenced their own action against the defendants in England in June 1989 for payment of reinsurance monies. Subsequently, in August 1989 the defendants asked the English courts to stay their proceedings in favour of New York *lis alibi pendens* as *forum conveniens*. It was common ground that the Convention governed the English action.

Judgment

As previously seen, Potter J. followed *Berisford* in finding against power to stay for *forum non conveniens* under s.49, this time for *lis alibi pendens* which was merely an aspect of the former—even in relation to non-Contracting State proceedings.

However, if he were wrong on this, Potter J. still did not consider New York to be clearly or distinctly the more appropriate forum and a stay of the English action would not be granted.

Foreign *lis pendens* was a factor in favour of stay (see *The Spiliada* [1987] AC 460, at 475–8), but not conclusive, especially if New York proceedings were only brought by the defendants in order to pre-empt the prospective English action of the plaintiffs. Furthermore, English law governed the reinsurance contracts concluded in London, evidence was accessible in England and costs in New York were unlikely to be less. Even if the costs would have been less in New York, the plaintiff would still lose a legitimate juridical advantage of being able to recover costs in England—important where, as here, the sums involved in the claim were relatively small.

3.   In the Court of Appeal in *Airbus Industrie GIE v Patel*, [1997] I.L.Pr. 230, 31 July 1996, on an application to restrain parties from suing anywhere outside India, which would have included courts of the applicant's French domicile (not that there appeared to be any actual intention to proceed there), Hobhouse L.J. indicated that to the extent that this would prevent French jurisdiction, the application would have to fail because the Convention accorded French courts jurisdiction under Art. 2 and there was no suggestion that France was *forum non conveniens*.

It is unclear whether Hobhouse L.J., previously the High Court judge in *Berisford*, see *supra*, meant to suggest that English courts could not possibly restrain Contracting State—here, French—jurisdiction in favour of competing non-Contracting State, on grounds including *forum non conveniens*. If he did, plainly this would be contrary to the rationale of *Re Harrods*, even taking into account the even more stringent requirements for restraint of a foreign action than those applied to stay of English proceedings.

Airbus

Facts

The case itself arose from the crash of an aircraft on landing in India in 1990 with large loss of life amongst the passengers and crew. An Indian inquiry indicated pilot error and lack of fire-fighting facilities of the airport as the cause, but no fault was found on the part of the aircraft's manufacturers, Airbus Industrie (AI), a company with its seat in France. The claimants for compensation were survivors and representatives of the deceased, mostly Indian but including a few British and American. In 1992, they sued the airline and Indian airport authorities in India, and also brought an action in Texas, where liability was strict and contingency fees available, against a number of parties including AI. AI itself brought an action in India in 1992 for an injunction to restrain the English claimants in India from suing outside India (in other words, in Texas), which was successful. However, since the Indian courts' jurisdiction over the claimants was based upon Order 11-type discretionary jurisdiction, the English courts themselves would not recognise and enforce the Indian judgment against the claimants (*Turnbull v Walker* (1892) 67 LT 767) and consequently AI sought the same injunctive relief from the English courts themselves, which was refused by Colman J. at first instance, on the ground that AI had failed to show that Texan proceedings against them would be unjust through being vexatious or oppressive—on the contrary, since there were no contingency fees available to the plaintiffs in India, possibly long delays in litigation there and fault-based liability, not strict as in Texas, the grant of an anti-suit injunction in favour of AI, confining claimants' proceedings to India, would not be appropriate. AI appealed.

Judgment (reversed by House of Lords, 2 April 1998)

The Court of Appeal upheld AI's appeal and granted the anti-suit injunction against claimants, prohibiting them from suing outside India other than in England or France, being the claimants' and AI's respective domiciles.

In the first place, there did exist the power in the English courts to grant such a restraint of foreign proceedings in spite of the fact that this was in favour of India, *not England* itself, as *forum conveniens*. This had never previously been held, but the principles underlying the case law on such injunctions in favour of English *forum conveniens* (or local *forum conveniens* in case of decisions of the Judicial Committee of the Privy Council—see *S.N.I. Aérospatiale v Lee* [1987] 1 AC 871) were equally applicable to restraint in favour of another country's jurisdiction as *forum conveniens*.

Secondly, as to discretion and whether suit outside India was shown to be unjust through vexation or oppression to AI, the Court of Appeal considered this to be the case: there were no significant connections with Texas, liability in Texas was strict and Texan courts at the time applied no doctrine of *forum non conveniens* which would otherwise have enabled AI to challenge jurisdiction in that state itself. However, as seen, in view of the French seat of AI, the anti-suit injunction would not also include France where the claimants would have a perfectly proper basis of jurisdiction over AI under Convention Art. 2 (see, however, criticism in 3, *supra*).

4. In *Re Polly Peck International plc*, *The Times*, 27 December 1996 High Court, 29 November 1996, Rattee J. in the Chancery Division of the High Court had before him a claim concerning trespass to land in Northern Cyprus as a non-Contracting State. The question of English courts' jurisdiction arose and this was found to exist under s.30(1) of the Civil Jurisdiction and Judgments Act 1982 (see *supra*, Case 102). National authorities in *British South Africa Co. v Companhia de Moçambique* [1893] AC 602 and *Hesperides Hotels v Aegean Turkish Holidays Ltd* [1979] AC 508 had previously held English courts to lack jurisdiction over actions for title to, possession of or trespass to foreign immovables. But, subsequently, s.30(1) had excluded trespass and other torts from this rule, which was thereafter confined to actions principally concerned with title to or possession of the property. In *Polly Peck*, Rattee J. in fact held that s.30(1) was satisfied. However, it had been argued in the alternative that even if the action were to be held to be principally concerned with title to or possession of the foreign immovables so that s.30(1) was not applicable so as to enable jurisdiction of the English courts, nevertheless, the latter could still possess jurisdiction under Art. 2 of the Convention, notwithstanding the foreign, non-Contracting State situation of the property. Rattee J. did not have to decide on this, given his finding that s.30(1) applied, but he did comment that such an argument for jurisdiction under Art. 2 appeared to face considerable difficulty in the light of the *Harrods* decision. In other words, the claims to jurisdiction of

non-Contracting States' courts, otherwise recognized under the national rules of the Contracting State forum, should not simply be ignored in such circumstances, whether in the area of stays for *forum conveniens* or title to or possession of foreign land.

The matter is discussed in Kaye, *Civil Jurisdiction and Enforcement of Foreign Judgments* pp. 880–3 and 973.

For converse considerations, note the non-Convention case of *Finance Ltd v Afribank Nigeria Ltd* [1995] 1 Lloyd's Rep. 134 High Court, 25 April 1994, where Longmore J. held possession of assets in a foreign Contracting State (Ireland) by the defendant non-Contracting State domiciliary to be material in favour of national English *forum conveniens* over the non-Contracting State's (Nigeria's) courts because of the ease of enforcement of any future English judgment against those foreign Contracting State assets under the Convention (p. 140 col. 2—meaning the Brussels Convention as between the UK and Ireland, rather than the Lugano as there mentioned by Longmore J.).

Case principle

4. Non-Contracting State proceedings against a defendant who is domiciled in a Contracting State and who is otherwise subject to a Contracting State's courts' jurisdiction will not be restrained by an anti-suit injunction simply on the ground of 'invasion' of the defendant's Convention-jurisdiction 'rights'.

Case

112 Société Commerciale de Réassurance v Eras International Ltd (No. 2) [1995] 2 All ER 278 High Court, 17 December 1993

Facts

See infra, Art. 6(1), Cases 188 and 190.

Judgment

In rejecting this ground for the stay of further pursuit of the Illinois proceedings in negligence against the French applicants, otherwise subject to French or English Convention jurisdiction under Arts 2 and 6(2) respectively, Potter J. himself questioned whether individuals possessed such direct 'rights' under the Convention's Preamble; and even if they did, *Re Harrods* had shown that Convention jurisdiction was intended to co-exist with competing non-Contracting States' jurisdiction, not to exclude the latter and, as a decision of the Court of Appeal, *Re Harrods* was to be followed.

Case principle

5. *Forum non conveniens* still applies as between courts of different parts of the UK in purely internal, non-international cases governed by 1982 Act, Sched. 4.

Case

Cumming v Scottish Daily Record and Sunday Mail Ltd, The Times, 8 June **113**
(1995) High Court, 30 March 1995

Facts

The plaintiff was a student at a Scottish university, who had lived for a short
period in England and intended to work as a journalist in England. He claimed
that he had been defamed by the defendant Scottish newspaper in both
England and Scotland. The Sunday Mail newspaper had a weekly circulation
of 850 000 copies of which 60 000 were sold in England and Wales. The
plaintiff wished to sue the defendants for damages in the English courts. The
defendant sought a stay of English proceedings in favour of Scotland as *forum
conveniens*. The dispute was not international, since all parties and facts were
confined to the United Kingdom and consequently the Convention was inapplicable. Sched. 4 to the 1982 Act, allocating jurisdiction between courts of
different parts of the UK (England and Wales, Northern Ireland and Scotland),
applied instead. Scottish courts would have jurisdiction under Sched. 4, Art. 2
on the ground of defendant's Scottish domicile; and English jurisdiction would
be sought to be founded upon Sched. 4, Art. 5(3), as place of harmful event in
the tort of defamation.

The essential question for the English court was whether it possessed the
power to stay proceedings for *forum non conveniens* when it was seised of the
action *under Sched. 4*? Schedule 4 itself made no express provision for this, yet
s.49 of the 1982 Act said that *nothing* in the Act was to prevent a UK court
from staying its proceedings on the ground of *forum non conveniens* or
otherwise, where to do so was not inconsistent with the 1968 Convention.

Judgment

Drake J. held that *forum non conveniens* continued to apply in relation to
courts in other parts of the UK under Sched. 4. The judge thought that its
exclusion might have been preferable, as being more in conformity with the
Convention itself, yet s.49 required such stays to be *inconsistent* with the
Convention for them to be excluded, and this they were not.

Comment

Drake J.'s judgment in *Cumming* was completely contrary to his finding a year
earlier in a case involving almost identical facts (see *Foxen, infra*). His explanation in *Cumming* was that he had changed his mind as a result of adverse
academic commentary upon his earlier decision (see 'Jurisdictional Discretion
in Intra-United Kingdom Cases' (1994) *Personal Injury Law and Medical
Review* 151; and 'International Jurisdiction: High Court Reverses Itself'
(1996) *Personal Injury Law and Medical Review* 19).

The position is, therefore, that there are two conflicting High Court decisions *by the same judge*—a situation which Drake J. himself regarded as

unique, were the *Cumming* case to have gone to the Court of Appeal. In the meantime, presumably, the later judgment in *Cumming*, delivered in full knowledge of the earlier, is likely to have the greater authority in practice.

The earlier case referred to was:

Foxen v Scotsman Publications Ltd, The Times, 17 February 1994 High Court, 4 February 1994

Facts

The plaintiff, who was domiciled in Scotland, wished to sue the defendant Scottish newspaper publisher in the English courts for damages for a defamatory article published in the defendant's newspaper *Scotland on Sunday*, which had 90 per cent of its circulation in Scotland and the remainder in England. The defendant challenged English Sched. 4, Art. 5(3) jurisdiction, on the ground that Scotland was *forum conveniens*: plaintiff and defendant were domiciled there, which was also where the main damage was suffered to the plaintiff's reputation and where the principal witnesses were to be found. Whereas, the English connection was that the newspaper report was about an English soil association of which the plaintiff was the chairwoman, most of the meat involved in the report was likely to have been sold in England rather than in Scotland where the cattle in question were to be found, and many of the plaintiff's witnesses were in England.

Judgment

As seen, Drake J. regarded *forum non conveniens* as inapplicable to Sched. 4 English jurisdiction, which could therefore not be so stayed—notwithstanding that, on balance, he would otherwise have considered Scotland to be *forum conveniens*.

The judge believed that the Convention's spirit, if not letter, excluding *forum non conveniens*, required the latter also to be displaced for purposes of Sched. 4. Operation of *forum non conveniens*, consequently, would be inconsistent with the Convention, in contravention of the 1982 Act s.49 (*supra*).

Comment

In *Cumming*, Drake J. recognized that Convention-international and Sched. 4-internal-UK spheres were related, but separate (see further, Kaye, *Civil Jurisdiction* pp. 216–26).

Furthermore, this approach has some consistency with the European Court's perception of Sched. 4 in its decision in *Kleinwort Benson Ltd v City of Glasgow District Council* Case C–346/93, in which the court declined jurisdiction to rule upon interpretation of Sched. 4's jurisdiction grounds, as opposed to those of the Convention, notwithstanding the close similarities of their provisions.

> " . . . staying . . . proceedings before it . . . "

General

Section 49 preserves stays of *English* proceedings where not inconsistent with the Convention.

English courts also have a national law power, only to be exercised with the utmost caution, to grant an injunction restraining a party from proceeding with a foreign action, on the ground of (probably not exhaustively) (i) foreign *forum non conveniens* (see *SNI Aérospatiale v Lee Kui Jak* [1987] 1 AC 871, PC: vexation or oppression also required; *Société Commerciale de Réassurance v Eras International Ltd (No. 2)* [1995] 2 All ER 278: party joined as third party can apply for restraint of foreign action; *Airbus Industrie GIE v Patel* [1997] I.L.Pr. 230, CA, 31 July 1996: anti-suit injunction need not be granted in favour of solely English courts, reversed by Lords 2 April 1998; *Deaville v Aeroflot Russian International Airlines* [1997] 2 Lloyd's Rep. 67, *infra*, Case 302: restraint of French action refused on the ground that it would be a breach of comity so to injunct pending determination of their own jurisdiction by the French courts—and English courts' Art. 57 jurisdiction stayed instead, under English courts' inherent powers to do so in the meantime), or (ii) breach of a jurisdiction or arbitration agreement, or (iii) unconscionability of bringing the foreign proceedings, through interference with English process or equitable defences (*British Airways Board v Laker Airways Ltd* [1985] AC 58; *South Carolina Insurance Co. v Assurantie NV* [1987] AC 24).

Are such powers exercisable in relation to foreign *Contracting* States' *Convention* proceedings?

Case principles

1. Injunctions *can* also be granted in order to restrain foreign Contracting States' proceedings.
2. Where the ground of restraint is that of breach of a jurisdiction or arbitration agreement, the traditional controls on exercise of the discretion may be relaxed.

Case

Continental Bank N.A. v Aeakos Compania Naviera S.A. [1994] 1 Lloyd's Rep. 505 Court of Appeal, 10 November 1993   **114**

Facts

See infra, Art. 17 'disputes in connection with'.

The Court of Appeal dealt with the first main issue of whether a contractual jurisdiction clause would also cover disputes in tort arising from the contract (*infra*), before proceeding to the matter of injunctions to restrain foreign Contracting States' proceedings.

Judgment

The Court of Appeal confirmed the first instance judge's decision to injunct the plaintiff in Greek proceedings against breach of an English jurisdiction agreement. Steyn L.J. considered that damages for breach of (jurisdiction) contract would be a relatively ineffective remedy when compared to an injunction, and the jurisdiction agreement would otherwise be valueless. This was a paradigm case for grant of an injunction.

Comment

See, however, *Marc Rich & Co. AG v Società Italiani Impianti PA (The "Atlantic Emperor") (No. 2)* [1992] 1 Lloyd's Rep. 624, in which the central issue was whether an Italian court's ruling upon arbitral-existence would be entitled to recognition, as a factor in deciding whether to grant the plaintiff's request for an injunction to restrain the defendants from continuing their Italian proceedings in alleged breach of an English arbitration agreement of which the existence was denied by the defendants. As it happened, the Court of Appeal concluded that the Italian judgment would have to be recognized— a finding strongly militating against granting the injunction to restrain the Italian action. Nevertheless, Neill L.J. did comment that even if the Italian ruling had not been required to be recognized, the proper decision would have been to refuse the injunction in any event, out of caution against exercise of the discretion (at 633 col. 2–634).

Case

115 Aggeliki Charis Compania Maritima S.A. v Pagnan S.p.A. (The 'Angelic Grace') [1995] 1 Lloyd's Rep. 87 Court of Appeal, 17 May 1994

Facts

See infra, Art. 17 'disputes in connection with'.

The Court of Appeal dealt with the first main issue of whether an arbitration clause also covered disputes in tort arising out of the contract, before proceeding to pronounce upon injunctions to restrain a foreign Contracting State's proceedings.

Judgment

The Court of Appeal followed *Continental Bank* in being prepared to issue an injunction against Italian proceedings in breach of a London arbitration clause in a charter party.

Millett L.J. explained furthermore that usual controls on exercise of the injunctive discretion would be relaxed where the party bringing foreign proceedings was in beach of its promise not to do so.

Comment

This decision was followed by Clarke J. in the High Court in *Kara Mara Shipping Ltd v Cereol Italia Srl* (unreported), 5 October 1995, in relation to the power to injunct United States court proceedings in breach of agreed London arbitration. *Aggeliki* was also referred to by the Court of Appeal in *Schiffahrtsgesellschaft Detlef von Appen GmbH v Wiener Allianz Versicherungs AG* (unreported), 16 April 1997, in which it was held that an injunction could be granted in order to restrain Brazilian court proceedings which had been brought in breach of a London arbitration clause by an insurer who was not an original party to the charterparty containing the arbitration clause, but a mere assignee thereof. Such an assignee was said to take the benefits and the burdens—here, in the circumstances, specifically in the shape of the arbitration clause—of the assigned rights (see *The Tilly Russ*, Case 71/83). (The court also dealt with effects of delays in applying for an injunction and with application of RSC Ord. 11, r.1(1)(d) to contractual assignees.)

Case principle

3.   Applications for injunctions to restrain foreign proceedings in breach of agreed jurisdiction or arbitration, or for declarations of arbitral validity with the same object, must not be brought after undue delays.

Case

Toepfer International GmbH v Molino Boschi Srl [1996] 1 Lloyd's Rep. 510   **116**
High Court, 17 January 1996

Facts

See infra, Arts 1, para. 2(4), 17, 18, 21 and 22.

English jurisdiction was established under Art. 17 over the plaintiffs' application for a declaration of validity of London arbitration and injunctions to restrain continuation of Italian proceedings in breach. The question for the English court, however, was whether it should exercise its discretion to grant such injunctive relief?

Judgment

Mance J. held that the plaintiffs were too late and refused the measures. They could have sought the declaration and injunctions in 1989 when the Italian proceedings were instituted by the defendant. Instead, they waited until October 1995 to bring the English application, apparently because their in-house lawyer had by then heard about *The Angelic Grace* and concluded that English courts would now be less cautious about restraint of foreign proceedings in breach of arbitration. Mance J. said that this was not a satisfactory reason for the delay. Defendants abroad should not be allowed to wait and see how the case went in the foreign courts and only at the last minute apply to the English courts for restraint if things were not going too well in the foreign action. The relief had to be requested promptly from the English courts.

Comment

See too *Schiffahrtsgesellschaft Detlef von Appen GmbH v Wiener Allianz Versicherungs AG* (unreported) Court of Appeal, 16 April 1997, *supra* Comment to Case 115.

Case principle

4.   The injunction should be able to be enforced against the defendant present or in possession of assets in England, or by the foreign court itself.

Case

117   Phillip Alexander Securities and Futures Limited v Bamberger, Theele, Kefer, Riedel, Franz and Gilhaus [1997] I.L.Pr. 73 Court of Appeal, 12 July 1996

Facts

The plaintiff English futures and options brokers were sued for losses in Germany by the six defendant customers. The plaintiffs pleaded London arbitration clauses as their defence in Germany. This was unsuccessful, since the German courts regarded the arbitration agreements as invalid according to mandatory consumer protection legislation. Furthermore, the German courts refused to serve or to enforce interim injunctions of the English courts which they regarded as an interference with German process, and proceeded to deliver judgment on the merits in five of the actions against the plaintiffs. The plaintiffs applied to the English courts for an injunction to prevent the sixth defendant from continuing to judgment in Germany (see too *infra*, Art. 1, para. 2(4) 'Arbitration', for the plaintiffs' further claim for declarations of arbitral validity against the other defendants).

Judgment

The Court of Appeal held that the arbitration agreements were inapplicable under the Consumer Arbitration Agreements Act 1988 s.1, which consequently ruled out the grant of the injunction requested.

   Nevertheless, Leggatt L.J. did comment *obiter* that, notwithstanding *The Angelic Grace*, grant of an injunction restraining breach of agreed jurisdiction or arbitration was not automatic: the injunction should be enforceable against the defendant personally or against his assets in England or enforceable in the foreign court itself.

Case principle

5. Art. 17 does not *oblige* chosen English courts to grant an injunction to
    restrain continuation of (Contracting or) non-Contracting State proceedings
    in contravention of the jurisdiction agreement. The remedy remains discre-
    tionary (*Continental Bank* and *The Angelic Grace* followed and applied).

Case

Ultisol Transport Contractors Ltd v Bouygues Offshore S.A. [1996] 2 Lloyd's   **118**
Rep. 140 High Court, 2 February 1996

Facts

See infra, Art. 17.

The defendant French company, Bouygues, commenced proceedings for damages for a lost barge in the South African courts against the plaintiff Bermudan
company, Ultisol, and others in 1994. In 1995, Ultisol requested the English
courts to grant an injunction to restrain Bouygues from continuing the South
African action in breach of an exclusive English jurisdiction clause in their
contract. Ultisol argued that as the English courts' jurisdiction was founded
upon Art. 17, they were obliged to grant the injunction thereunder and
possessed no discretion in the matter.

Judgment

Clarke J. held that Art. 17 imposed no obligation to restrain *non*-Contracting
States'—here South African—proceedings in breach of the exclusive English
jurisdiction clause. Art. 17 was intended to regulate competing Contracting—
not non-Contracting—States' jurisdiction (citing *Re Harrods* and *Kurz, infra*)
and national discretionary principles of restraint would therefore continue to
apply. Further, even in the case of contravening *Contracting* State proceedings,
Continental Bank and *The Angelic Grace* had shown that chosen courts had
a discretion in the matter; and even if Art. 17 had attempted to impose such a
mandatory requirement, injunctive relief was an *equitable* remedy and consequently would have remained discretionary.

   Thus, with regard to the principles for exercise of the discretion:

   (1)   On the one hand, *Continental Bank* and *Angelic Grace* had shown
         that English courts should not be reluctant to grant restraining
         injunctions as amounting to interference with foreign courts.
   (2)   On the other hand, grant would not be as a matter of course. The test
         was the same as for stays of *English* proceedings brought in breach
         of a foreign jurisdiction clause at national law: the burden was on the
         party in breach to show a strong case why the breach should be
         ignored and a stay (restraining injunction) refused. The court would
         look at all the circumstances, including parties' places of business,

applicable law, costs and place of evidence. The fact that there were other defendants in South Africa and the consequent risk of multiple proceedings was regarded by Clark J. as a strong factor against the grant of an injunction in favour of the plaintiff. However, on balance, he chose to award the injunction against the South African proceedings, in particular because Ultisol would otherwise have been denied a more favourable regime for limitation of damages in the agreed English jurisdiction and had undertaken to provide equivalent security for enforcement in England to that in South Africa.

Case principle

6.   English courts should not grant a restraining injunction on the ground that foreign Contracting States' courts have misapplied the Convention.

Case

118a In re European Patent (UK) No. 189958 in the name of Akzo Nobel NV/In re a Petition by Fort Dodge Animal Health Ltd. (1997) The Times, 24 October, High Court, 16th October 1997

Facts

The petitioners' request to the English courts was to restrain Akzo's action against them in the Dutch courts for alleged acts of infringement of Akzo's patents committed by them in England, on the ground that Dutch courts had erred in so treating the Convention as having made claims for infringement of foreign intellectual property rights justiciable (see *infra*, Article 1).

Judgment

Laddie J. expressed it to be repugnant to him to review the correctness or propriety of a foreign Contracting State's courts' assumption of Convention jurisdiction.

CONVENTION

ARTICLE 1, PARAGRAPH 1

"This Convention shall apply . . . "

Case principle

When an action is non-justiciable in the English courts, this is not affected by what is otherwise the existence of Convention jurisdiction (*obiter*).

(However, there are now stronger and more recent conflicting decisions at the same level—see Comment, infra.)

Case

Plastus Kreativ AB v Minnesota Mining and Manufacturing Co. [1995] RPC   **119**
438 High Court, 9 December 1994

Facts

The defendants, Minnesota, owned a European Patent for audio visual equipment in the UK, France and Germany and alleged that the Swedish plaintiffs, Plastus, had committed acts of infringement in the UK. The plaintiffs requested the defendants to acknowledge that the plaintiffs had not infringed the patent in the UK, France or Germany, and, on the defendants' refusal to do so, brought an action in the English courts for a declaration that they had not infringed the patent in the UK, France or Germany. The defendants asked the English court to strike out the claim in so far as this related to alleged infringement acts in France and Germany.

Judgment

Aldous J. in the Chancery Division of the High Court agreed to strike out the parts of the plaintiffs' claim concerning France and Germany, irrespective of the existence or not of Convention jurisdiction.

In the first place, specific provision for such declarations to be made under s.71 of the Patents Act 1977 was inapplicable, because s.60 expressly limited this power to acts carried out in the UK.

Secondly, with regard to the English courts' inherent powers to make a negative declaration of non-liability, these were only exercisable, according to the authorities, in relation to claims of right actually made by the defendants, and, as a matter of construction of the correspondence between the parties, Aldous J. accepted that the defendants had never sought to establish a claim in respect of acts of infringement in France and Germany, so that an action by the plaintiffs for a declaration of non-liability as to these could not be brought.

This was the *ratio decidendi* of the case.

However, Aldous J. made further comments, expressly of an *obiter* nature. The defendants had argued in the alternative that even if they *had* alleged infringement acts in France and Germany, they would not have been allowed to bring such a claim on foreign acts in the English courts in any event, because these were non-justiciable in England—cases of *British South Africa Company v The Companhia de Moçambique* [1893] AC 602 and *Tyburn Productions Ltd v Conan Doyle* [1991] Ch 75 had established the 'local' nature of land, copyright and patent actions. English courts could only deal with *English* infringement.

But, had the Convention brought about a change so that English courts should now accept Convention jurisdiction thereunder?

Aldous J., not needing to decide on this, indicated *obiter* that, as far as he was concerned, the position on non-justiciability remained the same for good policy reasons that patent 'monopolies' concerned relations between members of the public in the granting State and therefore Convention jurisdiction would be unavailable.

Comments

See 'The Private International Law of Tort and Product Liability' (1991) pp. 60–1, note 4 and 'International Trade Mark Infringement: Territorially Defined Torts and the Double Actionability Rule' (1990) 12 *European Intellectual Property Review* 28, for the writer's criticisms of the English non-justiciability rule in relation to patent infringement actions.

This case is now contradicted by the stronger decisions of Lloyd J. and Laddie J. in the Chancery Division of the High Court—also *obiter*, technically—of 7 and 26 March 1997 in *Pearce v Ove Arup Partnership Ltd* [1997] 3 All ER 31 and *Coin Controls Ltd v Suzo International (UK) Ltd* [1997] 3 All ER 45, respectively, in which the Convention was held to prevail over the traditional English non-justiciability approach in infringement of Dutch copyright, and German and Spanish patent, actions (see *infra*, *Recent Cases*, Art. 1, para. 1 Cases 386 and 387—and also *Mecklermedia Corporation v DC Congress GmbH* (unreported) 7 March 1997, on passing off; *In re European Patent* (1997) *The Times*, 24 October; and *Mother Bertha Music Limited v Bourne Music Limited* (1997) 21 March (unreported)).

> " . . . *civil and commercial* . . . "

Case principle

A petition to wind up a solvent foreign Contracting State company, brought by the Secretary of State for Trade and Industry in the public interest under s.124A of the Insolvency Act 1986, on the ground that this would be just and equitable, falls outside the Convention's scope, as not being a civil and commercial matter (*LTU* and *Rüffer* applied).

Case

120   Re a Company SHV Hanseatische Verwaltungsgesellschaft GmbH (unreported) High Court, 14 June 1996

Facts

Two German legal entities were carrying on business in the UK as a 'business club', inviting members of the public to join for the sum of £2,500. The British government authorities, following an investigation of the companies' affairs carried out under s.447 of the Companies Act 1985, petitioned the English courts to have them wound up in the public interest under s.124A of the Insolvency Act 1986.

The companies challenged English jurisdiction over the winding up: their seats were in Germany, which meant that German courts possessed exclusive jurisdiction under Art. 16(2).

Judgment

Sir Richard Scott V.-C., in the Chancery Division, held that a petition brought by the Secretary of State in the public interest under s.124A was not a civil and commercial matter within Art. 1, and, consequently, Art. 16(2) was inapplicable to accord exclusive jurisdiction to German courts under Arts 16(2) and 19.

The Vice-Chancellor followed the European Court's rulings in *LTU* Case 29/76 and *Rüffer* Case 814/79, according to which, action by the Secretary of State as a public law authority in the exercise of his public authority powers, as here, should not be considered to be 'civil and commercial' within the Convention.

(He also commented that *had* Art. 16(2) been applicable, the 'object' of the proceedings within the meaning thereof would have been the winding up and dissolution, not the different, broader object of *protection of the public*.)

" . . . *matters* . . . "

Case principle

The Convention's jurisdictional scope does not extend to proceedings themselves to establish merits *jurisdiction* over civil and commercial matters.

Case

The Canada Trust Co. v Stolzenberg *(No. 1)*, The Times, 1 May 1997 Court of Appeal, 28 April 1997, now reported in [1997] 4 All ER 983

121

Facts

The plaintiff trustees of Canadian pension funds alleged a series of massive frauds by the first defendant, implicating 36 others. They decided to proceed in the English courts on the basis that the first defendant was domiciled in the UK under Art. 2 of the Convention, through residence and substantial connection there by virtue of s.41 of the 1982 Act, and that the other defendants were then necessary or proper parties to the action against the first defendant.

The question arose as to whether the first defendant was in fact domiciled in the UK, which the defendants denied. The plaintiffs' primary evidence was the first defendant's past residence and continuing presence in London—and they applied to the English court to exercise its discretion to make orders under RSC Ord. 38, r.13 requiring banks and other bodies to produce documents providing evidence of the first defendant's address on relevant dates. It was in respect of the latter request to exercise the court's powers that Rattee J. at first instance in the High Court considered that, at that stage, it had not yet been established that the English court possessed jurisdiction over the plaintiffs' application to prove to the court's satisfaction that it possessed jurisdiction to try the substantive merits of the dispute. The plaintiffs appealed.

Judgment

The Court of Appeal (Millett, Nourse and Ward L.JJ.) unanimously held that the court possessed inherent 'jurisdiction' to decide upon matters connected with its own merits jurisdiction. Jurisdiction to decide on jurisdiction was part of the court's power to control its own process and existed even if the court was subsequently to find against its merits jurisdiction or to make an error of fact or law in relation to the latter.

Consequently, the English courts did not lack international jurisdiction to make RSC Ord. 38, r.13 orders to provide evidence of merits jurisdiction and the matter would be sent back to the High Court for exercise of the discretion or not.

Comment

Arguably, the concomitant of this finding, in effect, that Convention Title II is inapplicable to merits-jurisdiction enquiries, is that decisions reached in the course of the latter *upon jurisdiction* and ancillary matters in aid thereof, such as Ord. 38, r.13 orders, also fall outside the definition of 'judgment' in Art. 25 and outside Title III on recognition and enforcement—a view entirely in accord with the writer's expressed opinion.

ARTICLE 1, PARAGRAPH 2(1)

" . . . *succession* . . . "

Case principle

Proceedings are excluded from the Convention's scope when succession is the principal subject matter of the claim, not merely incidental.

Case

122 Re Hayward (deceased) [1997] 1 All ER 32 High Court, 28 March 1996

Facts

See infra, Art. 1, para. 2(2) 'bankruptcy', Case 123.

The applicant trustee further argued against Convention applicability (and consequent exclusive Spanish jurisdiction under Art. 16(2)—*see infra*), on the ground that since the defendant, whose title the trustee in bankruptcy denied, claimed to have acquired this on a transfer from the deceased bankrupt's widow, who was alleged to have inherited the transferred interest on his death intestate, the matter was one of excluded succession under Art. 1, para. 2(1).

Judgment

Rattee J., in the Chancery Division, held the matter not to be one of excluded succession and that the Convention consequently applied. Succession here was merely an incidental, not principal, issue in the proceedings, and this was insufficient for exclusion. The trustee's contention was that he owned a half share of the disputed property. The fact that the validity of the defendant's competing claim depended, ultimately, upon whether the deceased's widow had inherited, was not capable of constituting the main issue as one of succession.

ARTICLE 1, PARAGRAPH 2(2)

"Bankruptcy . . . "

Case principle

A trustee in bankruptcy's claim for a declaration of nullity of a deceased bankrupt's widow's transfer of the deceased's property to a third party held not, principally, to be an excluded matter of bankruptcy.

Case

Re Hayward (deceased) [1997] 1 All ER 32 High Court, 28 March 1996　　**123**

Facts

The deceased purchased an equal half-interest in a Spanish villa with the defendant in 1986. In 1987, the deceased went bankrupt and the plaintiff trustee in bankruptcy was appointed. When the deceased died intestate later in the same year, his widow, believing herself to have inherited his half-interest in the villa, purported to transfer this to the defendant in consideration for the cancellation of debts. The trustee then claimed declarations of title to the interest, voidness of the widow's transfer and rectification of the Spanish property register in the English courts. The defendant challenged English jurisdiction, on the ground that Spanish courts possessed exclusive jurisdiction under Art. 16(1)(a) and (3) (see *infra*).

However, the applicant trustee argued that the Convention was excluded from applying in this way, since the proceedings related to excluded bankruptcy under Art. 1, para. 2(2) (see too *supra*, Art. 1, para. 2(1) 'succession').

Judgment

Rattee J. held, in the Chancery Division, that the Convention applied and was not so excluded as relating to bankruptcy.

In *Gourdain* Case 133/78, the European Court had required proceedings to be *directly derived from* and *closely connected with* the bankruptcy, and the Jenard Report (pp. 10 and 12) emphasised that bankruptcy had to be the principal, not merely incidental, subject matter of the proceedings for these to be excluded. Here, the trustee's rights in bankruptcy were merely a preliminary to the main object of the proceedings, being to assert his title against that of the defendant and to have the latter's interest declared void—in the same way that enforcement of debts owed by third parties to the bankrupt would also not have fallen within the exclusion.

> " . . . *proceedings relating to the winding-up* . . . "

Case principle

1. Proceedings for avoidance of a transfer at an undervalue under s.238 of the Insolvency Act 1986 considered (*obiter*) to be excluded from the Convention's scope under Lugano Art. 1, para. 2(2).

Case

124   Aiglon Ltd and L'Aiglon S.A. v Gau Shan Co. Ltd [1993] 1 Lloyd's Rep 164 High Court, 23 June 1992

Facts

See supra, s.49 1982 Act and infra, Art. 5(3).

The claimant sought to argue that the doctrine of *forum non conveniens* applied to Convention jurisdiction between Contracting States.

Judgment

Hirst J. held that it did not; *but even if it had*, he doubted whether the Convention applied in any event, since such a claim was probably excluded under Art. 1, para. 2(2) (see Kaye, *Civil Jurisdiction* p. 137, in agreement).

Case principles

2. In assessing the nature of a plaintiff's claim in order to determine whether it is excluded from the Convention's scope under Art. 1, the court will only have regard to the facts as they have been pleaded.

3.   Where a pre-existing contractual obligation of payment becomes accel-
     erated as a result of the liquidation according to the law governing the
     latter, the claim so pleaded is excluded from the Convention's scope, as
     relating to the winding up, in accordance with the test of *directly derived
     from* and *closely connected with* the liquidation, as laid down by the
     European Court of Justice in *Gourdain* Case 133/78.

Case

Firswood Limited v Petra Bank (unreported) Court of Appeal, 13 December   **125**
1995

Facts

In 1987 the defendant Jordanian bank guaranteed payment of a debt of six
million Swiss francs owed by a principal debtor to an original creditor which
subsequently assigned its rights to the plaintiff in 1992. In 1990, the defendant
went into liquidation under Jordanian law, according to which the creditor
could claim payment of the entire debt notwithstanding that it had been
agreed that it would be paid in 10 instalments up to 1992 and that only three
had fallen due which were paid. The liquidator accepted the claim, but the
plaintiff, fearing that there would be insufficient assets to pay it, instituted proceedings in the English courts for payment by the defendant. The plaintiff
wished to serve the English writ upon the defendant outside the jurisdiction
without leave of the court. It could do this under RSC Ord. 11, r.1(2), *inter
alia*, if jurisdiction existed *under the Convention* (here, it would have to be by
virtue of an English jurisdiction agreement under Art. 17, in view of the defendant's non-Contracting State domicile, see *infra*, Art. 17). The defendant,
however, denied that the Convention applied: the proceedings related to winding up of the insolvent defendant bank and were consequently excluded from
the Convention's scope under Art. 1, para. 2(2). RSC Ord. 11, r.1(2) would
therefore not apply and r.1(1) would do so instead, requiring leave of the
English court to exercise its discretion to permit service out of the jurisdiction
on the ground that England was *forum conveniens* (naturally the defendant
would argue against England as such—and, as it happened, would go on to
succeed in both these respects, *infra*).

Judgment

The Court of Appeal unanimously held the Convention's application to be
excluded under Art. 1, para. 2(2) and went on to refuse to grant leave to serve
the writ outside the jurisdiction, considering Jordan, rather than England, to
be the most appropriate forum.
    The Court of Appeal applied the European Court's formula in *Gourdain* on
whether proceedings were excluded from the Convention as relating to winding
up under Art. 1, para. 2(2): they had to be directly derived from and closely
connected with the liquidation.

Here, in the first place, the Court of Appeal decided that it would only assess the facts as pleaded in the plaintiff's statement of claim. This had been done on the ground of the plaintiff's claim to the accelerated payment of the debt guaranteed under the Jordanian liquidation, and not on the purely contractual basis of the defendant's pre-existing debt.

Secondly, therefore, the claim, as pleaded, did derive directly from the liquidation and was closely connected therewith.

The proceedings were excluded from the Convention's scope under Art. 1, para. 2(2).

ARTICLE 1, PARAGRAPH 2(4)

" . . . 4. Arbitration"

Case principle

1. Arbitration-existence, as an incidental issue in main proceedings on contract not excluded from the Convention's scope, does not lead to the latter's exclusion from application to the main contracts issue, even if arbitral-existence itself were to be considered to be part of the Art. 1, para. 2(4) arbitration exclusion (*Marc Rich* Case C–190/89 applied).

Case

126 Marc Rich & Co. A.G. v Società Italiana Impianti P.A. (The Atlantic Emperor) (No. 2) [1992] 1 Lloyd's Rep. 624 Court of Appeal

Facts

The defendant Italian sellers of oil brought proceedings for a judgment of non-liability for breach of contract towards the plaintiff purchasers in the Italian courts in 1988. The plaintiffs, however, asserted an English arbitration agreement and applied to the English courts for appointment of an arbitrator in the absence of nomination by the defendants. The defendants denied any agreement on arbitration and requested the English courts to stay their arbitral-appointment proceedings under Art. 21 on the ground that Italian courts were first seised. The English High Court dismissed the defendants' application for a stay under Art. 21, on the ground that the subject matter of the proceedings was excluded arbitration and consequently that the Convention, including Art. 21, was inapplicable. The case went to the Court of Appeal, which requested a ruling on interpretation of Art. 1, para. 2(4) from the European Court of Justice. The European Court was successfully able to sidestep the crucial matter of whether a main issue concerning existence of arbitration agreement in the first place fell within the Art. 1, para. 2(4) 'arbitration' exclusion and ruled that, as an incidental question, its status as excluded or

148

otherwise would not affect that of the different main subject matter of the proceedings (see 'The Judgments Convention and Arbitration: Mutual Spheres of Influence' (1991) 7 *Arbitration International* 289 and 'The EEC and Arbitration: the Unsettled Wake of *The Atlantic Emperor*' (1993) 9 *Arbitration International* 27).

Subsequently, in the present English proceedings, the plaintiffs sought an injunction from the English courts to restrain the defendants from proceeding with their Italian action in breach of the alleged English arbitration agreement.

The issue which the Court of Appeal chose to treat as decisive as to grant of the injunction or not was whether an Italian judgment, including determination that arbitration had not been agreed to, would be required to be recognised in England (so as to give rise to an issue estoppel)? If so, the injunction would be refused.

For present purposes, it should suffice to say that in accordance with ss.32 and 33 of the 1982 Act, there are two relevant circumstances in which a foreign—here Italian—judgment in breach of an arbitration or jurisdiction agreement could be recognized:

(1) if the plaintiffs *submitted* to the Italian proceedings; or
(2) the Italian judgment would be entitled to recognition under the *Judgments Convention*.

Judgment

In respect of the former, the Court of Appeal held the plaintiffs, on the facts, to have submitted to the defendants' Italian action and consequently that an Italian judgment would be recognized at national English private international law, so that the injunction should be refused (see *infra*, Art. 18).

Strictly, therefore, the Court of Appeal did not need to consider whether an Italian decision would also be required to be recognized *under the Convention*—in particular, whether the Convention's applicability was excluded or not as relating to arbitration under Art. 1, para. 2(4) when the issue to be decided upon by the Italian court concerned arbitral-existence itself.

Nevertheless, the Court of Appeal could not resist passing some comment, which was mainly to confirm that the European Court's ruling on the matter had been inconclusive (see (1993) 9 *Arbitration International* 27). All that was clear therefrom was that, since here the *main* issue of contractual liability in the Italian proceedings was not excluded from the Convention's scope, this would remain the same and the overall Italian judgment consequently enforceable under the Convention, even if it were to be held that the incidental matter of arbitral-existence in the judgment would itself otherwise have been of excluded status under Art. 1, para. 2(4). As to the latter, the Court of Appeal declined to rule.

Comments

The further question arises as to whether arbitral-existence, *if* itself otherwise excluded from the Convention under Art. 1, para. 2(4), *remains* so excluded when merely an incidental issue in a judgment principally concerned with non-excluded matters of contract.

For criticism of an early English non-Convention case on 1982 Act ss.32 and 33, *Tracomin S.A. v Sudan Oil Seeds Co. Ltd* [1983] 1 WLR 662 High Court; affd [1983] 1 WLR 1026 Court of Appeal, see Kaye, *Civil Jurisdiction* pp. 1551–3 (note: footnote numbers on those pages are incorrectly printed as one behind the proper number!).

Case

127   The Xing Su Hai [1995] 2 Lloyd's Rep. 15 High Court, 22 February 1995

Facts

See supra, 1982 Act s.25(2), Case 96.

The defendants challenged English jurisdiction on the ground that they were domiciled in Germany. The plaintiffs responded, *inter alia*, that Convention jurisdiction was inapplicable because they *also* wished to assert arbitration against the defendants, and consequently, the Convention was excluded in relation to the court proceedings.

Judgment

Rix J. referred to the European Court's decision in *Marc Rich* and confirmed that an incidental issue of arbitral existence would not render the Convention inapplicable to the main question.

Case principle

2.   Principal issue of arbitration existence and validity said to fall within the Convention's scope and outside the Art. 1, para. 2(4) arbitration exclusion.

Case

128   The Heidberg [1994] 2 Lloyd's Rep. 287 High Court, 16 December 1993

Facts

The German shipowners' ship, Heidberg, collided with a jetty in France in 1991, causing damage to the cargo of maize. The cargo consignees' insurers brought proceedings against the shipowners in France in 1991, and in 1993 the French courts held the shipowners to be liable. The shipowners argued against French jurisdiction, on the ground that the bill of lading incorporated an English arbitration clause which was contained in the charterparty—an assertion rejected by the French court, which considered that there had been no such incorporation. The shipowners, however, had commenced English proceedings, alleging that the insurers were bound by English arbitration.

The central question which arose before the English courts, therefore, was whether the English courts were bound by the French court's ruling against arbitral existence?

Section 32 of the 1982 Act provides that an English court must refuse to recognize or to enforce a foreign judgment in breach of an arbitration (or jurisdiction) clause, *inter alia*, unless the Convention applies to require recognition or enforcement.

Hence, the question which faced the English court was: did a French judgment, part of which concerned *existence or validity* of an arbitration agreement, fall within the Convention's scope or was it excluded therefrom as 'arbitration' under Art. 1, para. 2(4)?

Judgment

Judge Diamond Q.C. noted that the European Court of Justice had omitted to deal with this matter *as a principal issue* in proceedings in its judgment in *Marc Rich* and further that Professor Schlosser had apparently changed his mind from his former view favouring exclusion in his Report.

Accordingly, Judge Diamond Q.C. found no help in the authorities and decided to reach a view based upon practicality and policy.

In so doing, he held that the Convention applied to arbitral existence and validity and that Art. 1, para. 2(4) consequently was inapplicable in any event, whether the arbitration aspect of the French judgment was regarded as principal or incidental.

Certainly, where it was preliminary to a main judgment on substance, in his opinion it was highly desirable that Convention recognition and enforcement of judgments over the substance of the case should also be accompanied by recognition of the decision upon the arbitration issue in order to avoid irreconcilable judgments with those of the arbitration-State's courts.

Furthermore, Art. 5(1) should be able to confer jurisdiction upon courts of an arbitration-State under the Convention if it applied to arbitration existence or validity as a main issue.

Comment

This was a first instance judgment by a judge who candidly and diffidently commented that he would have preferred to have left the decision on so difficult and perplexing a matter to Court of Appeal or European Court of Justice. The arguments in the case for and against Convention exclusion assuredly were in no way novel. It cannot be assumed that a higher court's decision or even judgments of courts on the same level would be the same.

The subsequent decision of Waller J. in the High Court in *Phillip Alexander Securities and Futures Limited v Bamberger, Theele, Kefer, Riedel, Franz and Gilhaus* (see *infra*, Case 130—the Court of Appeal in that case would have rejected the request for declarations in any event on national discretionary grounds) led to the same outcome on not dissimilar facts, but properly treated arbitration as merely incidental in the context, without drawing conclusions upon its status as a main issue had this been the case.

Case principle

3. Application for an injunction to restrain foreign court proceedings conducted in alleged breach of agreed arbitration held to fall outside Art. 1, para. 2(4) arbitration exclusion.

Case

129 Toepfer International GmbH v Molino Boschi Srl [1996] 1 Lloyd's Rep. 510
High Court, 17 January 1996

Facts

The defendants complained about short and defective delivery of Chinese soya meal to Italy by the plaintiffs in 1988 under a contract alleged to be subject to GAFTA 100 terms containing a London arbitration clause and they began Italian court proceedings for damages against the plaintiffs in 1988. The plaintiffs contested Italian jurisdiction, on the ground that the parties had agreed to London arbitration, which the defendants denied. That contest was still not resolved in the Italian courts by 1994, and in 1995 the plaintiffs requested the English courts to grant:

- a declaration that the defendants were obliged to arbitrate the dispute in London (although, the plaintiff would also claim that the defendants were now time-barred!); and
- injunctions to restrain the defendants from continuing with the Italian action in breach of the London arbitration agreement.

The defendants objected under RSC Ord. 12, r.8 that the English courts should decline or stay their proceedings under Art. 21 or 22, as the case may be, in favour of first-seised Italian proceedings (see *infra*, Arts 21 and 22), as well as denying English jurisdiction in the first place (see *infra*, Art. 18).

However, the plaintiffs asserted that the Convention was in fact inapplicable to the English restraint action, as it amounted to excluded arbitration under Art. 1, para. 2(4).

Judgment

Mance J. held the Convention to be assumed to be applicable and not to be excluded under Art. 1, para. 2(4).

(1) With regard to the declaration of arbitral obligation, he assumed *The Heidberg* to be correct, and, consequently, this was not excluded as integral to the arbitral process.

(2) In the case of the injunction against foreign proceedings in breach of arbitration, these were directed to stopping the Italian action rather than actually to bringing any arbitration into existence.

Case principle

4. Recognition of a foreign judgment in alleged breach of an arbitration agreement falls within the Convention's scope (*obiter*).

Case

Phillip Alexander Securities and Futures Limited v Bamberger, Theele, Kefer,   **130**
Riedel, Franz and Gilhaus [1997] I.L.Pr. 73 High Court, 15 May 1996; [1996]
I.L.Pr. 104, Court of Appeal, 12 July 1996

Facts

See supra, 1982 Act s.49, Case 117.

In the case of five of the six defendants, the German courts had ignored English courts' interim injunctions and, finding the English arbitration clauses to be invalid, proceeded to deliver judgment against the plaintiff.

The plaintiff, in an effort to forestall enforcement in England, applied for declarations of validity of the arbitration agreements.

Judgment

In the High Court, Waller J. held the arbitration agreements to be inapplicable under English law and this was upheld in the Court of Appeal (see *supra*, s.49).

However, the judge did go on to consider, *obiter*, whether the German judgments on substance would have been excluded from the Convention's scope as relating to arbitration under Art. 1, para. 2(4), on grounds that they were delivered in breach of arbitration, *had the arbitration agreements instead been valid* in the eyes of the English courts. He concluded that they would have fallen within the Convention's scope: reports on the Convention, on balance seemed to support this finding (see too Kaye, *Civil Jurisdiction* pp. 1555–6), and any separate but preliminary German judgment on arbitral invalidity, even if itself excluded (undecided by the European Court in *Atlantic Emperor*), would not, in accordance with the European Court's judgment in *The Atlantic Emperor*, affect the non-excluded status of the main judgment.

Nevertheless, Waller J. also considered that, notwithstanding such Convention application, recognition and enforcement of the German merits judgment thereafter would have been refused, on the ground that this was against public policy under Art. 27(1) where the defendants were aware of the English injunctions yet continued to proceed with their German actions to judgment.

Comments

In the Court of Appeal, Leggatt L.J. simply commented that had the matter been material, he would have favoured a reference to the European Court. As it was, a declaration of non-recognition was not appropriate in any event as a matter of declaratory discretion since the defendants had not yet actually even come to the English courts in order to apply for enforcement of the German judgments at that stage, which the plaintiff was attempting to pre-empt.

It will be recalled that in *The Heidberg, supra*, Judge Diamond Q.C. was able to avoid the question of whether recognition of a foreign Contracting State's judgment fell within the arbitration exclusion or not on similar facts because he regarded arbitral existence or validity, whether as main or incidental issue, *as itself not excluded from the Convention* by Art. 1, para. 2(4)—clearly a questionable presupposition.

See too *Zellner v Phillip Alexander Securities and Futures Ltd* [1997] I.L.Pr. 730 in the High Court on 17 February 1997, following the judgment in Case 130.

Case principle

5. In determining whether a claim is excluded from the Convention's scope as being integral to the arbitration process, courts should have regard to the substance of the claim as opposed merely to its form (*Marc Rich* applied).

Case

131 Union de Remorquage et de Sauvetage S.A. v Lake Avery Inc. (unreported) High Court, 4 November 1996

Facts

On 2 July 1996 the defendants' ship experienced difficulties in Dutch waters and the plaintiffs agreed to assist, which they did successfully. Prior to their intervention, the plaintiffs asked the captain of the defendants' ship to sign LOF 95 salvage forms containing a London arbitration clause, but the captain requested to deal with this later. Once the ship had been refloated, the captain refused to accept the LOF 95 forms: the defendants denied that the ship had grounded for salvage and claimed that they themselves had refloated it—and all that they had agreed to with the plaintiffs were other services, not salvage and not on LOF 95 terms.

On 3 July 1996 the plaintiffs had a Lloyd's arbitrator appointed under LOF 95 (hoping to secure higher rates for salvage than in Dutch courts) and thereafter on 20 August 1996 instituted proceedings in the Admiralty Division of the English High Court for a declaration that they had orally concluded a salvage agreement on LOF 95 terms with the captain as representative of the defendants on 2 July. The defendants requested the English courts to decline or to stay the proceedings under Art. 21 or 22 (or to refuse to grant discretionary leave to serve out under RSC Ord. 11, r.1(1)(d)(iii) if national rules governed in place of the Convention) in favour of Dutch courts which had been seised in the first place, on 5 or 11 July, of the defendants' application for a declaration of inapplicability of LOF 95, conceded to be between the same parties and to involve the same cause of action.

From this arose the dispute as to whether the plaintiffs' English action for a declaration that LOF 95, including its London arbitration clause, had been orally agreed upon, amounted to proceedings principally involving arbitration, in which case the Convention, including Arts 21 and 22, was alleged to be excluded from applying under Art. 1, para. 2(4), so that the second-seised English courts could then continue (subject to any national law discretion to stay).

Judgment

Clarke J. held the English action to be excluded arbitration under Art. 1, para. 2(4).

The basis for this finding was what he described as being the 'narrow grounds' that the claim was essentially *the same* as in *Marc Rich* itself: that is to say, notwithstanding that the form in which the plaintiffs' action was brought was, in effect, as to arbitration existence, the substance of the claim was that the plaintiffs wished to proceed with arbitration at the hands of a validly appointed Lloyd's arbitrator, and in *Marc Rich* the European Court had held that such a claim for arbitral appointment fell within the Art. 1, para. 2(4) arbitration exception.

There was, consequently, no need for Clarke J. to comment expressly upon whether a principal claim for arbitral existence or validity would also be excluded under Art. 1, para. 2(4), beyond noting the *Schlosser Report's* apparent support for its exclusion (para. 64) and the European Court's more limited finding in *Marc Rich* that, whatever its status as excluded or not, arbitral existence as a mere preliminary issue would not affect exclusion of a main question of arbitral appointment. He also reviewed the previous English cases on the question in order to demonstrate how thin the dividing line was between cases of exclusion or otherwise and the policy nature of decisions against mere casual designation as excluded arbitration.

Mance J.'s approach in *Toepfer International* was approved of, namely, that for exclusion, the action should be an integral part of the arbitration process—as Clarke J. had construed it to be on the facts before him.

Comment

Clarke J., having held the Convention and Arts 21 and 22 to be inapplicable, went on to find English courts to be *forum conveniens* at national English law, compared to the Dutch, on a balance of factors. Therefore, English service abroad under RSC Ord. 11 was good.

Case principle

6. Judgments enforcing arbitration awards as judgments are part of the arbitration exclusion in Art. 1, para. 2(4).

Case

132   Arab Business Consortium International Finance and Investment Co. v Banque Franco-Tunisienne [1996] 1 Lloyd's Rep. 485 High Court, 14 December 1995

Facts

The plaintiff obtained an arbitration award against the defendant for damages of over three million US dollars for breach of a contract to transfer shares, before the International Chamber of Commerce in Paris in 1987. French courts then gave a judgment making the arbitration award enforceable as a judgment of the French courts. The plaintiff sought to enforce the French judgment in England under the 1968 Convention.

Judgment

Waller J., in the Commercial Court, held that the French judgment fell within the arbitration exclusion from the Convention's scope under Art. 1, para. 2(4). Consequently, Convention Title III was inapplicable to enforcement. The award itself should be applied to be enforced under the Arbitration Act 1975, implementing the 1958 New York Convention.

The judge considered that there were cogent reasons for his decision: 1968 Convention drafters clearly intended to leave arbitration matters to existing international conventions, and this had been confirmed in the European Court's judgment in *Marc Rich*, as well as by the Advocate General's Opinion in those proceedings and by Jenard, Schlosser and Evrigenis/Kerameus Reports on the Convention—also in relation to enforcement of arbitration awards incorporated into judgments, not just to ancillary court decisions.

Case principle

7.   Where an arbitrator orders security for costs of the arbitration to be provided by one of the parties to the arbitration in the event that costs might eventually be awarded against that party, and in order to provide such security an undertaking to pay the costs is given by a third party who is not otherwise involved in the arbitration, an action to enforce that undertaking does not fall within the Art. 1, para. 2(4) arbitration exclusion.

Case

133   Lexmar Corporation and Steamship Mutual Underwriting Association (Bermuda) Ltd v Nordisk Skibsrederforening and Northern Tankers (Cyprus) Ltd [1997] 1 Lloyd's Rep. 289 High Court, 2 April 1996

Facts

In the course of a London arbitration in 1992 between the plaintiff time charterer, Lexmar, and the shipowner, Norrthon, pursuant to an arbitration clause in the charterparty agreement, the arbitrator ordered Norrthon to provide security for Lexmar's arbitration costs up to £135,000 in the event of an award being made against Norrthon in the arbitration. A Norwegian company, Nordisk, the first defendant in the English court proceedings, provided the plaintiff Lexmar with letters of undertaking to pay the costs in the event of such arbitration award against Norrthon. The undertakings contained an exclusive English jurisdiction agreement.

Subsequently, an arbitration award was made against Norrthon, but the defendant Nordisk refused to pay the agreed costs.

When the plaintiff brought English proceedings for payment against Nordisk under Lugano Convention Art. 17, the defendant challenged the English jurisdiction on the ground, *inter alia*, (see too *infra*, Arts 17, 21 and 22) that the Convention's application was excluded under Art. 1, para. 2(4) because the English proceedings were ancillary to arbitration in accordance with the European Court's judgment in *Marc Rich* Case C–190/89. Further, the defendant's defence on substance would be that it was unable to pay the costs because this would be in breach of a Norwegian court order of provisional attachment of its debt towards Lexmar, obtained by the second defendant, Northern Tankers: Northern Tankers had been granted American arbitration awards of 11 million US dollars against Lexmar, of which it had applied for enforcement in the Norwegian courts, and the Norwegian attachment was provisional upon such enforcement. Co-plaintiff in England, Steamship Mutual, which had financed Lexmar's costs in the London arbitration, disputed Northern Tankers' claim to the debt owed by Nordisk to Lexmar (itself now filing for bankruptcy in the United States).

Judgment

Colman J. held that the English proceedings fell outside the arbitration exclusion in Art. 1, para. 2(4) and, consequently, that Art. 17 applied so as to give English courts jurisdiction (see *infra*, Arts 17, 21 and 22 as to priorities between Arts 17, 21 and 22).

The Jenard Report, referred to by the European Court in *Marc Rich*, had explained the reason for exclusion of arbitration in its entirety from the Convention as being the pre-existence of international conventions on recognition and enforcement of arbitration awards, from which it followed that the exclusion comprised all procedures, including court proceedings, for the control, support and regulation of the arbitral process, which would have covered even an application to the court to order security for arbitration costs under s.12(6) of the Arbitration Act 1950, had the arbitrator himself not possessed such power so to order under the terms of the arbitration.

However, in spite of this broad scope of the arbitration exclusion, the debt owed by the defendant towards the plaintiff was derived from an undertaking agreement which was distinct from the arbitral process itself, albeit conditional upon its particular outcome.

Accordingly, the English court action was not ancillary to the arbitration, and the Convention, including Art. 17, applied so as to afford English courts jurisdiction.

See too infra, Arts 17, 21 and 22.

ARTICLE 2

" . . . *persons domiciled in a Contracting State shall . . . be sued . . .* "

Case principle

Purely English conceptions of the nature of *in rem* proceedings should not be allowed to affect the Convention classification thereof as involving actions in which the person 'sued' is the shipowner or, as the case may be, charterer.

Case

134   The Deichland [1990] 1 QB 361 Court of Appeal, 20 April 1989

Facts

The plaintiff cargo owners brought an English action *in rem* under national English jurisdiction rules in respect of damage to the cargo. German charterers challenged English jurisdiction, on the ground of their German— Contracting State—domicile under Art. 2 of the Convention. The plaintiffs' response was that Art. 2 could not apply in this way because, for purposes of Art. 2, the persons 'sued' in an action *in rem* were not the charterers but the ship itself.

Judgment

The Court of Appeal unanimously held that whatever the formal position was in the writ as to the *named defendant*, as the *ship*, the *reality*, in conformity with Convention policy favouring suit in the domicile, was that *the charterers* were the defendant against whom the underlying complaint was brought. It would be strange, therefore, if they were unable to challenge English jurisdiction under Art. 2; and consequently, the Convention should instead be interpreted according to the intentions of the drafters (who did not in fact originally include those from the UK, as a state which subsequently acceded). German charterers' domicile applied for purposes of Art. 2.

ARTICLE 4, PARAGRAPH 1

" . . . *law of that State.*"

Case principle

The national law referred to includes not only national connectional grounds of jurisdiction but also discretionary national rules of *forum non conveniens* and *lis alibi pendens*, even in relation to competing jurisdiction of foreign Contracting States.

Case

Sarrio S.A. v Kuwait Investment Authority [1996] 1 Lloyd's Rep. 650 High   **135**
Court, 12 October 1995; [1997] 1 Lloyd's Rep. 113 Court of Appeal, 12
August 1996

(See infra, Art. 21.)

ARTICLE 4, PARAGRAPH 2

" . . . *any person domiciled in a Contracting State may, whatever his nationality . . .* "

Case principle

A plaintiff domiciled in a Contracting State may use national jurisdiction grounds under Art. 4, para. 2, whether he is a national of a Contracting or non-Contracting State.

Case

The Po [1991] 2 Lloyd's Rep. 206 Court of Appeal, 17 April 1991   **136**

Facts

Plaintiff Americans wished to sue Italian defendants in England on national English jurisdiction grounds corresponding with those in an Art. 57 convention on particular matters. The defendants challenged English jurisdiction, *inter alia*, on the ground that Art. 4, para. 2 only extended national jurisdiction grounds to the advantage of plaintiffs who were Contracting State nationals.

Judgment

This was not the effect of Art. 4, para. 2 at all. It was available to plaintiff Contracting and non-Contracting State nationals alike.

ARTICLE 5

" ... may ... be sued ... "

Case principle

Special jurisdiction grounds in Art. 5 are independent and disjunctive and can be pleaded in the alternative.

Case

137 Twin Books (UK) Limited v Cronion S.A. (unreported) High Court, 9 July 1993

Facts

The plaintiff sued the Spanish defendant in the English courts for failure to return property, both in tort for wrongful retention and in breach of contract to redeliver the property, alternatively seeking to rely upon Art. 5(3) and (1) for English courts' jurisdiction. The defendant denied that both grounds could be pleaded in a cause of action arising from the same facts.

Judgment

Deputy High Court Judge J. Griffith Williams Q.C. held that Arts 5(1) and (3) could be relied upon in the alternative.

Comment

See too *infra, Atlas Shipping Agency (UK) Limited v Suisse Atlantique Société d'Armement Maritime SA* [1995] I.L.Pr. 600 High Court, 6 April 1995, Case 145.

ARTICLE 5(1)

"In matters relating to a contract ... "

Case principles

1. Following the European Court's ruling in *Effer v Kantner* Case 38/81, a bare assertion of contractual existence by the plaintiff is insufficient for contracts jurisdiction to exist under Art. 5(1).

2. However, the plaintiff need not prove disputed existence of contract con-
    clusively at the jurisdiction stage, and need only adduce evidence to satis-
    fy the court that there is a serious question of contractual existence for
    determination at the trial of substance (but see now *infra*, Comment to
    Case 143).

Case

Tesam Distribution Ltd v Schuh Mode Team GmbH and Commerzbank AG   **138**
[1990] I.L.Pr. 149 Court of Appeal, 20 October 1989

Facts

The plaintiff English company was an importer of shoes and the two defendants were German companies, a shoe exporter and the latter's bank respectively. The plaintiff sued the defendants for damages for breach of contract of
£174,040 in the English courts (and the second defendant, in the alternative,
for the tort of inducing the first defendant to breach the alleged contract, see
infra, Art. 5(3) 'matters relating to tort'), on the ground that the defendants
had failed to deliver the shoes as agreed. Negotiations between the parties had
taken place at meetings, on the telephone and by telex. The defendants denied
that a contract had ever finally been concluded. They further contested jurisdiction of the English courts under Art. 5(1) as place of contractual performance: according to *Effer v Kantner* in the European Court (para. 7), they
alleged that the plaintiff was required to adduce *conclusive* and relevant evidence of contractual existence if proceedings on a disputed contract were to be
regarded as involving *matters relating to a contract* for purposes of Art. 5(1)
jurisdiction. Since courts would require plaintiffs to satisfy this test where a
defendant failed to enter an appearance, under Art. 20, para. 1, it would be
wrong to place defendants who did enter an appearance to contest jurisdiction
in a worse position than the former by somehow reducing the burden on the
plaintiff where defendants made a challenge to contract.

Judgment

The Court of Appeal rejected the defendants' arguments.

True it is that, in accordance with *Effer v Kantner*, a bare assertion of contractual existence by the plaintiff would not be sufficient to establish Art. 5(1)
jurisdiction; but, on the other hand, the plaintiff should not have to prove existence of contract conclusively as if on substance at the preliminary jurisdictional stage when evidence would not be available from pleadings and discovery. Therefore, all that was required of the plaintiff was to show that there was
a genuine and real dispute over existence or otherwise of the contract and a
serious question calling for trial for its proper determination—the equivalent
of a good arguable case according to national English principles.

Thus, on the facts and circumstances of the case, the Court of Appeal considered that the plaintiff had satisfied the test of serious issue for trial: it was

arguable that a contract had come into existence and furthermore that the second defendant was party to it through the agency of the first defendant. Consequently, the proceedings amounted to *matters relating to a contract* for purposes of Art. 5(1) jurisdiction of English courts—and this was so even if it were subsequently to be held as a matter of substance that the contract had never entered into existence.

Comment

In later cases, the High Court and Court of Appeal elaborated upon the principle of good arguable case, as serious issue to be tried, for establishment of Art. 5(1) jurisdiction over disputed contractual existence, first put forward by the Court of Appeal in *Tesam*.

Case principles

3. Where contractual existence is disputed, the plaintiff must prove existence on 'a good arguable case' if Article 5(1) is to be available to confer jurisdiction.
4. A good arguable case exists:

    (1)   if the dispute is purely on a point of law—where there is a serious case to be tried (*Tesam*); and
    (2)   if the dispute is on *fact*—where the plaintiff will probably succeed in his substantive claim.

Case

139   Mölnlycke A.B. v Proctor & Gamble Ltd [1992] 1 WLR 1112, Court of Appeal, 27 June 1991

Facts

In these proceedings, the plaintiffs sued for liability in *tort* through alleged patent infringement. The Court of Appeal was called upon to decide, *inter alia*, whether tort jurisdiction existed under Art. 5(3) (see *infra*) where the defendants denied liability in tort.

Judgment

The Court of Appeal drew the analogy of defendants' contestation of contractual existence under Art. 5(1) in accordance with the European Court's judgment in *Effer* Case 38/81, and held that in both sets of circumstances plaintiffs must prove contracts or, as the case may be, torts existence as on a good arguable case. This meant a serious question to be tried, where the dispute was purely on *law*, but also a probability that the plaintiffs would win on the substantive claim, if *facts* of contracts or tort liability existence were in dispute.

See too infra, Art. 6(1), The Rewia, in the specific context of the latter provision.

Comments

As will also be seen in connection with Arts 5(3) and 6(1), the Court of Appeal went on to indicate that Arts 5 and 6 jurisdiction grounds could not be utilized where proceeding against a defendant would be an abuse of the process of the court—held not to be so in the case itself. As a principle of Convention jurisdiction—as opposed to domestic national procedure (see *Kongress Agentur Hagen GmbH* Case 365/88, in relation to Art. 6(2))—it is doubted whether this is correct (see further *infra*).

The *Tesam* test seems to accord with the House of Lords' national English law development in *Seaconsar*, Case 84, *supra*, as to standard of proof required to establish a good arguable case *on the merits of the claim* for discretionary service of a writ out of the jurisdiction (see *supra*, RSC Ord. 11, r.4(1)(b)).

Case

New England Reinsurance Corporation and First State Insurance Co. v   **140**
Messoghios Insurance Co. S.A. [1992] 2 Lloyd's Rep 251 Court of Appeal, 13 May 1992

Facts

The plaintiff American companies transacted with the defendant Greek company for a number of years but wished to terminate the relationship in 1986 through dissatisfaction with the defendant. A draft written agreement was drawn up on settlement terms, following which there were further communications by post, fax and telephone.

On the non-payment of the sum of 450000 US dollars by the defendant to the plaintiffs, alleged to have been agreed to, the plaintiffs sought to bring proceedings for breach of contract before the English courts. The Greek defendant contested English Art. 5(1) jurisdiction, on the ground that the parties had never finally concluded a settlement contract.

Judgment

The Court of Appeal upheld the jurisdiction challenge. *Tesam* and *Mölnlycke* were followed.

Thus, the test to be applied to determine whether a contract existed for Art. 5(1) jurisdiction was that there should be a serious issue to be determined at trial, as held in *Tesam* and *Mölnlycke*, to the exclusion of the higher level of proof laid down in the earlier, national law decision in *Attock Cement Co. Ltd. v Romanian Bank for Foreign Trade* [1989] 1 All ER 1189 that the plaintiff would *probably win at trial*, as the meaning of 'good arguable case'.

The burden was upon the plaintiffs to satisfy the court on this, and, on the facts, it was doubtful whether they had succeeded.

Comment

The court went on to find that the same level of proof applied to the requirement of England as *place of performance* of the alleged agreement; and even on the assumption that an agreement's existence could be established, the plaintiffs had failed also to prove that payment of the contractual sum was to take place in London rather than in Boston, Massachusetts, USA (see *infra*).

Case principles

5.   A plaintiff seeking to rely upon Art. 5(1) contracts jurisdiction must be prepared to prove the disputed existence of the alleged contract as a serious issue to be tried, taking into account the evidence of both plaintiff and defendant (following the Court of Appeal in *Tesam Distribution Ltd*, rather than in the earlier, national English law case of *Attock Cement* where it was indicated that the plaintiff had to show that he would *probably win* at trial).

6.   The same requirement for existential proof and the test to satisfy this apply where it is simply or also the alleged existence of the obligation in question which is at issue.

Case

141   Rank Film Distributors Limited v Lanterna Editrice Srl and Banca Nazionale del Lavoro [1992] I.L.Pr. 58 High Court, 4 June 1991

Facts

In 1988, the plaintiff, Rank, and the first Italian defendant's predecessor, Lanterna, made an agreement for Rank to supply films to the defendant in return for payment. One of the terms was that Lanterna would arrange for an irrevocable bank guarantee to be provided by the second defendant, the Italian bank, Banca Nazionale, in the sum of six and a half million US dollars. An additional term was that Rank and Lanterna would conclude a further, long-term agreement to take over from the original. The guarantee contract was issued by Banca to Rank in November 1988 and a day later the long-term agreement was concluded between Rank and Lanterna, providing for payment as in the original agreement, and to take place in London.

Subsequently, when Rank requested payment, neither Lanterna nor Banca complied. Lanterna even obtained an interim order from the Rome courts requiring Banca not to pay Rank under the guarantee. After that, Rank brought proceedings in the English courts against Lanterna and Banca for, *inter alia*, payment of the six and a half million US dollars agreed to.

Both defendants contested English Art. 5(1) jurisdiction.

Lanterna argued that because of Rank's own alleged breach of the agreement, Lanterna was not under any contractual obligation towards Rank and that consequently, Art. 5(1) did not apply. (It also contended that its contractual obligation was to organise the guarantee by Banca—which it had done—not also to pay, which the court rejected.)

Judgment

Saville J. held that if the existence of a contractual obligation upon Lanterna to pay the sum claimed was disputed, Rank would be required: (i) to establish the existence of such an obligation; and (ii) to do so by satisfying the court that there was a serious issue of its existence to be tried. The requirement was the same as that laid down in the *Tesam* case in respect of proof of contractual existence as a whole, where the latter was disputed. A plaintiff would not be stopped from satisfying the court merely through the bare assertions of the defendant, although the latter would also be taken into account alongside the plaintiff's own evidence.

On the facts, the court decided that Rank had established there to be a serious issue for trial of existence as to the obligation.

The issue with Banca was whether, as a matter of contractual construction, the guarantee contract had incorporated the London payment clause in the long-term agreement. Saville J. concluded that it had.

Thus, in the case of both Lanterna and Banca, the matter in dispute was held to relate to a contractual obligation for purposes of Art. 5(1) and place of performance of the payment obligation in question was London.

The English courts possessed jurisdiction under Art. 5(1).

Case principle

7. The *Tesam* meaning of the requirement of 'good arguable case' applies not only to disputed contractual existence under Art. 5(1), but also to disputed location of place of performance of the obligation in question.

Case

Twin Books (UK) Limited v Cronion S.A. (unreported) High Court, 9 July **142** 1993

Facts

The plaintiff English publishing company concluded an agreement in 1991 with the defendant Spanish printing company for the defendant to print books from tapes provided by the plaintiff and thereafter to return the tapes to the plaintiff. The defendant complained that the plaintiffs were slow payers and refused to return the tapes until sums due were paid. The plaintiffs brought proceedings in the English courts for breach of the contractual obligation of the defendants to return the tapes (and for the tort of wrongful detention), alleging that the defendants had received all payments due to them and claiming as damages the expenses of recreating the tapes. The defendants contested English Art. 5(1) jurisdiction, on the ground that their contractual obligation was to redeliver the tapes in Spain, not England (it was agreed that the 'obligation in question' for Art. 5(1) was that of redelivery of the tapes).

Judgment

Deputy High Court Judge J. Griffith Williams Q.C. held that English courts lacked Art. 5(1) place of contractual performance jurisdiction.

(1)   The burden was entirely upon the plaintiff to satisfy the court on a good arguable case that England was the place of contractual performance. The test for doing so was *Tesam*, namely, that there was a serious question to this effect for proper determination at trial.

(2)   Taking into account the contractual terms and surrounding circumstances, the defendant's obligation was to return the tapes to the plaintiff in Spain, not in England. Spain was the place of performance, therefore, and there was no real prospect for the plaintiff to argue successfully to the contrary.

Case principles

8.   The *Tesam* test of good arguable case, as meaning serious issue for determination at trial, applies to (*Tessili*) determination of the law governing the contract for the purposes of locating place of performance.

9.   It also applied to the question of whether a case fell within the *Ivenel* exception to *de Bloos*.

Case

143   Mercury Publicity Ltd v Wolfgang Loerke GmbH [1993] I.L.Pr. 142 Court of Appeal, 16 October 1991

Facts

The plaintiff English advertising company appointed the defendant to be its exclusive agent for Germany and wished to sue the defendant, for sums allegedly owed, in the English courts. The plaintiff asserted that English law governed the contract, according to which the payment was required to be made in England, place of performance for purposes of Art. 5(1). The defendant countered that German law, requiring payment in Germany as place of performance, governed the contract, and that, in any event, even if English law applied, a commercial agent in the position of the defendant was subject to the *Ivenel* exception to *de Bloos*, and consequently, the obligation in question was that which characterized the contract, being performance of the defendant agent's work in Germany, not payment of the sums in England.

Judgment

The Court of Appeal rejected the defendant's arguments and in so doing upheld English Art. 5(1) jurisdiction.

In its ruling, the Court of Appeal held that the defendant had failed to establish a good arguable case according to the *Tesam* test that German law or the

Ivenel principle applied, whereas the plaintiff had succeeded in relation to the application of English law to the contract.

Comment

In *The Canada Trust Co. v Stolzenberg (No. 2)* (1997) *The Times*, 10 November [Court of Appeal] 29 October 1997, [1998] 1 All ER 318, the defendants contested English Article 6(1) jurisdiction or Order 11 rule 1(1)(c), on the ground that the main defendant was not domiciled in England. The Court of Appeal held that the standard of proof for Article 6(1) conditions was that of good arguable case, not the ordinary civil standard of balance of probabilities (see too Langley J. at first instance in the High Court in *Sameon Co. SA v N.V. Petrofina SA*, Case 162 *infra*).

However, the court also went on to criticise the *Tesam/Mölnlycke* line of authority for applying the lower serious-issue-for-trial test to merits aspects of Convention jurisdiction grounds, rather than the higher 'good arguable case' ('strong case for argument') approach. The previous courts, it was said, should not have used the two expressions indiscriminately, because there was a difference: the national *Seaconsar* case (*supra*, Case 84) had now shown that the lower serious-issue standard only applied to the special national Order 11 rule 4(1)(b) requirement to show good cause of action on the merits in addition to a rule 1(1) jurisdiction head and rule 4(2) *forum conveniens*; and so far as rule 1(1) jurisdiction heads were concerned, these had to be established on a good arguable case, not merely as a serious issue—as to both *merits* and non-merits elements. Convention grounds, therefore, were to be treated in the same way: solely good arguable case. *Tesam and Mölnlycke* were excused from fault, as having been decided prior to the *Seaconsar* clarification when there was some confusion over whether serious-issue and good arguable case were interchangeable, and it was thought that had they been decided after *Seaconsar*, the courts would instead have used the expression 'good arguable case'. As to which of *Canada Trust (No. 2)* and *Tesam/Mölnlycke* future courts will follow, this remains to be seen—in particular at House of Lords and ECJ level (*Shevill* Case C–68/93 said standard was for national laws).

Case principle

10. A contract within Art. 5(1) must be that which is legally binding between the parties.

Case

Gamlestaden plc v Casa de Suecia SA and Hans Thulin [1994] 1 Lloyd's Rep **144** 433 High Court, 3 February 1993

Facts

In these proceedings, the argument was put that as a matter of construction, an alleged loan contract was merely an anticipation of contracts for the loan of money subsequently to be concluded as part of the facility.

Judgment

The judge rejected this interpretation of the facts. However, the implication of support for the view that a 'contract' within Art. 5(1) must be an agreement which is already binding rather than merely in anticipation of future contractual agreement may be drawn.

The approach of the Court of Appeal in *Mölnlycke*, Case 139, *supra*, was further apparently approved by the judge, Potter J.

Case principle

11. Enforcement by a third party of a trust of a contractual promise in favour of the third party falls within Art. 5(1) as 'matters relating to a contract'.

Case

145 Atlas Shipping Agency (U.K.) Limited v Suisse Atlantique Société d'Armement Maritime S.A. [1995] I.L.Pr. 600 High Court, 6 April 1995

Facts

The plaintiff English company acted as shipbrokers for the sale of two ships to the defendant Swiss buyers. The defendant buyers agreed with the sellers (co-defendants) to deduct a sum from the purchase price, to be paid as commission to the plaintiffs. The plaintiffs sued for the amount in the English courts and wished to rely upon Art. 5(1), since the parties were agreed that payment was required to be made in England, as the obligation in question.

The defendant buyers contested English Art. 5(1) jurisdiction: as under English law the doctrine of 'privity of contract' prevented a third party to the contract, in the position of the plaintiffs, in whose favour the contract had been made, from enforcing the contract, the plaintiffs were compelled to assert the existence of a trust of the sellers' promise to pay the plaintiffs under the contract, with the defendant buyers as trustees thereof (see *Les Affréteurs Réunis S.A. v Leopold Walford (London) Ltd* [1919] AC 801, HL), or alternatively with the sellers as constructive trustees. However, the defendants contended that this meant that the proceedings consequently fell outside the classification as 'matters relating to a contract' in Art. 5(1), citing the restrictive approach of the European Court of Justice in *Jakob Handte & Co. GmbH* Case C–26/91 (action by sub-buyer against manufacturer under French law not within Art. 5(1)), in preference to the broader treatment of the contractual conception in *Peters* Case 34/82 (action by an association against one of its members held to fall within Art. 5(1)).

Judgment

Rix J. held in favour of the contractual classification of the action as falling within Art. 5(1), and consequently English courts possessed jurisdiction. He recognized that in *Jakob* the Court of Justice had applied the restrictive interpretation of Art. 5(1), being in derogation of Art. 2. Nevertheless, the present action was different to *Jakob* because there could be a long contractual chain between manufacturer and ultimate plaintiff sub-buyer, in which event the manufacturer would be uncertain where it might eventually be sued as place of performance in relation to the sub-buyer, nor would it have voluntarily undertaken an obligation towards the plaintiff. Whereas, in the present case, the defendants knew precisely who the potential third party plaintiff was and had actually entered an obligation for the latter's benefit.

Furthermore, special jurisdiction grounds in Art. 5 were to be assumed to be disjunctive. Accordingly, simply because the (constructive) trust, alternatively alleged, fell outside the terms of Art. 5(6) specifically on trusts jurisdiction, this did not necessarily mean that Art. 5(1) could not then apply.

Thus, the claim fell within 'both the letter and the spirit of Article 5(1)' as a matter relating to a contract.

Comment

In the unreported case of *Twin Books (UK) Limited v Cronion S.A.*, 9 July 1993, deputy High Court Judge J. Griffith Williams Q.C. also made the point that Arts 5(1) and (3) were disjunctive, in the context of a wrongful retention of property, breach of contract, claim (see *supra*, Case 137).

It is certainly arguable that Rix J. was correct to conclude that, on the facts of *Atlas Shipping*, the plaintiffs had succeeded in cutting their way through the wire netting of the European Court's *Jakob Handte*.

Case principle

12. In an action for avoidance of a reinsurance contract and for an account and repayment of sums paid to the reinsured, through non-disclosure and misrepresentation in breach of the fiduciary duty of good faith, is the 'obligation in question' contractual for purposes of Art. 5(1)? There are conflicting decisions at **High Court** level.

Case

Trade Indemnity Plc v Försäkringsaktiebolaget Njord (in lig) [1995] 1 All ER   **146**
796 High Court, 7 July 1994

Facts

The plaintiffs made contracts in 1991 to reinsure the Swedish defendants against risks. Subsequently, that same year, the defendants went into liquidation in Sweden and were investigated by the Swedish securities authorities who found evidence of gross mismanagement and fraud.

The plaintiffs then brought two identical English actions against the defendants in October 1992 and February 1993, claiming avoidance of the contracts for misrepresentation and non-disclosure of risks and an account, and the return of sums paid. The defendants challenged English jurisdiction in both actions. In the first action, national English rules governed because, although the Lugano Convention entered into force on 1 May 1992 in the UK, Sweden only became a Contracting State on 1 January 1993. As for the second action, this had been instituted precisely in case the English court held against its national jurisdiction in the first action and here the Convention was now clearly applicable. The plaintiffs claimed that Art. 5(1) conferred English jurisdiction.

Judgment

Rix J. in the High Court held as follows.

In the first action, national English discretionary contracts jurisdiction under RSC Ord. 11, r.1(1)(d) would be set aside in favour of Swedish jurisdiction as clearly more appropriate *forum conveniens*.

As to the second action, Rix J. decided that Art. 5(1) was inapplicable to the claim for avoidance on grounds of non-disclosure and lack of fair representation of risks by the defendants.

Although *Peters v ZNAV* had held that the Convention Art. 5(1) concept of 'matters relating to a contract' would be extended to non-contractual relationships which nevertheless displayed similarities to contract, it was still a requirement that the obligation in question must be contractual. This was not the case here, where the obligation of disclosure arose prior to and independently of the contract.

Nor was it true to say that the obligation in question was that of payment of claims by the plaintiffs themselves. The *Ivenel* characteristic obligation method was confined to employment relationships, as shown by the European Court's ruling in *Shenavai* Case 266/85.

Case

147 Agnew and others v Lansförsäkringsbolagens AB [1996] 4 All ER 978 High Court, 30 July 1996

Facts

The plaintiffs reinsured elements of the Swedish defendants' risk under insurance of the supply of valves for use in the North Sea oil fields. The plaintiffs wished to bring English proceedings to avoid the contract for the defendants' lack of disclosure and false representations of risk in negotiations which took place in the plaintiffs' offices in London prior to contract. The defendants challenged English Art. 5(1) jurisdiction on the ground, in the *Trade Indemnity* case, that an obligation arising outside the contract was not an 'obligation' for purposes of Art. 5(1).

Judgment

Mance J. held that Art. 5(1) was satisfied in relation to the obligation to make fair representation and disclosure and that since England was the place of performance thereof, English courts had jurisdiction under Art. 5(1), for the following reasons.

(1) He expressly disagreed with Rix J.'s view in *Trade Indemnity*, *supra*, that obligations, such as those of disclosure and representation, having their source in equity outside the contract, did not qualify as 'obligations' for purposes of Art. 5(1).

(2) Mance J. was strongly influenced by the expansive approach of the Court of Appeal in *Kleinwort Benson*, decided earlier in the year, subsequent to *Trade Indemnity*, towards interpretation of the first component of Art. 5(1)—'matters relating to a contract' (see *infra*, Case 149).

(3) Since in *Kleinwort Benson* Art. 5(1) of Schedule 4 was applied to a claim that a contract was void *ab initio* for incapacity, he considered that an action for avoidance through misrepresentation should itself be held to satisfy that element—and that the mere fact that the duty arose prior to the contract itself should not be held to prevent it from amounting to an obligation for purposes of Art. 5(1).

(4) This was said to be in accordance with the Convention's system and objectives, to concentrate actions relating to contract in the most appropriate court, and with the expansive approach towards interpreting the contractual concept in Art. 5(1) in *Peters* and *Kleinwort Benson*.

Comment

Agnew was decided after the Court of Appeal's *Kleinwort Benson* judgment, whereas the latter was not available to Rix J. in *Trade Indemnity*. Mance J.'s judgment has been affirmed by the Court of Appeal on 31 July 1997 [1997] 4 All ER 937.

It might have been reasonable to conclude, therefore, and simply because, in any event, it was the later case, giving full consideration to *Trade Indemnity*, that *Agnew*, although of concurrent jurisdiction to *Trade Indemnity*, would have been the judgment preferred by later courts, until the Court of Appeal had had occasion to decide authoritatively.

However, a majority of the House of Lords has now overturned the Court of Appeal's judgment in *Kleinwort Benson* and found that a restitution claim for money paid under a contract which is void *ab initio* is not a matter relating to a contract within Schedule 4 Article 5(1) ((1997) *The Times* 31 October)!

(Notwithstanding which, shortly before this book went to print, the report of the Court of Appeal's judgment of 31 July 1997 in *Agnew* [1997] 4 All ER 937 appeared—affirming Mance J.'s first instance decision in preference to Rix J.'s treatment in *Trade Indemnity*.)

Case principle

13. Article 5(1) is applicable to a plaintiff's claim for a negative declaration *against* contractual existence (*Effer* applied).

Case

148 Boss Group Ltd v Boss France S.A. [1996] 4 All ER 970, Court of Appeal, 2 April 1996

Facts

The defendant French company was appointed sole French distributor of fork lift truck products of its English parent company, Lancer Boss Group Limited, in 1967, but in 1994 Lancer Boss went into administrative receivership and its business was sold to the plaintiff, which terminated the relationship with the defendant and appointed a new French distributor. The defendant brought provisional proceedings in France against the plaintiff, compelling the plaintiff to supply the defendant with the product and restraining the new French distributor from acting—subsequently in fact overturned by the Paris Court of Appeal. The plaintiff itself instituted proceedings in the English courts, following the first instance French decision, for a negative declaration that it was not and never had been in a contractual relationship with the defendant and it sought to rely upon Art. 5(1) for English jurisdiction. The defendant successfully contested English Art. 5(1) jurisdiction at first instance, on the ground that the plaintiff, seeking a declaration of contractual *non*-existence, was consequently necessarily unable to prove a good arguable case of contractual existence, as required according to *Tesam* following *Effer v Kantner*. The plaintiff appealed to the Court of Appeal.

Judgment

The Court of Appeal held in favour of English Art. 5(1) jurisdiction.

The court applied the underlying rationale of *Effer*, which, it considered, applied as much to where the *plaintiff* denied contractual existence, as to where the defendant did so. This was said to be self-evident and the contrary argument illogical and self-contradictory. The defendant should not at one and the same time assert contractual existence, and yet seek to rely upon its non-existence, alleged by the plaintiff, as the basis of inapplicability of Art. 5(1).

Case principle

14. Claim for restitution of money paid under a contract which was void *ab initio* held not to fall within Sched. 4, Art. 5(1) as matter relating to a contract. There has been disagreement between majorities at Court of Appeal and House of Lords levels.

Case

149 Kleinwort Benson Limited v City of Glasgow District Council [1996] I.L.Pr. 218 Court of Appeal, 25 January 1996

Facts

The plaintiff bank and defendant Scottish local authority entered into 'interest rate swap agreements' in 1982, whereby payments of interest on principal sums loaned were to be made at various times based upon differences between fixed and market rates. The problem was that in a test case in 1992 the House of Lords held such contracts to be void *ab initio* as being *ultra vires* the capacity of the local authorities. The plaintiff claimed repayment of the monies held by the defendant under the void transaction and wished to proceed to enforce the obligation in the English courts under Art. 5(1) (or Art. 5(3)) of 1982 Act, Sched. 4, governing internal, intra-UK jurisdiction (the case was purely internal to the United Kingdom, so that the Convention itself was inapplicable). However, the defendant, wishing to take advantage of shorter Scottish limitation periods, challenged English jurisdiction, on the ground that the claim for restitution was not a matter relating to a contract within the meaning of Art. 5(1) (nor tort under 5(3)—it was, nonetheless, common ground that England was Art. 5(1) and (3) place of contractual performance and harmful event in tort, respectively, if these were applicable). The defendants were successful at first instance. The plaintiff appealed to the Court of Appeal. The Court of Appeal asked the European Court of Justice to provide an interpretative ruling, which the European Court refused to do, on the ground that interpretation of Sched. 4 was beyond its jurisdiction (see Case C–346/93 and *infra*, 1971 Protocol). The Court of Appeal itself, therefore, was required to decide.

Judgment

A majority of the Court of Appeal (Millett and Roch L.JJ.) held that the plaintiff's claim for restitution of money paid under a void contract was a matter relating to a contract within the meaning of Art. 5(1)—at least where such a claim for unjust enrichment had a (void) contract as its source.

The majority considered that although Convention interpretation was not binding upon English courts applying Sched. 4, nonetheless, regard had to be had to the former in respect of the latter's meaning and effect (1982 Act s.16(3)(a)), especially where provisions were identical, and this meant that Sched. 4, Art. 5(1) too should be given an independent (Convention) meaning rather than that necessarily based upon a national law of a Contracting State. Furthermore, the European Court's ruling in *Peters* Case 34/82 showed that Convention Art. 5(1) would be extended to analogous situations where there were close links akin to contract, provided that the minimal element of consensuality was present.

On this basis, restitution, even for Sched. 4, not Convention Art. 5(1) as such, came within the extended meaning of 'matters relating to a contract' thereunder and applied so as to afford jurisdiction to the English courts.

In the minority, Leggatt L.J. differed in his reasoning and conclusion. A void contract was no contract at all; there was no contractual obligation in question and no place of performance of contract. Furthermore, Sched. 4 was not the Convention, and consequently national meanings could be resorted thereto. In English national law, as in most national laws, a distinction was drawn between contract, tort and restitution. So should it be under Sched. 4. In addition, it was important to avoid a different result according to the way in which a claim was pleaded—restitution being merely incidental if contractual avoidance was the main relief sought. In his view, neither Art. 5(1) nor Art. 5(3) (see *infra*, Art. 5(3)) applied.

Comment

The Court of Appeal's majority judgment was subsequently overturned on 30 October 1997, by a three to two majority in the House of Lords (Lords Goff, Clyde and Hutton—with Lords Mustill and Nicholls dissenting as to Sched. 4 Art. 5(1)) in (1997) *The Times* 31 October. For the majority, Lord Goff noted that European Court decisions on Convention Art. 5(1) had to be had regard to: these showed a restricted scope of Art. 5 special jurisdiction in derogation of Art. 2 and that obligation in question was that upon which the claim was based (*de Bloos*). In view of which it was very difficult to conclude that this restitution claim was based on a particular contractual obligation, since the contract had never existed. It was to be presumed that unjust enrichment was omitted from Art. 5 because the closest connection was in fact Art. 2 domicile in such cases. Dissenting, Lord Nicholls sought to demonstrate that Art. 5(1) jurisdiction was not to be confined to 'performance' disputes and that for reasons of obvious good sense and convenience Art. 5(1) should apply to the broader range.

When Art. 5(1) *of the Convention* next comes before the English courts on this issue, it is hoped that the European Court will be requested to choose between the conflicting views!

Case principle

15. A claim to avoid a reinsurance contract for non-disclosure and false misrepresentation constitutes a matter *relating to* a contract for purposes of Art. 5(1) (Court of Appeal in *Kleinwort Benson* applied).

Case

150 Agnew v Lansförsäkringsbolagens AB [1996] 4 All ER 978 High Court, 30 July 1996

Facts

The plaintiffs reinsured Swedish defendants' risks under insurance of valves for use in North Sea oil fields. The plaintiffs wished to avoid the contract for defendants' breach of the duty of good faith in disclosure and fair representation of risk and brought proceedings in English courts under Art. 5(1). The defendants challenged the latter, on the ground that the duty arose in equity outside the contract and consequently was not an 'obligation' for purposes of Art. 5(1).

Judgment

Mance J. held Art. 5(1) to be satisfied in relation to English jurisdiction (which place of performance, in fact, had been conceded by the defendants).

The whole gist and purpose of the action *related to* a contract, in the expansive sense which had been adopted by the European Court in *Peters* and by the Court of Appeal in *Kleinwort Benson* (see *supra*), notwithstanding that the duty of disclosure itself arose prior to the conclusion of the contract which it was sought to avoid.

Comment

The main content of Mance J.'s judgment concerned not the issue here of 'matters relating to a contract', but the second element of Art. 5(1), namely, even if the action on duties of disclosure and fair representation were matters relating to a contract, nonetheless, did they amount to 'obligations' for the purposes of Art. 5(1)—especially in view of the previous decision of Rix J. in the very similar *Trade Indemnity* case (prior to the Court of Appeal in *Kleinwort*) that such duties were *not* Art. 5(1) obligations (see *supra*, Case 146, and *infra*, Art. 5(1) 'obligation'). However, in view of the House of Lords' reversal of the Court of Appeal's *Kleinwort* decision on Art. 5(1) Sched. 4, Mance J.'s ruling on contracts classification loses some of its force for the time being.

Case principle

16. Disputes over contracts (or tort-liability) existence do not constitute submission to substance under Art. 18, if solely in order to challenge Art. 5(1) (or 5(3)) jurisdiction.

Case

Hewden Stuart Heavy Cranes Ltd v Leo Gottwald Kommanditgesellschaft   **151** (unreported) Court of Appeal, 13 May 1992

Facts

See infra, Case 154, and Art. 18.

Judgment

See supra, Case principle.

Comment

It would have seemed remarkable had this not been held to be the case and would have risked making Art. 5(1) and (3) (not to mention (6)) redundant!

> " . . . obligation in question . . . "

Case principle

1. In an action for damages against a supplier for breach of an exclusive distribution agreement through termination without reasonable notice required by the contract and for wrongful appointment of another distributor, the principal obligation in question is that of providing reasonable notice of termination (*de Bloos*, Case 14/76 and *Shenavai*, Case 266/85 applied).

Case

152 Medway Packaging Ltd v Meurer Maschinen GmbH & Co. KG [1990] 2 Lloyd's Rep. 112 Court of Appeal, 1 March 1990

Facts

The plaintiff English company concluded a contract in 1981 with the defendant German manufacturer of stretch-wrapping machines to be the exclusive distributor of the defendant's machines in the UK. It was an implied term of the agreement that either party could terminate it on giving reasonable notice. The plaintiff wished to sue the defendants in the English courts for damages of £269,000 in respect of the defendants' alleged breach of the agreement through appointment, in 1988, of a third party to act as their distributor in the UK and failure to give reasonable notice of termination to the plaintiff. The defendant contested Art. 5(1) jurisdiction of the English courts. The latter would depend upon identification of the 'obligation in question' under the exclusive distribution agreement (and upon its place of performance).

Judgment

The Court of Appeal held European Court case law to apply.

Thus, *de Bloos* required courts to determine the actual obligation upon which the plaintiff's claim was based (and referred to applicable law in order to determine whether a damages obligation was independent—and non-contractual—or merely representing the unperformed contractual obligation); *Ivenel* had applied the characteristic obligation in the case of employment contracts; and *Shenavai* had limited the latter protective doctrine to employment and confirmed *de Bloos* as the general rule. In addition, where a number of contractual obligations were in issue in the proceedings, the obligation in question was the *principal* obligation under the contract from amongst them.

Accordingly, the Court of Appeal concluded that:

(1) the reasonable notice obligation would be regarded as the principal obligation of the defendants in the case before it, because 'it is the

giving of proper notice which brings the whole contract to an end'
(so that place of performance thereof would have to be England for
Art. 5(1) jurisdiction to exist); but

(2)   nevertheless, had the 'obligation' sought to be enforced instead been
held to be that of exclusive distribution on the facts, this was said to
mean the defendant grantor's obligation so to act as to respect fully
the rights of the plaintiff grantee under the agreement.

Comment

See *infra*, 'place of performance', Case 159, for the Court of Appeal's decision on
this aspect.

Case principle

2.   The 'obligation in question' in a *voyage charter of a vessel to be nominated*, as opposed to the charter of a named vessel, is the obligation to
nominate, rather than the obligation to provide ship and crew at the loading port (*Shenavai v Kreischer* Case 266/85 applied).

Case

Union Transport plc v Continental Lines S.A. [1992] 1 WLR 15 (H.L.(E))   **153**
House of Lords, 12 December 1991

Facts

The plaintiffs claimed damages in the English courts against the defendant
Belgian shipowners for the alleged breach of a voyage charter of a vessel to be
nominated: the defendants had neither nominated a ship nor subsequently provided ship and crew at the loading port in Florida, USA. The contract, the existence of which the defendants were prepared to dispute, provided, *inter alia*,
for payment of commission in London, application of English law, nomination
of the ship in London and advance notice of its arrival at the loading port.

   The plaintiffs relied upon Art. 5(1) for jurisdiction of English courts over the
Belgian defendants: *nomination* of the ship was the *principal* obligation of the
defendants at issue in the proceedings and its place of performance was London,
England. The defendants objected: the principal contractual obligation was to
provide a ship at the loading port, in Florida, the place of its performance.

Judgment

The House of Lords unanimously upheld English Art. 5(1) jurisdiction. In
Shenavai v Kreischer, the European Court had confirmed the principle in *de
Bloos v Bouyer* Case 14/76, that it was the obligation forming the basis of the
legal proceedings which was to be taken into account for purposes of Art.
5(1)—*Ivenel v Schwab* Case 133/81, referring to the 'characteristic obligation'
under the contract, being limited to employment contracts; and the Court of

Justice had further held, in *Shenavai*, that where a number of contractual obligations were at issue in the proceedings, place of performance of the *principal* obligation would be referred to.

In this case, therefore, where the plaintiffs had pleaded breach of both the obligation of the defendants to nominate a ship and that of providing the vessel at the loading port, the House of Lords considered *nomination* to be the principal obligation. Since its place of performance was London, English courts possessed jurisdiction under Art. 5(1).

Comments

See too *infra*, 'place of performance', *Boss Group Ltd v Boss France S.A.*, Case 160.

In the Court of Appeal in *Royal Bank of Scotland plc v Cassa di Risparmio delle Provincie Lombard*, *The Financial Times*, 21 January 1992, CA, *infra*, Case 158, Mustill L.J. suggested that plaintiffs could not manipulate jurisdiction by tailoring their claims to ensure that a particular obligation was held to be the principal one for *Shenavai*.

Case principal

3.   In an action for damages for breach of contract to design, manufacture, supply, test and advise on use of heavy machinery, the obligation in question is the principal one to design and manufacture (consistent with *Shenavai*).

Case

154   Hewden Stuart Heavy Cranes Ltd v Leo Gottwald Kommanditgesellschaft (unreported) Court of Appeal, 13 May 1992

Facts

The plaintiff plant hire company wished to sue the German defendants on a contract to design, manufacture, supply, test and advise on use of a large crane, to be delivered to the plaintiff *ex works* Düsseldorf. The crane had collapsed when being used at an English port. The defendants contested English Art. 5(1) (and Art. 18) jurisdiction.

Judgment

Lloyd L.J. in the Court of Appeal, with whom the other two judges agreed, held that German, not English, courts possessed Art. 5(1) contracts jurisdiction.

The plaintiff had argued that the defendants' obligations to test the crane and to warn the plaintiff of any manoeuvres which might be dangerous were to be carried out in England. However, the court considered these to be merely ancillary obligations. The main obligation of the defendants was to design and to manufacture the crane and this was for performance in Germany. German courts were those of the place of performance.

Comment

The Court of Appeal did not expressly refer to *Shenavai v Kreischer*. Yet, their decision upon principal obligation in proceedings was completely consistent with the European Court's approach in that case.

Case principle

4.   In a contract for the financing of shipping operations through a bank, the principal obligation of the defendant bank was held to be the overall financing obligation of the bank, not the actual payment of money into the borrower's bank account (following *Union Transport Plc, supra* Case 153, 'the real ground of complaint').

Case

Ocarina Marine Ltd v Marcard Stein & Co [1994] 2 Lloyd's Rep. 524 High   **155**
Court, 13 May 1994

Facts

The plaintiff shipowning firms entered an agreement with the defendant German bank for the financing of their operations. Their earnings were to be paid into the defendant's London branch and debited with the defendant's fees. When the defendant terminated the contract in 1992, the plaintiffs sought damages and the return of monies in their account from the English courts. The defendant challenged English jurisdiction, on the ground that Germany, not England, was the place of performance of the obligation in question.

Judgment

Rix J. held for the defendant on Art. 5(1). The principal obligation of the defendant bank—its failure to be performed being the *real ground of the plaintiff's complaint*—was the defendant's overall obligation to provide finance in various forms, in Germany, not that of funding the plaintiffs' bank account kept in England.

Nevertheless, in respect of three of the five claims of the plaintiffs, English courts possessed jurisdiction on the ground of agreement to their jurisdiction under Art. 17 (see *infra*, Art. 17).

> " ... *place of performance* ... "

Case principle

1.   Determination of place of contractual payment as performance is for the private international law of the forum (*Tessili* Case 12/76 applied).

Case

156 Project XJ220 Limited v Comte d'Uze and Comte de Dampierre (unreported)
High Court, 19 November 1993

Facts

The French defendants ordered expensive motor cars from the plaintiff manufacturer and failed to make the second payment of £50,000 towards the price
when given nine months' notice of delivery, as had been agreed. The plaintiff
sued for payment in the English courts and the defendants challenged English
jurisdiction on the ground that France, not England, was the place of payment
as performance under Art. 5(1) and that French courts alone possessed jurisdiction over these 'consumer contracts' in any event under Art. 14, para. 2, as
those of the defendants' French domicile.

Judgment

Deputy High Court Judge Boyd Q.C. upheld Art. 5(1) jurisdiction of English
courts as those of the place of performance of the obligation in question.

In conformity with *de Bloos*, payment, on which the claim was based, was
the obligation in question. Place of payment, following *Tessili*, was for English
private international law to determine, according to which, English law
governed the contract. English law, in the absence of express or implied agreement, required payment to be made at the *creditor's* address, here, in England.
England was the place of payment and performance. English courts possessed
jurisdiction under Art. 5(1).

Article 14 was held to be inapplicable because the defendants were found
not to be consumers (see *infra*, Art. 13).

Case principle

2. The English rule of contractual performance, when applicable in accordance
    with *Tessili* Case 12/76, is that performance takes place at the creditor's
    establishment unless: (i) contrary provision is expressed in the contract, or
    (ii) contrary provision is implied through business efficacy or practice.

Case

157 Royal Bank of Scotland plc v Cassa di Risparmio delle Provincie Lombardi
[1991] I.L.Pr. 411 High Court, 5 December 1990

Facts

The plaintiff Scottish bank, through its London branch, confirmed letters of
credit for the defendant Italian banks, subject to ICC Uniform Customs and
Practice (UCP), to finance the purchase of a consignment of pears from
Argentina by Italian importers. It was a term of the agreement between
the plaintiff and defendants that the plaintiff should be reimbursed by an

intermediary American bank based in New York with which it had a New York bank account.

After the plaintiff had made payment to the seller of the pears, the Italian buyers discovered that the pears were non-existent and suspected fraud. They instructed the defendants not to reimburse the plaintiff and in turn the defendants withdrew authorization to do so from the New York bank.

The plaintiff wished to sue the Italian defendants for breach of contract in English courts under Art. 5(1), but the defendants challenged jurisdiction. The plaintiff relied upon the rule of English law that a debtor must pay at the creditor's place of business, in this case, London. The defendants countered that this rule was unsuitable for international banking practice, just as it was the case that an account holder with a surplus in his account had to seek repayment at the branch where the account was kept.

Judgment

Phillips J. agreed with the defendants and held New York, not London, to be the place of performance for purposes of Art. 5(1), so that English courts lacked jurisdiction.

The obligation in question was undoubtedly that of the defendants to reimburse the plaintiff, in accordance with *de Bloos* Case 14/76; and English law, applicable to the contract, governed its place of performance under the *Tessili* rule.

What was the English rule for place of contractual performance?

The general position, apparently, was that the debtor had to follow the creditor in order to pay.

However, this would give way whenever there was a contrary indication in the contract, which could be expressed or implied. Implication could be given rise to either through business efficacy or because, according to the nature of a particular type of transaction in practice, the general rule would be inappropriate.

It was the latter position which applied to the present case. Phillips J. examined the nature of the international banking transaction involved. Where an intermediary bank was used for purposes of reimbursement in this way in the absence of a direct account relationship between plaintiff and defendant banks, the place of performance of reimbursement was to be taken to be intended to be the place of business of the reimbursing bank in America. Furthermore, on the failure of reimbursement to be carried out in the manner agreed, America did not then cease to be the place of performance and the latter *revert* to the plaintiff's place of business in London under the general rule.

The plaintiff appealed to the Court of Appeal.

Case

Royal Bank of Scotland plc v Cassa di Risparmio delle Provincie Lombard, **158** The Financial Times, 21 January 1992 Court of Appeal, 19 December 1991

Facts

See supra.

Judgment

The Court of Appeal unanimously upheld the judgment of Phillips J. in the High Court.

No definitive view was expressed upon whether the English general rule of payment at a creditor's place of business was inappropriate for international banking transactions, although some scepticism was voiced.

The Court of Appeal based its decision against Art. 5(1) jurisdiction upon the simple, straightforward ground that there was but one obligation in question upon the defendants under the contract, being to *secure reimbursement of the plaintiff*; and, according to the contract, this obligation was agreed to be performed in the United States. In the event of its failure to be carried out, the place of performance was not thereafter transferred nor did it somehow 'revert' to London. It was always in New York, and in New York it stayed.

Case principle

3. In an exclusive distribution agreement providing for reasonable notice of termination by either side: a) place of performance of the grantor's notice obligation towards the grantee is that of the grantee's place of business; and b) place of performance of the exclusive distribution aspect is wherever the grantor must so act so as to comply fully with the grantee's rights under the agreement.

Case

159 Medway Packaging Ltd v Meurer Maschinen GmbH & Co. KG [1990] 2 Lloyd's Rep. 112 Court of Appeal, 1 March 1990

Facts

See supra, 'obligation in question', Case 152.

The plaintiff English company entered an agreement in 1981 for exclusive distribution in the UK of the defendant German company's stretch-wrapping machines. It was an implied term of the agreement that either party could terminate it by giving reasonable notice to the other. The plaintiff wished to sue the defendant in the English courts for damages of £269,000 in respect of alleged breach of the distribution agreement through termination by the defendant with insufficient notice and appointment of a third party as its UK distributor. Article 5(1) jurisdiction of the English courts would depend upon whether England was held to be the place of performance of those obligations.

Judgment

The Court of Appeal held that it was so.

First, in the case of the reasonable notice obligation, a requirement to give notice of termination to an English company carrying on its business in England had to be interpreted under the contract as being required to be performed at the company's place of business in England.

Secondly, the exclusive distribution obligation of the defendant German grantor so to act as to respect fully the rights of the plaintiff grantee under the agreement was performable in *both* England and Germany.

English Art. 5(1) jurisdiction, therefore, was satisfied in each case.

Comment

This judgment of Fox L.J., with which the other two judges agreed, suffered from a less than satisfactory degree of clarity in certain respects, and its final conclusion as to place(s) of performance of the exclusive distribution obligation is highly debatable.

Case principles

4. If a number of contractual obligations are in dispute, the obligation to be referred to is the principal obligation in the proceedings (following *Shenavai* Case 266/85 and *Union Transport*, Case 153, *supra*).
5. In an exclusive distribution agreement, the obligation of the manufacturer is both positive, to supply the distributor, and negative, not to supply anyone else.
6. Place of performance of the negative obligation is *everywhere* (following *Medway Packaging*, *supra* Case 159).

Case

Boss Group Ltd v Boss France S.A. [1996] 4 All ER 970, C.A. Court of Appeal, 2 April 1996   **160**

Facts

These were noted in connection with application of Art. 5(1) to contractual non-existence claims (see *supra*, 'matters relating to a contract', Case 148). The defendant French distributors challenging English jurisdiction under Art. 5(1) in the plaintiff English manufacturer's action in England for a declaration against existence of the sole distribution agreement alleged by the defendants, further questioned whether the place of performance of the obligation in dispute under the alleged French exclusive distribution agreement was performable at all in England rather than in France.

Judgment

The Court of Appeal considered that whether the principal obligation (of the plaintiff) in question was viewed as positive or negative—to *supply* the defendant or *not* to supply others, respectively—it was still to be performed in

England as: (i) delivery to the defendant distributors would have been at the plaintiff manufacturer's place of business in England; and (ii) supplies would have been required not to be made to third parties in England, as well as in France.

Case principle

7. The *Ivenel* exception to *de Bloos* is limited to employees' contracts and does not extend to commercial agents who enjoy close relations with the principal (consistent with *Shenavai*).

Case

161   Mercury Publicity Limited v Wolfgang Loerke GmbH [1993] I.L.Pr. 142 Court of Appeal, 16 October 1991

Facts

The plaintiff English company was appointed as advertising agent outside France for filling space in *Le Figaro* magazines. It, in turn, appointed the defendant German company as exclusive sub-agent—one of 15 in the world—for Germany. The plaintiff wished to sue the defendant in the English courts for payment of certain sums, which it said were payable in England as place of performance for purposes of Art. 5(1) according to applicable English law. The defendant contended—unsuccessfully as it turned out—that German law governed the contract, according to which, place of payment as performance was Germany so that English courts lacked jurisdiction. However, the defendant went on to argue that on the facts its relationship with the plaintiff was one of employment, and, consequently, the *Ivenel* exception to *de Bloos* applied: place of performance to be determined for Art. 5(1) was that of the 'characteristic obligation' under the contract and this was the performance of its (sub-)agent's duties under the contract by the defendant—*in Germany*.

Judgment

The Court of Appeal unanimously held against such application or extension of the *Ivenel* exception to *de Bloos* to a commercial agent in the position of the defendant.

The defendant had pointed to the fact that during the contract period, it had no authority to represent competitors of *Figaro*, documentation for orders received was prepared by the plaintiff, and the *Ivenel* exception was intended to cover a person who had been integrated within the organizational framework of an enterprise. In addition, under EC law, Art. 85 of the EC Treaty, prohibiting restrictive agreements between undertakings, would not be applied where a commercial agent was so integrated within the principal's undertaking as, in effect, not to amount to a separate entity.

The Court of Appeal rejected these arguments. Close though relations between plaintiff and defendant might be, the degree of freedom and independence enjoyed by the defendant in carrying out its functions, absence of any minimum level of obligation upon it and the lack of *unequal* bargaining power and of consequent need to protect the defendant as weaker party distinguished the situation from that of employment in *Ivenel* and prevented the latter's extension in the circumstances. With regard to the treatment of Art. 85, its purpose was different from that of *Ivenel*: the latter was intended to protect the employee party to the contract, whereas the single-integrated-corporate-entity concept in relation to Art. 85 was meant to limit that provision's protective effects to the appropriate third parties and effects, so that principles developed were not necessarily also suitable for Art. 5(1): objectives were, respectively, party-protective and macro-economic.

Ivenel was inapplicable and English courts possessed jurisdiction as those of place of performance of the payment obligation under Art. 5(1).

Case principle

8.   A clause in a standard form charterparty selecting a London adjuster for general average contribution to be settled was not also to be construed as an agreement to pay the contribution in London as place of performance of that obligation for purposes of Art. 5(1), in the absence of a trade practice to that effect.

Case

Sameon Co. S.A. v NV Petrofina S.A. ('World Hitachi Zosen'), The Times, **162** 8 April 1996 High Court

Facts

The plaintiff Panamanian shipowner wished to sue defendant Belgian cargo owners and their insurers in the English courts for general average contribution of almost one and a half million US dollars after the plaintiff's ship, World Hitachi Zosen, carrying the defendants' cargo of crude oil from Iran to Rotterdam, collided with another off the coast of Mauritania in 1992, so that the cargo had to be transhipped to another vessel in order to complete its voyage. The standard form charterparty incorporated into the bill of lading provided for adjustment of general average in London, but the parties were unable to agree on the adjustment.

The plaintiff argued that English courts possessed jurisdiction over the Belgian defendants under Art. 5(1), on the ground that agreement upon London as the place of 'adjustment' of general average also amounted to an implied agreement that the adjusted sum should then be *paid* in London as place of performance.

Judgment

Langley J. held that, as a matter of contractual construction, the choice of London adjustment did not also amount to agreement upon London as the place for payment of the general average. Adjustment simply referred to the non-binding assessment of the amount of general average contribution made by the London adjuster; and there was no trading practice whereby this was also to be taken to mean that the assessed sum should then be paid to the London adjuster as agent for the creditor.

Article 5(1), therefore, was inapplicable to confer jurisdiction upon the English courts as those of place of payment. More evidence than adduced was required in order to demonstrate existence of Art. 5(1) jurisdiction in derogation of Art. 2.

The plaintiffs appealed to the Court of Appeal.

Case

163   Sameon Co. SA v NV Petrofina SA (unreported) Court of Appeal, 30 April 1997

See too infra, Art. 17.

Judgment

The Court of Appeal unanimously (Staughton, Henry and Thorpe L.JJ.) upheld the lower court's judgment.

The plaintiffs had argued that it was expedient for all general average contributors to pay their contributions to the London adjuster, as a single channel for payments, and that this was standard practice.

However, the Court of Appeal disagreed with the plaintiffs' conclusions from this (even if it were to be accepted that the alleged practice existed) and as to their proposed construction of the parties' agreement: there was no binding obligation to pay in London; the adjuster was simply an experienced person brought in to calculate amounts, and parties would not always be pleased to pay over large sums to such person; and there could also be problems over matters such as set-off, if payment to the adjuster in London were to be treated as obligatory.

Consequently, payment was not required to be made to the adjuster, in London. English courts lacked Article 5(1) jurisdiction.

ARTICLE 5(3)

"In matters relating to tort . . . "

Case principles

1.   The plaintiff must prove existence of a cause of action in tort.
2.   However, the plaintiff need not adduce evidence which is conclusive as to substance, but merely that there is a serious issue to be tried as to existence of the cause of action in tort (but see *supra*, Comment to Case 143).

Case

Tesam Distribution Ltd v Schuh Mode Team GmbH and Commerzbank AG   **164**
[1990] I.L.Pr. 149 Court of Appeal, 20 October 1989

Facts

See *supra*, Art. 5(1) '*matters relating to a contract*', Case 138.

The plaintiff English company claimed to have made a contract with the defendant German companies, a shoe exporter and the latter's bank respectively, for the import of a quantity of shoes, delivery to take place in London. The defendants denied that the contract had been concluded, and the shoes were never supplied. In the alternative to breach of contract, the plaintiff alleged that if the second defendant was not party to the contract of sale with the first defendant, the second defendant had nevertheless committed the tort of inducing the first defendant to breach the contract with the plaintiff.

The second defendant contested English jurisdiction in contract and tort under Art. 5(1) and (3) respectively: where a defendant denied contractual existence, Art. 5(1) was inapplicable; and similarly, if the plaintiff failed to prove existence of the cause of action in tort, there could be no 'matters relating to tort' for purposes of jurisdiction under Art. 5(3).

Judgment

The Court of Appeal rejected the second defendant's objection to Art. 5(1) 'matters relating to a contract' and held there to be sufficient evidence of contractual existence for purposes of English jurisdiction thereunder (see *supra*, Art. 5(1)).

In the case of alternative tort jurisdiction under Art. 5(3) (in fact, unnecessary to decide, in view of the finding as to existence of Art. 5(1) contracts jurisdiction), the Lord Justice of Appeal who dealt with the issue, Nicholls L.J., agreed with by one of the other two, applied the same test to establish existence of a tort cause of action as in the case of contracts existence under Art. 5(1): that is to say, the plaintiff had to adduce evidence to establish that there was a *serious issue to be determined at full trial* as to whether the plaintiff had a cause of action in tort against the second defendant—but this need not be proved conclusively at the jurisdiction stage, just as this was not a requirement in the case of a good arguable case under RSC Ord. 11 at national English law (see *supra*, *Seaconsar*, Case 84).

On the facts, Nicholls L.J. considered that the plaintiff had *not* satisfied the standard of proof for Art. 5(3) torts jurisdiction: the events showed that either the second defendant might have authorized the first defendant to conclude the contract as agent on its behalf, in which case the cause of action against the second defendant would be in contract, not tort, or the second defendant had not consented, in view of which the sequence of events were hardly sufficient to support the conclusion that the second defendant had subsequently interfered with the contract made by the first defendant alone with the plaintiff so as to amount to a tort.

Accordingly, matters relating to tort for purposes of Art. 5(3) were not involved and jurisdiction thereunder would have been lacking.

Comment

In later cases, the Court of Appeal elaborated upon the principle of good arguable case as serious issue to be tried, first put forward by the Court of Appeal in *Tesam* as the condition for Art. 5(1) and (3) jurisdiction over disputed contractual and torts existence respectively.

Case principles

3. Where tort liability is disputed, the plaintiff must prove its existence for purposes of Art. 5(3) jurisdiction as on a 'good arguable case'.
4. A good arguable case means:
   (1) where the dispute is on a point of law—a serious case to be tried (*Tesam*); or
   (2) where the dispute is on *fact*—that the plaintiff is probably right.
5. Article 5(3) is not available where it is used for joinder of a defendant in circumstances amounting to an abuse of the courts' process.
6. The same principles apply to proof of contractual existence for purposes of jurisdiction under Art. 5(1) (see *supra*).
(In *Shevill* Case C–68/93, 7 March 1995, the ECJ ruled that, as with Art. 5(1) contracts, denial of tort liability did not make Art. 5(3) unavailable. Liability had to be proven according to standard of applicable national law, subject to overall Convention effectiveness.)

Case

165 Mölnlycke A. B. v Procter & Gamble Ltd [1992] 1 WLR 1112 Court of Appeal, 27 June 1991

Facts

Swedish and English plaintiffs brought English proceedings for infringement of a patent relating to babies' nappies against first, second and third defendants, English, American and German companies in a multinational group. The defendants denied liability and appealed against a decision of the first instance English judge that leave to serve the writ outside England and Wales was not required because this was permitted without leave where Convention jurisdiction grounds were satisfied.

Judgment

The Court of Appeal examined whether jurisdiction grounds in Arts 5(3) and 6(1) were established.

With regard to Art. 5(3) (see *infra*, for Art. 6(1)), as in the case of proof of contractual existence under Art. 5(1), in accordance with the European

Court's judgment in *Effer SpA v Kantner* Case 38/81, where existence of tort liability was disputed, this had to be shown by the plaintiff on a good arguable case, meaning: (i) a serious issue to be tried, if a pure question of law was involved; but (ii) that the plaintiff would probably succeed in the substantive claim, if the defendant contested the facts giving rise to tort liability.

Comments

The point was also made that for Art. 5(3) jurisdiction to be available, the joinder of the third defendants merely in order to obtain disclosure of certain documents from them, which could not be acquired from the others, must not be an abuse of the court's process—held not to be so on the facts.

It is questionable whether the Court of Appeal was correct to impose this condition upon the operation of Art. 5(3) (or of any other Convention jurisdiction ground), which, in contrast to national English jurisdiction rules, is mandatory not discretionary. It is difficult to find evidence in the Convention or in the European Court's jurisprudence to suggest that such a restriction exists, and if it does apply, this should be solely as a national, domestic English rule of procedure for the proper joinder of actions against several defendants, or otherwise for proceedings against a particular defendant (see *Kongress Agentur Hagen GmbH v Zeehaghe BV* Case 365/88, in relation to Art. 6(2)).

The *Tesam* test seems to accord with the House of Lords' national English law development in *Seaconsar*, as to standard of proof required to establish a good cause of action on the merits of the claim for discretionary service of a writ out of the jurisdiction (see *supra*, RSC Ord. 11, r.4(1)(b), Case 84).

Case principle

7.   The *Tesam* meaning of good arguable case, as serious issue of torts liability to be determined at trial, also applies to location of harmful event in tort under Art. 5(3).

Case

Twin Books (UK) Limited v Cronion S.A. (unreported) High Court, 9 July 1993   **166**
So held deputy High Court Judge J. Griffith Williams Q.C. (see *supra*, Art. 5(1)).

Case principle

8.   An action brought by one tortfeasor against another for a contribution towards damages paid by the first under a judgment obtained against him by the injured person, may not be able to be regarded as one in 'tort' for purposes of Art. 5(3).

Case

Sante Fe (UK) Limited v Gates Europe NV (unreported) Court of Appeal, 16   **167**
January 1991

Facts

An employee of the plaintiff English company was injured in an accident on an oil rig in Scottish waters of the North Sea through the rupture of a defective hose supplied by the defendant Belgian company. The employee successfully sued the plaintiff for negligence in the English courts. Two years later, the plaintiff wished to claim a contribution towards damages paid to the employee from the defendant in an action to be brought in the English courts. The defendant company contested English courts' jurisdiction: Art. 5(3) was said to be inapplicable because a contribution claim under legislation permitting such a third party action was not 'tort' within Art. 5(3).

Judgment

The Court of Appeal indicated agreement with the defendant. Although *Kalfelis v Schröder* Case 189/87 had held actions not related to contract within Art. 5(1) to amount to tort for purposes of Art. 5(3), that judgment of the Court of Justice had not itself been concerned with a contribution claim.

Comment

This was not, however, a conclusive view of the Court of Appeal, which declined to provide a definitive decision in the absence of full argument by the parties.

Case principle

9. An issue arises as to whether proceedings to establish liability of defendants as constructive trustees through misappropriation of corporate funds are matters relating to tort, delict or quasi-delict for purposes of Art. 5(3)?

Case

168 Polly Peck International plc v Citibank NA [1994] I.L.Pr. 71 High Court, 14 October 1993

Facts

See infra, Art. 21.

The main issue in this case involved dates of English and Swiss seisin for purposes of Art. 21.

Judgment

The judge, Vinelott J., agreed to adjourn the defendants' application for a stay of the English proceedings, so that Swiss courts would be able to decide upon the date of Swiss seisin.

However, prior to reference to the Swiss courts, legal counsel in the English proceedings were to be invited to address the English court upon whether the proceedings involved tort, delict or quasi-delict within the meaning of Art. 5(3), since there was some uncertainty over whether particular Swiss rules on seisin were applicable to 'tort'.

Case principles

10. Actions for breach of confidence not based upon a contractual undertaking of confidentiality under English law, were not founded upon implied contract but on a broad principle of equity not to disclose information received in confidence.
11. Like claims for restitution and unjust enrichment, it was doubtful whether the *Kalfelis* definition of tort was intended to include noncontractual breach of confidence actions.

Case

Kitechnology BV v Unicor GmbH Rahn Plastmaschinen [1994] I.L.Pr. 560 **169**
Court of Appeal, 28 April 1994

Facts

The plaintiff international group of companies invented a new method of manufacturing piping equipment. They entered agreements—containing English jurisdiction clauses—with two of the defendants to inspect the secret process and the latter undertook not to disclose the confidential information. Subsequently, the plaintiffs alleged that the defendants and six others who were their companies, employees and shareholders, were in breach of confidence through disclosing and using the information for the manufacture of pipes in Germany. All defendants were domiciled in Germany.

The two defendants party to the confidentiality agreements challenged English Art. 17 jurisdiction under their contracts (see *infra*, Art. 17).

The other defendants asserted that a non-contractual breach of confidence action against them under English law was not one in tort under Art. 5(3).

Judgment

Evans L.J. considered that actions for breach of confidence were based upon a principle of equity not to disclose information given in confidence, and he doubted whether the definition of tort in *Kalfelis* was intended also to cover such claims.

He regarded the position as similar to that of claims for restitution and unjust enrichment which he again doubted were covered by the tort definition. That matter was in fact before the European Court for an interpretative reference at the time—although, subsequently, the European Court of Justice declined to rule on the English Court of Appeal's reference, on technical jurisdictional grounds (see *Kleinwort Benson Ltd v City of Glasgow District Council* Case C–346/93).

Comment

In the event, it would not affect the outcome that English courts lacked Art. 5(3) jurisdiction, because the court went on to find that even if Art. 5(3) were to apply, the alleged harmful events of disclosure and damage had occurred in Germany, not England (see *infra*).

Case principle

12.   Claims for restitution for unjust enrichment held (*obiter* in the Court of Appeal) not to be tort or delict for Art. 5(3).

Case

170   Kleinwort Benson Limited v City of Glasgow District Council [1996] I.L.Pr. 218 Court of Appeal, 25 January 1996

Facts

See supra, Art. 5(1), Case 149.

Judgment

The majority of two to one judges of the Court of Appeal held the subject matter to be contractual and Art. 5(1) to apply, so that consideration need not (and could not, in accordance with *Kalfelis*) be given to Art. 5(3) (see *supra*, Article 5(1)).

The minority judge, Leggatt L.J., who held against Art. 5(1) contracts classification of the restitution claim, then went on to declare that restitution from unjust enrichment was also not tort and delict for purposes of Art. 5(3), notwithstanding the broad definition in *Kalfelis* Case 189/87 and *Reichert (No. 2)* Case C–261/90. He cited the European Court's judgment in *Kalfelis* (para. 14) in support, where, referring to breach of contract and unjust enrichment, the Court of Justice made the point that concurrent *non*-tortious claims would not be subject to the same Art. 5(3) jurisdiction as that in tort.

Comment

In the House of Lords proceedings on 30 October 1997, (1997) *The Times*, 31 October, the majority of three judges who held Sched. 4 Art. 5(1) to be inapplicable, also confirmed that Sched. 4 Art. 5(3) did not apply, because a claim based upon unjust enrichment did not, exceptional circumstances apart, presuppose either a harmful event or a threatened wrong. Obviously, the two dissenting Lords who held Art. 5(1) to apply could therefore also be taken, in accordance with *Kalfelis*, to agree that Art. 5(3) did not.

"In matters relating to . . . quasi-delict . . . "

Case principle

A claim of invalidity of transfer of assets at an undervalue in fraudulent preference of creditors under s.423 of the Insolvency Act 1986 *might* come within Art. 5(3) as a quasi-delict.

Case

Aiglon Ltd and L'Aiglon S.A. v Gau Shan Co. Ltd [1993] 1 Lloyd's Rep. 164   **171**
High Court, 23 June 1992

Facts

See supra s.49 of the 1982 Act, Case 109.

The claimant sought to base this aspect upon Lugano Art. 5(3), in the alternative to Art. 6(1).

Judgment

Since Art. 6(1) already applied, the matter was unnecessary to decide. However, the judge, Hirst J., thought that Art. 5(3) might well also be applicable as to quasi-delict.

Comments

Where such claims directly derive from and are closely connected with the winding up of an insolvent company, the Convention is probably inapplicable in the first place under Art. 1, para. 2(2) (see *supra*, Case 124).

If, however, these conditions are not satisfied and the Convention applies, in *Reichert (No. 2)* Case C–261/90, the European Court declined to regard the similar French *action paulienne* as falling within Art. 5(3) as a quasi-delict, because it affected dispositions even where a third party disponee was in good faith and had not committed a wrongful act. Hirst J.'s ruling, therefore, may be incorrect to the extent that s.423 may also apply to the third party in good faith, in which circumstance Art. 5(3) should be regarded as inapplicable.

> " . . . *place where the harmful event occurred.*"

Case principle

1. Where the causative event is split between more than one Contracting State ('double-locality' causative event), the place of causative act as optional harmful event in tort within *Bier* Case 21/76, is that in which the substance of the causal event occurred.

Cases

172 Minster Investments Ltd v Hyundai Precision and Industry Co. Ltd [1988] 2 Lloyd's Rep. 621 High Court, 25 January 1988

Facts

A defendant French company, with an office in Korea, made a contract with a Korean company to supervise and report on the manufacture of container products by the latter for the plaintiff English company. The French defendant duly issued an inspection certificate to the Korean company (in Korea or France), which was then sent to the plaintiff who was in England and who, in reliance upon the allegedly negligently prepared certificate, arranged for payment to be made to the Korean company in Korea. The plaintiff argued that English courts possessed jurisdiction over the French defendant as those of the place of harmful event in tort for Art. 5(3)—where the negligent certification was received, relied on and acted upon. The defendant responded that the causative act, within *Bier*, had occurred in Korea (or France) from which the certificate was sent by the French defendant, not in England (and, presumably, damage was payment of the Koreans, by the plaintiff, in Korea).

Judgment

Steyn J. held that *Bier* itself was inapplicable to the particular question of multi-State (double-locality) causative events, having been confined to a choice between single-States *causative event and damage*. Nevertheless, he decided to follow what he referred to as the 'broad approach' of the European Court of Justice in *Bier* and to base his decision on the very words of Art. 5(3) 'harmful event'.

Accordingly, he proceeded to determine the place in which the *substance* of the *Hedley Byrne* negligent misrepresentation action had occurred (irrespective of the manner in which it had been pleaded).

On the facts, Steyn J. concluded that the substance of the wrongdoing had occurred in England where the negligent advice was received and relied upon, not in Korea (or France) where the historical carelessness took place and from which the certificate was sent, which was too insubstantial.

English courts consequently possessed jurisdiction under Art. 5(3).

Comment

The decision is open to criticism, not for the result, but on the ground that the 'broad approach' of the European Court of Justice in *Bier* was to allow jurisdiction to be conferred upon more than one State's courts where more than one connection were to compete as harmful event—as in multi-state/double-locality causative event (see Kaye 'Private International Law of Tort' (1991) p. 19 *et seq*; and 'Place of Commission of International Torts', Chap. 8 in McLean ed., *Compensation for Damage: An International Perspective* (1993)).

In addition, Steyn J. did not make it entirely clear whether in such cases courts should refer to place of substance of the *tort as a whole* or merely of the double-locality *causal event itself.*

Case

Metall und Rohstoff AG v Donaldson Lufkin & Jenrette Inc. [1989] 3 WLR   **173**
563 Court of Appeal, 27 January 1989

Facts

The plaintiff Swiss company, trading on the London Metal Exchange, suffered losses through the fraud of one of its aluminium traders and wished to sue the defendant New York company for damages in the English courts in 1983 for torts including conspiracy, inducing breach of contract and abuse of process. Since the defendant was not domiciled in any Contracting State, Convention jurisdiction grounds were inapplicable and national English rules governed instead. The relevant ground of discretionary English torts jurisdiction was RSC Ord. 11, r.1(1)(f) (claim founded on a tort and damage sustained or resulted from an act committed within the jurisdiction). The problem was to determine where the *causative act* in the case of inducement of breach of contract had occurred?

It seemed that the relevant activities were split between London and New York: there were some acts of inducement and breaches of contract in New York; but other acts of inducement and the main breaches of contract took place in London.

Judgment

The Court of Appeal, delivering judgment through Slade L.J., first coined the expression 'double-locality' for such cases in which the causative event is divided between more than one country (or, presumably, damage is so in the alternative).

The court concluded that in these circumstances, the tort should be held to have been committed in the place in which the *substance* of the cause of action in tort occurred.

On the facts, it was considered that the substantial tortious wrongdoing had occurred in London, not New York.

Comments

The case was actually decided in relation to national English jurisdiction outside the Convention and not specifically on Art. 5(3). Yet, the principle enunciated consistently with *Minster*, Case 172 *supra*, is obviously usable in the latter context as well.

For the sake of completeness, it should be understood that the Court of Appeal's decision was only *indirectly* for the purposes of jurisdiction rather than choice of law. This was because it is a requirement for resort to RSC Ord. 11, r.1(1), that the plaintiff has a good cause of action on the merits of his claim, here in tort, under RSC Ord. 11, r.4(1)(b) (see *supra*). Accordingly, in laying down the double-locality approach, the court was in fact dealing directly with choice of law: it was looking into whether the plaintiff was likely to win on the merits and for this purpose it was necessary to determine applicable law of tort. Under previous English private international law of tort pre-1 May 1996, this would partly depend upon finding *locus delicti—place of commission* of the alleged tort—and it was for these latter purposes that the court would need to locate where causal event and damage had occurred and whether these were in the same state. Again, nevertheless, principles developed would be essentially transportable to the purely jurisdictional sphere, including Art. 5(3). (For criticism of *Metall und Rohstoff*, see Chap. 8 in McLean ed. *supra*).

In *Banque Paribas (Suisse) S.A. v Stolidi Shipping Company* (unreported) 24 August 1995, the Court of Appeal (Evans and Hutchinson L.JJ.) reserved its view upon whether the *Minster* 'substance' test was correct, in a case where a fax containing an alleged misrepresentation of risks was sent from Hamburg to the Swiss plaintiffs' London solicitors by the defendant German insurance brokers, because even if it was not the proper approach, the court considered that place of causative act for *Bier* was that of receipt of the fax in London by the plaintiffs' solicitors, rather than the place of its despatch, Hamburg. Had the substance test applied, the court made it clear that this would have been established at the plaintiffs' solicitors' place of business in London, where most of the communications were sent and the transaction took place, rather than in Geneva where the plaintiffs were based and to which the fax was forwarded. Although the solicitors were merely the agents of the plaintiffs, they were active agents and not just a postbox address.

In *Source Ltd v TUV Rheinland Holding AG* [1997] 3 WLR 365 Court of Appeal, 18 March 1997 (see *infra*, E. *Recent Cases*, Art. 5(1) and (3) Cases 388 and 389), the Court of Appeal (Staughton, Waite and Aldous L.JJ.) held— on similar facts to those in *Minster*, yet where the plaintiff claimed Art. 5(1) breach of contract and Art. 5(3) negligent certification in the alternative—that the principal (*Shenavai* Case 266/85) contractual obligation of the German defendant for Art. 5(1) was quality inspection, taking place in China and Taiwan, not the report on the inspection, to be performed in England, so that English Art. 5(1) jurisdiction was lacking. Of present relevance, Staughton L.J. went on to comment that he was not prepared to give a view upon whether the *Minster* approach to Art. 5(3) harmful event in tort was correct. However, he did state: (i) that even if it was adopted, it did not then also follow that the court should instead find Art. 5(1) principal contractual obligation in question to be the report rather than the inspection in order to achieve consistency with the Art. 5(3) result; and (ii) if the latter *were* said to be the required outcome, he would then simply refuse to follow the High Court in *Minster*.

Finally, the European Court's approach to Art. 5(3) damage jurisdiction in the case of international newspaper libel, in *Shevill* Case–68/93 (damage in each place of distribution) may be said to lend additional support to the arguments against the substance test for double-locality.

Case principle

2. In a claim for the tort of passing off, where the causal event, as optional harmful event in accordance with *Bier* under (Sched. 4) Art. 5(3), is split between more than one country (here England and Scotland)—double-locality—causal event is taken to have occurred in that jurisdiction in which the *substance* of the wrongdoing took place (*Minster Investments*, Case 172, followed).

Case

Modus Vivendi Ltd v The British Products Sanmex Co. Ltd [1997] I.L.Pr. 654   **174**
High Court, 24 June 1996

Facts

See infra, Art. 5(3) 'damage', Case 180.

The Scottish defendants' cigarette lighter refill cans were manufactured by a company in England and designed by a party from Hong Kong before being sent to the defendants' premises in Scotland for filling with gas lighter fuel. They were then transported to an English port for shipment to Hong Kong and China, in respect of which markets the plaintiff brought its passing off action and where *damage* was held to have occurred for Art. 5(3) (see *infra*).

The English plaintiff attempted to base English courts' jurisdiction over the Scottish defendants under Sched. 4, Art. 5(3) (applicable to the internal UK jurisdiction), *inter alia*, on the ground that the causal event had occurred in England.

Judgment

Knox J. held that the causal event had occurred in Scotland, where the defendants had carried out the can-filling process, not in England where the cans had been manufactured and printed to their order and from which they had subsequently been exported to Hong Kong and China.

Knox J. expressly followed Steyn J.'s approach in *Minster Investments*: where causal events are split between different countries, it would be wrong to dissect the causative element and to permit plaintiffs to opt to bring their actions in any of the states in which an act had taken place. Instead, causal event jurisdiction should be restricted to that territory in which the substance of the wrongdoing had occurred—and here, on the facts, Knox J. considered the substantial wrongdoing to have taken place in Scotland and not in England where the defendants' acts were regarded as subsidiary to those in Scotland.

Comment

See too *infra, Mecklermedia Corporation v D.C. Congress GmbH* [1997] I.L.Pr. 629 High Court, 7 March 1997, *E. Recent Cases.*

Case principle

3. In a claim for contribution to damages brought by one joint tortfeasor against another, on the assumption (thought not to be correct: see *supra*, Case 167) that the contribution action amounted to tort for purposes of Art. 5(3), the 'harmful event' within Art. 5(3) was the original accident to the injured person, not the judgment obtained by him against the contribution-claimant nor agreement to damages by the latter.

Case

175   Santa Fe (UK) Limited v Gates Europe NV (unreported) Court of Appeal, 16 January 1991

Facts

The plaintiff English company was successfully sued for damages in England by an employee who was injured by a defective hose on an oil rig in the Scottish part of the North Sea. Two years later the plaintiff sought to bring an action in the English courts claiming a contribution towards damages from the defendant Belgian company which had supplied the hose. The plaintiff argued that the 'harmful event' in a contribution claim was the judgment obtained against it by the injured employee—which had occurred in England for purposes of Art. 5(3). But the defendant challenged English jurisdiction on the ground that 'harmful event' in such a case was the original accident leading to liability of plaintiff and defendant—and that had occurred in Scottish territory, not in England.

Judgment

The Court of Appeal unanimously held that, on the plain wording of Art. 5(3), 'harmful event' must be held to mean the original set of circumstances which led to liability in tort, and not the judgment reached against the plaintiff, nor admission of liability by the plaintiff, nor agreement to pay compensation to the injured party by the plaintiff.

As a consequence, the harmful event in tort in the contribution proceedings occurred in Scottish territory, not English. English courts lacked jurisdiction over the Belgian defendant under Art. 5(3).

Case principle

4. In claims for breach of confidence not based upon a contractual duty of confidentiality, if Art. 5(3) is held to apply (see *supra*, Case 169), place of damage is where the commercial interests of the plaintiff are actually affected or threatened, not merely where its interests in the confidential information are entitled to protection.

Case

Kitechonology BV v Unicor GmbH Rahn Plastmaschinen [1994] I.L.Pr. 560   **176**
Court of Appeal, 28 April 1994

Facts

See supra, Case 169.

The plaintiffs claimed that breach of confidence proceedings against those
defendants not party to the confidentiality agreements satisfied Art. 5(3) jurisdiction of English courts as those of place of damage.

Judgment

The Court of Appeal disagreed.
   The German defendants had allegedly made the improper use and disclosure
of the secret information in Germany. There was no evidence, for example,
that the resulting products had been imported into England so as to reduce the
value of the plaintiffs' rights of licensing its process nor that its commercial
interests had otherwise been adversely affected in England. It was not sufficient that the plaintiffs merely had interests to protect in England or elsewhere,
since jurisdiction on this basis could amount in effect to that of plaintiffs'
domicile, in major derogation from Art. 2.

Case principle

5.   Consequential financial loss from a tort is not 'damage' as harmful event
     under Art. 5(3).

Case

Twin Books (UK) Limited v Cronion S.A. (unreported) High Court, 9 July   **177**
1993

Facts

The plaintiff English publishing company concluded a contract with the defendant Spanish publishing company in 1991 for the printing of books from tapes
supplied by the plaintiff, which were thereafter to be returned to the plaintiff.
The defendant complained that the plaintiff was a slow payer and therefore
refused to return the tapes until all payments had been made.
   The plaintiff denied that the defendant was owed any sums of money and
brought proceedings in the English courts for damages for the tort of wrongful detention of the tapes, relying upon Art. 5(3) for English jurisdiction (and,
in the alternative, for breach of contract founded upon Art. 5(1), see *supra*,
Cases 142 and 166).
   The defendant contested English jurisdiction, on the ground that the harmful event in tort had occurred in Spain, not England.

Judgment

Deputy High Court Judge J. Griffith Williams Q.C. upheld the defendant's jurisdiction challenge and declined to hear the case.

  (1) Causative event of failure to return the tapes had taken place in Spain, not England, because the defendant's contractual obligation was to redeliver the tapes to the plaintiff in Spain (see *supra*, Art. 5(1)).

  (2) The financial damage alleged by the plaintiff to have been suffered in England as a result of the wrongful detention of the tapes, through having incurred the expense of recreating the tapes, did not 'flow from' the causative act and was merely consequential. Accordingly, its location did not amount to place of occurrence of damage for purposes of Art. 5(3), as interpreted in *Bier*, and the plaintiff could not sue in England.

Comment

This decision seems consistent in principle with the general line of authority of the European Court of Justice in *Dumez* Case C–220/88 and *Marinari* Case C–364/93 against acceptance of consequential financial loss as being jurisdiction-conferring within Art. 5(3).

Case principles

  6. Harmful event in international newspaper libel is in every Contracting State in which the publication is distributed and in which the victim claims consequent injury to reputation, in respect of the harm there (applying ECJ's ruling on the reference in *Shevill* Case C–68/93).

  7. Article 5(3) applies, notwithstanding that according to applicable national law, actual damage to reputation is presumed rather than having to be pleaded and proved by the plaintiff.

Case

178 Shevill v Presse Alliance S.A. [1996] 3 All ER 929 House of Lords, 24 July 1996

Facts

In 1989, the first plaintiff, Miss Fiona Shevill, was an English student working for three months at a bureau de change in Paris run by the other plaintiff, Chequepoint SARL. In September 1989, an article appeared in the French defendant's newspaper, France Soir, claiming that the bureau de change had been involved in laundering drug-money and implicating the plaintiffs, who were named. The plaintiffs sought to sue the defendant for defamation in the

English courts in 1989, relying on Art. 5(3) for jurisdiction. The defendant contested English Art. 5(3) jurisdiction: France Soir had a wide circulation in France, but only 230 copies were sold in England and Wales, five in Yorkshire where Miss Shevill lived. There was no harmful event in England according to the defendant. The English High Court and Court of Appeal agreed.

However, the House of Lords referred the question of interpretation of Art. 5(3) to the European Court of Justice, which delivered its ruling in March 1995 in *Shevill* Case C–68/93, to the effect that international newspaper libel was a harmful event for Art. 5(3) in each Contracting State in which the *publication was distributed* and in which *the victim claimed to have suffered harm to reputation therefrom*—though limited to the damage in the particular Contracting State alone.

Yet, the Court of Justice did something else as well: it left the criteria as to whether 'harm' to the plaintiff existed, and as to the evidence required for this to be proven, if any, to applicable national substantive law under the private international law of the national court seised (provided that Convention effectiveness was not impaired).

Accordingly, when the case came back to the House of Lords from the European Court, the defendant argued that:

- required harm was a matter for national law; and
- there should be a special rule of evidence that for Art. 5(3) jurisdiction purposes, the law required proof of actual harm from libel even though the normal English rule was that this would be presumed and need not be pleaded and proved.

Consequently, in the absence of any such actual proof, Art. 5(3) was inapplicable. The plaintiff, Shevill, had been named in the defamatory publication, but she had not produced evidence of having been identified to a particular person; and the plaintiff, Chequepoint, itself had no actual reputation to lose in the United Kingdom.

However, the plaintiffs responded that this was precisely what the European Court had indicated was not required, since the Convention's purpose was not to alter national substantive laws.

Judgment

The House of Lords: (i) applied the European Court's ruling that Art. 5(3) conferred jurisdiction over harm to the plaintiff in England through publication there; and (ii) as to determination of existence of such harm and evidence required therefor, the Lords unanimously agreed with the plaintiffs, in accordance with the European Court's ruling, that it was for national substantive laws to decide upon such existence and evidence of harm, so that Art. 5(3) was not excluded simply because harm to reputation was presumed under applicable English substantive law of libel.

Case principle

8. In the tort of wrongful interference with goods, damage occurs where the goods are harmed or lost, not where the consequential financial loss is felt by the owners (*Marinari* Case C–354/93 applied).

Case

179 Bastone & Firminger Limited v Nasima Enterprises (Nigeria) Limited (unreported) High Court, 20 May 1996

Facts

The English plaintiffs delivered goods to a third party in Nigeria in respect of payment for which the Nigerian defendants became liable when the goods were lost in Nigeria without payment having been made.

The plaintiffs wished to serve an English writ for the tort of wrongful interference with goods upon the defendants in Nigeria under RSC Ord. 11, r.1(1)(f) on the ground that the damage had occurred (*been sustained*, under r.1(1)(f)) in England where the plaintiffs had their headquarters.

Judgment

Rix J. applied the Art. 5(3) Convention *Marinari* principle: damage occurred in Nigeria, where the initial harm to the goods took place, not in England where indirect financial consequences of the harm were felt by the plaintiffs. The latter would in effect be to afford jurisdiction to courts of the plaintiffs' domicile.

Case principle

9. In a claim for the tort of passing off, the *Bier* damage occurs where the plaintiff's sales or goodwill is adversely affected, not where financial consequences of the harm are suffered (*Shevill* Case C–68/93 applied).

Case

180 Modus Vivendi Ltd v The British Products Sanmex Co. Ltd [1997] I.L.Pr. 654, High Court, 24 June 1996

Facts

See supra, Case 174.

The plaintiff English cigarette gas light refill company, Modus Vivendi, wished to sue the Scottish defendants, Sanmex and their managing director, in English courts under the 1982 Act, Sched. 4, Art. 5(3), on the ground that the harmful event in tort had occurred in England. The claim was that the defendants had passed off their own gas lighter product as the plaintiff's in the latter's Hong Kong and China markets leading to the loss of sales there.

The defendants employed an English company to manufacture the cans, the design of which was the work of a customer in Hong Kong, and the cans were then sent to the defendants' premises in Scotland to be filled with the gas lighter fuel, following which the product was said to have been sent to Hong Kong and China from a port in England.

The plaintiff claimed that damage from the passing off in Hong Kong and China had been suffered in England through their lost profits. The defendants contended that damage had occurred in Hong Kong and China where the sales were lost or misrepresented as those of the plaintiff's product.

Judgment

Knox J., in the Chancery Division, held that the damage had occurred in Hong Kong and China, as the places in which the sales or goodwill were adversely affected.

Knox J. referred to European Court case law, in particular to *Shevill*, in which the two Advocates General had made explicit what was implicit in the Court's judgment, namely, that place of *occurrence* of damage was to be taken as harmful event, not place in which damage was merely *suffered*; and *Dumez* Case 220/88 and *Marinari* Case C–354/93 had already established too that place of ricochet damage to a victim or of financial loss to a plaintiff were not satisfactory to classify as Art. 5(3) damage.

Accordingly, since the deception had taken place in and had its alleged effects on sales or goodwill in Hong Kong and China, not in England, damage had not occurred in England for purposes of Sched. 4, Art. 5(3).

Comment

In *Mecklermedia Corporation v D.C. Congress GmbH* [1997] I.L.Pr. 629, in the High Court, 7 March 1997, Jacob J. followed and approved of *Modus Vivendi* as to place of damage (see *infra*, E. Recent Cases).

ARTICLE 6

" . . . *may also be sued* . . . "

Case principle

1. Article 6 jurisdiction is not available where the purpose of joinder of the defendant is an abuse of the process of the court.

Cases

The Rewia [1991] 2 Lloyd's Rep. 325 Court of Appeal, 20 June 1991   **181**

See infra, Art. 6(1).

182 Mölnlycke A. B. v Procter & Gamble Ltd [1992] 1 WLR 112 Court of Appeal
27 June 1991

Facts

See *supra*, Case 165.

Swedish and English plaintiffs alleged breach of a UK patent for babies' nappies on the part of first, second and third defendants (English, American and
German companies in a multinational group), which the defendants denied.

The defendants appealed against a decision by the first instance English
judge to allow them to be served with a writ outside England and Wales under
domestic English procedure permitting this without leave where international
jurisdiction of English courts could be founded upon the Convention's
grounds. The question for the Court of Appeal was whether Convention
grounds—in particular, Arts 5(3) and 6(1)—were satisfied?

Judgment

In relation to Art. 6(1), the Court of Appeal held that Art. 6(1) could not be
used where, as here, the purpose of joinder of the third defendant was to
obtain discovery of certain documents from them which had been unable to be
sought from the others, rather than principally to pursue the substantive claim
against the third defendant, since this would otherwise have been to allow an
abuse of the process of the English court.

Comment

It is considered that the Court of Appeal was incorrect to attach this condition
to the operation of Art. 6 (or to any other Convention ground) which nowhere
appears in the Convention nor in European Court jurisprudence thereon.

Instead, it is submitted, it may only be justified on narrow grounds as a rule
of domestic English procedure for joinder, or otherwise for proceeding against
a defendant (see RSC Ord. 18, r.19 as to striking out of pleadings). In the
European Court case of *Kongress Agentur Hagen GmbH v Zeehaghe BV* Case
365/88 [1990] ECR 1845, Art. 6(2) was held not to exclude national procedural rules on third party joinder, provided that these would not impair the
effectiveness of Convention provision for international jurisdiction.

Case principle

2.   Articles 5 and 6 special jurisdiction grounds are mandatory, not merely
permissive. Consequently, they are not subject to discretionary stays in
favour of other Contracting State jurisdiction as *forum conveniens*.

Case

Aiglon Ltd and L'Aiglon S.A. v Gau Shan Co. Ltd [1993] 1 Lloyd's Rep. 164   **183**
High Court, 23 June 1992

Facts

See supra, s.49, Case 109.

Claims were brought against a Swiss company under Lugano Art. 6(1) as a co-defendant with an English company in 1992. The Swiss defendant requested the English courts to stay their proceedings in favour of Switzerland as *forum conveniens.*

Judgment

Hirst J. refused. Convention special jurisdiction in Arts 5 and 6 was mandatory, not merely permissive, in the same way as Art. 2. Therefore, it was not subject to discretionary *forum non conveniens* which would be inconsistent with the Convention for purposes of 1982 Act, s.49 and consequently was excluded.

ARTICLE 6(1)

" . . . *where he is one of a number of defendants* . . . "

Case principle

1. If a person is to be joined as a co-defendant under Art. 6(1), there must be a real issue which the English court could reasonably be asked to try between the plaintiff and main defendant as a necessary or proper party to the proceedings.

Case

The Rewia [1991] 2 Lloyd's Rep. 325 Court of Appeal, 20 June 1991   **184**

Facts

The plaintiffs claimed for loss or damage to a cargo of nutmegs and mace, shipped on the ship *Rewia*, against the first defendant, the sub-charterer, domiciled in England, and the third defendant, the shipowner, domiciled in Germany. The only possible Convention jurisdiction ground available to English courts against the third defendant was that in Art. 6(1).

Judgment

The Court of Appeal held Art. 6(1) to be inapplicable on the facts of the case and, consequently, that English courts lacked jurisdiction over the third defendant.

The reason was that the court considered that for Art. 6(1) to apply, there had to exist a real issue between the plaintiffs and the first defendant. The court concluded that no such issue arose because, on a construction of events, it was the third defendant, the shipowner—not the first defendant, the sub-charterer—who had assumed liability towards the plaintiff under the bill of lading.

Since Art. 6(1) was inapplicable, the court declined jurisdiction.

Comment

It is considered that the Court of Appeal's decision was correct (see Kaye, *Civil Jurisdiction*, pp. 642–3) and generally consistent with the European Court's requirements for propriety of joinder in *Kalfelis* Case 189/87.

However, it could be argued that the validity of the judgment is nevertheless open to question, because the Court of Appeal appeared to justify its application of the condition of existence of real issue between plaintiff and main defendant under Art. 6(1) by reference to national English private international principles by way of analogy. This is not acceptable because Art. 3 of course excludes national rules.

On the other hand, however, the judgment could still be justified as the operation of domestic English procedural provision, permitted by the European Court, in *Kongress Agentur Hagen GmbH v Zeehaghe BV* Case 365/88 [1990] ECR 1845, to continue to apply in so far as this does not impair the effectiveness of Convention international jurisdiction provision. Clearly, this condition is satisfied by the limitation imposed in *The Rewia* and the latter should therefore continue to apply.

Note further that in *Canada Trust Co. Ltd v Stolzenberg (No. 2)* [1998] 1 All ER 318, the majority in the CA held that the main defendant need not have been served with the writ prior to issue or service of the proceedings upon the foreign defendants (in the minority, Pill, LJ did not regard Art. 6(1) as applicable in any event). See too *Petrotrade v Smith* [1998] 2 All ER 346.

Case

185 Holding Oil Finance Inc. v Marc Rich & Co. A.G. (unreported) Court of Appeal, 27 February 1996

Facts

The plaintiff Panamanian company alleged that it had concluded an agreement with the English and Swiss defendants to represent them in negotiations with the Iranian oil authorities in return for payment of commission. The commission was not paid and the plaintiff sought to bring proceedings against the defendants in the English courts in 1993, claiming payment of commission and tortious damages for conspiracy and inducement of breach of contract. The

Swiss defendants were said to be subject to English jurisdiction by virtue of Lugano Art. 6(1).

Both English and Swiss defendants asked for the action to be struck out or the writ's service to be set aside—the English, under RSC Ord. 18, r.19, on the ground that the action against them was an abuse of the English court's process, having only been commenced against them in order to bring in the Swiss defendants under Art. 6(1); and the Swiss, under RSC Ord. 12, r.8, referring to *Kalfelis* in the European Court, on the ground that Art. 6(1) did not apply if the action against the Art. 2 defendant was improperly brought.

Judgment

The Court of Appeal struck out the action against the English defendants under RSC Ord. 18, r.19, as an abuse of the court's process: there was no plausible case that the English defendants had concluded the alleged commission agreement (referring to the Irish case of *Gannon v British and Irish Steampacket Company* [1993] 2 I.R. 359) and the claims in tort against the English defendants for conspiracy and interference with contract were simply included for the purpose of bringing in the Swiss defendants.

Since the action against the English defendants had been struck out, there was no possibility to found jurisdiction over the Swiss defendants upon Lugano Art. 6(1) and the service of the writ upon them was set aside under RSC Ord. 12, r.8 as requested.

The Court of Appeal stated *obiter*, citing *Kalfelis*, that even if the action had not been applied to be struck out against the English defendants, Art. 6(1) nonetheless would still have been unavailable, since the sole object of the action against the English defendants had been to bring into English jurisdiction the Swiss defendants under Art. 6(1), which was not an acceptable use of the latter ground.

The court also went on to dismiss jurisdiction over the Swiss defendants under Art. 5(3) and (5): alleged conspiracy or contractual interference would have taken place in Switzerland, not England, and the English defendants were not a branch or agency of the Swiss.

Comment

As a point of general interest on the issue of striking out of proceedings subject to Convention jurisdiction under English procedure, an action for a negative declaration of non-liability is not vexatious nor an abuse of the English courts' process, provided that the intention is not to pre-empt competing jurisdiction (see *Charman v WOC Offshore B.V.* [1993] 2 Lloyd's Rep. 551, CA, *infra*, Art. 12, Case 197).

Case principle

2. A co-defendant joined to main proceedings under Art. 6(1) must also have a real interest in the action for the joinder to be proper.

Case

186 Chiron Corporation v Evans Medical Ltd and Others (unreported) High Court, 3 July 1996

Facts

The first defendant, an English company, subsidiary of another, obtained a patent for a vaccine, for which the third defendant, a Belgian company, became the exclusive worldwide licensee. The plaintiff Californian company wished to market a similar product in Europe and brought proceedings in the English courts for a declaration that it did not infringe the defendants' patent rights. The third defendant contested English jurisdiction under Art. 6(1).

Judgment

Robert Walker J. upheld English courts' jurisdiction over the third defendant under Art. 6(1).

    (1)   There was a requirement that, for such jurisdiction to be exercised, the claim against the third defendant should be genuine and that it should have a real interest in the proceedings.

    (2)   However, on the facts this was satisfied. As an exclusive world licensee of the patent rights, the third defendant had taken a combative attitude towards the plaintiff's claim and was a natural defendant with a real interest in the declaratory relief sought.

Case principles

3.   Common issues of fact in the claims against main defendant and co-defendant, and not solely common issues of law, may create a risk of irreconcilable judgments, for purposes of the required connection between claims.

4.   Special jurisdiction grounds in Arts 5 and 6 should not be interpreted more restrictively than is necessary or justified.

Case

187 Gascoine v Pyrah [1994] I.L.Pr. 82 Court of Appeal, 25 May 1993

Facts

The plaintiffs engaged the first defendant, domiciled in England, to find a suitable showjumping horse for purchase for their daughter and to procure a vet's report, which the first defendant did on finding a horse for potential acquisition. The vet's report was provided by the second defendant, domiciled in Germany, and disclosed a defect in the horse's right front foot. However, the first defendant alleged that when they spoke about this on the telephone, the second defendant had informed him that the defect was not serious, and, as a consequence the first defendant advised the plaintiffs that they could safely pay the asking price for the horse of £75000 which they did. Two months later the horse fell lame as a result of the defect in its foot and was worth only £3000. The plaintiffs sued the first defendant in the English courts in 1990 for damages for negligent advice. When the first defendant made his allegations about advice received from the second defendant, the plaintiffs sought to join the second defendant under Art. 6(1) a few months later. At first instance, deputy High Court Judge Richard Southwell Q.C. held that the European Court's requirement in *Kalfelis* of *connexité* between the claims against the two defendants, based upon the existence of a risk of irreconcilable judgments, was not satisfied and that special jurisdiction grounds should be applied very restrictively and subject to a heavy burden of proof upon the plaintiffs.

Judgment

The Court of Appeal unanimously held that the *Kalfelis* test was satisfied and that Art. 6(1) conferred jurisdiction over the second defendant.

(1)   The Court of Appeal agreed with the deputy High Court judge that risk of irreconcilability could arise from common issues of fact in the claims, not just of law. Here, there was such a factual question which was capable of being decided differently by courts of Contracting States so as to lead to inconsistent judgments: namely, *had* the second defendant orally assured the first defendant, in the course of their alleged telephone discussion, that the defect in the horse's foot bone was not serious? This would clearly affect liability in both cases.

(2)   Two of the Court of Appeal judges, Hirst and Roch L.JJ., considered that although they were exceptions to Art. 2, Arts 5 and 6 nonetheless should not be interpreted excessively restrictively so as to risk defeating their specific purpose of providing a particularly close jurisdictional connection between court and dispute (citing, in support, Purchas L.J. in *Mercury Publicity Ltd v Wolfgang Loerke* concerning Art. 5(1), see *supra* Case 143, and *Six Constructions Ltd*, Case 32/88 in the European Court of Justice). The third appeal judge, Glidewell L.J., preferred to reserve his position on the issue.

Case

Société Commerciale de Réassurance v Eras International Ltd (No. 2) [1995]   **188**
2 All ER 278 High Court, 17 December 1993

Facts

See infra, Case Principle 6.

The Illinois plaintiffs further contested application of Art. 6(1) English jurisdiction over them, on the ground that the English claim against the third party applicants was not sufficiently related to the claims made against them as defendants or third parties in the proceedings in Illinois.

Judgment

Potter J. disagreed with the applicants that *Kalfelis* irreconcilability, borrowed from Art. 22, para. 3, should be narrowly construed for Art. 6(1). Instead, it should cover common issues of fact or law or remedies on which irreconcilable findings might be reached.

Comment

In fact, this corresponds in any event with the European Court's subsequent treatment of related actions for Art. 22, para. 3 itself in *The Maciej Rataj* Case C–406/92, one year later on 6 December 1994, as essentially involving the same factual and legal issues, creating a risk of conflicting decisions, even if the legal consequences are not mutually exclusive.

Case principle

5. Conditions of operation of Art. 6(1), of existence of a real issue against the main defendant in England (see *supra, The Rewia*, Case 184) and of sufficient connection between claims (*Kalfelis* Case 189/87), must be satisfied at the later date of challenge to Art. 6(1) English jurisdiction, not merely at the earlier time of institution of proceedings.

Case

189   The Xing Su Hai [1995] 2 Lloyd's Rep. 15 High Court, 22 February 1995

Facts

See supra, 1982 Act, s.25(2), Case 96.

The plaintiffs tried to establish English courts' jurisdiction over the German co-defendants (and their controller), agents of the main defendant (Liechtenstein) charterers, by bringing in as fourth defendants a firm of brokers with a London place of business, and asserting Art. 6(1) jurisdiction over the former, on the basis of main jurisdiction against the latter. However, by the time of the German co-defendants' challenge to Art. 6(1) jurisdiction, it had become clear that there was no real case against the London brokers because it had mistakenly been thought that they were the charterers' brokers, which they were not.

Judgment

Rix J. held that it was not sufficient that the conditions of real issue and *connexité* appeared to be satisfied as at the date of commencement of the proceedings, if this was not also still the position at the subsequent date of assessment of Art. 6(1) jurisdiction.

Comment

See too, however, *Canada Trust Co. Ltd (No. 2) v Stolzenberg* [1998] 1 All ER 318, C.A., whereby date for satisfaction of defendant's domicile for Articles 2 and 6 is that of *issue* of the writ, not service thereof (Pill, LJ dissenting).

Case principle

6.   Article 6(1) is available to an applicant for anti-suit injunctions restraining 'plaintiffs' from conducting proceedings against him in a foreign country.

Case

Société Commerciale de Réassurance v Eras International Ltd (No. 2) [1995]   **190**
2 All ER 278 High Court, 17 December 1993

Facts

The applicants for an anti-suit injunction in the English courts were French reinsurers, SCOR, who were members of a pool providing insurance for United States companies against pollution liability. Plaintiff members of the pool brought proceedings in England against the managers of the pool for, *inter alia*, breach of contract and negligence in the course of management and the applicants were brought in by the defendants as third parties for an indemnity. The plaintiffs also instituted an action in the courts of Illinois in the United States in which the applicants were again defendants or third parties.

   Thereafter, the applicants sought an injunction in the English courts against the Illinois plaintiffs in order to prevent the further pursuit of the Illinois action, which they claimed was vexatious and oppressive towards them. The applicants relied upon Art. 6(1) for jurisdiction over the German and Swiss plaintiffs, since several of the other plaintiffs were domiciled in England.

   The Illinois plaintiffs opposed the application, on the ground that Art. 6(1) could not be used for 'procedural' claims for anti-suit injunctions and was limited to proceedings over substantive disputes.

Judgment

Potter J. held Art. 6(1) to apply.

   There was nothing in Art. 6(1) to suggest that it was limited as to the type of claim which was brought, and, in particular, to substantive as opposed to procedural claims, notwithstanding that the method of granting anti-suit injunctions may have been unknown under the legal systems of original Contracting States to the Convention.

   In addition, Art. 6(1) was considered to be available to third parties who were brought into English and/or foreign proceedings, in the applicants' position, not merely to those who were plaintiffs/defendants in England or defendants abroad.

ARTICLE 6(2)

" . . . *any other third party proceedings* . . . "

Case principles

1. Domestic procedural provisions for joinder of third parties do not qualify as 'any other third party proceedings' within Art. 6(2), unless they require a sufficient connection between the subject matter of or remedies for the plaintiff's claim against the defendant and the defendant's claim against the third party.
2. Exercise of discretion against allowing third party proceedings under domestic procedural law on the ground of English *forum non conveniens* would *not* be inconsistent with what would otherwise be Convention Art. 6(2) jurisdiction.

Case

191   Kinnear v Falconfilms NV [1994] I.L.Pr. 731 High Court, 27 January 1994

Facts

The British actor Roy Kinnear was severely injured in a fall from a horse while filming in Spain. He was taken to hospital in Madrid and died a day later. The plaintiff administrators of Kinnear's estate brought a claim for breach of contract and negligence in England against the defendant film company, producer and director. The defendants sought to issue third party proceedings in England against the Spanish hospital and the doctor who treated Kinnear, alleging medical negligence and claiming an indemnity for any liability of the defendants towards the plaintiffs. The third parties denied jurisdiction under Art. 6(2), on the ground that, in accordance with *Kalfelis*, Art. 6(2), in derogation of Art. 2, should receive a restrictive interpretation, and, consequently, the third party claim would not be *any other third party proceedings* within Art. 6(2) on the facts, because these related to the medical treatment, not to the horse riding accident.

Judgment

Phillips J. held that, in accordance with the European Court's *Kongress Hagen* Case C–365/88, the provision for third party joinder under national English domestic procedural law had to ensure that a sufficient nexus existed between plaintiff-defendant and defendant-third party claims for purposes of Art. 6(2); otherwise, the national provisions would prejudice the correct and proper operation of Convention jurisdiction.

On the facts, Phillips J. considered that the domestic English procedure *did* satisfy this test, in requiring for third party joinder that the third party claim was for substantially the same relief or remedy or for determination of any issue related to or connected with the subject matter of the main claim; and here, this would be so because both claims involved determination of causation of death by negligence.

The judge went on to hold that in the matter of exercise of domestic discretion to allow third party joinder or not under national English procedural law, whereas, in accordance with *Kongress Hagen*, the English court would not be permitted to exercise its discretion against such a third party claim on the ground of the third party's foreign Contracting State domicile, nevertheless, it would not be inconsistent with the Convention to do so on grounds that England was *forum non conveniens* for the defendant's claim against the third party (actually held not to be so on the facts).

Comment

This latter finding of Phillips J. must be open to question, since discretionary *forum non conveniens* is clearly excluded from the Convention's jurisdiction regime and accordingly ought not to be permitted to affect the functioning of Art. 6(2) in this manner if *Kongress Hagen* is to be adhered to (it is a different matter if *non*-Contracting State *forum conveniens* is in issue— this is not a question of mode of functioning of the Convention ground, but of its operation at all in the circumstances). See further, *infra* p. 404.

> " . . . *in the court seised of the original proceedings* . . . "

Case principle

Article 6(2) confers jurisdiction over third party contribution proceedings which are brought in the course of the main tort action against the contribution-claimant by the injured person, but not over subsequent contribution proceedings.

Case

Santa Fe (UK) Limited v Gates Europe NV (unreported) Court of Appeal, 16 **192**
January 1991

Facts

The plaintiff English company was sued for damages in negligence in the English courts by an employee who was injured by a defective hose on an oil rig in Scottish waters off the North Sea. Two years later, the plaintiff sought to bring English contribution proceedings against the defendant Belgian company which had supplied the hose. The defendant denied English jurisdiction under Arts 5(3) and 6(2).

Judgment

The Court of Appeal held against Art. 5(3) jurisdiction of the English courts (see *supra*, Art. 5(3), Case 175).

The case for English Art. 6(2) jurisdiction was not fully argued because the plaintiff had decided not to do so unless the proceedings were to have been referred to the European Court of Justice for interpretation of Art. 5(3), which had not taken place.

Nevertheless, the Court of Appeal still expressed the view that Art. 6(2) jurisdiction was unavailable in contribution proceedings brought *subsequently* to the main action in tort against the claimant.

ARTICLE 6a

" . . . *court . . . has jurisdiction in actions relating to liability* . . . "

Case principle

Limitation jurisdiction may be founded on Art. 6a even *before* the main liability action is commenced against the limitation claimants.

Case

193 The Falstria [1988] 1 Lloyd's Rep. 495 High Court, 5 November 1987

Facts

The Danish ship *Falstria*, chartered to the plaintiffs, collided with a quay and crane in an English dock in 1986, causing £1.5 million loss to the dock company.

The plaintiffs instituted liability limitation proceedings in the English courts in February 1987 when the higher limits in the 1979 merchant shipping legislation had not yet entered into force in contrast to the position in Denmark. A few days later the dock company commenced liability proceedings against the plaintiffs in the Danish courts and thereafter challenged the existence of English Art. 6a jurisdiction in respect of the liability limitation action, on the ground that the Art. 6a court must actually have been seised of the main liability proceedings at the time of institution of the limitation proceedings for Art. 6a to operate. If the dock company chose not to bring liability proceedings in England under Art. 5(3), but to do so in Denmark at the subsequent date under Art. 2 or 57, the plaintiffs should not have been permitted to pre-empt this decision through prior English Art. 6a proceedings.

Judgment

Sheen J. rejected the dock company's complaint. Limitation jurisdiction existed under Art. 6a, even *before* the date of commencement of a main liability action.

Comment

This conclusion receives some support from the non Convention case of *Caspian Basin Specialised Emergency Salvage Administration and Ultisol Transport Contractors Ltd v Bouygues Offshore SA, The Times*, 3 July 1997 High Court, 30 April 1997. The plaintiffs were the owners and charterers, respectively, of a tug which was towing a barge, owned by the defendant, lost off the coast of South Africa. The defendant commenced liability proceedings for damages of more than £50 million in both the South African and the English courts, while the plaintiffs, without admitting liability, began limitation actions in England, under the Merchant Shipping Act 1995, for a declaration of limitation of their liability to the amount of just over £500000, being the sum constituted as the limitation fund. The defendant claimed that a limitation declaration could not be granted unless the plaintiffs' liability had first been admitted or established. Rix J. in the High Court Admiralty Division held against the defendant's plea. There was nothing in the text of the Act or 1976 Limitation Convention on which it was based, nor in RSC Ord. 75, nor in principle, which could be taken to support the view that the court was unable to pronounce upon limitation while liability was still in issue. Determination of limitation amounts usefully enabled parties to calculate whether it was worthwhile going on with liability litigation if the different sums involved were not greatly at variance.

> " . . . also have jurisdiction over claims for limitation . . . "

Case principles

1. Shipowners' Convention Art. 6a liability limitation jurisdiction is subject to any inconsistent Art. 17 jurisdiction agreement concluded between the shipowner and a potential claimant.
2. But Art. 6a jurisdiction nevertheless continues in respect of limitation of liability, if there are *any other potential claimants* who are not bound by the Art. 17 jurisdiction agreement.

Case

Saipern SpA v Dredging V02 BV and Geosite Surveys Ltd (The Volvox **194** Hollandia) [1988] 2 Lloyd's Rep. 361 Court of Appeal, 18 April 1988; [1987] 2 Lloyd's Rep. 520 High Court, 1 May 1987

Facts

An English company, Conoco, contracted with the plaintiff Italian company, Saipern, in 1983 for the plaintiff to carry out work in the North Sea oil field. They mutually agreed to indemnify each other for damage to their respective equipment and property. English law and courts were chosen to govern any disputes.

The plaintiff subcontracted the work to the Dutch defendant, Dredging V02, which owned the suction dredger Volvox Hollandia. Again, English courts and law were chosen to regulate the subcontract.

In turn, the defendant, V02, subcontracted to the English co-defendant, Geosite Surveys Ltd, for provision of high-tech equipment, and English law and London arbitration were chosen.

The defendant V02 damaged Conoco's pipeline in 1984, allegedly causing £4.5 million damage.

In 1985, defendant V02 obtained a provisional Dutch liability limitation order under the 1957 Limitation Convention for a maximum sum of £375000.

Thereafter, Conoco and Saipern brought damages actions against defendants V02 and Geosite in England. Conoco claimed in tort; the plaintiff Saipern against V02 in contract and tort, and against Geosite in tort. Leave to serve the writ out of the jurisdiction was granted under RSC Ord. 11, r.1(1).

Defendant V02 challenged English courts' jurisdiction on the national English ground that Dutch courts previously seised of its liability limitation action were *forum conveniens* and English courts should stay the plaintiffs' liability action in favour of Dutch *lis pendens*. The plaintiffs argued that although Convention jurisdiction was transitionally inapplicable in England under Art. 34(1) of the 1978 Accession Convention because the English proceedings were instituted before 1 January 1987 when the Convention entered into force in the UK, nevertheless, the Convention's jurisdiction grounds were indirectly of relevance to the English courts' decision upon whether England or The Netherlands was *forum conveniens*, because, since English and Dutch judgments would be reached *after* the Convention's entry into force in the UK, the Convention would then apply to their recognition and enforcement under Art. 34(3) of the 1978 Accession Convention if jurisdiction had been based upon grounds corresponding with those in the Convention. For those indirect purposes, therefore, it was material to decide which of English and Dutch courts *would have* possessed jurisdiction under the Convention, so that consequent enforceability could then be taken into account as a factor in national *forum conveniens*.

Judgment

In the first place, Staughton J. in the High Court accepted the argument that in spite of its transitional inapplicability, Convention jurisdiction was indirectly relevant to national *forum conveniens*—except that Arts 21 and 22 could not, of course, apply as such (and if English courts were to exercise jurisdiction as well as the Dutch, Art. 27(3) would be available to deal with the problem of irreconcilable judgments).

Secondly, English jurisdiction would have been available against the defendants on a number of Convention grounds:

(1) against the English defendant Geosite, under Art. 2;
(2) against the Dutch defendant V02, under Art. 6(1); and
(3) against V02 in contract, under Art. 17 (and additionally, Staughton J. regarded the English forum clauses in contracts between Conoco and plaintiff Saipern and between plaintiff Saipern and defendant V02 as also relevant to the *forum conveniens* inquiry into national English *tort* jurisdiction in the claims by Conoco against V02 and Geosite and by Saipern against Geosite, which stemmed from the overall contractual arrangements).

Thirdly, although Dutch courts would have jurisdiction over the Dutch defendant V02's liability limitation claim under Art. 6a, nevertheless, in accordance with European Court of Justice rulings on the relationship between Arts 6(1), (2) and 17 in *Colzani* Case 24/76 and *Segoura* Case 25/76, English Art. 17 chosen jurisdiction should prevail over Dutch Art. 6a jurisdiction. Thus, the plaintiff Saipern and defendant V02 had agreed on Art. 17 English jurisdiction, so that in the ordinary course of events, English courts, not Dutch, would have Convention jurisdiction over the plaintiff's action.

However, Staughton J. made the further finding that Dutch Art. 6a jurisdiction should nonetheless continue where there were other potential claimants upon the Dutch limitation fund, with whom the defendant V02 had not agreed upon non-Dutch jurisdiction—and this was the case here where Conoco was also a potential claimant and had not agreed to English jurisdiction with V02.

Thus, English courts would have enjoyed Convention Art. 17 jurisdiction over defendant V02—but in the circumstances not exclusively, since Dutch liability limitation proceedings could have continued under Art. 6a.

In the event, England was held by Staughton J. to be *forum conveniens* on all the facts.

Comment

This case represents a most unusual situation, since Staughton J. considered that ordinarily the Dutch action should have been declined in relation to the *Art. 17 plaintiff in England* and continued only in relation to the other potential claimants. The problem with this, however, is the peculiar feature of a limitation fund, which is that by its very nature it is intended to be a global and universal limitation of the shipowner's liability—not just in relation to particular claimants. So how could it continue solely towards the latter and not also towards the Art. 17 claimant?

Thus, in *The Falstria*, Case 193 *supra*, Sheen J. held that a *second*-seised Art. 6a limitation action could not be stayed in relation to *actual* plaintiff, under Art. 21, where there were *other* potential claimants on the fund who were not also party to the first-seised liability proceedings and to whom Art. 21 was consequently inapplicable. The fund action cannot proceed in relation to only some of the claimants. It must stand or fall as a whole.

(See 'Jurisdiction in Shipowners' Liability Limitation Actions: *The Volvox Hollandia*' (1989) 10 *Business Law Review* 285).

The defendant V02 subsequently appealed the High Court's decision to the Court of Appeal in:

Case

195 Saipern S.p.A. v Dredging V02 B.V. and Geosite Surveys Ltd (The 'Volvox Hollandia' [1988] 2 Lloyd's Rep. 361 Court of Appeal, 18 April 1988

Facts

See supra, Case 194.

The Court of Appeal did not deal with the relationship between Arts 6a and 17—although, the first instance approach of Staughton J., to take account of 1978 Accession Convention Art. 34(3) post-entry-into-force Convention recognition and enforcement possibilities as a factor in the exercise of RSC Ord. 11 *forum conveniens* national discretionary jurisdiction, was confirmed in the Court of Appeal.

The case on appeal was in fact fought about the proper exercise of discretion by the first instance judge on the *forum conveniens* basis in RSC Ord. 11, r.4(2) (and specifically on grounds in r.1(1)(c) and (d)(i) and (iii)) and the scope of the Court of Appeal's limited power to review the judge's decision, in accordance with *The Spilidia* [1987] AC 460 principles.

The defendants realized that England was more likely to be justified as *forum conveniens* over liability limitation if the latter was included as one issue in proceedings alongside liability and quantum. So, in a change of tactics, they ceased to argue on appeal that the whole English action should be stayed in favour of Dutch limitation proceedings, and effectively conceded English *forum conveniens* over liability and quantum, by asking solely for stay of the plaintiffs' English application for a *negative declaration that the defendants were not entitled to limit their liability.*

Judgment

The Court of Appeal held by a majority of two (Kerr and Nicholls L.JJ.) to one (Dillon L.J.) that the first instance decision of Staughton J. should be overturned and England, rather than Dutch courts, held to be *forum non conveniens* for the determination of the liability limitation issue.

On *forum conveniens* itself, the majority took into account a number of factors: that the English proceedings were instituted one year later than the Dutch, and the existence of Dutch *lis pendens* required even greater caution from the English court before permitting service out under RSC Ord. 11, r.4(2); that the plaintiffs were not alleging that Dutch limitation amounts were too low or that Dutch courts lacked jurisdiction; and that they were incorrect to assert that the burden of proof in The Netherlands was unfavourable to them and that Dutch courts' disclosure powers were insufficient. Thus, the plaintiffs' real motives were thought to be not to safeguard their own English 'advantages' over Dutch proceedings, which did not in fact exist, but to subject the defendants to disadvantages from English proceedings if they could. Under *The Spiladia* approach, England had to be shown by the plaintiffs to be clearly the appropriate and natural forum for the case for justice to be done and this they had failed to do in relation to the liability limitation issue. It was a fundamental right of shipowners to choose the forum in which the limitation fund should be established.

Also, the majority considered that the restrictions in *The Spiladia* upon the Court of Appeal's power to interfere with the first instance judge's exercise of discretion on *forum conveniens* were easier to negotiate where the grounds of challenge were altered at the appellate stage as in this case—disagreed with by the minority judge, Dillon L.J. With all due diffidence to the first instance judge, the majority therefore formed the view that Staughton J. had misdirected himself and given insufficient weight to the existence of the pending Dutch limitation proceedings.

All three appeal court judges were extremely cautious about exercising a discretion to allow English proceedings for a *negative declaration*, in this case against liability limitation rights of the defendant—in particular, where the right or liability in question, which it was sought to have declared non-existent, was that of another person rather than of the plaintiff himself and specifically in the case of shipowners' liability limitation proceedings, where, as seen, the shipowner was the party who should be permitted to select the forum in which to establish the limitation fund. Only where there was merely one potential claimant—or where there were two, but they could effectively be viewed as one, as the minority judge, Dillon L.J., believed was the position in this case—might an ancillary claim for a negative declaration against limitation have been justified in order to be determined in the same forum as liability and quantum. In the circumstances, however, the majority of the Court of Appeal believed that the claims for negative declarations were improperly included in order to wrest the defendants from the natural Dutch forum and that their inclusion was indefensible for this reason.

Comment

One final point is that one of the majority judges in the Court of Appeal (Nicholls L.J., at 379 col. 1) indicated as a further factor against English jurisdiction over the limitation issue, the matter that, had the Convention applied to jurisdiction under the 1978 Accession Convention Art. 34(1) on the transitional position, English courts seised in the second place under Art. 17 to Dutch courts first-seised under Art. 6a, might have had to decline or to stay their jurisdiction under Art. 21 or 22. This subjection of Art. 17 to Arts 21 and

22, however, is contrary both: (i) to English authorities to the opposite effect (see *infra*, Arts 17 and 21); and (ii) to the point derived from Staughton J.'s first instance judgment in *The Volvox Hollandia* itself (see *supra*) that because of the very special nature of limitation fund proceedings, the latter could themselves proceed in any event, whether first- or *second*-seised, if there were other potential claimants on the fund, apart from the Art. 17 plaintiff himself.

ARTICLE 11, PARAGRAPH 1

" . . . *only in the courts . . . in which the defendant is domiciled . . .* "

Case principle

Section 3 of Title II, on jurisdiction matters relating to insurance, is not excluded from applying generally to business insurance.

See too Art. 17 and Art. 54, para. 3.

Case

196 New Hampshire Insurance Company v Strabag Bau AG and others [1992] 1 Lloyd's Rep. 361 Court of Appeal, 25 October 1991

Facts

The plaintiff American insurers insured the defendant German (and Austrian) companies for building work in Iraq in 1981. The defendants made substantial claims on the policy in 1989 through defects discovered in the construction. In September 1989, the plaintiffs sought a declaration from the English courts that they had validly avoided the insurance contract and were not liable thereunder. The defendants challenged English jurisdiction which the plaintiffs had sought to found on a number of grounds, one of which was that s.3 of Title II, on jurisdiction relating to insurance, Art. 11, para. 1 of which would state that the defendant insured could *only* be sued in its German domicile, was inapplicable to business insurance and to reinsurance because such parties did not need special jurisdictional protection of the type in s.3.

At first instance in the High Court, Potter J. rejected the plaintiffs' plea and agreed with the defendants that s.3 was not excluded from application to business insurance, according to its plain wording. Accordingly, the defendants were only to be sued in the German courts.

The plaintiffs appealed to the Court of Appeal.

Judgment

The Court of Appeal upheld Potter J.'s judgment that s.3 was not excluded from applying to business insurance.

First, the drafters of the 1978 Accession Convention had discussed exclusion of certain types of insurance on the ground that protection was not required; but solely shipping matters in Art. 12a were kept out, so that a wider purposive interpretation would not have been justified.

Secondly, if a parallel was sought to be drawn between business insurance and reinsurance, which latter Schlosser (para. 151) seemed to regard as excluded, the European Court had left open the question of reinsurance in its *Overseas Union Insurance* Case C–351/89 judgment, so that it was not clear that reinsurance *was* excluded from s.3 of Title II.

Thirdly, even if *reinsurance* was so excluded, this would not automatically mean that all business insurance should also therefore be so regarded as falling outside s.3.

Accordingly, German courts possessed exclusive Art. 11, para. 1 jurisdiction in relation to the German defendants.

Comment

(See 'Business Insurance and Reinsurance under the Judgments Convention' (1990) *JBL* 517 for commentary following Potter J.'s High Court judgment at first instance.) In the Court of Appeal proceedings in *Agnew v Lansförsäkringsbølagens AB* [1997] 4 All ER 937 on 31 July 1997, Schlosser's approach *supra*, excluding reinsurance from Title II Section 3, was approved of by Evans LJ (agreed with by the others): *inter alia*, reinsurance and insurance were conceptually distinct (p.944). In *Jordan Grand Prix Ltd v Baltic Insurance Group* (1997) *The Times* 14 Nov., the CA held on 24 Oct. 97 that Art. 11 was not limited to plaintiff insurers who were *Contracting* State domiciliaries.

ARTICLE 12(5)

' . . . *in so far as it covers* . . . "

Case principle

A jurisdiction clause covering insurance risks and interests, some of which are within and some outside risks and interests included in Art. 12a, is *wholly* ineffective.

Case

Charman v WOC Offshore B.V. [1993] 2 Lloyd's Rep. 551 Court of Appeal, **197** 19 July 1993

Facts

The plaintiffs, Lloyd's insurers, entered a contract with the defendant Dutch engineering company to insure the defendant against loss through failure to recover property it had hired to a Yugoslav company for the construction of a breakwater in Algeria. The plaintiffs subsequently brought proceedings in the English courts for avoidance of the insurance contract and alternatively for a declaration of non-liability. On the assumption that the insurance policy incorporated a choice of English jurisdiction clause common in the insurance trade, the defendants challenged English courts' jurisdiction, on the ground that the jurisdiction clause was wholly ineffective under Art. 12(5) because it related both to risks and interests within Art. 12a and to those outside it; and at least the jurisdiction agreement would only be given effect to in relation to risks and interests falling within Art. 12a and not also outside, on the ground that the words 'in so far as' in Art. 12(5) were to be construed as meaning 'to the extent that'. However, the plaintiffs argued to the opposite effect: namely, that risks and interests in the policy falling outside Art. 12a would also be subject to the jurisdiction clause if there were *some* falling within Art. 12a; and 'in so far as' meant 'if' or 'provided that'.

In *Jordan Grand Prix Ltd v Baltic Insurance Group* (1997) *The Times*, 14 November, the Court of Appeal held, on 24 October 1997, that Article II was not limited to plaintiff insurers who were Contracting State domiciliaries.

Judgment

The Court of Appeal held in favour of the defendants—although this was not on the alternative ground that 'in so far as' meant 'to the extent that'. The Court of Appeal's view, on policy and text, was that if non-Art. 12a risks and interests were included, the jurisdiction clause failed completely and would not even be applied to the Art. 12a risks and interests alone. The textual justification provided for this by the court was that the words 'and no other' were to be implied at the end of Art. 12(5).

Comment

As it happened, however, notwithstanding the Court of Appeal's ruling on ineffectiveness of the English jurisdiction clause, on the facts of the case the jurisdiction agreement would be given full effect, because the court had already held that *all* risks and interests in issue fell within Art. 12a (see *infra*, Case 198, Art. 12a).

ARTICLE 12a(4)

"Any risk or interest connected with any of those referred to in points 1 to 3 above."

Case principles

1. 'Interest' in Art. 12a(4) means types of *property*, not ownership interest or title.

2. 'Connected with' in Art. 12a(4) is to be literally construed so as to extend beyond risks and interests which are accessory or ancillary to marine or aircraft risks in Art. 12a(1)–(3) and to include land-based property, provided that: (i) this is not a major element of the insurance; and (ii) the connection is not too insubstantial.

Case

Charman v WOC Offshore B.V. [1993] 2 Lloyd's Rep. 551 Court of Appeal,   **198**
19 July 1993

Facts

See *supra*, Case 197.

The plaintiff Lloyd's insurers, entered a contract with the defendant Dutch engineering company covering risk of loss of property hired by the defendants to a Yugoslav company for the construction of a breakwater in Algeria. The property in question consisted of both sea-going items, such as a tugboat, and land-based, for example, a crawling crane. The plaintiffs brought English proceedings against the defendants for avoidance of the insurance policy and for a declaration of non-liability. The defendants challenged English courts' jurisdiction on the assumption—itself challenged by the defendants as a matter of contractual construction—that the contract of insurance did in fact incorporate an English jurisdiction clause: Art. 12(5) expressly only permitted jurisdiction clauses to be given effect to in relation to risks within Art. 12a (see *supra*, Case 197, Art. 12(5)); Art. 12a(1)–(3) was concerned with sea-going and aircraft, not land-based, risks and interests, and Art. 12a(4) included solely those risks and interests accessory to marine or aircraft insurance, and not land-based.

Judgment

The Court of Appeal examined the Schlosser Report and determined the objective of Arts 12(5) and 12a as somehow to limit the ability to depart by agreement from the protective provisions of Title II, s. 3 on insurance, solely to where the insured did not require protection. Thus, this latter *could* include land-based, as well as air or marine, insurance.

Accordingly, 'interest' in Art. 12a(4) was to be held to refer to types of *property*, such as land-based, and not to the abstract concept of title. Land-based property subject to the insurance policy could, therefore, fall within Art. 12a(4) and consequently also within the jurisdiction clause effective under Art. 12(5).

The proviso was, however, in accordance with Art. 12a(4), that such 'interest' had to be properly connected with marine and air risks in Art. 12a(1)–(3). The defendants argued for a narrow construction, that the Art. 12a(4) interests should be so relatively insignificant compared to the main marine risks as to be merely ancillary or accessory thereto. The Court of Appeal rejected this approach, in favour of a liberal and generous interpretation of Art. 12a(4):

provided that the other risk or interest was not major, it need not be so small as to be merely ancillary to the Art. 12a(1)–(3) risk. On the facts, the land-based property satisfied this test because its worth was only about 20 per cent of the total value of property involved.

ARTICLE 13, PARAGRAPH 1

" . . . *for a purpose which can be regarded as being outside his trade or profession* . . . "

Case principles

1. The purpose at the date of conclusion of the contract, and not any subsequent change of use, will be taken as determining the consumer nature of the contract.
2. The apparent purpose of acquisition should be taken into account.
3. Acquisition of a product for display on premises used for business of a different nature held to be for trade or business.
4. Acquisition of a product outside a trade or business, but for the purpose of transfer to a third party other than family member or non-business donee, is not a consumer contract within Art. 13.

Case

199 Project XJ220 Limited v Comte d'Uze and Comte de Dampierre (unreported) High Court, 19 November 1993

Facts

The plaintiff car manufacturer received orders for a very expensive model of vehicle independently from the two French defendants, Comte d'Uze and Comte de Dampierre, in 1990. The terms were that each would pay a deposit of £50,000 on acceptance of order and a further £50,000 on being given notice of delivery in nine months. The first but not the second sum was paid when they fell due. The plaintiff wished to sue the defendants in England on the ground of Art. 5(1) as place of contractual performance (see *supra*, Art. 5(1), Case 156). The defendants both challenged English jurisdiction and the applicability of Art. 5(1), on the ground that their transactions were consumer contracts under Art. 13 and that consequently they could only be sued in the courts of their French domicile under Art. 14, para. 2.

Judgment

Deputy High Court Judge Boyd Q.C. held Arts 13 and 14 to be inapplicable: the defendants were not consumers.

In the case of the Comte d'Uze, the facts were that he bought the car in order to display it on his estate where he ran a business offering conference and reception facilities, which the exhibition of the car could make more attractive. This meant that the purpose of acquisition could not be regarded as being outside his trade or profession. It was irrelevant that the original purpose at contract was subsequently abandoned and that in fact the car had simply been garaged on the estate. Furthermore, even if the latter had been the real, original purpose and the former only reasonably apparent to the plaintiff, this was sufficient to make Art. 13 inapplicable, on the Convention principle of good faith.

With regard to the Comte de Dampierre, he had acquired the car for the purpose of transferring it to a third party financing the deal, which he was contractually obliged towards that person to do, for no personal interest nor payment. He was therefore merely acting as an intermediary for the third party who was himself ineligible to make the purchase. Deputy Judge Boyd Q.C. referred to the European Court of Justice's decision in *Bertrand* Case 150/77 and to the reference therein to *final* consumers (para. 21) and to *Shearson* Case C–89/91 (p. 221) as well as to similar remarks in the Schlosser Report (para. 153). Only such ultimate transferees were supposed to be protected by s.4 of Title II, not a middleman like the Comte de Dampierre, unless the transfer was to a member of his family for their private use, or as a private gift, seemingly not the position in this case where the defendant Dampierre was simply allowing his name to be used for the benefit of another person who was the true final consumer.

Section 4 on consumer contracts did not apply to the Comte de Dampierre, who was not a consumer for the purposes.

ARTICLE 16

" . . . shall have exclusive . . . "

Case principle

Article 16 exclusive jurisdiction prevails over Art. 21.

Case

Kloeckner and Co. AG v Gatoil Overseas Inc [1990] 1 Lloyd's Rep. 177 High **200** Court, 31 July 1989

Facts

See infra, Art. 17, Case 273.

Judgment

The judge, Hirst J., clearly accepted this principle to be correct, although, the case itself was concerned with the relationship between *Art. 17* and Art. 21 (subsequently followed in *Denby v The Hellenic Mediterranean Lines Co. Ltd* [1994] 1 Lloyd's Rep. 321, *infra*).

Case

201 The Filiatra Legacy [1994] 1 Lloyd's Rep. 513 High Court, 9 April 1990

Facts

See infra, Art. 16(5), Case 211.

Judgment

A few months after *Kloeckner*, Saville J. reached the like conclusion (*obiter—* because neither Art. 16 nor 17 applied on the facts).

Comment

In *Overseas Union Insurance Limited v New Hampshire Insurance Company* Case C–351/89 [1991] ECR I-3317, Advocate General Van Gerven and the Court of Justice clearly contemplated that Art. 16 would prevail over Art. 21.

ARTICLE 16(1)

" . . . *have as their object* . . . "

Case principle

Article 16 rights *in rem* and tenancies must be the actual basis of the claim for them to be the 'object' of the proceedings thereunder. It is not sufficient that they are merely linked to or connected with the claim (*Reichert Case* C–115/88 and *Webb Case* C–294/92 applied).

Case

202 Jarrett v Barclays Bank Plc and another; Jones v First National Bank Plc; Peacock v First National Bank Plc [1997] I.L.Pr. 531 Court of Appeal, 31 October 1996

Facts

These are dealt with in detail below in connection with the meaning of 'tenancies' under Art. 16(1). The plaintiffs had purchased timeshare interests in

Portuguese and Spanish holiday apartments in 1989 and 1990, which were financed by loans to the plaintiffs of between £2,000 and £5,000 by the defendant banks under what were alleged to be 'debtor-creditor-supplier' agreements under the Consumer Credit Act 1974. Sections 56 and 75 enabled the plaintiff 'debtors' to sue the defendant 'creditor' banks for misrepresentation and breach of contract committed by the 'suppliers'—the timeshare sellers.

In a series of county court actions brought against them by the plaintiffs, the defendant banks contested English courts' jurisdiction on the ground that Portuguese or Spanish courts of the *situs* of the immovable property possessed exclusive jurisdiction under Art. 16(1)(a) (Brussels Convention Art. 16(1)(b) was inapplicable because the landlords were not natural persons as required thereunder) and that, consequently, English courts should decline under Art. 19.

The plaintiffs argued, however, that the timeshare transactions were not 'tenancies' within the meaning of Art. 16(1).

When this was unsuccessful before the Court of Appeal (see *infra*, Art. 16(1) 'tenancies', Case 204), the plaintiffs further contended that since the actions were against the creditor banks under debtor-creditor-supplier agreements to finance the purchases, as opposed to being against the sellers themselves, this meant that the foreign tenancies were not the 'object' of the proceedings for purposes of Art. 16(1), which was therefore inapplicable.

Judgment

The Court of Appeal unanimously agreed with the plaintiffs in this respect: the Portuguese and Spanish timeshare tenancies were not the object of the English court proceedings and consequently Arts 16(1) and 19 were inapplicable to deprive English courts of jurisdiction over the defendant British banks.

The Court of Appeal followed *Reichert* and *Webb* in the European Court. It was not enough for Art. 16(1) to apply that the foreign Contracting State rights *in rem*—or here tenancies—were linked to and connected with the claim. For them to be the 'object' of the proceedings, they were required to form the actual basis of the claim. This was not the case here where the actions were brought not against the sellers of the timeshare interests but against the financiers, the defendant banks, under alleged debtor-creditor-supplier agreements. The foreign tenancies were merely linked—not sufficient for Art. 16(1).

Comment

In *Re Polly Peck International Plc, The Times*, 27 December 1996 High Court, 29 November 1996, *infra*, Case 205, Rattee J., in the Chancery Division, dealt with the meaning of there not being 'principally' a question of the right to possession of foreign immovable property for national English torts jurisdiction to exist in non-Convention cases under s.30(1) of the 1982 Act (see *supra*, 1982 Act s.30(1), Case 102). Presumably, analogies can be drawn with Art. 16(1)(a)'s requirement that proceedings must have 'as their object' rights *in rem* in or tenancies of immovable property.

" . . . object rights in rem . . . "

Case principle

Proceedings by a trustee in bankruptcy to have a transfer of the (deceased) bankrupt's immovable property to a third party declared void have as their object rights *in rem* in the property.

Case

203 Re Hayward (deceased) [1997] 1 All ER 32 High Court, 28 March 1996

Facts

A deceased party purchased a villa in Spain in equal half-interests with the defendant in 1986. In 1987, the deceased went bankrupt and the plaintiff was appointed his trustee in bankruptcy. Later that year on the death intestate of the deceased, his widow purported to transfer his half-interest to the defendant in consideration for the release of debts. Subsequently, the trustee brought English proceedings for, *inter alia*, declarations that the transfer was void and that the deceased's interest had vested in the trustee on his appointment. The defendant challenged English courts' jurisdiction, on the ground that Spanish courts of the *situs* of the villa possessed exclusive jurisdiction over the action to enforce rights *in rem* under Art. 16(1)(a). The trustee countered that in *Webb v Webb* the European Court had held an action to establish a resulting trust of immovables to be *in personam*—so should the trustee's action here be so viewed.

Judgment

Rattee J., referring to the Schlosser Report (para. 166), distinguishing rights *in rem* and *in personam*, held in the Chancery Division that Art. 16(1)(a) applied to the trustee's application, having as its object rights *in rem* in the Spanish villa. *Webb* had been an action *to establish* equitable rights under a trust; here, however, the object was to enforce rights *already* existing, allegedly, in the trustee, in respect of immovable property. The widow had no right to transfer an interest in property which the trustee had previously had vested in him.

See too supra, Art. 1, para. 2(1) and (2) and infra, Art. 16(3).

" . . . tenancies . . . "

Case principle

Annual timeshare interests in foreign immovable property are not excluded from the independent Convention concept of 'tenancies'.

Case

Jarrett v Barclays Bank Plc and another; Jones v First National Bank Plc; Peacock v First National Bank Plc [1997] I.L.Pr. 531 Court of Appeal, 31 October 1996

204

Facts

The plaintiffs were purchasers of timeshare interests in Portuguese or Spanish holiday properties for one week a year annually—indefinitely, in perpetuity and for 80 years respectively, in 1989 and 1990. The plaintiffs paid a purchase price for the exclusive possession of the timeshare properties together with management and maintenance services, and in the case of the Jones, this was for shares in the timeshare company entitling them to their rights of occupancy. The plaintiffs borrowed the purchase monies, between £2500 and £5000 approximately, from the defendant banks under what were alleged to be debtor-creditor-supplier financing agreements within the meaning of s.12 of the Consumer Credit Act 1974.

The plaintiffs claimed that the timeshare sellers had misrepresented facts inducing them to enter the timeshare contracts and were further in breach of contract—in the Jones' case, it was claimed that the Spanish property never existed. With the Peacocks, the timeshare company had gone into liquidation without issuing the licence to occupy.

The plaintiffs brought actions in various English county courts for misrepresentation and breach of contract in respect of the deficiencies in the foreign timeshare properties, against the defendant banks which had financed the transactions. The plaintiffs were able to claim such liability on the part of the banks, on the ground that under s.56 of the Consumer Credit Act 1974 the sellers were treated as having conducted antecedent negotiations as agents for the creditor banks as well as on their own account for the purposes of liability for misrepresentations under debtor-creditor-supplier agreements; and s.75 also made the creditor jointly and severally liable with the seller for misrepresentation and breach of contract by the seller.

The banks challenged English courts' jurisdiction, on the ground that Portuguese or Spanish courts of the *situs* possessed exclusive jurisdiction over the tenancies of immovable property under Art. 16(1)(a) and that consequently English courts were obliged to declare against jurisdiction under Art. 19. The plaintiffs argued that timeshares were not 'tenancies' within the meaning of Art. 16(1)(a) (note that Brussels Convention Art. 16(1)(b) was inapplicable in any event because the landlords were not natural persons).

Before two of the county courts the banks' challenge succeeded, but failed in the third. The unsuccessful plaintiffs and bank respectively appealed.

Judgment

The Court of Appeal unanimously held in the first place that the timeshare transactions were 'tenancies' within the meaning of Art. 16(1)(a), as contended for by the defendant banks.

First, the concept of 'tenancy' was to be given an independent Convention meaning in accordance with European Court case law on Art. 16(1), rather than being referred to national *lex situs*.

Secondly, as it happened, European Court cases were of limited use in providing a detailed definition. *Sanders* Case 73/77, had set out the principles based upon the good administration of justice, also followed in *Rösler* Case 241/83 and *Hacker* Case C–280/90: tenancies were best left to courts of the *situs* which would carry out necessary local checks and enquiries and apply sometimes complex local legislation. Yet, beyond this, all that was known was that in *Sanders* the sub-letting of the flower business and in *Hacker* the overall accommodation and travel agreement fell outside Art. 16(1), whereas in *Rösler*, short-term holiday letting was nonetheless held to be a tenancy for purposes of Art. 16(1).

Consequently, taking its lead mainly from *Rösler* (and rejecting the idea that a tenancy could not be in perpetuity, in the case of the Jones), the Court of Appeal concluded that there was nothing in the authorities nor in Art. 16(1) to indicate that the timeshare agreements did not amount to tenancies for the purposes of Art. 16(1). Furthermore, such exceptions to Art. 16(1) would create uncertainty and unpredictability.

Comments

In the end, the Court of Appeal upheld English jurisdiction against Art. 16(1): the latter was inapplicable because although the timeshares were tenancies, they were not the principal object of the proceedings for Art. 16(1) (see *supra*, Case 202, 'object' Art. 16(1)).

The Court of Appeal declined to refer the matters concerning Art. 16 to the European Court for reasons of delay, cost, small amounts involved and doubts over whether any questions of interpretation existed in view of the clarity of existing European Court authorities.

> " . . . *of the Contracting State* . . . "

Case principle

Where the action involves rights *in rem* in or tenancies of immovable property situated in a non-Contracting State, Convention jurisdiction grounds should not prevail over national law of the forum according jurisdiction to the courts of the non-Contracting State *situs*.

Case

Re Polly Peck International Plc, The Times, 27 December 1996 High Court,   **205**
29 November 1996

Facts

See supra, 1982 Act s.49, Comment (4) to Re Harrods (Buenos Aires) Ltd,
Case 102 and Comments to 202.

Judgment

Rattee J. indicated *obiter* that Art. 2 jurisdiction of English courts would have
been unlikely to prevail over the claims of courts in Northern Cyprus had the
proceedings been held principally to involve matters of title to or possession of
immovable property in Northern Cyprus.

Comment

This approach could be supported on either of two grounds: (1) that, as a matter of principle, national English jurisdiction grounds should apply in this way
where the immovables are situated outside the Contracting States, since the
Convention no longer has an interest to apply thereto; or (2) on the basis of
Harrods itself, that non-Contracting State *situs* of the property makes the latter territory overwhelmingly *forum conveniens*, in favour of which the English
courts' Convention jurisdiction should be stayed.

For a discussion, see Kaye, *Civil Jurisdiction and Enforcement of Foreign
Judgments*, pp. 880–3 and 973.

ARTICLE 16(2)

" *. . . proceedings which have as their object the validity of the
constitution . . . or the decisions of their organs . . .* "

Case principles

1. Article 16(2) is to be narrowly construed as applicable, *inter alia*, to pro-
    ceedings having as their object the *validity* of the decisions of their organs,
    but not to those merely having as their object the decisions of their organs,
    the wide construction (*Newtherapeutics* and *obiter* in *Grupo Torras*).
2. Issues of whether directors taking a decision constituted a board as organ
    and of whether a board was required to be convened at all held to relate
    to *validity of* decisions of the company's organs (*Newtherapeutics*).
3. Whether narrow or wide construction were correct, there must at least
    have been a *decision of an organ* as the object of the proceedings, as the
    essential minimum requirement (*Grupo Torras*).

4. Claims against individual directors for breach of their fiduciary duties held to fall within Art. 16(2) in the absence of fraud, if carried out through a decision of the board (*Grupo Torras*—prevailing over *Newtherapeutics* according to which Art. 16(2) is inapplicable thereto).

Case

206 Newtherapeutics Ltd v Katz [1990] 3 WLR 1183 High Court, 5 March 1990

Facts

The plaintiff English company manufactured drugs to treat AIDS. Its main source of income was under an agreement with a French company whereby the latter financed the plaintiff's research operations in return for distribution rights. At a meeting in Paris in 1988 between the defendant directors of the plaintiff company, Katz and Lablanchy, and another director called Vich, on the one hand, and representatives of the French company on the other, it was agreed by the defendants on behalf of the plaintiff to reduce the amount of money paid to the plaintiff under the original agreement, although the director Vich refused to sign. Subsequently, the majority of the plaintiff's shareholders decided that the variation of the original agreement was not to the advantage of the plaintiff and sought to bring proceedings in the English courts against the defendant directors for breach of their directors' duties of good faith towards the plaintiff in entering the variation agreement on its behalf. The defendants contested English jurisdiction under RSC Ord. 12, r.8. The defendant Lablanchy was domiciled in a Contracting State outside the UK, namely France. The plaintiff asserted that English courts possessed exclusive jurisdiction over him under Art. 16(2), applicable regardless of his French domicile, on the ground that the plaintiff company's seat was situated in England and the proceedings *had as their object* the *decisions of their organs*, that is to say, of its board of directors, as prescribed thereunder. The defendants countered this by arguing, first, that the text of Art. 16(2) should be construed more narrowly, as requiring the proceedings to have as their object *the validity* of the decision of an organ, not merely any question concerning the decision, and, secondly, that what had occurred did not have as its object the validity of any such decision.

The issue arose out of a footnote in a commentary which queried the correct construction of the provision, as being wider or narrower (see Kaye, *Civil Jurisdiction* pp. 1019–20, n.289).

Judgment

Knox J. held that:

(1) Art. 16(2) applied to *validity of* decisions of organs—thereby favouring the narrower construction over the wider; but

(2) on the facts, the claim by the plaintiff did involve *validity of* the decision of the directors.

The first of the preceding conclusions was reached on the basis of a linguistic construction of foreign texts of Art. 16(2) even though the English version itself favoured the wider construction.

With regard to the second finding (departed from and modified by the Court of Appeal in *Grupo Torras*, see *infra*, Case 207), Knox J. considered from the pleadings whether the principal claim was that the directors' decision had not been taken in good faith or that in taking the decision they had not properly constituted themselves as the board when they ought to have done so: only if the latter was the case, would the proceedings concern validity of decisions of the plaintiff company's organs. Knox J. opted for the latter.

Comment

This decision is discussed and criticised by the author in 'Corporate Jurisdiction Under the European Judgments Convention' (1991) 10 *Civil Justice Quarterly* 220. The points there made include the following:

(1)   Knox J.'s textual construction of foreign versions of Art. 16(2) as supporting the narrower interpretation is disagreed with and further arguments in favour of the wider interpretation are presented;

(2)   breach of directors' individual duties of good faith, it is agreed, do not involve validity of decisions of organs, nor, it is submitted, even decisions of organs under the wider construction—although, in *Grupo Torras*, *infra*, the Court of Appeal in fact took the opposite view;

(3)   it is not necessarily correct to regard the question of whether a meeting of directors constituted the board, or of whether a board was required to be convened in the first place, as involving *validity* of its decisions—whereas, clearly, the matter of whether these are *decisions of the board* at all, under the wider construction, may be said to be the issue in such cases; and

(4)   in the subsequent proceedings in *Grupo Torras*, *infra*, the Court of Appeal sought to develop the *Newtherapeutics* analysis by sidestepping the need to choose between narrower and wider constructions of Art. 16(2), although nonetheless giving a certain support, incidentally, to the latter.

In actual fact, Knox J.'s treatment of Art. 16(2) in *Newtherapeutics* was strictly *obiter* in relation to the defendant Lablanchy who was subsequently held to be freed of all liability in any event by virtue of a waiver agreement entered into with the plaintiff company in return for his resignation as director of the plaintiff.

With regard to jurisdiction over co-defendant Katz, although he was domiciled in New York, Art. 16(2) still applied, irrespective of his non-Contracting State domicile—although, there was some confusion over whether leave was required for him to be served outside the jurisdiction or not, and, in the end, Knox J. chose to set aside leave against Katz through failure of the plaintiffs to disclose fully the material facts and because of doubts over whether grounds for leave were properly founded in the first place.

Case

207   Grupo Torras S.A. v Sheikh Fahad Mohammed Al Sabah [1995] I.L.Pr. 667
Court of Appeal, 26 May 1995

Facts

The plaintiff Spanish company sought to sue the 20 defendants, including Contracting and non-Contracting State domiciliaries, in the English courts for damages for breach of fiduciary duties towards the plaintiff and to account as constructive trustees. The defendants included directors of and advisors to the plaintiff company, as well as a network of off-shore companies. They were alleged to have fraudulently misappropriated the plaintiff's assets which were made to disappear into various 'black holes' and were lost to the plaintiff.

The defendants challenged English courts' jurisdiction, on the ground that the object of the proceedings was the decisions of the plaintiff Spanish company's organs, namely, the board of directors, and that Art. 16(2) consequently accorded exclusive jurisdiction to Spanish courts of the plaintiff's seat (and that even if Art. 16(2) did not apply, English courts should decline proceedings in favour of first-seised Spanish courts under Art. 21, see *infra*, Art. 21, Case 285).

The plaintiff responded that Art. 16(2) was inapplicable:

(1)   *Newtherapeutics* had held that the provision should be narrowly construed so as only to cover proceedings having as their object the *validity* of a company's decisions where its organs were concerned; and

(2)   that an action for breach of fiduciary duties of directors was therefore excluded from Art. 16(2).

Judgment

Stuart-Smith L.J. in the Court of Appeal held Art. 16(2) to be inapplicable, so that English courts possessed jurisdiction.

The *minimum* requirement was that there had to have been a *decision of an organ*. Here, it was considered that on the facts there had been none in view of the allegedly fraudulent and abusive nature of the directors' actions. Consequently, it was irrelevant whether narrow or wider construction of Art. 16(2) was adopted. The minimum, wider requirement was not even met. Nevertheless, Stuart-Smith L.J. did allow himself to pass comment on some of the issues:

(1)   he favoured the narrower construction in *Newtherapeutics* in the light of foreign texts and on a purposive approach to interpretation;

(2) although, he did not seem to think that the choice between *decisions* and *validity of decisions* would make a lot of difference in practice; and

(3) in disagreement with *Newtherapeutics*, though reserving his final view, he considered that an action for breach of directors' duties in the absence of fraud would fall within Art. 16(2) if effected through the decision of the board as organ on the facts.

(See *infra*, Case 285, Art. 21, for Court of Appeal's decision on whether to decline thereunder.)

ARTICLE 16(3)

" . . . *in public registers* . . . "

Case principle

The essential element of a 'public' register for the purposes of Art. 16(3) is access by the public rather than maintenance of the register by a public authority or official.

Case

Re Fagin's Bookshop plc [1992] BCLC 118 High Court, 24 May 1991   **208**

Facts

Section 352(1) of the Companies Act 1985 requires English registered companies to maintain a register of their members which, under s.356(1), is open to public inspection. The applicants to the High Court in these proceedings requested rectification of the Fagin company's members' register under s.359, in order to reduce the number of shares in the company listed as held by the defendant Luxembourg company, Banque Leu (Luxembourg) S.A., and for entry of another company as a shareholder.

The defendant challenged the English courts' jurisdiction, on the ground of its Luxembourg domicile under Art. 2. However, the applicants responded that the members' register was a 'public register' under Art. 16(3), required to be kept at its registered office in England and Wales under s.353(1), which meant that English courts possessed exclusive jurisdiction to rectify the register, regardless of domicile, under Art. 16(3). The defendant denied that a company's register of members, which was kept by the company itself—compared to, say, the register of company charges, maintained by the Registrar of Companies, a public official—was a 'public' register for the purposes of Art. 16(3).

Judgment

Harman J. held that the register of members of a company was a public register within the meaning of Art. 16(3). Consequently, English courts possessed exclusive jurisdiction over the application for rectification, irrespective of the defendant's Luxembourg domicile.

The essential feature of a public register for the purposes of Art. 16(3) was said to be not its maintenance by a public authority or official—which the company's members' register would fail to conform to—but public access to inspection, which it would satisfy. The judge compared the members' register to a 'public' park owned by a private person, or to a 'public' road where a private person owned the subsoil—nonetheless *public* in either case.

> " . . . object the validity of entries . . . "

Case principle

An action to order a third party transferee of an interest in property under a void transaction to obtain rectification of the ensuing entry in the public register falls within exclusive jurisdiction provision in Art. 16(3) (*obiter*).

Case

209   Re Hayward (deceased) [1997] 1 All ER 32 High Court, 28 March 1996

Facts

See supra, Art. 16(1)(a), Case 203.

As well as requesting declarations of the trustee's title and voidness of the transfer to the defendant of the deceased's half-interest in the Spanish villa, the trustee also claimed an order to obtain rectification of the Spanish property register. The trustee argued that this was *in personam* against the defendant.

Judgment

Rattee J. held (*obiter*, since it was already held that Art. 16(1)(a) applied, see *supra*) that Art. 16(3) would apply to this case. Rectification of the Spanish property register was not merely subsidiary and consequential but was essential to enable the trustee to deal with the interest in the Spanish property.

Spanish courts, therefore, possessed exclusive jurisdiction in respect of the Spanish property register entries and English courts had to decline under Art. 19.

ARTICLE 16(4)

" . . . *concerned with the registration or validity of patents* . . . "

Case principle

Proceedings for a declaration of non-infringement of patent rights (or for damages for infringement) do not fall within Art. 16(4), notwithstanding that the issue of the validity of the patent might arise as an incidental matter.

Case

Chiron Corporation v Evans Medical Ltd and Others (unreported) High **210** Court, 3 July 1996

Facts

See supra, Art. 6(1), Case 186.

Judgment

In the course of reaching his decision that a Belgian worldwide exclusive licensee of patent rights belonging to an English company and its parent had been properly joined to a plaintiff competitor's English action against the others for a declaration of non-contravention of the patent under Art. 6(1), Robert Walker J. in the English Patents Court confirmed that Art. 16(4) was inapplicable to (non-)infringement proceedings.

Comment

See, however, *Coin Controls Ltd v Suzo International (UK) Ltd* [1997] 3 All ER 45 (*infra*, Case 392 E. Recent Cases, Art. 16(4)): if validity of the patent is seriously in issue, as principal object of proceedings, whether or not by way of defence to an infringement claim, Art. 16(4) applies.

ARTICLE 16(5)

" . . . *proceedings concerned with the enforcement of judgments* . . . "

Case principle

Article 16(5) applies where the enforcement of a judgment is the object of proceedings, not merely where delivery of a judgment is a pre-condition of contractual liability sought to be enforced in the proceedings.

Case

211 The Filiatra Legacy [1994] 1 Lloyd's Rep. 513 High Court, 9 April 1990

Facts

The plaintiffs obtained judgment for more than one and a half million US dollars in English proceedings against the ship Filiatra Legacy for cargo shortage. Subsequently, the plaintiffs commenced English proceedings against the defendant insurers for payment of part of that sum under an insurance contract. The plaintiffs sought to base the English courts' jurisdiction upon Art. 16(5).

Judgment

Saville J. held that Art. 16(5) did not apply. The subject matter of the action was not enforcement of the judgment against the *Filiatra Legacy*, but the terms of the insurance contract. The judgment was merely the condition in the contract according to which payment by the defendants would fall to be made.

" . . . enforcement . . . "

Case principle

'Enforcement' may mean implementation of a judgment through force or constraint and possibly may not also include the holding of an inquiry into damages pursuant to a court order.

Case

212 Berkeley Administration Inc v McClelland [1995] I.L.Pr. 201 Court of Appeal, 18 February 1994

Facts

See infra, Art. 26 'Recognition', Case 347.

Judgment

The Court of Appeal agreed that the court order for an inquiry into damages to be held was itself a 'judgment' within Art. 25.

But since foreign proceedings were no longer pending, the court found it unnecessary to express a view on whether the inquiry amounted to 'enforcement' of the order for purposes of Art. 16(5), as argued by the defendants and denied by the plaintiffs (and see too *infra*, Art. 28(1), Case 355).

> " . . . *Contracting State in which the judgment has been or is to be enforced*"

Case principle

Courts lack jurisdiction to order independent, post judgment disclosure of (English or) foreign assets against a judgment debtor for purposes of enforcement of the judgment *in a foreign Contracting State.*

Case

Interpool Ltd v Galani [1988] QB 738 Court of Appeal, 23 June 1987   **213**

Facts

The plaintiff, Interpool, obtained registration in England of a French judgment for over eight million US dollars against the Greek defendant, Galani, under the Foreign Judgments (Reciprocal Enforcement) Act 1933 and thereafter applied to the English courts for an order under RSC Ord. 48, r.1(1) for the defendant to be examined orally as to his assets.

The defendant objected to such an examination in respect of assets situated outside England and Wales because the English courts lacked jurisdiction over *enforcement* of judgments in other Contracting States and consequently also *disclosure* powers in such cases.

Judgment

The Court of Appeal held that the English courts possessed jurisdiction to enforce judgments against assets abroad and therefore also to order disclosure, *where this was for enforcement in England.*

Comment

Balcombe L.J. made it clear (p. 743) that had the Convention been applicable to the preceding *pre-Convention* case, Art. 16(5) would have entailed that, to the extent that Ord. 48 disclosure of (English or) foreign assets were required for the purposes of enforcement of the judgment in a *foreign* Contracting State, English courts would have lacked jurisdiction under Arts 16(5) and 19 (see 'Examination of Judgment Debtors as to their Assets Abroad: Courts' Powers and Jurisdiction' (1989) *Lloyd's Maritime and Commercial Law Quarterly* 465, 470 *et seq.*). Such independent disclosure (even if *pre*-judgment), not ancillary to interim injunctive relief, would not itself qualify as Art. 24 provisional, including protective, relief. *Interpool* was cited with approval by Thomas J. at first instance in *Union Bank of Finland Ltd v Lelakis* [1996] 4 All ER 305 at 313 (see *supra*, 1982 Act s.25 and *infra*, Art. 17).

See infra, Art. 24 for 'provisional' enforcement jurisdiction.

ARTICLE 17, PARAGRAPH 1

" . . . parties . . . have agreed . . . "

Case principle

1. If existence of the agreement on jurisdiction is contested, the party alleging this is required to establish it.

Case

214 Kloeckner & Co AG v Gatoil Overseas Inc [1990] 1 Lloyd's Rep. 177 High Court, 31 July 1989

Facts and judgment

See *infra*, Case 273.

The judge considered that *Effer v Kantner* Case 38/81, decided by the European Court in relation to general contractual existence under Art. 5(1), applied by analogy to Art. 17 jurisdiction agreements.

Case principle

2. Agreement to jurisdiction under Art. 17 must be express, not implied.

Case

215 New Hampshire Insurance Company v Strabag Bau AG [1992] 1 Lloyd's Rep. 361 Court of Appeal, 25 October 1991

Facts

See supra, Art. 11, para. 1 and infra, Art. 54, para. 3.

The plaintiff insurers attempted to found English courts' jurisdiction over the defendant German insured, *inter alia*, on implied agreement to English jurisdiction, arising from substantial connections with the London insurance market.

Judgment

The Court of Appeal held that agreed Art. 17 jurisdiction had to be the subject of an express jurisdiction agreement (even if in a *form* of international trade or commerce). Consequently, it would not be implied.

Case principle

3. Plaintiffs must prove Art. 17 jurisdiction by showing a good arguable case
    that agreement on jurisdiction was reached with the defendant.

Case

Agrafax Public Relations Ltd v United Scottish Society Incorporated [1995] **216**
I.L.Pr. 753 Court of Appeal, 11 May 1995

Facts

The plaintiffs were the organizers of a tour of California by a Scottish military
band in 1991 and entered discussions with the defendant society based in
California for sponsorship of the band's expenses. There was a series of faxed
communications sent by the plaintiffs to the defendant over the terms of the
sponsorship, which was responded to, allegedly, by a telephone call from the
defendant. The defendants did not reply to the plaintiffs' faxed draft contract
containing an English jurisdiction clause and the tour then took place. On the
band's return, the defendants claimed that they had only agreed to pay a maximum sum of £60 000, which had been paid, and refused to pay a further £27 000
expenses claimed by the plaintiffs—the tour had been a financial failure.

The plaintiffs wished to sue the defendants in the English courts on the basis
of the alleged English jurisdiction agreement, but the defendants denied that
they had ever agreed to such.

Judgment

The Court of Appeal held that, in relation to Art. 17 (there were a number of
obiter comments concerning the alternative possibility of national English
jurisdiction over the non-Contracting State defendants, in the absence of agreement on jurisdiction under Art. 17), the existence of the jurisdiction agreement
had to be proven as on *a good arguable case*. This was not easy, given the poor
state of communications between the parties prior to the tour. In the end, however, the court considered that, notwithstanding the absence of express acceptance by the defendants, there was nonetheless a good arguable case that the
latters' failure to object to the plaintiffs' draft contract meant that the latter
had been accepted (referring to *Berghoefer* Case 221/84). The plaintiffs would
hardly have sent the band off on tour without such an understanding.

Comment

Presumably, the meaning of 'good arguable case' here is of a higher standard
than for contracts and torts jurisdiction—a serious issue for determination at
trial—under Art. 5(1) and (3) respectively (see *supra*), simply because the
matter is for determination solely by the court of jurisdiction and not trial
of substance (although, see *supra*, Comment to Case 143, as to possible
applicability of the 'good arguable case' standard generally now).

Case principle

4. A counterclaim does not constitute an agreement to jurisdiction within Art. 17.

Case

217 Rank Film Distributors Limited v Lanterna Editrice Srl and Banca Nazionale del Lavoro [1992] I.L.Pr. 58 High Court, 4 June 1991

Facts

The plaintiff sued the defendants to enforce a contract in England. Subsequently, the first defendant brought an action in Italy to terminate the contract. The plaintiff in England put in a defence and counterclaim in the Italian proceedings.

Judgment

Saville J. held that a counterclaim did not amount to a jurisdiction agreement within Art. 17. The defendants had argued that it did and that second-seised Italian Art. 17 jurisdiction overrode Arts 21 and 22 otherwise favouring first-seised English courts.

Comment

The present writer opposes the English case law giving precedence to Art. 17 over Arts 21 and 22 (see *infra*, 'exclusive jurisdiction'). Presumably, the plaintiff had nonetheless submitted to Italian jurisdiction under Art. 18. Since non-exclusive Art. 18 does not prevail over Art. 21 (see *infra*, Art. 18), and yet, in accordance with *Elefanten Schuh* Case 150/80, Art. 18 has precedence over Art. 17, the anomalous step of giving priority to Art. 17 over Art. 21 is further demonstrated!

Case principles

5. Effects of the parties' jurisdiction agreement are dependent upon the construction of their intentions.
6. If an agreement is expressly limited to provisional security proceedings or similar, it will include *in rem* proceedings for the arrest of a ship, to the extent that those proceedings are not then continued to judgment on the merits of the claim.

Case

218 Ultisol Transport Contractors Ltd v Bouygues Offshore S.A. [1996] 2 Lloyd's Rep. 140 High Court, 2 February 1996

Facts

The defendant in the English proceedings, the French company Bouygues, previously commenced proceedings *in rem* against the plaintiff Bermudan company, Ultisol, in South African courts for damages for the loss of the defendant's barge due to an accident in South African waters in 1994. The defendant had hired a tug from the plaintiff charterer of the tug, but the towline attached to the tug parted from the barge leading to its sinking. In the South African courts the defendant obtained attachment of the tug as security for its claims against the owner and attachment of bunkers on the tug as security for its claims against the plaintiff charterer, Ultisol.

Ultisol sought an injunction from the English courts in the present action, in order to restrain continuation of the South African proceedings on the merits, alleged to be in breach of an exclusive English jurisdiction agreement applicable between plaintiff and defendant under standard terms incorporated. The clause in question stated that English courts were to have exclusive jurisdiction over disputes, except where proceedings were brought elsewhere *in rem* to obtain conservatory seizure or similar remedy over a vessel or other property.

The defendant Bouygues argued that the exception in the jurisdiction clause for conservatory seizure or similar proceedings would include arrest and security *as part of* the process of institution of *in rem* proceedings, and further that since the very essence of those types of action was to obtain eventual judgment against the ship, it followed logically that even continuation of the South African proceedings on the merits was included in the exception to exclusive English jurisdiction in the jurisdiction clause. This was confirmed by the words 'No suit shall be *brought* in any other state' except for conservatory attachment proceedings: 'brought' was to be interpreted as merely meaning 'commenced', not also 'continued'—so, provided that the defendant Bouygues could bring itself within the conservative seizure exception to English jurisdiction, there was then no bar to *continuation* of such proceedings on the merits. It was solely *commencement* on the merits other than in England which was prohibited by the jurisdiction clause.

Judgment

Clarke J. in the Admiralty Court accepted the first, but not the ingenious second, part of the defendant Bouygues' argument.

(1) Arrest and attachment of a vessel, or similar, as security for a claim were to be construed as falling within the permitted exception to exclusive English jurisdiction under the agreement therefor, which was to be interpreted in its total context—it was certainly not in the least bit unusual for ships to be arrested and security to be retained for purposes of enforcement of arbitration awards or judgments on the merits in foreign court proceedings.

(2) But, if the South African proceedings were then to be continued to judgment on the merits, this would be in contravention of the

243

parties' jurisdiction agreement. The whole purpose of the latter was to confine merits to the English courts and yet to allow courts of other states to provide conservatory relief but no more. The defendant Bouygues' construction of the clause, and in particular of the word 'brought', was incorrect and too narrow. *Brought* meant commenced *and continued*, not merely the former—so merits continuation from permitted conservatory proceedings outside England was also prohibited, not just commencement *as* merits. This made sense. It was perfectly normal for attachment to take place as security in one state for merits proceedings in another.

Having thus established the partial applicability of the exclusive English jurisdiction agreement, Clarke J. then went on to consider, therefore, whether an injunction would in fact be granted against continuation of the South African proceedings on the merits and the principles involved in such a discretionary restraint (see *supra*, 1982 Act s.49).

See too *infra*, *The Bergen* [1997] 1 Lloyd's Rep. 380, Case 379.

Case principles

7. A sub-contractor who is also party to the main contractual agreement containing a jurisdiction clause is entitled to benefit from the latter under Art. 17.
8. An English company debentureholder's receiver who sues a party in a contractual relationship with the company is bound by a jurisdiction clause in the contract.

Case

219   Talbot v Edcrest Limited [1993] I.L.Pr. 786 High Court, 28 May 1993

Facts

An English car manufacturing company, Leyland, and its Dutch parent, DAF, entered into an agreement in 1991 with a Dutch company and its English subsidiary, Edcrest Limited, for the storage and transport of its finished vehicles. The English car company fell into financial difficulties in 1991 and a debentureholder appointed the plaintiff receiver. The receiver brought proceedings in England in 1993 against the Dutch and English storage and transport companies for repossession of vehicles worth about £24 million currently stored which the latter refused to supply until it was paid unpaid fees of nearly £4 million. The English storage company, Edcrest, contested English courts' jurisdiction, on the ground that the agreement for storage and transport contained a clause selecting Dutch jurisdiction. However, the plaintiff receivers responded first that Edcrest was merely a sub-contractor to the Dutch storage company and neither party was consequently subject to and entitled to benefit from the Dutch jurisdiction agreement, and secondly, that the plaintiffs themselves, as debentureholders' receivers, were not bound by their company's agreement to Dutch jurisdiction thereunder.

Judgment

The Vice-Chancellor of the Chancery Division of the High Court, Sir Donald Nicholls, rejected the plaintiff receivers' arguments and upheld the Dutch jurisdiction clause so as to decline English jurisdiction.

With regard to the entitlement of Edcrest to rely upon the jurisdiction agreement, as a matter of construction of the main storage and transport contract containing it, Edcrest, not merely its Dutch parent, was a party thereto. Accordingly, whatever the arrangements for performance might be as between parent and subsidiary themselves, Edcrest could take advantage of the Dutch jurisdiction agreement in relation to the other contracting parties, Leyland and DAF, in resisting English courts' jurisdiction.

Secondly, the device of an English debentureholder receivership over Leyland was purely procedural and did not operate as a transfer of substantive rights of the company under the main contract, nor of its property, to the receivers, who continued to hold office as agent for the company. Consequently, the receivers were not freed from the Dutch jurisdiction agreement and could not divest themselves of it. They were bound, as the company itself was, by the exclusive Dutch jurisdiction clause. English courts lacked jurisdiction.

Comment

On the first issue, the European Court's ruling in *Gerling* Case 201/82 in the insurance field would suggest that Edcrest would have been able to rely upon the Dutch jurisdiction clause under Art. 17 in any event, even if not personally party, where the clause had been inserted for its benefit.

As to the second finding, again, even if receivership were to have been regarded as substantive, not merely procedural, transfer of rights, the European Court's decision in *Tilly Russ* Case 71/83 may indicate that the plaintiff receivers would nonetheless have been bound by the Dutch jurisdiction clause under Art. 17.

Case principle

9. A third party assignee of contractual rights subject to a jurisdiction agreement can take the benefit of the latter (*The Tilly Russ* Case 71/83 and *Gerling* Case 201/82 applied and developed).

Case

Firswood Limited v Petra Bank (unreported) Court of Appeal 13 December **220** 1995

Facts

The plaintiff was the assignee of rights under a contract of guarantee concluded between the original creditor (the assignor) and the defendant Jordanian bank (guarantor) in 1987. The plaintiff wished to sue the defendant, by now in liquidation under Jordanian law, in the English courts in 1993. RSC Ord. 11, r.1(2) permitted the plaintiff to serve the writ outside England and Wales *without leave* of the English court, provided that *inter alia* the Convention applied and the defendant was party to a jurisdiction agreement under Art. 17.

The Court of Appeal had already held the Convention to be inapplicable to the proceedings classified as relating to winding up of the defendant bank (see *supra*, Case 125, Art. 1, para. 2(2)), but nevertheless decided to deal with the issue of Art. 17 since it had been argued upon by the parties.

The defendant contended that Art. 17 formalities could not be regarded as having been satisfied on the part of the plaintiff assignee of the original creditor's contractual rights. The plaintiff, on the other hand, pointed out that in *Gerling* the Court of Justice had held a third party, for whose benefit an insurance contract was concluded, to be entitled to take advantage of the jurisdiction clause therein; while in *The Tilly Russ*, a third party buyer of goods shipped was bound by a jurisdiction clause contained in the bill of lading issued by carrier to shipper of which the third party plaintiff became the holder.

Judgment

The Court of Appeal, acknowledging that the facts were not wholly identical to those in *Gerling* and *Tilly Russ* (not made for benefit and assignee wished to adopt, not oppose), nevertheless held that the underlying principles of justice and consensus in those cases were equally applicable to the present.

Consequently, the plaintiff assignee of the original creditor's rights could have taken the benefit of the English jurisdiction clause in the guarantee contract, had the Convention been held to apply. This would not have caused injustice to the defendant to be sued in the agreed forum, especially since such bank guarantees were frequently the subject of assignments in practice.

Comment

As seen, the facts and principle lie inbetween *Gerling* and *Tilly Russ*: (i) jurisdiction agreement not made for assignee's benefit; and (ii) assignee wishes to avail itself of jurisdiction agreement, not to oppose it.

" . . . *agreed* . . . *court* . . . *to have jurisdiction* . . . "

Case principle

1. An election of domicile for purposes of jurisdiction held *not* to amount to an agreement upon *jurisdiction* for purposes of Art. 17.

Case

221 The Kherson [1992] 2 Lloyd's Rep. 261 High Court, 6 April 1992

Facts

The plaintiff Dutch cargo owners wished to sue the Georgian owners of the ship *Kherson* in the English courts for damage to cargo carried on the sister-ship *Kerch*. Under a treaty between the USSR and The Netherlands, the defendants were permitted to elect a Dutch domicile for jurisdiction, which they agreed to do in return for the plaintiffs' agreement not to arrest the *Kerch*. Although, the defendants acknowledged service of the English writ, nevertheless they contested English jurisdiction, *inter alia* (see *infra*, Art. 21), on the ground that the plaintiffs' acceptance of elected Dutch domicile for the defendants amounted to an exclusive Dutch jurisdiction agreement within Art. 17 and English courts consequently ought to decline jurisdiction.

Judgment

Sheen J. held Art. 17 to be inapplicable to the Dutch domicile election: the latter was not an agreement on jurisdiction for the purposes of Art. 17. It was simply that the plaintiffs had accepted the right to sue the defendants in Dutch courts in return for giving up the option of arresting the *Kerch* in Rotterdam as security for their claim.

Such an arrangement was not affected by Art. 17.

Comment

The correctness of the preceding decision may have to be reconsidered in the light of the European Court's ruling in *Mainschiffahrts-Genossenschaft Eg (MSG) v Les Gravières Rhénanes SARL* Case C–106/95, *The Times*, 25 February 1997, in which a purely fictitious place of contractual performance agreement, for purposes of jurisdiction only, was held to be governed by Art. 17, not Art. 5(1) (see Kaye, *Civil Jurisdiction* p. 524, in agreement). In the present writer's opinion, therefore, subject to one possible qualification (see *infra*), it is now extremely doubtful whether Sheen J.'s decision can any longer be regarded as correct and it seems unlikely to be saved through an application of the previous *Zelger v Salinitri* Case 56/79 policy. In the latter, the parties' agreement upon place of performance was held to be subject to Art. 5(1), not Art. 17, jurisdiction because connectional policies underlying Art. 5(1) were still satisfied and consequently inappropriate to be replaced by subjective-intentions policies of Art. 17 jurisdiction. Whereas, in the case of purely fictitious deemed-domicile election of the type involved in *The Kherson*, it cannot be said that the fundamental connectional link underlying the primary Convention rule of defendant's domicile jurisdiction was in any way established. All that there really was to justify the jurisdiction asserted was Art. 17.

However, the qualification to the preceding view, previously mentioned, is simply this: if the effect of the particular rule of the treaty between USSR and The Netherlands was not merely to permit such domicile-for-jurisdiction agreements under their national laws, but *actually to accord the defendant a Dutch domicile for the purposes* on such election, then this would alter the position completely. The English forum would be quite justified in referring to Dutch law in order to determine such Dutch domicile, in accordance with Art. 52, para. 2 or Art. 53, para. 1—and the defendant would legitimately possess a Dutch domicile for the purposes of Art. 2, without reference to Art. 17 requirements for jurisdiction (although, how existence of defendant's registered office or central management and control in The Netherlands would be satisfied for purposes of 1982 Act s.42(6) seat remains a puzzle—deemed again, presumably!).

Case principle

2.   Provision in a standard charterparty form for general average to be 'adjusted in London' construed as not amounting to choice of jurisdiction of English courts.

Case

222   Sameon Co. S.A. v NV Petrofina S.A. ('World Hitachi Zosen'), The Times, 8 April 1996 High Court, 14 March 1996

Facts

The Panamanian plaintiff's ship collided with another ship off the coast of Mauritania and the cargo of crude oil being shipped from Iran to Rotterdam was transferred to another vessel to complete the voyage. The plaintiff was unable to agree general average contribution with the defendant Belgian cargo owners and their insurers and wished to sue through the English courts. They sought to base English jurisdiction on Art. 17: they argued that the provision for general average to be adjusted in London contained in the standard form charterparty, incorporated into the bill of lading, amounted to a choice of English jurisdiction on the merits.

Judgment

Langley J. disagreed with the plaintiffs and upheld the defendants' objection to English courts' jurisdiction. There had to be far stronger evidence of English jurisdiction agreement for purposes of Art. 17. Simply to provide for general average to be 'adjusted' in London, in the absence of contrary practice, did not also amount to choice of English *courts*. 'Adjustment' was merely the non-binding assessment by the London adjuster of the amount of general average contribution.

The plaintiffs appealed to the Court of Appeal.

Case

223   Sameon Co SA v NV Petrofina SA (unreported) Court of Appeal, 30 April 1997

Judgment

The Court of Appeal (Staughton, Henry and Thorpe L.J.J.) unanimously upheld Langley J.'s first instance judgment.

In the absence of contrary agreement, since 'the dawn of time' general average had been dealt with at the port of discharge—Rotterdam—and mere agreement to London adjustment did not amount to implied choice of the latter's courts instead.

See too supra, Art. 5(1), Cases 162 and 163.

Case principle

3.   Jurisdiction clause in commercial guarantee contracts construed so as to cover RSC Ord. 48 proceedings to examine a judgment debtor as to his assets for enforcement, and not as including solely the adjudicatory stage of the proceedings.

Case

Union Bank of Finland Ltd v Lelakis [1996] 4 All ER 305 Court of Appeal, 13   **224**
May 1996

Facts

The Greek defendant was sued in England in 1994 by the plaintiff bank for payment of 10 million US dollars under guarantees. Stay of execution pending the defendant's appeal having been refused, the plaintiff obtained an order for examination of the defendant as to his assets for execution, under RSC Ord. 48. The defendant, who was personally served with the order in Greece, contested that the order was properly served out of England and Wales without leave of the court. There was an English jurisdiction clause in the contracts, which could have enabled such service without leave under rules of court; but the defendant argued that this was merely an agreement to submit to the adjudication stage of the proceedings, not also to enforcement measures.

Judgment

The Court of Appeal agreed with the first instance judge that in a commercial contract, a purposive construction supported the conclusion that the jurisdiction clause was not intended to be limited solely to the adjudication stage and that it also covered proceedings for enforcement of any judgment delivered.

As to whether relevant rules of court then permitted service of the Ord. 48 order, obtained according to such contractual provision, to be served outside England and Wales without leave, the Court of Appeal held that this was the case under RSC Ord. 11, r.9(4), if the writ in the action itself, which led to judgment, *could have been* requested so to be served out without leave under Ord. 11, r.1(2), even if, on the facts, it was not served out, nor even in the form required for such service out (see *supra*, 1982 Act s.25, Comment to Case 87).

> " . . . disputes . . . in connection with a particular legal relationship . . . "

Case principle

1. Dual requirements for claims to be covered by a jurisdiction agreement
    are: (i) the claim must be able to be held to have arisen in connection with
    a particular legal relationship between the parties, as laid down by Art.
    17, para. 1; and (ii) in addition, the parties must have intended the claim
    to be covered by their agreement.

Case

225 Kitechnology BV v Unicor GmbH Rahn Plastmaschinen [1994] I.L.Pr. 560
Court of Appeal, 28 April 1994

Facts

The plaintiffs were an international group of companies which had developed
a new type of durable plastic pipe under secret processes. The defendants, all
German domiciliaries, included companies, together with certain of their
employees, which, in the course of negotiations concerning possible future
manufacture of the pipe, had entered into agreements with the plaintiffs
undertaking not to disclose confidential information regarding the piping
process gained during visits to and inspections at the plaintiffs' factories. The
agreement chose English courts and law in the event of a dispute.

Subsequently, the plaintiffs alleged, *inter alia*, breach of confidence (contract) and procurement of breach of contract (tort) against the defendants.

The question arose, *inter alia*, of whether jurisdiction was conferred upon
English courts under Art. 17 over all of the claims, including those in tort, or
solely over those in contract and solely for breach of the confidence agreement
in respect of information gained at the time of its conclusion, to the exclusion
of claims concerning much later use of the original information alongside further technological developments and processes?

Judgment

Evans L.J., delivering the main judgment of the Court of Appeal, believed that
for claims to be covered by the English jurisdiction agreement, they should satisfy, first, the requirement in Art. 17 that they must arise in connection with a
particular legal relationship—as to which the court gave very little guidance—
and secondly, the further condition that the claims must have been intended to
be covered by the jurisdiction clause as a matter of construction according to
its letter and spirit, as indicated by the European Court of Justice in *Meeth v
Glacetal* Case 23/78 [1978] ECR 2133.

In the case itself, Evans L.J. considered that reference in one of the confidence agreements to information 'developed henceforth' could be taken to prove the parties' intention that claims relating to subsequent, partial ulitisation of the original knowledge as later developed *would* be covered by their agreement and the jurisdiction clause therein; whereas another agreement omitting that formula would be beyond a claim in respect of the developed information.

Further, the judge did not exclude the possibility that any *connected tort claim relating to contractual performance* would also be included within the jurisdiction agreement.

Case principles

2. A jurisdiction clause should be construed as to its scope in a commonsense business manner.
3. The clause should be construed as including tortious, as well as contractual, actions arising from the contractual relations, where tort and contract are closely and inextricably interwoven.

Case

Continental Bank N.A. v Aeakos Compania Naviera S.A. [1994] 1 Lloyd's   **226**
Rep. 505 Court of Appeal, 10 November 1993

Facts

A jurisdiction clause in a loan contract between plaintiff and defendant stated that the defendants *submitted to the jurisdiction of English courts*. On the defendant's default, the defendant instituted proceedings for damages in tort against the plaintiff in the Greek courts, alleging bad faith in contractual performance by the plaintiff. The plaintiff requested English courts to grant an injunction against the defendant, restraining it from proceeding in Greece in contravention of the Art. 17 English jurisdiction clause. The defendant responded that the clause was limited to contractual claims.

Judgment

The Court of Appeal held the English jurisdiction agreement to apply to the Greek action, notwithstanding its tortious nature.

As with arbitration clauses, the courts would adopt a commonsense business construction if the literal, textual meaning would lead to an unrealistic conclusion.

Thus, submission to contractual jurisdiction would include an action for damages in tort, as in the Greek court, where it arose out of contractual performance.

See too *supra*, *Kitechnology BV v Unicor GmbH Rahn Plastmaschinen*, Case 225.

Case

Aggeliki Charis Compania Maritima S.A. v Pagnan S.p.A. (The 'Angelic   **227**
Grace') [1995] 1 Lloyd's Rep. 87 Court of Appeal, 17 May 1994

Facts

The plaintiff Panamanian shipowners chartered the ship *Angelic Grace* to defendant Italian charterers for carriage of grain from Rio Grande to the Italian Adriatic. Damage occurred to the ship and the plaintiffs commenced London arbitration pursuant to an arbitration clause in the charterparty applicable to all disputes from time to time arising out of the contract. The defendants contended that the arbitration agreement only covered contractual, not also tortious, disputes and instituted their own proceedings against the plaintiffs in the Italian courts.

The plaintiffs sought an injunction from the English courts in order to restrain the defendants from proceeding in the Italian courts in breach of the London arbitration agreement (see *supra* 1982 Act s.49, Case 115).

The question arose as to the scope of the arbitration clause: did it also cover claims for damages in tort such as that of the defendants in Italy in respect of the captain's alleged negligence?

Judgment

The Court of Appeal followed the *Continental Bank* case *supra*, applicable to construction of jurisdiction—here arbitration—agreements.

Where tort and contract claims were so closely interwoven that there was a risk of irreconcilable judgments, there existed almost a presumption of construction of the jurisdiction/arbitration clause in favour of 'one-stop adjudication' over both contract and tort in pursuance of the forum agreement.

> " . . . *shall have exclusive jurisdiction* . . . "

Case principle

1. Exclusivity or otherwise of chosen jurisdiction held to be a matter of contractual construction of parties' intentions in the first instance (apart from the *Kurz* principle—see *infra*, Case 229).

Case

228   S & W Berisford plc v New Hampshire Insurance [1990] 2 All ER 321 High Court, 27 November 1989

Facts

See supra, 1982 Act s.49, Comment to Case 111.

The question arose as to whether the English jurisdiction clause in the insurance policy was exclusive or non-exclusive, since the view of the judge,

Hobhouse J., was that even if *forum non conveniens* were able to operate in relation to Convention grounds (held not so in that case—see *supra*, s.49), there would be a difference in its scope of application, according to exclusivity or otherwise of the agreed jurisdiction:

(1) a very strong case would be required for such a stay of English proceedings if the clause was non-exclusive; and

(2) there would be little hope at all of a stay in practice if the clause was exclusive.

Judgment

Hobhouse J. followed the Court of Appeal in *Sohio Supply Co. v Gatoil (U.S.A.) Inc.* [1989] 1 Lloyd's Rep. 588, CA, to the effect that exclusivity was a matter of contractual construction, whether or not the word 'exclusive' was used (p. 591, col. 2). Staughton L.J. had pointed out that the contract there was made between sophisticated businessmen who specifically chose their words as to English jurisdiction, and was not a consumer contract on a printed form (pp. 591, col. 2 to 592, col. 1). Thus, it might be that in certain types of contract, such as insurance, there could be a reason for choosing non-exclusive English jurisdiction—but in *Sohio* there was no call for that construction of choice of English courts, in a contract for the sale of crude oil: ' . . . it may be that they wanted to join the 28 per cent of cases in the Commercial Court where both sides come from overseas; or it may be that they just wanted to choose a neutral forum' (p. 592, col. 1). Either way, the construction normally would be one of exclusive choice of jurisdiction between businessmen.

In the *S & W Berisford* case itself, the clause stated: 'This insurance is subject to English jurisdiction'. Hobhouse J. construed it to be non-exclusive, on the ground that a jurisdiction clause in an insurance policy was most likely, by the very nature of the transaction, to have contemplated actions brought by the policyholder against the insurer rather than the reverse and would therefore not have been intended to bind the policyholder exclusively to sue in the chosen forum, but to afford him an additional forum to those otherwise available.

Comments

Clearly, it would be possible to quarrel with this interpretation of the parties' contractual intention by the judge on the facts!

See too *Nike v Parker* (unreported) Court of Appeal, 31 October 1994.

Case principles

2. Article 17 applies to multiple-choice jurisdiction agreements (applying *Meeth v Glacetal* Case 23/78).

3. Article 17 also applies to a *non*-exclusive jurisdiction agreement.

4. The chosen court therefore has exclusive jurisdiction thereunder.

Case

229 Kurz v Stella Musical Veranstaltungs GmbH [1992] 1 All ER 630 High Court, 26 July 1991

Facts

The plaintiff entered into a share subscription agreement with the defendant German company, expressly subject to non-exclusive choice of English jurisdiction. The plaintiff wished to sue the defendant in the English courts for breach of the agreement. The defendant contested English jurisdiction on the ground, *inter alia*, that Art. 17 was inapplicable to non-exclusive choice of courts; and if it were to apply, so as to render the choice exclusive, this would be to override the parties' intention. The plaintiff countered that Art. 17 would already disregard the parties' will where prescribed formalities were not complied with.

Judgment

Hoffmann J. upheld the validity of the English jurisdiction clause under Art. 17. *Meeth v Glacetal* Case 23/78, in the European Court of Justice, had demonstrated that Art. 17 was not restricted to choice of a single jurisdiction and could encompass several, whether otherwise applicable or not, as specifically provided for in Art. 21. Concentration of jurisdiction was an important Convention object, yet so was respect for the parties' will which should not be overridden.

Article 17 applied. Choice of English jurisdiction was valid.

It does not appear unequivocally from Hoffmann J.'s judgment that the full effects of Art. 17, including exclusivity of the chosen jurisdiction, are to be applied to the non-exclusive jurisdiction agreement thereunder. Much of the judge's deliberation, however, suggests that this was the further implication of his decision.

Comment

This is a difficult judgment. It is quite right for the parties' non-exclusive choice to be given effect to. Yet, Art. 17 itself is clearly not drafted so as to contemplate such a situation; and if it were to be applied so as to confer exclusivity on the chosen jurisdiction, this would conflict with what the parties had agreed. Furthermore, the judge's reference to *Meeth* for support was a little disingenuous. *Meeth* did not sanction non-exclusivity of *jurisdiction* once chosen, but merely of *choice* itself from amongst alternatives available.

Nevertheless, the judge's finding remains consistent with the text: where parties choose jurisdiction, Art. 17 makes it exclusive.

A subsequent first instance decision appeared to confirm that *Kurz* had the effect that a jurisdiction clause to which Art. 17 applied was rendered exclusive.

Case

I.P. Metal Ltd. v Ruote O.Z. S.p.A. [1993] 2 Lloyd's Rep. 60 High Court,   **230**
9 December 1992

Facts

The parties concluded agreements subject to a jurisdiction clause stating 'competent forum London'. The defendants argued that the agreed jurisdiction was not stated to be exclusive and consequently, Art. 17 could not make it so.

Judgment

Waller J. rejected the defendants' challenge and upheld exclusivity of the London jurisdiction clause, on the basis of the following measured explanation: *Kurz* merely meant that if more than one jurisdiction was contemplated in the parties' agreement, Art. 17 would not *prevent* the clause from being valid and enforceable and *exclusionary of non-chosen courts* which would otherwise have possessed jurisdiction. Furthermore, if *one* jurisdiction was chosen, Art. 17, by its terms, made that jurisdiction exclusive.

In another subsequent case, the High Court once again accepted that Art. 17 applied so as to validate a non-exclusive agreement—although, on this occasion, the exclusive effects of Art. 17 were not at issue.

Case

Gamlestaden plc v Casa de Suecia S.A. and Thulin [1994] 1 Lloyd's Rep. 433   **231**
High Court, 3 February 1993

Facts

The parties to a loan contract agreed upon English or Swedish jurisdiction at the plaintiff's election. The defendants argued that *Kurz* was incorrect in holding Art. 17 to be applicable to non-exclusive jurisdiction clauses.

Judgment

Potter J. disagreed with the defendants. *Kurz* had been correct to hold Art. 17 to apply. Here, therefore, English courts would possess jurisdiction over the Spanish defendant by virtue of Art. 17, if English jurisdiction were not otherwise held to exist under Art. 5(1).

Case

Continental Bank N.A. v Aeakos Compania Naviera S.A. [1994] 1 Lloyd's   **232**
Rep. 505 Court of Appeal, 10 November 1994

Facts

See supra, 'particular legal relationship', Case 226.

The parties to the loan agreement included a jurisdiction clause providing that the defendants submitted to English jurisdiction whereas the plaintiffs could sue in other states' courts possessed of jurisdiction. The defendants argued that this did not confer jurisdiction *exclusively* upon the English courts and consequently they could bring proceedings in Greece against the plaintiffs.

Judgment

The Court of Appeal held that in the first instance the exclusive effects of a jurisdiction clause were a matter of contractual construction. Here, the plaintiffs had expressly been granted the contractual right to sue elsewhere rather than solely in England, whereas the defendants had not. Accordingly, applying the maxim *expressio unius exclusio alterius*, it was to be inferred that the defendants were bound to sue, not merely to be sued, exclusively in the English courts.

Because of this conclusion, the Court of Appeal considered it unnecessary to decide:

(1) whether, as argued by the plaintiffs, there was a presumption of exclusivity in the absence of unusual or exceptional circumstances; and

(2) whether the *Kurz* decision (see *supra*) was to be taken to mean that Art. 17 rendered a non-exclusive jurisdiction clause, satisfying its requirements, exclusive in any event.

Case principle

5. *Independent* set-off cannot be pleaded in defence to a main claim, if the set-off claim is subject to an inconsistent jurisdiction agreement which is valid under Art. 17; *transaction* set-off, however, is not so subject to Art. 17 (*obiter*).

Case

233 Aectra Refining and Marketing Inc v Exmar N.V. (The 'New Vanguard') [1995] 1 Lloyd's Rep. 191 Court of Appeal

Facts

The plaintiffs obtained English summary judgment under RSC Ord. 14 against the defendants for 77 million US dollars owed under a settlement agreed in 1988. The defendants sought leave to defend by way of set-off of an amount claimed for off-hire time under a charterparty when the ship, chartered by the plaintiffs, was unavailable for loading. However, the plaintiffs contested the defendants' right to defend on this basis, on the ground that the charterparty was subject to agreed arbitration.

Judgment

The Court of Appeal upheld the plaintiffs' objection to the set-off defence and in so doing treated arbitration agreements and agreements on foreign court jurisdiction, whether under Art. 17 or otherwise, as equivalent.

The court drew a distinction between two types of set-off: independent and transaction. The former involved unrelated claims and simply offered a procedural means to a defendant to settle all accounts with the plaintiff; whereas, the second type concerned related claims between the parties. Thus, if the claim made by way of *independent* set-off was subject to arbitration or to an inconsistent, foreign jurisdiction agreement, these latter would prevail (citing Advocate General Slynn in *Spitzley v Sommer Exploitation S.A.* Case 48/84, p. 793, in support). Not the same, however, in the case of *transaction* set-off, when the set-off would be permitted (and the European Court of Justice's decision in *Meeth v Glacetal* Case 23/78, permitting set-off in the German courts, notwithstanding chosen French jurisdiction for that claim, was also relied on, see Kaye, *Civil Jurisdiction* pp. 653–4).

In the proceedings before the Court of Appeal, the set-off was viewed as *independent* and was therefore refused by the court by way of defence, and arbitration would prevail.

Case principle

6. If a foreign Contracting State's courts exercise jurisdiction in contravention of an Art. 17 English jurisdiction agreement, the English courts can grant an injunction to restrain the plaintiff abroad from proceeding with the foreign action.

Case

Continental Bank N.A. v Aeakos Compania Naviera S.A. [1994] 1 Lloyd's **234** Rep. 505 Court of Appeal, 10 November 1993

See *supra*, Cases 226 and 232.

Facts

Plaintiffs and defendants entered a loan facility agreement containing an English jurisdiction clause. The defendants defaulted but instituted proceedings in Greek courts alleging bad faith in performance by the plaintiffs. As a preliminary to their own English action on the contract, the plaintiffs sought an injunction from the English courts restraining the defendants from proceeding with their Greek action in breach of the English jurisdiction clause. The defendants challenged that English courts should not interfere with foreign Contracting States' courts' proceedings.

Judgment

The Court of Appeal confirmed grant of the injunction. Damages to the plaintiffs from breach of the jurisdiction agreement would have been inadequate. The continuance of the Greek action in breach of Art. 17 was vexatious and oppressive and an injunction was the only effective remedy.

Case principle

7. Article 17 confers exclusive jurisdiction as between *Contracting* States. The chosen court is not obliged to issue an injunction to restrain contravening *non-Contracting* State proceedings—the matter is for national English discretionary principles.

Case

235 Ultisol Transport Contractors Ltd. v Bouygues Offshore S.A. [1996] 2 Lloyd's Rep. 140 High Court, 2 February 1996

Facts

See supra, 1982 Act s.49 and Art. 17 'agreed', Cases 118 and 218.

Judgment

It will be recalled that Clarke J. preferred to limit the influence of Art. 17 to that of competing Contracting State jurisdiction. This meant that the chosen English court was not obliged thereunder to grant an injunction restraining continuation of South African proceedings in contravention. Discretionary national English principles remained applicable.

Case principles

8. Where a shipowner brings proceedings in one Contracting State under Art. 6a for establishment of a liability limitation fund, the latter State's jurisdiction is subject to any inconsistent Art. 17 jurisdiction agreement with the claimant.

9. But if there is more than one potential claimant upon the fund, and not just the plaintiff in another Contracting State with whom the shipowner made an Art. 17 jurisdiction agreement, the court seised of the Art. 6a action to establish the limitation fund need not decline or stay jurisdiction in favour of the Art. 17 court, even if second-seised thereto under Art. 21 or 22. The fund action proceeds (*obiter*).

Case

236 Saipern S.p.A. v Dredging V02 BV and Geosite Surveys Ltd (The 'Volvox Hollandia') [1987] 2 Lloyd's Rep. 520 High Court; [1988] 2 Lloyd's Rep. 361 Court of Appeal, 18 April 1988

See supra, Art. 6, Cases 194 and 195. Note too *infra*, p. 404.

Case principle

10. Article 17 jurisdiction agreements prevail over Art. 21.

Case

Kloeckner & Co. AG v Gatoil Overseas Inc. [1990] 1 Lloyd's Rep. 177 High **237**
Court, 31 July 1989

Facts

See infra, Case 273.

Judgment

Hirst J. held that Arts 16 and 17 were equally as important as Art. 21 under
the Convention system and had a degree of paramountcy over Art. 21 (subsequently followed by the High Court in *Denby v The Hellenic Mediterranean
Lines Co. Ltd* [1994] 1 Lloyd's Rep. 320, Rix J., *infra*).

Case

The Filiatra Legacy [1994] 1 Lloyd's Rep. 513 High Court, 2 April 1991 **238**

Facts

See supra, Art. 16(5), Case 211.

Judgment

Saville J. reached the like conclusion (*obiter*—neither Art. 16 nor 17 was in
fact held to apply).

Case

Continental Bank N.A. v Aeakos Compania Naviera S.A. [1994] 1 Lloyd's **239**
Rep. 505 Court of Appeal, 10 November 1993

See *supra*, Cases 226, 232 and 234.

Facts

The plaintiff and defendant concluded a loan agreement including an English
jurisdiction clause. The plaintiffs wished to sue in England, but the defendants
had previously begun their action in the Greek courts and contested applicability of Art. 17 English jurisdiction in the plaintiff's application for an injunction
to restrain the Greek proceedings, on the ground that Art. 21 or 22 required or
enabled English courts to stay their own jurisdiction as second seised.

Judgment

The Court of Appeal held that Art. 17 prevailed over Art. 21 or 22. Hirst J. in
Kloeckner and Saville J. in *The Filiatra Legacy* were approved of (see *supra*,
Art. 17 and *infra*, Art. 22).

Comments

In *Overseas Union Insurance Limited v New Hampshire Insurance Company* Case C–351/89 [1991] ECR I-3317, both Advocate General Van Gerven and the Court of Justice itself seemed to contemplate that Convention exclusive jurisdiction—or, at least, that in Art. 16—would prevail over Art. 21.

Colman J. followed *Continental Bank, obiter*, in *Lexmar Corporation and Steamship Mutual Underwriting Association (Bermuda) Ltd v Nordisk Skibsrederforening and Northern Tankers (Cyprus) Ltd* [1997] 1 Lloyd's Rep. 289, in relation to prevalence of Art. 17 over Art. 21 (see *infra*, Arts 17 and 22).

In *The Bergen* (unreported), 20 November 1996, Clarke J. in the High Court followed and applied the reasoning in, *inter alia*, *Continental Bank*, confirming the overriding nature of Art. 17, in the course of justifying the latter's exclusion from application in relation to a case governed by the 1952 Brussels Arrest Convention under 1968 Art. 57, on the ground that Art. 17 would otherwise thereby have displaced 1952 jurisdiction, which would have been in contravention of Art. 57 (see *infra*, Art. 57).

Case principle

11(a).   Article 17 prevails over Art. 22.

Case

240   Continental Bank N.A. v Aeakos Compania Naviera S.A. [1994] 1 Lloyd's Rep. 505 Court of Appeal, 10 November 1993

Facts

See supra, Cases 226, 232, 234 and 239.

The plaintiff bank concluded an agreement with the defendants for provision of a loan facility, including an English jurisdiction clause. The defendants defaulted, but instituted proceedings in Greece against the plaintiff, claiming bad faith in performance. The plaintiffs sought an injunction from the English courts, as a preliminary to their own action on the agreement, restraining the Greek action in breach of the English jurisdiction agreement. The defendants challenged the English courts' Art. 17 jurisdiction as being second seised to the Greek under Art. 21 or 22.

Judgment

The Court of Appeal held that English Art. 17 jurisdiction was not subject to Art. 21 or 22.

This finding was said to follow from the very structure and system of the Convention: it would be absurd and against principles of party autonomy if a party to an Art. 17 jurisdiction agreement were to be able to escape its effects through institution of proceedings in a different country's courts at a prior date. Article 17 was in mandatory terms and, unlike national English jurisdiction, Convention grounds were not discretionary.

Comment

The Court of Appeal's decision is entirely consistent with the prevailing trend regarding relations between Arts 17 *and 21* (see *supra*); and in *Toepfer International GmbH v Molino Boschi Srl* [1996] 1 Lloyd's Rep. 510 (see *supra*, Case 129), Mance J. in the High Court followed the Court of Appeal in *Continental Bank v Aeakos*, in giving precedence to Art. 17 over Art. 22 (and 21).

However, in the case of Art. 22, there was a previous High Court judgment which did not go as far as *Continental Bank*, in merely raising a kind of *presumption* that Art. 17 prevailed over Art. 22, whatever the position as to Art. 21: *I.P. Metal Ltd v Ruote O.Z. S.p.A.* [1993] 2 Lloyd's Rep. 60, 9 December 1992.

Since the House of Lords or European Court of Justice will eventually be called upon to reach a definitive decision on the issue, it is instructive to consider the alternative approach adopted by Waller J. in the High Court in *I.P. Metal Ltd. v Ruote O.Z. S.p.A.*

Case principle

11(b). Article 17 is subject in principle to Art. 22. But the discretion will not be exercised in favour of a stay of chosen English jurisdiction, if *either* the foreign court is assumed to reach the same decision as to applicability of Art. 17 *or* in any event it would be unjust to order a stay because a defence would exist in the foreign court unavailable according to applicable law in the English proceedings.

Case

I.P. Metal Ltd v Ruote O.Z. S.p.A. [1993] 2 Lloyd's Rep. 60 High Court,   **241**
9 December 1992

Facts

The plaintiffs concluded seven contracts for the sale of aluminium to the Italian defendants. Six of the contracts were sued upon in England and Art. 17 held to apply. But Italian courts were first seised of the defendants' action against the plaintiffs on the seventh contract, held to be related within Art. 22, para. 3. The defendants requested the chosen English court to exercise its discretion to stay under Art. 22.

Judgment

Waller J. refused to stay the second-seised English action.

Cases on the relationship between Arts 17 and 21 were not in point, because it was Art 22, not 21, which was in issue.

Thus, in the first place, the English court would assume that an Italian judge would also find Art. 17 to be applicable and therefore decline in favour of exclusive English jurisdiction.

Secondly, even if this were to be disproved, a stay would be unjust to the plaintiffs in England because Italian courts would apply a different governing law to the contract, which would offer a defence unavailable to the defendant in the English proceedings.

Comment

Consequently, the principle which would have had to have been inferred from this case, but for its inconsistency with the subsequent Court of Appeal decision in *Continental Bank, supra*, would have been as follows:

(1)   Article 17 is subject in principle to Art. 22.
(2)   But the discretion will *not* be exercised in favour of a stay of chosen English jurisdiction, if *either* the foreign court is assumed to reach the same decision as to applicability of Art. 17 *or* in any event it would be unjust to order a stay because a defence would exist in the foreign court unavailable according to applicable law in the English proceedings.

There seems something not wholly satisfactory about a view which states that: (i) Art. 17 must prevail over Art. 21 because otherwise it *never* would, whereas; (ii) Art. 17 need not prevail over Art. 22 because it could, in effect, do so whenever the discretion was not exercised in favour of a stay under Art. 22. The priority of both Arts 21 and 22, or otherwise, should surely be a matter of Convention principle, if the doctrine is to remain consistent. The writer's view, against the English case law, is that Arts 21 and 22 prevail over Art. 17.

Notwithstanding which, *Continental Bank* was expressly followed and developed in the High Court in a subsequent case.

Case principle

12.   Article 17 prevails over Art. 22 even when the foreign related action was not brought by a party to the jurisdiction agreement.

Case

242   Lexmar Corporation and Steamship Mutual Underwriting Association (Bermuda) Ltd v Nordisk Skibsrederforening and Northern Tankers (Cyprus) Ltd [1997] 1 Lloyd's Rep. 289 High Court, 2 April 1996

Facts

See supra, Art. 1, para. 2(4) 'arbitration', Case 133.

The plaintiff, Lexmar, wished to sue the Norwegian defendant, Nordisk, in the English courts on the defendant's agreement to pay the plaintiff's costs of London arbitration to which the defendant itself was not a party, subject to an exclusive choice of English law and jurisdiction. The defendant contested English courts' Lugano Art. 17 jurisdiction, *inter alia* (see *supra*, Art. 1, para. 2(4)), on the grounds that Norwegian courts were first seised of a related action brought against the plaintiff by Northern Tankers in order to attach the debt owed by defendant to plaintiff, in payment of sums owed (from American arbitration) by the plaintiff to Northern Tankers.

The plaintiff argued that even if English and Norwegian actions were related, this was irrelevant because Art. 17 prevailed over Art. 22 in any event.

Judgment

Colman J. agreed with the plaintiff and expressly followed *Continental Bank*. Article 17 had to prevail over Art(s) 22 (and 21) according to the logic and structure of the Convention. Exclusive jurisdiction agreements reached according to the parties' free will could not be allowed to be undermined simply by bringing a pre-emptive action elsewhere, which would deprive Art. 17 *exclusivity* of much of its significance. Therefore, where Art. 17 applied, there was a blanket exclusion of Arts 21 and 22. This was no less the case where, as here, the (allegedly) related action in first-seised Norwegian courts was in fact brought by someone other than a party to the English jurisdiction agreement, namely, Northern Tankers.

Case principle

13. Article 17 is inconsistent with *in rem* arrest jurisdiction under the 1952 Brussels Arrest Convention and consequently is excluded under 1968 Convention Art. 57.

Case

The Bergen [1997] 1 Lloyd's Rep. 380 High Court, 20 November 1996   **243**

Facts and Judgment

See *infra*, Art. 57, Case 379.

Comment

The judge, Clarke J., commented that the outcome was unlikely to be any different in practice, since English courts were highly likely to exercise their national law discretionary power to stay *in rem* proceedings, in favour of chosen foreign jurisdiction, just as they would have been obliged to do had Art. 17 been held to be applicable.

ARTICLE 17, PARAGRAPH 1(a)

" . . . *in writing or evidenced in writing* . . . "

Case principle

Article 17 formal requirements operate to the exclusion of national rules of form.

Case

244 Denby v The Hellenic Mediterranean Lines Co. Ltd [1994] 1 Lloyd's Rep. 320 High Court, 29 October 1993

Facts

The plaintiff insurance underwriters brought English proceedings against the defendant shipowners for avoidance of the insurance policy through misrepresentation. Jurisdiction of the English courts under Art. 17 was sought to be founded upon an English jurisdiction clause incorporated into the signed slip contract by reference to the well-known MAR form of Lloyd's marine policy containing the clause. The defendants challenged jurisdiction, *inter alia* (see *infra*, Art. 21), on the ground that the Greek procedural code required such incorporation not only to be clear and express but also that the document containing the clause should be attached to the contract.

Judgment

Rix J. rejected the challenge to the English jurisdiction agreement. Article 17 was a self-contained code to decide whether parties had or had not agreed upon a jurisdiction clause (citing passages from the European Court's judgment in *Elefanten Schuh v Jacqmain* Case 150/80 [1981] ECR 1671, at 1687–1688). Consequently, Greek procedural law had no bearing upon the question.

> *" . . . in writing . . . "*

Case principle

An express reference in a written contract to general conditions containing a jurisdiction clause is sufficient to satisfy the 'in writing' requirement, in accordance with the European Court's judgment in *Salotti* Case 24/76, even if the general conditions are not, as in *Salotti*, printed on the reverse of the contract and are not otherwise made readily available at contract to the party upon whom they are sought to be imposed.

Case

245 Crédit Suisse Financial Products v Société Générale d'Entreprises [1997] I.L. Pr. 165 Court of Appeal, 4 July 1996

Facts

The plaintiff English company and defendant French company made an agreement by fax in 1994 for the sale of a bond-put-option by defendant to plaintiff. The plaintiff's faxed offer, thereafter accepted by the defendant by fax, referred to the International Swaps and Derivatives Association's General Conditions containing an English jurisdiction clause, by way of incorporation into the contract. The plaintiff subsequently wished to sue the defendant in England for payment of approximately 10 million French francs under the transaction, but the defendant denied that the English jurisdiction clause in the general conditions satisfied the Art. 17(1)(a) 'in writing' requirement.

Judgment

The Court of Appeal upheld the jurisdiction agreement as being in writing under Art. 17(1)(a).

The court followed the true consensus approach of the European Court of Justice in *Salotti v Rüwa*. In that case, explained the Court of Appeal, the requirement of communication of the general conditions to the addressee was restricted to where there was an onward reference to the general conditions in the document—there a prior offer—referred to in the written contract. It did not also apply where, as in the present case, the reference to the general conditions containing the jurisdiction clause was made in the written contract itself.

Thus, *provided that* the reference in the written contract was clear and *express*, and not indirect nor implied, this would satisfy the Art. 17(1)(a) in writing requirement and guarantee existence of the true consent to the jurisdiction clause.

Comments

See too supra, Denby v The Hellenic Mediterranean Lines Co. Ltd, Case 244.

It is not wholly clear from *Salotti* whether such mere reference directly to the general conditions containing the jurisdiction clause *is* sufficient. At least, the general conditions referred to should be able to be checked and the jurisdiction clause discovered by a party using reasonable care—and it is even possible that the general conditions must actually be communicated together with the document referring thereto. Simply because the situation in *Salotti*, requiring this, involved an indirect, onward reference, it need not necessarily follow that this would not also be required in the case of a direct reference to the other document containing the general conditions with jurisdiction clause (see Kaye, *Civil Jurisdiction* p.1039).

> " . . . *evidenced in writing* . . . "

Case principle

Where a party sends a telex containing general conditions including a jurisdiction clause by way of confirmation of previous oral acceptance of order and jurisdiction, there is sufficient written evidence and consensus to satisfy Art. 17 in the absence of objection by the recipient within a reasonable time (*Segoura Case 25/76 and Berghoefer Case 221/84 applied*).

Case

246 I.P. Metal Ltd v Ruote O.Z. S.p.A. [1993] 2 Lloyd's Rep. 60 High Court, 9 December 1992

Facts

The plaintiffs wished to sue the Italian defendants in England on contracts for the sale of aluminium to the defendants. The agreements were negotiated orally on the telephone and subsequently the plaintiffs telexed confirmation of acceptance, containing general conditions with an English jurisdiction clause.

The defendants contested English jurisdiction under Art. 17, on the ground that there was a lack of consensus as required by the Court of Justice in its case law on Art. 17.

Judgment

Waller J. upheld the English jurisdiction clause.

Article 17 formalities and consensus, in accordance with *Salotti*, *Segoura* and *Berghoefer*, were independent but with overlapping requirements.

Berghoefer had established that a recipient of unilateral confirmation in writing must raise an objection within a reasonable time of receipt if the confirmation is not to be regarded as sufficient written evidence of express oral agreement to jurisdiction for purposes of Art. 17, para. 1, which had not been carried out in the present case. *In addition*, as time went on and orders were performed, there was further evidence of consensus and of a continuing trading relationship subject to the jurisdiction clause, in accordance with *Segoura* (even if no prior express oral agreement on jurisdiction).

Comment

See Kaye, Civil Jurisdiction, pp. 1045–50.

ARTICLE 17, PARAGRAPH 1(c)

" . . . *in such trade or commerce is widely known to, and regularly observed by, parties . . .* "

Case

Denby v The Hellenic Mediterranean Lines Co. Ltd [1994] 1 Lloyd's Rep. 320   **247**
High Court, 29 October 1993

Facts

An insurance contract contained in a slip was drawn up by the defendant
shipowners' insurance brokers and was stamped and initialled by the plaintiff
insurance underwriters. The slip referred to the well-known MAR form of
Lloyd's marine policy, which contained an English jurisdiction clause. The
defendants questioned whether Art. 17 formalities had been satisfied.

Judgment

The court held that both sub-paras (a) and (c) of Art. 17, para. 1 were satisfied. The contract was in writing or evidenced in writing and in a well-known
form of international trade or commerce.

ARTICLE 17, PARAGRAPH 5 (LUGANO 4)

" . . . for the benefit of . . . "

Case principle

An English jurisdiction agreement between borrower and lender, expressed to
be for the lender's benefit, will be construed as applicable to proceedings in
which the borrower is plaintiff, not solely where he is defendant.

Case

Ocarina Marine Ltd v Marcard Stein & Co. [1994] 2 Lloyd's Rep. 524 High   **248**
Court, 13 May 1994

Facts

The plaintiff shipowners entered financing agreements with the defendant
German bank for the provision of loan facilities to a London branch bank
account. The relevant agreements chose English law and jurisdiction for the
settlement of any disputes and this was expressed to be 'for the benefit of
the lender'. When the defendant terminated the loans facility in 1992, the
plaintiffs sought to bring proceedings for damages and repayment of funds in
accounts before the English courts pursuant to the jurisdiction agreement
under Art. 17 (and on the ground of England as Art. 5(1) place of performance, see *supra* Art. 5(1) 'principal obligation'). The defendant challenged

English jurisdiction, on the ground that since the English jurisdiction agreement was expressed to be for its benefit, the agreement should be construed as limited in its effect to where the lender was plaintiff in England and the borrower the defendant—not also the reverse as in the current proceedings.

Judgment

Rix J. held against the defendants and consequently in favour of chosen English jurisdiction under Art. 17 as a matter of contractual construction in accordance with English applicable law.

The jurisdiction clause referred to English courts' power to settle *any* disputes, without confining this to those instituted by the lender. Had the parties wished for the latter, they could have stipulated this expressly.

Furthermore, although the jurisdiction agreement was expressed to be for the defendant bank's benefit, this had in fact borrowed the phrase from Art. 17, para. 5 (Lugano Art. 17(4)) and therefore related to the retention *by the benefited party of the ability to bring proceedings* in the chosen jurisdiction or elsewhere thereunder and consequently was not also concerned with the situation in which the benefited party was defendant. So, therefore, should the parties' jurisdiction clause be correspondingly construed.

Comment

Rix J.'s judgment is by no means secure from attack in the future, on grounds of construction and principle.

ARTICLE 18

" . . . *defendant enters an appearance* . . . "

Case principle

1. The procedural step of acknowledgement of service of a writ *in personam* held *not* to constitute entry of appearance for purposes of Art. 18.

Case

249 The Sydney Express [1988] 2 Lloyd's Rep. 257 High Court, 22 April 1988

Facts

The plaintiffs sued the defendant German shipowners for damage to cargo in transit. The defendants contested English *in personam* jurisdiction, on the ground of a German jurisdiction clause in the bill of lading. The plaintiffs asserted that the defendants had nonetheless submitted to English fora under

Art. 18 through their 'entry of appearance' to the English writ (which took precedence over agreed German Art. 17 jurisdiction according to *Elefanten Schuh* Case 150/80); and they further argued that since the defendants had merely sought a stay of the English proceedings, rather than requesting the English court to decline jurisdiction under RSC Ord. 12, r.8, their 'entry of appearance', consequently, was not solely to contest the English jurisdiction.

Judgment

Sheen J. ordered the English action to be stayed in favour of agreed German jurisdiction under Art. 17. The defendants had not 'entered an appearance' for purposes of Art. 18 simply through their acknowledgement of service, which was a neutral procedural step.

(Furthermore, even if acknowledgement of service had amounted to 'entry of appearance', the application to stay the English action *would* have shown that the former was solely to contest the English jurisdiction: see *infra*.)

Comments

Presumably, notice of intention to defend would have amounted to entry of appearance for Art. 18—although this might still have been solely in order to contest the jurisdiction (see *infra*).

See Kaye, *Civil Jurisdiction* p. 1117, for a contrary approach to Sheen J.'s, treating acknowledgement of service as entry of appearance.

The domestic rule of procedure in RSC Ord. 12, r.10, although not unequivocally transferable to the international, Convention Article 18 sphere, nonetheless supports the view in Kaye, p. 1117, by expressly providing that acknowledgement is to be treated as entry of appearance. In practice, acknowledgement will invariably be accompanied by notice of intention to defend.

Case principles

2. Acknowledgement of *issue* of a writ *in rem* against a ship held to amount to submission.
3. Provision of bail to avoid arrest or to obtain release of a ship amounts to submission to the jurisdiction.

Case

The 'Prinsengracht' [1993] 1 Lloyd's Rep. 41 High Court, 24 June 1992   **250**

Facts

Plaintiff cargo owners claimed against defendant Dutch shipowners in the English courts for damage to the cargo. In order to avoid arrest of their ship, the Prinsengracht, as it sailed towards an English port, the defendants issued a bail bond for the plaintiffs and acknowledged issue of the plaintiffs' writ *in rem*, not yet served. Subsequently, on the same day, the plaintiffs arrested the ship.

The defendants challenged English jurisdiction: (i) the arrest *following bail* was ineffective to confer *in rem* jurisdiction under the 1952 Arrest Convention by virtue of 1968 Convention Art. 57 and 1982 Act s.9(1) (see *infra*, Art. 57 and *supra*, s.9(1)); and (ii) neither Acknowledgement of Issue of the writ nor provision of bail amounted to submission to English jurisdiction (under Art. 18).

Judgment

The judge, Sheen J., dealt first with the question of submission: for even if Art. 57 were held to be unable to confer *in rem* jurisdiction, English courts might still be able to decide, on the ground of submission by the Dutch defendant.

Sheen J. held that the defendants had submitted to English jurisdiction in two ways, as follows.

(1) Acknowledgement of *issue* of the writ *before service*. The defendants did not have to do this. That they had done so was the clearest submission to the jurisdiction.

(2) Provision of bail. Historically, bail to avoid arrest was an undertaking by the defendant *to the court* to satisfy any judgment reached and it was considered to be an absurdity by Sheen J. that the defendant could thereafter nonetheless assert that it had not in fact submitted to the court's jurisdiction.

(Again, in *The Deichland infra*, the Court of Appeal had indicated that in the absence of effective arrest, the English courts might still possess jurisdiction through express agreement or submission by the defendant.)

Case

251 The Anna H [1994] 1 Lloyd's Rep. 287 High Court, 4 October 1993

Facts

The plaintiffs wished to proceed *in rem* in the English courts against German shippers of cargo from England and Wales to Barcelona, which arrived in a damaged condition. In order to avoid arrest, the defendants' P. & I. Club insurers undertook to the plaintiffs to provide bail and to acknowledge issue and service of the writ and entered a caveat against arrest for this purpose. Notwithstanding, the plaintiffs arrested the ship Anna H. for one hour before release, following which the P. & I. Club provided bail and the defendants acknowledged service.

The defendants contested English jurisdiction. German courts should instead hear the claim in accordance with Art. 2, as those of their domicile.

Judgment

Clarke J. upheld English jurisdiction.

This was, first, on the ground of arrest of the ship within the English jurisdiction, by virtue of Art. 57 (see *infra*).

Secondly, the decision was made that the German defendants had submitted to the English jurisdiction through provision of bail, following the judgment of Sheen J. in *The Prinsengracht*: as a matter of construction of the bail bond, the defendants, and not merely their P. & I. sureties, were submitting to the jurisdiction.

However, the judge did also find that:

(1) filing a caveat against arrest did not amount to submission by the defendants, because this was merely a revocable undertaking to take future steps;

(2) acknowledgement of 'service' of the writ (as opposed to *issue* in *The Prinsengracht*) was also not submission if, in accordance with Art. 18, this was solely for the purpose of contesting English jurisdiction; and

(3) if bail was given under protest (not so here), it would not amount to submission.

Comments

The advice generally to defendants, therefore, whether in *in rem* or in *in personam* actions, is to decline to acknowledge *issue* of the writ, since the latter will amount to entry of appearance if not required procedurally at that stage (although still possibly solely in order to contest jurisdiction, see *infra*).

Point (2) preceding may simply mean, consistent with *The Sydney Express supra*, that acknowledgement of *service* does not amount to entry of appearance in the first place for Art. 18—otherwise, there is a possible conflict between the two, unless the narrow issue of *in personam* and *in rem* nature of respective proceedings were to be taken to distinguish them.

In the Court of Appeal proceedings in *The Anna H* [1995] 1 Lloyd's Rep. 287 Court of Appeal, 26 May 1994 (see *infra*, Art. 57), Clarke J.'s first instance judgment was upheld. Procedural steps of mere acknowledgement of service or provision of bail, without more, were doubted as amounting to submission so as to preclude the shipowner from subsequently challenging jurisdiction.

> " . . . *solely to contest the jurisdiction* . . . "

Case principle

1. Entry of appearance followed by an application to stay in favour of agreed foreign jurisdiction is solely to contest the English jurisdiction.

Case

252   The Sydney Express [1988] 2 Lloyd's Rep. 257 High Court, 22 April 1988

Facts

See supra, Case 249.

Judgment

Sheen J. held that even if the defendants had been treated as having entered an appearance by reason of their acknowledgement of service of the English writ (see *supra*), this would still have been solely to contest the English court's jurisdiction, in view of their application for a stay of the action in favour of agreed German Art. 17 jurisdiction. He rejected the plaintiffs' argument that nothing less than an application to the English court to *decline* jurisdiction under RSC Ord. 12, r.8, rather than merely to *stay* on a procedural motion, would suffice to amount to contestation of jurisdiction under Art. 18. A request to stay was perfectly appropriate in the case of a foreign jurisdiction agreement.

Case principles

2.   A defendant who enters a merits defence contemporaneously with contesting jurisdiction, as required by national procedure, is treated as having entered appearance solely to contest the jurisdiction under Art. 18 (*Elefanten Schuh* and *Rohr* applied).
3.   Article 18 does *not* take priority over Arts 21 and 22.

Case

253   Rank Film Distributors v Lanterna Editrice Srl and Banca Nazionale del Lavoro [1992] I.L.Pr. 58 High Court, 4 June 1991

Facts

The English High Court was held to possess contracts jurisdiction over the Italian defendants under Art. 5(1). Subsequently, the first defendant had commenced proceedings in Italy against Rank for termination of the contract. Rank put in a defence and counterclaim at the same time as contesting jurisdiction of the Italian courts. The first defendant in England argued that Rank had thereby submitted to Italian courts' jurisdiction under Art. 18; and that Art. 18 took priority over Arts 21 and 22, so that although English courts were first seised under Art. 5(1), they would nevertheless have to concede jurisdiction to the Italian courts possessed of jurisdiction under Art. 18.

Judgment

Saville J. rejected this plea.

(1) In the first place, Art. 18 did not confer jurisdiction upon the Italian courts where Rank, as here, had entered an appearance solely in order to contest Italian jurisdiction.

(2) Secondly, in any event, even if Art. 18 had applied in Italy, it did *not* override Arts 21 and 22. English courts were first-seised and therefore took priority under these latter.

Case principle

4. A defendant who pleads to the merits for the first time at the same time as and no earlier than contesting jurisdiction does not submit to the jurisdiction within Art. 18, even though procedurally he was *not required* to defend the merits at that stage, provided that he only did so as a subsidiary and precautionary measure and that his primary purpose was to challenge the jurisdiction (*Elefanten Schuh* applied).

Case

Toepfer International GmbH v Molino Boschi Srl [1996] 1 Lloyd's Rep. 510   **254**
High Court, 17 January 1996

Facts

See supra, Arts 1, para. 2(4) and 17 and infra, Arts 21 and 22.

The defendants argued that English Art. 17 jurisdiction did not apply because the plaintiffs had submitted to the defendants' Italian proceedings under Art. 18 (see *Elefanten Schuh*) through putting in a defence to the merits alongside their challenge to Italian jurisdiction when they were not required to do so procedurally.

Judgment

Mance J. held that provided that the jurisdiction challenge was made at the same time as or prior to the defence on the merits, the plaintiffs had not submitted to the Italian court for purposes of Art. 18 where the pleadings made it abundantly clear that their primary purpose was to deny the Italian courts' jurisdiction and that the merits defence was merely a subsidiary and precautionary measure.

Case principle

5. An application by a defendant for extension of time to put in a defence on the merits does not amount to submission under Art. 18 and appearance can remain solely to contest jurisdiction (*Elefanten Schuh Case 150/80* applied).

Case

Kurz v Stella Musical Veranstaltungs GmbH [1992] 1 All ER 630 High Court,   **255**
26 July 1991

Facts

The German defendants to the English writ for breach of contract, sought discovery of documents and obtained an extension of the time for service of a defence, following their acknowledgement of service of the writ and notice of intention to defend. *Subsequently*, they initiated procedural steps to challenge English jurisdiction. The plaintiffs argued that the defendants had submitted to English jurisdiction under Art. 18: their 'entry of appearance' was not solely to contest the English courts' jurisdiction.

Judgment

Hoffmann J. held that the defendants had not submitted.

The defendants' application for discovery of documents mentioned in the plaintiff's statement of claim could be purely for purposes of a jurisdiction challenge, such as to determine place of performance of a contract.

Their application to extend the time for putting in a defence on the merits was not submission. In *Elefanten Schuh* the European Court of Justice had indicated that appearance could still be solely to contest jurisdiction under Art. 18, provided that the challenge was not made subsequently to the time of first defence according to national procedure. Here, this was satisfied by the defendant: applying for an extension was not the same as putting in the first defence, which meant stating what the defence was. At the time of the defendant's jurisdiction challenge, the defendant had not yet stated its defence.

See too *Hewden Stuart, infra*, Case 258.

Case principle

6. Application by a defendant for extension of time to comply with a disclosure order held not to amount to Art. 18 submission, where intention to contest jurisdiction was previously made clear in affidavit evidence.

Case

256   The Xing Su Hai [1995] 2 Lloyd's Rep. 15 High Court, 22 February 1995

Facts

See supra, 1982 Act s.25(2), Case 96.

The plaintiffs tried to assert that the German defendants had submitted to English jurisdiction because the order granted to extend their time for disclosure of assets did not include a repetition of their earlier declared intent to contest English jurisdiction.

Judgment

Rix J. rejected the plaintiffs' argument—there was sufficient evidence of the defendants' intention not to submit to English jurisdiction.

Case principle

7. Where the defendant contests jurisdiction so as not to submit to the merits, but subsequently, having lost the jurisdiction challenge, decides to defend the merits, he is thereby to be taken to have submitted to the proceedings on the merits.

Case

Marc Rich & Co. A.G. v Società Italiana Impianti P.A. (The Atlantic Emperor)   **257**
(No. 2) [1992] 1 Lloyd's Rep. 624 Court of Appeal

Facts

Swiss plaintiffs alleged breach of contract by the defendant Italian sellers of oil. The defendants commenced proceedings in Italy against the plaintiffs for a declaration of non-liability in 1988, subsequent to which the plaintiffs brought an English action for appointment of an arbitrator in England and challenged jurisdiction in Italy, requesting judgment in their favour on the merits in the event of failure on the jurisdiction point. The defendants sought a stay of the English proceedings as second-seised to the Italian under Art. 21. However, the first instance English judge held the Convention, including Art. 21, to be inapplicable to arbitration under Art. 1, para. 2(4), and the Court of Appeal referred to the European Court of Justice to decide whether arbitration-appointment proceedings fell within the Art. 1, para. 2(4) arbitration exclusion, notwithstanding the defendants' denial of any agreement upon arbitration (see *supra*). In the meantime, the plaintiffs' challenge to jurisdiction in Italy was rejected by the Italian court, following which they made further pleadings on the merits. After that the European Court ruled that an incidental issue of arbitral-existence would not affect the Convention's applicability or otherwise to the main subject matter of the proceedings. Accordingly, the Court of Appeal held the main application for appointment of an arbitrator to remain outside the Convention's scope, as excluded arbitration, whatever the status, as also excluded or otherwise, of the incidental arbitral-existence issue (*supra*). Under applicable discretionary national English principles of jurisdiction, therefore, the English courts declined to stay in favour of Italian jurisdiction, as had the Italians *vice versa*.

The subsequent stages of the dispute on jurisdiction which came before the English Court of Appeal were as follows.

(1) The plaintiffs requested an injunction from the English courts to restrain the defendants from proceeding with their Italian action.

(2) In respect of this application, the approach of the English courts was to refuse to grant the injunction if any Italian judgment on the issue of arbitral-existence would have to be recognized so as to create an issue estoppel in the English courts.

(3) This in turn meant that 1982 Act s.32 would have to be applied, according to which a foreign judgment in breach of an arbitration or jurisdiction agreement was to be refused recognition in prescribed circumstances. Recognition would not be refused thereunder *if the defendant submitted to the foreign jurisdiction*, within the meaning of s.33. Another circumstance in which the English court would not refuse recognition under s.32 was where the judgment was required to be recognized under the Judgments Convention (see *supra*).

There were, therefore, two main areas of dispute between the parties:

(1) had the plaintiffs *submitted* to Italian jurisdiction in accordance with s.33, so that an Italian judgment against arbitral-existence and contravention of allegedly agreed arbitration would nonetheless have to be recognized under s.32; and

(2) even if the plaintiffs had not submitted, would the Italian arbitral-existence ruling still have to be recognised *under the Judgments Convention*, in view of the European Court's ruling on scope?

Judgment

In respect of submission, the Court of Appeal applied principles laid down in relation to Art. 18 in *Elefanten Schuh*: namely, that defence on merits is not submission, if jurisdiction is also contested contemporaneously or prior thereto.

In the present proceedings, the plaintiffs initially only pleaded to Italian merits in order to be able to challenge Italian jurisdiction.

However, when the plaintiffs put in further defences to the merits, having already lost their challenge to Italian jurisdiction, their actions would then amount to submission to the Italian jurisdiction.

Accordingly, the injunction would be refused.

Comments

Although the Court of Appeal reached its decision primarily in relation to the meaning of submission in the *national* non-recognition context of ss.32 and 33 of the 1982 Act, the Court of Appeal clearly regarded its explanation and development of the *Elefanten Schuh* principle as equally applicable to Art. 18 itself.

In view of its conclusion as to submission, leading to recognition of any Italian judgment on arbitral-existence at national law, unhindered by s.32, it was unnecessary for the Court of Appeal to decide whether, as a result of the European Court's ruling in *Marc Rich*, the Convention would be applicable thereto so as to require recognition (submission or other jurisdiction not being a prerequisite to recognition thereunder) in which case s.32 non-recognition would be inoperative according to its terms (see *supra*, Art. 1, para. 2(4)).

(For a discussion and critique of the decision of the Court of Appeal, see 'Forensic Submission as a Bar to Arbitration' (1993) *Civil Justice Quarterly* 359.)

Case principle

8. Procedural responses by a defendant to the substance of a case do not amount to submission, if they go no further than is necessary to safeguard the defendant's substantive defence at the date of the challenge to jurisdiction (consistent with *Elefanten Schuh*).

Case

Hewden Stuart Heavy Cranes Ltd v Leo Gottwald Kommanditgesellschaft **258** (unreported) Court of Appeal, 13 May 1992

Facts

The plaintiffs wished to sue the German defendants in the English courts for damages for breach of contract to supply a crane, and sought to base English jurisdiction upon the defendants' alleged submission under Art. 18 (as well as upon Art. 5(1), *supra*, Case 154).

Judgment

The Court of Appeal held that the defendants had not submitted merely through: (i) seeking an extension of time to put in a defence, *without prejudice to the jurisdiction challenge* (see *Kurz*, *supra*); (ii) requesting security for costs *up to and including the jurisdiction hearing*; or (iii) challenging contractual or tortious existence *purely for the purpose of contesting applicability of Convention jurisdiction grounds* in contract or tort.

ARTICLE 21, PARAGRAPH 1

" . . . *involving the same cause of action* . . . "

Case principle

1. The same cause of action is involved where each party to an accident sues the other for negligence.

Case

The Linda [1988] 1 Lloyd's Rep. 175 High Court, 23 October 1987   **259**

Facts

The plaintiffs' ship, Arco Humber, collided with the defendants' ship, Linda, in international waters. The defendants arrested the Arco Humber in The Netherlands in April 1987 and subsequently released it on provision of security, whereupon they commenced their Dutch proceedings for damages against the plaintiffs. In May 1987, the plaintiffs themselves served an English writ *in rem* upon the Linda, subsequently released on security, and the defendants acknowledged service. Subsequently, the defendants challenged English jurisdiction under Arts 21 and 22, on the grounds of prior Dutch proceedings. The plaintiffs argued that Art. 21 did not apply, because English and Dutch causes of action (and parties—see *infra*) were not the same.

Judgment

Sheen J. held the causes of action to be the same for Art. 21. The subject matter of the two sets of proceedings—negligence causing damage through the collision—was the same, notwithstanding that the parties' respective roles in the litigation were reversed.

Case principle

2.   Where a shipowner personally appears to an action *in rem*, the proceedings become *in personam* as well as *in rem* and involve the same cause of action as foreign Contracting State *in personam* proceedings.

Case

260   The Nordglimt [1988] 1 QB 183 High Court

See infra, 'same parties' and 'shall . . . stay'; and supra, s.34, Case 101, Republic of India, Case 103 and Comments to Black v Yates, Case 104.

Comment

Hobhouse J. held that on the defendant shipowner's appearance, the initially *in rem* action became hybrid *in rem-in personam* with same parties and same cause of action from then—but, in the case of *parties*, not retrospectively to the date of the action's commencement, for Article 21.

However, in *The Kherson, infra*, Case 300, Sheen J. held that parties *were* the same for Article 21, notwithstanding initial *in rem* character of the proceedings.

In *The Maciej Rataj* the European Court confirmed the *Kherson* approach, as did the House of Lords, disapproving of *Nordglimt*, in *The Indian Endurance (No. 2), supra*, Case 106, and *infra* Case 261, in relation to 1982 Act, s.34, which it actually equated with Article 21 for these purposes.

Case

261   The Indian Endurance (No.2), Republic of India v India Steamship Co. Ltd [1996] 3 All ER 641 Court of Appeal, 23 April 1996

Facts

See infra, Art. 21 'same parties', Case 278.

The plaintiffs had argued that the cause of action, not just the parties, was not the same in Indian and English actions, so that s.34 of the 1982 Act would not apply so as to bar the English proceedings (bar on successful plaintiff abroad from bringing proceedings in England on same cause of action between same parties).

Judgment

The plaintiffs accepted at Court of Appeal level that the cause of action in the Indian *in personam* and English *in rem* (that is, subsequently hybrid *in rem-in personam*) proceedings was the same.

At first instance ([1994] 2 Lloyd's Rep. 331, at 354 col. 2), Clarke J. noted case authorities on Art. 21, including *Kherson* (see too *Nordglimt* pp. 201–2), finding the same cause of action, and saw no reason why the corresponding principles should not also apply to s.34 of the 1982 Act.

Comments

In the European Court of Justice's judgment in *The Owners of the Cargo lately Laden on Board the 'Tatry' v The Owners of the ship 'Maciej Rataj'* Case C–406/92 [1994] ECR I-5439 of 6 December 1994, on a reference from the English Court of Appeal, it was subsequently confirmed that Art. 21 conditions of *same cause of action* and *same parties* are capable of being satisfied, regardless of whether one set of proceedings is both *in rem* and *in personam*, or originally *in rem* and thereafter only *in personam*, while the prior *lis pendens* was solely *in personam*. Advocate General Tesauro, whose Opinion the European Court followed, actually cited *The Kherson* in support of the view that prior *in personam* proceedings for non-liability of a shipowner against cargo owners and the cargo owners' own subsequent liability claim against the shipowner, regardless of whether both *in rem* and *in personam* or now solely *in personam*, involved the same cause of action and parties for Art. 21.

Both the Court of Appeal and the House of Lords applied this in *The Indian Endurance* (see too *infra*, Art. 21 'same parties').

In the Court of Appeal proceedings in *The Maciej Rataj* [1992] 2 Lloyd's Rep. 552, at 559 col. 2 of 13 April 1992, Neill L.J. agreed with *The Nordglimt* that initially-*in rem* proceedings became hybrid *in rem-in personam* on acknowledgement of service. But, subsequently (at 561 col. 2), he differed, with great diffidence, from Sheen J. in *The Linda* and *The Kherson*, who had considered hybrid to become solely *in personam* on the release of the ship. Neill L.J. regarded the proceedings as continuing to be hybrid in such a case—although, his second question to the European Court expressed the two possibilities in the alternative, thereby explicitly demonstrating continuing uncertainty on the issue.

See too *supra*, s.34, *Republic of India* Case 103, for a finding by the House of Lords as to the meaning generally of 'cause of action' in s.34.

Case principle

3. Shipowner's liability limitation action and other party's liability proceedings held *not* to involve the same cause of action.

Case

262 The Falstria [1988] 1 Lloyd's Rep. 495 High Court, 5 November 1987

Facts

The plaintiff Danish ship charterer instituted English liability limitation proceedings in February 1987 in respect of damage caused by its ship to the defendant's property situated in an English dock. The defendant itself began liability proceedings against the plaintiff in the Danish courts and challenged English jurisdiction under Art. 21, on the ground that Danish courts were first-seised of the same cause of action between the parties.

Judgment

Sheen J., irrespective of which of English and Danish courts were considered to be first-seised, held that they did not involve the same cause of action: the English limitation proceedings involved the issue of maximum damages and conditions therefor, whereas in Denmark the question was one of liability in the first place.

Comment

One would have thought, nonetheless, that the actions ought to have been held to be related under Art. 22. An English judgment for limited damages, incorporating an admission of liability by the limitation plaintiff, would seem to be irreconcilable with a Danish judgment against his liability in the first place.

This was in fact the outcome of the next case, *The 'Happy Fellow'*, where the situation was the converse, namely, liability proceedings were also concerned with quantum (see *infra*, Art. 22, paras 1 and 3, Case 316).

Case

263 The 'Happy Fellow' [1997] 1 Lloyd's Rep. 130 High Court, 3 December 1996

Facts

There was a collision between two vessels, Darfur and Happy Fellow, at the mouth of the River Seine in France in 1995. The owners and operators of the Happy Fellow instituted an action in the French courts in December 1995 against the owners of Darfur, claiming damages for negligent steering. In March 1996, the owners of Darfur began limitation proceedings in the English courts for a fund of over £1.7 million against the owners and operators of Happy Fellow and against a company called Baco-Liner, the time-charterers of Darfur, who had previously commenced proceedings in the English courts against Darfur's owners for an indemnity in respect of their liability arising from the collision.

One of the Happy Fellow claimants, Sloman, applied to the English courts for a decline (or stay) of Darfur's English limitation proceedings under Art. 21

(or Art. 22), on the ground that these involved the same cause of action as first-seised French courts' liability proceedings (the other claimants and Baco-Liner indicated that they would join the application, if to do so was not held to amount to submission to the English jurisdiction). The plaintiffs, Darfur's owners, denied that the cause of action was the same.

Judgment

Longmore J. held that limitation and liability proceedings did not involve the same cause of action and that, consequently, Art. 21 was inapplicable.

He analysed the nature of limitation actions in the light of the authorities. Were these attached to and merely an incident of liability proceedings, or somehow distinct from the latter? In Longmore J.'s view, the second option was correct—limitation actions were a procedural restriction upon claimants' rights to enforce their claims, not in fact a reduction of those substantive rights themselves, even though liability was assumed or admitted.

Comments

The Falstria was not itself cited in *The 'Happy Fellow'* judgment.

Longmore J. went on to find the English and French proceedings nevertheless to be *related* for purposes of Art. 22 (see *infra*, Art. 22, para. 3 'related').

Unlike Sheen J. in *The Falstria*, Longmore J. did not also deal with the matter of 'same parties' for Art. 21.

Case principle

4. Proceedings for infringement of the same trade mark and passing off in two different Contracting States do not involve the same cause of action, because each is limited to facts and activities of infringement taking place in its own Contracting State.

Case

La Gear Incorporated v Gerald Whelan & Sons Limited [1991] FSR 670 High Court, 24 May 1991

264

Facts

The plaintiff sued the Irish defendant in England in February 1991 for infringement of its UK trade mark and passing off in respect of the words 'La Gear' relating to footwear.

The defendant contested English jurisdiction, *inter alia*, under Art. 21, on the ground that Irish courts were previously seised of the same cause of action in May 1990.

Judgment

Mummery J. held that the English and Irish causes of action were different and Art. 21 was inapplicable.

The subject matter differed because Irish courts—just like the English in the reverse situation—could not give a remedy for breach of a UK trade mark, which was territorially restricted to the UK (and this was why the complaint in the Irish action was that the defendant had enabled a third party to breach the trade mark, rather than that the defendant itself had committed the breach).

As for passing off, the acts complained of in England were sales in and import of products into the UK, but in the Irish action, sales in Ireland and exportation to the United Kingdom—different facts and subject matter.

Case principle

5. Proceedings for contractual or tortious liability and for non-liability respectively, involve the same cause of action (*Gubisch* Case 144/86 applied).

Case

265 Assurances Générales de France I.A.R.T. v The Chiyoda Fire and Marine Co. (U.K.) Ltd [1992] 1 Lloyd's Rep. 325 High Court, 1 October 1991

Facts

See infra, Case 295.

In respect of the French plaintiff reinsurers' action in England for non-liability against the Italian reassured, as well as the issue of respective dates of English and Italian seisin was that of whether Italian reassureds' contractual liability proceedings also involved the same cause of action as the English.

Judgment

Judge Diamond Q.C. held the English and Italian actions to have the same cause of action for Art. 21.

In accordance with the specific *Gubisch* definition and the broad interpretation approach in *Overseas Union* Case C–351/89, what were required to be the same were:

(1) cause of action
     ('*cause*'/*Maciej Rataj*
     facts and law in issue)   — the same contractual relationship; and
(2) subject matter
     ('*object*'/*Maciej Rataj*
     end in view)   — whether the reinsurance contract was binding and enforceable.

together amounting to the singular expression 'cause of action' in the English text.

Here, therefore, both were satisfied. Notwithstanding the formal differences between liability and non-liability claims, the subject matter/object at the heart of the two actions—the 'end in view' as stated in *Maciej Rataj*—was the same: contractual enforceability. The exact identity of claims was not required. Further, the cause (of action)—the alleged contractual relationship involving 'same facts and law in issue' as it was stated in *Maciej Rataj*—was likewise the same.

Comments

Note too *Overseas Union Insurance v New Hampshire Insurance*, *infra*, Case 266, which led to the reference to the European Court by the Court of Appeal and to the European Court's eventual ruling on applicability of Art. 21 to non-Contracting State defendants.

See also Neill L.J. in the Court of Appeal proceedings in *The Maciej Rataj* [1992] 2 Lloyd's Rep. 552, at 559 col. 1, of 13 April 1992, prior to reference to the European Court for interpretation.

Case

Overseas Union Insurance v New Hampshire Insurance [1991] I.L.Pr. 510   **266**
High Court, 9 September 1988

Facts

The defendant US insurance company brought a claim in French courts in 1988 for payment of sums due under a contract of reinsurance with the plaintiff Singapore insurers (and two English insurers). Subsequently in 1988, the plaintiffs brought English proceedings for a declaration of avoidance of the reinsurance policy for misrepresentation and non-disclosure by the defendant.

The defendant asked the English courts, *inter alia*, to decline jurisdiction in favour of first-seised French courts under Art. 21. The plaintiffs argued that Art. 21 was inapplicable because: (1) English and French causes of action were not the same, as they were required to be under Art. 21; and (2) Art. 21 did not apply to the defendant non-Contracting State (US) insurers in England.

Judgment

Hirst J. at first instance confirmed that Art. 21 applied.

First, the Court of Justice's ruling in *Gubisch AG v Palumbo* was applied, so that the first French action for contractual enforcement and subsequent English action for contractual avoidance involved the same cause of action.

Secondly, when Hirst J.'s decision went to the Court of Appeal, the Court of Appeal referred interpretation to the European Court which ruled in Case C–351/89 on 27 June 1991 that Art. 21 applied irrespective of Contracting or non-Contracting State domicile of the defendant—precisely as Hirst J. had done at first instance.

Comment

See (1992) Journal of Business Law 47, 51–8.

In *S & W Berisford Plc v New Hampshire Insurance* [1990] 2 All ER 321, Hobhouse J. in the High Court followed Hirst J.'s finding that Art. 21 applied equally to Contracting and to non-Contracting State domiciled defendants (see *supra*, 1982 Act s.49, Comment to Case 111).

Case principle

6. An action for a negative declaration of non-liability in negligence involves the same cause of action as proceedings to establish liability in negligence for a remedy under the Fatal Accidents Acts.

Case

267 Kinnear v Falconfilms NV [1994] I.L.Pr. 731 High Court, 27 January 1994

Facts

See supra, Case 191.

Judgment

Phillips J. so held in respect of earlier Spanish and subsequent English proceedings for non-liability and liability respectively, in line with the European Court's decision in *Gubisch v Palumbo*.

Comment

The finding was subsequently also confirmed by the European Court's ruling in December 1994 on the fifth question in the reference to the Court in *The Maciej Rataj* Case C–406/92.

Case

268 The Filiatra Legacy [1994] 1 Lloyd's Rep. 513 High Court, 9 April 1990

Facts

The plaintiff obtained judgment in England against the vessel *Filiatra Legacy* for over one and a half million US dollars in respect of cargo shortage. The plaintiff thereafter brought further English proceedings against the defendant insurers for payment of part of that sum under the insurance contract. Previously, the defendants themselves had begun an action in Italy against the plaintiff for a declaration that conditions of payment under the insurance letter of undertaking were not fulfilled. They sought a stay of the English action under Art. 21, in favour of first-seised Italian courts. The plaintiff argued that the two causes of action were not the same.

Judgment

Saville J. held that, in accordance with the European Court of Justice's ruling in *Gubisch v Palumbo*, he was bound to find the two sets of proceedings to involve the same cause of action—enforceability of the contract—and accordingly, he would stay the English action under Art. 21.

Case principle

7.   There must be the same 'subject matter' (object) as well as same 'cause' (of action) for Art. 21 to operate (*Gubisch* applied).

Case

Berkeley Administration Inc v McClelland [1995] I.L.Pr. 201 Court of Appeal, **269**
18 February 1994

Facts

See infra, Art. 26 'recognition', Case 347.

Judgment

The Court of Appeal unanimously applied the *same subject matter* (object) element of the *Gubisch lis pendens* definition as the test for issue estoppel from recognition of a French judgment in current English proceedings. (This was on the basis that the same policies applied in a Convention context.)

Views and approaches of the Lord Justices differed as to the nature of the subject matter of the two actions.

The current English proceedings were to assess whether the plaintiffs had abused English process in alleging breach of confidence by the defendants; whereas the French action had been concerned with their abuse of French process in bringing such a claim.

Dillon L.J. considered the subject matter to be the 'underlying question' in these actions, namely, whether the plaintiffs had had a credible claim against the defendants.

Stuart-Smith and Hobhouse L.JJ., however, regarded simply the claim for a remedy for abuse as the subject matter.

From all of which, a number of conclusions as to issue estoppel were drawn (see *infra*, Art. 26).

Case principles

8.   Same 'cause of action' in the English text means same 'cause' and same 'object' (following *Gubisch*).
9.   'Cause' means legal relationship, facts and rules of law relied on (*Gubisch, The Maciej Rataj*).
10. 'Object' means subject matter (*Gubisch*) and the end in view of the claim (*Maciej Rataj*).

Case

Sarrio S.A. v Kuwait Investment Authority [1996] 1 Lloyd's Rep. 650   **270**
High Court

Facts

See supra, 1982 Act s.49, Case 110, and infra, Art. 22 'related' Case 315.

The plaintiff sold its paper business through a transaction involving purchase and sale of corporate shares between the plaintiff and the defendant's Spanish subsidiaries.

In 1993, the plaintiff brought proceedings against the defendant in Spain, claiming unpaid sums on the share transactions for which it alleged the defendant itself was responsible through abuse of the corporate personality of its subsidiaries. Subsequently, in 1994 the plaintiff commenced a further action against the defendant in the English courts, claiming damages from the defendant for misstatement as to the value of the shares and alleged inducement to enter the contract of sale of the paper business.

The defendant contested English courts' jurisdiction, *inter alia*, on the ground that the English and Spanish proceedings involved the same cause of action and that consequently, since it was agreed that Spanish courts were first seised, English courts were obliged to decline to hear the case under Art. 21.

Judgment

Mance J. held Art. 21 to be inapplicable. The English and Spanish proceedings did not involve the same cause of action. Criteria of same 'cause' and 'object' in European Court of Justice decisions in *Gubisch* and *The Maciej Rataj* were followed and found not to be satisfied on the facts.

Cause meant the same legal relationship, relevant facts and legal rules: the relationship at issue in the English action was those direct relations in tortious misstatement between plaintiff and defendant; in Spain, it was the relationship between the defendant and its subsidiaries and the defendant's possible liability in contract towards the plaintiff for the subsidiaries' actions.

Object meant subject matter of the actions and the end and purpose in view: in England, the object was to obtain damages for the loss sustained by the plaintiff through the defendant's inducement to enter the contract; in Spain, the object was to obtain the sums initially owed by the defendant's subsidiaries.

On the other hand, Art. 22 was held to apply to the English and Spanish actions and Mance J. stayed the English proceedings as being related to the first-seised Spanish under Art. 22 (see *infra*, Art. 22, Case 327).

The plaintiffs appealed against this decision (*infra*) and the defendants cross-appealed against his finding against applicability of Art. 21.

Case

271 Sarrio S.A. v Kuwait Investment Authority [1997] 1 Lloyd's Rep. 113 Court of Appeal

Facts

See supra, Case 270.

Judgment

The Court of Appeal unanimously upheld Mance J.'s ruling upon Art. 21: Spanish and English causes of action were not the same and consequently Art. 21 did not apply.

Evans L.J. approved the approach of Mance J. at first instance: the relations (*Gubisch*) and facts and law at issue (*Maciej Rataj*) in Spain were those in contract (*cause*) and the end in view (*Maciej Rataj*) was to enforce contractual liability against the defendant (*object*); whereas, the equivalent in England were liability in the tort of negligent misrepresentation as between defendant and plaintiff (*cause*) and damages for inducement to conclude the contract and the loss caused thereby (*object*).

Case principle

11.   Causes of action are not the same merely because one of the actions *incidentally* raised a fact issue also involved—even centrally—in the other. The underlying questions must be the same.

Case

Berkeley Administration Inc. v McClelland [1996] I.L.Pr. 772 Court of **272** Appeal, 21 June 1996

Facts

In February 1989, the English courts granted the Chequepoint group, which ran bureaux de change worldwide, including Paris, an interlocutory injunction against its former employees, who had set up the Maccorp group in competition, from competing and using confidential information to acquire certain premises in the Champs Elysées, Paris, on Chequepoint's cross-undertaking to obey any damages award. Two months later, the injunction was discharged on Maccorp's agreement not to purchase the Paris premises. Then, in March 1990, Maccorp were released by the English court from the obligation not to buy the premises and an inquiry was ordered into their damages. In the meantime, in the period March–July 1989, Chequepoint had also unsuccessfully applied for an interlocutory injunction in the French courts to restrain breach of confidence by Maccorp and Maccorp companies, which had then sued Chequepoint for damages in France for unfair business practices and abuse of process through Chequepoint's own action. The latter suit failed in September 1990 and an appeal was pending at the time of current proceedings.

Over the next four years, from July 1990, Chequepoint made a number of unsuccessful applications to the English courts for a stay of the damages inquiry which had been ordered. The latter eventually took place before Mantell J., and in December 1994 he ordered Chequepoint to pay Maccorp £1.08 million damages, as representing the profits the latter would have earned had they not been prevented from acquiring the Paris premises.

Chequepoint appealed against Mantell J.'s judgment to the Court of Appeal on a number of grounds, including that the English damages inquiry should have been stayed under Art. 21 in favour of French courts first seised of Maccorp's claim (eventually unsuccessful and appealed against, see *supra*) for damages against Chequepoint for abuse of French procedure in bringing the Chequepoint action.

Judgment

The Court of Appeal unanimously upheld Chequepoint's appeal against the £1.08 million damages award to Maccorp.

The *ratio* of the decision was based upon the Court of Appeal's assessment *of the facts*: there was not sufficient evidence to establish that the owner of the Paris premises would have been willing to sell them to Maccorp even if Maccorp had not been prevented by the English interlocutory order from purchasing them, and, consequently, Maccorp had suffered no damage.

However, had this not been the case, the court took the view that Chequepoint had raised the objections based upon Art. 21 (and Art. 26 recognition and estoppel, *infra*) so late in the English proceedings that it would actually have been an abuse of process and oppressive to Maccorp to have allowed Chequepoint to plead that the English damages inquiry ought to have been stayed thereunder in favour of Maccorp's French action!

Even so, Vice-Chancellor Sir Richard Scott briefly considered *obiter* whether Art. 21 would have been satisfied had it been necessary and permitted to be pleaded. The answer was *no*, on all counts:

(1) English courts were first-seised in February 1989 to the French in July 1989.

(2) There was a party in the Maccorp group in the French proceedings not also party to the English action (see *Tatry*).

(3) The causes of action in English and French proceedings were not the same. It was not enough that they involved a common question of fact as to whether Maccorp would have been able to acquire the Paris premises but for the English injunction. The underlying question in both had to be the same, which it was not: the English damages inquiry action was on Chequepoint's *agreement* to pay damages caused by the injunction to Maccorp; the French was for damages for *abuse of French process* by Chequepoint in bringing its French action against Maccorp (object/subject matter/end in view not the same).

Comments

The preceding point on Art. 21 seems to be justified on the technical basis that English damages were for a contractual cause of action, whereas the French were for tortious abuse of French process—apart from which the underlying question in both might have been viewed as the same: abuse of process (see, however, *infra*, Art. 26, para. 1, for a further approach by C.A.).

The Court of Appeal also considered *obiter* whether the French court's dismissal of Maccorp's action in September 1990 would have estopped the English courts from deciding that Maccorp would have been able to acquire the Paris premises, had they been willing to hold this and had it not been too late for Art. 26 on recognition of the French judgment to be pleaded (see *infra*, Art. 26).

Case principles

12. Where two sets of Contracting State proceedings involve some, but not all, contracts in common, they only involve the same cause of action in relation to the common contracts.

13. Proceedings concerning the remaining contracts may be found to be related within Art. 22 if intricately interrelated; but if only on a minor scale in comparison with the others, the discretion to stay should not reasonably be exercised.

Case

Kloeckner & Co. AG v Gatoil Overseas Inc. [1990] 1 Lloyd's Rep. 177 High   **273**
Court, 31 July 1989

Facts

This case involved proceedings in England for damages arising out of contracts for the purchase and sale of oil, together with the underlying framework agreement providing for the former contracts, and German proceedings for wrongful termination of certain only of the oil contracts.

   The defendants sought a stay of English jurisdiction under Art. 21, but the plaintiffs argued that the latter did not apply because the cause of action was not on the same contracts in England and Germany.

Judgment

Hirst J. held, in any event, that English courts were first seised; but, *obiter*, had they not been, they would have been obliged to decline under Art. 21 in respect of the contracts subject to *both* English and German actions, as involving the same cause of action—but only in relation to those contracts.

   The remaining contacts were also said to be related, but since those in the German proceedings were on a far lesser scale, the discretion to stay the English action under Art. 22 in relation thereto would not reasonably have been exercised.

Comment

This is consistent with the European Court's 'partial' approach to same *parties* in *Maciej Rataj* Case C–406/92.

Case principle

14. Full proceedings in contract in one Contracting State held not to involve the same cause of action as *executory* process, leading to expedited

judgment, which can subsequently be overturned by a court of the same level in another.

Case

274 Gamlestaden Plc v Casa de Suecia SA and Thulin [1994] 1 Lloyd's Rep. 433 High Court, 3 February 1993

Facts

The plaintiff English company brought an action on contracts of loan and guarantee against Spanish and Belgian defendants in the English courts. Spanish executory process was also initiated, unsuccessfully for the plaintiff as it turned out.

Judgment

Potter J. held that English and Spanish actions did not involve the same cause of action because the Spanish executory judgment could form the subject of later proceedings in the same court, whereas the English action would lead to a final judgment on the substance of the case.

Case principle

15. An action in England to restrain a party from continuing with prior Italian breach of contract proceedings in alleged contravention of an English arbitration agreement held not to involve the same cause of action as the Italian claim, for purposes of Art. 21 (*Tatry* applied).

Case

275 Toepfer International GmbH v Molino Boschi Srl [1996] 1 Lloyd's Rep. 510 High Court

Facts

See supra, Art. 1, para. 2(4), Case 116.

The defendant argued (on the assumption that the Convention applied) that Italian courts were first-seised in 1989 of the defendant's breach-of-sales-contract damages claim against the plaintiff and that consequently the English court, seised in 1995 of the plaintiff's action for a declaration of English arbitral existence and injunction to restrain continuation of the defendant's Italian claim, should be obliged to decline its jurisdiction under Art. 21.

The plaintiff, on the other hand, contended that Art. 21 did not apply, because the cause of action was not the same in England and Italy.

Judgment

Mance J. held Art. 21 not to apply: the cause of action in English and Italian actions was not the same.

In the case of the English declaration and injunction, the principal *object/subject matter* of the English action, as 'the end it had in view' (*Maciej Rataj*), was to stop the Italian proceedings, whereas, the *object* of the latter was to obtain damages for breach of contract; and the principal *cause (of action)* in England, as legal relationship and 'facts and law relied on as the basis of the action' (*Maciej Rataj*), was the existence of the London arbitration agreement, whereas, in Italy, the *cause (of action)* was defective delivery of goods and performance under the sales contract.

Case principle

16. Applications for Art. 24 interim relief in one Contracting State and proceedings on substance in another Contracting State do not involve the same cause of action for the purposes of Art. 21.

Case

Republic of Haiti v Duvalier [1989] 2 WLR 261 Court of Appeal, 22 July **276** 1988

Facts

The plaintiffs sued the defendant for misappropriation of funds in the French courts and for interim '*Mareva*' relief (freezing assets) in England. The defendant argued that the English courts should decline jurisdiction as second seised under Art. 21.

Judgment

The Court of Appeal rejected this plea outright. Arts 24 and 21 dealt with different stages of proceedings and Art. 24 would be completely deprived of its effectiveness if Art. 21 were to be applied in such a way as to interrupt the English provisional proceedings (see too *supra*, 1982 Act s.25(1) Case 87).

> " . . . *between the same parties* . . . "

Case principles

1. Where a ship is not arrested, or is subsequently released following arrest, or the shipowner acknowledges service, the action is or proceeds *in personam* (as well as *in rem* in the latter case), and parties to an *in personam* action in a different Contracting State are the same (but see *Case principles*

four to eight *infra*, for a more detailed, post-*Maciej Rataj* confirmation by the Court of Appeal).

2.   Parties are the same even if their roles are reversed in the two actions (confirmed by *Gubisch*, paras 15 and 19).

3.   If the plaintiff's insurers are joined in one of the actions, the parties are still the same if the insurers are merely acting procedurally in subrogation to the rights of the plaintiff.

Case

277   The Linda [1988] 1 Lloyd's Rep. 175 High Court, 23 October 1987

Facts

See supra, 'same cause of action', Case 259.

The plaintiffs also tried to argue that the parties to English and Dutch proceedings were not the same, as was required for Art. 21 to apply: two different ships were involved as the defendants; the parties were not acting in the same capacity as plaintiff or defendant in each action; and the defendants' insurers were named as co-plaintiffs with the defendants in the Dutch proceedings.

Judgment

Sheen J. rejected each of the preceding arguments of the plaintiffs and held that English and Dutch proceedings were between the same parties for purposes of Art. 21.

As to the defendants in *in rem* proceedings, this was the ship if it remained arrested; the shipowner too if he acknowledged service, in which case the action was also *in personam* from that time; whilst the action was solely *in personam* if the ship was never arrested or was so but was later released on security.

With regard to the parties' roles as plaintiff or defendant, these did not have to be the same. Article 21 would have stated this had it been intended. This might not seem fair to the plaintiffs, but the primary objective of Art. 21 was to avoid the risk of irreconcilable judgments, just as likely where litigants' roles were reversed.

Finally, if the purpose of adding the defendants' insurers to the Dutch writ was a procedural requirement of Dutch law in order to protect the insurers' right of subrogation, it added nothing of substance and did not mean that the parties were now different in the two sets of proceedings.

Article 21 applied and English jurisdiction was duly declined.

Sheen J. added that if he were wrong on this, the two actions would certainly be related within Art. 22, para. 3 as being likely to lead to irreconcilable judgments—and it would then be 'absurd' not to decide to stay the English proceedings thereunder.

Comment

See too *The Nordglimt* [1988] 1 QB 183 High Court, *infra* 'shall . . . stay' and *The Kherson* [1992] 2 Lloyd's Rep. 261 High Court, *supra* 'same cause of action'.

In the European Court of Justice's judgment in *The Owners of the Cargo lately Laden on Board the 'Tatry' v The Owners of the ship 'Maciej Rataj'* Case C–406/92 [1994] ECR I-5439 of 6 December 1994, on a reference from the English Court of Appeal, it was subsequently confirmed that Art. 21 conditions of *same cause of action* and *same parties* are capable of being satisfied, regardless of whether one set of proceedings is both *in rem* and *in personam*, or originally *in rem* and thereafter only *in personam*, while the prior *lis pendens* was solely *in personam*. Advocate General Tesauro, whose opinion the European Court followed, actually cited *The Kherson* in support of the view that prior *in personam* proceedings for non-liability of a shipowner against cargo owners and the cargo owners' own subsequent liability claim against the shipowner, regardless of whether both *in rem* and *in personam* or now solely *in personam*, involved the same cause of action and parties for Art. 21.

The Court of Appeal and House of Lords thereafter adopted this principle in *The Indian Endurance* (see *infra*).

In the Court of Appeal proceedings in *The Maciej Rataj* [1992] 2 Lloyd's Rep. 552, at 559 col. 2 of 13 April 1992, Neill L.J. agreed with *The Nordglimt* that initially-*in rem* proceedings became hybrid *in rem-in personam* on acknowledgement of service (although, not also retrospectively to commencement in *The Nordglimt* in the case of *parties*). But, subsequently (561 col. 2), he differed, with great diffidence, from Sheen J. in *The Linda* and *The Kherson*, who had considered hybrid to become solely *in personam* on the release of the ship. Neill L.J. regarded the proceedings as continuing to be hybrid in such a case—although, his second question to the European Court expressed the two possibilities in the alternative, thereby explicitly demonstrating continuing uncertainty on the issue.

Case principles

4. *In rem* become hybrid *in rem* and *in personam* when the shipowner personally acknowledges service of the writ served on the ship.

5. Parties to foreign *in personam* and English hybrid *in rem-in personam* actions are the same.

6. *Deichland* had said that even in *in rem* proceedings the shipowner/charterer was a defendant for purposes of Art. 2. But this was a distinct issue from whether these also involved same parties for Art. 21.

7. Applying the European Court's ruling in *Maciej Rataj*, Art. 21 would apply to foreign *in personam* and English hybrid *in rem-in personam*, notwithstanding that only some of the parties (those *in personam*) were the same.

8. It was an open question whether hybrid *in rem-in personam* became solely *in personam* on release of a ship from arrest or discharge of security.

Case

278   The Indian Endurance (No. 2), Republic of India v India Steamship Co. Ltd
[1996] 3 All ER 641 Court of Appeal, 23 April 1996

Facts

See supra, 'same cause of action', Case 261.

This was in fact a *non-Convention* case, but where the English court drew
analogies with the position under Art. 21. In 1987, the plaintiff's cargo
was lost during carriage on the defendant's ship from Sweden to India and the
plaintiff obtained judgment *in personam* against the shipowners in the Indian
courts in 1989. An English writ *in rem* was served upon the defendant's ship
in an English port in 1990, which the defendant personally acknowledged and
provided an undertaking in order to prevent the ship's arrest.

The defendant raised a number of defences, based largely upon estoppel, on
which the proceedings went to the House of Lords. One of the bases of challenge to the English proceedings put forward by the defendants was that the
English proceedings were barred from being heard under s.34 of the 1982 Act
under which an action could not be brought in England where the plaintiff had
already succeeded on the same cause of action and between the same parties
in a foreign court. Therefore, since the plaintiffs, for the first time before the
Lords, proposed that neither cause of action nor the parties were the same for
s.34 in India and England because Indian proceedings had been *in personam*
whereas English had been brought *in rem*, the Lords ([1993] AC 410, at
424–5) remitted the case to be heard at first instance on the point ([1994]
2 Lloyd's Rep. 330, Clarke J.) and eventually it went to the Court of Appeal
(see *supra*, s.34, Case 106).

Judgment

The Court of Appeal held that on personal acknowledgement of *in rem* service, the English *in rem* became hybrid *in rem-in personam* proceedings and
that the *in personam* parties in the hybrid English *in rem-personam* were the
same as those in the Indian *in personam*.

In reaching this conclusion, Staughton L.J. delivering the Court of Appeal's
judgment, drew upon Art. 21 cases including *Nordglimt, Deichland, Linda*
and *Kherson* (see *infra*)—in addition to which, the European Court had ruled
in *Maciej Rataj* that not *all* parties to actions had to be the same for the Art.
21 condition of same parties to be satisfied in relation to the latter (so that the
in rem element could be discounted for the purpose).

The Court of Appeal rejected the argument that the word 'brought' in s.34
distinguished it from Art. 21: the latter also used that terminology and it could
not have been intended to mean that solely the English action's purely *in rem*
character at the time at which it was initially brought should be taken
into account for the purposes. English statutes, as well as the Judgments
Convention, should be interpreted purposively.

Comments

In the earlier case of '*The Sylt*' [1991] 1 Lloyd's Rep. 240, Sheen J. in the High Court appeared to ignore the difference between *The Nordglimt* and *The Deichland* (*supra*), and dubiously concluded as a consequence, in the national English law context of 1982 Act ss.26 and 34 (security retention on stays of action and bars on further proceedings in England by successful plaintiffs abroad, respectively), that, contrary to *The Nordglimt*, and in accordance with *The Deichland*, parties to an *in personam* action and to an *in rem* action were the same in substance *for purposes generally*, including s.34 and no doubt Art. 21—even *at the inception* of the *in rem* action and prior to any personal acknowledgement of service by shipowner or charterer. This was not of course what the Court of Appeal was saying in *The Deichland*, where the judgment was in relation to the specific issue of identification of a 'defendant' for purposes of ascription of domicile under Art. 2, not also necessarily for designation of such defendant as same 'party' for purposes of competing jurisdiction or estoppel (see *supra*, s.34). Notwithstanding which, Saville J. in the High Court subsequently picked up on and adopted Sheen J.'s *Sylt* judgment in *The Havhelt* [1993] 1 Lloyd's Rep. 523, in granting a stay of an English action *in rem* in favour of (pre-Lugano) prospective Norwegian *in personam forum conveniens* at national English law on the ground that there was no material distinction between the two. As to whether the narrower *Deichland* principle can be so extended in this way, and, in particular, into the Convention's Art. 21 sphere, so that *in rem* at inception is held to involve the same parties as *in personam* for those purposes, must await confirmation at appellate level and for the moment seems highly doubtful (although less so since the House of Lords' *Indian Endurance (No. 2)* decision of 16 October 1997, *supra*, Case 106).

With regard to *Case principle* eight, *supra*, it will also be recalled that in the Court of Appeal proceedings in *The Maciej Rataj* [1992] 2 Lloyd's Rep. 552 at 561 col. 2, Neill L.J. considered that the action remained hybrid on release of the ship—but the matter was uncertain (Sheen J. had indicated that proceedings would become solely *in personam* in such circumstances, in *The Linda* and in *The Kherson*, *supra*).

Case principle

9. Charterers' liability limitation proceedings against several actual or potential claimants are not between the *same* parties as the liability action brought against the charterers by *one* of those claimants.

Case

The Falstria [1988] 1 Lloyd's Rep. 495 High Court, 5 November 1987   **279**

Facts

Danish charterers of a ship brought Art. 6a liability limitation proceedings in England, followed by the institution of liability proceedings against them in Denmark brought by a claimant. The claimant challenged English jurisdiction, *inter alia*, on the ground of his existing (if it was first seised) *lis pendens* between the same parties under Art. 21.

Judgment

Sheen J. held that the parties were not the same in each action. The liability limitation proceedings involved potentially several claimants as defendants in the plaintiff charterer's English action; whereas, only one of the claimants was plaintiff against the charterers in the Danish liability proceedings.

Comments

See too *supra*, *The Falstria* and *The Happy Fellow*, as to Art. 21 'same cause of action', Cases 262 and 263.

As a result of the European Court's ruling in *Maciej Rataj*, strictly Art. 21 *should* now apply as between the common parties—plaintiff in England and Danish claimant (see *infra*, *Grupo Torras*, Case 280). The problem with a limitation fund action, however, is its all-or-nothing nature. Second-seised English courts could not simply suspend their action to establish the fund in relation to the first-seised Danish claimant alone—which is why, according to the Convention logic and system, Art. 6a should prevail over Arts 21 and 22 in such circumstances of partial actual claimants (see *supra*, Art. 6a).

Case principle

10.   Common parties in multiple-party actions are 'same parties' for Art. 21 (*Tatry v Maciej Rataj* applied).

Case

280   Grupo Torras S.A. v Sheikh Fahad Mohammed Al Sabah [1995] I.L.Pr. 667, [1996] 1 Lloyd's Rep. 7 Court of Appeal, 26 May 1995

Facts

See infra, Art. 21 'first-seised', Case 285.

Judgment

The Court of Appeal applied *Maciej Rataj* and overturned the first instance judge's finding that parties were not same parties for Art. 21 if not *all* were common to both English and foreign actions (the first judge had decided prior to the European Court's *Maciej Rataj* ruling). Common parties were same parties for Art. 21.

Comment

In any event, even though Art. 21 applied as the defendants had argued, English courts did not have to decline in favour of Spanish, because the English courts were held to be first seised (*see infra*, Art. 21 'first-seised').

Case

Deaville v Aeroflot Russian International Airlines [1997] 2 Lloyd's Rep. 67   **281**
High Court, 7 February 1997

Facts

See infra, Case 302, Art. 21 "shall . . . stay . . . ".

Judgment

Deputy High Court Judge Geoffrey Brice Q.C. held that common parties in
England and France would be subject to Art. 21 in principle, following *Maciej
Rataj*—but in fact this finding was *obiter*, because Art. 21 was considered to
have been displaced in any event by virtue of Art. 57.

Case principles

11.   In determining same parties, courts may look to substance rather than to
      mere formal identities of litigating parties.
12.   Multiple actions must be *between* the same parties for Art. 21 to oper-
      ate. It is not enough that those parties are merely involved in proceed-
      ings, but not in opposition to each other.

Case

Kinnear v Falconfilms NV [1994] I.I..Pr. 731 High Court, 27 January 1994   **282**

Facts (1)

The British actor Roy Kinnear was injured in a fall from a horse while filming
in Spain and died 24 hours after being taken to hospital. The Spanish police
opened an investigating action for possible criminal charges against the Spanish
hospital and doctor who had treated Kinnear, and Kinnear's wife sought to be
joined as civil plaintiff, in September 1988. In 1993, those proceedings were
abandoned. In 1991, the plaintiff administrators of Kinnear's estate brought an
English action against the defendant film company, producer and director for
breach of contract and negligence. The defendants wished to issue third party
proceedings against the Spanish hospital and doctor under Convention Art.
6(2). However, the third parties contested English courts' jurisdiction, on the
ground that Spanish proceedings had been instituted in the first place involving
the third parties and English courts consequently were obliged to decline under
Art. 21.

Judgment (1)

Phillips J. held that Art. 21 was inapplicable because the English and Spanish
actions were not between 'the same parties'. It was not sufficient that one
party—here the third party Spanish hospital and doctor—was involved as

common party in both sets of proceedings. There had to be at least two parties so involved in the two actions.

Comment

Where there are at least two common parties, the European Court of Justice in the *Maciej Rataj* Case C–406/92 ruled that Art. 21 does apply to the common parties in such actions, notwithstanding continuation of the proceedings (subject to Art. 22) in relation to the rest (see *supra, Grupo Torras*).

Facts (2)

In addition to the defendants' application to serve the Spanish third parties, the plaintiffs themselves wished to join the Spanish parties as co-defendants to the English proceedings, under Art. 6(1). However, previously in November 1993, the Spanish parties had instituted proceedings in Spain against the plaintiffs and Roy Kinnear's heirs, claiming that the Spanish parties were under no liability towards them, and consequently the Spanish parties contended that the English courts should decline jurisdiction in their favour under Art. 21.

The plaintiffs argued against this, on the ground that parties in English and Spanish actions were not the same.

Judgment (2)

Phillips J. was quite certain that the parties to both actions were 'the same' for purposes of Art. 21. Notwithstanding that solely Kinnear's administrators and agent were represented in the English action and not also his heirs and dependants, nonetheless the English claims under the Fatal Accidents Act were brought for the benefit of those heirs and dependants.

Facts (3)

The plaintiffs further argued that it was the Spanish action, not the English, which ought to be stayed as second-seised under Art. 21 because the defendants in the English action had sought to join the Spanish as third parties to the English proceedings at an earlier date.

Judgment (3)

Phillips J. rejected this. Article 21 required the two actions to be 'between' the same parties (not just to *involve* them). This was not so in the existing case where the Spanish parties had previously been joined to the English proceedings as third parties by the defendants, not as co-defendants by the plaintiffs.

> " . . . *courts of different Contracting States* . . . "

Case principle

Article 21 also operates in relation to non-Contracting State domiciled defendants subject to national jurisdiction grounds in Contracting States' courts under Art. 4.

Case

Kloeckner & Co AG v Gatoil Overseas Inc [1990] 1 Lloyd's Rep. 177 High   **283**
Court, 31 July 1989

Facts

See supra, Case 273.

Judgment

Hirst J. confirmed national jurisdiction of English courts over Panamanian defendants under RSC Ord. 11, r.1(1)(d) (contracts jurisdiction), and assumed Art. 21 to be applicable thereto in principle, even if not also on the facts.

The judgment preceded that of the European Court in *Overseas Union*, Case C–351/89, which confirmed the point.

Case

Deaville v Aeroflot Russian International Airlines [1997] 2 Lloyd's Rep. 67   **284**
High Court, 7 February 1997

Facts

See infra, Case 302, Art. 21, "shall . . . stay . . . ".

Judgment

Deputy High Court Judge Geoffrey Brice Q.C. accepted the applicability in principle of Art. 21 to the Russian (non-Contracting State) defendant, following *Overseas Union*, although this was an *obiter* finding in *Deaville*, since Art. 21 was held to have been displaced in any event by virtue of Art. 57.

> *" . . . court first seised . . . "*

Case principle

Definitive seisin is a matter for national procedural laws of English and foreign Contracting States' courts respectively (*Zelger v Salinitri (No. 2)* Case 129/83 applied).

Case

285 Grupo Torras S.A. v Sheikh Fahad Mohammed Al Sabah [1995] I.L.Pr. 667, [1996] 1 Lloyd's Rep. 7 Court of Appeal, 26 May 1995

Facts

The plaintiff Spanish company alleged that its 20 defendant directors and officers and their associated companies had fraudulently misappropriated funds and assets belonging to the plaintiff.

The plaintiff instituted joint criminal-civil proceedings in Spain and a civil action in England in the course of 1993.

Five of the defendants had commenced civil proceedings against the plaintiff in Spanish courts in 1992, alleging injurious falsehood. The defendants challenged English jurisdiction on a number of grounds (see *supra*, Art. 16(2), Case 207 as to arguments on exclusive Spanish jurisdiction in corporate matters—unsuccessful).

One ground of objection was that English courts were second-seised of the same cause of action between the same parties and consequently were obliged to decline jurisdiction under Art. 21.

The crucial question was whether English or Spanish courts were seised in the first place, on the assumption that parties and cause of action were the same (the former not in fact decided and the latter doubted, see *supra*)?

Judgment

Stuart Smith L.J., delivering judgment for the Court of Appeal, applied *Zelger v Salinitri (No. 2)* in order to determine English and Spanish seisin for purposes of Art. 21: English law of procedure would decide definitive English seisin, and Spanish procedure determined Spanish definitive seisin.

According to *Dresser U.K. Ltd v Falcongate Freight Management Ltd* (*infra* Case 287), the English court was seised at the date of service of the English writ upon the defendants rather than on the earlier date of issue.

With regard to the defendants' Spanish civil proceedings against the plaintiff, the Court of Appeal examined Spanish law and concluded on the evidence that: (i) Spanish courts' proceedings were *pending* at the earlier date of *filing* of the claim (an intermediate date of 'admission' of the claim was purely administrative and of no relevance in content); but (ii) they were only *definitively* seised at the subsequent date of its *service* according to Spanish doctrines of *lis pendens*.

Similarly, in the case of the Spanish joined criminal-civil action, it was only at the later stage of admission and sending for trial that the Spanish court was definitively seised, when the exact nature of the claim and the parties to it were known, not at the earlier times of filing or reference to an investigating judge.

In respect of neither set of Spanish proceedings, would the Court of Appeal accept that the Spanish seisin could retrospectively relate-back to the earlier date of filing of the Spanish actions.

Consequently, since the English writ was served upon the defendants before Spanish service in the Spanish civil action and before admission and sending to trial in the Spanish joined criminal-civil proceedings, the English courts were first seised prior to the Spanish and were not required to decline to hear the case under Art. 21.

Comment

The Court of Appeal applied the European Court's ruling in *Tatry v Maciej Rataj*, so that, although there were other defendants in England who were not also involved in the Spanish actions, Art. 21 was held to be applicable *in principle* in relation to the common parties to English and Spanish actions, as 'same parties' (see *supra*, Art. 21, 'same parties').

However, since the non-common and common defendants had been served with the English writ at different times—earlier in the former case than in the latter—the question arose whether in this situation the English court was seised in relation to all defendants on the date of first service upon *any* defendant, or whether it was only seised against each defendant when that defendant was served?

As things turned out, the Court of Appeal concluded that it was unnecessary for it to decide this issue because even if the last date of English service upon the common defendants were to be taken as the relevant date of English seisin for Art. 21, this was still prior to what was held to be Spanish seisin and consequently the English courts were first-seised in any event.

In *Fox v Taher* [1997] I.L.Pr. 441 Court of Appeal, 31 July 1996, Brooke L.J. (at 455) expressly approved the submission by counsel in *Grupo Torras* that seisin only existed over joined defendants from the date of their joinder, not from the earlier date of seisin in respect of the original defendant(s) (see *infra*, Art. 22, para. 1 ' . . . may . . . stay . . . ', Case 313).

See too infra, Assurances Generales de France I.A.R.T. v The Chiyoda Fire and Marine Co. (U.K.) Ltd [1992] 1 Lloyd's Rep. 325, 1 October 1991).

" *. . . seised . . .* "

General

The principles below were developed largely by the English Court of Appeal. Consequently, it is possible that a future judgment of the House of Lords will depart from them and take a different view. This *may* depend upon the particular membership of the House when it is called upon to decide such a case. As the House is presently constituted, this commentator's best guess is that the House will confirm the law as it has been developed by the Court of Appeal.

Case principle

1. Under English case law, following the UK's accession to the Brussels Convention, English courts are to be regarded as 'definitively seised' for Convention purposes, in accordance with the European Court's decision in *Zelger v Salinitri (No. 2)* Case 129/83, on the date upon which the document instituting the proceedings is *served*, not on the earlier date of its issue.

Case

286 The Freccia del Nord [1989] 1 Lloyd's Rep. 388 High Court, 29 November 1988

Facts

This involved an English Admiralty action *in rem* following a collision at sea. The English writ was issued, but not also served, on 25 June 1987. The defendants arrested the plaintiffs' ship in Rotterdam some 20 minutes later on the same day, and Dutch court process was served on 3 July 1987. The English writ was served on 9 July 1987.

Judgment

The judge in the English Commercial High Court, Sheen J., held, against the weight of English academic commentary favouring—or at least assuming—date of issue of a writ to be that of seisin, that definitive seisin in Admiralty actions *in rem* occurred at the date of *service* of the writ or of arrest of the ship, whichever was earlier, on the ground that a court could not be considered to be so 'seised' until it had been established that it possessed jurisdiction over the merits of the case.

Case

287 Dresser UK Limited v Falcongate Freight Management Limited [1992] 1 QB 502 Court of Appeal, 19 July 1991

Facts

Here, the principle of *service* as seisin was confirmed in relation to actions generally in the English courts, not merely those which were Admiralty actions *in rem*. The earlier, impressive judgment of Hirst J., as he then was, at first instance in *Kloeckner & Co. AG v Gatoil Overseas Inc.* [1990] 1 Lloyd's Rep. 177, upholding *issue* as date of definitive seisin generally, was disapproved of by the Court of Appeal in *Dresser*.

Plaintiff cargo owners issued a writ in the English High Court on 15 July 1988. In February 1989, liability limitation proceedings were initiated in The Netherlands by the defendants. It was only in July 1989 that the English writ was finally served upon the defendants. The defendants claimed, *inter alia*, that English courts should exercise their discretion to stay their proceedings on the ground that they were second-seised to the related proceedings in the Dutch courts under Convention Art. 22. The Court of Appeal unanimously held that *service*, not issue, was the date of English seisin, and consequently, Dutch procedure would be examined in order to determine whether English courts were second-seised to the Dutch.

There were three main reasons for the decision: policy and fairness to defendants, who were protected by the service rule; technicalities (mere issue of a writ was largely an administrative rather than a judicial act, and more substantial litigious process was definitively activated by service than in the case of issue); and there were some case law elements from a number of fields capable of being cited in support.

However, according to Bingham L.J. in the Court of Appeal, the rule of service as seisin was open to exceptions, for example, where, prior to service (and even issue), the court had actually exercised jurisdiction in order to grant interim protective relief (but see *infra*, *Neste Chemicals S.A.*, Case 288).

Comment

The principle in *Dresser* was subsequently followed and applied by the English High Court in *Polly Peck International Plc v Citibank SA* [1994] I.L.Pr. 71 (see *infra*) in relation to English seisin under Art. 21, para. 1 of the Lugano Convention—although, on the facts in that case English issue and service took place on the same date. Of additional interest, the English court questioned whether a pre-existing national law of the Swiss courts also seised, which appeared to indicate date of issue as possibly being that of definitive seisin, could continue to be regarded as applicable in the Convention context in view of the European Court's decision in *Zelger*—although the overall view of the English court was that Swiss, not English, courts should decide this and other matters concerned with the date of *Swiss* courts' seisin in any event as a matter of comity and in order to avoid conflicts of jurisdiction.

Not all English lawyers appear to appreciate the significance of the *Dresser* decision in the civil and commercial sphere. In *K v B (Brussels Convention)* [1994] 1 FLR 267, in the course of proceedings for child maintenance in the Family Division of the High Court, more than two years after the *Dresser* case, the court declared, in the course of applying Art. 21, that English courts were seised prior to the Italian because under English law, 'the English court is seised when proceedings are issued' (p. 269), whereas Italian courts were seised when proceedings were served on the defendant!

Case principle

2.   There are *no* exceptions to the rule of service as seisin.

Case

Neste Chemicals SA v DK Line SA [1994] 3 All ER 180 Court of Appeal, 25 **288**
March 1994

Facts

The plaintiff cargo owners obtained leave to issue their English writ out of
England and Wales in May 1992, but also issued and served process in the
Dutch courts in June 1992. It was in July 1992 that the English writ was even-
tually served upon the defendant shipowners for contamination of the cargo.
The defendants requested the English courts to decline jurisdiction, on the
ground that Dutch courts were seised first under Art. 21.

Judgment

The Court of Appeal unanimously held that English courts were seised on the
date of service in July 1992 and consequently they should decline jurisdiction
in favour of first-seised Dutch courts under Art. 21.

The principle of service as seisin pronounced upon by the Court of Appeal
in the previous decision in *Dresser* was confirmed, for reasons of fairness to
defendants, more significant procedural status of service than mere preliminary issue, and lack of inconsistent case law.

However, the Court of Appeal disagreed with the earlier judgment to the
extent that the Court of Appeal in the latter (Bingham L.J.), had admitted the
possibility of *exceptions* to the rule (see *supra*). The Court of Appeal in *Neste
Chemicals SA* unanimously decreed that the earlier court had been wrong to
state this. There was *no exception* to the rule of service as seisin, which, consequently, was the sole and exclusive date. There were two main reasons for
this: first, this was the more simple and certain solution, as prescribed by the
European Court in *Zelger v Salinitri*, rather than a rule subject to exceptions;
and secondly, it would be incorrect to assert that actual exercise of jurisdiction
prior to service (for example, in the *Neste* case itself, the English court's grant
of leave to serve out in May 1992) was effectively equivalent to definitive
seisin when this was only done in order to grant provisional measures, because
jurisdiction in respect of the latter would not necessarily also provide jurisdiction over the merits of the proceedings.

Comment

For a critique of the *Dresser* rule of service as definitive English seisin, see 'The
Date upon which an English Court becomes "Seised" of Proceedings under the
Brussels Convention: Issue or Service of Process?' (1995) *Journal of Business
Law* 217.

Case principles

3. In determining date of definitive seisin of a foreign Contracting State's
    courts under Lugano Art. 21, para. 1, as a matter of comity it is prefer-
    able to adjourn the application for stay of English proceedings thereunder
    until such time as the foreign court seised has itself decided upon that
    date, rather than for the English court itself to determine the latter, albeit
    in accordance with the foreign State's own procedural principles as
    required by *Zelger v Salinitri*. In that event, the foreign court should be

requested, and would be expected, to expedite its decision on this matter. If English courts were, however, to decide the issue, then in accordance with Art. 1 of Protocol No. 2 annexed to the Lugano Convention (given effect to in relation to the UK's own courts' obligations thereunder by Civil Jurisdiction and Judgments Act 1982 s.3B), Swiss courts would subsequently be required to pay due account to the principles laid down by the English courts when applying and interpreting the Convention's provisions, although they would not also be bound thereby.

4.   The European Court in *Zelger v Salinitri (No. 2)* is taken to have followed the Opinion of its Advocate General to the extent that the Convention had left date of definitive seisin for each national legal system to decide in relation to its own courts because of wide diversity—but the Court did not also agree that this should be *subject to* the objective criterion that such seisin should at least be excluded prior to the date of service.

Case

Polly Peck International Plc v Citibank NA [1994] I.L.Pr. 71 High Court, 14   **289**
October 1993

Facts

The plaintiffs informed the Swiss defendants that they would delay commencement of English proceedings for the tort of conversion of corporate funds, in order to give the defendants an opportunity to reach a compromise. On 8 February 1992, the defendants applied to a Swiss Cantonal official (known as a 'justice of the peace') in Zurich for the issue of a *Weisung*—a notification or certificate authorizing institution of proceedings (there for a declaration of non-liability towards the plaintiffs) in the District or Commercial Court. Normally, this would not be granted until an attempt at conciliation had failed, but this was not required where, as in *Polly Peck*, the plaintiff was domiciled abroad with no Swiss representative. The *Weisung* was therefore granted forthwith on 9 February 1992. On that same day, the plaintiffs issued and served their English writ. It was April 1992 when the Swiss proceedings for non-liability were issued and only much later that they were served on the English plaintiffs.

On 5 March 1993, the defendants requested the English High Court to decline jurisdiction under Lugano Art. 21, para. 1 in favour of Swiss courts first-seised—or to stay until prior Swiss jurisdiction had been established. However, the defendants also asked the English judge, Vinelott J., to adjourn their application for decline or stay until Swiss courts had decided whether they were first-seised, and it was the latter issue which was the subject of the *Polly Peck* judgment.

Judgment

In reaching his decision, Vinelott J. followed the Court of Appeal's judgment in *Dresser* in respect of service as English seisin—although, on the facts, issue and service had actually taken place on the same date, 9 February 1992. He interpreted the European Court's ruling in *Zelger v Salinitri* as leaving this to national courts to decide in accordance with their own laws, and considered the European Court to have disagreed with the Advocate General as to existence of a minimum objective requirement that this should at least not take place *prior to service*.

The real issue, therefore, in *Polly Peck* was whether the Swiss Cantonal Court of Zurich had been seised prior to the English court, on 8 February 1992 when proceedings for issue of the *Weisung* were instituted? Had it been left to Vinelott J., he would not have regarded the Swiss courts as properly seised on that date, which he regarded as equivalent to an English application for leave to issue proceedings or even to issue itself—not definitive seisin according to *Dresser*. However, the question was to be decided according to Swiss, not English, procedural principles—and, as a matter of comity, preferably by the Swiss courts, which hopefully would expedite their decision thereupon. The application for a stay of English proceedings under Art. 21, para. 1 was accordingly agreed to be adjourned pending the Swiss decision on Swiss courts' seisin in the case. Counsel were requested to address the court on questions to be submitted to the Swiss courts and upon certain preliminary issues, such as whether the proceedings fell within Swiss procedural laws as concerning tort, delict or quasi-delict.

Case principle

5.   Notwithstanding that a foreign Contracting State's courts were seised prior to the English, nevertheless, if the foreign proceedings were actually also *concluded before English seisin*, Arts 21 and 22 are inapplicable.

Case

290   Gamlestaden Plc v Casa de Suecia SA and Thulin [1994] 1 Lloyd's Rep. 433 High Court, 3 February 1993

Facts

See supra, Case 144.

The plaintiff English company sued Spanish and Belgian defendants in the English and Spanish courts on a loan agreement and guarantee. Executory Spanish proceedings were instituted in May 1991 and a writ in the English action issued in December 1991 and served in January/February 1992. In January 1992, prior to service of the English writ, the Spanish proceedings were concluded unsuccessfully for the plaintiff. The defendants challenged English jurisdiction under Arts 21 and 22.

Judgment

Potter J. held that Arts 21 and 22 were inapplicable because the action in firstseised Spanish courts had concluded and consequently was no longer pending, as it was required to be (expressly in Art. 22, par. 1), at the date of service—that is seisin—in the English proceedings.

Thus, English courts were not permitted to decline or to stay the action under Art. 21 or 22.

Comment

The defendants subsequently applied to the Court of Appeal for leave to appeal against Potter J.'s refusal to set aside the English writ, on a number of grounds. The Court of Appeal dismissed the application (unreported, 26 April 1993).

Inexplicably, Neill L.J. considered that the date to be had regard to, upon which Spanish proceedings were still required to be pending for Art. 21 to operate—and they were so—was that of *issue* of the English writ. Although Neill L.J. did in fact go on to hold Art. 21 to be inapplicable on policy grounds, since there was no longer any danger of parallel English and Spanish proceedings, which it was designed to prevent, nevertheless it seems rather strange—in view of previous authorities of *Dresser* and *Neste*—that he regarded date of *issue* of the English writ, rather than that of *service*, as the appropriate point in time to be considered for the purposes at hand!

Case principle

6.   If first-seised proceedings are later discontinued, the second-seised courts are no longer subject to Arts 21 and 22 (applying *Gamlestaden*).

Case

Internationale Nederlanden Aviation Lease B.V. (A Corporation established **291** under the laws of the Netherlands) and Others v The Civil Aviation Authority and Another (unreported) High Court, 13 June 1996

Facts

The defendant C.A.A. (Civil Aviation Authority), acting on behalf of Eurocontrol, detained an aircraft belonging to the plaintiffs when it was at Bournemouth airport in the South of England in 1993, proceeding under statutory powers in respect of air traffic control payments due to Eurocontrol from the aircraft's Turkish operators.

The plaintiffs commenced English proceedings in November 1993 for damages for alleged wrongful detention of the aircraft and subsequently too in the Belgian courts in August 1995. In the meantime, in October 1994 deputy High Court Judge Diamond Q.C. held, on a preliminary issue, that the plaintiffs were in fact liable for a proportion of the charges and that the defendant was entitled to sell the aircraft unless the relevant part of the debt was paid.

The current application made in 1996 was by the plaintiffs for the High Court's leave to discontinue the English action under RSC Ord. 21. The defendant opposed leave, on the ground that the plaintiffs were forum shopping. They had started in England and should not be permitted to switch to Belgium.

Judgment

Morison J. refused to exercise his discretion to grant leave to the plaintiffs to discontinue their English action.

(1)   One factor which the judge considered to be relevant was whether, if first-seised English proceedings were discontinued, Belgian courts, thitherto second-seised, would no longer regard themselves as subject to decline or stay under Art. 21 or 22 and would then proceed to hear the action—which might not be fair, as the defendant had argued.

   The judge was scrupulous to point out that he would in no way 'second-guess' the Belgian courts' likely actions in these events, which would be to interfere, contrary to the European Court's findings in *Overseas Union*. Nevertheless, the consideration was not wholly irrelevant and Morison J., following Potter J. in *Gamlestaden*, concluded that when a first-seised court discontinues, there is no longer the same policy reason for second-seised courts to be subject to Arts 21 and 22. Consequently, they would not be so.

(2)   Morison J. went on to conclude that he should not exercise his discretion in favour of grant of leave to discontinue, in all the circumstances. How far had the English action proceeded? It was wrong that having started in England, the plaintiffs should then be able to proceed in the Belgian courts which would probably, as seen, no longer regard themselves as second-seised for Art. 21 or 22. In particular, it was important that there had already been an English judgment on the preliminary matter of plaintiffs' liability for a proportion of the charges, which, effectively, had settled the common issue of lawfulness of the aircraft's detention and could not be 'unscrambled'. If leave to discontinue had been granted, therefore, it could only have been on the terms that the plaintiffs would not then proceed with the Belgian action.

Comment

In the non-Convention case of *Rofa Sport Management AG v DHL International (UK) Ltd The Times, 15 March 1989* Court of Appeal, 2 March 1989, Neill L.J. made the point that an action which had merely been stayed—on the facts, by consent following a settlement between the plaintiffs and first defendant—rather than dismissed or discontinued, technically remained in being (even though it could not be proceeded with without a court order); and consequently, the court could make an order under RSC Ord. 15, r.6(2)(b) for joinder of the second defendant on the latter's application.

Whether the preceding means that a mere stay of action in the first-seised court still does not prevent the latter from continuing to be regarded as being first-seised for purposes of Art. 21 is seriously open to question, since the policies and issues are quite different from those in the purely national context in *Rofa Sport Management*.

Perhaps it should be the case that in the circumstances the 'second-seised' court should, if not to proceed, at least merely stay its proceedings under Art. 21, para. 1 rather than decline under para. 2—on analogy with the situation in *Assurances Générales de France* (see *infra*) where power to stay until foreign *seisin* is established was confirmed by the High Court.

The doubts here expressed over the application of *Rofa* to the Convention context derive support from the *Solani* decision—see *infra*, *Case principle* nine.

Case principle

7. If a statute not only makes a contract void, but also procedurally bars its actionability and enforcement through the courts, the court before which such action is wrongly commenced ought not to be regarded as seised.

Case

Kloeckner & Co. AG v Gatoil Overseas Inc. [1990] 1 Lloyd's Rep. 177 High   **292**
Court, 31 July 1989

Facts

See supra, Case 273.

Judgment

Hirst J. in fact held that the contracts here in question were *not* gaming contracts made void and unenforceable under the gaming legislation.

However, he expressed the view that had they been held to be such, a court could not be said to be properly seised for purposes of Art. 21 of proceedings which were procedurally improper to be brought.

Case principle

8. A court merely provisionally seised of proceedings held not to be first-seised prior to another court subsequently seised of substance.

Case

Boss Group Ltd v Boss France S.A. [1996] 4 All ER 970 Court of Appeal,   **293**
2 April 1996

Facts

See supra, Art. 5(1), Case 148.

The defendants contended that English courts should decline in favour of French courts seised prior thereto.

309

Judgment

The Court of Appeal took the view that French courts were not first-seised for Art. 21, because their proceedings were merely provisional, whereas those before the English court were as to substance.

Comment

See too *supra*, *Gamlestaden* and earlier, Art. 21 'same cause of action'.

Case principle

9.   Where first-seised (pre-Lugano) English proceedings are stayed for national *forum non conveniens*, a foreign Contracting State's courts should not decline their *Lugano* jurisdiction as second-seised under Art. 21.

Case

294   Solani Bank v Bank Austria AG (unreported) Court of Appeal, 15 January 1997

Facts

The plaintiff Bangladeshi bank and defendant Austrian bank concluded an agreement to provide a mechanism for payments to be made under a trading agreement between companies in their respective countries, governed by Bangladeshi law. When the trading agreement came to an end in 1992, the plaintiff sued the defendant in England for payment of sums overdrawn of approximately 2.6 million US dollars. The defendants challenged English jurisdiction and sought a stay for *forum non conveniens* in the alternative.

Moore-Bick J. in the High Court upheld English jurisdiction on the ground that the defendants possessed an established place of business in London—but granted a stay in favour of Austria as *forum conveniens*.

The plaintiff sought leave to appeal against the judge's finding that England was *forum non conveniens*.

Judgment

The Court of Appeal (Evans and Otton L.JJ.) dismissed the appeal. Discretion was a matter for the judge, who had not erred in principle.

One of the plaintiff's arguments against stay was that Austria was now party to the Lugano Convention (since 1 September 1996), which it had not been at the time of the High Court proceedings. This meant that if the English courts were to stay, Austrian courts too were now obliged to decline under Art. 21 as second-seised, which made those courts, not the English, *forum non conveniens*.

The Court of Appeal rejected this.

In the first place, the plaintiff could simply discontinue its English action, in which event the Austrian court could then proceed.

Secondly, even in the absence of such a discontinuance, as a matter of Convention policy, it would be quite inappropriate for the Austrian courts to decline Lugano jurisdiction under Art. 21 in favour of national English *forum non conveniens*.

Comments

Evans L.J. also referred to the *Sarrio* decision (see Cases 270/1) for support.

See too *infra*, Lugano Art. 54, para. 1, Case 368, for transitional implications of the *Solani* case; and *supra*, Comment to Case 291. *Von Horn*, Case C–163/95 in the European Court means that Article 21 *could* apply in this type of situation (if the stayed English court were still to be regarded as 'seised').

> " . . . *other than the court first seised shall* . . . *stay* . . . *until* . . . *jurisdiction* . . . *is established.*"

Case principle

The obligation to stay proceedings until 'jurisdiction' of the foreign court first seised is established includes where it is seisin itself which is yet to be decided upon in the foreign court rather than jurisdiction pure and simple.

Case

Assurances Générales de France I.A.R.T. v The Chiyoda Fire and Marine Co. **295**
(U.K.) Ltd [1992] 1 Lloyd's Rep. 325 High Court, 1 October 1991

Facts

The plaintiffs were French and Belgian reinsurers and the defendants included the Italian reassured under a scheme of reinsurance for jewellery and furs arranged in 1988–9 and 1989–90. The French reinsurers' English writ for, *inter alia*, non-liability under the policies was served upon the defendants, including the Italians, in March 1990; and the Italian defendants served and entered their own proceedings in Italy upon the French and Belgian plaintiffs, claiming contractual enforcement, in June/July 1990. The Belgian plaintiffs' English writ was served in November 1990.

Subsequently, the French plaintiffs sought to introduce new claims and defendants. The defendants challenged English jurisdiction over both French and Belgian actions under Art. 21, on the ground that Italian courts were first-seised. The plaintiffs for their part had argued the converse in the Italian courts, whose proceedings were currently pending, waiting for future resumption.

Judgment

Judge Diamond Q.C. dealt with a number of issues.

(1) In relation to the defendants' challenge to Belgian plaintiffs' English action, in accordance with *Dresser*, English courts were seised on service in November 1990. As for Italian seisin, *Zelger* required this to be decided under Italian law (see *supra*). This said that the original service in June/July 1990 was invalid through incorrectly naming the Belgian plaintiffs. Consequently, it was only in February 1991 that the Italian court became seised in relation to the Belgian plaintiffs, on their entry of a defence thereto. This was subsequent to the English courts which were, therefore, first seised.

(2) Concerning the seisin of English courts over the French plaintiffs' application to reamend in February 1991, this was subsequent to Italian service in June/July 1990 and in accordance with *Gubisch*, causes of action were the same. This would mean that English courts should decline the reamendments under Art. 21. *However*, if the Italian court were to treat the reamendment proceedings *together with* the original, prior English process as related to the Italian action under Art. 22, then it could be concluded that English seisin *for the reamendments* was also that earlier date of original seisin in March 1990, so that even for the reamendments, English courts were first-seised for Art. 21.

(3) As it happened, since the Italian courts themselves were expected to decide the issue of Art. 22 relatedness, seisin and jurisdiction, Judge Diamond Q.C. considered that it would be wrong to pre-empt the Italian courts' decision on these matters and thereby indirectly to interfere with it, contrary to Convention principles. The provision for stay of the proceedings and of Art. 21 plea for decline thereunder *did also apply to where it was seisin of the foreign court*, not merely jurisdiction itself, which was awaited to be established—yet, under the old pre-1989 Art. 21(2) applicable to the case, there was a *discretion* to stay, rather than an obligation under the current Art. 21(1), and the judge preferred not to exercise it in favour of a stay in view of the time it was likely to take (over two years) for the Italian courts to resume proceedings. Instead, therefore, he chose to dismiss the French plaintiffs' application to reamend entirely, with leave to reapply when the Italian courts had decided on their jurisdiction and the other matters.

> " . . . *shall* . . . *stay* . . . "

Case principle

1. Arts 16 and 17 held to prevail over Art. 21, notwithstanding the mandatory terms of the latter.

Case

Kloeckner & Co. AG v Gatoil Overseas Inc. [1990] 1 Lloyd's Rep. 177 High   **296**
Court, 31 July 1989

Facts

See supra, Case 273.

Judgment

Hirst J. held that Arts 16 and 17 were just as important as Art. 21 within the
Convention system and were paramount over Art. 21. On the facts, English
courts were actually found to be first-seised (a decision no longer to be regarded
as correct: see *supra*, Case 287). Had they not been so, they would *not* have been
obliged under Art. 21 to decline in favour of German courts also seised, since
English courts were agreed to by the contracting parties under Art. 17.

Case

The Filiatra Legacy [1994] 1 Lloyd's Rep. 513 High Court, 9 April 1990   **297a**

(Decided in 1990 some months after *Kloeckner*).

Facts

See supra, Case 211.

Judgment

Saville J. held that Arts 16 and 17 must prevail over Arts 21 and 22 by virtue
of the exclusive nature of jurisdiction conferred under the former provisions.

His finding was *obiter* because he went on to conclude that neither Art. 16
nor Art. 17 in fact applied to the case.

Case

Denby v The Hellenic Mediterranean Lines Co. Ltd [1994] 1 Lloyd's Rep. 320   **297b**
High Court, 29 October 1993

(In this judgment, Rix J. followed and applied the previous High Court decision in *Kloeckner* and held Art. 17 to prevail over Arts 21 and 22.)

Facts

The plaintiff insurance underwriter issued and served English proceedings
upon the defendant shipowners in August 1993 for avoidance of an insurance
contract through misrepresentation. Previously, the defendants had commenced proceedings in Greece against the plaintiff in June 1993, claiming
monies due under the policy. The insurance contract was subject to an English

jurisdiction clause. The defendants requested English courts to decline jurisdiction as second-seised under Art. 21.

Judgment

The court held that Art. 17, as well as Art. 16, prevailed over Art. 21.
Consequently, English courts retained jurisdiction. Passages from the
European Court's judgment in *Overseas Union Insurance Ltd* Case C–351/89
(para. 13) were cited in support.

Comment

In *Overseas Union*, Advocate General Van Gerven and the Court of Justice
itself clearly contemplated that Convention exclusive jurisdiction—or at least
in particular, Art. 16—would prevail over Art. 21.

*See too infra, Rank Film Distributors Limited v Lanterna Editrice Srl and
Banca Nazionale del Lavoro, Art. 22, para. 1, Case 305.*

Case

298   Continental Bank N.A. v Aeakos Compania Naviera S.A. [1994] 1 Lloyd's
Rep. 505 Court of Appeal, 10 November 1993

Facts

Greek courts were first-seised before the English over proceedings covered by
an English jurisdiction clause.

Judgment

The Court of Appeal approved of Hirst J. in *Kloeckner* and of Saville J. in *The
Filiatra Legacy, supra*: Art. 17 exclusive jurisdiction prevailed over Art. 21
and, consequently, English courts retained their jurisdiction.

Comments

Continental Bank was expressly followed, *obiter*, by Colman J. in the High
Court in *Lexmar Corporation and Steamship Mutual Underwriting
Association (Bermuda) Ltd v Nordisk Skibsrederforening and Northern
Tankers (Cyprus) Ltd* [1997] 1 Lloyd's Rep. 289, in April 1996, in relation to
(Lugano) Art. 21 (see *supra*, Art. 17 and *infra*, Art. 22). Clarke J. in the High
Court in *The Bergen* (unreported) 20 November 1996, also 'borrowed' the
reasoning in *Continental Bank* in order to confirm the mandatory nature of
Art. 17 for purposes of insisting upon its exclusion as otherwise contravening
Art. 57 in the circumstances (see *supra*, Art. 17 and *infra*, Art. 57).

Case principles

2.   Article 57 particular conventions have priority over rules in the
Judgments Convention.

3. Judgments Convention provisions do not apply to the extent that they are inconsistent with the rules or overall scheme and relationship between particular conventions and the Judgments Convention.
4. National English *in rem* grounds based upon those in the 1952 Arrest Convention not otherwise implemented in England, can be treated as if they had priority afforded the latter by Art. 57; and, effectively, Art. 57 has the effect of indirectly incorporating the 1952 Convention into municipal English law for Convention purposes in any event.
5. In principle, consequently, Art. 21 can continue to apply to an Art. 57 particular convention, including English *in rem* jurisdiction derived from the 1952 Arrest Convention, if Art. 21 conditions are satisfied.
6. At the inception of an English *in rem* action, the defendant is the ship and, consequently, the proceedings were not between the same parties as in a foreign *in personam* action on the same claim at that date. However, if and when the shipowner chooses to defend the *in rem* action (or at least to acknowledge service in), he then becomes subject to potential *in personam* liability, and on such entry of appearance by the defendant shipowner, the initially *in rem* action becomes hybrid *in rem-in personam* and parties are the same for purposes of Article 21 (*House of Lords in Indian Endurance (No. 2), supra Case 106, disapproving of Hobhouse J. in The Nordglimt, infra, who had previously held that although parties became the same 'as from' such hybrid character of the proceedings, through defendant's entry of appearance, nonetheless, for Article 21, parties were not the same retrospectively, by reason of the initial in rem nature of the proceedings*). On release of the ship, the action is thought to become solely *in personam*.

Case

The Nordglimt [1988] 1 QB 183 High Court, 31 July 1987   **299**

Facts

Barley carried on board the Danish ship Nordkap from Antwerp to Jedda in Saudi Arabia was defective on arrival. The cargo's Saudi Arabian receivers and their insurers brought *in personam* proceedings for damages in the Belgian courts in 1985 against the Danish shipowners and Canadian charterers. In 1987, the Saudi Arabians and the Liechstenstein shippers brought further proceedings *in rem* in the English courts: the Nordkap's sister ship, Nordglimt, was arrested and security given for its release. The shipowner challenged the arrest and main English *in rem* jurisdiction on a number of grounds, including that second-seised English courts should stay proceedings in favour of the earlier Belgian action under Art. 21.

Judgment

Hobhouse J. held that there would be no stay.

In the first place, Art. 57 particular conventions had priority over the Judgments Convention's provisions—and although English *in rem* jurisdiction was actually based upon rules of domestic English legislation, ss.20 and 21 of the Supreme Court Act 1981, rather than on the 1952 Brussels International Arrest Convention to which the UK was party but had not actually specifically implemented, nevertheless, the domestic provisions were very similar and Hobhouse J. considered that the effect of Art. 57 itself, in the overall scheme and context of the 1952 Arrest–1968 Judgments Convention as a whole, was *indirectly* to incorporate the 1952 Arrest Convention into English law for purposes of such priorities.

Secondly, Art. 57 particular conventions did not bring about a blanket exclusion of the Judgments Convention—the latter was only excluded to the extent that it was inconsistent with individual provisions or the general structure and object of the former conventions.

As to whether Art. 21 was so inconsistent in the case of the 1952 Convention, Hobhouse J. believed this to be the position in respect of English 1982 Act s.26–1952 Convention Art. 7 retained arrest and security jurisdiction, since Art. 21 would destroy the whole point of these (see *supra*, s.26, Case 101).

Yet, with regard to such consistency of Art. 21 with general *in rem* merits jurisdiction under or derived from the 1952 Convention, Hobhouse J. did not in fact have to decide conclusively, since he considered Art. 21 to be inapplicable according to its terms in any event: unless and until the shipowner decided to enter a defence (presumably meaning 'acknowledged service'), English *in rem* proceedings were to be treated at their inception as brought against the defendant ship, whatever the named parties on the writ, whereas the Belgian *in personam* action was against the shipowners and charterers. Therefore, the proceedings were not between the same parties, as required by Art. 21, and the latter was inapplicable. Hobhouse J., however, thought it likely that Art. 22 on related actions could have applied.

Comment

Hohhouse J. considered that initially *in rem* proceedings would become hybrid *in rem-in personam* on the defendant shipowner's personal appearance and that parties would be the same as from the later time. But he went on to conclude that even this would not be sufficient to make parties the same for purposes of Art. 21, because they were not also the same *initially*, whereas, he thought, it would be Article 22 which should properly be applied, if at all (compare cause of action which he *seemed* to say *was* even initially the same, pp. 201–2, although see p. 203).

Subsequently to Hobhouse J.'s judgment, however, such inapplicability of Article 21 became subject to great doubt following the ECJ's contrary ruling in *Maciej Rataj* Case C–406/92, and in *Indian Endurance (No. 2)*, *supra*, Case 106, on 16 October 1997, the House of Lords, equating Article 21 and 1982 Act s.34 for the purposes, confirmed that parties *were* the same for estoppel or *lis pendens* where proceedings thus became hybrid, and expressly disapproved of *Nordglimt* to the contrary (cause of action was by then conceded by the parties to be the same; see *supra*, *ibid*.).

These conclusions had earlier also been reached in the High Court at the same level as *The Nordglimt*, by Sheen J. in *The Kherson*, *infra*, Case 300 (actually referred to in *The Maciej Rataj*, by Advocate General Tesauro [1994] ECR I-5439, at p. 5452).

Case

The Kherson [1992] 2 Lloyd's Rep. 261 High Court, 6 April 1992   **300**

Facts

Dutch cargo owners wished to sue Georgian shipowners in the English courts for damage to the cargo. A writ *in rem* was issued and the defendants' ship *Kherson* arrested. The defendants acknowledged service of the writ and their P. & I. Club provided security, following which the *Kherson* was released. However, prior to the arrest, the plaintiffs had already commenced proceedings against the defendants personally in the courts of Rotterdam. The defendants therefore argued that English courts were obliged to decline jurisdiction, as being second-seised to the Dutch under Art. 21. The plaintiffs responded that Art. 21 was inapplicable because English *in rem* and Dutch *in personam* proceedings did not involve the same cause of action, as required by Art. 21.

Judgment

Sheen J. rejected the plaintiffs' plea against applicability of Article 21 on the facts on this ground. Although *in rem* and *in personam* were different, the English proceedings became *in personam* as well as *in rem* when the defendants acknowledged service (following *The Nordglimt* to this extent)—and solely *in personam* on release of the ship.
   Consequently:

   (1)   the cause of action was the same in the English proceedings as in the Dutch; and
   (2)   the parties were too.

   This was so not just when the English action became solely *in personam* on release of the ship, but also when they were *in personam* as well as *in rem* because of the defendants' acknowledgement of service. At this stage, the only differences were in the remedies available to a successful plaintiff and the procedures to be followed to obtain them.
   English courts would therefore be obliged to decline jurisdiction in favour of the first-seised Dutch under Art. 21.

Case

The Linda [1988] 1 Lloyd's Rep. 175 High Court, 23 October 1987   **301**

Facts

See infra, Art. 57, Case 376.

Judgment

Sheen J. held Art. 21 to continue to apply to 1952 Arrest Convention juris-diction, which itself contained no corresponding *lis pendens* provision. Consequently, application of Art. 21 to jurisdiction thereunder was not in con-travention of Art. 57 of the 1968 Convention.

Case

302 Deaville v Aeroflot Russian International Airlines [1997] 2 Lloyd's Rep. 67 High Court, 7 February 1997

Facts

In 1994, an Aeroflot international flight crashed in Siberia en route from Moscow to Hong Kong, with the loss of all 63 passengers and 12 crew, allegedly caused by pilot error and the aircraft manufacturers' failure to pro-vide warning systems.

In March 1996, 44 of the relatives of the deceased passengers commenced proceedings in French courts against the Russian carrier, Aeroflot, the French manufacturer, Airbus Industrie, and two other defendants, and later in that year 22 of the relatives began an action in England against Aeroflot in order to preserve English time limits should French courts eventually decide against their own jurisdiction. The latter was challenged by the defendants in France, on the ground that the Warsaw Convention on air carriage gave jurisdiction to English, Russian and Hong Kong courts but not also to the French. The plaintiffs wished to fight that challenge, because French courts could grant moral damages and adopt a more favourable interpretation of the Warsaw Convention than the English.

In the English proceedings:

(1) the plaintiffs requested a stay of the English action, either under Art. 21 as being second-seised to the French, or, should Art. 21 be held to be inapplicable, under the English courts' inherent power of stay; and

(2) the defendants sought
—a declaration that French courts lacked jurisdiction under the Warsaw Convention, and
—an anti-suit injunction restraining continuation of the French proceedings.

Judgment

Deputy High Court Judge Geoffrey Brice Q.C. held that Art. 21 was inapplicable.

The Warsaw Convention was a particular convention under Art. 57—actually one of those listed in the Jenard Report.

Thus, although Art. 21 could continue to apply in principle alongside an Art. 57 convention if not incompatible with the latter, in this case its operation would be so incompatible, because first-seised French courts might not possess jurisdiction under the Warsaw Convention at all, whereas the second-seised English courts were known to do so.

Comment

Brice Q.C. went on:

(1) to refuse to grant the defendants' application for (a declaration and) an anti-suit injunction restraining the French action (see *supra*, 1982 Act s.49, *General*); and

(2) to agree to the plaintiffs' request to stay their English proceedings under the English courts' inherent power, pending determination of French jurisdiction by the French courts.

Case principles

7. Notwithstanding that conditions of stay and decline in Art. 21 are not satisfied, nevertheless, national English principles of discretionary stays for *forum non conveniens* continue to apply, even in relation to competing foreign *Contracting* State jurisdiction, when jurisdiction is exercised on national grounds over non-Contracting State defendants under Art. 4.

8. The same applies in respect of national stays for *lis alibi pendens*, including *lis pendens* in another Contracting State.

Case

Sarrio S.A. v Kuwait Investment Authority [1996] 1 Lloyd's Rep. 650 High   **303** Court, 12 October 1995

Facts

See supra, 'same cause of action', Cases 270 and 271.

The plaintiff Spanish company commenced proceedings against the Kuwaiti defendant in respect of the sale of the plaintiff's paper business, in the courts of Spain in 1993 and of England in 1994. The defendant contested English courts' jurisdiction, *inter alia*, on the ground of discretionary common law *forum non conveniens*, including *lis alibi pendens* in favour of Spain, in the event that Art. 21 was inapplicable to require English courts to decline.

The plaintiff argued that these English common law doctrines were inapplicable in relation to competing foreign Contracting State jurisdiction, even where English jurisdiction was founded upon national grounds under Art. 4.

Judgment

Mance J. held for the defendant on this point: there was no distinction between national jurisdiction 'grounds' and discretionary national rules on 'appropriateness' of jurisdiction for the purposes of Art. 4—both types were preserved thereunder. Nor was it true to say that *forum non conveniens* applied, but national *lis alibi pendens* did not. The latter was merely one aspect of the former, not independent thereof.

Case

304 Sarrio S.A. v Kuwait Investment Authority [1997] 1 Lloyd's Rep. 113 Court of Appeal, 12 August 1996

Facts

The plaintiff appealed against Mance J.'s preceding findings, on the ground that the Convention's system impliedly excluded application of national *lis pendens* in relation to foreign Contracting State Art. 4 proceedings.

Judgment

The Court of Appeal disagreed with the plaintiff and upheld Mance J.'s judgment at first instance in favour of continued availability of national English powers of discretionary stays for *lis alibi pendens* in the circumstances. Nor would there be any risk of negative jurisdictional conflicts from operation of *forum non conveniens* to Art. 4 situations in circumstances in which English courts had instead been first-seised and Art. 21 applicable on the facts, because *either* second-seised foreign Contracting States' courts would not have regarded stayed English proceedings as 'established' for purposes of decline under Art. 21, *or* even if they were to have done so, an English court should not then have regarded such a foreign court as *forum conveniens* so as to lead the former to have stayed its proceedings in the first place.

The Court of Appeal then went on to find that, on balance, England was *forum conveniens* on the facts, in particular, in view of the delays which might otherwise ensue in Spain if the stayed English action were sought to be accumulated with the Spanish proceedings in Spain. Accordingly, a stay would be refused (see *infra*, Art. 22, para. 1 'discretion'—Mance J. at first instance reached the opposite conclusion in exercising his discretion to stay under Art. 22, held inapplicable by the Court of Appeal).

ARTICLE 22, PARAGRAPH 1

" . . . *any court other than the court first seised* . . . "

Case principle

1. Article 2 domicile jurisdiction is *not* an exception to Arts 21 and 22.

Case

Rank Film Distributors Limited v Lanterna Editrice Srl and Banca Nazionale   **305**
del Lavoro [1992] I.L.Pr. 58 High Court, 4 June 1991

Facts

See supra, Case 253.

The English court had upheld its jurisdiction under Art. 5(1) and the Italian
defendants had failed to persuade it that second-seised Italian courts were possessed of jurisdiction over the plaintiff under Art. 18 and that Art. 18 would
prevail over Arts 21 and 22. So, the defendants tried again. This time they
argued that since the plaintiff had brought a counterclaim against them in the
Italian action and the Italian court would have jurisdiction to hear that counterclaim under Art. 2, Italian Art. 2 jurisdiction would—as the *pre-eminent*
Convention jurisdiction ground—prevail over English Art. 5(1) jurisdiction,
and Art. 2 thereby, in effect, amounted to an exception to Arts 21 and 22.

Judgment

Saville J. dismissed these submissions and held that Art. 2 was not an exception to Arts 21 and 22. His view in *The Filiatra Legacy*, *supra* Art. 21, Case
238, had been that Arts 16 and 17 were such exceptions, but this was due to
the fact that those provisions—unlike Art. 2—conferred *exclusive* jurisdiction.

Case principle

2.   Article 22 (or Art. 21) overrides Art. 18.

Case

Rank Film Distributors Limited v Lanterna Editrice Srl and Banca Nazionale   **306**
del Lavoro [1992] I.L.Pr. 58 High Court, 4 June 1991

Facts

See supra, Art. 18, Case 253.

Judgment

Saville J. held that Art. 18 was not an exception to Arts 21 and 22. The priority of the first-seised court continued to apply over competing, second-seised
Art. 18 jurisdiction.

Case principle

3.   English Art. 57 *in rem* jurisdiction derived from 1952 Arrest Convention
     held to be subject to Art. 22.

Case

307 The Linda [1988] 1 Lloyd's Rep. 175 High Court, 23 October 1987

Facts

See supra, and infra, Art. 57.

Judgment

Application of Art. 22 to 1952 Arrest Convention-derived jurisdiction would not contravene Art. 57 of the 1968 Convention, according to Sheen J.

Case principle

4.   Article 22 is inapplicable to Art. 17 jurisdiction.

Case

308 Continental Bank N.A. v Aeakos Compania Naviera S.A. [1994] 1 Lloyd's Rep. 505 Court of Appeal, 10 November 1993

Facts and Judgment

See supra, Art. 17, Case 239.

Comment

The case succeeded upon a slightly different approach, based on a mere *assumption* of prevalence of Art. 17, adopted by Waller J. in the High Court in *I.P. Metal Ltd v Ruote O.Z. S.p.A.* [1993] 2 Lloyd's Rep. 60 (see *supra*, Art. 17, Case 241). Waller J. had held that in principle, Art. 17 jurisdiction *could* be stayed in favour of first-seised Art. 22 related jurisdiction—but the discretion was not to be exercised if *either* the first-seised foreign court was to be assumed to decline in favour of Art. 17 *or* even if not, if it would be unjust to stay Art. 17 jurisdiction.

Mance J. in the High Court in *Toepfer International GmbH v Molino Boschi Srl* [1996] 1 Lloyd's Rep. 510 followed *Continental Bank v Aeakos* in giving precedence to Art. 17 over Art. 22 (and Art. 21).

Colman J. in the High Court in *Lexmar Corporation and Steamship Mutual Underwriting Association (Bermuda) Ltd. v Nordisk Skibsrederforening and Northern Tankers (Cyprus) Ltd* [1997] 1 Lloyd's Rep. 289, in April 1996, expressly followed *Continental Bank*, in according precedence to (Lugano) Art. 17 over Art(s) 21 and 22, in conformity with the structure and logic of the Convention including where the plaintiff in the first-seised foreign related action was not itself party to the inconsistent jurisdiction agreement (see Case 242 *supra*, Art. 17).

> " . . . *pending at first instance* . . . "

Case principle

Where judgment has already been delivered by a foreign Contracting State's courts, the latter are no longer (first-) seised and the action is no longer pending.

Case

Gamlestaden Plc v Casa de Suecia SA and Thulin [1994] 1 Lloyd's Rep. 433   **309**
High Court, 3 February 1993

Facts

See supra, Art. 21 *'same cause of action' and 'seised'*, Case 290.

Judgment

The court held that conditions for stay and decline of jurisdiction under Art. 21 were not satisfied.

In addition, Art. 22 would also not apply, because Spanish proceedings had been concluded all the way through to judgment and consequently they were no longer *pending* on the date upon which English courts became seised.

> " . . . *may . . . stay* . . . "

Case principles

1. Actions may be related where they involve intricately interrelated contracts which are part of an overall network contemplated by a framework agreement.
2. *But* the discretion to stay should not reasonably be exercised if those contracts which are the subject of the first-seised foreign Contracting State proceedings are on a minor scale compared with those in the forum.

Case

Kloeckner & Co. AG v Gatoil Overseas Inc. [1990] 1 Lloyd's Rep. 177 High   **310**
Court, 31 July 1989

Facts

See supra, Art. 17, Case 273 and *infra* Case 319.

Judgment

English proceedings involved an entire network of intricately interrelated contracts, whereas the German action only comprised certain of these.

Case principle

3. *Forum non conveniens* considerations, specifically, juridical advantage, are not factors to be taken into account in exercise of the discretion to stay or not under Art. 22.

Case

311 The Linda [1988] 1 Lloyd's Rep. 175 High Court, 23 October 1987

Facts

See supra, Art. 21, Case 259.

English jurisdiction was declined under Art. 21.

Judgment

Sheen J. stated that had Art. 21 been held to be inapplicable to the English proceedings, English and Dutch actions would still have been related within Art. 22 and the discretion to stay the former would have been exercised thereunder.

However, in so doing, he commented that the Convention system in Arts 21 and 22 was one of time priority and that consequently, the doctrine of *forum non conveniens* had no relevance to Arts 21 and 22.

Case

312 Virgin Aviation Services Limited v CAD Aviation [1991] I.L.Pr. 79 High Court, 21 January 1990

Facts

The plaintiffs sued the defendant, their agent, in the English courts in 1989 for payment of £36,000, as the balance of money in their mutual trading account arising from their dealings. Prior to that, the defendant had commenced proceedings in the Dutch courts against the plaintiffs, claiming damages of £100 000 for wrongful termination of the agency contract by the plaintiffs. The defendant requested the English court to stay the plaintiffs' action under Art. 22, as being related to the first-seised Dutch. The plaintiffs objected on the grounds that if the English proceedings were to be stayed, they would be deprived of the juridical advantage that RSC Ord. 14 summary judgment would be available in respect of part of their action, whereas this was not possible under Dutch procedure.

Judgment

Ognall J. dismissed the plaintiffs' objections and granted the stay of the English action under Art. 22. Cases on juridical advantage pre-dated the entry into force of the Convention in the United Kingdom, and it would be quite contrary to the Convention's spirit if it were to be concluded that one Contracting State's procedures were inferior or superior to another's as the basis for stay under Art. 22. The impression given by the Jenard Report (p. 41) was that there should be a strong presumption in favour of granting a stay on an application to do so under Art. 22.

Comments

See *infra*, however, *E. Recent Cases*, Art. 1, para. 1, Comment to Case 387.

Thus, it may be that if the Convention has had the effect of making actions for infringement of *foreign* intellectual property rights justiciable in Contracting States' courts, English courts will still be reluctant to stay in favour of first-seised foreign courts, in the context of Art. 22, para. 1 stays discretion, preferring to view the English courts as the appropriate fora to determine English copyright and passing off *et alia* (see *infra*, *Pearce v Ove Arup* and *Mecklermedia Corporation v DC Congress GmbH*). See *infra*, too, *Case principle* 4.

Case principle

4. *Forum conveniens* may be relevant where Art. 22 is *indirectly* applicable in connection with national joinder discretion.

Case

Fox v Taher [1997] I.L.Pr. 441 Court of Appeal, 31 July 1996   **313**

Facts

The plaintiff, Fox, was an Irish solicitor who claimed to be owed £1.2 million by the Taher defendants as percentage fees for representing them in litigation, an amount disputed by the Tahers.

In April 1995, the plaintiff served English proceedings upon the Taher defendants' English solicitors, Orchards, in order to restrain the solicitor defendants from paying funds in their possession to the Taher defendants and for a lien on those funds. The Taher defendants were to be 'notified' of the writ in Ireland.

Subsequently, the plaintiff decided to pursue proceedings in Ireland instead and succeeded in serving Bon Meats, a company associated with the Tahers, on 20 July 1995. Later on the same day, the English court was applied to by the Taher defendants to be joined as parties to the English proceedings against Orchards under RSC Ord. 15, r.6(2)(b) (intervention by non-party in order to determine all issues). Sir Michael Davies held that 'notification' of the action to the Taher defendants in Ireland in April had amounted to good service upon them and duly exercised his discretion to join them. The plaintiff appealed.

Judgment

The Court of Appeal unanimously (Leggatt, Morritt and Brooke L.JJ.) held against joinder of the Taher defendants. The reason was that, without the Taher defendants, neither Art. 21 (not the same parties) nor Art. 22 (not related actions, because judgments would not be conflicting) applied; but if the Tahers were joined in England, the English and Irish actions would thereby become related within Art. 22, para. 3, since Fox's claims against Bon Meats and the Tahers were both as to the substantive issue in dispute, whereas the application against the English solicitors was merely for conservatory measures. Consequently, it would be wrong to join the Tahers, because:

(1) Art. 22 would become applicable; and
(2) since Ireland was overwhelmingly *forum conveniens*, it would be appropriate for the Art. 22 discretion to stay to be exercised in respect of the English action in relation to the Tahers, as being second-seised (see *supra*, Art. 21, para. 1 '. . . *court first-seised* . . . ', *Grupo Torras*, Case 285 to the related Irish action against Bon Meats.

The Court of Appeal could so interfere with the first instance judge's exercise of discretion in this way because this had apparently been carried out without him having knowledge of the earlier establishment of substantive Irish seisin against Bon Meats on the same day as that of his own decision.

Comment

The result appears quite justified. Had Art. 22 applied, English courts would have stayed as second-seised (the Court of Appeal disagreed with the first instance judge's finding that mere 'notification' of the Tahers of the English proceedings in April 1995 amounted to service): and this was clearly relevant to the national joinder discretion.

But, where the Court of Appeal is respectfully dissented from by the present writer is in its apparent assumption that Art. 22 stay would only have been granted because Ireland would have been *forum conveniens*, whereas not also so if it were otherwise the case. It is submitted in this respect that the *forum conveniens* factor ought properly to have played little, if any, part in any such consideration. Article 22 stays should be granted irrespective of *forum conveniens* investigations, subject to a heavy burden of proof upon the opponents of stays to persuade a court of good reasons in justice for a stay to be refused in any particular case.

Case principle

5. If a party bringing proceedings in a foreign Contracting State's courts, first-seised of the action, seeks a stay of a related English action against

him under Art. 22, the court may refuse to grant the stay if it appears that the applicant misled the plaintiffs in England in order to trick them into delaying commencement and seisin in England until the foreign courts had become first-seised.

Case

The Filiatra Legacy [1994] 1 Lloyd's Rep. 513 High Court, 9 April 1990   **314**

Facts

The plaintiffs brought proceedings in England against the defendant insurers, claiming sums payable under an insurance contract. Previously, the defendants had instituted a related action in Italy against the plaintiffs for a declaration of non-liability. The defendants in England requested a stay of proceedings in favour of first-seised Italian courts under Arts 21 and 22.

Judgment

Saville J. agreed to stay the English proceedings under Art. 21.

He went on to comment *obiter*, however, that if he had needed to exercise his discretion under Art. 22, and had found that the defendants had caused the plaintiffs, by sharp practice, to delay instituting the English proceedings, he would either have dismissed the defendants' application to stay in England, as an abuse of the process of the English courts, or at least have exercised his discretion against granting a stay under Art. 22.

Comment

If treated as an abuse of the court's process, an application to stay and decline under Art. 21 itself presumably would also have to be struck out.

Case principle

6. The second-seised court should show caution before refusing to exercise the discretion to stay its related action (*Owens v Bracco* Case C–129/92 applied and *Grupo Torras* followed).

Case

Sarrio S.A. v Kuwait Investment Authority [1996] 1 Lloyd's Rep. 650 High Court   **315**

Facts

These were seen in connection with Art. 21, held to be inapplicable, and are again dealt with *infra* with regard to the definition of 'related action' under Art. 22, para. 3 (an aspect on which the High Court's ruling was reversed by the Court of Appeal in [1997] 1 Lloyd's Rep. 113, CA).

The plaintiffs opposed a stay of the English action under Art. 22, para. 1, on grounds of likely delays in the Spanish proceedings, strength of English connections and location of witnesses and documents.

Judgment

Mance J. granted the stay.

He referred to AG Lenz in *Owens v Bracco* and to his own words in *Grupo Torras* requiring caution before refusal to exercise the discretion to stay on the ground of other factors, once the definition of related actions in Art. 22, para. 3 had been held to be satisfied.

Thus, the delays in Spain were unlikely to cause major hardship to the plaintiffs, especially since the defendant was prepared to undertake to help speed up the process by abandoning possible procedural objections; Spanish connections and the desirability of common issues being decided in one court outweighed the English; and details of the negotiations and communications, centrally relevant to the English action, were to be found in evidence in Spain. However Mance J. also made the point that he would not compare the superior(!) English discovery of evidence procedures with those in Spain because this would be invidious, as being merely one of many differences between common law and civil law procedure.

Viewed overall, therefore, the judge concluded that there was nothing which came anywhere near to justifying a refusal to stay or to decline English jurisdiction.

Finally, in view of certain doubts over consolidation of the English action with the Spanish, the judge preferred a stay under Art. 22, para. 1 to irrevocable decline under para. 2, until it were to be established that consolidation had taken place (see *infra*, Art. 22, para. 2).

Comment

This aspect of the *Sarrio* decision is here regarded as suspect for two reasons. First, the Court of Appeal, which held Art. 22, para. 3 *not* to be satisfied in the first place (see *infra*, [1997] 1 Lloyd's Rep. 113, CA), reached the opposite conclusion on the facts: in applying *national English* discretionary principles: England, not Spain, was *forum conveniens*, in particular in view of possible delays in Spain in any procedure to accumulate the English action with the Spanish (see *supra*, Art. 21 'court other than the court first seised shall . . . '). Secondly, Mance J. appeared to be taking into account *forum non conveniens* factors in the operation of Art. 22, which arguably is inappropriate and contrary to national case law trends (see *supra*).

Note, however, that Mance J.'s first instance judgment was subsequently restored—although converted from stay to decline—by the House of Lords on 13 November 1997, (1997) *The Times*, 17 November.

Case principle

7. A stay of liability limitation proceedings is not refused just because only one of the claimants applied for it.

Case

The 'Happy Fellow' [1997] 1 Lloyd's Rep. 130 High Court, 3 December 1996   **316**

Facts

See supra, Art. 21 'same cause of action' and infra, Art. 22, para. 3 'related', Cases 263 and 320.

Although the judge held English limitation and prior French liability proceedings to be 'related' within Art. 22, the plaintiff in England argued that the English court should not exercise its discretion to stay under Art. 22, because: (i) only one of the liability claimants in France had applied for the English stay; and (ii) the plaintiff would not obtain justice in French courts, which habitually exceeded the 1976 Limitation Convention's damages limits by allowing those limits to be broken where there was *merely* gross negligence, even if no intent or recklessness (or by fishing for facts to show these latter). The defendants argued that it was against comity to assess the probity of French courts' actions.

Judgment

Longmore J. held in favour of a stay of the English limitation action.

The fact that only one claimant had applied for this was not a bar to a stay of related proceedings.

As for the complaint about injustice, the court would examine French courts' practice in view of the seriousness of the alleged treaty contravention. But, on doing so, the judge concluded that French courts were not proven to be treaty-breakers: thus, different interpretative practices were not automatically to be viewed as being incorrect and in breach of treaties.

ARTICLE 22, PARAGRAPH 2

" . . . *and the court first seised has jurisdiction over both actions.*"

Case principle

The first-seised court must have local jurisdiction over the proceedings before the second-seised court for the latter to be able to decline to hear the action under Art. 22, para. 2. It is not sufficient that courts generally of the first-seised Contracting State merely have general, international jurisdiction, if the first-seised court itself lacks local jurisdiction over the related proceedings of the second-seised court.

Case

317   Jose Cardoso De Pina v MS 'Birka' Beutler Schiffahrts KG [1994] I.L.Pr. 694
High Court, 5 May 1993

Facts

The plaintiff was a seaman of Portuguese origin who fell off the German
defendants' boat when it was moored in Devon, England. He brought an
action against the 'German Compensation Board for Seamen' before the Social
Court in Germany and subsequently against his defendant employers in the
English courts for damages in the tort of negligence.

The defendants applied for a stay or decline of jurisdiction over the English
proceedings under Art. 22, paras 1 and 2 respectively, on the ground that the
actions were related within Art. 22, para. 3.

Judgment

With regard to Art. 22, para. 2, the deputy High Court judge held that it was
not sufficient for it to be shown by the defendants that German courts as a
whole would possess jurisdiction over the related English action. For the
English court to be permitted to decline jurisdiction thereunder, it was necessary for it to be established that the first-seised German court also had local
jurisdiction over the defendant. Here, this was not the case: the German
Sozialgericht, seised of the first type of claim, was not also competent to hear
the English negligence action against an employer. Consequently, the English
court would not decline its proceedings under Art. 22 para. 2.

See too *infra* as to the meaning of 'related' under Art. 22, para. 3, Case 324.

> *" . . . may also . . . decline jurisdiction . . . "*

Case principle

Since decline of jurisdiction is irrevocable, the second-seised court should stay
in the first instance under Art. 22, *para. 1* if there are any doubts about consolidation in the first-seised court, until consolidation is finally established to
have taken place.

Case

318   Sarrio S.A. v Kuwait Investment Authority [1996] 1 Lloyd's Rep. 650 High Court

Facts

*See infra, Art. 22, para. 3 'related actions' Cases 327 and 328 and supra, Art.
22, para. 1 'stay discretion', Case 315.*

Judgment

The judge preferred to stay the English proceedings in the first instance under Art. 22, para. 1 rather than to take the irrevocable step of declining under Art. 22, para. 2, since: (i) there were possible procedural difficulties over consolidation in Spain; and (ii) the defendant was an unusual organization, which might be entitled to sovereign immunity.

Thus, there would be a decline subsequently, on application, following completion of consolidation in Spain. As seen *supra*, in Comment to Case 315, this was actually ordered by the House of Lords.

ARTICLE 22, PARAGRAPH 3

" . . . *related* . . . "

Case principle

1. If different contracts, forming the subject matter of different Contracting State proceedings between the same parties, are closely intertwined, they may be held to be related actions.

Case

Kloeckner & Co. AG v Gatoil Overseas Inc. [1990] 1 Lloyd's Rep. 177 High   **319**
Court, 31 July 1989

Facts

English proceedings involved a claim for damages in respect of a network of contracts for the purchase and sale of oil, subject to an overall framework agreement contemplating the other contracts. German proceedings for wrongful termination, brought by the defendants to the English action, concerned only certain of the contemplated contracts.

Judgment

Hirst J. held English and German actions to be related for purposes of Art. 22—although it still would not have been reasonable to exercise the discretion to stay the English proceedings thereunder, had English courts not been held to be first seised, because the scope of the German action was on a much narrower scale (see *supra*, Art. 22, para. 1, Case 310).

Case principle

2. Where parties conclude seven contracts subject to identical terms and one of them sues in one Contracting State on six of the contracts and the other

sues in a different Contracting State on the seventh contract, the actions are treated as related for Art. 22, but not as the same cause of action for Art. 21.

Case

320   I.P. Metal Ltd v Ruote O.Z. S.p.A. [1993] 2 Lloyd's Rep. 60 High Court, 9 December 1992

Facts and judgment

See supra, Case 241.

Case principle

3.   Limitation proceedings and liability action are related where the liability action includes quantum as well as bare liability issues.

Case

321   The 'Happy Fellow' [1997] 1 Lloyd's Rep. 130 High Court, 3 December 1996

Facts

See supra, Art. 21 'same cause of action', Case 263, and Art. 22, para. 1 'discretion', Case 316.

The English limitation and French liability actions did not involve the same cause of action for Art. 21 (*supra*). But were they 'related' for Art. 22?

Judgment

Longmore J. held that, on the facts, they were related, because the French court would not deal simply with the issue of bare liability and duty of care, but also with matters of damages and remedies overlapping with English limitation proceedings.

Comments

The court then went on to decide that it would exercise its discretion to stay in favour of first-seised French liability proceedings under Art. 22 (see *supra*, Art. 22, para. 1 'discretion', Case 316).

Conversely, presumably, even if French courts were for some reason to be concerned solely with liability, the actions would nonetheless still be related if English limitation proceedings were held to involve an admission of liability on the part of the plaintiff shipowners.

> " . . . *expedient to hear and determine them together to avoid the risk of irreconcilable judgments . . .* "

Case principles

1. Provisional and final judgments on a contract are not to be considered 'irreconcilable'. They are not related.
2. Even if they are irreconcilable, it would not be expedient to hear and determine them together in the first-seised court of the provisional proceedings. Consequently, they are not related actions.

Case

Rank Film Distributors Limited v Lanterna Editrice Srl and Banca Nazionale del Lavoro [1992] I.L.Pr. 58 High Court, 4 June 1991 **322**

Facts

See supra, Art. 5(1), Case 141.

The defendants requested second-seised English courts to stay final merits proceedings for breach of contract under Art. 22 in favour of prior Italian provisional proceedings for an interim order against contractual performance.

Judgment

Saville J. refused to stay. The proceedings were not related for purposes of Art. 22, para. 3 because the Italian action was only for an interim judgment. This meant that *either* the Italian interim and final English judgments were not irreconcilable *or*, even if they were, it was not expedient to hear and determine them together in the Italian interim action.

Case principle

3. Actions in different Contracting States for infringement of a UK trade mark and passing off cannot be related for Art. 22, because they are beyond the scope of adjudication of courts outside the UK and the rights are only exercisable in the latter.

Case

La Gear Incorporated v Gerald Whelan & Sons Limited [1991] FSR 670 High Court **323**

Facts and judgment

See *supra* Art. 21, Case 264. Having failed to persuade the English court that English and Irish causes of action were the same for Art. 21, the defendants sought to argue that they were related within Art. 22, para. 3 and that second-seised English courts should exercise their discretion to stay in favour of the Irish. Mummery J. held that the two actions were not related. Since it was not *possible* for the Irish court to hear an action concerning breach of a UK trade mark in England—a 'territorially-defined right' (see Kaye, 'International Trade Mark Infringement: Territorially Defined Torts and the Double Actionability Rule' (1990) 12 *European Intellectual Property Review* 28)—it followed too that it was unable to be found that it would be *expedient* for the two actions to be heard together in Ireland in accordance with Art. 22, para. 3. But see now recent case law suggesting that foreign intellectual property rights *are* justiciable through the Convention's operation—*supra* Comment to Case 119 and *infra* Cases 386 and 387. *However*, this still does not mean that an English judge would be especially keen to exercise the discretion to stay in favour of first-seised foreign courts over English intellectual property!

Case principle

4. Actions are not related within the meaning of Art. 22, para. 3 if the first-seised court does not possess local as well as international jurisdiction over the second action, because Art. 22, para. 3 requires it to be expedient to hear and determine the two actions together, which implies that this must be possible.

Case

324 Jose Cardoso De Pina v M.S. Birka Beutler Schiffahrts KG [1994] I.L.Pr. 694 High Court, 5 May 1993

Facts

The plaintiff seaman, of Portuguese origin, fell off his employers' ship while it was moored in Devon, England and was severely injured. He brought an action against the 'German Compensation Board for Seamen' before the Social Courts in Germany and subsequently instituted proceedings claiming negligence against his employers in the English High Court.

The defendant employers applied to the High Court in England to stay or decline its process, as being related to the action before the first-seised German courts, under Art. 22, paras 1 and 2 respectively.

The outcome of the plaintiff's application under Art. 22, para. 2 was previously considered (see *supra*, Case 317).

Judgment

Deputy Judge Richard Buxton Q.C. concluded that the actions were not related, on the basis of the wording of Art. 22, para. 3 and Convention policy: the phrase 'expedient to hear and determine them together' pre-supposed that this had to be possible. In the case in question, it was not, since the German Social Courts would not hear a claim brought against an employer, which was in fact said to be extinguished by the proceedings against the Compensation Board.

(Nor would refusal of stay lead to irreconcilable English and German judgments in any event, because parties in the actions were not identical).

Comment

The judgment, it is submitted, should be regarded with some suspicion, not because it was that of a *deputy* judge, but because it is quite contrary to the purpose of Art. 22, para. 1, which is not specifically to consolidate related actions (compare the special provision made for this under Art. 22, para. 2—*lex specialis*) but to stay second-seised proceedings in appropriate cases for such exercise of the discretion, pending the outcome of the first-seised related action.

" . . . expedient to hear and determine them together . . . "

Case principle

5. An English action for an injunction to restrain prior foreign Contracting State proceedings for damages for breach of a sales contract brought in alleged contravention of an English arbitration agreement, is not related to the foreign proceedings within the meaning of Art. 22, para. 3.
6. An English claim for a declaration of arbitral validity is related to the foreign action where the same plea is brought as a defence to the foreign action.

Case

Toepfer International GmbH v Molino Boschi Srl [1996] 1 Lloyd's Rep. 510 **325**
High Court, 17 January 1996

Facts

See supra, Art. 21, Case 275.

Judgment

Mance J. held as follows in relation to Art. 22. In so far as the English claim for an injunction to restrain the Italian proceedings was concerned, this was not related to the Italian action and it would not be expedient for these proceedings to be heard and determined together: since the whole purpose of the English action was to *stop* the Italian proceedings, how could there be a risk of irreconcilable judgments? Even if the defendant and the Italian court were to ignore the English injunction and to proceed to judgment, their decision would then be refused recognition in England and probably elsewhere under Art. 27(1) on public policy grounds.

As for the English declaration, however, this was different. The purpose was to establish that the Italian claim should be brought in London arbitration, as was the plaintiff's plea by way of defence to this effect in the Italian proceedings. Consequently, the basic issue was the same in both actions and these were related: it was expedient to hear and determine them together to avoid the risk of irreconcilable judgments on the issue.

Comment

As to whether the discretion should be exercised in favour of a stay of the English claim for a declaration, there were arguments for and against according to Mance J.

However, in the end he did not find it necessary to decide because there was also an exclusive English jurisdiction clause in the terms incorporated into the sales contract—and, in accordance with the Court of Appeal's decision in *Continental Bank N.A. v Aeakos Compania Naviera S.A.* (see *supra*, Art. 17, Case 240), Art. 17 chosen English jurisdiction prevailed over the Art. 22 discretion to stay.

Notwithstanding, the plaintiffs did not in fact achieve their aim on the substantive relief because Mance J. chose not to exercise his discretion to grant the requested declaratory and injunctive measures. He considered that the plaintiffs had waited too long to apply (see *supra*, 1982 Act s.49, Case 116).

> " . . . *risk of irreconcilable judgments* . . . "

Case principles

1. Risk of irreconcilability is not absent just because English and foreign Contracting States' courts are likely to decide in the same way on one of the issues involved in the first-seised proceedings.
2. Therefore, mere partial stay of proceedings should not be ordered under Art. 22 in such circumstances.

Case

326 Virgin Aviation Services Limited v CAD Aviation Services [1991] I.L.Pr. 79 High Court, 21 January 1990

Facts

The plaintiff brought proceedings against the defendant, its cargo sales promotion agent, in the English High Court in 1989 for repayment of the balance of £36 000 outstanding on their trading account. However, prior to that, the defendants had themselves begun an action in the Dutch courts claiming

£100000 from the plaintiff for breach of contract through premature termination of the agency contract. The defendants also obtained provisional attachment of their debt towards the plaintiff under the trading account, to the extent of £28000 which they admitted, as security for any damages awarded against the plaintiff by the Dutch court, which was thereby enabled to investigate the trading account liability issue. The defendants sought a stay of the English proceedings as being related and—as agreed between the parties—second-seised to the Dutch, under Art. 22. The plaintiff countered, *inter alia* (see *supra*, Art. 22, para 1, 'discretion' Case 312), that since the defendants had admitted £28000 of the plaintiff's English claim on the trading account, there was only a risk of irreconcilability *beyond that* up to £36000. Consequently, the actions were only related for purposes of Art. 22, para. 3 *beyond that*, and, therefore, the English action should only be stayed partially, that is, in respect of the sum claimed between £28000 and the full £36000.

Judgment

Ognall J. dismissed the plaintiff's arguments against the power to stay the English proceedings in their entirety.

First, Art. 22 did not contemplate a partial stay of proceedings. Actions would be stayed in their totality under the Convention, or not at all.

Secondly, the English and Dutch actions were related in their entirety. The Dutch court might decide that the defendants were indebted towards the plaintiff to a different amount between £28000 and £36000 from that held to be owed in the English court. There was thus a risk of irreconcilable judgments and a stay should be possible.

(The plaintiff then sought to argue, unsuccessfully, that the English court should exercise its discretion against granting a stay of its proceedings, see *supra*, Art. 22, para. 1 'discretion', Case 312.)

Case principles

3. (At first instance) judgments may be irreconcilable if there is a risk of conflict, even if they can be separately enforced and their legal consequences are not mutually exclusive (*The Maciej Rataj*, Case C–406/92 applied).
4. (Court of Appeal) only primary, not mere secondary, issues of fact and law, essential to the decision, are to be taken into account in determining whether there is a risk of irreconcilability. Now reversed by the House of Lords.

Case

Sarrio S.A. v Kuwait Investment Authority [1996] 1 Lloyd's Rep. 650   **327**
High Court

Facts

These are as set out for Art. 21 (held inapplicable, see *supra*, Cases 270 and 271, and also 303 and 304).

The prior Spanish action was to hold the defendant liable for the payment obligations of its subsidiaries towards the plaintiff under the transaction to purchase the plaintiff's paper business, on the ground of the defendant's use of their corporate personality, as to which the plaintiff argued that the defendant was liable for its subsidiaries' acts. The subsequent English claim was for damages through alleged misstatement inducing contract to sell the paper business to the subsidiaries. The defendant requested a stay of the second-seised English proceedings, *inter alia*, under Art. 22 on the ground that the two actions were related in accordance with Art. 22, para. 3, as risking irreconcilable judgments.

Judgment

Mance J. held English and Spanish actions to be related under Art. 22, para. 3.

It was true to say that their legal consequences might not be mutually exclusive and that they could be separately enforced.

However, the important point for the judge was that both English and Spanish courts could be called upon to decide the issue of whether the defendant was bound by the communications of its subsidiaries and representatives in the course of the paper business sale negotiations—in the English proceedings because this was the actual matter forming the basis of the claim, and in the Spanish because it was highly relevant, though not indispensable, to the overall inquiry into the general relationship between the defendant and its subsidiaries and of whether it was bound by their activities, including, via this route, the paper sale transaction, through its use of their corporate personality. On this question, Mance J. held that there *was* a risk of conflicting judgments, according to the broad interpretation approach of the Court of Justice in *The Maciej Rataj*, paras 52 and 53, and consequently English and Spanish actions were related within the meaning of Art. 22, para. 3.

Case

328 Sarrio S.A. v Kuwait Investment Authority [1997] 1 Lloyd's Rep. 113 Court of Appeal [reversed by HL, 13 Nov. 1997: see *infra*, p. 404]

Facts

The plaintiff, Sarrio, appealed against Mance J.'s finding that the Spanish and English proceedings were related leading to stay under Art. 22.

Judgment

The Court of Appeal reversed Mance J.'s decision and held that Spanish and English proceedings were not related under Art. 22, para. 3, for two main reasons.

First, only primary issues of fact and law which were essential to the decision were to be taken into account in determining existence of the risk of irreconcilability, not merely secondary issues.

Secondly, the Court of Appeal disagreed with Mance J. as to the factual and legal issues primarily involved: the question of whether the negotiator of the contract of sale in England with the plaintiff was acting on behalf of the defendant in concluding that contract was held *not* to be in issue in the Spanish action, whereas representation of the defendant by the negotiator in inducing the plaintiff to enter the contract was not only in issue but central to the plaintiff's claim in the English proceedings.*

Comment

See *Deaville v Aeroflot Russian International Airlines* [1997] 2 Lloyd's Rep. 67 High Court, 7 February 1997, *supra*, Art. 21, Case 302, in which Deputy High Court Judge Geoffrey Brice Q.C. accepted Case principle three *supra*, from *Maciej Rataj* (*obiter*, since Arts 21 and 22 were displaced by Art. 57).

ARTICLE 24/1982 ACT SECTION 25(1)

" . . . *provisional, including protective, measures . . .* "/
" . . . *interim relief . . .* "

Case principle

1. Security for costs does not amount to provisional, including protective, measures within Art. 24 of the Judgments Convention, nor to interim relief for purposes of s.25(1) of the Civil Jurisdiction and Judgments Act 1982, implementing the Convention in the UK. Consequently, English courts have neither international jurisdiction (Art. 24) nor the procedural power (s.25) to make orders for plaintiffs to provide security for defendants' costs in relation to main proceedings on substance conducted in Contracting (or non-Contracting) States outside the UK.

Case

329

Bank Mellat v Helliniki Techniki SA [1984] 1 QB 291 Court of Appeal

This view was stated *obiter* by Kerr L.J. in the Court of Appeal, and, therefore, is not yet binding law.

Case principle

2. Article 24 provisional measures are not the same cause of action as the main proceedings on substance for purposes of Art. 21.

*See *Stop Press* on p. 404 at the end of this chapter.

Case

330   Republic of Haiti v Duvalier [1989] 2 WLR 261 Court of Appeal, 22 July 1988

Facts

See supra, Case 88.

Judgment

As Case principle two, supra.

Case principle

3.   Provisional proceedings should not be regarded as related through being irreconcilable, nor expedient to be heard and determined together, with final proceedings on the same subject matter for purposes of Art. 22, para. 3.

Case

331   Rank Film Distributors Limited v Lanterna Editrice Srl and Banca Nazionale del Lavoro [1992] I.L.Pr. 58 High Court, 4 June 1991

Facts

These are as set out *supra*, Case 322, in relation to Art. 22, para. 2: first-seised Italian interim proceedings to prevent contractual performance; and subsequent final English proceedings to enforce the contract. The defendants in England requested a stay of the latter under Art. 22.

Judgment

Saville J. held that since the Italian proceedings were merely for a provisional judgment, the two actions would not be held to be related for purposes of Art. 22, para. 3.

> " . . . even if, under this Convention, the courts of another Contracting State have jurisdiction as to the substance . . . "

Case principle

1.   Extraterritorial (worldwide) *Mareva* injunctions and any ancillary disclosure orders, in aid of final enforcement in foreign Contracting States, are within the provisional and protective jurisdiction of the forum under Art. 24.

Case

Babanaft International Co. S.A. v Bassatne [1990] 1 Ch 13 Court of Appeal,   **332**
29 June 1988

Facts

The plaintiff company obtained an English judgment against its defendant
directors for over 15 million US dollars owed under shipping transactions. The
defendants challenged the making of a post-judgment *Mareva* injunction and
ancillary (in fact, RSC Ord. 48) disclosure order in respect of assets situated
worldwide, as being beyond the powers and jurisdiction of the English courts.

Judgment

The Court of Appeal, referring to the increased reciprocity of international
recognition and enforcement under the Brussels Convention and to the cases
of *Interpool Ltd v Galani* (confirming jurisdiction over independent disclosure
proceedings in proper circumstances—see *supra*, Art. 16(5), Case 213) and
Maclaine Watson & Co. Ltd v International Tin Council (No. 2) [1988] 3
WLR 1190, CA (confirming post-judgment disclosure ancillary to mandatory
payment injunction—see IPRAX (1989) 179), held that previous English practice against exercising the discretion to grant *Mareva* relief under s.37 (1) of
the Supreme Court Act 1981 in *Ashtiani v Kashi* [1987] 1 QB 888, CA, in relation to assets situated outside England and Wales, should be reversed in favour
of making such orders, albeit exceptionally, in appropriate cases.

  With regard to *jurisdiction*, the Court of Appeal concluded that to the
extent that such extraterritorial post-judgment *Mareva* and ancillary disclosure relief was required for *foreign* Contracting State enforcement, Art. 16(5)
exclusive enforcement jurisdiction (see *supra*, *Interpool Ltd v Galani*) was not
contravened, because Art. 24 gave the English court provisional, including
protective, jurisdiction (alongside the 1982 Act s.25(1) power, see *supra*, Case
91, *Crédit Suisse Trust SA v Cuoghi* (unreported) 14 December 1995) over the
Mareva and ancillary disclosure measures, in relation to foreign Contracting
State main enforcement proceedings.

Case

Republic of Haiti v Duvalier [1990] 1 QB 202 Court of Appeal, 22 July 1988   **333**

Facts

The plaintiffs sued the defendants, former rulers of Haiti, in the French courts
for 120 million US dollars allegedly embezzled and were granted worldwide
Mareva and ancillary disclosure orders by the English courts. The defendants
challenged the English orders on a number of grounds relating to procedural
powers of English courts (see *supra*, 1982 Act s.25, Case 88 and Art. 21,
Case 276).

Judgment

In the course of rejecting the defendants' objections to its possession and exercise of procedural powers to grant the relief requested, the Court of Appeal upheld its Art. 24 jurisdiction to award such pre-judgment interim relief in respect of French main proceedings on substance.

Comment

These cases, confirming English courts' power and jurisdiction to grant (extraterritorial) *Mareva* and ancillary disclosure relief, pre- and post-judgment, under Art. 24 without contravening Art. 16(5), were succeeded by *Derby & Co. Ltd v Weldon (No. 1)* [1990] Ch 48, CA; *(Nos 3 and 4)* [1990] 1 Ch 65 CA; *(No. 6)* [1990] 1 WLR 1139, CA; and *Rosseel N.V. v Oriental Commercial and Shipping (UK) Ltd* [1990] 3 All ER 545, CA, concerning the scope of the extraterritorial powers, yet at the same time upholding the underlying Art. 24 jurisdiction.

See Kaye, Private International Law of Tort and Product Liability, 1991, pp. 113–73 for a detailed consideration of the line of decisions.

Case principle

2. Article 24 held subject to transitional provision in Art. 34(1) 1978 Accession Convention and inapplicable to Dutch main proceedings instituted before the Convention's entry into force as between the UK and The Netherlands.

Case

334 Alltrans Inc. v Interdom Holdings Limited [1993] I.L.Pr. 109 Court of Appeal, 30 January 1991

Facts

See supra, 1982 Act s.25(1), Case 94, and infra, 1978 Accession Convention Art. 34(1), Case 381.

Judgment

Article 24 required Dutch main proceedings to have been instituted *following* the Convention's entry into force in the UK on 1 January 1987 (not so 1982 Act s.25(1), however—see *supra*, Case 94).

ARTICLE 25

" . . . *any judgment given by a court* . . . "

Case principle

Dutch court order for provisional attachment of a debt claimed, as security for damages claim by debtor against creditor, stated (*obiter*) not to be a 'judgment' for Art. 25.

Case

Virgin Aviation Services Limited v CAD Aviation Services [1991] I.L.Pr. 79 **335** High Court 21 January 1990

Facts

See supra, Art. 22, paras 1 and 3, Cases 312 and 326.

The defendants in England argued that even at the stage of provisional attachment by the Dutch courts of the sum claimed by the plaintiffs in England, there was a risk of irreconcilable 'judgments'.

Judgment

Ognall J. doubted that this was correct. His tentative view was that 'judgments' within Art. 25 did not include interlocutory orders and that Art. 25 would only 'bite upon' some final determination, permanently definitive of the substantive rights of the parties under the matter in dispute.

Comment

The above seems inconsistent with the European Court's decision in *Denilauler* Case 125/79, only excluding judgments from Title III where these were delivered *ex parte* without prior service; and see *infra*, Art. 26, *Profer AG v The Owners of the Ship 'Tjaskemolen' now renamed 'Visvliet'* (unreported) 5 November 1996, Case 350, for a finding, on the other hand, that an interlocutory order, *discharging* provisional security, *was* a judgment within Art. 25!

> " . . . as well as the determination of costs or expenses by an officer of the court."

General

English rules of procedure give courts a discretion to order a plaintiff to provide security for the defendant's costs of the action where the plaintiff is ordinarily resident outside England and Wales, if, having regard to all the circumstances of the case, the court thinks it just to do so (RSC Ord. 23, r.1(1)(a)).

In *Firma Mund & Fester v Firma Hatrex International Transport*, Case C–398/92 of 10 February 1994 [1994] ECR I–467 the European Court held that a national German rule of civil procedure authorizing precautionary seizure of a defendant's German assets where an eventual judgment would require to be enforced abroad in a foreign—including EU—country, whereas in other cases, such seizure could only take place if it could be shown that enforcement was likely to be impossible or fundamentally difficult, was in contravention of EC Treaty Art. 6 (previously Art. 7)

- as an example of covert *nationality* discrimination prohibited thereunder, since more non-Germans than Germans were likely to be affected by the rule as defendants; and
- such discrimination was not considered to be justified by objective factors. In particular, enforcement in foreign EU countries under the Convention was regarded on policy as no more difficult or risky than if enforcement was to take place in Germany. (Even prior to this, in *Hubbard v Hamburger* Case C–20/92 of 1 July 1993 [1993] ECR I–3777, the European Court had held the German rule of security to be incompatible with freedom to supply professional services under specific EC Treaty Arts 59 and 60, as a nationality-based barrier to such provision of services in Germany.)

Case principle

Previous English practice as to discretion to order security for costs against plaintiffs ordinarily resident in the EU was to the contrary: not covert nationality discrimination—or at least, objectively justified if it was such.

Case

336 Porzelack KG v Porzelack (UK) Ltd [1987] 1 WLR 420 (Ch D) High Court, 20 January 1987

Facts

The plaintiff German company claimed an injunction against use of a similar name to its own by an unconnected English company and the defendant sought security for costs of £19000.

Judgment

The Vice-Chancellor of the Chancery Division of the High Court, Sir Nicolas Browne-Wilkinson V.-C., rejected the argument that the plaintiff's foreign *ordinary residence* requirement in RSC Order 23 amounted to *nationality* discrimination within Art. 6 of the EC Treaty in relation to a foreign EU—here German—ordinary resident.

Case

337 De Bry v Fitzgerald [1990] 1 All ER 560 Court of Appeal, 1 November 1988

Facts

The plaintiff, resident in France, sued for damages in England for breach of a contract of sale of a valuable sculptor's 'modello' said to be by Michelangelo. The defendants sought security for costs of £270 000.

Judgment

In the Court of Appeal, Lord Donaldson M.R. held, without hearing argument from counsel, that where an order for security was granted, this would not amount to nationality discrimination within EC Treaty Art. 6.

Case

Berkeley Administration Inc. v McClelland [1991] I.L.Pr. 45 Court of Appeal,   **338**
13 February 1990

Facts

The plaintiffs were ordinarily resident outside England and Wales in Panama, the British Virgin Islands and France. The Court of Appeal ordered security for costs in the sum of £150 000.

Judgment

Art. 6 of the EC Treaty was held not to be contravened by the ordinary residence condition in the rules of procedure, which operated regardless of the plaintiffs' nationality. The three appeal court judges agreed that European Court jurisprudence admitted the possibility that conditions of residence and the like *could* amount to covert nationality discrimination. However, they were of the view, first, that in spite of the fact that plaintiffs who were foreign EU ordinary residents were all the more likely also to be foreign EU nationals, nevertheless, ordinary residence and nationality were still not equivalent so as covertly to amount to the same; and secondly, even if ordinary residence were to be held covertly to be equivalent to nationality and consequently required not to be differentiated therefrom, nevertheless, there would not be *discrimination* on such grounds for purposes of EC Treaty Art. 6, if *either* the ordinary residence criterion was actually advantageous to the plaintiffs in all of the circumstances overall, *or* could be objectively justified on policy grounds not offending principles of equality of treatment.

Case principle

Furthermore, under the developing English practice, although ease of foreign enforceability of English costs awards under the Judgments Convention was a factor against an order for security for costs, it was not conclusive.

Case

Porzelack KG v Porzelack (UK) Ltd [1987] 1 WLR 420 (Ch D) High Court,   **339**
20 January 1987

Facts

See supra, Case 336.

Judgment

The High Court held Convention enforceability of a costs order to be a factor of considerable importance to be taken into account *against* exercise of the discretion to order security, but that nonetheless this was not to be treated as decisive and conclusive. The court should assess the precise level of difficulty of enforcement likely to be experienced in individual cases, in deciding whether to decline to order security against a plaintiff ordinarily resident in a foreign Judgments Convention Contracting State. In this case, enforcement of costs against the plaintiff in Germany would be sufficiently easy and an order for security was refused.

Case

340 De Bry v Fitzgerald [1990] 1 All ER 560 Court of Appeal, 1 November 1988

Facts

See supra, Case 337.

Judgment

Porzelack was confirmed by the Court of Appeal. It would be wrong to order security against the plaintiff resident in France in view of ease of Convention enforcement in France.

Case

341 Berkeley Administration Inc. v McClelland [1991] I.L.Pr. 45 Court of Appeal, 13 February 1990

Facts

See supra, Case 338.

Judgment

Porzelack was again confirmed. Ease of foreign enforcement in an individual case was a powerful factor against security, and security was frequently refused where plaintiffs were resident in foreign Convention States. In the event, however, the Court of Appeal decided as a matter of their general discretion that security of £150000 should be ordered because, by reason of the manner in which the plaintiffs had ordered their affairs, any costs order against them would be likely to be enforceable only by a significant expenditure of time and money, and the plaintiffs were companies capable of shifting money from one to the other and from one country to another. Convention enforceability was, therefore, relevant but not conclusive against security.

Case

Thune and Roll v London Properties Ltd [1991] I.L.Pr. 66 Court of Appeal, **342**
20 February 1990

Facts

The plaintiffs were Norwegian trustees in bankruptcy of a deceased's estate who sought to claim back through the English courts assets of the deceased which they alleged had come into the defendants' hands. The defendants applied for security of £500 000.

Judgment

The Court of Appeal agreed with the preceding cases that ease of enforcement of the English costs order in Norway—at the time not yet party to the Lugano Convention—was relevant though not decisive nor the sole consideration against ordering security for costs to be provided by the plaintiffs. As it happened, the Court of Appeal decided that in all the circumstances, it would be appropriate for security to be ordered against the plaintiffs notwithstanding relative ease of enforcement in Norway because there could be many competing claims against the plaintiff trustees in Norway. The defendants should not be put to such risk.

Comment

However, as a result of the European Court of Justice's decision in *Firma Mund, supra*, the English Court of Appeal thereafter decreed a change of practice from the previous cases. This will represent the law unless the highest court, the House of Lords, were to disagree in a later judgment. The principles thenceforth to be applied, therefore, were as follows.

Case principles

1. Provision for discretionary security for costs to be ordered against a plaintiff on the ground of his ordinary residence in a foreign EU State amounts to covert nationality discrimination under Art. 6 of the EC Treaty and is forbidden to be exercised (applying the European Court of Justice's ruling on the different German procedural rule in *Firma Mund* Case C–398/92, *supra*).
2. Exceptionally, however, the discretion may be exercised if there is very cogent evidence of substantial difficulty in enforcing the costs order in the foreign EU State.

Case

Fitzgerald v Williams [1996] 2 WLR 447 Court of Appeal, 20 December 1995   **343**

Facts

The plaintiffs in the English courts were Irish citizens resident in the Republic of Ireland and claimed damages from the defendant for fraudulent misrepresentation. The defendant applied for an order for security for costs against the plaintiffs under RSC Ord. 23, r.1(1)(a).

Judgment

Sir Thomas Bingham M.R., with whom the other Court of Appeal judges agreed, reviewed previous English case law which had held Ord. 23 not to amount to covert nationality *discrimination* under EC Treaty Art. 6. Those authorities now had to be reconsidered in the light of the Court of Justice's decision in *Firma Mund*. The view of the Court of Appeal was that:

(1)   Order 23 *did* amount to a *covert nationality* provision, because most EU plaintiffs ordinarily resident outside the United Kingdom would be non-UK EU nationals; and

(2)   *in view of ease of enforcement of English costs orders elsewhere in the EU by virtue of the Judgments Convention*, there was no objective justification for such differentiation on covert nationality grounds under Ord. 23 and accordingly,

- the English procedural rule was held to be discriminatory in breach of EC Treaty Art. 6 and consequently the English courts should never exercise their discretion against an EU plaintiff,
- at least in the absence of very cogent evidence of substantial difficulty in enforcing the costs order elsewhere in the EU.

In the case itself, it was considered that no such difficulty existed over Irish enforcement and security was refused.

The judgment was stated to be limited to plaintiffs who were individuals rather than insolvent companies, and to those ordinarily resident in the EU, not outside.

Comment

This is a binding judgment of the Court of Appeal which stands unless reversed by the House of Lords or in conflict with a European Court of Justice ruling (see *infra*).

The Court of Appeal described it as a modification of English practice as to exercise of the discretion to order costs against an EU plaintiff. While the judgment stands, no such order will be made, other than in exceptional cases of very cogent evidence of substantial difficulty of enforcement in the foreign EU state of the plaintiff—unlikely in view of Judgments Convention applicability.

The exact scope of the Court of Appeal's judgment is not wholly clear (the court appeared to indicate that the plaintiff should also actually be a national of the foreign EU state of ordinary residence, for Ord. 23 to be in breach of Art. 6 of the EC Treaty!).

Furthermore, the principle in *Porzelack*, *de Bry*, *Berkeley* and *Thune supra*, that ease of Judgments Convention enforceability of English costs orders is a powerful factor, though not conclusive, against exercise of the Ord. 23 discretion to order security for costs, remains in relation to plaintiffs who are ordinarily resident in EFTA states to which the Lugano Convention applies. Obviously, Art. 6 of the EC Treaty has no effect in such cases. See too *R v Hereford Book Society, ex p. O'Neill* (unreported) High Court, 27 March 1995.

Case principles

3. RSC Ord. 23 r.1(1)(a) is not *invalidated* under Art. 6 of the EC Treaty following *Mund*. The effects of *Mund*, according to *Fitzgerald*, is to *control exercise of the discretion* under r.1(1)(a): in relation to plaintiff individuals who are foreign EU ordinary residents, the discretion must not be exercised solely on the ground of the plaintiff's foreign ordinary residence, which would be discriminatory in contravention of Art. 6.
4. Where the plaintiff is a foreign EU *company*, availability of security under r.1(1)(a) is also not discriminatory, because s.726(1) of the Companies Act 1985 enables security to be ordered against English companies.

Case

Chequepoint SARL v McClelland [1996] I.L.Pr. 602 Court of Appeal, 5 June **344** 1996

Facts

The French plaintiff, Chequepoint, wished to sue the defendant, Mr. McClelland, for allegedly republishing a defamatory newspaper article concerning money-laundering activities alleged to have been conducted through the plaintiff's bureaux de change in Paris. The defendant obtained an order for security for costs against the plaintiff from the High Court under r.1(1)(a). The plaintiff appealed on the ground that, following *Mund* and *Fitzgerald*, such an order made against a foreign EU plaintiff was discriminatory in contravention of Art. 6 of the EC Treaty.

Judgment

The Court of Appeal, including Bingham L.C.J., who had himself delivered judgment in *Fitzgerald* as Master of the Rolls, upheld the order for security.

First, the judgment in *Fitzgerald* was not that r.1(1)(a) was invalidated against foreign EU plaintiffs; it was merely to prohibit exercise of the discretion solely on grounds of the plaintiff's foreign EU nationality or ordinary residence. This condition of security had been considered to be satisfied by the High Court judge in the current proceedings by reason of the fact of the plaintiff's impecuniosity and the possibility that it would be unable to pay the defendant's costs if the defendant succeeded in his defence.

Secondly, where the foreign EU plaintiff was not an individual but, as here, a company, existence of the discretion under r.1(1)(a) would not be discriminatory contrary to Art. 6 of the EC Treaty in any event, because English companies themselves were subject to orders for security on the ground of impecuniosity under s.726(1) of the Companies Act 1985.

Comment

The position reached by the English Court of Appeal on a combination of *Fitzgerald* and *Chequepoint* was as follows:

> (1) a very strong presumption that security for costs against a foreign EU plaintiff individual would be in contravention of Art. 6, able to be rebutted by cogent evidence of substantial difficulties of enforcement or reasons other than solely foreign residence or nationality; but
>
> (2) no such contravention of Art. 6 exists in the case of plaintiff foreign EU ordinarily resident companies.

These findings, however, now have to be considered in the light of the European Court's decision of September 1996 in *Data Delecta Aktiebolag and Forsberg v MSL Dynamics Limited* Case C–43/95 [1996] I.L.Pr. 738. There the Court ruled that a Swedish law which required plaintiffs who were non-Swedish nationals to provide security for costs, which would not also be ordered against plaintiffs who were Swedes, was in contravention of Art. 6.

The European Court provided no reasoning for this aspect of its judgment (which also dealt with applicability in principle of Art. 6 in the first place in relation to national rules of a procedural, rather than substantive EC Treaty, nature—held to be so where the national procedure at least *indirectly* affected substantive EC law, as in the case of security for costs, reducing foreign plaintiffs' ability to enforce substantive EC rights and consequently also the desirability of taking advantage of free movement of goods so as to export to Sweden).

Questions remain, therefore. Does the *Data Delecta* judgment also apply to *disguised* nationality discrimination such as under the English Ord. 23 rule ostensibly based upon ordinary residence?

If it does, did *Data Delecta* exclude any exceptions to or mere presumptions of discrimination-contravention of Art. 6 as have hitherto existed in England according to *Fitzgerald* and *Chequepoint*? Are such exceptions even excluded in the case of a purely nationality-based security for costs rule, such as existed under Swedish law in *Data Delecta*? The European Court simply did not elaborate, one way or the other.

Is the current inapplicability of Art. 6 to orders for security against plaintiff *companies* ordinarily resident in a foreign EU state now displaced by the *Data Delecta* ruling which was also expressed in relation to companies? This seems most unlikely, given the absence of any discrimination in favour of English resident companies in the first place (see *supra*).

No one will have been surprised by the essence of the European Court's ruling in *Data Delecta* that a Swedish security for costs rule based solely upon the foreign nationality of the plaintiff was in contravention of Art. 6; nor by the fact that in March 1997, the European Court confirmed its *Data Delecta* ruling in a very similar case relating to a German rule on security (see *Hayes v Kronenberger GmbH* Case C–323/95 [1997] I.L.Pr. 361—also *Saldanha v Hiross Holding AG*, Case C–122/96, of 2 October 1997). But as for the rest, more questions than answers.

Case principle

5.   General impecuniosity of the plaintiff is a relevant factor in favour of ordering security for costs to be provided, but not conclusive.

Case

De Bry v Fitzgerald [1990] 1 All ER 560 Court of Appeal, 1 November 1988   **345**

Facts

See supra, Case 337.

Case

Thune and Roll v London Properties Inc. [1991] I.L.Pr. 66 Court of Appeal,   **346**
20 February 1990

Facts

See supra, Case 342.

Judgments

The Court of Appeal in these cases held that a plaintiff's lack of funds was never in itself enough to justify an order for security, but that courts could and should consider this as a factor in the exercise of their discretion. This was contrary to the earlier finding of the High Court in *Porzelack KG v Porzelack (UK) Ltd* [1987] 1 WLR 420, Case 336, that a plaintiff's impecuniosity had no effect upon the question of whether to order security for costs because the purpose of the latter was to ensure that there was a fund within the jurisdiction out of which a defendant's costs could be satisfied, not to safeguard a defendant generally against the risk that a penurious plaintiff might not be able to satisfy an eventual costs order, which was the same whether the plaintiff was ordinarily resident in a foreign country or not. This aspect too of the High Court's *Porzelack* decision can therefore be regarded as no longer good law, in the light of the Court of Appeal's later judgments in *De Bry* and *Thune*.

Comments

For discussion of preceding developments, see 'Security for Costs in International Cases' (1995) 2 *Personal Injury Law and Medical Review 118*;

'Orders against Foreign EU Plaintiffs to Provide Security for Defendants' Costs: a breach of European Law?' (1996) *Personal Injury* 221; Security for Costs in International Cases: A Further Instalment (1997) *Personal Injury* 75. In *Allied General Holdings Limited v Sorsky* [1997] I.L.Pr. 315 of June 1996, the Court of Appeal balanced the risk that security ordered might stifle the Isle of Man plaintiff's claim, against protection of the defendants' right to afford a first class defence, and decided in favour of the latter.

ARTICLE 26, PARAGRAPH 1

" . . . *shall be recognized* . . . "

Case principle

1. Issue estoppel from a foreign Contracting State's judgment recognized under Art. 26 depends upon the test of 'same subject matter' (object/end in view) laid down by the European Court of Justice in *Gubisch* and *Maciej Rataj* (alongside same 'cause' (of action)/relationship/facts and law in issue) as one of the elements for *lis pendens* under Art. 21.

Case

347 Berkeley Administration Inc. v McClelland [1995] I.L.Pr. 201 Court of Appeal, 18 February 1994

Facts

See supra, Cases 269 and 272.

The plaintiff company, whose business was to run bureaux de change, alleged that the defendant English and French companies, Maccorp G.B. and Maccorp France, set up by its ex-employees, had made use of confidential information gained from the plaintiff as to business premises and opportunities available in Paris. English proceedings for misuse of confidential information were instituted in 1989 and interlocutory restraint orders were made against the defendants. Parallel proceedings were brought in France but interlocutory orders were refused. The defendants, the Maccorp companies, then instituted proceedings in France against the plaintiff for the tort of abuse of process. They alleged that the plaintiff's intention in bringing the claim had been to give the defendants a bad reputation and to harm their business prospects as rivals.

In April 1990, Wright J. held against the plaintiff in the English action and ordered an inquiry into damage suffered by the defendants from the earlier interlocutory orders, in accordance with the plaintiff's undertaking to pay. Subsequently, in September 1990, the French court dismissed the defendants' claim for abuse of process.

The current English proceedings were the damages inquiry ordered by Wright J. The plaintiff argued that since the French judgment of September 1990 was entitled to recognition in England under Art. 26, this created an issue estoppel as to whether the plaintiff was in abuse of process or not—held by the French not to be the case, as seen—as a factor in the English damages assessment. The defendants argued against issue estoppel, on the ground that the issues in the English and French proceedings were not the same—they were abuse of *English* and *French* process respectively.

Judgment

The English Court of Appeal held by a majority of two (Dillon and Stuart-Smith L.JJ.) to one (Hobhouse L.J.) that issue estoppel operated on the facts.

There was unanimity amongst the judges that the test of the *same issue* for these estoppel purposes in a Convention context was that of *same subject matter* as one of the two elements (the other being same 'cause' (of action)) laid down by the European Court of Justice for the operation of Art. 21 in this respect in *Gubisch*. It was logical that the same policies should apply.

In the majority, however, Dillon L.J. considered the English and French subject matter to be the same—to establish whether the plaintiff had had a credible claim as to misuse of confidential information by the defendants—whereas Hobhouse L.J., in the minority, regarded the subject matter as different—remedies for abuse of English and French process respectively. In the majority, Stuart-Smith L.J., like Hobhouse L.J., considered the subject matter of English and French actions to be to recover for abuse of process; but unlike Hobhouse L.J., he took the view that even though the French court had only taken account of the alleged English abuse *as evidence of the French* rather than actually also adjudicating upon the English as part of the French judgment, nevertheless, the former factor still made the English abuse part of the subject matter of the French, as well as the English, proceedings and the English damages court was consequently estopped as to this issue by the earlier French judgment.

Case principle

2.   Article 26 is limited to recognition. *Effects* of recognition in estoppel is for national law of the recognition-State (*obiter* inferred).

Case

Berkeley Administration Inc. v McClelland [1996] I.L.Pr. 772 Court of **348** Appeal, 21 June 1996

Facts

See supra, Art. 21 '*same cause of action*', Cases 269 and 272.

It will be recalled that the English Court of Appeal took the view on the facts that Maccorp would not have been able to acquire the Paris premises in any event and therefore suffered no such damage from the English injunction.

This meant that Chequepoint had no need to rely upon Art. 21 *lis pendens* or Art. 26 recognition of and issue estoppel from the French judgment dismissing Maccorp's abuse of process action against Chequepoint.

Furthermore, even if the English court's view of the facts had not so been in Chequepoint's favour, the Court of Appeal considered that it was too late in the English proceedings for Chequepoint to have pleaded Art. 21 or 26 without being oppressive to Maccorp.

However, would the English court have been estopped by Art. 26 recognition of the French judgment dismissing Maccorp's action against Chequepoint for damages for abuse of process and unfair business practice, had it been necessary and possible for Chequepoint to plead this?

Judgment

The Vice-Chancellor Sir Richard Scott held that the fact that the French judgment was required to be recognized under Art. 26 did not also mean that it would create an issue estoppel in England. The French court had left open the question whether Maccorp could have purchased the Champs Elysées premises and this 'non-finding' would not create an issue estoppel under domestic English law.

Comment

The inference is clear. Article 26 is confined to recognition. Further effects in estoppel are for the recognition-State's law—another inevitable qualification to the *Hoffmann v Krieg* Case 145/86 principle of governing effects by the judgment-State's law, aside from the exception in *Hoffmann v Krieg* itself concerning priority, under the enforcement-State's law, of a divorce decree of the enforcement-State outside the Convention's scope in the context of Art. 27(3).

Case principle

3.   An English court is not estopped by a foreign Contracting State's courts' determination of location of Art. 5(1) place of contractual performance, if the foreign judgment was merely provisional.

Case

349   Boss Group Ltd v Boss France S.A. [1996] 4 All ER 970 Court of Appeal, 2 April 1996

Facts

These have been noted in connection with Art. 5(1) 'contracts existence', Case 148, and 'place of performance of principal obligation in dispute', Case 160.

The defendants further objected to English Art. 5(1) jurisdiction, on the ground that French courts had earlier held place of performance to be located in France.

Judgment

The Court of Appeal considered that as the French court's finding was merely provisional and not binding upon French courts of substance, an English court would not be estopped as to the French determination of place of performance.

Comment

It seems unlikely, in any event, that Convention recognition should operate in relation to such purely jurisdictional decisions of foreign courts in the first place (to which this writer would also add matters of Convention *scope*—see *supra*, Art. 1, para. 2(4) and *infra*, Art. 31 *CFEM Façades SA v Bovis Construction Limited* [1992] I.L.Pr. 561, Case 358).

Case principle

4. Scope of a foreign judgment for recognition must be construed for its intended limits.

Case

Profer AG v The Owners of the Ship 'Tjaskemolen' now named 'Visvliet'   **350**
(unreported) High Court, 5 November 1996

Facts

The plaintiffs arrested the defendants' ship in the Netherlands, following which, pre-judgment security for its release was provided by the defendants, which the Dutch courts subsequently discharged. Thereafter, the defendants opposed an English court's further order for security for the release of the same ship, which had been arrested in Liverpool for the plaintiffs' English proceedings *in rem* in relation to the same claim. One of the defendants' grounds of opposition to English security was that English courts were bound to recognize the previous Dutch court order releasing security in the Dutch proceedings.

Judgment

Clarke J. in the English Admiralty Court rejected this ground of opposition by the defendants to the order of security.

On the one hand, a Dutch interlocutory order was a 'judgment' within the meaning of Art. 25 (see *supra*, comment upon *Virgin Aviation Services Ltd v CAD Aviation Services* [1991] I.L.Pr. 79, Case 335, and Kaye, *Civil Jurisdiction* pp.1350–1 excluding from Art. 25 interlocutory decisions concerning further conduct of proceedings, but not those also intended to govern legal relationships; however, even if provisional, protective orders are covered by Art. 25, they fall outside Title III enforcement, if *ex parte*, see *Denilauler* Case 125/79, and further, *infra* Case 358).

But, on the other hand, the Dutch court's order of discharge could not have been intended to apply other than to *Dutch* security, just as an English court's order for release of a ship arrested in English *in rem* proceedings would only apply to an English arrest.

Comment

The latter seems quite consistent with the European Court's judgment in *Hoffmann v Krieg* Case 145/86.

ARTICLE 27(1)

" . . . *recognition is contrary to public policy* . . . "

Case principles

1. Public policy includes allegations of fraud in obtaining the foreign judgment.
2. If the judgment-court itself dealt with the issue of fraud, the English enforcement-court is prohibited from reviewing the substance of the judgment-court's findings by Art. 29 and Art. 34, para. 3.
3. If the judgment-court did not assess the matter of fraud, the English enforcement-court can only do so if there is fresh evidence of fraud since the trial which was not available at the earlier date, although exceptionally, even if the latter condition is not satisfied, the English court may agree to examine the issue of fraud if justice so requires.

Case

351 Interdesco S.A. v Nullifire Ltd [1992] 1 Lloyd's Rep. 80 High Court, 1 May 1991

Facts

The plaintiff French paint manufacturer, Interdesco S.A., appointed the defendant English company, Nullifire Ltd, to be its exclusive distributor of its fire-resistant paint in the United Kingdom for a period of five years. About halfway through that time, the defendant terminated the agreement on the ground that the paint's quality failed to meet British standards. The plaintiff brought proceedings against the defendant in France for breach of contract, claiming that the defendant's real intention was to steal the plaintiff's market. The French courts accepted the plaintiff's experts' test results rather than the defendant's experts' reports and awarded damages to the plaintiffs of six and a half million francs. The plaintiff's judgment was ordered to be registered for enforcement in England under the Convention in 1990. The defendants appealed against the order, on the ground that the plaintiffs had obtained their French judgment by fraud—that they had misled the French court in their pleadings by falsely asserting that they had not conducted a test of the paint in England which had shown it to be sub-standard. The defendant's line of argument was that fraud was an aspect of public policy. Consequently, it would be contrary to public policy for an English court to recognize and enforce a French judgment obtained by fraud and recognition should be refused under Art. 27(1).

Judgment

Phillips J., although willing to accept that the defendants had made out a prima facie case as to the misleading of the French court, nonetheless refused to set aside the order to register the French judgment, under Art. 27(1).

(1)   At national English private international law, English courts were prepared to hear allegations of fraud upon the foreign judgment-court, irrespective of whether the foreign court itself had dealt with the issue or could have been requested to (see *Abouloff v Oppenheimer* [1882] 10 QBD 295; *Vadala v Lawes* [1890] 25 QBD 310; *Syal v Heyward* [1948] 2 KB 443; *Jet Holdings Inc. v Patel* [1990] 1 QB 335; *Owens Bank Ltd v Bracco* [1991] 4 All ER 833, CA, affd [1992] 2 WLR 621, HL) although if the foreign court's finding against fraud was reached in separate and second proceedings, themselves untainted by fraud, the enforcement-court is not permitted to review the same question of fraud, and the foreign judgment is conclusive through operation of estoppel (see *House of Spring Gardens Ltd v Waite* [1991] 1 QB 241 Court of Appeal).

(2)   However, although in principle Art. 27(1) public policy was broad enough to encompass fraud, Phillips J. considered that the national English approach, as being based essentially upon mistrust of foreign courts, was totally inappropriate for and contrary to the spirit of the Convention.

(3)   Accordingly, if the allegations of fraud were already made before the French judgment-court, English enforcement-courts should not rehear them. Article 29 and Art. 34, para. 3 stated that under no circumstances should recognition and enforcement-courts review a foreign judgment as to its substance.

(4)   If the judgment-court had not examined the question of fraud, it was best to leave it to do so if it had equivalent procedures to the English; and as in the case of English judgments alleged to be tainted by fraud, the English court itself should not conduct a review, in the absence of fresh evidence coming to light since the trial, unless justice otherwise required.

In the case itself, these conditions of English re-examination were not satisfied and French courts alone were appropriate to deal with the issue of fraud in the *recours en révision* proceedings.

ARTICLE 27(2)

" . . . duly served . . . "

Case principle

1. Due *transmission* of the document instituting proceedings to the defendant in a foreign Contracting State is required to be carried out in accordance with international conventions on transmission where these are applicable as between the relevant Contracting States, by virtue of annexed Protocol/Lugano Protocol No. 1 Art. IV, para. 1.

Case

352 Thierry Noirhomme v David Walklate [1992] 1 Lloyd's Rep. 427 High Court, 15 April 1991

See infra, Art. IV, para. 1, Case 380.

Case principle

2. It may be that where the defendant challenged due service in adversary proceedings in the judgment-court, the enforcement-court is bound by the judgment-court's finding as to due service.

Case

353 Coverbat SA v Jackson (unreported) Court of Appeal, 31 January 1997

Facts

The plaintiff obtained judgment in default against the defendant in Belgian courts in 1993 in respect of damage to a motor car from pieces of glass which fell from the window of the defendant's rented flat in Belgium.

The Belgian judgment was registered for enforcement in England in 1995, but the defendant applied for leave to appeal against enforcement under Art. 27(2) on the ground that he had never been served with Belgian process. The plaintiff alleged that the document was served upon the defendant by delivery to his address in Belgium, but the defendant said that this was not in accordance with Belgian law.

Judgment

There was no evidence that the Belgian courts themselves had dealt with the matter of due service. However, the two judges of the Court of Appeal concluded that there was a proper case for consideration of whether an enforcement-court was bound by a judgment-court's decision as to due service, where this finding had been made in adversary proceedings in which the defendant had participated for the purpose of objecting to service.

Accordingly, leave to appeal against enforcement was granted, together with a stay of execution of judgment.

Comment

See Kaye, *Civil Jurisdiction* pp. 1467–8, for the view from the European Court's case law that enforcement-courts are *not* bound by judgment-courts' decisions as to due service.

ARTICLE 27(3)

" . . . *irreconcilable with a judgment* . . . "

Case principle

A foreign interim maintenance order is irreconcilable with a (subsequent) final decree of divorce in the enforcement-State and recognition and enforcement of the maintenance award must therefore be refused under Art. 27(3) (*Hoffmann v Krieg* Case 145/86 applied).

Case

Macaulay v Macaulay [1991] 1 WLR 179 High Court, 22 November 1990   **354**

Facts

A wife received an interim maintenance award from the Irish courts against her husband who had left to live in England. Subsequently, the husband obtained a final divorce decree from the English courts, but nearly three years later, in 1990, the wife had the Irish maintenance order registered for enforcement against the husband in an English magistrates' court under national legislation giving effect to the Hague Convention of 1973 on the Recognition and Enforcement of Decisions Relating to Maintenance Obligations, which is optionally available to a maintenance applicant alongside the Judgments Convention itself, by virtue of Art. 57 of the latter (see Kaye, pp. 527–8). The husband challenged registration, *inter alia*, on the ground that the Irish maintenance order was irreconcilable with the English divorce: Art. 6(5) of the

1972 maintenance enforcement legislation was equivalent to Art. 27(3) of the Judgments Convention which required recognition to be refused where the foreign judgment was irreconcilable with a judgment between the same parties in the recognition-State.

The magistrates' court upheld the husband's challenge and set aside registration of the Irish order. The wife appealed to the High Court.

Judgment

The High Court (Booth J.) agreed with the magistrates: the Irish and English judgments were irreconcilable and the Irish maintenance award would therefore be denied enforcement and its registration set aside.

Although the Judgments Convention was not applicable as such, the judge considered that its principles still applied in respect of construction of the applicable 1972 maintenance enforcement legislation, in order to preserve uniformity wherever possible and appropriate.

Thus, the relevant Judgments Convention decision was that in *Hoffmann v Krieg* (which would have been binding had the Judgments Convention been chosen to apply), the facts of which were virtually identical and in which the European Court of Justice had held a German maintenance award, of which enforcement was requested in The Netherlands, to be irreconcilable with a subsequent Dutch divorce between the parties and consequently not entitled to recognition and enforcement under the Convention, through operation of Art. 27(3).

The judge believed that the wife would suffer no injustice from this unsuccessful outcome to her enforcement application, because she could still request financial relief from the English divorce court.

ARTICLE 28, PARAGRAPH 1

" . . . conflicts with the provisions of . . . "

Case principle

The exceptional jurisdiction ground contravened must have been as to a principal issue in the judgment-court's proceedings, not merely incidental.

Case

355 Berkeley Administration Inc. v McClelland [1995] I.L.Pr. 201 Court of Appeal, 18 February 1994

Facts

See *supra*, Case 347.

Judgment

The defendants argued that a French judgment should be refused recognition under Art. 28, para. 1, if Art. 16(5) had conferred exclusive jurisdiction upon English, not French, courts.

The Court of Appeal indicated that this was not the case. The alleged *English* 'enforcement' was not a principal issue in the French proceedings leading to judgment (see *supra*).

ARTICLE 30, PARAGRAPH 1

" . . . may stay the proceedings . . . "

Case principle

See infra, Art. 38, para. 1 " . . . may . . . stay the proceedings . . . " Case Principle 1.

Case

Thierry Noirhomme v David Walklate [1992] 1 Lloyd's Rep. 427 High Court,   **356**
15 April 1991

See infra, Case 361.

" . . . may stay . . . if an ordinary appeal . . . "

Case principle

A French *recours en révision* is not an 'ordinary appeal' if it can be lodged at any time following judgment, with no maximum period prescribed (*Industrial Diamond Supplies* Case 43/77 applied).

Case

Interdesco S.A. v Nullifire Ltd [1992] 1 Lloyd's Rep. 180 High Court, 1 May   **357**
1991

Facts

See Cases 351 and 362.

The defendant also sought a stay of English enforcement of a French judgment, on the ground of pending French *recours en révision*.

Judgment

Phillips J. refused. According to the European Court of Justice, an 'ordinary appeal' for Arts 30 and 38 was that which may result in annulment or amendment of the judgment *and* which had to be lodged within a certain period of time after the judgment. The French *recours en révision* was said to be unable to satisfy the latter of these criteria.

ARTICLE 31, PARAGRAPH 1

"A judgment given in a Contracting State . . . "

Case principles

1. Judgments on procedural directions fall within the Convention's civil and commercial scope of main proceedings under Art. 1 and within the definition of judgment in Art. 25, but outside the scope of operation of Title III on enforcement.
2. Procedural matters excluded from Title III are those decided in the course of main proceedings which do no more than regulate procedure and neither govern parties' legal relationships nor affect their proprietary rights.

Case

358 CFEM Façades SA v Bovis Construction Limited [1992] I.L.Pr. 561 High Court, 29 January 1992

Facts

The plaintiffs were engaged to design and supply internal walls for an office building in London. They contracted the defendants, including British, French, Dutch and Belgian companies, to supply designs and contribute to the works. Following complaints about the quality of the work, the plaintiffs began provisional proceedings against the defendants in the French courts and obtained an order for the appointment of two experts to inspect the building and report after listening to what people involved had to say; to reach a view on quality and any steps needed to remedy defects; decide on responsibility and settle accounts between parties; authorise emergency repairs and try to mediate on this. The French order was initially registered for enforcement in England under Art. 31, but the defendants subsequently challenged this on a number of grounds.

Judgment

Deputy High Court Judge Simon Goldblatt Q.C. reached the following conclusions.

(1) Foreign procedural judgments fell outside Title III. There was nothing in the text of Art. 1 or 25 to indicate that foreign courts' orders on procedural directions were, as such, outside the Convention's civil and commercial scope under Art. 1 or outside the definition of 'judgment' in Art. 25. Nevertheless, his view was that they were inappropriate for enforcement under Title III and the precedent for this approach was the Court of Justice's decision in *Denilauler* Case 125/79, in relation to *ex parte* orders.

(2) Excluded procedure defined. The deputy judge based his definition upon a passage in the Jenard Report (p. 10) referring to the *proprietary* scope of the Convention. Consequently, he concluded that a foreign judgment would be excluded from Title III as procedural if it was:

- interlocutory in the course of main proceedings; and
- did no more than regulate procedural matters and neither governed the parties' legal relationships nor affected their property rights.

In the case before him, therefore, the deputy judge considered that those parts of the French order concerning the questioning of witnesses and the preparation of accounts and costs fell within the meaning given to excluded procedure; whereas, appointment of experts and associated authorization of plaintiffs to carry out emergency work were not excluded—these would possibly affect legal relations and proprietary rights. The latter aspects of the French order, but not the former, would thus be registered for enforcement in England under Art. 31, and such partial enforcement was expressly authorised by Art. 42 (see *infra*, Case 364).

Comment

The judge involved was a deputy High Court judge who initially appeared to be not highly experienced in Convention law—some of the reasoning was pedestrian and a little tenuous, especially regarding interpretation of and reliance upon the Jenard Report.

Nevertheless, his eventual mastery of policy and text and construction of a workable solution to the complex problem is greatly to be applauded.

> " . . . and enforceable in that State . . . "

Case principle

An *ex parte* judgment delivered without the defendant having been summoned to appear, does *not* fall outside Title III in accordance with *Denilauler* Case 125/79, unless it was also intended to be *enforced* without first being served upon the defendant.

Case

359 E.M.I. Records Ltd v Modern Music Karl-Ulrich Walterbach GmbH [1992] 1 QB 115 High Court, 19 April 1991

Facts

The German respondents óbtained an injunction from the German courts prohibiting the appellant English company from reproducing and distributing the master tapes of a pop group. The German judgment was initially registered for enforcement in England, but the appellant appealed against registration, on the ground that the *ex parte* injunction fell outside Title III and therefore could not be enforced. *Denilauler* was relied upon. The respondents countered this by saying that in *Denilauler*, the European Court of Justice not only required a foreign judgment to have been *delivered ex parte* for it to be held to fall outside Title III; it also had to be one which was *intended to be enforced* without prior service upon the appellant. The respondents argued that the latter was not the position where it was possible for the appellant to apply to have the German judgment set aside at any time; and when they did, the pre-enforcement service requirement would be retrospectively satisfied.

Judgment

Hobhouse J. held against registration of the German judgment and allowed the appeal to have it set aside. Title III was inapplicable.

(1) He accepted the German respondents' argument that *Denilauler* prescribed *both ex parte* nature of proceedings *and* intention to enforce prior to service for Title III to be excluded.

(2) *But* he completely rejected their arguments about *ex post facto* displacement of the second *Denilauler* condition above through defendants' subsequent ability to apply to set aside the judgment following notice (and he also indicated *obiter*, in relation to Art. 27(2), that notice of proceedings was required at the date thereof, not retrospectively, following judgment). Thus, the German injunction had not been suspended; it was enforceable before the notice was served upon the appellants enabling them to apply to have it set aside, and, therefore, on the facts, *Denilauler* was satisfied. The German judgment fell outside Title III and registration for its enforcement in England would be set aside.

ARTICLE 38, PARAGRAPH 1

"... *may* ... *stay the proceedings* ... "

Case principle

1. Discretion to stay under Art. 38, para. 1 or to enforce on security under Art. 38, para. 3 is unfettered and exercised according to the facts of a particular case so as equitably to protect judgment creditor and judgment debtor. There is no presumption in favour of enforcement on security under para. 3 as the most appropriate exercise of discretion.

Case

Petereit v Babcock International Holdings Ltd [1990] 1 WLR 350 High Court, **360** 28 November 1989

Facts

The plaintiff official receiver of an insolvent German company obtained a German judgment in 1988 ordering the defendant to pay to the plaintiff 40 million DM owed by the defendant under a share subscription agreement. The judgment was made provisionally enforceable in Germany on provision by the plaintiff of bank guarantees for 49 million DM by way of security. In November 1988, the defendant appealed against judgment in Germany. Subsequently, however, the plaintiff registered the German judgment for enforcement in England under Art. 31. The defendant appealed against English enforcement and requested a stay of its enforcement-appeal in England under Art. 38, para. 1 or, alternatively, enforcement subject to provision of security by the plaintiff under Art. 38, para. 3.

Judgment

Deputy High Court Judge Anthony Diamond Q.C. chose to exercise his discretion to stay the enforcement-appeal proceedings under Art. 38, para. 1 rather than to grant enforcement subject to plaintiff's provision of security under Art. 38, para. 3.

The deputy judge pointed to a number of criteria which would influence his decision:

(1) likelihood or otherwise of a successful appeal against judgment in Germany—the greater the likelihood of success, the more powerful the arguments for a stay under para. 1;

(2) the discretion to stay under para. 1 was general and unfettered, notwithstanding the Convention policy in favour of fast and effective enforcement;

(3) both paras 1 and 3 were intended to protect judgment-debtors against unjustified enforcement, and their respective applicability depended upon the detailed circumstances of the case;

(4) exercise of the discretion under Art. 38, para. 1 could be made subject to provision of security to be provided by the defendant in order to protect the plaintiff against loss of use of his money, for which mere interest might not fully compensate (although the plaintiff might be asked to provide the defendant with security for the costs incurred by the defendant in providing the plaintiff with such security); and

(5) the fact that the judgment-court itself made enforcement of the judgment conditional upon provision of security by the plaintiff was a strong factor against stay under para. 1 or a further order of security under para. 3.

Thus, applying these principles the deputy judge took the following steps.

(1) The enforcement-appeal proceedings were stayed under para. 1, because: (i) the defendant could suffer greatly from unnecessarily having to pay the large sum of £17 million claimed, whereas the plaintiff's company was insolvent—consequently interest would not compensate the defendant for unjustified enforcement, whereas it would compensate the plaintiff for delays in receipt; and (ii) the German court's order for the plaintiff to provide security for enforcement would not prevent a stay under para. 1, since the sum of 49 million DM ordered as security was considered wholly inadequate.

(2) The defendant was ordered to provide security for the stay, in the form of a bank guarantee sufficient to pay the principal sum of 40 million DM at 5 per cent interest from judgment to stay of the enforcement-appeal and at a rate thereafter according to the plaintiff's reasonable earnings from the funds if they had been paid to the plaintiff on the date of stay, together with the plaintiff's legal costs and his costs of providing security guarantees ordered by the German courts. Further, if the plaintiff were released from his German guarantee, he should then provide security in the English proceedings for the defendant's costs of appealing against judgment in Germany and of providing the English security guarantee.

The plaintiff was to undertake not to seek enforcement of the German judgment anywhere else in the world until final determination of the German judgment-appeal.

Comments

It is uncertain from European Court case law whether Art. 38 courts ought to take account of prospects of a successful appeal against judgment in the judgment-State or not.

In *Van Dalfsen* Case C–183/90, the Court of Justice seemed to indicate that such factors should *not* be considered. Advocate General Van Gerven was less categorical and appeared willing for judgment-State appeal prospects to be assessed, so long as the substance of the action was not reviewed contrary to Art. 29 and Art. 34, para. 3. Subsequently, in *SISRO* Case C–432/93, Advocate General Léger was quite unequivocal in his view that judgment-State appeal prospects (as well as refusal to stay enforcement by judgment-State's courts) were relevant, although never decisive, as to exercise of the Art. 38 discretion to stay. The European Court itself did not have to decide the matter and declined to comment.

The principles for exercise of discretion under Art. 38 set forth and applied by the deputy judge in *Petereit* may be judged and accepted or rejected on their own merits. Independently of this, the judgment may be criticised for the questionable application of Art 38 in the first place, in a situation in which it is not immediately apparent that the defendants had put forward any justiciable grounds of appeal against enforcement under the Convention at all (see 'Stay of Enforcement Proceedings under the European Judgments Convention: Factors Relevant to the Exercise of Discretion' (1991) *Journal of Business Law* 261).

In *SISRO*, Advocate General Léger seemed to think that this would not affect a court's powers under Art. 38—although the Court of Justice itself found this unnecessary to decide.

Case principles

2. An applicant for a stay should provide evidence of the time left to appeal against judgment in the judgment-State if that appeal has not yet been brought.
3. Even if the stay is refused or unavailable, the enforcement-court retains a national law power to stay *execution* of the judgment.

Case

Thierry Noirhomme v David Walklate [1992] 1 Lloyd's Rep. 427 High Court, **361** 15 April 1991

Facts

The appellant appealed against registration of a Belgian judgment against him in England (unsuccessfully under Art. 27(2): see *infra*, annexed Protocol/ Protocol No. 1 Art. IV, para. 1, Case 380). He sought a stay of the enforcement-appeal proceedings under Art. 38.

Judgment

Deputy High Court Judge Michael Kershaw Q.C. refused to stay.

No appeal had been lodged in Belgium and the appellant had adduced no evidence as to the time, if any, available for appeal in Belgium. Since the Belgian judgment had been delivered 18 months earlier, it was highly unlikely that the time for appealing had not yet expired.

The court retained its national law power to stay *execution* of the registered Belgian judgment because, under Convention implementing legislation, registered foreign judgments were to be treated as if they were UK judgments (1982 Act s.4(3)). However, on the facts, a discretionary stay of execution would not be granted in order to enable the appellant to investigate the possibilities of an appeal in Belgium, because he had done nothing in this respect since the Belgian judgment was delivered.

> " . . . *if an ordinary appeal has been lodged* . . . "

Case principle

A French *recours en révision* is not an 'ordinary appeal' within the uniform Convention meaning, to the extent that it may be lodged at any time following judgment, with no limit on that period (*Industrial Diamond Supplies* Case 43/77 applied).

Case

362 Interdesco S.A. v Nullifire Ltd [1992] 1 Lloyd's Rep. 180 High Court, 1 May 1991

Facts

See supra, Cases 351 and 357.

The defendant sought a stay of its enforcement-appeal proceedings against registration in England of a French judgment, pending determination of the *recours en révision* in French courts.

Judgment

Phillips J. refused. The *recours en révision* could be lodged at any time following judgment, according to French procedure, and, consequently, was not an 'ordinary appeal' for Convention purposes.

> **ARTICLE 38, PARAGRAPH 3**
>
> " . . . *may also make enforcement conditional on the provision of such security* . . . "

Case principle

If the judgment creditor *undertakes* to the enforcement-court to repay damages in the event that the foreign judgment-court were to reverse or to reduce the award made in his favour, an order for provision of security may not be appropriate.

Case

Interdesco S.A. v Nullifire Ltd [1992] 1 Lloyd's Rep. 180 High Court, 1 May 1991   **363**

See *supra*, Case 362.

Facts

The defendant unsuccessfully sought to stay an appeal against enforcement of a French judgment for damages in England. In the alternative, the defendant requested the English enforcement-appeal court to order the plaintiff to provide security for enforcement in the event that the defendant were to succeed in its appeal against judgment in the French courts.

Judgment

Phillips J. refused. It was not appropriate to order security, since the plaintiff had already offered to provide an undertaking to repay damages to the defendant if the French judgment-court were to reverse or to reduce the award.

```
ARTICLE 42

" . . . given in respect of several matters . . . "
```

Case principle

'Matters' in Art. 42 include both those excluded and those not excluded from the scope of the Convention or, as the case may be, of Title III.

Case

CFEM Façades SA v Bovis Construction Limited [1992] I.L.Pr. 561 High Court, 29 January 1992   **364**

Facts

See supra, Art. 31, para. 1, Case 358.

The plaintiffs obtained a judgment in France which was partly procedural, and they applied for registration for enforcement of the judgment in England.

Judgment

The deputy High Court judge held that:

(1) procedural aspects (as defined, see *supra*, Case 358) of the foreign judgment were excluded from Title III; but

(2) non-procedural parts could be enforced—Art. 42 permitted partial enforcement.

ARTICLE 50, PARAGRAPH 1

" . . . *formally drawn up . . . as an authentic instrument* . . . "

Case principle

Formal acknowledgement of debt, enforceable without court action, is authentic instrument.

Case

365 S. & T. Bautrading v Nordling (unreported) Court of Appeal, 29 July 1996

Facts

See supra, 1982 Act s.25(1), Case 93.

Judgment

The Court of Appeal noted that there had been no appeal from the first instance deputy High Court Judge's finding that a German *Schuldanerkenntnis* —a formal acknowledgement of a debt by the debtor towards the creditor, capable of being executed under German law without the need to sue in court or to prove any underlying debt—was an authentic instrument within Art. 50.

ARTICLE 53, PARAGRAPH 1

" . . . *in order to determine that seat, the court shall apply its rules of private international law.*"

1982 ACT SECTION 42(3)(b)

" . . . *central management and control* . . . "

Case principle

Under English private international law for Convention purposes, a company's seat is

    (1)   in the case of seat in the United Kingdom: founded upon *either* incorporation and registered office *or* exercise of central management and control (Civil Jurisdiction and Judgments Act 1982 s.42(3)); and

    (2)   in the case of seat in another Contracting State: as in the case of United Kingdom seat, except that courts of the foreign Contracting State must also regard the company as having its seat in that State (s.42(6) and (7)).

Case

The Rewia [1991] 2 Lloyd's Rep. 325 Court of Appeal, 20 June 1991   **366**

Facts

See supra, Case 184.

Judgment

In this decision, the Court of Appeal concluded that a company incorporated in Liberia, nevertheless had its seat and, therefore, domicile in Germany, on the ground that its central management and control were exercised in Hamburg.

Although the shipowning company in the claim for loss and damage to cargo was managed on a day-to-day basis by a management company in Hong Kong, the court held that central management and control existed in Hamburg for the following reasons: all directors were German and resident in Germany; all shares in the company were beneficially owned or controlled by German companies; major policy decisions were made in Hamburg; directors met in Hamburg; the management agreement with the Hong Kong company was expressly subject to German law and courts and reserved major policy decisions to the directors of the shipowning company.

Comment

Consequently, the determining factors of central management and control appear to be:

- director control;
- shareholder ownership and control; and
- any other consistent elements referring to the place of central control.

LUGANO ARTICLE 54, PARAGRAPH 1

" . . . *apply only to legal proceedings instituted . . . after its entry into force in the State of origin . . .* "

General

See too *infra*, 1978 Accession Convention, Article 34(1), for equivalent provision to Article 54, para. 1.

Case principle

1. In legal proceedings instituted prior to the (Lugano) Convention's entry into force, the Convention's provisions nevertheless apply to co-defendants joined or to claims amended *after* its entry into force.

Case

367 Aiglon Ltd and L'Aiglon S.A. v Gau Shan Co. Ltd [1993] 1 Lloyd's Rep. 164 High Court, 23 June 1992

Facts

See supra, 1982 Act s.49, Case 109.

The Swiss party, against which amended claims were made under Art. 6(1), argued that the Lugano Convention should be held to be inapplicable to those amended claims under Art. 54, since the English proceedings had been *instituted* prior to the Lugano Convention's entry into force in the UK on 1 May 1992.

Judgment

Hirst J. held that Art. 54 should be regarded as satisfied because the date of the amendment to the claims fell after that of the Convention's entry into force in the UK. This was sufficient.

Case principle

2. Article 21 applies in principle where second-seised proceedings are instituted after entry into force of the Lugano Convention in the second-seised State, even if first-seised proceedings were instituted prior to that date of entry into force.

Case

368 Solani Bank v Bank Austria AG (unreported) Court of Appeal, 15 January 1997

Facts and Judgment

See supra, Art. 21, Case 294.

Comments

This principle was not expressed in the judgment—it was merely implicit in the Court of Appeal's willingness to examine whether the second-seised Austrian courts would be obliged to decline under Art. 21 in favour of first-seised English courts deciding under pre-Lugano rules as part of their investigation into English *forum non conveniens*. The Court of Appeal's decision was that in the particular circumstances of the case, Austrian courts would not decline, in view of the fact that English courts were considered to be *forum non conveniens*. The decision seems not wholly inconsistent with the European Court's ruling in *Von Horn v Cinnamond*, Case C–163/95 of 9 October 1997 in relation to the equivalent Article 29 of the 1989 San Sebastian Spain/Portugal Accession Convention—even though, in *Solani* it was the Contracting State (UK) which was first seised prior to entry into force in the thereafter (to be) second-seised and previously non-Contracting State (Austria), whereas in *Von Horn*, the non-Contracting State (Portugal) was first seised prior to entry into force therein and the Contracting State (UK) second seised, subsequent to the Convention's entry into force in the first. The European Court ruled that Article 21 applied if the first-seised court's judgment would be transitionally entitled to Title III recognition and enforcement under Article 29(2) (1978 34(3)/54 para. 2) in the second-seised State; otherwise Article 21 was inapplicable. Of course, to the extent that the Court of Appeal is taken to suggest that there is any discretion in the operation of Article 21 (even transitionally), this is quite incorrect. Article 21 is mandatory, not subject to *forum conveniens* considerations.

ARTICLE 54, PARAGRAPH 3

(Old Art. 35 of the 1978 Accession Convention, now deleted)

" . . . *had agreed in writing* . . . "

Case principle

1. Agreement in writing on applicable law does not include an oral agreement subsequently confirmed in writing.

Case

Lombard Continental Insurance Co. Plc v Claeys Luck S.A. (unreported) **369**
Court of Appeal, 22 November 1988

Facts

Plaintiff English insurers wished to sue the defendant French insured in the English courts, notwithstanding absence of Convention grounds. The defendants contested English 1978 Article 35 transitional jurisdiction.

Judgment

At first instance, Phillips J. in the High Court held 1978 Accession Convention Art. 35 to be inapplicable, because the agreement on English law was not in writing, merely oral and subsequently confirmed in writing.

Case principle

2. Pre-Convention agreements on choice of law under 1978 Accession Convention Art. 35 are restricted to express agreements on applicable law and may not be implied.

Case

370 New Hampshire Insurance Company v Strabag Bau AG [1992] 1 Lloyd's Rep. 361 Court of Appeal, 25 October 1991

Facts

See supra, Art. 11, para. 1, Case 196.

The plaintiff American insurers insured the defendant German (and Austrian) construction companies in 1981 in respect of building work in Iraq. In 1989, the defendants claimed between £20 million and £60 million relating to faults in the building work. The plaintiffs brought an action before the English courts for a declaration of avoidance of the insurance policy. The German defendants challenged English jurisdiction, on the ground that the courts of their German domicile possessed jurisdiction in insurance matters under Art. 11, para. 1 (see *supra*, Art. 11, para. 1, Case 196).

However, the plaintiffs sought to justify English jurisdiction, *inter alia*, on the ground that there had been an implied choice of English law to govern the contract in 1981 and that, accordingly, Art. 35 required such pre-Convention (that is, pre-1 January 1987 in the UK) choice of English law to be given effect to as founding national English jurisdiction, whether the law agreement was express *or implied*. This argument failed before Potter J. at first instance in the High Court: Art. 35 was limited to express agreements on choice of law. The plaintiffs appealed to the Court of Appeal.

Judgment

The Court of Appeal upheld Potter J.'s decision: Art. 35 only preserved national English jurisdiction based upon express agreements on choice of English law.

The plaintiffs had tried to argue that *implied* choice of law should also be permitted to found such transitional English jurisdiction, because the basis of such at national law was discretionary RSC Ord. 11, r.1(1)(d)(iii), which provided for jurisdiction over a contract by its terms *or by implication* governed by English law. Lloyd L.J. could not accept this argument, because it ignored the words in Art. 35 'agreed in writing'—this meant that the choice of law itself, not merely the overall contract from which an implication as to choice of law could be drawn, must be so expressly agreed. There had to be an express choice of law clause.

Comment

(See 'Business Insurance and Reinsurance under the European Judgments Convention: Application of Protective Provisions?' (1990) *Journal of Business Law* 517, for discussion of the first instance decision; and 'Transitional Scope of the Jurisdiction and Judgments Convention' (1988) 7 *Civil Justice Quarterly* 53, 55–8, for argumentation in support of restricting Art. 35 to express choice of law, prior to the *Strabag Bau* decisions. Note too 'Jurisdiction of English Courts Based Upon Choice of English Law' (1989) 133 *Solicitors' Journal* 1537).

ARTICLE 57(1)

"This Convention shall not affect any conventions to which the Contracting States are or will be parties . . . "

Case principles

1. Where national English law *implements* an Art. 57 convention, the English rule receives priority over the 1968 Convention under Art. 57, by virtue of s.9(1) of the 1982 Act—but only *to the extent that* the English statute implements the Art. 57 convention.
2. If it goes further than the latter in conferring jurisdiction, *to the extent of the excess the English rule receives no Art. 57 priority.*

Case

The Deichland [1990] 1 QB 361 Court of Appeal, 20 April 1989   **371**

Facts

See supra, 1982 Act s.9(1), Case 85.

The plaintiff cargo owners brought national *in rem* proceedings for damages in the English courts for damage to cargo, which the defendant German charterers asserted should have been brought in their German domicile under Art. 2 of the Convention. The plaintiffs claimed that national English *in rem* jurisdiction laid down in ss.20 and 21 of the Supreme Court Act 1981, implementing the 1952 Brussels Arrest Convention to which the UK and Germany were parties, had priority over the 1968 Convention under Art. 57, by virtue of s.9(1) of the 1982 Act equating implementing legislation with the Art. 57 conventions themselves (see *supra*, s.9(1)).

Judgment

The Court of Appeal held that ss.20 and 21 had only implemented 1952 Convention arrest jurisdiction to the extent that they conferred *in rem* jurisdiction upon English courts on the basis of actual arrest, as laid down in the 1952 Convention. Where, however, as in the present case, the defendants' ship merely *could have been* arrested but for provision of security or an undertaking to prevent arrest, this basis of 1981 Act jurisdiction went beyond that in the 1952 Convention and could not enjoy Art. 57 priority under s.9(1). Consequently, such national rule was excluded by 1968 Convention Art. 3, and Art. 2 applied so as to confer jurisdiction upon courts of the defendant charterers' German domicile.

Comments

Compare the subsequent Court of Appeal decision in *The Po*, Case 372, where *The Deichland* was distinguished because the former involved the 1952 Brussels *Collision* Convention. The Collision Convention *did* include jurisdiction where the ship *could have been* arrested. The problem in *The Po*, however, was that the particular rule of English law had not been enacted *specifically* in order to implement the Collision Convention, as seemed to be required by s.9(1). The Court of Appeal, nonetheless, held the national rule's *existence* to be enough for Art. 57 to be available (see *infra*).

In addition, in *The Havhelt* [1993] 1 Lloyd's Rep. 523, Saville J. in the English Admiralty Court held there to be no material distinction in the context between English *in rem* and Norwegian *in personam* proceedings such as to dissuade him from granting a stay of the English action in favour of chosen Norwegian jurisdiction as *forum conveniens* in 1992 (the Lugano Convention entered into force subsequently in Norway in 1993). The judge expressly followed *The Deichland*, *The Kherson* and *The Sylt*, see *supra*, Arts 21 and 57).

More generally, in *Harrison & Sons Ltd v RT Steward Transport Ltd* (unreported) 30 July 1992, Gatehouse J. in the High Court held the 1956 CMR Convention, given effect to in the UK by the Carriage of Goods by Road Act 1965, to be a Convention to which Art. 57 applied.

Case principle

3. National UK laws *corresponding to* jurisdiction grounds in a Convention on particular matters to which the UK is party, enjoy priority over the

1968 Convention by virtue of Art. 57 thereof, as if they were provisions of the particular Convention itself.

Case

The Po [1991] 2 Lloyd's Rep. 206 Court of Appeal, 17 April 1991   **372**

Facts

See *supra*, Case 86.

The Italian defendants' ship, The Po, collided with the American plaintiffs' ship, Bowditch, in Brazilian waters in 1987. The plaintiffs wished to sue The Po for damages in England and served on it a writ *in rem* when it was in English waters in 1988. The Po was not arrested because security was undertaken to prevent this.

The defendants objected to national English *in rem* jurisdiction on two grounds. First, England was *forum non conveniens* for the trial of the action. Brazil was clearly and distinctly the more appropriate forum.

Secondly, the national English rules were excluded by Convention Art. 3 and the defendants had to be proceeded against in the courts of their Italian domicile under Art. 2. Although the UK and Italy were parties to the 1952 Brussels Convention on Collisions, which permitted jurisdiction where a ship had been arrested or *could have been* arrested but for security, Art. 57 would not give priority to corresponding English *in rem* jurisdiction on the ground that The Po could have been arrested, because this particular aspect of English law had not been formulated specifically in order to implement the relevant 1952 Collision Convention provision. Section 9(1) of the 1982 Act, specifying that statutory provisions and rules of law having such implementation effect, were to be accorded the same priority under Art. 57 as the convention on particular matters themselves, demonstrated that national rules not introduced for implementation purposes fell outside Art. 57.

Judgment

First, by a majority of two to one, the Court of Appeal held England to be *forum conveniens*, and that the ruling of the first instance judge to this effect ought not to be disturbed, so that a stay of proceedings would not be granted on this ground in favour of Brazil.

Secondly, with regard to Art. 57, the Court of Appeal unanimously rejected the defendants' arguments against application of Art. 57 to the English rule of jurisdiction over a ship which could have been, but was not, arrested. Section 9(1) of the 1982 Act merely *confirmed* that in the UK where international conventions were transformed into national laws in order to have internal effect, the internal provisions themselves would enjoy Art. 57 priority. It did not, however, mean that national rules which had not been introduced specifically in order to implement provisions of the particular convention—such as that of English law on jurisdiction over ships which could have been arrested, which already existed—were excluded from Art. 57, if they, nonetheless, *corresponded with and gave effect to* the particular convention's relevant provisions. Such was the position with regard to arrest jurisdiction in the 1981 Act, only part of which gave effect to the 1952 Collision Convention in the UK (see Supreme Court Act 1981 s.21).

Accordingly, national English *in rem* jurisdiction, based upon security to avoid arrest, took priority over German 1968 Convention Art. 2 jurisdiction under Art. 57. The previous Court of Appeal decision in *The Deichland*, Case 371 *supra*, was distinguished on the ground that that case had involved the 1952 *Arrest* Convention, which permitted jurisdiction on the basis of arrest of a ship—but not also where it merely could have been arrested. Consequently, national English *in rem* jurisdiction to this extent went beyond the Art. 57 convention and could not itself therefore derive priority from Art. 57 (see *supra*).

Case principle

4. Arrest of a ship confers jurisdiction *in rem* upon the English court under the 1952 Brussels Arrest Convention by virtue of 1968 Convention Art. 57, even if arrest is *subsequent* to provision of bail by the defendant, not just if it takes place prior thereto.

Case

373 The 'Prinsengracht' [1993] 1 Lloyd's Rep. 41 High Court, 24 June 1992

Facts

The plaintiff cargo owners claimed for damage to the cargo in the English courts against the defendant Dutch shipowners. The defendants provided bail and acknowledged issue of the writ as the defendants' ship, Prinsengracht, sailed towards an English port, but when it arrived shortly afterwards the plaintiffs (doubtless mindful of *The Deichland* decision, *supra*) had the ship arrested for a small amount of time.

The defendants challenged English jurisdiction *in rem* on the ground that the arrest had taken place *after* bail had been provided and was therefore invalid to confer arrest jurisdiction under the 1952 Convention.

Judgment

Sheen J. dismissed the defendants' objections: arrest was valid whenever it took place. It had lasted less than one day and was not vexatious or oppressive—*a fortiori* if the provision of bail by the defendants would not (contrary to the judge's view) otherwise confer jurisdiction upon the English court on the ground of submission (see *supra*, Art. 18, Case 250).

Case principle

5.   Arrest also confers Art. 57 jurisdiction upon English courts notwithstanding that it takes place following an undertaking to provide bail (and to acknowledge service) as security for satisfaction of judgment.

Case

The Anna H [1994] 1 Lloyd's Rep. 287 High Court, 4 October 1993   **374**

Facts

The plaintiffs were British shippers and Spanish consignees of steel shipped by the German defendants from England and Wales to Barcelona in 1990. The cargo arrived in Barcelona in a damaged condition and the plaintiffs prepared to institute proceedings *in rem* in the English courts. In order to avoid arrest, the defendants' P. & I. Club undertook to acknowledge issue and service of a writ and to provide bail as security for judgment. However, the plaintiffs proceeded to arrest the defendants' ship, The Anna H, releasing it after one hour, following which the defendants' P. & I. Club provided bail and the defendants acknowledged service of the writ.

    The defendants contested English *in rem* jurisdiction on the ground that an arrest following an undertaking by defendants to provide bail was not an arrest within the meaning of the 1952 Arrest Convention and consequently 1968 Convention Art. 57 was inapplicable to displace German domicile under 1968 Convention Art. 2.

Judgment

Clarke J. upheld English 1968 Convention Art. 57 *in rem* jurisdiction under Supreme Court Act 1981 ss.20 and 21 giving effect to the 1952 Arrest Convention. Notwithstanding the prior undertaking by the defendants' P. & I. Club to provide bail, the arrest remained a measure 'to secure a maritime claim' within the definition in the 1952 Convention and regardless of the plaintiffs' motive to ensure existence of English *in rem* jurisdiction (see *supra*, *Deichland*, Case 371, and Art. 18, Case 251).

Case

The Anna H [1994] 1 Lloyd's Rep. 287 Court of Appeal, 26 May 1994   **375**

Facts

The defendants appealed to the Court of Appeal against Clarke J.'s decision.

Judgment

The Court of Appeal unanimously upheld Clark J.'s first instance judgment and dismissed the appeal.

First, 1952 Arrest Convention jurisdiction based on arrest prevailed over 1968 Convention Art. 2. Article 7(1) of the 1952 Convention stated as one of the conditions of jurisdiction of the arresting State thereunder the existence of jurisdiction under the 'domestic law' of that State. This did *not* include 1968 Convention Art. 2 (recall defendants were *German*, not English, domiciliaries), which was 'treaty law' not 'domestic law' in this context.

Secondly, the defendants were incorrect to argue that the plaintiffs' obvious motivation for the arrest, being to obtain English jurisdiction, was insufficient to amount to an 'arrest' as defined in the 1952 Convention, being detention *in order to secure* a maritime claim. Motivation was irrelevant and existence of sufficient security already for the plaintiffs from the defendants' P. & I. Club quite apart from arrest was not enough to prevent the arrest from being valid for the purposes.

> " . . . *shall not affect* . . . "

Case principle

1. English jurisdiction *in rem* derived from the 1952 Arrest Convention and applicable under 1968 Convention Art. 57 is subject to Arts 21 and 22 of the 1968 Convention.

Case

376   The Linda [1988] 1 Lloyd's Rep. 175 High Court, 23 October 1987

Facts

The plaintiffs' ship, Arco Humber, collided with the defendants' ship, The Linda, and the plaintiff commenced English proceedings *in rem* against the defendants in May 1987. The defendants challenged English jurisdiction under Arts 21 and 22 of the 1968 Convention, on the ground that the defendants had previously begun their own action against the plaintiffs in the Dutch courts. However, the plaintiffs sought to rely upon Art. 57 of the 1968 Convention: English *in rem* jurisdiction was derived from the 1952 Brussels Arrest Convention, which had priority over the 1968 Convention, *including Arts 21 and 22*, under Art. 57. Therefore, Arts 21 and 22 did not apply.

Judgment

Sheen J. held that Arts 21 and 22 applied to the 1952 Arrest Convention. *Existence* of jurisdiction thereunder was not 'affected' by Arts 21 and 22 within the meaning of Art. 57, even if its *exercise* was so.

Comment

This was clearly a policy decision, as opposed to one flowing ineluctably from the wording of the provisions!

See too infra, Nordglimt, Case 377.

Case principles

2. Judgments Convention provisions can only apply to the extent that they are not inconsistent with the rules or system of an Art. 57 convention on particular matters.
3. In the case of the 1952 Arrest Convention, Art. 21 would *not* require courts seised solely *in rem* thereunder to stay and decline jurisdiction in favour of foreign courts first-seised *in personam*, because at its inception an action *in rem* does not involve the same parties as the foreign action *in personam*, as required by Art. 21.
4. However, if the owner of the arrested ship chooses to acknowledge service and to defend the *in rem* action, at that point he becomes party *in personam* to the proceedings, which are converted into hybrid *in rem–in personam*, and solely *in personam* on release of the ship—in either of which events, parties *would* (partially) be the same. Although, according to Hobhouse J. in *The Nordglimt*, such conversion to same parties would not however operate retrospectively so as to satisfy Article 21, the High Court subsequently held that it would do so in *The Kherson, infra* Case 378 which was itself confirmed by the European Court in *Maciej Rataj* Case C–406/92—and *The Nordglimt* was thereafter expressly disapproved of for this aspect by the House of Lords in the analogous context of 1982 Act s.34 in *The Indian Endurance (No. 2)* (see *supra*, Cases 103–6, 260, 261, 277, 278, 299 and 300).

Case

The Nordglimt [1988] 1 QB 183 High Court, 31 July 1987   **377**

Facts

See supra, Arts 21 and 22.

Saudi Arabian receivers of damaged cargo and their insurers sued the Danish shipowners and Canadian charters *in personam* for the damage to the cargo in Belgian courts. Subsequently, *in rem* proceedings were brought against a ship of the same owner in the English courts.

The defendant in England requested a stay of proceedings under Art. 21.

Judgment

Hobhouse J. refused.

(1) Although the 1952 Arrest Convention had never *formally* been made a part of national English law, provisions in the Supreme Court Act 1981 were closely based on it—and it was even arguable that by virtue of Art. 57 of the Judgments Convention and of the latter's structure and system generally, the 1952 Convention *was* to that extent indirectly incorporated into English law, so that 1981 Act jurisdiction *in rem* effectively fell within Art. 57.

(2) As to whether Art. 21 was inconsistent with the 1952 Arrest Convention, this was unnecessary to decide, since Art. 21 was inapplicable in any event: the parties to the actions were not the same, as they were required to be. At least at its inception, the ship was the defendant to an *in rem* proceeding—only if and when the owner decided to acknowledge service and defend would his potential *in personam* liability be added (too late, for Hobhouse J., now disapproved).

Comment

See too *Deaville v Aeroflot Russian International Airlines* [1997] 2 Lloyd's Rep. 67 High Court, 7 February 1997, as to the relationship between Arts 57 and 21 (*supra*, Art. 21, Case 302).

Case

378   The Kherson [1992] 2 Lloyd's Rep. 261 High Court, 6 April 1992

Facts

See supra, Arts 21 and 22.

Plaintiff Dutch cargo owners instituted proceedings *in rem* through arrest of the Georgian defendants' ship *Kherson*, claiming damages for contamination of cargo. Following issue of the writ, but prior to the arrest, the plaintiffs began *in personam* proceedings against the shipowners in Dutch courts. Thereafter, the *Kherson* was released when the defendants acknowledged service of the English writ and their P. & I. Club provided security. The defendants challenged English jurisdiction on the ground that they were second-seised to Dutch courts of the same cause of action under Art. 21. The plaintiffs argued that the causes of action in English and Dutch proceedings respectively were not the same, as they were required to be under Art. 21.

Judgment

Sheen J., referring to the words of Hobhouse J. in *The Nordglimt*, held that once the defendants had entered an appearance through acknowledgement of service of the writ, the action became *in personam* as well as *in rem*—and solely *in personam* on release of the ship. Consequently, not only was the cause of action the same, but also the parties thereto at either stage (hybrid *in rem-in personam*, or subsequent solely *in personam*).

Comments

In the European Court of Justice's judgment in *The Owners of the Cargo lately Laden on Board the 'Tatry' v The Owners of the ship 'Maciej Rataj'* Case C–406/92, of 6 December 1994, on a reference from the English Court of Appeal, it was subsequently confirmed that Art. 21 conditions of *same cause of action* and *same parties* are capable of being satisfied, regardless of whether one set of proceedings is both *in rem* and *in personam*, or originally *in rem* and thereafter only *in personam*, while the prior *lis pendens* was solely *in personam*. Advocate General Tesauro, whose Opinion the European Court followed, actually cited *The Kherson* in support of the view that prior *in personam* proceedings for non-liability of a shipowner against cargo owners and the cargo owners' own subsequent liability claim against the shipowner, regardless of whether both *in rem* and *in personam* or now solely *in personam*, involved the same cause of action and parties for Art. 21.

The Court of Appeal and the House of Lords subsequently applied this in *The Indian Endurance (No. 2)* in relation to 1982 Act s.34 (*supra*).

In the Court of Appeal proceedings in *The Maciej Rataj* [1992] 2 Lloyd's Rep. 552, at 559 col. 2 of 13th April 1992, Neill L.J. agreed with *The Nordglimt* that initially-*in rem* proceedings became hybrid *in rem-in personam* on acknowledgement of service. But, subsequently (at 561 col. 2), he differed, with great diffidence, from Sheen J. in *The Linda* and *The Kherson*, who had considered hybrid to become solely *in personam* on the release of the ship. Neill L.J. regarded the proceedings as continuing to be hybrid in such a case—although his second question to the European Court expressed the two possibilities in the alternative, thereby explicitly demonstrating continuing uncertainty on the issue.

Case principles

5. 1968 Convention is only excluded to the extent that it is inconsistent with the Art. 57 convention on particular matters (*Maciej Rataj* Case C–406/92 applied).

6. 1968 Convention Art. 17 jurisdiction, unlike Arts 21 and 22 (*Maciej Rataj*), is inconsistent with the 1952 Brussels Arrest Convention's arrest jurisdiction and with national grounds derived therefrom or corresponding thereto.

Case

The Bergen [1997] 1 Lloyd's Rep. 380 High Court, 20 November 1996   **379**

Facts

The plaintiff cargo owners wished to sue the defendant German shipowners in the English courts for damages of £230 000 for fire damage to a cargo of wood pulp carried on the defendants' ship 'Bergen' in 1994 from America to Aberdeen in Scotland. The defendants contested English courts' jurisdiction, on the grounds of an exclusive German jurisdiction clause in the bills of lading, valid under Art. 17.

The plaintiffs argued that Art. 17 was inapplicable and that merely discretionary national English principles governed instead, because Art. 57 excluded the 1968 Convention provisions where inconsistent with a convention on particular matters conferring jurisdiction. This was so here: English *in rem* arrest jurisdiction under ss.20(2) and 21(4) of the Supreme Court Act 1981 corresponded with Art. 7 of the 1952 Brussels Arrest Convention, with which 1968 Convention Art. 17 jurisdiction would be in conflict. The defendants protested that Art. 17 would have no such effect as claimed because, provided that English courts were seised first of *in rem* jurisdiction, then, unlike in the case of contravention of Art. 16, Art. 19 did not require courts to declare against jurisdiction contravening Art. 17 of their own motion; and furthermore (and rather crucially in view of the defendants' *perilous* resort to the preceding point *in order to negate Art. 17's 'mandatory'*, and consequently *inconsistent, force*), 1968 Convention Arts 21 and 22 had been preserved in relation to the 1952 Brussels Arrest Convention, so why not Art. 17?

Judgment

Clarke J. upheld the plaintiffs' case for exclusion of Art. 17 by virtue of Art. 57 and entirely rejected the defendants' objections.

(1) Drawing upon the previous judgment in *Continental Bank* where Art. 17 had been found to prevail over Arts 21 and 22 (see *supra*, Case 239), and on that in *The Anna H* (*supra*, Cases 374 and 375), it was not true to say that Art. 17 was anything less than mandatory. If it applied, it most certainly would have the effect of overriding 1952 *in rem* jurisdiction if inconsistent as here.

(2) The effect of *Maciej Rataj* was indeed that Arts 21 and 22 could continue to apply to the 1952 Arrest Convention notwithstanding Art. 57. *But* Art. 17 was different from Arts 21 and 22, in that it turned upon whether the court possessed original jurisdiction on a ground which was inconsistent with or missing from the Art. 57 convention, not on whether it was permissible to apply a 1968 procedural solution to the problem of *lis pendens* under the 1952 Convention if the latter itself made no provision for this issue.

**ANNEXED PROTOCOL/LUGANO PROTOCOL NO. 1
ARTICLE IV, PARAGRAPH 1**

" *. . . in accordance with the procedures laid down in the conventions . . .* "

Case principle

Permitted methods of transmission of documents abroad for service under Art. IV, para. 1 of the annexed Protocol/Protocol No. 1 do not just include those specifically referred to in international service conventions, but also other—including national law—methods preserved and provided for thereunder.

Case

Thierry Noirhomme v David Walklate [1992] 1 Lloyd's Rep. 427 High Court,   **380**
15 April 1991

Facts

See *supra*, Case 361.

The plaintiff Belgian property owner successfully sued the English defendant for damage caused during a letting of the former's house and obtained registration for enforcement in England of the Belgian judgment in default under Art. 31.

The defendant appealed against enforcement under Art. 27(2) on the ground that service of the Belgian writ had been sent by post to the defendant at his address in England, whereas, the defendant claimed that in accordance with Art. IV of the annexed Protocol/Protocol No. 1, such transmission abroad had to be that 'laid down in' the relevant convention, being the 1965 Hague Convention on Service Abroad of Judicial and Extrajudicial Documents in Civil and Commercial Matters. Article 5 of the 1965 Convention provided for a method of transmission through the Central Authority of the state addressed, *but* other provisions referred to continuation of *national law* methods, *including postal*, as alternatives.

Judgment

Deputy High Court Judge Michael Kershaw Q.C. held that service had been duly effected and enforcement would not be refused and registration set aside under Art. 27(2) (see *supra*, Case 352).

The reason was that the words 'laid down' in Art. IV had to be interpreted purposively rather than literally. This meant that they included:

- not just the specific method of transmission through Central Authorities, introduced by Art. 5 of the 1965 Hague Convention;
- but also the other methods of transmission—including post—preserved and provided for under the 1965 Convention. This was the wider sense in which the expression 'laid down in' in Art. IV of the annexed Protocol/Protocol No. 1 was to be understood.

Accordingly, transmission in this case had been properly carried out in accordance with Art. IV, and Art. 27(2) was not contravened. Registration would remain.

1971 INTERPRETATION PROTOCOL ARTICLE 3(2)

" . . . that court may . . . request . . . "

Case principle

The discretion to refer might not be exercised in favour of a reference where the judge has formed a firm view on all the issues.

Case

381a Mölnlycke A.B. v Procter & Gamble Ltd [1992] 1 WLR 1112 Court of Appeal, 27 June 1991

Facts

See supra, Art. 5, Case 139.

This was the explanation given for failure to refer interpretation of Arts 5 and 6 in the appeal proceedings.

1978 ACCESSION CONVENTION ARTICLE 34(1)

" . . . legal proceedings instituted . . . after the entry into force . . . "

General

See too *supra*, Article 54, para. 1, for equivalent Brussels/Lugano provision to 1978 Accession Convention Article 34(1).

Case principle

Article 24 treated as inapplicable to English application for provisional relief in aid of Dutch main proceedings instituted prior to entry into force of the Convention in the UK (and of the 1978 Accession Convention in The Netherlands in relation to the UK).

Case

381b Alltrans Inc. v Interdom Holdings Limited [1993] I.L.Pr. 109 Court of Appeal, 30 January 1991

Facts

See supra, 1982 Act s.25(1), Case 94.

Judgment

Article 34(1) expressly requires the proceedings to have been instituted after entry into force of the Convention. However, Dutch main proceedings were commenced in February 1986, whereas the 1978 Accession Convention entered into force almost one year later as between The Netherlands and the UK.

Comment

It seems questionable whether the decision would survive a purposive construction of the European Court's ruling of 9 October 1997 in *Von Horn v Cinnamond*, Case C–163/95 in relation to transitional operation of *Article 21* (see *supra*, Comment to Case 368). *Textually*, Article 24 can be distinguished from Article 21 for these purposes, because (1) the former expressly states that substance jurisdiction must be possessed "under this Convention" (not just the transitionally ambiguous reference to *Contracting* State in Articles 21 and 24), and (2) the "legal proceedings" referred to in Article 34(1) could also be taken to include those in the State of substance in Art. 24, not just those for provisional relief in the Art. 24 State itself, which should *both* have been instituted after entry into force of the Convention in those States. However, provided that in accordance with *Von Horn* conditions, the substance judgment would be entitled to transitional recognition and enforcement under Title III, this seems precisely the case in which, as a matter of Convention enforcement policy, Article 24 ought to be held to apply if *Von Horn* is to be given its full purposive scope.

ARTICLE 34(3)

" . . . *founded upon rules which accorded with the provisions of Title II . . .* "

Case principle

Where Convention jurisdiction grounds are transitionally inapplicable to proceedings instituted prior to the Convention's entry into force in the UK, hypothetical existence of Convention jurisdiction has nonetheless been held to be relevant to the discretionary decision by English courts to proceed or to stay their jurisdiction under national principles of *forum conveniens* outside the Convention, because if Convention jurisdiction *would have* been available to English courts had the Convention been in force in the UK at the date of institution of proceedings, then under Art. 34(3) the English judgment will be required to be recognized and enforced in other Contracting States in accordance with Convention Title III if given after the Convention's entry into force—and clearly this is a factor in favour of continuation of English proceedings as national *forum conveniens*.

Case

382 Saipern S.p.A. v Dredging V02 BV and Geosite Surveys Ltd (The 'Volvox Hollandia') [1987] 2 Lloyd's Rep. 520 High Court, 1 May 1987

Facts

The Dutch defendants brought liability limitation proceedings in the Dutch courts in 1985 and the plaintiff commenced a liability action against the defendants in England subsequently, in 1985. The defendants contested English jurisdiction as being *forum non conveniens* under national English principles on discretionary stays of action.

Judgment

Staughton J. held the Convention's jurisdiction grounds to be inapplicable to the English proceedings commenced before 1 January 1987 when the Convention entered into force in the UK, in accordance with 1978 Accession Convention Art. 34(1).

However, Convention jurisdiction was *indirectly* relevant, from the point of view that if it existed, other Contracting States would have to recognize and enforce the English judgment under the Convention by virtue of Art 34(3) where judgment was delivered after the Convention's entry into force in the United Kingdom.

Thus, on the facts English courts would have possessed Convention jurisdiction as those agreed to under Art. 17 (although unusually, not exclusively of Dutch Art. 6a jurisdiction—so that Art. 27(3) would possibly be needed, see *supra*, Cases 194 and 195). Accordingly, English courts were held to be *forum conveniens* at national law.

Comment

The English judge plainly treated satisfaction of Convention jurisdictional connections as the precondition for Convention recognition and enforcement under 1978 Accession Convention Art. 34(3), rather than actual exercise of national English jurisdiction on grounds formally corresponding to those in the Convention, notwithstanding that Art. 34(3)'s wording ('was founded upon rules which accorded with the provisions of Title II') *could* be taken to indicate the latter. It is submitted that the judge was correct (see Kaye, *Civil Jurisdiction* pp. 240–2).

The defendant V02 appealed the decision of Staughton J. to the Court of Appeal.

Case

Saipern S.p.A. v Dredging V02 BV and Geosite Surveys Ltd (The 'Volvox **383**
Hollandia') [1988] 2 Lloyd's Rep. 361 Court of Appeal, 18 April 1988

Facts

The appeal was fought out on the issue of proper exercise of discretion by the
first instance judge.

Judgment

In the event, a majority of two to one judges of the Court of Appeal reversed
the decision of Staughton J. to exercise English jurisdiction over the liability
claim. In the course of doing so, the Court of Appeal adopted Staughton J.'s
approach of taking into account the possibilities of post-Convention's entry
into force recognition and enforcement of judgments in other Contracting
States under 1978 Accession Convention Art. 34(3).

E.   RECENT CASE LAW*

1982 ACT SECTION 25(2)

" . . . *makes it inexpedient for the court to grant it.*"

Case principles

1. Courts should consider whether the defendant is resident in England and
   Wales or not, as a factor in the exercise of their discretion in relation to
   s.25(1) extraterritorial orders, under s.25(2).
2. If the s.25(1) order is also extraterritorial in scope, the s.25(2) element of
   discretion remains dependent upon expediency of grant of an order thereunder and there is no *increased* requirement of exceptionality of circumstances for grant by reason of the lack of substantive English jurisdiction,
   beyond that already required for the extraterritoriality element.
3. The likely reaction of the foreign courts of main proceedings on substance
   and of *situs* of assets to be affected is highly material to the exercise
   of discretion.

Case

Crédit Suisse Fides Trust SA v Cuoghi, The Times, 3 July 1997, [1997] 3 All **384**
ER 724, Court of Appeal, 11 June 1997

---

*Possibly taken from reports which may be less detailed or less accurate than
mainstream series.

Facts, Judgment and Comments

See supra, s.25(1), Case 92.

SECTION 49

" . . . not inconsistent with the 1968 Convention."

Case principle

In principle, 'territorially-defined' torts may no longer be excluded from English courts under the Convention's system as being non-justiciable, nor even consequentially on grounds of *forum conveniens*.

Case

385 Pearce v Ove Arup Partnership Ltd, The Times, 17 March 1997, [1997] 3 All ER 31, High Court, 7 March 1997

Facts

See Case 386 *infra*.

The action in England was for breach of Dutch copyright. The defendants challenged the English courts' jurisdiction, notwithstanding English domicile of the main defendant, on grounds that: (i) actions over foreign copyright were non-justiciable, through being local according to *British South Africa Co. v Companhia de Moçambique* [1893] AC 602; and (ii) even if heard by the court, the action would fail on the merits if English law were to be applied, since it too was locally limited (*Def Lepp Music v Stuart-Brown* [1986] RPC 273). For these reasons too, England was *forum non conveniens*.

Judgment

Lloyd J. held *obiter*:

(1) breach of copyright actions were civil and commercial within Convention Art. 1;

(2) they also fell within Art. 5(3), and, but for English domicile of the defendant, The Netherlands was the place of the harmful event in tort in an action for breach of Dutch copyright;

(3) Art. 2 was a fundamental Convention rule of jurisdiction, to which *forum conveniens* was not an exception;

(4) nor was either the *Moçambique* rule of non-justiciability any longer an exception to English jurisdiction where the Convention applied,

nor the *Def Lepp* principle a reason therefor (especially since s.10 of the Private International Law (Miscellaneous Provisions) Act 1995 had abolished automatic application of *lex fori* to international torts as from 1 May 1996). This was because, although these were not strictly *jurisdiction* rules, nonetheless, 'Each of them, to the extent that they would preclude the English court from hearing such an action, would impair the effectiveness of the Convention by frustrating the operation of the basic rule in Art. 2, and therefore had to give way to allow the jurisdictional rules of the Convention to have their proper effect'. According to Lloyd J., this was the first English case in which the point had been raised.

Comment

However, these findings were in fact *obiter*. This was because, although thenceforth non-justiciability would not be permitted to interfere with Convention jurisdiction in the manner explained, the English action would still be struck out as being an abuse of the court's process, since the provisions of the 1995 Torts Act apparently were transitionally inapplicable and consequently the action on Dutch copyright was bound to fail to the extent that English *lex fori* were to continue to be applied under the old 'double-actionability' rule in the private international law of tort.

CONVENTION ARTICLE 1, PARAGRAPH 1

"This Convention shall apply . . . "

Case principle

1. In principle, 'territorially-defined' torts may not be excluded from English courts under the Convention's system as being non-justiciable (nor even consequentially on grounds of *forum conveniens*).

Case

Pearce v Ove Arup Partnership Ltd The Times, 17 March 1997, [1997] 3 All   **386**
ER 31, High Court, 7 March 1997

Facts

See *supra*, Case 385.

The action in England was for breach of Dutch copyright. The defendants challenged the English courts' jurisdiction, notwithstanding English domicile of the main defendant, on grounds that: (i) actions over foreign copyright were non-justiciable, through being 'local' according to *British South Africa Co. v Companhia de Moçambique* [1893] AC 602; and (ii) even if heard by the court, the action would fail on the merits if English law were to be applied, since it too was locally limited (*Def Lepp Music v Stuart-Brown* [1986] RPC 273). For these reasons too, England was *forum non conveniens*.

Judgment

Lloyd J. held *obiter*:

(1)   breach of copyright actions were civil and commercial within Convention Art. 1;

(2)   the also fell within Art. 5(3), yet, but for English domicile of the defendant, under Article 2, Convention jurisdiction would be lacking in the English courts because The Netherlands was the place of harmful event in tort in an action for breach of Dutch copyright;

(3)   Article 2 was a fundamental Convention rule of jurisdiction, to which *forum conveniens* was not an exception;

(4)   nor was the *Moçambique* rule of non-justiciability any longer an exception to English jurisdiction where the Convention applied, nor the *Phillips v Eyre* double-actionability choice of law principle a reason therefor (especially since s.10 of the Private International Law (Miscellaneous Provisions) Act 1995 had abolished automatic application of English *lex fori* to international torts as from 1 May 1996). This was because, although these were not strictly *jurisdiction* rules, nonetheless, each of them, to the extent that they would preclude the English court from hearing such an action, would impair the effectiveness of the Convention by frustrating the operation of the basic rule in Art. 2, and therefore had to give way to allow the jurisdictional rules of the Convention to have their proper effect. According to Lloyd J., this was the first English case in which the point had been raised.

Comments

However, these findings were in fact *obiter*. This was because, although non-justiciability would not be permitted to interfere with Convention jurisdiction in the manner explained, the English action would still be struck out as being an abuse of the court's process, since the plaintiff's claim was considered to be purely speculative and furthermore the choice of law provisions of the 1995 (Torts) Act apparently were transitionally inapplicable and consequently the action on Dutch copyright was bound to fail on the merits, to the extent that English *lex fori* were to continue to be applied under the old double-actionability rule in the private international law of tort.

Nevertheless, the decision is rather stronger than the earlier High Court judgment of Aldous J. in *Plastus Kreativ AB v Minnesota Mining and Manufacturing Co.* [1995] RPC 438, *supra*, Case 119, to the opposite (*obiter*) effect.

Case principle

2.   Actions for infringement of foreign patents are no longer non-justiciable in Convention cases.

Case

Coin Controls Ltd v Suzo International (UK) Ltd [1997] 3 All ER 45 High   **387**
Court, 26 March 1997

Facts

The plaintiff wished to bring proceedings in the English courts for alleged infringement of identical European Patents as to coin-dispensing machinery for the UK, Germany and Spain, jointly against defendant English, Dutch and German members of the Suzo group of companies, in respect of infringements in England, Germany and Spain. The defendants alleged, *inter alia*, non-justiciability of the claims relating to the German and Spanish patents, even if Convention jurisdiction were otherwise to exist.

Judgment

Laddie J. in the Chancery Division of the High Court followed Lloyd J. in *Pearce*, decided three weeks earlier in respect of foreign copyright, and held that the mandatory nature of Convention application meant that actions for infringement of foreign intellectual property rights, including patents, were no longer non-justiciable.

Aldous J.'s contrary judgment in *Plastus Kreativ, supra* Case 119, was disagreed with.

(1)   The *Def Lepp Music* difficulties over English *lex fori* as applicable law no longer existed, since s.10 of the Private International Law (Miscellaneous Provisions) Act 1995 abolished *Phillips v Eyre* double-actionability.

(2)   The *Moçambique* problem of localized justiciability over actions on immovable and, by way of analogy, intellectual, property, still remained. Patents were quasi-monopolies, developed in order to protect local industries, in which the public in the locality had an interest; and s.30 of the 1982 Act, expressly removing non-justiciability of torts against foreign immovables, was not also applicable to intellectual property.

However, the Convention itself was to be taken to have overridden the disability. Adjudication over foreign intellectual property might produce inconveniences; but the Convention had no doctrine of *forum non conveniens* and any problems had to be borne for the sake of its unificationist aims. Thus, courts of Contracting States possessed of Convention jurisdiction over infringement of foreign intellectual property were required to exercise it.

Comments

(1) The decision adds further weight to that in *Pearce* against *Plastus Kreativ*, *supra*, at the same High Court level (see too *infra*, Case 818 Sweden).

Again, it is arguable that the *Coin Controls* decision was *obiter*, because Laddie J. went on to find that although Arts 2 and 6(1) (see *infra*) jurisdiction might exist against English and foreign Contracting State defendants respectively, nonetheless, since the principal object of the proceedings was in fact not infringement, but validity of the patents, German and Spanish courts possessed exclusive jurisdiction under Art. 16(4) and English courts were required to decline under Art. 19 in any event.

As to whether English courts nevertheless possessed interlocutory jurisdiction under Art. 24, Laddie J. did not need to decide this, because the parties had agreed to a very early trial date, so that interim relief was not considered to be appropriate in the circumstances.

(2) In *In re European Patent (UK) No. 189958 in the name of Akzo Nobel NV/In re a Petition by Fort Dodge Animal Ltd* (1997) *The Times*, 24 October, Laddie J. in the High Court Chancery Division, on 16 October 1997, refused to grant an injunction restraining an application to Dutch courts in respect of patent infringement acts in England, on the ground that it would be repugnant so to review and possibly interfere with a foreign Contracting State's Convention application. As to whether Dutch courts were correct to regard foreign intellectual property rights as having become justiciable under the Convention, Laddie J. gave no view other than to note that international patent litigation and competition for jurisdiction was currently in some disarray.

(3) In derogation from the trends in *Pearce* and *Coin Controls Ltd*, *supra*, however, in *Mecklermedia Corporation v DC Congress GmbH* (unreported) 7 March 1997 (see *infra*, Arts 5(3), 21 and 22), Jacob J., having held Art. 22 to be inapplicable, nevertheless discussed *obiter* whether, if it had applied, the English court would have exercised its discretion to stay its *English* passing off proceedings in favour of German courts first-seised of the German trade mark infringement action. Although unnecessary to decide whether the Convention had made it possible and justiciable for the English claim to be heard in Germany (as a factor relevant to discretion), even if it had, Jacob J. indicated that he might have been reluctant to stay: English courts were best placed to deal with English passing off and English trade marks, especially if deceptive resemblance and English language were involved. Consequently, it may now be that foreign intellectual property is no longer non-justiciable in the English courts in Convention cases; but, there are circumstances, namely those of Art. 22 as in *Mecklermedia*, in which the English courts might still decide to show their 'disapproval' of the inconveniences involved, by declining to exercise their discretion to stay, where the Convention itself exceptionally allows such latitude.

(4)   In *Mother Bertha Music Limited v Bourne Music Limited (1997) 21st March (unreported)*, the American songwriter, Phil Spector, claimed an account for royalties through breach of worldwide copyright (except North America) in a popular song, against the defendant English company, Bourne Music, in the Chancery Division of the English High Court.

    The judge, Ferris J., held that:

(a)   infringement of foreign intellectual property rights was non-justiciable in the English courts; and

(b)   this also applied to a claim for an account of sums acquired by the English defendant as a result of the copyright infringement and paid into an English bank account, where, essentially, the action remained one of infringement.

Nevertheless, at a late stage in the preparation of his judgment, the judge became aware of the *Pearce* decision, and he expressly acknowledged that this might in future, if followed, render justiciable claims for breach of foreign copyright—as to which, however, he himself would not provide even a provisional view in relation to the case with which he was concerned, given the absence of argumentation on the question.

ARTICLE 5(1)

          " . . . *obligation in question* . . . "

Case principle

In an action for breach of contract through negligent report on quality of goods, principal obligation held to be inspection, not delivery of report (*Shenavai* Case 266/85 and *Union Transport, supra* Case 153, applied).

Case

Source Ltd v TUV Rheinland Holding AG, The Times, 28 March 1997, [1997]   **388**
3 WLR 365, [1997] I.L.Pr. 514, Court of Appeal, 18 March 1997

Facts

The plaintiffs wished to import promotional toy products from China and Taiwan and to pay by letter of credit, for which they required a certificate of quality. They engaged the German defendants to inspect and report on the products, which they did, allegedly, negligently. The plaintiffs wished to sue the defendants in England for breach of contract to use reasonable care and skill (as well as, in the alternative, in tort for negligent misstatement—see *infra*, Art. 5(3), Case 389). The defendants challenged English Art. 5(1) and (3) jurisdiction.

Judgment

The Court of Appeal sought to determine the place of performance of the principal obligation, where, as here, more than one obligation was breached, in accordance with judgments of the European Court in *Shenavai* Case 266/85 and the House of Lords in *Union Transport Plc v Continental Lines SA* [1992] 1 WLR 15. Here, the principal obligation was held to be *inspection* of the products in China and Taiwan, not delivery of the reports in England.

Consequently, England was not the place of performance of the obligation in question for Art. 5(1).

Comment

See, too, comment to *Minster Investments Ltd v Hyundai Precision & Industry Co. Ltd* [1988] 2 Lloyd's Rep. 621, *supra*, Case 172. Staughton L.J. in *Source* considered that the judgment in *Minster*, concerning place of harmful event in tort for purposes of Art. 5(3) on very similar facts, would not affect the decision in *Source* as to principal *contractual* obligation in question for Art. 5(1).

> ### ARTICLE 5(3)
>
> " . . . *relating to tort, delict or quasi-delict* . . . "

Case principle

The *Kalfelis* Case 189/97 independent definition of tort as excluding matters relating to a contract within Art. 5(1) meant that where the facts gave rise to claims in *both* Art. 5(1) contract and tort, the latter did not also fall within Art. 5(3).

Case

389 Source Ltd v TUV Rheinland Holding AG The Times, 28 March 1997, [1997] 3 WLR 365, [1997] I.L.Pr. 514, Court of Appeal, 18 March 1997

Facts

The plaintiffs wished to import products from China and Taiwan, for which they required a certificate of quality in order to open a letter of credit to pay the sellers. They engaged the German defendants to inspect the goods and to provide a report, which they alleged was inaccurate as a result of negligent inspection, leading to many complaints about quality.

The plaintiffs brought claims against the defendants for breach of contract to use reasonable care and skill in preparing the report and in tort for negligent misstatement.

The defendants challenged English jurisdiction under Art. 5(3) (and Art. 5(1)—see *supra*, Case 388), on the ground that the claim was outside the definition of tort in *Kalfelis* Case 189/87.

Judgment

The Court of Appeal agreed with the defendants. In *Kalfelis*, the European Court had autonomously defined Art. 5(3) tort, delict and quasi-delict as being all actions which seek to establish the defendant's liability *and are not related to a contract* within the meaning of Art. 5(1). Accordingly, said Staughton L.J. (agreed with by Waite and Aldous L.JJ.), since the claim *could* also be (indeed, had been—unsuccessfully on jurisdiction) brought in contract on the same facts, it was related to a contract within the meaning of Art. 5(1) and thus was not within the concept of tort in Art. 5(3).

English courts therefore lacked jurisdiction over the German defendants.

Comment

This seems a very strange decision. If there was a separate claim in tort, it should surely have been held to fall within Art. 5(3). The *Kalfelis* definition could not have been intended to cover such a situation where the same facts give rise to two separate causes of action which are otherwise indisputably in contract and in tort respectively—but solely where the nature of just one of the claims, or of the sole claim, as being tortious or not, is uncertain and requires to be defined. Thus, if one of the claims is otherwise tortious, it should not somehow be besmirched simply because it is *also* possible to bring a claim in contract on the same facts. At national English law, existence of a contractual claim will have a certain *inhibiting* effect upon the ability to proceed in tort (although no longer, it would seem, a *paralysing* effect as in the past: see Kaye, *An Explanatory Guide to the English Law of Torts* pp. 123–30). However, this inflection has no justification for spilling over into the international jurisdictional sphere, where quite different policies may be expected to be in play.

> " . . . *harmful event occurred.*"

Case principle

In a passing off action, damage occurs where the goodwill is harmed.

Case

Mecklermedia Corporation v D.C. Congress GmbH, The Times, 27 March 1997, [1997] I.L.Pr. 629 High Court, 7 March 1997　　**390**

Facts

The plaintiffs alleged the tort of passing off by the German defendants in relation to use of the words 'Internet World', in which the plaintiffs owned the goodwill, as a result of which, damage to the plaintiffs was said to have occurred in England and Wales. The defendants challenged English jurisdiction, on the ground that Germany, whence the defendants sent the offending material to England, was the place of harmful event for Art. 5(3).

Judgment

Jacob J. held England and Wales to be the place of harmful event, which was the harm done to the plaintiffs' goodwill there and its effect upon the plaintiffs' reputation in England and Wales.

Consequently, English courts possessed jurisdiction over the defendants.

See too infra, Art. 21 'involving the same cause of action', Case 393.

Comment

Jacob J. purported to follow Knox J. in *Modus Vivendi*, Case 174 *supra*, of which he expressed approval.

However, whereas Knox J. regarded causal event as occurring in the place whence the offending products were sent, it is possible (although rather unclear) that Jacob J. viewed this as also being in England, not Germany—that is, place of circulation rather than despatch.

If so, this seems far less appealing than Knox J.'s approach in such respect.

ARTICLE 6(1)

" . . . one of a number of defendants . . . "

Case principle

Claims against foreign Contracting State defendants for infringement of foreign patents, held to satisfy the *Kalfelis* Case 189/87—Art. 22, para. 3 *connexité* test, so as to enable the defendants to be brought into an English action against the main English defendant for infringement of a UK patent, where the patents were identical, derived from a single application to the European Patent Office and had not subsequently been amended so as to diverge (*obiter*).

Case

391 Coin Controls Ltd v Suzo International (UK) Ltd [1987] 3 All ER 45 High Court, 26 March 1997

Facts

See supra, Art. 1, para. 1, Case 387, and infra, Art. 16(4), Case 392.

The English defendant, which was sued in respect of infringement of the English patent, was subject to English jurisdiction by virtue of Art. 2. However, the plaintiff argued that the claim against the German defendant for infringement of the German patent should be able to be brought in under Art. 6(1) and similarly in the case of the claim against the Dutch defendant for infringement of the German and Spanish patents, on the ground that the European Court's *Kalfelis connexité* test was satisfied.

Judgment

As things turned out, Laddie J. subsequently held exclusive Art. 16(4) to apply in relation to the German and Spanish patents, which were said principally to involve validity, so that the English court was required to decline such jurisdiction as it would otherwise have possessed in respect of these, under Art. 19 (see *infra*, Art. 16(4)).

However, prior to this, the judge did examine the question of Art. 6(1) jurisdiction, *obiter*.

He concluded that since the English, German and Spanish patents were all identical and originally derived from a single application to the European Patent Office, even though thereafter distilled into the respective national patent systems ('cuttings taken from the European patent stock and planted in the national soil'), they were so closely interrelated that the Art. 22, para. 3 test to be applied to Art. 6(1) required *connexité*, in accordance with the European Court's ruling in *Kalfelis* (paras 11 and 13)—that it was expedient to hear and determine them together to avoid the risk of irreconcilable judgments resulting from separate proceedings—was satisfied.

It would have been a different matter, according to Laddie J., had the patents been materially different, whether through subsequent amendment or original application separately through the national patent offices.

ARTICLE 16(4)

" *. . . concerned with . . . validity . . .* "

Case principle

Article 16(4) applies if invalidity of the patent is the principal object of the proceedings, even if it is only raised as a defence to a patent infringement claim.

Case

392   Coin Controls Ltd v Suzo International (UK) Ltd [1997] 3 All ER 45 High Court, 26 March 1997

Facts

See supra, Art. 1, para. 1, Case 387, and Art. 6(1), Case 391.

The plaintiff sought to argue that even though the defendants had challenged the validity of the German and Spanish patents, the principal object of the proceedings should be determined according to the plaintiff's own claim, which was one for infringement, not validity.

Judgment

Laddie J. in the Chancery Division rejected this. If a defendant raised validity as a defence to infringement—as would frequently, but not always, be the case—the principal issue in the proceedings would thereupon be the validity of the patent, and consequently Art. 16(4) would apply. Here, this was so, and the English courts were required to decline in favour of exclusive German and Spanish patents jurisdiction, under Art. 19.

Comments

Laddie J. conceded that the treatment of intellectual property was far from perfect under the Convention: Art. 16(4) applied to registered, but not to unregistered, rights; defendants could forum shop by raising the invalidity defence; even European Patent Office patents would be subject to diverse jurisdiction.

The case may be distinguished from that of *Chiron Corporation v Evans Medical Ltd* (unreported) 3 July 1996, High Court, (*supra*, Art. 16(4), Case 210), where, on the facts, the issue appeared to be one of patent differentiation for purposes of (non-)infringement, rather than one of validity.

As a matter of additional interest, in *Coin Controls* the further question arose of the mutual scope of Arts 24 and 16—could an English court exercise provisional jurisdiction to grant interim injunctions under Art. 24 in aid of exclusive Art. 16(4) German and Spanish main substantive jurisdiction, or was Art. 24 limited to non-exclusive cases? Laddie J. declined to decide, since the parties had accepted a very early date for the hearing and consequently such interlocutory relief would have been inappropriate in any event.

ARTICLE 21, PARAGRAPH 1

" *. . . involving the same cause of action . . .* "

Case principle

Passing off in England and alleged German trade mark infringement in Germany held not to involve the same cause of action.

Case

Mecklermedia Corporation v D.C. Congress GmbH The Times, 27 March 1997, [1997] I.L.Pr. 629 High Court, 7 March 1997   **393**

Facts

See supra, Art. 5(3), Case 390.

The defendant had previously brought proceedings in the German courts against a licensee of the plaintiff for alleged infringement of the German trade mark registration and argued that the English courts ought therefore to have declined jurisdiction in favour of first-seised German courts under Art. 21.

Judgment

Jacob J. held Art. 21 to be inapplicable.

First, applying the European Court's *Maciej Rataj* Case C–406/92, English passing off and German trade mark infringement were not the same cause of action.

Secondly, the parties were not the same: the plaintiff's licensee was not the plaintiff itself.

> " . . . between the same parties . . . "

Case principle

A party's licensee of intellectual property rights is not the same party as the former, the licensor.

Case

Mecklermedia Corporation v DC Congress GmbH, The Times, 27 March 1997, [1997] I.L.Pr. 629 High Court, 7 March 1997   **394**

Facts

See supra, 'same cause of action', Case 393.

Judgment

Jacob J. conceded, in accordance with *Berkeley Administration Inc v McClelland*, *supra*, Cases 272 and 347, that it would have been a different matter if the licensee had been the wholly-owned subsidiary of the licensor.

> ## ARTICLE 22, PARAGRAPH 1
>
> " . . . *pending at first instance* . . . "

Case principle

If there are interim proceedings as a preliminary stage to the main substantive action, the latter may be treated as pending for purposes of stays.

Case

395 Mecklermedia Corporation v DC Congress GmbH, *The Times*, 27 March 1997, [1997] I.L.Pr. 629 High Court, 7 March 1997

Facts

See supra, Arts 5(3), Case 390, *and 21*, Cases 393 and 394.

Judgment

Jacob J. reached no conclusion on the issue of pendency through the interim nature of the German trade mark action, having already held Art. 22 to be inapplicable (see *infra*, Art. 22, para. 3, Case 396).

However, he did regard it as being perfectly arguable that the main proceedings in Germany were commenced thereby and pending at the interim stage: even though, procedurally, the application for the injunction in Germany took place 'outside' the main proceedings, the defendant could require the successful plaintiff to begin the main action, and it would be wrong to make distinctions from the English system on the basis of such procedural features. If the application for the injunction were to be unsuccessful, on the other hand, a second-seised related English action which had been stayed under Art. 22 could thereupon simply be resumed.

> ## ARTICLE 22, PARAGRAPH 3
>
> " . . . *irreconcilable* . . . "

Case principle

1. English passing off and German trade mark infringement actions held not to give rise to a risk of irreconcilable judgments (*Maciej Rataj* Case C–406/92 applied).

Case

Mecklermedia Corporation v DC Congress GmbH, *The Times*, 27 March **396**
1997, [1997] I.L.Pr. 629 High Court, 7 March 1997

Facts

See supra, Arts 5(3), Case 390, *21*, Cases 393 and 394 *and 22, para. 1*, Case 395.

Judgment

Jacob J. considered there to be no risk in conflict of law or fact between the
English and German actions. The feature of such international intellectual
property disputes was the extent to which they were founded upon *local* goodwill and use.
  Consequently, the actions were not related and Art. 22 was inapplicable.

Comment

Jacob J. did also discuss whether the English passing off claim would be
justiciable in the first-seised German courts as a result of the Convention, as
an element which would have been pertinent to exercise of the discretion to
stay or not, had Art. 22 been held to be applicable (see *supra*, Art. 1, para. 1,
Pearce v Ove Arup Partnership Ltd, Case 386 and Comment 3 to Case 387).

Case principle

2. Claims against German and Spanish defendants for infringement of
    German and Spanish patents are said to satisfy Art. 22, para. 3 criteria in
    relation to a claim against an English defendant in the English courts for
    infringement of an *identical* English patent deriving from the *same* appli-
    cation to the European Patent Office.

Case

Coin Controls Ltd v Suzo International (UK) Ltd [1997] 3 All ER 45 High   **397**
Court, 26 March 1997

Facts and Judgment

See supra, Arts 1, para. 1, Case 387, *6(1)*, Case 391, *and 16(4)*, Case 392.

Comment

The finding was *obiter* and was in fact made not in relation to Art. 22 itself as
on an application to stay thereunder, but in application of the criteria laid
down therein to Art. 6(1) required *connexité* between claims in accordance
with the European Court's ruling in *Kalfelis* Case 189/87 (paras 11 and 13).

Note Case 30 *supra*.

Stop Press (see page 339)

The Court of Appeal's decision itself has subsequently been reversed by the House of Lords and Mance J.'s order restored (although para. 1 stay converted to para. 2 decline in view of litigation events in Spain), on 13 November 1997, see (1997) *The Times*, 17 November. Lord Saville explained that there was nothing in *Maciej Rataj* to support the alleged distinction between primary and secondary issues. Instead, there was to be a broad, commonsense approach to interpretation of the related definition in Art. 22, para. 3, applying the simple wide test therein (in the light of the Convention's objective to prevent litigation from being more expensive and time-consuming than necessary, through multiple actions) and refraining from an over-sophisticated analysis. Thus, the wide words of Art. 22 were against the Court of Appeal's limitation: they were intended to cover both cases where actions were virtually identical, yet outside Art. 21, and those where the connection was simply close enough, extending beyond primary or essential issues.

Stop Press (see pages 213 and 258)

A further development has been in *Hough v P.&O. Containers Ltd., Blohm & Voss Holding AG* (1998) *The Times* 6 April. Rix J. in the High Court on 25 March 1998 held Article 17 agreements between defendant and third party to prevail over inconsistent Article 6(2) jurisdiction.

5

FINLAND

Professor Risto Koulu

A. LEGAL SYSTEM

Courts

The general courts have three levels: District Courts, Appeal Courts and the Supreme Court. In 1993, the two different types of lower courts were replaced by a uniform system of District Courts which covers the whole country. There are currently 69 District Courts, and the country is divided into an equivalent number of court districts. The number of inhabitants within the districts varies a great deal: with a population of nearly 500 000, the District Court of Helsinki has the largest district, whereas the smallest districts may have only 70 000 people.

The District Courts hear all civil cases for which the law does not provide differently; they have general jurisdiction. The proceedings before a District Court are partly hearings and partly conducted in writing. In principle, a District Court decides civil cases with a panel of three judges, but the majority of cases are resolved by a single judge, a procedure which the parties may request. The District Courts also serve as *exequatur* (enforcement authorisation) courts under the Lugano Convention: they are the first instance to decide whether a foreign judgment may be enforced in Finland. In *exequatur* cases the District Court is always composed of a single judge.

The decisions of District Courts are appealable to the Appeal Courts, of which there are six. This also applies to decisions in *exequatur* cases. Both applications which have been granted and those which have been refused may be appealed. There are no limitations on the appeal to the appeal court; a proposal to make appeal subject to permission has, however, recently been submitted to Parliament and is being debated. A division of the Appeal Court decides on the appeals, and the proceedings are usually in writing. A division consists of three judges. Cases which have significance on the level of principle are examined in full session.

The highest instance is the Supreme Court. It is exclusively for setting precedents. Appeal is subject to permission by the court. Permission is granted in cases which are important for the court to hear for the development of the law or for the consistency of legal practice.

Enforcement (exécution)

An independent public enforcement official is entrusted with the exclusive powers of enforcement. The enforcement official is independent of the rest of the system of jurisdiction, and courts do not have immediate jurisdiction over enforcement (such as a right to issue orders on the details of the measure of enforcement). The official has a special title (*kihlakunnanvouti*, roughly: county bailiff) and works in the county office or, in large cities, in a separate enforcement office. There are a total of 90 county offices and 13 enforcement offices. The measures and decisions of the public enforcement official are appealable to the District Court: in such cases the court may issue orders to suspend the measure of enforcement. An appeal may also be lodged on the grounds that the official refused enforcement without reason.

Consumer Complaint Board

The Consumer Complaint Board is a public board. It issues recommendations in disputes between consumers and businesses. While its decisions are not formally binding they are largely respected. A fair number of minor disputes are thus settled with a final decision taken by the Board, (see *infra*, Case 400).

B. IMPLEMENTATION OF THE LUGANO CONVENTION

The Lugano Convention was implemented in Finland by an Act on the Approval of the Convention on Jurisdiction and the Enforcement of Judgments in Civil and Commercial Matters and of the Protocols Related to it (16 April 1993 No. 612). This is a so-called blanket law to make the provisions of the Lugano Convention part of the Finnish legal order. More detailed provisions on the implementation of the Lugano Convention were given in a Decree by the same title (28 June 1993 No. 613). This Decree also provides for the entry into force of the said implementation Act (and of the Lugano Convention); the Convention came into force in Finland on 1 July 1993.

The Decree lacks more specific provisions; it has five Articles. Article 2 provides for the national central authority under Protocol 2 of the Convention to ensure and be responsible for the exchange of information on the Lugano Convention (judgments by national courts). This authority is the Ministry of Justice. The system for the exchange of information remains to be introduced.

Article 3 states that the *exequatur* authority in Finland—in deviation from the original text of the Convention—is the District Court. Paragraph 1 of the Article says that an application for *exequatur* must be made to the District Court in whose jurisdiction the party against whom enforcement is sought is domiciled. If that party is not domiciled in Finland, the application must be lodged with the District Court in whose jurisdiction 'the enforcement will take place'.

Paragraph 2 requires that the Act relating to non-contentious proceedings in lower courts (*HakKäsL*, 307/86) be applied to *exequatur* proceedings, unless provisions in the Convention require otherwise. Consequently, *exequatur* proceedings are part of summary, non-contentious jurisdiction. A reference to the above Act permits both proceedings on the basis of documents in the judge's chambers and hearings by the court in session. The Convention, however, supersedes the principle that the opposite party must be heard which otherwise applies to non-contentious jurisdiction. In addition to the above references, the Act also refers to other provisions on legal proceedings in civil cases. As a result of multiple references, the exact nature of proceedings in *exequatur* cases remains ambiguous in so far as not specifically governed by the Lugano Convention.

Article 4 of the Decree allows the applicant exemption from finding out which District Court has territorial jurisdiction over that particular case. Under the Article, the applicant may submit his application to the Ministry of Justice, and it is for the Ministry to establish which is the competent District Court and to transmit the documents to that court. None of the applicants so far have used this service by the Ministry of Justice.

The general law on enforcement (*exécution*), the Enforcement Act, does not contain provisions on the enforcement of foreign judgments. This means that the same provisions are applied to foreign judgments as to domestic judgments. A foreign creditor has to lodge the usual application with the competent enforcement official; it must be accompanied by the foreign judgment and the *exequatur* decision by the Finnish court. A decision on *exequatur* does not guarantee that enforcement proceedings are undertaken. Even if the District Court has declared that a foreign judgment is enforceable, the official may refuse to enforce it unless it fulfils the criteria set out in the Enforcement Act.

Article 21(4), Chap. 3 of the Enforcement Act, requires a foreign creditor seeking enforcement in Finland to have a representative there. The requirement also applies to a creditor who bases his application on the Lugano Convention. Thus, in the actual enforcement proceedings—although not yet in the *exequatur* proceedings—the applicant is under an obligation to use a representative. The representative in Finland need not be a lawyer or other legal professional.

C. OVERVIEW OF CONVENTION CASE LAW

No Supreme Court decisions, on public record, exist on Titles I (Scope of application), II (Jurisdiction) and III (Recognition and Enforcement) of the Lugano Convention. This is probably explained by the fact that the Convention has been in force in Finland for only four years. Legal proceedings where interpretation of the Articles in the Convention governing jurisdiction has become necessary are yet to reach the highest instance. The Supreme Court has the first civil case before it at the moment.

All but one of the decisions summarized below in the text have been rendered by Appeal Courts. They have been collected from the registrars of the Appeal Courts. The majority relate to Articles under Title II of the Lugano Convention.

Decisions by courts of first instance on Title III (*Recognition and Enforcement*) have been collected for a study. They are decisions on applications for *exequatur* and therefore do not carry the weight of precedent. Taken as a whole, however, they give an idea of the general attitude of the Finnish courts to cross-border jurisdiction.

By the spring of 1997 about 20 applications for *exequatur* had been submitted to District Courts in Finland, most of them based on the Lugano Convention. The foreign applicants usually had a Finnish representative—a lawyer or a staff member of a collection agency. The line of interpretation adopted by the District Courts was in favour of foreign applicants—a rare finding in comparative law. With few exceptions, the applications were granted and the foreign judgments declared enforceable in Finland. Full evidence of the enforceability of the foreign judgment in the judgment-State was not required in every case.

Exequatur cases are decided on the basis of documents provided in chambers; a hearing is permitted, but it was not arranged in any of the cases. This is because unilateral proceedings usually do not necessitate a session of the court. Also, a hearing can only be given if this is in the applicant's interest: in this case, the proceedings in a court session are an alternative to refusal. It is a drawback that applications for *exequatur* take a long time to be decided by the District Courts: a decision is rarely rendered 'without delay' as required by the Lugano Convention; rather, the proceedings usually take two to four weeks.

Instances of appeal against decisions on *exequatur* are few; the collected material only contained one case of appeal. It will be discussed later.

Not all *exequatur* decisions lead to application for enforcement (*exécution*). Enforcement officials have received only a handful of applications. Some have been refused on the grounds that the foreign judgment did not define the enforceable obligation with sufficient accuracy. As far as is known, not a single case of refusal by the enforcement official has led to appeal. It may be said that in this regard the enforcement of foreign decisions in Finland faces obstacles totally unknown elsewhere in Europe. It may well be that the problems evident at the enforcement (*exécution*) stage are part of the explanation for the relatively few applications for enforcement.

D. CASES

LUGANO ARTICLE 5(1)

"*. . . matters relating to a contract . . .*"

Case principle

The autonomous Convention concept of contracts includes unilateral, not just bilateral, contracts.

Case

The Appeal Court of Helsinki, ruling of 29 August 1996. No. 4418, case No. **398**
S 96/292 (not *res judicata*, since the case is before the Supreme Court)

Facts

Defendant P, a Dutch company, had provided the plaintiffs, two companies domiciled in Finland, with a guarantee for the debt of N, another Dutch company. The plaintiffs brought an action against P in the District Court of Loviisa in Finland. On the basis of the guarantee, they demanded payment for fairway dues and forwarding charges which they had been forced to pay on behalf of a vessel owned by N. At the request of the plaintiffs the vessel had been seized.

The District Court of Loviisa held that it lacked international jurisdiction in the case, because the plaintiffs did not have any obligation to provide a counter-performance for P. Therefore, the case did not come under Art. 5(1) of the Lugano Convention ('matters relating to a contract'): no contract existed between the defendant and the plaintiffs.

The District Court also considered whether the case fell within the definition of maritime claim referred to in Art. 54a of the Convention. If so, the jurisdiction of the District Court could have been founded on that Article. The Article could not, however, be applied, because P did not own the vessel.

Judgment

The Appeal Court ruled that the guarantee obligation constituted a contract under Art. 5(1). The fact that the guarantee was interpreted as a contract did not require reciprocity between the plaintiffs and the guarantor. As the payment obligation inherent in the guarantee had to be fulfilled in Loviisa, Finland—under Finnish law payments had to be made in the creditor's domicile—the District Court of Loviisa had jurisdiction in the case. Therefore, the Appeal Court returned the case to the District Court.

The question of interpretation of Art. 54a of the Lugano Convention did not arise before the Appeal Court.

The defendant has sought permission to appeal to the Supreme Court, but this is as yet undecided.

Comment

The prevailing opinion is that the concept of ' . . . matters relating to a contract . . . ' in Art. 5(1) of the Lugano Convention is autonomous. The ruling of the District Court was based on an artificial differentiation between bilaterally binding legal transactions (or contracts) and unilateral expressions of will. If accepted, this interpretation would lead to a more narrow scope of application of Art. 5(1); it would deviate from the broad line of interpretation adopted by the European Court of Justice when setting precedents for the interpretation of the corresponding Article in the Brussels Convention (*Arcado S.A. v Haviland S.A.* Case 9/87, for example).

The decision of the Appeal Court was a consistent application of the broad line of interpretation. There is no rational reason for special treatment of unilateral obligations. Also, it may be difficult to define which obligations are reciprocal and which are unilateral. Thus, in this case it would also have been possible to claim that the plaintiffs had *de facto* undertaken to perform a kind of obligation: they had promised to release the vessel on receipt of the guarantee.

There is reason to assume that the Supreme Court will uphold the Appeal Court ruling.

> ### LUGANO ARTICLE 22, PARAGRAPH 1
>
> " . . . *may . . . stay . . .* "

Case principle

In the exercise of its discretion, the court assesses advantages and disadvantages to parties involved and the needs of justice.

Case

399 The Appeal Court of Kouvola, ruling of 4 September 1996 No. 1277 S 96/88

Facts

A Russian company S had undertaken to transport a container of tobacco from Holland to Russia via Finland. In the freight documents, not only T but also H, the Finnish agent of S, were named as the carriers. The container was damaged in Holland, and T and H were sued in a Dutch court for damages. Then H initiated declaratory proceedings in a Finnish court for a decision that he had not acted as carrier of the damaged container. The defendant T demanded that the Finnish proceedings be stayed on the basis of Art. 22 of the Lugano Convention.

The District Court dismissed T's demand for a stay of the proceedings.

Judgment

Similarly to the District Court, the Appeal Court held that the two actions were related and Art. 22, para. 1 of the Lugano Convention became applicable. When considering a stay of the proceedings, the court had to take account of the advantages and disadvantages for the parties. A key factor was the protection of the defendant. In this situation, it was appropriate that the position of H was solved as a preliminary question, before the proceedings for damages in Holland. The Appeal Court upheld the District Court's ruling.

Comment

The position adopted by the Finnish court is economically rational. The act of noting H as carrier in the documents took place in Finland (this fact was specifically mentioned by the District Court in the reasoning). It could therefore be presumed that the appropriateness of that act could best be assessed in Finland.

It may be added that H won the case in Finland. The final decision stated that in the carriage of the container, H had acted merely as an agent (and not as a carrier).

LUGANO ARTICLE 25

" . . . *judgment given by a court or tribunal . . .* "

Case principle

Recommendation of a public consumer body, not binding, held to be akin to a judgment of a court for Convention jurisdiction purposes.

Case

The Consumer Complaint Board (full session), decision of 11 March 1996,   **400**
94/36/2379

Facts

A Finnish consumer had ordered postage stamps by mail from a Danish mail order company. As the price charged on the Visa card exceeded the amount earlier given, the consumer demanded, before the Consumer Complaint Board, that the Danish company was obliged to return the amount of the price which the company had refused to refund voluntarily.

The consumer protection legislation does not contain provisions on the international jurisdiction of Finnish consumer protection authorities. Therefore, the Board had to consider whether it had jurisdiction over the case.

Judgment

The Consumer Complaint Board stated that, because of its independence, it could be partly compared to a court of law. Therefore, it was appropriate that the principles contained in the Lugano Convention were followed, specifically, Arts 13 *et seq.* of the Convention, in S.4 of Title II (Jurisdiction over consumer contracts).

In accordance with Art. 14 of the Convention, a consumer could bring an action against a trader either in a court of the Contracting State in which the trader was domiciled or in the Court of the Contracting State in which the consumer himself was domiciled. On the latter ground, the Consumer Complaint Board had jurisdiction over a dispute between the Finnish consumer and the Danish trader and was competent to give a recommendation to solve it.

There was no appeal against the decisions of the Consumer Complaint Board.

Comment

In this case the Articles of the Lugano Convention governing jurisdiction were, somewhat surprisingly, applied to proceedings before a public board. The interpretation improves the protection of consumers: protection is afforded in the country where subsequent legal proceedings are likely to take place. As the decision given by the Board is a recommendation, it will be up to the trader to decide whether to comply with it or to wait for possible legal proceedings— to which the Lugano Convention would apply in any case.

LUGANO ARTICLE 27(2)

" . . . sufficient time . . . "

Case principle

Service by post can be sufficient, if evidence is provided of receipt on the part of the defendant.

Case

401   The Appeal Court of Helsinki, ruling of 4 March 1997 No. 690 S 96/1261

Facts

Upon application by a Dutch applicant, the District Court declared a French judgment enforceable in Finland. The Finnish debtor (a forwarding company) appealed against the decision on *exequatur* to the Appeal Court on the grounds that the document initiating the proceedings had not been served upon it duly and in sufficient time to allow the company to prepare a defence, as required by Art. 27(2) of the Lugano Convention.

The proceedings were started in a French court on 17 March 1993 and the case was postponed until public proceedings on 21 July 1994. The defendant had been served with the document initiating the proceedings by post in December 1992, in accordance with French law. An attempt had been made to serve the documents personally on the defendant company; a representative of the company had refused to accept them because they had been drawn up in French and there was no translation in Finnish.

Judgment

The Appeal Court stated that the defendant had been notified of the trial properly by being served with the documents initiating the proceedings by post and also having refused to accept the documents offered by the server. The company did not give a legal reason for its refusal to accept the documents, neither had the company taken any measures on subsequently being served with the French judgment, even though it had the possibility to appeal.

In its reasoning, the Appeal Court also referred to the Convention on the Taking of Evidence Abroad in Civil or Commercial Matters, Art 10 of which stated that the Convention did not preclude the service of documents relating to legal proceedings by mail, unless the receiving state objected to this.

The appeal was dismissed.

Comment

The conclusion that may be drawn from the ruling is that service of documents initiating proceedings by post would not alone be sufficient if no evidence was provided that the company had actually received the letter. On the other hand, the fact that documents had not been translated into the official languages (Finnish and Swedish), in theory gives the Finnish defendant a right to refuse acceptance—which means that appropriate service under Art. 27(2) of the Lugano Convention is precluded. In this case the Finnish authorities expressly stated that the defendant knew enough French. As the company was engaged in forwarding business, this was a natural conclusion to draw.

LUGANO ARTICLE 55

" . . . shall . . . supersede . . . "

Case principle

Enforcement applications for judgments delivered after entry into force of the Lugano Convention take place according to the latter.

Case

402 The Appeal Court of Rovaniemi, ruling of 20 August 1996 No. 0910, U 96/20

Facts

SS, a Swedish citizen, applied for the enforcement of a judgment of a Swedish court under the 1977 Nordic Convention on the Recognition and Enforcement of Judgments. He submitted an application for *exequatur* to the provincial board (which at the time was the *exequatur* authority referred to in the 1977 Convention). The Provincial Board declared the Swedish judgment enforceable, whereupon SS applied to the enforcement official for enforcement proper to recover a debt from the debtor ES. The enforcement official seized the shares owned by ES, who appealed the seizure to the Appeal Court.

Judgment

The Appeal Court held that the Lugano Convention had, in accordance with Art. 55, replaced the Nordic Convention. Consequently, the Swedish judgment had to be enforced in Finland according to the Lugano Convention. The application for *exequatur* should have been submitted to the District Court. The Provincial Board should not have considered the case admissible, because it did not have jurisdiction in the case. The Appeal Court quashed the decision taken by the Provincial Board and transmitted the case to the District Court under Chap. 10, Art. 29 of the Code of Judicial Procedure (the District Court was the court of *exequatur* under the Lugano Convention).

Comment

The ruling shows a great degree of 'judicial activism'. First, the replacement of the Nordic Convention by the Lugano Convention was taken into account *ex officio*, although ES had not invoked the matter. Secondly, ES did not even appeal against the decision on *exequatur*, but against the later measure of seizure which in principle constituted the execution of the Swedish decision. The Appeal Court interpreted the appeal to mean that ES also contested the correctness of the decision rendered by the Provincial Board in the *exequatur* case.

Chapter 10, Art. 29 of the Code of Judicial Procedure states that a higher court may transfer a case to the right court if it notices that the lower court, where the proceedings were initiated, is not the appropriate court. The case may be transferred either at the request of the party in question (which was not the case here) or 'for special reasons'. The Appeal Court considered it a special reason that the application of the Lugano Convention ensured a 'surprise effect of enforcement'.

The ruling by the Appeal Court meant *de facto* that international enforce-ment jurisdiction was brought into the scope of the appropriate convention. This in turn favoured SS, the foreign applicant. A traditional procedure would have been for the application of SS to be merely dismissed. In that case, it would have been for SS to submit the right kind of application, to the right court and under the right Convention.

The ruling of the Appeal Court is questionable in principle. However, exten-sive judicial activism may be defended on the ground that in the end it led to a fair outcome. Also, the Appeal Court succeeded in balancing the interests of the applicant and of the judgment debtor.

6

FRANCE

Professor Yves Tassel

A. LEGAL SYSTEM

Courts

The French courts of general jurisdiction—the Tribunaux de Grande Instance, the Cours d'Appel and the Cour de Cassation—are composed of professional judges, who reach decisions in collegiate fashion. The courts are within a hierarchy. At the bottom there are the first instance courts (Tribunaux de Grande Instance), followed by a second or appeal level (Cours d'Appel) and finally, at the top, the Cour de Cassation. The latter is not strictly a third level of appeal court, as it only hears appeals on points of law, not fact.

There is at least one Tribunal de Grande Instance for each Département. It is composed of both trial judges (juges du siège) who try cases, and prosecuting judges (juges du parquet), whose role is to represent society in cases coming before the court.

There are 30 Cours d'Appel, the jurisdiction of each one covering several Départements. These too are composed of both trial judges and prosecuting judges. It is always possible to appeal by way of a rehearing against a judgment of a lower court to the Cours d'Appel. This is the fundamental 'two levels of court' rule.

There is just one Cour de Cassation for the whole of France. It is, however, made up of six divisions; five civil divisions and one criminal division. The civil divisions are as follows: 1st, 2nd, 3rd Civil divisions; the Commercial and Financial division; and the Social division. They contain both trial and prosecuting judges.

The importance of the Cour de Cassation within this hierarchy is evident. However, its hierarchical role is not enforced through a doctrine of precedent: the Cours d'Appel are free to decide a case contrary to the case law of the Cour de Cassation. Moreover, the Tribunaux de Grande Instance may also refuse to follow the case law of the Cours d'Appel.

Alongside the courts of general jurisdiction there are a number of specialist courts, amongst the most important of which are the Tribunaux de Commerce. They are composed of judges who are not members of the career judiciary, but business people elected by their peers. Appeal always lies against their judgments to the Cour d'Appel within whose jurisdiction they are situated.

B. IMPLEMENTATION OF CONVENTIONS

International conventions are negotiated by the President of the Republic or by the body recognized as having power to do so (1958 Constitution, Art. 52). The international Convention must then be ratified by the President of the Republic. Ratification is the act by which the head of state solemnly consents to France being legally bound by the said convention.

An international convention does not necessarily come into effect at the same time in domestic law as in international law. Indeed, the international convention comes into effect in domestic law only when an additional formality has been carried out (Constitution, Art. 54). This formality, which normally takes place after ratification has occurred, is the publication of the international agreement in the *Official Journal of the French Republic*. Such publication is ordered by decree of the President of the Republic. The international agreement is only applicable in domestic law after having been published in the Official Journal.

However, Parliament has a role to play in this procedure. In effect, Parliament authorizes the ratification. However, the difference between authorization and ratification should be noted. Even if the Act authorizing ratification has been passed by Parliament and promulgated, the President of the Republic does not immediately have to ratify the treaty. Thus, the ratification of the European Convention on Human Rights, which was signed on 4 November 1950 and authorized by an Act of 31 December 1973, was not ratified until 3 May 1974.

The Brussels Convention of 27 September 1968, was published in France by Decree No. 73–63 of 13 January 1973, and the Lugano Convention of 16 September 1988 was published by Decree No. 92–111 of 3 February 1992. The San Sebastian amendments to the Brussels Convention entered into force in France on 1 February 1991, and the Lugano on 1 January 1992.

C. CASES

ARTICLE 1, PARAGRAPH 1(2)

" . . . proceedings relating to the winding-up . . . "

Case principle

Action to enforce personal liability of directors is excluded from Convention's scope when founded upon company winding-up as a condition precedent to the action.

Case

Pierrel v Ergur, D (1991) IR 130 Paris Court of Appeal, First Emergency   **403**
Chamber, 13 March 1991

Facts

An action for an administration order was commenced against the director of a company on the basis of Art. 182 of the French law of 25 January 1985. The issue was whether this action fell within the scope of the application of the Convention?

Judgment

The action derived directly from the insolvency, and fell closely within the framework of a liquidation procedure or a voluntary arrangement approved by the court in the sense of the Convention and also within the community concept of insolvency, because the putting into effect of an administration order against the company was a necessary condition precedent of the commencement of such proceedings against its director.

This action was very closely linked to the principal action against the company in respect both of the conditions of its exercise and its legal regime (the same court having competence, the date of the cessation of payment, the uniformity of the limitation rules) and of its effects (the liability of the director covering not only his personal liability but also that of the company).

Accordingly, this action, the legal basis of which was derived from the law of insolvency as interpreted in the Convention, was excluded from the Convention's scope.

ARTICLE 2, PARAGRAPH 2

" . . . shall be governed by the rules of jurisdiction applicable to nationals of that State."

Case principle

Election of internal domicile within France applies to foreign registered companies with real seat in France.

Case

404   Bruno v Société Citibank, D (1991) IR 285 Cour D'Appel de Versailles, First Emergency Chamber, 26 September 1991

Facts

A foreign company had an establishment in France for which it obtained registration on the commercial register.

The case brought against it did not relate to the activity of this establishment.

Were the French courts competent to hear the litigation?

Judgment

The answer was in the affirmative.

The Court of Appeal referred to Art. 2, para. 2 of the Convention, according to which persons who were not nationals of the State in which they were domiciled were governed by the rules of jurisdiction applicable to nationals of that State, and considered that the fact that companies were deemed to elect domicile at the address of their branches or secondary establishments was a sufficient application of the aforementioned rule.

ARTICLE 4, PARAGRAPH 1

" . . . determined by the law of that State."

Case principle

National private international law governs jurisdiction over defendants who are not domiciled in any Contracting State.

Case

Société Atlas Halicilik Islemtmesi v Société Anonyme Alecto et autres, D   **405**
(1996) IR 246 Paris Appeal Court, First Civil Chamber, 26 September 1996

Facts

A company subject to Turkish law and one subject to French law entered into
a contract under the terms of which the Turkish company granted to the
French company, for an indeterminate period, the 'exclusive right to import
and distribute' its products on the French and Belgian markets.

Was the French court territorially competent to hear litigation relating to the
performance of the contract brought in France by the French plaintiff?

Judgment

When the defendant is not domiciled in the territory of a Contracting State,
Art. 4 of the Convention provided for the determination of jurisdiction by reference to the French international rules of jurisdiction.

Art 14 of the French Civil Code only applied where no other French jurisdiction ground was available.

The Commercial Court was therefore correct to hold itself competent in
respect of the defendant, the Turkish company, by application of Art. 42(2) of
the New Civil Procedure Code which conferred on the plaintiff, in both French
law and international law, the possibility of suing several defendants in the
court of the place where one of them lived, where the co-defendants would be
domiciled abroad, since the registered office of the French company which had
benefited from the direct delivery of products of the Turkish company was situated within the area of territorial competence of that Commercial Court.

Comment

Jurisdiction was to be identified under the rules of French internal law, because
the defendant was domiciled in Turkey, a non-Contracting State.

However, as one of the usual criteria of territorial jurisdiction in France was
met, the jurisdictional privilege of Art. 14 of the Civil Code would not
be applied.

The jurisdiction of the French court in this case was based on the cumulative
application of the dispositions of Arts 42 and 46 of the New Civil Procedure
Code, according to which, in contractual matters, the plaintiff may seise the
court of the place of the effective delivery of the goods.

It has been held for a long time that Art. 42 applies despite the fact that
some of the defendants reside overseas (Cour de Cassation, Civil Chamber, 26
December 1899, DP (1900) I 900).

However, this case law is contrary to that in which the Cour de Cassation
held that the rule set out in Art. 42(2) does not allow defendants to be sued in
a court whose jurisdiction in respect of one of them is based on reasons other
than territorial ones, and which particularly would only be competent because

of the provisions of Art. 46(2) (Cour de Cassation, Commercial Chamber, 20 July 1981, Bull IV 324).

ARTICLE 5(1)

" . . . *obligation in question* . . . "

Case principle

1. Where there are several obligations forming the basis of a claim, the principal obligation is taken for Art. 5(1) (*Shenavai* Case 266/85 applied).

Case

406 Meyer v Société Charles Wednesbury Ltd, D (1996) SC 167, note Audit Paris Appeal Court, 13 September 1995

Facts

The claim against a British company was essentially to do with the payment of an indemnity for rescission and damages for breach of contract entered into by the parties. There was also a claim for commission.

The question was which was the obligation on which the action was based?

Judgments

The obligation on which the action was based was the obligation of the company to provide its manufactured products to its agent.

As this obligation was to be performed in France, in particular in Paris, where the plaintiff was domiciled, the Paris Commercial Court had jurisdiction to hear the case.

Comment

The implicit rejection of the reasoning based automatically on the place of payment of a sum of money can be justified by the European Court's decision in *de Bloos* Case 14/76.

Case principle

2. Contractual guarantee of guarantor's *own* performance to be assessed as distinct or not from obligation guaranteed, in accordance with law governing contract.

Case

407 Société Comptoir des Plastiques de l'Ain v Société Novamec et autre, D (1994) IR 58 Cour de Cassation, First Civil Chamber, 9 October 1994

Facts

The litigation related to performance of a contract of sale, specifically the execution of the vendor's obligation of guarantee or warranty.

The contract stated that the sale was to be 'free ex factory', the latter being situated in Italy.

The question was whether the litigation came within the jurisdiction of the French or Italian courts?

Judgment

The Court of Cassation criticized the Court of Appeal for having held that the case fell within the jurisdiction of the Italian courts on the ground that the place of delivery of the merchandise was in Italy and that the vendor's obligation of guarantee or warranty was a corollary of the delivery obligation.

The Court of Cassation held that the Court of Appeal should have determined:

(1) which was the law applicable to the vendor's obligations;

(2) whether, under this law, the obligation of guarantee or warranty claimed was or was not distinct from the delivery obligation; and

(3) if the obligation of guarantee or warranty was distinct from the delivery obligation, the place where the former obligation was to be performed.

Case principle

3. Obligation in question of principal under agency contract in claim for damages for breach of contract held to be to allow agent to perform duties.

Case

Pierre v Société de Droit Italien Vetrolan, D (1992) SC 164, note Audit, Paris **408** Court of Appeal, First Emergency Chamber, 22 May 1991

Facts

A demand for the payment of commission was made at the same time as the contract was repudiated. The amount claimed was much lower than the amount sought for wrongful breach of contract.

Which was the competent jurisdiction?

Judgment

In French law, the claim by a commercial agent for damages for breach of contract was based on the failure to comply with the contract.

The facts of this case revealed that in the eyes of the plaintiff, the principal object of the litigation was the claim for damages for breach of the contract, which was regarded as located in the country where the agent carried on his activities, rather than the improperly executed duty to perform the contract by payment of agent's commission.

The competent jurisdiction was therefore that of the country where the commercial agent carried out his activities.

Comment

By deciding that the right to an indemnity takes precedence over the improperly executed contractual obligation to pay commission, and that the former was to be regarded as located in France, the decision failed properly to identify the obligation referred to. It could be said that this was the obligation to continue to uphold the agent's agency, and this could be regarded as being localized in the place where the agent carried out his activities.

The solution is not perhaps free from criticism; but it has the practical merit of granting jurisdiction to the forum of the place of performance of the obligation which is characteristic of the contract.

> " . . . *place of performance* . . . "

Case principle

1. Transport by sea is performed at the place of delivery, not of loading.

Case

409 Réunion Européenne Corporation et autres v Spiethoff Corporation and the Captain of the ship *Alblasgracht*, DMF (1995) 554, note Tassel, Paris Court of Appeal, Fifth Chamber, 16 November 1994

Facts

Merchandise transported by sea to The Netherlands under a bill of lading deteriorated during the journey. The insurer chose to pursue a claim against the shipowner in the Crétail Commercial Court. The defendant argued that the court was not competent to hear the case, on the basis of Arts 2 and 5(1) of the Convention.

Judgment

The French court lacked jurisdiction.

Effectively, the litigation came within the jurisdiction of the Amsterdam court, the place where the defendant was domiciled.

Because of Art. 5(1), it also came within the jurisdiction of the Rotterdam court, the place where the obligation which was the subject matter of the dispute, was to be performed.

Comment

It is an accepted part of French law that, in respect of the transport of merchandise, the place of performance of the obligation which is the subject matter of a dispute is the place where the service under the transport contract is to be performed. This place is the place where the merchandise is unloaded, and not where it is taken on board.

Case principle

2. Guarantee or comfort letter relating to obligations of payment of primary debtor held performable where primary debtor had to make payment.

Case

Société Svedex Holging BV v Banque Nationale de Paris et autre, Bull. Civ.IV, **410** n.101; D (1993) SC 61, note Audit. Cour de Cassation, Commercial Chamber, 3 March 1992

Facts

Two French subsidiaries of a Dutch parent company obtained loans from two credit institutions.

The latter obtained, from the parent company, a letter of comfort in the following terms: 'In accordance with our policy, we confirm that we will make every effort to ensure that the two subsidiaries have sufficient funds to enable them effectively to fulfil their obligations towards lending institutions, and this during the entire period of loans made to our subsidiaries'.

Both subsidiaries became subject to a voluntary arrangement approved by the courts, and the parent company was said to be liable to compensate the credit institutions.

The question was whether the French courts had jurisdiction to hear the case?

Judgment

The French courts had jurisdiction, because the promises given by the parent company to the credit institutions were to be given effect by material or legal acts carried out in France and which would produce their effects in France.

Comment

At issue here was the determination of the place of performance of a comfort letter in the light of Art. 5(1).

Case principle

3. Applicable law decides place of performance (*Tessili*, Case 12/76 applied).

425

Case

411   Société Promac SPRL v Société Anonyme Sogeservice, D (1992) SC 167, note
Audit. Paris Court of Appeal, Fourth Chamber, 16 May 1991.

Facts

The vendor of land situated in France approached a Belgian company to find
a purchaser. The latter, in its turn, and by a separate contract (entered into, it
appears, with the agreement of the vendor), came to an agreement with a
French company, according to which any eventual commission would be
shared equally between them.

Despite the French intermediary's success in obtaining a purchaser, the vendor failed to pay to the Belgian company the commission as agreed.

The latter company, therefore, sued the vendor in the Belgian courts, but
found that it was itself sued in the Paris Commercial Court by the French
company.

The Belgian company objected to the French courts' jurisdiction.

Judgment

The Court of Appeal held the competent court to be that of the place of performance of the obligation in question. As the text of Art. 5(1) referred to the
obligation and not to the contract, it was appropriate to take into account
what was the basis of the action.

As the claim was for the payment of the agent's commission and as the purpose of the agency was the sale of a building situated in France, the country in
which the research and the dealings between the agent and the purchaser effectively took place, the agency contract was subject to French law, according to
which the issue of the place of payment was to be determined.

In French law, as in Belgian law, payment of commission due from the
Belgian agent to the French property agent had to take place at the registered
office of the former company. As this was situated in Belgium, the Belgian
court for the area had jurisdiction in respect of the performance of the
contractual obligation.

Comment

In respect of the determination of the applicable law to the agency, the court
could, without changing the result, have referred to the Hague Convention of
14 March 1978 on the law applicable to contracts of intermediaries and representatives, which is not in force, but has been ratified by France. However,
in the absence of a clear choice of the applicable law, the said Convention des-
ignates the internal law of the State in which the intermediary has its principal
establishment at the time of the creation of the relationship of representation
(Art. 6(1)).

ARTICLE 5(3)

" . . . *place where the harmful event occurred.*"

Case principle

The plaintiff can choose between place of act or damage (*Bier*, Case 21/76).

Case

Schimmel Pianoforte Fabrik GmbH v Bion, D (1991) IR 37 Court of **412**
Cassation, First Civil Chamber, 8 January 1991

Facts

A manufacturer domiciled in Germany complained about the refusal of a
French importer to sell.

Judgment

The criterion for determining which jurisdiction is competent is 'the place
where the harmful event occurred'.

In Art. 5(3) of the Convention this expression covers both the place where
the loss occurred and the place of the causal event, and when these two places
are not one and the same, the defendant can be sued in the courts of either of
these two places, at the sole discretion of the plaintiff.

ARTICLE 5(5)

" . . . *arising out of the operations* . . . "

Case principle

Where a plaintiff's complaint is that a particular branch ought to have been
involved but was not, the dispute did not arise out of the latter's operations.

Case

Ben Lassin v Payne et autre, D (1994) IR 127 Court of Cassation, First Civil   **413**
Chamber, 27 April 1994

Facts

A cover note issued by a London insurance company noted a broker from Lichtenstein, but not the Parisian broker who had issued the note, nor, *a fortiori*, his address. The victim of the theft was insured for various risks throughout Europe, and was domiciled in Geneva.

Were the French courts competent to hear the action by the assured against the London insurance company for failing to perform its duty to advise the general agent in France of the said company and of the insurance broker?

Judgment

The answer was in the negative.

(1) The claim did not relate to the 'operation'—in the sense of Art. 5(5)—of the general agency of the London company; and none of the heads of competence set out in Art. 8 applied.

(2) Article 6(1) was inapplicable to insurance matters—Art. 7 only preserved Arts 4 and 5(5).

(3) By reason of Art. 3, neither the rules of internal law of Art. 42(2) of the New Civil Procedure Code nor Art. R.114–1 of the Insurance Code could be invoked.

(4) The insurance which was the subject matter of the litigation was not a French matter in the sense of Art. R.321–10 of the Insurance Code.

> " . . . *branch, agency or other establishment* . . . "

Case principle

These must have sufficient apparent links, yet with autonomy from the parent company.

Case

414 Société Comebo v Société Strafor Développement et autres, D (1996) SC 167, note Audit. Paris Court of Appeal, 5 July 1995

Facts

This case involved a conflict between an Italian company and a French company which had its registered office in Strasbourg, France. However, the contract, the subject of the litigation, was managed by a secondary establishment situated in Paris, by a person who was specially recruited for this purpose and who had complete responsibility for the said contract. Furthermore, the secondary establishment paid the bills and informed the other contracting party of the decision not to renew the said contract.

The question was whether the Paris Commercial Court had jurisdiction?

Judgment

The branch, agency or other establishment was characterized, in the sense of Art. 5(5) of the Convention, by a centre of operations appearing to act with a degree of permanence, as an extension of the parent company, although enjoying a sufficient degree of autonomy to be able to conclude deals with third parties in a way which enabled the latter, whilst knowing that a legal relationship would be created with the parent company situated elsewhere, to dispense with dealing directly with the parent company and to enter into contracts at the centre of operations of the subsidiary.

The Paris Commercial Court thus possessed jurisdiction.

Comment

This case brings attention to a mistake which is often made concerning the relationship between Arts 2 and 5 of the Convention.

Article 5 never has the effect of granting jurisdiction to a court in the State in which the defendant is domiciled: only the internal jurisdiction rules of the said State can determine which court has jurisdiction.

It follows that there were no grounds for Article 5(5) to apply. For Art. 5(5) to have applied in the present case, the Italian plaintiff would have had to have tried to sue the French companies in Italy on the grounds that they had a branch there: or, again, on the grounds that that was where the obligation forming the subject matter of the litigation was to be carried out under Art. 5(1).

ARTICLE 6

" . . . may also be sued . . . "

Case principle

Article 6 is inapplicable to insurance contracts within s.3 of Title II.

Case

Ben Lassin v Payne et autre, D (1994) IR 127 Court of Cassation, First Civil **415** Chamber, 27 April 1994

Facts

A cover note of an insurance broker issued from a London insurance company noted a broker from Lichtenstein, but not the Parisian broker who had issued the note, nor *a fortiori*, his address. The victim of the theft was insured for various risks throughout Europe, and was domiciled in Geneva.

Were the French courts competent to hear the action by the assured against the London insurance company for failing to execute its duty to advise the general agent in France of the insurance?

Judgment

The court held against French jurisdiction, particularly on the question of the plurality of the defendants, because Art. 6(1) did not apply to insurance matters, Art. 7 being without prejudice only to Arts 4 and 5(5).

ARTICLE 6(1)

" . . . *where any one of them is domiciled.*"

Case principle

Claims to rescind linked contracts where one is not performed are sufficiently connected for Art. 6(1).

Case

416 Société Oskar Fech GmbH v Sart Fondal et autre, D (1995) IR 54 Court of Cassation, Commercial Chamber, 31 January 1995

Facts

A machine, purchased on lease-credit from French company A, could only produce mechanical items of a particular type with a mould provided by German company B, with whom the purchaser of the machine placed an order.

The litigation resulted from company B's failure to deliver the mould.

The purchaser sued company A to rescind the contract for purchase of the machine and company B for rescission of the mould contract before the courts of the place in which the registered office of company A (the seller of the machine) was situated.

The question was whether those courts had jurisdiction under Art. 6(1) to deal with the issue of the annulment of the contract of sale of the mould?

Judgment

It was held that the courts possessed such jurisdiction. The Court of Appeal had properly held that there was only one solution to the litigation resulting from the failure to deliver the mould which would impact on all parties to the case. The Court of Appeal had considered there to be sufficient connection between the two requests for the annulment of the sales, and thus had legal foundation for the decision to uphold, in respect of the two sales, the jurisdiction of the courts in whose jurisdiction the registered office of company A (the seller of the machine) was situated.

ARTICLE 6(2)

" . . . may also be sued . . . As a third party . . . "

Case principle

Article 6(2) is subject to an inconsistent jurisdiction agreement between the third party and main defendant valid under Art. 17.

Case

Société De Groot Nijkerk Machinefabrieck BV v Sart Maschinenefabrick **417** Rhenania et autres, Bull.civ.IV, 179; JDI (1993) 151, 2eme esp, obs Huet; D (1993) SC 348, obs Audit, Court of Cassation, Commercial Chamber, 12 May 1992

Facts

A French purchaser, subject to a voluntary arrangement under judicial supervision, commenced an action—seemingly on the basis of Art. 5(1)—against the Dutch seller of an allegedly defective machine. The defendant brought in, on a guarantee action, the German supplier of part of the machine. The latter sought to invoke a Dutch jurisdiction clause.

Did Art. 6(2) enable the Dutch jurisdiction clause to be ignored?

The Court of Appeal, whose decision was appealed against, held that it could not be ignored, regardless of the validity of the jurisdiction clause invoked.

Judgment

The Court of Cassation criticized the decision of the Court of Appeal, on the grounds that only a valid jurisdiction clause would enable the third party to avoid a guarantee action within the jurisdiction of the court seised of the original proceedings. Thus, if valid, Article 17 prevailed over Art. 6(2).

Comment

By Art. 333 of the New Civil Procedure Code, French internal law gives priority to the rule of third party jurisdiction over the jurisdiction clause, preventing the third party brought in on the guarantee from using the jurisdiction clause.

However, the opposite conclusion has prevailed in respect of the interpretation of the Brussels Convention (Cour de Cassation, First Civil Chamber, 12 July 1982, D (1982) IR 145, obs Audit; JCP (1983) II 20015, note Bourel; JDI (1983) 405, obs Holleaux; Rev.Crit.DIP (1983) 659, notes Lagarde; see too Kaye, *Civil Jurisdiction* p. 650).

> *" . . . seised of the original proceedings . . . "*

Case principle

The main defendant need not have been proceeded against on *Convention* jurisdiction grounds.

Case

418 Veenbrink v Banque Internationale pour l'Afrique Occidentale et autre, Bull.Civ.I, 134; JDI (1993) 151, 1ere esp obs Huet; D (1993) SC 348, obs Huet
Court of Cassation, First Civil Chamber, 14 May 1992

Facts

The question was whether under Art. 6(2) a defendant domiciled in the territory of a Contracting State, could, in the case of an action on a guarantee or warranty or third party proceedings, be sued in the court seised of the original proceedings, even when, in respect of those proceedings, the jurisdiction of the court was not based on the rules set out in the Convention?

Judgment

The Court of Cassation confirmed that this was the case.

Comment

This position, which has been supported in France by several commentators on the Convention, is not self-evident. It could well be thought that the application of the rule of derived competence necessitates a competent forum according to the Convention, either under Art. 2 itself, or under one of the special jurisdiction rules of Art. 5, or even by virtue of a jurisdiction clause under Art. 17, otherwise the court seised of the original proceedings might have exercised jurisdiction on the basis of the normal rules of international jurisdiction, including in France the exorbitant rule contained in Art. 14 of the Civil Code.

This case, therefore, makes Art. 6(2) of the Convention into an autonomous procedural disposition of community law. Practically, it extends the impact of the cases of exorbitant jurisdiction, to the detriment of a defendant domiciled in the Community.

For a contrary view, see Kaye, *Civil Jurisdiction* p. 648.

ARTICLE 6(3)

" . . . may also be sued . . . On a counter-claim . . . "

Case principle

If the plaintiff brings proceedings in breach of an Art. 17 jurisdiction agreement and the defendant submits, Art. 6(3) confers jurisdiction over the defendant's counter-claim.

Case

Société Proma di Franco Gianotti v Société d'Exploitation des Établissements   **419**
Montuori, D (1994) 245, concl Jeol Court of Cassation, Plenary Chamber, 18
February 1994

Facts

The Italian company Proma granted the French company Montuori the exclusive right to distribute its products in France. The exclusive distribution agreement contained a clause assigning jurisdiction to the Geneva courts. Despite this clause, Proma sued the concessionary in the Tarascon Commercial Court in France for the payment of a bill of exchange.

Montuori did not contest the jurisdiction of the court nor the existence of the debt, but did issue a counterclaim against Proma for damages for breach of the exclusive concession agreement.

The court accepted both plaints, and deciding between the competing claims, held that Proma should pay the concessionary the measure of damages above the amount due under the letter of credit.

Was the Tarascon court competent to hear the counterclaim despite not being competent to hear the principal claim prior to the defendant's submission under Art. 18?

Judgment

The Court of Cassation held that French courts had jurisdiction under Art. 6(3): the lower French court had been seised in respect of the principal proceedings by the Italian company, so that it also had jurisdiction to hear the counterclaim of the French company.

Editor's Comment

Arguably, French courts' jurisdiction over Montuori's counterclaim ought to have been based upon Art. 18 if anything rather than on Art. 6(3), on the ground that Proma had implicitly submitted to French courts under the former, since Art. 6(3) should be held to be subject to Art. 17 (see Kaye, *Civil Jurisdiction* pp. 662–3). However, on the facts, it has to be said that it seems highly doubtful whether Proma could be taken so to have impliedly submitted to French jurisdiction over the counterclaim.

ARTICLE 10, PARAGRAPH 2

" . . . *Articles 7, 8 and 9 shall apply to actions brought by the injured party directly against the insurer* . . . "

Case principle

A jurisdiction agreement between insured and insurer does not bind the third party in his direct action against the insurer.

Case

420 Société Lutz et autre v Société Frasgo et autres, D (1991) SC 285 Paris Court of Appeal, Fifth Chamber, 12 November 1991

Facts

The policyholder signed a contract with a jurisdiction clause which assigned all litigation relating to the execution of the contract to the Munich District First Instance Court.

Could this jurisdiction clause be invoked by the insurance company against the victim who was exercising a direct action because of a tortious act by the assured which took place on French territory?

Judgment

The Court of Appeal held that it could not, on the basis that the victim who was exercising a direct action could not be subject to a jurisdiction clause which, by definition, he had not been able to negotiate, and indeed which he was not aware of.

ARTICLE 16(1)(a)

" . . . *have as their object rights in rem* . . . "

Case principle

An action in contract for work carried out to immovable property falls outside Art. 16(1).

Case

Fondation Solomon R Guggenheim v Consorts Helion et autres, D (1996) IR   **421**
201 Court of Cassation, First Civil Chamber, 3 July 1996

Facts

A foundation, the registered office of which was situated in the U.S. (in New York State), was also registered in Italy, where it owned property.

The action involved work carried out to a building owned by the foundation, and situated in Italy.

Was Art. 16(1) to be applied?

Judgment

The court held that it was not, because the action, the purpose of which was to enforce compliance with a contractual obligation and to obtain indemnification for a moral loss, did not put in issue a right *in rem* in immovable property in the sense of Art. 16(1).

ARTICLE 16(4)

" . . . *proceedings concerned with the registration or validity* . . . "

Case principle

Article 16(4) also applies to forfeiture actions.

Case

Société Douwe Egberts France v Société Eden-Waren DJI (1993) 153, note   **422**
Huet; D (1993) 349, note Audit, Paris Court of Appeal, First Emergency Chamber, 15 April 1992

Facts

The plaintiff started an action in France against a German corporation which owned certain French trademarks, for forfeiture of some of these and partial annulment of others.

The defendant requested that the two categories of action be separated, arguing that the German courts had jurisdiction over the forfeiture actions in accordance with the fundamental rule of Art. 2 of the Convention, notwithstanding exclusive French Article 16(4) jurisdiction in respect of the annulment claims.

Was such separation to be permitted?

Judgment

It was held that it should not. The Court of Appeal adjudged that in the interpretation of Art. 16(4) it was appropriate to refer not just to the internal law of one or other of the States concerned, but to an autonomous definition applying uniformly throughout the EC, and which recognized the exclusive jurisdiction of the courts of the State of the deposit or issuing of a certificate for all actions in respect of the validity, the existence *or the forfeiture* of the latter.

ARTICLE 17, PARAGRAPH 1

" . . . court or the courts . . . "

Case principle

Article 17 applies to an agreement under which a plaintiff must choose from amongst a number of possible fora.

Case

423 Société Hantarex Spa v Société Digital Research Public D (1991) IR 218, Paris Court of Appeal, First Emergency Chamber, 10 July 1991

Facts

The jurisdiction clause gave a plaintiff the choice between 'The Paris courts' or another court which had competence under the rules of the Convention.
  Was the clause valid?

Judgment

The court held that the clause was valid, and that it afforded the parties the greatest of choices and furthermore was agreed between commercial corporations and was specified in a very clear way in the general conditions of the contract. Once chosen, the court would have exclusive jurisdiction under Art. 17.

ARTICLE 17, PARAGRAPH 1(a)

" . . . in writing . . . "

Case principle

A jurisdiction clause in a bill of lading not signed by the shipper does not satisfy the 'in writing' requirement in relation to the shipper.

Case

Société Nedlloyd Lines and the Captain of the ship Isla de la Plata v UAP, **424** Cabinet Burbach and Primel SNC, DMF (1995) 357, note Tassel, Court of Cassation, Commercial Chamber, 15 November 1994

Facts

Following loss during transportation by sea, the Primel Corporation and its insurers sued the carrier in the Commercial Court of Le Havre. The defendants argued against jurisdiction because of a jurisdiction clause in the bill of lading in favour of Dutch courts. However, the bill of lading was not signed by the shipper.

Was the jurisdiction clause applicable in favour of the defendants?

Judgment

The Court of Cassation upheld the Court of Appeal's refusal to apply the clause, on the grounds that the shipper had not signed the bill of lading, and that the carrier could not produce a written document signed by the shipper confirming that he had signed the clause, and that the carrier had not proved, nor even alleged, that there was an agreement in a form admitted by recognized international usages and which the parties knew or were deemed to know of.

Comment

It is considered that the question could have been a different one: that of whether the absence of a signature on the bill of lading was in accord with usage, in which case the jurisdiction clause in an unsigned bill of lading would take a form which was in conformity with the usages of international commerce and known to the contracting parties?

> " . . . shall have exclusive jurisdiction . . . "

Case principle

Article 17 prevails over Art. 6(2).

Case

425   Société Bretonne de Construction Navale v Nanni Diesel Société, MB Marine
Société and Société Marine Drive Units, DMF (1995) 283, note Tassel, Court
of Cassation, Commercial Chamber, 18 October 1994

Facts

The litigation concerned the supply of a propulsion unit for a ship. The unit
was ordered by the SBCN Corporation from the Nanni Diesel Corporation,
who bought it from Marine Drive Units Ltd, who had themselves ordered it
from the Breda Marine Corporation.

When the unit proved to be faulty, the SBCN Corporation commenced an
action against the Nanni Diesel Corporation. The latter brought in the Breda
Marine Corporation on a guarantee action. The latter argued that the French
courts had no jurisdiction, based on a jurisdiction clause in favour of the
Italian courts. This clause was part of the general conditions of sale annexed
to the order confirmation which had been signed and sealed by the Nanni
Diesel Corporation.

Was the clause determining jurisdiction enforceable against the Nanni Diesel
Corporation?

Judgment

The Court of Cassation held that it was, judging that 'by so acting, the Nanni
Diesel Corporation had thereby accepted that it had notice of the jurisdiction
clause'. The Court of Appeal's decision on this basis was therefore legally correct.

ARTICLE 17, PARAGRAPH 5/LUGANO ARTICLE 17(4)

" . . . for the benefit of only one of the parties . . . "

Case principle

This does not follow from choice of a party's domicile alone.

Case

426   Société Edmond Coignet v Banca Commerciale Italiana, Bull.Civ.1, 2731;
Rev.crit.DIP (1991) 613, note Gaudemet-Tallon; D (1992) SC 244, Court of
Cassation, First Civil Chamber, 4 December 1990

Facts

Two Italian companies, one of which was the subsidiary of the French
company Edmond Coignet Corporation, entered into a subcontracting

arrangement with a Libyan company. First-demand guarantees were granted to the Libyan company by the Libyan Wada Bank. The latter obtained a counter-guarantee from the Banca Commerciale Italiana, which covered the risk by a guarantee under the French Civil Code from the Edmond Coignet Corporation. The latter obligation stated its execution 'to be subject solely and uniquely to the jurisdiction of the Milan Court'.

The guarantees were called in. The Banca Commerciale Italiana paid the Wada Bank, and sued the Edmond Coignet Corporation, not in the Milan Court, but in the Paris Commercial Court, which held that it had jurisdiction.

The question was whether, when jurisdiction was granted to the court of the place where the bank was domiciled, was the jurisdiction agreement to be considered as concluded for the benefit of the bank, so that the latter could waive it and seise any other court which had jurisdiction under the Convention?

Judgment

It was held that this was not necessarily so.

Indeed, according to the interpretation given by the ECJ in *Anterist v Crédit Lyonnais* Case 22/85, a jurisdiction agreement must not be regarded as only having been concluded in favour of one of the parties on the basis that the parties agreed that the courts which should have jurisdiction were those in whose jurisdiction that party was domiciled. There had to be a clearly expressed common intention to give an advantage to one of the parties, either in the terms of the clause itself, or from a combination of indicia in the contract or in the circumstances surrounding the conclusion of the contract.

ARTICLE 21, PARAGRAPH 1

" . . . *seised* . . . "

Case principle

A French court is seised not on issue of the writ but when a copy of the writ is presented to the court clerk.

Case

Jacky Maeder GmbH v Société Maritime d'Affrètement, D (1994) IR 255, **427**
Court of Cassation, Commercial Chamber, 4 October 1994

Facts and Judgment

The French court, in deciding to reject the plea of *lis alibi pendens* before the Belgian courts, should not have regard to the date when the writ was issued, but rather to the date on which a copy of the writ was *presented to the court clerk.* This is because, in effect, under Art. 857 of the New Civil Procedure Code, the Commercial Court is seised of a matter when a copy of the writ is presented to the court clerk.

ARTICLE 25

" . . . *judgment* . . . "

Case principle

A judgment cannot be recognized and enforced under Part III where it was given without the person who was found liable having been called to appear, even where it is by itself capable of execution without having been previously notified (Denilauler Case 125/79 applied).

Case

428   Micciche v Banco di Silicia, Rev.Crit.Dip (1994) 688, note Ancel; D (1994) IR.147, Court of Cassation, First Civil Chamber, 18 May 1994

Facts

An action for payment was brought by an Italian bank against several debtors. The president of the court found the latter jointly liable to pay. He specified that the debtors could appeal against the default judgment within 21 days from the date of notification, the judgment being provisionally enforceable.

Should an order for enforcement of this decision be granted?

Judgment

The Paris Court of Appeal felt that it could confirm that it was enforceable on the basis that the right to appeal had been mentioned in the judgment, and the latter had been notified to the defendants, who had not appealed.

The Court of Cassation overturned the decision of the Court of Appeal for not taking into account the circumstance that the Italian judgment was enforceable even before its notification to a debtor who was not called to appear before the court.

ARTICLE 27

" . . . *shall not be recognized* . . . "

Case principles

1. The enforcement of a judgment granted in respect of maintenance payments does not require a previous order for enforcement of the declaratory judgment on which it is based.
2. The role of the enforcement-court is to be carried out within the bounds of Arts 27 and 28, which exclude the matters of applicable law.

Case

X v Y, Rev.Crit.DIP (1995) 69, note Ancel; D (1994) IR 214, Court of   **429**
Cassation, First Civil Chamber, 12 July 1994

Facts

R was found liable by the German courts to pay, from 1 February 1989, sums by way of maintenance to S, of whom he was legally declared the father in 1985.

The Court of Appeal ordered the enforcement of this judgment under the Convention on 16 May 1989.

R objected, first, on the ground that although judgments in respect of maintenance payments would benefit from a simplified regime of execution under the Convention, this was on condition that they were completely autonomous on the matter of the scope of the Convention; and, secondly, on the ground that the French Court of Appeal was in breach of Art. 27 of the aforesaid Convention and Arts 3 and 342 of the Civil Code when it affirmed that the German law permitting the amount of the maintenance payments to be determined solely on the basis of the creditor's needs was not contrary to French public policy; and also because the decision which had affirmed the rights also required the payment of arrears for a period prior to the demand.

Judgment

The enforcement of a judgment granted in respect of a demand for maintenance payments did not require a previous order for enforcement of the declaratory (paternity) judgment on which it was based.

The role of the judge from whom *exequatur* was requested under the Convention was to be carried out within the bounds of Arts 27 and 28 thereof, which excluded the matter of the law applied by the German court.

ARTICLE 27(1)
" . . . *contrary to public policy* . . . "

Case principle

1. The court cannot quash an order for enforcement of a costs order on the ground of contravention of public policy by the *substantive judgment,* without examining whether the order for costs itself was contrary to French public policy.

Case

430 Société Times Newspapers v Pordea, D (1993) IR 136, Court of Cassation, First Civil Chamber, 5 May 1993

Facts

Judgments relating to the fixing of costs were reached in the UK after 1 January 1987, in relation to actions commenced before that date.

The question was whether these judgments relating to the fixing of the costs of the action could be subject to an order for enforcement?

The president of the Higher First Instance Court held that they could, and issued an enforcement order.

The Court of Appeal quashed the decision of the president of the Higher First Instance Court, for the reason that the substantive judgment was contrary to French public policy.

Judgment

The Court of Cassation quashed the judgment of the Court of Appeal, criticizing the judges for not having examined whether the order for costs itself was contrary to French public policy.

Case principle

2. Public policy does not require, when the defendant has knowledge of the foreign action, the notification of the judgment to include an indication of the appeals which are possible in the judgment-State.

Case

431 Roche v Direction Générale des Aéroports de l'Etat d'Ankara, D (1996) IR 210, Court of Cassation, First Civil Chamber, 10 July 1996

Case principle

3. Except for the purpose of determining the genuineness of the writ, Art. 27 does not permit the court to examine whether or not the foreign civil procedure was in accordance with the requirements of public policy in the recognition-State.

Case

Société Anonyme Eurosensory v Société F.J. Tieman BV et autre, D (1994) IR **432**
66, Paris Court of Appeal, First Civil Chamber, 28 January 1994

ARTICLE 27(2)

" . . . to enable him to arrange for his defence."

Case principle

The document instituting the proceedings, which must be properly served
under Art. 27(2), must, by definition, include sufficient details on the subject
matter of the claim, if the rights of the defence are to be respected.

Case

Société Polypetrol v Société Générale Routière, Rev.Crit.DIP (1992) 516, note **433**
Huet, Court of Cassation, First Civil Chamber, 9 October 1991

ARTICLE 27(3)

" . . . irreconcilable . . . "

Case principle

Judgments held not irreconcilable if, in recognition-State proceedings, contract
was also annulled but on different grounds.

Case

Société Simod, Rev.Crit.DIP (1990) 550, note Huet, Paris Higher First **434**
Instance Court (President), 31 May 1989

Facts and Judgment

The judgment of an Italian court annulling a contract between an Italian corporation and a French corporation through the wrongful actions of the latter,
could not be regarded as irreconcilable with a French judgment, which had
annulled the same contract, but on the grounds of the wrongful actions
of the Italian corporation.

ARTICLE 27(4)

" . . . concerning . . . succession . . . "

Case principle

Excluded matters are those relationships governed by rules of law specific to the excluded area.

Case

435 Paris Court of Appeal, First Chamber, D (1995) IR 259, 2 November 1995

Facts and Judgment

A judgment for the repayment of a loan taken out by the deceased, obtained by the lender against the deceased's estate, was not affected by the law of succession, as it was an ordinary action for repayment which could have been brought against the deceased himself before his death.

ARTICLE 28, PARAGRAPH 1

" . . . conflicts with . . . Sections . . . 4 . . . "

Case principle

Consumers are protected through jurisdictional review.

Case

436 Tonnoir v Société Anonyme Vanherf, Jnl.Dr.Int. (1991) 161, note Huet, Douai Court of Appeal, Eighth Chamber, 9 February 1989

Case principle

In accordance with Art. 28, a foreign judgment cannot be recognized where it failed to respect Arts 13 and 14 of the Convention (s.4 of Title II), granting mandatory protection to consumers.

Facts

A French woman domiciled in the Nord Département purchased, following an 'exhibition in a shopping gallery in Petit Forêt (France)', a door, a veranda and a window from the Belgian Vanherf Corporation. She paid a deposit, but not the remaining sums due, and was sued in the Belgian civil court, apparently on the basis of a jurisdiction clause which was contained in the contract of sale.

Judgment

The Douai Court of Appeal, unlike the President of the Higher First Instance Court of Valenciennes, refused to accept the Belgian judgment, for contravention of Art. 14, para. 2 and Art. 15.

Comment

This is the correct solution if, at least, the jurisdiction rules set out in the Brussels Convention in respect of consumer contracts were indeed applicable to the present case. However, not all of these conditions in Art. 13 para. 1 appear to have been present.

ARTICLE 29

"Under no circumstances . . . be reviewed as to its substance."

Case principle

Challenge to the amount of damages awarded is review of substance.

Case

Société Anonyme Compagnie Française BK v Hatzatz Hae, d'Umin, D (1996) **437** SC 169, note Audit, Paris Court of Appeal, 21 September 1995

Facts

A French company contracted with an Israeli company to provide an industrial installation. The latter was unhappy with the installation, and commenced an action in the Israeli courts, in which the French company was ordered to pay damages.

The French company sought to contest the enforcement of the judgment in France, arguing that it was contrary to international public policy on the basis that it failed to respect the contractual limitation of responsibility, thereby 'leading the foreign judge to award damages which were unreasonable and even punitive'.

Judgment

The argument was rejected on the grounds that the appellant, by arguing that the foreign judgment was contrary to international public policy, was in reality undermining the foreign judgment, and it is forbidden for the court enforcing the judgment to review the merits of the foreign judgment.

Comment

It is true that the examination of the amount of damages awarded by a foreign court is a *characteristic* of review of the merits. However, not every intervention on this ground of public order can be ruled out.

In the present non-Convention case, the problem of reconciling public policy and refusal to review the merits did not appear to be sufficiently examined.

ARTICLE 33, PARAGRAPH 2

" . . . *must give an address for service* . . . "

Case principle

According to the ECJ's interpretation of Art. 33, para. 2, the requirement to choose a domicile must be carried out according to formalities laid down by the law of the State in which enforcement is sought; and where that law is silent as to the moment when this formality is to be carried out, then the latest time shall be the moment when the order granting enforcement is served (*Carron*, Case 198/85).

Case

438a Office des Affaires Sociales et de la Jeunesse de la Ville de Karlsruhe v D, D (1990) 146, note Rémery, Court of Cassation, First Civil Chamber, 18 April 1989

Facts

The Court of Appeal annulled an enforcement order which authorized the execution in France of a formal document issued in the Federal Republic of Germany on the grounds that the election of domicile at the moment of application for an enforcement order was irregular, as it was carried out in lawyers' chambers outside the area of jurisdiction of the court which had been seised, and a subsequent election of domicile, carried out at the practice of a process-server who attended to the notification of the application, was inoperative.

Judgment

The decision of the Court of Appeal was quashed on the basis of the principle set out above, and because French law is silent as to the time when an election of domicile must take place.

ARTICLE 38, PARAGRAPH 1

" . . . may . . . stay . . . "

Case principle

1. The purpose of Art. 38 is to make it possible to prevent judgments from being automatically recognized and enforced in other Contracting States when there is still the possibility that they will be quashed or amended in the State of origin.

Case

Société Anonyme La Médicale Equipex v Société Farmitalia Erba SRL Fice, D   **438b**
(1989) IR 64, Court of Appeal of Versailles, 25 January 1989

Facts and Judgment

Therefore, a request for a stay is not contrary to Art. 34, para. 3, which prohibits the enforcement-court from reviewing the merits of the foreign judgment, where the latter is appealed against in the State of origin.

The enforcement-court may thus reserve its decision whenever there is a reasonable doubt as to the final outcome of a judgment in the State of origin.

Case principle

2. The enforcement-court has a discretion under Art. 38 to order a stay: it should examine whether there is a reasonable doubt as to the final outcome of a judgment in the State of origin.

Case

Société Protis v Société Cidue, Rev.Crit.DIP (1992) 126, note Gaudemet-   **439**
Tallon, Court of Appeal of Versailles, 21 June 1990

Facts

An Italian corporation, Cidue, obtained judgment in the Venice Court against a French corporation, Protis, in the sum of 463342.47 French francs.

The decision of the Venice Court was appealed against to the Venice Court of Appeal.

The Cidue Corporation sought from the President of the Higher First Instance Court of Nanterre an order for the recognition of the judgment of the Venice Court, and this was duly granted.

The Protis Corporation requested that the decision of the court be suspended until the Venice Court of Appeal had reached its decision.

Judgment

It was appropriate to examine whether the issues put forward by the Protis Corporation were sufficient to raise a reasonable doubt as to the final outcome of the judgment of the Venice Court in the Venice Court of Appeal.

ARTICLE 46(1)

" . . . *shall produce . . . a copy of the judgment . . .* "

Case principle

The recognition of a foreign judgment for which reasons were not given is contrary to the French conception of international public policy, when supporting documents are not produced to fill the lacuna left by the absence of grounds.

Case

440 Société Polypetrol v Société Générale Routière, Rev.Crit.DIP (1992) 516, note Huet, Court of Cassation, First Civil Chamber, 9 October 1991

Facts

In the decision appealed against, the French court refused to enforce the judgment of the Landgericht Saarbrücken, a default judgment, in which the Société Générale Routière was held liable to pay the Germany Polypetrol Corporation the equivalent in Deutschmarks of 231256.61 French francs, on the grounds that the supporting documents produced were not sufficient to enable the French court to determine whether the conditions necessary for enforcement had been met.

The French court's decision was criticized on the ground that it was for the person who alleged an irregularity of a judgment to prove that the lack of reasoning concealed a breach of the rules of the Convention.

Judgment

It was for the person seeking enforcement to produce the documents to fill the lacuna left by the absence of grounds. He had to produce a duplicate of the German judgment, in accordance with Art. 46 of the Convention. The Court of Appeal had no duty, as part of its role of supervision, to fill the gaps left by the plaintiff and to request the latter to produce the appropriate elements of proof.

> ## ARTICLE 47(1)
>
> " . . . *according to the law of the State of origin* . . . "

Case principle

The law of the judgment-State regulates the effectiveness of the notification of the judgment.

Case

De Wouters d'Oplinbter v Cts Janson, D (1993) IR 38, Paris Court of Appeal, **441** First Chamber, 5 October 1992

Facts

A Belgian process-server, a ministerial officer in the State of origin, sent a copy of a Belgian judgment to a French process-server by post. He also posted a copy of the judgment to the judgment debtor.

The French process-server gave notification of the foreign judgment without mentioning in the document the dispositions of Art. 680 of the New Civil Procedure Code.

Was this notification effective?

Judgment

The Court of Appeal held that it was, on the grounds that Art. 680 of the New Code of Civil Procedure, which provides that the document of notification must contain, in a way which is clear and certain, a number of matters, was not applicable to the service of a *foreign* judgment. Belgian law applied instead.

> ## ARTICLE 50, PARAGRAPH 1
>
> " . . . *authentic instrument* . . . "

Case principle

In the same way that a certificate of civil status is conclusive until judicially declared invalid in an action commenced by any interested party, any voluntary recognition of paternity of a natural child and agreement to pay maintenance made in a foreign country has full legal effect without the need for the document which contains the recognition to be subjected to further, original proceedings in the recognition-State.

Case

442   Tonon v Office Cantonal de la Jeunesse de Tuttlingen, Rev.Crit.DIP (1994)
557, note Pamboukis, D(1990) IR 108, Court of Cassation, First Civil
Chamber, 12 January 1994

Facts

Tonon, a French national, recognized the paternity of his son TT, and agreed
to pay him maintenance.

The judgment which was being appealed against had held that the documents which contained the recognition of paternity and the agreement to pay
maintenance could be enforced.

Judgment

The appeal was rejected on the ground that an instrument, voluntarily agreed,
but nonetheless possessing formal legal status in the judgment-State, qualified
as an authentic instrument under Art. 50.

> " . . . *contrary to public policy* . . . "

Case principles

1.   Authentic instruments which are drawn up and enforceable in a
     Contracting State may be declared enforceable in another Contracting
     State on condition only that such enforcement is not contrary to the pub-
     lic policy of the State in which execution is requested.
2.   This disposition applies only to instruments which come within the scope
     of the Convention, from which is excluded the status and capacity of
     natural persons, but which includes the duty to maintain, even when
     collateral to an issue of the status of a person.

Case

443   Office de Prévoyance pour la Jeunesse de Bodenseekreis v X Jnl.Dr.In (1991)
162, obs Huet; D (1990) IR 108, Paris Court of Appeal, 22 February 1990

Facts and Judgment

An order to pay maintenance in accordance with German civil procedure was
not contrary to French public policy, which itself also imposed an obligation
to maintain children in this area. This order was therefore to be enforced
in France.

ARTICLE 53, PARAGRAPH 1

" . . . shall apply its rules of private international law."

Case principle

French private international law refers to the law of the country of the registered office of a foundation in order to determine its seat.

Case

Fondation Solomon R. Guggenheim v Consorts Hélion et autres, D (1996) IR **444**
201, Cour de Cassation, First Civil Chamber, 3 July 1996

Facts

A foundation, which had its registered office in New York State in the USA was registered in Italy where it held property.

Did this registration mean that the foundation could be regarded as being domiciled in Italy?

Judgment

The Court of Cassation answered in the negative. A foundation could not be regarded as being domiciled in Italy simply on the basis of its registration there. Its registered office was in New York State, the law of which had never granted it the possibility of having another registered office in a foreign State in which it held property.

7

GERMANY

Professor Thomas Rauscher[*]

A. LEGAL SYSTEM

Courts

First instance civil and commercial cases are decided by local courts (Amtsgericht—AG) or District Courts (*Landgericht*—LG), depending upon the value of the claim: the AG has—with certain exceptions—jurisdiction up to 10000 DM, the LG has jurisdiction for higher claims and is divided into civil divisions each with three judges and commercial divisions each with one judge and two merchant judges.

Appeals (*Berufung*), which again depend on the value of the claim, are to the LG, if the AG was the court of first instance, and to Court of Appeal (*Oberlandesgericht*—OLG 'higher court of a region'), if the LG was the court of first instance.

Judicial Appeal (*Revision*), which can only be brought against an OLG's judgment if the value of the appellant's claim of inadequacy of award is of more than 60000 DM or if Revision is expressly permitted in the OLG's judgment, is to be decided by the Federal Civil Court (*Bundesgerichtshof*—BGH). The BGH is the only Federal Court for ordinary civil and commercial matters, as all other courts are State courts. Therefore, in the German judicial system there is a unique jurisdiction of the State courts in the first two instances beneath the Bundesgerichtshof, rather than double competencies of State and Federal Courts as in the US.

*Professor at Leipzig University, Law Faculty, Chair for Private International Law, Comparative Law and Civil Law

Only a few cases falling within the material scope of the Brussels Convention (Art. 1) are not decided on *action* in the instances described above but on *application* with a slightly different order of instances.

Labour Law cases are decided by special Labour courts (*Arbeitsgericht*), appeals going to the State Labour Court (*Landesarbeitsgericht*) and Revision to the Federal Labour Court (*Bundesarbeitsgericht*).

The Bundesgerichtshof and *Bundesarbeitsgericht* are Supreme Federal Courts which, according to Art. 2, para. (1) of the Protocol of 3 June 1971, are entitled and are under an obligation to refer questions of the Brussels Convention's interpretation to the European Court of Justice. The German Constitutional Court (*Bundesverfassungsgericht*) is not included within the meaning of 'Supreme Federal Courts' and therefore is not entitled to refer such questions.

The *Landgericht, Oberlandesgericht* and *Landesarbeitsgericht* may refer such questions to the European Court of Justice according to Art. 2, para. 2 of the said Protocol, but the Landgericht can only do so when deciding on appeal.

B. IMPLEMENTATION OF CONVENTIONS

The Brussels Convention has been in force in Germany since 1 February 1973. The First (1978) Accession Convention has been in force in Germany since 1 November 1986, the Second (1982) Accession Convention since 1 April 1989, including the New Federal Countries (former GDR) since 3 October 1990. The Third (1989) Accession Convention came into force on 1 December 1994. The *implementation law* of 29 July 1972 does not contain any significant issues, nor do the *implementation laws* for the Accession Conventions.

There is a law concerning the execution of recognition and enforcement (*Anerkennungs- und Vollstreckungsausführungsgesetz*—AVAG) of 30 May 1988, replacing a former law for the same purpose and containing specific executory prescriptions which also apply to cases under the Brussels Convention in the German courts. Contrary to the method of implementation of the Brussels Convention in the UK by the Civil Jurisdiction and Judgments Act 1982, German implementation laws merely declare the applicability of the respective convention. The AVAG contains procedural rules concerning the application for enforcement according to Art. 32 of the Convention which is under the jurisdiction of the presiding judge of a chamber of the Landgericht; for the appeal with the *Oberlandesgericht*, according to Arts 37 and 40 of the Convention; and for the special appeal (Rechtsbeschwerde) to the Bundesgerichtshof, according to Art. 41.

C. OVERVIEW OF CONVENTION CASE LAW

German courts are often concerned with the Convention's application, a fact which is shown by the great number of questions which have been presented to the European Court of Justice during the last 20 years.

With few exceptions, the case reports *infra*, contain only judgments which have been published in the 1990s. Preference is given to decisions of the *Bundesgerichtshof*, which are almost completely reported below for this period and decisions of the courts of *Oberlandesgericht*, which are reported only if deciding on crucial questions.

Although the *Landgerichts'* decisions are rarely reported, this should not give rise to the impression that the Brussels Convention cases are not decided in this instance. But it seems that in most cases when difficult questions concerning the application of the Brussels Convention were involved, there was an appeal to the *Oberlandesgericht*.

D. CASES

PREAMBLE, PARAGRAPH 4

" . . . *international jurisdiction* . . . "

Case principle

Convention inapplicable to a purely domestic case.

Case

OLG of Hamm 26 June 1990 (7 U 16/90) NJW–RR (1992) 499   **445**

Facts

The holder of a cheque, signed in Mallorca (Spain) and payable in Münster (Germany) sued the German domiciled drawer according to s.605a of the German Code of Civil Procedure (ZPO).

Judgment

The court left undecided whether Convention Art. 2(1) was to be applied in the present case or whether the jurisdiction of German courts resulted from national German law (ss.605a, 603(1) of the ZPO). The court explained that the case was a 'purely domestic case', for which type, according to the prevailing opinion in Germany, the Convention was not to be applied.

Comment

The court should have determined the jurisdiction according to the rules of the Brussels Convention. No doubt, the Convention in principle deals only with questions of *international jurisdiction* (see preamb para. 4), and only partly (*e.g.* Art. 5) with *local jurisdiction*. One opinion concludes the Convention is not applicable in purely domestic cases (*Piltz* NJW (1979) 1071). This opinion might only be followed as far as there is only a theoretical question for the international competence if the facts have no relationship to another country at all (in a similar sense, *Kropholler*, before Art. 2, para. 7). But in such cases, the international jurisdiction—assuming the Convention is applicable as to the matter in dispute (see Art. 1(2))—is not to be examined according to national law, but exists without any problem. If there is any doubt, on the other hand, about international jurisdiction, this question is governed by the Convention.

From a more dogmatic view, in *any* case—also in purely domestic cases—the question concerning international jurisdiction must be answered and therefore the Convention is also applicable to such cases (*Zöller/Geimer* Appendix, Art. 2, para. 14). In consequence, the international jurisdiction could result, without any problem, from the Convention in cases having no relation to any other country, but the local jurisdiction could follow the Convention's rules and not national law as far as the Convention deals with local jurisdiction. This problem does not arise for Convention jurisdictional provisions which presuppose a connection with more than one Contracting State (for example Art. 5). But it is a different matter if a provision presupposes a connection with only one Contracting State (for example, Art. 6 of the Brussels Convention).

This case, in any event, has sufficient foreign connections, as the cheque was drawn in a country other than the country of the plaintiff's domicile. Undoubtedly Art. 2(1) of the Brussels Convention should have been applied.

ARTICLE 1, PARAGRAPH 1

" . . . civil and commercial matters . . . "

Case principle

A claim for damages in a criminal court is a civil matter under Art. 1.

Case

446 BGH 16 September 1993 (IX ZB 82/90) NJW (1993) 3269

Facts

Both the parties were domiciled in Germany. The plaintiffs' son, a schoolboy, had been killed in an accident during a school excursion in Italy. The defendant, the teacher who had accompanied the schoolboys, was sentenced by the criminal Corte d'Appello of Bolzano in Italy for negligent manslaughter. The same judgment granted the plaintiffs, who had joined the criminal proceedings, damages of 20 MIO Lit and compensation for their expenses in the proceedings in the amount of 984 000 Lit. They applied to enforce the Italian judgment in Germany according to Art. 31 ss of the Brussels Convention. In the Italian proceedings, the defendant/accused had replied only to the criminal charge but not to the civil claim.

Judgment

The judgment was the final judgment following the ruling of the European Court in *Sonntag* Case C–172/91. The Bundesgerichtshof held, according to the binding decision of the European Court, that the claim for civil damages and compensation in a criminal court against the teacher of a public school fell within the scope of the Convention as a 'civil matter' within the meaning of Art. 1. Furthermore, the Bundesgerichtshof held that the claim for compensation for the plaintiffs' expenses in the criminal proceedings (discovery and trial) and their costs of taking part in the criminal proceeding as a civil party, were also to be treated as a civil matter.

See too infra, Case 521.

ARTICLE 1, PARAGRAPH 2(1)

" . . . *rights in property arising out of a matrimonial relationship* . . . "

Case principle

1. Claims under BGB ss.1301 and 530 for compensation after breach of engagement are excluded from the Convention.

Case

BGH 28 February 1996 (XII ZR 181/93) NJW (1996) 1411   **447**

Facts

The plaintiff, a German citizen residing in Germany, sued the defendant, his former fiancée, a Brazilian citizen living in Spain, for restitution of engagement gifts, including a Mercedes car, 245 000 DM in cash and the funds for a house in Spain.

Judgment

The court declined to apply the Brussels Convention for reasons of its transitional and subject matter inapplicability (see *infra*, Case 563). The Convention was not applicable, as the claim was based on ss.1301 and 530 of the BGB—special claims of unjust enrichment in German law for the restitution of gifts after the breach of an engagement (s.1301) and the restitution of gifts in the case of severe offence or ingratitude of the donee (s.530). The court gave no reason for its decision that such claims were outside the scope of the Brussels Convention and that German rules of jurisdiction consequently were applicable.

Comment

The decision is wrong on this point. Maybe the court wanted to explain that the Convention did not provide a *German forum* for this action, when remarking that Art. 5, para. 1 was not to be applied to unjust enrichment cases. But the consequences of a *non-application* of the entire Convention according to its material scope of applicability, on the one hand, and the lack of jurisdiction of the German courts in *application of the Convention*, on the other hand, are different. To find the case outside the scope of the Convention means to apply the national rules of jurisdiction, as the Bundesgerichtshof actually did in the case in question. Whereas if the Convention applies but does not provide a German forum, the German courts are then incompetent, without the possibility of reference to national law of civil procedure instead.

Case principle

2. Convention applicable to a dispute between spouses concerning property held in common.

Case

448 LG of Stuttgart of 23 August 1995 (19 O 689/94) IPRax (1996) 140

Facts

The parties, Greek spouses living separately, had a dispute over a common bank account in Greece. The account was in the names of both parties; the defendant had withdrawn the balance.

Judgment

The court applied the Convention, reasoning that the exception in Art. 1, para. 2(1), concerning matrimonial property, did not apply to an account held by a married couple. The prerequisite was that Greek law had a system of separate property. Therefore, the account was not held as some kind of common property and the claim was not based on matrimonial property law.

Comment

The decision is correct. In addition, it seems necessary to remark that Greek matrimonial property law provides a system of separate property, combined with a claim for participation in any increase in a spouse's assets during marriage whenever the marriage ends. In theory, the system is similar to German *Zugewinnausgleich*, but is more flexible as to the amount of participation. Such a claim for participation according to matrimonial property law undoubtedly *would* fall within the scope of Art. 1, para. 2(1) and, therefore, would be excluded from the application of the Convention.

ARTICLE 1, PARAGRAPH 2(2)

" . . . proceedings relating to the winding-up of insolvent companies . . . "

Case principle

1. Proceedings according to s.30 *et seq.* Konkursordnung are excluded from application of the Convention.

Case

BGH 11 January 1990 (IX ZR 27/89) NJW (1990), 990; WM (1990) 326. **449**
IPRax (1991) 183; EWiR (1990) 257; ZIP (1990), 246; ZZP (1990) 221

Facts

On 24 November 1986, a proceeding according to Chap. 11 of the US Bankruptcy Code was instituted over the property of USL, a US company limited by shares. On 28 November 1986, the Amtsgericht of Bremen, on application of the defendant, a Netherlands company domiciled at Rotterdam, had ordered an arrest (s.917 of the German Code of Civil Procedure—ZPO) over the estate of USL situated in the Federal Republic. In performance of this arrest, the Amtsgericht of Bremen had seised a claim of USL against S—GmbH, a German limited company domiciled in Bremen, for the payment of freight costs and delivery of bunkered gas. In December 1986, the defendant suspended prosecution of the arrest in respect of the bunkered gas, in exchange for securities given by the owner of the vessel, on behalf of whom company M of New York, residing in Frankfurt, gave a guaranty in the arrest proceedings up to the maximum amount of 118000 US dollars, payable on presentation of enforceable judgments of a German or foreign court against USL. On 3 March 1987, bankruptcy proceedings according to the German law of bankruptcy (*Konkursordnung*—KO) were instituted against the chattels of USL—the branch in Bremen. The liquidator contested the above mentioned seizures in arrest according to s.30(1), (2) and (37) of the KO (contestation of transactions which are disadvantageous for creditors of the bankrupt). The petition of the liquidator against the defendant in the Landgericht of Bremen was for renunciation by the defendant of its rights under the order of arrest and under the guaranty of company M.

Judgment

The Bundesgerichtshof's starting point was that proceedings according to s.30 ss KO were excluded from the scope of the Brussels Convention according to Art. 1, para. 2(2). According to the principles from the *Gourdain* Case 133/78 in the European Court of Justice, the decision over the trustee's claims was entirely connected with the bankruptcy. The trustee was the only one to bring the action in the interest of the community of creditors in order to give them a partial fulfilment of their claims, taking into account the privileges and general equality of the creditors.

Comment

Article 1, para. 2(2) of the Brussels Convention refers to 'Bankruptcy, proceedings relating to the winding up of insolvent . . . and analogous proceedings'. When drafting the Convention, there was an expectation that these terms would be entirely defined by a European Convention on bankruptcy in the very near future. Because to date there were only proposals for this Convention (see Kegel/Thieme *Vorschläge und Gutachten zum Entwurf eines EG-Konkursübereinkommens* (1988), (proposals and opinions on the project of an EC Bankruptcy Convention), the Bundesgerichtshof followed the definition of such proceedings provided by the European Court of Justice (*Gourdain* Case 133/78). Section 29 ss of the KO covers particular proceedings of bankruptcy law which cannot be defined homogeneously other than in terms of the bankruptcy proceeding itself. The European Court ruled that the subsection in question covered such types of proceedings which 'derive directly from the bankruptcy or winding up and are closely connected with the proceedings for the *"liquidation des biens"* or the *"règlements judiciaires"'*.

The Bundesgerichtshof applies this formula to all legal cases of contestation provided by s.29 ss of the KO. The reasoning is not absolutely convincing: the fact that only the trustee in bankruptcy can bring the claims according to s.29 ss of the KO is not decisive for the said 'close connection'. It is simply that, until institution of the bankruptcy proceedings, the bankrupt cannot raise any judicial claim, regardless of the existence of this claim *before* the institution of the bankruptcy proceeding (s.6 of the KO). The second argument, according to which the claim is to the advantage of all creditors, does not meet the point, because this argument is true for any other claim of the bankrupt. Nevertheless, the Bundesgerichtshof's decision may be followed for s.30 of the KO. The claim, based on this rule, depends on the bankruptcy proceeding's very existence. On the other hand, that cannot be said for other legal rules dealing with contestation. According to one opinion (see Baur/Stürner

Zwangsvollstreckungs-, Konkurs- und Vergleichtsrecht, Vol. II (1990)) s.18, ss.31 and 32 of the KO only continue the pre-bankruptcy claims of s.3 of the German Contestation Law (*Anfechtungsgesetz*). Some authors conclude that these claims are not of a specifically bankruptcy nature. This argument could be convincing, especially if one tends to interpret the European Court's formula with regard to the Advocate General's opinion in Case 133/78, which talks of a 'characterizing' 'closed material connection with a bankruptcy proceeding'. Nevertheless, it should be given preference over an autonomous interpretation with regard to the EC Bankruptcy Convention project. This interpretation should avoid the discussion over the character of national bankruptcy regulations. In consequence, any dispute on the validity, in relation to the creditors, of any transaction managed by the bankrupt (without regard to the time the transaction had taken place and without regard to any pre-bankruptcy possibility of contestation) should fall within the scope of Art. 1, para. 2(2) of the Brussels Convention, which means that the Convention is not applicable for such proceedings (see s.15 (1) of the EC Bankruptcy Convention 2nd Project. In the same sense: *Schmidt* EuZW (1990) 220; *Balz* EWiR (1990) 257; *Thode* WuB VII B 1 Art. 1 EuGVÜ 1.90; *Taupitz* ZZP 105 (1992) 221).

Case principle

2. The Convention is not applicable to claims arising after institution of bankruptcy proceedings, notwithstanding judicial approval according to Art. 475 of the Belgium Commercial Code.

Case

OLG of Zweibrücken 30 June 1992 (3 W 13/92) EuZW (1993) 165   **450**

Facts

On 20 February 1979, a Belgium court had decreed an adjudication of bankruptcy against X GmbH & Co KG, a German corporation. On 25 April 1990, the creditors obtained a final Belgian decree for payment against one of X's debtors. The decreed amount consisted of (i) claims resulting from deliveries before the time of adjudication of bankruptcy, (ii) claims for deliveries during bankruptcy which were based on special agreement with the trustee in bankruptcy and authorization by the court according to Art. 475 of the Belgium Commercial Code. Furthermore there were included (iii) claims concerning products which had not been produced completely and delivered in consequence of the adjudication of bankruptcy. The creditors applied for enforcement of the Cour d'Appel's final decree.

Judgment

The Oberlandesgericht of Zweibrücken granted enforcement only partially as far as claims arose during the time *before* bankruptcy was declared. The court applied Arts 31 *et seq*. of the Brussels Convention, because these claims did not arise during a bankruptcy proceeding. On the other hand, the court affirmed the criterion of close connection to the bankruptcy proceedings in the sense of Art. 1(2), para. 2, as far as the business of the bankrupt had been continued with judicial approval according to Art. 475 of the Belgian Commercial Code. This ruling was founded on the interpretation of the said Belgium regulation (referring to Cour Commerciale of Gent 11 February 1980) and on the interpretation of the similar German prescription in s.17 of the bankruptcy law (*Konkursordnung*). In addition, the court explained that this interpretation was in accordance with Art. 15(8) of the EC Bankruptcy Convention Project. This prescription would exclude any dispute concerning the termination or continuation of contracts based on regulations of bankruptcy law from the scope of the Brussels Convention. Article 1(4) of the German–Belgium Convention (see Art. 56(1) of the Brussels Convention) does not apply to decisions of this type during a bankruptcy proceeding.

Comment

The decision is to be followed. Claims arising from the continuation of the business by the liquidator, with the judicial approval necessary in accordance with the applicable bankruptcy law, are necessarily based upon and entirely connected with the bankruptcy proceeding. The interpretation with regard to the EC Bankruptcy Convention Project makes sure that the scope of both Conventions will be harmonized as soon as possible (see *supra*, Comments to Case 449).

Case principle

3. Claims for manager's responsibility in French law outside the scope of the Convention.

Case

451 OLG of Hamm 26 February 1993 (20 W 3/93) EuZW (1993) 519; RIW (1994) 62

Facts

On 7 February 1990, the applicant was granted a final judgment by the Cour de Commerce of Marennes (France) against the defendants (X, Y, Z), which deemed that errors of management by the defendants had been the reason for the insolvency of S, a French company. The judgment stated, furthermore, that X, Y and Z were responsible for S's debts in the amount of 4 012 520 French francs according to Art. 180 law of 25 January 1985.

Judgment

The Oberlandesgericht of Hamm refused enforcement, because the French judgment was outside the scope of Art. 1 of the Brussels Convention. Article

180 of the said French law replaced—concerning bankruptcy proceedings instituted after 1 January 1986—the rule of Art. 99 of the Law of 13 July 1967 which was concerned in the European Court's decision in *Gourdain* Case 133/78. The French court's main reason was that all the elements of the managers' responsibility, according to Art. 99, which had been decisive for the European Court to apply Art. 1, para. 2(2) of the Brussels Convention, remained unchanged in the new Art. 180. The bankruptcy court was *competent* for the proceedings under both prescriptions; it could extend the bankruptcy proceedings to affect the property of the liable manager; the *limitation* of action (in French law) ran from the day of the judgment concerning liability; and the *amount* recovered from the manager was to benefit all creditors equally. The changes in the new version—namely, the extension of the *right* to apply, to the representatives of the creditors, and a change in the *burden of proof* by elimination of the presumption of fault against the managers—did not justify another interpretation.

Comment

The decision correctly qualifies Art. 180 as a rule of bankruptcy law in the sense of Art. 1, para 2(2) of the Brussels Convention. Aside from involvement in the bankruptcy proceeding, this qualification should be based less on the equal protection of the creditors (on this point see comment to Case 449) than on the exclusively bankruptcy nature of the claim. The changes between Art. 99 of the 1967 Law and Art. 180 of the 1985 Law have no influence on this point.

Nevertheless, the court's comparison of the *particular elements* of both Laws is not convincing. The only decisive criterion for the application of Art. 1, para. 2(2) of the Brussels Convention is the bankruptcy nature of the claim: thus the liability according to Art. 180 is based on a '*redressement judiciaire*' *v* '*liquidation judiciaire*', *i.e.* it is not independent from a bankruptcy proceeding. Furthermore, it only arises if during this proceeding the estate of the bankrupt is found to be insufficient.

ARTICLE 1, PARAGRAPH 2(3)

" . . . 3. *Social security.*"

Case principle

A claim for restitution of social security payments is excluded from Convention.

Case

OLG of Köln 29 September 1990 (13 W 67/90) EuZW (1991) 64   **452**

Facts

The Dutch Kantongericht of Heerlen (The Netherlands), in a judgment of 19 July 1985, ordered the defendant according to Art. 58(b) of The Netherlands' Social Security Law (*Algemene Bijstandswet*—ABW) to restore social security payments which had been improperly granted. The applicant applied for authorization of enforcement in Germany.

Judgment

The Oberlandesgericht of Köln refused enforcement. The Brussels Convention was not applicable because of Art. 1, para. 2(3). Undoubtedly, the *granting* of social security payments fell within the scope of 'social security' within the meaning of Art. 1. However, even though this claim was not a matter concerning such grant, but a claim for restitution of social security payments which had been granted improperly, nonetheless, it should be interpreted as belonging to the scope of social security, due to the narrow factual and legal connection with the granting of such payments.

Comment

The decision does not discuss the nature of the restitution in Art. 58(b) of The Netherlands' Social Security Law. Without such a discussion it cannot be decided whether the claim is sufficiently close to the granting of social security payments. The exception from the scope of the Brussels Convention works only for disputes which result directly from the *relationship* between the National Insurance and the subject entitled to social security. Generally, the decision can be accepted as far as claims for *repayment* have to be considered as belonging to the scope of 'social security', as long as their granting belongs there (in the same sense: *Bundessozialgericht*, 26 January 1983 BSGE 54, 250, Kropholler Art. 1 n.36).

The result is not the same, however, if the claim concerns any regulation which entitles the National Security authorities to obtain restitution from other persons (not the person entitled), for example, in the case of tort (Kropholler Art. 1 n.36) or in the case of recourse against somebody who has to maintain, according to family law, the person entitled to social security payments. In such cases, the granting of payments in the social security system is not involved in the proceedings for reimbursement.

As to the nature of Art. 58(b) of the ABW, the prescription deals with the possibility of obtaining reimbursement of the social security payments from the entitled person himself ('Op de betrokkene zelf kunnen worden verhaald . . . b. Kosten van bijstand . . . '). That is the reason that the result of the case was correct: Art. 58(b) deals with a claim against the entitled person and not with recovery from a third person according to regulations of civil law.

ARTICLE 1, PARAGRAPH 2(4)

"Arbitration."

Case principle

Excluded 'arbitration' extends to court proceedings for the appointment of an arbitrator pending in a foreign court.

Case

OLG of Hamburg 21 September 1995 (6 U 178/94) NJW–RR (1996) 510;   **453**
RIW (1996) 862

Facts

The plaintiff, a Panamanian resident company, sued for a declaration of enforceability of an English High Court decision on the costs of an adjournment. In the course of arbitration in England, the plaintiff had brought an action in the High Court for the appointment of the arbitrator, to which the defendant had objected, arguing that she was not bound by the arbitration clause.

Judgment

The decision was enforceable under the German-British Convention of 1960 as the Brussels Convention was excluded by its Art. 1, para. 2(4). Notwithstanding that the decision had been made by a court in a Contracting State rather than by an arbitration tribunal, its purpose was to support an arbitration procedure by appointing an arbitrator.

ARTICLE 2

" . . . domiciled in a Contracting State . . . "

Case principle

1. The Convention is applicable to a maintenance claim, notwithstanding citizenship of a non-Contracting State and divorce in the state of citizenship.

Case

OLG of Hamm 11 July 1988 (10 WF 285/88) IPRax (1989) 107   **454**

Facts

A Moroccan citizen sued her husband, another Moroccan citizen, for maintenance during separation and for child support for the parties' child. Both parties were domiciled in Germany; the child was living with the plaintiff. The defendant objected to German jurisdiction, on the ground that he had divorced his wife by *talaq* according to Muslim law in Morocco. Moroccan courts should have maintenance jurisdiction.

Judgment

The court exercised jurisdiction under Art. 2 of the Convention.

Comment

The decision is correct. According to Art. 2, the courts of the Contracting State where the defendant has his domicile are internationally competent. For the application of this rule the only prerequisite is that a question concerning international jurisdiction is to be answered. On this point, there are some controversies concerning so-called 'pure domestic cases' (see *supra*, Case 445). A further connection of the case with another Contracting State is not necessary (Kropholler before Art. 2, n.7), as the rule does not expressly require such a connection.

Case

455   OLG of Stuttgart 4 October 1988 (17 UF 131/88) IPRax (1990) 93

Facts

The plaintiff, a Japanese citizen, domiciled in Japan, sued her husband, another Japanese citizen, domiciled in Germany for information on his income in preparation for an application for maintenance.

Judgment

The court assumed international jurisdiction according to Art. 2.

Case principle

2.   The Convention held inapplicable if defendant is domiciled in a non-Contracting State.

Case

456   OLG of München 28 September 1989 (24 U 391/87) IPRax (1991) 46; EuZW (1991) 59

Facts

The plaintiff, a German firm, sued the defendant domiciled in Canada, for payment for the delivery of goods (for further questions concerning this case, see *infra*, Art. 17, Case 486).

Judgment

The court held the Convention to be inapplicable, the defendant not being domiciled within the territory of a Contracting State, which, in the opinion of the court, was a general prerequisite for the application of the Convention.

Comment

The court was creating unwritten prerequisites: every rule of the Convention concerning jurisdiction defines its own scope of application. There is no general rule that the Convention was only applicable in cases with one party, or even just the defendant, being domiciled in one of the Contracting States (Kropholler before Art. 2, n.11). However, if restricted to the denial of jurisdiction based on Art. 2 of the Brussels Convention, the decision is correct, since Art. 2 confers jurisdiction only for proceedings against a defendant domiciled in one of the Contracting States.

ARTICLE 5(1)

" . . . *matters relating to a contract* . . . "

Case principle

Article 5(1) is applicable to a claim for damages when a contract was not effectively concluded, through lack of power of representation.

Case

OLG of Saarbrücken 2 October 1991 (5 U 21/91) NJW (1992) 987; RIW **457** (1992) 670; IPRax (1992) 165

Facts

A firm named B.E., domiciled in France, ordered shop equipment from the plaintiff, domiciled in Germany. The equipment was to be delivered and installed in B.E.'s place of business in France. B.E. was represented by the defendant. The owner of B.E. was H.B.E. S.a.r.l., a French stock company, of which the managing director was the defendant. The plaintiff was not informed about these facts during negotiations. The plaintiff sued the defendant as 'apparent owner' of B.E. for payment under the contract. It relied on its general conditions which were printed on the reverse side of the order form signed by the defendant and which contained a choice of German law and an agreement as to the place of performance at the plaintiff's place of business (for further details see *infra*, Art. 17, Case 488).

Judgment

The court applied Art 5 (1). It started from the standpoint that the parties to the action had not become parties to a contract, because the defendant was not the owner of the contracting firm B.E. The contract was to be interpreted as concluded in the name of the owner of business of B.E. In consequence, the plaintiff had not agreed with the defendant about a binding German place of performance. From the circumstances the place of performance in a contract of this kind was the place where the equipment was to be installed—France. Article 5(3) could not be applied, because liability based on apparent ownership did not fall within the scope of that provision.

Comment

The judgment unnecessarily narrows the scope of Art. 5(1). If one agrees with the court as to the fact that the defendant assumed the appearance that it—not H.B.E. S.a.r.l.—was the owner of B.E., the question then arises whether claims based on liability for such appearance, against the apparent party to the contract, are to qualify as 'matters relating to a contract' in the sense of Art. 5(1). This should be affirmed and the meaning of 'contract' should be given a wide interpretation for the purposes of Art. 5(1), so as to provide a possibility to submit all obligations arising from a narrow contractual or quasi-contractual connection with one and the same court (see the European Court of Justice's decision, *Peters* Case 34/82). The decision ignores this aim, denying, on one hand, any contractual obligation in the sense of Art. 5(1), yet, on the other hand, not applying Art. 5(3), the case being concerned with an obligation flowing from a contract in the sense of Art. 5(1) and therefore, according to the autonomous interpretation, not being of a delictual nature. Consequently, the obligation in question should be subsumed under Art. 5(1), whereas the court denied both Art. 5(1) and (3).

It remains necessary to decide on the place of performance. That is the other area where the judgment is unsatisfactory. On one hand, it denied the contractual nature of the obligation, yet on the other hand, it argued that the relevant place of performance was that of the contractual obligation to install the equipment. Therefore the correct question was whether somebody, responsible for any apparent negotiation, is bound by an *agreement* on place of performance, which he himself agreed to, acting for a firm but appearing as its owner. Again the answer should be affirmative: the defendant is bound by such an agreement concerning the place of performance for the contractual obligation, the agreement is valid in other aspects and the defendant is responsible for these obligations as apparent owner (see *Rauscher* IPRax (1992) 143 at 147).

> " . . . *place of performance* . . . "

Case principle

1.   Place of performance is for applicable national law (*Tessili* Case 12/76 applied).

Case

BGH 31 January 1991 (III ZR 150/88) WM (1991) 1009; ZZP 104 (1991)   **458**
449; WuB VII B 1, 1.91

Facts

The plaintiff, a German lawyer, sued a husband and wife, both French citizens domiciled in France, for the payment of lawyer's fees which the parties had agreed to pay in Germany for their defence in a criminal action brought against the husband in a German court.

Judgment

The Bundesgerichtshof exercised jurisdiction under Art. 5(1). The court ruled that place of performance had to be determined according to the *Tessili* decision of European Court of Justice (Case 12/76). The obligation in question was the obligation to pay the lawyer's fees which was to be considered according to German law made applicable by German private international law. In German law, the place of performance for obligations resulting from an agreement to take over the legal representation of accused is determined at the place of the lawyer's office, according to s.269 Civil Code (BGB).

Comment

The Bundesgerichtshof confirmed the general rules laid down by the European Court in the *Tessili* case. The judgment is correct. The lawyer and his client are bound by the terms of a contract (of service). The determination of law applicable corresponds to Art. 4 of the Rome Convention. But the facts of the case give reason to modify the general rule, as the European Court began to do in *Ivenel* Case 133/81 and continued in *Humbert* Case 32/88. It would have been desirable if the court had determined the place of performance by an autonomous interpretation of the Convention, making possible a uniform interpretation in all Contracting States (see recently *Thode* WuB VII B 1 Art. 5 EuGVÜ-7.91, 937). The European Court in *Shenavai* Case 166/85 refused to extend the *Ivenel* exception for employees to independent working professional men, but the case here once again shows that the determination of the place of performance according to national law is inadequate. In German law it is controversial whether the place of performance for obligations to pay remuneration to professional men is the place of the office. There are objections that this way of ruling leads to a *forum actoris*, inconvenient under the Convention (Schack, *Der Erfüllungsort im deutschen, ausländischen und internationalen Privat- und Zivilprozeßrecht*, (1985) n.79, fn 228). Whether to accept or to deny such forum is a question of interpretation of the Brussels Convention itself, which should be solved in a uniform—that is autonomous— way. In the concrete case, such a forum seems to be convenient, since the office of the lawyer is the place where all characteristic activities of the lawyer are concentrated. But this forum should not be determined—by chance—in application of any national law, but by means of a uniform interpretation of the Convention in all Contracting States (see *Roth* ZZP 104 (1991) 462).

For further information see *infra* BGH 11 February 1988 (I ZR 201/86), Case 468, Art. 5(3).

Case principle

2.   The place of performance is determined according to ULIS, as part of German law.

Case

459   BGH 13 May 1992 (VIII ZR 154/91) NJW (1992) 2428

Facts

The defendant, domiciled in the Netherlands, sold filters for vacuum cleaners in the Netherlands and—through a subsidiary company—in France. The plaintiff, domiciled in Germany, produced these filters. The parties had business relationships since 1969. The plaintiff firm's general conditions ruled that for contracts with foreign customers private international law should be applied in addition to the agreements. According to a rewriting of the general conditions in 1982, German law was to be applicable. The defendant asked the plaintiff for an explanation of these changes in the general conditions, to which the plaintiff gave no reply.

The general conditions further contained the following rules:

'(1)   The place of performance for delivery, performance and payment is H (official residence of the plaintiff).

(2)   A forum may be created—besides H—in the official residence of the principal, too, if we decide in this sense.'

After the proceedings in the German court, which ended with a compromise, a further dispute arose between the parties. The plaintiff brought an action at Landgericht of H for payment of accounts, damages, etc.

Judgment

The Bundesgerichtshof founded jurisdiction of the German courts on Art. 5(1) following the *Tessili* decision of the European Court Case 12/76. It determined the place of performance according to German law, applicable to the contract. The court explained that the uniform law on sales (*i.e.* the German transformation of the 1964 Hague Convention on Sales—ULIS) was applicable as a part of German law, because the contracts had been concluded before 1 January 1991, the date when the membership of the Federal Republic in ULIS was terminated. The determination of the law applicable led—if the plaintiff's general conditions did not contain a clear denial—to the application of ULIS. The mere election of German law gave no evidence to the contrary, because ULIS was part of German law.

Article 59(1) of the ULIS provided that the obligations which gave rise to the cause of action had to be performed at the place of the *seller's* residence (*i.e.* the plaintiff's). Article 59(1) 2 did not apply in the absence of an agreement to pay the price against the handing over of the goods.

Comment

See too *infra*, Case 460.

Case

BGH 26 March 1992 (VII ZR 258/91) EuZW (1992) 514   **460**

Facts

The plaintiff, a limited company of Bielefeld (Germany), sued for remuneration under a contract for sale of manufactured goods. The defendant was a limited company domiciled in London. The contract in dispute was the first one between the parties and was made verbally after negotiations in English. The plaintiff confirmed the contract in writing in English. The letter contained the formula 'subject to our terms of sale . . . '. The plaintiff's general conditions which were enclosed—in a German version—said in s.8:

> 'Place of performance and jurisdiction for any disputes arising from this contract between the parties is Bielefeld, as far as the buyer is a merchant (*Vollkaufmann*)'.

Judgment

The Bundesgerichtshof referred the following questions concerning Art. 5(1) to the European Court of Justice (for those concerning Art. 17 see *infra*, Case 499):

'(1a)   Does the rule that the place of performance mentioned in Art. 5(1) must be determined according to the national law which applies to the obligation in question according to the private international law of the deciding court, apply to a manufacturer's action against the buyer for payment of remuneration arising from a contract to manufacture and sell goods? Does it apply if this contract, in accordance with the private international law of the court, is governed by a uniform sales law which determines, as the place of performance of the obligation, the official residence of the plaintiff seller?

(1b)   In the event that the Court of Justice gives a negative answer to question no. 1a: in which way should the place of performance in Art. 5(1) be determined in such a case?'

The Bundesgerichtshof argued that German law was applicable, including the uniform law of sales (1964 Hague Convention on Sales—ULIS—see *supra*, Case 459). According to the *Tessili* decision of the European Court of Justice (Case 12/76), in application of Art. 59(1) 1 half-sentence no 1, the courts of the plaintiff's residence had jurisdiction. With regard to the controversy on this point in Germany, the Bundesgerichtshof raised the question whether such *forum actoris* did not inappropriately benefit the plaintiff? The Bundesgerichtshof suggested an exception to the *Tessili* rule, if the law applicable according to private international law of the court was not a national one but any uniform sales law. The same problem would be posed under the 1980 United Nations Convention on Uniform Law for International Sales, in force in the Federal Republic on 1 January 1991.

Comment

In older judgments, the Bundesgerichtshof and other German courts (see *supra*, Case 459 and references in the comment) have assumed the position that Art. 59(1) of the EKG (ULIS) governed the determination of the place of performance in similar cases. The discussion on this point which led the Bundesgerichtshof to refer this problem to the European Court of Justice, has several aspects: first of all there is the question whether the place of performance in application of Art. 5(1) should be determined applying any national law at all. The European Court unfortunately decided in the *Tessili* Case 12/76 against an autonomous interpretation and never moved from this position essentially (see *supra*, Case 458). The wide demand to apply the principles of an autonomous interpretation of the 'place of performance' if the case falls into the scope of any uniform law of sales is based on the argument that both ULIS and CISG (Art. 57(1)(a)) determine the seller's place of business to be the place of performance for the obligation to pay. This obligation might be disadvantageous to essential procedural interests of the buyer. This view, now followed by the Bundesgerichtshof, is a first step towards abandoning the *Tessili* rule.

This way of solving the problem is essentially more satisfactory than another approach that has recently been suggested. The rules concerning the place of performance in national contract law cannot be reformed with regard to procedural interests of the party (in this sense *Rennpferdt, Die internationale*

Harmonisierung des Erfüllungsrechts für Geldschulden (1993) 167 s). When determining the place of performance in contract law, material interests of the parties are to be taken into consideration, which might lead to other solutions than procedural interests would.

On the other hand, there is no convincing reason to restrict the Bundesgerichtshof's idea to cases within the scope of uniform sales laws. A *forum actoris* is acceptable or unacceptable regardless of whether it results from the application of uniform sales laws or from the application of any national contract law applicable according to the *Tessili* rule. Therefore, the most convincing solution can only be to give up the *Tessili* rule and to accept a system of autonomous interpretation of the place of performance for purposes of Art. 5(1). This solution will give the possibility to link the place of performance and the place of business of the party executing the characteristical obligation of the contract, if there exists a strong connection with this place, as, for example, the European Court of Justice decided for the contract of employment. But this solution should not be restricted solely to this type of contract. Undoubtedly, there are other contracts, for example, the contract of sale as a mere exchange-contract, for which there are good arguments against a *forum actoris* at the place of business of the seller, although, strictly speaking, the seller performs the characteristic obligation.

As things turned out, the European Court of Justice answered question (1a) in the affirmative sense, again declining the options mentioned above (in *Custom Made Commercial Ltd* Case C–288/92).

Case principle

3. The validity of an oral agreement between merchants concerning the place of performance.

Case

BGH 6 March 1995 (II ZR 37/94) RIW (1995) 410; EuZW (1995) 714; NJW **461** (1996) 872

Facts

The plaintiff, a navigation cooperative, sued the defendant, a French company, for damages. The defendant had chartered the plaintiff's vessel for transportation of goods on the River Rhine, the destinations exclusively being in France. The damage in dispute had been caused during unloading.

As to jurisdiction of the German courts, the plaintiff referred to an oral agreement between the parties which determined the plaintiff's domicile (Würzburg, Germany) to be the place of performance as well as the place of jurisdiction for the contractual obligations.

Judgment

With reference to the European Court of Justice's decision in the *Zelger* Case 56/79, the court presented another question to the European Court concerning the validity of an agreement as to the place of performance for purposes of application of Art. 5(1). Agreements like the one in the case in issue are very common in German practice. Merchants, who, in application of national rules of international civil procedure, are free to agree on places of performance and jurisdiction, usually conclude place of performance agreements, which do not actually have an influence on the *material* place of performance. Their only purpose is the creation of a *forum contractus* in the agreed place of performance. The BGH put the question whether such an abstract agreement of place of performance could create a *forum contractus* in application of Art. 5(1) or whether it was invalid as far as the prerequisites of Art. 17 have not been observed?

According to the opinion of the BGH, this question had not been answered by the European Court of Justice in *Zelger* Case 56/79, and the court noted the controversy on this point in German jurisdiction and writings. There was a certain sympathy tending towards a restriction of the validity of such agreements in cases of misuse.

Comment

The problem seems to be a special German one. Unlike the systems in Arts 17 and 5(1) of the Brussels Convention, German national law of civil procedure contains severe restrictions as to agreements concerning jurisdiction, which, in general, are not allowed to be used by parties which are not merchants in the sense of the German Commercial Code. This rule also applies to agreements on the place of performance, whether such agreements really do decide the material place of performance, or are only made to circumvent the severe restrictions concerning jurisdictional agreements. From this point of view, the European Court's decision in *Zelger* against the application of Art. 17's formal restrictions concerning place of performance agreements was astonishing. However, according to the prevailing opinion in Germany, the European Court of Justice's decision gave preference to a clear and simple interpretation of Art. 5(1), consciously undergoing the risk of facilitating mere fictitious agreements with the intention of circumventing the Art. 17 restrictions.

Formally, the question seemed to be open, because the European Court did not pronounce on this point, although the Advocate General, in the former proceeding, had discussed the possibility of misuse. Nevertheless, the creation of an exception would cause a severe impact on the Convention's aim of clear and certain jurisdictional rules. In almost every agreement concerning the place of performance, there may be found some doubt whether it is really a material one.

On the other hand, the case does show that the free, even oral, possibility of place of performance agreements creates a jurisdictional risk, which should not be underestimated. According to the Brussels Convention, such an agreement is valid even if the defendant is not a merchant (which does not, on the other hand, fall within the scope of consumer protection in Art. 13 *et seq.* of the Brussels Convention). A solution to this problem cannot be found by having an exceptional rule, but by implementing the formal prerequisites of Art.

17 in relation to place of performance agreements under Art. 5(1), a solution which has to be discussed on the legislative level, not the judicial.

In the meantime, the European Court of Justice (Case 106/95) answered the question, altering its former position and following the BGH's approach: an agreement concerning the place of performance is not valid under Art. 5(1), if the only purpose of such an agreement is prorogation (see *MSG*, Case C–106/95).

Case principle

4. Breach of lawyer's contractual duties by ignoring the applicability of the Convention.

Case

OLG of Koblenz 9 June 1989 (2 U 1907/87) NJW (1989); IPRax (1991), 116   **462**

Facts

The plaintiff sued the defendant, her lawyer, a German citizen domiciled in Germany, for damages which she had suffered as a result of mistakes the defendant had made during a process against the plaintiff's debtor, a Netherlands firm. The defendant, ignoring the Brussels Convention, on 25 June 1984, had brought an action in the Landgericht of Mainz against the said Dutch firm for payment of goods delivered by the plaintiff. The court informed the lawyer of its doubts over jurisdiction. In consequence, the lawyer withdrew the action on 30 November 1984. During January/February 1985 the Netherlands firm went into liquidation. The plaintiff could not realize her claim in the bankruptcy proceedings.

Judgment

The court held that in 1984, a German lawyer was under an obligation to know that the Brussels Convention was in force. Ignoring the Convention could lead to an obligation from a 'positive breach of contract' (*positive Vertragsverletzung*). Nevertheless, in this case the Landgericht of Mainz had jurisdiction under the Convention: the place of performance had to be determined according to Art. 59(1) EKG (ULIS), in consequence whereof the action had been brought in the competent court and the lawyer had not in fact made a mistake in this respect.

The court left open the position whether the defective withdrawal of the action in late November 1984 would have amounted to a breach of contract. In any event, this breach had not caused any damage, because at this time the plaintiff's claim had no further chance of being realized, owing to the Dutch debtor's insolvency at the beginning of 1985.

Comment

For the application of Art. 59(1) EKG (ULIS) see *supra*, Case 460. The decision is satisfactory as far as an obligation of a German lawyer to have knowledge of the Convention was in dispute. The court applied the standard for knowledge of German laws. Any German lawyer is under an obligation to know German laws, whilst there is no obligation to know foreign law, applicable in a certain case, but only an obligation to obtain information on such law or to seek assistance from a competent foreign lawyer.

To treat the Brussels Convention like German law for these purposes might be doubtful for formal reasons. From a strictly formalistic point of view, the Convention must be treated as an international treaty. That is the reason why one opinion would base the obligation of knowledge on the mere effect of ratification and publishing in the Federal Republic's official gazette (*Bundesgesetzblatt, Tepper* IPRax (1991) 99). It seems more convenient to deduce such obligation from material facts. The Convention was in force—as between the original Contracting States—from 1 February 1973. It had been commented upon in several commentaries to the German Code of Civil Procedure (ZPO). A German lawyer is under an obligation to be completely familiar with important legal publications. With regard to the importance of the Convention and the easy possibility of access to information in standard commentaries, the lawyer undoubtedly was under an obligation of knowledge as part of his obligation to advise his client. (*Tepper* IPRax (1991) 99).

Case principle

5. German courts have jurisdiction over a claim in respect of a labour contract executed in Germany.

Case

463 LAG of München 22 August 1990 (8 SA 766/83) IPRax (1992) 97

Facts

The plaintiff, an Italian citizen, was employed with the defendant, a branch of the Italian Labour Union (ITAL) since 1970. From 1973, he was working in Munich for his employer. On 22 June 1977 the plaintiff brought an action against the validity of his dismissal which the defendant had expressed to be effective from 30 April 1977.

Judgment

The court applied the Convention, arguing that the defendant changed its judicial nature by Law No. 112 of 27 March 1980, formerly being a non-commercial corporation of public law, now to be treated as an artificial person of private law.

Jurisdiction was founded on Art. 5(1). The obligation in question arising from the labour contract was the obligation to work, being the characteristic obligation of the contract, which had to be performed in Munich.

Comment

With regard to the time at which the action was brought, the Convention was to be applied in its original pre-1989 version (Art. 54(1)). The court referred to the *Ivenel* decision (Case 133/81) of the European Court of Justice. Since there were not several claims in question, but only the validity of the dismissal, strictly, it could not be based on that decision. But it is in accordance with the development in *Six Constructions* Case 32/88 towards a forum at the working place for all actions concerning a contract of employment. This development in judicial reasoning has been accepted in Art. 5(1) of the Brussels Convention as amended by the Third Accession Convention of 26 May 1989 (San Sebastian).

Case principle

6.   Place of performance for German manufacturer in Germany.

Case

OLG of Schleswig 4 June 1992 (2 U 78/91) NJW–RR (1993) 314; RIW (1993) **464** 669; IPRax (1993) 95

Facts

A German manufacturer sued the Dutch defendant for remuneration from a contract for dying and ironing clothing articles at the German party's factory in Flensburg, Germany. When the articles were delivered in Flensburg, the remuneration, contrary to their agreement, was not paid.

Judgment

The court determined the place of performance of the concrete obligation in question, according to *Tessili*, by applying the law governing the contract, which was German law according to Art. 28 of the Introductory Law to the BGB (EGBGB), which corresponds to Art. 4(1) of the Rome Convention. Applying s.270 of the BGB the payment had to be performed at the debtor's residence. The mere agreement that the payment had to take place when collecting the goods only produced an obligation to send the money to the creditor at that time and did not change the place of performance.

In the opinion of the court, the place of performance had not been changed by an implied agreement to transmit the remuneration. The court declined to connect the place of performance of the obligation to pay with the place of performance of the obligation to work. In German law, such uniform place of performance is restricted to contracts entirely connected with one place through the immovability of the work (for example, contracts for construction of a building).

Comment

The general position of the court is in accordance with the *Tessili* decision. Concerning the place of performance in German law, the decision reflects the disagreement over whether an agreement to pay cash should be interpreted as an agreement relating to the place of performance. Moreover, the German courts have developed a narrow exception to the rule laid down in German law: the place of performance of the obligation to pay has to be determined separately from the places of performance of other contractual obligations. There are only selected types of contracts for which the obligation to pay has the same place of performance as the characteristic obligation. In determining the place of performance, the decision is not convincing: neither can it be said that an agreement to pay cash on delivery did not change the place of performance for the payment, nor can the mere concession to pay by distance be interpreted as giving up an agreement upon place of performance advantageous to the manufacturer. The decision is not even persuasive from the point of view of the prevailing German judgments dealing with the question whether to connect the place of performance of payment with that of work. German courts assume this position not only for contracts for construction but also for a contract to repair movables (especially cars: see *Vollkommer*, IPRax (1993) 80).

The more general point of criticism is that this case again shows the necessity of an autonomous interpretation of the place of performance, because the application of Art. 5(1) should not depend upon the interpretation of national law, which is highly debated in national courts as well as in the literature. There are many good reasons to make differences between different types of contracts in order to choose the characteristic forum for one type and to avoid the *forum actoris* for other types. There is no good reason against the uniform application of these differentiations, independently of the material law applicable to the contract (for further comments on this point see cases *supra*, and *infra*, Case 466).

Case principle

7.   Agreement in general conditions concerning the place of performance for all contractual duties is valid.

Case

465   OLG of Hamm 28 June 1994 (19 U 179/93) RIW (1994) 877; NJW–RR (1995) 188

Facts

The plaintiff sued the defendant for payment of the price for delivery of textiles which the London domiciled defendant had ordered from the plaintiff through the plaintiff's English commercial representative. The plaintiff had sent a confirmation referring to general conditions for delivery and payment, containing: 's.1. The place of performance for all duties to be performed under this contract is our residence in S'; and 's.2. When the prerequisites for a prorogation according to s.38 of the German Code of Civil Procedure (ZPO), are given, the court having jurisdiction for the seller is agreed to be competent'. Moreover the confirmation contained an endorsement written in English whereby the confirmation was only valid when a copy was signed and returned. Furthermore, following the signatures on the confirmation there was written: 'Competent forum: s.38 of the ZPO (commercial residence of plaintiff)'. The defendant had returned a signed copy. It objected to jurisdiction of the Landgericht of Münster.

Judgment

As far as Art. 5(1) was concerned, the court assumed that the plaintiff's general conditions had become part of the contract, since the defendant had signed a copy of the confirmation. The general conditions had been printed on the reverse side and there was a statement on the front side referring to them.

An agreement fixing the place of performance for all duties under a contract was held to be valid. Incidentally the court explained that if the general conditions would not have become part of the contract, the place of performance for the duty in dispute had to be determined according to Art. 59(1) of the Hague Sales Convention, as at the plaintiff's commercial domicile.

Comment

The decision achieved the correct result, although the reasoning concerning the question whether the general conditions had become a part of the contract was not perfect. This question must be decided differently according to whether either Art. 5(1) or Art. 17 is concerned. With regard to Art. 5(1), implementation of general conditions is governed by the law applicable to the contract, because—unfortunately—the European Court refers to this national law when determining the place of performance. But the court also adopted this solution for purposes of Art. 17 (for further information see *infra*, Case 495, Art. 17).

Case principle

8.   Action for payment from a contract of sale of a medical practice not necessarily at the place where the practice is situated.

Case

OLG of Hamm 28 January 1994 (29 U 147/95), NJW–RR (1995) 187   **466**

Facts

Both the parties were dentists and citizens of The Netherlands, where the defendant was domiciled. The plaintiff sold his medical practice, situated in

Germany, to the defendant. The defendant refused to perform the contract. The action was for performance and for damages.

Judgment

According to the general rule in *Tessili* the court determines the place of performance according to the law applicable under the forum's Conflicts Law—here German law. The general rule in s.269 of the BGB says that the place of performance for obligations in money is at the debtor's residence. The actual agreement saying that the defendant had to pay only against delivery of the practice did not change the place of performance. The court rejected the view that bilateral obligations which have to be fulfilled at the same time as the other have a common place of performance. The court adopted the prevailing opinion that such common place of performance only existed under special circumstances, for example, if the payment had to be made in cash. The court further rejected the theory of the characteristic obligation as place of performance for both the bilateral obligations. The delivery of the medical practice, including taking over of employees' contracts, which *both* took place in Germany, was not so characteristic as also to constitute the place of performance for the other contractual obligations.

Comment

This is a decision in accordance with other German judgments on this point (see *supra*, Case 464). According to the European Court's practice, the decision whether a characteristic obligation can attract places of performance of other obligations is given to the national law applicable by rules of conflict. Therefore, it is correct to answer this question by applying German law; yet, this case again shows the fundamental lack of an autonomous determination of the place of performance as inefficient.

ARTICLE 5(2)

" . . . *maintenance creditor is domiciled* . . . "

Case principle

Continuation of student's domicile according to German law.

Case

467 OLG of Hamm 13 March 1989 (10 WF 76/89) IPRax (1990) 58

Facts

A German student, studying in the UK sued her German father, a UK resident, for maintenance. She herself was domiciled continuously in Germany.

Judgment

The court applied Art. 5(2). If the plaintiff continued to be domiciled in Germany, the courts of her domicile were locally and internationally competent. Whether the plaintiff really had a domicile in Germany was to be determined applying German law according to Art 52, para. 1. The court held that a student usually did not acquire a domicile at her place of study.

Comment

The decision is correct in principle. But from the point of view of German law, it is not generally true what the court held concerning domicile, because a student can acquire a domicile at a place where he/she is studying. Nevertheless, the decision is correct, because in German law a person may have *more than one* domicile/residence. In consequence, acquiring a domicile at the place of studying is not an objection to retention of home domicile in the sense of s.7 of the German Civil Code (BGB). Such secondary residence at the place of study is sufficient to give jurisdiction to the courts there in the sense of Art. 5(2).

ARTICLE 5(3)

" . . . *tort, delict or quasi-delict* . . . "

Case principle

1. German courts have jurisdiction over a claim for unfair competition and trade mark infringement committed in Germany.

Case

BGH 11 February 1988 (I ZR 201/86) IPRax (1989) 98   **468**

Facts

The plaintiff, with a place of business in Berlin, was trading in products for cars and motorcycles. Since 1956, for the purposes of his business, the trade mark 'AGIAV' was registered for bicycles and parts thereof. Since 1967, the plaintiff was the general distributor in Germany of the defendant's business domiciled in Italy and selling, amongst other things, crash helmets and clothing for motorcycles using the sign 'AGV'.

When, in 1975, the defendant started distributing its business products in Germany through a recently founded branch, a dispute arose between the parties and it was contested whether a new contractual agreement had been made by a letter of intent.

The plaintiff, in preparation for a claim for damages, sued for information on the defendant's deliveries to Germany under the sign 'AGV'. He also claimed to be entitled to benefits from the 1967 representation contract. The defendant, using the sign 'AGV', was alleged to have breached the trade marks registered for the plaintiff's business.

Judgment

The Bundesgerichtshof declined international jurisdiction of the German courts as to obligations arising in contract. According to the *Tessili* decision, the court applied German law, applicable to the contract, to determine the place of performance. Section 269 of the BGB prescribed residence of the debtor as place of performance of the obligation of information and payment in question. The court rejected reference to the characteristic obligation of the defendant.

However, the Bundesgerichtshof extended the scope of Art. 5(3) to the defendant's contravention of competition regulations alleged by the plaintiff. Section 16 of the German Law Against Unfair Competition (UWG) and s.24 of German Trade Mark Law (WZG) raised the preliminary question of whether by agreement (1967—contract or letter of intent) the defendant was entitled or not to use the trade mark? This question could also be decided in the tort forum of Art. 5(3). Solving this preliminary question did not necessarily lead to a decision on contractual obligations, which the court had no competence to decide upon.

The Bundesgerichtshof again left undecided (see BGHZ ss.98, 263, 276) whether in the Art. 5(3) forum there could also be jurisdiction over contractual claims based on the same facts because of close connections between these facts. In the German Code of Civil Procedure (s.32 ZPO, which is similar to Art. 5(3) of the Brussels Convention) this jurisdiction is rejected. In any event, this would not create jurisdiction for German courts, because the claims on the contract and the claims for damages from using the mark 'AGV' were based upon different facts.

Comment

The Bundesgerichtshof classifies claims based on unfair trading as delictual in the sense of Art. 5(3) of the Brussels Convention (Kropholler Art. 5 n.36) according to an autonomous qualification in line with the prevailing opinion now confirmed by the European Court of Justice (*Kalfelis* Case 189/87). The Bundesgerichtshof could leave this question unanswered, because the same result follows from applying German law as *lex causae*, which qualifies unfair trading as delictual (s.24 of the UWG).

Another question the Bundesgerichtshof left undecided—jurisdiction over contractual claims connected to tort actions—has been decided in the meantime by the European Court of Justice in *Kalfelis*: Art. 5(3) of the Brussels Convention extends only to claims for damages not arising from a contract in the sense of Art. 5(1). The court, having jurisdiction under Art. 5(3), is not competent to decide non-delictual aspects.

On the other hand, in cases like this, the Art. 5(3) courts remain competent for delictual claims, although there might be conflicting contractual obligations. The European Court of Justice dealt with the situation of tort claims and contract claims in concurrence, which arose from one and the same business relationship to a bank.

The complementary question of whether a court having jurisdiction under Art. 5(1) is competent to decide a tort claim based on the same facts remains unsolved. Interpreting the European Court of Justice's point of view in the *Kalfelis* case, the system of *fora* being appropriate to the matters of fact probably will not allow such a solution, although economy of process would be achieved where a court was competent to decide both aspects (tort *and* contract). Interpreting Art. 5(1) and (3) as a system of fora, of which one excludes the other, means that the only forum to bring all the claims concerning the same case is the general one in Art. 2.

The decision is also to be followed concerning preliminary questions to the tort claim of a contractual nature: the jurisdiction must be based on the nature of the claim in question. Objections against the tort claim, which arise from an agreement, can make the actions of the defendant lawful and exclude the unfair trading claim. But that does not change the *nature* of the tort claim. The decision on such preliminary contractual questions, furthermore, will not be *res iudicata*: courts of the *forum contractus* are not estopped *per rem judicatam* (see *Mansel* IPRax (1989) 86).

Case principle

2.   Article 5(3) is also available for a preliminary injunction against a threatened tort.

Case

BGH, 17 March 1994 (1 ZR 304/91) RIW (1994) 591; RIW (1994) 678 and **469** OLG of Bremen 17 October 1991 (2 U 34/91) RIW (1992) 231

Facts

The German plaintiff and the Italian defendant were in dispute over the trade mark 'B'. The plaintiff sued for breach of trade mark and unfair competition according to s.24 of the German Trademark Law (WZG) and s.16 of the Unfair Competition Law (UWG). The defendant had applied, at the competent Italian authority, for international registration of the trademark 'B' at the international authority in Geneva, which registration should also be valid in Germany. The defendant brought another action at the court of his domicile in Italy against the plaintiff in the present proceeding, concerning the same dispute.

Judgment

The only jurisdictional rule in dispute was Art. 5(3). The OLG held that jurisdiction could be based on this norm for claims from s.16 of the UWG or s.24
of the WZG. The application for registration, which had taken place abroad,
was not a breach of s.16 of the UWG (using a trademark as sign), because registration would take place in Geneva and not via the Geneva authority with
the National Patent Offices. For the same reasons, the domestic publication of
the application for registration was not a breach of s.24 of the WZG and s.16
of the UWG.

Therefore, the claim was only for a preliminary injunction. The court left
undecided whether such an injunction could fall within the scope of Art. 5(3),
if a breach had taken place and the injunction was claimed in order to prevent
continuation. In any event, as far as the OLG was concerned, Art. 5(3) did not
apply to an injunction against a threatened breach, according to the clear
wording of the rule, because there was no tort, delict or quasi-delict which had
'*occurred*': instead of the place where the harmful event *occurred* in this case
the rule would have to be applied to the place where the harmful event was
expected to occur.

The Bundesgerichtshof upheld the decision in so far as OLG of Bremen did
not deal with breaches within the Federal Republic, confirming the opinion
that a violation of trade marks would fall within the scope of Art. 5(3).

On the other hand, contrary to the Oberlandesgericht's view, the
Bundesgerichtshof held that Art. 5(3) *could* create a forum for a preliminary
injunction. Neither the wording nor the intention of Art. 5(3) were contrary
to this interpretation. Therefore, the Bundesgerichtshof referred this question
to the European Court of Justice.

Comment

It does not seem to be convincing to interpret Art. 5(3), as did the OLG, only
according to its wording. As to the purpose of the rule, it seems to be preferable to include claims for an injunction against a threatened tort within Art.
5(3), as far as the law applicable provides for such claim (*Kropholler* Art. 5,
n.37; *Geimer/Schütze* vol l 1, 621). The reasons for creating a *forum delicti* are
of the same importance. Since Art. 5(3) gives jurisdiction to the courts at the
place where the tortious facts occur as well as to the courts of the place where
the damage was suffered, for an injunction one can rely on all places where the
concrete facts exist which are necessary for such an injunction. For claims concerning an offence against trademark or unfair competition regulations, in any
event the place of business of the trademark owner is within the range, because
the threatened tort would cause damage to him.

Therefore, the question should be answered in the manner indicated by the
Bundesgerichtshof, namely, that Art. 5(3) is applicable to a preliminary
injunction and gives jurisdiction to the court of the place where the tort is
expected to be committed.

Case principle

3. No jurisdiction under Art. 5(3) if a claim for damages is connected with a contract between the parties.

Case

OLG of München 8 March 1989 (15 U 5989/88) RIW (1989) 901; WM **470** (1989) 602; ZZP 103 [103] (1990) 91; WuB VII B 1 Art. 17 EuGVÜ 1,89

Facts

The plaintiff sued the defendant, a subsidiary company of German X bank, domiciled in Luxembourg, for damage to property, and embezzlement of shares. The plaintiff, in accordance with an agreement to pledge, dated 1–13 August 1984, had placed all his negotiable papers on deposit at the defendant's office as security for all the plaintiff's obligations towards the defendant arising from their business relationship. The agreement contained the clause: 'competent forum is Luxembourg'. In December 1984, the plaintiff handed over 9567 shares of X bank to X bank to be sent to the defendant to be kept there in its deposit. The defendant left the shares to be kept by its parent company in Munich, which placed them on deposit with Y, an independent depositor of negotiable papers. Some days later, the plaintiff signed an approval on a copy of the defendant's general conditions, which said in No. 26, Part 1: 'The office of the bank is the place of performance for both parties. For all actions arising from this business connection between the customer and the bank, the bank can only be sued in the forum of the place of performance'.

The plaintiff claimed that the defendant, contrary to its unambiguously declared intention, had, through its parent company, withdrawn shares from its deposit and handed them over to third persons which had acquired ownership in good faith. It therefore claimed damages.

Judgment

The court declined jurisdiction under Art. 5(3). From *Kalfelis* Case 189/87, the claim for damages could not be brought in the forum if it was connected with a contract in the sense of Art. 5(1). An embezzlement of shares was doubtless possible without an express contract of custody having been concluded. But in the present case the embezzlement had taken place exclusively in the course of performance of such a contract.

Comment

The court was incorrect to refer to the *Kalfelis* decision in this way, which, contrary to the court's interpretation, precisely held that tort claims based on a contract could not be brought under Art. 5(3). The facts of *Kalfelis* related to a breach of an obligation of information and claims for fraud and immoral damage, which was a comparable situation (*Roth*, IPRax (1992) 68). There is no question in the reasoning of that decision as to existence of *forum delicti* and tort claims. The European Court of Justice only denied an *extension* of that forum to accessory contractual claims. No doubt the solution of the Oberlandesgericht of München avoids problems as to litispendence and res *iudicata* that could arise, if in one forum the case can only be decided under *one* of the several grounds of action (see *Geimer* NJW (1989) 3090). But such a solution offends the purpose of the special jurisdictions of the Brussels Convention (*Coester-Waltjen* WuB VII B 1 Art. 17 EuGVÜ 1/89, 1086).

For further information on this case, concerning prorogation, see *infra*, Art. 17, Case 497, decision six.

" . . . harmful event . . . "

Case principle

Breach of duty to conclude a term-contract can also be a harmful event.

Case

471   OLG of Düsseldorf 8 March 1996 (17 U 179/95) IPRax (1997) 118

Facts

The plaintiff sued a London Limited Company (defendant 1), which was engaged in brokerage of term contracts for German customers at foreign stock exchanges. The action was for damages arising from term contracts. Defendant 2, a German resident, was the chairman of defendant 1's board of directors. Several independent German investment firms were engaged in promotional activities of defendant 1's business.

   The contract between the plaintiff and defendant 1 was made by one of the latter. The first defendant challenged the German courts' jurisdiction.

Judgment

According to s.53(2) of the German stock exchange law (*Börsengesetz*), the ability of a person who is not a merchant to perform term contracts depends upon provision of detailed information concerning the risks of such kind of investment. A broker, bank or investment firm contracting with somebody without providing such information can be liable for damages under German tort law (s.826 of the Civil Code (BGB)). Starting from these principles, the OLG of Düsseldorf assumed jurisdiction under Art. 5(3). The place where the harmful event occurred was situated in Germany, because defendant 2's activities, as well as the promotional activities of the investment firm promoting the contract, occurred in Germany and the damage to the plaintiff occurred in Germany as well.

Moreover, the court assumed jurisdiction under Art. 5(5), arguing that the investment firms were an agency of defendant 1. The mere fact of legal independence of this 'agency' did not prevent the application of Art. 5(5). The court explained that usually the activities of such investment firms in Germany, acting for English brokers, were not restricted to the mere making of the contract, but included activities to prevent the customer from withdrawing his initial profits and to motivate him to continue the investments despite severe losses.

Comment

As far as Art. 5(3) is in question, it seems to be doubtful whether an action for damages from a contract can be brought before the *forum delicti*. In German law, such claims for damages can be based on *culpa in contrahendo* as well as on tort. Some authors suggest a restriction of the *forum delicti* to claims arising from breach of duties of care, whereas the breach of a duty to inform the other party to a contract should fall within the scope of Art. 5(1) rather than Art. 5(3) (see Kropholler Art. 5 n.51). Even if this opinion was correct, such a restriction could not prevent the *forum delicti* from deciding the case under tort law (*i.e.* s.826 of the BGB) which the court actually did. The opposite opinion (*Thorn*, IPRax 1997 101) would lead to the result that a victim of a tort was prevented from using the *forum delicti* when the harmful act in addition amounted to a breach of contract.

The decision has been criticized for applying Art. 5(5), thereby exceeding the scope of the terms 'branch' or 'agency' in the European Court of Justice's decisions (*Thorn* IPRax 1997) 98 *et seq.*).

However, although usually an investment firm does promote several brokers, there seems to be a necessity to extend the term 'agency' to such independent firms. For the judicial relationship between the customer and the broker it makes no difference if the agent is acting for one or more masters, as far as he materially acts like an agent.

> " . . . *place where the harmful event occurred.*"

Case principle

Article 5(3) covers claims from fair trade regulations.

Case

OLG of München 17 June 1993 (29 U 6063/92) NJW–RR (1994) 190   **472**

Facts

The plaintiff residing within the jurisdiction of the Landgericht of München II and the defendant residing in Milan (Italy) were competing in the market of producing and distributing 'who's who' type literature concerning persons of public interest within the Federal Republic of Germany. In the past, both parties had claimed the other party's edition to be plagiaristic. Therefore, an employee of the plaintiff made a telephone call from the plaintiff's firm to the defendant with the intention of checking the defendant's behaviour. The employee, speaking in English, introduced herself as a 'Mrs H' from a London publisher. During the conversation concerning the differences between both parties' publications, the plaintiff's employee asked for certain information by fax, giving a London fax number. After having been directly asked, the defendant's employee allegedly answered: 'Ours is called: "who is who in European Institutions, etc." and that's a Sutter's group original publication'. The plaintiff sued the defendant in respect of this last part of the sentence which, according to the plaintiff, was contrary to fair trade regulations.

Judgment

The court held Art. 5(3) to include actions based on fair trade regulations.

On the other hand, the determination of *locus delicti* constituted a restriction upon the general rule whereby both the places where the damaging act was completed and where the damage occurred created a forum at the plaintiff's discretion: Art. 5(3) was only applicable to a place in which the wrongdoer would expect the damage to occur. Since the plaintiff's employee had created circumstances under which the defendant's employee had been persuaded to assume that her calling partner was in London, she had no duty to expect that her statements would reach a person within the jurisdiction of the court.

The court left undecided whether a tort committed in another country (Italy—or putatively—Great Britain) could result in a *forum delicti* with respect to the risk of committing the same tort in Germany. There was no evidence that the plaintiff expected the defendant to repeat her statements in Germany.

Comment

The assumption that claims concerning fair trade regulations fall within the scope of application of Art. 5(3) is in accordance with the prevailing opinion. It is the same when it determines the applicable law. In German private international law there is a restriction on that place when the interests of the competing parties are in conflict.

The restriction created by the court seems convincing. There is no reason to assume a tort to be committed in a place where the wrongdoer actually did not want his statement to arrive and where it arrived only through a 'victim's' malpractice.

The European Court of Justice has confirmed that the plaintiff can elect a *forum delicti* out of several places where the damaging facts occurred (*Fiona Shevill* Case C–68/93). But it denied the existence of a *forum delicti* in a place where merely financial damage to the estate, but not a damaging act, had taken place (*Marinari* Case C–364/93).

Concerning the question whether a preliminary injunction can be decided in the Art. 5(3) forum—left undecided in this case—see *supra*, Case 469.

ARTICLE 5(5)

" . . . *branch, agency or other establishment* . . . "

Case principle

1. Article 5(5) is applicable to legally independent companies trading like a defendant's branch.

Case

OLG of Düsseldorf 26 May 1995 (17 U 240/95) WM (1995) 1349   **473**

Facts

Defendant No. 1 was a London domiciled broker company trading in term contracts and options. Defendant No. 2, domiciled in Germany, negotiated defendant No. 1's contracts. The plaintiff, a medical doctor domiciled in Germany, made an agreement with defendant No. 1 by negotiation with defendant No. 2 and sued the defendants for damages caused by the loss of almost his entire funds given to defendant No. 1 under the contract. The contract contained a choice of English law and an arbitration agreement to non-domestic arbitration to be nominated by the London Court of International Arbitration.

Judgment

The court exercised jurisdiction under Art. 5(5) for the action against defendant No. 1. Article 5(5) was not only applicable to dependent agencies, but also to judicially independent companies which in fact were trading like a defendant's branch for the Contracting State where the action was brought.

The arbitration clause and the election of English law were not valid, as being contrary to German public policy including the rules of ss.53, 58, 61 of the Börsengesetz (Stock Exchange Law), protecting German customers undergoing term contracts.

Comment

The decision is in accordance with the prevailing opinion in Germany as far as the applicable law and the arbitration clause are in dispute. This is not a question entirely connected with the Convention, but has to be answered in applying German law.

As to Art. 5(5) of the Brussels Convention, the decision is in accordance with the European Court of Justice's ruling in *Schotte* Case 218/86. The question whether an agency acting on behalf of the defendant in a Contracting State falls within the scope of Art. 5(5) cannot be answered by reference to criteria of legal or structural organization. Neither a formal independence in a legal sense nor independence in fact in the internal organization structure can prevent the application of Art. 5(5), if the independent company is acting like an agent and on behalf of the 'mother' company in their business relationship (see *Kropholler* Art. 5(85)).

See too supra, Case 471.

Case principle

2.   Article 5(5) only applies to permanent branches.

Case

474   LG of Berlin 28 September 1995 (30 O 206/95) IPRax (1996) 416

Facts

The plaintiff sued the defendant, an Italian corporation (S.A.), under a contract of construction. The defendant had an independent branch in Munich until May 1995 and a field agency in Berlin.

Judgment

Berlin courts had no jurisdiction under Art. 5(5) as this rule only applied to *permanent* branches or agencies contracting independently of the main branch. An agency which had been installed temporarily for the purpose of a specific construction project in Berlin was not sufficient to give jurisdiction to Berlin courts for an action against the main branch, particularly as most of the negotiations had been carried out by the defendant's Munich branch.

Comment

See *Rüßmann* IPRax (1996) 402.

ARTICLE 6(3)

" . . . *may also be sued . . . On a counter-claim* . . . "

Case principle

1. Jurisdiction under Art. 6(3) derogated from by an agreement under Art. 17.

Case

OLG of Koblenz 17 September 1993 (2 U 1230/91) RIW 1993 934   **475**

Facts

The defendant was the exclusive sales agent of the French plaintiff in Germany. The contract contained a term that actions arising from this contract had to be brought at the domicile of the respective defendant. The plaintiff sued for the balance of its accounts. The defendant brought a counterclaim concerning damages for breach of the exclusive sales rights.

Judgment

The court held that jurisdiction under Art. 6(3) was derogated from by an agreement under Art. 17, just as jurisdiction could be based on Art. 18 on a defendant's appearance without contesting jurisdiction for the counterclaim.

Comment

The decision is correct (and the conflicting finding in Case 476 *infra*, incorrect). Jurisdiction over a counterclaim is not named as one of the express and exclusive exceptions in Art. 17, para. 4. Therefore, it can be derogated from, according to Art. 17(1) (*Kropholler* Art. 17, n.93). On the other hand, Art. 18 is applicable in place of exclusive jurisdiction based on agreement. The exception in Art. 18 applies only to exclusive jurisdiction under Art. 16 (*Elefanten Schuh* Case 150/80).

Case principle

2. Article 6(3) held to prevail over inconsistent Art. 17 jurisdiction agreement.

Case

LG of Berlin 19 March 1996 (102 O 261/95) RIW (1996) 960   **476**

Facts

The plaintiff, domiciled in Italy sued the defendant for payment under a contract of sale which had been made under the plaintiff's general conditions of sales contracts including a prorogation to the courts of Treviso (Italy) and a right of choice for the seller to sue the buyer at the buyer's place of business as well.

The defendant counterclaimed for compensation and damages from a contract of commercial agency.

Judgment

The defendant's compensation claim in the German court was not prevented by the prorogation of Italian courts in the plaintiff's general conditions. Referring to the European Court of Justice's decision in the *Meeth* Case 23/78, the court held that this clause was not to be interpreted so as to prevent a counterclaim in another court even though the prorogation was only in favour of one party to the contract.

The court applied Art. 6(3) and in fact denied jurisdiction thereunder to decide the validity of the compensation claim in so far as this did not arise from the same contract.

Comment

See comment to Case 477 *infra*.

Editor's Comment

The correctness of this decision of the Berlin District Court must be open to question—see *supra*, Case 475.

" . . . *counter-claim* . . . "

Case principle

A court having jurisdiction under Art. 2 can only decide on obligations in 'set-off' if competent for an action concerning such obligations.

Case

477 BGH 12 May 1993 (VII ZR 110/92) NJW (1993) 2753; RIW (1993) 846; EuZW (1993) 577; EWiR (1993) 877

Facts

The plaintiff, an Italian company, domiciled in Italy, sued the defendant, a Munich merchant, for payment under a contract of sale. The obligation was not in dispute. But the defendant had claimed to set-off several claims of R, the plaintiff's former agent in Germany, which had assigned them to the defendant up to an amount equivalent to the claim in question (see the OLG of München 25 March 1992 7 U 6176/91/91; RIW (1992) 672, Court of Appeal in the same case).

Judgment

The Bundesgerichtshof exercised international jurisdiction over the claim in the action under Art. 2 of the Brussels Convention. The court explained that the obligation in the set-off could only be decided if the German courts would have had jurisdiction to decide on this obligation when pleaded in an action. The Bundesgerichtshof relied on s.322(2) of the German Code of Civil Procedure (ZPO) whereupon the decision concerning an obligation in set-off can be *res iudicata*. Such jurisdiction was given if German courts had jurisdiction over the obligation in the set-off. The Bundesgerichtshof denied jurisdiction under Art. 5(1).

The Bundesgerichtshof left undecided whether Art. 6(3) could be applied to set-off by analogy. The facts did not support it, because the cause of action and the claim in set-off were based on different contracts and facts. To what extent a court, not having jurisdiction for certain claims, was nevertheless competent to decide on a set-off, was not clear from the European Court of Justice's decisions in *Meeth* Case 23/78, *Spitzley* Case 48/84 and *ABS Autoteile Service* Case 220/84. Here, the question arose whether the German courts, having jurisdiction for the claim in the action, could have heard *counterclaims*. The Bundesgerichtshof thought not, according to general principles of the Brussels Convention. If the counterclaim was not allowed, *a fortiori* the set-off should not be. This result, the court said, was so obvious that the case was not to be brought to the European Court of Justice.

Comment

The Bundesgerichtshof's *a fortiori* conclusion is not convincing (in contrary sense: *Otte* EWiR (1993) 877): set-off is a defence, counterclaim is an independent procedural attack irrespective of whether the obligation and set-off is contested or not (in the contrary sense: *op. cit.*). The defendant must be given more freedom for defences, whereas jurisdiction for a counterclaim is restricted to situations of connexity to the cause of action.

The problem must be seen in the context of set-off of claims for which another forum has been prorogated. This question has been decided by the European Court (*Meeth* Case 23/78, *Spitzley* Case 48/84). For those claims, the European Court does not assume the set-off to be excluded, but orders this question to be decided on interpretation of the prorogation agreement. For this interpretation, the Bundesgerichtshof (NJW (1979) 2477), in application of national German law of civil procedure, has established a presumption that the prorogation would lead to an exclusion of set-off, if the counterclaim was contested. This opinion cannot be followed (in the contrary sense: in *Kropholler* Art. 27, n.95). Decisive on this point is the idea of *equity of arms*: the defendant, drawn into the process, must be entitled to raise any appropriate defence. Although set-off is subject to different regulations in the national laws of civil procedure, it should be given an autonomous interpretation for purposes of the Brussels Convention (*MunchKomm* [ZPO]. *Gottwald* Art. 17 EuGVÜ (58)).

For the case in question the aspect of *equity in arms* is also decisive: the plaintiff generally is at risk of being sued for the claim in set-off only in a forum supplied by the Brussels Convention. But when *he* brings an action against the creditor concerning another obligation, this protection is reduced, because he must suffer the burden of pursuing process (including the burden of defending against a set-off) in a forum which he has freely elected (in the same sense: *Wolf* note to BGH *op.cit.* LM EGÜbk 39(4). Moreover, this solution will promote procedural economy, which the European Court of Justice has always affirmed to be a main purpose of Brussels Convention (see *Wolf op.cit.*).

German courts have never seen this problem differently, as far as local jurisdiction is concerned. The Bundesgerichtshof's opinion is based on the different attitude of the German International Law of Civil Procedure, whereby the plaintiff submits only to German jurisdiction for set-offs with connected counterclaims (see *Geimer* IPRax (1986) 208. *MünchKomm* [ZPO]–*Peters* s.145, n.37: this opinion has been contested in German law, too—in different sense: *Stein/Jonas/Leipold* ZPO 145(39)). But this aspect cannot be decisive for the Brussels Convention member states, because the Brussels Convention is a uniform system of jurisdiction applicable in all member states.

Finally, *litispendence* and *res iudicata* as to the claim in set-off do not prevent this solution: in the German Law of Civil Procedure, set-off does not have the effect of *litispendence* and the claim can be brought in another forum. This is a further argument against a jurisdictional test for set-off. As far as the set-off leads to *res iudicata* (in German law according to s.322(2) of the ZPO as far as set-off was pleaded), recognition of such judgment can give rise to a conflict under Art. 27(3), if the claim in set-off was brought to the courts of the second State and was decided in a different way. In this case, Art. 21 would not prevent the second court deciding on this claim, because set-off does not lead to *litispendence* as a cause of action does in the sense of Art. 21. This conflict can be solved when enforcement is sought and the decision concerning set-off has no enforceable content, because set-off is only brought as a defence. As far as the main claim was denied as a consequence of set-off, there is no enforceable content either. If the claim was decided in the same way, recognition of the first decision must be an impediment to the enforcement of the second as far as the claim was made by way of set-off.

Consequently, set-off unconnected with the claim in the action is only prevented by an express agreement excluding the set-off or by a prohibition of set-off or compensation in the law applicable according to private international law of the forum; whereas, a set-off as a mere instrument of defence against an action does not depend on the jurisdictional prerequisites of Art. 6(3) (in the same sense, see *Danvaern AS* Case C–342/93).

Finally, the case in question excludes denial of set-off as being contrary to good faith because the situation enabling the defendant to plead a set-off had been brought about by the assignment (*Wolf op. cit.*).

ARTICLE 13, PARAGRAPH 1

" . . . "the consumer" . . . "

Case principle

Article 13 does not protect a consumer who is not personally party to the action.

Case

BGH 20 April 1993 (XII ZR 17/90) NJW (1993) 2687; RIW (1993) 670;   **478**
EuZW (1993) 517; ZIP (1993) 1000; IPRax (1995) 98

Facts

As to the facts, see the European Court's judgment in *Shearson Lehmann Hutton Inc* Case C-189/91.

Judgment

The present case is the final decision following *Shearson Lehmann Hutton Inc* Case C-89/91. The Bundesgerichtshof held against international jurisdiction over the defendant, a broker, domiciled in New York, based on s.23 sentence 1 of the German Code of Civil Procedure (ZPO). Jurisdiction could not be based on Art. 13 of the Brussels Convention, because, in accordance with the binding interpretation of the European Court of Justice, this rule only protected the consumer if he *personally* was the plaintiff or the defendant.

Comment

Concerning Art. 13, the decision does not go beyond the reasoning of the European Court's decision.

It is in dispute whether, in a case like this, besides Art. 13, which does not apply in the case, the jurisdictional rules of the German Code of Civil Procedure do apply. Generally, according to Art. 4, international jurisdiction over a defendant not domiciled in a Contracting State shall be determined by national law. Article 3 of the Brussels Convention does not exclude s.23 of the ZPO in this situation. Article 13 is applicable only if the defendant is domiciled in a Contracting State. If the defendant has a branch, agency or an establishment in a Contracting State (in this case: Germany), then Article 13, para. 2 prescribes the application of the consumer jurisdiction rules. According to the prevailing opinion, this excludes the application of Art. 4, *i.e.* national law concerning jurisdiction is excluded (*Kropholler* Art. 14, n.12, Art. 8, n.5. See also *Thode* WUB VII B 1 Art. 13 EuGVÜ 1/91).

The priority of Art. 13 can only exist as far as the material and personal scope of this rule is satisfied. According to the interpretation by the European Court of Justice, where the qualification of a party as a consumer is missing, the case is outside the scope of the rule, as in this case.

Due to such reasoning, the decision is correct on the facts, although wrong as to the principles. Sections 21 and 23 of the ZPO are only considered, if Art. 13 does not apply according to its personal or material scope of application.

> ## ARTICLE 13, PARAGRAPH 2
>
> *" . . . not domiciled in a Contracting State . . . "*

Case principle

1. Investor in a 'term contract' as consumer under Art. 13-contract for the supply of services. Whether precontractual obligations included?

Case

479 BGH 25 May 1993 (XI ŻR 45/91 and XI ZR 59/9) RIW (1993) 671; WM (1993) 1215; ZIP (1993) 993; EuZW (1993) 518; EWiR (1993) 675

Facts

The decision concerned two actions which the Bundesgerichtshof submitted to the European Court of Justice. The plaintiff B was an independent joiner and the plaintiff N an employed textile technician. Both plaintiffs had, beyond their professional activities, charged the defendant, a New York broker, to carry out term contracts on commission. A Frankfurt agency was involved (it was contested, whether this agency should only arrange, or independently conclude, transactions). The plaintiffs sued for repayment of lost investments, based on damages for breach of contractual and precontractual obligations, tort damages for 'charge-chopping by churning' and/or unjust enrichment.

Judgment

The Bundesgerichtshof started from the standpoint that international jurisdiction of German courts could only result from Arts 13 and 14. It considered the investor in a term contract to be a 'consumer' in the sense of Art. 13, para. 1 and presented the following questions to the European Court.

    (1)   Whether Art. 14(1) and (2) of the Brussels Convention depended on the fact that the other party to the contract was in fact domiciled in another Contracting State or it was also sufficient that he was to be treated as being domiciled there according to Art. 13, para. 2?

The Bundesgerichtshof doubted whether the fact that the defendant was domiciled outside the Contracting States excluded applicability of Art. 14 at all or whether the alternative of the jurisdiction of the courts of consumer's domicile was preserved in such circumstances.

    (2)   Did Commission contracts of this type fall within the meaning of 'contract for the supply of services' in the sense of Art. 13, para. 1(3) of the Brussels Convention?

The Bundesgerichtshof tended towards this interpretation, because such contracts, according to German law, were classified as contracts for negotiation (Geschäftsbesorgungsverträge).

(3)   Did the wording 'proceedings concerning a contract' include claims for the breach of precontractual obligations (*culpa in contrahendo*) and for unjust enrichment by the performance of contractual obligations?

The Bundesgerichtshof reasoned that even if Art. 13, para. 1 was to be interpreted in accordance with the autonomous interpretation of the meaning of 'contract' in Art. 5(1), it remained ambiguous whether *culpa in contrahendo* and unjust enrichment fell within this conception.

(4)   Did Art. 13, para. 1 confer ancillary jurisdiction over non-contractual claims?

The Bundesgerichtshof agreed with the opinion widely found in literature, which said that the court had jurisdiction over extra-contractual claims. The Kalfelis decision (Case C–89/87) did not prevent such a funding.

Comment

Question one dealt with a similar problem as in the final decision of the Bundesgerichtshof in *Shearson Lehmann Hutton Inc* Case C–89/91 (for the Bundesgerichtshof's decision, see *supra*, Case 478). In that case, the European Court did not deal with this question (which had been denied by the OLG of München, *infra*, Case 481), because the European Court denied the application of Art. 13 to a company suing on an assigned claim.

The Brussels Convention jurisdiction rules generally do not apply to defendants domiciled outside the Contracting States (Art. 4) as far as there is no special prescription (Art. 16 or 17). According to the wording, the defendant's domicile in a Contracting State is necessary for application of Art. 14 of the Brussels Convention. Article 13, para. 2 provides an additional argument for this interpretation.

But such an understanding is hardly in accordance with the intention of *forum consumptoris* in Art. 14(1): a consumer requires protection even more when the contracting party is domiciled outside the Contracting States. The problems arising when a businessman is doing business from abroad in the Contracting States' territories are solved by Art. 13, para. 2 of the Brussels Convention in a very inadequate way: if one accepts consumer protection as a purpose of the Convention (critical on this point *Geimer* EWiR Art. 14 EuGVÜ 1/93, 676), then it is improper to differentiate between the deciding State and other States. This protection should be based on the aspect of preparing the contract within the territories of the Contracting States, as under Art. 5(2) of the Rome Convention. Article 13, para. 1(3) does not cover the problem at all, because in connection with Art. 4 and Art. 13, para. 2, the protection is only granted against contracting parties or agencies from Member States. It is doubtful whether the protection necessary can be provided by interpretation.

In the event, the European Court decided (*Brenner, Noller/Dean Witter Reynolds* Case C–318/93) not to adopt the idea of the Bundesgerichtshof creating a *forum actoris* for the consumer based on Art. 14, para. 1 of the Brussels Convention. As the contract had not been made by the defendant's Frankfurt agency, and the representative which had made the contract, was not an agent in the meaning of Art. 13, para. 2, there was no jurisdiction of German courts. This result does not seem to be satisfactory, since a broker residing outside the Contracting States should not be protected against European consumer protection regulations, when doing business within Europe. Interpreting the intention of Arts. 13 and 14 of the Brussels Convention in an economic way, it makes no difference whether a company out-of-Europe is doing business within Europe by a dependent agency or giving power of contracting to an independent company.

As the European Court answered the first question in a negative way, the Bundesgerichtshof's further questions remained undecided.

There is also controversy over the classification of term contracts as consumer contracts (in contrary sense see *Schütze* EWiR s.61 BörsG 1/89, 681). The Bundesgerichtshof did not discuss this point. The question whether such contracts are 'for the supply of services' should not be answered according to national laws. In an autonomous interpretation, this conception should be given a wide scope of application (as Art. 5(1) of the Rome Convention) covering all investments, independent of their speculative character (in this sense, OLG of Düsseldorf WM (1989) 50 and WM (1994) 376).

Questions three and four give an opportunity to develop not only Art. 13 forum jurisdiction, but also the *forum contractus* in Art. 5(1). After *forum delicti* (Art. 5(3)) was restricted to delictual claims in the *Kalfelis* case, this question was highly discussed. The best argument for drawing concurring claims from tort and delict into the *forum contractus* is the idea of a uniform forum. That is not convincing. As long as the European Court of Justice insists that it is not necessary to decide contractual obligations from one and the same contract in a unique *forum contractus*, the idea that a contractual relationship attracts any *other* claim is not satisfactory. There always remains the *forum domicilii* in Art. 2 to bring all actions against the defendant. On the other hand, claims of a precontractual nature or unjust enrichment, following a failed performance of contract, should be decided in the contractual fora, either of Art. 5(1) or Art. 13 *et. seq.*

Case principle

2. Section 32 of the Zivilprozessordnung is applicable to action against a New York broker.

Case

480 BGH 22 November 1994 (XI ZR 45/91) IPRax (1995) 316

Facts

The decision in question is the final decision to Case 479 *supra*, following the European Court's *Dean Witter Reynolds* Judgment.

Judgment

The Bundesgerichtshof consequently did not apply Arts 13 and 14 of the Brussels Convention, but applied the German Code of Civil Procedure. Although German rules of international jurisdiction did not contain any consumer-protecting jurisdictions, the court assumed German courts' international jurisdiction from s.32 of the ZPO (German Code of Civil Procedure). As there were not only contractual claims in dispute, but also a tort (the plaintiff claimed that the defendant had done 'churning'), the claim could be decided in the *forum delicti*.

Comment

The decision shows that the narrow interpretation of Arts 13 and 14 given by the European Court of Justice creates the possibility that courts occasionally will find solutions in an equitable manner. It seems to be preferable to achieve a wide interpretation to be applied by all EC courts rather than creating different national solutions which might be based on the so-called 'exorbitant jurisdictions' (Art. 3 of the Brussels Convention).

Case principle

3. Article 13 is not applicable to an action against a New York broker when a German resident company acting for this broker was an independent company.

Case

BGH 24 November 1992 (XI ZR 72/92) not published. OLG of München **481** 21 January 1992 (25 U 2987/91) NJW–RR (1993) 701

Facts

The plaintiff, residing in Germany, had contracted with the defendant, a New York resident broker, on term contracts. The contract had been made on forms provided by a Munich resident, 'Kapitalanlage-GmbH' (a limited company), which had been given these forms by the defendant, but was a formally independent company. The plaintiff relying on Arts 13 para. 2 and 14 para. 1, sued the defendant for repayment of his lost stock.

Judgment

The Oberlandesgericht of München did not assume the Munich GmbH to be a branch of the New York defendant, but a German company having a different personality and management. Although the activities of the Munich GmBH had led to a contract without an immediate contact between the parties, this was not enough to treat it as a branch, because the Munich firm dealt with German investors not only for the defendant but for other companies as well.

Comment

The case seems to be rather similar to Case 479 (*supra*) which was referred to the European Court. From the Bundesgerichtshof's point of view, the decisive point was that in the former case there was the Frankfurt agency of the defendant involved. As the European Court did not rely on this point in the former case, the present case has been decided in accordance with the later European Court decision *a fortiori*.

From our point of view, both cases were not decided correctly according to the intention of Art. 13. Even an independent agency, contracting for several brokers, should be treated as a branch for the purposes of Art. 13, if a broker provides this agency with contractual forms and leaves all the contracting necessities to the responsibility of this agency. This argument also extends to the prerequisites of Art. 13 para. 1(1) and (3)(a): the offer and the promotion arranged by the Munich agency, economically meant that the defendant was 'doing business' in Germany (for further information, see *supra*, Comment to Case 479).

ARTICLE 16(1)(a)

" . . . *have as their object* . . . "

Case principle

1. Article 16(1) does not apply to a consumer protection association's action against a German company renting flats in Spain for abstaining from the use of mandatory general conditions of contract.

Case

482 BGH 12 October 1989 (VII ZR 339/88) NJW (1990) 317; WM (1989) 1936; EuZW (1990) 36; IPRax (1990) 318

Facts

The plaintiff was a consumer protection association which sued the defendant, a limited liability company domiciled in Germany, professionally trading in the lease of flats and houses for holidays, situated in Spain and France, according to s.9 and 13 of the Law concerning General Conditions (AGBG), for abstaining from the use of general conditions, which led to delays in the repayment of security after performance.

Judgment

The BGH exercised international jurisdiction under Convention Art. 2 (as to French situated houses) and under s.14(1) of the AGBG (as to Spain situated houses—Spain being a *non*-Contracting State at the relevant date). In both cases, in the Bundesgerichtshof's opinion, Art. 16(1) was not applicable: the provision was not to be interpreted in a wider sense than was necessary for its purpose. According to the European Court's rulings, Art. 16(1) dealt with the regulation of property and compulsory rules on tenancies. The proceedings according to ss.13 ss AGBG, so called 'consumer-protection-association-action' (*Verbandsklage*), had the purpose of protecting German business against the use of illegal general conditions. This did not touch the purpose of Art. 16(1). Thus, the consumer-protection-association-action could only be brought before the German courts thereunder.

Therefore, the controversial question whether Art. 16(1) would apply to non-Contracting States could be left open. The Bundesgerichtshof declined to refer the question to the European Court, because the interpretation was obvious.

Comment

It was not correct to determine the international jurisdiction of German courts concerning the Spanish situated flats and houses according to s.14 of the AGBG. Article 2 was applicable, because it was not necessary that the case related to another Contracting State. The only criterion is the defendant's domicile (*Nagel* EuZW (1990) 38 *Kropholler* Art. 2 n.15, see *supra*, Art. 2, Cases 445 and 454).

In relation to a non-Contracting State (Spain), Art. 16 does not apply. It would be contrary to its intention, so to create an exclusive jurisdiction of a court situated outside any Contracting State. Article 16 is made to determine the court of a Contracting State, being most proximate to the facts of the case, but not to exclude the jurisdiction of all courts within the Contracting States (*Kropholler* Art. 16 n.8). A different view (*MünchKomm*-[ZPO]/*Gottwald* Art. 16 EuGVÜ n.5 *Grundmann* IPRax (1985) 249 *et. seq.*) is to accept the exclusive jurisdiction of a non-Contracting State as a *reflex* of Art. 16. This opinion can not be followed: the Brussels Convention works like an internal system of jurisdictions, making the Contracting States a closed territory of jurisdictions. Therefore, the Convention only says whether courts of a Contracting State have jurisdiction or not; and it is a principle of any regulation of international jurisdiction to rule only upon the forum's, and not upon foreign jurisdiction. The most decisive question in the case was decided correctly (*Schwerdtner* EWiR Art. 16 EuGVÜ 1/90, 903): the purpose of Art. 16(1) is to grant effective legal protection whenever a lease is in dispute, because there normally exist special rules. Whereas the control of a professional agent's general conditions, not related to a certain contract of lease, does not fall within this intention.

The further question is whether these general conditions may be used in German business (*Nagel* EuZW (1990) 38). Where the flats leased under these general conditions are situated, whether in one or several States, is relevant. If several States are involved, there would not even be *one* court having exclusive jurisdiction (*Lorenz* IPRax (1990) 294). On the other hand, Art. 16(1) would be applicable, if the validity of the general condition included in a single contract of lease was in dispute (*Lorenz* IPRax 1990, 294), provided that the contract itself fell under Art. 16(1) (see *infra*, for commercial lease).

It must be remarked that the Bundesgerichtshof faced this question only because the European Court declined in *Rösler* Case 241/83 to except the lease of flats for holidays, in a restrictive interpretation, from the scope of Art. 16(1) (on this point now, see the exception in Art. 16(1)(b) of the 1989 Accession Convention—Donostia/San Sebastian and Art. 16 Lugano Convention). Subsequently, the European Court exempted the *commercial* lease of flats for holidays not belonging to the lessor from the scope of Art. 16(1) (*Elisabeth Hacker* Case C–280/90, see *infra*, Case 483).

Case

483 BGH 9 July 1992 (VII ZR 7/92) NJW (1992) 1239; RIW (1992) 1025; IPRax (1993) 244

Facts

The defendant, a company domiciled in Düsseldorf (Germany), commercially offered houses and flats for holidays in south and west European countries. The plaintiff was an association for consumer protection. The plaintiff sued the defendant according to s.13 of the German Law of General Conditions (AGBG) to abstain from using several clauses in its general conditions in a catalogue concerning flats in Spain, France, Italy and Portugal.

Judgment

The Bundesgerichtshof confirmed international jurisdiction under Art. 2 and its decision concerning jurisdiction for actions brought by consumer protection associations (see *supra* Case 482). An additional reasoning was based on *Hacker* Case C–280/90, according to which this case does not fall within the scope of Art. 16(1) because the leasor was a commercial travel agent, negotiating other people's flats.

Comment

It again seems to be doubtful whether the Bundesgerichtshof agreed with the reasoning of the Court of Appeal, referring to s.14(1) of the AGBG, as far as flats not situated in a Contracting State were concerned, where there is only Art. 2 to apply (see *supra*, Case 482, *Lindacher* IPRax (1993) 229).

The *Hacker* decision circumvents the problem in most cases, because there is no 'lease' in the sense of Art. 16. The question remains decisive, however, whenever there is a lease of the general condition users' own flats for holidays.

Case principle

2. Article 16(1) does not apply to an action for compensation for use of a flat situated in France.

Case

OLG of Frankfurt/Main 10 June 1992 (19 U 253/89) EuZW (1993) 776   **484**

Facts

The counterclaimant sued the defendant to the counterclaim for compensation for the use of a flat situated in France. In 1978 the counterclaimant had agreed with the defendant on the transfer of property in this flat to the defendant. The agreement later appeared to be invalid as to the form after the defendant to the counterclaim had had possession of the flat for almost nine years.

Judgment

The court asked the European Court whether compensation for possession and use after a failed transfer of property fell within the scope of the application of Art. 16(1)?

The court explained that the compensation in dispute could arise, on the one hand, from the termination of the failed contract and, on the other hand, as a compensation for using another's property ('owner-possessor-relationship', *Eigentümer—Besitzerverhältnis*). An argument to subsume such a claim for compensation under the conception of 'rights *in rem*' was a necessity to determine the value of using the flat at the place of its situation. Such interpretation was doubtful because of the European Court of Justice's tendency towards a restrictive interpretation.

Comment

Article 16(1) only covers actions aiming to determine the extent or the existence of any ownership in immovable property or other rights *in rem* and to protect the owner as to his real rights (*Reichert* Case 115/88). According to Schlosser (para. 162), actions for damages for a breach of real rights cannot be founded on Art. 16(1). A claim for damages is only an indirect consequence of ownership. Its aim is not the realization of ownership but a mere compensation for unjustified use. The argument of proximity of the dispute to the court is valid as much as for contractual or other damages which would also lead to Art. 5(1) and (3). But the exclusiveness of the *real forum* can not only be founded on the proximity to the case. Of greater relevance is the *familiarity* of the court of the *situs* with regulations concerning real property and the necessity to *enforce* such rights at the place of situation. These aspects, however, are not valid for a monetary compensation claim.

In the event, the European Court of Justice (*Lieber* Case C–292/93 of 9 June 1994) clearly affirmed the view expressed here: Art. 16 prevails only for rights *in rem* but not for personal obligations concerning improper use. The OLG of Frankfurt's argument concerning the calculation of the value of using the flat was not enough reason to apply Art. 16(1).

Case principle

3.   Spanish courts have exclusive jurisdiction in time sharing cases related to a holiday club situated in Spain.

Case

485   LG of Darmstadt 23 August 1995 (9 O 62/95) EuZW (1996) 191; IPRax 1996, 87

Facts

The plaintiff, an Isle of Man registered private company limited by shares, managing a holiday club in Spain, sued the defendants for payment under a contract of sale for time-sharing-rights in the said club.

Judgment

German courts had no jurisdiction, as the court applied Art. 16(1)(a): a contract of sale for time-sharing-rights, without an option to acquire property rights, was a type of tenancy. Therefore, Spanish courts had exclusive jurisdiction. The plaintiff's obligation to provide services and the defendants' right freely to sell or to lease the time-sharing-right was not an impediment to interpretation of the contract as a tenancy by nature.

Comment

The decision is concerned with a new and problematic type of contract, as far as EU-consumer protection rules are evaded by choosing the law of the Isle of Man or by incorporating a company there, while doing business in Spain in the manner described.

The decision is correct.

Article 16(1) is applicable if the real property is situated in a Member State, even if the parties or one of them is domiciled in a non-Contracting State. As far as Art. 16(1)(b) does not restrict the exclusiveness of the jurisdiction of the courts where the immovable is situated, Art. 16(1) has to be interpreted in a functional sense. Therefore, a contract granting use of a specific immovable should be interpreted as a contract having as its object a tenancy rather than the property itself.

There may, however, be exceptional time-sharing-contracts, granting special services or membership of an association owning several real properties and giving the right to elect to use one of them each year and therefore not falling within the scope of Article 16 (see *Mankowski* EuZW (1996) 177).

ARTICLE 17, PARAGRAPH 1

" . . . *one or more of whom is domiciled in a Contracting State* . . . "

Case principle

Article 17 not applicable to choice of a Contracting State's courts when the defendant is domiciled in a non-Contracting State.

Case

OLG of München 28 September 1989 (24 U 391/87) EuZW (1991) 59; IPRax   **486**
(1991) 46

Facts

See *supra*, Case 456.

The defendant's orders had been made in writing and, with a few exceptions, in English. The confirmations of the plaintiff contained general selling conditions on the reverse side, according to which exclusive jurisdiction and place of performance was at Neu-Ulm (Germany).

Judgment

The Oberlandesgericht of München declined to apply the Brussels Convention, which was not applicable since the defendant was domiciled in Canada, not a Contracting State. Article 17 would only apply if a party was domiciled in a Contracting State, jurisdiction of the courts of a Contracting State was prorogated and there was a relationship to at least one other Contracting State.

Comment

The decision concerns the basic question of the unwritten prerequisites of the application of the Brussels Convention, and especially that of Art. 17. According to the clear wording and to the intention to make a homogeneous system of jurisdiction, such prerequisites should not have been asserted (concerning the case, see *Geimer* IPRax (1991) 31 and comment to Case 456 *supra*.

" . . . *have agreed* . . . "

Case principles

1. Scope of the jurisdiction agreement initially a matter of contractual construction.
2. Valid prorogation according to Art. 17 extends to claims from trade restriction regulations, notwithstanding restrictions of prorogation agreements in German law.

Case

487 OLG of Stuttgart 9 November 1990 (2 U 16/90) EuZW (1991) 125; IPRax (1992) 86

Facts

The plaintiff, a Germany domiciled company, a subsidiary of a firm domiciled in Bozen (Italy), imported into the Federal Republic sporting cars of the defendant, an Italian manufacturer and distributor of luxury-class sporting cars from 1983. The relationship was based on a contract of distribution dated from 7 October 1983, changed on 1 March 1986, and written in the Italian language, providing 'Modena (Italy) courts have exclusive jurisdiction for any disputes arising from the present contract. Italian law is applicable'. After revision of the contract by the defendant, the plaintiff sued for damages under s.26(2), 35 of the German Code against Trade Restrictions (*Gesetz gegen Wettbewerbsbeschränkungen*-GWB). It claimed that its business was harmed by the defendant not granting an appropriate time to organize its dealings with regard to valuable investments and its distribution of the defendant's sporting cars. The defendant earlier had brought a declaratory (non-liability) action in Italy. The plaintiff itself had brought a counterclaim in Italy in the event of dismissal of its own claim in Germany.

Judgment

The court held that the German courts lacked international jurisdiction by reason of Art. 17.

The form of Art. 17(1) was not in dispute. As in the situation of concurring delictual claims, it was a matter of interpretation whether the prorogation extended to claims based on s.26(2), 35 GWB. The wording of the clause was to be interpreted objectively. Therefore, it not only extended to disputes resulting from the execution of the contract, but to all disputes arising in any connection with the contract between the parties. The choice of Italian law was evidence that delictual claims and claims resulting from laws against restrictions on competition were to be decided exclusively according to Italian law by Italian courts.

Article 17(1) prevailed over restrictions against a derogation according to national German law: no doubt the prorogation of foreign courts was excluded according to s.98(2), 1 of the GWB for matters underlying this code; and such matters were to be decided exclusively according to German law. But Art. 17(1) was an exhaustive regulation which did not allow the application of any such national restriction.

Comment

The court could leave undecided whether Art. 21 of the Brussels Convention was to be applied, dismissing the action for valid derogation according to Art. 17(1). There is no ranking in application of Arts 17 and 21.

The interpretation of the prorogation's scope is correct: if the parties to a contract agree to such an exhaustive prorogation, this prorogation must be interpreted in the sense that it also extends to the delictual claims.

It is also agreed that Art. 17(1) prevails over national restrictions on prorogation. As far as it is applicable for several situations (Arts 12, 17(3) and Art. 17(5)), the fact that the Convention follows its own policy of derogation restrictions is a good argument for its prevalence against restrictions in national laws, especially if such restrictions extend to situations for which the Brussels Convention does not contain any respective restriction (*Zöller/ Geimer* Art. 17, n.2; Schlosser in: *Essays in honour of Steindorff*, 1389 *Roth* IPRax (1992) 68).

In any event, it must be remembered that not only will such national restriction on derogation be inapplicable, but also a mandatory German law against competition restrictions will not be applied by the Italian courts, whereas it would have been applied by German courts having jurisdiction under Art. 5(3). But that is a logical consequence of any derogation, which could only be prevented by the Convention itself extending the above-named derogation restrictions to the advantage of the economically 'weaker' party, to law of competition.

Case principle

3.   Application of national German law rather than Art. 17 to the substantive existence and validity of the agreement upon jurisdiction.

Case

OLG of Saarbrücken 2 October 1991 (U 21/91) NJW (1992) 987; RIW (1992)   **488**
670; IPRax (1992) 165

Facts

See supra, Art. 5(1), Case 457.

The plaintiff's general conditions were printed on the reverse side of the order form signed by the defendant. They contained a provision whereby the courts of the plaintiff's domicile had jurisdiction, if the buyer was domiciled abroad.

Judgment

The court left undecided whether the formal requirements of Art. 17(1) were satisfied, because the material prerequisites of an agreement were for the national law applicable under the court's private international law, and, applying German law, the prorogation had *not* been agreed with the defendant. The agreement was only valid against the owner of B.E.'s business in France. Any responsibility from apparent ownership according to German law did not put the defendant in the position of a party to the contract.

Comment

The decision is incorrect in determining the law applicable to the agreement. Whether an agreement has been made or not and towards whom it extends must be decided in application of Art. 17 of the Convention in an autonomous interpretation according to the European Court of Justice's principles (*Rauscher* IPRax (1992) 145, with references).

Thus, in the present case only the form of evidence in writing (second alternative) could be fulfilled. As in the case of an agreement in writing (*Colzani* Case 24/76), written evidence exists if the prorogation clause has been printed on the reverse side of writing, signed by one party and containing an express reference to the general conditions. The intention of Art. 17 to ensure the agreement is—at least—preserved, if, in the case of written evidence, one contracting party has signed the other's order form containing the reference and the prorogation on the reverse side, since in this situation the party signing the document was able to have knowledge of the clause through exercising reasonable diligence. The decision does not explain whether such reference had been made. The effect of the prorogation toward third persons must also be decided by an autonomous interpretation of the Convention (*Gerling,* Case 201/82). Such an effect towards the defendant should be assumed in the present case: the court held that according to the applicable German law of contract, responsibility according to the theory of apparent ownership was possible. Therefore, the intention of Art. 17 would lead to jurisdiction of the prorogated forum. The form of Art. 17 is fulfilled in relation to the defendant, since it itself signed the document containing the prorogation in accordance with Art. 17(1).

> " . . . *in connection with a particular legal relationship* . . . "

Case principle

Prorogation included in the constitution of a company does not extend to *non-corporate* obligations of shareholder.

Case

489 BGH 11 October 1993 (II ZR 155/92) NJW (1994) 51

Facts

The case was referred to the European Court of Justice by the Oberlandesgericht of Koblenz *(Powell Duffryn* Case C–214/89). The Oberlandesgericht of Koblenz (31 July 1992 6 U 1946/87; WM (1992) 1736; RIW (1993) 141; EWiR (1992) 989; ZIP (1992) 1234; WuB VII B Art. 17

EuGVÜ 1.93; EWiR Art. 17 EuGVÜ 2/92, 990) which ruled that the clause contained in the company's constitution ('s.4: by signing or acquiring shares or scripts the shareholder accepts the ordinary forum of the company for all disputes with the company or its executives') was generally valid as to form according to the European Court of Justice's case law. But the OLG of Koblenz held the clausula not to be *particular enough*, because it extended to any dispute between shareholders and company, not only arising from the membership but also from any other legal relationship.

Judgment

The BGH did not accept this view that, as a matter of construction, the pro rogation clause was limited to corporate disputes. The wording, which was not restricted to disputes arising from membership, did not convincingly lead to the interpretation adopted by the Oberlandesgericht of Koblenz, even though since the prorogation only became operative on signing the contract or acquiring shares, it made more probable an interpretation that only disputes arising from membership were included in this prorogation.

Comment

The decision is generally acceptable. The Oberlandesgericht of Koblenz had interpreted the clausula—as prescribed by the European Court of Justice—but had only taken into consideration the wording and not a teleological construction. Systematically, the clausula, as a part of the constitution should be restricted to membership disputes under company law.

As to Art. 17(1), the decision of the Oberlandesgericht of Koblenz on the first view is in harmony with the decision of the European Court of Justice. The court had not immediately decided on the formal requirements of the prorogation clausula. The requirement of such a clausula to be restricted to a *particular legal relationship* was fulfilled, in the opinion of the European Court of Justice, whenever such clausula was restricted to all controversies arising from the legal relationship between the company and its shareholders. Whether a prorogation has a wider range and consequently is not particular enough must be decided through interpretation by national courts. But this does not include—as Bundesgerichtshof showed—that such interpretation will follow *national* law. The prorogation being contained in the constitution of a company subject to a national law of the company does not necessarily lead to an interpretation of this clausula in accordance with the law applicable to the company. The Bundesgerichtshof omitted any reasoning on autonomous principles of interpretation of such a prorogation clausula by reference to Art. 17. But this might be the opinion of the European Court of Justice too, because an interpretation according to autonomous principles based on Art. 17 would not have been subject to national law. A material argument in favour of an interpretation applying the company's domestic law could be that the definition of *relations arising from membership*, in contrast to other contractual relations, is entirely connected with the very nature of the company's statutes which are to be interpreted according to the company's domestic law.

ARTICLE 17, PARAGRAPH 1(a)

" . . . in writing . . . "

Case principle

1. A juristiction agreement is in writing if contained in the general conditions on the reverse side of the contractual confirmation.

Case

490 BGH 31 October 1989 (VIII ZR 330/88) WM (1989) 1941; IPRax (1991) 326; WuB VII B 1. Art. 17 EuGVÜ 1.90 and OLG of Hamm 10 October 1988 (2 U 196/87) IPRax (1991), 324

Facts

The plaintiff was trustee in bankruptcy of G company, domiciled in Germany. Since 1985 G had business relationships with the defendant, domiciled in England. The language of negotiation and contracting was exclusively English. Every order of the defendant had been confirmed by G in English, referring to the general conditions printed in German on the reverse side and containing a prorogation of courts in Dortmund (Germany). The defendant had counter-signed the letters of confirmation.

Judgment

The Oberlandesgericht of Hamm applied Art. 17, which was also applicable according to Art. 54 of the Brussels Convention to prorogations stipulated before it came into force.

The court held that there was an agreement in writing. For integration of a prorogation clause in general conditions, a reference in the signed text of the contract was necessary, referring to the general conditions, but not necessarily also referring to the prorogation itself. This reference had to be in the language of the contract, even though the prorogation could be in another language. In any event, it was sufficient that the defendant had expressly accepted the general conditions in German, notwithstanding that no one in the defendant's office was able to understand these general conditions.

The Bundesgerichtshof did not accept the defendant's appeal. The interpretation, according to which the defendant had expressly accepted the general conditions, concerned merely the facts of the case and therefore was excluded from review by the Bundesgerichtshof. Because of the express acceptance, the agreement was clearly valid and, therefore, the question was not to be referred to the European Court of Justice.

Comment

The transitional application of the 1978 Accession Convention is in accordance with the *Sanicentral* decision of the European Court of Justice (Case 25/79).

Concerning Art. 17(1), the Oberlandesgericht of Hamm improperly deduced its interpretation from the rules concerning general conditions in German law. Article 17(1) of the Brussels Convention is to be interpreted in an autonomous way (*Kohler* IPRax (1991) 299 *et. seq.*). Therefore, contrary to the opinion of the Bundesgerichtshof, the question should have been referred to the European Court of Justice (*Kohler* IPRax (1991) 301; *Welter* WuB VII B 1 Art. 17 EuGVÜ 1.90).

The reference to the *Colzani (Estasis Salotti)* decision (Case 24/76) is doubtful, because, in that case, not only was the express reference in the signed written contract required (as an *element of form*), but also the possibility of knowledge (as an *element of the agreement*). As the European Court of Justice does not hold the 'blind' agreement of a party to the other party's general conditions to be sufficient, it might be rather doubtful to assume such a position, if the general conditions are in another language (*Kohler* IPRax 1991, 301) and therefore have not been understood. Therefore, the solution in the present case might preferably have been found in application of the third alternative of Art. 17(1), *i.e.* a trade practice (*Kohler* IPRax (1991) 301) or in the exception proposed by the European Court of Justice in the *Segoura* decision (Case 25/76) as *evidence in writing* in a case of a continuing business relationship. Nevertheless, such subsidiary solutions seem unnecessary. For an autonomous interpretation it should be clear that a contracting party expressly agreeing to general conditions, although knowing they are in a foreign language, is bound by this agreement without regard to course of dealing or trade practices.

Case principle

2. Prorogation is invalid when made by reference to general conditions not referred to during the negotiations.

Case

BGH 28 March 1996 (III ZR 95/95) EuZW (1996) 473   **491**

Facts

The German plaintiff sued the French domiciled defendant with reference to the former's general conditions containing an agreement providing for jurisdiction of German courts. The agreement had neither been part of the negotiations nor been included in the plaintiff's catalogues which had been sent to the defendant.

Judgment

The agreement was not validly included in the contract. With reference to the European Court of Justice's decision in *Colzani* Case 24/76, the Bundesgerichtshof held that a jurisdiction agreement in general conditions was only valid under Art. 17(1) if the opposite party had the opportunity of knowledge when acting with reasonable care. Despite the possibility that the general conditions had been included in *former* catalogues during the parties' course of dealing, it would have been essential for validity that the plaintiff had expressly referred the other party to these general conditions.

Particularly, a confirmation in the contract form, presented by the plaintiff and signed by the defendant, according to which the defendant had read and entirely understood the conditions of the contract, did not create an *agreement* necessary under Art. 17.

Comment

The decision is perfectly in accordance with the European Court of Justice's decisions on Art. 17. There is no agreement without a clear reference to the general conditions, although the jurisdiction clause itself does not need to be expressly referred to.

Case principle

3. Agreement in general conditions is invalid if printed in excessively small type.

Case

492   OLG of Stuttgart 18 July 1988 (5 U 85/87) IPRax (1989) 174

Facts

(Appeal to Landgericht of Rottweil, IPRax 1989, 45) The plaintiff, domiciled in Germany, sued for payment for producing, delivering and assembling doors and windows for a building situated in France, which were ordered by the defendant domiciled in France. The order was given on the plaintiff's form, written in German, which contained the plaintiff's conditions for delivery and payment on the reverse side in German. The order form had been signed by both the parties.

Judgment

The Oberlandesgericht of Stuttgart held the prorogation to be invalid according to Art. 17. The clause was not discoverable with normal diligence because of small print. The whole form contained about 120 lines in small print and two columns. (According to s.2 of the German Code of General Conditions (AGBG) too, the clause would not have been part of the contract, despite reasonable possibility of knowledge.)

Comment

The *Segoura* decision of the European Court of Justice (Case 25/76) dealt only with the clearness *of the reference* to a prorogation contained in general conditions. In this case, the clearness of the clause itself was decisive. There is no doubt that a special reference to the prorogation within the general conditions is not necessary (*MünchKomm*-[ZPO]-*Gottwald* Art. 17 EuGVÜ, n.18). But from the point of view that Art. 17(1) extends to all aspects of the agreement, excluding contractual incorporation rules under national law, it is necessary to develop autonomous criteria not only for the clearness of the reference but also for the form of the clause being referred to (*Jayme* IPRax (1989) 174). A clear reference to an unreadable clause cannot prove sufficient agreement.

Case principle

4.   There is no valid agreement in writing, when prorogation is contained in a sticker fixed on the face of the contractual deed.

Case

OLG of Düsseldorf 6 January 1989 (16 U 77/88) NJW–RR (1989) 1330   **493**

Facts

The plaintiff, a shoeseller, domiciled in Germany, sued the defendant, domiciled in Italy, for payment under a contract of sale of shoes, which the plaintiff alleged was concluded at the international shoe fair in Bologna. The plaintiff had fixed a sticker on the order form, which said: 'foro competente Remscheid', before the representative of the defendant completed and signed the form. In its upper part, the sticker had information about the firm in large print, while the general conditions in the lower two thirds were printed in small letters.

Judgment

The court held against a valid agreement in writing. No doubt the clause was contained in a document signed by both parties, which resulted from fixing the sticker on the form before signing. But there was no 'agreement' in the sense of the European Court of Justice's definition. The decision in *Colzani* Case 24/76 dealt with the form only (reference to general conditions on the reverse), but not with the 'agreement'. To this, the Oberlandesgericht of Düsseldorf applied national (German) contract law applicable by private international law of the forum. In German law the clause did not become part of the contract, under s.3 of the German Code of General Conditions (AGBG), owing to the failure to bring sufficient attention to the sticker. In Italian law Art. 1341(1) of the Codice Civile also worked against validity, because the defendant would not know of the clause applying ordinary diligence.

Comment

The decision is unsatisfactory. The requirement of a valid agreement, contained in Art. 17 of the Brussels Convention, according to the ruling of the European Court of Justice must be examined as an autonomous criterion. National laws are *not* to be applied. Article 17(1) of the Brussels Convention does not only provide prescriptions as to mere form—like Art. 1341(2) of the *Codice Civile* which requires a special signature under general conditions. Article 17(1) also excludes any control of integration of general conditions in a contract, especially by rules like s.3 of the AGBG.

Therefore, the case should have been decided applying only Art. 17(1). Still, the judgment can be supported in its results, although the arguments are not convincing: the European Court of Justice understands writing in the sense of Art. 17(1) as evidence for the existence of an agreement. This evidence is even stronger if the prorogation is contained in signed writing as in *Colzani*—such as where there is a reference to general conditions printed on the reverse side. Accordingly, the argument of the Oberlandesgericht of Düsseldorf, distinguishing the present case is not convincing. Nevertheless, the validity of an agreement may be questioned if the prorogation is contained in signed writing, but this writing, exceptionally, does not amount to evidence that the other party had knowledge of it. It must remain undecided whether such doubt was justified in this case.

Case principle

5. **No written agreement without express reference to general conditions in the text of the contractual deed.**

Case

494 OLG of Hamm 20 January 1989 (29 U 155/86) NJW (1990) 652

Facts

The plaintiff, domiciled in Germany, undertook, under an exclusive sales contract, to allow its products to be sold in France exclusively by the defendant domiciled there, whereas the defendant was under an obligation to permit all articles produced by it to be sold in Germany only by the plaintiff. The plaintiff sued the defendant for payment of a contractual penalty for breach of this obligation. The general buying conditions of the plaintiff contained the clause 'Place of performance for delivery is . . . Löhne (Germany) for both parts . . . Bad Oeynhausen (Germany) is the competent forum'. The defendant had received these general conditions together with deliveries and had not objected to them for more than one year.

Judgment

The court held against the existence of a written agreement, because there was no express reference to the general conditions in the written text of the contract. Receiving the general conditions without any objection for more than one year was not an agreement in writing in accordance with Art. 17(1) of the Brussels Convention, because there was no confirmation in writing in the past.

Comment

The judgment was correct. Prorogation clauses are not integrated into the written contract without an express reference.

However, the reasoning does not support the opinion that there was no *evidence in writing* according to the *Segoura* decision (Case 25/76). Sending the general conditions amounts to written evidence. Only the *agreement* might be doubtful. An agreement cannot be based on receiving without any objection—except that in the course of a permanent business relationship such receiving without objection *is* sufficient. Nevertheless, in the present case there was no valid prorogation: no doubt there could have been *current* business relationships, underlying the plaintiff's general conditions. But the claim in the action resulted from the primary exclusive sales contract, which had not been concluded in the course of the business relationship, but at its very beginning. Therefore, the agreement concerning general conditions could not embrace this contract.

Case principle

6. An agreement in general conditions signed by the other party unable to read and understand the language of said conditions may still be valid if that party did not act with due care.

Case

OLG of Hamm 28 June 1994 (19 U 179/93) RIW (1994) 877   **495**

Facts

See supra, Art. 5(1), Case 465.

Judgment

The court considered the plaintiff's general conditions to have become part of the contract, as explained (see *supra*, Art. 5(1), Case 465).

The plaintiff could not rely on a misinterpretation of the general conditions. As it had signed and returned a copy, it had shown its agreement though ignoring the content. Otherwise it should not have signed. Therefore, it could not rely on the fact that it could only understand English when signing and returning completed the written form of Art. 17(1) of the Brussels Convention.

The reference to s.38 of the ZPO was only a kind of legal condition in the event that the parties were merchants (to whom s.38 restricts the possibility of prorogation in German Code of Civil Procedure). Therefore, the agreement was valid, although Art. 17 was applicable, not s.38 of the ZPO.

Comment

The decision might be correct in its result, but is not correct in considering Art. 17(1) only to be a rule as to form, and not also as to the entire agreement. The court should not have decided the existence of an agreement according to German law as the law applicable to the contract. According to the European Court of Justice, the signing of a written contract which contains a reference to a general condition printed on the reverse side is sufficient evidence for the existence of an agreement and not only for fulfilment of the written form.

The interpretation of the prorogation clause itself seems to be doubtful: the reference to s.38 should be interpreted as a restriction upon the prorogation. Therefore, although under Art. 17 a prorogation would be valid even if one of the parties was not a merchant, the prorogation itself states very clearly that it should only be valid against a merchant.

> " . . . *evidenced in writing* . . . "

Case principle

1. Whether general conditions containing a jurisdiction clause, subsequently sent, where allowed as part of a continuing business relationship, *substitute* for previous oral agreement or are additional thereto?

Case

496 BGH 9 March 1994 (VIII ZR 185/92) RIW (1994) 508; StR (1994) 347

Facts

Between the plaintiff, domiciled in Germany, and the defendant, domiciled in Belgium, there existed a business relationship for several years. The plaintiff sold textiles to the defendant. Several contracts were subject to the plaintiff's general conditions, determining the jurisdiction of the courts at the plaintiff's residence. The matter in dispute started with a defendant's offer containing detailed description of the merchandise and requesting confirmation, but not referring to any general conditions. The plaintiff confirmed in a letter containing the plaintiff's general conditions on the reverse side. The defendant did not accept the merchandise because of some difference between offer and acceptance, and the plaintiff sued for damages at Landgericht D.

Judgment

It was decisive whether a contract had actually been made. The court did not assume the prerequisites of Art. 17(1) to be completed. According to the European Court of Justice the forms of Art. 17 should show unambiguously that there was a consent of the parties. There was not a written form, because neither parties' declarations nor even the offer expressly referred to general conditions. Only the plaintiff's acceptance contained such reference. To create the written form, an express and written consent of the defendant would have been necessary.

Neither was there written evidence. For this alternative, consent of both parties was necessary. This could be fulfilled in a course of dealing underlying the general conditions (*Segoura*), but, in this event, the written confirmation of one side had to be *preceded* by an oral agreement. *In casu*, the plaintiff's confirmation did not follow the agreement, but *was* the acceptance, *creating* the agreement itself.

The prerequisites of the third alternative of Art. 17(1) were not satisfied either. The plaintiff's confirmation was not a merchant's written confirmation (*kaufmännisches Bestätigungsschreiben*). The situation that during a course of dealing general conditions of one party had been applicable without the other party's objection, could not be treated in the same way.

Comment

The court's opinion concerning the second alternative (written evidence) seems to be doubtful, since the European Court of Justice has decided that an express reference to general conditions containing the prorogation is not necessary, if these general conditions have been applicable in a course of dealing. The proof of an oral consent of both parties is *substituted* by this course of dealing. Therefore, it should not make any difference whether the contract in dispute has been made before or after a party's written confirmation, which is merely a formal prerequisite in this case.

Case principle

2.   Confirmation in writing when using the words 'read and agreed'.

Case

OLG of München 8 March 1989 (15 U 5989/88) WM (1989) 602; ZZP 103   **497**
(1990) 84; RIW (1989) 901; WuB VII B 1. Art. 17 EuGVÜ 1.89

Facts

See supra, Art. 5(3), Case 470.

Judgment

The court found an agreement evidenced in writing. The plaintiff had confirmed in writing his knowledge of the clause and given his consent, using the words 'read and agreed'. This was sufficient for the form of a confirmation in writing. Furthermore, the parties had had a current business relationship for a long-time, underlying the general conditions.

The reference to an agreed place of performance, in the opinion of the court, was an express prorogation and did not only create the forum of the place of performance.

Section 12 of the German Code of General Conditions (AGBG) was not an impediment to the prorogation. Generally, it was doubtful whether the prorogation could be examined applying ss.2, 3, 5, 9 to 11 of the AGBG, because Art. 17 of the Brussels Convention was an exhaustive regulation for the validity of prorogations, autonomously of national law. The court did not decide definitely on this point, because it was not proved that the plaintiff was a German resident.

Article 1, para. 2 of the Protocol to the Brussels Convention was not an impediment, either. No doubt the defendant was domiciled in Luxembourg. But it had produced the general conditions itself and implemented them in the course of business. Therefore, there existed an express declaration of the defendant.

Furthermore, the prorogation was sufficiently specific. It was enough that the legal relationship in dispute could be individualized at the moment of contracting as to its type and subject. This presumption was fulfilled by the immediate connection with the 9567 shares.

The Art. 17-forum not only covered contractual, but also delictual, causes of action. From the viewpoint of the German Code of Civil Procedure (ZPO) there was only one matter in dispute, because it was only one claim for damages.

Comment

The decision has been criticized, because Art. 17 was applied without any connection with another Contracting State. Both the general forum of Art. 2 and the special one of Art. 5(1) were situated in Luxembourg, whereas the plaintiff was domiciled in Spain (*Schmidt* ZZP 103 (1990) 94). But the application of Art. 17 only depends upon a prorogation of the courts of a Contracting State. There are no further unwritten requirements (*Coester-Waltjen* WuB VII B 1 Art. 17 EuGVÜ 1.89, 1085). Moreover, Art. 17 is applicable if the chosen forum coincides with the forum which was otherwise applicable. In such a case, there always remains the *derogating effect* ('exclusive'), decisive in the case of the Oberlandesgericht of München. The action was to be dismissed for lack of jurisdiction of the Munich court.

The decision correctly affirms that—at least—the conditions of Art. 17(1) for a written confirmation were fulfilled according to the European Court of Justice's rulings. The effectiveness of the elected courts is not prejudiced by the reference to the place of performance in the agreement. Such reference only confirms the alternative forum of the place of performance, but chooses it as an exclusive one.

Only the treatment of the general conditions is doubtful: Art. 17(1) probably does prevail over the control of *integration* of general conditions in national law (see *supra*, Cases 487 and 488, and *infra*, Comment to Case 499), but not necessarily over the control of *content* according to ss.9 to 11 of the AGBG.

The arguments concerning the scope of the agreement are also able to be contested. A prorogation connected with a contract must be interpreted so that, if there is no clear wording, an interpretation should prevail which extends the prorogation to concurrent delictual claims (*Coester-Waltjen ab. cit.*, 1086).

ARTICLE 17, PARAGRAPH 1(c)

" . . . accords with a usage . . . "

Case principle

Is the mere silence of a merchant sufficient under the third alternative of Art. 17?

Case

BGH 6 March 1995 (II ZR 37/94) RIW (1995) 410; EuZW (1995) 714   **498**

Facts

See supra, Art. 5(1), Case 461.

Judgment

The question is to be answered only if the European Court of Justice would restrict the scope of application of Art. 5(1) to agreements concerning the place of performance actually governing the material place of performance and not only to create a *forum contractus* (on this point see *supra*, Art. 5(1)). The court has again asked (for details see *supra*, BGH 26 March 1992, Case 499 *infra*), whether the mere silence of a merchant to a written confirmation containing a prorogation, which actually has never been made before (a practice of trade which is common under German law), creates a valid prorogation under Art. 17, third alternative?

The European Court of Justice (C–106/95 *Mainschiffahrtsgesellschaft*) has now answered this question affirmatively on certain conditions: such behaviour leads to a valid agreement if, and only if, there exists a practice in trade in the parties' branch of business and the silent party is aware or is presumed to be aware of this practice. There are many questions remaining, particularly as to how to prove such practices. The most important clarification by this judgment seems to be that the third form of agreement can replace not only the formal requirements of Art. 17, but also the essential prerequisite of prior agreement.

> " . . . ought to have been aware . . . "

Case principle

Prorogation by general conditions included in written confirmation in another language after contract verbally made?

Case

499   BGH 26 March 1992 (VII ZR 258/91) EuZW (1992) 514

Facts

See *supra*, Art. 5(1), Case 460.

Judgment

For the questions concerning Art. 5(1) see *supra* Art. 5(1), Case 460.

Concerning Art. 17, the Bundesgerichtshof referred the following questions to the European Court of Justice.

> (2a)   Can a prorogation, according to Art. 17, be validly agreed on where a seller, after the contract being orally concluded, confirms the contract by writing, including his general conditions for the first time, which contains a prorogation clause, and the buyer does not object, if, at the buyer's domicile, there is no trade practice considering silence in response to such written confirmation as an agreement, the buyer is not aware of such practice in trade and the contract in question is the first business transaction between the parties?
>
> (2b)   In the event that the court affirms question no (2a): is this also true when the general conditions containing the prorogation are written in a language different from the language of negotiations on contract and not known to the buyer and if the confirmation in writing, written in the language of negotiation and contract points only globally to the general conditions but not specifically to the prorogation?
>
> (3)   If both questions are to be answered affirmatively: does Art. 17, if there exists a clause in general conditions sufficient for a valid prorogation, prevent the court from examining, additionally, whether the clause has been validly inserted into the contract according to national laws made applicable by private international law of the court?

The Bundesgerichtshof explained as to question (2a) that neither the requirement for 'writing' nor for 'evidence in writing' were satisfied, because no written contract expressly pointed to the general conditions. The general conditions sent to the buyer after conclusion of the contract had not been accepted in writing, and silence—with the exception of contracting in a course of dealing—could not be interpreted as acceptance. Therefore, Art. 17(1) in the 1978 Accession Convention's version was to be interpreted: the interpretation of this rule was ambiguous. Its purpose was to enable a valid prorogation by silence to a commercial confirmation in writing. In the opinion of the court, this should be restricted to cases where the addressee of such writing was aware of such practice according to the laws of his domicile.

Concerning questions (2b) and (3) the Bundesgerichtshof explained the opinions in dispute (below).

Comment

The decision deals with several most important problems. Due to the affirmative answer concerning question (1a) (see *supra*, Case 460), the European Court of Justice did not deal with these aspects (see *Custom Made Commercial Ltd* Case C–288/92).

The third 'form' allowed by the 1978 version of Brussels Convention was intended to give validity to prorogations in general conditions sent to the other party together with a confirmation in writing. By this regulation, Art.17 became more than a prescription concerning 'form'. The intention could only be realized by reducing the requirements not only as to form, but as to the material *agreement*. For this purpose, the European Court of Justice developed very strict requirements. Consequently, trade practice became another way of reaching an *agreement*, not only another *form* of agreement. But the existence of a trade practice must have a double relationship with the parties: first not *any* trade practice is sufficient, but only a practice recognized by the law applicable to the contract (see *Rauscher* ZZP 104 (1991) 294 s. in a different sense: *Kropholler* Art. 17, n.42). Another possibility would be to assume an autonomous reference from Art. 17 to the laws in force at the addressee's domicile.

The most decisive point is the *knowledge* test: any trade practice recognised under a material law applicable must be known to the addressee (different opinion: *MünchKomm*-[ZPO]-*Gottwald* Art. 17 EuGVÜ, n.30). The criterion, that the parties are aware or ought to be aware of such practice can, for the purposes of Art. 17(1) be decided in conformity with Art. 8(2) of the Rome Convention (in the same sense: *Kropholler* Art. 17 n.43). Therefore, it is decisive whether such practice is in use at the addressee's domicile in any event, and the mere fact of having business contacts with a German businessman cannot produce an obligation to have knowledge of the practice of commercial confirmation in writing in German commercial law (for another opinion: see Kohler IPRax 1991, 301).

The problem of languages, arising in question (2b), the European Court of Justice had approached in the *Elefanten Schuh* decision (Case 150/80), when the Court denied the applicability of a rule in a national code, which prevented any prorogation in a foreign language, which was only a question of prevalence of Art. 17 in relation to a national Code of Civil Procedure. The first two alternatives of Art. 17(1) do not necessarily depend upon the language of contract. Anybody, *signing* a reference to general conditions (which means the form of 'in writing' according to *Colzani*, Case 24/76), or who *accepts* general conditions after having concluded a contract (amounting to 'evidence in writing' according to *Segoura*, Case 25/76) has to bear the risk of misunderstanding. As to the third alternative of an agreement in trade or commerce, the addressee undertakes a bigger risk: Is a prorogation clausula valid against him without a reference in an understandable language? This question should be answered by the law which is applicable to existence of the trade practice and to its validity as against the addressee, *i.e.* the law of his domicile.

Question (3) is related to Art. 27(1) and control of general conditions according to national law. The German Code of General Conditions (AGBG) uses two different methods of control, control of integration of the clausula (*Einbeziehungskontrolle*—s.2 ss of the AGBG) and control of contents of the clausula (*Inhaltkontrolle*—s.9 ss of the AGBG). This dual method of control makes the problem clear. The question whether a general condition becomes part of a contract means a type of control over whether there is an *agreement*. In this respect, Art. 17, as interpreted by the European Court of Justice, prevails and does not leave any scope for the application of national laws. On the other hand, the control of contents is concerned with the question whether the single clausula is appropriate according to good faith. This aspect is not necessarily withdrawn from national law by Art. 17, which is only concerned with the form and the essentials of the agreement (for particular discussion, see: *Rauscher* ZZP 104 (1991) 295 ss).

ARTICLE 18

" . . . *enters an appearance* . . . "

Case principle

1.   Jurisdiction from Art. 18 when a defendant enters an appearance.

Case

500   BAG 24 August 1989 (2 AZR 3/89) IPRax (1991) 407

Facts

The plaintiff, a British citizen, domiciled in the UK, made a contract of employment with the first defendant, an English company, domiciled in Sheerness (UK). The first defendant owned ferry landing slots in the port of

Sheerness and did the catering for the second defendant's vessels. The plaintiff sued in an action in the Labour Court (*Arbeitsgericht*) of Hamburg on 20 August 1987, objecting to its dismissal against the first defendant.

Judgment

The Bundesarbeitsgericht (Federal Labour Court) assumed jurisdiction based on Art. 18 without any problem as to the facts. The 1978 Accession Convention was to be applied, since according to its Art. 34, the Convention was in force for the UK for an action brought after 1 January 1987.

Case principle

2. German courts have jurisdiction to decide on a claim in set-off, when the plaintiff has entered an appearance without contesting jurisdiction over the defendant's claim.

Case

BGH 4 February 1993 (VII ZR 179/81) NJW (1993) 1399   **501**

Facts

The plaintiff, a merchant domiciled in Belgium, had carried out building work for the defendant, domiciled in Germany, on the basis of an oral agreement. He sued for payment. The defendant declared an eventual set-off, claiming for damage to this building and other buildings constructed by the defendant.

Judgment

The Bundesgerichtshof allowed the set-off without declining jurisdiction. The plaintiff had entered an appearance, without contesting jurisdiction over the set-off, sufficient according to *Spitzley* Case 48/84.

Comment

The decision follows the European Court of Justice's *Spitzley* case. For jurisdictional questions in the case of set-off, see *supra*, Art. 6(3), Case 477.

Case principle

3. Jurisdiction of German courts for a claim to set-off notwithstanding a derogation, if the plaintiff did not contest jurisdiction for the set-off when bringing his own action.

Case

OLG of Stuttgart 15 February 1989 (9 U 207/88) IPRax (1989) 247   **502**

Facts

An Italian company sued a German company for payment under a contract of sale. The existence of the contract was in dispute. The defendant declared set-off of commissions under an alleged sales-agency contract. The sales contract contained a choice of foreign courts.

Judgment

The court referred to a decision of the Bundesgerichtshof from 1972 (BGHZ 60/86) that the prorogation was ineffective against a set-off through the plaintiff's entry of an appearance without contesting jurisdiction. The plaintiff could avoid such result only by an anticipated contestation of jurisdiction for set-off together with his action.

Comment

The decision is concerned with the relationship between Arts 18 and 17: the court decided correctly that entering an appearance under Art. 18 would de-activate an Art. 17 prorogation (see *Elefanten Schuh* Case 150/80).

However, the decision is not satisfactory in respect of the point at which jurisdiction under Art. 18 arose. No doubt for the defendant, jurisdiction can be based on Art. 18 as soon as he enters an appearance concerning the material questions of the claim. But this time limit cannot bind the plaintiff as far as jurisdiction for a set-off is concerned. The plaintiff is not under an obligation to contest such jurisdiction in anticipation, at the date of commencing the action. Contestation is brought in time if this is before defending the set-off on the merits (*Jayme* IPRax (1989) 247).

Another question is whether the plaintiff is allowed to contest the set-off jurisdiction by virtue of the prorogation, on the one hand, but, on the other hand, to rely on Art. 18 for his own action? It seems to be contradictory behaviour, and therefore not in accordance with good faith, to disregard a prorogation for one's own action and yet to insist on it as to the other party's set-off!

Case principle

4. Jurisdiction for claim in a set-off when the plaintiff does not contest such jurisdiction, even if contestation would not have been successful.

Case

503 OLG of Koblenz 23 December 1988 (2 U 809/87) RIW (1989) 384

Facts

The plaintiff, a joint stock company domiciled in Belgium, and the German firm P, had business relationships for several years. The plaintiff, using P as an intermediary, delivered wire-products to the defendant for further delivery to Iran. There were no direct relationships between the parties until the plaintiff became aware that P was insolvent. After negotiations, a contract of sale was made between the plaintiff and the defendant for 119 tons of fine-wires, stored in a deposit in Germany. The defendant objected that the property in these wires had been transferred to it after payment to P and therefore it had bought its own property twice. Eventually, it set-off damages, arising from the fact that the plaintiff had seized the defendant's property contrary to law.

Judgment

The court based its international jurisdiction for the action on Art. 2 of the Brussels Convention; and jurisdiction to decide on the set-off resulted from Art. 18.

Comment

It is correct that the court had jurisdiction for the set-off, since the plaintiff had not contested such jurisdiction.

Such contestation, nevertheless, would not have been successful: the defendant had the possibility of suing for damages for interference with the property in the movables being the object of the contract of sale, by a *counterclaim* according to Art. 6(3). Therefore, the same claim could be brought by set-off under Art. 18.

Case principle

5. Jurisdiction of German courts notwithstanding a prorogation agreement when defendant enters an appearance.

Case

OLG of Koblenz 3 March 1989 (2 U 1543/87) RIW (1989) 310   **504**

Facts

The plaintiff, domiciled in Italy, sold marble flags to the defendant, domiciled in Germany, and sued for payment. The defendant declared set-off with damages. The plaintiff's general sales conditions, printed on the plaintiff's accounts, contained a prorogation in favour of Verona (Italy) courts.

Judgment

The court had jurisdiction under Art. 18, since entering an appearance prevailed over the Art. 17 prorogation. That was also true for the set-off.

Comment

The decision is in harmony with the European Court of Justice's decisions, see comments *supra*; in the same sense: OLG of Koblenz 3 May 1991 (2 U 1645/87) RIW (1992) 59.

ARTICLE 21, PARAGRAPH 1

" . . . *involving the same cause of action* . . . "

Case principle

No identity of causes of action when a contractual claim was pending in German proceedings, whereas foreign proceedings were for damages to be calculated including the same contractual claim as set-off.

Case

505   OLG of München 10 April 1987 (23 U 6422/86) RIW (1989) 57

Facts

The plaintiff, domiciled in Germany, sued the defendant, domiciled in Italy, for commission under a contract of commercial agency. The court of first instance (Landgericht) ordered international service. After the return of the Italian communication of service, the Landgericht granted a default judgment and ordered substituted service according to ss.175, 213 of the German Code of Civil Procedure (ZPO) by post. In the enforcement-proceedings, the communication of service was translated, showing that the writ had not been served upon the defendant. After re-commencement of the procedure by service of the writ on 19 August 1986, the defendant objected *res judicata*. Moreover, it had itself brought an action for damages against the plaintiff on 16 April 1986. This action, in the defendant's view, involved the same cause of action because the Milano court had to decide on whether the commission was yet due, which was a material prerequisite for the claim in the present action. Moreover, in Milano there were claims in set-off, which could only be decided when the existence or non-existence of the obligations against which the set-off should operate, was clear.

Judgment

The court assumed international jurisdiction. The default judgment had not been validly served according to ss.175, 213 of the ZPO, since this method of service was only applicable if the defendant had not fulfilled its obligation to appoint a representative for service within the court's jurisdiction. Such obligation did not arise, because the order to appoint such representative had not been served together with the writ. Despite service, the default judgment was not even in existence, since there was not an oral procedure but a procedure in writing, and, according to s.310(3) of the ZPO, after such a procedure a default judgment only became valid by service upon both the parties. Otherwise such judgment had no *res iudicata* effect.

Neither was jurisdiction to be declined with respect to the Milano proceedings according to Art. 21. It had to be decided whether the causes of action were identical by applying the national Codes of Civil Procedure of both the states concerned. The Milano action was only for damages, and the defendant had merely asked to deduct the amount of commission due when measuring the damages. It could not be decided which commissions from which contracts were in dispute. Consequently, there were not even indirectly the same causes of action. Moreover, from the point of view of German law, there was no identity in causes of action between suing for payment and set-off.

A stay of proceedings, according to Art. 22, para. 1, was not to be considered, *since this provision only applied to courts of first instance.*

Comment

The decision is correct as to existence and validity of the default judgment. This question is outside the scope of the Brussels Convention. Moreover, no question of recognition was concerned, since the judgment did not even exist according to the laws of the judgment-State (Germany).

Identity of the causes of action must be defined according to an autonomous interpretation according to the European Court of Justice in *Gubisch* Case 144/86; in the same sense, in *Tatry* Case C–406/92. The old views applied in the present judgment, have been overruled. As the European Court of Justice decided on a wide interpretation, Art. 21 must be applied—contrary to theory of *lis alibi pendens* in German law—if in both procedures there has to be decided the same preliminary question, *e.g.* the existence of a contract. The main action concerning the obligation is in conflict with an action for payment concerning the same obligation in the sense of Art. 21. The mere announcement of a main declaratory action which, according to the court's evaluation of the facts, had taken place in the Italian proceedings, is not sufficient. Neither is any deduction of commissions from damages sufficient, even if the commissions have been sued for elsewhere. It would be a different matter if, in both proceedings, the validity of the contract itself was in dispute.

The exact time of litispendence cannot be determined in an autonomous way. This decision must be for the national Code of Civil Procedure. Therefore, litispendence in Milano exists from the same time of '*notificazione della citazione*' (Art. 39(3) of the *Codice di Procedura Civile*—Italian Code of Civil Procedure).

The pronouncement upon Art. 22 was correct. A stay of procedure according to this provision can be ordered only as long as both proceedings are at first instance. The material assumptions of Art. 22 would have been satisfied in the case of obligations arising under the same contract, as far as there is a risk of contradictory decisions. In the present case, it depends on the identity of the claims for commissions sued for in Germany and the commissions in set-off in Italy (*e.g.* see: *Kropholler* Art. 22, n.2, *MünchKomm [ZPO]— Gottwald* Art. 22, n.2).

> " . . . *courts of different Contracting States* . . . "

Case principle

Article 21 applies to actions pending in courts of different Contracting States notwithstanding that (some of) plaintiffs and defendants are domiciled in non-Contracting States.

Case

506 OLG of Köln 13 February 1990 (*5 W 57/90*) NJW (1991) 1427; IPRax (1992) 89

Facts

An Austrian and two German constructors sued 13 insurers who were, with the exception of two, domiciled in England, for determination of their obligations under insurance contracts. The plaintiffs had agreed on the insurances with the defendants, covering their liabilities for the construction of an airport in Basrah (Iraq). The defendants brought an action in the English courts for rescission of the policies. Those proceedings were pending on appeal after the English court declined jurisdiction according to Art. 11 (see *supra*, Case 196).

Judgment

The Landgericht of Köln stayed the proceedings under (1978 version) Art. 21, para. 2. The plaintiffs appealed: the Landgericht of Köln had improperly used its discretion given by Art. 21, para. 2. Although it was to be expected that the English Court of Appeal would decline jurisdiction according to Art. 11, the proceedings should have been continued, because even if an English judgment were to have been delivered, it would not have been recognizable according to Art. 21, para. 1.

The Oberlandesgericht of Köln applied Art. 21 to all parties to the proceedings. It was irrelevant that some plaintiffs and defendants were not domiciled within the Contracting States. The only requirement of Art. 21 was that there were actions pending *in courts of different Contracting States*. Generally, (1978 version) Art. 21, para. 1 made decline of jurisdiction compulsory. Although worded '*may stay*', Art. 21, para. 2 gave no discretion over stay: stay of the proceedings was the only alternative to decline under para. 1 (see Kaye, *Civil Jurisdiction*, pp. 1219–1220). Stay of the proceeding was compulsory if—as in the present case—there was some possibility that the other court would decline jurisdiction. A calculation as to possibility of future refusal of recognition was not admissible, because Art. 26 excluded this.

There was only one exception: if there was exclusive jurisdiction of the court seised second according to Art. 16, jurisdiction of the first court was to be examined for purposes of Art. 23. If the second court was the only one having jurisdiction, it had to continue its proceedings.

Comment

The decision is in harmony with the later *Tatry* decision Case C–406/92, confirming that an action for (negative) declaration of non-existence of a claim can be an obstacle to an action for performance based on the same claim. It is also in harmony with the later *Overseas Union Insurance* decision in Case C–351/89. Article 21 of the Brussels Convention must be applied without regard to the parties' domicile, and Art. 21, para. 2 (now para. 1) does not allow an examination of the first court's jurisdiction. The further considerations are also correct: if the second court has exclusive jurisdiction according to Art. 16, the first court's jurisdiction must exceptionally be examined. One reason is Art. 23 requiring decline of jurisdiction, (*only*) if both courts have *exclusive* jurisdiction. The second reason is, that—otherwise than in the situation of Art. 21, para. 2 (now para. 1)—recognition may be taken into consideration: the foreign judgment, if pronounced later, would not be recognized because of Art. 21, para. 1 (now para. 2) and Art. 16 in any Contracting State (*Kropholler* Art. 21, n.12; *Rauscher/Gutknecht* IPRax (1993) 21). Therefore, the proceeding need not be declined.

> " . . . *first seised* . . . "

Case principle

Foreign court not first-seised when foreign action pending from the same day as German action.

Case

OLG of Koblenz 30 November 1990 (2 U 1072/89) EuZW (1991) 158   **507**

Facts

The plaintiff, a German firm, by a contract of distribution and delivery agreed upon in 1973, gave the right of exclusive sales of preparation 'S' in Belgium to the defendant. The defendant was under an obligation not to sell competing producers' products. The contract contained a choice of the Landgericht of Koblenz to decide any disputes. The plaintiff sued the defendant for payment of balances for deliveries of products.

The defendant brought an action against the plaintiff at the Cour de Commerce Nivelles (Belgium) for compensation.

Judgment

The court assumed international jurisdiction under Art. 17 or 18. The *lis pendens* defence was rejected.

Article 21, as amended by the 1978 Accession Convention, was not applicable. Following *Gubisch*, the court autonomously determined the scope of litispendence so as to avoid decisions which would not be recognizable according to Art. 27(3). On a wide interpretation, the claims for damages under the exclusive sales agreement were involved in both proceedings as a part of the calculation of damages. Nevertheless, Art. 21 dealt only with *actions*. In the present case, damages were sued for in the Belgian proceedings whilst they were only in set-off in Germany. The court left undecided whether this was satisfied for Art. 21, since the Belgian court was not 'first seised'. The court determined the time of litispendence according to the *Zelger* decision (Case 129/83) applying the respective national Codes of Civil Procedure. The present action was pending after service, the Belgian action on the same day by arrival of the notice concerning *remise au parquet* at the German court of first instance. When both actions were brought on the same day, Art. 21 could not be applied and both the courts had to continue their proceedings.

Comment

The result was correct, leaving undecided the validity of the prorogation. When there is an exclusive prorogation of one court, but in the sense of Art. 21 another court is seised earlier, there exists the risk of a negative conflict of jurisdiction, which stay under Art. 21 para. 1 now helps to avoid. In the 1978 version this was achieved by a stay of proceedings under para. 2, if jurisdiction of the other court was contested (*Overseas Union Insurance*, Case C–351/89), until the second court denied its jurisdiction. Even if the Cour de Commerce of Nivelles had been seised earlier, the Oberlandesgericht of Koblenz would not have been allowed to examine and to deny the other court's jurisdiction, but could only stay according to 1978 Art. 21(2) (the Belgian court could have based jurisdiction on Art. 18). The new version in the San Sebastian Accession Convention improves the situation, because the contestation of the other court's jurisdiction is no longer necessary.

The decision is also correct as to the identity of both claims in the actions, because the requirements are met if the same damages are relevant for the decision in both the proceedings. The question left open by the court was whether the concurrence of set-off with the same claim made Art. 21 applicable? This should be denied. No doubt Art. 21 is to be interpreted widely, but one of the prerequisites must be that the claim is *pending* in both courts, which is not so in the case of set-off. Application of Art. 22 remains possible for this conflict.

The solution found by the court for the problem of accidental contemporaneity of both actions is the only logical one: if none of the actions prevails according to Art. 21, both proceedings have to be continued. Thereafter Art. 27(3) will prevent recognition if the decisions are irreconcilable.

> *" . . . seised . . . "*

Case principle

Definitive seisin is for relevant national laws to decide (*Zelger*, Case 129/83).

Case

OLG of Hamm 3 December 1993 (12 U 18/92), IPRax (1995) 104   **508**

Facts

The plaintiff sued for a declaration that it was not under an obligation for damages or warranty under a contract with the defendant. The defendant was sued for damages in a French court by third parties to whom the defendant had delivered products which it had received from the plaintiff under that contract.

Judgment

In accordance with *Gubisch*, the court applied Art. 21 in the case of conflict between a declaratory action and an action for performance and damages. There were detailed deliberations concerning the question at which stage of a proceeding an action was pending for Art. 21 under the French Code of Civil Procedure. The action was not pending when it was brought to the French court, nor at the time when the defendant was served or refused to be served with the action as long as the action had not been filed in the court's register of actions. As the defendant in the German action had been served with the action in the meantime, causing definitive litispendence in German law, the German action was earlier in the sense of Art. 21.

Comment

The court has been criticized for not referring the case to the European Court of Justice. The case shows that that court's preference for national Codes of Civil Procedure as far as litispendence must be determined can cause competition between the parties to try to beat each other's action. The application of French law by the court seems to be correct (see: *Rüßmann* IPRax (1995) 77), but the registration of the action in French commercial courts (*mise au rôle*) is effected in French practice at a very late stage of procedure, mostly several days before trial. Therefore, the decision is correct in application of the European Court of Justice's rules. But these rules are unsatisfactory and should be overruled by a unique and autonomous determination of litispendence for purposes of Art. 21. This could be either at the moment when the action is brought to the court or at the time of service. From a German point of view, the time of service is preferred, but the time of first delivery of the action to the court seems to be preferable in the European context, as it does not depend upon risks and delays in international service. For the solution of the problem, it is not decisive which stage of procedure to choose if there is only one unambiguous solution for any action brought to a court of a Contracting State.

> " . . . *shall* . . . *stay* . . . "

Case principle

1. Application of Art. 21 is not prevented even though a foreign judgment is expected not to be recognized under the Convention.

Case

509 BGH 8 February 1995 (VII ZR 14/94), NJW (1995) 1758; RIW (1995) 413; EuZW (1995) 378, EWS (1995) 169; IPRax (1996) 192

Facts

The parties were commercial companies domiciled in Italy. In a written agreement, the defendant had agreed to assign shares held in two German companies to the plaintiff in return for payment of 1 000 000 DM. A notarial deed was to be made after complete payment. For disputes concerning interpretation and performance of the agreement, the courts in Munich were chosen.

In June 1983, the plaintiff brought an action in Treviso (Italy) to affirm the invalidity of the agreement through misrepresentation and error and repayment of 200 000 DM which it had already paid under the contract. The Italian Corte Cassazione affirmed the jurisdiction of the Italian courts. Subsequently, the parties failed to pursue the Italian proceedings.

After the defendant in the Treviso proceedings had been served with the action, it brought an action in Munich for payment of the agreed price. This action was rejected because of invalidity of the contract through formal invalidity. The judgment was recognized in Italy under Art. 26.

In late 1985, after the Munich court's decision, the plaintiff brought an action in Bolzano (Italy) for affirmation of invalidity of contract due to formal invalidity and repayment of 200 000 DM. In 1988, the Bolzano court decided that the contract was formally valid. The appeal has not yet been decided.

In the present action, brought in January 1987 before the Landgericht of München, the plaintiff sued again for repayment of 200 000 DM, with reference to the former Munich decision, finding invalidity of the contract. The defendant objected on grounds of litispendence in Italy, *i.e.* the Bolzano-procedure.

Judgment

The Bundesgerichtshof left expressly undecided whether the claim for repayment was still pending in the Bolzano court, which was doubtful because the plaintiff no longer expressly asked for payment in the latter. Identity of actions was also satisfied in the sense of Art. 21 between the action for a declaration of invalidity in Italy and the action for payment in Germany.

Neither was it decisive whether the declaratory action was the action for performance. Article 21 applied even if in both proceedings plaintiff and defendant were in the same role.

Nor was the application of Art. 21 in favour of the Italian proceedings prevented by the following argument: the plaintiff argued that an Italian decision affirming the validity of the contract would be irreconcilable with the former Munich decision affirming invalidity. Therefore, any Italian decision, being not in accordance with the former valid Munich decision, would not be recognized according to Art. 27(3). The Bundesgerichtshof rejected this argument, because it was not a prerequisite of Art. 21 that the foreign judgment would be expected to be recognized.

Comment

In general, the decision is in accordance with the European Court of Justice's rulings. Article 21 does not depend on *formal* identity of the claims in either proceeding, and is interpreted in a wide sense to prevent conflicting decisions in the sense of Art. 27(3).

But that is exactly the reason why the last argument produced by the Bundesgerichtshof cannot be right. If the court states, and, in so far as it does so, absolutely correctly, that Art. 21 is to prevent situations of an Art. 27(3)-type, the obvious unenforceability of the judgment which will result from the earlier proceeding abroad cannot be neglected, as the judgment says that it can.

The 1989 version of the Brussels Convention, which was not applicable in this case brought before 1 December 1994 when the new Convention came into force in Germany, gives more flexibility, avoiding the obviously unsatisfactory result that the action brought in Germany has to be rejected for lack of jurisdiction.

But not even the solution of the 1989 version of the Brussels Convention would prevent all the problems which the Bundesgerichtshof's decision produces for the plaintiff. Nor would the possibility of staying the procedure and waiting for the result in the Italian proceedings be helpful at all.

There are two possible answers to the present problem. The first one does not depend on the specific conflict produced by several decisions made on the same subject in this special case. The mere fact that an appeal against the Bolzano decision was pending in the Italian Corte d'Appello for more than six years must lead to the question of whether it is acceptable to suspend a German proceeding and deny protection to the plaintiff for several years. The case, with regret, shows again that judicial standards are not the same in all Contracting States.

The second solution is based on the specific case. The Bolzano action which was brought after the first Munich action was in conflict with this German proceeding in the sense of Art. 21. As the later of both these actions, the Bolzano proceedings should have been declined according to Art. 21. But then it is not compulsory for one Contracting State's courts to observe the Art. 21

rule in relation to proceedings which, vice versa, did not observe this rule in the same case. Indeed, the question whether the Italian judgment could be recognized one day in Germany arises from the Italian court's failure to decline the proceedings through conflict with the Munich judgment which had even been formally recognized in Italy.

Case principle

2. No stay of procedure according to Art. 21 if German courts do not have jurisdiction under Art. 2.

Case

510   OLG of Bremen 17 October 1991 (2 U 34/91) RIW (1992) 231

Facts

See supra, Art. 5(3), Case 469.

Judgment

The court denied the international jurisdiction of German courts. Therefore, a stay of proceedings in favour of the action pending in Italy was not to be granted. Dismissal for lack of jurisdiction prevailed over stay and decline of proceedings under Art. 21.

The court did, however, make certain remarks as to Art. 21. The dispute was over which party had the right to use the word 'B' as a trademark and firm name in Germany and to exclude the other party from doing so. Article 21 applied if a judgment pronounced in the foreign proceedings could be in conflict with the German and therefore refused recognition according to Art. 27(3).

The Landgericht of Bremen was the first court seised: and the retroactivity of s.270(3) of the German Code of Civil Procedure (ZPO) could not change the rank of litispendences fixed in autonomous interpretation. The earlier Italian service (Art. 163 of the Italian Code of Civil Procedure—*Codice di Procedura Civile*) had not taken place within a 90 days term between service and the term for the trial and was therefore invalid (Art. 163bis, 164). This was not saved by the defendant entering an appearance to the Italian procedure because the Landgericht of Bremen's priority in litispendence was already previously established.

Comment

In accordance with the purpose of Art. 21, a stay of the proceedings can be ordered only if the court has jurisdiction. If jurisdiction of the other court is not yet established, Art. 21 is to be applied. But the second court must decline if there is no jurisdiction of the second court at all.

The interpretation of 'same cause of action' with respect to Art. 27(3) was also correct. Article 21 is intended to ensure the recognizability of judgments (*Kropholler* Art. 21, n.6; *MünchKomm* ZPO-*Gottwald* Art. 21 EuGVÜ, n.4).

Case principle

3. Article 21 priority in time operates in favour of forum even if under national procedure priority otherwise lapses where forum's proceedings are merely for negative declaratory relief.

Case

BGH 11 December 1996 (VIII ZR 154/95) NJW (1997) 870; WiB (1997) 329   **511**

Facts

The plaintiff, a sweetness producer domiciled in Germany, sued the French domiciled defendant, a chocolate factory, for a (negative) declaration that the plaintiff was under no obligations arising from warranty. The defendant sued to enforce the same contract of sale at the Tribunal de Grande Instance de Strasbourg. The action in Germany was served on 17 March 1992; the action in France, following a preliminary proceeding which started in 1991, was brought subsequently in May 1992.

The defendant denied jurisdiction of German courts, arguing that under German law there was no longer a legal interest for a negative declaration, as soon as the action for damages was pending.

Judgment

In German law, a legal interest is a necessary prerequisite for an action for a declaration (s.256 of the *Code of Civil Procedure* (ZPO)). An action for specific performance prevailed over an action for negative declaration concerning the same obligation, even if the latter had been brought earlier. Nevertheless, some restrictions applied to this rule: the legal interest lapsed in this situation if and only if the plaintiff for negative declaration could be sure that all claims of the other party would be decided in the proceedings for specific performance.

However, if, under the Brussels Convention, the action for a declaration pending before the courts of one Contracting State and the action for performance brought in another Contracting State were related in the sense described in Art. 22, the rule of priority under this Article applied, notwithstanding that the first action was (merely) for negative declaratory relief. Although the German courts were not allowed to negate the French court's jurisdiction—which under Art. 21 may only be done by the second court itself—a German court must not reject the action for lack of the said legal interest, being seised first and therefore having priority under Art. 21 to decide the case.

Comment

The decision is a necessary consequence of the unanimous opinion that under Art. 21 the action for a declaration is equal to an action for performance between the same parties. Therefore, the national Code of Civil Procedure must not lead to a situation that one action might be rejected under Art. 21 as second-seised and the other under the national Code of Civil Procedure for *lack of a legal interest.*

ARTICLE 24

" . . . *available under the law of that State . . .* "

Case principle

Article 24 only gives jurisdiction for arrest under s.919 of the Zivil-prozessordnung, when German courts have jurisdiction over the main action.

Case

512 OLG of Koblenz 23 February 1990 (2 U 1795/89) IPRax (1991) 241. ZIP (1991) 1098

Facts

The plaintiff in an arrest proceeding, a German wine firm, sued the defendant, an Italian domiciled wine trading company, for damages for the delivery of wine and applied for an order of arrest (s.917 of the German Code of Civil Procedure, ZPO) and seizure of the defendant's assets.

Judgment

The court rejected the application for arrest. Article 24 made the German Code of Civil Procedure applicable, but there was no power of the German courts according to s.919 of the ZPO, especially where the defendant had no property in Germany (s.919, second alternative of the ZPO). Although the main action was *pending* in the court (s.919, first alternative of the ZPO), this could not create jurisdiction for arrest since the court had no *jurisdiction* to decide the main action. In application of s.919, first alternative of the ZPO, within the scope of Art. 24, German international jurisdiction over the main action was necessary.

Thus, German courts neither had main jurisdiction under Art. 2 nor Art. 5(1) or (3). Whether s.23 of the ZPO could create jurisdiction for the main action for the purpose of Art. 24, by virtue of Art. 4, was a highly discussed question, in the light of Art. 3, para. 2, but it could be left undecided, since the defendant had no funds in Germany in any event.

Comment

Article 24 has the purpose of giving the creditor the benefit of national Codes of Civil Procedure measures. In the present case, only s.919, first alternative of the ZPO was in issue. If national law determines the power of arrest through requiring international jurisdiction over the main action, there is a dispute as to whether this jurisdiction can only be based on the Brussels Convention or also on national jurisdictional rules, applicable under Art. 4, especially those excluded by Art. 3, para. 2 of the Brussels Convention. The court did not decide this point, because s.23 of the ZPO's requirements were not satisfied. The prevailing opinion in Germany is generally in favour of such a (fictitious) application of national German Code of Civil Procedure within the scope of Art. 24 of the Brussels Convention. No doubt it seems to be more logical to decide the jurisdiction for the main action according to the rules of the Brussels Convention, which are to be applied in fact to the action. But the purpose of Art. 24 is to ensure effective protection of rights in preliminary matters. Such protection becomes more efficient if the court can apply its national jurisdictional rules as a whole, without regard solely to the Brussels Convention (*Hanisch* IPRax (1991) 216, *Kropholler* Art. 24, n.8 *MünchKomm* [ZPO]-*Gottwald* Art. 24 EuGVÜ, n.5).

The decisive question in the present case was whether jurisdiction of the court where the main action was pending was possessed, according to s.919, first alternative of the ZPO. Generally, the court does not examine its jurisdiction when applying s.919 and it seems doubtful that there should be another rule if *international* jurisdiction is in question, as the decision seems to require (in the same sense *Zöller/Vollkommer* ZPO s.919 n.8). The efficiency of the arrest proceeding makes it necessary to avoid difficult questions of jurisdiction (*Otte* ZIP (1991) 1048).

The court did not also deal with whether an arrest could legally be based on the necessity of enforcement of the judgment in another Contracting State (s.917(2) of the ZPO) without contravening EC Treaty Art. 6, a question in the meantime decided by the European Court of Justice (*Mund & Fester*, C–398/92) in a negative sense.

ARTICLE 25

" *. . . any judgment . . .* "

Case principle

Article 25 does not apply to a French order for discovery.

Case

OLG of Hamm 14 June 1988 (20 W 24/88) RIW (1989) 566   **513**

Facts

The applicant, domiciled in France, was the plaintiff in an action in France against the defendant, a French entity not party to the German procedure. In France the plaintiff obtained a provisionally enforceable order (*ordonnance de référé*) by which a French expert was ordered and authorized to inspect a technical installation in Essen, Germany, to inquire into evidence there and to investigate which changes in the installation had taken place and to interrogate persons for this purpose. The applicant applied to the Landgericht of Essen for recognition of this French order.

Judgment

The court held the French order to fall outside Art. 25 and consequently the order was neither recognizable nor enforceable. (A discovery ordered by a court in a foreign State nevertheless would fall within the Hague Convention of 18 March 1970 on international judicial assistance.)

Comment

The decision has been criticized because the French ordonnance, according to Art. 145, 484 of the New Code of Civil Procedure, was not pronounced on an *ex parte* application but after trial. The European Court of Justice did not apply the Convention to two cases concerning discoveries (*De Cavel [1]* 143/78. C.H.W., 25/81), because both cases concerned proceedings for divorce, not falling within the scope of application of the Convention. Therefore, it did not solve the problem generally. For example, a German order for securing evidence, if decided after trial, would be recognizable as a judgment in the sense of Art. 25 of the Brussels Convention (*Bloch* RIW (1989) 567).

These objections are partly correct: generally, orders for discovery are not enforceable according to the Convention. This result accords with the prevailing opinion in the Schlosser Report (No 187). Article 25 could not be applied to decisions which the parties could not comply with without co-operation of the court (*Kropholler* Art. 25, n.25).

An exception is not necessary where a decision in discovery proceedings is ordered *after* trial. Article 25 must be applied to all decisions deciding provisionally or finally on *obligations* between the parties. Thus, the present ordonnance in this sense contained not only an order *to the expert*, but also imposed a material obligation on the defendant to permit the visit to the installation and the interrogation of its employees (*MünchKomm* [ZPO]-*Gottwald* Art. 25 EuGVÜ, n.15).

> " . . . *given by a court or tribunal of a Contracting State* . . . "

Case principle

The enforceability of a foreign judgment granting enforceability of an arbitration award.

Case

OLG of Hamburg 5 November 1991 (6 W 43/91) RIW (1992) 939; NJW–RR **514**
(1992) 568

Facts

The applicant sued for partial declaration of enforceability of a British court order enforcing an arbitration award of the Board of Appeal of the Grain and Feed Trade Association. It explained that it had been necessary to apply for enforcement in England in order to obtain an enforceable judgment according to s.20 of the Arbitration Act 1950. The English decision granted interest on the interest ordered in the award.

Judgment

The court generally permitted authorization of enforcement of a foreign exequatur ('double-exequatur'), under the conditions stated by the Bundesgerichtshof (27 March 1984, IPRax (1985), 157), which were present in the case: the English judgment contained not only a declaration of enforceability of the GAFTA award, but an independent order for payment, including interest after the arbitration award was decreed (for further information concerning this case, see *infra*, Case 523).

Comment

Generally, a double-exequatur for decisions of *non*-Contracting States cannot be pronounced according to Art. 25: only judgments from Contracting States enjoy the privileges of recognition according to Art. 25. A recognition according to the national law of one Contracting State must not make a non-Contracting State decision recognizable in this indirect manner (*Kropholler* Art. 25, n.16. *MünchKomm* [ZPO]-*Gottwald* Art. 25, n.10). The Convention is not even applicable to proceedings in different Contracting States which are concerned with the same non-Contracting State decision to be recognized in each of those states.

Therefore, the court's opinion is to be followed only for foreign arbitration awards, which have been recognized or confirmed in their state of origin. The Oberlandesgericht of Hamburg is not correct when referring to the Bundesgerichtshof *op cit.*, because that case was concerned with a New York arbitration with an exequatur of the New York Supreme Court. For the scope of Art. 25 the solution must take account of the Convention's purposes. Recognition of an exequatur of an arbitration award may be granted according to Art. 25 if the award is *replaced* by the exequatur according to the Code of Civil Procedure of the country of origin. In this situation, the exequatur amounts to a first and original judgment under a Member State's Code of Civil Procedure and therefore is recognizable according to Arts 25 *et seq.*

" *. . . as well as the determination of costs . . .* "

Case principle

Costs of 'execution' of a judgment held not a 'judgment' within Art. 25, unless contained in a court order.

Case

515   OLG of Saarbrücken 11 August 1989 (5 W 71/89) IPRax (1990) 207

Facts

Under a binding final judgment of the Tribunal d'Instance of Boulay (France) on 10 April 1987, the defendant had been ordered to pay the costs of the procedure. By the same court's order of 10 September 1987, these costs, payable to the applicant, were fixed at 1241,39 French francs. The applicant applied for authorization of enforcement of the judgment, dated 10 April 1987, and of the order fixing the costs of 10 September 1987, including the costs caused by the judgment's service in France and the costs caused by execution in France (23045 and 32108 French francs).

Judgment

The Oberlandesgericht of Saarbrücken confirmed the granting of enforcement for both the judgment and the order fixing the costs according to Arts 25 and 31. The court rejected the application for enforcement in the amount of another 23045 and 32108 French francs, because there was no decision of a Contracting State's court containing an enforceable obligation against the defendant. The bailiff's bills could not be considered as a 'judgment' on these costs.

Comment

The decision is correct. Decisions concerning the costs of the proceeding or fixing the amount of the costs generally fall within the recognition—and enforcement—rules of the Brussels Convention as far as the judgment on the merits falls within the scope of Art. 1 (*Kropholler* Art. 25, n.12). But, necessarily, there must be a 'judgment' containing a decision, enforceable in the judgment-State (Art. 31). In the present case, none of the judgments adjudicated enforcement of the bailiff's costs. The applicant should have applied in a French procedure according to Art. 704 of the New Code of Civil Procedure for a '*certificat de vérification*' concerning the costs. Such certificate, if not contested by the defendant and if noted by the court's clerk, becomes an enforceable decision (*Schütze* IPRax (1990) 208). Therefore, there was no enforceable judgment as to these costs in France either.

ARTICLE 26, PARAGRAPH 1

" . . . *shall be recognized* . . . "

Case principle

1. French *ordonnance de non conciliation* granting maintenance is *res judicata* when action for new type of maintenance is brought in Germany which could have been, but was not, ordered in the French proceedings.

Case

OLG of Karlsruhe 19 May 1994 (II UF 179/93) NJW–RR (1994) 1286   **516**

Facts

The parties had been divorced by Tribunal de Grande Instance of Strasbourg (France). The defendant had been ordered to pay monthly maintenance of 3000 French francs. Both parties were French citizens. During the divorce procedure in France the same court granted the plaintiff an allowance of 1600 DM monthly and 800 DM for the parties' child. The plaintiff sued the defendant for a separation payment of 2000 DM monthly. The defendant objected that the French decision during the divorce procedure, an *ordonnance de non conciliation contradictoire*, had been the only procedure to decide on this type of maintenance. Therefore, the latter now gave rise to the objection of *res judicata* towards the present action.

Judgment

The court dismissed the claim owing to *res judicata*. The French decision was enforceable according to Art. 26 and therefore prevented a new action in Germany. Both actions had the same intention and the same type of *res judicata* effect. This effect was to be determined for each procedure according to the law of the country where the award was made. According to French law, the *ordonnance* was not merely a preliminary award but continuing for the whole period until the divorce procedure ended. The description of this *ordonnance* as '*provisoire*' was no impediment to such an interpretation since its only purpose was to describe the *ordonnance's* relationship to and dependency upon the divorce action.

Comment

The decision is to be followed when applying Art. 26 to the *ordonnance*. It is also correct that a final decision, even if made only for a certain period of time, should prevent another action concerning the same matter (see Art. 21 of the Brussels Convention).

Case principle

2. Under national German law, a foreign judgment is no reason for inadmissibility of a second action in Germany, if enforceability of the former in Germany is contested.

Case

517   OLG of München 24 July 1996 (7 U 2651/96) RIW (1996) 856

Facts

The plaintiff, a Greek carrier, sued the defendant, an insurance company, for coverage under CMR. In 1987, the plaintiff had brought an action for the same claim in Greece and had been granted a default judgment in 1993. The defendant argued that the Greek judgment was unenforceable in Germany due to a prorogation agreement giving exclusive jurisdiction to Munich courts.

Judgment

According to several judgments of the BGH, a foreign judgment, even if enforceable in Germany, did not render inadmissible an action in German courts. In such a case, German courts had to grant a judgment which, due to the effect of *res judicata*, did not deviate materially from the foreign judgment.

The court left it undecided whether or not this national rule applied to judgments enforceable under the Brussels Convention: the reason for the BGH's rule is strongly connected to the problems a party to a foreign process faces when applying for enforceability—problems that are excluded by the principles of Art. 26.

Nevertheless, the court did not reject the action as inadmissible, as the enforceability was contested by the defendant and the application of the Brussels Convention was doubtful because the action in Greece had been brought before the Brussels Convention was in force for Greece. Although the court held that Greek courts had jurisdiction under the German-Greek Enforcement Convention, the mere contestation of this result by the defendant and a difficult legal situation led to the conclusion that legal certainty and the protection of the plaintiff justified a new judgment.

Comment

The decision is vague and ambiguous. If the Greek decision was recognizable and enforceable under the Brussels Convention, the court should not have left the issue undecided. Under the Brussels Convention, one of the most important outcomes of recognition is the effect of *res judicata*, which means that a new action in another Contracting State must be dismissed (see Case 42/76 *De Wolf*).

Particularly, the court had the authority to clarify doubts about applicability of the Brussels Convention and enforceability of the Greek decision. The applicability of the Brussels Convention to Greek judgments was not governed by Art. 54. Article 12(1) of the Accession Convention with Greece of 25 October 1982 clearly says that in general the Convention applied only to actions brought after the Convention came into force in the judgment-court's state. According to Art. 12(2), the scope of application extended to the recognition of judgments resulting from earlier proceedings, if the courts of the judgment-state had jurisdiction under rules in accordance with the Brussels Convention or bilateral conventions in force between the judgment-state and the state of recognition.

Therefore, the Greek judgment was to be recognized under Arts 26 *et seq.* if Greek courts had jurisdiction under the German-Greek Convention—as the court assumed.

Obviously, there was no impediment to recognition under Art. 27: particularly, jurisdiction of the foreign court is not a prerequisite for recognition under the Brussels Convention. Therefore, the defendant's objection was only decisive for Art. 12(2) of the Accession Convention (jurisdiction of Greek courts under German-Greek Convention), not for recognition under Art. 26. Exclusive jurisdiction of German courts under Art. 17 would not prevent recognition under Art. 28, para. 1, as Art. 17 is not protected by this rule.

ARTICLE 27(1)

" . . . contrary to public policy . . . "

Case principles

1. Article 27(1) is inapplicable for mere mistake in application of the laws of civil procedure in the judgment-State.
2. Article 27(2) is inapplicable to violation of the defendant's right of audience after the commencement of foreign proceedings.

Case

BGH 21 March 1990 (XII ZB 71/89) NJW (1990) 2201; EuZW (1990) 257; **518** IPRax (1992) 33

Facts

The parties, Italian citizens, married in Italy in 1960. The defendant did not enter an appearance to the divorce procedure at Tribunale di Ancona. By a judgment of the Corte d'Appello di Ancona, of which recognition was applied for, the defendant was ordered to make a monthly payment of 200 000 LIT to the plaintiff. The plaintiff had not made an application for maintenance in the Italian procedure.

Judgment

The Bundesgerichtshof first discussed Art. 27(2) which it held to be inapplicable because it only protected the defendant's audience in the matter of institution of the proceedings. Other violations of a party's audience could exceptionally fall under Art. 27(1). A mere violation of the judgment-State's Code of Civil Procedure was not contrary to public policy in the state where recognition was requested. Public policy was only violated, if the judgment did not result from a legally conducted and constituted procedure. Ordering a so-called 'divorce-payment' without an application having been made, or ordered through the mistaken belief of the Italian court that an application had been made, did not amount to such a violation. The Bundesgerichtshof took into account that the defendant had had the opportunity to bring an objection of a violation of public policy in the Italian proceedings.

Comment

The decision is satisfactory as to public policy. Only a violation of fundamental principles of civil procedure can amount to a violation of public policy. The constitutional guaranty of an audience in the court (Art. 103(1) of the German Constitution—*Grundgesetz*) belongs to these general principles.

    The Bundesgerichtshof's opinion has to be agreed with that the defendant is under an obligation to use the opportunity granted to him to challenge erroneous decisions in the judgment-State (same opinion *Geimer* IPRax (1992) 14). This is not the same situation as in the case of Art. 27(2) where the defendant to whom audience was *not* given from the beginning is under no obligation to secure this audience by his own efforts. Nevertheless, if the Italian court decided without any application for maintenance, the defendant had no chance to avoid this decision by challenging an application. Therefore, the Bundesgerichtshof should not have left undecided whether there was an application in the Italian proceedings or not.

Case principle

3.   Indefinite amount of interest in a French judgment does not prevent enforcement in Germany, if interest can be calculated by application of published laws of the judgment-State.

Case

BGH of 5 April 1989 (IX ZB 68/89) NJW (1990) 3084; WM (1990) 1122;   **519**
WuB VII B 1 Art. 31 EuGVÜ 1.90

Facts

In 1983, the applicant, a French enterprise, applied for enforceability of a
French judgment against the defendant, a German company, for payment of
a certain amount of money plus legal interest from the day of bringing the
action. As a consequence of the court's direction that the judgment was not
determined as to the interest, the applicant partially withdrew its application
and enforceability was granted for the rest.

In December 1988, the applicant applied for a declaration of enforceability
of the French judgment for legal interest.

The defendant objected on the ground of fraud of the applicant during the
French proceedings.

Judgment

The Bundesgerichtshof found no contravention of public policy under Art.
27(1). The alleged fraud was not to be taken into account because it had
allegedly *arisen* before the judgment was delivered.

Neither was the indefinite nature of the interest an impediment to recognition: Art. 31 did not prevent a declaration of enforceability, since the decision
was also enforceable in France as to the legal interest. Since the foreign judgment was to be recognized according to the Brussels Convention, enforcement
should not be prevented by the fact that the obligation was not to be measured
by the judgment itself, but according to procedures of the law of the judgment-
State. The French judge could only award 'legal interest', because the *rate* of
interest depended on the discount of the Banque de France. In France, such a
judgment was enforceable if the rate of legal interest was proved to the bailiff.
Therefore, the judgment was sufficiently definite. Only the finalization could
not be left to the German bailiff, but had to be made by the court: the judge
deciding on enforceability was entitled to calculate the concrete obligation
resulting from the judgment by adding the amount of interest.

Comment

The only ground for denying recognition and enforcement because of the indefinite nature of a foreign judgment for interest could have been Art. 27(1).
Some German courts have decided this way (OLG München IPRspr
1980 no 170. OLG München IPRax 1988, 291). However, so far the
Bundesgerichtshof's decision confirms a prevailing opinion amongst most courts
of appeal (OLG of Celle RIW (1988) 565; OLG of Stuttgart RIW (1988) 302;
also, overruling its own opinion: OLG of Hamm RIW (1993) 764, see *infra* Art.
27(2). A judgment granting a legal rate of interest, without specifying the
percentage, is not contrary to German public policy. Therefore, there is no
impediment to recognition in the sense of Art. 27(1). This result is satisfactory:
practice of recognition between the Member States must support the different

national procedural rules as far as possible to ensure an efficient practice of recognition. The decision is important not only for French but also for Belgian Luxembourg and Italian judgments. Its general principles can also be applied to maintenance decisions under an indexation (*Roth* IPRax (1992) 15 s).

The Bundesgerichtshof empowered the court competent under Arts 31 and 32 to make the concretization necessary for enforcement in Germany. This solution does not give rise to any problems if the factors for calculation lying outside the judgment are not subject to changes. In the present case, the legal interest in French law was fluctuating. The concretization during the enforcement procedure risks that a later enforcement will not be in conformity with later changes concerning the percentage of interest (*Münch* RIW (1989) 21). Nevertheless, the decision must also be followed on this point: the judicial decision at least makes sure that the calculation is correct (*Roth* IPRax (1989) 16).

The Bundesgerichtshof's arguments denying the relevance of the alleged fraud were not convincing: the Bundesgerichtshof referred to s.17 of the German Code of Execution of Recognition Conventions (AVAG), whereby objections against the obligation decided by the judgment for which recognition is sought were excluded. But the allegation of fraud in process is not an objection to the substantive obligation, but against due process. Fraud in a process *can* amount to a violation of German public policy (BGH WM (1986) 1370. IPRax (1987) 236); and, on this issue, Art. 27(1) does extend to facts which arose *before* the foreign judgment was delivered (*Thode* WuB VII B 1. Art. 31 of the Brussels Convention 1.90, 1175).

Case principle

4. Italian judgment is not contrary to German public policy when including legal interest of more than 30 per cent per annum, but where Italian currency was devalued in relation to Deutschmark, so that interest, when calculated in Deutschmarks, was only 9.5 per cent.

Case

520   BGH 4 March 1995 (IX ZB 55/92) NJW (1993) 1801; LM EGÜbk Nr 38

Facts

The applicant was granted a judgment of the Tribunale Genoa against the defendant for payment of over 21 million Italian Lire plus interest. The defendant brought a *Rechtsbeschwerde* (appeal on point of law) under Art. 37 against enforcement, since the applicant's claim calculated on the revaluation basis ordered for interest was more than four times as high as the original obligation, which amounted to a rate of interest of more than 30 per cent per annum, contrary to good faith in German law.

Judgment

The Bundesgerichtshof rejected the defendant's complaint. A foreign judgment was only contrary to German public policy if the result led to a fundamental conflict with elementary ideas of justice. The increase in the amount granted in the judgment substantially resulted from the revaluation of currency. However, calculated *in Deutschmarks*, there was only an increase of 9.5 per cent per annum and revaluation of currency itself was not contrary to German public policy, especially with respect to s.3 of the German Currency Code (*Währungsgesetz*—WährG). A revaluation of obligations was not forbidden for creditors domiciled abroad (ss. 49(1), 4(1), 3 Foreign Trade Code— *Außenwirtschaftsgesetz*—AWG) and for obligations in other currencies than the Deutschmark.

But the judgment as authorized for enforcement was not sufficiently certain as to the revaluation of currency and legal interest. The court had to describe unambiguously the content and the limits of enforceability. The official concerned with the enforcement could only tolerate less important ambiguities. This separation of functions between the court and the official concerned with enforcement also applied to foreign judgments. That did not make recognition and enforcement impossible. The German court had to suggest an appropriate method of concretization of amounts. As in the case of judgments granting maintenance under an indexation, or granting interest at a legal rate, the revaluation of currency, automatically applicable according to the foreign law, had to be given effect to in Germany by concretization in the Art. 31 procedure.

The Bundesgerichtshof expressly rejected a solution proposed by some authors, to leave open the concretization of judgments for payment until the enforcement proceedings. The judgment-court had to give clear instructions for the calculation which could also take into consideration any developments after granting enforceability and before enforcement.

Comment

See also supra.

The decision is correct to have rejected the objection of usury. Certain rates of interest which are counted as usury in German law cannot be assessed without reference to the currency in question. They are only valid for obligations in Deutsche Mark or currencies with similar stability.

As to the concretization of foreign judgments, the Bundesgerichtshof confirmed its former decision (see *supra*, Case 519). If a foreign judgment is not concrete as to certain amounts, this is not necessarily contrary to German public policy (*Geimer* LM note to EGÜbk 1995, n.38). But the *German declaration of enforceability* must be as concrete as German judgments have to be. It is also proper that the Bundesgerichtshof did not follow the opinion whereby enforceability can be granted without concrete calculation. Such calculation does not fall within the functions of the execution process. The decision also gives an approach to the practical problem that fluctuation of amounts in the judgment does not end at the moment of declaration of enforceability. The authorization of enforcement may not only calculate the exact amount enforceable; it can describe the method of calculation in order to enable the official carrying out enforcement to calculate—as in the case of a mere calculation of interest at a fixed rate in German judgments—the exact amount which is to be enforced.

Case principle

5. Foreign judgment not contrary to German public policy when the defendant was performing official services and the judgment exceeded the limits of responsibility under the German Constitution and German federal insurance law.

Case

521   BGH 16 September 1993 (IX 82/90) NJW (1993) 3269

Facts

See supra, Art. 1(1), Case 446.

Judgment

The Bundesgerichtshof discussed several aspects of German public policy: s.1(1) of the German ordinance concerning injuries to German citizens abroad of 7 December 1942, which leads to the application of German law to torts caused by a German citizen to another German citizen. Only the material result was decisive to German public policy.

Freedom of an official from responsibility towards third persons was not part of the fundamental principles of German law of state officials. Nevertheless, the Federal Republic's obligation to safeguard its officials was part of these principles. But this obligation could be performed by the state guaranteeing the obligation of officials towards third persons.

As to all damages, the Italian judgment might offend German public policy, since the regulations in ss. 636 and 637 of the Federal Insurance Order (Reichsversicherungsordnung), excluding responsibility for personal injuries towards people insured against accidents in employment and school, were a fundamental element of the system of legal insurance against accidents. Actions brought abroad should not defeat this principle. This regulation was also applicable against foreign tort law. Insurance in case of accidents, according to the law of the country of origin during short-term professional stays within the EU, indirectly supported freedom of movement. The Bundesgerichtshof did not decide whether this measure of public policy was to be determined by the national courts or—in an autonomous fashion—by the European Court of Justice. In both cases, ss.636 *et seq.* of the Insurance order had to be considered.

Article 27(2) was not an impediment to recognition. The debtor had entered an appearance in the civil action by responding to the joined criminal action, although during the trial he had only answered the criminal action.

Comment

With respect to Art. 27(2) the decision follows the European Court of Justice's *Sonntag* ruling in Case C–172/91.

As to Art. 27(1) it must be reviewed from the point of view of the recognition-State's public policy. There is not a European 'public policy'. Nevertheless, the scope of public policy must be strictly interpreted for the purposes of the Brussels Convention (*Kropholler* Art. 27, n.4).

It might be doubted whether or not the release of an official from responsibility towards third persons is part of the general principles of German law of officials, and therefore part of public policy. This principle is stated in Art. 34, sentence 1 of the German Constitution (Grundgesetz) and should not be seen as merely general and exemptable. But although it is true that the obligation to safeguard officials is of great importance, nonetheless, this obligation was not contravened in the present case, since the Federal Republic could restore the damages to the defendant.

The decision is correct as to ss.636 *et seq.* of the Federal Insurance Order: principles of social security in the national law of the state where recognition is sought must not be circumvented by bringing an action abroad under the application of foreign tort law.

Case principles

6. French court deciding without a professional judge is not contrary to German public policy if composition of court was correct under French law.
7. Public policy cannot be opposed to enforceability if defendant did not exhaust all procedural remedies in the state of origin.

Case

OLG of Saarbrücken 3 August 1987 (5 W 102/87) NJW (1988) 3100. IPRax **522**
(1989) 37

Facts

The applicant obtained a preliminarily enforceable judgment of the Court of Commerce of Paris (France) against the defendant—decided by only one lay judge—for payment of about 2.3 million French francs with interest on the contractual rate from 18 June 1986, with a deduction of interest to be made between specified dates, 29 June 1984 and 19 February 1986. The judgment held that the guarantor was under an obligation of repayment of several loans with contractual interest, which was to be cancelled under certain conditions. The defendant objected that the judgment was indefinite, the court was not duly composed, the trial was not public and the applicant had committed fraud during the process. Further, the obligation had been partly performed before the judgment was made and there was no dispute on this point during the procedure for enforceability.

Judgment

The Landgericht of Saarbrücken granted enforceability and concretised the French judgment by determining the interest as resulting from the French court's reasoning. The Oberlandesgericht of Saarbrücken partly reversed this for contravention of Art. 27(1).

The composition of the French court was not contrary to German public policy. The judgment-State's law of civil procedure and judicial constitution applied and only an infringement of fundamental principles of German law would affect German public policy. Such infringement was generally excluded, because all Contracting States' laws were on a constitutional level.

Publicity of trial was also a principle of German civil procedure. But this principle was not unrestricted, even in the German Code of Civil Procedure.

Moreover, the court explained that the defendant, not having exhausted all legal remedies in the judgment-State, could not rely on public policy in the recognition-State.

But there was the necessity for enforceable content of the judgment, since otherwise the applicant had no interest in legal protection through authorization of enforcement, which would later be impossible due to indefinite character. In the present case, the judgment was not sufficiently determined as to the interest and as to the deduction of interest not calculated in the judgment but described in the court's reasoning. A concretization was not possible through merely applying the amounts and rates of interests described in the reasoning. An examination of the foreign court's reasoning was impossible, since this method could amount to an inadmissible review of substance, révision au fond (Art. 34, para. 3), by an inadmissible supplement to the judgment. In any event, a description of the deductible interest, running between 29 June 1984 and 19 February 1986, was impossible, since the rate of interest could not even be ascertained from the judgment or its reasoning. However, that was no impediment to enforcement of the obligations under the loan *excluding the interest* which was not clearly ascertainable from the judgment. Article 42, para. 1 allowed this separation.

Then, the defendant's alleged partial performance was to be considered. Although it happened before delivery of judgment for which recognition was sought, the court did not consider this to be an inadmissible *révision au fond*. It interpreted the lack of objection of the parties as a negative acknowledgement (s.397(2) of the German Civil Code—BGB) and as an agreement restricting enforceability, both having occurred after the judgment was made.

Comment

The reasoning on differences between the French organization of courts and German law is not wholly satisfactory. Generally, there may be an assumption that other EU States' laws are in accord with principles of a constitutional state. But this is not an impediment against a State's applying its own public policy to particular questions, just as in any national system the *general* confidence in Parliament's constitutionality is not an impediment against finding that particular laws are unconstitutional. The composition of a court with only one lay judge seems problematical (in the same sense, OLG of Saarbrücken: *Roth* IPRax (1989) 17; *Kropholler* (Art. 27, n.11), but must be accepted, because the defendant did not appeal to higher courts with professional judges. The court's opinion that the defendant had to exhaust all legal remedies in the state of origin before raising the objection of German public policy must also be restricted: such an obligation can only exist, as far as the offence against public policy in the state where enforcement is sought amounts to a mistake in the first state's procedure, which can make such remedy successful. In other cases, when the procedure and the judgment are in complete harmony with the judgment-State's laws, the judgment nevertheless *may* be contrary to the recognition-State's public policy, when it cannot be successfully attacked by legal remedies in the first state.

The court's reasoning on the problem of concretization of the judgment as to interest seems artificial in the light of separate functions of court and the enforcement official in German law (see *Comment supra*, Case 519, *Roth* IPRax (1989) 15).

Starting from the Bundesgerichtshof's principles for the concretization of indefinite judgments during later enforcement procedures, in the present case there is a further problem that the rate of 'contractual' interest was not expressly stated in the reasoning, but had to be calculated from criteria given in the French judgment's reasoning. Such calculation is inadmissible in an enforcement proceeding (*Roth* IPRax (1989) 16).

The court's construction considering the performed part of the obligation seems to be acceptable, especially from the point of view of economy of process. Undoubtedly, performance of an obligation while the action was pending is irrelevant if recognition of the judgment is later sought. Such satisfaction occurring *before* judgment cannot be considered during the procedure for authorization of enforcement. On the other hand, the defendant could raise the issue as an objection against execution itself. Therefore, it seems more economical to allow this objection during the earlier procedure for enforceability.

Case principle

8. English judgment granting compound interest not contrary to German public policy.

Case

OLG of Hamburg 5 November 1991 (6 W 43/91) NJW–RR (1992) 568; RIW   **523**
(1992) 939

Facts

See supra, Art. 25, Case 514.

Judgment

In the opinion of the court, German public policy was not affected by the English judgment granting compound interest for delay. Such interest was contrary to s.289, sentence 1 of the German Civil Code (BGB), but the German-British Convention for Recognition and Enforcement of 14 July 1960, in force until 31 December 1986, had allowed such interest according to s.17 of the Judgments Act 1838 (Art. IX(3), sentence 1 of the German-British Convention). The Brussels Convention did not change the permissibility of such interest in relation to the UK.

Comment

The result is correct because s.289, sentence 1 of the BGB is not part of German public policy. Moreover, s.289 grants compound interest for delay if the debtor is in delay with interest. But the reasoning of the court is not convincing: an obligation not to insist on public policy in general or in part, which had been contained in a Convention no longer in force, has no influence on the interpretation of Art. 27(1) since this Convention's rules expressly allow refusal of recognition where contrary to public policy.

Case principle

9. French judgment is not contrary to German public policy when granting interest at legal rate annually fixed according to the situation on the capital market.

Case

524 OLG of Hamburg 18 June 1993 (6 W 21/93, 6 W 57/92) RIW (1994) 424

Facts

The applicant, an insurance company, applied for partial enforceability of a French court's judgment and—with an additional application—for concretization concerning interest. The judgment ordered: 'the defendant's firm to pay to the plaintiff:—73865,76 French francs including interest at the legal rate from the day of payment of the obligations due to temporary inability to work—78488,09 French francs including interest at the legal rate from the payment of overdue amounts and—to pay amounts due or becoming due after 15 September 1983 corresponding to a part of due amounts equal to a debt of 12821449 French francs, according to the time of becoming due with interest at the legal rate'.

The defendant had paid a part of the amount. The applicant applied for enforceability of the rest including legal interest and costs of the proceeding. It asserted that legal interest had to be calculated according to the French interest law in the amount of discount of Banque de France. In an additional application, the applicant calculated the amounts of interest.

Judgment

The court held the judgment to be enforceable and not to be contrary to German public policy. An annual refixing of legal interest according to the situation on the capital market was not contrary to public policy.

However, the judgment could only be enforced within the limits of the French court's decree, which could neither be changed nor supplemented by a German court.

Thus, the French judgment was not definite enough to be enforced in Germany as far as legal interest was granted. There was a necessity of con-cretization of the amount of interest during the enforcement procedure. However, this was possible, according to German law, since the rate of inter-est resulted from French laws, *i.e.* generally accessible sources.

Comment

The decision is in accordance with the prevailing opinion in Germany. For further information see Bundesgerichtshof *supra*, Case 519.

Case principles

10. Violation of an arbitration clause does not prevent enforceability.
11. French judgment granting interest according to variable legal rate not contrary to German public policy.

Case

OLG of Hamm 28 December 1993 (20 W 19/93) RIW (1994) 243; NJW-RR   **525**
(1995) 189

Facts

The applicant requested enforceability of an *ordonnance de référé de Tribunal de Commerce Nanterre* ordering the defendant to pay about 185 million French francs with legal interest from 1 January 1993 and a further 100 000 French francs according to Art. 700 of the New Code of Civil Procedure. After the applicant had specified the amount of legal interest, the Landgericht grant-ed enforceability. The defendant raised several objections, including that the French court had ignored an arbitration clause.

Judgment

As to Art. 27(1) the court held that even if the French court had exercised juris-diction contrary to an existing arbitration clause, it was not an impediment to enforceability, according to German public policy. This resulted *a fortiori* from Art. 28, para. 3, whereby a violation of jurisdiction could not prevent enforce-ability. Moreover, the decision was a preliminary one and therefore from a German point of view not within the jurisdiction of an arbitration tribunal.

The order on interest was not contrary to public policy, since it could be concretizised in application of French laws. On the other hand, the decision was not enforceable as to the costs, since the amount could not be determined by mere application of law.

Comment

Concerning the concretization of the interest, the decision is in accordance with the prevailing opinion in Germany (see *supra*, Case 514).

The arguments are convincing concerning the arbitration clause: the question had to be decided in accordance with German law, since only German public policy could prevent enforceability. It was not decisive whether the decision was contrary to French law.

For further discussion, see Art. 27(2) and Art. 38, para. 1, *infra*, Cases 543 and 551.

Case principle

12.   Even if a foreign court was incorrect to disregard an arbitration agreement, a German court must not decline enforcement for such reason, not stated in Arts 27 and 28.

Case

526   OLG of Hamburg 5 August 1993 (6 W 92/89) IPRax (1995) 391

Facts

The applicant sought enforcement of a judgment of the Cour d'Appel of Rennes (France). The defendant objected that French courts had no jurisdiction owing to an arbitration agreement in the contract.

Judgment

The court rejected this objection: Arts 27 and 28 listed exclusively the grounds of refusal of recognition and enforcement. That prevented the court from applying German public policy to a jurisdictional question, even if it arose from an arbitration agreement.

Comment

The question whether a decision of the judgment-court concerning existence or non-existence of an arbitration agreement is binding on the recognition-court has been discussed. When the UK became a Member State, its view was that the court of the State of enforcement was free to decide whether the Convention was applicable or not, according to Brussels, Art. 1, para. 2(4) and if not, within the rule in s.32(1) of the Civil Jurisdiction and Judgments Act 1982 providing for refusal of recognition of a contravening court judgment in the circumstances.

The prevailing opinion in Germany is the opposite: arbitration, which is excluded by Art. 1, para. 2(4), only means proceedings of an arbitration tribunal. It does not extend to preliminary questions for a judge of ordinary jurisdiction to answer. As far as Art. 1, para. 2(4) does not prevent a court of ordinary jurisdiction from deciding on questions arising from an arbitration agreement in a contract, this decision must be binding for the courts in another Contracting State, *i.e.* for the enforcement procedure. Therefore, the recognition-court is not entitled to deny applicability of the Convention by using the argument that the first court was wrong in applying the Convention. Accordingly, the decision is to be followed.

Case principle

13. Enforceability of foreign judgments is not prevented by Art. 27(1) for incorrect decision on substance or violation of principles of fair process.

Case

OLG of Düsseldorf 13 November 1996 (3 W 347/96), EuZW (1997) 284   **527**

Facts

The defendant argued that recognition of an Italian judgment was prevented by German public policy, because the Italian court had not granted legal audience to, and reached its decision ignoring facts and proof offered by the defendant.

Judgment

Article 34, para. 3 prevented the court from reviewing the correctness of the substance of the foreign decision. Therefore, even if the decision was based on wrong facts this could not prevent recognition under public policy.

As far as the defendant argued that the Code of Civil Procedure had been violated, these violations did not lead to the conclusion that the Italian decision was not made in a legal and ordinary procedure; such violations gave grounds to appeal in Italy, which had already been brought, but did not prevent recognition.

The court also refused stay of proceedings according to Art. 38, para. 1 as the success of the appeal in Italy was doubtful, the Italian court of appeal had not granted a stay of enforcement during the appeal, and security measures according to Art. 38, para. 3 were sufficient to protect the defendant.

Comment

See too supra, Case 518.

ARTICLE 27(2)

" . . . *duly served* . . . "

Case principle

1. Service is not duly performed under Art. 5(2) of the 1965 Hague Convention or under the German-French Convention, if carried out upon another (substitute) person rather than the addressee willing to accept.

Case

528 BGH of 20 September 1990 (IX ZB 1/88) NJW (1991) 641; WM (1990) 1936; WuB VII B 1. Art. 27 EuGVÜ 1.91

Facts

The judgment is the final decision in the *Lancray* Case C–305/88 of the European Court of Justice. The applicant, a stock company (société anonyme) domiciled in France, and the defendant, a German Limited Partnership (KG), had business connections, for which the jurisdiction of the Tribunal de Commerce of Nanterre was agreed. The applicant obtained a preliminary injunction of Amtsgericht E against the defendant. Later it brought an action in the Tribunal de Commerce of Nanterre for a confirmation of Amtsgericht E's order. French process for trial on 18 November 1986 was served on 18 August 1986 by handing it to a secretary in the defendant's office. For a further hearing on 16 December 1986 the process was sent to the defendant in the French language in a registered letter. The defendant did not enter an appearance. The French court granted the plaintiff a default judgment.

Judgment

The Bundesgerichtshof determined sufficiency of time by assessing the time which the defendant actually had for preparing its defence. Three months was considered enough for the defendant to appreciate the content of the document served and written in French by means of a translation.

But service was not *duly* carried out according to the Hague Convention of 15 November 1965. Simple delivery was—with the exception of subs.1(b)—generally permissible according to Art. 5(2), but could only take place by handing the notice to the addressee himself who was ready to accept. Service on another person was subject to the necessity of a translation according to s.3 of the German Code of 22 December 1977. Under the agreement of 6 May 1961, between the governments of the Federal Republic and France for further simplification of service according to the Hague Convention of 1 March 1954, the service was not correct either. The requesting authority had not asked for service in the form of the national law of the requested authority. According to the agreement's Art. 3(1) service could have been performed by handing process to the addressee prepared to accept. But here there was formal service in the form of substituted service upon another person. Therefore, a translation was necessary according to Art. 3(2) of the Hague Convention of 1 March 1954.

Thus, according to the decision of the European Court of Justice, it was not decisive whether service was in time, since the service was not duly performed

according to the laws of the judgment-State, including those on international contracts. In particular, service by simple mailing was not possible when the service
had to be performed in Germany, since the Federal Republic had objected to such
service according to Art. 10 of the Hague Convention of 1965.

Comment

Although the Bundesgerichtshof was bound by the European Court of Justice's
decision, there remained several questions concerning the validity of service. It
is correct that the Hague Convention prevails over the national French law of
service. Invalidity was based on the lack of a German translation. There are
objections against this argument, however (*Stade* NJW (1993) 185) that the
requirement of a translation did not result from Art. 5(3) of the Hague
Convention of 1965, giving a discretion to the requested authority,
nor resulted from the bilateral German-French agreement. Section 3 of the
German Code of 22 December 1977—prescribing such translation—was
doubtless binding for the German judge, but from the point of view of French
law it was not incorrect service if the German judge did not follow this prescription. Yet, this objection itself is incorrect: whenever service on the
addressee (Art. 5(2)) is impossible and a special form according to Art. 5(1)(b)
is not requested, the service can only be performed under Art. 5(1)(a)
according to the requested state's law of service; and the prescription of s.3,
requiring a translation, is part of the applicable German law.

According to the European Court of Justice, the ability to rectify incorrect
service generally is for the judgment-State's law. It is correct that international
conventions on service prevail over these national rules for rectification of incorrect service. But s.187 of the German Code of Civil Procedure (rectification
through actual knowledge of the addressee) was applicable in the present case:
whenever the service must be performed according to Art. 5(1)(a) of the Hague
Convention of 1965, *i.e.* in the requested state's forms, the rectification of incorrect service was for the same law. The Convention's purpose to decide homogeneously on recognition in all Contracting States is not an impediment, since in the
case of Art. 5(1)(a) the national law of service of the addressee's state is also relevant.

Although the Bundesgerichtshof's opinion that Art. 10 of the Hague
Convention of 1965 is a rectification rule seems to be incorrect, since it is a
simple rule for the forms of service, the application of Art. 10 is correct in its
result. There are several decisions denying recognition of judgments from
Contracting States familiar with this kind of service (such as the UK and The
Netherlands), since the documents to be served had been mailed by ordinary
or registered post to Germany. Such service does not comply with the Hague
Convention, since Germany validly has objected to Art. 10.

Case principle

2. Substituted service, being incorrect according to s.182 of the
    Zivilprozessordnung when the defendant is a legal entity with a place of
    business, prevents enforceability, notwithstanding an incorrect certificate
    issued by German court verifying service.

Case

529   BGH 18 February 1993 (IX ZB 87/90) NJW (1993) 2688; WM (1993) 1352;
RIW (1993) 673; EWiR (1993) 981; EuZW (1993) 579; IPRax (1993) 396

Facts

The case is the final decision in *Minalmet* Case C–123/91 of the European
Court of Justice. The applicant, domiciled in London, applied for authorization of enforcement of a default judgment of the English High Court of Justice.
The writ of summons had been transmitted to the Amtsgericht of Düsseldorf
for service according to Art. 5(1)(a) of the Hague Convention of 1965. The
post office, failing to find anyone in the defendant's place of business, effected
substitute service according to s.182 of the German Code of Civil Procedure
(deposition at the post office, making a record, leaving a notification in the
addressee's letter box). The Amtsgericht of Düsseldorf recorded the certificate
according to Art. 6 of the Hague Convention. The defendant did not enter an
appearance to the hearing in England and claimed incorrect service.

Judgment

The Bundesgerichtshof refused enforcement through lack of due service. The
Amtsgericht of Düsseldorf had incorrectly given the certificate, since the defendant was a legal entity, having a place of business, and therefore substituted
service according to s.182 of the ZPO did not apply (ss.195(1) and 184(2) of
ZPO). No doubt the English court would not know of these rules of German
civil procedure.

Rectification of the mistake was impossible, because in the application of
the Hague Convention, only a rectification according to Art. 15(2) was to be
considered. According to English law, the only possibility of rectification was
if the document in fact reached the addressee, which was disputed. Only a correct service, not merely a certificate erroneously given, gave a reason for the
presumption that the document had reached the addressee.

The defendant was, in accordance with the European Court of Justice's decision, not estopped from relying on Art. 27(2), although it had not brought an
appeal in England.

Neither was the application successful in resort to Art. V(1), s.1 and Art.
III(1) of the German-British Convention of 14 July 1960. According to Art.
56, para. 1 of the Brussels Convention, the former Convention was no longer
applicable within the material scope of the Brussels Convention, *i.e.* for recognition and enforcement.

Comment

The decision is generally in accordance with the *Lancray* decision of the
European Court of Justice, Case C–305/88. It is true that an incorrect service
cannot be rectified by the competent authority of the requested state giving
a certificate.

The question whether the defendant is under an obligation to bring proceedings for legal remedies in the state of origin, having been in dispute in Germany for a long time (for the different opinions see *Geimer* EuZW (1991) 447 and *Rauscher* IPRax (1991) 156) has now been decided by the European Court of Justice in the *Minalmet* decision (Case C–123/91).

Some problems still exist with respect to rectification: in the present case an examination of English law was incorrect. As far as the Hague Convention is applicable, it prevails over rules of service and rectification of incorrect service under the Code of Civil Procedure of the judgment-State. On the other hand, when applying rules of service of the requested state (Art. 5(1)(a) of the Hague Convention), the rectification rules of this state are also to be applied. In this case, s.187 of the ZPO (*Rauscher* IPRax (1993) 379) was applicable, but did not validate the service.

Case principle

3. A defendant was not duly served, but having applied for adjournment, could not prevent enforcement by application of Art. 27(2).

Case

OLG of Köln 8 December 1989 (2 W 118/89) IPRax (1991) 114   **530**

Facts

The applicants applied for authorization of enforcement of a Belgium default judgment of 9 February 1984 and of a Belgium judgment of 4 October 1984. During the procedure leading to the judgment of October 1984, the defendant had requested an adjournment of trial because of the absence of its lawyer, but had not objected to the validity of service. The summons to the trial which led to the default judgment of February 1984, had been served by deposition at the police station at the defendant's former domicile in K, Belgium. Defendant K, at the time of service, was domiciled in Germany and was no longer officially registered in Belgium. Defendant H, who was served in the same manner, was 'officially resident' in K, according to the record of service.

Judgment

The court granted enforcement of the Belgian judgment of 4 October 1984. The defendant *had entered an appearance* by asking for an adjournment for reasons not concerned with the validity of service.

Enforcement of the default judgment of February 1984 was denied with respect to defendant K. The service had to be made in accordance with the German-Belgium agreement of 25 April 1965 and the 1954 Hague Convention, since the defendant was domiciled in Germany. Therefore, service in Belgium was incorrect. With respect to the defendant H, the Oberlandesgericht remitted the case to the Landgericht to ascertain the defendant's residence and to decide whether the service was in accordance with Belgian law or not.

Comment

The decision is correct as far as there was an appearance in the sense of Art. 27(2). In an autonomous interpretation, an 'appearance' means any behaviour by which the defendant shows that he has knowledge of the procedure and could arrange for his defence, besides a mere objection to the validity of service (*Kropholler* Art. 27(22), *Linke* IPRax (1991) 92). The contrary opinion (*Geimer* IPRax (1988) 271) whereby the defendant cannot rely on Art. 27(2), if he appeared during the original proceeding, even when only objecting to incorrect or late service, cannot be followed, especially in view of the development of the European Court of Justice opinion in the *Lancray* decision. The defendant is under no obligation to participate in a proceeding begun by absence of due service, and his bona fide notice to the court about mistakes in the service, must not be disadvantageous to him.

As for the service in the default proceedings, service according to the Hague Convention of 1965 and therefore according to the German-Belgian agreement (see Art. 31 of the Hague Convention) was only necessary if a document was to be transmitted abroad for reasons of service (Art. 1(1)) and the address of the document's addressee was known (Art. 1(2)). The Belgian court had to determine, according to Art. 40 *Code Judiciaire* (Code of Civil Procedure), if the defendant had a remaining residence or domicile of choice in Belgium. If resident abroad, the court would carry out service by *remise au parquet* or by public service in accordance with national Belgian law. In the result, the decision is only correct if service was not carried out in sufficient time in the sense of Art. 27(2) (*Linke* IPRax (1991), 94 see *supra*). Furthermore, the defendant could be estopped from relying on Art. 27(2) because he did not notify the registration office of his change of residence (see *infra*, Case 538).

Case principle

4. Translation of the summons to trial in a French court was not necessary under given circumstances.

Case

531   OLG of Koblenz 3 December 1990 (2 U 42/90) EuZW (1991) 157

Facts

The applicant requested enforcement of a default judgment of a French Commercial Court of 27 November 1987. The summons to the trial of 20 November 1987, had been handed to the defendant's managing director between 3 September and 15 September 1987, with acknowledgement.

Judgment

The court examined whether the service was duly carried out according to the Hague Convention of 1965. The service was valid according to Art. 5(2), since a special form of service (Art. 5(1)(b)) had not been requested. A translation according to Art. 3(2) of the German-French agreement of 6 May 1961, was not necessary for this kind of service. The service was in time since the defendant had more than two months to prepare for its defence at the Commercial Court.

Comment

The decision is acceptable. For the question relating to translation of the document to be served, see *supra*, Case 528.

Case principle

5.   Service of writ by ordinary post held to be invalid according to Germany's reservation to Art. 10 of the Hague Convention.

Case

OLG of Frankfurt/Main 21 February 1991 (20 W 154/90) IPRax (1992) 90   **532**

Facts

The applicant applied for enforcement of an English judgment. The writ had been posted to the defendant on 18 March 1988, by ordinary mail. After the writ had not been returned as undelivered by 15 April 1988, the English court entered a default judgment.

After being requested to pay the adjudicated amount, the defendant engaged English lawyers, who were granted an order allowing the defendant a reopening following the defendant's undertaking to provide security. When the defendant did not furnish the securities, the judgment was declared unconditionally enforceable.

Judgment

The Oberlandesgericht of Frankfurt determined the validity of service according to the Hague Convention of 1965. According to Art. 5(1)(a) or (b), service had not been duly carried out. As the Federal Republic had objected to the application of Art. 10, it was not decisive that service of the writ by ordinary post was regular according to national English law, because such service was not valid when effected in Germany.

The objection under Art. 10 was not an impediment to applying any method of service under bilateral agreements. However, the German-British Convention of 20 March 1928, did not allow this method, although this convention's Art. 6 permitted the transmission of documents by mail if this was in accordance with the laws of the country where the document was executed. But the Hague

Convention of 1965 was part of the relevant English law. Therefore, such service was not admissible.

Comment

As to the interpretation of bilateral agreements, the decision cannot be followed: by Art. 24 of the Hague convention of 1965, additional agreements to the 1905 and 1954 conventions remain in force if there is no contrary agreement. The convention between the UK and Germany is not such an additional agreement. But it is not affected by the Hague Convention of 1965 according to its Art. 25. That means that provisions in the UK-German agreement prevail over restrictions on methods of service in the 1965 Hague Convention. The objection to Art. 10 is such a restriction: systematically, this method of service is admissible (Art. 10). Due to the objection, such service does not apply to an addressee in Germany. But by the bilateral agreement, this method of service can be reopened (Art. 24). This has been done in relation to the UK as far as this method of service is in accordance with English law. At this stage, logically, the measure can only be national English law, since the bilateral convention prevails over Art. 10 of the Hague Convention (*Rauscher* IPRax (1992) 72). Nevertheless, the result is correct, since in English law personal service is necessary for the writ of summons.

Case principle

6. Translation of the summons to trial in Belgium held not necessary under given circumstances.

Case

533   OLG of Saarbrücken 15 June 1992 (5 W 21/92) NJW-RR (1992) 1534

Facts

The applicant requested authorization of enforcement of a Belgian default judgment of 21 March 1990. The summons to the trial of 14 June 1989, had been served on the defendant without a German translation, by handing it to an employee, having power of representation, on 11 May 1989. The defendant did not enter an appearance in Belgium.

Judgment

The court held service to be valid according to Art. 5(2) of the Hague Convention of 1965 and that a translation was not necessary. The service was also in accordance with the German-Belgian Convention.

   As the service was effected more than one month before the trial, service was in sufficient time, since the term was two weeks for notice in German law and, moreover, arrangement of a defence was possible within one month.

Comment

The decision is satisfactory. A translation is not necessary for service according to Art. 5(2) of the Hague Convention. Service upon a representative is not a substituted service and therefore is admissible by application of Art. 5(2) (see *supra*, Case 528).

As to the timeliness of the service, this was very short: the periods for notice in German law can only be considered as the minimum for protection of the defendant. In the present case, there should have been taken into consideration the fact that the defendant had to arrange a translation of the documents (see *infra*). There are additional difficulties compared with procedures in the country of domicile, arising from the need to engage a lawyer abroad. Therefore, all particular circumstances of the case must be considered, whereas under normal circumstances one month should be sufficient.

Case principle

7.   Service by mailing to Germany held not valid.

Case

OLG of Hamm 25 September 1992 (20 W 27/92) RIW (1993) 70; IPRax   **534**
(1993) 376

Facts

The applicant applied for authorization of enforcement of a default judgment entered by the English High Court. The writ of summons was mailed by ordinary post to the defendant. The default judgment was entered when the document was not returned as undelivered. The defendant asserted that he never had any knowledge of the writ.

Judgment

The court refused enforcement because ordinary postal service was insufficient proof of service. Simple mailing was contrary to the German objection to Art. 10 of the Hague Convention. The defendant's assertion that he had no knowledge was not disproved.

Comment

The decision is correct, at least in the result, although it does not discuss validity of service according to the UK-German Convention. This Convention's Art. 6 generally allows transmission by mail as far as the state of origin's laws provide for this; and this rule is not excluded by the German objection to Art. 10 of the Hague Convention (see *supra*, Case 532).

Nevertheless, the court was correct to apply Art. 27(2), since personal service is necessary for the writ of summons according to English law. The argument is of more general interest that where service has not been recorded, as with service by mere mailing, the proof of service required by Art. 47(1) cannot be replaced by the mere proof of the document having been posted.

Case principle

8. Service not valid when summons not accepted by defendant and document not left at the place of service according to s.186 of the Zivilprozessordnung.

Case

535   OLG of Saarbrücken 1 October 1993 (5 W 96/93–56) NJW-RR (1994) 636

Facts

By a judgment of the Tribunal de Grande Instance Chateauroux, the defendants had been ordered to pay 215 000 French francs. The judgment became valid by service and was declared enforceable in France. From the judgment there was evidence that the defendants had refused to accept the documents of service and had not been represented in the procedure. On the request for enforcement, the defendants objected that there was no documentary proof of service of the writ commencing the action required under Art. 46.

Judgment

The court refused enforcement under Art. 27(2). The defendants had not been duly served with a writ and the only written document commencing the action could, therefore, be the notification of trial, which the defendants had not accepted. As the French court had not asked for a specific form of service, it had to be performed according to German laws or to Art. 5(2) of the 1965 Hague Convention, by personal delivery. As the defendants had not accepted the documents, the only possibility of valid service was according to German law. If a person who is personally served refuses to accept without good reason, then according to s.186 of the German Code of Civil Procedure, the document must be left at the place of service and the document concerning service must explain this. Obviously such service had not been performed. The applicant's objection that the defendant had denied service in a fraudulent manner was rejected.

Comment

The decision is to be followed. Whether due service was effected must be decided according to the laws regulating service according to the Hague Convention. Whether fraudulent refusal to accept the documents results in a valid service must also be answered according to these laws. As in this case, most laws of service provide for remedies for this situation which must be followed.

For further information concerning this case see *infra* Art. 31, para. 1, Case 546.

Case principle

9. Service according to Belgian rules (*remise au parquet*—prerequisites described) valid, notwithstanding later lack of notification of trial.

Case

OLG of Köln 6 October 1994 (7 W 34/94), NJW–RR (1995) 446; EuZW   **536**
(1995) 381

Facts

The applicant applied for enforcement of a judgment given by the commercial court of Antwerp against the defendant, domiciled in Germany. The defendant did not participate in the Belgian proceedings. He had been served with the summons (dagvaarding) by personal service together with a translation in the German language. He had not been served with a notification of trial. The defendant did not avail himself of legal remedies against the Belgian decision.

Judgment

The service was correct according to the Belgian Code of Civil Procedure as a *remise au parquet*. The service had been effected in accordance with the Hague Convention including the German translation, which is necessary for service in Germany. The fact that there was a sufficient time, which complied with the Belgian Code of Civil Procedure, only between the *fictitious* service effected by *remise au parquet* and the trial and not between the *actual* time of service and trial, did not affect due and sufficient service. The question whether service was in time or not had only to be decided in application of the second criterion in Art. 27(2). Timeliness was for the enforcement-court, not judgment-court, to decide.

   That the defendant had not been notified *of the trial* did not prevent enforceability under Art. 27(2), because this rule was restricted to the service of the document commencing the procedure. Neither did it prevent enforceability under Art. 27(1) (public policy), because the term for trial had been fixed and notified during the first hearing.

Comment

The decision is in accordance with prevailing opinions. Only the finding of service in sufficient time seems to be doubtful. Theoretically, the rules of civil procedure of the judgment-State are not decisive for Art. 27(2). Nevertheless, a violation of these rules, *i.e.* a term between service and trial which is too short according to the internal rules of the judgment-court, normally leads to the result that this term cannot be sufficient for a defendant residing in another state and not familiar with the first court's law. On this point, the decision seems to be rather restrictive, holding that three weeks were enough to find a German-speaking lawyer in Antwerp and to prepare the defence.

Case principle

10.   An applicant for enforcement has the burden of proof of due service.

Case

537   OLG of Karlsruhe 22 January 1996 (13 W 220/92) IPRax (1996) 426

Facts

The applicant had been granted an enforceable judgment in France and applied for enforceability in Germany. The defendant opposed, arguing that he had not been duly served during the entire proceedings.

Judgment

The court rejected the application for enforcement. As the Hague Convention was applicable to service from France to Germany, the applicant had the *burden of proof* of ordinary service under this Convention and Art. 27(2). Enforcement could not be granted, because the applicant had not produced any proof of service, and there was a probability that service might have been made by *remise au parquet*.

Comment

The decision is perfectly correct. Article 47(2) provides an additional argument concerning the burden of proof of due service.

> *" . . . in sufficient time . . . "*

Case principle

1.   Service at the last known address of the defendant is presumed to be in sufficient time.

Case

538   BGH 2 October 1991 (IX ZB 5/91) NJW (1992) 1239; RIW (1992) 56; IPRax (1993) 324

Facts

The plaintiff was granted a default judgment against the defendant by a Belgian court. The writ for trial of 9 September 1986, had been served on the defendant at a German address, named by the plaintiff, where the defendant was officially registered since 1982. The German court, requested for service, replied that service had not been successful because the addressee was said to be in Africa and was expected to return at the end of 1986.

Judgment

The Oberlandesgericht refused recognition of the Belgian default judgment according to Art. 27(2) since the service was duly performed according to Belgian law, but the defendant had not had sufficient time to arrange for its defence.

However, the BGH adopted the presumption that service at the last known address was in time. Therefore, the possibility of knowledge was sufficient. The court of the state where enforcement was sought could also take into consideration the defendant's behaviour as a relevant factor in the examination of sufficiency of time. In European civil procedure, public—and therefore fictitious—service had to be possible in order to prevent the defendant from escaping legal prosecution by changing his place of residence. The decisive question was whether the defendant's present address could be discovered by the plaintiff when using all generally and easily accessible information, and that the defendant had not informed the plaintiff about its change of address.

Comment

The decision is questionable. Obviously service had taken place by public service because of impossibility of personal service in Germany. Actual knowledge, presupposed by the European Court of Justice (*Klomps* Case 166/80) for sufficiency of time in the sense of Art. 27(2), therefore, was excluded. According to this interpretation, logically, public service could never be in time (*Linke* IPRax (1993) 296).

Nevertheless, the central idea of the decision seems to be understandable. It is that in European law of civil procedure the defendant must not be allowed to escape by changing his address. An application of Art. 27(2) according to the wording and to the European Court of Justice's decision referred to, would always be an impediment to recognition of the judgment in such cases. The question is whether the defendant may be precluded by his own fault from relying upon Art. 27(2). The decisions in *Pendy Plastic* Case 228/81 and *Debaecker* Case 49/84 show that the European Court of Justice contemplates such a possibility, if the plaintiff made all reasonable efforts to effect service. This makes an examination of the facts of the particular case necessary and therefore makes the application of Art. 27(2) uncertain. The case shows that this uncertainty cannot be avoided when the defendant is absent from his regular domicile for a longer, but determined time. A higher degree of certainty in the application of Art. 27(2) would be achievable, if the correctness of service according to the law of the judgment-State was assessed as well as its conformity with the law of the state where service was performed. If the service is subject to the Hague Convention of 1965, this idea can be based on Art. 5(1)(a)—service according to the law of the requested state. Generally, such provision requires that any addressee has to accept the regulations of his domicile's law. In the present case, there would be the result that at least a substituted service by lodging the document at the post office and putting notice in the addressee's letter box would have been necessary before public service could apply (see *Linke* IPRax (1993) 296).

Case principle

2.   Service after trial was late even if *remise au parquet* was correct under Belgian laws.

Case

539   OLG of Köln 12 April 1989 (13 W 73/88) NJW-RR (1990) 127

Facts

The applicant was granted a default judgment against the defendant by a Belgian Commercial Court. The summons for the trial on 21 January 1986, had been served on the defendant on 21 February 1986. The reason for the delay was that the address given was incorrect and that no translation was enclosed, so the German court had to arrange a translation before service.

Judgment

The court refused enforcement under Art. 27(2), since the defendant was served after the trial and after the default judgment was delivered. It was not sufficient under Art. 27(2) that according to Belgian law, the *remise au parquet* was valid at the earlier time of service upon the German authorities.

Comment

The judgment is correct: Art. 27(2), according to the European Court of Justice, requires actual knowledge in sufficient time, subject to exceptions. The Hague Convention of 1965 is not applicable to *remise au parquet*, because there is no document to be transmitted abroad for reasons of service (Art. 1). Only a notice has to be transmitted after service has been made. But this can only correct a service, not also ensure that the service is in time.

Case principle

3.   Public service which was duly made is not invalidated by later knowledge of the defendant's address.

Case

540   OLG of Koblenz 19 June 1990 (2 U 706/89) EuZW (1990) 486; IPRax (1992) 35

Facts

The applicant applied for enforceability of a Luxembourg default judgment for divorce, as far as the ancillary maintenance order was concerned. The writ could not be served on the defendant under the Hague Convention of 1954 because the defendant was no longer resident at the known address in Germany. Therefore, public service was carried out according to Art. 69 no 8 Luxembourg Code of Civil Procedure (*Code de Procédure Civile*). The defendant learnt of the proceedings only when he was requested for payment after the judgment had been delivered.

Judgment

Whether service was duly carried out the court decided according to Luxembourg law under Art. 69(8) of the Code of Civil Procedure. The service was not invalidated when the applicant later discovered the defendant's new address. Concerning timeliness, the court only considered the amount of time between service and trial and held more than two weeks to be sufficient. That the defendant had no actual knowledge of the service was not an impediment to recognition.

Comment

The decision does not give effect to the European Court of Justice's guidelines concerning timeliness in application of Art. 27(2). Generally, actual knowledge is necessary (see *supra*, Case 538). The court was incorrect to calculate from the time of fictitious service (*Geimer* IPRax (1992) 11). Furthermore, the court did not appreciate the statement made in *Pendy Plastic* Case 228/81 that, in application of Art. 27(2), circumstances are also to be taken into consideration which occurred after further service took place, especially when the plaintiff obtained knowledge of the defendant's new address. The court should also have examined whether the failed service at the old address estopped the defendant from relying on Art. 27(2) when considering all particulars of the case (see *supra*, Case 538).

Case principle

4. Service in sufficient time when made one month before default was decreed and six weeks before judgment was delivered in an English court.

Case

OLG of Hamm 5 August 1992 (20 W 11/92) RIW (1993) 148   **541**

Facts

The applicants requested enforcement of a default judgment of the English High Court. The writ of summons had been served on the defendant's representative on 22 July 1991, together with a German translation. On 23 August 1991 the defendant's default was decreed and a default judgment was entered on 4 September 1991.

Judgment

The court held service to be valid according to Art. 5 of the Hague Convention of 1965. The service was in time since there was a period of one month until default was decreed or six weeks until the judgment was entered. This was sufficient, especially since the writ was accompanied by a translation and consequently the defendant could enter its defence without the help of a translator. Furthermore, it was decisive that according to the statement in the writ, a default judgment could be set aside through submission of a defence within three weeks. Only as an additional argument, the court referred to the even shorter periods of German law (s.276(1) of the ZPO).

Case principle

5. Service in sufficient time when made about four months before trial in Belgian court.

Case

542   OLG of Hamm 18 June 1993 (20 W 28/92) RIW (1993) 764

Facts

The application was for authorization of enforcement of a Belgian default judgment of 17 January 1990. The defendant was personally served with the writ on 26 September 1989.

Judgment

The court held service to have been duly carried out and in sufficient time. The period between late September 1989 and 17 January 1990, was sufficient to enable a defendant to arrange his defence.

Comment

There is no problem here. Service was correct according to Art. 5(2) of the Hague Convention of 1965 (see *supra*, Case 528). Without any examination of the particular facts, a time period of almost four months is sufficient even if translations have to be made and legal advice sought (see *supra*, Cases 528 and 541). Nevertheless, the time to be considered is not always the time until the default judgment was granted. Only the date of the hearing should be relevant, because later he would not have had a possibility to be heard. Thus, if the hearing was for an earlier time, it could be an impediment to his defence.

Case principle

6. Article 27(2) does not prevent enforcement when the defendant responded to the action, notwithstanding the fact that it did so only in order to protect its property in the judgment-State.

Case

OLG of Hamm 28 December 1993 (20 W 19/93) RIW (1994) 243   **543**

Facts

See supra, Art. 27(1), Case 525.

Judgment

The court left undecided whether the defendant had been duly served and in sufficient time. In any event, it had answered the action. It could not rely on the fact that it was required to answer the action in order to avoid a default judgment and to protect its property in France from enforcement. As it knew that service was not correctly performed, it had to decide whether to accept a default judgment and enforceability in France in order to prevent enforceability in Germany according to Art. 27(2), or to participate in the procedure and avoid a default judgment, but with the consequence of enforceability in all the Contracting States.

Comment

The decision is to be followed. Article 27(2) only has the purpose of protecting the defendant from service not duly carried out in sufficient time. If a defendant did participate in the procedure, Art. 27(2) does not give a sanction for a mere violation of rules of service *which did not prevent the defendant from participating in the procedure.*

ARTICLE 27(3)

" . . . with a judgment . . . "

Case principle

1.   Whether compromises are included in Art. 27(3).

Case

BGH 5 November 1992 (IX ZB 15/92) EuZW (1993) 195   **544**

Facts

The applicant, domiciled in Italy, had been granted damages for breach of a contract for delivery of goods against the defendant, domiciled in Germany, by the Corte d'Appello M (Italy). The judgment had been authorized for enforcement in Germany. On the defendant's appeal, the parties entered a compromise at the Oberlandesgericht of Stuttgart on 24 February 1978, expressly declaring all further obligations arising from their business contacts to be finished. During the pendency of this procedure, the parties dealt with obligations arising from breach of rights to name and unfair competition on appeal at the Corte d'Appelo B. This procedure ended with a judgment ordering the defendant to pay damages. The Italian court explained that the compromise at the Oberlandesgericht of Stuttgart was not an impediment, since this compromise had not been authorized for enforcement in Italy and moreover did not relate to obligations arising from tort. A proceeding concerning the amount of damages followed, which ended with a judgment against the defendant. The applicant requested enforcement of this judgment in Germany.

Judgment

The Bundesgerichtshof referred several questions to the European Court of Justice concerning the quality of a compromise as a judgment with which the judgment sought to be enforced might be irreconcilable in the sense of Art. 27(3). These questions were decided in *Solo Kleinmotoren GmbH* Case C–414/92 in a negative sense.

The Bundesgerichtshof had put forward some arguments for inclusion of compromises in Art. 27(3). However, not even the fact that a judgment in the sense of Art. 27(3) need not be *res iudicata* provides an argument for treating compromises as a judgment, since not *every* instrument for enforcement can be treated as a judgment.

Comment

Neither is the parallel drawn with Art. 21 convincing: if one of the proceedings under Art. 21 ends with a compromise before one of the courts declines jurisdiction, the litispendence of the finished procedure ends and therefore Art. 21 is no longer applicable. If one of the procedures was stayed according to Art. 21 after a compromise, the procedure which has not been terminated can be continued without regard to whether it was the procedure to be stayed according to Art. 21 or the other one. Only in the event that a procedure was declined according to Art. 21, will it not revive if the other procedure ends by compromise. Therefore, in the case of Art. 21, a compromise in one of the procedures does not stop the other procedure, from which it can be argued that in the situation of recognition, the compromise is not an impediment to the recognition and enforcement of a judgment concerning the same matter. Therefore, the European Court of Justice's reference to the systematic distinction between judgments (Art. 26) and compromises (Art. 51) is the correct solution (*Kropholler* Art. 25(17); and Advocate General *Gulman's* final statement of 22 March 1994).

ARTICLE 31, PARAGRAPH 1

" . . . given in a Contracting State . . . "

Case principle

Judgment of the Royal Court of Jersey is not within the Convention's scope.

Case

BGH 27 October 1994 (IX ZB 39/94) EuZW (1995) 96   **545**

Facts

The applicant applied under Art. 31 for enforcement of a judgment of Royal Court of Jersey.

Judgment

The Judgment of the Royal Court of Jersey was not within the scope of application of Art. 31 according to Art. 60, para. 1 and 3, because the UK had not notified the applicability of the Convention to the Channel Islands.

The court did not have to decide the question whether Art. 55 overruled the German-British Convention of 14 July 1960 as far as this related to territories which were not within the scope of application of the Brussels Convention. This was because the German-British agreement did not extend to Jersey.

Finally, an application under Art. 31 could not be decided according to national German law, because enforcement of foreign judgments under the German Code of Civil Procedure (ZPO) is by means of an action (s.722 of the ZPO) and not a mere application.

" . . . shall be enforced . . . "

Case principle

1. Proceedings for enforcement not interrupted by bankruptcy proceeding against defendant.

Case

OLG of Saarbrücken 1 October 1993 (5 W 96/93–56) NJW–RR (1994) 663   **546**

Facts

See supra Art. 27(2), Case 535.

Judgment

The procedure of enforceability was not interrupted by opening a bankruptcy proceeding concerning the defendant's property. The Brussels Convention did not admit of such interruption. This was not a question which had to be answered according to German law. There was no reason to apply s.240 of the Code of Civil Procedure (ZPO) that a civil procedure was interrupted by a party's bankruptcy, because s.240 of the ZPO did not concern a procedure on enforceability of a foreign judgment even in German law.

There was no necessity to stop this procedure for other reasons. The mere fact that an enforcement could not take place during bankruptcy was not a permanent impediment to any enforcement and therefore did not prevent the applicant from preparing for later enforcement by application for enforceability.

Comment

The difference between a declaration of enforceability and enforcement itself seems to be correct. Declaration of enforceability has no immediate influence on the bankruptcy procedure. The procedure according to Art. 31 only prepares for actual enforcement. Neither the liquidator's nor the creditors' rights to object to an applicant's claim during bankruptcy are prevented by a declaration of enforceability. Only the defendant himself is precluded from raising an objection against the claim if it is not raised during the procedure for enforcement.

Case principle

2.   If a foreign judgment itself is not precise enough to be enforced in Germany (other than by reference to other documents), recognition is not prevented if clarification can be made during the proceeding for enforcement.

Case

547   OLG of Düsseldorf 18 September 1996 (3 W 264/96), RIW (1996) 1043

Facts

The applicant requested enforcement of a Belgian judgment ordering the defendant to pay 12 per cent interest on each bill from its date until the day of effective payment.

Judgment

In German law, enforcement of a judgment required the content of the judgment to be able to be determined on its face. The court granted enforcement notwithstanding the fact that the period for which the interest ran was not comprehensible from the Belgian judgment itself but made it necessary to refer to other documents. Since, following a declaration of enforceability, the decision to be enforced was the decision according to Art. 34 rather than the original judgment, the court was entitled to clarify the content of the foreign judgment and to include this clarification in its decision granting enforceability. Therefore, the mere fact that the foreign judgment itself would not be sufficiently clear to be enforced in Germany was not an impediment to recognition.

ARTICLE 32(2)

" . . . jurisdiction of local courts . . . place of domicile of the party
against whom enforcement is sought . . . "

Case principle

A German court has no jurisdiction under Art. 32 when the defendant has no
domicile in the court's district. Section 16 of the Zivilprozessordnung is
excluded by the aforesaid Convention rule.

Case

OLG of Saarbrücken 24 September 1992 (5 W 84/91) RIW (1993) 672; NJW-   **548**
RR (1993) 190

Facts

The applicant applied for enforcement of a French Tribunal d'Instance's judgment applied to the Landgericht of Saarbrücken. The Landgericht of
Saarbrücken rejected the application, since it had no jurisdiction under Art.
32(2). The applicant's *Beschwerde* of 16 April 1991 could not be served on the
defendant, because he had left his residence in the Landgerichts' district for an
unknown destination (according to the post office information, it was thought
that he had moved to France on 28 September 1989, his residence in France
being unascertainable).

Judgment

The court confirmed the Landgericht of Saarbrücken's decision. There was no
jurisdiction according to Art. 32(2). The defendant had no residence in the
court's district. Contrary to the applicant's opinion, Art. 52, para. 1 did not
point to s.16 of the German Code of Civil Procedure (ZPO), *giving jurisdiction* to the court of the defendant's *last* residence in Germany. Section 16 of
the ZPO was applicable only if a person had no residence at all. Furthermore,
Art. 32(2) prevailed over s.16 of the ZPO.

The second alternative in Art. 32(2) (place of enforcement) was not available
in the court's district, since the applicant had not notified the court of any possibilities for enforcement.

Comment

The decision is correct. But the explanations concerning s.16 of the ZPO are
not exact: Art. 52 only refers to the law applicable to the determination of
domicile. Article 52 does not also prescribe the application *of national jurisdictional rules*. Local enforcement jurisdiction is determined exclusively by
Art. 32(2). If the defendant has no residence at all, s.16 of the ZPO cannot be
applied, and only the second alternative of Art. 32(2) is applicable.

ARTICLE 36, PARAGRAPH 1

" . . . *may appeal* . . . "

Case principle

If an enforcement-court incorrectly applies the Convention to enforcement falling beyond its scope, an appeal may be brought under the Convention itself as well as under national law of civil procedure.

Case

549 OLG of Frankfurt/Main 25 May 1993 (20 W 435/92) NJW-RR (1993) 958

Facts

The applicant had been granted a declaration of enforceability in respect of an Austrian judgment. The decision on enforcement was expressly based on s.7 of the AVAG (German law concerning the application of the Brussels Convention). The defendant had not been heard.

He appealed against enforcement under Arts 36 and 37.

Judgment

If the law had been properly applied, the Brussels Convention would have been held to have been inapplicable. Therefore, the decision of enforceability had to be based on the German-Austrian Convention on Enforcement in Civil Matters. Against such a decision, the correct remedy was not a *Beschwerde* under the Brussels Convention Arts 36 and 37 themselves, but a *Widerspruch*, under s.1042c(2) of the Code of Civil Procedure (ZPO). Nevertheless, the *Beschwerde* was admissible, since the court's error could not result in a party's loss of remedy.

Comment

The decision is in accordance with the prevailing opinion whereby when a decision is in the wrong form or based on a wrong rule, both remedies against the substantive decision and against the formal decision are given.

ARTICLE 37(2)

" . . . *judgment given on the appeal* . . . "

Case principles

1. Rechtsbeschwerde is not available through the mere fact of non-application of Art. 38.
2. Partial performance after the foreign judgment was delivered can give a reason for Rechtsbeschwerde.

Case

BGH 21 April 1994 (IX ZB 8/94), IPRax (1995) 243   **550**

Facts

The applicant obtained a judgment of the Commercial Court of Mons (Belgium) against the defendant residing in Germany. The defendant appealed in the Belgian courts. Enforcement was granted in Germany and an application to stay the proceedings during the Belgian appeal according to Art. 38, para. 1 was rejected. The defendant brought a *Rechtsbeschwerde* according to Art. 37(2), arguing that the Oberlandesgericht had not decided according to Art. 38(1) and (3) and that under the Belgian judgment a deposit of 3.3 million BEF had been paid to the applicant on account of the debt.

Judgment

The mere fact that the Oberlandesgericht had not applied Art. 38 was not a ground for a Rechtsbeschwerde under Art. 37(2).

The second objection, that the claim in the action had been partially performed after the foreign judgment was given, could provide a reason for a Rechtsbeschwerde. The question whether performance under a preliminarily enforceable judgment was a material performance had to be decided by reference to the law of Belgium in the present case. The same law had to decide whether a partial performance was on account of the claim, the interests or the costs. Therefore, the Bundesgerichtshof reversed the decision of the Oberlandesgericht.

The Bundesgerichtshof further advised on Art 38. Since Art. 38(3) had the intention of protecting the debtor from prejudice resulting from enforcement of preliminarily enforceable judgments, the court had to exercise its discretion and had to include all arguments concerning the case and not only the probability of the debtor's success on appeal. In the present case, the (even enforced) payment of 3.3 million BEF was a relevant argument under Art. 38(3) if the applicant creditor was in financial difficulties and repayment of the enforced amount was doubtful.

Comment

As the European Court of Justice decided in *Van Dalfsen* Case 183/90, the refusal of the court to order a stay of procedure according to Art. 38(1) or security under Art. 38(3) does not found a Rechtsbeschwerde under Art.

37(2). The case shows that there is a certain risk of discretional error in the application of Art. 38, because the Oberlandesgericht is the first and last instance to apply these rules. Nevertheless, there are good reasons for restrictive use of Rechtsbeschwerde according to Art. 37(2). According to the Jenard Report, the principle of free enforcement of judgments of Contracting States must not be restricted by legal remedies which only serve the purpose of prolonging the proceedings. On the other hand, the arguments of the Bundesgerichtshof in its additional explanations must be considered. As there is no further control, the Oberlandesgericht has a heavy burden of responsibility to avoid prejudice to the debtor. An order under Art. 38(3) should be the rule when ordering enforcement of a preliminary enforceable judgment—as it is for most cases of preliminary enforceability under the German Code of Civil Procedure.

Considering Art. 38(1), the Bundesgerichtshof adopted the prevailing opinion in favour of a stay of proceedings under Art. 38(1) for reasons which could not be raised in the original proceedings. This opinion is not convincing. Article 38(1) is an exceptional remedy, while Art. 38(3) should be the rule, since a stay of proceedings is only to be ordered if securities are not sufficient to protect the debtor and his interest goes beyond the mere interest of securing his possible claim for repayment. But if there is any reason to apply Art. 38(1), the question whether this reason has been discussed in the original proceedings is not important, because this proceeding is still pending through the appeal brought by the debtor, which is the basic condition of Art. 38 application in the first place. The decision whether Art. 38(1) has to be applied or not should not be made too difficult, for example, by making it conditional upon whether a certain argument can be brought or is excluded on appeal in the foreign proceedings (see *Grunsky* IPRax (1995) 218; *Stadler* IPRax (1995) 220).

ARTICLE 38, PARAGRAPH 1

" . . . if an ordinary appeal . . . "

Case principle

Arbitration is not an ordinary appeal within the meaning of Art. 38, para. 1.

Case

551   OLG of Hamm 28 December 1993 (20 W 19/93) RIW (1994) 243

Facts

See supra, Art. 27(1), Case 525.

Judgment

The defendant's application to stay the appeal against enforcement under Art. 38, para. 1, because of pending arbitration procedure, was not successful. Arbitration was not an ordinary appeal within the meaning of Art. 38.

For further information on this case see *supra*, Arts 27(1) and 27(2), Cases 525 and 543.

ARTICLE 39, PARAGRAPH 1

" . . . other than protective measures . . . "

Case principle

A creditor held not entitled to take *any* measures of enforcement before the judgment was served, because Art. 39 prevents enforcement as long as the term in Art. 36 is running.

Case

OLG of Saarbrücken 5 January 1994 (5 W 397/93–199), IPRax (1995) 244   **552**

Facts

The applicant requested enforcement of a French order for payment, which it intended to enforce against the debtor's income from employment in Germany. After enforcement had been authorized, the Landgericht tried to serve the debtor with this decision at his place of employment in Germany. When this failed, the Landgericht ordered service in France. The creditor's application for provisional enforcement, before service had been completed, was refused. Therefore, the applicant raised a *Beschwerde*.

Judgment

The *Beschwerde* was not successful under Art. 40, because enforcement had been granted and the applicant only sought provisional execution. In the German Code of Civil Procedure (ZPO), *Beschwerde* would be possible if this application were rejected. The court left undecided whether within the scope of the Brussels Convention, this rule in the national Code of Civil Procedure (s.567(1) of the ZPO) could be applied. The Oberlandesgericht also held that Art. 39, para. 1 restricted enforcement as long as the term in Art. 36, para. 1 was still running. Since this term did not start before the debtor had been served with the decision granting enforcement, the creditor was not entitled to take *any* measures of enforcement before the decision was served.

Comment

The interpretation given by the Oberlandesgericht is in accordance with general principles of German law of enforcement (s.750 of the ZPO, providing proof of service before enforcement). According to the wording of Arts 39 and 36, this interpretation seems also to be correct.

Nevertheless, the interpretation given by the court is not the only possible one. The wording and the intention of Art. 39 obviously exclude an unlimited enforcement before service. After service, enforcement is restricted by Art. 39, para. 1 as long as the term of Art. 36 is running. But, theoretically, there is a possibility to allow provisional, protective enforcement even before the debtor has been served with the decision. In national cases, there is no need for such a solution, because service normally can be made within a few days. With respect to the international implications of the Brussels Convention, however, this case shows the creditor may have an interest in obtaining enforcement before service. This is because the debtor has a good chance to prevent a successful enforcement, if he knows that enforcement has been granted, but service, which may be rather time-consuming, has not yet been carried out. There is no rule that under the Brussels Convention the decision granting enforcement in another Contracting State must be served by order of the court. If under the Brussels Convention service can also be made by the creditor, the decision is obviously wrong, because the creditor can only serve an instrument which he has in his possession.

Moreover, the Oberlandesgericht's decision is not necessary to protect the debtor from prejudice. Obviously, Art. 39, para. 1 does not allow a final execution but only preliminary measures of execution until the Art. 36, para. 1 term has run out; and the preliminary character of the execution will be sufficient to protect the debtor on the one hand and to protect the creditor's interests on the other (see *Haas* IPRax (1995) 223).

ARTICLE 41

" . . . judgment given on appeal . . . "

Case principle

Rechtsbeschwerde is admissible whenever the Oberlandesgericht deviates from the European Court of Justice's decision, notwithstanding that Rechtsbeschwerde was not admitted by the Oberlandesgericht according to s.621d of the Zivilprozessordnung.

Case

553 BGH 21 March 1990 (XII ZB 71/89) IPRax (1992) 33

Facts

See supra, Art. 27(1) Case 518.

The Oberlandesgericht had denied enforceability because the Italian courts, according to the Corte Cassazione's jurisprudence, must not grant maintenance without an application. Furthermore, the Oberlandesgericht explained that the prerequisites of a *Rechtsbeschwerde* according to s.17(1) of the AVAG (the German law concerning the application of the Brussels Convention) (see *supra*, Case 548, Art. 32) were not satisfied.

Judgment

The Bundesgerichtshof held a *Rechtsbeschwerde* to be admissible. In a family action, this remedy depended on the Oberlandesgericht's permission (s.621d(1) of the Code of Civil Procedure (ZPO)) but s.38 of the AVAG gave the legal remedy of *Rechtsbeschwerde* whenever the Oberlandesgericht deviated from a decision of the European Court of Justice. This rule was not immediately applicable to the present procedure, pending before 8 June 1988 (the day of coming into force of AVAG), but was to be considered in interpreting the former law on application of the Brussels Convention. Thus, in deviation from the European Court of Justice's decision, the Oberlandesgericht had examined whether an Italian court could grant maintenance without an application.

Comment

The decision seems artificial. But it gives the only solution to the problem arising under s.38 of the AVAG. Strictly speaking, there was no deviation by the Oberlandesgericht from a *European Court of Justice decision*, but the decision was contrary to Art. 34, para. 3 (prohibition of review of substance) and the European Court of Justice's interpretation thereof in a judgment.

Correctly, the *Rechtsbeschwerde* should be available in maintenance cases according to general rules, even if the maintenance was granted in a divorce judgment. Section 17(1) of the AVAG permits the *Rechtsbeschwerde* as far as appeal (revision) would be given in the case of a final judgment. Therefore, such maintenance decisions ancillary to a divorce judgment underly s.621d of the ZPO, which provides that revision in family matters is only given if permitted by the Oberlandesgericht. Since only the maintenance decision is to be recognized according to the Brussels Convention (Art. 1(2)), for the purposes of Art. 41, only the maintenance judgment (as a partial decision) should be considered, *i.e.* revision is not restricted.

ARTICLE 46(1)

" . . . *shall produce* . . . "

Case principle

1. No valid application for enforcement without original or certified true copy of documentary proof of service.

Case

554 OLG of Köln 12 April 1989 (13 W 73/88) NJW-RR (1990) 127

Facts

See supra, Art. 27(2), Case 539.

The applicant could not present a document proving the service of the writ.

Judgment

The court held that there was no formally valid application for authorization of enforcement. Together with the application, the original or a certified copy of a document would have to be presented, showing that the document which instituted the proceedings or an equivalent document had been served upon the party in default of appearance. The documents named in Arts 46 and 47 could be presented as long as the procedure was still pending on appeal (see too next two cases).

Case principle

2. Document proving service can be presented during the proceedings.

Case

555 OLG of Koblenz 19 June 1990 (2 U 706/89) EuZW (1990) 486, IPRax (1992) 35

Facts

See supra, Art. 27(2), Case 540.

The applicant presented the documents proving service in the proceedings of *Rechtsbeschwerde* at the Oberlandesgericht.

Judgment

The Oberlandesgericht held that the Landgericht should have applied Art. 48. This defect was cured by presentation of the document later (see too case preceding, and following).

Case principle

3. Document proving service can be presented during *Beschwerde*.

Case

OLG of Koblenz 3 December 1990 (2 U 42/90) EuZW (1991) 157   **556**

Facts

See supra, Art. 27(2), Case 531.

The applicant for enforcement only presented the copy writ, but not a document proving service. The court had consulted the records of service.

Judgment

The court held that generally enforcement could not be authorized if the necessary documents were not presented. But, under Art. 48, the documents could be presented while the *Beschwerde* was pending. The court considered it to be sufficient that the documents on file proved service—although the applicant did not present the document.

Comment

The decisions in this and the preceding two cases are in harmony with the prevailing opinion and the purpose of the Convention. The presentation of documents is mandatory for the application. Without sufficient proof in writing, Art. 48 of the Brussels Convention is to be applied. But these provisions do not imply any special formalism. Articles 46 and 47 are only intended to provide proof of an enforceable judgment's existence. Therefore, the presentation of the documents is possible during proceedings for remedies. However, this does not extend to the actual carrying out of service at this later time (see Art. 46(2)).

Case principle

4. Res judicata is not an impediment to a new proceeding, if a decision was validly made in Germany but without service of the application and therefore could not be enforced in The Netherlands under the Convention, Arts 27(2) and 46(2).

Case

OLG of Hamm 12 December 1994 (23 W 221/94) IPRax (1996) 414   **557**

Facts

Party 1, a German lawyer who had formerly acted for party 2, had obtained a decree fixing his fees according to s.19 of the German Attorney's Fees Regulation (*Bundesrechtsanwaltsgebührenordnung*). As party 2, domiciled in The Netherlands, had not been formally served with the application for this proceeding in compliance with German law, party 1 applied for a second decree containing the same decision based on a formal service of the application. The argument of party 1 was that the decision was not enforceable in The

Netherlands under Art. 27(2) for lack of proof of formal service according to Art. 46(2).

Judgment

The court granted a new proceeding despite *res judicata*. Although, under German law, the first decree was not only valid and therefore *res judicata* but also perfectly correct under German law, the court decided that according to Art. 46(2) formal service had been necessary in order to ensure enforceability in the country where the other party was domiciled.

Comment

The decision is not completely correct. According to Art. 46(2), formal service is necessary even if German laws allow a simplified proceeding without such service. As both The Netherlands and Germany are Contracting States to the Hague Convention on international service, such service has to be made according to this Convention, including Art. 10 (service by mail), because this type of service is not excluded for services *from* Germany to abroad whenever the destination country has not declared a reservation against this rule.

On the other hand, there is no rule in German law that a decision might be revoked after becoming *res judicata*, for the mere default of enforceability abroad (see *Tepper* IPRax (1996) 398).

See too *infra*, Case 558.

Case principle

5. A foreign decree, validly made under The Netherland's laws without service of the application on a German defendant, held not enforceable.

Case

558 OLG of Düsseldorf 23 August 1995 (3 W 176/95) IPRax (1996) 415

Facts

The applicant, a lawyer domiciled in The Netherlands who formerly acted for the defendant, applied for enforcement of a costs decree granted by the president of the *Arrondissenmentsrechtbank Utrecht* for the lawyer's fees.

Judgment

Enforcement was not granted. The court left undecided whether the decree, which was not a 'determination of costs' as referred to in Art. 25, following a decision on the merits and merely fixing the amount of costs due rather than a completely new and independent decision, was a 'judgment' under Art. 25. In any event, Art. 46(2) not only applied to default judgments in a technical sense, but also to *ex parte* decisions without appearance of the defendant. As there was no proof of ordinary service, and according to Article 10 of the Hague Convention service by simple mail was invalid *into* Germany, Art. 46(2) prevented enforceability.

Comment

The decision is entirely correct: although national law may allow proceedings for the fixing of lawyers' fees without notification to the debtor, such decisions are not enforceable under the Convention if there is no proof of ordinary service under Arts 46(2) and 27(2).

ARTICLE 47(1)

" . . . judgment . . . has been served . . . "

Case principle

1. *Remise au parquet* is valid service as the Hague Convention only applies to international service and not to this type of national French service.

Case

OLG of Oldenburg 22 August 1991 (1 W 74/91) NJW (1992) 3113.　　　**559**

Facts

The applicant requested enforcement of a French judgment of 17 November 1987. The defendant was represented by a lawyer in both instances in France. An enforceable copy of the judgment was handed to the Cour d'Appel and at the same time another enforceable copy in French was posted to the defendant (Arts 684 and 685 of the New French Code of Civil Procedure). The defendant objected that the judgment had not been duly served upon him.

Judgment

The court held that the requirements of Art. 47(1) were satisfied. The applicant had presented a document proving due service of the judgment according to the law of the state where the judgment was entered, *i.e.* French law. The *remise au parquet* was not subject to the Hague Convention of 1965. According to Art. 1(1), the Convention was only applicable to service abroad, and such service was not necessary according to French law. There was no obligation of Contracting States to effect service upon a person abroad according to the Convention.

Comment

The Hague Convention of 1965 does not prevent a *remise au parquet*. The prescriptions of Arts 15 and 16 are not applicable, because they are only applicable in the situation in which a document was to be transmitted abroad 'according to this convention for service'. Article 20, para. 2 of the 1968 Convention is applicable, as far as the defendant does not enter an appearance. In the present case, the defendant had appeared, and therefore neither the first procedure was to be stayed according to Art. 20, para. 2 nor was there ground for refusal of recognition according to Art 27(2). For the purpose of Art. 47(1) an ordinary *remise au parquet* was sufficient.

Case principle

2.   Lack of service under German law can be cured, according to s.187 of the Zivilprozessordnung, by the defendant's actual knowledge.

Case

560   OLG of Hamm 5 August 1992 (20 W 11/92) RIW (1993) 148

Facts

See supra, Art. 27, Case 541.

The English judgment had been posted immediately to the defendant by the applicant's German lawyers.

Judgment

The court held that service did not comply with the regulations concerning service of judicial documents abroad, which had to be proved in writing according to Art. 47(1). This was not an impediment to *recognition*. Article 47 only extended to authorization of enforcement.

It could be left open whether service had to be repeated before granting enforcement. The defect was cured according to s.187 of the Code of Civil Procedure (ZPO) by the defendant's knowledge. Article 47(1) of the Brussels Convention only had the purpose of making it possible for the debtor to pay voluntarily.

Comment

It is correct that Arts 46 and 47 only apply to enforcement. The impediments to recognition are exclusively ruled on in Art. 27. But, to cure service for Art. 47(1), there cannot be applied any principles other than those resulting from the judgments on Art. 27(2). In the present case, service was to be effected according to the Hague Convention of 1965, or according to the German-British Convention (see *supra*, Art. 27(2), Case 541). Section 187 of the ZPO was not applicable to cure, since service according to German law had not even been tried although it would have been possible by Art. 5(1)(a) of the Hague Convention. The only consideration could be whether service through the post was valid according to Art. 6 of the German-British Convention. But such service was not valid, since the judgment was not posted from England but to England. German law does not allow service through the post.

As long as the judgment has not been served, enforcement cannot be authorized, because otherwise Art. 47(1) would be undermined. Whether the service could be carried out during the proceedings for enforcement depends on whether the purpose of enabling a voluntary payment could be achieved. For a default judgment, this seems to be impossible, as such judgments come to the defendant's knowledge only by service (*Kropholler* Art. 47, n.2).

Case principle

3. If service of the judgment is not a necessary requirement in the state of origin, service arranged by the plaintiff is sufficient under Art. 47.

Case

OLG of Düsseldorf 7 December 1994 (3 W 277/94), RIW (1995) 324   **561**

Facts

The defendant had been ordered to pay an amount in Netherlands Guilders by a preliminary enforceable judgment of the *Kantongerecht of Arnhem* (The Netherlands). After the judgment had been sent to the defendant by ordinary post, the defendant was later formally served with the judgment.

Judgment

There were several objections made by the defendant to enforceability of the judgment.

The objection that The Netherlands court had no jurisdiction in the case did not prevent enforceability. The German court was not entitled to check the judgment-court's jurisdiction.

That the judgment resulted from a special type of proceeding in Netherlands law (Art. 1639 BW) not providing any legal remedy against this decision, was not an impediment to enforceability under German public policy. There were also German proceedings without legal remedies.

The application of Netherlands law in the case could not be an impediment to enforceability, even if this application was not correct.

The fact that the judgment had been sent to the defendant merely by ordinary mail and that service was effected later was no impediment either. According to Art. 47(1), the applicant must produce a document proving service. Since the Code of Civil Procedure in the state of origin (The Netherlands) did not provide for a formal service, for the purpose of Art. 47(1), service by the court was not necessary and service at the plaintiff's instigation, effected by the court bailiff, was sufficient.

GREEK ACCESSION CONVENTION 1982 ARTICLE 12(1)

" . . . *legal proceedings instituted . . . after the entry into force of this Convention . . .* "

Case principle

Convention held not applicable to action brought before the Accession Convention entered into force in country in which action brought.

Case

562   BGH 14 November 1991 (IX ZR 250/90) RIW (1992) 142; NJW (1993) 1070; EuZW (1992) 123; ZZP (1992) 330; IPRax (1992) 377

Facts

The plaintiff, domiciled in Germany, was granted an order (*Mahnbescheid*) against the defendant, domiciled in Greece, for an obligation arising under a guarantee, which was served on the defendant on 8 December 1988. On 28 February 1989, the proceeding was given to the competent court for the action and the action was served before 1 April 1989. The plaintiff asserted international jurisdiction of the German courts according to Arts 5(1) and 17.

Judgment

The Bundesgerichtshof held that the action was pending before 1 April 1989 by service of the action. Article 12 of the Greek Accession Convention of 1982 provided that the Accession Convention with Greece was applicable only to actions which were brought *after* the Convention came into force in the judgment-State. For Germany this was 1 April 1989.

Comment

The decision is correct. In the national German law of international civil procedure, international jurisdiction is assessed as at the time of the *final* hearing in the proceedings. But such a principle is not known to the Accession Convention. Article 12 of the Accession Convention of 1982, in the same manner as Art. 54 of the Brussels Convention and Art. 34(1) of the Accession Conventionof 1978, expressly regulates the transitional application from the moment of bringing the action. According to the clear wording, later events cannot create jurisdiction.

> ## SPAIN–PORTUGAL ACCESSION CONVENTION 1989 ARTICLE 29(1)
>
> " . . . *legal proceedings instituted . . . after the entry into force of this Convention . . . "*

Case principle

Convention held not applicable to action brought before the Accession Convention entered into force in country in which action brought.

Case

BGH 28 February 1996 (XII ZR 181/93) NJW (1996) 1411   **563**

Facts

See supra, 1968 Convention Art. 1(2), Cases 447 and 562.

The action had been brought before 1 December 1994 when the 1989 Convention came into force between Germany and Spain, the country of the defendant's domicile.

Judgment

The Bundesgerichtshof held that the Brussels Convention was not applicable to actions brought before the Convention entered into force for the state of the defendant's domicile. Therefore, the jurisdiction of German courts was to be decided according to the national Code of Civil Procedure (ZPO).

Comment

The decision does not state the correct reasoning. As far as the primary jurisdiction is concerned, the Convention is applicable if the action was brought after the Convention entered into force in the state of the judgment-court, which means Germany for the case in question. Article 29(2) does not extend to this question, but only to recognition and enforcement of member states' decisions.

Since the pre-1989 Convention *was* in force in Germany at the date of institution of the proceedings, the Brussels Convention should have been held to be temporally applicable, even if its jurisdiction grounds themselves were displaced by national German grounds in relation to the *non-Contracting* State domiciled (Spanish) defendant under Art. 4: as the defendant had its domicile in Spain, and Spain was not a Contracting State when the action was brought, the German Code of Civil Procedure applied rather than Convention grounds.

8

GREECE

Dr Elina Moustaira

A. LEGAL SYSTEM

One-member District Courts are first instance courts.

Three-member District Courts are also first instance courts, but they are all appellate courts as regards appeals against the decision of the justices of the peace (the latter are first instance courts for cases of small importance).

Courts of Appeal, of which there are 13 in Greece, are second instance courts and deal with questions of both law and fact.

The Supreme Court (*Areios Pagos*) sits in Athens and only reviews questions of law.

D. CASES

ARTICLE 3, PARAGRAPH 1

" . . . only by virtue of . . . "

Case principle

National jurisdiction grounds based upon the presence of a defendant's assets are excluded in Convention cases.

Case

564 Three-member District Court of Thessaloniki 585/1993, Harmenopoulos
(1994) 308

Facts

A person domiciled in the USA brought an action against four companies, to one
of which, domiciled in Hamburg, the Brussels Convention was applicable. The
plaintiff had lent sums of money to two companies which had their seats in
Monrovia, Liberia. One of them, a defendant in the present case, sought to make
the satisfaction of the plaintiff's claim impossible by transferring its only asset,
namely, the ownership of a cargo vessel with the Bahamas flag, to another defendant company, with its seat in Liberia. The latter also transferred the ownership
of the cargo vessel to another defendant company, with its seat in Limassol,
Cyprus. Under an agreement, a German company, also a defendant in this case,
registered a (maritime) mortgage on the ship. The plaintiff brought an action
claiming a declaration of invalidity of the abovementioned transfers and of the
mortgage's registration, as having been carried out in fraud of creditors, and for
ancillary payment of damages in tort.

Judgment

The action was brought in the Greek courts because one of the defendants had
assets in Greece (Art. 40 of the Code of Civil Procedure) and on the basis of
connexity in the case of the other defendant companies—the ship was moored
in Thessaloniki's harbour. As regards the German defendant company, as
already mentioned, the Convention was applicable to jurisdiction of the Greek
courts. None of the defendant companies had its seat in Greece. Consequently,
the Greek courts did not have jurisdiction under Art. 6(1). Certainly, the court
did not have international jurisdiction, based on assets, over the German
company, given the fact that Art. 3 explicitly excluded exorbitant heads of
jurisdiction. The allegedly tortious acts had taken place in the Bahamas, by
registration of the transfers of the ownership of the ship and of its mortgage.
Therefore, the Greek courts had no international jurisdiction based on tort
under Art. 5(3).

The plaintiff also invoked the fact that he had filed a charge against
the German company before the Public Attorney of the Police Court of
Thessaloniki. But no criminal proceedings had yet been instituted against the
German company, and consequently the Greek court had no jurisdiction based
on the civil claim under Art. 5(4). Moreover, more importantly, according to
Art. 5(4), it is the penal court before which the civil claim is brought which has
jurisdiction over it and not the civil court which corresponds to the penal court.

Thus, the court held that it had no international jurisdiction over the defendant German company. So it dismissed the action as far as that company was
concerned, according to Art. 4 of the Code of Civil Procedure. As regards the
other defendant companies, over which national Greek jurisdiction existed, it

ordered the plaintiff to produce information about the law of the Bahamas, which the court held was the applicable substantive law.

ARTICLE 5(1)

" . . . *obligation in question* . . . "

Case principle

Obligation in question is that upon which the plaintiff's claim is based (*de Bloos*, Case 14/76).

Case

Court of Appeals of Thessaloniki 2253/1994, Harmenopoulos (1995) 204   **565**

Facts

In this case, the plaintiff (thereafter appellant) claimed damages from the defendant for breach of accessory contractual obligations, in the context of a contract of publication. According to the plaintiff, the defendant Italian company was owner of the exclusive copyright on a series of eight books assigned to the plaintiff by a contract concluded in Thessaloniki, the copyright on those books being in Greece and in the Greek language, without any time limit for their publication. Subsequently, in breach of its contractual obligation not to conclude other contracts of copyright on the same work, where these contracts could prejudice the plaintiff's right, the defendant purported to transfer copyright on these books for four years, in Greek, and the rights to their sale in Greece, to another publisher.

The defendant alleged that the action should be rejected as inadmissible for lack of international jurisdiction of the Greek courts, because its seat was in Ozzano, Italy. The contract of publication had been concluded there, and Italy was the place of performance of the payment obligation by the plaintiff.

Judgment

The court rejected this objection as groundless. The Italian courts had general (international) jurisdiction because of the defendant's seat (Art. 2 and Art. 53, para. 1). But Thessaloniki was the place of performance of the defendant's initial contractual obligation, which was the transportation and delivery of the works and of the films to the plaintiff. Given that the ancillary compensatory obligations were attracted to the place of performance of the initial contractual obligations, the Greek courts, and more specifically the courts of Thessaloniki, had concurrent specific (international) jurisdiction on the ground of the place of performance of the defendant's obligation (Art. 5(1)).

Greek law was considered applicable, since the essential function of the contract of publication would take place in Greece (Art. 25 of the Civil Code and Art. 4, para. 5 of the 1980 Rome Convention on Applicable Law on Contractual Obligations). The court went on to hold that the action, which had been properly and admissibly brought before Thessaloniki's courts, was legal as regards the application for damages, but not legal and, therefore, inadmissible as regards the second request for pecuniary satisfaction for moral damage. It also held that the ancillary petition of the plaintiff for the pronouncement of personal arrest against the legal representative of the defendant company was not legal and therefore should be dismissed.

> " . . . place of performance . . . "

Case principle

1.   Place of delivery of goods shipped held to be place of performance.

Case

566   Three-member District Court of Piraeus 22/1994, Epitheorissi Naftiliakou Dikaiou (1995) 372

Facts

This decision was given on reopening the default decision 276/1992.

In the initial action, it was mentioned that a sale contract had been concluded through the mediation of the Commercial Bank of Greece between the plaintiff and the Kuwait commercial house Ahmed M. Al Najdi TRDG EST. for 1167 paper boxes of frozen shrimps, of gross weight 21.500kgs and net weight 14.004kgs. For the transportation of this merchandise, the seller had concluded with the defendant Dutch company, a charter contract, according to which the defendant would carry the merchandise from Kuwait to Piraeus, on the ship Norasia Arabia Voy 004; and for the execution of that contract the merchandise was loaded on the abovementioned ship on 12 April 1990, at the Kuwait port, destination Piraeus where, notwithstanding the fact that according to the agreement they had to arrive in 25 days, they arrived on 8 June 1990 on the ship N.S., because of successive reloading and repeated changes of route. The delivery to the plaintiff, who had become legal holder of the bill of lading, No. 736–003776 issued in Kuwait by the defendant's agents, took place on 18 June 1990. The plaintiff claimed that the delay in the transportation and delivery of the merchandise by the defendant caused it damage, and because of this the plaintiff failed to sell the merchandise at a price which would cover the import costs and the wholesale gain. According to its estimations, the damage was 13 611 173 drachmas.

The defendant demanded a reopening of the default action, claiming either that it had never been served with the writ in the action or that the writ had been served legally and in time but that since it was in default during the first hearing, it had the right to demand a reopening.

Judgment

The court held the reopening to be legal (Art. 501, para. 1; Art. 502, para. 1 and Art. 506, para. 1 of the Code of Civil Procedure). It also held that the defendant was legally served in time with the process in Rotterdam, Holland, according to the provisions of the Hague Convention of 15 November 1965, ratified in Greece by the Law 1334/1983, also in force in Holland. Therefore, it held that the defendant was indeed in default, and dismissed as unfounded the principal reason for reopening the default action, but admitted the right of reopening.

The Dutch defendant alleged that the court had no international jurisdiction to try the case, because the only factor connecting it with Greece was that Pireaus was the place of delivery. The court rejected the challenge to the Greek courts' international jurisdiction as groundless: according to Art. 5(1), they had jurisdiction, since Pireaus was the place of performance of the contract—where the merchandise was delivered.

Case principle

2. The place of performance is for applicable law under private international law (*Tessili*, Case 12/76).

Case

Three-member District Court of Thessaloniki 15252/1995, Harmenopoulos **567** (1996) 223.

Facts

The plaintiff corporation, with its seat in Thessaloniki, Greece, made ready-to-wear clothes. The defendant, a company with its seat in Dusseldorf, Germany, also made and sold clothes. At the beginning of 1992, the defendants, through their joint agent in Germany, ordered clothes from the plaintiff, the subject of the action, and agreed that the price, calculated in German marks per piece, would be paid in Thessaloniki. The plaintiff was under an obligation to deliver the clothes in instalments in Thessaloniki from February to April 1992. According to the plaintiff, it performed its obligations in time and the defendant had to pay the sum of 435,783 DM. The defendant paid, successively, 406,841.60 DM, so there was a balance due of 28 941.40 DM, which had to be paid for the last delivery of the merchandise. Therefore, the plaintiff asked the defendant to pay the balance in drachmas, the equivalent of 28,941.60 DM, plus the legal interest, and to pay the plaintiff's court costs.

Judgment

The court concluded that the law applicable to the contract was Greek law, since it was in Greece that the clothes had been made, the dispatch invoices issued, the company making them had its seat and the agreed price to be paid. Thus, under Greek law, the place where the obligation of the defendant was to be performed was Greece. Consequently, according to Art. 5(1), the court had jurisdiction to try the case.

Case

568 Three-member District Court of Thessaloniki 1900/1991, Harmenopoulos (1992) 374

Facts

The action concerned a contract of agency which the plaintiff, a Greek man, had concluded with the first defendant, a German company with its seat in Munich. After some time, when there were no problems whatsoever in the performance of the contract, the German company agreed with the second defendant, domiciled in Athens, that the latter should act as its agency in Attica and, eventually, in other parts of Greece.

The first agent considered this act to be a breach of the contract and brought an action for an account by the defendant in respect of the amounts due to him. In case the company would not state the accounts in due time, the plaintiff asked for the defendants to be held jointly and severally liable to pay damages for unfair competition and tort as ancillary relief.

Judgment

Since the principal debt of the first defendant was non-monetary, its place of performance was where it had its seat, that is, Germany. Therefore, according to Art. 5(1) the first defendant was not subject to the jurisdiction of the Greek courts. Nevertheless, since the action brought against the second defendant, domiciled in Greece, was based on tort, according to Art. 6(1), the action could be brought against both of them, before the court of the domicile of the second, that is the three-member District Court of Athens.

So the Thessaloniki court declared itself territorially incompetent and referred the action to the three-member district court of Athens (Art. 46 of the Code of Civil Procedure).

Editor's Comment

Compare the decision as to place of performance of the principal's non-monetary agency obligation under Greek law with that under English decisions—*supra*, Case 159.

ARTICLE 5(2)

" . . . where the maintenance creditor is domiciled or habitually resident . . . "

Case principle

The maintenance creditor must be domiciled or habitually resident in the district of the national court seised, not merely in the Contracting State.

Case

One-member District Court of Thessaloniki 2175/1984, Harmenopoulos **569**
(1986) 803

Facts

A minor, represented by his mother, brought a maintenance action against his father. The action was brought in the one-member District Court of Thessaloniki where, allegedly, the defendant was domiciled.

The defendant alleged that the Greek court had no international jurisdiction because he had become an employee of the European Community, and, therefore, his domicile was in Brussels, not in Thessaloniki.

Judgment

The court rejected this objection and invoked Art. 5(2) of the Brussels Convention, which had not yet come into force in Greece, to support its decision.

Comment

The court in fact applied Art. 5(2) incorrectly, since the plaintiff was domiciled in Athens, not Thessaloniki, so that the courts in Thessaloniki would not have international jurisdiction to try the case.

ARTICLE 5(3)

" . . . harmful event occurred."

Case principle

In an action for damages through supply of defective products, place of *use* of product held to be that of *Bier* causative act.

Case

570   Court of Appeals of Piraeus 351/1994, Nomiko Vima (1996) 658

Facts

This decision was rendered on the defendant's appeal against the first instance decision. The plaintiff, a company with its seat in Monrovia, Liberia (represented in Greece by another company, with an establishment in Piraeus), owned a Greek ship which was navigating in the Mediterranean Sea and in the seas of North Europe. It had agreed with the defendant, a company with its seat in Mortsel, Belgium, to buy from it about 400 tons of fuel oil (IFO–180), according to British Standards M6, at 14950 US dollars per ton and about 70 tons of Diesel MDO oil, at 248 US dollars per ton, deliverable in Antwerp, Belgium. When these fuels were used by the ship, it was found that they were not of the agreed type and quality, a fact that the defendant was aware of, and so they caused damage to the ship's engines, which was discovered when the plaintiff's ship sailed into the harbour of Elefsis, where the damage had to be repaired. The plaintiff sued the defendant for 17821900 drachmas. The first instance decision, favourable to the plaintiff, was rendered in default of the defendant's appearance, who then appealed.

Judgment

The court of appeal held that it had international jurisdiction according to Art. 5(3), since the damaging act, that is, the use of unsuitable fuel, took place on a Greek ship and in Greek territorial waters.

Comment

The defendant/appellant company also asked the appeal court to apply Arts 21 and 22 and stay the proceedings, since it had brought an action in Antwerp, Belgium, against the Greek company, for 7726192 US dollars, that is, the price of the oil mentioned in the action.

The appellate court rejected a stay: this was not a case of *lis alibi pendens* since, in its view, neither the parties nor the subject matter of the actions were the same. Besides, under Art. 22, para. 1, both actions had to be pending at first instance and that was not the case here.

ARTICLE 6(1)

" . . . *one of a number of defendants* . . . "

Case principle

Sufficient connection exists between claims against primary debtor for payment and against surety of his performance.

Case

Three-member District Court of Thessaloniki 31543/1995, Harmenopoulos **571**
(1996) 361 and 615

Facts

The plaintiff Greek company, with its seat in Thessaloniki, claimed that under
two consecutive sale contracts which it had concluded with the first defendant
company, its seat in Germany, through the mediation of the second defendant
company, its seat in Thessaloniki, acting as the plaintiff's agent, it sold to the
first defendant products for 52,800 DM and 12,400 DM respectively, payable
on delivery. The first defendant refused to take delivery of the merchandise and
to pay the total price of 65,200 DM, plus the cost for storage of the merchandise in storehouses in Germany, estimated at 566 DM. Moreover, the
plaintiff maintained that the second defendant company, under a contract concluded between them, had agreed that it would be jointly and severally liable
with the first defendant for the non-performance or defective performance
of the first defendant's obligations arising from the above mentioned sales
contracts. The plaintiff, therefore, sued both defendants jointly and severally
for the total sum of 65,766 DM.

Judgment

The court held that it possessed jurisdiction over the first defendant under
Art. 6(1).
   The first defendant alleged that the Greek courts had no international juris-
diction since its seat and the place of performance of the obligation was in
Germany. The court rejected this allegation, saying that its jurisdiction was
founded on Art. 6(1).

ARTICLE 8, PARAGRAPH 1(2)

" . . . *place where the policy-holder is domiciled* . . . "

Case principle

The policy-holder is the party who concluded the contract of insurance with
the insurer.

Case

Three-member District Court of Piraeus 422/1994, Dikaio Epicheirisseon & **572**
Etairion (1995) 82

Facts

The plaintiffs, companies incorporated in Monrovia, Liberia, with their real seats in Piraeus, Greece, where their business activity took place, each bought a ship, on 27 July 1990 and on 6 August 1990, respectively, in Rio de Janeiro, Brazil, from local companies. The ships were insured through brokers in Piraeus, by the defendants, Lloyd's of London Syndicates, against war risks. One contract concerned both ships and contained the Insurance Rules for War, Strikes, Agitations, Social Hostilities and Malevolent Damage, based on the War and Strikes Rules of 1 October 1983 of the London Insurers' Institute.

The ships had been illegally detained for more than a year and had been totally stripped of their equipment by the company, Score Shipyard, in the refitting base in Rio de Janeiro, where they had been tugged to be refitted. Consequently, the ships were considered constructive total loss. Nevertheless, although the insured risk had already happened, the defendant foreign Syndicates refused under various pretexts to pay the plaintiffs their insurance monies of half-a-million and one million US dollars, respectively.

The plaintiffs claimed that the dispute was regulated by the abovementioned English rules according to which the detention of a ship for 12 months continuously, created the right of the insured to ask for damages for constructive total loss of the ship. They also claimed that the Greek courts had international jurisdiction based on Art. 8, para. 1(2).

Judgment

The court held that the action obviously concerned a contract of ship's insurance concluded in London, where the defendants, Lloyds Syndicates, had their seat, according to the usual practice of English law on mediation of broker companies. It further held, however, that the plaintiffs had not determined, as they should, the contracting parties, and especially who had concluded a contract with the insurers, how they had acquired the right to the insurance amount, or whether *the brokers concluding the contract* had acted as agents for the plaintiffs. These elements were absolutely necessary in this case, since the plaintiffs invoked only Art. 8, para. 1(2) to establish the international jurisdiction of the Greek courts: and for the application of this provision, the determination of the party who concluded the contract with the insurer—the 'policy-holder'—was indispensable.

Therefore, the Greek court dismissed the present action as inadmissible.

ARTICLE 10, PARAGRAPH 2

" . . . *where such direct actions are permitted.*"

Case principle

1. Direct actions against insurers are permitted under Greek procedures.

Case

One-member District Court of Serres 59/1990, Harmenopoulos (1992) 375   **573**

Facts

This was an action for damages for tort (a car accident), against the tortfeasor and the insurance company.

Judgment

In the case of car insurance for civil liability, Law 489/1976 provides for the possibility of bringing a direct action against the insurer.

Case

Court of Appeals of Athens 1579/1991, Dike (1995) 504   **574**

Facts

On 7 April 1989, in Isthmia, a crash took place between the car of the first of the plaintiffs (which was driven by himself and in which was also his wife—mother of the second and third plaintiffs and daughter of the fourth plaintiff) and a car insured by the first defendant—and appellant—an insurance company with its seat in Italy, for which car a green card had been issued. The driver of the second car was exclusively responsible for the car crash. The second defendant was the Greek Office of International Insurance, authorized representative of the first. The car crash caused the death of all four people in the second car and of the wife of the driver of the first car and the serious injury of the driver himself.

On 16 November 1989 an action was filed, seeking damages.

Judgment

Jurisdiction was admitted by the court. This was a direct action against the insurer, according to Art. 10, para. 2.

Case principle

2. Conditions for bringing direct actions against insurers are for the national law of the court seised.

Case

Court of Appeal of Athens 7455/1993, Elliniki Dikaiossyni (1995) 389   **575**

Facts

The plaintiff instituted proceedings against an English insurance company claiming compensation for damage caused to his car in a collision with a truck on a Greek road due to the negligence of the truck driver—insured by the English company.

International jurisdiction of Greek courts in cases of actions against insurance companies with their seat in a Contracting State but no branch in Greece, for road accidents which happened in Greece and where the responsible car was insured by the company are based on Art. 5(3) and Art. 10, para. 2—which latter refers to Arts 7, 8 and 9.

The defendant, and later appellant, insurance company contested the international jurisdiction of the Greek courts.

Judgment

The Court of Appeal upheld Greek territorial jurisdiction—but since the action was imprecisely pleaded under Greek law, it had to be dismissed because there was no evidence of the place where the truck responsible was habitually parked or of whether it was equipped with a certificate of international insurance or if the defendants had a branch in Greece, which would have concluded the insurance in question, so that the defendant would have capacity to be sued.

ARTICLE 16(1)(a)

" . . . have as their object . . . "

Case principle

Immovables must be *a principal* object of proceedings.

Case

576 Three-member District Court of Kavala 175/1995, Harmenopoulos (1995) 925

Facts

The defendant company with its seat in Germany, had agreed on 9 August 1983 with a Greek citizen to lend him 619286.56 DM. On 29 August 1983, the German company had filed, before the one-member District Court of Kavala, Greece, an application for a note of mortgage on immovables of the other party, in Thassos (an island off Kavala), for the amount of 500000 DM, owed to it under the loan contract. The Greek man alleged that on 31 December 1986 the claim of the German company had been extinguished by payment and that it was, therefore, in bad faith that the German company later obtained conversion of the above note of mortgage into a mortgage. The Greek plaintiff brought an action for redemption of the mortgage before the one-member court of Kavala. In this action, he asked for declarations: (i) that the defendant's claim had been extinguished by payment; (ii) that no loan contract had been concluded between him and the defendant; and (iii) that the German company had never had the legal form of a corporation.

Judgment

The court, without examining the case on its merits, dismissed it for lack of international jurisdiction over the German defendant. At first, it enquired as to whether it was possible to found jurisdiction on the place of the immovable (Art. 16(1)) but concluded against this, since the plaintiff's principal claim was that no contract had been concluded and that, consequently, there was no obligation of the plaintiff towards the defendant company arising from such a contract. The fact that a note of mortgage, later converted into a mortgage, had been registered in the mortgage books of the Mortgage Office of Thassos, did not transform the action *principally* into an action *in rem* for purposes of Art. 16(1).

ARTICLE 17, PARAGRAPH 1(a)

" . . . in writing . . . "

Case principle

A jurisdiction agreement in writing should be signed and dated, and not merely a printed set of conditions handed by one party to the other.

Case

Court of Appeals of Piraeus 389/1994, Dikaio Epicheirisseon & Etairion **577** (1995) 84; Dike (1995) 353

Facts

A Greek company, with its seat in Kallithea, Attica, on 23 January 1992, bought from an Italian company, its seat in Palermo, liquid chemical products, namely: 314.467 kgs trichloraethylenium for 0,38 US dollars per kg. In order to carry this amount from the Italian port of Marghera to the Greek port of Perama, Piraeus, the buyer, on 23 January 1992, concluded a contract of carriage by sea with the defendant (appellant), in performance of which contract, on 26 January 1992, the above amount of trichloraethylenium was loaded onto a ship owned by the defendant, of Panamanian flag. On the same day, the captain of the ship issued a bill of lading to the order of the consignor who thus was at the same time consignee of the cargo. When the ship arrived at the destination port on 1 February 1992, a deficit of 10.500 kgs in the cargo was ascertained, due to gross negligence of the captain and crew of the ship. The value of the lost amount, estimated on the basis of the value of goods of the same kind and amount at the time the unloading began, was up to 33926 US dollars. The plaintiff, an insurance company who had insured the whole cargo for all maritime risks, was subrogated to the consignee's rights against the defendant, after having paid to it insurance damages of 764155 drachmas.

Based on the above, the plaintiff asked the defendant to pay 764155 drachmas, or the equal amount in drachmas, at the time of payment, of 33926 US dollars.

Judgment

The defendant (appellant) alleged that the Greek court had no international jurisdiction over the dispute, because at the time at which the contract of carriage was concluded, it had agreed with the Greek consignor-consignee that for the resolution of disputes arising out of the contract, the English courts would have jurisdiction and that, therefore, this agreement was also binding upon the plaintiff subrogated to the rights and obligations against the defendant. Thus, a fax had been sent in Piraeus on 23 January 1992 to the consignor, containing a summary of the terms of the contract, and the fax in reply, of 23 January 1992, of the consignor, accepted those terms. A printed paper, unsigned, undated, with blanks needing completion, and containing only printed general terms of a charterparty, mentioned that the English courts would have jurisdiction over any dispute arising from the contract.

The Court of Appeals held that, according to bona fides, trade customs and the real will of the contracting parties (Arts 173 and 200 Civil Code), it could not be accepted that the contracting parties wished the terms as to jurisdiction, of the abovementioned paper, to have validity and to bind them as a charterparty, without their signature and its due completion. There was no agreement to jurisdiction in writing.

" . . . evidenced in writing . . . "

Case principle

For confirmation following contract to amount to evidence in writing through lack of objection thereto, there must have been a preceding oral agreement as to jurisdiction, in the absence of a (*Segoura,* Case 25/76) continuing trading relationship dispensing therewith (*Berghoefer,* Case 221/84).

Case

578 Areios Pagos (Supreme Court) (D section) 1309/1991, Elliniki Dikaiossyni (1992) 1181; Dike (1992) 1050; Ephimeris Ellinon Nomikon (1993) 99

Facts

In this case the court, in order to support its decision, referred to Art. 17, even though the Convention was not applicable since the action had been brought in the court of first instance before the Convention's entry into force in Greece.

The case concerned a dispute between foreign companies, which arose from a sales contract concluded in Athens. The action had been brought in the three-members District Court of Athens which had international jurisdiction to try the case, in accordance with Art. 3, para. 1 and Art. 33 of the Code of Civil Procedure. According to Art. 3, para. 1, Greek civil courts have jurisdiction over both Greeks and foreigners, on the condition that a Greek court is competent. According to Art. 33, disputes which concern the existence or the validity of a juridical act done *in vivo* and all the rights which emanate from it, may be brought before the court in the district of which the contract was concluded. The above Articles, combined with Arts 42, 43 and 44 of the Code of Civil Procedure, provide that a relevant agreement of the parties can preclude the international jurisdiction of the Greek civil courts—also for future disputes which will arise from a particular legal relation. In order for the agreement to be valid, it has to be in writing. According to Art. 17, not only a written agreement is permitted for the prorogation of the international jurisdiction of a court or of courts of a Contracting State, but even an oral one, under the condition that its written acknowledgement will follow.

The defendant, during the trial before the courts of first and second instance, and even before Areios Pagos (the Supreme Court), pleaded that in a registered letter served on the plaintiff, it had proposed the specific agreement that the disputes arising from the sales contract would be tried by the Commercial Court of Paris or by the Arbitration Court of Paris and that, consequently, the agreement of prorogation of those courts' jurisdiction had been concluded, since the plaintiff had not refused it explicitly.

Judgment

Areios Pagos held that no such valid agreement had been concluded, either according to the provisions of the Code of Civil Procedure, since the letter did not meet the prerequisite of a written agreement, or according to Art. 17—which, as it was held, was not applicable to the present case—given the fact that the defendant did not invoke a preceding oral agreement for the prorogation of international jurisdiction, of which oral agreement the letter would have been written evidence.

ARTICLE 18

" *. . . to contest the jurisdiction . . .* "

Case principle

Contestation of jurisdiction is active, not mere non-participation in the proceedings.

Case

579 Court of Appeals of Thessaloniki 754/1991, Harmenopoulos (1992) 368

Facts

The plaintiff, a company with its seat in Thessaloniki, which made and sold clothes abroad, had concluded four contracts with the defendant, a company with its seat in Amstelveen, The Netherlands, in performance of which the merchandize was sent to the defendant with bills of lading. The plaintiff company was not paid. It brought an action for the debt before a Greek court for payment of the sum owed plus interest. It claimed that the Greek courts had international jurisdiction according to Arts 5(1) and 18.

Judgment

Before the court of first instance, the defendant contested the international jurisdiction of the Greek courts. The court dismissed this objection. Under Art. 18 it was provided, as an exception to the rule established in the first sentence, that the appearance of the defendant before the court in which the action was brought did not imply the tacit prorogation of the international jurisdiction of this court, when the defendant had limited itself to contestation of that jurisdiction.

The Court of Appeals held that because the defendant did not adduce evidence before the court to challenge the international jurisdiction of the court of first instance, the latter, based on the evidence which the plaintiff had brought, was right to accept that it had international jurisdiction. Contestation under Art. 18 is active, not merely passive.

ARTICLE 20, PARAGRAPH 3

" . . . shall be replaced by . . . Article 15 of the Hague Convention . . . "

Case principle

Article 15 requires due and sufficient service upon the defendant in time for organization of a defence.

Case

580 Three-member District Court of Thessaloniki 2133/1990, Harmenopoulos (1990) 1210

Facts

In this decision, Art. 20, para. 3 was applied, that is, in this sense, Art. 15 of the Hague Convention of 1965 on the Service Abroad of Judicial and Extrajudicial Documents in Civil and Commercial Matters.

The action brought was one for damages and there were three defendants. One of them, a company with its seat in Munich, Germany, was in default of appearance.

Judgment

In order that the legality of the company's default be investigated and, given the fact that the requirement of civil or commercial nature of the dispute was met, the court held that it was not Art. 136, para. 1 Code of Civil Procedure establishing fictitious service which should be applied, but the provisions of the Hague Convention. Consequently, the handing of the writ to the public attorney for service, as Art. 136, para. 1 Code of Civil Procedure dictated, according to the court was not enough. Satisfaction of the requirements of Art. 15, para. 1 of the Hague Convention was necessary, namely, the due and timely service of the writ upon the defendant company. Since that service had not taken place, the hearing of the action as regards this defendant was declared inadmissible.

ARTICLE 24

" . . . as may be available under the law of that State . . . "

Case principle

The scope of national laws is limited to procedural conditions and does not also cover national rules of international jurisdiction.

Case

One-member District Court of Thessaloniki 3115/1991, Harmenopoulos   **581**
(1992) 377

Facts

This was an application for provisional measures (Art. 682 Code of Civil Procedure) ordering damages against an English surgeon and an English hospital, filed by the wife and daughter of a Greek man, operated on for a heart by-pass, who died after the operation, according to the applicants, as a result of the surgeon's negligence. The English courts had international jurisdiction to try the case, since the defendant was domiciled in England and it was there that the damaging act took place (Art. 5(3)). The applicants, however, invoked urgency and danger from the postponement of adjudication of damages for the loss they had sustained due to the fact that they had been deprived of maintenance from the deceased. They asked the Greek court to order provisional measures, according to Art. 24.

Judgment

The court referred to the two approaches adopted by courts of the Contracting States: (i) that under Art. 24 a kind of unlimited international jurisdiction of the Contracting States' courts to order provisional measures is established; or (ii) that the Article refers to the national laws also as regards the conditions for the exercise of international jurisdiction over cases of provisional measures. The Greek court held the first opinion to be correct, reasoning that, first, from the text of Art. 24, the second approach did not appear to be correct, and secondly, the intention of the drafters of the Brussels Convention was to assist the Contracting States' inhabitants in those cases where the national laws would not have adequate rules of international jurisdiction permitting the courts to order provisional measures in private international disputes. Thus, only the first approach made it possible to recognize that the Greek courts had international jurisdiction to order provisional measures. If the other approach was accepted, then the Greek courts could not order provisional measures, since neither the principal claim could be tried in Greece, nor could provisional measures be executed in Greek territory.

Finally, the court held that there was in fact no urgency, given that the petition had been filed after two years had passed since the deceased had died and, therefore, they could temporarily afford their living costs (it also dismissed the petition because no pretrial evidence had been produced as to the applicable law in the case, which was English law since the alleged tort had taken place in London—Arts 26 Civil Code and Art. 5(3) of the Brussels Convention).

> " ... even if ... courts of another Contracting State have jurisdiction
> as to the substance ... "

Case principle

Article 24 is available even where substantive jurisdiction does not exist for domestic procedural reasons.

Case

582 One-member District Court of Athens 18.185/1992, Harmenopoulos (1995) 60

Facts

A Swiss company, with its seat in Geneva, asked the Greek court to order, because of imminent danger, the conservatory seizure of the assets of the defendant, the Central Service of Administration of Domestic Products (CSADP), with its seat in Athens, for the amount of 7853628571 drachmas. Its claim against CSADP was based on two grounds: first, CSADP owed 40000000 Swiss francs to the Swiss company, on the basis of tort. For this reason, the Swiss company had instituted main proceedings before a Swiss court which had issued a judgment ordering the parties to supply evidence; secondly, CSADP was in default as regards its contractual obligation to the Swiss company for the sale of 50000 M.T. of Greek corn, with the result that the Appellate Commission of the Union for the Trade of Cereals and Animal Supplies awarded to the Swiss company in arbitration, a sum of 185223751 drachmas.

Judgment

The Greek court held that it had international jurisdiction to try the case under Art. 24, even though it lacked jurisdiction on substance through domestic *res judicata*.

As far as the second part of the application was concerned, during the hearing another Swiss company intervened, alleging that the applicant had assigned to it the claim against CSADP by an assignment contract signed in Geneva and governed by Swiss law—and that the assignment had been notified to CSADP. The intervening Swiss company asked for the conservatory seizure of assets of CSADP, situated both in Greece and abroad, to secure its foreign arbitral award not yet declared enforceable in Greece.

The court held that it had international jurisdiction to order the conservatory seizure of the assets of CSADP situated *abroad*, only in so far as the injunction was to be enforced in countries of the EU.

According to the leading opinion in Greece, Greek civil courts have international jurisdiction to order conservatory measures only if these measures are to be enforced in Greece, given the fact that such an order is an administrative order, and that its enforcement in another country would offend the principle of sovereignty. To this rule there are exceptions, such as under some bilateral conventions and the Brussels Convention. According to the latter, judgments ordering conservatory measures are considered the same as the judgments issued in the main proceedings: that is, their recognition and enforcement by the other Contracting States is facilitated without review of the international jurisdiction and the applicable substantive law of the judgment-State.

ARTICLE 25

" . . . *as well as . . . costs . . .* "

Case principle

Determination of costs falls within Title III enforcement.

Case

583 One-member District Court of Thessaloniki 33114/1995, Harmenopoulos (1996) 363

Facts

This was an application for the German courts' judgment to be enforced in Greece (the seat of the debtor company). By a Tübingen first instance court, the defendant company was ordered to pay to the applicant 35,428.55 DM, plus interest at 10 per cent as from 15 March 1994. Under the same judgment, the applicant was ordered to pay to the defendant 12,415 DM, plus interest at 5 per cent as from 6 February 1994. The decision was declared provisionally enforceable for the above sums, on the condition of paying a guarantee. It was also ordered that the defendant would pay 9/10 of the costs, whereas the applicant would pay 1/10. Accordingly, the defendant owed to the applicant, as costs, 8,347.46 DM, plus interest at 4 per cent on the sum of 6,255.76 DM as from 26 May 1995 and the sum of 2,091.70 DM as from 3 July 1995.

The defendant appealed, but the Court of Appeal of Stuttgart dismissed the appeal. Therefore, the first instance decision became final and executable, without the condition of guarantee. It was also ordered that the defendant had to pay all the costs of the second instance trial, that is 2,642.50 DM, plus interest at 4 per cent as from 13 March 1995.

Judgment

The Greek court held recognizable and enforceable the German judgment (and only dismissed the applicant's request that the debtor pay her court costs, on the ground that the application had been filed in the interests of the applicant) (Art. 746a of the Code of Civil Procedure).

Case

584 One-member District Court of Kavala 135/1991, Epitheorissi Trapezikou—Axiografikou Chrimatistiriakou Dikaiou (1995) 92

Facts

An 'order of enforcement' (Vollstreckungsbescheid) was issued in 1990 by Stuttgart's local enforcement court (Amtsgericht) to be enforced in Greece. The debtor was then domiciled in Germany and was obliged to pay to the petitioner 50939 DM plus 15 per cent interest on the sum of 50000 DM which was the principal claim (289 DM: court costs; 650 DM: interest).

Judgment

This order, according to Art. 25, was held to constitute a *judgment*. The enforcement petition was filed with the Greek court in the district in which the debtor was by that time domiciled. The Greek court held that the requirements for the German order to be enforced in Greece were met.

ARTICLE 27(1)

" . . . *contrary to public policy* . . . "

Case principle

Absence of reasoning in the foreign judgment held not contrary to Greek public policy.

Case

Court of Appeals of Piraeus 419/1994, Elliniki Dikaiossyni (1995) 421   **585**

Facts

This was an appeal against the order declaring a judgment of the English High Court of Justice to be enforceable in Greece. The foreign judgment obliged the appellant, domiciled in Piraeus, to pay to the party against which the appeal had been filed, an English bank, the amount of 714999.89 US dollars plus interest. There were three objections: (i) the appellant had not been summoned to the hearing of the application before the court, and therefore he had been deprived of the opportunity to put forward any defence; (ii) the declaration of enforceability of the foreign decision was contrary to Art. 20 of the Greek Constitution and to Greek public policy, because the right of the appellant to be heard had been offended against, and also for lack of reasoning of the foreign judgment; and (iii) the appellant had not been served with the foreign judgment and consequently 'he had been deprived of his legal rights to institute legal remedies'.

Judgment

According to Art. 34, para. 1, the proceedings at the enforcement stage were *ex parte*. The Greek appellate court stressed the fact that Art. 34 aimed at the rapid and surprise declaration of enforceability, in order that a defendant be deprived of the chance to conceal his assets so as to protect himself against execution.

The court stressed that the non-contentious stage of enforcement proceedings did not offend the right of the defendant to be heard, since he could appeal against the order declaring the enforceability of the foreign judgment and that the appeal was contentious.

Nor was the fact that the foreign judgment contained no or insufficient reasoning judged contrary to Greek public policy, since the lack of reasoning did not render invalid a decision of a Greek court either. Finally, the appellant debtor had been duly summoned before the foreign court in sufficient time to be heard and defend himself. Moreover, as was proved by the relevant report of service and notwithstanding his contrary allegation, he had been served with the foreign judgment and consequently had not been deprived of his legal rights to legal remedies. Given the fact that there was a certificate of the English court proving that the foreign judgment was enforceable according to the law of the country of origin, the Greek appellate court concluded that there were no reasons to deny recognition and enforcement according to Arts 27, 28 and Art. 34, para. 2.

Therefore, the court rejected as unfounded the three objections put forth in the appeal.

Case

586   Court of Appeals of Athens 10415/84, Archeion Nomologias (1985) 425

Facts

This decision was rendered on an appeal against the order declaring an English judgment enforceable in Greece. The English judgment obliged the appellants to pay their debt to a bank in US dollars or English sterling, and it had been issued in default of an appearance by the defendants.

Judgment

The Greek appellate court rejected the assertion of the appellants that the Brussels Convention was applicable to the judgment's enforcement in Greece, since the Convention would only come into force after its ratification and at that time it had not yet been ratified. Therefore, it held that the requirements for the judgment's enforcement in Greece were set by the Greek Code of Civil Procedure's provisions. It rejected the allegation of the appellants that the lack of reasoning of the foreign judgment and also the obligation to pay in foreign currency were contrary to Greek public policy—a contract was valid when it was agreed that payment in foreign currency would take place abroad—as in this case in which the contract had been concluded in London, where the payment would take place.

The court dismissed the appeal against enforcement as unfounded.

ARTICLE 28, PARAGRAPH 3

" . . . jurisdiction . . . may not be reviewed . . . "

Case principle

The 1978 Accession Convention, Art. 34(3) is a further exception to the prohibition upon examination of judgment-court jurisdiction.

Case

Court of Appeals of Athens 2667/1994, Nomiko Vima (1995) 252   **587**

Facts

An English company had brought an action in England against a Greek corporation, claiming to be paid the remainder of the agreed purchase price, plus interest, for the dying machine it had sold to the defendant, and had obtained a favourable judgment.

The English court's judgment was declared enforceable in Greece in accordance with the provisions of the Brussels Convention. The defendant appealed against this decision under Art. 36, para. 1. The reasons for the appeal were: (i) that the writ instituting the English proceedings had not been duly served and in sufficient time on the defendant; and (ii) that the English court had no international jurisdiction.

Judgment

According to Art. 28, para. 3, 'the jurisdiction of the court of the State of origin may not be reviewed', although 'subject to the provisions of the first paragraph'. This case was a further exception to the prohibition of review: namely, the transitional rule of law, contained in Art. 54 of the 1968 Convention, Art. 34 of the Accession Convention 1978, Art. 12 of the Convention for the Accession of Greece 1982—the latter was applicable here—and Art. 29 of the Accession Convention 1989. According to this rule, the Greek courts apply the Brussels Convention for recognition and enforcement of a judgment given after the entry into force of the Convention in Greece, that is, after 1 April 1989 (1 October 1989 for the UK), even if the action had been instituted before that date.

In a case like this, as it was pointed out in the Greek court, the provisions of the Brussels Convention which govern the direct international jurisdiction of the courts of the Contracting States may apply as rules of *indirect* international jurisdiction. That is to say, the Greek court proceeded to a review of the international jurisdiction of the English court, because the latter's jurisdiction was founded not on the Brussels Convention but on a rule equivalent to the provisions of an Article in Title II of the Convention—Art. 5(1).

Thus, since the remainder of the purchase price claimed had to be paid by the defendant, by an irrevocable credit on security, to the plaintiff's bank branch in Nottingham, England, the Greek court came to the obvious conclusion that the place of performance of the defendant's contractual obligation in question was Nottingham and that therefore the *English* court had international jurisdiction.

As regards the other ground for the appeal—absence of due and sufficient service of the English writ on the defendant—the following must be said: by order of the English court, the plaintiff English company had issued a writ of summons to be served on the defendant Greek company and a time limit of 21 days from the service of this writ was set for the defendant to announce to the court that it had been served with it. A copy of the writ, together with the form for the acknowledgement of service and the order for the service of the writ out of the jurisdiction, were legally served on the defendant within the time limit set by English law. The defendant engaged legal counsel who, representing it, completed the document for the acknowledgement of service of the writ and filed a defence to the action.

Afterwards, the English court issued an order, according to which the defendant had to file its counterclaim in a time limit of 14 days from the notification of this order. After the lapse of this time limit, the plaintiff obtained an order for the striking out of the defendant's defence and counterclaim and for a judgment in default in favour of the plaintiff, which was declared enforceable in Greece.

Clearly, the argument of the defendant concerning lack of due and sufficient service could not be accepted by the Greek court. Therefore, it was right to dismiss the appeal as groundless.

ARTICLE 34, PARAGRAPH 1

" . . . not . . . entitled to make any submissions . . . "

Case principle

If the party against whom enforcement is sought in fact makes submissions on the enforcement application, the enforcement-court may take account of these.

Case

588 One-member District Court of Thessaloniki 511/1994, Harmenopoulos (1994) 1409

Facts

A company, with its seat in Germany, applied to the Greek courts for enforcement in Greece of a foreign judgment. Since it had no domicile in Greece, it should appoint an attorney with special authority to accept service of legal documents (Art. 33), which it did not. The defendant, a company with its seat in Thessaloniki, alleged that this fact would cause it damage if the enforcement were to be allowed, because it would be obliged, in order to appeal under Art. 36, to serve the necessary documents abroad. According to Art. 159(3) of the

Code of Civil Procedure: 'The violation of a provision which governs the procedure and especially the form of some procedural act, has as a consequence its nullity . . . when the judge estimates that the violation caused harm to the party invoking it, which cannot be restored otherwise than by a declaration of nullity'.

Judgment

The court, based on the above, declared the enforcement application inadmissible.

Comment

It must be pointed out that, notwithstanding the fact that Art. 34, para. 1 forbids, explicitly, the party against whom enforcement is applied for, from making any submissions during the application for enforcement (*ex parte*), in the present case the party against whom enforcement was applied for was in fact summoned and alleged harm. The Brussels Convention does not impose sanctions in the event that the defendant participates at this stage and that the court, judging admissible his participation, takes account of his allegations—as it did in the present case.

The European Court of Justice has already ruled that the prerequisites for the appointment of an authorized representative, according to Art. 33, para. 2, as well as the consequences of its omission, are governed by *lex fori*, so long as this is not opposed to the aims of the Convention (*Carron*, Case 198/85). The view here is that the obligation to appoint an authorized attorney functions as a prerequisite for the admissibility of the application, which, if not met, would have as a direct consequence the dismissal of the application as inadmissible. This decision will be final, so that the applicant will either file a new application, having, in the meantime, legally appointed an attorney, or will appeal according to Art. 40. The difference between this opinion and the one chosen by the court in the case here, is that the decision which declares the hearing of the application as inadmissible is interlocutory, with the result that a new, similar application cannot be tried because of litispendence. The applicant has to bring back the same application to be tried, taking care that an authorized representative has been appointed.

9

ICELAND

Professor Eiríkur Tómasson

A.   LEGAL SYSTEM

Courts

The main structure of the Icelandic court system is as follows.

There are only two judicial instances, the lower instance being formed by eight District Courts and the superior instance by the Supreme Court. Almost all civil cases must start before the District Courts, whose judgments can, in most instances, be appealed to the Supreme Court.

The main rule is that each case is heard by one professional District Court judge, although some cases are heard by three judges, either three professional judges or one professional judge and two lay judges, specialized in certain fields other than law. In the Supreme Court, cases are normally heard by three or five professional judges—although simple cases can be heard by only one judge and in extraordinary circumstances a case may be subject to a hearing in plenary, with all nine judges participating.

In both instances, there will be rendered a written judgment, identifying the parties and issues at stake, with a summary of the arguments presented by the parties, as well as the court's reasons for its decision.

Enforcement proceedings

The courts do not concern themselves with matters other than those which are defined by law as judicial. Therefore, the execution of judgments and orders has been entrusted to magistrates. Iceland is divided into 27 administrative districts, and in each of them is a magistrate who is a lawyer by training and has other functions as well, such as being commissioner of police and public prosecutor in certain criminal cases.

B. IMPLEMENTATION OF THE LUGANO CONVENTION

Iceland, being a member of the European Free Trade Association (EFTA) as well as of the European Economic Area (EEA), ratified the Lugano Convention with effect from 1 December 1995. Nationally, the Convention, with the three Protocols, was implemented by the Act of 10 March 1995, No. 68, on the Lugano Convention on jurisdiction and the enforcement of judgments in civil and commercial matters.

Section 2 of this Act provides that the Convention and the three Protocols apply as formal law in Iceland. The full text of the Convention and the Protocols are attached to the Act as annexes.

Section 3 reads as follows:

'Judgments rendered in another Convention State at a venue according to Articles 5(1) and 16(1)(b) of the Lugano Convention, shall be recognized and enforced in Iceland even though the relevant State has made a reservation that it will not recognize or enforce Icelandic judgments in similar circumstances.

Judgments which need not be recognized or enforced according to Article II, Subsection 2 of Protocol No. 1 to the Convention, are not legally binding and enforceable in Iceland.'

C. OVERVIEW OF CONVENTION CASE LAW

Until now, no cases regarding the Lugano Convention have come before the Icelandic courts.

10

IRELAND

Professor Peter Kaye

A.   LEGAL SYSTEM

The Irish system is completely separate from that of the UK but historically influenced by the common law nonetheless. It has a written Constitution (*Bunreacht na hÉireann*) dating from 1937. Binding case law precedent applies and since 1964 the highest court, the Supreme Court, has been able to overrule its past judgments. English cases can be cited as persuasive authority.

The three levels of first instance court are District, Circuit and High Court. The former two have jurisdiction up to a certain financial amount.

The High Court sitting in Dublin has no financial limit and takes appeals from the Circuit Court. The High Court normally sits with one judge (of which there are 15 and a President) without a jury in civil cases.

The highest court is the Supreme Court, consisting of the Chief Justice and five other Supreme Court judges. It is the final court of appeal. Usually three judges sit in civil proceedings, but five will do so in constitutional or other important cases.

A judge's status is very high and equivalent to that in the English system.

There are also procedural Masters of the High Court to deal with matters arising during certain stages of trials.

B.   IMPLEMENTATION OF THE CONVENTIONS

The Brussels Convention entered into force in Ireland in pursuance of the 1978 Accession Convention on 1 June 1988 by virtue of the Jurisdiction of

Courts and Enforcement of Judgments (European Communities) Act 1988. The San Sebastian Convention on the Spanish/Portuguese Accession came into force on 1 December 1993, and the 1988 Lugano Convention also did so on 1 December 1993 by virtue of the Jurisdiction of Courts and Enforcement of Judgments Act 1993.

C. OVERVIEW OF CONVENTION CASE LAW

Article 1, para. 2(2) and Art. 5(1) decisions faithfully apply European Court principles, with some useful additional insight in particular respects as to the nature of an 'obligation in question' in the latter case.

As to Art. 5(3), Ireland's possession of a written constitution has led to case developments on the meaning of 'tort' unlikely to appear in the English legal system.

With regard to place of occurrence of the harmful event in tort, there is an interesting application of the European Court's *Shevill* principle to where the defendant is the *reported* rather than the reporter.

The drafting of Art. 16(2) continues to exercise the courts' prowess at construction.

In respect of Art. 17, the question of non-exclusive jurisdiction clauses not surprisingly has also presented itself in Ireland, but fortunately and with the benefit of the unsatisfactory English experience, the High Court dealt with the issue with somewhat greater clarity than Hoffmann J. had done so in the English *Kurz* decision (see *supra*, Case 229).

Article 18 introduces the theme of the role and scope of national procedural laws within the Convention's regime, as do certain of the Convention's enforcement provisions.

Articles 21 and 22 have given rise to comparatively little case law, although again there is brought to light the question of the factors properly to be taken into account in the exercise of the Art. 22 discretion to stay.

With regard to Art. 25 and security for costs, Irish courts have followed the English Court of Appeal's response to the European Court's rulings as to prohibition of covert nationality discrimination in relation to foreign EU plaintiffs and, if anything, seem to have gone rather further than the English in their pronouncements in this respect.

ABBREVIATIONS

J	Judge
CJ	Chief Justice
IR	Irish Reports

ILRM   Irish Law Reports Monthly
RSC   Rules of the Superior Courts

D. CASES

LUGANO ARTICLE 1, PARAGRAPH 2(2)

" . . . *proceedings relating to the winding-up of insolvent companies* . . . "

Case principle

An action brought under the general law not modified for purposes of
winding-up, in order to avoid a transaction for the assistance of a company to
purchase its own shares, is not within the Lugano Art. 1, para. 2(2) exclusion
simply because the company is in insolvent winding-up at the date of the
proceedings (*Gourdain v Nadler* Case 133/78, applied).

Case

Crédit Suisse & Crédit Suisse Canada v CH (Ireland) (In Liquidation) (unre-   **589**
ported) High Court, 2 February 1996

Facts

The liquidator of an insolvent Irish company sought directions from the Irish
courts as to invalidity of transactions made between the company and its associated Swiss and Canadian banks, which were alleged to be in contravention
of Irish legislation prohibiting the latter from assisting in the company's purchase of its own shares. The Swiss and Canadian banks applied to the Irish
High Court for a stay of the liquidator's action, on grounds that:

(1)   in the case of the Swiss bank, Swiss courts of its seat possessed
      exclusive jurisdiction under Lugano Art. 16(2); and
(2)   with regard to the non-Contracting State Canadian bank, Ireland
      was *forum non conveniens* under national Irish private internation-
      al law rules, since all relevant documents were located in
      Switzerland and Irish courts lacked jurisdiction over the Swiss bank
      (see (1) *supra*).

The liquidator sought to undermine this line of argument by asserting that
the Lugano Convention was excluded from applying by virtue of Art. 1, para.
2(2), since the proceedings related to the winding-up of an insolvent company;
and it was further contended that Ireland was *forum conveniens* under applicable national Irish conflicts.

Judgment

Keane J. held as follows.

(1) In relation to the Swiss bank, in *Gourdain* (although not binding in respect of the Lugano Convention, nonetheless said to be of the highest persuasive authority) the European Court had held that proceedings which were directly derived from and closely connected with a winding-up, as explained in Kaye, *Civil Jurisdiction* pp. 131 *et seq.*, fell within the Art. 1, para. 2(2) exclusion, and this was considered *not* to be the position in the case of the present action, governed by legal regulations applicable whether a winding up was in progress or not, notwithstanding the overall insolvency context in which the proceedings were brought. Consequently, the Lugano Convention and, in particular, Art. 16(2) thereof, applied so as to accord exclusive jurisdiction to Swiss courts over the Swiss bank, and Irish courts were obliged to decline in relation to the Swiss bank under Art. 19. It would have been a different matter, according to Keane J., had the question of jurisdiction related, for example, to the winding up petition itself or to directors' personal liability for the company's debts in a winding-up by reason of their fraudulent trading: these would have been excluded under Art. 1, para. 2(2) (see Kaye, pp. 137–8).

(2) As to the Canadian bank, a stay was refused by Keane J. in accordance with national Irish private international law rules of jurisdiction. Ireland was held to be *forum conveniens*, since Irish law governed the validity of the transactions, the Irish liquidation was already in progress and the Canadian bank had in fact proved as a creditor in it.

ARTICLE 5(1)

" . . . *obligation in question* . . . "

Case principle

1. In an action for breach of an agreement to assign exclusive performing rights, the obligation in question is that of execution of the assignment of the rights, not of compliance with exclusivity of the rights to be assigned.

Case

590 Olympia Productions Ltd v Mackintosh, Cameron Mackintosh (Overseas) Ltd, Cameron Mackintosh Ltd [1992] I.L.R.M. 204 High Court, 9 October 1991

Facts

The plaintiff Irish theatre owning company wished to sue the English defendant for breach of an agreement to execute an assignment of the exclusive right to perform 'Les Misérables' in Ireland. The defendant contested Art. 5(1) jurisdiction.

Judgment

Costello J., applying *de Bloos* Case 14/76, held that, on the facts of the claim, the obligation in question of the defendant was not that of respecting exclusivity of rights assigned, performable in Ireland, but to proceed with the agreed formal assignment thereof in the first place—which was to be carried out in England.

Therefore England, not Ireland, was the Art. 5(1) place of performance. Irish courts lacked jurisdiction.

Case principle

2. Obligation in question is the principal contractual obligation in the proceedings, determined according to contractual terms (*Shenavai,* Case 266/85 applied).

Case

Hanbridge Services Limited v Aerospace Communications Limited [1993] **591**
I.L.Pr. 778 Supreme Court, 10 March 1993

Facts

In its action for non-acceptance, the plaintiff Irish company alleged existence of a contract with the defendant UK company for the sale of 8000 computers to be manufactured by the plaintiff, who also asserted that Ireland was the place of manufacture and delivery. The defendant contested Irish jurisdiction, on the ground that the obligation in question was not that of acceptance of the delivery of the computers in Ireland, but to place orders with the plaintiff up to the agreed numbers of computers and that such communications would take place in the UK, not Ireland, as place of performance.

Judgment

Finlay C.J., construing Art. 5(1) in accordance with the European Court's ruling in *Shenavai* Case 266/85, held that the principal obligation of the defendant in dispute was, as the latter had argued, that of placing orders for the 8000 computers, which was the essential prerequisite to performance of the other obligations under the contract.

As to its place of performance, on a construction of the contractual terms, this was located outside Ireland, the courts of which consequently lacked jurisdiction under Art. 5(1) (see further *infra*, 'place of performance', Case 594).

Case

592 Ferndale Films Limited v Granada Television Limited [1994] I.L.Pr. 180
Supreme Court, 20 July 1993

Facts

In 1993, the plaintiff Irish company sued the defendant English company for breach of their 1988 agreement under which the plaintiff made the film 'My Left Foot' for the defendant.

The defendant contested Irish Art. 5(1) jurisdiction.

Judgment

The Supreme Court held against Irish jurisdiction under Art. 5(1). Applying *de Bloos* and *Shenavai*, Blayney J. construed the agreement: the defendant was responsible for the marketing of the film outside the UK and Ireland and for the sharing of gross receipts, breach of each of which obligations was the subject of the claim. The plaintiff argued that the payment obligations were the principal obligations, to be performed in Ireland, but the Supreme Court took the contrary view, namely, that distribution and exploitation of the film were the principal obligations of the defendant in the claim—and these were not performable in Ireland.

Comment

In the High Court, where payment *was* assumed to be the obligation in question, Carney J. had held that the principal part of that obligation was payment—in Ireland—for Art. 5(1) purposes and that its collection—outside Ireland—was merely a mechanical, ancillary aspect.

> " . . . *place of performance* . . . "

Case principle

1. In an action for wrongful termination by the principal of an exclusive distribution agreement and appointment of another person as distributor, place of performance of the principal's negative obligation not to contravene exclusivity is wherever distribution is agreed to take place (English *Medway Packaging* case followed).

Case

593 Carl Stuart Ltd v Biotrace Ltd [1993] I.L.R.M. 633 High Court, 4 February 1993

Facts

In 1990, the plaintiff Irish company was appointed exclusive distributor in Ireland of the defendant English company's hygiene testing products, but claimed that in 1992 the defendant had wrongfully terminated the agreement. The plaintiff wished to sue the defendant in the Irish courts for damages for breach of contract and for an injunction to restrain the defendant from appointing another distributor for Ireland and Northern Ireland. The defendant contested Irish Art. 5(1) jurisdiction.

Judgment

Barron J. upheld the Irish courts' jurisdiction as those of the place of performance under Art. 5(1). The judge applied the principles of *de Bloos* and *Shenavai* decided upon in the European Court and, in particular, also followed the judgment of Hobhouse J. in the English High Court in *Medway Packaging Ltd v Meurer Maschinen GmbH & Co. KG* [1990] 1 Lloyd's Rep. 383 (see *supra*, Case 159 for Court of Appeal's decision in that case), to the effect that where the action was for breach of exclusivity of distribution by the principal, as opposed to damages for the supply of defective goods thereby, the place of performance of the defendant principal's negative obligation to do nothing to harm or to impede exclusivity was in all places in which the distribution was agreed to be carried out. In the present case, this would include Ireland, the courts of which consequently possessed jurisdiction under Art. 5(1).

Thus, although the place of actual supply of the product to the plaintiff by the principal was Wales, nevertheless, in accordance with *Shenavai*, compliance with exclusivity was the principal obligation in question of the defendant principal, whereas supply, although necessary to continuation of exclusivity, was merely subsidiary to the latter (*aliter* had the action been for damages for defects in the goods).

Case principle

2. In the absence of provision in the applicable law, the contract must still be construed in order to determine place of performance and the plaintiff has to discharge the burden.

Case

Hanbridge Services Limited v Aerospace Communications Limited [1993] **594**
I.L.Pr. 778 Supreme Court, 10 March 1993

Facts

See supra, 'obligation in question', Case 591.

Judgment

The Supreme Court found nothing express in the contract about the place of communication of the defendant's orders.

However, since most of the negotiations had been face to face in England, it was not inconceivable that the Irish plaintiff's representatives would attend at the defendant's offices in England in order to obtain the orders.

Consequently, as there was no rule of applicable law specifying the seller's place of business as that of communication of orders in the absence of express or implied stipulation in the agreement, and since the burden was on the plaintiff to prove Irish Art. 5(1) place of performance, this was not discharged and Irish courts lacked jurisdiction thereunder.

Comment

The court further intimated that for Art. 5(1) jurisdiction to exist, the plaintiff had to prove that the obligation in question *must*—not merely *can*—be performed in the forum in accordance with the contract.

ARTICLE 5(3)

" . . . *matters relating to tort* . . . "

Case principle

Breach of a constitutional right, or of EC law, giving rise to a claim for damages, is a tort (*obiter*).

Case

595 Norburt Schmidt v Home Secretary of the Government of the United Kingdom [1995] 1 I.L.R.M. 301 High Court, 22 November 1994

Facts

The plaintiff claimed damages for, *inter alia*, false imprisonment and breach of constitutional rights and of EC Treaty principles of the freedom of movement against the defendant British police authorities.

Judgment

The defendants were held by Geoghegan J. to be entitled to sovereign immunity against suit.

However, if this finding were found to be wrong, the judge regarded the matters complained of as relating to 'tort' for purposes of Art. 5(3) jurisdiction and national leave of court was not therefore required for service of process outside the jurisdiction. Geoghegan J. took the view that if breach of statutory duty was a tort as a result of judge-made law, there was no reason why breach of constitutional rights or of EC law giving rise to a damages claim should not also be treated as such (see Kaye, *Private International Law of Tort and Product Liability*, pp. 17–18).

Comments

The Supreme Court, on appeal on 24 April 1995 (unreported), upheld the High Court's decision conferring sovereign immunity. No finding was made upon the further element of the latter judgment as to the Convention's and Art. 5(3)'s applicability; and in addition, expression of views was said to be unnecessary upon whether procedural rules for leave to serve process outside Ireland could also validly be used in Convention proceedings for which service without such leave was provided (Lynch J.—see English Cases *Republic of Haiti* and *X v Y*, Cases 88 and 89 *supra*).

In *Short v Ireland, AG, British Nuclear Fuels* (unreported), 24 October 1996, however, the Supreme Court considered the action against British Nuclear Fuels Plc for, *inter alia*, breach of the Irish Constitution and of EC Environmental Directives and for compensation for resulting damage clearly not to be a 'commercial' dispute. As to whether the Convention's scope was wide enough for the action nonetheless to be regarded as civil and tortious when it was for alleged breach of constitutional rights or EC Directive, this was left for further discussion—although it was felt that the Convention could be invoked when an action was essentially based upon some civil wrong but also contained minor elements of administrative law (Barrington J.).

> " . . . *harmful event occurred.*"

Case principles

1. In international newspaper libel, Art. 5(3) courts have jurisdiction over such harm as occurred within their territory (*Shevill* Case C–68/93 applied).
2. Not only Art. 2 courts of the defendant's domicile, but also Art. 18 courts have jurisdiction over *all* of the harm, wherever it occurred.

Case

Murray v Times Newspapers Ltd (unreported) High Court, 12 December 1995   **596**

Facts

The plaintiff wished to sue the defendant publishers of *The Times* newspaper in the Irish courts for damages for libel, in respect of harm suffered in Ireland and elsewhere, in 1991. Somewhat late in the pleadings, the defendants challenged Irish jurisdiction under Arts 5(3) and 18, in respect of harm alleged to have been suffered by the plaintiffs outside Ireland.

Judgment

Barron J. upheld Irish jurisdiction.

(1) With regard to Art. 5(3), following *Shevill* in the European Court, Irish courts would only possess jurisdiction in respect of the harm alleged to have occurred in Ireland.

(2) *However*, the defendants were considered to have entered an unconditional appearance for the purposes of Art. 18 in any event (see *infra*, Art. 18, Comments to Case 604), in view of which, Irish courts would possess jurisdiction over the entire damage wherever it occurred.

Case principle

3. In the case of negligent misrepresentation, causal event is where the representation is received by the victim and damage where relied upon.

Case

597 James Casey v Ingersoll-Rand Sales Company Limited (unreported) High Court, 12 July 1996

Facts

The Irish plaintiff wished to sue the defendant English company in the Irish courts for damages for negligent misrepresentation concerning the sale of a product to the plaintiff. The defendant denied Irish courts' jurisdiction under Art. 5(3).

Judgment

Shanley J. held against Irish Art. 5(3) jurisdiction on the facts. Applying the dual test for harmful event's occurrence in *Bier* Case 21/76, it was concluded that:

(1) as to causal event—the defendant's representations were at no time received by the plaintiff while he was in Ireland; and

(2) with regard to damage as harmful event—it seemed that the plaintiff's principal business operation was in the United Arab Emirates, which was therefore where he would have placed reliance upon the misrepresentations.

Case principle

4. In international television broadcast libel, if the defendant maker of a defamatory statement, televised in one Contracting State and broadcast to another, is capable of being liable according to applicable law on the ground that such broadcast was the natural and probable result of making the statement, the damage, as harmful event, may be taken to have occurred in the second Contracting State (*Shevill* applied).

Case

Ewins, Collins, McBride v Carlton Television Ltd (unreported) High Court,   **598**
3 March 1997

Facts

The plaintiffs in Ireland wished to sue the defendant English and Northern
Irish television broadcasting companies in the Irish courts for allegedly defamatory broadcasts which were made in London and Belfast but which were
nevertheless picked up by about 100 000 viewers in Ireland who had tuned
into the broadcasts by turning their aerials in the appropriate direction. The
defendants contested Irish courts' jurisdiction, on the ground that harmful
event had taken place in London and Belfast where the libellous statement was
published, not in Ireland where the broadcasts were received.

Judgment

Barr J. held in favour of Irish jurisdiction under Art. 5(3) in relation to harm
suffered in Ireland as place of harmful event, applying the European Court's
ruling in *Shevill*.

The distinction proposed by the defendants for these purposes, between
publication and distribution of the defamatory statements, was rejected in
accordance with a Northern Irish case, *Turkington v Baron St. Oswald* (unreported), 6 May 1996 (*infra*, Case 754), in which Carswell L.J. had found that
the defendant's defamatory statement at a televised press conference in
London, which was also broadcast in Northern Ireland where the plaintiffs
lived, was capable of founding a cause of action against the defendant in
respect of the libellous broadcast, as a repetition, according to applicable law
(in addition to the original slanderous statement made to the reporters in
London) where the repetition was the natural and probable result of the initial statement, and, consequently, it could amount to harmful event in
Northern Ireland for purposes of Art. 5(3) jurisdiction.

So too, therefore, would the original London and Belfast broadcasts be able
to found Irish jurisdiction under Art. 5(3) in *Ewins v Carlton Television*.
Ireland was an additional *Shevill* place of 'distribution'.

ARTICLE 6(1)

" . . . one of a number of defendants . . . "

Case principle

1. There must be a real and genuine claim against the main defendant for
    Art. 6(1) to operate.

Case

599 Valerie Gannon v B. & I. Steam Packet Co. Ltd [1994] I.L.Pr. 405 Supreme Court, 5 November 1992

Facts

The plaintiff was injured in a road crash between the second and third defendants, English coach and lorry drivers respectively, on a coach trip in England in 1989, organized by the first defendant, an Irish travel agent.

The English defendants challenged Irish courts' Art. 6(1) jurisdiction, on grounds that the Irish defendant had only been proceeded against in order to bring in the English defendants, and further that the claims against Irish and English defendants were in contract and tort respectively.

Judgment

The Supreme Court held as follows.

> (1) Although Art. 6(1) was to be interpreted restrictively, as being in derogation of Art. 2, it was, nevertheless, the case that tort and contract claims against different defendants could still satisfy the *Kalfelis* Case 189/87 *connexité* test.
>
> (2) However, on the facts, the requirement that the main Irish defendant should be a real defendant against whom there was a genuine claim was not satisfied here. Thus, there had to be a prima facie plausible claim against the Irish main defendant, which there was not: there was no evidence to suggest that the Irish defendant was somehow in breach of an implied contractual obligation towards the plaintiff to ensure that the coach driver was qualified and the coach roadworthy—indeed, the main cause of the accident seemed to have been that the lorry was doing a U-turn in the road and possibly also that the coach driver might have been travelling too fast.

Thus, there was no Irish Art. 6(1) jurisdiction over the second and third defendants—and, consistently with this, the action against the Irish first defendant was dismissed, as being in abuse of the Irish courts' process.

Case principle

2. It does not also have to be established that the action against the main defendant is certain to succeed.

Case

600 Kelly v McCarthy [1994] I.L.Pr. 29 High Court, 14 January 1993

Facts

The plaintiff beauty therapist was injured when the Irish defendant took her for a sailing trip in a yacht on the French Riviera. In response to the plaintiff's claim for negligence, the defendant argued that he had only been sued so that the plaintiff could bring in the French owner of the yacht under Art. 6(1) and that there was no real claim against the defendant under applicable French law, which would regard the owner as being strictly liable. Consequently, the action against the defendant was requested to be stayed under Irish procedural rules.

Judgment

Morris J. upheld Irish Art. 2 jurisdiction over the defendant and refused a stay.

First, in accordance with *Gannon*, the plaintiff did possess a real and genuine claim against the defendant.

Secondly, there was no requirement to show that the plaintiff would definitely succeed on the merits, nor did it affect the existence of jurisdiction over the Irish defendant that the foreign defendants were willing to admit liability.

Comment

Although the actual basis of the High Court's decision was in relation to the operation of Irish procedural process, the implication and context—*a fortiori* in view of the reference to *Gannon*—was that the principles elaborated upon were also to relate to the propriety of joinder of any foreign defendants under Art. 6(1)—the mirror image of *Gannon*, itself principally concerned with the latter rather than with procedural consequences in relation to continuation of the action against the Irish main defendant.

ARTICLE 16(2)

" . . . *decisions of their organs* . . . "

Case principle

If the conduct of an organ of a corporate shareholder in another company is objected to on the ground of improper exercise of the organ's powers as an organ of the shareholding company, the object of the proceedings is the decisions of the organ as organ *of the shareholding company*, and not of the company in which the shares are held.

Case

Papanicolaou v Thielen and Euro Mediterranean Estates SAH [1997] I.L.Pr. **601** 37 High Court, 1 March 1996

Facts

The second defendant Luxembourg company, Euro Med, was set up to promote tourism in Southern Europe, and the first defendant, Thielen, was appointed by the Luxembourg courts to be its provisional administrator when its affairs became paralysed over a dispute between shareholders as to which class could appoint the board of directors. The second defendant was a 95 per cent shareholder in a group of Irish companies and the first defendant convened meetings of the latter in order to cast the 95 per cent vote to remove the plaintiff, as director of the Irish companies, on the ground that he was not acting in their best interests and had misused his position.

The plaintiff denied the allegations and applied to the Irish courts to restrain the defendants from convening and voting at the meetings on grounds that the first defendant had exceeded his powers under the Luxembourg court's appointment.

The defendants contested Irish jurisdiction, arguing that Luxembourg courts possessed exclusive jurisdiction under Art. 16(2), since the object of the proceedings was the validity of the decisions of the first defendant as an organ of the second defendant with its seat in Luxembourg. The plaintiff challenged this, saying that it was the decisions of the organs of the Irish companies, not of the Luxembourg, which were the object of the application to the Irish courts and that consequently the latter had exclusive jurisdiction under Art. 16(2).

Judgment

Keane J. expressed no doubt that the object of the action was the propriety of the first defendant's behaviour as an organ *of the second defendant Luxembourg company* in convening a meeting of the Irish companies to vote down the plaintiff.

Accordingly, Luxembourg courts had exclusive jurisdiction over the claim, by virtue of Art. 16(2), and Irish courts were required to decline under Art. 19.

Comment

Keane J. also remarked that the result would have been the same whether the 'narrower' construction of Art. 16(2) ('validity' in the first line also governing "the decisions of their organs") or the 'wider' construction ('validity' not doing so) were to have been adopted. Nonetheless, the judge expressed agreement with the English Court of Appeal in *Grupo Torras v Al-Sabbah* [1996] 1 Lloyd's Rep. 7 (see *supra*, Case 207) that the Convention should be interpreted in a purposive manner, without too much fine-tooth combing of the grammatical and syntactical minutiae. Thus, it was abundantly clear to Keane J. that the proceedings were not to be determined by the Irish courts.

ARTICLE 17, PARAGRAPH 1

" . . . shall have exclusive jurisdiction . . . "

Case principle

Agreements for non-exclusive jurisdiction are valid under the Convention, but are not converted into exclusive jurisdiction thereby (*Meeth* Case 23/78 followed and English case *Kurz supra* Case 229 partially applied).

Case

G.P.A. Group Plc v Bank of Ireland and Eurocontrol [1992] 2 I.R. 408 High **602** Court, 30 October 1992

Facts

The plaintiff Irish aircraft company agreed with the Belgian second defendant, Eurocontrol, to pay for certain air route charges and, in order to do so, made an agreement with the first defendant, the Bank of Ireland, to open a letter of credit for this purpose. Subsequently, however, the plaintiff took the view that the arrangement with Eurocontrol, derived from international treaty, was unconstitutional in Ireland and sought to bring an action in the Irish courts for cancellation of the charges and for an injunction restraining the Irish bank from making payment to Eurocontrol under the credit. The bank contested Irish jurisdiction on the ground that there was an English jurisdiction clause in the credit agreement which would have exclusive effect under Art. 17.

The plaintiff denied this: the English jurisdiction was expressly non-exclusive and stated that it would not prevent proceedings from being brought elsewhere where jurisdiction was possessed. Article 17 did not have the effect of converting this into an exclusive jurisdiction agreement.

Judgment

Keane J. upheld Irish (Art. 2) jurisdiction. The non-exclusive English jurisdiction clause was valid, but not exclusive in its effects, under Art. 17.

The judge followed the European Court in *Meeth* in seeking to give effect to the parties' intentions as to jurisdiction, and also purported to apply the judgment of Hoffmann J. in the English High Court in *Kurz v Stella Musical Veranstalltungs GmbH* (see *supra*, Case 229), to the extent that the English judge had found that Art. 17 also applied to uphold non-exclusively *chosen* jurisdiction—although Keane J., fortunately, did not go to the same lengths as Hoffmann J. in *Kurz* of appearing to conclude that Art. 17 exclusivity *of effects* would also then apply. Quite the contrary: in view of *non*-exclusivity of chosen English jurisdiction, Irish courts of the defendant bank's domicile could continue to decide.

Comments

Two further findings were made by Keane J.

(1)   The defendant bank had tried to argue that the jurisdiction clause should be construed as being solely for its benefit within Art. 17,

para. 5 (Lugano para. 4), so that it alone was entitled thereunder to bring proceedings other than in England, whereas the latter remained exclusive for the plaintiff's actions. Keane J. rejected this construction of the clause which he found instead to have been intended to be equally for the benefit of all participants to the transaction.

(2) As to the discretionary grant of the interlocutory injunction requested against the bank, this was refused in view of the great importance of payment under documentary credits in international commerce.

ARTICLE 17, PARAGRAPH 1(a)

" . . . in writing . . . "

Case principle

A contract concluded by telex without containing a jurisdiction agreement is not subject to a jurisdiction clause contained in general conditions subsequently supplied as part of a party's formal order referred to in the telex.

Case

603 Unidare Plc and Unidare Cable Ltd v James Scott Ltd [1991] 2 I.R. 88 Supreme Court, 8 May 1991

Facts

The plaintiff Irish electrical companies made a contract by telex in 1988 with the defendant Scottish engineering company for the supply of cabling conductors to the defendant, whom the plaintiffs subsequently sought to sue in the Irish courts under Art. 5(1).

The defendants challenged Irish courts' jurisdiction, *inter alia*, on the ground that their telexed acceptance of terms referred to what was to be their subsequent provision of a formal order of purchase, which was duly transmitted containing an exclusive English jurisdiction clause.

Judgment

The Supreme Court unanimously held the jurisdiction clause to be ineffective under Art. 17 and the Irish courts were consequently allowed to adjudicate. The contract for purchase had been concluded at the date of exchange of telexes and the subsequent inclusion of the jurisdiction clause in the formal general conditions provided, was not part of the agreement in writing.

Comment

The court further rejected the defendants' contention, as a matter of construction of the contract, that place of payment as Art. 5(1) place of performance, was England, where the defendants' cheques would have been cashed by the plaintiffs, rather than Dublin to where they were required to be sent to the plaintiffs.

ARTICLE 18

" . . . solely to contest the jurisdiction . . . "

Case principle

For appearance to be held to be solely to contest jurisdiction, the defendant should signify this intention according to the procedural forms provided, or, if there is none, in any other manner sufficient to make his intention clear to the plaintiff at the time of entry of appearance or immediately afterwards (*Elefanten Schuh* Case 150/80 applied).

Case

Campbell International Trading House Ltd and Nature Pure Ltd v Peter **604** Van Aart and Natur Pur GmbH [1992] 2 I.R. 315 Supreme Court, 28 January 1992

Facts

The plaintiff Irish company entered an agreement with the defendant German company to incorporate joint venture companies in Ireland and Germany, whereby the former would purchase food products in Ireland for distribution by the latter to customers in Germany, the profits thereafter to be sent back to the Irish company for distribution according to the terms of the agreement.

In the plaintiffs' Irish action for breach of contract by the defendants, the latter contested Irish jurisdiction.

Judgment

The Supreme Court considered the response of the defendants to the plaintiffs' claim and pleadings and held that although there was no specific form in Irish superior court procedure for a defendant to signify his appearance solely in order to contest jurisdiction, it was nonetheless possible for a defendant so to indicate to the plaintiff, by some method, such an intention on entering an appearance, even if not exactly contemporaneously—for example, by a letter (or notice of motion) accompanying the appearance or immediately following it.

This would in no way prevent the defendant from defending the case on the merits if the jurisdiction challenge were subsequently to fail or to be abandoned.

Thus, on the facts, the defendants had done nothing of this nature to indicate that they intended anything other than a plain and unconditional appearance for purposes of Art. 18. Irish courts possessed jurisdiction thereunder.

Comments

It is uncertain what the position would be if there *were* prescribed procedural forms for signifying that appearance was solely to challenge jurisdiction, but these were not utilized and informal methods adopted instead. The view here is that in these circumstances the result should depend upon the facts: if the informal method used by the defendant ought reasonably to have been understood by the particular plaintiff as indicating a lack of acceptance of jurisdiction by the defendant, it ought to be sufficient to negate Art. 18 submission—but, mindful of the possible principled objections which may be made to this proposal (see *Lancray v Peters* Case C–305/88 on Art. 27(2) and *infra*, Case 613 on Art. 36, para. 1 by way of analogy), the burden on the defendant to prove such understanding should be considerable.

The court also intimated that a defendant in the circumstances might seek to prove that an unconditional appearance was in fact entered by mistake or owing to a misunderstanding as to the nature of the plaintiff's claim. This was followed subsequently by Barron J. in the High Court in *Murray v Times Newspapers Ltd* (unreported), 12 December 1995 (see *supra*, Art. 5(3) 'harmful event occurred', Case 596), who, however, refused to accept the defendants' reasons for delay in contesting appearance as being that they had not realized that the plaintiff's claim was not confined to harm within Ireland—it had long been clear that this was so and the plaintiff alleged that the defendants had simply waited until the statute of limitations had expired in the UK before making their challenge (see too *O'Neill v Ryan* [1993] I.L.R.M. 557). Consequently, Irish courts possessed jurisdiction under Art. 18 (although as to whether the pleadings were sufficient to support the claim for damages in respect of harm occurring other than in Ireland, this was a matter of substantive merits for decision by the trial judge).

ARTICLE 22, PARAGRAPH 1

" . . . *seised* . . . "

Case principle

Seisin *in rem* under (Irish and) Belgian law held to take place through proceedings for the arrest of a ship even if the court dealing with arrest is not also competent to decide upon the merits of the claim.

Case

The MV 'Turquoise Bleu': Medscope Marine Ltd v MTM Metal Trading and   **605**
Manufacturing Ltd [1996] 1 I.L.R.M. 406 High Court, 28 July 1995

Facts

The plaintiff Cypriot shipowner chartered the ship 'Turquoise Bleu' to a
Belgian company for the carriage of steel to the Far East and the Belgians sub-
chartered it to the Irish defendant for wire rods to be delivered to Vietnam. A
dispute arose between the plaintiff and the Belgian charterer over salvage, as
a result of which the plaintiff refused to allow the ship to leave Antwerp for
Vietnam. The defendant, therefore, brought proceedings in the Antwerp First
Instance Court for the arrest of the ship in January 1994 as security for its
claim for damages against the plaintiff, which came on in the Antwerp
Commercial Court in May 1994. In the meantime, the plaintiff had commenced the present proceedings in the Irish High Court in February 1994,
claiming a lien over the defendant's cargo on board the ship in respect of the
Belgian company's breach of charterparty.

The defendant requested the Irish courts to stay their proceedings in favour
of the first-seised related action in the Antwerp courts.

The plaintiff denied that Antwerp courts were seised before the Irish: the
January application for arrest in Antwerp did not amount to seisin for purposes of Art. 22, because the arrest-judge had no competence under Belgian
rules of judiciary to decide upon the substantive merits of the dispute.
Consequently, Belgian courts were only seised in May when the substantive
proceedings were commenced in the Antwerp Commercial Court and by then
the Irish High Court had already become seised.

Judgment

Barr J. held that Belgian courts were first-seised at the time of the January
arrest application (and the judge went on to exercise the discretion to stay in
favour of Antwerp courts under Art. 22—see *infra*, Case 606).

The judge examined the nature of the Belgian process and found it to be
broadly similar to the Irish itself: the arrest stage was not independent and
complete in itself, but merely a first step in the overall substantive claim in
order to obtain security for the latter—a step in larger proceedings concerning
a claim against the shipowner. Consequently, the *overall* Belgian action was
commenced through the arrest application in Antwerp in January, not at the
subsequent date of the substantive hearing in May.

Comments

The defendant's Belgian proceedings concerned the alleged breach of obligation by the plaintiff under the contract of carriage evidenced by the bills of lading, which would require to be construed; and in the plaintiff's Irish action, it
would have to be shown that terms of the charterparty between the plaintiff

and Belgian charterer were incorporated into a contractual relationship between plaintiff and defendant in accordance with the bills of lading providing for this.

Accordingly, Irish and Belgian proceedings were regarded as related within the meaning of Art. 22, para. 3, as being capable of leading to irreconcilable judgments.

Of further interest, Barr J. also commented that had Irish courts been found to have been first-seised, there would have been no possibility under the Convention of granting a stay in favour of Belgian courts as *forum conveniens* according to inherent powers of the Irish courts.

> " ... *may* ... *stay* ... "

Case principle

Administration of justice advantages taken into account in the course of exercise of discretion to stay under Art. 22, para. 1.

Case

606 The MV 'Turquoise Bleu': Medscope Marine Ltd v MTM Metal Trading and Manufacturing Ltd [1996] 1 I.L.R.M. 406 High Court, 28 July 1995

Facts

See supra, Art. 22, para. 1 'seised', Case 605.

Judgment

Barr J. not only held the Belgian courts to be first-seised in relation to the Irish, and the Belgian and Irish actions to be related for Art. 22, but also detailed those factors which had led the court unhesitatingly to conclude it to be proper to exercise its discretion to stay under Art. 22, as follows:

(1) the defendant was in reality an Austrian company, which was only registered in Ireland for tax reasons, and the case had no other Irish connection;

(2) all the witnesses resided outside Ireland;

(3) Belgian courts would be reluctant to recognize an Irish interlocutory order for sale of the cargo on board ship at Antwerp and the plaintiff could easily have sought the same relief by way of counterclaim in the Belgian proceedings but had failed to explain why it had not done so;

(4) the defendant had paid all sums due and appeared to have no direct legal relationship with the plaintiff; and

(5) Antwerp courts were already familiar with the facts and issues from their own proceedings.

Comment

English case law trends are *not* to take into account *forum non conveniens* type factors in the exercise of the discretion to stay under Art. 22, which should almost be presumed on satisfaction of Art. 22, para. 3 unless there is some strong reason against doing so (*e.g.* the plaintiff in the foreign proceedings has acted unreasonably in causing delays in their progress).

ARTICLE 24

" . . . *available under the law of that State* . . . "

Case principle

Irish courts possess the statutory power to grant interim protective relief in aid of substantive proceedings in foreign Contracting States.

Case

Oblique Financial Services Ltd v The Promise Production Co. Ltd [1994]   **607**
I.L.R.M. 74 High Court, 24 February 1993

Facts

The plaintiff UK financings company made a contract with the defendants to obtain sources of finance for production of a film. The agreement contained a confidentiality clause which the plaintiff alleged had been breached by the defendants' disclosure of the identity of an investor and the plaintiff requested an interim injunction from the Irish courts restraining the defendants from publishing the information in a magazine, pending substantive proceedings on the merits of the claim to be brought in the English courts.

Judgment

Keane J. held that Irish courts possessed the procedural powers to make Art. 24 protective orders in aid of substantive proceedings in foreign Contracting States, under s.11 of the Jurisdiction of Courts and Enforcement of Judgments (European Communities) Act 1988 (equivalent to the English s.25(1) of the Civil Jurisdiction and Judgments Act 1982).

The national Irish condition for grant of interim relief, of serious issue to be tried on the merits, was found to be satisfied, and the measure would not amount to a breach of the defendants' constitutional rights of communication.

The protective relief was ordered.

ARTICLE 25

" . . . as well as the determination of costs . . . "

Case principle

Plaintiffs resident in foreign EU Contracting States must not be ordered to provide security for costs (*Mund* Case 398/92 applied).

Case

608 Maher v Phelan (unreported) High Court, 3 November 1995

Facts

The English plaintiff had conceded that the defendant had a pleadable defence, and the normal Irish rule was that in such circumstances the Irish court had a discretion to order the foreign plaintiff to provide security for costs (*Fares v Wiley* [1994] 1 I.L.R.M. 465).

However, the plaintiff argued that since the European Court's decision in *Mund* (see *supra*, General comment preceding Case 336), the Irish procedural rules and practice could no longer apply to a foreign Contracting State plaintiff.

Judgment

Carroll J. agreed with the plaintiff: *Mund* showed that such a practice, in the light of the Convention, would be covert nationality discrimination in breach of EC Treaty Art. 6; and, consequently, an order for security could not be made against the English plaintiff, as it could not be so against an Irish resident plaintiff individual. Pre-*Mund* English cases to the contrary were no longer apposite.

Comment

The judge went on to remark that even if an order had been possible, it would not have been appropriate for it to be granted: the Convention made enforcement comparatively easy; the plaintiff was not impecunious; and there was no suggestion that he was arranging his affairs so as to render himself 'judgment-proof'.

Case

Proetta v Neil (unreported) High Court, 17 November 1995   **609**

Facts

The plaintiff had dual British and Spanish citizenship. At the time of proceedings, she was living and working in Spain and shared an apartment in Gibraltar.

Judgment

Murphy J., applying *Mund* to Irish Ord. 29 on security, refused to order security to be provided.

Case

Pitt v Bolger & Barry (unreported) High Court, 2 February 1996   **610**

Facts

The plaintiff, a livestock breeder in the Isle of Man, sued the defendants in the Irish courts for fraud and negligence. The allegation, strongly denied, was that the first defendant horse trainer had advised the plaintiff to enter into a partnership with the second defendant horse breeder for the purpose of selling the plaintiff's horse, sired by Mill Reef, to an American for £400,000. As it turned out, according to the plaintiff, the horse was in fact secretly sold to a Dubai purchaser for £800,000. The defendants sought security for costs from the plaintiff.

Judgment

Keane J. refused to order security against the plaintiff.

The judge expressly followed the two preceding cases and the decision of the English Court of Appeal in *Fitzgerald v Williams* (see *supra*, Case 343): as a result of *Mund*, EC Treaty Art. 6 would be contravened if an order for security were to be made on the ground of a plaintiff's foreign EU nationality or ordinary residence treated as such.

In this case, the plaintiff was both a UK citizen (it was explained by Keane J. that the Isle of Man was not part of the UK but a British possession whose citizens were also British); and, apparently, the plaintiff was also considered to be ordinarily resident in England, having purchased a substantial house there. Consequently, security on the ground of her ordinary residence in a foreign EU Contracting State was contrary to *Mund* and prohibited by Art. 6 EC Treaty.

Comments

The English case of *Fitzgerald v Williams* referred to was succeeded by further English and European Court case law (see *supra*, Chapter 4), which must now also be taken into account.

The preceding account is what is believed to be the most *benign* construction of Keane J.'s judgment. There are, in fact, some elements of the latter which may be less than satisfactory. It is not at all certain that Keane J. *did* regard the plaintiff as ordinarily resident in England as opposed to the Isle of Man. If the latter, how could her UK nationality have been discriminated against, if a plaintiff *Irish* national, ordinarily resident in the Isle of Man, could also have been subjected to an order for security? There was also a worrying suggestion by Keane J. that Convention enforceability of costs orders as between Ireland and the UK, on the one hand, and under reciprocal arrangements between the UK and the Isle of Man, on the other hand, would amount, in effect, to such as between Ireland and the Isle of Man—that is, *enforcement on enforcement* (*exécution exécution*), being quite contrary to Convention principles.

ARTICLE 27(1)

" . . . contrary to public policy . . . "

Case principle

Recognition of a foreign judgment upholding a transaction in breach of Irish exchange control legislation required to be removed under EC law, is not contrary to public policy under Art. 27(1).

Case

611   Westpac Banking Corporation v Dempsey [1993] 3 I.R. 331 High Court, 19 November 1992

Facts

The plaintiff bank obtained an English judgment for almost £500 000 against the defendant in 1991 on a loan and guarantee transaction, which the plaintiff then sought to enforce in Ireland. The defendant appealed against enforcement on the grounds that the transaction was void as being in contravention of Irish exchange control legislation, and unenforceable by virtue of the Bretton Woods Agreement incorporated into Irish law, and that consequently the English judgment ought to be refused recognition as being against public policy under Art. 27(1) for these reasons.

Judgment

Morris J. rejected these objections to enforcement.

First, breach of the criminal laws on exchange control did not automatically mean that offending transactions themselves were null and void.

Secondly, as to Bretton Woods, this should have been raised in the English proceedings and to do so now was to embark upon a review of substance of the foreign judgment, prohibited by Art. 29 and Art. 34, para. 3.

Finally, with regard to the use of Art. 27(1) to request refusal of recognition on the ground that to grant recognition in the face of such alleged contravention would be against public policy, Morris J. refuted this, pointing out that the exchange controls in question were merely temporary and already required to be removed under EU laws on free movement of money.

ARTICLE 33, PARAGRAPH 2

" . . . applicant must give an address for service . . . "

Case principle

The address must be in the application for enforcement, if in accordance with national implementing procedures, not necessarily also on the face of the enforcement order served upon the judgment debtor (*Carron* Case 198/85 applied).

Case

Rhatigan v Textiles Y Confecciones Europeas SA [1992] I.L.Pr. 40 Supreme **612** Court, 31 May 1990

Facts

The judgment creditor obtained an English judgment against an English company and its controller for almost £1.5 million in 1988 and gave its Dublin solicitors as its address for service in its successful application for Irish enforcement in December 1988 served on the judgment debtor on the same day.

The judgment debtor appealed against enforcement on the principal ground that the judgment creditor's address for service under Art. 33, para. 2 had not appeared on the face of the enforcement order served upon the judgment debtor.

Judgment

The Supreme Court held that Art. 33, para. 2 only required the address for service to be given in the application for enforcement and not also on the order itself.

Griffin J. commented that the Convention was intended to ensure fast and simple enforcement with minimal formalities, and procedures were generally left to the national laws if not inconsistent with this objective.

In *Carron v Germany* Case 198/85 [1986] ECR 2437, the European Court ruled that notice of the address was to be given *no later than* at the time of service of the enforcement authorization upon the judgment debtor, which the Supreme Court held to be quite inconsistent with the judgment debtor's assertion that notice *had to* accompany such service.

Comments

The Supreme Court made the following findings.

(1) Again in accordance with *Carron*, since there was no Convention rule requiring the enforcement order to disclose on its face that it was in respect of a Contracting State judgment, it was for national Irish law to determine any sanction for such non-disclosure. Griffin J. had no doubt that, on the facts, the failure would not affect enforcement under Irish law, since the judgment debtor had fully participated in the English proceedings and could not have had the slightest doubt as to the source of the judgment referred to in the enforcement order.

(2) Of transitional interest, under the 1978 Accession Convention, Art. 34(3) not only must the enforcement application have been brought *after* the date of the Convention's entry into force in Ireland on 1 June 1988—which it was—but also there had to be evidence that the English proceedings were instituted after 1 January 1987 when the Convention entered into force in the UK—which there was. This is quite incorrect. Under Art. 34(3), it is not required that proceedings were instituted after entry into force in the state of origin, whether or not also so in the state addressed for enforcement. The Irish Supreme Court ought to have assessed English jurisdiction in accordance with the conditions laid down in Art. 34(3), since the Convention was not yet in force *as between Ireland and the UK* at the date of institution of the English action.

(3) *Foskett v Deasy* (unreported) Supreme Court, 3 June 1997 may be noted for an interesting illustration of application of national procedural principles to an application for enforcement of an English judgment and for the significance of distinguishing between, on the one hand, an application for enforcement of a judgment as a trustee for others who were *also* represented in the English action and, on the other hand, an application as a mere representative of the judgment creditor.

ARTICLE 36, PARAGRAPH 1

" . . . *of service* . . . "

Case principle

The implied Convention obligation of service of the enforcement order upon the judgment debtor under Art. 36 must be duly carried out in accordance with procedures—including as to time and manner—of the enforcement-State. It is not acceptable for this to be performed by a different method, even if it affords the judgment debtor a sufficient opportunity to respond within one or two month periods for appealing thereunder.

Case

Barnaby (London) Ltd v Mullen (unreported) Supreme Court, 25 April 1997   **613**

Facts

The plaintiff obtained an English judgment for over £250 000 damages against the defendant in 1992 and Irish courts authorized enforcement in 1993. The defendant appealed against enforcement, on the ground that the Irish enforcement order had not been properly served upon him personally in accordance with Irish procedural rules. The order had been served at an address in Dublin but the defendant had not lived there for years and was separated from his wife and family who still resided there. There was much uncertainty over whether the defendant still had lines of communication open with his family, but the plaintiffs argued that since the order had evidently come to the defendant's notice at some stage in any event for him to have been able to make the current objection, this should be regarded as good enough for purposes of service.

Judgment

The Supreme Court drew the analogy with due and sufficient service of the document instituting proceedings in default of appearance by the defendant for purposes of Art. 27(2). In *Lancray v Peters* Case C–305/88, the European Court had held that such service in sufficient time to defend was nonetheless not adequate thereunder: there also had to be service *duly* carried out.

So too, therefore, in the case of Art. 36 service of the enforcement order, Murphy J. considered that there were good reasons for service to be carried out properly in accordance with the enforcement-State's procedural law of personal service, where substituted service had—curiously—not been applied for: service was not simply to enable the defendant to respond, but also to set a date from which such response by way of an appeal against enforcement was to run under Art. 36 and to give effect to documentary requirements for issuing execution on judgments which had been declared to be enforceable. This was why service was necessary to comply with enforcement-State procedure and it was not good enough to show that the judgment debtor had somehow managed to become aware of it. Proper evidence of dates and methods was needed, and defects would not retrospectively be deemed to be removed through such later knowledge.

ARTICLE 39, PARAGRAPH 2

" . . . shall carry with it the power to proceed to any such protective measures."

Case principle

Protective measures under Art. 39 are mandatory on authorization of enforcement (*Capelloni v Pelkmans* Case 119/84 applied). Consequently, if refused by the High Court Master, an application may be made to the High Court for an order of *mandamus* to compel the grant of such relief.

Case

614 Elwyn (Cottons) Limited v The Master of the High Court [1990] I.L.Pr. 196 High Court, 16 March 1989

Facts

An application was made to the Master for enforcement of an English judgment for over £13 000, together with protective measures restraining the defendant from reducing its assets to below that sum. The Master granted the former but refused the latter.

Judgment

O'Hanlon J. in the High Court held as follows.

First, in accordance with the European Court in *Capelloni*, the Master should not have refused protective measures under Art. 39.

Secondly, *mandamus* could and, in the circumstances, would be made against the Master, to compel the grant, notwithstanding that he was an officer of the court—although opinion was reserved as to whether the previous finding of Carroll J. in the proceedings was correct, to the effect that *mandamus* and judicial review were the only remedy against the Master's decision in the circumstances because neither the Convention nor Irish implementation rules made any provision for an appeal to be made against refusal.

ARTICLE 52, PARAGRAPH 1

" . . . apply its internal law."

Case principle

The Irish Convention-Art. 52 meaning of domicile of an individual as 'ordinary residence' is in place of the traditional Irish concept, not in addition thereto in any particular case.

Case

Deutsche Bank Aktiengesellschaft v Anthony Murtagh and Dagmar Murtagh   **615**
[1995] 1 I.L.R.M. 381 High Court, 16 December 1994

Facts

The plaintiff German bank claimed from the defendant husband and wife one million DM under guarantees made and to be performed in Germany. The defendants, who were not Irish citizens but currently lived in a property in Tipperary, Ireland, contested Irish courts' jurisdiction.

Section 13 of the Jurisdiction of Courts and Enforcement of Judgments (European Communities) Act 1988 defines Irish domicile (and non-Contracting State domicile) for purposes of Art. 52 as 'ordinarily resident'.

The plaintiff argued that ordinary residence was intended to denote a much weaker connection than the traditional common law concept of domicile and was closer to the civilian meaning of domicile, referring to the Schlosser Report (para. 73) for support.

The defendants, on the other hand, asserted that the ordinary residence stipulation in s.13 was *additional* to that of traditional domicile, because s.13 began with the words 'Subject to Article 52', not 'to give effect to Article 52' or 'in pursuance of Article 52', which former therefore indicated that ordinary residence had been superimposed upon Irish internal rules of domicile, as a *further* requirement.

Judgment

Costello J. rejected the contentions of the defendants and held that traditional rules of Irish domicile of individuals were *replaced* by the ordinary residence meaning and that the Schlosser Report approach had thereby been given effect to.

As to the meaning of ordinary residence, the authorities showed that this was to be its *ordinary* meaning, construed and applied in relation to the facts of the particular case by reference to the intentions underlying the particular statute in which it was used (see Kaye, *Civil Jurisdiction* pp. 353–61).

The facts here were that the defendant husband was British and raised in the UK, but had lived in Germany during adulthood, then in Ireland with his wife and children for the previous 12 months. There was no certainty about their remaining in Ireland, which would depend upon whether a further business opportunity were to arise there or in Germany, to which the defendant would willingly return with his defendant German wife. Thus, at the relevant time, neither defendant had any residence outside Ireland and they had been living for one year in their substantial home in Ireland, where they had a number of bank accounts and where their children attended school.

Costello J. concluded that, according to the ordinary meaning of 'ordinarily resident' and to the context in which it appeared in the 1988 Act, the defendants were ordinarily resident in Ireland on the relevant date of institution of proceedings and Irish courts consequently possessed jurisdiction under Art. 2. The fact that the defendants had formed no intention to remain permanently or indefinitely in Ireland might have prevented them from acquiring a domicile in Ireland according to the traditional common law principles, but this did not have the same effect when deciding upon s.13 ordinary residence as Art 52 domicile.

Comment

The judge went on to confirm that the Irish courts possessed similar powers to the English to order *Mareva* injunctions and ancillary disclosure in respect of assets situated outside, as well as within, the jurisdiction.

LUGANO ARTICLE 54, PARAGRAPH 1

" . . . *apply only to legal proceedings instituted . . . after its entry into force . . .* "

Case principle

Date of transitional *institution* of proceedings held to be that of issue of process for service outside Ireland, not the earlier date of application for leave to serve out. Consequently, the Lugano Convention applied if it had entered into force prior to issue, even if subsequently to the application therefor.

Case

616 United Meat Packers (Ballaghaderreen) Ltd (In Receivership) v Nordstern Allgemeine Versicherungs-AG (unreported) Supreme Court, 24 June 1997

Facts

Throughout 1992 and for most of 1993, the plaintiffs were in the process of claiming for losses of stock in trade destroyed in a fire at premises in Ireland, under an insurance policy with the defendant Swiss or German insurers (it was not clear in which of those States the insurers had their seat).

In November 1993, the plaintiffs applied to the Irish High Court for leave to serve the defendants with process outside Ireland under the Rules of the Superior Courts, Ord. 11, r.1(e)(ii), on the ground that the action was on a contract made by or through the defendants' agent trading or residing within Ireland. In January 1995, the defendants challenged Irish jurisdiction, arguing that the plaintiff should have proceeded under r.1(e)(iii)—contract by its terms or implication governed by Irish law or breached in Ireland—not r.1(e)(ii).

The plaintiff responded that the mistake was irrelevant, because by the date of issue of the process on 2 December 1993, the Lugano Convention had already entered into force in Ireland, on 1 December 1993, in relation to the Swiss defendant (specifically, Arts 5(5), 7 and 8(2) would be relied upon) and accordingly, leave for service out was not required in any event, by virtue of Ord. 11A.

Judgment

The Supreme Court held that service was valid on two grounds, explained by O'Flaherty J.

(1) In the first place, the High Court judge had been incorrect to refuse to allow the plaintiff to amend the proceedings so that they would fall under r.1(e)(iii) instead of (ii) if the former was satisfied, as it clearly was (and O'Flaherty J. also noted that in *Doran v Power*, Case 618 *infra*, the Supreme Court had permitted amendment so as to bring proceedings under the 1952 Collision Convention instead of the Judgments Convention).

(2) Furthermore, since the Lugano Convention had entered into force in Ireland at the time of *issue* of the proceedings, even though not also on the earlier date of application therefor, the former was that of institution within the meaning of Lugano Art. 54, para. 1 and, consequently, the Convention was properly applicable, which meant that leave to serve out was not required in any event.

(3) Third party proceedings are transitionally instituted when leave to issue the third party notice is granted, not when it is subsequently served upon the third party.

Case

International Commercial Bank Plc v The Insurance Corporation of Ireland **617** Plc (Meadows Indemnity Co. Limited, Third Party) [1990] I.L.Pr. 356 Supreme Court, 15 June 1989

Facts and Judgment

This was decided in the context of the corresponding 1978 Accession Convention Art. 34(1): see *infra*, Case 619.

ARTICLE 57(1)

" . . . *shall not affect* . . . "

Case principle

Jurisdiction must be founded upon grounds in the convention on particular matters, even if there are equivalent grounds in the Judgments Convention.

Case

618 Gerard Doran v Tracey Power [1996] 1 I.L.R.M. 55 Supreme Court, 26 July 1995

Facts

In a collision between James Power's boat and the French defendant's vessel, Power and a member of his crew, Doran, were drowned. Power's Irish personal representative, Tracey Power, and the French company were sued in Ireland by Doran's father, and Tracey sued Kenneth Pierce, an Irish crew member on watch at the time of the accident, and the French company. The latter argued that the plaintiffs had been incorrect to base Irish jurisdiction upon Judgments Convention Art. 6(1), because Ireland and France were parties to the 1952 Collision Convention which applied instead under Art. 57.

Judgment

The Supreme Court unanimously agreed with the French defendant that Irish jurisdiction over it ought to have been based upon the joinder ground in the 1952 Convention, not Art. 6(1).

Nevertheless, since the effect was the same, the action should not be struck out, merely amended.

Comment

Blayney J. made two further points of interest.

(1)   The reference to joinder possibility under national laws in the relevant provision of the 1952 Convention (Art. 3(3)) meant *domestic* procedural rules of joinder—and therefore was not also a *renvoi* to international jurisdiction rules of the State of the main defendant, such as Art. 6(1) itself.

(2)   The 1952 joinder was not confined to where the main defendant was the owner of one of the ships involved in the collision and consequently included Tracey's action against main defendant Pierce, since this arose from the collision between two ships.

1978 ACCESSION CONVENTION ARTICLE 34(1)

" . . . *instituted* . . . "

Case principle

1. Third party proceedings are instituted when leave to issue a third party notice is granted, not when it is subsequently served upon the third party.

Case

International Commercial Bank Plc v The Insurance Corporation of Ireland **619** Plc (Meadows Indemnity Co. Limited, Third Party) [1990] I.L.Pr. 356 Supreme Court, 15 June 1989

Facts

The plaintiff English company sued the defendant Irish company for 11.5 million Swiss francs under a guarantee and in 1988 the defendant issued a third party notice against a Guernsey company under a reinsurance contract made in London, which was granted by the Irish courts on the ground that the third party was a necessary and proper party to the action under national Irish private international law rules in Rules of the Superior Courts Ord. 11 in respect of the non-Contracting State third party.

After institution of the Irish action, but before issue of the third party notice therein, the third party had commenced proceedings in the English courts in October 1987 against the defendant to avoid the reinsurance contract and the plaintiff had been brought into those English proceedings as a third party.

The third party in the Irish proceedings, therefore, argued that since Irish courts were seised of the third party proceedings against it after the English courts were first-seised of the third party's own proceedings there, Irish courts were obliged to decline under Art. 21.

Judgment

The Supreme Court held the Convention and Art. 21 to be transitionally inapplicable and accordingly refused to decline thereunder. The date on which the Irish proceedings were *instituted* against the third party was *May* 1988 when leave to join was given, not on the date of actual service on 14 June 1988. This timing was crucial because the Convention had entered into force in Ireland on 1 June 1988. All of which meant that the Irish third party proceedings were instituted *before* entry into force of the Convention in Ireland. Consequently, according to the clear terms of 1978 Convention Art. 34(1), the Convention, including Art. 21, was inapplicable in the Irish proceedings.

The court then went on to decide against exercise of the national discretion to stay in favour of prior English courts, since it was appropriate for the third party claim to be dealt with at the same time as the main action in Ireland.

Case principle

2. Proceedings are transitionally instituted on the date of issue of proceedings for service outside Ireland, not on the earlier date of application for leave.

Case

620 United Meat Packers (Ballaghaderreen) Ltd (In Receivership) v Nordstern Allgemeine Versicherungs-AG (unreported) Supreme Court, 24 June 1997

Facts and Judgment

This was decided in the context of the corresponding Art. 54, para. 1 of the Lugano Convention: see *supra*, Case 616.

11

ITALY

Professor Bruno N. Sassani

A. LEGAL SYSTEM

The Italian legal system belongs to the civil law area. It is a system based upon the supremacy of statutory law in which the courts are not considered a source of law in the sense of *Stare Decisis* doctrine: judges are required to connect the case to a specific text, and not to decide in accordance with a precedent (nevertheless, Supreme Court judgments have, naturally, a leading role for lower courts, which in practice very often follow its guidelines).

It rests, firstly, upon a written Constitution which establishes the basic powers of the State and its legal order and their limitations (whose observance is under the control of a Constitutional Court). Systematic collections of rules are the so-called 'four codes': civil and commercial matters are found in the civil code (*codice civile*); civil procedure is mainly regulated by a civil procedure code (*codice di procedura civile*, greatly modified in 1990); a code regulating criminal matters (*codice penale*) and a code regulating criminal proceedings (*codice di procedura penale*) are in force as well.

The judicial system in the field of civil and criminal matters is based upon a pyramid organization of territorial courts, with a Supreme Court (*Corte di Cassazione*) at the top.

The courts of first instance are scattered throughout the country. They are: (i) the Justice of the Peace (a lay magistrate who deals, as sole judge, with small claims and car accident disputes); (ii) the *pretore*, a magistrates' court constituted by professional judges; (iii) the *tribunale*, a court traditionally deciding as a collective body, and now transformed—in most cases—into a sole judge, following the reform of the civil procedure code in 1990. Administrative competence is conferred upon special courts: administrative regional tribunals

(*Tribunali amministrativi regionali*) at first instance; a Supreme Administrative Court sits at second instance (*Consiglio di Stato*).

The judgments of the *Tribunale* can be appealed to the Court of Appeal, whereas the same *Tribunale* acts—always as a collective body—as an appellate court against the judgments of Justices of the Peace and those of the magistrate's court. The *Corte di Cassazione* has its seat in Rome: it is a court of last resort which decides further appeals against second instance judgments and deals with questions of law—interpretation and application—instead of matters of fact. Moreover, the Supreme Court often deals with the jurisdiction issue in the first instance proceedings, by means of a special application— provided by Art. 41 of the Code of Civil Procedure, called *Regolamento di giurisdizione*—by which each party may request a final decision upon jurisdiction, binding the future judgment of the court before which the proceeding is pending. The Supreme Court deals with the *Regolamento* as a particularly solemn body called *Sezioni Unite* (united benches). Most cases shown in this chapter consist of judgments rendered by the Supreme Court in the *Regolamento di giurisdizione* sitting.

B. IMPLEMENTATION OF THE CONVENTIONS

The Brussels Convention was implemented in Italy by the law 804/1971 and came into effect on 1 February 1973. Following accessions by other countries extending the Convention's scope, there were subsequent implementation laws: the law 967/1980 for the new version consequent upon the accession of Denmark, Ireland and the UK; the Law 756/1984 for the new version consequent upon accession of Greece; the Law 339/1991 for the new version consequent upon the accession of Spain and Portugal, with effect from 1 May 1992.

The Luxembourg Protocol of 3 June 1971 (establishing the competence of the European Court of Justice upon the interpretation of the Convention), was implemented by the law 180/75.

The Lugano Convention of 16 September 1988 was implemented by the Law 198/1992, with effect from 1 December 1992.

C. OVERVIEW OF CONVENTION CASE LAW

With reference to the Italian courts' response to the Brussels Convention, it is quite important to remark that the Convention met an Italian legal order preoccupied with the concept of nationality of the parties: in the language of the Code of Civil Procedure, the main characters of jurisdiction, judgment-recognition and implementation provisions were the *straniero* (the foreigner) and the *cittadino* (the Italian citizen). Thus, the nationalistic attitude of the courts led, at the very beginning, to an ambiguous (more than strict) interpretation of the Convention, sometimes effected by recourse to the *passe-partout* formula of 'public policy'.

Things have progressively changed to the point that the Law 218/95, a major reform of Italian private international law, recently introduced an impressive set of modifications as to its jurisdiction rules and the recognition and enforcement of any foreign judgment. The Brussels Convention constituted the first point of reference of the reform, in the sense that the general Italian system of jurisdiction rules and of foreign judgment recognition and enforcement is now in line with the principles of the Convention. Particularly as to jurisdiction, the defendant's domicile has become the new leading principle. As to recognition, any special recognition proceeding has been eliminated so as to integrate the foreign judgment into the domestic order (only in the case of a challenge to automatic recognition on grounds of violation of the rights of defence in the foreign court or of public policy etc., is a special recognition proceeding allowed, and competence is allocated to the Court of Appeal).

The present case law shows a rather limited number of proceedings where the courts have dealt with the Convention (compared to the very high number of proceedings in civil matters generally). Courts have a good understanding of the basic principles of the Convention and regularly use European Court of Justice references in uncertain cases, with whose rulings they loyally comply.

D. CASES

ARTICLE 1, PARAGRAPH 2(2)

" . . . *relating to the winding up* . . . "

Case principle

1. Setting aside of transactions in bankruptcy is excluded from the field of application of the Convention.

Cases

Corte di Cassazione sez. un., 21 April 1989, 1905   **621**
Corte di Cassazione sez. un., 23 February 1990, 1396   **622**

Facts

In both cases, the plaintiff receivers sued a company located in a Contracting State other than Italy, before an Italian judge for the revocation of a payment, and invoked the application of Art. 5(1). The defendant challenged the

Convention's application, on the ground of the insolvency nature of the case, and raised the issue before the Supreme Court through the special procedure called *Regolamento di giurisdizione* (see *supra*, A. *LEGAL SYSTEM*).

Judgment

In both cases, the Supreme Court held that proceedings to set aside transactions were those relating to winding up for the purposes of Art. 1, para. 2(2), since the so called *revocatorie fallimentari* provided by Art. 67 of Italian 'Legge fallimentare' displayed the features of bankruptcy proceedings according to *Gourdain v Nadler* Case 133/78 (the facts of being provided for by a national bankruptcy law and regulated exclusively by its rules; and that the action was confined to the receivership in the name and for the benefits of the bankrupt estate).

Case principle

2.   The Convention only applies to actions derived from or closely connected in some way to bankruptcy, even when they are not strictly dependent upon it.

Cases

623   Tribunale Milano, 30 January 1989
624   Tribunale Torino, 13 May 1989
625   Tribunale Milano, 7 January 1985

Facts

In the first case, the plaintiff receiver sued a debtor, domiciled in a different Contracting State, for the fulfilment of an obligation assumed towards the receiver itself, under Art. 5(1). In the second case, the plaintiff receiver sued a third party, civilly liable for the fulfilment of an obligation undertaken by the bankrupt entrepreneur before the declaration of insolvency (again under Art. 5(1)). The third case was similar to the previous one: the plaintiff receiver brought an action against a third party for recovery of money deposited in other Contracting States. In all cases, the defendants invoked Art. 1, para. 2(2), on the ground that the actions substantially belonged to the bankruptcy field. Consequently they contested the possibility of applying the Convention and, in particular, Art. 5(1).

Judgment

The courts held that the actions neither belonged to the bankruptcy proceedings nor strictly derived from bankruptcy, because they were independent actions only incidentally connected with it. Accordingly, they concluded in favour of the application of the Convention and its jurisdiction grounds argued for by the plaintiffs.

> **ARTICLE 5(1)**
>
> " . . . *obligation in question* . . . "

Case principle

In a claim for an account and payment of sums disclosed as being owed as a result of such account, the place of performance must be determined with regard to the first obligation as the principal. Consequently, according to Italian law, the specific place of performance is the debtor's domicile (*de Bloos*, Case 14/76 and *Shenavai*, Case 266/85 applied).

Case

Corte di Cassazione sez. un., 22 May 1986, 3411   **626**

Facts

The plaintiff sued a Dutch company under a contract of agency, whereby the defendant agent had produced an account displaying several wrong entries. The claim was for a new account and for payment by the defendant of the sums stated by the court on judicial examination of the account. The defendant contested Italian jurisdiction: assuming production of the correct account to be the specific 'obligation in question' for the purposes of Art. 5(1), the place of performance was not in Italy, because the obligation was to be performed—according to Art. 1182(2) of the Civil Code—in the place of domicile of the defendant in The Netherlands. The defendant appealed to the Supreme Court through the *Regolamento di giurisdizione* procedure.

Judgment

The court held that the place of performance, to be established in accordance with Italian law, was the domicile of the debtor. In accordance with *de Bloos* Case 14/76, according to which the obligation to be taken into account for the purposes of Art. 5(1) was not any obligation under the contract, but that obligation which corresponded to the main claim upon which the action was based, the court acknowledged that the principal obligation in the case was the production of the account. Accordingly, the court held that the place of performance was the debtor's domicile in The Netherlands. Indeed, Italian law provided that the creditor's domicile was to be considered as the place of performance only when the obligation consisted in the payment of a sum of money (Art. 1182(1) of the Civil Code). Conversely, Art. 1182(2) of the Civil Code provided that, in any other case, the debtor's domicile constituted the place of performance.

> " . . . *place of performance* . . . "

Case principle

The general rule of the defendant's domicile provided by Art. 2 takes the place of the special rule of Art. 5(1) where the place of delivery of the goods is the place of performance of the obligation arising from a sale, and this is located in a non-Contracting State (see *Six Constructions*, Case 32/88).

Case

627 Corte di Cassazione sez. un., 15 May 1990, 4198

Facts

The plaintiff purchaser of goods sued a German company for non-delivery. The Italian court had been seised as the court for the place of performance of the obligation in question under Art. 5(1). The first instance court declined jurisdiction in favour of the German judge, but the appellate court upheld Italian jurisdiction. Owing to the fact that the sale was to be considered a 'documentary sale' and that the price should be paid 'on delivery of documents' in the place of destination of the goods, the court concluded that Art. 5(1) was applicable since this place was located in Italy. The defendant appealed to the Supreme Court.

Judgment

The court held that although the contract contained the clause *Kasse gegen Dokumente* (payment against documents), the sale was not a documentary sale, and since the goods were unascertained and not yet existent at the time of the contract, the place of performance was instead to be considered the place where the goods were delivered to the carrier and the place of destination in Italy had no relevance. Thus, since the place of delivery was not located in any Contracting State (carriage was from California), Art. 5(1) was inapplicable. The only rule applicable was Art. 2, and since the domicile of the defendant was in Germany, Italian jurisdiction was declined in favour of German.

ARTICLE 5(2)

> " . . . *proceedings concerning the status of a person* . . . "

Case principle

Incidental determination of paternity, involved in an action for a declaration of non-existence of a maintenance obligation, does not constitute 'proceedings concerning the status of a person' which, according to Art. 5(2), would allow the plaintiff to bring an ancillary maintenance claim in the court which, according to its own law, has jurisdiction to entertain the status proceedings. Consequently, the fact that the Italian courts would have jurisdiction to entertain the proceedings concerning the status of the parties is irrelevant for determining jurisdiction in an action brought by an Italian national against a person domiciled in another Contracting State.

Case

Corte di Cassazione, 28 April 1993, 4992   **628**

Facts

An Italian national domiciled in Italy, sued a German minor before an Italian court for a declaration of non-existence of any maintenance obligation in favour of the latter. The court of first instance rejected as inadmissible the claim, without considering any jurisdiction question. The court of appeal upheld the judgment on grounds other than jurisdiction. The plaintiff lodged a further appeal to the *Corte di Cassazione*, and the defendant invoked lack of Italian jurisdiction on the grounds that the defendant maintenance creditor was habitually resident in Germany, and that there was a *Zahlungsvaterschaft* pending suit before a German court between the same parties.

Judgment

The Supreme Court first solved the question of the reportedly pending suit for *Zahlungsvaterschaft* in Germany. Though acknowledging in principle the possibility of applying the provision for *lis pendens* under Art. 21 between such a proceeding and a trial for maintenance, the court actually denied the application of the provision because, in the meantime, the German proceeding had come to an end.

Further, the court held that the case did not fall within the provision of Art. 5(1), because the matter did not relate to a contract, so that the connecting factor of the place of performance of the obligation could not apply.

The plaintiff had also argued for Italian jurisdiction on the ground that the maintenance proceeding was ancillary to determination of paternity for purposes of Art. 5(2). In rejecting the plea, the Supreme Court held that the fact that maintenance litigation could involve a matter of status did not automatically constitute the former as merely ancillary for the purposes of Art. 5(2), so long as the main proceedings on status were not actually pending. With regard to the initial ground in Art. 5(2) conferring jurisdiction on the courts of the place where the maintenance creditor is domiciled or habitually resident, since the creditor was resident in Germany, the Supreme Court declared in favour of jurisdiction of German, not Italian, courts.

ARTICLE 5(3)

" . . . harmful event occurred . . . "

Case principle

The place where the harmful event occurred is not where indirect financial damage is suffered by the victim of a transaction between other parties (*Dumez*, Case 220/88, and *Marinari*, Case C-364/93 applied).

Case

629   Corte di Cassazione, sez. un., 27 November 1996, 10524

Facts

The plaintiffs were shareholders of a bankrupt Italian company. They sued the holding company on the ground that, in a contract of share transfer, the holding company had accepted a ruinous set-off, instead of determining the right price of the shares, as a consequence of which the plaintiffs suffered serious damage through the resulting bankruptcy of the controlled company. Jurisdiction was based on the fact that the bankruptcy had been declared in Italy. The defendant challenged jurisdiction, on the ground that the share transfer contract had been performed in Switzerland, and that, consequently, Art. 5(3) was inapplicable to the case, because the place where the event had occurred coincided with the place where the obligation under the contract had been performed.

Judgment

The Supreme Court declined jurisdiction. It held that the place where the event had occurred was to be determined as the place where the contractual obligation had been performed. The court excluded the place where a third party suffered financial damage from an event occurring in a different place between two other parties. The court followed the line of the European Court of Justice (particularly *Dumez* Case 220/88) stating that not any damage could be considered as the harmful event for the purposes of Art. 5(3) and specifically not the indirect financial damage suffered by the victim of an act between other parties.

ARTICLE 5(4)

"As regards a civil claim for damages or restitution which is based on an act giving rise to criminal proceedings, in the court seised of those proceedings, to the extent that that court has jurisdiction under its own law to entertain civil proceedings".

Case principle

The initial stage of preliminary investigation following a mere accusation does not satisfy the conditions necessary for the existence of the criminal proceeding which, according to Art. 5(4), allows a person to be sued for civil damages or restitution in a State other than that of his domicile before the court seised of criminal proceedings.

Case

Corte di Cassazione sez. un., 1991, 13300   **630**

Facts

The plaintiff had sued an English lawyer for damages before an Italian court, arguing that since the complaint was based on an act giving rise to a criminal proceeding, Art. 5(4) was to be applied. The defendant challenged Italian jurisdiction and the assumption which had been made that a criminal proceeding was pending in Italy because there was only an 'information' against the defendant. The Supreme Court was asked to rule on jurisdiction by means of the *Regolamento di giurisdizione*.

Judgment

The Supreme Court upheld the defendant's challenge, and ruled that the mere 'information'—an accusation without indictment—was not enough to apply Art. 5(4). The court held that only the formal bringing of a prosecution by which the defendant was brought to trial could satisfy the conditions necessary to establish the existence of a criminal proceeding for the purposes of Art. 5(4).

ARTICLE 6(1)

" . . . one of a number of defendants . . . "

Case principle

Although the Convention says nothing about the mutual position of the defendants for the purposes of Art. 6(1), the mere fact of being one of a number of defendants is insufficient for jurisdiction thereunder, since a *connection* between the respective causes of action is required (in the case the connection was identified in the common element of defamation upon which the actions were founded) (see *Kalfelis v Schröder* Case 189/87).

Case

631   Corte di Cassazione sez. un., 6 August 1990, 7935

Facts

The plaintiff, a Brazilian national, claimed to have been defamed by a book first published in England, then translated into Italian and put into circulation in Italy. He sued the author, a British national, the publisher and the printer, both British companies, the Italian publisher and the Italian printer before an Italian court. The British companies challenged Italian jurisdiction and appealed to the Supreme Court, by means of the *Regolamento di giurisdizione*, on the ground that an Italian court could not be the court of the place where the event occurred for the purposes of Art. 5(3) (printing and circulation of the book occurred in England, personal damage in Brazil), nor could Art. 6(1) be used because the claims against the English defendants were not connected to the actions brought against the Italian defendants in the sense of Art. 4(3) of the Italian *Codice di Procedura Civile*.

Judgment

The Supreme Court held the Italian courts to be able to deal with the actions brought against the British companies. First, it stated that, although the Convention said nothing about the mutual position of the defendants for the purposes of Art. 6(1), the mere fact of being one of several defendants should be considered insufficient for jurisdiction, since a *connection* between the causes of action was required. In the case, however, the claims were sufficiently connected because—although the respective causes of action were not the same—all the complaints shared the common element of defamation. Thus, the court stated that the case fell within the scope of Art. 6(1) and confirmed the jurisdiction of the Italian courts as those of the place where some of the defendants were domiciled. Accordingly, it was unnecessary to examine the issues raised concerning Art. 5(3).

ARTICLE 8, PARAGRAPH 2

" . . . *in disputes arising out of the operations of the branch, agency or establishment* . . . "

Case principle

The fact that an insurer not domiciled in a Contracting State has a branch, agency or other establishment in Italy confers Italian jurisdiction only with regard to disputes related to insurance policies issued by the branch, agency or establishment.

Case

Corte di Cassazione sez. un., 13 February 1993, 1820   **632**

Facts

In a dispute on third party liability in automobile insurance, an Italian national plaintiff as the injured party in an accident occurring abroad, sued the person responsible and his insurer before an Italian court. Both the policy-holder and the insurer were not domiciled in a Contracting State, but, considering that the latter had a branch in Italy, the plaintiff asserted that the insurer was to be deemed to be domiciled in Italy according to Art. 8, para. 2. The defendant insurer argued that Art. 8 was inapplicable, and raised the issue before the Supreme Court by means of the *Regolamento di giurisdizione* in order to have jurisdiction definitively ruled upon.

Judgment

The Supreme Court held that Italian jurisdiction should be declined, because Art. 8 was to be interpreted in a strict manner. Accordingly, the mere location in Italy of a branch of the non-Contracting State insurance company did not confer jurisdiction under Art. 8 if the dispute did not arise out of the operations of such a branch.

ARTICLE 17, PARAGRAPH 1(a)

" . . . *in writing or evidenced in writing* . . . "

Case principle

1. The expression 'in writing or evidenced in writing' requires the party to produce a document specifically containing the written prorogation agreement (either the original or a copy). The party is not allowed to refer to evidence of such an agreement in the form of a previous court ruling.

Case

Corte di Cassazione sez. un., 23 January 1991, 597   **633**

Facts

The plaintiff company sued two people domiciled in Germany before an Italian court for payment of the price of the transfer of property. Italian jurisdiction was sought to be founded upon Italy as the place where the obligation was to be performed. The defendants challenged jurisdiction through the *Regolamento di giurisdizione* to the Supreme Court. They invoked Art. 17, since the contract included the clause *Erfüllungsort und Gerichtsstand ist Köln* (place of performance and jurisdiction, Cologne). No written text of such a contract was submitted to the court, but the defendants asserted that the terms of the agreement should be considered as proved in previous proceedings between the same parties (never terminated through failure to proceed by the parties). The written evidence would be in the form of a Supreme Court judgment ruling on jurisdiction in that proceeding, but not to be considered as *res judicata* in the proceedings currently before the courts.

Judgment

The Supreme Court held that the fact that the alleged judgment referred to the clause was irrelevant, since Art. 17 required strict interpretation (*Salotti* Case 24/76). Thus, the expression 'in writing or evidenced in writing' had to be understood as requiring the party to produce either the original document containing the clause or a copy. Therefore, any document or deed which only *refers* to the written clause is deemed to be insufficient for the purposes of Art. 17 written requirements.

Case principle

2. An agreement conferring jurisdiction does not require to be *specifically* undersigned, provided that it is in writing.

Case

634   Corte di Cassazione, 28 March 1987, 3030

Facts

An Italian Court of Appeal had refused to review its previous recognition of a German default judgment given in an agency matter. The unsuccessful party filed an appeal to the Supreme Court on the ground that the prorogation agreement upon which German jurisdiction had been founded, was invalid, as it did not comply with Art. 1341 of the Italian Civil Code, which provides that, in a printed form, a simple signature below the form containing the clause may not suffice, because the clause should be approved specifically (in the sense of an additional signature), which had not occurred in the case. As a basic rule of domestic law, Art. 1341 of the Civil Code should supplement Art. 17, so that the simple written form provided there would not be sufficient for the purpose.

Judgment

The court rejected the appeal and held—in accordance with previous cases (which had overcome the initially nationalistic interpretation of the Convention by the Italian Corte di Cassazione)—that the essential requirement of being 'in writing' is satisfied by a single mutual signature of the deed, on the sole condition that, when the clause is printed on the reverse side of the sheet, it is to be expressly referred to within the undersigned text (*Salotti* Case 24/76).

ARTICLE 18

" . . . *defendant enters an appearance* . . . "

Case principle

The defendant's application for an interlocutory measure to a court of a Contracting State other than the one where he is domiciled, cannot be regarded as conferring jurisdiction on the former court as to the substance of the matter, since jurisdiction on the merits does not automatically coincide with jurisdiction over provisional measures.

Case

Corte di Cassazione sez. un., 13 February 1993, 1821   **635**

Facts

An Italian publisher filed a petition to obtain a declaration of the right to use and exploit the name of a magazine and for the right to publish and distribute it all over the world by virtue of a previous use of the masthead. The defendant was a German publisher who challenged jurisdiction by invoking Art. 2. The first instance court declined jurisdiction, as did the Court of Appeal subsequently. A further appeal was lodged by the plaintiff with the Supreme Court. He argued that since the defendant had applied for a provisional measure to the magistrate's court in Milan, and since such an act was intended as ancillary to an application for enforcement of a judgment upon the substance of the matter, the defendant was to be considered as having chosen Italian jurisdiction instead of the jurisdiction founded upon its domicile.

Judgment

The Supreme Court rejected the appeal. It stated that the mere fact of applying for an interlocutory measure did not confer merits jurisdiction upon the court seised. Since Art. 24 clearly distinguished between interlocutory measures—as provided by the law of a Contracting State—and the substance of the action, so that an interlocutory measure could be rendered by a judge other than the one having jurisdiction over the substantive subject matter, the court held that the fact of requesting such a measure was not to be regarded as an act conferring jurisdiction as to the merits.

See too *infra*, Case 636.

> " . . . *solely to contest the jurisdiction.* "

Case principle

1. The rule by which the defendant's appearance solely to contest the jurisdiction does not confer jurisdiction upon the court before which he so appears, applies even if there are substantive pleas, if these are brought not principally but solely in the event of a finding in favour of jurisdiction.

Case

636   Corte di Cassazione sez. un., 13 February 1993, 1821

Facts

An Italian publisher filed a petition to obtain a declaration of the right to use and exploit the name of a magazine and for the right to publish and distribute it all over the world by virtue of a previous use of the masthead. The defendant was a German publisher which contested jurisdiction by invoking Art. 2. The first instance court declined jurisdiction, as did the subsequent judgment of the court of appeal. A further appeal was lodged by the plaintiff with the Supreme Court, on the ground that the defendant had raised substantive pleas so that its appearance could not be considered as being limited to contestation of jurisdiction, under Art. 18 (see *supra*, Case 635).

Judgment

The court held against Italian jurisdiction, on the basis of the final provision of Art. 18. The court held that the rule that a court of a Contracting State before which a defendant entered an appearance should have jurisdiction, could not apply in the case, despite the submission of substantive pleas. In fact, the existence of the defendant's substantive pleas was regarded as not being capable of conferring jurisdiction upon the court, for such pleas were brought only in the event of a possible finding in favour of jurisdiction. The defendant's appearance was to be considered as being limited to the sole contestation of jurisdiction, even when accompanied by such substantive pleas, in the circumstances (*Gerling* Case 201/82 referred to).

Case principle

2.   The rules provided by Art. 18 can affect a plaintiff as well when a negative declaration is pursued and aims to prevent the defendant from bringing his action before a court of a different country.

Case

Corte di Cassazione sez. un., 2 February 1991, 999   **637**

Facts

The plaintiffs were two companies, the French parent company and its Italian associated firm. They jointly sued an employee before an Italian judge for a declaration that the defendant's period of temporary attachment in Italy was at an end and that the Italian firm was under no obligation towards him. They asserted that their acceptance of Italian jurisdiction was limited to the claim made, and that under no circumstances should this amount to an acceptance of jurisdiction over any claim brought by the defendant. Since the defendant had filed a counterclaim for the declaration that he had the status of an employee of the Italian company, the plaintiffs resorted to the Supreme Court to have jurisdiction decided by *Regolamento di giurisdizione*. They submitted to the court a clause in writing, by which, in accordance with Art. 17, the parties had agreed that French courts were to have exclusive jurisdiction to settle any disputes which might arise in connection with their relationship.

Judgment

The Supreme Court held that Art. 17 was not applicable, because the case fell within the scope of Art. 18 (see *Elefanten Schuh* Case 150/80). It was true— the court stated—that Art. 18 referred to the *defendant* entering an appearance; but its provision also governed *a fortiori* the case in which a party sued a person before a court to prevent the defendant from bringing his action before courts of a different country. The fact that the plaintiffs had declared their non-acceptance of jurisdiction over the possible counterclaim did not alter the position, because, claiming that the Italian firm was not party to the relationship, they had submitted the whole litigation to the same judge, so that no separation was possible between the substantive question of the standing of the Italian firm and the rest of the dispute.

Editor's Comment

Article 18 was needed to be relied upon for jurisdiction over the counterclaim against the French and Italian plaintiffs, because Art. 17 would otherwise prevail over Arts 6(3) and 2, respectively.

ARTICLE 21, PARAGRAPH 1

" . . . *first seised* . . . "

Case principle

The determination of the moment at which the court becomes definitively seised for the purposes of Art. 21 is to be made according to the rules of the national procedural law in force for *that* court (*Gubisch* Case 144/86 applied).

Case

638 Corte di Cassazione, sez. un., 12 October 1990, 10014

Facts

A company had requested a *Mahnbescheid* in Germany. After obtaining it, but before it was served on the defendant, the latter had sued the company before an Italian court in an action with the same cause. The defendant raised the *lis alibi pendens* issue. The court refused to stay its proceedings under Art. 21, on the ground that the proceedings before the German judge were to be considered as having become pending only from the moment of service on the defendant, so that the court first-seised, for the purposes of Art. 21, was the Italian. The decision was upheld by the appellate court.

Judgment

The Supreme Court decided in a different way. Following *Gubisch* Case 144/86, definitive seisin, for the purposes of Art. 21, is to be determined according to the rules of the national procedural law in force for the judge applied to. Thus, the Supreme Court held that, in compliance with paras 253 and 261 of the German Code of Civil Procedure (ZPO), the *Rechtshängigkeit* was determined at the time of the submission of the petition to the judge (*Einreichung*), and not by the service (*Zustellung*)—contrary to Art. 39 of the Italian Code of Civil Procedure, according to which the so-called *prevenzione* (determination of the court first-seised) is established by the service of the summons.

Accordingly, the Supreme Court held that the Italian court was not the court first-seised, and reversed the previous judgment, so that the Italian court had to decline its jurisdiction in favour of the German court.

ARTICLE 27(2)

" . . . *given in default of appearance* . . . "

Case principle

Any investigation of regularity of the service of process is precluded on the part of the recognition-court, if the defendant entered an appearance in the proceeding before the judgment-court.

Case

Corte di Cassazione, 28 April 1990, 3598   **639**

Facts

An Italian Court of Appeal had recognized a Dutch judgment upholding a claim brought by a Dutch company against an Italian entrepreneur, for recovery of sums due. The losing party appealed on a point of law to the Supreme Court, contesting recognition on the ground that, in the original Dutch proceedings, the plaintiff had actually sued the wrong party. In fact, the plaintiff had sued and served an Italian company; whereupon the defendant, assuming the non-existence of such a company, had entered an appearance, hoping that he would subsequently be able to invoke the provision of Art. 27(2), that is, so as to be able to contest that *he* was duly served with the document which instituted the proceedings.

Judgment

The Supreme Court rejected the appeal. It stated that the position of the Italian Court of Appeal was in accordance with the Convention recognition system, under which a Contracting State's courts' judgment should not be recognized under Art. 27(2) where given *in default of appearance*. The court held that the defendant's appearance was sufficient for him to be considered as having been properly brought before the Dutch court. The fact that the lawsuit was formally addressed to a party other than the correct one (*i.e.* the person obliged to perform under the contract) was considered irrelevant, and any question about the service of process could only arise in default of the defendant.

ARTICLE 27(3)

" . . . *with a judgment* . . . "

Case principle

Although irreconcilable with a subsequent judgment given in a dispute between the same parties in another Contracting State, an Italian judgment cannot impede the recognition of the latter if the Italian judgment has been appealed and therefore is not yet enforceable (*res judicata*).

Case

640   Corte di Cassazione, 12 November 1994, 9554

Facts

After the Court of Appeal of Venice had recognized a German judgment definitively upholding a previous judgment, the unsuccessful party appealed on a
point of law to the Supreme Court contesting recognition on the ground that
a judgment *inter partes* had been previously delivered by an Italian court, and
that such judgment was to be considered as irreconcilable with the German
judgment for the purposes of Art. 27(3).

Judgment

The Supreme Court rejected the appeal against enforcement. It agreed that the
Italian and subsequent German judgments were mutually incompatible, but
held that, in order to prevent the recognition of the German judgment, the
Italian judgment had to be either a final decision or an effective one. It was
true, the Court affirmed, that Art. 27(3) simply referred to 'a judgment' with
no special features, but this 'judgment' could not be one which was still devoid
of effects. Thus, the Italian judgment invoked as irreconcilable was a first
instance decision which had been appealed and was not yet enforceable for
lack of the executive clause required by the Civil Procedure Code to execute
judgments. Further, in rejecting the appellant's application to make a reference
to the European Court of Justice, the Supreme Court declared compliance
with *Hoffmann v Krieg* Case 145/86, in which the European Court had
stated that irreconcilability must be acknowledged when the two judgments
generated effects which were mutually exclusive. Accordingly, in this case the
Supreme Court held that a judgment which was neither enforceable nor final
could not be considered to give rise to *any* substantive effects (as actually regulating duties, rights or obligations), as long as such a state persisted, which it
would for as long as the appeal was pending against it (although it should be
added that, owing to the recent reform of civil procedure—see *supra A. Legal
System*—first instance judgments which are not enforceable have become more
unusual in the Italian legal system, since decisions under appeal *can* be executed as a rule).

12

LUXEMBOURG

Monsieur Jean-Claude Wiwinius

A. LEGAL SYSTEM

The law of 7 March 1980, as modified on a number of occasions, establishes the judicial organization, and, in particular, the functioning and the composition of the different jurisdictions in the Grand Duchy of Luxembourg. Chaps I, II and III of Title I (On the judicial power) deal with the Justices of the Peace, the Tribunaux d'arrondissement and the Superior Court of Justice, respectively.

The Tribunal d'arrondissement has jurisdiction in relation to civil law in Luxembourg. According to Art. 17 of the preliminary Title to the Civil Procedure Code, the 'Tribunal d'arrondissement'—in its collegiate jurisdiction, made up of three judges—has jurisdiction, in civil and commercial matters, over all cases in which competence is not expressly allocated to another jurisdiction because of the nature or the amount of the claim. There is no specific commercial court.

It is important to note that the Justice of the Peace—as sole judge—may have jurisdiction over all claims inferior or equal to 400 000 Flux (±10 000 ECU).

There are two 'Tribunaux d'arrondissement' in the Grand Duchy, one in Luxembourg City and the other in Diekirch.

There are three Justices of the Peace, that is to say, in Luxembourg City (16 judges), in Esch-sur-Alzette (7 judges) and in Diekirch (3 judges).

It is the president of the Tribunal d'arrondissement with territorial jurisdiction who has jurisdiction over claims in *exequatur*, as provided by Art. 32 of the Brussels Convention of 27 September 1968.

The Tribunal d'arrondissement has appellate jurisdiction in relation to the decisions taken by the Justice of the Peace.

The Court of Appeal—at present composed of nine divisions (chambers) each made up of three judges—has jurisdiction over all appeals from the judgments of the two Tribunaux d'arrondissement and from the decisions of the two presidents of the Tribunaux d'arrondissement ruling on claims in *exequatur*.

At the top of the judicial hierarchy there is the Court of Cassation—made up of five judges—which forms, together with the different divisions of the Court of Appeal, the Superior Court of Justice. The Court of Cassation may be seised only of disputes relating to law or procedure. It no longer has jurisdiction over facts, which are exclusively considered by the judge having jurisdiction as to the substance of the matter.

B. IMPLEMENTATION OF THE CONVENTIONS

Luxembourg is one of the six original Member States of the European Union. The Brussels Convention of 27 September 1968 has been applicable amongst the six States, in its original version, from 1 February 1973.

The law of approval of Luxembourg is dated 8 August 1972 (*cf*. Mémorial, *i.e. Journal Officiel de la Législation Nationale Luxembourgeoise* 1972 p. 1364).

The First Accession Convention dated 9 October 1978 with Denmark, Ireland and the UK, was approved in Luxembourg by a law dated 18 January 1981 (*cf*. Mémorial 1981, p. 1153). From 1 November 1986, this Convention was applicable amongst the six original States and Denmark, from 1 January 1987 for the UK and, in the end, from 1 June 1988 for Ireland.

The Second Accession Convention of 25 October 1982, with Greece, was approved in Luxembourg by a law dated 28 February 1984 (*cf*. Mémorial 1984, p. 262). This Convention came into force on 1 April 1989 for the six original States, Denmark, Ireland and Greece and on 1 October 1989 for the UK.

The Third Accession Convention of 26 May 1989, with Spain and Portugal, was approved in Luxembourg by a law dated 31 July 1991 (*cf*. Mémorial 1991, p. 1153). This Convention came into force on 1 February 1992 for Luxembourg.

As far as the interests of the inhabitants of Luxembourg are specifically concerned, it is necessary to refer to Art. I, para. 2 of the Protocol annexed to the Brussels Convention which states that jurisdiction agreements shall not have effect in relation to a person domiciled in Luxembourg unless this person has 'expressly and specifically so agreed'. This disposition seemed essential to the drafters of the Convention, taking account of the fact that a large number of contracts concluded by people with residence in Luxembourg were international contracts.

The parallel Lugano Convention of 18 September 1988 was ratified in Luxembourg by a law of 31 July 1991 (*cf*. Mémorial 1991, p. 1154). That law came into force on 1 February 1992.

C. OVERVIEW OF CONVENTION CASE LAW

The first comment that may be made after reading the different decisions taken by the courts, either at first or second instance, is that the law of Luxembourg is not particularly original. However, this should not be considered a criticism. On the contrary, the courts of Luxembourg, in their decisions, faithfully follow the law of the European Court of Justice in that not only do they have a perfect knowledge of the case law through the easy access to that law, given the proximity of that institution, but also they accept, such as should be the case everywhere, the role of harmonization and coordination in matters of which the European Court is in charge.

A recent consultation of the courts of Luxembourg, in the framework of the revision projects of the Brussels and Lugano Conventions, put forward by the European Commission, revealed that Luxembourg has not met any major difficulty in the application of these Conventions and that no modification shall be suggested.

Examination of the decisions listed also indicates that—no longer surprisingly—most of the litigation concerning *conflicts of jurisdiction* relate to the application of Art. 5(1) of the two Conventions, concerning contract law. Connected with this issue are the problems relating to Art. 17 on jurisdiction clauses and Art. I of the annexed Protocol concerning acceptance of those clauses by people domiciled in Luxembourg.

In relation to the *enforcement of foreign judgments*, most of the problems relate, on one hand, to the control of the jurisdiction of the judge of origin. On this matter we have made some comments about the courageous decisions of the courts of Luxembourg in refusing that control even in case of a violation of Art. I of the Protocol by the judge of origin. On the other hand, it is necessary to mention those problems derived from the alleged contravention of the defendant's right to notice of the document instituting proceedings.

In all these matters, the law of Luxembourg is consistent and, as has been stated above, in conformity with the law of the European Court of Justice.

D. CASES

ARTICLE I, PARAGRAPH 2(2)

> *"2. Bankruptcy, proceedings relating to the winding-up . . . and analogous proceedings: . . . "*

Case principle

Actions not affected by bankruptcy are not excluded.

Case

641 Endres v Royco Investment and Abinger Southfield Fiduciary Services 769/92, Tribunal d'arrondissement of Luxembourg, 2 December 1992

Facts

Endres had invested some money in a small fund managed by the Royco company set up in the Dutch Antilles. Since Royco, which had, in the meantime, gone into liquidation in accordance with the English Insolvency Act 1986, had not provided Endres with the relevant fund certificates, the latter sued Royco before the tribunal d'arrondissement of Luxembourg for repayment of the invested amount. Royco pleaded lack of jurisdiction.

Judgment

Proceedings under the Insolvency Act 1986 fell within Art. 1, para. 2(2) of the Brussels Convention. The exclusion under that rule applied only to those proceedings which were based on suspension of payment, insolvency or withdrawal of the credit and required intervention of the judicial authorities leading to compulsory liquidation or to an administration on the part of that authority. Civil actions not modified by the bankruptcy remained within the Convention. Consequently, the Convention was held to apply.

ARTICLE 5(1)

" . . . *In matters relating to a contract* . . . "

Case principle

Article 5(1) applies even when contractual existence is disputed.

Case

642 Martens-Fashion v Burg-Martin 7625, Court of Appeal, 12 June 1985

Facts

Burg-Martin sued the Martens-Fashion company for a declaration relating to the existence of a contract based on the purchase of clothing and for the payment of damages incurred through faulty execution of the contract. The defendant pleaded lack of Luxembourg jurisdiction. The defendant contested, in particular, the existence of the contract invoked by Burg-Martin to support the claim.

Judgment

In relation to Art. 5(1), jurisdiction of the judge seised to decide questions relating to a contract included assessment of the existence of the contract itself, and such an assessment was essential to allow the judge to verify jurisdiction in accordance with the Convention. Consequently, according to Art. 5(1), a plaintiff can rely upon Art. 5(1) even though the creation of the contract in question was disputed by the defendant.

" . . . *obligation in question* . . . "

Case principle

1. The obligation in question is that on which the plaintiff's claim is based (*de Bloos*, Case 14/76 applied).

Case

Gondert v Pultz, Pasicrisie t. 24, p. 168 Court of Appeal, 7 June 1978   **643**

Facts

Under a contract of sale, Pultz sold to Gondert, domiciled in Germany, some iron goods. After delivery of a certain amount of goods, Gondert informed Pultz that he would not perform the rest of the contract. Pultz sued Gondert in the Tribunal d'arrondissement of Luxembourg for the payment of the TVA on the iron goods which had been provided and for damages for breach of contract. Gondert pleaded lack of Luxembourg jurisdiction.

Judgment

The term 'obligation' in Art. 5(1) refers to the contractual obligation on which the action is based.

The determination of the place of performance of that obligation has to be carried out according to the law applicable to the contractual relationship in question.

When the obligation, the enforcement of which is claimed by the plaintiff, consists of a payment of a balance relating to the goods delivered in execution of a sale in cash and the parties recognize that the law applicable to the juridical relationship in question is the law of Luxembourg, the determination of the place of payment, which had not been specified at the time of the contract, has to be carried out according to Art. 1651 of the Civil Code of Luxembourg, which states that, if nothing has been agreed on this matter during the sale, the buyer has to pay in the place and at the time where the delivery has to take place.

Consequently, when, in accordance with the contract, the delivery of the goods has to be made in Luxembourg, the courts of Luxembourg have jurisdiction.

When the litigation relates to the consequences of breach of his obligations by the buyer, as in the case of the payment of damages for the breach of the contract of sale, the obligation to which it is necessary to refer, in order to apply Art. 5(1), is that of the buyer upon which the claim for damages is based.

Comment

This old decision, which referred to the Court of Justice's ruling in *De Bloos*, has been used as a precedent in various later decisions (*cf.* Court of Appeal, 26 September 1980, Pasicrisie 25, p. 134; Court of Appeal, 21 December 1983, 6187; Court of Appeal, 12 June 1985, 7625; Court of Appeal, 16 March 1987, 9259; Court of Appeal, 8 March 1994, 14785; Court of Appeal, 10 May 1994, 15664, as well as various decisions of first instance).

Case

644 Ruckert v Karmann 12898 Court of Appeal, 26 November 1991

Facts

See too *infra*, Case 660

Under a contract of works, Karmann, who lived in Germany, was retained to repair the roof of Ruckert's house situated in Luxembourg. The latter sued Karmann in summary proceedings for the payment of damages for the faulty performance of the contract. Karmann pleaded lack of Luxembourg jurisdiction.

Judgment

In the case of a claim for damages relating to a contract, the obligation which has to be referred to for the application of Art. 5(1) is that on which the plaintiff's claim is based.

As the obligation assumed by Karmann consisted of the provision of a repaired and waterproof roof having to be carried out in Luxembourg, the courts of Luxembourg had jurisdiction over the claim.

Case principle

2. The obligation in question for wrongful termination of exclusive distributorship is that of giving reasonable notice of termination.

Case

645 Peckels v Deuter 174/88 Tribunal d'arrondissement of Luxembourg, 21 April 1988

Facts

Peckels sued the German company Deuter in the Tribunal d'arrondissement of Luxembourg for damages for an abusive breach of an exclusive distribution agreement for leather articles. The defendant challenged Luxembourg jurisdiction. The plaintiff wished to rely upon Art. 5(1).

Judgment

The obligation in question for Art. 5(1) is that on which the claim is based.

When, in the case of a breach of a contract of representation, the sales representative, judging the breach as wrongful, claims payment for damages, the obligation in question is not that of payment of a sum of money (in the debtor's domicile), but that of providing reasonable notice of termination: here in Luxembourg.

Case

Thill v Ragolds 157/87, Tribunal d'arrondissement of Luxembourg, 27 March   **646**
1987

Facts

Thill sued the German company Ragolds for the payment of damages for abusive breach of a contract of concession. The defendant pleaded that the courts of Luxembourg did not have Art. 5(1) jurisdiction and questioned the existence of any contract of representation. He argued that since the obligation of delivery within the framework of the individual contracts of sale had to be carried out in Germany, Germany was place of performance.

Judgment

The court first decided that the contract between the parties had as its object the concession given to the plaintiff for the distribution of the goods of the defendant in Luxembourg and that the contract had had its effects in Luxembourg.

The obligation to which it was necessary to refer for the application of Art. 5(1) was that on which the claim was founded.

When, in the case of breach of a contract of representation, the sales representative, considering the breach as wrongful, claims payment of damages, the obligation in question was not that of paying a sum of money (in the debtor's German domicile), but that of providing reasonable notice of termination in Luxembourg.

Comment

A similar decision was reached in a judgment of the Tribunal d'arrondissement in Luxembourg on 19 February 1987 (*Comptoir des Tabac-Fixmer v Interland* 90/87).

Case principle

3. Where several obligations are in dispute, the principal obligation is chosen (*de Bloos* Case 14/76 and *Shenavai* Case 266/85 applied).

Case

647 Vesque v Badischer Winzerkeller 14785 Court of Appeal, 8 March 1994

Facts

Vesque was linked to the Badischer Winzerkeller company by a contract of representation and consultancy. Following the termination of the contract, Vesque sued the Badischer Winzerkeller company for unpaid commissions and various indemnities.

The jurisdiction of the Tribunal d'arrondissement was sought, *inter alia*, on the basis of Art. 5(1) (see too *infra*, Case 653). The German defendant challenged the Luxembourg jurisdiction.

Judgment

The court seised on the basis of Art. 5(1) has to determine, in accordance with its own rules of conflict of laws, which is the law applicable to the juridical relationship in question and to specify, in accordance with that law, the place of performance of the obligation in question.

In order to determine which is the applicable law, it is required to refer to the Convention of Rome of 19 June 1980, introduced by the law of 27 March 1986 and which stipulates, in Art. 3(1) that the contract is governed by the law chosen by the parties.

Once the law applicable to the contract, in this instance German law, has been decided upon, it is necessary to determine, in accordance with that law, the place of performance of the obligation in question.

When the litigation relates to various obligations resulting from a same contract, the court seised, in order to determine its jurisdiction, will focus on the principle according to which the secondary follows the primary. In other words, it will be the place of performance of the *principal* obligation, amongst various obligations in question, which will establish its competence.

The principal obligations here, being obligations to pay, were, in accordance with applicable German law, to be performed in the headquarters of the German company. Consequently, the courts of Luxembourg had no jurisdiction over the claim.

Comment

The Court of Appeal correctly applied, expressly, the European Court's judgments in *de Bloos* and *Shenavai*.

Case principle

4. Characteristic obligation of work applied in employment contract (*Ivenel* Case 133/81, pre-1989 amendments).

Case

Républicain Lorrain v Mancini, Pasicrisie, t. 29, p. 30 Court of Appeal,   **648**
3 December 1992

Facts

Under a contract of employment, signed in France, Mancini was employed as
a journalist by the French company Le Républicain Lorrain. During the whole
period of his employment, the place where the work was carried out by
Mancini was Luxembourg. After being dismissed, Mancini sued his employer
in the industrial tribunal in Luxembourg claiming damages. Le Républicain
Lorrain challenged the Luxembourg jurisdiction.

Judgment

In matters relating to a contract of employment, the place of performance of
the obligation in Art. 5(1) was that where the characteristic services under the
contract were carried out, *i.e.* where the work was done, which in this case
was Luxembourg.

Comment

This is now express in the 1989-amended text.

" . . . place of performance . . . "

Case principle

The place of performance is for national law applicable under private international law (*Tessili*, Case 12/76 applied).

Case

Maschinen-Lauer v Faillite Fabriart 9259 Court of Appeal, 16 March 1987   **649**

Facts

Maschinen-Lauer sued the Fabriart company, set up in Luxembourg, for the
payment of the balance for various goods which had been sold and delivered.
Following the bankruptcy of Fabriart (before a decision on that claim), the
trustee in bankruptcy and Maschinen-Lauer agreed that the latter would buy
the machines back for the price of 500 000 Flux, but that the price was payable
only after the decision of the courts on the reservation of ownership invoked
by Maschinen-Lauer in the first case. As this decision was against Maschinen-
Lauer, the trustee sued the latter for payment of the sum of 500 000 Flux.
Maschinen-Lauer pleaded lack of jurisdiction of the Luxembourg courts.

Judgment

In the case of a claim for the payment of the balance of the price due for the delivery of goods and breach of a contractual stipulation, the place for the payment for the goods delivered in execution of a contract governed by the law of Luxembourg is determined according to Art. 1651 of the Civil Code of Luxembourg, so that the court of the place of delivery of the goods has jurisdiction, that is, the place where the goods were at the time of the 'sale': Luxembourg.

Consequently, the courts of Luxembourg possessed jurisdiction.

Case

650 Couverture and Ferblanterie du Centre v Lauterbach 15664 Court of Appeal, 10 May 1994

Facts

The Couverture et Ferblanterie du Centre company sued Lauterbach, who lived in Germany, in the Luxembourg courts for payment for services. Lauterbach pleaded lack of jurisdiction. As to the application of Art. 5(1), which was not being contested, the question was to find out which law determined the place where the obligation was or had to be performed.

Judgment

The place of performance of the obligation which determined international jurisdiction would not be determined under the *lex fori*, but according to the law which governed the obligation in question according to the rules of the conflict of laws of the court seised.

In determining such law governing the obligation in question, reference would be made to the Convention of Rome of 19 June 1980 relating to the law applicable to contractual obligations, introduced into the law of Luxembourg by a law of 27 March 1986.

Under paras 1 and 2 of Art. 4 of the Rome Convention, the contract was governed by the law of the country with which it had the closest links and it is presumed that the contract had its closest connections with the country where the party which had to carry out the characteristic obligation had, at the moment of conclusion of the contract, its habitual residence.

What was characteristic in the synallagmatic contract was not the payment which, generally, is made in cash, but the service for which the payment was made.

As this service consisted in this case in the work carried out by the plaintiff, whose headquarters were situated in the Grand Duchy, consequently, Luxembourg law applied.

Under applicable Luxembourg law, payment was, under Art. 1247 of the Civil Code of Luxembourg, required to be made in Germany, which led to jurisdiction of the German courts under Art. 5(1).

Case

FISTA v IBC 16651 Court of Appeal, 20 June 1995   **651**

Facts

The IBC company sued the Swiss company FISTA in the court of summary jurisdiction in Luxembourg for payment of a certain sum for goods which had been sold and delivered. On appeal, FISTA denied Luxembourg jurisdiction under Lugano Art. 5(1).

Judgment

The place of performance under Lugano Art. 5(1) is determined in accordance with the law governing the contract, itself determined in accordance with the rules of conflict of laws of the seised jurisdiction. In Luxembourg the law governing the contract will be decided by reference to the Convention of Rome of 19 June 1980 on the law applicable to contractual relations, introduced in our internal law by a law of 27 March 1986.

In synallagmatic contracts, it is not the payment which is the characteristic obligation for applicable law, but the service for which payment is to be made.

Thus, turning to jurisdiction, according to applicable Luxembourg law, performance of the payment obligation in question, as the basis of the claim, was to be carried out in Switzerland where the debtor was domiciled.

The courts of Luxembourg, therefore, lacked jurisdiction over the claim.

Comment

This is the only decision given by the Court of Appeal concerning the application of the Lugano Convention.

ARTICLE 5(3)

" . . . *place where the harmful event occurred.*"

Case principle

Place of causal act held to be that of the harmful event.

Case

Valmorbida v CNAMO and MAAF 313/87 Tribunal d'arrondissement of   **652**
Luxembourg, 2 July 1987

Facts

Mr and Mrs Valmorbida sued the insurance company MAAF in the Tribunal d'arrondissement of Luxembourg, claiming compensation for the harm suffered after the loss of their son who died after a traffic accident which took place in France and which was caused by the negligence of the person insured by the MAAF. The Caisse de Maladie CNAMO was sued as a third party.

The MAAF contested Luxembourg jurisdiction under Art. 5(3).

Judgment

In the case of road traffic accidents, there was no doubt that the place where the harmful event occurred was the 'place where the accident occurred', in accordance with the phrase used in Art. 3 of the Hague Convention on the law applicable to road traffic accidents, signed on 4 May 1971, and not the place where the damage was done.

As a matter of fact, the intention of those who signed the Convention was to bring together, in the same court, all actions concerning the same event wherever the harm was done.

Consequently, the Tribunal d'arrondissement of Luxembourg declined jurisdiction in relation to the claim.

Comment

This judgment is now not wholly correct as a result of the European Court's decision in *Bier*, Case 21/76, enabling plaintiffs to choose place of causal event or *damage*. See too *infra*, Case 654.

ARTICLE 5(5)

"A person domiciled in a Contracting State may, in another Contracting State, be sued: . . . dispute arising out of the operations of a branch, agency or other establishment . . . "

Case principle

Article 5(5) is for third parties to sue the principal, not for actions between principal and agency/branch.

Case

653 Vesque v Badischer Winzerkeller 14785 Court of Appeal, 8 March 1994

Facts

Vesque, who lived in Luxembourg, was linked to the German company Badischer Winzekeller by a contract of representation and consultancy. Following the conclusion of the contract, Vesque sued Badischer Winzerkeller for payment of the unpaid commissions and various indemnities.

It was sought to base the jurisdiction of the Tribunal d'arrondissement, *inter alia*, on Art. 5(5) (see too *supra*, Case 647).

Judgment

Article 5(5) of the Convention was held not to apply to the relationship between the headquarters and the branch, but only permitted a third party who dealt with the branch to sue at the place of the latter.

It is therefore correct that the courts of Luxembourg declined jurisdiction over the claim.

ARTICLE 6(1)

"A person domiciled in a Contracting State may also be sued:
. . . where any one of them is domiciled."

Case principle

There must be a genuine claim against the main defendant.

Case

Valmorbida v CNAMO and MAAF 313/87 Tribunal d'arrondissement of   **654**
Luxembourg, 2 July 1987

Facts

Mr and Mrs Valmorbida sued the French insurance company MAAF in the Tribunal d'arrondissement of Luxembourg, claiming compensation for the harm suffered after the loss of their son who died after a traffic accident which took place in France and was caused by the negligence of the person insured by the MAAF. The Luxembourg Caisse de Maladie CNAMO was also sued.

Initially, the court declared itself to lack jurisdiction over the claim against MAAF under Art. 5(3) (see *supra*, Case 652).

The question was raised whether it may, nevertheless, have had jurisdiction under Art. 6(1), since the plaintiff's social security insurers (CNAMO) were asked to intervene.

Judgment

Jurisdiction over the defendant insurers of the party liable was not determined by the fact that the action was also brought against the Luxembourg social security scheme of the victim, as the latter had only been brought in for the purpose of achieving Luxembourg Art. 6(1) jurisdiction over the former.

ARTICLE 16(1)(a)

" . . . *proceedings which have as their object rights in rem in immovable property or tenancies of immovable property* . . . "

Case principle

Article 16(1)(a) is inapplicable to proceedings on a contract for the sale of immovable property.

Case

655   Van Elsken and Newman v Giquel 15593 Court of Appeal, 10 January 1996

Facts

See too *infra*, Case 661.

Giquel, the purchaser of a commercial site situated in Tenerife (Spain) and residing in Luxembourg, decided to terminate an agreement of sale concluded with Van Elsken and Newman, living in Belgium, and to request a refund of the advanced amounts because the sale could not be carried out any more, as the sellers had transferred half of the immovable property to a third person. Giquel effected an attachment on the bank accounts of Van Elsken in Luxembourg.

Jurisdiction of the Luxembourg courts was contested, in particular under Art. 16(1)(a) on the ground that Spanish courts had exclusive jurisdiction.

Judgment

'Mixed' proceedings, such as those for rescission of a contract for the sale of immovable property, were held to be excluded from the mandatory provisions of Art. 16 of the Convention.

ARTICLE 17

" . . . *shall have exclusive jurisdiction* . . . "

Case principle

Article 17 prevails over both general Art. 2 and specially connected Art. 5 jurisdiction.

Case

656   IMAC v STRAFE 16671 Court of Appeal, 3 May 1995

Facts

IMAC Co. sued STRAFOR Co. in the Tribunal d'arrondissement of Luxembourg claiming payment of a certain sum as damages for the breach of a contract of exclusive agency. The court declined jurisdiction over the claim, on the basis of a clause in the contract conferring jurisdiction upon the courts of Strasbourg in France.

On appeal, the IMAC company sought to base Luxembourg jurisdiction upon Art. 5(1).

Judgment

Article 17 of the Convention, which provides for the exclusive jurisdiction of the court agreed between the parties, displaces both the general rules of jurisdiction, provided in Art. 2 of the Convention, and the special rules, provided in Art. 5 of the same Convention, and removes all the objective elements of connection between the litigious relationship and the designated court. French, not Luxembourg, courts possessed jurisdiction.

ARTICLE 21

" . . . same parties . . . "

Case principle

Direct action against an insurer of a person responsible for injuries held not to involve same parties as action against latter himself.

Case

François v Winterthur 126/87 Tribunal d'arrondissement of Luxembourg,   **657**
12 March 1987

Facts

François sued the insurance company Winterthur in the Tribunal d'arrondissement of Luxembourg claiming compensation for injuries suffered in a traffic accident which had taken place in Belgium, and for which the person insured by Winterthur was responsible. The latter had also been criminally charged in the Belgian courts for breach of traffic regulations and for causing involuntary injuries, in which proceedings François intervened as civil party.

Winterthur pleaded the defence of *litispendentia* and that of related actions.

Judgment

There was identity of object, cause and parties between, on the one hand, the claim for damages by the victim of a road accident against the perpetrator in the criminal courts by way of the constitution of 'partie civile' and, on the other hand, the claim for compensation for the same damage made by the victim in the civil court, to the extent that this was directed against the person responsible for the accident. These conditions of *litispendentia* were not, however, fulfilled in the case because the civil court action was directed against the *insurer* in accordance with the insurance contract made between the insured and the insurance company, whereas the Belgian 'action civile' was against the person responsible himself: not the same parties nor cause.

In contrast, there was a connection between the claim for damages presented by way of constitution of *partie civile* before the Belgian criminal court against the perpetrator of the harmful event and the claim for compensation for damage brought in the Luxembourg civil court by way of direct action against his insurer, as the two claims had the same object. Accordingly, Art. 21 was inapplicable, but Art. 22, not requiring same parties, could apply.

ARTICLE 24

" . . . *such provisional, including protective, measures* . . . "

Case principle

1. Article 24 includes proceedings concerning validity of an attachment as well as its imposition.

Case

658 SMAC v Thielen, Pasicrisie 25, p. 134 Court of Appeal, 26 September 1980

Facts

Thielen sued the SMAC company, located in France, in the Tribunal d'arrondissement of Luxembourg for the payment of a certain sum due as expenses arising from the execution of a mandate and for the validation of an attachment. SMAC pleaded lack of jurisdiction of the Luxembourg courts to judge the claim.

Judgment

After having ascertained that the Luxembourg courts did not have jurisdiction over the substantive claim for payment, the court held that the judge did, however, have jurisdiction to authorize an attachment against a debtor domiciled abroad and to secure a contractual obligation which was outside its substantive jurisdiction. That jurisdiction was considered as extending to the action for the validity of the attachment, since that action was part of the procedure of the attachment. The rule of jurisdiction stated in Art. 24 of the Convention prevailed over the internal law of Luxembourg, with the effect that Art. 567 of the Code of Civil Procedure did not apply, as it provided that the creditor had to make his claim relating to validity of the attachment in the courts of the domicile of the party whose assets were seized.

Comment

This decision has been cited on various occasions, by the courts of first instance (*cf.* Tribunal d'arrondissement of Luxembourg, 13 July 1988, 380/88; 30 November 1988, 568/88 and 2 December 1992, 768/92).

Case principle

2.   If an application for provisional measures requires a certain level of proof of the substantive case at national law, the former may fall outside Art. 24.

Case

Ruckert v Karmann 12898 Court of Appeal, 26 November 1991   **659**

Facts

See *supra*, Case 644.

Under a contract for services, Karmann, who lived in Germany, was engaged to repair the roof of Ruckert's house situated in Luxembourg. The latter sued Karmann in summary proceedings for payment of damages for defective performance of the contract. Karmann pleaded lack of Luxembourg jurisdiction. The plaintiff had, *inter alia*, utilized Art. 24 of the Convention.

Judgment

Article 24 of the Convention rigorously distinguished between provisional and protective measures on the one hand, and substance on the other, so that its application was excluded whenever the measure required from the judge was a measure which related to substance and which, therefore, could not be classified as a provisional or a protective measure in accordance with Art. 24. Thus, since Art. 807, para. 2 of the Code of Civil Procedure did not permit the judge in chambers to grant provisional payment to the creditor unless the existence of the obligation attached was not seriously opposable, that provision seemed, to that extent, to relate to the substance of the matter. It followed that a claim for provisional payment would not be classified as a provisional measure in accordance with Art. 24 and that it was consequently not governed by the rule of jurisdiction stated in that Article, but by Convention grounds applicable to substance instead.

> " . . . *courts of another Contracting State have jurisdiction* . . . "

Case principle

Article 24 provisional, protective jurisdiction even applies to exclusive Art. 16 proceedings.

Case

660 Van Elsken and Newman v Giquel 15583 Court of Appeal, 10 January 1996

Facts

See *supra*, Case 655

Giquel, the purchaser of a commercial site situated in Tenerife (Spain) and residing in Luxembourg, decided to terminate an agreement of sale concluded with Van Elsken and Newman, living in Belgium, and to request refund of the advanced amounts because the sale could not be carried out any more, as the sellers had transferred half of the immovable property to a third person. Giquel effected an attachment on the bank accounts of Van Elsken in Luxembourg.

Jurisdiction of the courts of Luxembourg was contested, in particular, in relation to Art. 16(1)(a).

Judgment

According to Art. 24 of the Convention, a court always had jurisdiction to take provisional or protective measures provided by the internal law, even where, in accordance with the Convention, courts of another Contracting State were to have had exclusive jurisdiction as to the substance of the matter.

> **ARTICLE 27(1)**
>
> " . . . *contrary to public policy* . . . "

Case principle

1. Public policy is to be interpreted restrictively. It does not apply to require refusal of recognition of a foreign judgment to which contentious procedural rules were applied incorrectly.

Case

Plewa v Graziani 8739 Court of Appeal, 14 May 1986   **661**

Facts

Plewa filed an appeal against a ruling of the President of the Tribunal d'arrondissement who had declared enforceable in Luxembourg a judgment of the criminal court of Grasse (France) which had found Plewa liable to pay the 'partie civile', Graziani, a certain sum as repayment of a bad cheque and damages. Plewa argued, in particular, that the judgment in question had been incorrectly classified as *inter partes*, despite the absence of the defendant, in application of Art. 410 of the Code of Criminal Procedure, a specific Article in French legislation, and that consequently the decision was contrary to the public policy of Luxembourg which required that a judgment which has been classified as being *inter partes* shall be a judgment given after hearing the parties or their representatives.

Judgment

The notion of public policy provided in the Convention was imprecise and had to be interpreted restrictively, since otherwise the Convention would lose an important part of its aim to maximize the circulation of judgments. Therefore, recognition of the decision of the French court, decided in accordance with French procedural rules for contentious proceedings in relation to a person validly served by a summons but who did not attend, was not contrary to the public policy of Luxembourg.

Case principle

2.   Public policy is international public policy, not purely internal of the recognition-State.

Case

Rey v Berteau 17052 Court of Appeal, 15 March 1995   **662**

Facts

Berteau requested recognition of a Belgian judgment which gave him retrospectively, on the day of attaining majority, maintenance from his parents. By invoking the principle of Luxembourg law according to which 'maintenance is not deferred' the appellant against enforcement argued that Berteau should surrender his maintenance, as the Belgian decision would otherwise violate the aforementioned principle of public policy of Luxembourg and should not be recognized.

Judgment

The principle is that where recognition is sought, essentially the question is whether the law applied to the substance by the judge of origin was compatible with international public policy. In this respect, the idea of re-establishing, under the cover of public policy, additional grounds of refusal of recognition and enforcement must immediately be rejected, because in the end it would be nothing but a re-examination of the substance of the matter. Therefore, the *exequatur* has to be granted, even when the law applied by the judge of origin is not the law which the judge where recognition is sought would have applied, nor equivalent. Since it is a question of giving effect in Luxembourg to rights acquired abroad, public policy will apply only with mitigated effect and should be less demanding than it would be if the application was to acquire these rights themselves in Luxembourg. It is not in the power of the enforcement-court to review the compatibility of the foreign judgment with the public policy of his country, but only to verify whether recognition and enforcement of that judgment are of such a nature as to attract public policy. It is not, therefore, the *internal* policy of the country where the judgment is invoked which is dealt with in Art. 27(1), but its *international* public policy, that is, all that concerns the essential laws of the administration of justice or the accomplishment of contractual obligations, *i.e.* all that is considered as essential to the established moral, political and economic policy. To have the *exequatur* refused, the judgment, in its result, will have to offend against those fundamental principles of the law applicable to international relations, at the moment when the judge is seised. In this case, the court concluded that the misunderstanding by the judge of origin of the principle 'maintenance is not deferred' did not offend against the international public policy of Luxembourg as the country where recognition was sought.

ARTICLE 27(2)

" . . . *document which instituted the proceedings . . .* "

Case principle

Document which instituted the proceedings is that which *initiates* the process leading to binding judgment.

Case

663 Schmit v Kreissparkasse Saarlouis 17675 Court of Appeal, 13 July 1995

Facts

The Kreissparkasse Saarlouis obtained enforcement of a warrant of enforcement (Vollstreckungsbescheid) delivered by a German Amtsgericht and which allowed the enforcement of an injunction to pay (Mahnbescheid) delivered by the same Amtsgericht.

On appeal, Schmit argued that the document which instituted the proceedings (the Mahnbescheid) had not been duly served in sufficient time.

Judgment

'Document which instituted the proceedings' meant every procedural
document destined to lead to the submission of the case to the judge and to
give rise to a judicial decision. The injunction to pay (Zahlungsbefehl or
Mahnbescheid of German law) was therefore a 'document which instituted the
proceedings' when its notification allowed the applicant to obtain, in case of
default of appearance of the defendant, a decision capable of being recognized
and executed according to the Convention. In contrast, the authorization
of enforcement (Vollstreckungsbescheid) did not fall within the concept of
'document which instituted the proceedings', even when, according to the
Convention, it is enforceable. Accordingly, the fact that the
Vollstreckungsbescheid mentioned that the Mahnbescheid had been served,
was not sufficient for the court to consider as fulfilled the conditions of Art.
27(2) in the absence of the Mahnbescheid itself from the file.

Comment

This decision followed two similar judgments of the same Court on 22 April
1992 (13247) and 22 March 1995 (16732).

> " . . . in sufficient time . . . "

Case principle

1. The notion of service 'in sufficient time' is for the enforcement-court to
    decide upon on independent Convention principles, not on those of
    national laws of judgment- or recognition-State.

Case

Sassalle v Comptagest 18710 Court of Appeal, 4 April 1996   **664**

Facts

Comptagest obtained enforcement of a ruling (injunction to pay) given by
a French court. On appeal, Sassalle argued that he had not known of the action
against him in France, so that he could not prepare his defence in a proper way.

Judgment

The need for notice 'in sufficient time' implies that the defendant has acknowledged the procedure started against him and has had sufficient time to prepare
his defence. The problem of ascertaining whether the defendant in default of
appearance was given the chance to know about the procedure in sufficient

time, has no meaning, at the risk of rendering illusory the particular protection of the defendant in default of appearance desired by the signatories of the Convention, unless, in the area of the procedure of *exequatur*, the control of regularity of the notification of the document which instituted the proceedings is submitted both to the judge of the State of origin and to the judge of the State addressed; and the judge addressed is bound neither by the laws applied by the judge of origin, nor by those in effect in the addressed state.

Comment

The same Court of Appeal gave a similar judgment where, in application of the same principles, it decided that it was superfluous to consult the authorities of the State of origin to know if, in accordance with their own law, a notification of the document which instituted the proceeding was in sufficient time (*cf. Boehm v Krause* 175596 Court of Appeal, 2 May 1996).

Case principle

2. A document instituting proceedings written in a foreign language held sufficient for defence when accompanied by translation.

Case

665 Koch v Danielle 7994 Court of Appeal, 13 March 1985

Facts

The Danielle company had requested and obtained enforcement of a Belgian judgment in default which had found Koch liable to pay the sum of 38 145 French francs.

On appeal against enforcement, Koch, a national of Luxembourg, argued that in his country of origin his rights to a defence had not been respected, in particular, because the writ, written in Flemish language, was incomprehensible to him.

Judgment

Since the writ in Flemish was accompanied by a French translation, the Luxembourg defendant was able effectively to prepare his defence.

ARTICLE 28, PARAGRAPH 1

" . . . *if it conflicts with the provisions of Sections 3, 4 or 5 of Title II . . .* "

Case principle

A judgment reached against a consumer defendant in the courts of a Contracting State other than that of his domicile in contravention of Art. 14, para. 2 must be refused recognition and enforcement.

Case

Weber v Eurocard, Pasicrisie 28, p. 157 Court of Appeal, 15 May 1991   **666**

Facts

See *infra*, Case 670.

Weber was held liable to refund Eurocard the amounts due for the use of two credit cards, one for private use and the other for professional use.

In the enforcement proceedings, a question was raised in relation to the jurisdiction of the court of origin over the claim concerning the credit card for private use.

Judgment

A dispute concerning the use of a credit card which *was made available for private use* and consequent upon advertising in Luxembourg was within the exclusive jurisdiction of the court where the defendant owner of the card was domiciled under Art. 14, para. 2, even when the latter worked as a business-man. A foreign judgment in conflict with these rules of jurisdiction was held not enforceable.

ARTICLE 28, PARAGRAPH 3

" . . . may not be reviewed . . . "

Case principle

The special protective rules of jurisdiction for Luxembourg domicilaries in annexed Protocol Art. I are *not* exceptions to the prohibition of jurisdictional review in Art. 28, para. 3.

Case

Europe Trade v Rinkfensterblock 14069 Court of Appeal, 3 February 1993   **667**

Facts

The Europe Trade company lodged an appeal against enforcement of a judgment of the Landgericht of Limburg/Lahn (RFA) in litigation with the German company Rinkfensterblock.

In support of its appeal, Europe Trade submitted that the German Landgericht should have declared itself *ex officio* to lack jurisdiction in accordance with paras 1 and 2 of Art. I of the Protocol annexed to the Brussels Convention, on the ground that the defendant was domiciled in Luxembourg and had not expressly and specifically agreed to the jurisdiction of the court of Limburg/Lahn.

Judgment

Article 28, para. 3 of the Brussels Convention decrees that jurisdiction of the court of the State of origin must not be reviewed by the courts of an addressed State, except in those limited cases when it applies to matters for which ss.3, 4 and 5 of Title II fix the rules of mandatory and exclusive jurisdiction. To prevent avoidance, that Article also states that, outside these limited cases, the rule of public policy referred to in Art. 27(1) should not be applied to jurisdiction. In other words, it is not allowed to verify, by recourse to public order of the State addressed, the jurisdiction of the judge of origin.

It follows that the enforcement-court may not refuse to order enforcement of a foreign judgment because the judge of origin may have violated Article I of the Protocol annexed to the Convention.

Comment

This case, which admits that control of the jurisdiction of the judge of origin by the judge addressed has been definitively suppressed by the Brussels Convention, may be qualified as 'courageous' to the extent that it is contrary to the interests of people domiciled in Luxembourg and is one of a line of judgments all to the same effect (*cf.* Court of Appeal, 5 March 1974, Pasicrisie 22 p. 425; Court of Appeal, 11 November 1975, Pasicrisie 23 p. 230; Court of Appeal, 30 March 1988, 9963; Court of Appeal, 3 July 1985, 7747; Court of Appeal, 30 March 1988, 9963; in the same sense *cf.* once again Court of Appeal, 22 March 1995, 16732).

ARTICLE 31, PARAGRAPH 1

" . . . enforceable in that State . . . "

Case principle

For enforcement, the foreign judgment must still be enforceable in the judgment-State at the time of enforcement(-appeal) proceedings in the enforcement-State.

Case

668 Verhoestraete v Kempische Verzekeringsmakelaars 16336 Court of Appeal, 13 July 1995

Facts

The Kempische Verzekeringsmakelaars company obtained enforcement of a Belgian judgment reached in default of appearance against Verhoestraete, for payment of a certain sum of money.

On appeal against enforcement, Verhoestraete argued that the judgment had lost its enforceability in Belgium, because it had lapsed.

Judgment

Article 31 of the Convention establishes that the foreign decision must be enforceable in the country where it was made, a condition which is sufficient even if it is still open to an appeal. The *exequatur* has to be refused if the judgment has lost its enforceable character in that country owing to its expiration.

ARTICLE 34, PARAGRAPH 3

"Under no circumstances may the foreign judgment be reviewed as to its substance."

Case principle

Proof of payment of a debt ordered cannot be adduced on appeal against enforcement.

Case

Grazzioli v Farago, Pasicrisie 28, p. 146 Court of Appeal, 20 February 1991   **669**

Facts

Grazzioli appealed against enforcement of a German judgment which ordered him to pay Farago a certain sum of money. In support of his appeal, Grazzioli contested the existence of the debt invoked by Farago, stating that he had paid the sum claimed.

Judgment

The defence was rejected, because, in accordance with Art. 34, para. 3 of the Brussels Convention, the foreign judgment may not be reviewed as to its substance.

Comment

The following cases may be cited to the same effect: Court of Appeal, 3 June 1987, 9680 and 22 March 1995, 16732. The same principle has allowed the

Court of Appeal to exclude appeals based on the *exceptio non adimpleti contractus* (*cf.* Court of Appeal, 3 February 1993, 14069).

ARTICLE 42, PARAGRAPH 1

" . . . *given in respect of several matters* . . . "

Case principle

Partial enforcement is not available where recognizable and non-recognizable parts of the foreign judgment are *not severable.*

Case

670   Weber v Eurocard, Pasicrisie 28, p. 157 Court of Appeal, 15 May 1991

Facts

See *supra*, Case 666.

Weber had been ordered by a court to repay Eurocard the amount due for the use of two credit cards, one for private use and the other for professional use.

In the enforcement proceedings, the Luxembourg court decided (under Art. 28, para. 1), on the one hand, that the Belgian courts did not have jurisdiction over the card for private use, and, on the other hand, that the Belgian courts were to be taken to have possessed jurisdiction in relation to the card for professional use. The question of a partial enforcement was, therefore, in issue in Luxembourg.

Judgment

Partial enforcement of a foreign judgment implies several heads of claim and likewise elements of judgment. Consequently, it is not possible if the judgment has a global and inseparable character.

ARTICLE 50, PARAGRAPH 1

" . . . *enforceable in one Contracting State* . . . "

Case principle

It is not a condition of its enforcement that the authentic instrument is valid under the law of the State of origin.

Case

Lindner v Tillman 12720 Court of Appeal, 25 November 1992   **671**

Facts

On an application by Tillman, the Luxembourg courts declared enforceable in
the Grand Duchy a contract of sale notarized by a German notary and concluded between Tillman as the seller and Lindner as the buyer.

On appeal, Lindner submitted that Tillman had unilaterally terminated the
sale, thereby depriving it of its enforceability.

Judgment

Enforcement of an authentic foreign instrument does not depend upon its
validity, as Art. 50, para. 1 of the Brussels Convention does not require the
judicial act to be valid. The reason is that validity or nullity of the document
is a question relating to its substance which is a matter for the judgment-court.

ANNEXED PROTOCOL ARTICLE I, PARAGRAPH 2

" . . . expressly and specifically . . . agreed."

Case principle

Express and specific agreement of a party domiciled in Luxembourg requires
a separate clause, signed by that party (*Porta-Leasing*, Case 784/79 applied).

Case

ENI-Verbeeck v Comat, Conter and Cie. 4677 Court of Appeal, 26 November   **672**
1980

Facts

Comat, Conter and Cie sued ENI and Verbeeck in the Tribunal d'arrondissement of Luxembourg for the payment of a certain sum. The defendants argued
that the court did not have jurisdiction, because of a contractual clause conferring exclusive jurisdiction on Belgian courts.

It was known that the agreement signed between the parties, concerning the
location of a concrete-pump, stated in Dutch that the order was made under
the general conditions of the defendant companies. On the back of this written document there was a clause in Dutch conferring exclusive jurisdiction
upon the courts of Anvers in Belgium. In an addendum, which was an integral
part of the contract, written in French, once again there was a reference to the
general conditions of the defendants, but this was only in a particular section
concerning the installation of the rented material.

Judgment

Even if, in principle, on the basis of Art. 17 of the Brussels Convention, jurisdiction agreed between the parties had to be either in writing or in an oral agreement evidenced in writing, it seemed, however, indispensable to the authors of the Convention that, having regard to the fact that various contracts made by people living in the Grand Duchy of Luxembourg were international contracts, clauses giving jurisdiction over people living in Luxembourg should be subjected to even more rigorous conditions than those in Art. 17.

For this reason, Art. I, para. 2 of the Protocol annexed to the Convention of 27 September 1986, provides that an agreement conferring jurisdiction shall not have effect in relation to a person domiciled in Luxembourg, unless this person has 'expressly and specifically' agreed to it. These special conditions are in addition to those already provided for in Art. 17 of the Convention.

This provision has to be interpreted in the sense that a clause conferring jurisdiction shall not be considered as expressly and specifically accepted by a person domiciled in Luxembourg unless, besides the written form required by Art. 17 of the Convention, that clause is contained in a section which is particularly and expressly related to it and which has been especially signed by the party domiciled in Luxembourg—the signature of the whole contract not being enough for these purposes. It may not, however, be necessary for that clause to be mentioned in a document *distinct* from that which is the 'instrumentum' of the contract.

In this case, the choice of jurisdiction appearing in the general conditions, to which both the contract and the inserted addendum referred, did not comply with the requirements of Art. I, para. 2 of the Protocol, since its acceptance was not the object of a provision which was particularly and exclusively devoted to it and which had been especially signed by the party domiciled in Luxembourg.

Comment

This judgment is in accordance with the European Court's decision in *Porta-Leasing* Case 784/79 of 6 May 1980.

Similar judgments of the Court of Appeal were 12 June 1985 (7625) and 15 May 1991 (Pasicrisie 28, p. 157).

The Tribunal d'arrondissement of Luxembourg has added in a judgment of 2 February 1988 (60/88) that mere silence following the receipt of a written order on the back of which there is a written clause giving jurisdiction together with a number of other clauses, is not proof of expressed and specific agreement.

13

THE NETHERLANDS

Professor Maurice V. Polak and Lilian F.A. Steffens*

A.   LEGAL SYSTEM

Courts

Adjudication of civil and commercial matters in The Netherlands is entrusted to the 'ordinary' judiciary. The relevant Act on Judicial Organization calls for a four-tier system: the *Kantonrechter* or Justice of the Peace (of which there are 61), the *Arrondissementsrechtbank* or District Court (of which there are 19), the *Gerechtshof* or Court of Appeal (in Amsterdam, Arnhem, 's-Gravenhage, 's-Hertogenbosch and Leeuwarden) and the *Hoge Raad* or Supreme Court (in 's-Gravenhage).

The Justice of the Peace has competence in civil cases if the claim is for less than 5000 DFL. In employment disputes, for claims based on individual labour contracts or collective agreements, and some other areas, the Justice of the Peace has competence irrespective of the amount claimed. The Justice of the Peace also has competence in various non-contentious proceedings. Appeal from decisions rendered by the Justice of the Peace is usually possible in claims for more than 2500 DFL and must be brought before the District Court. For

*Maurice V. Polak, LL.B. Leiden '83, LL.M. Columbia '84, LL.D. Leiden '88, is Professor of Private International and Comparative Law, Leiden University. Lilian F.A. Steffens, LL.B. Amsterdam '92, LL.D. Leiden '97, is an Attorney-at-law at Loeff Claeys Verbeke, Amsterdam. The first author wrote the introductory remarks and documented the cases on Arts 17 *et seq*. The second author dealt with the case law on Arts 1 to 16 and 24. Both authors gratefully acknowledge the helping (collecting) hand of Pepijn P.J. van Ginneken, LL.B. Leiden '95, Attorney-at-law, De Brauw Blackstone Westbroek, Amsterdam. The manuscript for this contribution was completed in December 1996.

decisions not subject to such ordinary appeal, appeal in cassation to the Hoge Raad is limited.

The District Court is the basic court of first instance for contentious and non-contentious proceedings, provided no other court has special competence. The District Court is also the appellate court against judgments given by the Justice of the Peace. A District Court's decision at first instance is generally subject to appeal to the Court of Appeal. The President of the District Court has competence to issue provisional and protective measures in summary proceedings, which do not prejudice the principal dispute. The President's decisions in summary proceedings are also subject to appeal to the Court of Appeal. Moreover, the President of the District Court is the authority charged, pursuant to Art. 32(1) of the Brussels and Lugano Conventions, with the authorization of a judgment's enforcement. According to Art. 37(1) of both Conventions, the District Court hears appeals against the President's decisions authorizing enforcement.

The Court of Appeal is the appellate institution for judgments delivered by the District Court and has a limited first instance competence of its own. The Court of Appeal is the highest court dealing with factual questions; in general no further appeal on a question of fact is possible. The Court of Appeal is also the court which, pursuant to Art. 40(1) of the Brussels and Lugano Conventions, decides on appeal against the President of the District Court's refusal to authorize a judgment's enforcement.

The Hoge Raad is the highest court in The Netherlands for, *inter alia*, civil and commercial cases. It deals exclusively with questions of law, taking factual issues as they have been established by the lower courts. The Hoge Raad can only rescind a lower court's decision if it is incompatible with formalities, amongst which the formality that a decision be reasoned ranks as number one, or if it is incompatible with 'the law'. The latter concept covers both statutory and non-statutory Dutch law, whereby public and private international law—whether or not contained in conventions—is also considered Dutch law. However, the law of foreign States is expressly excluded. The Hoge Raad is the court mentioned in Arts 37(2) and 41 of the Brussels and Lugano Conventions, dealing with the appeal in cassation against certain decisions given by the lower courts in the framework of both Conventions.

The Act on Judicial Organization is currently being revised. One of the major changes proposed is the integration of the Justice of the Peace and the District Court into a new and general Court of First Instance. This integration has been severely criticised and, subsequently, postponed in the course of 1997. At later stages, changes relating to appeal and to appeal in cassation are to be expected.

B.   IMPLEMENTATION OF THE CONVENTIONS

The Brussels Convention of 1968 entered into force for The Netherlands on 1 February 1973. The entry into force for The Netherlands of the First, Second and Third Accession Conventions took place on 1 November 1986, 1 April 1989 and 1 February 1991, respectively.

The Brussels Convention, as amended, is in The Netherlands accompanied by implementing legislation. The relevant Act of 4 May 1972, published in (1972) *Staatsblad* 240, has been amended twice: by Act of 14 September 1978, published in (1978) *Staatsblad* 468, and by Act of 25 October 1989, published in (1989) *Staatsblad* 490. The Act, as amended, only contains 10 provisions, providing additional rules on the procedural aspects of the enforcement of foreign judgments pursuant to Arts 31 *et seq.* of the Brussels Convention.

The Lugano Convention of 1988 entered into force for The Netherlands on 1 January 1992. In The Netherlands, the Lugano Convention is also accompanied by implementing legislation. The relevant Act of 26 March 1992, published in (1992) *Staatsblad* 141, contains one provision, stipulating that the Act implementing the Brussels Convention also covers the procedural aspects of the enforcement of foreign judgments pursuant to Arts 31 *et seq.* of the Lugano Convention.

C. OVERVIEW OF CONVENTION CASE LAW

The cases selected for this contribution are just a fraction of the total amount of reported case law on the Brussels and Lugano Conventions. However, the authors believe that their selection will be interesting for foreign lawyers. Their selection contains, on the one hand, cases which provide a succinct account of the prevailing trends in the Dutch case law, and, on the other hand, cases which are interesting precisely because they deviate from these prevailing trends. The selection concentrates on the more recent years and does not contain cases which are clearly 'outdated' in view either of more recent decisions of the European Court of Justice or of later amendments to the text of the Brussels Convention.

Abbreviations

In the references to the cases, the court reports are abbreviated as follows:

ECR	European Court Reports
KG	Kort Geding (cited to case number)
NILR	Netherlands International Law Review
NIPR	Nederlands International Privaatrecht (cited to case number)
NJ	Nederlandse Jurisprudentie (cited to case number)
RvdW	Rechtspraak van de Week (cited to case number)
S&S	Schip en Schade (cited to case number)

D. CASES

ARTICLE 1, PARAGRAPH 2(1)

" . . . *rights in property arising out of a matrimonial relationship* . . . "

Case principle

1. The decisions of a Belgian court determining the amount one spouse has to pay to the other as his or her share in the costs of the common household cannot be enforced under the Brussels Convention as it falls outside the substantive scope of the Convention as defined in Art. 1. This duty flows directly from the marital bond and thus falls under the exclusion in Art. 1, para. 2(1).

Case

673   X v Y, (1980) NJ 515, District Court of 's-Hertogenbosch, 4 January 1980

Facts

X, domiciled in Belgium, applied to the District Court, for the enforcement—within the meaning of Art. 31 of the Brussels Convention—of a decision of a Belgian court, in which Y had been ordered to: (i) pay a sum of 30,087 Belgian francs to X, by way of contribution to the costs of the common household, and (ii) half of the costs of the proceedings before the Belgian court.

Judgment

The District Court held that the judgment of a Belgian court determining the amount one spouse has to pay to the other as his or her share in the costs of the common household cannot be enforced under the Brussels Convention as it falls outside the substantive scope of the Convention as defined in Art. 1. This duty flows directly from the marital relation between parties and thus falls under the exclusion in Art. 1, para. 2(1).

Comment

Presumably, the District Court did not characterize the contribution to the costs of the common household as an issue of *maintenance*, as referred to in Art. 5(2), which *would* be covered by the Brussels Convention.

Case principle

2. Not all disputes relating to property between (former) spouses fall outside the substantive scope of the Brussels Convention. The facts of the case and the questions put before the court are decisive.

Case

X v Y, (1981) NJ 555, Court of Appeal of Amsterdam, 29 May 1981, *revers-*   **674**
ing District Court of Amsterdam

Facts

A dispute arose between former spouses, who had been married under the separate estate arrangement, concerning immovable property situated in France.
The spouses had acquired this immovable property in joint-ownership during
their marriage. The question was whether this immovable property should,
pursuant to the wishes of one of the joint-owners, be sold publicly, even
against the wishes of the other joint-owner. The Court of Appeal, in order to
determine whether the Dutch courts had jurisdiction, had to decide whether
this matter fell within the substantive scope of the Brussels Convention.

Judgment

The Court of Appeal held: 'This matter can be considered to be a civil matter
within the meaning of Art. 1(1). Considering that the dispute has no connection with the marriage or matrimonial property regime of the parties, but only
with their joint purchase of the immovable property, the applicability of the
Brussels Convention is not excluded pursuant to Art. 1, para. 2(1). Pursuant
to Art. 16, the French courts have exclusive jurisdiction as the courts of the
place where the immovable property is situated.'

Case principle

3. Where a claim of a spouse against the other spouse is based on the
    alleged ownership of certain property, it does not concern a matter of
    matrimonial property law, but a matter of ordinary property law and is
    thus not excluded from the Convention's substantive scope pursuant to
    Art. 1, para. 2(1).

Case

X v Y, (1988) NIPR 510, District Court of Alkmaar, 8 September 1988   **675**

Facts

Parties of Moroccan nationality and domiciled in The Netherlands, married
on 23 March 1976 in Amsterdam. By judgment of the District Court of
Alkmaar of 27 November 1986, they were divorced. During their marriage the
parties had a joint household, to which both made financial contributions. In
November 1985, when the parties were still living together, a fire broke out in
the marital home in Alkmaar, in which the household goods were damaged.
The property concerned was insured against damage by fire by the Dutch
insurance company Nationale Nederlanden. In connection with the fire,
Nationale Nederlanden paid damages in the amount of 14687 Dfl, which was

paid to the husband. In these proceedings, the wife claimed payment of half of the said amount from her former husband, alleging that she owned half of the property damaged by the fire.

Judgment

The District Court held: 'The Court is of the opinion that the claim for the payment of insurance money paid because of damage to household goods cannot be qualified as a matter of matrimonial property law. As the claim is based on the ownership rights, which the wife allegedly possessed when the harmful event occurred, it should be qualified as a matter of ordinary property law. This leads to the conclusion that the matter in dispute falls within the substantive scope of the Brussels Convention.'

ARTICLE 2

" . . . domiciled in a Contracting State . . . "

Case principle

Domicile is the sole criterion for the determination of jurisdiction under Art. 2 of the Brussels Convention: actual residence is irrelevant.

Case

676 Klaassen v Driessen, (1977) NJ 480, District Court of Roermond, 15 April 1976, *reversing* Justice of the Peace of Venlo, 20 August 1974

Translation taken from: 23 NILR 357 (1976), note Verheul.

Facts

In 1972 and 1973, Driessen was employed as a factory worker in Klaassen's factory in Grefrath (West Germany). Driessen's action for payment of 1404 Dfl, by way of statutory minimum holiday pay, based on Dutch mandatory statutory provisions, was allowed by the Justice of the Peace Venlo. On appeal, Klaassen produced certified copies of entries in the civil registers of Venlo (The Netherlands) and Issum (West Germany), showing that, as from 1962, he was registered as domiciled in Issum, where, moreover, he owned a house in the neighbourhood of the factory. The heirs of Driessen (who had died in the meantime) alleged that Klaassen had his actual residence in The Netherlands, so that the Justice of the Peace had jurisdiction under Art. 126(2) of the Code of Civil Procedure, stipulating: 'The defendant who has no known domicile in the Kingdom shall be sued before the court of his actual residence.'

Judgment

The District Court held: 'According to German law—decisive on this point—the said circumstances clearly show that Klaassen was domiciled in Issum-Sevelen, West Germany. A possible actual residence in The Netherlands is irrelevant, as the self-executing jurisdiction provisions of the Brussels Convention use domicile as the sole criterion, which, as appears from the Jenard Report, was adopted consciously.'

Jurisdiction on the ground of Art. 5(1) was rejected, because the obligation in question had to be performed in Germany. Art. 18 did not provide a basis either, because Klaassen had appeared before the court solely to contest jurisdiction.

The judgment of the Justice of the Peace was reversed, and it was held that no jurisdiction existed.

> **ARTICLE 5(1)**
>
> " . . . *obligation in question* . . . "

Case principle

1. The 'obligation in question' is the obligation on the breach of which the claim is based.

Case

Souer v Roba Music Verlag, (1986) NIPR 487, District Court of Amsterdam, **677** 2 April 1986

Facts

On 23 November 1979, Souer entered into a written agreement with Roba, in which Souer committed himself to grant to Roba the exclusive publication rights of all the compositions and texts which he would make from 1 January 1980 to 31 December 1982. The agreement contained a choice of Dutch law and a choice of forum for the court in Amsterdam. In September 1982, Souer and Roba talked about the continuation of their agreement after 31 December 1982, and Souer received a written confirmation of the result of these talks on 8 October 1982. Subsequently, both parties negotiated the text of a written contract and sent each other draft contracts. Souer assigned the copyrights he had on compositions written by him, after 1 January 1983 to Roba, under the condition 'only valid when contract is signed and validated'. In the course of 1984, the negotiations were terminated.

Souer primarily claimed rescission of the contract, which, according to him, had been made, plus damages, and alternatively, damages for the wrongful termination of the negotiations. Roba contested the jurisdiction of the court. The District Court of Amsterdam assumed jurisdiction and found for the defendant Roba.

Judgment

The District Court held, in determining the question of jurisdiction, that an investigation had to be held concerning the question of whether a contract had been made between the parties.

In accordance with Dutch private international law, the question whether a contract existed was to be answered by the law applicable to the contract, in the event that it did indeed exist. This was Dutch law.

In support of his position that a contract had been concluded, Souer referred to the letter of 8 October 1982. From the fact that the letter existed, the District Court concluded that there were, in accordance with *Effer v Kantner*, Case 38/81, convincing and relevant circumstances from which to conclude that a contract had been made.

On the question whether the District Court had jurisdiction in this matter, it assumed the existence of a contract. Souer based his claim on the breach of just one obligation. That was the obligation to pay. Pursuant to Art. 5(1), the court of the place of performance of the obligation to pay had jurisdiction, and not, as Roba had argued, the place of performance of the obligation characterizing the contract.

The District Court assumed jurisdiction on the basis of Art. 5(1).

Comment

For determining whether the District Court had jurisdiction, the court first construed the existence of a contract in order for Art. 5(1) to be applicable. The existence of the contract was 'construed', because, on appeal of the main issue—the claim for damages—the Court of Appeal Amsterdam, 1 February 1990, (1990) NIPR 453 (*reversing* District Court of Amsterdam, 10 February 1988) found for Souer concerning the alternative claim—damages for the wrongful termination of negotiations by Roba. This meant that Souer was entitled to damages concerning an action *in the pre-contractual phase*. The question was whether this obligation arose out of contract and thus fell under Art. 5(1)—the obligation in question then being the obligation of Roba to continue the negotiations—or whether the termination was a tort, in which case the jurisdiction should be based on Art. 5(3). The Court of Appeal, however, did not get the chance to review the matter of jurisdiction.

A second comment concerns the way in which the District Court determined the place of performance. Apparently it applied Dutch law—which according to the court was the applicable law—as the obligation to pay had, pursuant to Dutch law (Art. 1429 old Civil Code, Art. 116, Book 6 New Civil Code), to be performed at the place of business of the creditor.

Case

Letex Sylvia v Mégisserie Jean Martin Estrabaud, (1988) NJ 31, Court of **678**
Appeal of 's-Hertogenbosch, 12 December 1986, *affirming* District Court
of Breda, 10 January 1984

Facts

In 1982, Letex entered into two contracts, through an agent, with Estrabaud
concerning the sale of two bulks of leather to Letex by Estrabaud. The clause
'franco frontière française' was included in both contracts.

Letex alleged that delivery of the leather was late and that the quality of the
leather left a lot to be desired. Letex claimed damages and restitution of the
purchase price. Estrabaud contested the jurisdiction of the court.

The District Court of Breda declined jurisdiction, stating that the obligation
in question was the obligation of Estrabaud to deliver the goods and not, as
Letex claimed, the obligation to pay damages and pay back the purchase-
money. Letex appealed.

Judgment

The Court of Appeal held: 'Letex claims that pursuant to Art. 5(1) the Dutch
courts have jurisdiction, considering the fact that the claim concerns an obligation relating to contract which has to be performed in The Netherlands.'

This last point of view cannot be accepted. The obligation meant in Art. 5(1)
is the obligation in dispute. In this case that was the obligation to deliver.

Because the sale was Franco-French-border, the delivery had to take place in
France. The clause Franco-French-border did not just include a regulation concerning the costs of transport but also a stipulation for delivery. Thus, the
obligation in question had, by stipulation, to be performed in France.

The Court of Appeal confirmed the judgment of the District Court.

Comment

These judgments are in accordance with European Court of Justice's decisions
in *De Bloos v Bouyer* Case 14/76 and *Shenavai v Kreischer* Case 266/85.

Case principle

2. When the claim for damages is based on the non-performance of the
    obligation to provide a ship for transport, the 'obligation in question' for
    Art. 5(1) may consist of the obligation to carry and deliver the goods to
    the port of destination.

Case

Italmare Shipping v Verenigde Pharmaceutische Fabrieken, (1982) NJ 22, note **679**
Schultsz, (1981) S&S 99 Hoge Raad, 12 June 1981, *affirming* Court of Appeal
of 's-Gravenhage, *affirming* District Court of Rotterdam.

Translation taken from: 30 NILR 251 (1983), note Verheul.

Facts

The Verenigde Pharmaceutische Fabrieken (VPF), a company incorporated in The Netherlands, chartered the ship Calypso N for the carriage of poppies from Calcutta to Rotterdam, from the Italian company Italmare Shipping. In the charter, VPF stipulated its right to annul the agreement if the ship was not ready on time. In fact, it was not, and VPF sued for damages against Italmare for substitute transport. The writ of summons specified that the non-performance consisted of the fact that Italmare had not placed the ship at VPF's disposal on time in Calcutta.

Italmare contested the jurisdiction of the Dutch courts. The District Court assumed jurisdiction on the basis of Art. 5(1), as did the Court of Appeal. Italmare appealed to the Hoge Raad.

Judgment

The Hoge Raad noted that the Court of Appeal had interpreted the writ of summons as dealing with the non-performance by Italmare of two obligations, namely: (i) the obligation to have the ship available at the agreed place and time; and (ii) the obligation to carry the goods to the agreed place of destination and to deliver them there.

According to the Hoge Raad, the Court of Appeal had understood the interrelation between both non-performances in the sense that the carrier must be deemed also to be in breach of his obligation to carry and to deliver. Starting from this premise, the Court of Appeal, notwithstanding Art. 458 of the Code of Commerce, could correctly conclude that the claim was based on the non-performance of the obligation to carry.

The charter being governed by Dutch law—in the opinion of the parties and the Court of Appeal—the Supreme Court held the Court of Appeal's statement, that the place where this obligation should be performed was the place of destination, to be correct.

Comment

To read the 'obligation to carry' into the 'obligation to provide for a ship at the agreed time and place', is possible, provided that the company from which the ship is chartered can also be regarded as the carrier of the goods. Of course, this is not necessarily always the case.

Case principle

3. In cases concerning agency contracts where the principal has terminated the contract unilaterally and the agent claims damages, the obligation in question within the meaning of Art. 5(1) is the obligation of the principal to observe a term of notice and during that time to allow the agent to do his work, without any infringement on the part of the principal.

Case

Readicut v Hendriks, (1988) NIPR 187, Court of Appeal of Amsterdam,   **680**
24 September 1987, *affirming* District Court of Amsterdam, 8 January 1986

Facts

On 1 May 1970, the French company Readicut, as principal, and Hendrix, as
agent, entered into an agency contract for a period ending on 31 March 1973.
The contract was, however, implicitly continued after this date. Then, in a
letter dated 6 May 1983, Readicut rescinded the contract as from 30 June 1983,
without Hendrix's approval, and opened a branch in The Netherlands to take
over Hendrix's work. Hendrix claimed, *inter alia*, damages and compensation
for goodwill. Readicut contested the jurisdiction of the court. The District Court
assumed jurisdiction and found for the plaintiff. Readicut appealed.

Judgment

The Court of Appeal held: 'As Hendrix has based his claim on the non-
performance of the agency contract entered into by Readicut and himself, it
concerns matters relating to contract, within the meaning of Art. 5(1).

Hendrix's claim is based on the non-performance by Readicut of obligations
arising out of the agency contract.

To determine whether the District Court can assume jurisdiction pursuant
to Art. 5(1) concerning the claim for damages, the obligation in question is the
obligation arising out of the agency contract of which the non-performance
justifies the claim.

That obligation consists of the duty of Readicut to allow Hendrix, in conformity with the agreed term of notice, to work in The Netherlands, and to
refrain from opening a branch during that term. The place of performance of
that obligation is The Netherlands, so that the court of the place of domicile
of Hendrix has jurisdiction concerning the claim for damages.'

In connection with the other claim—compensation for goodwill—the Court
of Appeal was of the opinion that the obligation of Readicut as stated above
could be considered to be the *principal* obligation. The claim for compensation
for goodwill could be considered to flow directly from the non-performance of
the principal obligation, so that the District Court also had jurisdiction concerning the claim for compensation for goodwill.

Case principle

4.   The obligation in question, where a concession-holder claims damages for
      breach of the concession-agreement, is the main obligation arising from
      that concession-agreement for the concession-grantor, namely, to allow the
      concession-holder, to the exclusion of all others, to sell and distribute goods
      in the State to which the concession applies, for as long as the concession-
      agreement has not been terminated in accordance with the law. According
      to Dutch law, if the concession-holder is incorporated in the State to which

the concession applies, this obligation has to be performed in that State. Pursuant to Art. 5(1), the courts of that State then have jurisdiction.

Case

681   Häcker Küchen v Bosma, (1991) NJ 676, note Schultsz, Hoge Raad, 24 May 1991, *affirming* Court of Appeal of Leeuwarden, 3 May 1989, (1989) NIPR 466, *reversing* District Court of Assen, 16 April 1985

Facts

In this case, the Dutch company Bosma claimed damages from the German company Häcker, for breach of contract, claiming that the Dutch court had jurisdiction pursuant to Art. 5(1). In support of this, Bosma submitted that Häcker had entered into a contract with Bosma on 22 February 1972, under which Häcker granted Bosma the sole-import and sole-sales right in The Netherlands of Häcker's goods. The parties agreed that the contract should be characterized as a concession-agreement. The resulting relationship between the parties continued to exist until its unilateral termination by Häcker, who then started to distribute its goods via other intermediaries. Häcker contested the jurisdiction of the Dutch courts, submitting that the obligation in question did not have to be performed in The Netherlands, so that jurisdiction could not be based on Art. 5(1). The District Court of Assen found for Häcker and declined jurisdiction. Bosma appealed and the Court of Appeal of Leeuwarden found for Bosma in deciding that the District Court did have jurisdiction pursuant to Art. 5(1). Häcker appealed to the Hoge Raad.

Judgment

The Hoge Raad held: 'The Court of Appeal has inquired: (1) on which obligation or obligations Bosma bases its claim for damages, (2) which law, pursuant to Dutch private international law, is applicable to the concession-agreement and (3) what, according to the applicable law, is the place of performance of the obligations referred to under (1)?

The Court of Appeal first of all held that there was a three-fold breach by Häcker on which Bosma based its claim. Bosma claimed damages because: Häcker had unilaterally terminated the contract; was selling its goods in The Netherlands through other intermediaries; and refused to sell and deliver the goods to Bosma.

The Court of Appeal, by listing (just) two obligations, on which the claim was based and which Häcker should have performed, only wished to express the fact that these were connected obligations, of which the two listed by the Court of Appeal determined the nature and gravity of the alleged breach. It may be concluded that the Court of Appeal intended to hold that the obligation on which Bosma had based its claim, was the principal obligation arising from the concession-agreement, namely, the obligation to allow Bosma, to the exclusion of all others, to sell and distribute Häcker's goods in The

Netherlands, for as long as the concession-agreement had not been terminated in accordance with the law (that is to say, by observing the term of notice and on legally valid grounds).

This was also the obligation on which Bosma based its claim: "the obligation arising from the said contract, namely to allow, guarantee and continue the concession"'.

Both the Court of Appeal and the Hoge Raad came to the conclusion that Dutch law determined the place of performance of the obligation in question, this being the law applicable to the concession-agreement in accordance with Dutch private international law.

The Court of Appeal correctly established that pursuant to Dutch law, Häcker's obligation to allow Bosma, to the exclusion of all others, to sell and distribute Häcker's goods in The Netherlands, for as long as the concession-agreement has not been terminated in accordance with the law, had to be performed in The Netherlands.

The Court of Appeal had thus correctly assumed that where the concession-holder was incorporated in the State to which the concession applied, the main obligation arising from the concession-agreement for the concession-grantor had to be performed in that State.

Case

Isopad v Huikeshoven, (1992) NJ 422, note Schultsz, Hoge Raad, 1 **682** November 1991, *affirming* Court of Appeal of Arnhem, 7 November 1989, *affirming* District Court of Arnhem, 24 November 1988

Translation taken from: 40 NILR 241 (1993), note Pellis.

Facts

Huikeshoven, incorporated in The Netherlands, entered into an outline contract with Isopad, incorporated in the UK, in 1962. In that contract, it was agreed that Huikeshoven and Isopad were to work together in selling apparatus produced by Isopad in England, in the sales territory of The Netherlands. The agreement contained a term of notice of three months.

Isopad terminated the outline contract unilaterally on 7 September 1987, taking effect immediately. Huikeshoven claimed damages for the alleged wrongful termination of the outline contract by Isopad, the latter not having respected the agreed term of notice, plus compensation for the clientele with which Huikeshoven had provided Isopad.

Isopad contested the jurisdiction of the District Court of Arnhem. The District Court, however, assumed jurisdiction on the basis of Art. 5(1). It took the view that under Dutch law, applicable to the outline contract, the obligation of Isopad to respect a reasonable term of notice had to be performed in The Netherlands. Isopad appealed, but the Court of Appeal affirmed the judgment, stating that the obligation in question within the meaning of Art. 5(1), was the obligation of Isopad to continue the outline contract during the term of notice. Isopad appealed to the Hoge Raad.

Judgment

The Hoge Raad held: 'The unlawful manner of termination of the outline contract by Isopad must be seen as the basis of Huikeshoven's claim, in respect of which the jurisdiction of the Dutch courts has to be examined.

The judgment of the Court of Appeal must be understood in the sense that the obligation in question is the obligation arising out of the outline contract for Isopad to continue the contract during the term of notice, and that the breach of that obligation by Isopad forms the justification of Huikeshoven's claim for damages.

The judgment was a correct application of Art. 5(1).

According to the Court of Appeal, the termination of the contract takes effect in The Netherlands and, moreover, Huikeshoven was incorporated in The Netherlands, "so that the declaration of the termination by Isopad had to be received there". The judgment of the Court of Appeal amounted to the following: according to Dutch law, applicable to the outline contract, the obligation in question—to continue the contract during the term of notice—had to be performed in The Netherlands.

Isopad contended that the obligation in question was the obligation not to terminate the contract otherwise than in a lawful manner, which was an obligation to refrain from doing something and could not be located.

The Court of Appeal, however, made clear that the obligation in question within the meaning of Art. 5(1), was the obligation of Isopad to continue the outline contract during the lawfully agreed term of notice.'

The Hoge Raad rejected the appeal against the judgment of the Court of Appeal of Arnhem.

> " . . . *place of performance* . . . "

Case principle

1. Place of performance is determined by reference to the private international law of the court seised.

Case

683 Algemene Verzekeringsmaatschappij Diligentia van 1890 v Transport Dubois, (1990) NIPR 508, District Court of Haarlem, 22 May 1990

Facts

Dubois, incorporated in France, had been involved in the transport of a bulk of tracksuits from Casablanca (Morocco) via Marseilles by sea and next on to Lisse (The Netherlands) by road. Bills of lading had been issued in

Casablanca for this transport on or about 22 October 1985. During the delivery of the tracksuits to the consignee in Lisse, Bizerta Sport, it was established that there was a shortage and that the tracksuits had been damaged. Diligentia, incorporated in The Netherlands, compensated Bizerta in accordance with the insurance contract between Diligentia and Bizerta. Claiming to be subrogated to the rights of Bizerta against Dubois, Diligentia claimed damages from Dubois. Dubois contested the District Court's jurisdiction, stating that it was the shipping-agent and not the transporter, pursuant to a contract which it had entered into with Sogetimar in Casablanca, to which it had transferred the goods. The jurisdiction could therefore not be based on the Convention on the Contract for the International Carriage of Goods by Road of 1956 (CMR) and there were no other grounds for jurisdiction of the Dutch courts. Diligentia contested that Dubois was just the shipping-agent, stating that Dubois had been appointed 'successive transporter' in the bills of lading.

Judgment

The District Court held that Dubois could be considered the successive transporter and that the Dutch courts thus had jurisdiction based on the CMR Convention.

Moreover, Diligentia correctly stated that the District Court could (also) base its jurisdiction on Art. 5(1).

The claim in this case was based on the contract of transport of goods, to which Dubois, in the opinion of Diligentia, had become a party as successive transporter. Pursuant to Art. 5(1), in matters relating to a contract, the court of the place of performance of the obligation in question could also claim jurisdiction. The place of performance had to be determined by the law applicable to the contract, according to the rules of private international law of the adjudicating court, in this case, therefore, according to the rules of Dutch private international law.

The District Court concluded that Dutch law was applicable to the contract of transport. Also, in accordance with the decision of the Hoge Raad, 12 June 1981, (1982) NJ 222, Case 679, the place of performance, according to Dutch law, of the obligation to transport goods to a certain destination and deliver them at that destination, was the place of destination. In this case the place of destination was Lisse, which meant that pursuant to Art. 5(1), the Dutch courts had jurisdiction.

Case principle

2. If the rules of private international law lead to the applicability of a convention containing uniform substantive rules, the provisions of that convention determine the place of performance of the obligation in question within the meaning of Art. 5(1). If the parties have stipulated the place of performance of the obligation in question in the contract, then that constitutes the place of performance within the meaning of Art. 5(1), provided such stipulation is in accordance with the applicable uniform rules.

Case

684   Bombardieri v Esta Trust Reg., (1980) NJ 512, Court of Appeal of 's-Hertogenbosch, 27 March 1979, *affirming* District Court of Maastricht

Translation taken from: 30 NILR 253 (1983), note Verheul.

Facts

A purchaser, Esta Trust Reg., incorporated in Liechtenstein, sued a seller, Bombardieri, domiciled in Italy, in the District Court of Maastricht for rescission of a contract of sale and for damages. The contract required delivery of ice-machines, destined for a business in Maastricht, and the plaintiff, Esta Trust, alleged that the machines had been delivered in a defective condition. The defendant, Bombardieri, contested the jurisdiction of the court.

Judgment

The Court of Appeal held that the District Court of Maastricht had jurisdiction. Italian law governed the contract of sale, and this law declared the Uniform Law on the International Sale of Goods of 1964 to be applicable. The parties had deviated from Art. 19(2) thereof and had agreed upon delivery Franco-Maastricht. The transport had been carried out under the supervision of the defendant and on his responsibility. Consequently, the delivery had to take place, and had taken place, in Maastricht. Thus, the place of performance within the meaning of Art. 5(1), was Maastricht.

Case

685   Jungmann Nutzfahrzeuge v Terhaag Bedrijfsauto's, (1995) NIPR 261, Court of Appeal of 's-Hertogenbosch, 26 October 1994, *reversing* District Court Roermond, 4 November 1993

Facts

In 1992, the Dutch company Terhaag sold and delivered two trucks to the German company Jungmann. Terhaag sued Jungmann in the District Court of 's-Hertogenbosch for payment of a certain sum of money. This claim apparently related to the payment of part of the purchase price and/or the payment of the indebted VAT. Jungmann contested the jurisdiction of the District Court. Terhaag alleged that the District Court had jurisdiction on the basis of Art. 5(1) and the District Court assumed jurisdiction on that basis. Jungmann appealed.

Judgment

The Court of Appeal held that the first question to be answered was where the obligation, which was the basis of Terhaag's claim, had to be performed?

The obligation underlying Terhaag's claim was the obligation to pay for the two trucks delivered by Terhaag. Terhaag had sold and delivered these trucks to Jungmann in November 1992, and had undertaken the export to Germany, whilst Jungmann had only partly performed its obligation to pay.

The claim therefore concerned the question whether Jungmann should have paid for the obligations performed by Terhaag.

The question whether Jungmann should have paid, had to be answered by looking at the contracts entered into by Jungmann and Terhaag. Both contracts were governed by the United Nations Convention on Contracts for the International Sale of Goods of 1980 (CISG). Pursuant to Arts 53 and 57(1) first sentence CISG, Jungmann should have paid at the place agreed in the contract.

In the contracts it was agreed—in accordance with Art. 57(1)(b) CISG—that Jungmann had to pay on delivery, that is to say in Germany. In the contract as well as on the invoice it said: 'The truck which has been delivered to you . . . Frei Haus . . . Bezahlung mit Bank bestätigte Cheque bei Abnahme'.

The conclusion on the basis of the foregoing was that the obligation underlying Terhaag's claim had to be performed in Germany. This meant that Art. 5(1) did not provide the Dutch courts with jurisdiction in the case.

Accordingly, the Court of Appeal reversed the judgment of the District Court, holding that the Dutch courts could not assume jurisdiction.

Comment

These decisions are in conformity with the European Court of Justice's decision in *Custom Made v Stawa Metallbau* Case C–288/92.

Case principle

3. A breach of the obligation to ensure that a piece of property is free from any security rights at the time of the transfer, is performed where the property is situated. In determining whether a court has jurisdiction under the Brussels Convention, it must consider the facts as they are presented by the plaintiff.

Case

Van der Bij v Heerkens Thijssen, (1987) NIPR 461, Court of Appeal of **686** 's-Gravenhage, 27 March 1987, *affirming* District Court of 's-Gravenhage, 4 September 1985

Facts

Hasenpflug, domiciled in The Netherlands, by notary deed of 1 June 1983, purchased the tenure of a piece of land situated in 's-Gravenhage, from Van der Bij, domiciled in Belgium. The deed stipulated that Van der Bij was under a duty to free the tenure from mortgage. At the time of the transfer, however, there appeared to be a mortgage on the piece of land securing a debt which Van der Bij owed to the tax collector in 's-Gravenhage. This debt was paid by Hasenpflug. Heerkens, incorporated in The Netherlands, allegedly provided the money to Hasenpflug for the payment of the debt and Hasenpgluf allegedly assigned the right to damages based on the breach of contract against Van der Bij to Heerkens. Heerkens sued Van der Bij for the said damages in the District Court of 's-Gravenhage. Van der Bij contested the jurisdiction of the District Court. The District Court, however, assumed jurisdiction on the basis of Art. 5(1), judging that the claim was based on breach of contract, concerning the obligation to ensure that the piece of land situated in 's-Gravenhage would be transferred free from mortgages. Thus, the obligation in question had to be performed in 's-Gravenhage, because that was the place where the piece of land was situated, where the transfer of property took place and where the purchaser was domiciled. The District Court found for Heerkens.

Van der Bij appealed and alleged that the District Court did not have jurisdiction, because the relationship between Van der Bij and Hasenpflug was of a different nature than was put forward by Heerkens.

Judgment

The Court of Appeal held: 'The jurisdiction of the District Court, under the Brussels Convention, is determined by the facts as they have been stated by the plaintiff and not by the relation as it existed in reality'.

Case principle

4.   If the creditor has designated a place of performance for the payment of a debt—that being the obligation in question—then, according to Dutch law, this is considered to be the place of performance of the obligation in question within the meaning of Art. 5(1). Even if the provision of Art. 5(1) leads to the jurisdiction of the court of the place of domicile of the plaintiff, that court has jurisdiction under the Brussels Convention, without prejudice to the rule laid down in Art. 2.

Case

687   Tramp Oil and Marine v Joss Handelsonderneming, (1995) NIPR 372, Court of Appeal of 's-Gravenhage, 28 February 1995, *affirming* District Court of Rotterdam, 25 March 1994

Facts

In December 1992 and January 1993, the Dutch company Joss purchased, in its own name, two bulk loads of lubricating oil. The bulk was transported from Buenos Aires to Rotterdam and delivered on 4 February 1993. Joss paid for the purchase and storage of the bulk.

Joss claimed payment from the English company Trampoil before the District Court of Rotterdam, alleging that the purchase of the lubricating oil took place on the basis of an outline agreement, which Joss allegedly entered into with Trampoil in December 1992. The costs, profits or losses arising from this agreement would be shared on a 50/50 basis.

Trampoil contested the jurisdiction of the court. The District Court, however, assumed jurisdiction on the basis of Art. 5(1), holding that the obligation in question—payment by Trampoil—was, according to the applicable Dutch law, to be performed in The Netherlands.

Trampoil appealed, claiming that payment could also be performed in England. The fact that Joss did not have a bank account in England was, in the opinion of Trampoil, of no importance, because it might and was able to make the payment to Joss's bank account in Rotterdam by ordering its English bank to make the remittance.

Judgment

The Court of Appeal held: 'The District Court has held that the place of performance of the obligation underlying Joss's claim, should be determined by Dutch law. There is no evidence that this judgment is incorrect nor has it been contested on appeal. The dispute between the parties concerns the question whether, in accordance with Dutch law, the place of performance of the obligation in question is in The Netherlands exclusively or can also be in England. Trampoil argues that because the remittance can very well be made in England, from an English bank account, regardless of whether Joss had a bank account in England or not, The Netherlands is not the sole place of performance and it must be presumed that the English courts have jurisdiction in this case. Any other opinion in this case would, according to Trampoil, be in conflict with Art. 3 of the Brussels Convention, containing the provision that exorbitant grounds for jurisdiction found in some of the national legislation—like the domicile/seat of the plaintiff—cannot be applied when the defendant has his domicile in a Contracting State.

Trampoil's argument must fail. Pursuant to the applicable Dutch law, the payment of a money-debt has to be performed at the place of domicile (or seat) of the creditor and/or any other place designated by the creditor. Taking into account that Joss has designated Rotterdam as the place of payment on the invoice, Rotterdam is considered to be the place of performance of the obligation in question. The fact that Trampoil can order its own bank in England to remit the indebted sum to Joss's designated account in Rotterdam does not lead to a different conclusion.

Trampoil's argument that the jurisdiction of the Dutch courts conflicts with the rule laid down in Art. 3 of the Brussels Convention must fail. That Article expresses that the jurisdiction grounds listed in the Convention, including the special jurisdiction ground of Art. 5(1), are exhaustive. The jurisdiction ground laid down in Art. 5(1) is thus valid, *even if* this leads to the jurisdiction of the court of the plaintiff's place of domicile, without prejudice to the main rule laid down in Art. 2 that the court of the defendant's place of domicile has jurisdiction.'

ARTICLE 5(3)

" . . . *matters relating to tort, delict or quasi-delict* . . . "

Case principle

For the question of whether jurisdiction can be based on Art. 5(3), it is important to ascertain that all claims which seek to establish the liability of the defendant fall within the term 'tort, delict or quasi-delict', and that they are not related to a contract within the meaning of Art. 5(1).

Case

688   Kater v SVT Strategic Design, (1996) NIPR 269, Court of Appeal of Amsterdam, 23 November 1995, *reversing* District Court of Amsterdam, 11 January 1995, (1996) NIPR 269

Facts

SVT, a Dutch company, sued Kater, domiciled in Belgium, before the District Court of Amsterdam. The claim was based on Art. 203, s.3 of Book 2 of the Dutch Civil Code, concerning joint liability for the damage suffered by SVT, caused by the fact that Prestige Holding—of which Kater was joint-promoter—left invoices unpaid. The invoices concerned the execution of the design of the interior and exterior of the 'Prestige' kitchen and bathroom showproject. The confirmation of the order was—as stated by SVT—signed by Kater on behalf of Prestige Holding, which at that moment was not yet founded. SVT submitted that the District Court of Amsterdam had jurisdiction based on the choice of forum clause contained in SVT's General Conditions, which were applicable to the agreement between SVT and Prestige. Kater contested the jurisdiction of the court, by stating that SVT had based its claim on Art. 203, s.3 of Book 2 Dutch Civil Code, which in the opinion of Kater was a type of tort. Thus, SVT could not rely on the choice of forum clause included in the General Conditions applicable to the contract.

SVT submitted that it had based its claim on breach of contract, for which Kater was jointly liable in accordance with Art. 203, s.3 of the Dutch Civil Code.

The District Court found for the plaintiff, and assumed jurisdiction on the basis of the choice of forum clause contained in the General Conditions. Kater appealed the decision.

Judgment

The Court of Appeal held: 'For the question whether jurisdiction can be based on Art. 5(3) it is important to ascertain that all claims which seek to establish the liability of the defendant fall under the term "tort, delict or quasi-delict", as long as there is no relation to a contract within the meaning of Art. 5(1).

Taking the above into consideration, the claim based on Art. 203, s.3 of Book 2 of the Dutch Civil Code is clearly related to a contract, so that jurisdiction cannot be based on Art. 5(3).

It is, however, not a matter relating to a contract *within the meaning of Art. 5(1)*, because liability which flows from Art. 203, s.3 of Book 2 of the Dutch Civil Code constitutes an obligation *ex lege* and not a contractual obligation.

The District Court, therefore, cannot base its jurisdiction on the choice of forum clause. There are no other grounds, nor have they been stated, on which the court could have based its jurisdiction.'

The Court of Appeal accordingly reversed the decision by the District Court and declined jurisdiction.

Comment

This decision seems to be in conformity with the case law of the European Court of Justice in *Kalfelis v Schröder* Case C–189/87. The above case is in some ways remarkable, because it denies application of Art. 5(3) based on the fact that the action is *related* to a contract within the meaning of Art. 5(1). On the other hand, the action is held not to be based on a contractual obligation, which accounts for the inapplicability of Art. 5(1). The Court of Appeal seems to apply a more narrow interpretation of 'tort' and/or 'matters relating to contract', than the European Court of Justice.

> " . . . *harmful event occurred.*"

Case principle

1. The place where the harmful event occurred, within the meaning of Art. 5(3), does not include the place where the financial loss was suffered.

Case

Mecoma v Stahlhandel Lübeck, (1979) NJ 368, Court of Appeal of   **689**
's-Hertogenbosch, 31 October 1978, *affirming* District Court of Breda, 21 June 1977

Translation taken from: 25 NILR 81 (1978), note Verheul.

Facts

Mecoma, domiciled in The Netherlands, sued Stahlhandel, domiciled in Germany, for damages, alleging failure to conclude a definite contract in conformity with preparatory talks between the parties concerning the construction by Mecoma of a hall with an office in Germany. Stahlhandel did not enter an appearance, but the District Court of Breda held that it did not have jurisdiction because neither the place of performance of a contractual obligation nor a harmful event were located within the court's jurisdiction. Mecoma appealed, claiming that it had sustained financial damage to its business located in The Netherlands.

Judgment

The Court of Appeal confirmed the decision of the District Court and held that 'harmful event' may, according to the interpretation given by the European Court of Justice in *Bier v Mines de Potasse* Case 21/76, comprise the original act as well as the damage but not, however, the financial loss, which may obviously be located anywhere in the world.

Case

690 Takaztex v Eldo, (1993) NIPR 171, District Court of Amsterdam, 18 November 1992

Facts

On 13 March 1992, the Dutch company Takaztex sued the Italian company Eldo in the District Court of Amsterdam for the payment of a sum of money, arguing that Eldo had committed a tort by violating the interests of the agent Takaztex engaged by Eldo's subsidiary G.F.B., incorporated in Germany. On this ground Eldo had to compensate Takaztex for the damage it had suffered.

Eldo claimed that, because the alleged harmful events occurred either in Germany and/or Italy, the District Court of Amsterdam could not assume jurisdiction and Eldo should have been summoned before the Italian courts pursuant to Art. 2.

Takaztex argued that the tortious action on which it based its claim might well have taken place in Germany, but the fact that it was incorporated in Amsterdam (The Netherlands) meant that this was also the place where it suffered the damage, so that the District Court of Amsterdam could assume jurisdiction pursuant to Art. 5(3).

Judgment

The District Court held: 'The argument of Takaztex must fail. A distinction has to be made between the event which may give rise to liability in tort, the material consequences (the damage caused by that event) and the property in which the financial loss, caused by that event, is felt, which property can be situated all over the world.

In the European Court of Justice's decision *Bier v Mines de Potasse* Case 21/76, the Court of Justice expanded the jurisdiction ground of Art. 5(3). The courts of *both* the place where the event giving rise to the liability in tort occurred and the place where the material consequences, the damage, occurred can assume jurisdiction pursuant to Art. 5(3). This expansion, however, does not extend to the place where the financial loss in property is suffered, as is put forward in this case.

As neither the event giving rise to the liability in tort nor the material consequences can be said to have occurred in The Netherlands, the District Court must decline jurisdiction.'

Comment

Both decisions are in conformity with the case law of the European Court of Justice: *Dumez v France and Tracoba* C–220/88, CJ.Eur.Comm., 11 January 1990; *Marinari v Lloyd's Bank plc.* C–364/93, CJ.Eur.Comm., 19 September 1995 42 NILR 420.

Case principle

2.   In matters concerning product liability, the place where the harmful event occurred is the place where the product was introduced on the market.

Case

Seatrade Groningen v Sulzer Escher Wyss, (1996) NIPR 447, District Court of **691** Rotterdam, 20 June 1996

Facts

Under commission of Seatrade, a Dutch company, six ships were built by two shipyards in Waterhuizen (The Netherlands). Both ships were equipped with a so called 'controllable pitch propeller' (hereafter: cpp-installations). The manufacturer of the cpp-installations, a German company SEW, had supplied both shipyards with these installations under identical conditions.

Seatrade claimed that it had suffered damage because of the inferior quality of the cpp-installations. Seatrade claimed that SEW had acted in a tortious manner by introducing an inferior product on the market. SEW contested that the District Court had jurisdiction on the basis of Art. 5(3).

Judgment

The District Court held: 'In this case the harmful event is the introduction of the cpp-installations, which it is submitted were of inferior quality, onto the market. This introduction onto the market took place in The Netherlands, because the installations were delivered by SEW to the shipyards in Waterhuizen (The Netherlands), in order to be—to SEW's knowledge—installed in the ships being built for Seatrade.

This should lead to jurisdiction for the District Court of Groningen. However, SEW has informed the Rotterdam Court that in case the Dutch Courts have jurisdiction under Art. 5(3), it will not have to decline jurisdiction in favour of another District Court. This leads to the conclusion that the District Court of Rotterdam has jurisdiction to decide this matter.'

Comment

It can be deduced from this case that under Dutch law, product liability is a tort which should fall within the scope of Art. 5(3). This, however, is not the case in some other European legal orders. The European Court of Justice in *Jakob Handte v Societé Traitements*, Case C–26/91, has so far only decided that product liability does not fall within the scope of Art. 5(1). It has not yet decided whether product liability falls within the scope of Art. 5(3).

ARTICLE 6(1)

" . . . one of a number of defendants . . . "

Case principle

Article 6(1) continues to apply where proceedings against one of the defendants are terminated, but continued against the other defendant(s).

Case

692 Llambes v Bayllon, as trustee in bankruptcy, and Van Gend & Loos, (1981) NJ 540, Court of Appeal of 's-Hertogenbosch, 24 February 1981, *reversing* District Court of 's-Hertogenbosch

Translation taken from: 30 NILR 255 (1983), note Verheul.

Facts

The plaintiff Llambes, incorporated in Spain, sued Bayllon, a Belgian trustee in bankruptcy, and the Dutch company Van Gend & Loos in the District Court of 's-Hertogenbosch, on the basis of Art. 6(1). The action sought a declaration that the plaintiff was the owner of certain goods in the hands of Van Gend & Loos, a transport firm, who held them on behalf of the bankrupt Belgian company. The plaintiff also sought an order for the defendants to deliver those goods to him. The parties agreed to a sale of the goods, and the action against Van Gend & Loos was consequently terminated. The action continued against the trustee in bankruptcy, however, with regard to the proceeds of sale. The trustee contested the jurisdiction of the District Court.

Judgment

The Court of Appeal held that Art. 6(1) jurisdiction continued for the action against the trustee in bankruptcy.

Comment

The Court of Appeal did not pay attention to the fact that the action was instituted against a trustee in bankruptcy. In fact, the proceedings did not 'arise directly from the bankruptcy' within the meaning of Art. 1, para. 2(2), so that the application of the Brussels Convention by the Court of Appeal was justified.

ARTICLE 6(2)

" . . . *may also be sued . . . As a third party . . .* "

Case principle

In judging whether a request to sue a third party on a warranty should be granted, the court must weigh the plaintiff's interests against the defendant's interests. The consideration that the request to sue a third person on the warranty may delay the main proceedings is of particular interest. The fact that the third party is domiciled outside the State of the court cannot, in connection herewith, be taken into consideration as being a particularly delaying factor.

There are no special reasoning requirements—in a judgment in respect of a procedural 'incident'—for such a weighing of interests.

Case

Kongress Agentur Hagen v Zeehaghe, (1991) NJ 558, note Schultsz, Hoge **693** Raad, 12 December 1990, decision following answers by the European Court of Justice, 15 May 1990 (C–365/88); (1990) ECR 1845, to preliminary questions put to it by the Hoge Raad, 9 December 1988, (1991) NJ 556

Facts

The German company Hagen made reservations for hotel rooms with the Dutch company Zeehaghe. This agreement was subsequently cancelled by Hagen. Zeehaghe sued Hagen in the District Court of 's-Gravenhage for payment of the costs caused by the cancellation. Hagen contested the jurisdiction of the court. In the event that the court were to assume jurisdiction, Hagen requested the court to permit it to sue the German cooperative association Garant Schuhgilde, its principal, on a warranty. Zeehaghe challenged this request.

The District Court assumed jurisdiction pursuant to Art. 5(1) and declined Hagen's request to permit it to sue Garant Schuhgilde on a warranty. On appeal Hagen contested this last decision with the argument that Art. 6(2) makes it mandatory upon the court competent for the original claim, to allow a third party to be sued on a warranty, providing that the exception mentioned in that provision does not occur. The Court of Appeal of 's-Gravenhage

(9 January 1987, (1987) NIPR 262) dismissed that argument and affirmed the judgment of the District Court. The Court of Appeal stated that Art. 6 did not contain a duty for the court, but only provided for the possibility to allow such a request to sue a third party on a warranty. The Hoge Raad Court put three preliminary questions to the European Court of Justice concerning the interpretation of Art. 6(2).

The European Court of Justice held: 'Art. 6(2) must be interpreted as meaning that it does not require the national court to accede to the request for leave to bring an action on a warranty or guarantee and that the national court may apply the procedural rules of its national law to determine whether that action is admissible, provided that the effectiveness of the Convention in that regard is not impaired and, in particular, that leave to bring the action on the warranty or guarantee is not refused on the ground that the third party resides or is domiciled in a Contracting State other than that of the court seised of the original proceedings.'

Judgment

The Hoge Raad held: 'The grounds for the appeal in cassation add up to the argument that the Court of Appeal has based its refusal of the request to sue Garant Schuhgilde on a warranty, on incorrect or at least on insufficient grounds.

The challenged decision of the Court of Appeal must be understood in the following way. The Court of Appeal has weighed Zeehaghe's interest to continue the proceedings without further delay against Hagen's interest to be allowed to sue its principal on a warranty, whereby Zeehaghe's interest prevailed. By agreeing with the District Court's judgment, the Court of Appeal only wanted to express that Hagen aimed at linking the main proceedings to the proceedings on the warranty, and that this might delay the main proceedings.

In its reference to the delay "generally" connected to "a procedure to sue on a warranty", the Court of Appeal has not considered the fact that the third party is domiciled outside The Netherlands as a particular delaying factor in this weighing of interests, which, had it done so, would have been contrary to the European Court's ruling. Hagen's claim to that effect must therefore fail.

Hagen's claim that the Court of Appeal should have provided reasoning as to why it allowed Zeehaghe's interest to prevail over Hagen's interest must also fail, because such a reasoning requirement is too strict for a judgment in respect of a procedural "incident" based as it is on the weighing of conflicting interests.'

The Hoge Raad dismissed the appeal.

ARTICLE 6(3)

" . . . *may also be sued . . . On a counter-claim* . . . "

Case principle

Article 6(3) is applicable, regardless of whether the original claim falls within the substantive scope of the Brussels Convention, provided that the counter-claim does so and that the defendant to the counterclaim is domiciled in a Contracting State.

Case

District Court of Leeuwarden, 31 May 1979, 28 NILR 74 (1981)   **694**

Translation taken from: 28 NILR 74 (1981), note Verheul.

Facts

A German creditor lodged a claim against a bankrupt person with the trustee in bankruptcy, who did not recognize the claim. According to Dutch bank-ruptcy law, the dispute was referred to the court for so-called 'verification' of the claim. In the proceedings that followed, the trustee instituted a counter-claim based on the same agreement which was the basis for the claim lodged by the German creditor.

Judgment

The District Court held: 'The Court has jurisdiction to judge the *original claim*, since it concerns a verification dispute in a bankruptcy adjudicated by this court. As for the *counterclaim*, in the court's view it does not arise direct-ly from the bankruptcy, for the bankrupt could have instituted the action him-self were he not adjudicated bankrupt. Consequently, Art. 1, para. 2(2) of the Brussels Convention does not apply and thus the counterclaim is governed by the jurisdiction rules of the Convention. Art. 6(3) provides that a counterclaim arising from the same contract on which the original claim was based, may be instituted in the court in which the original claim is pending.

Comment

The original claim did not fall under the substantive scope of the Convention, pursuant to Art. 1, para. 2(2). 'Verification' proceedings are generally consid-ered to be a matter of bankruptcy within the meaning of that provision. The question was whether Art. 6(3) still applied when the original claim fell out-side the scope of the Convention. In our opinion, the court rightly applied Art. 6(3), because the matter concerned the question of jurisdiction for the coun-terclaim. As the court held, the counterclaim fell within the substantive scope of the Convention and the defendant to the counterclaim was domiciled in a Contracting State. Article 6(3) gives an alternative court to Art. 2, for the plaintiff of the counterclaim. The only other condition for its applicability is that both claims arise from the same contract, regardless of the character of or of the applicability of the Convention to the original claim.

ARTICLE 6a

" . . . *has jurisdiction in actions relating to liability* . . . "

Case principle

1. Article 6a stipulates that the owner of a ship may bring his (independent)
    claim for limitation of liability, arising from the use or operation of that
    ship, before the national court competent for that purpose, provided that
    this court can (also) assume jurisdiction over the claim for damages of the
    victim. In order for the national court to assume jurisdiction in matters
    concerning the limitation of liability, it is not required that the main claim
    for damages is or will actually be brought before that court.

Case

695   Maersk Olie og Gas v Firma M. de Haan en W. de Boer, De Haan and De Boer,
(1988) NJ 766, Court of Appeal of Leeuwarden, 6 January 1988, *affirming*
District Court of Groningen, 27 May 1987

Facts

On 14–15 June 1985, a cutter owned by the Dutch company De Haan and De
Boer and registered in Groningen (The Netherlands), whilst fishing in the
Danish part of the Continental Shelf, caused damage to pipelines situated on
the bottom of the Shelf, belonging to the Danish company Maersk.

On 23 April 1987, De Haan and De Boer requested the District Court of
Groningen to determine a maximum amount for their liability pursuant to Art.
740a of the Code of Commerce and Arts 320 *et seq.* of the Code of Civil
Procedure. On 27 May 1987, the District Court set the maximum amount for
liability, which was far below the actual amount of damages. On 19 June 1987
Maersk sued De Haan and De Boer for damages in a Danish court.

On 24 June 1986, Maersk appealed from the decision of the District Court,
in so far as the decision confirmed the assumption of jurisdiction over De
Haan and De Boer's application.

Judgment

The Court of Appeal held: 'Pursuant to Art. 2, the court of the place of domicile of De Haan and De Boer has jurisdiction concerning claims against De
Haan and De Boer.

Pursuant to Art. 320a of the Code of Civil Procedure, the court of the place
of registration of the cutter has jurisdiction concerning the claim for limitation
of liability.

Article 6a stipulates that the owner of a ship may bring his (independent) claim for limitation of liability, arising from the use or operation of that ship, before his national court competent for that purpose, provided that this court can (also) assume jurisdiction concerning the claim for damages of the victim. In order for the national court to assume jurisdiction in matters concerning the limitation of liability, it is not required that the main claim for damages is or will actually be brought before that court.

The fact that the Danish courts can also assume jurisdiction for the main claim for damages pursuant to Art. 5(3), does not affect the competence of the District Court of Groningen concerning the request for the limitation of liability.

No rule of law obliges the District Court to stay the proceedings concerning the limitation of liability or decline jurisdiction in favour of the Danish court.'

The Court of Appeal confirmed the judgment of the District Court concerning the assumption of jurisdiction.

Comment

See also District Court of 's-Gravenhage, 1 February 1985, *infra*, Art. 22, Case 719.

Case principle

2.   Article 6a neither implies that a request for limitation can *only* be brought before the court competent for a claim against petitioners, nor that that court has *exclusive* jurisdiction to judge a claim concerning the limitation of liability.

Case

Jeeninga & Zonen and Hullmann's Aalaufzucht v Die Kasse zur Versicherung **696** von Fischereifahrzeugen and Hamann, (1991) NIPR 237, District Court of Rotterdam, 5 February 1990

Facts

On 28 December 1988, a collision occurred within Dutch territorial waters between the fishingboat Vertrauen-NB 2, registered in Germany and belonging to Hullmann's Aalaufzucht, and the fishingboat Paloma I-SC 28, also registered in Germany and belonging to Hamann. Due to this collision the Paloma sunk and one of its crew died. The petitioners wished to limit their liability pursuant to Arts 740a *et seq.* of the Code of Commerce and Arts 320a *et seq.* of the Code of Civil Procedure. The defendants contested the jurisdiction of the Dutch courts.

Judgment

The District Court held: 'Petitioners wish to limit their liability, which, in their opinion, they are able to do pursuant to Art. 740a of the Code of Commerce. They allege that the Dutch company Jeeninga & Zonen exploited the

Vertrauen and that, in accordance with Dutch law, Jeeninga & Zonen and Hullmann's Aalaufzucht are liable in respect of the damage arising from the collision.

Pursuant to Art. 320a of the Code of Civil Procedure in conjunction with Art. 740a of the Code of Commerce, the interested parties concerning a ship that is not registered in The Netherlands, may bring their request for the limitation of liability before the District Court of Rotterdam.

The Dutch courts have jurisdiction in this matter and the District Court of Rotterdam is the competent court.

Contrary to what the defendants apparently believe, the opposite does not follow from any provision of the Brussels Convention, Art. 6a in particular. This provision neither implies that the request at issue can only be brought before the German court, which would be competent for a claim against petitioners, nor that this German court has exclusive jurisdiction to judge a claim concerning the limitation of liability.'

ARTICLE 13, PARAGRAPH 1(3)(a)

" . . . specific invitation . . . "

Case principle

A visit to a consumer's home by the seller's agent can be considered a 'specific invitation' from the seller within the meaning of Art. 13, para. 1(3)(a), regardless of whether the consumer was *already* interested in entering into a contract with that seller.

Case

697 Kuipers v Van Kesteren, (1994) NIPR 160, District Court of Amsterdam, 24 April 1993

Facts

Kuipers (seller), domiciled and incorporated in Twist, Germany, claimed payment from Van Kesteren (buyer/consumer), domiciled in The Netherlands, on account of a breach of contract for the delivery and installation of a kitchen.

Van Kesteren contested the jurisdiction of the District Court, referring to the—non-contested—applicability of Kuipers's standard conditions to the contract, which stipulated: 'Regardless of whether the purchaser is Dutch or German, the parties agree that any dispute arising from or in connection with the contract will be brought before the Amtsgericht Meppen'.

Kuipers alleged that this clause was invalid in contravention of Art. 14, para. 2, requiring consumer defendants within Art. 13 to be sued in their domicile.

Judgment

The District Court held that according to the statements made by both parties, the contract was entered into in The Netherlands. Furthermore, Van Kesteren stated—uncontested and therefore established—that 'an agent of Kuipers Möbel had visited Van Kesteren at his home and subsequently entered into a contract with Van Kesteren'. The condition of specific invitation in Art. 13, para. 1(3)(a), in conjunction with (b), was thus fulfilled. The circumstance, as alleged by Van Kesteren, that an acquaintance had previously mentioned Kuipers Möbel to Van Kesteren, did not undermine the fact that the subsequent visit by the said agent could be seen as the 'specific invitation' within the meaning of that provision.

Pursuant to Art. 14, para. 2, the Dutch courts had jurisdiction in this matter and the inconsistent jurisdiction clause was ineffective by virtue of Art. 15. Whether the choice of forum in the standard conditions had been made in conformity with Art. 17 could therefore remain unanswered.

The District Court could assume jurisdiction.

ARTICLE 16(1)

Case principle

1. A claim for the payment of a penalty in case of default, agreed on in a contract of sale concerning real property, does not fall within the exclusive jurisdiction provision of Art. 16(1), as it does not concern the ownership of—a right *in rem* in—the real property.

Case

La Société Civile Immobilière de Bourgogne and La Société Civile Particulière **698** et Immobilière 'Azuréenne' v Raat, (1977) NJ 251, District Court of Amsterdam, 25 November 1975

Translation taken from: 23 NILR 366 (1976), note Verheul.

Facts

The plaintiffs, two French corporations, sold a piece of land situated in France, to the defendant Raat, domiciled in The Netherlands. The agreement, a notarial instrument, contained a clause that the transfer of title should take place on a fixed date, two months later, and that on that same date Raat should pay the first part of the purchase price, on a penalty of 100 000 French francs. Raat did not pay the first part of the purchase price and was sued by the plaintiffs in the District Court of Amsterdam for payment of the penalty.

Judgment

The District Court of Amsterdam held: 'This Court has jurisdiction to deal with this matter, since the defendant is domiciled in The Netherlands, and the case does not concern the ownership of the real property situated in France, but the contractual obligation to pay the agreed penalty in case of default by Raat.'

Case principle

2. A claim for damages based on the non-performance of a contract of sale of real property is to be classified as a personal claim and does not fall within the scope of Art. 16(1).

Case

699 Stas v Kapoen, Nijland and Hendrickx, (1993) NIPR 459, District Court of Zwolle, 9 June 1993

Facts

Stas, domiciled in Belgium, claimed damages, *inter alia*, on the basis of breach of a contract of sale concerning real property situated in Belgium between himself and Kapoen and Nijland, both domiciled in The Netherlands.

Judgment

In deciding whether it had jurisdiction, the District Court applied Art. 2 of the Brussels Convention. It stated that this matter did not fall within the scope of Art. 16(1) concerning exclusive jurisdiction in matters relating to real property, because the claim for damages brought by Stas on the basis of breach of a contract of sale was first and foremost a personal claim and did not directly concern a right *in rem*.

Case principle

3. Attachment of assets in The Netherlands (which would give the Dutch courts jurisdiction on the basis of Art. 767 of the Code of Civil Procedure) can under no circumstances set aside the exclusive jurisdiction of the court of the Contracting State in which the immovable property is situated under Art. 16(1)(a) of the Brussels Convention.

Case

700 Club Torre Vella v Stevens, (1995) NIPR 559, District Court of 's-Gravenhage, 19 April 1995

Facts

A Spanish company, Club Toree Vella, claimed payment from Stevens, domiciled in The Netherlands. Club Toree Vella based its claim on the fact that

Stevens had decided not to lease the catering establishment 'Club Torre Vella' situated in Spain. According to Club Torre Vella, Stevens's decision not to lease was in breach of the lease contract concluded between the parties.

Stevens contested the jurisdiction of the District Court.

Club Torre Vella denied that Art. 16(1)(a) of the Brussels Convention was applicable by stating the following:

(1)   the lease contract was concluded in The Netherlands;
(2)   Stevens was domiciled in The Netherlands; and
(3)   assets situated in The Netherlands had been attached, so that the Dutch court had jurisdiction in accordance with Art. 767 of the Code of Civil Procedure.

Judgment

The District Court of 's-Gravenhage held: 'The arguments put forward by Club Torre Vella did nothing to detract from the main rule that in cases such as the one at issue the court of the place where the immovable property is situated has jurisdiction. The attachment of assets situated in The Netherlands did not alter this rule. It had to be concluded that Art. 16(1)(a) of the Brussels Convention was applicable and thus that the District Court did not have jurisdiction in this case.'

ARTICLE 17, PARAGRAPH 1

" . . . *arise in connection with a particular legal relationship* . . . "

Case principle

Damages for subsequent defective inspection of machinery sold are covered by a jurisdiction clause in the sales contract.

Case

Stork v Cacolac, (1995) NIPR 258, Court of Appeal of Amsterdam, 6 October **701** 1994, *reversing* District Court of Amsterdam, 14 July 1993

Facts

In 1977, Stork Inter France, the French subsidiary of the Dutch company Stork Amsterdam, made an offer to the French company Cacolac for the delivery of machinery. The offer contained a reference to Stork Amsterdam's general conditions, including a choice of forum clause in favour of the courts in Amsterdam. Later that year, Stork Amsterdam confirmed Cacolac's purchase in a letter which also referred to its general conditions. Both in 1987 and 1988,

Stork Amsterdam issued purchase confirmations for the delivery of some components for the original machinery. In both instances, reference was again made to Stork Amsterdam's general conditions. When Stork initiated proceedings in Amsterdam, the District Court declined jurisdiction. Stork appealed.

Judgment

The Court of Appeal held that the way in which the 1977 transaction was made constituted a choice of forum clause 'in writing', as was then required by the prevailing text of Art. 17(1) of the Brussels Convention. Cacolac had not only received a written offer and a written purchase confirmation, both referring to the general conditions, it had also (i) received a copy of these conditions, (ii) ordered the machinery pursuant to the offer, and (iii) signed and returned the purchase confirmation to Stork Inter France.

The contract, made in 1987, also contained a valid choice of forum clause, under the text of Art. 17(1) then prevailing: Cacolac had not sufficiently contested Stork's argument that general conditions accorded with a usage in the particular trade or commerce concerned and that Cacolac ought to have been aware of such a usage.

Disputes concerning damages sustained after an inspection of the machinery in 1988 were also covered by the general conditions and the choice of forum clause, because such disputes arose directly from 'a particular relationship', created by the contracts made in 1977 and 1987.

Stork's claim for a declaratory judgment to the effect that it was not liable for damages sustained after 1988 constituted a dispute arising 'in connection with a particular legal relationship' (Art. 17(1)), because this claim related to the question of whether Stork was liable for damages concerning machinery it had delivered and inspected.

The Court of Appeal reversed the District Court's judgment and held that the District Court had jurisdiction to entertain the case.

Editor's Comment

Two things should be distinguished.

First, whether *as a matter of contractual construction*, a tortious or other further claim following upon the contract should be held to fall within the jurisdiction clause. Secondly, if that is the case, whether *as a matter of interpretation of Art. 17*, such other, non-contractual disputes should be considered to satisfy the "any disputes" and "particular legal relationship" conditions under Art. 17, so as to require Art. 17 formalities to be satisfied as a condition of the jurisdiction agreement's validity in relation thereto and so as also to attract exclusive effects prescribed by Art. 17.

ARTICLE 17, PARAGRAPH 1(a)

" *. . . in writing . . .* "

Case principle

Dutch courts apply the requirements as to the formal validity of a choice of forum clause, as set forth in Art. 17, para. 1(a), (b), and (c), in a strict manner.

Case

Plaumann v Van der Linden, (1985) NJ 786, District Court of Middelburg, **702**
4 July 1984

Facts

The distributorship contract between Plaumann, domiciled in Germany, and Van der Linden, incorporated in The Netherlands, was confirmed in a letter from Van der Linden to Plaumann. This letter was written in German on Van der Linden's letterhead. The letterhead contained a preprinted clause in English, referring to Van der Linden's general conditions. These general conditions referred all disputes to the District Court of Middelburg.

Judgment

The formal requirements of Art. 17 sought to guarantee that the choice of forum clause was based on the parties' true consent, which was clearly and precisely expressed. In the original German contract the oral agreements were spelt out in detail, without a choice of forum clause. Van der Linden's wish to vest jurisdiction in the District Court of Middelburg could only be inferred from the reference on the letterhead. Plaumann was justified in assuming that the German text contained a full account of all the parties' agreements and did not have to pay attention to a preprinted reference in another language. His consent to the German text did not include a consent to the English reference, not even implicitly. The same is true for any later correspondence between the parties.

Comment

The case was decided under the Brussels Convention before the entry into force of the First Accession Convention of 1978.

Case

Kunstveilingen Erasmus v Salamon, (1986) NJ 557, Court of Appeal **703**
of Amsterdam, 25 April 1985, *affirming* District Court of Amsterdam,
12 October 1983

Facts

During one of its auctions, held in Germany, Kunstveilingen Erasmus, a company incorporated in The Netherlands, sold a collection of tapestries to Salamon, domiciled in Germany. Kunstveilingen Erasmus sued Salamon for payment in the District Court of Amsterdam on the basis of a choice of forum clause inserted in its auction conditions. These conditions were read aloud in both German and Dutch at the auction's outset and were also displayed during the auction. After the auction, Salamon had signed a partly preprinted bond, in which he declared in German that he was aware of the conditions and agreed to them. Salamon did not appear before the District Court of Amsterdam. The District Court held that it had no jurisdiction. Kunstveilingen Erasmus appealed.

Judgment

The Court of Appeal held that the choice of forum clause did not comply with the strict requirements set out in Art. 17. The bond referred to the auction conditions in general, but did not expressly mention the choice of forum clause. This fact by itself evidenced that there was no agreement in writing. Nor was there an oral agreement evidenced in writing. Although the auction conditions were read aloud in German and Dutch and displayed, Kunstveilingen Erasmus had neither argued that Salamon had actually taken cognizance of the specific clause nor brought forward any other facts which could demonstrate an oral agreement upon the District Court's jurisdiction. The Court of Appeal affirmed the District Court's decision that it had no jurisdiction.

Comment

The case was decided under the Brussels Convention before the entry into force of the First Accession Convention of 1978.

Case

704 Opree v Interrent Europcar Autovermietung, (1995) NJ 219, District Court of Maastricht, 16 December 1993, *affirming* Justice of the Peace of Maastricht, 19 June 1991

Facts

Opree, domiciled in The Netherlands, was sued by Interrent, a German company, for payment of the lease of an automobile. On appeal, Opree invoked a choice of forum clause in Interrent's general conditions, conferring jurisdiction on the courts in Hamburg.

Judgment

Whereas a choice of forum clause inserted in general conditions, printed on the contract's back is on its own insufficient, nevertheless, a clear reference in the contract, signed by both parties, to the general conditions, containing the choice of forum clause, met the requirements of Art. 17(1). Here, the contract was signed by both parties and referred to the general conditions on the back, in particular to the choice of forum clause. The District Court agreed that there was a valid choice of forum clause.

Comment

The case is also discussed under Art. 17(4), *infra* Case 712.

Case

705 Foppen a.k.a. MJM Productions v Tissage Impression Mécanique, (1995)

NIPR 278, District Court of Maastricht, 26 January 1995, *reversed on other grounds*, Court of Appeal of 's-Hertogenbosch, 9 October 1995, (1996) NIPR 118, affirmed Hoge Raad, 26 September 1997 (1997) RvdW181

Facts

Foppen, domiciled and doing business in The Netherlands, ordered textiles from Tissage, incorporated in France. When sued in the District Court of Maastricht for damages, Tissage, *inter alia*, invoked a choice of forum clause inserted in its general conditions.

Judgment

The District Court referred to the European Court of Justice's case law, holding that Art. 17 of the Brussels Convention did not cover general conditions printed on the back of purchase confirmations or invoices. In such situations, there was no guarantee whatsoever that the other party had actually consented to these conditions. A different approach was only called for if a previous, oral agreement between the parties specifically related to the choice of forum clause, or if the purchase confirmation formed part of long-standing business relationships between the parties, provided that these relationships as a whole were covered by the general conditions containing the choice of forum clause. The District Court determined that neither the first nor the latter condition was fulfilled. Moreover, the purchase confirmations and invoices contained no reference to the general conditions, while the general conditions on the specific purchase confirmation were crossed out. This led the District Court to disregard the general conditions and the choice of forum clause contained therein.

Comment

See also *Centurion Accumulatoren v A & A Lohmann*, (1996) NIPR 279, Court of Appeal of 's-Hertogenbosch, 20 October 1995.

ARTICLE 17, PARAGRAPH 1(c)
" . . . *accords with a usage* . . . "

Case principle

Previous dealing between businessmen can constitute a usage of international trade.

Case

Smit Ovens v Airsec, (1993) NIPR 300, District Court of Arnhem, **706**
24 December 1992

Facts

Smit Ovens, incorporated in The Netherlands, purchased two dryers from Airsec, incorporated in Spain. In the written purchase confirmations, sent by Smit Ovens to Airsec, reference was made to Smit Ovens's conditions of purchase. Airsec signed and returned these confirmations to Smit Ovens. Smit Ovens's conditions of purchase contained a choice of law clause in favour of Dutch law and a choice of forum clause referring all disputes to the courts of Smit Ovens's place of business. In previous years, the parties had done business in the same manner.

When sued before the District Court of Arnhem, Airsec argued, *inter alia*, that the conditions were not printed on the orders' back nor were they sent to Airsec, whereas a reference to them in the purchase confirmations did not entail a valid choice of forum clause.

Judgment

The District Court started from the premise that the choice of forum clause, were it to be binding, should meet the formal requirements set out in Art. 17(1) of the Brussels Convention, as amended by the Third Accession Convention, in particular subss. (b) and (c). Citing the Schlosser Report on the First Accession Convention, the District Court held that a choice of forum clause in general conditions was specifically covered by subs. (c). As to the parties' dispute on the question of whether Smit Ovens's conditions formed part of the contracts between the parties, the District Court held that prior to the contracts in dispute, Smit Ovens used to refer to its conditions. Airsec had never protested against this reference. Therefore, Smith Ovens could assume—and Airsec as a professional trading partner should have been aware of this—that the conditions formed part of their contractual relationship. The fact that the conditions were probably never sent to Airsec was irrelevant; Airsec could have asked for them. According to 'Community' law, the District Court continued, the conditions thus formed part of the contracts in dispute. The same was true under Dutch law, which would be applicable to this question pursuant to Art. 8(1) of the Rome Contracts Convention, which *Bale-press*, (1992) NJ 750, 42 NILR 259 (1995), note Hudig-Van Lennep, Hoge Raad, 25 September 1992, had applied by way of anticipation. Since the parties were used to doing business with each other in this manner, the choice of forum clause was 'in a form which accords with practices which the parties have established between themselves' (Art. 17(1)(b)). Moreover, it was widely known that in international trade, general conditions between manufacturers were used, also in the parties' particular sector. International trade could not function without conditions and choice of forum clauses. It was essential—said the Schlosser Report—that a contract could be concluded swiftly, accompanied by the insertion of general conditions. This was also the reason why Art. 17(1) was 'liberalized'. Thus, the formal validity of the choice of forum clause also met the requirements of Art. 17, para. 1(c). The District Court had jurisdiction to entertain the case.

Case

Christie's Amsterdam v Alazraki and Zelig, (1994) NIPR 159, District Court **707**
of Amsterdam, 10 February 1993

Facts

Christie's Amsterdam sued Alazraki, domiciled in Italy, and Zelig, an Italian
company, for payment of auctioned items before the District Court of
Amsterdam, this court being referred to in Christie's Amsterdam's general conditions. Alazraki and Zelig argued that the District Court had no jurisdiction.

Judgment

The District Court referred to Art. 17, para. 1(c). Further, the District Court
established that Christie's Amsterdam's general conditions were printed in its
catalogues, that Christie's Amsterdam had presented extensive information
that in the auction trade the use of general conditions by auctioneers was customary and that Alazraki and Zelig, as professional parties active in the international art trade, were aware or should have been aware of this usage. Thus,
the District Court held that it had jurisdiction.

Case

Extenso and Combi v Royal Mail Lines, (1994) S&S 115, District Court of **708**
Rotterdam, 17 June 1994

Facts

Royal Mail Lines, incorporated in the UK, transported containers with frozen
meat from Brazil to Rotterdam. The relevant bills of lading were transferred
to Extenso and Combi, two companies incorporated in The Netherlands.
Clause 25 in the bills of lading referred all disputes thereunder to the English
courts and provided for the application of English law. Extenso and Combi
initiated proceedings against Royal Mail Lines in Rotterdam, arguing, *inter
alia*, that the choice of forum clause was invalid as to its form.

Judgment

The District Court first decided that the clause was covered by Art. 17 of the
Brussels Convention, as amended by the Third Accession Convention. This
provision could not be overridden by any reference to Dutch or Brazilian
law. Should the choice of forum clause be validly contracted between Royal
Mail Lines and the consignor, it would also be valid as between Royal Mail
Lines and Extenso and Combi as third party holders of the bills of lading
(see *Tilly Russ*, Case 71/83). Since the choice of forum clause was inserted
in the bills of lading, the requirement of Art. 17, para. 1(c) was fulfilled. The
District Court concluded that it had no jurisdiction.

Case

709   Nematron Europa v Procon Engineering und Consulting, (1996) NIPR 112,
Court of Appeal of Amsterdam, 2 February 1995, *reversing* District Court of
Utrecht, 23 March 1994, (1996) NIPR 112

Facts

Nematron, a Dutch company, sued Procon, a German company, before the
District Court of Utrecht, claiming payment of 80326.85 DM plus interest.
Procon contested the jurisdiction of the court, stating that parties expressly
agreed that payment should take place in Düsseldorf (Germany). Thus, the
District Court could not base its jurisdiction on Art. 5(1). The District Court
found for the defendant Procon and declined jurisdiction.

Nematron appealed, stating that Procon's applicable general conditions contained a valid choice of forum clause for the Dutch courts. Procon contested
applicability of its general conditions.

Judgment

The Court of Appeal held that a choice of forum clause contained in (applicable) general conditions was a form which was customary in international
trade and apparently not unknown to the parties. Jurisdiction could thus be
based on Art. 17, if it could be established that Procon's general conditions
were in fact applicable.

Procon had explicitly stipulated that its general conditions were applicable.
There was nothing to imply, nor had it been stated, that Nematron had
objected to the applicability of Procon's general conditions. It therefore had
to be concluded that Nematron accepted the applicability of those conditions,
regardless of whether Nematron was familiar with the contents of those conditions, as was stated by Procon.

Nematron could therefore rely on the choice of forum clause in favour of
the District Court of Utrecht contained in the general conditions.

Comment

If in this case *Procon* had relied on the choice of forum clause in its general
conditions, the Court of Appeal would no doubt have been less lenient (see the
cases discussed *supra*)!

> ## ARTICLE 17, PARAGRAPH 5/LUGANO PARAGRAPH 4
>
> *" . . . for the benefit of only one of the parties . . . "*

Case principle

Interpretation of the choice of forum clause: was the choice made for the benefit of only one of the parties?

Case

MMV v Aerts, (1993) NIPR 162, Court of Appeal of 's-Hertogenbosch, **710**
2 December 1992, *reversing* District Court of Roermond, 28 November 1991

Facts

MMV, a German company, sued Aerts, domiciled in The Netherlands, for payment under a surety contract in the District Court of Roermond. The contract contained a clause attributing jurisdiction to the courts in Koblenz 'according to MMV's choice'. Aerts argued that the District Court of Roermond had no jurisdiction, since the choice of forum clause was not made for MMV's benefit, but also for that of Aerts. The District Court held that there were insufficient grounds to decide that the clause was only made for MMV's benefit and declined jurisdiction. MMV appealed.

Judgment

The Court of Appeal referred to the European Court of Justice's decision in *Anterist v Crédit Lyonnais* Case 22/85 of 24 June 1986, holding that it had to be established whether the parties had a common intention to confer an advantage on one of them, from the terms of the choice of forum clause, from all the evidence to be found in the contract, or from the circumstances in which the contract was concluded. Here, the text of the clause demonstrated such a common intention, since it enabled only MMV to use the courts in Koblenz. The Court of Appeal found no evidence that the parties' choice of the courts in Koblenz was also made in Aerts's interest. The clause's text did not allow for an interpretation other than that it was for MMV, and MMV alone, to choose to proceed before the courts in Koblenz rather than in the Dutch courts. The Court of Appeal reversed the District Court's judgment and held that the latter court had jurisdiction to hear the case.

Case

Van Morkhoven v Van Kleef, (1994) NIPR 297, Court of Appeal of **711**
's-Hertogenbosch, 31 January 1994, *affirming* District Court of 's-Hertogenbosch, 18 September 1992

Facts

In 1987, Van Morkhoven, domiciled in Spain, made a contract with Van Kleef, domiciled in The Netherlands, for the sale of a piece of land in Spain and the construction of a house on it. The contract contained a choice of forum clause for the local Spanish courts. Van Morkhoven sued Van Kleef in the District

Court of 's-Hertogenbosch for payment of the remaining part of the agreed price. The District Court held that, in view of the clause, it had no jurisdiction. Van Morkhoven appealed.

Judgment

The Court of Appeal held that the mere fact that the parties had chosen the courts of the State in which one of them was domiciled, did not justify the conclusion that the choice was made for the benefit of that party alone. Moreover, Van Kleef had explicitly denied that the parties had a common intention to that effect and there were no other facts to support Van Morkhoven's argument based on Art. 17, para. 5(4). Neither the fact that Van Kleef, at the time when the contract was made, was domiciled in The Netherlands and would probably keep his domicile there, nor the fact that the Spanish courts had not been given exclusive jurisdiction, were sufficient grounds to lead the Court of Appeal to another interpretation. On the contrary, since the house was located in Spain and Van Kleef wanted to defend himself against Van Morkhoven's claim, Van Kleef had a legitimate interest in the local courts' jurisdiction. Finally, the Court of Appeal said that Van Kleef's behaviour did not constitute an 'abuse of rights'. The District Court's decline of jurisdiction was affirmed.

Comment

See also *1. Stinnes; 2. Hofka Sampermans v Vredestein Nederland*, (1995) NIPR 556, District Court of Arnhem, 13 April 1995.

Case

712   Opree v Interrent Europcar Autovermietung, (1995) NJ 219, District Court of Maastricht, 16 December 1993, *affirming* Justice of the Peace of Maastricht, 19 June 1991

Facts

See *supra*, Case 704.

Opree, domiciled in The Netherlands, was sued by Interrent, a German company, for payment of the lease of an automobile. On appeal, Opree invoked a choice of forum clause in Interrent's general conditions, conferring jurisdiction on the courts in Hamburg.

Judgment

The District Court held that the relevant clause was explicitly written for the situation where the lessee of an automobile, at the time when the lease was entered into or thereafter, was not domiciled in Germany or had no known domicile or residence. For these situations, the clause departed from the general rule that disputes were to be brought before the courts identified by either statute or convention. In other words, the clause's rationale was that Interrent wished to attribute jurisdiction to the German courts for itself in all possible situations. Thus, the clause was made solely for Interrent's benefit. Opree's interest to be able to bring a suit in Germany was considered merely a fortuitous circumstance. Since the clause was inserted in Interrent's general conditions, the District Court would only decide differently if the parties' common intention was to make the clause for their mutual benefit. However, there was insufficient evidence supporting the latter view. The District Court held that the Dutch courts had jurisdiction.

ARTICLE 18

" . . . solely to contest . . . "

Case principle

Article 18 enables a defendant to contest jurisdiction, without exclusion of his right to present his substantive defences after his jurisdictional argument has been rejected. If necessary, Art. 18 prevails over national law.

Case

Bata v Beugro, (1984) NJ 745, Court of Appeal of Leeuwarden, 4 April 1984,   **713**
reversing District Court of Groningen, 16 October 1981, and 30 July 1982

Facts

In a dispute brought by the Dutch company Beugro against the French company Bata before the District Court of Groningen, Bata contested the District Court's jurisdiction under the Brussels Convention. The District Court rejected this argument and held that it had jurisdiction to entertain the case. Subsequently, the District Court held that Art. 154 of the Code of Civil Procedure—stipulating that a defence as to lack of jurisdiction shall be raised before all other defences—was not applicable here. Since Bata's statement of defence only raised the issue of jurisdiction, the District Court held that Bata was now precluded from presenting its substantive arguments against Beugro's claim. Bata appealed, *inter alia*, against this interpretation of Art. 154 of the Code of Civil Procedure.

Judgment

The Court of Appeal started with a reference to the European Court of Justice's decision of 24 June 1981 in *Elefanten Schuh v Jacqmain* Case 150/80, holding that a defendant *may*, under certain conditions, combine his claim for lack of jurisdiction with his substantive arguments. The question before the Court of Appeal was whether a defendant *must* combine both defences, if national (Dutch) law so required? The Court of Appeal answered this question negatively, for the following reasons:

(1) The Dutch, as well as most of the other foreign texts of Art. 18, and the European Court's decision, led to the conclusion that the defendant could always choose merely to present his jurisdictional defence.

(2) If (non-uniform) national law were to govern this issue, this could result in the situation that judgments rendered in the State of origin without a fair hearing on the merits of the case, were to be recognized and enforced in other States.

(3) Even if national law were to govern this issue, this did not affect the principle that the Convention directly governed the issue of jurisdiction.

Therefore, Art. 154 of the Code of Civil Procedure had to be interpreted in such a way as to allow a defendant merely to present his arguments as to lack of jurisdiction, without precluding his right to present his substantive arguments, should his jurisdictional defence be rejected.

ARTICLE 20, PARAGRAPH 1

" . . . of its own motion . . . "

Case principle

If the defendant objects to a default judgment and claims lack of jurisdiction, the plaintiff may still present his argument that the court has jurisdiction in conformity with the Brussels Convention. The court hearing the objection may also take account of facts other than those contained in the original writ of summons.

Case

714 Rathglade v Studio Press Holland, (1994) NJ 770, Court of Appeal of Amsterdam, 10 February 1994, *affirming* District Court of Amsterdam, 16 October 1991, and 18 November 1992

Facts

Studio Press Holland, a Dutch company, sued Rathglade, an English company, in the District Court of Amsterdam. This court rendered a default judgment against Rathglade. The latter party initiated proceedings before the District Court against the default judgment in accordance with Dutch law and invoked the District Court's lack of jurisdiction under the Brussels Convention. The District Court, deciding on Rathglade's objections against the default judgment, rejected Rathglade's jurisdictional argument. Thereupon, Rathglade appealed to the Court of Appeal against the latter decision.

Judgment

The Court of Appeal held that where Studio Press Holland's original writ of summons did not contain a basis for jurisdiction under the Brussels Convention, the District Court should have applied Art. 20, para. 1 since Rathglade had not entered an appearance. On the other hand, Studio Press Holland's omission could still be rectified in the present proceedings brought by Rathglade against the District Court's default judgment. The Court of Appeal also held that, in order to decide—which decision, pursuant to Arts 20, para. 1 and 1(1), was to be made *ex officio*—on the issue of jurisdiction, the courts should not only look at the original writ of summons, but also at other facts and evidence, brought forward by either party.

ARTICLE 21

" . . . *same cause of action* . . . "

Case principle

1. The Dutch courts will stay the proceedings and decline jurisdiction in conformity with Art. 21, if the foreign and Dutch proceedings involve the same cause of action and the same parties.

Case

MMS Europe v Gruas, (1993) NIPR 169, District Court of Amsterdam,   **715**
28 October 1992

Facts

MMS Europe, a Dutch company, sued Gruas, a Spanish company, in the District Court of Amsterdam for payment for delivery under a distributorship agreement. The agreement contained a choice of forum clause in favour of the courts in Amsterdam. Gruas invoked Art. 21, arguing that the District Court should decline jurisdiction or stay its proceedings, since Gruas had already started proceedings against MMS Europe in the Tribunal de Barcelona under the same distributorship agreement. MMS Europe replied that the two sets of proceedings did not involve 'the same cause of action' as required by Art. 21 and that in the Spanish proceedings it had already argued lack of jurisdiction for the Tribunal de Barcelona on the basis of the Dutch choice of forum clause.

Judgment

The District Court held that where both claims were based on the distributorship agreement, the two sets of proceedings did involve the same cause of action. Therefore, the District Court should stay its proceedings until the Tribunal de Barcelona, which was the court first seised, had decided on the issue of its jurisdiction. The District Court then stayed the proceedings, ordering MMS Europe to present a copy of the decision of the Tribunal de Barcelona.

Case

716   Ampersand Ltd and Ampersand Software BV v Sisro, (1996) NJ 259, Hoge Raad, 10 November 1995, *affirming* Court of Appeal of Amsterdam, 26 May 1994, (1995) NIPR 256, *reversing* District Court of Amsterdam, 22 August 1990, (1991) NIPR 220

Facts

Sisro, a French company, alleged that Ampersand Ltd, a company incorporated on the Isle of Man, and Ampersand Software BV, a Dutch company (both companies hereinafter jointly referred to as Ampersand), infringed upon Sisro's copyright on the computer program called Cortex. Sisro initiated proceedings against Ampersand in the Tribunal de Grande Instance Paris, which awarded damages to Sisro. Ampersand lodged an appeal against this decision, which was still pending. Meanwhile, Sisro attached assets belonging to Ampersand, which were located in The Netherlands. In the case before the District Court of Amsterdam, Sisro claimed validation of the attachment, pending the outcome of the proceedings in Paris. By way of counterclaim, Ampersand demanded a declaratory judgment to the effect that it had not infringed upon Sisro's copyright. Sisro alleged that this counterclaim was covered by Art. 21. The District Court rejected Sisro's argument based on Art. 21. Sisro appealed from this decision. The Court of Appeal followed Sisro's argument as to Art. 21 and reversed the District Court's ruling. Thereupon, Ampersand lodged an appeal in cassation.

Judgment

The District Court had held that the declaratory judgment sought by Ampersand could only concern Sisro's copyright in The Netherlands, whereas the courts in Paris could only take cognizance of the alleged infringement of Sisro's copyright in France. Therefore, the two sets of proceedings did not involve 'the same cause of action' as required by Art. 21.

The Court of Appeal had held that—notwithstanding the territorial effect of a copyright under both French and Dutch law—the Tribunal de Grande Instance Paris had also paid attention to the alleged copyright infringement in The Netherlands and had included this infringement in the total amount of damages awarded to Sisro. The Court of Appeal established that the declaratory judgment sought by Ampersand was completely modelled upon the French proceedings and essentially concerned the same infringement already reviewed by the French court. Therefore, the counterclaim in The Netherlands was covered by Art. 21 and the Dutch courts were not permitted to rule on the merits of the alleged infringement in The Netherlands. However, since Ampersand had lodged an appeal against the decision of the Tribunal de Grande Instance Paris, which was still pending, the jurisdiction of the French courts as to the Dutch infringement was not yet finally established. The Court of Appeal therefore referred the case to the District Court with the instruction to stay its proceedings until the French courts' jurisdiction was finally established.

The Hoge Raad cited the European Court of Justice's decision in *Maciej Rataj* Case C–406/92 of 6 December 1992, [1994] ECR I–5439, holding that Art. 21 was to be interpreted in such a way that proceedings for a judgment to the effect that the defendant was liable for damages involved 'the same cause of action' as proceedings lodged by this defendant aimed at a declaratory judgment to the effect that he was not liable for those damages.

The Hoge Raad continued: 'In this case, the Court of Appeal started from the premise that the issue put forward in Ampersand's counterclaim was totally covered by and did not concern anything but the issue presented by Sisro in its claim before the French courts. This issue concerns the question of whether Ampersand, through the use and exploitation of a certain computer program, infringed upon Sisro's copyright on the Cortex program. Contrary to what Ampersand argued, the fact that the parties answered this question in opposite ways, as evidenced by their respective claims, did not justify the conclusion that the proceedings concerned different causes of action. On this basis and taking into account the above mentioned interpretation of Art. 21, the Court of Appeal, in its judgment, did not apply the law in an incorrect manner.'

Ampersand's appeal in cassation was dismissed.

Case principle

2.   Article 21 does not affect the Dutch courts' jurisdiction to issue provisional and protective measures pursuant to Art. 24, if the foreign proceedings relate to the merits of the case.

Case

Trade Link v Selettra, (1992) NIPR 419, Court of Appeal of Amsterdam, 16 **717** July 1992, *reversing* President District Court of Utrecht, 23 April 1991

See infra, Art. 24, Case 720.

Case

718   Box Doccia Megius v Wilux International, (1992) NIPR 420, Court of Appeal
of Amsterdam, 16 July 1992, *reversing* President District Court of Utrecht,
16 April 1992, (1992) KG 189

See infra, Art. 24, Case 721.

ARTICLE 22, PARAGRAPH 3

" . . . risk of irreconcilable judgments . . . "

Case principle

Article 22 may be given a broad interpretation so as to avoid irreconcilable
judgments. Before eventually declining jurisdiction in favour of the court first-
seised, the court subsequently seised should ascertain whether the court first-
seised will actually hear the case and, pending the latter court's decision on this
issue, stay its proceedings.

Case

719   SCA v HAM, (1985) S&S 95, District Court of 's-Gravenhage, 1 February
1985

Translation taken from: 34 NILR 108 (1987), note Verheul.

Facts

During a hurricane in 1979, two seagoing ships of HAM went adrift in the
harbour of Fort de France, Martinique, and damaged the plant of SCA established there. SCA commenced an action for damages in the District Court of
Fort de France in 1980, which was still pending. In 1983, the District Court
of 's-Gravenhage, upon HAM's petition, limited HAM's liability on the basis
of Arts 740a *et seq.* of the Code of Commerce and Arts 320a *et seq.* of the
Code of Civil Procedure (the statutory provisions implementing the
Convention relating to the limitation of the liability of owners of seagoing
ships of 1957, providing for a procedure with one judge, the *rechter-commissaris*, and a receiver, similar to the procedure in bankruptcy). In the course of
the allocation of the liability fund, HAM contested SCA's claim, whereupon
the dispute was referred to the full court. Before the full court, SCA raised a
plea of no jurisdiction and, in the alternative, demanded that the case be
referred to the District Court of Fort de France for *lis pendens* or related
actions (Arts. 21 and 22 respectively).

Judgment

The District Court held that contested claims referred by the *rechter-commissaris* to the full court were ordinary proceedings governed by the Brussels Convention; that the creditor of the ship (SCA) took the place of the plaintiff and the shipowner the place of the defendant; and that accordingly this court had jurisdiction as being the court of HAM's registered office by virtue of Art. 2 of the Convention.

Further, the District Court considered that the action before it concerning the limitation of liability, and the action before the District Court of Fort de France concerning liability itself, were related actions, and that there was a risk of conflicting decisions. A decision by this court would necessarily entail a decision on the question of fault and the measure of damages. Besides, this court, when deciding whether HAM could limit its liability, had to face the question of 'personal fault', which could not be done without establishing and evaluating the same facts which were to be judged by the District Court of Fort de France in view of the question of liability. The risk of conflicting decisions, as well as the desirability to leave complex factual situations such as this to the court most acquainted with local circumstances, induced the court to stay the case on the basis of Art. 22. Therefore, it could be left undecided whether the court was *obliged* to stay the case of its own motion on the basis of *Art. 21* because of the identity between the 'incidental questions' in this Court (liability and measure of damages) and the principal questions in the District Court of Fort de France.

Since it was not absolutely certain the the District Court of Fort de France would be prepared and allowed to deal with this case, the court merely stayed the proceedings. As soon as the District Court of Fort de France were to take the case, the case could then be definitively deleted from the cause list of this court.

Comment

At the time this decision was rendered, the Brussels Convention did not yet contain Art. 6a. The Convention relating to the limitation of the liability of owners of seagoing ships of 1957 has been superseded, for The Netherlands as of 1 September 1990, by the Convention on limitation of liability for maritime claims of 1976. The Arts 740a *et seq.* of the Code of Commerce and Arts 320a *et seq.* of the Code of Civil Procedure were amended accordingly, with effect from 1 September 1990.

ARTICLE 24

" . . . *even if* . . . *the courts of another Contracting State have jurisdiction as to the substance* . . . "

Case principle

1. The fact that Art. 21 may cause the court ultimately to decline jurisdiction as to the substance of the matter, does not mean that until that time the President cannot assume jurisdiction in summary proceedings to take provisional measures. The court in summary proceedings may, even if the court of another Contracting State has jurisdiction concerning the substance of the matter, base its jurisdiction on national law. In answering the question whether the requested provisional measures should be granted, account must be taken of the proceedings pending before the court of another State concerning the substance of the matter. In deciding whether permission for attachment of property should be granted, it must be taken into consideration whether or not the property is situated in The Netherlands and whether or not the requested attachment must be enforced in another State, especially when proceedings concerning the substance of the matter are pending before a court of that State. In addition, a special interest is needed to request the permission for attachment in The Netherlands of property situated elsewhere.

Case

720 Trade Link v Selettra, (1992) NIPR 419, Court of Appeal of Amsterdam, 16 July 1992, *reversing* President District Court of Utrecht, 23 April 1991

Facts

In October 1989, the Dutch company Trade Link entered into an outline contract with the Italian company Selettra, in which it was agreed that for a trial period of up to 30 June 1990, Trade Link would deliver used engines to Selettra, which Selettra would then resell to Italian companies on its own account and risk. Five different contracts of sale were entered into under this outline-agreement, each on the following conditions: (i) delivery to be performed at the place of destination; (ii) conditions for delivery C.I.F; and (iii) payment due 30 days after delivery. Selettra left part of several purchase prices unpaid.

Trade Link started summary proceedings before the District Court of Utrecht on 18 April 1991 against Selettra and claimed: payment of the unpaid purchase prices; alternatively, in order to secure the main claim, permission to attach Selettra's bank account in Italy and permission for the attachment of property belonging to Selettra situated in Italy; alternatively, a bank guarantee from Selettra. Trade Link based its claim on breach of contract by Selettra through non-performance of the obligation to pay. Trade Link was of the opinion that Dutch law governed the contract and that the Dutch courts had jurisdiction in this matter. Selettra contested the jurisdiction of the District Court. The President found for the defendant and declined jurisdiction for all three claims. Trade Link appealed.

Meanwhile a procedure between the parties was pending in Italy, initiated by Selettra through a writ of summons dated 16 November 1990 and served on Trade Link on 11 December 1990, summoning Trade Link to appear before the Court of Monza on 27 June 1991. Selettra claimed rescission of the contract plus damages and the determination of the amount of the debt owed by Selettra to Trade Link with a view to a set-off against the damages Trade Link owed to Selettra.

Judgment

The Court of Appeal held that the dispute concerned the question whether the President could assume jurisdiction concerning the different claims brought by Trade Link. These claims were the following: (i) payment, by way of a provisional measure, of the purchase price left unpaid by Selettra; (ii) permission for attachment; and (iii) security for the claim under (i).

(i) The claim for payment

From the facts of the case it could not be inferred that the parties had agreed on a place of performance for the payment of the purchase price. The clause in the contract stating: 'payment 30 days after delivery' did not in any clear way designate a place of performance. It therefore had to be assumed that parties had not set aside the provision of Art. 59(1) of the Uniform Law on the International Sale of Goods of 1964 (which Article uncontestedly governed the relations between the parties). This Article stipulated that the purchaser was to pay at the place of domicile/establishment of the seller, in this case in The Netherlands. This meant that the Dutch courts could assume jurisdiction pursuant to Art. 5(1). The President had thus unjustly declared himself incompetent to issue a provisional measure pending the proceedings before the court judging the substance of the matter.

The above was, however, without prejudice to the fact that proceedings were pending before the Court in Monza (Italy), which had been requested to determine the amount of the unpaid purchase price owed by Selettra to Trade Link. According to the case law of the European Court of Justice (*Gubisch v Palumbo* Case 144/86 of 8 December 1987), this was a matter involving the same cause of action within the meaning of Art. 21. It was true that this would mean that the Dutch courts, in a procedure started by Trade Link concerning the substance of the matter, would have to stay the proceedings until the jurisdiction of the Court of Monza had been determined and in that event decline jurisdiction. This, however, did not mean that until that time the President could not assume jurisdiction in summary proceedings to take provisional measures. It had to be taken into consideration that in connection with Art. 24, it was to be assumed that the court in summary proceedings, even if the court of another Contracting State had jurisdiction concerning the substance of the matter, could base its jurisdiction on national law.

In answering the question whether the requested provisional measures should be granted, account had to be taken of the procedure pending before the Court of Monza.

The President had thus unjustly declined jurisdiction. The question whether the requested provisional measures in the summary proceedings should be granted was, however, dependent on whether they were to take effect in The Netherlands. This was not the case. Together with the fact that a Dutch court would probably have to decline jurisdiction as to the substance of the matter in favour of the Court of Monza, this led to the conclusion that the provisional measures could not be granted.

(ii) *Permission for attachment*

Pursuant to the Dutch interpretation of Art. 24, the President should have assumed jurisdiction based on provisions of Dutch internal law, which provided for jurisdiction in summary proceedings for the President of the District Court which could assume jurisdiction concerning the substance of the matter.

This, however, would probably not be of any use to Trade Link. It is true that the decision of the European Court of Justice in *Denilauler v Couchet Frères* Case 125/79 of 21 May 1980, in connection with Arts 24 and 25 *et seq.*, did not exclude the possibility that, under certain circumstances, permission for attachment taking effect in another State could be given, but in judging whether such permission should be granted, special caution had to be taken, because the attachment would be enforced in another State and the court of that State would probably be in the best position to judge which provisional or protective measures were appropriate.

In this case, the requested permission for attachment was declined, for lack of a sufficient legal basis. It was thereby taken into consideration that none of the property for which permission of attachment was requested, was situated in The Netherlands and the requested attachment had to be enforced in Italy, where a procedure as to the substance of the matter was pending. In addition, nothing was put forward to suggest that there was a special interest to request permission for attachment in The Netherlands.

(iii) *Security*

Although, in the light of the above, the President should have assumed jurisdiction in this matter, the request would, for lack of a sufficient legal basis, as set out above, be declined.

The judgment of the President of the District Court had to be reversed, because the President had unjustly declined jurisdiction. The requested provisional measures and the permission for attachment would, however, be refused.

Case principle

2. Article 24 creates a separate jurisdiction regime to the extent that, even if a court of another Contracting State has jurisdiction as to the substance of the original claim, the court of a Contracting State may claim jurisdiction—as far as provisional measures are concerned—on the basis of its

national law. The fact that the latter court will also look into the substance of a claim already pending in the first court, does not affect this interpretation of Art. 24.

Case

Box Doccia Megius v Wilux International, (1992) NIPR 420, Court of Appeal **721**
of Amsterdam, 16 July 1992, *reversing* President District Court of Utrecht,
16 April 1992, (1992) KG 189

Facts

In 1984, the Italian firm Megius entered into an oral agreement with the Dutch firm Willux, concerning the resale by Willux of shower cubicles, manufactured by Megius in Europe, with the exception of Italy and France. Megius started proceedings before the Italian District Court of Padua on 12 March 1992, demanding payment by Willux of the unpaid invoices and a declaratory judgment that an exclusivity-agreement had never existed between it and Willux. In the summary proceedings before the President of the District Court of Utrecht, instigated by Willux against Megius on 17 March 1992, Willux alleged that an exclusive resale-agreement did exist between it and Megius, that Megius was in breach of contract and now directly supplied its new sole reseller, undercutting market prices, which was detrimental to Willux. On these grounds, Willux claimed that Megius should perform the contract as agreed and demanded an order prohibiting Megius from selling shower cubicles to the other/new reseller. The President of the District Court of Utrecht declared himself competent and entered judgment for Willux. Megius appealed to the Court of Appeal of Amsterdam, claiming, amongst other things, that the President of the District Court should have declined jurisdiction under Art. 21.

Judgment

The Court of Appeal held that Art. 24 created a separate jurisdiction regime to the extent that, although a court of another Contracting State had jurisdiction as to the substance of the matter, the court of a different Contracting State could claim provisional jurisdiction on the basis of its national law. The fact that the latter court would look into the substance of a claim already pending in the first court, did not affect this interpretation. Megius seemed to overlook the fact that the court in the provisional proceedings only rendered a provisional judgment and just took provisional measures by which the competent court as to the substance of the matter was not bound.

This meant that the Dutch court did not have to decline jurisdiction or to stay the proceedings, within the meaning of Art. 21.

Comment

The judgment of the Court of Appeal leads to the conclusion that Art. 21 does not apply, when two sets of proceedings between the same parties and concerning the same cause of action have been started, if one set is concerned with provisional measures within the meaning of Art. 24 and the other set concerns the substance of the matter.

See *supra*, Cases 88, 276 and 330

Case principle

3. Jurisdiction in summary proceedings—based on Art. 24—concerning the infringement of a trade mark, does not need to be founded upon earlier infringement or other tortious action within the district of the court, but it may be based on an imminent threat of such an infringement or tortious action taking place in the future within the district.

    However, Art. 24 does not provide jurisdiction when provisional measures, such as an order to prohibit certain conduct, have been demanded for the whole territory of the European Union, thus including the district of the court, without there being other connecting factors to justify the jurisdiction of *that* court. A court cannot, under Art. 24, be made competent by extending the scope of the provisional measures requested, without there being other connecting factors to justify its competence.

Case

722 Microfilm Diffusion Belgium v Hyosung Deutschland and HS Electronics Corporation, (1993) KG 200, President District Court of Arnhem, 19 April 1993

Facts

The Belgian firm MDB sold fax machines and was the Benelux trade mark owner of the word and logotype Cafax. International registration took place on 23 May 1990. The Korean firm HS produced fax machines of the Cafax type and deposited this type as a trade mark on 6 March 1989, in Korea. The official registration of this deposit took place on 10 August 1990. The German firm Hyosung distributed these machines in Europe and Northern Africa. MDB was the exclusive distributor of the fax machines delivered to it by Hyosung from the end of 1989 to mid–1991. In this lawsuit, MDB started summary proceedings against Hyosung and demanded, *inter alia*, a prohibition of any further infringement of the trade mark in all the countries mentioned in its international depot and in the member States of the European Union.

Judgment

The District Court held, in the matter of jurisdiction, that for jurisdiction in summary proceedings it was irrelevant whether, in the district concerned, an infringement of a trade mark had occurred in the past, but only whether such infringement was likely to occur there in the future and that provisional measures were required there. Although the infringement of a trade mark in a certain place in the past could very well justify the fear of such infringements occurring there in the future, this was not the case in these proceedings.

The fact that the competent court could issue an order, prohibiting any further wrongful acts, which also had effect outside The Netherlands, did not of course mean that a court could be made competent by demanding a prohibition order with such a wide scope when there were no other connecting factors for the court's competence. Thus, Art. 24 did not confer jurisdiction in this case.

The conclusion was that the President of the District Court did not have jurisdiction.

Case principle

4. For jurisdiction under Art. 24, it is not enough that the court has jurisdiction under national law, when that jurisdiction is solely based on the place of domicile of the plaintiff. There must be other connecting factors to justify its jurisdiction. The *forum non conveniens* rule must be applied. The fact that the requested provisional measures will have effect in the State of the issuing court is sufficient to fulfil the requirements imposed by the *forum non conveniens* rule.

Case

Deco-Line and Determann v Van Uden Maritime, (1995) KG 449, Court of **723** Appeal of 's-Gravenhage, 11 October 1994, *reversing* President District Court of Rotterdam, 21 July 1994, (1994) KG 334

Facts

In March 1993, Van Uden and Deco-Line entered into a 'slot/space charter agreement'. Under that agreement Van Uden had to supply Deco-Line with cargo space on board ships which Van Uden either exploited itself or did so in collaboration with others in connection with a scheduled service between North/Western Europe and the Ivory Coast. Deco-Line had the duty to pay the agreed price for the charter of the supplied cargo space. As a consequence of the fact that Deco-Line left certain invoices unpaid, Van Uden started arbitration against Deco-Line, in conformity with Art. 10 of the agreement. Arguing that Deco-Line was delaying in the selection of arbitrators and that non-payment endangered its financial position, Van Uden started summary proceedings before the President of the District Court of Rotterdam, claiming payment of several invoices.

Deco-Line contested the jurisdiction of the President of the District Court. The President, however, considered himself competent and found for the plaintiff. On appeal Deco-Line again contested the jurisdiction of the President.

Judgment

The Court of Appeal held that the President of the District Court, referring to Art. 24, had based his jurisdiction on Art. 126(3) of the Code of Civil Procedure, which stipulated that the court of the place of the plaintiff's domicile was competent, when the defendant was not domiciled within The Netherlands.

Pursuant to Art. 24, such provisional measures as may be available under the law of a Contracting State could be issued by the courts of that State, even if, under the Brussels Convention, the courts of another Contracting State had jurisdiction as to the substance of the matter. This meant that, in a petition for provisional measures, the Dutch courts could base their jurisdiction on the rule laid down in Art. 126(3) of the Code of Civil Procedure.

The President, however, was of the opinion that for international jurisdiction, it was not sufficient that he had been given jurisdiction by convention or statute, when the basis for that jurisdiction lay solely in the fact that the *plaintiff* had his domicile in The Netherlands. In that case, there had to be other factors, *i.e.* sufficient connections with the Dutch legal sphere, to justify the assumption of international jurisdiction. The Court of Appeal shared this opinion.

The system of the Brussels Convention, which assumed that provisional measures had to be requested before the court of the place where the measures were to take effect, did not allow the court to assume jurisdiction in matters of provisional measures solely on the basis of the place of domicile of the plaintiff.

This meant that the question of whether the President had international jurisdiction concerning the provisional measures had to be answered according to whether the measures were to take effect in The Netherlands.

While the President was of the opinion that this was the case, the Court of Appeal did not think so. The Court of Appeal decided that there were not sufficient grounds on which the international jurisdiction of the Dutch court could be based and reversed the judgment of the President of the District Court of Rotterdam.

Comment

Van Uden Maritime appealed the decision of the Court of Appeal of 's-Gravenhage to the Hoge Raad, 8 December 1995, (1995) Rvd W 262, (1996) NIPR 107. The Hoge Raad put eight questions, concerning the interpretation of Art. 24 (specifically whether summary proceedings fell within the scope of Art. 24), to the European Court of Justice for a preliminary ruling in Case C-391/95.

Case principle

5.   The court in summary proceedings can claim jurisdiction under Art. 24 if the requested measures are to take effect within the district of the court *or* if the defendant is domiciled in the district of the court.

Case

724   Interform v Krupp Maschinenbau, (1995) NIPR 560, President District Court of Haarlem, 21 July 1995

Facts

On 25 January 1995, the German company Krupp made a written offer for the sale of a machine to the Dutch company Interform, with its seat in

Haarlem. Subsequently, Interform found a buyer for the machine and informed Krupp on 14 April and 2 May 1995, that it accepted the offer. On 18 May 1995, Krupp informed Interform that the machine had in the meantime been sold and that it withdrew its offer.

Interform claimed in summary proceedings primarily that Krupp should be ordered to deliver the machine to it and to issue a letter of credit for its benefit from a Dutch or German bank, and, subsequently to prohibit Krupp from selling and/or delivering the machine to others.

Judgment

The President of the District Court held that in accordance with the provisions of Art. 5(1) and (3) of the Brussels Convention, the German court had jurisdiction as to the substance of the original claim, so that the President could not base his jurisdiction on those provisions.

Subsequently, the President had to determine whether he had jurisdiction on the basis of Art. 24.

In accordance with the prevailing opinion, the President could take jurisdiction under Art. 24 if the requested measures were to take effect within his district or if the defendant was domiciled within his district.

The President concluded that neither one of the conditions was fulfilled so that he could not base his jurisdiction on Art. 24.

Comment

Looking at all the cases discussed above, it could hardly be argued that there was a prevailing opinion in The Netherlands on the interpretation of Art. 24. The decision has been appealed.

See, however, for a similar decision: *Becker v Spaan*, President District Court of Arnhem, 11 October 1994, *reversed on other grounds by* Court of Appeal of Arnhem, 10 January 1995, *then later affirmed by* Hoge Raad, 19 January 1996.

> **ARTICLE 25**
>
> " . . . *any judgment given by a court or tribunal* . . . "

Case principle

A German *Kostenrechnung* is not to be considered a judgment as referred to in Art. 25.

Case

Zilken and Weber v Scholl, (1982) NJ 466, President District Court of **725**
Maastricht, 11 November 1981

The case is discussed infra, under Art. 50, Case 740.

ARTICLE 26, PARAGRAPH 1

" . . . shall be recognized . . . "

Case principle

The recognition of a foreign judgment implies that the judgment must have the same effects in the State addressed as it does in the State of origin.

Case

726 X v Y, (1979) NJ 399, note Schultsz, Hoge Raad, 26 January 1979, *affirming* District Court of Maastricht, 23 February 1978, *affirming* President District Court of Maastricht, 2 June 1977

Translation taken from: 28 NILR 84 (1981), note Verheul.

Facts

A wife, domiciled in Belgium, had obtained from the Justice of the Peace of Maasmechelen (Belgium) a decree authorizing her to receive 60 per cent of her husband's social insurance allowance. The husband was domiciled in Maastricht (The Netherlands) and so was the social insurance office charged with payment of the allowance. The decree was based on Art. 221 of the Belgian Civil Code which reads as follows:

> Each spouse contributes to the charges of the marriage according to his/her capacity.
> When one of the spouses does not fulfil this obligation, the other (...) may have him-/herself authorized by the Justice of the Peace to receive his/her revenue (...) as well as any other amounts of money owed to him/her by third persons, under the conditions and the extent as determined in the decree.
> The decree may be invoked as against any present or future third person-debtor, after notification by the court clerk on the request of the petitioner (...).
> If afterwards a petition for divorce or separation is filed, the authorization nevertheless continues to be enforceable until the decision of the court, or of the president in summary proceedings.

As the 'third person-debtor' was domiciled in The Netherlands (the social insurance office in Maastricht), the wife sought and obtained an order for enforcement from the President of the District Court of Maastricht. The husband appealed to the District Court, but was unsuccessful. Thereupon, the husband lodged an appeal in cassation with the Hoge Raad. He invoked, *inter alia*, the following argument. The Belgian Justice of the Peace had given two decisions: (i) the authorization to receive 60 per cent of the social insurance allowance for the maintenance of the wife and two children; and (ii) an order directed to the social insurance administration in Maastricht, to pay the said 60 per cent directly to the wife as from 1 January 1977. However, the order for enforcement was granted by the President of the District Court of Maastricht only as regards the former decision mentioned under (i). This authorization as such, not complemented by an order directed to the social insurance office, was not liable to enforcement, since it did not lay any obligation on that office. Granting the order for enforcement on the decision (i) alone had no clear effect in The Netherlands, led to confusion and procedural complications, and was therefore contrary to Dutch public policy.

Judgment

The Hoge Raad held that the order for enforcement implied that the Belgian decision should be recognized in full in the sense of Art. 26 of the Brussels Convention. The order for enforcement had significance owing to this implied determination, which meant that the authorization granted to the wife, even on the basis of Art. 221 of the Belgian Civil Code, had to have effect as such in The Netherlands as well. That meant that the social insurance office in Maastricht was not legally discharged by paying out to the husband as far as the said percentage was concerned.

Comment

The Hoge Raad's decision seems to be in line with the European Court of Justice's ruling in *Hoffmann v Krieg* Case 145/86 of 4 February 1988, which also indicated that a judgment must in principle have the same effects in the State addressed as it does in the State of origin. The Hoge Raad's decision is also discussed under Arts 27(1) and (3), *infra*, Cases 728 and 734.

ARTICLE 26, PARAGRAPH 2

" . . . *interested party* . . . "

Case principle

Article 26 only provides for a decision to recognize a foreign judgment, not also for a declaratory decision that a foreign judgment *cannot* be recognized. A party opposing the enforcement of a foreign judgment should make use of the appeals procedure of Arts 36 *et seq*.

Case

727 Van den Broek v Ranieri, (1994) NIPR 157, Court of Appeal of 's-Hertogenbosch, 17 December 1993, *affirming* President District Court of Breda, 31 August 1993

Facts

Van den Broek, a Dutch company, petitioned the President of the District Court of Breda to: (i) declare that two judgments rendered against Van den Broek by the Pretura circondariale Catanzaro (Italy) could not be recognized; or (ii) to recognize these judgments notwithstanding Van den Broek's objections against them. The President held that Van den Broek's application could not be received in this petition. Van den Broek appealed.

Judgment

The Court of Appeal held that both judgments were rendered against Van den Broek. Article 26 only provided for the application for a decision that a judgment be recognized, for the purposes of enforcement, and did not permit the party against whom the judgment was rendered to address the court for a decision on the possibilities of its recognition. Thus, Van den Broek could not be considered an 'interested party' as referred to in Art. 26(2). The Court of Appeal pointed out that Van den Broek could make use of the procedure of Art. 36 *et seq.*: an appeal against the decision to authorize the judgment's enforcement, which procedure Van den Broek had meanwhile commenced. For the same reason, the Court of Appeal refused to stay its proceedings until a decision was rendered on the appeal against the enforcement authorization.

Comment

See Kaye, Civil Jurisdiction, pp. 1395–8 in agreement.

ARTICLE 27(1)

" . . . *contrary to public policy* . . . "

Case principle

The public policy provision of Art. 27(1) is interpreted narrowly, lest the court addressed for recognition or enforcement engage in a review as to the foreign judgment's substance.

Case

728 X v Y, (1979) NJ 399, note Schultsz, Hoge Raad, 26 January 1979, *affirming* District Court of Maastricht, 23 February 1978, *affirming* President District Court of Maastricht, 2 June 1977

Translation taken from: 28 NILR 84 (1981), note Verheul.

Facts

See *supra*, Case 726.

A wife, domiciled in Belgium, had obtained from the Justice of the Peace of Maasmechelen (Belgium) a decree authorizing her to receive 60 per cent of her husband's social insurance allowance. The husband was domiciled in Maastricht (The Netherlands) and so was the social insurance office charged with payment of the allowance. Faced with the enforcement of the Belgian decree, the husband argued, *inter alia*, that the maintenance figure of 60 per cent of the social insurance allowance (1330 Dfl. a month) substantially exceeded the husband's financial capacity, was irreconcilable with Dutch mandatory rules concerning the influence of the debtor's capacity on the amount of maintenance and anyway *in casu* was contrary to Dutch public policy.

Judgment

The Hoge Raad held that the circumstance that the husband's financial capacity was substantially exceeded, did not entail that the recognition of the decision was contrary to Dutch public policy in the sense of Art. 27(1). The interest of 'free circulation of judgments' within the EU, served in this case by recognition, weighed so heavily that the consequence of that recognition (*i.e.* that the husband might become dependent upon social assistance) should be accepted.

Comment

See the *Comment infra, Hupperichs v Dorthu*, Case 729, and *infra*, Case 734.

Case

Hupperichs v Dorthu, (1987) NJ 481, note Schultsz, Hoge Raad, 2 May 1986, **729** *affirming* District Court of Maastricht, 20 September 1984, *affirming* President District Court of Maastricht, 21 January 1982

Facts

The President of the District Court of Maastricht declared two Belgian judgments enforceable. Hupperichs appealed against this decision, and his appeal was rejected. Thereupon, Hupperichs contested this decision by an appeal in cassation.

Judgment

The Hoge Raad first established that Hupperichs had based his appeal against the decision which permitted enforcement of the Belgian judgments, on Art. 27(1), alleging that these judgments did not comply with 'minimal requirements of fair justice'. In particular, Hupperichs had argued that the experts' reports, called for by the Belgian courts, contained various omissions, as did the judgments themselves.

The Hoge Raad then agreed with the District Court that the Brussels Convention sought to achieve a 'free circulation of judgments' so that Art. 27(1)—according to its drafters—could only be applied in exceptional situations.

The Hoge Raad also agreed with the District Court that an application for enforcement could only be refused on grounds—to be scrutinized within the limits of Art. 34, para. 3—which amounted to such a violation of the principles of fair justice as were considered fundamental principles within the Dutch legal order, so that recognition and enforcement could not be permitted.

Finally, the Hoge Raad agreed with the District Court that this condition was not fulfilled in the present case. Hupperichs's alleged omissions in the Belgian judgments all came down to the Belgian courts' refusal to let Hupperichs present evidence on the cash payment for deliveries. However, Hupperichs's offer to present such evidence had been refused in well-reasoned decisions, presumably in accordance with the relevant Belgian rules. Hupperichs's statement that the Belgian courts' reasoning was 'completely unfair' was based on facts already reviewed by the Belgian courts and was thus non-reviewable under the 'no review as to the substance' rule of Art. 34, para. 3.

The Hoge Raad rejected the appeal in cassation against the District Court's decision.

Comment

Both decisions would seem to be in line with the European Court of Justice's decision in *Hoffmann v Krieg* Case 145/86 of 4 February 1988, which indicates that the public policy clause must be applied restrictively. See also *N v B*, (1996) RvdW 198 Hoge Raad, 11 October 1996, which is discussed under Art. 27(2), Case 733.

ARTICLE 27(2)

" . . . *to enable him to arrange for his defence."*

Case principle

1. The Dutch courts vary in opinion as to whether Art. 27(2) requires that the defendant be notified that a civil claim for damages will be lodged during criminal proceedings.

Case

730 CSM and Mathijssen v De Deugd, (1983) NJ 308, note Schultsz, Court of Appeal of 's-Hertogenbosch, 25 June 1981, *reversing* President District Court of Breda, 17 June 1980

Facts

Within the framework of criminal proceedings, the District Court of Turnhout (Belgium) had awarded damages to the victims, the Dutch corporation CSM and Mathijssen, domiciled in The Netherlands. The application for enforcement as against De Deugd, also domiciled in The Netherlands, was refused by the President of the District Court of Breda, because De Deugd had not been sufficiently notified that the victims would present a civil claim for damages during the criminal proceedings. CSM and Mathijssen appealed.

Judgment

The Court of Appeal held that Art. 27(2) did not require that the document which instituted the proceedings should also inform the defendant that the victims, such as CSM and Mathijssen, in their capacity of plaintiffs under civil law, would lodge a civil claim for a certain amount of damages during the criminal proceedings against the defendant De Deugd.

Comment

See *infra, Comment* to *Municipality of Hemikshem v Holleman and Den Haan*, Case 731.

Case

Municipality of Hemikshem v Holleman and Den Haan, (1985) NJ 441,   **731**
President District Court of 's-Hertogenbosch, 3 August 1984

Facts

A criminal court in Antwerp had awarded damages, in a default judgment rendered on a civil claim brought by the Municipality of Hemikshem (Belgium) against a Dutch company. The Belgian judgment was presented for authorization of enforcement.

Judgment

The President held that where the document which instituted the criminal proceedings in Antwerp in no way mentioned the possibility that a third party could bring a civil claim for damages (even orally) during the criminal trial, the defendant's interests would be jeopardized if the judgment, whereby the civil claim was awarded, were to be recognized and enforced. The President held that the requirement of Art. 27(2) was not fulfilled.

Comment

Neither the Court of Appeal nor the President paid attention to Art. II of the Protocol annexed to the Brussels Convention, which would seem to be relevant here. See, on Art. II of the Protocol, European Court of Justice's *Rinkau* Case 157/80 of 26 May 1981, and *Sonntag*, Case C–172/91 of 21 April 1993.

Case principle

2.   Article 27(2) aims to protect the rights of the defendant. Those rights are not violated by the simple fact that the document instituting the proceedings failed to mention the complete name of the defendant, if that defendant has admitted that he received the document and has in fact responded to it.

Case

732   Weisz Uurwerken v Caymex, (1995) NIPR 553, District Court of Amsterdam, 14 June 1995

Facts

The District Court of Antwerp rendered a judgment in default of appearance against Weisz on 4 September 1991, ordering Weisz to pay to Caymex the amount of 150000 Belgian francs. On 18 October 1991 notice of this judgment was served upon Weisz. On 21 July 1993, Caymex applied to the President of the District Court of Amsterdam for enforcement of the judgment rendered by the Court in Antwerp. An order for enforcement was issued by the President on 26 November 1993.

Weisz appealed against enforcement, claiming that she was not duly served with the document instituting the proceedings.

Judgment

The District Court held that Art. 27(2) aimed to protect the rights of the defendant. The simple fact that the document instituting the proceedings failed to contain the complete name 'S. Weisz Uurwerken B.V.', was insufficient for it to be concluded that the rights of the defendant were violated, considering that Weisz had not denied that the address stated in the document was correct nor that she had received the document. Moreover, she had admitted that she responded to the document. Therefore, it had to be concluded that Weisz was duly served with the document instituting the proceedings in Antwerp, within the meaning of Art. 27(2).

Case principle

3.   Article 27(2) does not require evidence of the fact that the document instituting the proceedings actually reached the defendant. When it has been established that, in accordance with the law of the court of origin, the defendant has been duly served with the document and in sufficient time, the court addressed for recognition and enforcement can only examine whether, in the specific case before it, there are exceptional circumstances which may lead to the conclusion that the document, although duly served, has not been served in such a manner as to enable the defendant to prepare for his defence.

Case

N. v B., (1996) RvdW 198, Hoge Raad, 11 October 1996, *reversing* President **733**
District Court of Almelo, 4 July 1995, *affirming* Court of Appeal of Arnhem,
9 January 1996

Facts

On 7 October 1992, within the framework of divorce proceedings, B (the wife)
requested the Justice of the Peace of Canton B, Belgium, to award her maintenance in the amount of 20 000 Belgian francs per month. N (the husband) had
already left the marital home, but had left no forwarding address. Both parties
were summoned to appear before the Justice of the Peace on 20 October 1992
to be heard in connection with the request for maintenance. Both court sum-
monses were served at the marital home. In its decision of 20 October 1992,
the Justice of the Peace, after having considered that N, 'although he had been
duly served', did not appear before the court, granted the request for maintenance in default of appearance, including several measures, one of which was to
order N to pay the maintenance of 20 000 Belgian francs.

As N had, in the meantime, moved to The Netherlands, B applied to the
President of the District Court of Almelo for enforcement of the maintenance
order. The President refused the enforcement order, because in his opinion the
defendant had not been duly served with the document instituting the proceedings, because he had already left the marital home at that time. B appealed
the decision, submitting that under Belgian law, N was duly served.

The Court of Appeal stated that the question of whether the document had
been duly served in time, was in principle to be determined by the law of the
court of origin, in this case by Belgian law. Parties agreed that under Belgian
law the document instituting the proceedings was indeed duly served. Belgian
law therefore did not obstruct the enforcement order.

However, the court deciding on enforcement, should in each specific case
check all circumstances of the case to decide whether the defendant was served
with the document in sufficient time to prepare for his defence.

This question could not be answered affirmatively, regardless of whether or
not the defendant was duly served under Belgian law, if there were exceptional
circumstances which stood in the way of enforcement. Such a circumstance
could be the fact that B had knowledge of the habitual residence of N. The
Court of Appeal was of the opinion that such was not the case, and that
enforcement of the judgment of the Justice of the Peace could not be denied on
the basis of Art. 27(2), nor on any other ground.

The Court of Appeal reversed the decision of the President and authorized
the enforcement.

N appealed, submitting that the Court of Appeal had violated the provision
of Art. 27(2), since it had been established, in retrospect, that the document
did not reach N and that the Justice of the Peace had not taken notice of the
fact that N had already left the marital home.

Judgment

The Hoge Raad held that N misjudged the fact that Art. 27(2) did not require evidence of the fact that the document instituting the proceedings had actually reached the defendant. When it had been established that the defendant had been duly served in time with the document instituting the proceedings in accordance with Belgian law, the court addressed for enforcement could only examine whether, in the specific case before it, there were exceptional circumstances which could lead to the conclusion that the document, although duly served, had not been served *in such a manner* as to enable the defendant to prepare for his defence and, thus, for the time period in Art. 27(2) to commence. The Court of Appeal had checked whether such circumstances occurred and had come to the conclusion that there were no such circumstances.

The Hoge Raad affirmed the decision of the Court of Appeal.

ARTICLE 27(3)

" . . . *irreconcilable* . . . "

Case principle

The court deciding on the application for enforcement is not bound to examine *ex officio* whether the foreign judgment is irreconcilable with a judgment rendered in the State addressed.

Case

734 X v Y, (1979) NJ 399, note Schultsz, Hoge Raad, 26 January 1979, *affirming* District Court of Maastricht, 23 February 1978, *affirming* President District Court of Maastricht, 2 June 1977

Translation taken from: 28 NILR 84 (1981), note Verheul.

Facts

See *supra*, Case 726.

A wife, domiciled in Belgium, had obtained from the Justice of the Peace of Maasmechelen (Belgium) a decree authorizing her to receive 60 per cent of her husband's social insurance allowance. The husband was domiciled in Maastricht (The Netherlands) and so was the social insurance office charged with payment of the allowance. The husband, *inter alia*, invoked Art. 27(3). In divorce proceedings between the parties pending before the District Court of Maastricht, the wife had sought provisional maintenance for herself and her children. The petition was, however, rejected and the husband's maintenance obligation fixed at *nihil* by an order of 19 February 1975, thus earlier than the decree of the Belgian Justice of the Peace (7 January 1977). Consequently, there was an irreconcilable judgment concerning the same parties in the sense of Art. 27(3) of the Brussels Convention and the District Court should have refused to uphold the order for enforcement.

Judgment

The Hoge Raad rejected the husband's argument. It did not appear from the pleadings that the husband had already invoked the decree of 19 February 1975 in the *exequatur* appeal proceedings before the District Court. He could not do this for the first time before the Hoge Raad, since the plea required an examination of a factual nature. The District Court was not obliged to examine *ex officio* whether in the divorce proceedings an earlier irreconcilable judgment had been rendered.

Comment

The case is also discussed *supra*, under Arts 26 and 27(1), Cases 726 and 728.

ARTICLE 27(4)

" . . . *conflicts with a rule of the private international law of the State in which the recognition is sought* . . . "

Case principle

If a foreign court does not observe the Dutch conflicts rules on divorce, the foreign court's decision as to maintenance will not be recognized in The Netherlands.

Case

X v Y, (1977) NJ 132, Court of Appeal of Amsterdam, 19 February 1976, **735** *affirming* District Court of Amsterdam, 10 January 1974

Facts

In 1973, the Tribunal de Grande Instance Créteil (France) had granted a divorce decree between two spouses with Dutch nationality. The French court had based its decision on French law, in particular Art. 232 of the Civil Code, which provided for divorce in case of 'injure grave'. The District Court held that the French divorce decree could not be recognized in The Netherlands under Dutch private international law, which—at that time—only permitted the recognition of a foreign divorce decree, rendered between two spouses who both possessed solely Dutch nationality, if the divorce was based on grounds or facts which would suffice as grounds or facts under Dutch divorce law. According to the District Court, the 'injure grave' did not qualify as a ground for divorce under Dutch law. The court then turned to the French court's decision that the husband was no longer obliged to pay maintenance to his ex-wife.

Judgment

The Court of Appeal stated that the French divorce decree was covered by the Brussels Convention as far as it contained a decision as to maintenance. The fact that both parties, at the time when the divorce procedure was commenced, lived in France, did not affect the Convention's applicability. The Court of Appeal then referred to Art. 27(4) and held that the French court, by applying French law to the divorce, had violated the Dutch conflicts rule on the applicable divorce law. Had the Dutch conflicts rule been observed, Dutch divorce law would have been applied, with the result that the husband's claim for divorce would have been rejected and the husband's obligation to pay maintenance would have continued to exist. Thus, the French court's decision that the husband was no longer obliged to pay maintenance could not be recognized in The Netherlands.

ARTICLE 36, PARAGRAPH 1

" . . . *may appeal against* . . . "

Case principle

If the party against whom enforcement is sought, has not made use of the appeals procedure of Arts 36 *et seq.*, this party may still ask for a stay of the foreign judgment's execution, but the grounds upon which the stay will be granted are very limited.

Case

736 Huberts v Belmat (1990) KG 319, President District Court of Arnhem, 18 September 1990

Facts

The Commercial Court of Nijvel (Belgium) had rendered a judgment against the Dutch company Huberts. Huberts had appealed against this judgment in accordance with Belgian law, which appeal was still pending. Meanwhile, Belmat had obtained an authorization for the judgment's enforcement in The Netherlands and had attached Huberts' bank account in The Netherlands. Huberts had not appealed against this authorization pursuant to Art. 36. In the present summary proceedings, Huberts sued Belmat before the President of the District Court of Arnhem for a provisional order not to proceed with the execution of the Belgian judgment, pending the appeal against it, provided that

Huberts issued a bank guarantee. Huberts argued, *inter alia*, that the Belgian judgment was incorrect and suffered from lack of jurisdiction.

Judgment

The President held that, notwithstanding Huberts' omission to lodge an appeal in conformity with Art. 36, proceedings to stay the foreign judgment's execution were still possible. However, the President's decision could neither be based on grounds which could not have been brought forward under Art. 36 nor on grounds which should have been presented under Art. 36. A different approach would jeopardize the system of appeals and time limits under the Brussels Convention and under national law as well as the parties' need for legal predictability and certainty.

The President held that none of the grounds of Arts 27 or 28(1) were at stake here and refused to look into issues of substance and jurisdiction, as put forward by Huberts, since such issues, pursuant to Arts 28(3) and 29, could not be reviewed in proceedings under Art. 36.

However, subsequently, the President indicated that the court deciding on the appeal against an enforcement authorization and on the staying of the appeal proceedings under Art. 38, would nevertheless not be able to escape from looking—albeit very superficially and very marginally—at the issues mentioned in Arts 28(3) and 29 nor from making a guess as to whether the foreign judgment would be reversed in the State of origin. Thus, such and similar issues as brought forward by Huberts could again have been presented under Art. 36.

The President concluded that where Huberts had omitted to initiate the appeal under Art. 36, it could not object to the Belgian judgment's enforcement on the grounds it now presented. In this connection the President remarked that since an appeal under Art. 36 automatically suspended further enforcement (Art. 39), the party against whom enforcement was sought should make use of these procedures and not wait until the real enforcement commenced.

The President decided that Huberts' application could not be admitted.

Comment

The President's decision that proceedings to stay the judgment's enforcement were possible, even if the party against whom enforcement was sought, had omitted to lodge an appeal pursuant to Art. 36, would seem to be in line with the European Court of Justice in *Hoffmann v Krieg* Case 145/86 of 4 February 1988. In its decision, the European Court of Justice also held that this party could only base its objection against enforcement on grounds that could not have been presented under Art. 36. The President's decision that the court deciding on the appeal against the enforcement authorization and on the staying of the appeal proceedings under Art. 38, would not be able to escape from looking at the issues mentioned in Arts 28(3) and 29 nor from making a fair guess as to the chances of the original judgment being reversed, would seem to be incompatible with the Court of Justice in *Van Dalfsen v Van Loon* Case

C–183/90 of 4 October 1991, holding that it was *not* permitted to take those factors into account within the framework of Art. 38.

ARTICLE 38, PARAGRAPH 1

" . . . *appeal under Article 37(1)* . . . "

Case principle

Article 38 is presumably limited to an appeal against the enforcement of a court judgment and does not cover the enforcement of an authentic instrument pursuant to Art. 50.

Case

737 Bertrand v CDE, (1992) NIPR 455, District Court of Roermond, 27 August 1992

See *infra*, Case 742.

ARTICLE 43

" . . . *finally determined by the courts* . . . "

Case principle

1. A claim for the determination of the final amount of a periodic payment by way of a penalty, with a view to its enforcement abroad under Art. 43, may be brought by way of a counterclaim in summary proceedings concerning the enforcement of the penalty, litigated in the court which, in previous summary proceedings, ordered the periodic payment by way of a penalty.

Case

738 Du Pont de Nemours v Rienstra, (1983) NJ 406, Court of Appeal of Leeuwarden, 7 April 1982, *reversing* President District Court of Leeuwarden, 12 June 1980

Facts

In summary proceedings before the President of the District Court, Rienstra claimed that the President should stay the enforcement of a penalty ordered by the same President in earlier summary proceedings. By way of counterclaim Du Pont de Nemours asked for the final determination of the amount of the payment, with a view to its later being enforced in other Contracting States in accordance with Art. 43 of the Brussels Convention.

Judgment

The Court of Appeal held that it would be inefficient if, as was the case here, the question of whether and, if so, to what extent Rienstra had forfeited the penalty, could be fully addressed by the President in the (second) summary proceedings, to force Du Pont de Nemours to sue Rienstra in separate proceedings (for the determination of the final amount). Now that Rienstra had started proceedings to stay the enforcement and to lift the attachment, an efficient way of doing justice entailed that the very President, who in the earlier summary proceedings had ordered the periodic payment by way of a penalty, was also empowered to entertain Du Pont de Nemours' counterclaim (based on Art. 611c of the Code of Civil Procedure) for the final determination of the amount of payment.

Case principle

2. The procedure of Art. 43 aims at the enforcement of the penalty and does not affect the procedure under national law whereby the penalty may be lifted or revised.

Case

Moksel v KVV, (1992) NIPR 422, Court of Appeal of 's-Gravenhage, 21 May **739** 1992, *reversing* President District Court of Middelburg, 4 April 1990, (1990) KG 153

Facts

The President of the District Court of Middelburg ordered Moksel, a German company, to deposit certain documents with a Dutch civil law notary, and ordered a periodic payment by way of a penalty in case of non-compliance. Subsequently, KVV started proceedings for purposes of Art. 43 before the District Court of Middelburg, as a step towards enforcement of the penalty in Germany. Thereupon, Moksel brought proceedings under Art. 611d of the Code of Civil Procedure before the President of the District Court of Middelburg, to lift and revise the penalty on the ground of *force majeure*. The President rejected the claim under Art. 611d. Moksel appealed.

Judgment

The President held that Art. 43 of the Brussels Convention involved a different procedure from that of Art. 611d of the Code of Civil Procedure. The former was aimed at the enforcement of penalties already forfeited and did not affect the decision whereby the penalty was ordered. The latter was aimed at the revision of (the order for) the penalty. Thus, those procedures could be entertained simultaneously by different courts. Nevertheless, if the penalty was revised under Art. 611d, this fact could be relevant for the court determining the amount forfeited under Art. 43. It was for the latter court to decide to what extent it was bound by the decision on the penalty's revision.

The Court of Appeal in fact reversed the President's decision *on other grounds.*

ARTICLE 50, PARAGRAPH 1

" . . . as an authentic instrument . . . "

Case principle

1. A German 'Kostenrechnung' is not to be considered an 'authentic instrument' as referred to in Art. 50.

Case

740 Zilken and Weber v Scholl, (1982) NJ 466, President District Court of Maastricht, 11 November 1981

Facts

Zilken and Weber, two German civil law notaries, applied for the enforcement of a *Kostenrechnung*, covering the costs of services rendered by them for their client Scholl, domiciled in The Netherlands. Zilken and Weber had provided the Kostenrechnung with a *Zwangsvollstreckung* pursuant to German law, with the result that the Kostenrechnung was enforceable in Germany.

Judgment

The President held that the Kostenrechnung was not a judgment as referred to in Art. 25, since it was neither a decision given by a court or tribunal nor a determination of costs or expenses by an officer of the court. Nor was the Kostenrechnung to be considered an authentic instrument pursuant to Art. 50. An authentic instrument contained the written statement of an agreement reached between the relevant parties, in the presence of a person with official authority, who himself is not a party to the agreement. The Kostenrechnung, on the other hand, was nothing but a statement of the costs drawn up by the civil law notaries for themselves. The fact that German law considered this Kostenrechnung as an enforceable instrument, was not sufficient for it to qualify as an authentic instrument under Art. 50.

Case principle

2. A German 'Urkunde' is to be considered an 'authentic instrument' as referred to in Art. 50.

Case

Raad voor de Kinderbescherming Middelburg v X, (1986) NJ 512, note   **741**
Schultsz, Court of Appeal of 's-Gravenhage, 18 October 1985, *reversing*
District Court of Middelburg, 17 July 1985, (1985) NIPR 389

Facts

The Raad voor de Kinderbescherming (Child Protection Board) of Middelburg applied for enforcement of an 'Urkunde', drawn up by the Bezirksamt Zehlendorf von Berlin. According to the document, X had agreed to pay monthly maintenance to the minor Y. The document had been drawn up after a session of the Bezirksamt or one of its departments or staff members, during which session X had been present. X had signed the document.

In its petition the Raad voor de Kinderbescherming had not mentioned the Brussels Convention, but merely the Hague Convention concerning the recognition and enforcement of decisions relating to maintenance obligations towards children of 1958. Faced with the fact that the latter Convention, pursuant to its Art. 1, was only applicable to court judgments, the Raad voor de Kinderbescherming, during the court hearing on its petition, amended it so as to request enforcement under the Brussels Convention.

The District Court dismissed the application on the ground that such a revision of the petition could not be admitted during the proceedings. By way of *obiter dictum*, the District Court added that the document did not constitute a judgment, as required in Art. 25 Brussels Convention.

The Raad voor de Kinderbescherming appealed, arguing, *inter alia*, that the document was to be considered an authentic instrument, as provided for in Art. 50.

Judgment

The Court of Appeal held that the Urkunde could be considered as an authentic instrument, provided for in Art. 50 of the Brussels Convention. Furthermore, the Court of Appeal held that 'in view of the nature of the dispute', the District Court, after the Raad voor de Kinderbescherming had changed its petition during the proceedings, should have decided upon the revised petition accordingly.

> " . . . *contrary to public policy* . . . "

Case principle

The public policy clause in Art. 50 is to be interpreted in a strict manner. It opposes the enforcement of an authentic instrument containing provisions which violate the public policy of the State addressed and does not allow a revision of the instrument's material validity.

Case

742 Bertrand v CDE, (1992) NIPR 455, District Court of Roermond, 27 August 1992

Facts

CDE, a French company, had obtained authorization for enforcement in The Netherlands of an authentic instrument, drawn up by a French civil law notary. Bertrand, domiciled in France, appealed against this authorization.

Judgment

The District Court first established that the parties agreed that the authentic instrument complied with the formal requirements mentioned in Art. 50 and that Bertrand's appeal against the authorization could therefore only be based upon the public policy clause in Art. 50. The District Court held that this public policy clause only envisaged the situation where enforcement was sought of an instrument containing provisions which violated Dutch public policy. However, Bertrand had merely argued that the contract, embodied in the instrument, was entered into in violation of mandatory rules of Dutch law and thus was contrary to Dutch public policy. The District Court held that such an argument was of a different nature and that the present appeal proceedings did not permit a review of the contract's validity. If Bertrand had initiated an ordinary suit in France to have the contract declared invalid, the District Court could have stayed the appeal pursuant to Art. 38. Bertrand's request for a stay under Art. 38 was, however, in no way a well-reasoned request and was therefore to be rejected. Moreover, Art. 38 was presumably limited to an appeal against the enforcement *of court decisions* and did not cover the enforcement of authentic instruments. The District Court rejected the appeal and refused to stay the proceedings.

ARTICLE 52

" . . . is domiciled . . . "

Case principle

Domicile is the sole criterion for the determination of jurisdiction under the Brussels Convention: actual residence is irrelevant.

Case

Klaassen v Driessen, (1977) NJ 480, District Court of Roermond, 15 April **743**
1976, *reversing* Justice of the Peace of Venlo, 20 August 1974

The case is discussed *supra*, under Art. 2, Case 676.

ARTICLE 53, PARAGRAPH 1

" . . . *apply its rules of private international law.*"

Case principle

In determining a company's domicile pursuant to Art. 53, the Dutch courts,
applying Dutch private international law, establish the company's *registered
seat*, in conformity with either statutory provisions or the company's articles
of association or by-laws.

Case

Interlloyd v Sevasti and Marmaras, (1992) NIPR 439, District Court of **744**
Amsterdam, 1 July 1992

Facts

Interlloyd, a Dutch company, together with several other plaintiffs, sued
Sevasti and Marmaras, two Liberian companies, before the District Court of
Amsterdam for damages sustained during sea transport. The defendants
argued that the District Court had no jurisdiction.

Judgment

In determining whether Brussels Convention jurisdiction grounds were applicable, the District Court had to establish whether Sevasti and/or Marmaras
were domiciled, as they alleged, in Piraeus (Greece). Pursuant to Art. 53, this
question of domicile had to be answered by reference to Dutch private international law, *i.e.* in accordance with the law of the place where the companies
had their registered seats, in conformity with either statutory provisions or
their own articles of association or by-laws. Both defendants had their
registered seats in Monrovia (Liberia) and they had not presented any information or facts to support their view that their domicile under Art. 53
was also located in Piraeus. The District Court decided that Brussels
Convention grounds were not applicable.

Comment

This decision is in conformity with case law and literature concerning a company's domicile under Dutch private international law. See R. van Rooij and M.V. Polak, *Private International Law in The Netherlands* 170 (1987), and Supplement 105–106 (1995).

ARTICLE 55

"*. . . supersede the following conventions . . .*"

Case principle

The Brussels Convention and its Dutch implementing statute prevail over the Convention of 1925 between Belgium and The Netherlands.

Case

745 Owel v Immobiles, (1993) NIPR 163, Court of Appeal of 's-Hertogenbosch, 11 January 1993, *reversing* District Court of Breda, 12 July 1991

Facts

The Liechtenstein company Owel sued the Dutch partnership Immobiles under a loan agreement before the Commercial Court of Turnhout (Belgium). The court delivered a default judgment in favour of Owel. Owel petitioned the President of the District Court of Breda for permission to enforce the Belgian judgment in conformity with the Convention of 1925 between Belgium and The Netherlands. The District Court of Breda, to which the application had been transferred in conformity with Arts 985 *et seq.* of the Code of Civil Procedure, refused the application for enforcement under the bilateral Convention of 1925. Owel appealed.

Judgment

The Court of Appeal held that Owel's application for enforcement was to be decided pursuant to the Brussels Convention rather than the bilateral Convention of 1925. First, the case concerned a civil and commercial matter as referred to in Art. 1, para. 1 of the Brussels Convention and did not fall under one of the exceptions mentioned there. Secondly, the subject matter of the case was not one for which Arts 55 and 56 of the Brussels Convention provide that the bilateral Convention of 1925 remains applicable, since the recognition and enforcement in one Contracting State of a judgment rendered in another Contracting State is provided for in Title III of the Brussels Convention. Pursuant to Art. 2(1) of the Dutch implementing statute to the

Brussels Convention, Arts *985 et seq.* of the Code of Civil Procedure are set aside in situations covered by Art. 31 of the Brussels Convention. According to Art. 32 of the Brussels Convention, the application for enforcement must be submitted to the President of the District Court rather than to the District Court, while the President shall review the application under the Brussels Convention and the implementing statute. Thus, the District Court's decision had to be reversed and the application transferred to the President of that Court. Since both parties based their arguments on the bilateral Convention of 1925, the Court of Appeal decided to set-off the respective parties' costs of the appeal.

ARTICLE 56, PARAGRAPH 1

" . . . continue to have effect in relation to matters to which this Convention does not apply."

Case principle

The interpretation of the Convention of 1925 between Belgium and The Netherlands should follow, as closely as possible, the interpretation of the Brussels Convention.

Case

Molenschot v Molenschot, (1992) NJ 189, note Schultsz, Hoge Raad, 30   **746**
November 1990, *affirming* Court of Appeal of 's-Hertogenbosch, 19 January 1990, *affirming* District Court of Breda, 29 September 1989

Facts

Both the District Court and the Court of Appeal agreed with the parties that the application for enforcement of a Belgian decree was not covered by the Brussels Convention, since the case concerned a matter of 'wills and succession' (Art. 1(2)(a)), and that, in view of Arts 55 and 56 of the Brussels Convention, the Convention between Belgium and The Netherlands governed the application. In all three instances, the case concerned the interpretation of the latter Convention.

Judgment

The Hoge Raad observed: 'Now that (pursuant to Arts 55 and 56 of the Brussels Convention) the bilateral Convention of 1925 has, for most of its scope of application, been superseded by the Brussels Convention and only remains in force for matters not covered by the latter Convention, it is appropriate to interpret the provisions of the bilateral Convention of 1925 as much as possible in the same way as the provisions of the Brussels Convention which deal with the same issues.'

The Hoge Raad then referred to the European Court of Justice's decision in *Denilauler v Couchet Frères* Case 125/79 of 21 May 1980, to interpret the bilateral Convention of 1925.

ARTICLE 57(1)

" . . . in relation to particular matters . . . "

Case principle

The Benelux Convention on compulsory liability insurance for automobiles of 1966 is a special convention as referred to in Art. 57 of the Brussels Convention and its Art. 7 prevails over the fora mentioned in the Brussels Convention.

Case

747 Geerdink v GMF, (1993) NIPR 306, District Court of 's-Hertogenbosch, 16 April 1993

Facts

Geerdink, domiciled in The Netherlands, was involved in an automobile accident in France. Being the victim he claimed damages from GMF, the insurer of the other automobile, in the District Court of 's-Hertogenbosch. GMF argued that the District Court should decline jurisdiction under Arts 2 and 5(3) of the Brussels Convention. Geerdink, on the other hand, invoked Art. 7 of the Benelux Convention on the compulsory liability insurance for automobiles of 1966, which enabled a victim to sue the tortfeasor's insurer in the courts of the place where the accident occurred, *in the courts of the victim's domicile*, or in the courts of the insurer's domicile.

Judgment

The District Court held that the Benelux Convention was a convention concerning a particular matter, as referred to in Art. 57 of the Brussels Convention, in the version as amended by the 1978 First Accession Convention. The Benelux Convention created the right of the victim of a car accident to bring a direct action for his damages against the tortfeasor's insurer in the courts of the victim's domicile. Such was the situation. The fact that GMF had acknowledged its liability and that the dispute would be limited to the nature and the amount of damages, did not affect the basis of the claim upon which the Dutch courts' jurisdiction was founded, *i.e.* the insurer's tort liability. Therefore, the District Court decided that it had jurisdiction by virtue of Art. 57 of the Brussels Convention and Art. 7 of the Benelux Convention, it being the court of the victim's domicile.

The District Court saw no reason to decline jurisdiction on grounds of judicial efficiency. Rejecting GMF's view in this respect, the District Court decided that—referring to (unspecified) case law and literature—jurisdiction provisions contained in special conventions prevailed over those contained in the Brussels Convention, even if only one Contracting State had acceded to the special convention. In this particular case, the District Court found no grounds to depart from this principle: here, the issue of damages was closely connected with Geerdink himself, so that there was an objective reason to litigate that issue in The Netherlands.

The District Court also rejected GMF's argument that its decision would stimulate 'forum shopping'. Indeed, the decision as to jurisdiction would not affect the issue of the applicable law, which would be the French law of tort. On the other hand, Geerdink would benefit from the procedural advantages of litigating in his own country, such as the use of his native language, the short distance to the court and the use of his Dutch attorney; but creating such advantages for the victim was precisely the Benelux Convention's aim.

Finally, the District Court attached no importance to the fact that it would have to apply French law. Within the framework of the Brussels Convention, the issue of the applicable law had no relevance whatsoever to the issue of jurisdiction. Although the French courts would have more knowledge of French law, the Dutch court found itself to be sufficiently equipped to obtain information on French law and to decide the case on that basis.

The District Court rejected GMF's argument that it had no jurisdiction.

14

NORTHERN IRELAND

Professor Brice Dickson

A. LEGAL SYSTEM

Northern Ireland has a legal system which is separate from those in the rest of the UK. In many respects, the content of the law is identical to that in England and Wales, but on numerous matters there are significant differences. Very often the law is the same but the source of the law is different.

Northern Ireland has its own system of courts and tribunals. Criminal cases are heard first in a magistrates' court: those charged with minor offences can appeal to a county court and then to the Court of Appeal; those charged with serious offences are committed by a magistrates' court to a Crown Court for trial and the defendant can appeal from there to the Court of Appeal. Provided certain conditions are satisfied, there can be a further appeal from the Court of Appeal, in both minor and more serious cases, to the House of Lords in London, England.

Civil cases are heard first in a magistrates' court, a county court or the High Court, depending on the type of claim and, sometimes, on the monetary value of the claim. The High Court has three Divisions, the Queen's Bench Division, the Family Division and the Chancery Division. Appeals from a magistrates' court are to a county court and then to the Court of Appeal. Appeals from a county court are to the High Court and then to the Court of Appeal. Appeals from the High Court are to the Court of Appeal, and then, if leave is given, to the House of Lords.

Applications for judicial review are heard by the Queen's Bench Division of the High Court. Appeals in civil matters are to the Court of Appeal and then to the House of Lords. Appeals in criminal matters go directly to the Lords.

The top judge in Northern Ireland is the Lord Chief Justice, currently Sir Robert Carswell. There are three Lords Justices and seven Justices. The county courts are staffed by 14 judges and the magistrates' courts by 15 'Resident Magistrates'. District judges assist county court judges; there are also many deputy county court judges and deputy resident magistrates.

Northern Irish courts are not bound by English precedents, but they invariably follow them. Decisions of the House of Lords are binding when given in a case emanating from Northern Ireland. The doctrine of precedent operates within the court system of Northern Ireland itself.

B. IMPLEMENTATION OF THE BRUSSELS CONVENTION

The law implementing the Brussels Convention in Northern Ireland is the same as in the rest of the UK, namely the Civil Jurisdiction and Judgments Act 1982 (as supplemented by the same Act of 1991). The 1982 Act, and the relevant amendments to the Rules of the Supreme Court (Northern Ireland), came into force on 1 January 1987. The version of the Brussels Convention now applying in Northern Ireland is that included in Sched. 1 to the Civil Jurisdiction and Judgments Act 1982 (Amendment) Order 1990 (1990/2591).

C. OVERVIEW OF CONVENTION CASE LAW

All of the seven cases so far decided by Northern Irish courts, where the Brussels Convention has been mentioned, have been ones where the question at issue was the effect of the Convention, if any, on jurisdictional conflicts within the UK or between Northern Ireland and the Republic of Ireland. The most common scenario is where a defendant domiciled in England has been sued in Northern Ireland and then applies to have that action stayed on the grounds of *forum non conveniens*. The Northern Irish courts have affirmed on several occasions that that common law doctrine has survived the passing of the 1982 Act, at least for intra-UK cases. In four cases, the courts have denied a stay, or refused to set aside a writ, because the defendant has been unable to make a convincing enough argument for these orders within the principles laid down by the House of Lords in *Spiliada Maritime Corp v Consulex Ltd* [1987] AC 460.

In three other cases, the Northern Irish courts have upheld the validity of a contract's jurisdiction and choice-of-law clause conferring jurisdiction on English courts, and so have granted a stay to a defendant from England or Ireland who has been sued in Northern Ireland.

The courts have affirmed that interim relief can be granted to a plaintiff even though proceedings might be pending in another jurisdiction.

D.   CASES

> **1982 ACT SECTION 49**
>
> " . . . *not inconsistent with the 1968 Convention.*"

Case principle

Forum non conveniens applies in intra-UK cases.

Case

Macrete v Guardian Royal Exchange plc and others [1988] NI 332, [1988] 13   **748**
NIJB 1, High Court, 10 April 1987

Facts

The plaintiff ran a business in Northern Ireland manufacturing and supplying
concrete products. It was the object of claims from Ireland and Scotland
regarding the supply of allegedly defective products, but when it claimed from
its insurance company, the latter denied liability, on the ground of material
non-disclosure of certain circumstances. To pursue its claim for breach of the
insurance contract, the plaintiff served a writ on the defendant company,
domiciled in England, at a branch in Northern Ireland and sought leave to
serve concurrent writs out of the jurisdiction on underwriters in England. The
defendant sought to have the writ set aside because England was a more
appropriate forum.

Judgment

The court refused to set aside the writ, applying the principles enunciated in
Spiliada Maritime Corp v Consulex Ltd [1987] AC 460, and it did not prevent
service of concurrent writs out of the jurisdiction, since to do so would be
contrary to common sense when there was already a properly commenced
action against one of the defendants within Northern Ireland. As the proceedings in Northern Ireland were not brought under the 1982 Act or the
amended Rules of the Supreme Court—they came into force after the first writ
was served—the judge did not find it necessary to decide whether that Act
would have made any difference to the result in the case.

Case

Buchanan (trading as Warnocks) v Brook Walker & Co Ltd [1988] NI 116   **749**
High Court, 20 May 1988

Facts

The plaintiff business, operating in Northern Ireland, issued proceedings in Northern Ireland against the defendant company, domiciled in England, for breach of contract. The defendant moved to have the action stayed on the ground that the agreement between the plaintiff and defendant contained a clause saying that the agreement was to be governed by English law.

Judgment

The court held that, even if the court's discretion to apply the *forum non conveniens* doctrine still existed now that the 1982 Act was in force, this was not a proper case in which to apply it, because there was no difference between the relevant laws in Northern Ireland and England and there was no reason to suppose that the plaintiff was seeking a procedural advantage or that the defendant would be disadvantaged. A stay was refused.

Case

750 Walker (trading as The Country Garage) v BMW (GB) Ltd [1990] 6 NIJB 1
High Court, 14 May 1990

Facts

The plaintiff company, domiciled in Northern Ireland, sold and serviced BMW cars under a series of agreements with the defendant company, domiciled in England. The defendant company purported to exercise a contractual right to terminate that agreement, but the plaintiff disputed the existence of this right and sought a declaration from the court to this effect.

Judgment

The judge held that, as this was an intra-UK dispute, the rules of the Brussels Convention did not apply. He upheld the validity of the jurisdiction clause in the contract ('This Agreement shall be governed by and construed in all respects in accordance with the law of England and the Dealer hereby submits to the jurisdiction of the English courts') and, although willing to consider the applicability of the doctrine of *forum non conveniens*, concluded that the plaintiff had not made out a strong enough case for resisting a stay in accordance with the jurisdiction clause. He followed *The Eleftheria* [1970] P 94.

Case

751 Norbrook Laboratories Ltd v Export Credits Guarantee Department, Court of Appeal, 13 October 1992

Facts

The plaintiff company, domiciled in Northern Ireland, issued a writ in Northern Ireland against the defendant, a UK government department, claiming money due under a contract with that department. Two weeks later, the defendant issued a writ in England against the plaintiff for a much larger sum allegedly due under the contract. The defendant sought an order staying the proceedings in Northern Ireland. At first instance the judge granted a stay.

Judgment

The Court of Appeal held that Arts 21 and 22 of the Brussels Convention, dealing with proceedings involving the same cause of action between the same parties, or related actions, brought in the courts of different Contracting States, did not apply to intra-UK cases. There was nothing in s.16(3) or (4) of the 1982 Act to require the application of those Articles in intra-UK disputes. The court also held that s.49 of the 1982 Act, allowing the continued operation of the *forum non conveniens* doctrine, could apply here because it was not inconsistent with the 1968 Convention. The Court of Appeal reversed the High Court's decision to grant a stay, saying that the defendant had failed to discharge the burden resting on it to show that a trial elsewhere than in Northern Ireland was clearly more convenient.

Case

Smith (trading as Adair Smith Motors) v Nissan Motor (GB) Ltd, High Court,   **752**
19 May 1993

Facts

The plaintiff car dealer, in Northern Ireland, sued the defendant car manufacturing company, domiciled in England, for breach of contract. The defendant sought to have the writ set aside or the action stayed because of a jurisdiction clause in the contract ('This Agreement shall be governed by and construed in accordance with the laws of England. The Dealer submits to the jurisdiction of the English courts for all purposes relating to this Agreement').

Judgment

The judge considered that this was an *exclusive* jurisdiction clause. He went on to hold that this did not mean that the plaintiff could not rely upon the doctrine of *forum non conveniens* but that on the facts the plaintiff had not discharged the burden of establishing the necessary strong case for resisting the grant of a stay. He followed *The Eleftheria* [1970] P 94.

Case

McCartan, Turkington, Breen v Baron St Oswald and the BBC (unreported)   **753**
High Court, 2 May 1996

Facts

The plaintiff in Northern Ireland claimed damages for defamation from the defendants in England. The first defendant applied to have the plaintiff's writ set aside on the ground that Northern Ireland was *forum non conveniens*. The High Court Master acceded to the application, but the plaintiff appealed, relying on Art. 5(3) of the Brussels Convention as reproduced in Sched. 4 to the 1982 Act (which deals with intra-UK cases).

Judgment

The judge held that by s.16(3) of the 1982 Act, any question as to the meaning of any provision in Sched. 4 had to be determined by having regard to any relevant principles laid down by the European Court of Justice. He then applied the *Bier* decision, Case 21/76, saying it was unnecessary to decide whether the *Shevill* decision (Case C-68/93) applied to intra-UK cases. He observed that s.49 of the 1982 Act expressly preserved the doctrine of *forum non conveniens* in intra-UK cases 'where to do so is not inconsistent with the 1968 Convention'. He then applied the principles laid down by the House of Lords in *Spiliada Maritime Corp v Cansulex Ltd* [1987] AC 460, denying a stay to the first defendant, because he had not shown a sufficient case in favour of a stay, and if a stay were granted it would lead to the unacceptable result that an action against the second defendant would continue in Northern Ireland while another action would proceed against the first defendant in England.

ARTICLE 17

" . . . *shall have exclusive jurisdiction* . . . "

Case principle

A duty to decline in favour of chosen courts is mandatory under Art. 17.

Case

754 Coca Cola Bottlers (Ulster) Ltd v Concentrate Manufacturing Co of Ireland (trading as Seven-Up International) [1990] 3 NIJB 84 High Court, 6 April 1990

Facts

The plaintiff company, domiciled in Northern Ireland, sought a court order restraining the defendant company, domiciled in the Republic of Ireland, from authorizing any person other than the plaintiff to sell or distribute the mineral drink 'Seven-Up' in Northern Ireland. The defendant applied to have the writ set aside because under Art. 17 of the Brussels Convention the English courts had exclusive jurisdiction by virtue of Clause 28 of the contract between the plaintiff and defendant ('This agreement and its validity, construction, effect, performance and termination shall be governed and construed in accordance with English law and any disputes hereunder shall be submitted to the courts of England').

Judgment

The judge gave leave to the defendant to serve a summons to set aside the plaintiff's action but adjourned the hearing. At the adjourned hearing the plaintiff conceded that Clause 28 conferred exclusive jurisdiction on English courts and the judge stayed the plaintiff's action. Until that point the judge had been prepared to grant interim relief (in the form of a temporary injunction) to the plaintiff under s.25 of the 1982 Act, which allowed such relief to be granted by the High Court in Northern Ireland even where proceedings had been or were to be commenced in a Contracting State other than the UK (subsequently extended *inter alia* to *non*-Contracting States, under S.I 1997, No. 302) or in another part of the UK.

15

NORWAY

Professor Thor Falkanger

A. LEGAL SYSTEM

Courts

The main structure of the Norwegian court system on the civil side (as opposed to criminal procedure) is set out below.

There are 87 District Courts. Important cases start in the District Court (debt cases may start at a lower level in the so-called conciliation court). Each case is heard by one professional judge; in addition there may be two lay judges if one of the parties so demands or the professional judge so decides.

From the District Court there is a right of appeal to one of the six Courts of Appeal. In the Court of Appeal the case is heard by three professional judges, but also here there is a possibility of two or four lay judges in addition to the professional ones. Cases concerning minor issues (measured in money) cannot be appealed unless the President of the Court of Appeal gives his permission.

At the top of the court system there is the Supreme Court, sitting in Oslo. Ordinarily, a case is heard by five judges; in extraordinary circumstances a case may be subject to a hearing in plenary, with all 18 judges participating. The right of appeal against a decision by a Court of Appeal is limited.

In all three instances there will be given a written judgment, identifying the parties and the issues, with a summary of the views presented by the parties, as well as the court's reasons for its decision.

The Interlocutory Appeals Committee

In addition, there are some special courts and tribunals, whereof only one merits mentioning in the present context: the Interlocutory Appeals Committee of

787

the Supreme Court, which is not only an appeal selection committee, but has in addition jurisdiction in a number of important procedural matters. Each issue is decided by three Supreme Court judges on the basis of written pleadings.

B. IMPLEMENTATION OF THE LUGANO CONVENTION

Norway, being a member of the European Free Trade Association (EFTA), ratified the Lugano Convention with effect from 1 May 1993. Nationally, the Convention, with the Protocols, was implemented by an Act of 8 January 1993 No. 21, which entered into force on 1 May 1993. Section 1 of the Act provides that the Convention 'applies as formal law'. The text of the Convention and the Protocols is not repeated in the Act; a reference to the Convention is considered sufficient.

The following qualifications appearing from s.1, subs. 2 to 3 should be noted:

> 'Judgments rendered in another Convention State at a venue mentioned in the Convention Arts 5(1) and 16(1)(b) shall be recognized and enforced in Norway even though the State has made reservation that it will not recognize or enforce Norwegian judgments in similar circumstances.
> Judgments which need not be recognized or enforced according to Protocol No. 1 Article II, have not 'rettskraft' and 'tvangskraft' in Norway' (not legally binding and not for enforcement in Norway).

C. OVERVIEW OF CONVENTION CASE LAW

This summary is limited to decisions by the Supreme Court and the Interlocutory Appeals Committee of the Supreme Court.

D. CASES

Decisions by the Supreme Court or its Appeals Committee are reported in Norsk Retstidende (Rt.) (= Norwegian Supreme Court Reporter).

LUGANO ARTICLE 1, PARAGRAPH 2(2)

" . . . winding-up of insolvent companies . . . "

Case

Norsk Hydro AS and Hydro Aluminium As v Alumix S.p.A., Rt. 1996 p. 25   **755**
Supreme Court

Facts

The Italian buyer, a subsidiary of an Italian concern being liquidated in accordance with a specific Italian government resolution and specific Italian legislation, was sued in a Norwegian court for payment of the purchase price (*cf.* Lugano Convention Art. 5(1)).

Judgment

Even though bankruptcy did not preclude a judgment on claims outside the bankruptcy state, in this instance the Norwegian court would have to make decisions on a number of typical bankruptcy questions regulated by the Italian rules. Therefore, the case was, by a majority of three to two judges, dismissed by the Norwegian courts by reference to the bankruptcy exception in Lugano Convention Art. 1, para. 2(2). The Lugano Convention had priority over the Civil Procedure Act, s.25.

LUGANO ARTICLE 5(1)

" . . . *in matters relating to a contract . . .* "

Case principle

Contractual existence must be clear on the evidence for Article 5(1), but need not be *conclusively* established as if on substance.

Case

Deutsche Bank SAE v Den norske Bank AS, Rt. 1996 p. 822 Appeals   **756**
Committee

Facts

Deutsche Bank SAE, Barcelona, claimed—unsuccessfully—that the Lugano Convention Art. 5(1) was not applicable and that the case in Norway should be dismissed.

Judgment

The Committee remarked that it was somewhat unclear how strict the requirement of the Convention is in respect of establishing that a contractual relationship exists (*cf.* the European Court of Justice's decision in *Effer v Kantner*, Case 38/81).

In order that a case can be brought under Art. 5(1), there have to be comparatively clear indications that a contractual relationship existed. In the present circumstances, it was necessary to go into the substance of the case in order to establish, with final effect, whether the requirements for commencing a case were present. The Court of Appeal was, however, of the opinion that it was not necessary that all possible questions of a contractual relationship were fully clarified before allowing the commencement of the case. The possibility that the court might finally, after having heard arguments and considered all the evidence, find that the case was incorrectly commenced, could not in itself be sufficient ground to deny jurisdiction.

LUGANO ARTICLE 5(3)

" . . . *harmful event occurred . . .* "

Case principle

Place in which harm to reputation occurred founds jurisdiction under Art. 5(3).

Case

757 Sveriges Television AB v Gudmund Skogvik et al, Rt. 1994 p. 675 Appeals Committee

Facts and Judgment

Norwegian jurisdiction in a case of compensation for alleged defamation in a Swedish television programme depended upon the construction of the Civil Procedure Act s.29. The litigation was started prior to the entry into force of the Lugano Convention (see Art. 5(3) giving the claimant the choice between the place where the act was done and the place where the results occurred). The Committee remarked that there was no reason for a restrictive interpretation of s.29 when it, according to its wording, led to results compatible with internationally accepted rules. It was also remarked that Art. 5(3) had no particular rules in respect of compensation claims originating from expression of opinions.

Case

758 Gudmund Skogvik et al v Norsteds Forlag Ab, Rt. 1996 p. 875 Supreme Court

Facts and Judgment

Norwegian courts were held to be competent, in respect of a claim for defamation brought by Norwegian sealhunters against a Swedish book publisher (*cf.* Civil Procedure Act s.29), as courts of the place 'where the harmful event occurred'. The case was instigated before the Lugano Convention became binding in Norway. But the Supreme Court found that the interpretation of s.29 was supported by the Brussels Convention Art. 5(3) and the parallel stipulation in the Lugano Convention Art. 5(3) (*cf.* the European Court of Justice's decision in *Fiona Shevill v Presse Alliance S.A.* Case C–68/93). It was a factor of importance when applying s.29, as a rule on international jurisdiction, that it was in practice in conformity with jurisdiction rules in countries with which Norway, to a great extent, had a common legal tradition.

LUGANO ARTICLE 6(1)

" . . . also be sued . . . "

Case principle

1. *Plaintiffs* need not have a Contracting State domicile.
2. Art. 6(1) jurisdiction continues, even if action against main defendant is terminated.

Case

Kjell Tore Skjevesland v Geveran Trading Company Ltd, Rt. 1995 p. 1244   **759**
Appeals Committee

Facts and judgment

The plaintiff, domiciled in a non-Convention State (Cyprus), was held to be entitled to instigate proceedings in accordance with the venue rules of the Convention. The domicile of the plaintiff did not restrict the applicability of Art. 6(1).

Article 6(1) jurisdiction continues even if the action against the main defendant is terminated.

Case

Kjell Tore Skjevesland v Geveran Trading Co. Ltd Rt. 1996 p. 328 Appeals   **760**
Committee

Facts and judgment

Co-debtors A and B were rightly sued in Norway on the basis of A's domicile in Norway, (*cf.* Lugano Convention Art. 6(1)). After the case against A was settled, the court still had jurisdiction in respect of B. This followed from the Courts Act s.34, which was applicable also in instances where the initial jurisdiction was based upon the Lugano Convention.

> ## LUGANO ARTICLE 17(1)
>
> *" . . . shall have exclusive jurisdiction . . . "*

Case principle

Jurisdiction clause in charterparty satisfies written requirements.

Case

761 Nordic American Shipping AS v KS AS Manhattan Tankers, Rt. 1995 p. 391 Appeals Committee

Facts

A time charterparty provided that all disputes were to be decided by English courts 'to whose jurisdiction the parties hereby agree'.

Judgment

A question of general average in respect of an incident during the contract period could not be brought before a Norwegian court. The clause was within the requirements of the Civil Procedure Act s.36, and the Committee remarked that, according to the Lugano Convention Art. 17(1)(a), it could validly be agreed that English courts had sole jurisdiction to decide matters arising under the charterparty.

> ## LUGANO ARTICLE 17(4)
>
> *" . . . for the benefit of only one . . . "*

Case principle

Mere agreement upon courts of a particular contracting party's Contracting State domicile is not sufficient for it to be held that the jurisdiction agreement was concluded for the benefit of only that party.

Case

762 Societa per azioni commerciale iniziative spettacolo (SACIS) v Elliso AS, Rt. 1993 p. 1583 Appeals Committee

Facts

The contract stated: 'Applicable law: Italian, and the parties hereto submit to the jurisdiction of the Italian Courts.'

Judgment

The Appeals Committee said that, in construing clauses of this type, it was correct to have the principles internationally accepted as a starting point. If a jurisdiction clause was made part of the contract in the interest of one of the parties only, this was an argument for the construction that the clause did not prevent that party from suing in the courts of another country which according to general rules was competent. But the fact that the clause established jurisdiction in the country where a party had his domicile or his place of business, was not sufficient to declare that the clause was solely in the interests of that party. For the latter, the Committee found support in Art. 17 of the Lugano Convention.

LUGANO ARTICLE 27

" . . . *shall not be recognised* . . . "

Case principle

National law objections to execution proper of foreign judgments of which enforcement is authorized are not limited to those in Arts 27 and 28.

Case

Petter Samuelsen v Nilsen Brokers Ltd AS, Rt. 1996 p. 447 Appeals **763** Committee

Facts

Costs awarded by an English court, when dismissing a case, were used as the basis for execution in Norway against the Norwegian debtor. The proper authority was the court of enforcement (Lugano Convention Art. 32), and such court should give its decision without delay. The party against whom enforcement was sought was not at this stage of the proceedings entitled to make any submissions on the application—but the application could be refused for reasons specified in the Lugano Convention Arts 27 and 28 (Art. 34). If the court found that the application was to be accepted, there was a right of appeal.

Judgment

The Committee stated that, in addition to the objections specified in Arts 27 and 28, the debtor could submit objections related to the basis of enforcement execution and to its actual validity as against the debtor. Thus, an objection based upon set-off could be considered by the court of enforcement, but only in relation to execution, and not in the initial stage of authorisation of enforcement (*i.e.* of the English decision—*exequatur*). In the present case, the enforcement-court as well as the Court of Appeal had—incorrectly—given a decision which seemed to rule out all the objections of the debtor, without in fact having tried all of them.

LUGANO ARTICLE 27(1)

" . . . contrary to public policy . . . "

Case principle

Existence or otherwise of ordinary or extraordinary remedies against judgments in the judgment-State would be taken into account in order to determine whether recognition of a foreign judgment was against public policy.

Case

764 Nilsen Brokers Ltd AS v Rolf Kval, Rt. 1996 p. 502 Appeals Committee

Facts

Costs awarded by an English court when dismissing a case were used as a basis for a demand of execution in Norway against Rolf Kval, who, without his knowledge, had been named as co-claimant in the English case and who was not aware of the costs decision until enforcement proceedings were instigated in Norway.

Judgment

The Committee remarked that a person incorrectly made party would have to use the ordinary judicial remedies; if time for an appeal had expired when he became aware of the alleged error, he would have to use extraordinary remedies, *i.e.* apply for extraordinary leave to appeal or for a reopening of the case. If he did not act, enforcement could take place on the basis of the decision. This applied to foreign decisions as well. The starting point was that, to the extent that a foreign decision could be challenged on the basis of extraordinary remedies, it would *not* be contrary to public policy to allow enforcement against a person who did not utilize those remedies.

16

PORTUGAL

Judge Rui Manuel Moura Ramos*

A.   LEGAL SYSTEM

Courts

The main structure of the Portuguese court system—this expression covering the judicial courts only (tribunais judiciais)—comprises three categories of courts: the first instance courts, the second instance courts (Tribunais da Relação) and the Supreme Court (Supremo Tribunal de Justiça) (Art. 211(1)(a) of the Constitution).

The Supreme Court is the superior organ of the judicial courts hierarchy (Art. 212 of the Constitution). The Tribunais da Relação sit in the main judicial districts (Art. 38(1) of the Organic Law of Judicial Courts (Lei Orgânica dos Tribunais Judiciais—Law 38/87, 23 December), and currently there are four: Lisboa, Porto, Coimbra and Évora.

The Constitution also establishes a Constitutional Court, several courts dealing with administrative and fiscal matters, a Court of Auditors and Military Courts, and allows for the existence and activity of Arbitration Courts (Art. 211 of the Constitution).

There is a right of appeal against the decisions of first instance courts to the Tribunais da Relação. However, these latter courts exercise first level jurisdiction in some matters, for example, as regards the recognition and enforcement of foreign judgments outside the scope of the Brussels and Lugano Conventions (Art. 1095 of the Civil Procedure Code). Against the decisions of

---

*Member of the Institute of International Law; Professor, Law Faculty, University of Coimbra, Portugal; Judge of the Court of First Instance of the European Communities

the Tribunais da Relação, an appeal can be made to the Supreme Court, but only where infringement of procedural or substantive legal requirements is at issue (Art. 722 of the Civil Procedure Code).

The judicial courts of first instance are organized according to different criteria. According to the territorial area where they exercise their jurisdiction, there are *tribunais de comarca* (in general, the first instance courts), *tribunais de círculo* and *tribunais de distrito*. Depending on the subject matter of the cases which they decide, they may be courts of general jurisdiction and courts of specialized jurisdiction (civil matters, criminal matters, family matters, minors and guardianship, labour matters, maritime matters (admiralty) and sentencing).

According to the applicable procedural rules, there are courts of specific jurisdiction and courts of mixed jurisdiction.

Finally, as regards their structure and organization, they may be single courts, collective courts and jury courts (Arts 45 to 83 of the Organic Law of Judicial Courts).

B. IMPLEMENTATION OF THE CONVENTIONS

A member of the European Community since 1 January 1986, Portugal ratified the 1989 San Sebastian Accession Convention to the Brussels Convention on 15 April 1992 and thus acceded to the Brussels Convention with effect from 1 July 1992. The Lugano Convention was ratified by Portugal on 14 April 1992 and took effect in Portugal also on 1 July 1992 (see the communications of the Portuguese Minister of Foreign Affairs 95/92 and 94/92, respectively, published in the Portuguese Official Journal (Diário da República) Iª Série-A, 157, 10 July 1992, p. 2369).

In Portugal, rules of properly ratified or approved international treaties are in force in the domestic legal order after their official publication, provided that they are internationally binding on the Portuguese State (Art. 8(2) of the Constitution). Therefore, there is no need for a legislative Act of implementation of any convention, and such an Act has not been enacted in respect of these two Conventions.

The Portuguese text of the two Conventions was published in the Portuguese Official Journal, Iª Série-A, 250, 30 October 1991, p. 5588 *et seq.* (concerning the Lugano Convention) and p. 5588 *et seq.* (concerning the Brussels Convention).

These Conventions do not contain any transitional provision applying specially to Portugal, nor do they supersede any convention previously concluded between Portugal and another State.

C. OVERVIEW OF CONVENTION CASE LAW

The Portuguese case law applying the Brussels and Lugano Conventions is of a fragmentary character and, because of its recent nature, the decisions which have been published still do not cover the majority of the Convention's provisions. Furthermore, some problems specific to the Portuguese judiciary have led to difficulties in the application of the Conventions.

Many cases deal, naturally, with transitional provisions and with problems concerning the scope of application of the Conventions. Portuguese courts have had difficulties with the cumulative nature of the conditions in Art. 54, para. 1 and it appears that the Portuguese version of this provision could have been written in a clearer way; the application of para. 2 has given rise to some problems too. Although it may seem odd, the relationship between the two Conventions has been frequently misunderstood. As regards the scope of application *ratione materiae*, on the other hand, the courts have until now experienced no difficulties in the application of the relevant provisions.

Dealing with rules of jurisdiction, the courts have not always understood the real nature of the changes brought by the Conventions to the application of domestic rules, sometimes viewing the Conventions' provisions as ancillary to the application of domestic rules. That was the case in a decision of the Tribunal da Relação do Porto of 9 February 1993 (*Borge Mouritsen Trading, Ega A/S v Pinho & Dâmaso, Lda,* Colectânea de Jurisprudência (1993) t. I, p. 230–231), where Art. 28 was held not to exclude the recognition of a judgment dealt with exclusively under national Portuguese rules. But Portuguese courts do seem to have applied rather well the relationship between general and specific criteria of Convention jurisdiction and prorogation of jurisdiction thereunder.

In the field of recognition and enforcement, the position has been confused in several situations through the lack of certainty over the location of the court to which the application for enforcement should be submitted under Art. 32 of the Conventions (the tribunal judicial de círculo), until the matter was settled (tribunal de comarca). On the other hand, grounds for refusing enforcement (which are not very different from those contained in national law) have not been a problem, and one judgment even dealt with the interesting question of the effect of an appeal against the decision authorizing enforcement.

D. CASES

LUGANO ARTICLE 1, PARAGRAPH 1

" . . . *civil and commercial matters* . . . "

Case principle

Recognition of judgments relating to employment contracts is covered by the Lugano Convention.

Case

765 José de Castro v Sociedade Prestasals de Fernando Martins, Colectânea de Jurisprudência (1995) t. I, p. 229 Tribunal da Relação do Porto, 27 February 1995

Facts

The applicant, a Portuguese worker resident in France, sought, according to the rules of the national Portuguese law on recognition of foreign judgments (Art. 1094 *et seq.* of the Civil Procedure Code), recognition of a French judgment, dated 15 October 1993, against his employer whereby, pursuant to an employment contract, the latter was ordered to pay compensation to the former. In a preliminary ruling, the court dismissed the application, on the grounds of lack of jurisdiction *ratione materiae*. The court held that, since the recognition of decisions on employment matters was covered by the Lugano Convention, recognition should have been automatically granted (and the court which had jurisdiction for enforcement was the tribunal judicial de círculo) (Arts 26, 29, 31, 32 and 37).

Against this decision, and before the same court, the applicant appealed against refusal of enforcement, on the ground that judgments on individual employment contracts were not covered by the Convention, since they were not expressly mentioned in its text.

Judgment

The Court confirmed its first ruling on the basis of a Community interpretation of the wording of Art. 1, which required employment contracts to be treated as matters of private law. It recalled that the Court of Justice had supported such an interpretation in Case 25/79 (*Sanicentral v René Collin*) concerning the identical Article of the Brussels Convention and that the same interpretation expressly resulted from the wording of Arts 3 (in the part concerning Portugal) and 5(1) of the Convention.

Comment

The judgment is correct, except for the fact that the court ought to have applied the Brussels Convention and not the Lugano Convention, since the foreign judgement was that of a State, France, which had also ratified the former Convention, and at the time of the judgment, the San Sebastian Accession Convention had already been in force in that State since 1 February 1991. A reference to the Lugano Convention makes no sense in such a case (see Art. 54B). Besides, the court should not have considered that it lacked jurisdiction *ratione materiae*, but rather because the application should have been addressed to a lower court (Art. 101 of the Civil Procedure Code). Finally, the judgment does not enable us to know whether the conditions of Art. 54 concerning the temporal scope of application of the Brussels Convention (in particular, the condition concerning its entry into force in the State of origin of the foreign judgment (France) on the date at which the legal proceedings were instituted), had been met (as to which, see Dário Moura Vicente, 'Da Aplicação no Tempo e no Espaço das Convenções de Bruxelas de 1968 e de Lugano de 1988 (Anotação de Jurisprudência)', *Revista da Faculdade de Direito da Universidade de Lisboa* (1994) p. 461 *et seq.*, especially p. 484–5).

```
┌─────────────────────────────────────────────────────────────────┐
│                                                                   │
│   LUGANO ARTICLE 2, PARAGRAPH 1                                   │
│                                                                   │
│    " . . . persons domiciled in a Contracting State shall . . . " │
│                                                                   │
└─────────────────────────────────────────────────────────────────┘
```

Case principle

1. Convention jurisdiction grounds are mandatory and override national rules.

Case

Biscuiterie Confiserie Lor SA/Doce Alimentar v Productos Alimentares, Lda,   **766**
Colectânea de Jurisprudência (1995) t. 4, p. 217–18 Tribunal da Relação do Porto, 16 October 1995

Facts

A French company sued a Portuguese company in Portugal for damages arising from the non-payment of the price of goods delivered in Portugal in performance of a contractual relationship. The defendant contested jurisdiction of the Portuguese courts, and the court of first instance dismissed the action under national jurisdiction grounds.

Judgment

On appeal, the court of second instance annulled this decision: since France and Portugal were Contracting States to the Lugano Convention, it had preeminence over the national rules of jurisdiction of the Portuguese courts.

It added that the same result (jurisdiction of Portuguese courts) would have been reached under national Portuguese law since, by the principle of causality, the Portuguese courts had jurisdiction if the *causa petendi* had taken place in Portugal (Art. 65(1)(b) of the Civil Procedure Code—see Moura Ramos, 'A recente reforma do direito processual civil internacional em Portugal', *Liber Amicorum Vicente Marotta Rangel*, São Paulo (1997) (in course of publication), n. 6.). The court considered that the contract had been concluded in Portugal because the proposal made by the Portuguese buyer had been accepted implicitly by the French seller when the latter delivered the goods in Portugal. For this purpose, the court applied Portuguese domestic rules concerning formation of contracts, which regard a contract as concluded when acceptance of the offer is communicated to the other contracting party (Art. 224 of the Civil Code).

Comment

First, the court should have applied the Brussels Convention, not the Lugano Convention, since the two Conventions were already in force in Portugal when the legal proceedings were instituted (Article 54—the judgment does not mention this moment, but since the goods were delivered on 15 June 1993 and legal proceedings for lack of payment were instituted necessarily thereafter, these were subsequent to the entry into force of the two Conventions in Portugal on 1 July 1992)—and Article 54B(1) of the Lugano Convention provides that it shall not prejudice the application of the Brussels Convention by Community Member States.

Secondly, it was unnecessary and misleading to have examined Portuguese rules of jurisdiction, after establishing the jurisdiction of Portuguese courts on the basis of the solely applicable Brussels Convention. It is useful to make a comparison, on this point, with the judgment of the Tribunal da Relação de Lisboa from 24 January 1991 (in Colectânea de Jurisprudência (1991) t. 1, p. 149–51), *Importex Representações v Solido SA*. In this decision, which also dealt with jurisdiction of Portuguese courts in a similar case, the court stressed expressly that it was not bound by the jurisdiction rules of the Brussels Convention which, in that case, attributed jurisdiction to Portuguese courts on the basis of its Art. 2. However, in fact Portugal had still not ratified the Brussels Convention. In these circumstances, it applied Portuguese domestic law, which also granted jurisdiction to Portuguese courts according to the principle of coincidence, since the place of performance of the contract was Portugal (Art. 65(1)(a)) (see *supra*, Moura Ramos, *op.cit*).

Case

767 Jangaard Export AS v J. Gil e Cª Lda, Colectânea de Jurisprudência, 1996, t. V, p. 44–6 Tribunal da Relação de Coimbra, 17 December 1996

Facts

A Norwegian company sued a Portuguese company in the Tribunal Judicial de Círculo da Covilhã for damages arising from the non-payment for goods delivered pursuant to a contract of sale. The defendant contested the jurisdiction of the Portuguese courts (also alleging that partial payment had already been made and that Norwegian courts, not Portuguese, had jurisdiction). An appeal was brought against the preliminary ruling by which the judge had upheld Portuguese jurisdiction, following which, the second instance court had gone on to hold the defendant liable.

Judgment

The Court of Appeal of Coimbra held that, since the Lugano Convention was in force in Portugal, it superseded the Portuguese Civil Procedure Code and that, pursuant to the Convention's provisions, Portuguese courts had jurisdiction on the basis of the domicile of the defendant (Art. 2), even if, according to Art. 5(1) of the same Convention, courts of the country where the place of performance of the obligation in question was located also had jurisdiction. The court explained that, even if the Convention had not been in force in Portugal, the result would have been the same. In fact, the domestic law (Art. 65(1)(a) of the Civil Procedure Code) embodied the principle of coincidence, and Portuguese courts had territorial jurisdiction in contractual matters on the basis of the place of performance (Art. 74(1) of the Civil Procedure Code). Thus, in the case *sub judice*, according to Portuguese substantive law (Art. 885 of the Civil Procedure Code), although payment should have been made in the place of domicile of the creditor (Norway), nonetheless, the defendant had not established that Portuguese law should be applied and, in accordance with the choice of law rule (Art. 42(2), of the Civil Procedure Code) which considered the law of the place of contracting to be the governing law in the case, Portuguese law would not have been applied. Consequently, pursuant to Portuguese rules of jurisdiction, the Portuguese courts would have been deemed to have jurisdiction because some of the elements of the *causa petendi* had taken place in Portugal.

Comment

The court correctly applied the Lugano Convention—and its excursion into Portuguese domestic rules of jurisdiction was quite unnecessary!

Case principle

2.   Special jurisdiction provided for in Art. 5 of the Brussels Convention does not exclude general jurisdiction based on the domicile of the defendant under Art. 2.

Case

Claim 400/95—5th Section, Boletim do Ministério da Justiça (1995) No. 448, **768** p. 430 (just the summary) Tribunal da Relação do Porto, 19 June 1995

Judgment

Since special jurisdiction provided for in Art. 5 of the Brussels Convention was not mandatory nor exclusive, in contractual matters, when relying on the place of performance, persons domiciled in a Contracting State could, pursuant to Art. 2, still be sued in the courts of that State.

Comment

The decision should be approved because it stresses the alternative character of specific criteria of jurisdiction embodied in Art. 5.

ARTICLE 3, PARAGRAPH 2

"In particular . . . "

Case principle

Articles 2 and 3 of the Brussels Convention held not to supersede Art. 65(1)(b) of the Portuguese Civil Procedure Code.

Case

769 Manuel Pereira Puga v Maison Ranoux, Colectânea de Jurisprudência (1995) t. V, p. 131 Tribunal da Relação de Lisboa, 5 December 1995

Facts

The Portuguese plaintiff sued the defendant French company for damages arising from the defective performance of a contract. The defendant argued that the Portuguese courts lacked jurisdiction, since, according to Arts 2 and 3 of the Brussels Convention, persons domiciled in a Contracting State had to be sued in the courts of that State and could be sued in the courts of another Contracting State only by virtue of the rules set out in ss.2 to 6 of Title II. The judge of first instance, considering France to be the place of performance, held that the Portuguese courts had no jurisdiction according to Arts 2, 3 and 5(1) of the Brussels Convention. On appeal, the plaintiff argued that the contract had been concluded in Portugal, that its performance had taken place in Portugal and that damages had been suffered there for purposes of Art. 5(1) of the Brussels Convention.

Judgment

The court held that the Portuguese courts had jurisdiction on the basis of the principle of causality under national Portuguese law (Art. 65(1)(b)), since the place of contracting and the place of performance were located in Portugal. With regard to applicability of the Brussels Convention, it stated that since Art. 65(1)(b) of the Portuguese Civil Procedure Code had not been mentioned in Art. 3 of the Convention, it had not been superseded by the Brussels

Convention. In addition, it emphasized that Portuguese law was the law applicable to the contract, since the place of contracting and place of performance were located in Portugal and that legal order had the strongest connection with the contract.

Comment

The court of first instance (Tribunal Judicial de Círculo de Loures) correctly decided the question of the applicability of the Brussels Convention. In fact, even though the defendant's domicile was not located in Portugal, the place of performance of the obligation in question (the delivery of the goods) ought to have been held to be Portugal, and consequently the Portuguese courts should have had jurisdiction according to Art. 5(1). However, contrary to the view expressed by the Court of Appeal, the lack of mention of a domestic provision in Art. 3, para. 2 of the Convention does not mean that these provisions can be applied against a defendant domiciled in a Contracting State. It is simply the case that, as stated in Art. 4, they can be applied (subject to the provisions of Art. 16) when the defendant is not domiciled in a Contracting State. (In addition, the Court of Appeal misunderstood Art. 4 of the Rome Contracts Convention.)

ARTICLE 17, PARAGRAPH 1(a)

" . . . *an agreement conferring jurisdiction shall be . . . in writing or evidenced in writing . . .* "

Case principle

An agreement conferring jurisdiction included in the general conditions of sale appearing on the reverse of a document confirming an order does not meet the formal requirements of Art. 17, para. 1(a).

Case

Tribunal da Relação de Lisboa, 7 November 1996, Colectânea de   **770**
Jurisprudência (1996) t. V, p. 85–88

Facts

A German company, following non-payment for goods delivered to a Portuguese company in performance of a contract of sale, sued the latter in Portugal.

The judge of first instance dismissed the application, considering that an agreement conferring jurisdiction on the courts of the place of establishment of the seller, which was inserted in the general conditions of sale included on the reverse of a document sent by the seller to the buyer by way of confirmation of the order (*vertragsbestätigung*) was valid under Portuguese law. The seller appealed.

Judgment

The Tribunal da Relação held that, since the Brussels Convention had been in force in Portugal from 1 July 1992, its provisions were applicable and the jurisdiction agreement was therefore invalid, since it did not meet the formal requirements of Art. 17, para. 1(a). In these circumstances, the seller could sue the buyer in Portugal according to Art. 2, since the jurisdiction of the courts of the place of performance of the obligation established by Art. 5(1) was just an option available to the applicant. Furthermore, the court stressed that even if the agreement were deemed to be valid, the result would be the same since it had been concluded for the benefit of only one of the parties (the seller), who consequently retained the right to bring proceedings in any court having jurisdiction under the Convention (Art. 17, para. 5/Lugano (4)).

Comment

As was underlined by the Tribunal da Relação, the Brussels Convention regime, under which the Portuguese courts were to assess jurisdiction, provided that proceedings had been instituted after the entry into force of the Convention in Portugal (such a date is not mentioned in the judgment). As regards the formal validity of the agreement, the court might have sought to assess it under Art. 17, para. 1(c). If the agreement were to have been considered valid, the only courts which could have exercised jurisdiction would have been the chosen German courts, since jurisdiction established on the basis of an agreement should be deemed exclusive in accordance with Art. 17, para. 1.

   The assertion that the agreement should be regarded as concluded for the benefit of only one of the parties was not sufficiently reasoned and seems to contradict the case law of the European Court of Justice, which stresses that such a qualification must result from the common intention of the parties at the moment of concluding the contract and that this is not necessarily the case when the parties confer jurisdiction on the courts of the State where one of them is domiciled (see judgment of 24 June 1986, *Anterist* Case 22/85 [1985] ECR 1951, Kohler, 'Pathologisches im EuGVÜ: Hinkende Gerichtsstandsvereinbarungen nach Art. 17 Abs. 3', IPRax (1986) p. 340 *et seq.*).

ARTICLE 18

" . . . *solely to contest the jurisdiction* . . . "

Case principle

Jurisdiction deriving from appearance of the defendant is excluded if appearance was entered solely to contest court jurisdiction.

Case

Alba Radio Lda v Cerqueira & Moreira, Lda, Colectânea de Jurisprudência **771**
(1995) t. III, p. 146–7 Supremo Tribunal de Justiça, 7 December 1995

Facts

A Portuguese company was ordered by the English High Court to pay a sum
of money to a UK company. The creditor made an application for enforcement
in Portugal (Tribunal da comarca de Matosinhos), which was authorized on
the basis of the Brussels Convention. An appeal was lodged by the debtor with
the Tribunal da Relação do Porto, which annulled the authorization for
enforcement, but this judgment was in turn contested by an appeal on a point
of law to the Supremo Tribunal de Justiça.

Judgment

The court held that, under Art. 54, para. 1 of the Convention, enforcement of
the English court's decision could only be governed by the Convention if this
instrument were already in force in the State of origin and in the State
addressed when legal proceedings were instituted. This was not in fact the
case, since the Spain/Portugal Accession Convention had entered into force in
the UK on 1 December 1991 and legal proceedings had been instituted in that
country not later than 7 May 1991.

However, even if the Convention had been applicable, the court stressed that
the appearance of the defendant before the English court had not been a
proper basis for exercising jurisdiction, since such an appearance was entered
solely in order to contest the jurisdiction.

Comment

The court correctly considered matters of temporal scope of application of the
Convention dealt with in Art. 54, para. 1; and it may be presumed from the
silence of the decision that applicability of Art. 54, para. 2 was not put
forward. The interpretation given to Art. 18 of the Convention is equally
appropriate: although the Portuguese enforcement-court ought not in fact to
have concerned itself—albeit *obiter*—with review of jurisdiction of the English
judgment-court at the enforcement stage (Art. 28, para. 3).

LUGANO ARTICLE 32(1) AND (2)

*"The application shall be submitted . . . in Portugal, to the Tribunal
Judicial de Círculo . . . The jurisdiction of local courts shall be
determined by reference to the place of domicile of the party against
whom enforcement is sought . . . "*

Case principle

If, in the place of domicile of the party against whom enforcement is sought, there is no Tribunal Judicial de Círculo, application must be made to the Tribunal Judicial de Comarca of the same place.

Case

772   Adolf Burger v Alexandre Casal ou Alexandre Baumann Casal, Colectânea de Jurisprudência (1993) t. V, p. 51–2 Tribunal da Relação de Coimbra, 14 December 1993

Facts

According to rules of Portuguese law (Art. 1095 of the Civil Procedure Code), the enforcement of a decision of a German court against a party domiciled in Portugal was requested in the Tribunal da Relação de Coimbra.

Judgment

In a preliminary ruling by the judge rapporteur, later confirmed by the court, it was considered that, according to the Lugano Convention, the court having jurisdiction was the Tribunal Judicial de Círculo de Aveiro.

Applicability of the Lugano Convention was justified on the basis that it was already in force when enforcement proceedings had been instituted, even though the judgment of which recognition was being sought had been delivered prior (17 December 1991) to the entry into force of that Convention in Portugal (1 July 1992).

However, since the Tribunal Judicial de Círculo de Aveiro (the latter being the place of domicile of the party against whom enforcement had been requested) had not yet been constituted, the judgment ruled that application for enforcement should be addressed to the Tribunal da Comarca de Aveiro, notwithstanding that invocation of the latter jurisdiction of the Tribunal da Relação under the Convention is otherwise limited to appeals.

Comment

It is worth drawing attention to three points in this judgment.

First, it ignored Art. 54B of the Lugano Convention, according to which this Convention does not prejudice the application of the Brussels Convention by the EU Member States.

Secondly, concerning the scope of application *ratione temporae*, it ruled that the Lugano Convention applied to recognition, since the enforcement proceedings were instituted after the entry into force of the Convention in the State addressed; the court, however, overlooked that the Convention should also have been in force in the State of origin at the relevant time (in Germany, 1 March 1995).

Finally, the court dealt with a very important practical question in Portugal which concerns the effect of the lack of constitution of several Tribunais

Judiciais de Círculo, precisely those courts to which application for enforcement should be addressed. The Tribunal da Relação ruled convincingly that, in such cases, the Tribunal Judicial de Comarca of the place of domicile of the party against whom enforcement is sought, as the general jurisdiction court, should retain jurisdiction in this respect.

ARTICLE 34, PARAGRAPH 2

"The application [for enforcement] may be refused only for one of the reasons specified in Articles 27 and 28."

Case principle

Failure to produce documents establishing, pursuant to Art. 47(1), that, according to the law of the State of origin, the judgment is enforceable and has been served, does not constitute a reason for refusing an application for enforcement.

Case

Banco Pinto & Sotto Mayor, SA v Manuel dos Santos Portela e Maria de   **773**
Fátima do Couto, Colectânea de Jurisprudência (1995) t. IV, p. 35–8 Tribunal da Relação de Coimbra, 17 December 1995

Facts

Following a decision of the Tribunal de Círculo de Leiria, authorizing enforcement of two judgments of the French courts dated 26 November 1991 and 9 November 1993, ordering two Portuguese citizens to pay a sum of money to a bank established in Portugal, an appeal was made to the Tribunal da Relação de Coimbra. The parties against whom enforcement had been sought contested the applicability of the Brussels Convention and argued that application for enforcement should have been refused because the court addressed lacked territorial jurisdiction.

Judgment

The Tribunal da Relação considered, in accordance with Art. 54 of the Brussels Convention and Art. 54B of the Lugano Convention, that the Brussels Convention was applicable, since the request for enforcement had been subsequent (24 November 1994) to the entry into force of the Convention in the State addressed (Portugal: 1 July 1992) and the court of origin had applied the jurisdiction rules provided for in Arts 2 to 6 of the Brussels Convention.

As regards the material scope of application, the court rejected the argument of the persons against whom enforcement had been sought. It stressed that the circumstances in which an order against a legal person involved in proceedings analogous to bankruptcy had also been part of the same judgment was not relevant so as to exclude the applicability of the Convention, since enforcement was not being sought against that person and the judgment was not related to the above-mentioned proceedings.

As regards the requirements for refusal of recognition (set out in Arts 27 and 28 of the Convention), the court underlined that the rights of defence had been duly respected and that the enforceability of the judgment emerged from its text. Moreover, it observed that the Convention did not require the judgment to be final, since the courts of the addressed State could stay the proceedings under Art. 30 if an appeal against the judgment was brought.

Comment

Although the judgment misunderstood the transitional provisions of Art. 54, paras. 1 and 2 (*delivery* of judgment must be post-entry into force, not merely the *application* for its enforcement), it dealt satisfactorily with the material scope of application of the Convention and with the satisfaction of the conditions for rejecting the appeal against the decision authorizing enforcement (see the decision of the European Court of 14 March 1996 in *Roger Van der Linden v Berufsgenossenschaft der Feinmechanik und Elektrotechnik* Case C–275/94 [1996] ECR I-1393, for a type of confirmation).

ARTICLE 39, PARAGRAPH 1

" . . . *no measures . . . other than protective . . .* "

Case principle

Appeal against the decision authorizing enforcement has a suspensive effect, the only exception being the protective measures which may be taken against the property of the party against whom enforcement is sought.

Case

774 Alba Radio Ltd v Cerqueira & Moreira Lda, Colectânea de Jurisprudência, 1994, t. III, p. 228 *et seq.* Tribunal da Relação do Porto, 7 June 1994

Facts

An English company applied to enforce a judgment, given by the Queen's Bench Division of the High Court in London, ordering a Portuguese company to pay a sum of money. Enforcement having been authorized, the party against whom it had been sought lodged an appeal.

Judgment

The court held that such an appeal had the effect of staying the enforcement proceedings and based its ruling on Art. 39 of the Convention which provides that pending the appeal only protective measures against the property of the party against whom enforcement is sought are permitted.

Comment

The judgment, which addressed the effects of appeals against the decision authorizing enforcement, correctly applied the system of the Convention (for further commentaries, see Miguel Teixeira de Sousa, 'A Concessão de *Exequatur* a uma decisão estrangeira segundo a Convenção de Bruxelas', *Revista da Faculdade de Direito da Universidade de Lisboa* (1994) p. 445 *et seq*).

ARTICLE 54, PARAGRAPH 1

"The provisions of the Convention shall apply . . . after its entry into force in the State of origin and . . . in the State addressed."

Case principle

The Brussels Convention is not applicable to recognition proceedings instituted before the entry into force of the Convention in the State addressed.

Case

Supremo Tribunal de Justiça, 26 May 1993, Colectânea de Jurisprudência   **775**
(1993) t. 2, p. 126–127.

Facts

Application was made to the Tribunal da Relação de Coimbra under Portuguese procedural law, for recognition of a Belgian judgment of 5 June 1989 ordering a party to pay a sum of money. The court dismissed the application in accordance with Portuguese law and an appeal was made to the Supreme Court.

Judgment

In its decision, the Supreme Court considered the applicability of the Brussels Convention (which, in the meantime, had entered into force in Portugal), but excluded it on the ground that the application for recognition had been lodged prior to the entry into force of the Convention in the State addressed (contrary to what is required by Art. 54 of the Convention). The court therefore applied Portuguese law to the recognition proceedings.

Comment

The result is basically correct, to the extent that it concerns the non-applicability of the Brussels Convention. Nevertheless, the question should have been considered under Art. 29 of the San Sebastian Accession Convention and the court should have discussed whether the Convention was already in force in the State of origin at the time the proceedings were instituted. It should also have referred to Art. 54B of the Lugano Convention, which provides that, in such case, the Brussels Convention supersedes the Lugano Convention (see also Moura Vicente, *op. cit.,* n. 1, p. 480).

LUGANO ARTICLE 54, PARAGRAPH 2

" . . . shall be recognised . . . in accordance with . . . Title III . . . "

Case principle

The Lugano Convention's provisions can grant enforcement of a judgment given after its entry into force in the State addressed in respect of actions instituted before its entry into force between that State and the State of origin, if the defendant was domiciled in the latter State.

Case

776 Banque Franco Portugaise, SA v Pedro Severo Lopes, Colectânea de Jurisprudência (1994) t. IV, p. 28–30 Tribunal da Relação de Coimbra, 12 July 1994

Facts

A French bank requested recognition under national Portuguese law of a French judgment ordering a Portuguese citizen (at the time domiciled in France and now residing in Anadia, Portugal) to pay a sum of money.

Judgment

The court held that the Lugano Convention superseded the Portuguese system and that the Tribunal da Relação thus lacked enforcement jurisdiction. It noted that the Convention had entered into force in Portugal before enforcement of the judgment had been requested and was already in force in France when the judgment was delivered, even if it was not in force when proceedings had been instituted in that State. In these circumstances, the court decided that the Convention was applicable, since the French decision had been rendered taking into consideration all the relevant criteria of jurisdiction in France and, in particular, in accordance with one of the rules of jurisdiction embodied in the Lugano Convention—namely, the general provision of Art. 2, which refers to the domicile of the defendant. Accordingly, the court dismissed the request for enforcement, ruling that proceedings should have been instituted in the Tribunal Judicial de Círculo de Anadia pursuant to the Lugano Convention.

Comment

This judgment also misunderstood the respective scope of application of the Lugano and Brussels Conventions, overlooking Art. 54B of the former and the entry into force of the Brussels Convention in Portugal.

However, the court appears to have construed correctly the essential contents of the transitional provision of Art. 54, para. 2. In fact, this rule allows for recognition of decisions rendered after the entry into force of the Convention between the State of origin and the State addressed in proceedings instituted before that date, if jurisdiction of the court in question was founded upon rules which accorded with those provided for in Title II of the Convention—and the domicile of the defendant certainly fulfils this requirement. But the court overlooked that this provision also implies, as a condition for enforcement, that the *judgment* must be subsequent to the entry into force of the Convention in the State addressed. This was not the case, since the judgment was rendered on 9 January 1992 and the Convention had only entered into force in Portugal on 1 July 1992 (see also Moura Vicente (*op. cit., supra,* n. 1, p. 484).

Editor's Comment

The case, interestingly, also brings attention to the fact that Art. 54, para. 2 is mandatory: Title III applies if the conditions there set out are fulfilled. There is no question of being able to pick and choose between Title III and national enforcement procedures according to whichever would give the best chance of a successful outcome to the application for enforcement (see *Kaye, Civil Jurisdiction,* pp. 238–243).

17

SCOTLAND

Angus Glennie, Advocate (Q.C., England and Wales)

A.   LEGAL SYSTEM

The Scottish court system is comprised of inferior and superior courts. In ascending order the relevant civil courts are: the Sheriff Courts, both before the sheriff and the sheriff principal; the Outer House of the Court of Session; the Inner House of the Court of Session; and the House of Lords.

The inferior courts are the Sheriff Courts. There are six sheriffdoms in Scotland, each sheriffdom being divided into a number of Sheriff Court districts where the Sheriff Court is held. Each sheriffdom has one or more sheriffs, the largest being Glasgow and Edinburgh, in that order. Each sheriffdom is presided over by a sheriff principal. The jurisdiction of these courts is territorial. They have a wide jurisdiction over civil matters, such as actions for debt and damages, without pecuniary limit. There is an appeal from the sheriff to the sheriff principal. A dissatisfied party may also appeal to the Inner House of the Court of Session, either directly from the sheriff or from the sheriff principal. It should be noted that the Sheriff Courts also have a criminal jurisdiction.

The superior court, the Court of Session, is a court both of first instance and of appeal. It is divided into the Inner House and the Outer House. All judges of the Court of Session enjoy the same rank, as Senators of the College of Justice and Lords of Council and Session. In the Outer House a judge is referred to as a Lord Ordinary. The Outer House acts as a court of first instance. The Lord Ordinary sits alone to hear a case. Very occasionally in civil matters there is a jury. A party dissatisfied with a decision of the Outer House may reclaim to the Inner House. In certain types of cases leave (permission) to reclaim is necessary. The Inner House is divided into two divisions, the First and Second Division, presided over respectively by the Lord President and the

Lord Justice-Clerk. Occasionally, an Extra Division may be convened to deal with Inner House Business. In addition to acting as a court of appeal from the Sheriff Court and on a reclaiming motion from the Outer House, the Inner House has a limited original jurisdiction.

There is a right of appeal from a decision of the Inner House to the House of Lords. In some cases leave to appeal is necessary.

B. IMPLEMENTATION OF THE CONVENTIONS

Section 2 of the Civil Jurisdiction and Judgments Act 1982 gave the 1968 Brussels Convention 'the force of law' in the UK, including Scotland. The English text of the Convention is set out in Sched. 1 to the Act. Section 3 of the Act allows reference to be made to the Jenard and Schlosser Reports in ascertaining the meaning and effect of any provision of the Convention. The Act has been modified and amended in various respects by statutory instrument, under powers contained in s.14 of the Act (the most relevant Orders are S.I. 1989 No. 1346, S.I. 1990 No. 2591), in particular in the light of subsequent accession to the Convention by Greece, Spain and Portugal. In the Act, as amended, the term 'Brussels Conventions' is used to mean not only the 1968 Convention but also the 1971 Interpretation Protocol and the Accession Conventions of 1978, 1982 and 1989. Section 3 of the Act has been amended to allow reference, in ascertaining the meaning or effect of the Conventions, also to the Reports on the 1982 and 1989 Accession Conventions. More significantly, in 1991 the Act was amended by s.1 of the Civil Jurisdiction and Judgments Act 1991 to give the force of law to the Lugano Convention. This is effected by s.3A of the 1982 Act, as amended.

In addition to giving the Brussels and Lugano Conventions the force of law in the UK, the opportunity was taken in the 1982 Act: (i) to legislate for the allocation of jurisdiction in civil proceedings within the UK in Part II, ss.16–19 and Sched. 4, (*e.g.* between England and Scotland); and (ii) substantially to codify the circumstances in which a person (or company) may be sued in the Scottish courts, under Part III, ss.20–23 and Scheds 8 and 9. The relevant courts are the Court of Session or a Sheriff Court. These provisions for allocating jurisdiction between courts in the UK and for conferring jurisdiction on the Scottish courts apply the scheme of Title II of the 1968 Brussels Convention with certain modifications. Schedule 4, entitled 'Title II of 1968 Convention as Modified for Allocation of Jurisdiction within UK' adopts the format and wording of the Convention with only very minor changes. Schedule 8, entitled 'Rules as to Jurisdiction in Scotland' has a different format and there are many more changes—but the Schedule contains marginal references to Articles of the Convention and certain heads of jurisdiction are identical or virtually identical. It is specifically provided by ss.16(3) and 20(5) of the Act that in determining any question as to the meaning or effect of any provision in Scheds 4 and 8, derived to any extent from Title II of the 1968 Convention, regard shall be had to decisions on the Convention itself and to the Jenard, Schlosser and other Reports mentioned in s.3 of the Act. A number of cases in the Scottish Courts have been decided in relation to these Schedules, and it has been thought appropriate to include reference to such decisions in this Chapter where they raise the same question as could arise under the comparable section in the Brussels Convention itself. When noting such cases, reference has been made not only to the specific rules in Sched. 4 or 8, but also to the comparable Article of the Convention. Cases in which the wording of the particular Rule or Article of Sched. 4 or 8 is different in material respects from the equivalent Article in the Convention, or which turn substantially on procedural rules, have not been noted. For example, cases under Art. 17 of Sched. 4 to the Act (Prorogation of Jurisdiction) where the word 'exclusive' has been deliberately omitted from the end of the first paragraph. So also it has not been thought helpful to note cases on the application of Art. 18 of the Convention and its equivalent in Scheds 4 and 8 to the Act, which effectively turn on domestic procedural rules.

The cases noted in this Chapter cover the period from 1 January 1987 to 30 May 1997. They are predominantly decisions of the Court of Session, both the Outer House and the Inner House, there having been no relevant Scottish appeals to the House of Lords during this period. There have, in addition, been a number of Sheriff Court decisions, but they carry little weight as precedents and have been noted briefly only where they raise points of interest on the application of the Convention or the Act to particular circumstances.

The cases are noted by reference to the Sections and Articles of the Convention to which they relate.

C. OVERVIEW OF CONVENTION CASE LAW

Decisions of the House of Lords and of the Inner and Outer Houses of the Court of Session in this area are to be found mainly in the following series of reports, listed in order of precedence: Session Cases (*e.g.* 1995 SC 27); Scots Law Times (*e.g.* 1993 SLT 173); and in the Scottish Civil Law Reports (*e.g.* 1994 SCLR 316). The SLT and SCLR also report some decisions in the Sheriff Courts and other tribunals. In addition, reference may be made to *Current Law* and to *Green's Weekly Digest* for notes of recent cases, many of which are not otherwise reported.

D. CASES

ARTICLE 5(1)

"In matters relating to a contract . . . "

Case principle

Action founded upon *a statutory right of contribution towards* breach of contract damages towards a third party held to fall within Art. 5(1) as matters relating to a contract.

Case

777 Engdiv Ltd v G. Percy Trentham Ltd 1990 SC 53, 1990 SLT 617 Outer House

Facts

The pursuers had, in an earlier action, been held liable to a manufacturing company for defects in the construction of a new production plant, in respect of which they had provided architectural and design services. In this action the pursuers sought contribution from the defenders, who had been the main contractors in the construction of the plant. Their claim was brought under s.3(2) of the Law Reform (Miscellaneous Provisions) Act 1940. In terms of that Act, they contended that the defenders were a person 'who, if sued, might also have been liable [to the manufacturing company] in respect of the loss or damage'. They claimed that the defenders would have been liable to the manufacturing company for breach of contract. Since that contract was performed in Scotland where the plant was constructed, they asserted that the Scottish courts had jurisdiction over their claim since they were 'the courts for the place of performance of the obligation in question'. Since the issue was as to allocation of jurisdiction within the UK, the case was decided under Art. 5(1) of Sched. 4 to the 1982 Act, but the wording is identical in this respect to Art. 5(1) of the Brussels Convention.

Judgment

The pursuers' argument was accepted. Lord Prosser, while dismissing the action on other grounds, held that jurisdiction could be established on this basis. Although the defenders were not being sued for breach of contract, they were being sued 'in matters relating to a contract'. The contract was not merely background.

Comment

This case is to be contrasted with *Davenport*, Case 781, noted under Art. 5(3), *infra*. Note also the following Sheriff Court decision which is of some interest in this respect. In *Strathaird Farms Ltd v G.A. Chattaway & Co.* 1993 SLT (Sh. Ct.) 36 the Sheriff Court was concerned with a contract for the supply of goods and services. The pursuer brought an action of *condictio indebiti* (in effect a claim for money overpaid by him under the contract under a mistake of fact) and sought to found jurisdiction on the basis that this was a matter 'relating to a contract', and therefore within Art. 5(1) of Sched. 4 to the Act. In rejecting this argument and declining jurisdiction, the court held that 'in matters relating to a contract' meant 'in proceedings based upon a contract'. Since these proceedings were not based on a contract, the attempt to found jurisdiction under this head failed. The court applied the approach in *Davenport* (*infra*).

In *O'Neill v Tebbett* 1994 SLT 752 (Outer House), the pursuer raised an action against her former husband, now resident in Florida, seeking an increase in terms of a minute of agreement concluded earlier between the parties providing for aliment (maintenance) for the children of the family. In a dispute as to the jurisdiction of the Scottish courts, Temporary Judge R.G. McEwan Q.C., held that the claim was a *matter relating to a contract*, and that since the place of performance in the minute of agreement was Scotland, the Scottish courts had jurisdiction—presumably, given the authorities cited to him, on the basis of the rule that a debtor seeks out his creditor. Since the defender was not in a Convention country, the only question in fact was whether the Scottish courts had jurisdiction *under rule 2(2)* of Sched. 8 to the 1982 Act, but the wording is identical in this respect to Art. 5(1) of the Brussels Convention.

" . . . place of performance . . . "

Case principle

1. Obligation of supervisory control is performed at place of decisions rather than of effects thereof.

Case

Bank of Scotland v Investment Management Regulatory Organisation Ltd **778** 1989 SC 107; 1989 SLT 432 Inner House

Facts

This case concerned an application by the Bank of Scotland for judicial review and reduction of a decision by IMRO not to waive one of its rules as to the carrying on of investment business. It was alleged that IMRO had erred in law in failing to take into account relevant considerations and that its decision was irrational and unreasonable. It was contended, and for the purpose of the argument accepted, that the rules under which IMRO acted were contractual (the Bank being a member of IMRO) and that therefore IMRO was in breach of contract in so erring. IMRO's registered office was in London. The Bank sought to found Scottish jurisdiction on the basis that Scotland was the place of performance of IMRO's obligation, because that was where the main effect of IMRO's decision would be felt under Sched. 8, rule 2(2) of the 1982 Act, the wording of which is the same as that in Art. 5(1) of the Convention.

Judgment

An Extra Division of the Inner House declined jurisdiction, on the ground that the place of performance of the obligation in question would be London, where IMRO had made the decision and ought to have taken into account the relevant considerations. The fact that IMRO's failure (if proved) to perform its obligation had its main *effect* in Scotland did not make Scotland the place of performance. It was also held that this head of jurisdiction was not the appropriate head, since these were proceedings which had as their object the decision of an organ of a company or other legal person within Sched. 8, rule 2(12) of the 1982 Act, in materially identical terms to Art. 16(2) of the Convention, and consequently were required to be heard where IMRO had its seat, namely, in England.

Comment

This decision is interesting in identifying the place of performance of the obligation, where the obligation is to *make a decision* in a particular way. But it is likely to be of only marginal relevance in relation to the Convention itself since, as was noted in the opinion of Lord Cullen in the Outer House, both parties agreed that the subject matter of these proceedings fell within the description of 'administrative matters' which are excluded from the scope of the Convention by Art. 1, but are not excluded from that of Sched. 8 to the 1982 Act.

Case principle

2. Place of performance of guarantee of bank's credit is at place where account guaranteed is kept.

Case

779 Bank of Scotland v Seitz 1990 SLT 584 Inner House

Facts

A German national domiciled in Germany was sued by the Bank of Scotland for payment under guarantees granted by him in favour of the bank in respect of bank accounts of two companies holding accounts at the Glasgow branch of the bank. The guarantees were silent as to the place of payment thereunder. The defender argued that the Scottish court had no jurisdiction over him, since the Brussels Convention laid down a primary rule that a party should be sued in the courts of his domicile. He argued further that for Art. 5(1) to apply there had to be a single place of performance of the obligation to make payment under the guarantees, and that since the Bank of Scotland had places of business in Scotland and England, the pursuers could not say that Scotland was the place of performance of the obligation so as to enable them to establish jurisdiction in Scotland.

Judgment

The Inner House, First Division, held that Scottish courts possessed jurisdiction and rejected the defender's argument. Article 2 was not a primary rule to be applied in the absence of an express provision in the contract. Article 2 stated the general rule, but the rules of special jurisdiction with regard to particular matters, such as Art. 5, were of equal weight where they applied. In such cases, the pursuer had a choice. The language of Art. 5(1) strongly appeared to assume a single place of performance, but the court was concerned not with the place or places where the obligation *may* be performed but with where it *must* be performed. The fact that a creditor had more than one place of business was irrelevant if he could insist on performance at only one of them. Under Scots law, in the absence of any express provision in the contract, a debtor is bound to tender payment to the creditor at his residence or place of business. In the present case, the relevant place of business was Glasgow, since that was where the accounts were held. The guarantees were so intimately connected with the accounts that that was the place of performance under the guarantees.

Comment

This decision is unexceptional, but it does suggest a solution to the problem of a contract which has more than one possible place for performance of the obligation in question.

Case principle

3. Place of performance of payment under Scottish law is where the creditor receives payment at its place of business, not where payment is transmitted.

Case

Waverley Asset Management Ltd v Saha 1989 SLT 87 (Sh. Ct.) 87, Sheriff Court   **780**

Facts

The court was concerned with a claim by the pursuers for specific implement of a contract whereby (so they alleged) the defender, domiciled in England, had agreed to buy from them units in a unit trust. Under the contract, the defender was required to complete certain registration details on a form and return the form to Edinburgh together with payment.

Judgment

The court, in accepting jurisdiction under Art. 5(1) of Sched. 4 to the Act, held that the place of performance of the relevant obligations was Edinburgh, where the defender had to return the documents. Even if he entrusted the documents to the Post Office, fulfilment of the obligation was only complete on delivery to the pursuers.

ARTICLE 5(3)

"In matters relating to tort, delict . . . "

Case principle

Statutory claim against a motorist's insurer for unpaid damages is not a matter of tort or delict for Art. 5(3).

Case

781 Davenport v Corinthian Motor Policies at Lloyds 1991 SC 372, 1991 SLT 774
Inner House

Facts

In 1983, the pursuer was injured in a road traffic accident. In 1986, the pursuer raised an action in the Glasgow Sheriff Court against the other driver and obtained decree against him. She received no payment from him. Accordingly, in 1989 she raised an action against his English insurers in terms of s.151 of the Road Traffic Act 1988 which, in brief, requires an insurer, subject to certain conditions, to pay the amount of an unsatisfied judgment. The pursuer sought to found jurisdiction on the provisions of Art. 5(3) of Sched. 4 to the 1982 Act, since this was a dispute as to jurisdiction within the UK, the accident having occurred within the jurisdiction of the Glasgow Sheriff Court. Art. 5(3) of Sched. 4 is identical in material respects to Art. 5(3) of the Brussels Convention.

Judgment

The Extra Division of the Inner House declined jurisdiction: the matter was not one relating to tort or delict. Article 5, as a derogation from the general principle of jurisdiction based on domicile, had to be construed restrictively. Although the pursuer's earlier action against the driver was based on tort or delict, and the decree based on the tort or delict of negligence was an essential pre-requisite to the action against the insurers, the action against the insurers was based on the statutory provision and upon nothing else.

ARTICLE 5(4)

" . . . court seised of those proceedings . . . "

Case principles

1. The criminal proceedings in question must still be pending.
2. Civil and criminal proceedings must be heard together, not merely by the same court.

Case

Davenport v Corinthian Motor Policies at Lloyds 1991 SC 372; 1991 SLT 774   **782**
Inner House

Facts

The facts are set out in Art. 5(3), *supra*, Case 781. In addition, the pursuer attempted to found jurisdiction on Art. 5(4) of Sched. 4 to the 1982 Act. The relevant wording is the same as in the Convention. In 1984, criminal proceedings were brought in the Glasgow Sheriff Court against the driver of the other vehicle. It was argued for the pursuer that jurisdiction over the insurers in the 1989 action in the Glasgow Sheriff Court could be based on the fact that the court was seised of the criminal proceedings.

Judgment

The court rejected this argument: (i) the court in 1989 was not *still* seised of the criminal proceedings disposed of in 1984; and (ii) the Sheriff Court exercising its civil jurisdiction was not the *same* court as the Sheriff Court exercising its criminal jurisdiction.

ARTICLE 13, PARAGRAPH 1

" . . . outside his trade or profession . . . "

Case principle

A contract by a hotel owner to obtain hotel marketing services held to fall outside his trade or profession, so that hotel owner was a consumer.

Case

Chris Hart (Business Sales) Ltd v Niven 1992 SLT (Sh. Ct.) 53 Sheriff Court   **783**

Facts

In this case, a hotel owner had contracted with the pursuer for marketing the hotel. The pursuer raised an action for payment for his services, relying for jurisdiction on a clause prorogating the exclusive jurisdiction of the Sheriff Court at Glasgow. The defender, who was domiciled outside the jurisdiction of that court, challenged jurisdiction under the equivalent of Art. 13, contending that he was a consumer. The relevant provision was rule 3 of Sched. 8 of the 1982 Act. The wording is in material respects the same.

Judgment

The court held, in accepting this argument and declining jurisdiction, that since the defender's trade was the sale of liquor, not the marketing of licensed premises, he was concluding a contract for a purpose outside his trade or profession and the contract was a consumer contract.

ARTICLE 13, PARAGRAPH 1(3)

" . . . for the supply of services . . . "

Case principle

1.   Solicitor's client held consumer.

Case

784   Lynch & Co v Bradley 1993 SLT (Sh. Ct.) 2 Sheriff Court

Facts

This case concerned an action by a firm of solicitors against their client for payment of fees.

Judgment

In declining jurisdiction, the court held that the client was a consumer and the contract was a contract for the supply of services within the equivalent of Art. 13. The relevant provision was rule 3 of Sched. 8 to the 1982 Act. The wording is in material respects the same.

Case principle

2.   Unit trusts held not goods or services.

Case

785   Waverley Asset Management Ltd v Saha 1989 SLT (Sh. Ct.) 87 Sheriff Court

Facts

See *supra*, Case 780.

In this case the defender also challenged the jurisdiction of the Scottish courts on the basis that the contract for the sale of units in a unit trust, was a contract for the 'supply of goods' within Art. 13, para. 1(3) of Sched. 4 to the 1982 Act and that he had therefore under Art. 14 to be sued in the courts of his domicile.

Judgment

The court, in rejecting this argument, held that incorporeal moveables such as units in unit trusts were not 'goods'. The case, therefore, did not fall within Art. 13, para. 1(3).

ARTICLE 16(1)(a)

" . . . *have as their object* . . . "

Case principle

Rights *in rem* or tenancies must be directly in issue for exclusive jurisdiction to apply, not merely indirectly involved.

Case

Barratt International Resorts Ltd v Martin 1994 SLT 434 Outer House   **786**

Facts

The pursuers had appointed the defender to be manager of a timeshare development in Spain. He lived and worked on the premises but had no tenancy or rights of occupancy. His contract was terminated by the pursuers, who brought an action for declarator as well as for a decree of summary ejection.

Judgment

In rejecting an argument that the action for ejection from the property in Spain was caught by Art. 16(1), the court (Lord Sutherland) held that the object of the proceedings was the termination of the defender's appointment as manager, and the case did not fall within Art. 16(1). To come within Art. 16(1), the proceedings must relate directly to rights *in rem* or tenancies and not to a situation where this was only an indirect consideration.

Comment

A decision of the Sheriff Court may be noted here. In *Ferguson's Trustee v Ferguson* 1990 SLT (Sh. Ct.) 73, a trustee in sequestration sought to interdict against the bankrupt from selling or interfering with any property vested in the trustee and with any property *qua* director of any limited company in which he was a director. Amongst the property which the bankrupt or his companies had, were properties in Spain. The court held, applying Art. 16(1) of the Convention, that it had no jurisdiction to interdict the bankrupt from selling or interfering with the Spanish property.

ARTICLE 16(2)

" . . . *have as their object . . . the decisions of their organs* . . . "

Case principle

Action to annul a corporate decision falls within exclusive companies jurisdiction.

Case

787 Bank of Scotland v Investment Management Regulatory Organisation Ltd 1989 SC 107, 1989 SLT 432 Inner House

Facts

For the facts see *supra*, Case 778.

Judgment

The Court, in declining jurisdiction, held that the action for judicial review and reduction of a decision by IMRO not to waive certain of its conditions, was a proceeding which had as its object the decision of a legal person within the meaning of the equivalent of Art. 16(2)—Rule 2(12) of Sched. 8 to the 1982 Act—there are differences in the wording, but not material. Part of Art. 16(2) appears in Rule 2(12), and the remainder in Rule 4(1)(b).

ARTICLE 17

" . . . *have agreed* . . . "

Case principle

Agreement includes implied agreement under a general contractual renewal period.

Case

Barratt International Resorts Ltd v Martin 1994 SLT 434 Outer House   **788**

Facts

See *supra*, Case 786.

In addition, the contract as originally agreed between the parties prorogated the non-exclusive jurisdiction of the Scottish Courts. After its termination, the parties agreed a probationary renewal of the contract on the same terms. The letter from the pursuers setting out the terms of this renewal, which the defender accepted, provided that 'terms as to payment and obligations, proper law etc. during the proposed probationary period will be the same in all respects [as in the original agreement'.

Judgment

In accepting jurisdiction over the claim, the court (Lord Sutherland) held that the word 'etc.' in context was sufficient to carry forward into the probationary period the prorogation agreement, so as to confer jurisdiction on the Scottish courts.

> " . . . *shall have exclusive jurisdiction* . . . "

Case principles

1. Article 17 held to prevail over Arts 21 and 22 where prorogation contravened by party to it.
2. Parties not the same for Art. 21 where no issue joined between them.

Case

Bank of Scotland v SA Banque National de Paris 1996 SLT 103 Outer House   **789**

Facts

This case raises the important question of the relationship between Art. 17, on the one hand, and Arts 21 and 22, on the other. The facts were in summary as follows. The pursuers (BOS) raised an action in the Scottish courts against the defenders (BNP) for payment under a guarantee issued by BNP. The guarantee was in respect of the indebtedness to BOS by a Scottish company. The Scottish company was a subsidiary of a French company, which company had instructed BNP to issue the guarantee in favour of BOS. The guarantee was expressly governed by Scots law and provided for the exclusive jurisdiction of the Scottish courts. Before the raising of the Scottish action, the French company had raised proceedings in France against both BOS and BNP, seeking an injunction restraining BNP from paying BOS under the guarantee, a declaration that no money was owed by BNP under the guarantee, a declaration that a guarantee by the French company in favour of BNP was null and void and damages against BOS. The position adopted by the French bank in the French proceedings was in essence neutral. BOS challenged jurisdiction in the French action. That jurisdictional challenge had been dismissed in the French courts but was under appeal to the Cour de Cassation. The matter now came before the court in Scotland on a motion by BNP to sist (stay) the Scottish action on a number of grounds including: (i) that the French court was the court first-seised of the issues and that a sist was therefore mandatory under Art. 21; and (ii) that the court should in its discretion sist the action under Art. 22.

Judgment

Lord Penrose, in refusing the motion to sist the Scottish proceedings, held: (i) that in a simple case where a party to a prorogation agreement brought pre-emptive proceedings in another Convention country in breach of that agreement, Art. 17 ought to have priority over Art. 21, so that even if the court first-seised wrongly accepted jurisdiction despite the prorogation agreement, the court selected by the parties to the prorogation agreement should rule in favour of its own jurisdiction; (ii) that the position was more complicated where the proceedings in the court first-seised involved a number of parties, some of them parties to the prorogation agreement and some not; (iii) in such cases the court would not enforce the prorogation agreement against persons who were not parties to it; (iv) a conflict between Art. 17 and Art. 21 can only arise where the parties to the prorogation agreement are properly identified as 'parties' relative to each other in the proceedings before the court first-seised, in other words, when there is an issue between them in such proceedings—it is not sufficient simply that they are parties to the same action brought by another against them both; (v) in the instant case in France, it was not shown that BNP had done other than adopt a position of neutrality—they had not put in issue their liability under the guarantee. Accordingly, the conditions for the application of Art. 21 ('proceedings involving the same cause of action between the same parties') had therefore not been satisfied and no conflict with Art. 17 arose; if there had been identity of issues between the same parties in the French courts, that would have been because of BNP's breach of the prorogation clause and the Scottish court would have asserted its exclusive jurisdiction over the dispute between BNP and BOS by refusing the sist. It was also held that Art. 22 did not apply, since the proceedings in Scotland were at first instance whilst those in France were not, having gone on to appeal. There was therefore no discretion to sist the Scottish action under Art. 22. A sist would in any event have been refused.

Comment

In addition to the decision clarifying the relationship of Arts 17, 21 and 22, the case is interesting for the lengthy discussion in the judgment about the difficulties that can arise where, on the one hand, there is a prorogation agreement between two parties and, on the other hand, multi-party proceedings are commenced in another country by a third party, so that the courts of that other country (first-seised) accept jurisdiction over parties to the prorogation agreement pursuant to Art. 6. There is also discussion of what appears to be a lacuna in the Convention in that no provision is made for what is to happen when the court first-seised wrongly refuses to decline jurisdiction in favour of the court chosen by the parties.

ARTICLE 21

" . . . *between the same parties* . . . "

Comment

The relationship between Arts 21 and 22 and Art. 17 has been considered in detail in *Bank of Scotland v SA Banque National de Paris* 1996 SLT 103, *supra*, Case 789.

ARTICLE 24

" . . . *as may be available under the law of that State* . . . "

General

Article 24 is given statutory effect so far as concerns Scotland by s.27 of the 1982 Act which is in the following terms:

'27.—(1) The Court of Session may, in any case to which this subsection applies—(a) subject to subsection (2)(c), grant a warrant for the arrestment of any assets situated in Scotland; (b) subject to subsection (2)(c), grant a warrant of inhibition over any property situated in Scotland; and (c) grant interim interdict.

(2) Subsection (1) applies to any case in which—(a) proceedings have been commenced but not concluded, or, in relation to paragraph (c) of that subsection, are to be commenced, in another Contracting State or in England and Wales or Northern Ireland; (b) the subject-matter of the proceedings is within the scope of the 1968 Convention as determined by Article 1; and (c) in relation to paragraphs (a) and (b) of subsection (1), such a warrant could competently have been granted in equivalent proceedings before a Scottish Court; . . . '

Questions relating to the application of this section have been raised before the Scottish courts on a number of occasions during this period. The questions have included: what relief can a Scottish court give when exercising such powers, in particular is it limited to a remedy available according to Scots domestic law? Further questions have involved a consideration of how this power fits in with Art. 57 of the Convention which says that the Brussels Convention shall not affect certain other conventions.

Case principle

1. Measures available are those possible under the law of the forum applied to for provisional relief, even if not also available under the law of the foreign Contracting State hearing substance of proceedings.

Case

790   Stancroft Securities Ltd v McDowall 1990 SC 274; 1990 SLT 746 Inner House

Facts

The petitioners, having commenced substantive proceedings in England and obtained in England an interim *Mareva* injunction against the respondents restraining them from dealing with or diminishing their assets save in so far as their value exceeded £240,000, petitioned in Scotland under s.27 of the 1982 Act for a warrant for arrestment and inhibition on the dependence of the action and for interim interdict on similar terms to the English order. Lord Morison granted interim interdict but refused the *ex parte* application for warrant to arrest and inhibit.

Judgment

The Second Division of the Inner House held that the appeal against the refusal to grant a warrant to arrest and inhibit would be allowed. The Lord Ordinary was wrong to attach importance to the fact that the protection sought in Scotland differed from that available in England. Article 24 and s.27 of the 1982 Act made it clear that the protective measures which could be applied for under s.27 were protective measures available under the law of Scotland and it did not matter whether those measures differed from those which were available in the country in which the proceedings on substance were commenced.

Case principle

2. Conversely, a party applying for interim or protective relief is not confined to where a substantive remedy would be available under the law of Scotland itself.

Case

791   G v Caledonian Newspapers 1995 SLT 559 Outer House

Facts

In this case, the petitioners had obtained an injunction in England restraining disclosure of their identity and the identity of their children who had been born to them as a result of an implant procedure in Italy. They sought interim interdict in similar terms in Scotland under s.27. It was common ground that there was 'no substantive remedy' available in Scots law comparable to that to which effect was given by the English judgment.

Judgment

Lord Marnoch held that interdict would be granted in terms replicating the English order. In exercising the power under s.27 to grant relief ancillary to substantive proceedings outside Scotland, it would normally be sufficient that, as far as grounds of action were concerned, a prima facie case is made out according to the jurisprudence of the foreign court. Nothing in *Stancroft* (Case 790, *supra*) nor in the terms of Art. 24 required the court to apply Scots substantive law.

> " . . . *courts of another Contracting State have jurisdiction as to the substance* . . . "

Case principle

Article 24 can apply to Art. 57 conventions where not inconsistent (here through national statutory modification of the latters' implementation and application).

Case

Clipper Shipping Co Ltd v San Vincente Partners 1989 SLT 204 Outer House   **792**

Facts

The question was raised in this case of the relationship between the Brussels Convention, as reflected in s.27 of the 1982 Act, and the 1952 Arrest Convention. The International Convention relating to the Arrest of Seagoing Ships signed at Brussels on 10 May 1952, to which effect was given in the UK by the Administration of Justice Act 1956: see *Gatoil Inc. v Arkwright-Boston Co.* 1985 SC (HL)I. The 1956 Act has been replaced so far as concerns England and Wales by the Supreme Court Act 1981, but remains in force so far as concerns Scotland. The Arrest Convention limits the right to arrest ships to certain defined maritime claims. This is set out in Art. 1(1) of the Convention, and followed closely in s.47 of the 1956 Act. In this case the charterers of a ship raised an action against shipowners in Denmark for damages. The charterers presented a petition in Scotland under s.27 of the 1982 Act for a warrant of arrestment and arrested the shipowners' vessel. The shipowners moved to recall the arrestment of the vessel. One of their arguments was that the Arrest Convention, as given effect by s.47 of the Administration of Justice Act 1956, implied that there must be substantive proceedings in Scotland before warrant to arrest a vessel could be granted. They relied on Art. 57 of the Brussels Convention which provides that the Brussels Convention shall not affect other Conventions 'including the Arrest Convention' to which Contracting States are parties. They argued that the court should not allow the arrest of a vessel under s.27 of the 1982 Act without there being substantive proceedings in Scotland, since this *would* be contrary to the limits on the power of arrest of vessels in the Arrest Convention.

Judgment

Lord Coulsfield rejected this argument, stating that the court was prepared to accept that s.47 of the 1956 Act itself, giving effect to the Arrest Convention, assumed that a warrant to arrest would only be granted when the substantive action was proceeding in Scotland (though it noted that this limitation was not implicit in the Arrest Convention itself). *But* s.27 of the 1982 Act clearly *extended* that power of arrest to cases where substantive proceedings were taking place in a Convention country.

ARTICLE 27

" . . . shall not be recognized . . . "

Case principle

If recognition is once refused, a subsequent application for recognition of an appeal court's judgment in the same proceedings must be brought afresh, the original request being spent.

Case

793   Selco Ltd v Mercier 1996 SLT 1247

Facts

This was an appeal against registration of a Belgian judgment.

Judgment

The appeal was allowed by Lord Coulsfield, under Art. 27(2), on the ground that the Belgian proceedings had not been properly served on the respondent (the defendant to the Belgian proceedings). The decision turned entirely on findings of fact by the court. On a later motion by the petitioners for registration of the Belgian judgment as subsequently affirmed by the Belgian courts (either by way of appeal or further application), Lord Coulsfield ruled that the original petition was fully disposed of by the allowing of the appeal against enforcement and the expiry of the reclaiming days, and that any application based on the new decision of the Belgian courts would have to be the subject of a new petition.

ARTICLE 27(1)

" . . . contrary to public policy . . . "

Case principle

Fraud in obtaining judgment is not a ground of refusal for public policy.

Case

Arctic Fish Sales Co Ltd v Adam (No. 2) 1995 SLT 970 Outer House   **794**

Facts

The petitioners, an Irish company, obtained a decree in absence in Ireland against an individual (Adam) arising from a contractual dispute with a company of which Adam had been a director. Adam appealed against registration in Scotland of the decree in absence. Amongst his grounds of objection to registration were allegations: (i) that the decree had been obtained in circumstances where it was clear that he should not have been held liable; and (ii) that there had been no due service on him in sufficient time to enable him to arrange for his defence.

Judgment

Lord Cameron of Lochbroom, in allowing the appeal against registration, held that even if it had been the case that the decree was obtained by fraud, that was not a ground for reduction in the Scottish courts but was a matter for the Irish courts. The public policy exception to recognition in Art. 27(1) did not cover such a case but was concerned with the substantive issue of whether recognition of the decree, *because of its nature* or the nature of the action giving rise to it, would offend against public policy.

But in the highly unusual circumstances of the present case, where Adam at no time traded on his own account, had no reason to anticipate that he would be called as an individual and did not personally receive the court documents, even though service was *duly* effected for the purposes of the Convention, it was *insufficient* for the purpose of causing the time within which Adam as defender was to be enabled to arrange for his defence to begin under Art. 27(2) and consequently recognition should be refused thereunder.

18

SPAIN

Professor Julio D. González Campos* and Professor Alegría Borrás**

A. LEGAL SYSTEM

Courts

The Spanish Constitution of 1978 structured a non-unified legal system and, accordingly, both the State Parliament (*Cortes Generales*) and the Assemblies of the Autonomous Communities may enact laws in matters of their respective competence. However, the Constitution has established a unified system of courts and tribunals, the central organs of the State being competent, in general, with regard to the judiciary (Art. 149, para. 1(5) of the Constitution). So, the organization of the judiciary, the functions of the courts and tribunals and the status of judges are determined by an Act of the Parliament, the Law 6/1985, of 1 July 1985, on the judiciary (*Ley Orgánica del Poder Judicial*). As an autonomous constitutional organ, the General Council of the Judiciary (*Consejo General del Poder Judicial*) is the governing body of judges and it nominates the members of the judiciary to courts and tribunals, also having disciplinary power over them.

The Supreme Court (*Tribunal Supremo*—TS) is the highest judicial organ in all matters, except for constitutional questions and the protection of fundamental rights, matters which are assigned to the Constitutional Court (Art. 123(1) of the Constitution). In each of the 17 autonomous communities there is a High Court of Justice (*Tribunal Superior de Justicia*—TSJ) as the superior judicial organ of the territory and, at a lower level, the Provincial Courts

*Of the Autonomous University of Madrid and Judge at the Spanish Constitutional Court.
**Of the University of Barcelona.

(*Audiencia Provincial*—AP). Judges of first degree (*Juzgados de Primera Instancia*—JPI), who sit alone, are the ordinary judicial organs in civil, criminal, labour and administrative matters (competence over these four areas of law is distributed amongst the judges of First Degree of each district and also amongst the sections of the Provincial and High Courts and, finally, the Supreme Court).

Jurisdictional functions are exclusively vested in the judiciary, who are independent and subject to the rule of Law (Art. 117(1) of the Constitution). Access to the jurisdiction of courts by individuals, the right to a fair process for the parties and the right to the execution of judgments, in accordance with legal rules on competence and proceeding, are fundamental rights guaranteed by Art. 24 of the Constitution. If they are denied by a court, the individual may have redress first, by appeal to the Superior Court and, in the last resort, applying to the Constitutional Court by the means established for the protection of fundamental rights (*recurso de amparo*). Judicial decisions must be executed according to their terms—Art. 118 of the Constitution imposes this duty, first, on the organs of the Judiciary. Provisions for the execution of judicial decisions are included in the Law of Proceedings in Civil Matters of 1881 (*Ley de Enjuiciamiento Civil*).

B. IMPLEMENTATION OF THE BRUSSELS CONVENTION

Spain is party to the Convention on the Accession of Spain and Portugal to the Brussels Convention of 1968, concluded in San Sebastian on 26 May 1989. The implementation started with the signature of the Spanish instrument of ratification on 29 October 1990 and, after the authorization of the Parliament in accordance with Art. 94(1) of the Constitution, the 1989 Convention (with the texts of previous Conventions modifying the Brussels Convention from 1978 onwards) were published in the Official Journal (*Boletín Oficial del Estado*) of 28 January 1991. The 1989 Brussels Convention entered into force for Spain on 1 February 1991.

It should be noted that in Spanish law, no particular Act of incorporation of the provisions of the Brussels Convention was required. International treaties are part of the law of the land after their acceptance by Spain at the international level and the subsequent official publication of the instrument of ratification of the treaty in the Official Journal, as provided in Art. 96(1) of the Constitution and Art. 1(5) of the Civil Code.

In the Spanish official text, it is to be noted that the publication made in the Spanish Official Journal includes, separately, the previous instruments of the Brussels Convention from 1968 onwards and that of the Convention on Accession by Spain and Portugal of 1989. A non-official 'consolidated text' in Spanish and in the other languages of the Member States, published in the Official Journal of the European Communities No. C189, of 28 July 1990, may also be consulted, however.

On 1 July 1997, parties to the 1989 Convention with Spain, were Germany, Denmark, France, the UK, Greece, Italy, Ireland, Luxembourg, The Netherlands and Portugal.

Spain is also party to the Luxembourg Protocol of 3 June 1971, on the interpretation by the Court of Justice of the European Communities of the Brussels Convention of 1968, as modified by the above mentioned 1989 San Sebastian Convention on Accession of Portugal and Spain. The Protocol was published in the Spanish Official Journal on the same date, 28 January 1991, being from then a part of Spanish Law. On 1 July 1997, parties to the 1971 Protocol, as well as Spain, were Germany, Belgium, Denmark, France, UK, Greece, Ireland, Italy, Luxembourg, The Netherlands and Portugal.

C. OVERVIEW OF CONVENTION CASE LAW

The Spanish case law on the Brussels Convention is not very extensive, owing to the fact that Spain has only been a party to the Convention since 1991. However, more than 40 judicial decisions, both published and not published, have been reached.

Some of the judicial decisions reported made reference to the Brussels Convention before its entry into force in Spain and, therefore, they have not been included. Also excluded are those decisions applying the Convention to purely domestic cases.

In respect of the decisions rightly applying the Convention, it is to be noted, first, that many of them make reference to the case law of the Court of Justice of the European Communities—although some of them may merit criticism from the point of view either of the results reached or of the reasoning leading to these. Secondly, reference to the provisions of the Brussels Convention is sometimes coupled with those of the 'parallel' Lugano Convention of 1988, in force for Spain from 1 November 1994. Thirdly, some exclusions *ratione materiae* could have been solved *ratione temporis*. Lastly, it may be taken into account that the reform of the *national* Spanish rules on international jurisdiction of the Courts (Law 6/1985, of 1 July 1985, on the judiciary, Arts 21 and 22) incorporated many aspects of the Brussels Convention's provisions, but it diverged from them in other respects. The application of the Brussels Convention by the Spanish courts has contributed to modification of previous solutions, mainly in the matter of choice of courts.

A shortened account of certain Spanish decisions is included hereunder, prior to the more detailed case presentations which are set out in Section D below.

ARTICLE 1, PARAGRAPH 1(1)

" . . . status . . . "

Provincial Court of Madrid, 26 September 1995, COLEX

A French decree of divorce would only be declared enforceable in Spain pursuant to the bilateral convention between Spain and France, because divorce was excluded from the scope of the Brussels Convention.

ARTICLE 1, PARAGRAPH 1(2)

"Bankruptcy . . . "

First Instance Court of Ibiza, 27 November 1992, R.E.D.I. (1994) 2 854

The Convention was held to be inapplicable to enforcement of a French bankruptcy decree.

ARTICLE 2

" . . . persons domiciled in a Contracting State shall . . . be sued in the courts of that State."

Provincial Court of Barcelona, 30 May 1994, RGD 1994, No. 603, 1339; Actualidad civil, 1994, 4, No. 2775; COLEX

In a case involving a harmful event occurring in France, and where the plaintiffs were Spanish and resident in Spain and the defendants domiciled in Spain, the court upheld Spanish jurisdiction.

Comment

The court referred to Arts. 24 and 117 of the Constitution, guaranteeing rights of access to and protection afforded by Spanish courts.

Corresponding jurisdiction was exercised on similar facts by the Provincial Court of Valladolid, 24 February 1995, RGD No. 616–617, 1996, 1534–1535; R.E.D.I. Art. 2 was sufficient for Spanish jurisdiction and it was unnecessary to refer to Art. 6(1).

ARTICLE 6(1)

"Where he is one of a number of defendants . . . "

Provincial Court of Alava, 9 March 1995 (Actualidad civil, 1995–4, No. 1588; COLEX)

The court held that it possessed jurisdiction over the English defendants under Art. 6(1), where the Spanish main defendant was a school which had organised a visit to England for the plaintiff, one of its students, for the purposes of a stay with the defendant English family in whose care the plaintiff had suffered injuries. There was a sufficiently credible claim against the Spanish defendant for Art. 6(1) to be able to be used.

ARTICLE 17

" . . . shall have exclusive jurisdiction . . . "

Provincial Court of Madrid, 25 March 1996; COLEX

The court of appeal overturned the judge of first instance's acceptance of Spanish jurisdiction: the contracting parties had agreed upon French courts to decide any disputes.

ARTICLE 21, PARAGRAPH 1

" . . . involving the same cause of action . . . "

Provincial Court of Bilbao, 22 July 1993, R.E.D.I. (1994) 2 820

Where the same plaintiff sued the same defendant before French and subsequently Spanish courts, the Spanish court decided against decline of its jurisdiction, because the causes of action were not the same before Spanish and French courts.

Comment

The Spanish court in fact referred to national Spanish law on *lis pendens*, which is far more restricted than Art. 21 and the latter's interpretation by the European Court.

ARTICLE 34, PARAGRAPH 1

" . . . the party . . . shall not . . . be entititled to make
any submissions . . . "

First Instance Court of Madrid, 17 September 1993, R.E.D.I. (1994) 2 861

The court rejected the defendant's plea that the enforcement order was a nullity because he had not been heard on the enforcement application. Under the Convention's system, the method of objecting to the foreign judgment was to appeal against enforcement under Art. 36 (here, on the ground of lack of due and sufficient service of the document instituting proceedings upon the defendant).

ARTICLE 39, PARAGRAPH 1

"During the time specified for an appeal . . . "

First Instance Court of Madrid, 16 July 1993, R.E.D.I. (1994) 2 860

Foreign protective attachment order enforced by Spanish court held only to be in force for the time limit prescribed by Art. 39.

Editor's Comment

Strictly, Art. 39 is supposed to apply to the *enforcement*-court's protective measures pending final enforcement of the foreign judgment—not also to a foreign provisional order itself, enforcement of which is appealed against.

First Instance Court of Madrid, 21 July 1993, R.E.D.I. (1994) 2 861

Where attachment is ordered by a foreign court, the Spanish judge assesses whether it complies with *lex fori*.

D. CASES

ARTICLE 1, PARAGRAPH 2(1)

" . . . status . . . "

Case principle

1.   The Convention, *including Art. 21*, is inapplicable to divorce.

Case

Provincial Court of Barcelona, 20 July 1991, R.E.D.I. (1992) 2 642   **795**

Facts

The plaintiff Spanish national domiciled in Spain, sought a decree of divorce
in Spain in October 1989 against her husband, an Italian national domiciled
in Rome, from whom she was previously separated by decision of an Italian
Court. The latter had himself petitioned for divorce in Rome in September
1989 and challenged Spanish jurisdiction: the matrimonial domicile was in
Rome and, in addition, the Italian Court was first-seised of *lis pendens*.

Judgment

The Barcelona Court held the Convention, including Art. 21, to be inapplicable to divorce proceedings under Art. 1, para. 2(1).

Comment

The Court was of course right to deny the application of the Convention on
the basis of the nature of the action. However, the same result might have been
reached by taking into account the date of the proceedings, given that the
Convention only entered into force in Spain on 1 February 1991 (Art. 54).

Case principle

2.   A judgment for costs in excluded divorce proceedings is not itself also
     excluded when separately sought to be enforced (under Art. 42).

Case

Judge of First Instance Court of Benidorm, 5 July 1996, not yet published   **796**

Facts

Following the grant of a divorce in the UK, the wife asked for the enforcement
of the judgment in Spain against the husband resident in Spain under the
Convention, only in so far as the part relating to costs or expenses was concerned.

Judgment

The court held first, that it was *not* a question related to divorce or to matrimonial property and that, in consequence, it was not excluded from the
material scope of the Convention. Secondly, the court refused the request for

enforcement, because on applying for enforcement, the wife had not produced documents establishing that, according to the law of the state of origin, the judgment was enforceable and had been served.

> " . . . *arising out of a matrimonial relationship* . . . "

Case principle

Property rights derived from a matrimonial regime nonetheless are not excluded when the latter is not the subject of the dispute.

Case

797 Provincial Court of Barcelona, 27 May 1995, R.J.C. (1995) IV 1304–5

Facts

A married couple, the wife being Spanish and the husband German, but both residing in Germany, owned immovable property in Spain, which was part of the matrimonial regime of community. After their divorce, the wife sued the husband in the Spanish courts for division of the common property. The husband contested the jurisdiction of Spanish courts, arguing that the Convention, and, in particular, Art. 16(1), was inapplicable by virtue of Art. 1, para. 2(1).

Judgment

The Court held that the Spanish courts had jurisdiction under Art. 16(1), because the object of the proceedings was rights *in rem* in immovable property situated in Spain.

Editor's Comment

Although the *source* of the wife's alleged rights to the property was a matrimonial property regime, excluded under Art. 1, para. 2(1), the actual dispute appeared to relate to aspects of *resulting* property rights, with the source not in contention—a thin dividing line indeed! The opposite result was reached in the following case.

Case

798 Provincial Court of Baleares, 18th July 1995, R.G.D. (1997) 628–9, 1161–63; Cuadernos de Jurisprudencia balear, 3 14–7; Aranzadi civil (1995) 1306; R.E.D.I. (1996) 2, pp. 266–269

Facts

A French woman and a British man, habitually resident in Spain during their marriage, acquired immovable property in Spain. After divorcing in the UK, the wife, resident in France, sued the husband, resident in the UK, in Spain, claiming half of the benefits obtained by the tenancies of immovable property and expenses incurred in maintaining the property.

Judgment

The court held the Convention to be inapplicable because the matter related to rights in property arising out of a matrimonial relationship.

Comment

It is doubted whether the broad qualification of the question as related to matrimonial property was correct—although it would be justified if the dispute directly concerned rights of ex-spouses under the British Matrimonial Causes Act 1973.

ARTICLE 1, PARAGRAPH 2(2)

"Bankruptcy . . . "

Case principle

Bankruptcy of a debtor as a defence to a claim for a debt is excluded from the Convention, as not being merely incidental to the main debt claim.

Case

First Instance Court of Ibiza, 30 January 1993, R.E.D.I. (1994) 2 858   **799**

Facts

A French bankruptcy decision was pleaded as a defence to a claim against the debtor, and recognition was requested of the Spanish court.

Judgment

The French bankruptcy decision was excluded from the Convention even though it was only invoked by a party by way of a defence.

ARTICLE 5(1)

" . . . place of performance . . . "

Case principle

Place of performance determined by private international law rules of the forum (*Tessili*, Case 12/76 applied).

Case

800 Provincial Court of San Sebastian (Sección 2), 16 April 1993 R.E.D.I. (1994) 1 283

Facts

The plaintiff Spanish firm agreed with the defendant French firm for a distribution of the former's products in France by the defendant. The plaintiff sued the defendant in San Sebastián for termination of the obligation assumed by the defendant without payment to the latter, who pleaded lack of jurisdiction of the Spanish courts.

Judgment

The court held that, notwithstanding Art. 2, Art. 5(1) was also applicable, given that the obligation assumed was to be performed in Spain. In accordance with the jurisprudence of the European Court of Justice (*Tessili v Dunlop* Case 12/76 and *de Bloos v. Bouyer* Case 14/76), the place where the obligation was to be performed was determined by the choice-of-law rules of the forum. Thus, Arts. 10(5) and 1262 of the Spanish Civil Code applicable to the contract, referred to the place where the offer was made—Spain.

ARTICLE 8, PARAGRAPH 1(1)

" . . . State where he is domiciled . . . "

Case principle

A direct action can be brought by an injured party against an insurer in the latter's domicile.

Case

801 Provincial Court Castellón, 3 March 1995, R.G.D. 608 (1995) 6127–9; R.E.D.I. (1996) 2, pp. 263–265

Facts

A vehicle driven by the Spanish defendant was involved in an accident in Portugal with another vehicle driven by the Portuguese plaintiff domiciled in

Switzerland. The plaintiff sued the defendant's Spanish insurer in the Spanish courts. The defendant's insurers contested the jurisdiction of the Spanish courts on the basis that the accident had occurred in Portugal.

Judgment

The court held in favour of Spanish jurisdiction under Art. 2.

Comment

Although the decision is correct in its outcome, it is worth noting: (i) that the court, surprisingly, incorrectly quoted not only the Brussels Convention, but also the Lugano Convention, and mixed them up with a non-existent Geneva Convention! and (ii) that jurisdiction over the defendant's Spanish insurer ought properly to have been founded upon Art. 8, para. 1(1) and Art. 10, para. 2.

ARTICLE 16, PARAGRAPH 1(a)

" . . . have as their object . . . "

Case principle

Personal liability of a subscriber towards the unincorporated association for its debts does not fall within exclusive jurisdiction provision in Art. 16(2) (*Peters v ZNAV*, Case 34/82 applied).

Case

Provincial Court of Zaragoza, 12 July 1994, R.E.D.I. (1996) 2, pp. 258–261 **802**
COLEX

Facts

A Spanish cooperative society sued one of the partners, domiciled in Belgium, for debts owed by the society, under Art. 16. The defendant contested Spanish jurisdiction under Art. 16(2).

Judgment

The court held that the obligations of a partner in a cooperative society did not fall within Art. 16(2) because they had the character of contractual obligations according to the case law of the European Court of Justice. However, for the same reason, it was still possible to sue the defendant in Spain under Art. 5(1), since the place of performance of the obligation under Spanish applicable law was the domicile of the plaintiff creditor in Spain.

ARTICLE 17, PARAGRAPH 1

" . . . *shall have* . . . "

General

Spanish courts have incorrectly applied national laws alongside Art. 17.

Case principle

1. Article 17 excludes national laws on validity of jurisdiction agreements.

Case

803   Provincial Court of Barcelona, 15 February 1994, R.G.D. (1994) 598–9, 8588–92; R.E.D.I. (1995) 1 211–217

Facts

A Spanish firm acquired goods in Bangkok, undertaking the costs of the transport, to be performed by a French shipowner. The bill of lading contained an agreement conferring jurisdiction upon French courts. On their arrival in Spain, the goods were found to be in a defective condition and the buyer's insurance company only agreed to payment in return for an indemnity from and subrogation to the buyer's rights against the defendant shipowner, against whom proceedings were commenced. The shipowner argued lack of jurisdiction of the Spanish courts.

Judgment

Taking into account that the domicile of the plaintiff and of the shipowner's agent was in Barcelona, that the port of origin was Bangkok and that the final destination of the goods was Barcelona, the court held the French jurisdiction agreement to be invalid, because there was no material connection with Marseilles.

Comment

Derogatio fori is not expressly accepted in Spanish laws, and there is a doctrinal debate on the subject. In this case, the court concentrated upon this internal situation, forgetting that the position differs under the Convention. Although it can be argued that Art. 17 cannot operate when both parties are domiciled in the same Contracting State, in this case there *was* an international transport from Bangkok to Barcelona and the domicile of the shipowner was Marseilles.

Case principle

2. National rules of German applicable law ought not to be applied to the effectiveness of jurisdiction clause alongside Art. 17.

Case

Supreme Court 20 July 1992, R.E.D.I. (1993) 1 445, Arts 2, 3, 5(1) and 17   **804**

Facts

The defendant Spanish firm domiciled in Madrid undertook, under an exclusive sales contract, to sell the products of the plaintiff firm, domiciled in Belgium, who sued the defendant in Madrid for the resulting debt. The general conditions of the contract contained a clause choosing the jurisdiction of German courts and German law. The defendant pleaded lack of jurisdiction of the Spanish courts on the basis of Art. 17.

Judgment

The Supreme Court held that Spanish courts had jurisdiction under Arts 2 and 5(1). In respect of the clause of the contract choosing the jurisdiction of German Courts, it concluded that Art. 17 was not applicable, given that the clause also made a choice of German law: under Art. 10(5) of the Civil Code, a choice of jurisdiction in a contract lacking any connection with Germany was ineffective.

Comment

References to rules on jurisdiction in internal law are inappropriate. Article 17 alone governs effectiveness of choice of jurisdiction, to the exclusion of national rules. Furthermore, the decision used the rule on the choice of law for choice of jurisdiction.

ARTICLE 17, PARAGRAPH 4 (LUGANO 17(3))

" . . . *no legal force if . . . exclusive jurisdiction by virtue of Art. 16.*"

Case principle

Article 16 prevails over Art. 17.

Case

First Instance Court of Madrid, 15 November 1993, R.E.D.I. (1994) 2 861   **805**

Facts

A time-share contract concerning immovable property in Spain included a choice of jurisdiction clause in favour of the courts of the Isle of Man. The defendant, domiciled (as was the plaintiff) in Spain, pleaded lack of jurisdiction of the Spanish courts.

Judgment

The defence was rejected. Article 16 attributed exclusive jurisdiction to the Spanish courts in respect of immovables situated in Spain.

Case

806 Provincial Court of Málaga, 31 December 1994, (La Ley, (1995) 1, 467–70; R.G.D. (1996) No. 619 4761–62; Actualidad civil (1995) 3; COLEX

Facts

An agreement on jurisdiction of the courts and tribunals of Paris was contained in a finance contract between a French bank and a Spanish company. Later, in a written acknowledgement of debt and constitution of mortgage on immovable property situated in Spain, a clause giving jurisdiction to Spanish courts was included. The bank wished to rely upon the agreement included in the contract, but the Spanish firm argued that the valid agreement was the one included in the constitution of the mortgage, since it was subsequent in time and modified the previous one.

Judgment

The court held in favour of jurisdiction of Spanish courts, *but not on the basis of the parties' agreements*. For the court, the decisive argument was that the action related to a mortgage and, in that sense, had as its object rights *in rem* in immovable property, as to which, agreements on jurisdiction were not allowed since the property, the object of the mortgage, was situated in Spain, Spanish courts had exclusive jurisdiction.

ARTICLE 18

" . . . *shall have jurisdiction* . . . "

Case principle

Article 18 prevails over Art. 17 (*Elefanten Schuh* Case 150/80 applied).

Case

Provincial Court of Barcelona, 12 April 1994, R.G.D. No. 601–602 (1994), **807**
11447–50; R.E.D.I.; (1996) 2, pp. 251–257 COLEX

Facts

Notwithstanding a clause in the contract subject to the plaintiff German firm's
general conditions, choosing the jurisdiction of German courts, the plaintiff
sued the Spanish defendant in Spain.

Judgment

Despite the defendant's objection to the jurisdiction of the Spanish courts on
the basis of Art. 17, the court considered Art. 18 to be applicable, which prevailed over Art. 17 in any event.

Comment

The court was incorrect to apply Article 18 on the facts, since merely to appear
in order to contest jurisdiction, was not, according to *Elefanten Schuh*,
submission under Art. 18.

Case

Provincial Court of Alicante, 4 October 1995, R.E.D.I. (1996) 2, pp. 269–273 **808**

Facts

An agreement to the jurisdiction of the Luxembourg courts was included in a
contract made in Luxembourg. The plaintiff sued the defendant in Spain, the
jurisdiction of whose courts the defendant contested.

Judgment

The court held that the defendant had previously submitted to Spanish jurisdiction under Art. 18, which prevailed over express agreement under Art. 17.

ARTICLE 24

" . . . *available under the law of that State* . . . "

Case principle

Procedural powers to grant provisional measures are for *lex fori*.

Case

809   Provincial Court of Seville, 20 July 1993, R.E.D.I. (1994) 2 295

Facts

The plaintiff French firm sued the French defendant in France in respect of the defendant's failure to pay for construction of the roof for the railway station in Seville. The plaintiff asked for a pre-judgment protective measure before the Spanish courts to attach funds of the defendant in the hands of a Spanish public entity.

Judgment

In contrast to a previous decision of a lower court, the Audiencia Provincial declared that it had jurisdiction to grant the measure on the basis of Art. 24. But the application was finally rejected, considering that the measure did not comply with the conditions established by Arts 1400, 1401, 1410 and 1429 of the Spanish Code of Civil Procedure.

ARTICLE 27(2)

" . . . *in default of appearance* . . . "

Case principle

An appeal against enforcement cannot be made on the ground of lack of sufficient time to defend under Art. 27(2) if the defendant actually entered an appearance.

Case

810   Provincial Court of Vizcaya, 19 June 1996, not yet published

Facts

A Dutch firm sought enforcement of a Dutch judgment in Spain, ordering the Spanish defendant to pay an amount of money. The judge at first instance declared the judgment enforceable. The Spanish firm appealed against the decision authorizing enforcement, arguing, on the one hand, that the judgment-court founded jurisdiction on exorbitant fora excluded by Art. 3, and, on the other hand, that in the proceedings in The Netherlands, it had not received the documents instituting the proceedings in sufficient time to enable it to arrange for its defence.

Judgment

The court held that the defendant had never contested international jurisdiction of the Dutch courts, but only the subject matter jurisdiction of the Dutch court seised, jurisdiction then being based on Art. 18. The court also concluded that Art. 27(2) was not applicable, given that the defendant had entered an appearance by means of a legal representative who never raised the question of international jurisdiction.

Comment

Although the proceedings were instituted before the entry into force in Spain of the Convention, the latter applied because the circumstances of Art. 54, para. 2 (1989 Accession Convention Art. 29(2)) existed.

" . . . not duly served . . . "

Case principle

Judgments in default of appearance are enforceable if the writ was duly served in sufficient time for a defence.

Case

Provincial Court of Lugo, 31 October 1994, R.E.D.I. (1995) 2 412   **811**

Facts

Enforcement was sought of a judgment given in default of appearance in Scotland against a Spanish firm.

Judgment

The court declared the judgment enforceable, taking into account that, although given in default of appearance, it was clear that the defendant had been duly served.

ARTICLE 31, PARAGRAPH 1

" . . . shall be enforced . . . "

Case principle

1. A foreign *inter partes* Art. 24 measure must be enforced, even if it would not have been available under the law of the enforcement-State itself.

Case

812 First Instance Court of Palma de Mallorca, 30 November 1992, R.E.D.I. (1994) 2 856

Facts

Pre-judgment protection measure (attachment) ordered by an English court to be executed in Spain.

Judgment

Article 24 directly attributes to the Spanish court jurisdiction to enforce the measure, notwithstanding the limits of internal law on attachment when the measure is incidental to the principal proceeding.

Comment

Reference is made to the European Court of Justice Case 213/89, *Factortame*, to support the decision that limits resulting from Art. 1412 of the Code of Civil Procedure on incidental attachment may not exclude the enforcement of the measure adopted by the English court.

Case

813 First Instance Court of Madrid, 9 July 1993, R.E.D.I. (1994) 2 860

Facts

Attachment of goods in Spain was ordered by an Italian Court.

Judgment

The Italian decision being in due form was to be executed in Spain as the place of enforcement and the protective measures requested to that end were also ordered.

Comment

The Italian pre-judgment protective measures were ordered by the Spanish court not on the basis of Art. 24 but on that of Title III, on recognition and enforcement.

Case principle

2. It is implicit in Art. 47(1), concerning documentary requirements, that

enforcement must not be granted unless the judgment has been served upon the defendant.

Case

First Instance Court of Córdoba, 10 June 1993, R.E.D.I. (1994) 2 859   **814**

Facts and Judgment

Enforcement of a foreign judgment was refused: even though a letter of request was sent to the Spanish Ministry of Foreign Affairs, there was no evidence that the judgment was actually served on the defendant, so that he did not have sufficient time to appeal.

Case principle

3. Assessment of proper jurisdiction is for appeal in the judgment-State, not for enforcement-courts.

Case

Provincial Court of Toledo, 21 November 1993, R.G.D. (1996) No. 620   **815**
6269–72; Actualidad civil (1995)

Facts

A Dutch court delivered judgment against a Spanish firm, declared enforceable at first instance. The Spanish firm appealed on grounds that it had not been duly served and that the Dutch courts lacked jurisdiction.

Judgment

The court rejected both grounds—the first because, on the evidence, the defendant had been duly served and in sufficient time according to the Hague Convention of 15 November 1965 on the Service Abroad of Judicial and Extrajudicial Documents in Civil or Commercial Matters; and the second ground was also refused, since review of jurisdiction at the enforcement stage was generally prohibited.

> ### ARTICLE 53, PARAGRAPH 1
>
> " . . . *apply its rules of private international law.*"

Case principle

Seat, according to Spanish conflicts of law, is the centre of business direction or legal centre of a firm, not a mere delegation or agency.

Case

816 Provincial Court of Barcelona, 2 June 1994, R.G.D. (1995) No. 604–5; 1100–3; R.J.C. (1994) IV, 1025–28

Facts

A Spanish firm sued an American firm, in Spain, on the ground that the American firm had unilaterally repudiated their exclusive distribution agreement without justification. The American firm had a branch in London, where the documents instituting the proceedings were transmitted.

Judgment

The court considered that Art. 5(1) was inapplicable because the domicile of the American firm was not in London, where there was only a delegation or agency, but not also the centre of direction or legal centre of the firm. Consequently, the defendant's seat, as domicile, was not situated in any Contracting State.

1989 ACCESSION CONVENTION ARTICLE 29(1)

" . . . *legal proceedings instituted . . . after the entry into force . . .* "

Case principle

If proceedings were instituted prior to entry into force of the Convention, even Art. 21 of the latter is inapplicable.

Case

817 Provincial Court of Oviedo, 17 December 1991, R.E.D.I. (1992) 2 634

Facts

A Belgian firm sued the defendant Belgian national domiciled in Spain, in 1990 before the Spanish court for the payment of a commercial debt, assumed by the latter in a document signed in Spain. The defendant challenged Spanish jurisdiction on the ground of *lis alibi pendens*.

Judgment

The court held that Art. 21 was not applicable to the case: taking into account the date when the action was brought before the Spanish court, the Convention was not in force in Spain at that date.

Comment

See now the European Court's *Von Horn* Case C–163/95, for transitional implications.

19

SWEDEN

Professor Lennart Pålsson, University of Lund

A. LEGAL SYSTEM

Ordinary civil cases are heard by a District Court (*tingsrätt*). There are nearly 100 such courts in the country, each with jurisdiction within a specified geographical area. The court of second instance is a Court of Appeal (*hovrätt*), which hears appeals from the District Courts, in certain cases subject to leave being granted by the former court. There are six Courts of Appeal in the country. The oldest and biggest of them is *Svea hovrätt* in Stockholm, which is entrusted with important functions in regard to the recognition and enforcement of foreign judgments under the Lugano Convention. The court of last instance is the Supreme Court (*Högsta domstolen*), which hears appeals from judgments rendered by the Courts of Appeal. This is subject to leave being granted by the Supreme Court itself. Such leave will normally only be given in cases of major significance, such as precedents.

In addition, there are some special courts with jurisdiction to hear particular classes of cases. One such court of great importance is the Labour Court (*Arbetsdomstolen*). It is a court of first and last instance for the whole country in disputes concerning the interpretation and enforcement of collective agreements. In some other labour cases, it hears appeals from the District Courts. Another special court for the whole country is the Market Court (*Marknadsdomstolen*), whose jurisdiction covers, *inter alia*, cases involving legislation on free competition and unfair marketing methods.

There is also a hierarchy of administrative courts. Those courts, however, are of limited interest in the present connection.

Applications for the enforcement of foreign judgments under the Lugano Convention are submitted to Svea hovrätt (Art. 32 of the Convention), which is the sole court competent to handle such applications. At the initial stage, the court consists of a single judge. Appeals under Art. 37(1) or Art. 40 are heard by the same court, at this stage consisting of a full division (normally three judges, the judge whose decision is challenged being disqualified). The decision given on appeal may be contested by an appeal to the Supreme Court in accordance with Art. 37(2) and Art. 41, though only if leave is granted by that court.

The most important series of case reports is Nytt juridiskt arkiv (cited NJA), which contains reports of cases decided by the Supreme Court.

Other series of case reports include:

Arbetsdomstolens domar (cited AD), containing cases decided by the Labour Court;

Marknadsdomstolens avgöranden (cited MD), containing cases decided by the Market Court;

Nordiske domme i sjøfartsanliggender (cited ND), which is common to Denmark, Finland, Iceland, Norway and Sweden and which contains reports of maritime cases, including decisions in such matters given by lower courts; and

Rättsfall från hovrätterna (cited RH), containing a selection of cases decided by the Courts of Appeal.

B. IMPLEMENTATION OF THE LUGANO CONVENTION

Sweden is a party to the Lugano Convention but, at the time of writing (December 1996), not yet to the Brussels Convention. The Lugano Convention came into force for Sweden on 1 January 1993. In accordance with Art. IV, para. 2 of Protocol No. 1 to the Convention, Sweden has declared that it objects to the method of service described there. No other reservation has been made.

The Lugano Convention has been incorporated into Swedish law by Act 1992/794. That Act also contains some supplementary provisions to the Convention. Most of these are concerned with details of the procedure for obtaining an enforcement order pursuant to s.2 of Title III of the Convention.

C. OVERVIEW OF CONVENTION CASE LAW

The number of reported Swedish cases dealing with the Lugano Convention is so far rather limited. These cases concern a variety of questions and do not form any coherent pattern or allow any distinct trends to form.

Nevertheless, the general impression is that Swedish courts, in cases involving the Convention, have sought to follow the interpretations given by the European Court of Justice (ECJ) in its preliminary rulings with regard to the Brussels Convention. Whether they have been successful in so doing is another question which may occasionally give rise to doubts. There are also some decisions on issues which have not yet reached the European Court of Justice. A rather interesting example is *G.N. Preziosi di Gori & Nibi S.d.f. v Schweiziska Guldimporten AB i konkurs, infra*, Case 825.

The relative paucity of reported cases does not warrant the conclusion that the Convention should not have had any major impact on Swedish law. There are many cases involving the interpretation of the Convention which have been settled without resort to judicial proceedings or which have been decided by lower courts and have not been reported. This holds true particularly in the case of the provision in Art. 5(1) on the *forum solutionis*, which appears to be the single provision of the Convention most frequently giving rise to problems of interpretation and controversy.

It may also be noted, in this connection, that the Convention has had a 'contagious' effect on national Swedish law. The rules governing the jurisdiction of Swedish courts in matters not covered by the Convention are in the main uncodified and in many instances uncertain. This being so, both the Supreme Court and the Labour Court have sought guidance in the provisions of the Convention: see *Nordic Water Products AB v Sven H*, Case 818 and *Tjänstemannaförbundet HTF and another v Premiair A/S*, Case 821, *infra*.

D.   CASES

LUGANO ARTICLE 2

" . . . persons domiciled in a Contracting State shall . . . be sued in the courts of that State."

Case principle

1.   Swedish courts have jurisdiction to hear an action brought against a person domiciled in Sweden and concerning the right to an employee's invention in respect of which patent protection had been applied for both in Sweden and in a number of foreign countries.

Case

Nordic Water Products AB v Sven H, NJA (1994) 81 (English translation in **818** [1995] I.L.Pr. 766) Högsta domstolen, 23 February 1994

Facts

The plaintiff was the former employer of the defendant who, during his employment, had made an invention in respect of which patent protection was applied for both in Sweden and abroad. There was no information regarding the foreign countries in or for which such protection had been sought. The dispute concerned the right to the invention. Both parties seem to have been domiciled in Sweden. Did the Swedish courts have jurisdiction to hear the case in so far as the foreign applications were concerned?

Judgment

The court noted that there was no general provision in Swedish law governing jurisdiction in cases involving the right to patent applications made abroad. Of interest, however, was the Act 1978/152 implementing the Recognition Protocol to the European Patent Convention of 1973, under which Swedish courts would have jurisdiction to hear a dispute of the present type when the patent had been applied for in a Convention State. The same conclusion followed from Art. 2 of the Lugano Convention, according to which the action in such a dispute must be brought in the courts of the State of the defendant's domicile. Citing the decision of the European Court of Justice in *Duijnstee v Goderbauer* Case 288/82, the court also referred to Art. 16(4) of that Convention, but only in order to rule out its application.

The court went on to state that the Lugano Convention could be regarded as giving expression to what were now internationally accepted principles relating to disputes over jurisdiction between courts in different countries. It was therefore possible to extend the jurisdiction of the Swedish courts to cover a dispute of the present type, even if it involved a patent application in a non-Convention State. In consequence, Swedish courts had jurisdiction to hear the dispute in respect of all the foreign applications.

Comment

Unfortunately, the report of this case does not indicate in which countries the defendant had applied for the grant of a patent. If he had applied for a European patent, then the Recognition Protocol to the European Patent Convention was the proper instrument to apply, and the Lugano Convention would yield to it (see Art. 57(1) of the latter Convention). If, on the other hand, the case did not involve a European patent application, then the Lugano Convention was applicable, more particularly—as the court rightly held—Art. 2 and not Art. 16(4). The court, however, seems to have considered the Lugano Convention to be directly applicable only in respect of patent applications lodged in Convention States. As regards applications made in other States, the jurisdiction of the Swedish courts was apparently based on an unwritten rule of autonomous Swedish law which was inspired by, in fact identical to, Art. 2 of the Convention. It is questionable whether there was any need for such a distinction to be drawn. It may well be that the Lugano

Convention should properly have been regarded as applicable even concerning the latter applications. This depends on the view taken of the general—and controversial—question as to whether the sphere of application of the Convention is or is not limited to cases presenting a link with more than one Contracting State.

Case principle

2.   Swedish courts have jurisdiction to hear an action for the repayment of a loan brought against a person domiciled in Sweden. Whether the defendant is so domiciled must be determined by Swedish law.

Case

RH (1996) 86, Göta hovrätt, 11 October 1995   **819**

Facts

A French bank sued two Danish spouses, claimed to be domiciled in Sweden, for the repayment of a loan. The defendants contested the jurisdiction of the Swedish court on the grounds that they were domiciled in England and that the loan agreement contained a prorogation clause conferring exclusive jurisdiction on French courts. In the latter respect, the bank contended that the clause only meant that disputes concerning the agreement were to be resolved in accordance with French law, and not that jurisdiction was vested in French courts.

Judgment

The reference to French law in the loan agreement was only a choice-of-law clause and did not amount to a prorogation to the French courts.

Irrespective of whether the defendants were domiciled in Sweden or in the UK, the Lugano Convention applied, since both States were parties to the Convention at the time when the proceedings were instituted (Art. 54). The court's jurisdiction being contested, that issue had to be examined by reference to the rules of the Convention, even though those rules had not been invoked by the parties (who had proceeded on the basis of Swedish national law). No other provisions—in particular that contained in s.3 of Chapter 10 of the Swedish Code of Judicial Procedure (sanctioning the *forum patrimonii*), on which the court below had relied—could be applied unless the Convention so permitted.

The main rule of the Convention being that the defendant must be sued in the courts of the State of his domicile (Art. 2), it only remained to decide whether the defendants were domiciled in Sweden. Pursuant to Art. 52, para. 1, that question was determinable by Swedish law. Applying this test the court found that the defendants were domiciled in Sweden and that, accordingly, it had jurisdiction.

LUGANO ARTICLE 5(1)

" . . . in matters relating to a contract . . . "

Case principle

Jurisdiction may be assumed under Art. 5(1), even if the defendant denies the existence of the contract on which the plaintiff's claim is based.

Case

820 Trollship SA and Carflow International Inc. v Cool Carriers AB, ND (1994) 22, Svea hovrätt, 30 September 1994

Facts

Under a charterparty a Swedish shipping company (CC) undertook to transport cars from Belgium to Argentina. The charterer was a Panamanian company (C), on whose behalf the charterparty was signed by a Swiss company (T) acting 'as agents only'. The freight was payable in Stockholm. There was a clause in the charterparty according to which 'any dispute arising under this bill of lading shall be decided in the country where the carrier has his principal place of business' (which was in Sweden).

Before any performance had taken place, the charterer rescinded the contract. CC then sued both C and T claiming payment of dead freight. As regards jurisdiction, CC relied, *inter alia*, on Art. 5(1) of the Lugano Convention and on the prorogation clause. C objected that the Convention was not applicable since C was not domiciled in a Contracting State. T objected that there was no contractual relationship between CC and T, since T had acted solely as a broker. Both defendants contested the validity of the prorogation clause on various grounds.

Judgment

Regarding the action against T, the fact that T denied the existence of any contract with CC was irrelevant for the purpose of applying Art. 5(1) of the Convention. That provision was applicable and, since the freight was payable in Stockholm, led to the question of jurisdiction being answered in the affirmative.

See *infra*, Art. 17(1), Case 822, as to the action against C.

Comment

The court followed the decision of the European Court of Justice in *Effer v Kantner*, Case 38/81.

> *"in matters relating to individual contracts of employment, this place is
> that where the employee habitually carries out his work . . . "*

Case principle

In the case of a transfer of undertaking, Art. 5(1) applies to a dispute between
former employees of the transferor and the transferee, even though there is no
contract of employment between the parties to the dispute.

Case

Tjänstemannaförbundet HTF and another v Premiair A/S, AD (1995) 120,   **821**
Arbetsdomstolen, 4 October 1995

Facts

The Danish air company Premiair (P) was formed following the dissolution of
the Swedish consortium Scanair (S). For our purposes here, it was found as a
fact that a transfer of undertaking was involved, S being the transferor and P
the transferee. The employees of S had been dismissed. Many, but not all of
them, were re-employed by P. A Swedish trade union representing those who
had not been re-employed sued P claiming damages on the ground that P had
failed to respect their statutory right to priority for re-employment by the
transferee. Did the court have jurisdiction to hear the case although the defendant was domiciled in Denmark?

Judgment

Since at the critical time Denmark had not ratified the Lugano Convention,
that Convention was not directly applicable. Citing the decision of the
Supreme Court in the *Nordic Water* case (Case 818, *supra*), however, the
Labour Court said that the Convention undoubtedly expressed what was now
internationally accepted with regard to international jurisdiction. There were
therefore strong reasons for assuming that the (unwritten) rules of
autonomous Swedish law had been adapted to those of the Convention, with
the consequence that a dispute concerning a contract of employment which,
pursuant to Art. 5(1) of the Convention, could be brought before the court
of the place of performance, could also be so brought under autonomous
Swedish law. In any event, this conclusion was justified in the case of the defendant being domiciled in Denmark, where the same rule applied, since
Denmark was a party to the *Brussels* Convention.

In the opinion of the court, the present dispute did indeed concern a contract of employment. For, although the claimants were no longer employees,
their rights to priority for re-employment as well as its sanction, *i.e.* the

employer's obligation to pay damages in case of violation of that right, were derived from and based on their contracts of employment with S.

Finally, the court found that, under those contracts, the ex-employees had habitually carried out their work at various places in Sweden. It followed that the court would have jurisdiction pursuant to Art. 5(1) of the Lugano Convention. Jurisdiction was therefore held also to exist under autonomous Swedish law.

Comment

Like the *Nordic Water* case, *supra*, Case 818, the present case tends to demonstrate the impact of the Lugano Convention on Swedish law even outside its immediate sphere of application. The interpretation placed by the court on the relevant provision of the Convention is, however, rather extensive and questionable. As is well known, the judgments of the ECJ are rather marked by a tendency to interpret all exceptions to the main rule in Art. 2, including those contained in Art. 5, restrictively.

LUGANO ARTICLE 17(1)

"If the parties, one or more of whom is domiciled in a Contracting State, have agreed . . . "

Case principle

Where a party domiciled in Sweden brings proceedings both against a party domiciled in another Contracting State and against a party domiciled in a non-Contracting State, Art. 17 of the Convention applies only in respect of the former action.

Case

822 Trollship SA and Carflow International Inc. v Cool Carriers AB, ND (1994) 22, Svea hovrätt, 30 September 1994

Facts

See supra, Art. 5(1), Case 820.

Judgment

As regards the action against C, there was no valid objection to the prorogation clause, which conferred jurisdiction on the Swedish court. To that extent the decision was based on national Swedish law.

Concerning the action against T—in respect of whom the court had jurisdiction under Art. 5(1), see *supra*—jurisdiction could also be based on the prorogation clause in accordance with Art. 17 of the Lugano Convention, provided that it was found (by the court below, to which the case was referred for consideration of its merits) that an agreement existed between CC and T.

Comment

The court drew a distinction between the two defendants, holding Art. 17 of the Convention to apply to the action against T, who was domiciled in a Contracting State, but not also to the action against C, who was not so domiciled. This distinction is open to question. According to its wording, it is sufficient for Art. 17 to apply if *one* of the parties—not necessarily the defendant—is domiciled in a Contracting State. That requirement was met since the plaintiff was domiciled in Sweden. The decision may be explained on the footing that the court endorsed the view—although doubtful and controversial— that the Convention only applies in cases presenting a connection with more than one Contracting State (see *supra*, Art. 2, Comment to Case 818).

LUGANO ARTICLE 21, PARAGRAPH 1

"Where proceedings involving the same cause of action and between the same parties are brought in the courts of different Contracting States . . . "

Case principle

Where proceedings, involving the same cause of action and between the same parties, have been brought first in a foreign Contracting State and then in Sweden, but where the former proceedings have subsequently been withdrawn, those proceedings no longer constitute a bar to the exercise of jurisdiction by the Swedish court.

Case

Sveriges Fartygsbefälsförening v Sveriges Redareförening and Safe Service AB, **823**
AD (1995) 97, Arbetsdomstolen, 11 August 1995

Facts

A number of employees who had been working on dwelling platforms stationed in the British part of the continental shelf of the North Sea had been dismissed by their employer, a Swedish company (SS), which was one of the defendants in the present case. The plaintiff (SF), a trade union representing the employees, claimed, *inter alia*, that the dismissals should be declared invalid. Before this action was instituted, SF had brought proceedings involving the same cause of action against, amongst others SS, in an English court. SS contested the jurisdiction of the Swedish court on grounds of *lis pendens* pursuant to Art. 21 of the Lugano Convention. Before the court came to rule on this objection, however, SF withdrew its English action against SS. SF then claimed that there was no longer any bar to the exercise of jurisdiction by the Swedish court.

Judgment

The court shared SF's view. Whilst recognizing that the pendency of the English suit originally constituted a bar to its own jurisdiction, the court found that the withdrawal of SF's English action had had the effect of removing that bar.

LUGANO ARTICLE 25

" . . . *as well as the determination of costs* . . . "

Case principle

A foreign plaintiff, even if domiciled in a Member State of the European Union, can be required to lodge security for costs of judicial proceedings in accordance with Swedish law where the action brought has no connection with the exercise of fundamental freedoms guaranteed by Community law. The Lugano Convention and the Swedish statute implementing it contain nothing of relevance for this question.

Case

824   Ronny Forsberg v MSL Dynamics Ltd, NJA (1996) 668, Högsta domstolen, 13 November 1996

Facts

An English company (MSL) brought an action against a Swedish company (which was subsequently declared bankrupt and which no longer figured as a party in the present proceedings) and a Swedish national, claiming payment for the supply of goods which had been delivered in the years 1990 and 1991. The defendants applied for security to be furnished by MSL to cover the costs of the proceedings, pursuant to the Swedish Act 1980/307 on the obligation of foreign plaintiffs to lodge security for costs of judicial proceedings. The District Court and the Court of Appeal refused to grant the application, mainly on the ground that Act 1980/307 was considered to be contrary to Act

1992/794, by which the Lugano Convention was incorporated into Swedish law, and that the latter Act took precedence in accordance with the *lex posterior* rule. The Supreme Court decided to refer a question to the European Court of Justice for a preliminary ruling. That question was whether it was contrary to the EC Treaty, primarily Art. 6, to require a plaintiff who was a UK legal person to lodge such a security when no such security could be demanded from Swedish legal persons. The European Court answered the question in the affirmative, in so far as the action brought by the foreign plaintiff was connected with the exercise of fundamental freedoms guaranteed by Community law: see *Data Delecta & Forsberg v MSL Dynamics* Case C-43/95. The case then went back to the Swedish Supreme Court for decision.

Judgment

The court pointed out that the plaintiff's claim for payment was in respect of goods which had been supplied at a time before Sweden became a member of the EU. Therefore, the action had no connection with the exercise of any fundamental freedom guaranteed by Community law. Nor was this a case in which Community law claimed to be given retrospective effect. It followed that the preliminary ruling given by the European Court was not applicable to the facts of the present case.

The court further noted that there was no provision in the Lugano Convention dealing with the question of security for the costs of judicial proceedings. Contrary to the opinion of the courts below, therefore, the Convention afforded no support for setting aside the Swedish Act 1980/307. As the requirements of that Act were met, the plaintiff was held liable to provide security.

LUGANO ARTICLE 34, PARAGRAPH 3

"Under no circumstances may the foreign judgment be reviewed as to its substance."

Case principle

The execution of a foreign sequestration order, which has been declared enforceable in Sweden, can only take place in accordance with the methods allowed by Swedish law as the *lex fori*. The foreign court cannot decide on such questions with binding effect in Sweden.

Case

G.N. Preziosi di Gori & Nibi S.d.f. v Schweiziska Guldimporten AB i konkurs, **825**
NJA (1995) 495, Högsta domstolen, 12 September 1995

Facts

An Italian company (P) brought an action against a Swedish company in an Italian court concerning the ownership of some machinery which was in the latter company's possession in Sweden. On the application of P, the Italian court made an order for sequestration (*sequestro giudiziario*) of the property in question and, in accordance with Italian law (*Codice di Procedura Civile* Art. 676), appointed P as custodian of the property. The Italian order was declared enforceable in Sweden pursuant to the Lugano Convention. P then sought execution of the order and demanded the property be handed over and placed in P's custody, as provided by the Italian court. The Swedish enforcement authority officer did not accede to the latter request, but executed the order in accordance with Swedish law by taking the property into his own custody. P appealed.

Judgment

The Supreme Court, by a majority of three justices to two, affirmed the decisions of the courts below to the effect that the enforcement officer's action should be upheld. In so far as P was appointed as custodian of the property, the Italian order was held to concern the method of its enforcement. There was no support in the Lugano Convention for the proposition that the courts of the State of origin could decide on such questions with binding effect in the State of enforcement of the order. Instead, the Italian order had to be treated in the same way as a corresponding Swedish security measure, as provided by the Swedish Act 1992/794 incorporating the Convention. Thus, the nearest counterpart (there being no exact equivalent) in Swedish law to the Italian type of order was an order for *kvarstad* (provisional attachment), which is executed by the property in question being placed in the enforcement officer's custody.

The minority would have allowed P's claim to succeed. In their view, the appointment of P as custodian formed an integral part of the substance of the Italian order and, therefore, under the Lugano Convention, had to be respected in Sweden. It was argued, *inter alia*, on the strength of the decision of the European Court of Justice in *Hoffmann v Krieg* Case 145/86, that a judgment recognized under the Convention, in principle, had to have the same effects in the State of enforcement as it had in the State of origin. The minority also pointed out that the Swedish Enforcement Code (*utsökningsbalken*) gave scope for arrangements of the type prescribed by the Italian court.

Comment

It is common ground that the execution of a foreign judgment or order, which is enforceable by virtue of the Brussels or Lugano Convention, is governed by the law of the State in which execution is sought (see, *e.g. Deutsche Genossenschaftsbank v Brasserie du Pêcheur* Case 148/84, para. 18). Pursuant to Art. 16(5) of the Convention, such questions come within the exclusive jurisdiction of the courts of the State in which the judgment has been or is to be enforced.

As illustrated by the present case, however, it is not always easy to draw the line between such provisions of the foreign judgment or order as affect the substance of the case and those relating to its enforcement. Both the majority and the minority opinion in the present case contain extensive reasoning bearing on this issue.

20

SWITZERLAND

Professor Kurt Siehr

A.   LEGAL SYSTEM

Courts

The court system of Switzerland is not uniform. Each of the 26 Cantons has its own court system. The Swiss Federal Court in Lausanne is the only common court for all Swiss Cantons. The Canton of Zürich is the most populous Swiss Canton.

The court system of the Zürich Canton may serve as an example for a Swiss court system. There are 11 district courts (Bezirksgerichte), a court of appeal (Obergericht) and a court of cassation (Kassationsgericht). There are also special courts for commercial cases (Handelsgerichte), for labour relations (Arbeitsgerichte) and for landlord and tenant cases (Mietgerichte).

The District Court serves as a court of first instance, except for cases to be heard by one of the special courts for commercial cases, labour relations or landlord and tenant cases. However, before starting court proceedings, there must be an attempt at conciliation with a Justice of the Peace (Friedensrichter). If this fails, the Justice of the Peace issues a document (Weisung) whereby the plaintiff may start court proceedings within three months. If court proceedings are not commenced in time, there must be a new preliminary proceeding with the Justice of the Peace.

The District Court sits with a single judge in cases involving less than 8000 Swiss francs. If the amount in dispute exceeds 8000 Swiss francs, three judges decide and against their decision there is an appeal to the Court of Appeal, sitting with a bench of five judges. In commercial cases, with an amount in dispute of more than 8000 Swiss francs, two judges of the Court of Appeal and three commercial judges sit as the Commercial Court. The Cantonal Court of Cassation may hear appeals against decisions of the Court of Appeal and of the Commercial Court. A final appeal lies to the Swiss Federal Court if the amount in dispute exceeds 8000 Swiss francs.

B. IMPLEMENTATION OF THE LUGANO CONVENTION

Switzerland is a member of the European Free Trade Association (EFTA) and ratified the Lugano Convention with effect from 1 January 1992. As is usual in Switzerland, the Federal Parliament passed a resolution approving the Convention and empowering the Federal Council (government) to ratify it with two reservations mentioned in Arts Ia and IV(2) of Protocol 1, annexed to the Convention, until the end of the century. Switzerland will not recognize foreign judgments based only on Art. 5(1) of the Convention if the defendant was domiciled in Switzerland at the time of introduction of proceedings and raises an objection to the recognition of the judgment and has not previously waived the benefit of the Swiss declaration for the protection of defendants domiciled in Switzerland.

C. OVERVIEW OF CONVENTION CASE LAW

Most decisions of the Swiss Federal Court are reported in the official trilingual collection: Entscheidungen des Schweizerischen Bundesgerichts (BGE)/Arrêts du Tribunal Fédéral Suisse (ATS)/Decisioni del Tribunale federale svizzero (DTF).

D. CASES

LUGANO ARTICLE 1, PARAGRAPH 2(1)

" . . . *the status or legal capacity of natural persons, rights in property arising out of a matrimonial relationship* . . . "

Case principle

Although maintenance falls within the Convention's scope, a request merely for interim protective maintenance, ancillary to an excluded main status and matrimonial property application, held not governed by the Convention.

Case

BGE 119 II 167 (R.c.R)   **826**

Facts

In March 1992, Klara R petitioned the District Court of Zürich for an application for a marital protective order for maintenance, custody of the child and sole occupation of the matrimonial home. The court refused her request owing to a lack of jurisdiction—both petitioner and respondent were domiciled in France. In September 1992, the Court of Appeal of the Canton of Zürich upheld the lower court's decision. Klara R appealed to the Swiss Federal Court.

Judgment

The court declined jurisdiction under the Swiss Private International Law Act because of a lack of domicile of both parties in Switzerland.

The petitioner argued that the court must exercise jurisdiction under Art. 18 of the Lugano Convention. The court noted that under Art. 1, para. 2(1), the Convention did not apply to 'the status or legal capacity of natural persons, rights in property arising out of a matrimonial relationship, wills and succession.' Thus, although the Art. 1, para. 2(1) exclusion of matrimonial and child law did not also cover maintenance obligations, nevertheless, this was not also the case where maintenance obligations were only a subsidiary part of the application in which the petitioner had requested an order 'for the separation of goods'. The court held that while maintenance obligations were a part of the request, they alone did not justify exercising jurisdiction under the Lugano Convention Art. 18. The Federal Court upheld the decisions of the lower courts.

Comment

This is a dubious decision, which seems to transgress the European Court's ruling in *de Cavel (No. 2)* Case 120/78 [1980] ECR 731.

LUGANO ARTICLE 5(1)

" . . . place of performance . . . "

Case principle

The place of performance, which determines jurisdiction in accordance with Art. 5(1), is, in international purchase agreements, governed by the Vienna Sales Convention of 1980, and in the absence of a contrary agreement, the seller's place of business, or in the event of payment on delivery, at the place where delivery occurs.

Case

827 BGE 122 III 43 (Firma T. S.r.l. gegen Firma S. AG)

Facts

In February 1991, a Swiss corporation sent a written sales offer to a company in Italy for an exhaust gas cleaning unit. After the Swiss corporation had sent a second, revised offer in March 1991, the Italian company accepted the offer, which was confirmed by the Swiss corporation. Following delivery and installation of the unit, the Italian company claimed a series of defects and, by written notification, dated 3 March 1993, announced the cancellation of the contract. The Swiss corporation sued the Italian company in the Commercial Court for the Canton of Zürich, requesting the payment of 3149300 Swiss francs plus interest and court costs. The defendant argued that the contract called for payment on the handing over of goods and that consequently, Swiss courts, in accordance with Art. 5(1) of the Lugano Convention, did not have jurisdiction in this matter. The Commercial Court rejected the defendant's plea. The defendant appealed to the Federal Court.

Judgment

The Swiss Federal Court held that, with regard to bilateral contracts, the Lugano Convention provided a special jurisdiction for each obligation. Since the disputed obligation in this case was the payment of the sale price for the cleaning unit, the defendant had argued that payment was due at the time and place of delivery in Italy.

The Federal Court noted that the place of performance had to be fixed according to the law governing the contract. In this case Art. 57(1)(a) of the Vienna Sales Convention of 1980 applied: the contract required payment of 30 per cent of the sale price when ordering the unit, 30 per cent at the beginning of installation and 30 per cent at the completion of the installation, and the remaining 10 per cent upon commissioning the unit, and consequently the contract did not qualify as a cash sale under Art. 58 of the Vienna Sales Convention. Accordingly, the defendant's obligation to make payment for the goods to be delivered was to be performed at the seller's place of business in Switzerland under Art. 57(1)(a) of the Vienna Sales Convention and the Swiss courts therefore possessed jurisdiction under Art. 5(1) of the Lugano Convention.

APPENDIX

A. RULES OF THE SUPREME COURT OF ENGLAND AND WALES

Order 6, rule 7—Issue of writ

7.—(1) No writ which is to be served on a defendant out of the jurisdiction shall be issued for such service without the leave of the court unless it complies with the following conditions, that is to say—

    (a)   each claim against that defendant made by the writ is either—

        (i)   one which by virtue of the Civil Jurisdiction and Judgments Act 1982 the Court has power to hear and determine, or

        (ii)   one which by virtue of any other enactment the Court has power to hear and determine notwithstanding that the person against whom the claim is made is not within the jurisdiction of the Court or that the wrongful act, neglect or default giving rise to the claim did not take place within its jurisdiction;

        and

    (b)   where a claim made by the writ against that defendant is one which the Court has power to hear and determine by virtue of the Civil Jurisdiction and Judgments Act 1982, the writ is indorsed before it is issued with a statement that the Court has power under that Act to hear and determine the claim against that defendant, and that no proceedings involving the same cause of action are pending between the parties in Scotland, Northern Ireland or another Convention territory.

Order 11, rule 1—Principal cases in which service out of jurisdiction is permissible

1.—(1) Provided that the writ does not contain any claim mentioned in Order 75, r.2(1) and is not a writ to which paragraph (2) of this rule applies, service of a writ out of the jurisdiction is permissible with the leave of the Court if in the action begun by the writ—

- (a) relief is sought against a person domiciled within the jurisdiction;
- (b) an injunction is sought ordering the defendant to do or refrain from doing anything within the jurisdiction (whether or not damages are also claimed in respect of a failure to do or the doing of that thing);
- (c) the claim is brought against a person duly served within or out of the jurisdiction and a person out of the jurisdiction is a necessary or proper party thereto;
- (d) the claim is brought to enforce, rescind, dissolve, annul or otherwise affect a contract, or to recover damages or obtain other relief in respect of the breach of a contract, being (in either case) a contract which—
  - (i) was made within the jurisdiction, or
  - (ii) was made by or through an agent trading or residing within the jurisdiction on behalf of a principal trading or residing out of the jurisdiction, or
  - (iii) is by its terms, or by implication, governed by English law, or
  - (iv) contains a term to the effect that the High Court shall have jurisdiction to hear and determine any action in respect of the contract;
- (e) the claim is brought in respect of a breach committed within the jurisdiction of a contract made within or out of the jurisdiction, and irrespective of the fact, if such be the case, that the breach was preceded or accompanied by a breach committed out of the jurisdiction that rendered impossible the performance of so much of the contract as ought to have been performed within the jurisdiction;
- (f) the claim is founded on a tort and the damage was sustained, or resulted from an act committed, within the jurisdiction;
- (g) the whole subject-matter of the action is land situate within the jurisdiction (with or without rents or profits) or the perpetuation of testimony relating to land so situate;
- (h) the claim is brought to construe, rectify, set aside or enforce an act, deed, will, contract, obligation or liability affecting land situate within the jurisdiction;
- (i) the claim is made for a debt secured on immovable property or is made to assert, declare or determine proprietary or possessory rights, or rights of security, in or over movable property, or to obtain authority to dispose of movable property, situate within the jurisdiction;

(j)   the claim is brought to execute the trusts of a written instrument being trusts that ought to be executed according to English law and of which the person to be served with the writ is a trustee, or for any relief or remedy which might be obtained in any such action;

(k)   the claim is made for the administration of the estate of a person who died domiciled within the jurisdiction or for any relief or remedy which might be obtained in any such action;

(l)   the claim is brought in a probate action within the meaning of Order 76;

(m)   the claim is brought to enforce any judgment or arbitral award;

(n)   the claim is brought against a defendant not domiciled in Scotland or Northern Ireland in respect of a claim by the Commissioners of Inland Revenue for or in relation to any of the duties or taxes which have been, or are for the time being, placed under their care and management;

(o)   the claim is brought under the Nuclear Installations Act 1965 or in respect of contributions under the Social Security Act 1975;

(p)   the claim is made for a sum to which the Directive of the Council of the European Communities dated 15th March 1976 No. 76/308/EEC applies, and service is to be effected in a country which is a member State of the European Economic Community;

(q)   the claim is made under the Drug Trafficking Offences Act 1986;

(r)   the claim is made under the Financial Services Act 1986 or the Banking Act 1987;

(s)   the claim is made under Part VI of the Criminal Justice Act 1988;

(t)   the claim is brought for money had and received or for an account or other relief against the defendant as constructive trustee, and the defendant's alleged liability arises out of acts committed, whether by him or otherwise, within the jurisdiction;

(u)   the claim is made under the Immigration (Carriers' Liability) Act 1987.

(2) Service of a writ out of the jurisdiction on a defendant is permissible without the leave of the Court provided that each claim against that defendant made by the writ is either:—

(a)   a claim which by virtue of the Civil Jurisdiction and Judgments Act 1982 the Court has power to hear and determine, made in proceedings to which the following conditions apply—

(i)   no proceedings between the parties concerning the same cause of action are pending in the courts of any other part of the United Kingdom or of any other Convention territory, and

(ii)   either—
       the defendant is domiciled in any part of the United Kingdom or in any other Convention territory, or
       the proceedings begun by the writ are proceedings to which Article 16 of Schedule 1, 3c or 4 refers, or the defendant is a

party to an agreement conferring jurisdiction to which Article 17 of Schedule 1, 3c or 4 to that Act applies,

or

(b)   a claim which by virtue of any other enactment the High Court has power to hear and determine notwithstanding that the person against whom the claim is made is not within the jurisdiction of the Court or that the wrongful act, neglect or default giving rise to the claim did not take place within its jurisdiction.

(3) Where a writ is to be served out of the jurisdiction under paragraph (2), the time to be inserted in the writ within which the defendant served therewith must acknowledge service shall be—

(a)   21 days where the writ is to be served out of the jurisdiction under paragraph (2)(a) in Scotland, Northern Ireland or in the European territory of another Contracting State, or

(b)   31 days where the writ is to be served under paragraph (2)(a) in any other territory of a Contracting State, or

(c)   limited in accordance with the practice adopted under r.4(4) where the writ is to be served under paragraph (2)(a) in a country not referred to in sub-paragraphs (a) or (b) or under paragraph (2)(b).

(4) For the purposes of this rule, and of r.9 of this Order, domicile is to be determined in accordance with the provisions of sections 41 to 46 of the Civil Jurisdictions and Judgments Act 1982 and "Convention Territory" means the territory or territories of any Contracting State, as defined by s.1(3) of that Act, to which, as defined in s.1(1) of that Act, the Brussels or the Lugano Convention apply.

Order 11, rule 4—Application for, and grant of, leave to serve writ out of jurisdiction

4.—(1) An application for the grant of leave under rule 1(1) must be supported by an affidavit stating—

(a)   the grounds on which the application is made,

(b)   that in the deponent's belief the plaintiff has a good cause of action,

(c)   in what place or country the defendant is, or probably may be found, and

(d)   where the application is made under rule 1(1)(c), the grounds for the deponent's belief that there is between the plaintiff and the person on whom a writ has been served a real issue which the plaintiff may reasonably ask the court to try.

(2) No such leave shall be granted unless it shall be made sufficiently to appear to the Court that the case is a proper one for service out of the jurisdiction under this Order.

(3) Where the application is for the grant of leave under rule 1 to serve a writ in Scotland or Northern Ireland, if it appears to the Court that there may be a concurrent remedy there, the Court, in deciding whether to grant leave shall have regard to the comparative cost and convenience of proceeding there or in England, and (where that is relevant) to the powers and jurisdiction of

the sheriff court in Scotland or the county courts or courts of summary jurisdiction in Northern Ireland.

(4) An order granting under rule 1 leave to serve a writ, out of the jurisdiction must limit a time within which the defendant to be served must acknowledge service.

Order 11, rule 8A—Applications for interim relief under section 25(1) of the Civil Jurisdiction and Judgments Act 1982

8A.—(1) Service of an originating summons out of the jurisdiction claiming interim relief under section 25(1) of the Civil Jurisdiction and Judgments Act 1982 (as extended by Order in Council made under section 25(3)) is permissible with the leave of the Court.

(2) An application for the grant of leave under paragraph (1) must be supported by an affidavit stating—

(a)   the grounds on which the application is made;

(b)   that in the deponent's belief the plaintiff has a good claim to interim relief;

(c)   in what place or country the defendant is, or probably may be, found.

(3) The following provisions of this Order shall apply, with the necessary modifications, where service is to be effected under this rule as they apply where service is effected under rule 1:

Rule 1(3) (time limited for acknowledging service),

Rule 4(2), (3) and (4) (grant of leave),

Rule 5 (service of writ abroad: general),

Rule 6 (service of writ abroad through foreign governments, etc.), and

Rule 8 (undertaking to pay expenses of service).

B.   CIVIL JURISDICTION AND JUDGMENTS ACT 1982

Provisions supplementary to Title VII of 1968 Convention

9.—(1) The provisions of Title VII of the 1968 Convention and, apart from Article 54B, of Title VII of the Lugano Convention (relationship between the Convention in question and other conventions to which Contracting States are or may become parties) shall have effect in relation to—

(a)   any statutory provision, whenever passed or made, implementing any such other convention in the United Kingdom; and

(b)   any rule of law so far as it has the effect of so implementing any such other convention,

as they have effect in relation to that other convention itself.

(1a) [Application of Lugano Art. 54B].

(2) Her Majesty may by Order in Council declare a provision of a convention entered into by the United Kingdom to be a provision whereby the United Kingdom assumed an obligation of a kind provided for in Article 59 (which allows a Contracting State to agree with a third State to withhold recognition in certain cases from a judgment given by a court in another Contracting State which took jurisdiction on one of the grounds mentioned in the second paragraph of Article 3).

Allocation within U.K. of jurisdiction in certain civil proceedings

16.—(1) The provisions set out in Schedule 4 (which contains a modified version of Title II of the 1968 Convention) shall have effect for determining, for each part of the United Kingdom, whether the courts of law of that part, or any particular court of law in that part, have or has jurisdiction in proceedings where—
  (a) the subject-matter of the proceedings is within the scope of the 1968 Convention as determined by Article 1 (whether or not that or any other Convention has effect in relation to the proceedings); and
  (b) the defendant or defender is domiciled in the United Kingdom or the proceedings are of a kind mentioned in Article 16 of the 1968 Convention (exclusive jurisdiction regardless of domicile).

(2) In Schedule 4 modifications of Title II of the 1968 Convention are indicated as follows—
  (a) modifications by way of omission are indicated by dots; and
  (b) within each Article words resulting from modifications by way of addition or substitution are printed in heavy type.

(3) In determining any question as to the meaning or effect of any provision contained in Schedule 4—
  (a) regard shall be had to any relevant principles laid down by the European Court in connection with Title II of the 1968 Convention and to any relevant decision of that court as to the meaning or effect of any provision of that Title; and
  (b) without prejudice to the generality of paragraph (a), the reports mentioned in section 3(3) may be considered and shall, so far as relevant, be given such weight as is appropriate in the circumstances.

(4) The provisions of this section and Schedule 4 shall have effect subject to the 1968 Convention and the Lugano Convention and to the provisions of section 17.

Interim relief in England and Wales and Northern Ireland in the absence of substantive proceedings*

25.—(1) The High Court in England and Wales or Northern Ireland shall have power to grant interim relief where—

(a) proceedings have been or are to be commenced in a Brussels or Lugano Contracting State other than the United Kingdom or in a part of the United Kingdom other than that in which the High Court in question exercises jurisdiction; and

(b) they are or will be proceedings whose subject-matter is within the scope of the 1968 Convention as determined by Article 1 (whether or not that or any other Convention has effect in relation to the proceedings).

(2) On an application for any interim relief under subsection (1) the court may refuse to grant that relief if, in the opinion of the court, the fact that the court has no jurisdiction apart from this section in relation to the subject-matter of the proceedings in question makes it inexpedient for the court to grant it.

(3) Her Majesty may by Order in Council extend the power to grant interim relief conferred by subsection (1) so as to make it exercisable in relation to proceedings of any of the following descriptions, namely—

(a) proceedings commenced or to be commenced otherwise than in a Brussels or Lugano Contracting State;

(b) proceedings whose subject-matter is not within the scope of the 1968 Convention as determined by Article 1;

(c) arbitration proceedings.

(4) An Order in Council under subsection (3)—

(a) may confer power to grant only specified descriptions of interim relief;

(b) may make different provision for different classes of proceedings, for proceedings pending in different countries or courts outside the United Kingdom or in different parts of the United Kingdom, and for other different circumstances; and

(c) may impose conditions or restrictions on the exercise of any power conferred by the Order.

(5) An Order in Council under subsection (3) which confers power to grant interim relief in relation to arbitration proceedings may provide for the repeal of any provision of section 12(6) of the Arbitration Act 1950 or section 21(1) of the Arbitration Act (Northern Ireland) 1937 to the extent that it is superseded by the provisions of the Order.

(6) Any Order in Council under subsection (3) shall be subject to annulment in pursuance of a resolution of either House of Parliament.

(7) In this section "interim relief", in relation to the High Court in England and Wales or Northern Ireland, means interim relief of any kind which that court has power to grant in proceedings relating to matters within its jurisdiction, other than—

(a) a warrant for the arrest of property; or

(b) provision for obtaining evidence.

*Order in Council S.I. 1997 No. 302 made under s.25(3)(a) and (b), effective 1 April 1997.

S.25(3)(c) and (5) repealed by s.107(2) of and Sched. 4 to Arbitration Act 1996 as from 31 January 1997. S.44 of 1996 Act confers interim and protective powers in support of arbitration proceedings, extending to foreign arbitrations, under s.2(3).

Security in Admiralty proceedings in England and Wales or Northern Ireland in case of stay, etc.*

26.—(1) Where in England and Wales or Northern Ireland a court stays or dismisses Admiralty proceedings on the ground that the dispute in question should be submitted to arbitration or to the determination of the courts of another part of the United Kingdom or of an overseas country, the court may, if in those proceedings property has been arrested or bail or other security has been given to prevent or obtain release from arrest—

    (a) order that the property arrested be retained as security for the satisfaction of any award or judgment which—

        (i) is given in respect of the dispute in the arbitration or legal proceedings in favour of which those proceedings are stayed or dismissed; and

        (ii) is enforceable in England and Wales or, as the case may be, in Northern Ireland; or

    (b) order that the stay or dismissal of those proceedings be conditional on the provision of equivalent security for the satisfaction of any such award or judgment.

(2) Where a court makes an order under subsection (1), it may attach such conditions to the order as it thinks fit, in particular conditions with respect to the institution or prosecution of the relevant arbitration or legal proceedings.

(3) Subject to any provision made by rules of court and to any necessary modifications, the same law and practice shall apply in relation to property retained in pursuance of an order made by a court under subsection (1) as would apply if it were held for the purposes of proceedings in that court.

*By virtue of s.107(2) of and Schedule 4 to the Arbitration Act 1996, the references to stays or dismissals in favour of *arbitration* have been removed from s.26 and are now contained in the specially dedicated s.11 of the 1996 Act substantially reproducing 1982 Act s.26 in relation to arbitration—and s.2(2) of the 1996 Act expressly provides that *inter alia* s.11 also applies to arbitrations having their seats outside England and Wales or Northern Ireland

Proceedings in England and Wales or Northern Ireland for torts to immovable property

30.—(1) The jurisdiction of any court in England and Wales or Northern Ireland to entertain proceedings for trespass to, or any other tort affecting, immovable property shall extend to cases in which the property in question is situated outside that part of the United Kingdom unless the proceedings are principally concerned with a question of the title to, or the right to possession of, that property.

(2) Subsection (1) has effect subject to the 1968 Convention and to the Lugano Convention and to the provisions set out in Schedule 4.

Overseas judgments given in proceedings brought in breach of agreement for settlement of disputes

32.—(1) Subject to the following provisions of this section, a judgment given by a court of an overseas country in any proceedings shall not be recognised or enforced in the United Kingdom if—

(a)   the bringing of those proceedings in that court was contrary to an agreement under which the dispute in question was to be settled otherwise than by proceedings in the courts of that country; and

(b)   those proceedings were not brought in that court by, or with the agreement of, the person against whom the judgment was given; and

(c)   that person did not counterclaim in the proceedings or otherwise submit to the jurisdiction of that court.

(2) Subsection (1) does not apply where the agreement referred to in paragraph (a) of that subsection was illegal, void or unenforceable or was incapable of being performed for reasons not attributable to the fault of the party bringing the proceedings in which the judgment was given.

(3) In determining whether a judgment given by a court of an overseas country should be recognised or enforced in the United Kingdom, a court in the United Kingdom shall not be bound by any decision of the overseas court relating to any of the matters mentioned in subsection (1) or (2).

(4) Nothing in subsection (1) shall affect the recognition or enforcement in the United Kingdom of—

(a)   a judgment which is required to be recognised or enforced there under the 1968 Convention or the Lugano Convention;

(b)   a judgment to which Part I of the Foreign Judgments (Reciprocal Enforcement) Act 1933 applies by virtue of section 4 of the Carriage of Goods by Road Act 1965, section 17(4) of the Nuclear Installations Act 1965, section 13(3) of the Merchant Shipping (Oil Pollution) Act 1971, section 5 of the Carriage by Railway Act 1972, section 5 of the Carriage of Passengers by Road Act 1974 or section 6(4) of the Merchant Shipping Act 1974.

Certain steps not to amount to submission to jurisdiction of overseas court

33.—(1) For the purposes of determining whether a judgment given by a court of an overseas country should be recognised or enforced in England and Wales or Northern Ireland, the person against whom the judgment was given shall not be regarded as having submitted to the jurisdiction of the court by reason only of the fact that he appeared (conditionally or otherwise) in the proceedings for all or any one or more of the following purposes, namely—

(a)   to contest the jurisdiction of the court;

(b)   to ask the court to dismiss or stay the proceedings on the ground that the dispute in question should be submitted to arbitration or to the determination of the courts of another country;

    (c)   to protect, or obtain the release of, property seized or threatened with seizure in the proceedings.

(2) Nothing in this section shall affect the recognition or enforcement in England and Wales or Northern Ireland of a judgment which is required to be recognised or enforced there under the 1968 Convention or the Lugano Convention.

Certain judgments a bar to further proceedings on the same cause of action

34. No proceedings may be brought by a person in England and Wales or Northern Ireland on a cause of action in respect of which a judgment has been given in his favour in proceedings between the same parties, or their privies, in a court in another part of the United Kingdom or in a court of an overseas country, unless that judgment is not enforceable or entitled to recognition in England and Wales or, as the case may be, in Northern Ireland.

Domicile of individuals

41.—(1) Subject to Article 52 (which contains provisions for determining whether a party is domiciled in a Contracting State), the following provisions of this section determine, for the purposes of the 1968 Convention, the Lugano Convention and this Act, whether an individual is domiciled in the United Kingdom or in a particular part of, or place in, the United Kingdom or in a state other than a Contracting State.

(2) An individual is domiciled in the United Kingdom if and only if—

    (a)   he is resident in the United Kingdom; and

    (b)   the nature and circumstances of his residence indicate that he has a substantial connection with the United Kingdom.

(3) Subject to subsection (5), an individual is domiciled in a particular part of the United Kingdom if and only if—

    (a)   he is resident in that part; and

    (b)   the nature and circumstances of his residence indicate that he has a substantial connection with that part.

(4) An individual is domiciled in a particular place in the United Kingdom if and only if he—

    (a)   is domiciled in the part of the United Kingdom in which that place is situated; and

    (b)   is resident in that place.

(5) An individual who is domiciled in the United Kingdom but in whose case the requirements of subsection (3)(b) are not satisfied in relation to any particular part of the United Kingdom shall be treated as domiciled in the part of the United Kingdom in which he is resident.

(6) In the case of an individual who—

    (a)   is resident in the United Kingdom, or in a particular part of the United Kingdom; and

    (b)   has been so resident for the last three months or more, the requirements of subsection (2)(b) or, as the case may be, subsection (3)(b) shall be presumed to be fulfilled unless the contrary is proved.

(7) An individual is domiciled in a state other than a Contracting State if and only if—

    (a)   he is resident in that state; and

    (b)   the nature and circumstances of his residence indicate that he has a substantial connection with that state.

Domicile and seat of corporation or association

42.—(1) For the purposes of this Act the seat of a corporation or association (as determined by this section) shall be treated as its domicile.

(2) The following provisions of this section determine where a corporation or association has its seat—

    (a)   for the purpose of Article 53 (which for the purposes of the 1968 Convention, or, as the case may be, the Lugano Convention, equates the domicile of such a body with its seat); and

    (b)   for the purposes of this Act other than the provisions mentioned in section 43(1)(b) and (c).

(3) A corporation or association has its seat in the United Kingdom if and only if—

    (a)   it was incorporated or formed under the law of a part of the United Kingdom and has its registered office or some other official address in the United Kingdom; or

    (b)   its central management and control is exercised in the United Kingdom.

(4) A corporation or association has its seat in a particular part of the United Kingdom if and only if it has its seat in the United Kingdom and—

    (a)   it has its registered office or some other official address in that part; or

    (b)   its central management and control is exercised in that part; or

    (c)   it has a place of business in that part.

(5) A corporation or association has its seat in a particular place in the United Kingdom if and only if it has its seat in the part of the United Kingdom in which that place is situated and—

    (a)   it has its registered office or some other official address in that place; or

    (b)   its central management and control is exercised in that place; or

    (c)   it has a place of business in that place.

(6) Subject to subsection (7), a corporation or association has its seat in a state other than the United Kingdom if and only if—

    (a)   it was incorporated or formed under the law of that state and has its registered office or some other official address there; or

    (b)   its central management and control is exercised in that state.

(7) A corporation or association shall not be regarded as having its seat in a Contracting State other than the United Kingdom if it is shown that the courts of that state would not regard it as having its seat there.

(8) In this section—

"business" includes any activity carried on by a corporation or association, and "place of business" shall be construed accordingly;

"official address", in relation to a corporation or association, means an address which it is required by law to register, notify or maintain for the purpose of receiving notices or other communications.

Seat of corporation or association for purposes of Article 16(2) and related provisions

43.—(1) The following provisions of this section determine where a corporation or association has its seat for the purposes of—

(a) Article 16(2) of the 1968 Convention or of the Lugano Convention (which confers exclusive jurisdiction over proceedings relating to the formation or dissolution of such bodies, or to the decisions of their organs);

(b) Articles 5A and 16(2) in Schedule 4; and

(c) Rules 2(12) and 4(1)(b) in Schedule 8.

(2) A corporation or association has its seat in the United Kingdom if and only if—

(a) it was incorporated or formed under the law of a part of the United Kingdom; or

(b) its central management and control is exercised in the United Kingdom.

(3) A corporation or association has its seat in a particular part of the United Kingdom if and only if it has its seat in the United Kingdom and—

(a) subject to subsection (5), it was incorporated or formed under the law of that part; or

(b) being incorporated or formed under the law of a state other than the United Kingdom, its central management and control is exercised in that part.

(4) A corporation or association has its seat in a particular place in Scotland if and only if it has its seat in Scotland and—

(a) it has its registered office or some other official address in that place; or

(b) it has no registered office or other official address in Scotland, but its central management and control is exercised in that place.

(5) A corporation or association incorporated or formed under—

(a) an enactment forming part of the law of more than one part of the United Kingdom; or

(b) an instrument having effect in the domestic law of more than one part of the United Kingdom,

shall, if it has a registered office, be taken to have its seat in the part of the United Kingdom in which that office is situated, and not in any other part of the United Kingdom.

(6) Subject to subsection (7), a corporation or association has its seat in a Contracting State other than the United Kingdom if and only if—

(a) it was incorporated or formed under the law of that state; or

(b) its central management and control is exercised in that state.

(7) A corporation or association shall not be regarded as having its seat in a Contracting State other than the United Kingdom if—

(a) it has its seat in the United Kingdom by virtue of sub-section (2)(a); or

(b) it is shown that the courts of that other state would not regard it for the purposes of Article 16(2) as having its seat there.

(8) In this section "official address" has the same meaning as in section 42.

Saving for powers to stay, sist, strike out or dismiss proceedings

49. Nothing in this Act shall prevent any court in the United Kingdom from staying, sisting, striking out or dismissing any proceedings before it, on the ground of *forum non conveniens* or otherwise, where to do so is not inconsistent with the 1968 Convention or, as the case may be, the Lugano Convention.

C. BRUSSELS CONVENTION

Instruments as set out in the Schedules to the 1982 Act, as amended.

CONVENTION
on jurisdiction and the enforcement of judgments in civil and commercial matters

PREAMBLE

THE HIGH CONTRACTING PARTIES TO THE TREATY
ESTABLISHING THE EUROPEAN ECONOMIC COMMUNITY,

Desiring to implement the provisions of Article 220 of that Treaty by virtue of which they undertook to secure the simplification of formalities governing the reciprocal recognition and enforcement of judgments of courts or tribunals;

Anxious to strengthen in the Community the legal protection of persons therein established;

Considering that it is necessary for this purpose to determine the international jurisdiction of their courts, to facilitate recognition and to introduce an expeditious procedure for securing the enforcement of judgments, authentic instruments and court settlements;

Have decided to conclude this Convention and to this end have designated as their Plenipotentiaries;

(*Designations of Plenipotentiaries of the original Six Contracting States*)

WHO, meeting within the Council, having exchanged their Full Powers, found in good and due form,

HAVE AGREED AS FOLLOWS:

TITLE I
SCOPE
Article 1

This Convention shall apply in civil and commercial matters whatever the nature of the court or tribunal. It shall not extend, in particular, to revenue, customs or administrative matters.

The Convention shall not apply to—

1. The status or legal capacity of natural persons, rights in property arising out of a matrimonial relationship, wills and succession.

2. Bankruptcy, proceedings relating to the winding-up of insolvent companies or other legal persons, judicial arrangements, compositions and analogous proceedings.

3. Social security.

4. Arbitration.

TITLE II
JURISDICTION
Section 1
General provisions
Article 2

Subject to the provisions of this Convention, persons domiciled in a Contracting State shall, whatever their nationality, be sued in the courts of that State.

Persons who are not nationals of the State in which they are domiciled shall be governed by the rules of jurisdiction applicable to nationals of that State.

Article 3

Persons domiciled in a Contracting State may be sued in the courts of another Contracting State only by virtue of the rules set out in Sections 2 to 6 of this Title.

In particular the following provisions shall not be applicable as against them—

— in Belgium: Article 15 of the civil code (Code civil—Burgerlijk Wetboek) and Article 638 of the judicial code (Code judiciaire—Gerechtelijk Wetboek),

— in Denmark: Article 246(2) and (3) of the law on civil procedure (Lov om rettens pleje),

— in the Federal Republic of Germany: Article 23 of the code of civil procedure (Zivilprozeßordnung),

— in Greece: Article 40 of the code of civil procedure (Κώδικας Πολιτικής Δικονομίας),

— in France: Articles 14 and 15 of the civil code (Code civil),

— in Ireland: the rules which enable jurisdiction to be founded on the document instituting the proceedings having been served on the defendant during his temporary presence in Ireland,

— in Italy: Articles 2 and 4, nos 1 and 2 of the code of civil procedure (Codice di procedura civile),

— in Luxembourg: Articles 14 and 15 of the civil code (Code civil),

884

— in The Netherlands: Articles 126(3) and 127 of the code of civil procedure (Wetboek van Burgerlijke Rechtsvordering),
— in Portugal: Article 65(1)(c), article 65(2) and Article 65A(c) of the code of civil procedure (Código de Processo Civil) and Article II of the code of labour procedure (Código de Processo de Trabalho),
— in the United Kingdom: the rules which enable jurisdiction to be founded on:
  (a) the document instituting the proceedings having been served on the defendant during his temporary presence in the United Kingdom; or
  (b) the presence within the United Kingdom of property belonging to the defendant; or
  (c) the seizure by the plaintiff of property situated in the United Kingdom.

Article 4

If the defendant is not domiciled in a Contracting State, the jurisdiction of the courts of each Contracting State shall, subject to the provisions of Article 16, be determined by the law of that State.

As against such a defendant, any person domiciled in a Contracting State may, whatever his nationality, avail himself in that State of the rules of jurisdiction there in force, and in particular those specified in the second paragraph of Article 3, in the same way as the nationals of that State.

Section 2
Special jurisdiction
Article 5

A person domiciled in a Contracting State may, in another Contracting State, be sued—

1. In matters relating to a contract, in the courts of the place of performance of the obligation in question; in matters relating to individual contracts of employment, this place is that where the employee habitually carries out his work, or if the employee does not habitually carry out his work in any one country, the employer may also be sued in the courts for the place where the business which engaged the employee was or is now situated.

2. In matters relating to maintenance, in the courts for the place where the maintenance creditor is domiciled or habitually resident or, if the matter is ancillary to proceedings concerning the status of a person, in the court which, according to its own law, has jurisdiction to entertain those proceedings, unless that jurisdiction is based solely on the nationality of one of the parties.

3. In matters relating to tort, delict or quasi-delict, in the courts for the place where the harmful event occurred.

4. As regards a civil claim for damages or restitution which is based on an act giving rise to criminal proceedings, in the court seised of those proceedings, to the extent that that court has jurisdiction under its own law to entertain proceedings.

5. As regards a dispute arising out of the operations of a branch, agency or other establishment, in the courts for the place in which the branch, agency or other establishment is situated.

6. As settlor, trustee or beneficiary of a trust created by the operation of a statute, or by a written instrument, or created orally and evidenced in writing, in the courts of the Contracting State in which the trust is domiciled.

7. As regards a dispute concerning the payment of remuneration claimed in respect of the salvage of a cargo freight, in the court under the authority of which the cargo or freight in question—

  (a) has been arrested to secure such payment, or

  (b) could have been so arrested, but bail or other security has been given;

provided that this provision shall apply only if it is claimed that the defendant has an interest in the cargo or freight or had such an interest at the time of salvage.

Article 6

A person domiciled in a Contracting State may also be sued—

1. Where he is one of a number of defendants, in the courts for the place where any one them is domiciled.

2. As a third party in an action on a warranty or guarantee or in any other third party proceedings, in the court seised of the original proceedings, unless these were instituted solely with the object of removing him from the jurisdiction of the court which would be competent in his case.

3. On a counter-claim arising from the same contract or facts on which the original claim was based, in the court in which the original claim is pending.

4. In matters relating to a contract, if the action may be combined with an action against the same defendant in matters relating to rights *in rem* in immovable property, in the court of the Contracting State in which the property is situated.

Article 6a

Where by virtue of this Convention a court of a Contracting State has jurisdiction in actions relating to liability from the use or operation of a ship, that court, or any other court substituted for this purpose by the internal law of that State, shall also have jurisdiction over claims for limitation of such liability.

Section 3
Jurisdiction in matters relating to insurance
Article 7

In matters relating to insurance, jurisdiction shall be determined by this Section, without prejudice to the provisions of Articles 4 and 5 point 5.

Article 8

An insurer domiciled in a Contracting State may be sued—

1. in the courts of the State where he is domiciled, or

2. in another Contracting State, in the courts for the place where the policy-holder is domiciled, or

3. if he is a co-insurer, in the courts of a Contracting State in which proceedings are brought against the leading insurer.

An insurer who is not domiciled in a Contracting State but has a branch, agency or other establishment in one of the Contracting States shall, in disputes arising out of the operations of the branch, agency or establishment, be deemed to be domiciled in that State.

Article 9

In respect of liability insurance of immovable property, the insurer may in addition be sued in the courts for the place where the harmful event occurred. The same applies if movable and immovable property are covered by the same insurance policy and both are adversely affected by the same contingency.

Article 10

In respect of liability insurance, the insurer may also, if the law of the court permits it, be joined in proceedings which the injured party had brought against the insured.

The provisions of Articles 7, 8 and 9 shall apply to actions brought by the injured party directly against the insurer, where such direct actions are permitted.

If the law governing such direct actions provides that the policy-holder or the insured may be joined as a party to the action, the same court shall have jurisdiction over them.

Article 11

Without prejudice to the provisions of the third paragraph of Article 10, an insurer may bring proceedings only in the courts of the Contracting State in which the defendant is domiciled, irrespective of whether he is the policy-holder, the insured or a beneficiary.

The provisions of this Section shall not affect the right to bring a counter-claim in the court in which, in accordance with this Section, the original claim is pending.

Article 12

The provisions of this Section may be departed from only by an agreement on jurisdiction—

1.   which is entered into after the dispute has arisen, or

2.   which allows the policy-holder, the insured or a beneficiary to bring proceedings in courts other than those indicated in this Section, or

3.   which is concluded between a policy-holder and an insurer, both of whom are domiciled in the same Contracting State, and which has the effect of conferring jurisdiction on the courts of that State even if the harmful event were to occur abroad, provided that such an agreement is not contrary to the law of that State, or

4.   which is concluded with a policy-holder who is not domiciled in a Contracting State, except in so far as the insurance is compulsory or relates to immovable property in a Contracting State, or

5.   which relates to a contract of insurance in so far as it covers one or more of the risks set out in Article 12a.

Article 12a

The following are the risks referred to in point 5 of Article 12—

1.   Any loss of or damage to—

(a) sea-going ships, installations situated offshore or on the high seas, or aircraft, arising from perils which relate to their use for commercial purposes;

(b) goods in transit other than passengers' baggage where the transit consists of or includes carriage by such ships or aircraft.

2. Any liability, other than for bodily injury to passengers or loss of or damage to their baggage—

(a) arising out of the use or operation of ships, installations or aircraft as referred to in point 1(a) above in so far as the law of the Contracting State in which such aircraft are registered does not prohibit agreements on jurisdiction regarding insurance of such risks;

(b) for loss or damage caused by goods in transit as described in point 1(b) above.

3. Any financial loss connected with the use or operation of ships, installations or aircraft as referred to in point 1(a) above, in particular loss of freight or charter-hire.

4. Any risk or interest connected with any of those referred to in points 1 to 3 above.

Section 4
Jurisdiction over consumer contracts
Article 13

In proceedings concerning a contract concluded by a person for a purpose which can be regarded as being outside his trade or profession, hereinafter called "the consumer", jurisdiction shall be determined by this Section, without prejudice to the provisions of Article 4 and point 5 of Article 5, if it is—

1. a contract for the sale of goods on instalment credit terms, or

2. a contract for a loan repayable by instalments, or for any other form of credit, made to finance the sale of goods, or

3. any other contract for the supply of goods or a contract for the supply of services, and

(a) in the State of the consumer's domicile the conclusion of the contract was preceded by a specific invitation addressed to him or by advertising; and

(b) the consumer took in that State the steps necessary for the conclusion of the contract.

Where a consumer enters into a contract with a party who is not domiciled in a Contracting State but has a branch, agency or other establishment in one of the Contracting States, that party shall, in disputes arising out of the operations of the branch, agency or establishment, be deemed to be domiciled in that State.

This Section shall not apply to contracts of transport.

Article 14

A consumer may bring proceedings against the other party to a contract either in the court of the Contracting State in which that party is domiciled or in the courts of the Contracting State in which he is himself domiciled.

Proceedings may be brought against a consumer by the other party to the contract only in the courts of the Contracting State in which the consumer is domiciled.

These provisions shall not affect the right to bring a counter-claim in the court in which, in accordance with this Section, the original claim is pending.

Article 15

The provisions of this Section may be departed from only by an agreement—

1. which is entered into after the dispute has arisen, or

2. which allows the consumer to bring proceedings in courts other than those indicated in this Section, or

3. which is entered into by the consumer and the other party to the contract, both of whom are at the time of conclusion of the contract domiciled or habitually resident in the same Contracting State, and which confers jurisdiction on the courts of that State, provided that such an agreement is not contrary to the law of that State.

Section 5
Exclusive jurisdiction
Article 16

The following courts shall have exclusive jurisdiction, regardless of domicile:

1. (a) in proceedings which have as their object rights *in rem* in immovable property or tenancies of immovable property, the courts of the Contracting State in which the property is situated;

    (b) however, in proceedings which have as their object tenancies of immovable property concluded for temporary private use for a maximum period of six consecutive months, the courts of the Contracting State in which the defendant is domiciled shall also have jurisdiction, provided that the landlord and the tenant are natural persons and are domiciled in the same Contracting State.

2. In proceedings which have as their object the validity of the constitution, the nullity or the dissolution of companies or other legal persons or associations of natural or legal persons, or the decisions of their organs, the courts of the Contracting State in which the company, legal person or association has its seat.

3. In proceedings which have as their object the validity of entries in public registers, the courts of the Contracting State in which the register is kept.

4. In proceedings concerned with the registration or validity of patents, trade marks, designs, or other similar rights required to be deposited or registered, the courts of the Contracting State in which the deposit or registration has been applied for, has taken place or is under the terms of an international convention deemed to have taken place.

5. In proceedings concerned with the enforcement of judgments, the courts of the Contracting State in which the judgment has been or is to be enforced.

Section 6
Prorogation of jurisdiction
Article 17

If the parties, one or more of whom is domiciled in a Contracting State, have agreed that a court or the courts of a Contracting State are to have jurisdiction to settle any disputes which have arisen or which may arise in connection with a particular legal relationship, that court or those courts shall have exclusive jurisdiction. Such an agreement conferring jurisdiction shall be either—

(a) in writing or evidenced in writing, or

(b) in a form which accords with practices which the parties have established between themselves, or

(c) in international trade or commerce, in a form which accords with a usage of which the parties are or ought to have been aware and which in such trade or commerce is widely known to, and regularly observed by, parties to contracts of the type involved in the particular trade or commerce concerned.

Where such an agreement is concluded by parties, none of whom is domiciled in a Contracting State, the courts of other Contracting States shall have no jurisdiction over their disputes unless the court or courts chosen have declined jurisdiction.

The court or courts of a Contracting State on which a trust instrument has conferred jurisdiction shall have exclusive jurisdiction in any proceedings brought against a settlor, trustee or beneficiary, if relations between these persons or their rights or obligations under the trust are involved.

Agreements or provisions of a trust instrument conferring jurisdiction shall have no legal force if they are contrary to the provisions of Articles 12 or 15, or if the courts whose jurisdiction they purport to exclude have exclusive jurisdiction by virtue of Article 16.

If an agreement conferring jurisdiction was concluded for the benefit of only one of the parties, that party shall retain the right to bring proceedings in any other court which has jurisdiction by virtue of this Convention.

In matters relating to individual contracts of employment an agreement conferring jurisdiction shall have legal force only if it is entered into after the dispute has arisen or if the employee invokes it to seise courts other than those for the defendant's domicile or those specified in Article 5(1).

Article 18

Apart from jurisdiction derived from other provisions of this Convention, a court of a Contracting State before whom a defendant enters an appearance shall have jurisdiction. This rule shall not apply where appearance was entered solely to contest the jurisdiction, or where another court has exclusive jurisdiction by virtue of Article 16.

Section 7
Examination as to jurisdiction and admissibility
Article 19

Where a court of a Contracting State is seised of a claim which is principally concerned with a matter over which the courts of another Contracting State have exclusive jurisdiction by virtue of Article 16, it shall declare of its own motion that it has no jurisdiction.

Article 20

Where a defendant domiciled in one Contracting State is sued in a court of another Contracting State and does not enter an appearance, the court shall declare of its own motion that it has no jurisdiction unless its jurisdiction is derived from the provisions of the Convention.

The court shall stay the proceedings so long as it is not shown that the defendant has been able to receive the document instituting the proceedings or an equivalent document in sufficient time to enable him to arrange for his defence, or that all necessary steps have been taken to this end.

The provisions of the foregoing paragraph shall be replaced by those of Article 15 of the Hague Convention of 15th November 1965 on the service abroad of judicial and extrajudicial documents in civil or commercial matters, if the document instituting the proceedings or notice thereof had to be transmitted abroad in accordance with that Convention.

Section 8
Lis pendens—related actions
Article 21

Where proceedings involving the same cause of action and between the same parties are brought in the courts of different Contracting States, any court other than the court first seised shall of its own motion stay its proceedings until such time as the jurisdiction of the court first seised is established.

Where the jurisdiction of the court first seised is established, any court other than the court first seised shall decline jurisdiction in favour of that court.

Article 22

Where related actions are brought in the courts of different Contracting States, any court other than the court first seised may, while the actions are pending at first instance, stay its proceedings.

A court other than the court first seised may also, on the application of one of the parties, decline jurisdiction if the law of that court permits the consolidation of related actions and the court first seised has jurisdiction over both actions.

For the purposes of this Article, actions are deemed to be related where they are so closely connected that it is expedient to hear and determine them together to avoid the risk of irreconcilable judgments resulting from separate proceedings.

Article 23

Where actions come within the exclusive jurisdiction of several courts, any court other than the court first seised shall decline jurisdiction in favour of that court.

Section 9
Provisional, including protective, measures
Article 24

Application may be made to the courts of a Contracting State for such provisional, including protective, measures as may be available under the law of that State, even if, under this Convention, the courts of another Contracting State have jurisdiction as to the substance of the matter.

TITLE III
RECOGNITION AND ENFORCEMENT
Article 25

For the purposes of this Convention, "judgment" means any judgment given by a court or tribunal of a Contracting State, whatever the judgment may be called, including a decree, order, decision or writ of execution, as well as the determination of costs or expenses by an officer of the court.

Section 1
Recognition
Article 26

A judgment given in a Contracting State shall be recognized in the other Contracting States without any special procedure being required.

Any interested party who raises the recognition of a judgment as the principal issue in a dispute may, in accordance with the procedures provided for in Sections 2 and 3 of this Title, apply for a decision that the judgment be recognized.

If the outcome of proceedings in a court of a Contracting State depends on the determination of an incidental question of recognition that court shall have jurisdiction over that question.

Article 27

A judgment shall not be recognized—

1. If such recognition is contrary to public policy in the State in which recognition is sought.

2. Where it was given in default of appearance, if the defendant was not duly served with the document which instituted the proceedings or with an equivalent document in sufficient time to enable him to arrange for his defence.

3. If the judgment is irreconcilable with a judgment given in a dispute between the same parties in the State in which recognition is sought.

4. If the court of the State of origin, in order to arrive at its judgment, has decided a preliminary question concerning the status or legal capacity of natural persons, rights in property arising out of a matrimonial relationship, wills or succession in a way that conflicts with a rule of the private international law of the State in which the recognition is sought, unless the same result would have been reached by the application of the rules of private international law of that State.

5. If the judgment is irreconcilable with an earlier judgment given in a non-Contracting State involving the same cause of action and between the same parties, provided that this latter judgment fulfils the conditions necessary for its recognition in the state addressed.

Article 28

Moreover, a judgment shall not be recognized if it conflicts with the provisions of Sections 3, 4 or 5 of Title II, or in a case provided for in Article 59.

In its examination of the grounds of jurisdiction referred to in the foregoing paragraph, the court or authority applied to shall be bound by the findings of fact on which the court of the State of origin based its jurisdiction.

Subject to the provisions of the first paragraph, the jurisdiction of the court of the State of origin may not be reviewed; the test of public policy referred to in point 1 of Article 27 may not be applied to the rules relating to jurisdiction.

Article 29

Under no circumstances may a foreign judgment be reviewed as to its substance.

Article 30

A court of a Contracting State in which recognition is sought of a judgment given in another Contracting State may stay the proceedings if an ordinary appeal against the judgment has been lodged.

A court of a Contracting State in which recognition is sought of a judgment given in Ireland or the United Kingdom may stay the proceedings if enforcement is suspended in the State of origin, by reason of an appeal.

Section 2
Enforcement
Article 31

A judgment given in a Contracting State and enforceable in that State shall be enforced in another Contracting State when, on the application of any interested party, it has been declared enforceable there.

However, in the United Kingdom, such a judgment shall be enforced in England and Wales, in Scotland, or in Northern Ireland when, on the application of any interested party, it has been registered for enforcement in that part of the United Kingdom.

Article 32

1. The application shall be submitted—
— in Belgium, to the tribunal de première instance or rechtbank van eerste aanleg,
— in Denmark, to the byret,
— in the Federal Republic of Germany, to the presiding judge of a chamber of the Landgericht,
— in Greece, to the Μονομελές Πρωτοδικείο,
— in Spain, to the Juzgado de Primera Instancia,
— in France, to the presiding judge of the tribunal de grande instance,
— in Ireland, to the High Court,
— in Italy, to the corte d'appello,
— in Luxembourg, to the presiding judge of the tribunal d'arrondissement,

— in The Netherlands, to the presiding judge of the arrondissementsrechtbank,
— in Portugal, to the Tribunal Judicial de Círculo,
— in the United Kingdom—
 (a) in England and Wales, to the High Court of Justice, or in the case of maintenance judgment to the Magistrates' Court on transmission by the Secretary of State;
 (b) in Scotland, to the Court of Session, or in the case of a maintenance judgment to the Sheriff Court on transmission by the Secretary of State;
 (c) in Northern Ireland, to the High Court of Justice, or in the case of a maintenance judgment to the Magistrates' Court on transmission by the Secretary of State.

2. The jurisdiction of local courts shall be determined by reference to the place of domicile of the party against whom enforcement is sought. If he is not domiciled in the State in which enforcement is sought, it shall be determined by reference to the place of enforcement.

Article 33
The procedure for making the application shall be governed by the law of the State in which enforcement is sought.

The applicant must give an address for service of process within the area of jurisdiction of the court applied to. However, if the law of the State in which enforcement is sought does not provide for the furnishing of such an address, the applicant shall appoint a representative *ad litem*.

The documents referred to in Articles 46 and 47 shall be attached to the application.

Article 34
The court applied to shall give its decision without delay; the party against whom enforcement is sought shall not at this stage of the proceedings be entitled to make any submissions on the application.

The application may be refused only for one of the reasons specified in Articles 27 and 28.

Under no circumstances may the foreign judgment be reviewed as to its substance.

Article 35
The appropriate officer of the court shall without delay bring the decision given on the application to the notice of the applicant in accordance with the procedure laid down by the law of the State in which enforcement is sought.

Article 36
If enforcement is authorized, the party against whom enforcement is sought may appeal against the decision within one month of service thereof.

If that party is domiciled in a Contracting State other than that in which the decision authorizing enforcement was given, the time for appealing shall be two months and shall run from the date of service, either on him in person or at his residence. No extension of time may be granted on account of distance.

Article 37

1.   An appeal against the decision authorizing enforcement shall be lodged in accordance with the rules governing procedure in contentious matters—
— in Belgium, with the tribunal de première instance or rechtbank van eerste aanleg,
— in Denmark, with the landsret,
— in the Federal Republic of Germany, with the Oberlandesgericht,
— in Greece, with the Εφετείο,
— in Spain, with the Audiencia Provincial,
— in France, with the cour d'appel,
— in Ireland, with the High Court,
— in Italy, with the corte d'appello,
— in Luxembourg, with the Cour supérieure de justice sitting as a court of civil appeal,
— in The Netherlands, with the arrondissementsrechtbank,
— in Portugal, with the Tribunal de Relação,
— in the United Kingdom—
  (a)   in England and Wales, with the High Court of Justice, or in the case of a maintenance judgment with the Magistrates' Court;
  (b)   in Scotland, with the Court of Session, or in the case of a maintenance judgment with the Sheriff Court;
  (c)   in Northern Ireland, with the High Court of Justice, or in the case of a maintenance judgment with the Magistrates' Court.
2.   The judgment given on the appeal may be contested only—
— in Belgium, Greece, Spain, France, Italy, Luxembourg and in The Netherlands, by an appeal in cassation,
— in Denmark, by an appeal to the højesteret, with the leave of the Minister of Justice,
— in the Federal Republic of Germany, by a Rechtsbeschwerde,
— in Ireland, by an appeal on a point of law to the Supreme Court,
— in Portugal, by an appeal on a point of law,
— in the United Kingdom, by a single further appeal on a point of law.

Article 38

The court with which the appeal under Article 37(1) is lodged may, on the application of the appellant, stay the proceedings if an ordinary appeal has been lodged against the judgment in the State of origin or if the time for such an appeal has not yet expired; in the latter case, the court may specify the time within which such an appeal is to be lodged.

Where the judgment was given in Ireland or the United Kingdom, any form of appeal available in the State of origin shall be treated as an ordinary appeal for the purposes of the first paragraph.

The court may also make enforcement conditional on the provision of such security as it shall determine.

Article 39

During the time specified for an appeal pursuant to Article 36 and until any such appeal has been determined, no measures of enforcement may be taken other than protective measures taken against the property of the party against whom enforcement is sought.

The decision authorizing enforcement shall carry with it the power to proceed to any such protective measures.

Article 40

1. If the application for enforcement is refused, the applicant may appeal—
   — in Belgium, to the cour d'appel or hof van beroep,
   — in Denmark, to the landsret,
   — in the Federal Republic of Germany, to the Oberlandesgericht,
   — in Greece, to the Εφετείο,
   — in Spain, to the Audiencia Provincial,
   — in France, to the cour d'appel,
   — in Ireland, to the High Court,
   — in Italy, to the corte d'appello,
   — in Luxembourg, to the Cour supérieure de justice sitting as a court of civil appeal,
   — in The Netherlands, to the gerechtshof,
   — in Portugal, to the Tribunal de Relação,
   — in the United Kingdom—
      (a) in England and Wales, to the High Court of Justice, or in the case of a maintenance judgment to the Magistrates' Court;
      (b) in Scotland, to the Court of Session, or in the case of a maintenance judgment to the Sheriff Court;
      (c) in Northern Ireland, to the High Court of Justice, or in the case of a maintenance judgment to the Magistrates' Court.

2. The party against whom enforcement is sought shall be summoned to appear before the appellate court. If he fails to appear, the provisions of the second and third paragraphs of Article 20 shall apply even where he is not domiciled in any of the Contracting States.

Article 41

A judgment given on appeal provided for in Article 40 may be contested only—
   — in Belgium, Greece, Spain, France, Italy, Luxembourg and in The Netherlands, by an appeal in cassation,
   — in Denmark, by an appeal to the højesteret, with the leave of the Minister of Justice,
   — in the Federal Republic of Germany, by a Rechtsbeschwerde,

— in Ireland, by an appeal on a point of law to the Supreme Court,
— in Portugal, by an appeal on a point of law,
— in the United Kingdom, by a single further appeal on a point of law.

Article 42

Where a foreign judgment has been given in respect of several matters and enforcement cannot be authorized for all of them, the court shall authorize enforcement for one or more of them.

An applicant may request partial enforcement of a judgment.

Article 43

A foreign judgment which orders a periodic payment by way of a penalty shall be enforceable in the State in which enforcement is sought only if the amount of the payment has been finally determined by the courts of the State of origin.

Article 44

An applicant who, in the State of origin has benefited from complete or partial legal aid or exemption from costs or expenses, shall be entitled, in the procedures provided for in Articles 32 to 35, to benefit from the most favourable legal aid or the most extensive exemption from costs or expenses provided for by the law of the State addressed.

However, an applicant who requests the enforcement of a decision given by an administrative authority in Denmark in respect of a maintenance order may, in the State addressed, claim the benefits referred to in the first paragraph if he presents a statement from the Danish Ministry of Justice to the effect that he fulfils the economic requirements to qualify for the grant of complete or partial legal aid or exemption from costs or expenses.

Article 45

No security, bond or deposit, however described, shall be required of a party who in one Contracting State applies for enforcement of a judgment given in another Contracting State on the ground that he is a foreign national or that he is not domiciled or resident in the State in which enforcement is sought.

Section 3
Common provisions
Article 46

A party seeking recognition or applying for enforcement of a judgment shall produce—

1. a copy of the judgment which satisfies the conditions necessary to establish its authenticity;

2. in the case of a judgment given in default, the original or a certified true copy of the document which establishes that the party in default was served with the document instituting the proceedings or with an equivalent document.

897

Article 47

A party applying for enforcement shall also produce—

1. documents which establish that, according to the law of the State of origin the judgment is enforceable and has been served;

2. where appropriate, a document showing that the applicant is in receipt of legal aid in the State of origin.

Article 48

If the documents specified in point 2 of Articles 46 and 47 are not produced, the court may specify a time for their production, accept equivalent documents or, if it considers that it has sufficient information before it, dispense with their production.

If the court so requires, a translation of the documents shall be produced; the translation shall be certified by a person qualified to do so in one of the Contracting States.

Article 49

No legalization or other similar formality shall be required in respect of the documents referred to in Articles 46 or 47 or the second paragraph of Article 48, or in respect of a document appointing a representative *ad litem*.

TITLE IV
AUTHENTIC INSTRUMENTS AND COURT SETTLEMENTS
Article 50

A document which has been formally drawn up or registered as an authentic instrument and is enforceable in one Contracting State shall, in another Contracting State, be declared enforceable there, on application made in accordance with the procedures provided for in Article 31 *et seq*. The application may be refused only if enforcement of the instrument is contrary to public policy in the State addressed.

The instrument produced must satisfy the conditions necessary to establish its authenticity in the State of origin.

The provisions of Section 3 of Title III shall apply as appropriate.

Article 51

A settlement which has been approved by a court in the course of proceedings and is enforceable in the State in which it was concluded shall be enforceable in the State addressed under the same conditions as authentic instruments.

TITLE V
GENERAL PROVISIONS
Article 52

In order to determine whether a party is domiciled in a Contracting State whose courts are seised of a matter, the Court shall apply its internal law.

If a party is not domiciled in the State whose courts are seised of the matter, then, in order to determine whether the party is domiciled in another Contracting State, the court shall apply the law of that State.

Article 53

For the purposes of this Convention, the seat of a company or other legal person or association of natural or legal persons shall be treated as domicile. However, in order to determine that seat, the court shall apply its rules of private international law.

In order to determine whether a trust is domiciled in the Contracting State whose courts are seised of the matter, the court shall apply its rules of private international law.

TITLE VI
TRANSITIONAL PROVISIONS
Article 54

The provisions of the Convention shall apply only to legal proceedings instituted and to documents formally drawn up or registered as authentic instruments after its entry into force in the State of origin and, where recognition or enforcement of a judgment or authentic instruments is sought, in the State addressed.

However, judgments given after the date of entry into force of this Convention between the State of origin and the State addressed in proceedings instituted before that date shall be recognized and enforced in accordance with the provisions of Title III if jurisdiction was founded upon rules which accorded with those provided for either in Title II of this Convention or in a convention concluded between the State of origin and the State addressed which was in force when the proceedings were instituted.

If the parties to a dispute concerning a contract had agreed in writing before 1st June 1988 for Ireland or before 1st January 1987 for the United Kingdom that the contract was to be governed by the law of Ireland or of a part of the United Kingdom, the courts of Ireland or of that part of the United Kingdom shall retain the right to exercise jurisdiction in the dispute.

Article 54a

For a period of three years from 1st November 1986 for Denmark and from 1st June 1988 for Ireland, jurisdiction in maritime matters shall be determined in these States not only in accordance with the provisions of Title II, but also in accordance with the provisions of paragraphs 1 to 6 following. However, upon the entry into force of the International Convention relating to the arrest of sea-going ships, signed at Brussels on 10th May 1952, for one of these States, these provisions shall cease to have effect for that State.

1.   A person who is domiciled in a Contracting State may be sued in the Courts of one of the States mentioned above in respect of a maritime claim if the ship to which the claim relates or any other ship owned by him has been arrested by judicial process within the territory of the latter State to secure the claim, or could have been so arrested there but bail or other security has been given, and either—

(a)   the claimant is domiciled in the latter State, or

(b)   the claim arose in the latter State, or

(c)   the claim concerns the voyage during which the arrest was made or could have been made, or

(d)   the claim arises out of a collision or out of damage caused by a ship to another ship or to goods or persons on board either ship, either by the execution or non-execution of a manoeuvre or by the non-observance of regulations, or

(e)   the claim is for salvage, or

(f)   the claim is in respect of a mortgage or hypothecation of the ship arrested.

2.   A claimant may arrest either the particular ship to which the maritime claim relates, or any other ship which is owned by the person who was, at the time when the maritime claim arose, the owner of the particular ship. However, only the particular ship to which the maritime claim relates may be arrested in respect of the maritime claims set out in (5)(o), (p) or (q) of this Article.

3.   Ships shall be deemed to be in the same ownership when all the shares therein are owned by the same person or persons.

4.   When in the case of a charter by demise of a ship the charterer alone is liable in respect of a maritime claim relating to that ship, the claimant may arrest that ship or any other ship owned by the charterer, but no other ship owned by the owner may be arrested in respect of such claim. The same shall apply to any case in which a person other than the owner of a ship is liable in respect of a maritime claim relating to that ship.

5.   The expression "maritime claim" means a claim arising out of one or more of the following—

(a)   damage caused by any ship either in collision or otherwise;

(b)   loss of life or personal injury caused by any ship or occurring in connection with the operation on any ship;

(c)   salvage;

(d)   agreement relating to the use of hire of any ship whether by charterparty or otherwise;

(e)   agreement relating to the carriage of goods in any ship whether by charterparty or otherwise;

(f)   loss of or damage to goods including baggage carried in any ship;

(g)   general average;

(h)   bottomry;

(i)   towage;

(j)   pilotage;

(k)   goods or materials wherever supplied to a ship for her operation or maintenance;

(l)   construction, repair or equipment of any ship or dock charges and dues;

(m)   wages of master, officers or crew;

(n)   master's disbursements, including disbursements made by shippers, charterers or agents on behalf of a ship or her owner;

(o)   dispute as to the title to or ownership of any ship;

(p)   disputes between co-owners of any ship as to the ownership, possession, employment or earnings of that ship;

(q)   the mortgage or hypothecation of any ship.

6.   In Denmark, the expression "arrest" shall be deemed as regards the maritime claims referred to in 5(o) and (p) of this Article, to include a "forbud", where that is the only procedure allowed in respect of such a claim under Articles 646 to 653 of the law on civil procedure (lov om rettens pleje).

TITLE VII
RELATIONSHIP TO OTHER CONVENTIONS
Article 55

Subject to the provisions of the second subparagraph of Article 54, and of Article 56, this Convention shall, for the States which are parties to it, supersede the following conventions concluded between two or more of them—

— the Convention between Belgium and France on jurisdiction and the validity and enforcement of judgments, arbitration awards and authentic instruments, signed at Paris on 8th July 1899,

— the Convention between Belgium and The Netherlands on jurisdiction, bankruptcy, and the validity and enforcement of judgments, arbitration awards and authentic instruments, signed at Brussels on 28th March 1925,

— the Convention between France and Italy on the enforcement of judgments in civil and commercial matters, signed at Rome on 3rd June 1930,

— the Convention between the United Kingdom and the French Republic providing for the reciprocal enforcement of judgments in civil and commercial matters, with Protocol, signed at Paris on 18th January 1934,

— the Convention between the United Kingdom and the Kingdom of Belgium providing for the reciprocal enforcement of judgments in civil and commercial matters, with Protocol, signed at Brussels on 2nd May 1934,

— the Convention between Germany and Italy on the recognition and enforcement of judgments in civil and commercial matters, signed at Rome on 9th March 1936,

— the Convention between the Federal Republic of Germany and the Kingdom of Belgium on the mutual recognition and enforcement of judgments, arbitration awards and authentic instruments in civil and commercial matters, signed at Bonn on 30th June 1958,

— the Convention between the Kingdom of The Netherlands and the Italian Republic on the recognition and enforcement of judgments in civil and commercial matters, signed at Rome on 17th April 1959,

— the Convention between the United Kingdom and the Federal Republic of Germany for the reciprocal recognition and enforcement of judgments in civil and commercial matters, signed at Bonn on 14th July 1960,

— the Convention between the Kingdom of Greece and the Federal Republic of Germany for the reciprocal recognition and enforcement of judgments, settlements and authentic instruments in civil and commercial matters, signed in Athens on 4th November 1961,

— the Convention between the Kingdom of Belgium and the Italian Republic on the recognition and enforcement of judgments and other enforceable instruments in civil and commercial matters, signed at Rome on 6th April 1962,

— the Convention between the Kingdom of The Netherlands and the Federal Republic of Germany on the mutual recognition and enforcement of judgments and other enforceable instruments in civil and commercial matters, signed at The Hague on 30th August 1962,

— the Convention between the United Kingdom and the Republic of Italy for the reciprocal recognition and enforcement of judgments in civil and commercial matters, signed at Rome on 7th February 1964, with amending Protocol signed at Rome on 14th July 1970,

— the Convention between the United Kingdom and the Kingdom of The Netherlands providing for the reciprocal recognition and enforcement of judgments in civil matters, signed at The Hague on 17th November 1967,

— the Convention between Spain and France on the recognition and enforcement of judgment arbitration awards in civil and commercial matters, signed at Paris on 28th May 1969,

— the Convention between Spain and Italy regarding legal aid and the recognition and enforcement of judgments in civil and commercial matters, signed at Madrid on 22nd May 1973,

— the Convention between Spain and the Federal Republic of Germany on the recognition and enforcement of judgments, settlements and enforceable authentic instruments in civil and commercial matters, signed at Bonn on 14th November 1983,

and, in so far as it is in force—

— the Treaty between Belgium, The Netherlands and Luxembourg on jurisdiction, bankruptcy, and the validity and enforcement of judgments, arbitration awards and authentic instruments, signed at Brussels on 24th November 1961.

Article 56

The Treaty and the conventions referred to in Article 55 shall continue to have effect in relation to matters to which this Convention does not apply.

They shall continue to have effect in respect of judgments given and documents formally drawn up or registered as authentic instruments before the entry into force of this Convention.

Article 57

1. This Convention shall not affect any conventions to which the Contracting States are or will be parties and which in relation to particular matters, govern jurisdiction or the recognition or enforcement of judgments.

2. With a view to its uniform interpretation, paragraph 1 shall be applied in the following manner—

(a) this Convention shall not prevent a court of a Contracting State which is a party to a convention on a particular matter from assuming jurisdiction in accordance with that Convention, even where the defendant is domiciled in another Contracting State which is not a party to that Convention. The court hearing the action shall, in any event, apply Article 20 of this Convention;

(b) judgments given in a Contracting State by a court in the exercise of jurisdiction provided for in a convention on a particular matter shall be recognized and enforced in the other Contracting State in accordance with this Convention.

Where a convention on a particular matter to which both the State of origin and the State addressed are parties lays down conditions for the recognition or enforcement of judgments, those conditions shall apply. In any event, the provisions of this Convention which concern the procedure for recognition and enforcement of judgments may be applied.

3. This Convention shall not affect the application of provisions which, in relation to particular matters, govern jurisdiction or the recognition or enforcement of judgments and which are or will be contained in acts of the institutions of the European Communities or in national laws harmonized in implementation of such acts.

Article 58

Until such time as the Convention on jurisdiction and the enforcement of judgments in civil and commercial matters, signed at Lugano on 16th September 1988, takes effect with regard to France and the Swiss Confederation, this Convention shall not affect the rights granted to Swiss nationals by the Convention between France and the Swiss Confederation on jurisdiction and enforcement of judgments in civil matters, signed at Paris on 15th June 1869.

Article 59

This Convention shall not prevent a Contracting State from assuming, in a convention on the recognition and enforcement of judgments, an obligation towards a third State not to recognize judgments given in other Contracting States against defendants domiciled or habitually resident in the third State where, in cases provided for in Article 4, the judgment could only be founded on a ground of jurisdiction specified in the second paragraph of Article 3.

However, a Contracting State may not assume an obligation towards a third State not to recognize a judgment given in another Contracting State by a court basing its jurisdiction on the presence within that State of property belonging to the defendant, or the seizure by the plaintiff of property situated there—

1. if the action is brought to assert or declare proprietary or possessory rights in that property, seeks to obtain authority to dispose of it, or arises from another issue relating to such property, or

2. if the property constitutes the security for a debt which is the subject-matter of the action.

TITLE VIII
FINAL PROVISIONS
Article 60
[Deleted]

Article 61
This Convention shall be ratified by the signatory States. The instruments of ratification shall be deposited with the Secretary-General of the Council of the European Communities.

Article 62
This Convention shall enter into force on the first day of the third month following the deposit of the instrument of ratification by the last signatory State to take this step.

Article 63
The Contracting States recognize that any State which becomes a member of the European Economic Community shall be required to accept this Convention as a basis for the negotiations between the Contracting States and that State necessary to ensure the implementation of the last paragraph of Article 220 of the Treaty establishing the European Economic Community.

The necessary adjustments may be the subject of a special convention between the Contracting States of the one part and the new Member States of the other part.

Article 64
The Secretary-General of the Council of the European Communities shall notify the signatory States of—
    (a)   the deposit of each instrument of ratification;
    (b)   the date of entry into force of this Convention;
    (c)   [Deleted]
    (d)   any declaration received pursuant to Article IV of the Protocol;
    (e)   any communication made pursuant to Article VI of the Protocol.

Article 65
The Protocol annexed to this Convention by common accord of the Contracting States shall form an integral part thereof.

Article 66
This Convention is concluded for an unlimited period.

Article 67
Any Contracting State may request the revision of this Convention. In this event, a revision conference shall be convened by the President of the Council of the European Communities.

Article 68

This Convention, drawn up in a single original in the Dutch, French, German and Italian languages, all four texts being equally authentic, shall be deposited in the archives of the Secretariat of the Council of the European Communities. The Secretary-General shall transmit a certified copy to the Government of each signatory State.

(Signatures of Plenipotentiaries of the original six Contracting States)

ANNEXED PROTOCOL

The High Contracting Parties have agreed upon the following provisions, which shall be annexed to the Convention.

Article I

Any person domiciled in Luxembourg who is sued in a court of another Contracting State pursuant to Article 5(1) may refuse to submit to the jurisdiction of that court. If the defendant does not enter an appearance the court shall declare of its own motion that it has no jurisdiction.

An agreement conferring jurisdiction, within the meaning of Article 17, shall be valid with respect to a person domiciled in Luxembourg only if that person has expressly and specifically so agreed.

Article II

Without prejudice to any more favourable provisions of national laws, persons domiciled in a Contracting State who are being prosecuted in the criminal courts of another Contracting State of which they are not nationals for an offence which was not intentionally committed may be defended by persons qualified to do so, even if they do not appear in person.

However, the court seised of the matter may order appearance in person; in the case of failure to appear, a judgment given in the civil action without the person concerned having had the opportunity to arrange for his defence need not be recognized or enforced in the other Contracting States.

Article III

In proceedings for the issue of an order for enforcement, no charge, duty or fee calculated by reference to the value of the matter in issue may be levied in the State in which enforcement is sought.

Article IV

Judicial and extrajudicial documents drawn up in one Contracting State which have to be served on persons in another Contracting State shall be transmitted in accordance with the procedures laid down in the conventions and agreements concluded between the Contracting States.

Unless the State in which service is to take place objects by declaration to the Secretary-General of the Council of the European Communities, such documents may also be sent by the appropriate public officers of the State in which the document has been drawn up directly to the appropriate public officers of the State in which the addressee is to be found. In this case the officer of the State of origin shall send a copy of the document to the officer of the State applied to who is competent to forward it to the addressee. The document shall be forwarded in the manner specified by the law of the State applied to. The forwarding shall be recorded by a certificate sent directly to the officer of the State of origin.

Article V

The jurisdiction specified in Articles 6(2) and 10 in actions on a warranty or guarantee or in any other third party proceedings may not be resorted to in the Federal Republic of Germany. In that State, any person domiciled in another Contracting State may be sued in the courts in pursuance of Articles 68, 72, 73 and 74 of the code of civil procedure (*Zivilprozeßordnung*) concerning third-party notices.

Judgments given in the other Contracting States by virtue of point 2 of Article 6 or Article 10 shall be recognized and enforced in the Federal Republic of Germany in accordance with Title III. Any effects which judgments given in that State may have on third parties by application of Articles 68, 72, 73 and 74 of the code of civil procedure (*Zivilprozeßordnung*) shall also be recognized in the other Contracting States.

Article Va

In matters relating to maintenance, the expression "court" includes the Danish administrative authorities.

Article Vb

In proceedings involving a dispute between the master and a member of the crew of a sea-going ship registered in Denmark, in Greece, in Ireland or in Portugal, concerning remuneration or other conditions of service, a court in a Contracting State shall establish whether the diplomatic or consular officer responsible for the ship has been notified of the dispute. It shall stay the proceedings so long as he has not been notified. It shall of its own motion decline jurisdiction if the officer, having been duly notified, has exercised the powers accorded to him in the matter by a consular convention, or in the absence of such a convention has, within the time allowed, raised any objection to the exercise of such jurisdiction.

Article Vc

Articles 52 and 53 of this Convention shall, when applied by Article 69(5) of the Convention for the European patent for the common market, signed at Luxembourg on 15th December 1975, to the provisions relating to "residence" in the English text of that Convention, operate as if "residence" in that text were the same as "domicile" in Articles 52 and 53.

Article Vd

Without prejudice to the jurisdiction of the European Patent Office under the Convention on the grant of European patents, signed at Munich on 5th October 1973, the courts of each Contracting State shall have exclusive jurisdiction, regardless of domicile, in proceedings concerned with the registration or validity of any European patent granted for that State which is not a Community patent by virtue of the provisions of Article 86 of the Convention for the European patent for the common market, signed at Luxembourg on 15th December 1975.

Article VI

The Contracting States shall communicate to the Secretary-General of the Council of the European Communities the text of any provisions of their laws which amend either those articles of their laws mentioned in the Convention or the lists of courts specified in Section 2 of Title III of the Convention.

(Signatures of Plenipotentiaries of the original six Contracting States)

SCHEDULE 2
TEXT OF 1971 PROTOCOL, AS AMENDED
Article 1

The Court of Justice of the European Communities shall have jurisdiction to give rulings on the interpretation of the Convention on jurisdiction and the enforcement of judgments in civil and commercial matters and of the Protocol annexed to that Convention, signed at Brussels on 27th September 1968, and also on the interpretation of the present Protocol.

The Court of Justice of the European Communities shall also have jurisdiction to give rulings on the interpretation of the Convention on the accession of the Kingdom of Denmark, Ireland and the United Kingdom of Great Britain and Northern Ireland to the Convention of 27th September 1968 and to this Protocol.

The Court of Justice of the European Communities shall also have jurisdiction to give rulings on the interpretation of the Convention on the accession of the Hellenic Republic to the Convention of 27th September 1968 and to this Protocol, as adjusted by the 1978 Convention.

The Court of Justice of the European Communities shall also have jurisdiction to give rulings on the interpretation of the Convention on the accession of the Kingdom of Spain and the Portuguese Republic to the Convention of 27th September 1968 and to this Protocol, as adjusted by the 1978 Convention and the 1982 Convention.

Article 2

The following courts may request the Court of Justice to give preliminary rulings on questions of interpretation—

1. — in Belgium: la Cour de Cassation—het Hof van Cassatie and le Conseil d'État—de Raad van State,

— in Denmark: højesteret,
— in the Federal Republic of Germany: die obersten Gerichtshöfe des Bundes,
— in Greece: the ανώτατα δικαστήρια,
— in Spain: el Tribunal Supremo,
— in France: la Cour de Cassation and le Conseil d'État,
— in Ireland: the Supreme Court,
— in Italy: la Corte Suprema di Cassazione,
— in Luxembourg: la Cour supérieure de Justice when sitting as Cour de Cassation,
— in The Netherlands: de Hoge Raad,
— in Portugal: o Supremo Tribunal de Justiça and o Supremo Tribunal Administrativo,
— in the United Kingdom: the House of Lords and courts to which application has been made under the second paragraph of Article 37 or under Article 41 of the Convention.

2.   The courts of the Contracting States when they are sitting in an appellate capacity.

3.   In the cases provided for in Article 37 of the Convention, the courts referred to in that Article.

Article 3

1.   Where a question of interpretation of the Convention or of one of the other instruments referred to in Article 1 is raised in a case pending before one of the courts listed in point 1 of Article 2, that court shall, if it considers that a decision on the question is necessary to enable it to give judgment, request the Court of Justice to give a ruling thereon.

2.   Where such a question is raised before any court referred to in point 2 or 3 of Article 2, that court may, under the conditions laid down in paragraph 1, request the Court of Justice to give a ruling thereon.

Article 4

1.   The competent authority of a Contracting State may request the Court of Justice to give a ruling on a question of interpretation of the Convention or of one of the other instruments referred to in Article 1 if judgments given by courts of that State conflict with the interpretation given either by the Court of Justice or in a judgment of one of the courts of another Contracting State referred to in point 1 or 2 of Article 2. The provisions of this paragraph shall apply only to judgments which have become *res judicata*.

2.   The interpretation given by the Court of Justice in response to such a request shall not affect the judgments which gave rise to the request for interpretation.

3.   The Procurators-General of the Courts of Cassation of the Contracting States, or any other authority designated by a Contracting State, shall be entitled to request the Court of Justice for a ruling on interpretation in accordance with paragraph 1.

4. The Registrar of the Court of Justice shall give notice of the request to the Contracting States, to the Commission and to the Council of the European Communities; they shall then be entitled within two months of the notification to submit statements of case or written observations to the Court.

5. No fees shall be levied or any costs or expenses awarded in respect of the proceedings provided for in this Article.

Article 5

1. Except where this Protocol otherwise provides, the provisions of the Treaty establishing the European Economic Community and those of the Protocol on the Statute of the Court of Justice annexed thereto, which are applicable when the Court is requested to give a preliminary ruling, shall also apply to any proceedings for the interpretation of the Convention and the other instruments referred to in Article 1.

2. The Rules of Procedure of the Court of Justice shall, if necessary, be adjusted and supplemented in accordance with Article 188 of the Treaty establishing the European Economic Community.

Article 6
[Deleted]

Article 7

This Protocol shall be ratified by the signatory States. The instruments of ratification shall be deposited with the Secretary-General of the Council of the European Communities.

Article 8

This Protocol shall enter into force on the first day of the third month following the deposit of the instrument of ratification by the last signatory State to take this step; provided that it shall at the earliest enter into force at the same time as the Convention of 27th September 1968 on jurisdiction and the enforcement of judgments in civil and commercial matters.

Article 9

The Contracting States recognize that any State which becomes a member of the European Economic Community, and to which Article 63 of the Convention on jurisdiction and the enforcement of judgments in civil and commercial matters applies, must accept the provisions of this Protocol, subject to such adjustments as may be required.

Article 10

The Secretary-General of the Council of the European Communities shall notify the signatory States of—

(a) the deposit of each instrument of ratification;
(b) the date of entry into force of this Protocol;
(c) any designation received pursuant to Article 4(3);
(d) [Deleted].

Article 11

The Contracting States shall communicate to the Secretary-General of the Council of the European Communities the texts of any provisions of their laws which necessitate an amendment to the list of courts in point 1 of Article 2.

Article 12

This Protocol is concluded for an unlimited period.

Article 13

Any Contracting State may request the revision of this Protocol. In this event, a revision conference shall be convened by the President of the Council of the European Communities.

Article 14

This Protocol, drawn up in a single original in the Dutch, French, German and Italian languages, all four texts being equally authentic, shall be deposited in the archives of the Secretariat of the Council of the European Communities. The Secretary-General shall transmit a certified copy to the Government of each signatory State.

SCHEDULE 3
TEXT OF TITLES V AND VI OF THE ACCESSION CONVENTION, AS AMENDED
TITLE V
TRANSITIONAL PROVISIONS
Article 34

1. The 1968 Convention and the 1971 Protocol, with the amendments made by this Convention, shall apply only to legal proceedings instituted and to authentic instruments formally drawn up or registered after the entry into force of this Convention in the State of origin and, where recognition or enforcement of a judgment or authentic instrument is sought, in the State addressed.

2. However, as between the six Contracting States to the 1968 Convention, judgments given after the date of entry into force of this Convention, in proceedings instituted before that date shall be recognised and enforced in accordance with the provisions of Title III of the 1968 Convention as amended.

3. Moreover, as between the six Contracting States to the 1968 Convention and the three States mentioned in Article 1 of this Convention, and as between those three States, judgments given after the date of entry into force of this Convention between the State of origin and the State addressed in proceedings instituted before that date shall also be recognised and enforced in accordance with the provisions of Title III of the 1968 Convention as amended if jurisdiction was founded upon rules which accorded with the provisions of Title II, as amended, or with provisions of a convention concluded between the State of origin and the State addressed which was in force when the proceedings were instituted.

Article 35
[Deleted]

Article 36
[Deleted]

TITLE VI
FINAL PROVISIONS
Article 37

The Secretary-General of the Council of the European Communities shall transmit a certified copy of the 1968 Convention and of the 1971 Protocol in the Dutch, French, German and Italian languages to the Governments of the Kingdom of Denmark, Ireland and the United Kingdom of Great Britain and Northern Ireland.

The texts of the 1968 Convention and the 1971 Protocol, drawn up in the Danish, English and Irish languages, shall be annexed to this Convention. The texts drawn up in the Danish, English and Irish languages shall be authentic under the same conditions as the original texts of the 1968 Convention and the 1971 Protocol.

Article 38

This Convention shall be ratified by the signatory States. The instruments of ratification shall be deposited with the Secretary-General of the Council of the European Communities.

Article 39

This Convention shall enter into force, as between the States which shall have ratified it, on the first day of the third month following the deposit of the last instrument of ratification by the original Member States of the Community and one new Member State.

It shall enter into force for each new Member State which subsequently ratifies it on the first day of the third month following the deposit of its instrument of ratification.

Article 40

The Secretary-General of the Council of the European Communities shall notify the signatory States of—
    (a)   the deposit of each instrument of ratification;
    (b)   the dates of entry into force of this Convention for the Contracting States.

Article 41

This Convention, drawn up in a single original in the Danish, Dutch, English, French, German, Irish and Italian languages, all seven texts being equally authentic, shall be deposited in the archives of the Secretariat of the Council of the European Communities. The Secretary-General shall transmit a certified copy to the Government of each signatory State.

SCHEDULE 4
Section 2(2)

SCHEDULE 3B
TEXT OF TITLES VI AND VII OF 1989 ACCESSION CONVENTION
TITLE VI
TRANSITIONAL PROVISIONS
Article 29

1.   The 1968 Convention and the 1971 Protocol, as amended by the 1978 Convention, the 1982 Convention and this Convention, shall apply only to legal proceedings instituted and to authentic instruments formally drawn up or registered after the entry into force of this Convention in the State of origin and, where recognition or enforcement of a judgment or authentic instrument is sought, in the State addressed.

2.   However, judgments given after the date of entry into force of this Convention between the State of origin and the State addressed in proceedings instituted before that date shall be recognized and enforced in accordance with the provisions of Title III of the 1968 Convention, as amended by the 1978 Convention, the 1982 Convention and this Convention, if jurisdiction was founded upon rules which accorded with the provisions of Title II of the 1968 Convention, as amended, or with the provisions of a convention which was in force between the State of origin and the State addressed when the proceedings were instituted.

TITLE VII
FINAL PROVISIONS
Article 30

1.   The Secretary-General of the Council of the European Communities shall transmit a certified copy of the 1968 Convention, of the 1971 Protocol, of the 1978 Convention and of the 1982 Convention in the Danish, Dutch, English, French, German, Greek, Irish and Italian languages to the Governments of the Kingdom of Spain and of the Portuguese Republic.

2.   The texts of the 1968 Convention, of the 1971 Protocol, of the 1978 Convention and of the 1982 Convention, drawn up in the Portuguese and Spanish languages, are set out in Annexes II, III, IV and V to this Convention. The texts drawn up in the Portuguese and Spanish languages shall be authentic under the same conditions as the other texts of the 1968 Convention, the 1971 Protocol, the 1978 Convention and the 1982 Convention.

Article 31

This Convention shall be ratified by the signatory States. The instruments of ratification shall be deposited with the Secretary-General of the Council of the European Communities.

Article 32

1.   This Convention shall enter into force on the first day of the third month following the date on which two signatory States, of which one is the

Kingdom of Spain or the Portuguese Republic, deposit their instruments of ratification.

2. This Convention shall take effect in relation to any other signatory State on the first day of the third month following the deposit of its instrument of ratification.

Article 33

The Secretary-General of the Council of the European Communities shall notify the signatory States of—

(a) the deposit of each instrument of ratification;

(b) the dates of entry into force of this Convention for the Contracting States.

Article 34

This Convention, drawn up in a single original in the Danish, Dutch, English, French, German, Greek, Irish, Italian, Portuguese and Spanish languages, all 10 texts being equally authentic, shall be deposited in the archives of the General Secretariat of the Council of the European Communities. The Secretary-General shall transmit a certified copy to the Government of each signatory State.

D. LUGANO CONVENTION. SELECTED PROVISIONS

Instruments as set out in Schedule 1 to the Civil Jurisdiction and Judgments Act 1991.

CONVENTION
ON JURISDICTION AND THE ENFORCEMENT OF JUDGMENTS IN CIVIL AND
COMMERCIAL MATTERS
PREAMBLE

The High Contracting Parties to this Convention,

Anxious to strengthen in their territories the legal protection of persons therein established,

Considering that it is necessary for this purpose to determine the international jurisdiction of their courts, to facilitate recognition and to introduce an expeditious procedure for securing the enforcement of judgments, authentic instruments and court settlements,

Aware of the links between them, which have been sanctioned in the economic field by the free trade agreements concluded between the European Economic Community and the States members of the European Free Trade Association,

Taking into account the Brussels Convention of 27 September 1968 on jurisdiction and the enforcement of judgments in civil and commercial matters, as amended by the Accession Conventions under the successive enlargements of the European Communities,

Persuaded that the extension of the principles of that Convention to the States parties to this instrument will strengthen legal and economic co-operation in Europe,

Desiring to ensure as uniform an interpretation as possible of this instrument,

Have in this spirit decided to conclude this Convention and

Have agreed as follows:

Article 3

Persons domiciled in a Contracting State may be sued in the courts of another Contracting State only by virtue of the rules set out in Sections 2 to 6 of this Title.

In particular the following provisions shall not be applicable as against them:

— in Belgium: Article 15 of the civil code (Code civil—Burgerlijk Wetboek) and Article 638 of the judicial code (Code judiciaire—Gerechtelijk Wetboek),

— in Denmark: Article 246(2) and (3) of the law on civil procedure (Lov om rettens pleje),

— in the Federal Republic of Germany: Article 23 of the code of civil procedure (Zivilprozeßordnung),

— in Greece: Article 40 of the code of civil procedure (Κώδικας πολιτικής δικονομίας),

— in France: Articles 14 and 15 of the civil code (Code civil),

— in Ireland: the rules which enable jurisdiction to be founded on the document instituting the proceedings having been served on the defendant during his temporary presence in Ireland,

— in Iceland: Article 77 of the Civil Proceedings Act (lög um meðferð einkamála í héraði),

— in Italy: Articles 2 and 4, Nos 1 and 2 of the code of civil procedure (Codice di procedura civile),

— in Luxembourg: Articles 14 and 15 of the civil code (Code civil),

— in The Netherlands: Articles 126(3) and 127 of the code of civil procedure (Wetboek van Burgerlijke Rechtsvordering),

— in Norway: Section 32 of the Civil Proceedings Act (tvistemålsloven),

— in Austria: Article 99 of the Law on Court Jurisdiction (Jurisdiktionsnorm),

— in Portugal: Articles 65(1)(c), 65(2) and 65A(c) of the code of civil procedure (Código de Processo Civil) and Article 11 of the code of labour procedure (Código de Processo de Trabalho),

— in Switzerland: le for du lieu du séquestre/Gerichtsstand des Arrestortes/foro del luogo del sequestro within the meaning of Article 4 of the loi fédérale sur le droit international privé/Bundesgesetz über das internationale Privatrecht/legge federale sul diritto internazionale privato,

— in Finland: the second, third and fourth sentences of Section 1 of Chapter 10 of the Code of Judicial Procedure (oikeudenkäymiskaari/rättegångsbalken),

— in Sweden: the first sentence of Section 3 of Chapter 10 of the Code of Judicial Procedure (Rättegångsbalken),

— in the United Kingdom: the rules which enable jurisdiction to be founded on:

(a) the document instituting the proceedings having been served on the defendant during his temporary presence in the United Kingdom; or

(b) the presence within the United Kingdom of property belonging to the defendant; or

(c) the seizure by the plaintiff of property situated in the United Kingdom.

Article 5

A person domiciled in a Contracting State may, in another Contracting State, be sued:

1. in matters relating to a contract, in the courts for the place of performance of the obligation in question; in matters relating to individual contracts of employment, this place is that where the employee habitually carries out his work, or if the employee does not habitually carry out his work in any one country, this place shall be the place of business through which he was engaged.

Article 16

The following courts shall have exclusive jurisdiction, regardless of domicile:

1. (a) in proceedings which have as their object rights *in rem* in immovable property or tenancies of immovable property, the courts of the Contracting State in which the property is situated;

(b) however, in proceedings which have as their object tenancies of immovable property concluded for temporary private use for a maximum period of six consecutive months, the courts of the Contracting State in which the defendant is domiciled shall also have jurisdiction, provided that the tenant is a natural person and neither party is domiciled in the Contracting State in which the property is situated.

Article 17

1. If the parties, one or more of whom is domiciled in a Contracting State, have agreed that a court or the courts of a Contracting State are to have jurisdiction to settle any disputes which have arisen or which may arise in connection with a particular legal relationship, that court or those courts shall have exclusive jurisdiction. Such an agreement conferring jurisdiction shall be either:

(a) in writing or evidenced in writing, or

(b) in a form which accords with practices which the parties have established between themselves, or

(c) in international trade or commerce, in a form which accords with a usage of which the parties are or ought to have been aware and which in such trade or commerce is widely known to, and regularly observed by, parties to contracts of the type involved in the particular trade or commerce concerned.

Where such an agreement is concluded by parties, none of whom is domiciled in a Contracting State, the courts of other Contracting States shall have no jurisdiction over their disputes unless the court or courts chosen have declined jurisdiction.

2. The court or courts of a Contracting State on which a trust instrument has conferred jurisdiction shall have exclusive jurisdiction in any proceedings brought against a settlor, trustee or beneficiary, if relations between these persons or their rights or obligations under the trust are involved.

3. Agreements or provisions of a trust instrument conferring jurisdiction shall have no legal force if they are contrary to the provisions of Article 12 or 15, or if the courts whose jurisdiction they purport to exclude have exclusive jurisdiction by virtue of Article 16.

4. If an agreement conferring jurisdiction was concluded for the benefit of only one of the parties, that party shall retain the right to bring proceedings in any other court which has jurisdiction by virtue of this Convention.

5. In matters relating to individual contracts of employment an agreement conferring jurisdiction shall have legal force only if it is entered into after the dispute has arisen.

Article 28

Moreover, a judgment shall not be recognised if it conflicts with the provisions of Section 3, 4 or 5 of Title II or in a case provided for in Article 59.

A judgment may furthermore be refused recognition in any case provided for in Article 54B(3) or 57(4).

In its examination of the grounds of jurisdiction referred to in the foregoing paragraphs, the court or authority applied to shall be bound by the findings of fact on which the court of the State of origin based its jurisdiction.

Subject to the provisions of the first and second paragraphs, the jurisdiction of the court of the State of origin may not be reviewed; the test of public policy referred to in Article 27(1) may not be applied to the rules relating to jurisdiction.

Article 32

1. The application shall be submitted:
— in Belgium, to the tribunal de première instance or rechtbank van eerste aanleg,
— in Denmark, to the byret,

— in the Federal Republic of Germany, to the presiding judge of a chamber of the Landgericht,

— in Greece, to the μονομελές πρωτοδικείο,

— in Spain, to the Juzgado de Primera Instancia,

— in France, to the presiding judge of the tribunal de grande instance,

— in Ireland, to the High Court,

— in Iceland, to the héraðsdómari,

— in Italy, to the corte d'appello,

— in Luxembourg, to the presiding judge of the tribunal d'arrondissement,

— in The Netherlands, to the presiding judge of the arrondissementsrechtbank,

— in Norway, to the herredsrett or byrett as namsrett,

— in Austria, to the Landesgericht or the Kreisgericht,

— in Portugal, to the Tribunal Judicial de Círculo,

— in Switzerland:

(a) in respect of judgments ordering the payment of a sum of money, to the juge de la mainlevée/Rechtsöffnungsrichter/giudice competente a pronunciare sul rigetto dell'opposizione, within the framework of the procedure governed by Articles 80 and 81 of the loi fédérale sur la poursuite pour dettes et la faillite/Bundesgesetz über Schuldbetreibung und Konkurs/legge federale sulla esecuzione e sul fallimento;

(b) in respect of judgments ordering a performance other than the payment of a sum of money, to the juge cantonal d'exequatur compétent/zuständiger kantonaler Vollstreckungsrichter/giudice cantonale competente a pronunciare l'exequatur,

— in Finland, to the ulosotonhaltija/överexekutor,

— in Sweden, to the Svea hovrätt,

— in the United Kingdom:

(a) in England and Wales, to the High Court of Justice, or in the case of a maintenance judgment to the Magistrates' Court on transmission by the Secretary of State;

(b) in Scotland, to the Court of Session, or in the case of a maintenance judgment to the Sheriff Court on transmission by the Secretary of State;

(c) in Northern Ireland, to the High Court of Justice, or in the case of a maintenance judgment to the Magistrates' Court on transmission by the Secretary of State.

2. The jurisdiction of local courts shall be determined by reference to the place of domicile of the party against whom enforcement is sought. If he is not domiciled in the State in which enforcement is sought, it shall be determined by reference to the place of enforcement.

Article 37

1. An appeal against the decision authorising enforcement shall be lodged in accordance with the rules governing procedure in contentious matters:

- in Belgium, with the tribunal de première instance or rechtbank van eerste aanleg,
- in Denmark, with the landsret,
- in the Federal Republic of Germany, with the Oberlandesgericht,
- in Greece, with the ἐφετείο,
- in Spain, with the Audiencia Provincial,
- in France, with the cour d'appel,
- in Ireland, with the High Court,
- in Iceland, with the héraðsdómari,
- in Italy, with the corte d'appello,
- in Luxembourg, with the Court supérieure de justice sitting as a court of civil appeal,
- in The Netherlands, with the arrondissementsrechtbank,
- in Norway, with the lagmannsrett,
- in Austria, with the Landesgericht or the Kreisgericht,
- in Portugal, with the Tribunal de Relação,
- in Switzerland, with the tribunal cantonal/Kantonsgericht/tribunale cantonale,
- in Finland, with the hovioikeus/hovrätt,
- in Sweden, with the Svea hovrätt
- in the United Kingdom—
  - (a) in England and Wales, with the High Court of Justice, or in the case of a maintenance judgment with the Magistrates' Court;
  - (b) in Scotland, with the Court of Session, or in the case of a maintenance judgment with the Sheriff Court;
  - (c) in Northern Ireland, with the High Court of Justice, or in the case of a maintenance judgment with the Magistrates' Court.

2. The judgment given on the appeal may be contested only:
- in Belgium, Greece, Spain, France, Italy, Luxembourg and in The Netherlands, by an appeal in cassation,
- in Denmark, by an appeal to the højesteret, with the leave of the Minister of Justice,
- in the Federal Republic of Germany, by a Rechtsbeschwerde,
- in Ireland, by an appeal on a point of law to the Supreme Court,
- in Iceland, by an appeal to the Hæstiréttur,
- in Norway, by an appeal (kjæremål or anke) to the Hoyesteretts Kjæremålsutvalg or Hoyesterett,
- in Austria, in the case of an appeal, by a Revisionsrekurs and, in the case of opposition proceedings, by a Berufung with the possibility of a Revision,
- in Portugal, by an appeal on a point of law,
- in Switzerland, by a recours de droit public devant le tribunal fédéral/staatsrechtliche Beschwerde beim Bundesgericht/ricorso di diritto pubblico davanti al tribunale federale,
- in Finland, by an appeal to the korkein oikeus/högsta domstolen,
- in Sweden, by an appeal to the högsta domstolen,
- in the United Kingdom, by a single further appeal on a point of law.

Article 40

1. If the application for enforcement is refused, the applicant may appeal:
    — in Belgium, to the cour d'appel or hof van beroep,
    — in Denmark, to the landsret,
    — in the Federal Republic of Germany, to the Oberlandesgericht,
    — in Greece, to the ἐφετείο,
    — in Spain, to the Audiencia Provincial,
    — in France, to the cour d'appel,
    — in Ireland, to the High Court,
    — in Iceland, to the héraðsdómari,
    — in Italy, to the corte d'appello,
    — in Luxembourg, to the Cour supérieure de justice sitting as a court of civil appeal,
    — in The Netherlands, to the gerechtshof,
    — in Norway, to the lagmannsrett,
    — in Austria, to the Landesgericht or the Kreisgericht,
    — in Portugal, to the Tribunal de Relação,
    — in Switzerland, to the tribunal cantonal/Kantonsgericht/tribunale cantonale,
    — in Finland, to the hovioikeus/hovrätt,
    — in Sweden, to the Svea hovrätt,
    — in the United Kingdom:
        (a) in England and Wales, to the High Court of Justice, or in the case of a maintenance judgment to the Magistrates' Court;
        (b) in Scotland, to the Court of Session, or in the case of a maintenance judgment to the Sheriff Court;
        (c) in Northern Ireland, to the High Court of Justice, or in the case of a maintenance judgment to the Magistrates' Court.

2. The party against whom enforcement is sought shall be summoned to appear before the appellate court. If he fails to appear, the provisions of the second and third paragraphs of Article 20 shall apply even where he is not domiciled in any of the Contracting States.

Article 41

A judgment given on appeal provided for in Article 40 may be contested only:
    — in Belgium, Greece, Spain, France, Italy, Luxembourg and in The Netherlands, by an appeal in cassation,
    — in Denmark, by an appeal to the højesteret, with the leave of the Minister of Justice,
    — in the Federal Republic of Germany, by a Rechtsbeschwerde,
    — in Ireland, by an appeal on a point of law to the Supreme Court,
    — in Iceland, by an appeal to the Hæstiréttur,
    — in Norway, by an appeal (kjæremål or anke) to the Hoyesteretts kjæremålsutvalg or Hoyesterett,
    — in Austria, by a Revisionsrekurs,

— in Portugal, by an appeal on a point of law,
— in Switzerland, by a recours de droit public devant le tribunal fédéral/ staatsrechtliche Beschwerde beim Bundesgericht/ricorso di diritto pubblico davanti al tribunale federale,
— in Finland, by an appeal to the korkein oikeus/högsta domstolen,
— in Sweden, by an appeal to the högsta domstolen,
— in the United Kingdom, by a single further appeal on a point of law.

Article 44

An applicant who, in the State of origin, has benefited from complete or partial legal aid or exemption from costs or expenses, shall be entitled, in the procedures provided for in Articles 32 to 35, to benefit from the most favourable legal aid or the most extensive exemption from costs or expenses provided for by the law of the State addressed.

However, an applicant who requests the enforcement of a decision given by an administrative authority in Denmark or in Iceland in respect of a maintenance order may, in the State addressed, claim the benefits referred to in the first paragraph if he presents a statement from, respectively, the Danish Ministry of Justice or the Icelandic Ministry of Justice to the effect that he fulfils the economic requirements to qualify for the grant of complete or partial legal aid or exemption from costs or expenses.

Article 54

The provisions of this Convention shall apply only to legal proceedings instituted and to documents formally drawn up or registered as authentic instruments after its entry into force in the State of origin and, where recognition or enforcement of a judgment or authentic instrument is sought, in the State addressed.

However, judgments given after the date of entry into force of this Convention between the State of origin and the State addressed in proceedings instituted before that date shall be recognized and enforced in accordance with the provisions of Title III if jurisdiction was founded upon rules which accorded with those provided for either in Title II of this Convention or in a convention concluded between the State of origin and the State addressed which was in force when the proceedings were instituted.

If the parties to a dispute concerning a contract had agreed in writing before the entry into force of this Convention that the contract was to be governed by the law of Ireland or a part of the United Kingdom, the courts of Ireland or of that part of the United Kingdom shall retain the right to exercise jurisdiction in the dispute.

Article 54A

For a period of three years from the entry into force of this Convention for Denmark, Greece, Ireland, Iceland, Norway, Finland and Sweden, respectively, jurisdiction in maritime matters shall be determined in these States not only in accordance with the provisions of Title II, but also in accordance with the provisions of paragraphs 1 to 7 following. However, upon the entry into force of the International Convention relating to the arrest of sea-going ships, signed at Brussels on 10 May 1952, for one of these States, these provisions shall cease to have effect for that State.

1. A person who is domiciled in a Contracting State may be sued in the courts of one of the States mentioned above in respect of a maritime claim if the ship to which the claim relates or any other ship owned by him has been arrested by judicial process within the territory of the latter State to secure the claim, or could have been so arrested there but bail or other security has been given, and either:
   (a) the claimant is domiciled in the latter State; or
   (b) the claim arose in the latter State; or
   (c) the claim concerns the voyage during which the arrest was made or could have been made; or
   (d) the claim arises out of a collision or out of damage caused by a ship to another ship or to goods or persons on board either ship, either by the execution or non-execution of a manoeuvre or by the non-observance of regulations; or
   (e) the claim is for salvage; or
   (f) the claim is in respect of a mortgage or hypothecation of the ship arrested.

2. A claimant may arrest either the particular ship to which the maritime claim relates, or any other ship which is owned by the person who was, at the time when the maritime claim arose, the owner of the particular ship. However, only the particular ship to which the maritime claim relates may be arrested in respect of the maritime claims set out in 5.(o), (p) or (q) of this Article.

3. Ships shall be deemed to be in the same ownership when all the shares therein are owned by the same person or persons.

4. When in the case of a charter by demise of a ship the charterer alone is liable in respect of a maritime claim relating to that ship, the claimant may arrest that ship or any other ship owned by the charterer, but no other ship owned by the owner may be arrested in respect of such claim. The same shall apply to any case in which a person other than the owner of a ship is liable in respect of a maritime claim relating to that ship.

5. The expression 'maritime claim' means a claim arising out of one or more of the following:
   (a) damage caused by any ship either in collision or otherwise;
   (b) loss of life or personal injury caused by any ship or occurring in connection with the operation of any ship;
   (c) salvage;
   (d) agreement relating to the use or hire of any ship whether by charterparty or otherwise;
   (e) agreement relating to the carriage of goods in any ship whether by charterparty or otherwise;
   (f) loss of or damage to goods including baggage carried in any ship;

(g)   general average;

(h)   bottomry;

(i)   towage;

(j)   pilotage;

(k)   goods or materials wherever supplied to a ship for her operation or maintenance;

(l)   construction, repair or equipment of any ship or dock charges and dues;

(m)   wages of masters, officers or crew;

(n)   master's disbursements, including disbursements made by shippers, charterers or agents on behalf of a ship or her owner;

(o)   dispute as to the title to or ownership of any ship;

(p)   disputes between co-owners of any ship as to the ownership, possession, employment or earnings of that ship;

(q)   the mortgage or hypothecation of any ship.

6.   In Denmark, the expression 'arrest' shall be deemed, as regards the maritime claims referred to in 5.(o) and (p) of this Article, to include a 'forbud', where that is the only procedure allowed in respect of such a claim under Articles 646 to 653 of the law on civil procedure (lov om rettens pleje).

7.   In Iceland, the expression 'arrest' shall be deemed, as regards the maritime claims referred to in 5.(o) and (p) of this Article, to include a 'lögbann', where that is the only procedure allowed in respect of such a claim under Chapter III of the law on arrest and injunction (lög um kyrrsetningu og lögbann).

Article 54B

1.   This Convention shall not prejudice the application by the Member States of the European Communities of the Convention on Jurisdiction and the Enforcement of Judgments in Civil and Commercial Matters, signed at Brussels on 27 September 1968 and of the Protocol on interpretation of that Convention by the Court of Justice, signed at Luxembourg on 3 June 1971, as amended by the Conventions of Accession to the said Convention and the said Protocol by the States acceding to the European Communities, all of these Conventions and the Protocol being hereinafter referred to as the 'Brussels Convention'.

2.   However, this Convention shall in any event be applied:

(a)   in matters of jurisdiction, where the defendant is domiciled in the territory of a Contracting State which is not a member of the European Communities, or where Article 16 or 17 of this Convention confers a jurisdiction on the courts of such a Contracting State;

(b)   in relation to a *lis pendens* or to related actions as provided for in Articles 21 and 22, when proceedings are instituted in a Contracting State which is not a member of the European Communities and in a Contracting State which is a member of the European Communities;

(c)   in matters of recognition and enforcement, where either the State of origin or the State addressed is not a member of the European Communities.

3.   In addition to the grounds provided for in Title III recognition or enforcement may be refused if the ground of jurisdiction on which the judgment has been based differs from that resulting from this Convention and recognition or enforcement is sought against a party who is domiciled in a Contracting State which is not a member of the European Communities, unless the judgment may otherwise be recognised or enforced under any rule of law in the State addressed.

Article 55

Subject to the provisions of the second paragraph of Article 54 and of Article 56, this Convention shall, for the States which are parties to it, supersede the following conventions concluded between two or more of them:

—   the Convention between the Swiss Confederation and France on jurisdiction and enforcement of judgments in civil matters, signed at Paris on 15 June 1869,
—   the Treaty between the Swiss Confederation and Spain on the mutual enforcement of judgments in civil or commercial matters, signed at Madrid on 19 November 1986,
—   the Convention between the Swiss Confederation and the German Reich on the recognition and enforcement of judgments and arbitration awards, signed at Berne on 2 November 1929,
—   the Convention between Denmark, Finland, Iceland, Norway and Sweden on the recognition and enforcement of judgments, signed at Copenhagen on 16 March 1932,
—   the Convention between the Swiss Confederation and Italy on the recognition and enforcement of judgments, signed at Rome on 3 January 1933,
—   the Convention between Sweden and the Swiss Confederation on the recognition and enforcement of judgments and arbitral awards, signed at Stockholm on 15 January 1936,
—   the Convention between the Kingdom of Belgium and Austria on reciprocal recognition and enforcement of judgments and authentic instruments relating to maintenance obligations, signed at Vienna on 25 October 1957,
—   the Convention between the Swiss Confederation and Belgium on the recognition and enforcement of judgments and arbitration awards, signed at Berne on 29 April 1959,
—   the Convention between the Federal Republic of Germany and Austria on the reciprocal recognition and enforcement of judgments, settlements and authentic instruments in civil and commercial matters, signed at Vienna on 6 June 1959,
—   the Convention between the Kingdom of Belgium and Austria on the reciprocal recognition and enforcement of judgments, arbitral awards

and authentic instruments in civil and commercial matters, signed at Vienna on 16 June 1959,

— the Convention between Austria and the Swiss Confederation on the recognition and enforcement of judgments, signed at Berne on 16 December 1960,

— the Convention between Norway and the United Kingdom providing for the reciprocal recognition and enforcement of judgments in civil matters, signed at London on 12 June 1961,

— the Convention between the United Kingdom and Austria providing for the reciprocal recognition and enforcement of judgments in civil and commercial matters, signed at Vienna on 14 July 1961, with amending Protocol signed at London on 6 March 1970,

— the Convention between the Kingdom of The Netherlands and Austria on the reciprocal recognition and enforcement of judgments and authentic instruments in civil and commercial matters, signed at The Hague on 6 February 1963,

— the Convention between France and Austria on the recognition and enforcement of judgments and authentic instruments in civil and commercial matters, signed at Vienna on 15 July 1966,

— the Convention between Luxembourg and Austria on the recognition and enforcement of judgments and authentic instruments in civil and commercial matters, signed at Luxembourg on 29 July 1971,

— the Convention between Italy and Austria on the recognition and enforcement of judgments in civil and commercial matters, of judicial settlements and of authentic instruments, signed at Rome on 16 November 1971,

— the Convention between Norway and the Federal Republic of Germany on the recognition and enforcement of judgments and enforceable documents, in civil and commercial matters, signed at Oslo on 17 June 1977,

— the Convention between Denmark, Finland, Iceland, Norway and Sweden on the recognition and enforcement of judgments in civil matters, signed at Copenhagen on 11 October 1977,

— the Convention between Austria and Sweden on the recognition and enforcement of judgments in civil matters, signed at Stockholm on 16 September 1982,

— the Convention between Austria and Spain on the recognition and enforcement of judgments, settlements and enforceable authentic instruments in civil and commercial matters, signed at Vienna on 17 February 1984,

— the Convention between Norway and Austria on the recognition and enforcement of judgments in civil matters, signed at Vienna on 21 May 1984, and

— the Convention between Finland and Austria on the recognition and enforcement of judgments in civil matters, signed at Vienna on 17 November 1986.

Article 57

1.   This Convention shall not affect any conventions to which the Contracting States are or will be parties and which, in relation to particular matters, govern jurisdiction or the recognition or enforcement of judgments.

2.   This Convention shall not prevent a court of a Contracting State which is party to a convention referred to in the first paragraph from assuming jurisdiction in accordance with that convention, even where the defendant is domiciled in a Contracting State which is not a party to that convention. The court hearing the action shall, in any event, apply Article 20 of this Convention.

3.   Judgments given in a Contracting State by a court in the exercise of jurisdiction provided for in a convention referred to in the first paragraph shall be recognised and enforced in the other Contracting States in accordance with Title III of this Convention.

4.   In addition to the grounds provided for in Title III, recognition or enforcement may be refused if the State addressed is not a contracting party to a convention referred to in the first paragraph and the person against whom recognition or enforcement is sought is domiciled in that State, unless the judgment may otherwise be recognised or enforced under any rule of law in the State addressed.

5.   Where a convention referred to in the first paragraph to which both the State of origin and the State addressed are parties lays down conditions for the recognition or enforcement of judgments, those conditions shall apply. In any event, the provisions of this Convention which concern the procedures for recognition and enforcement of judgments may be applied.

Article 60

The following may be parties to this Convention:
(a)   States which, at the time of the opening of this Convention for signature, are members of the European Communities or of the European Free Trade Association;
(b)   States which, after the opening of this Convention for signature, become members of the European Communities or of the European Free Trade Association;
(c)   States invited to accede in accordance with Article 62(1)(b).

Article 61

1.   This Convention shall be opened for signature by the States members of the European Communities or of the European Free Trade Association.

2.   The Convention shall be submitted for ratification by the signatory States. The instruments of ratification shall be deposited with the Swiss Federal Council.

3.   The Convention shall enter into force on the first day of the third month following the date on which two States, of which one is a member of the European Communities and the other a member of the European Free Trade Association, deposit their instruments of ratification.

4. The Convention shall take effect in relation to any other signatory State on the first day of the third month following the deposit of its instrument of ratification.

Article 62

1. After entering into force this Convention shall be open to accession by:
   (a) the States referred to in Article 60(b);
   (b) other States which have been invited to accede upon a request made by one of the Contracting States to the depositary State. The depositary State shall invite the State concerned to accede only if, after having communicated the contents of the communications that this State intends to make in accordance with Article 63, it has obtained the unanimous agreement of the signatory States and the Contracting States referred to in Article 60(a) and (b).

2. If an acceding State wishes to furnish details for the purposes of Protocol No. 1, negotiations shall be entered into to that end. A negotiating conference shall be convened by the Swiss Federal Council.

3. In respect of an acceding State, the Convention shall take effect on the first day of the third month following the deposit of its instrument of accession.

4. However, in respect of an acceding State referred to in paragraph 1(a) or (b), the Convention shall take effect only in relations between the acceding State and the Contracting States which have not made any objections to the accession before the first day of the third month following the deposit of the instrument of accession.

Article 63

Each acceding State shall, when depositing its instrument of accession, communicate the information required for the application of Articles 3, 32, 37, 40, 41 and 55 of this Convention and furnish, if need be, the details prescribed during the negotiations for the purposes of Protocol No. 1.

Article 64

1. This Convention is concluded for an initial period of five years from the date of its entry into force in accordance with Article 61(3), even in the case of States which ratify it or accede to it after that date.

2. At the end of the initial five-year period, the Convention shall be automatically renewed from year to year.

3. Upon the expiry of the initial five-year period, any Contracting State may, at any time, denounce the Convention by sending a notification to the Swiss Federal Council.

4. The denunciation shall take effect at the end of the calendar year following the expiry of a period of six months from the date of receipt by the Swiss Federal Council of the notification of denunciation.

Article 65

The following are annexed to this Convention:

— a Protocol No. 1, on certain questions of jurisdiction, procedure and enforcement,
— a Protocol No. 2, on the uniform interpretation of the Convention,
— a Protocol No. 3, on the application of Article 57.
These Protocols shall form an integral part of the Convention.

Article 66

Any Contracting State may request the revision of this Convention. To that end, the Swiss Federal Council shall issue invitations to a revision conference within a period of six months from the date of the request for revision.

Article 67

The Swiss Federal Council shall notify the States represented at the Diplomatic Conference of Lugano and the States who have later acceded to the Convention of:
(a) the deposit of each instrument of ratification or accession;
(b) the dates of entry into force of this Convention in respect of the Contracting States;
(c) any denunciation received pursuant to Article 64;
(d) any declaration received pursuant to Article Ia of Protocol No. 1;
(e) any declaration received pursuant to Article Ib of Protocol No. 1;
(f) any declaration received pursuant to Article IV of Protocol No. 1;
(g) any communication made pursuant to Article VI of Protocol No. 1.

Article 68

This Convention, drawn up in a single original in the Danish, Dutch, English, Finnish, French, German, Greek, Icelandic, Irish, Italian, Norwegian, Portuguese, Spanish and Swedish languages, all fourteen texts being equally authentic, shall be deposited in the archives of the Swiss Federal Council. The Swiss Federal Council shall transmit a certified copy to the Government of each State represented at the Diplomatic Conference of Lugano and to the Government of each acceding State.

PROTOCOL No. 1

ON CERTAIN QUESTIONS OF JURISDICTION, PROCEDURE AND ENFORCEMENT

The High Contracting Parties have agreed upon the following provisions, which shall be annexed to the Convention:

Article Ia

1. Switzerland reserves the right to declare, at the time of depositing its instrument of ratification, that a judgment given in another Contracting State shall be neither recognised nor enforced in Switzerland if the following conditions are met:
(a) the jurisdiction of the court which has given the judgment is based only on Article 5(1) of this Convention; and

    (b)   the defendant was domiciled in Switzerland at the time of the intro-
          duction of the proceedings; for the purposes of this Article, a
          company or other legal person is considered to be domiciled in
          Switzerland if it has its registered seat and the effective centre of
          activities in Switzerland; and
    (c)   the defendant raises an objection to the recognition or enforcement
          of the judgment in Switzerland, provided that he has not waived the
          benefit of the declaration foreseen under this paragraph.

2.   This reservation shall not apply to the extent that at the time recognition or enforcement is sought a derogation has been granted from Article 59
of the Swiss Federal Constitution. The Swiss Government shall communicate
such derogations to the signatory States and the acceding States.

3.   This reservation shall cease to have effect on 31 December 1999. It may
be withdrawn at any time.

Article Ib

Any Contracting State may, by declaration made at the time of signing or of
deposit of its instrument of ratification or of accession, reserve the right,
notwithstanding the provisions of Article 28, not to recognise and enforce
judgments given in the other Contracting States if the jurisdiction of the court
of the State of origin is based, pursuant to Article 16(1)(b), exclusively on the
domicile of the defendant in the State of origin, and the property is situated in
the territory of the State which entered the reservation.

Article IV

Judicial and extrajudicial documents drawn up in one Contracting State
which have to be served on persons in another Contracting State shall be
transmitted in accordance with the procedures laid down in the conventions
and agreements concluded between the Contracting States.

Unless the State in which service is to take place objects by declaration to
the Swiss Federal Council, such documents may also be sent by the appropriate public officers of the State in which the document has been drawn up
directly to the appropriate public officers of the State in which the addressee
is to be found. In this case the officer of the State of origin shall send a copy
of the document to the officer of the State applied to who is competent to
forward it to the addressee. The document shall be forwarded in the manner
specified by the law of the State applied to. The forwarding shall be recorded
by a certificate sent directly to the officer of the State of origin.

Article V

The jurisdiction specified in Articles 6(2) and 10 in actions on a warranty or
guarantee or in any other third party proceedings may not be resorted to in the
Federal Republic of Germany, in Spain, in Austria and in Switzerland. Any
person domiciled in another Contracting State may be sued in the courts:
    —   of the Federal Republic of Germany, pursuant to Articles 68, 72, 73
         and 74 of the code of civil procedure (Zivilprozeßordnung) concerning
         third-party notices,

— of Spain, pursuant to Article 1482 of the civil code,
— of Austria, pursuant to Article 21 of the code of civil procedure (Zivilprozeßordnung) concerning third-party notices,
— of Switzerland, pursuant to the appropriate provisions concerning third-party notices of the cantonal codes of civil procedure.

Judgments given in the other Contracting States by virtue of Article 6(2) or Article 10 shall be recognised and enforced in the Federal Republic of Germany, in Spain, in Austria and in Switzerland in accordance with Title III. Any effects which judgments given in these States may have on third parties by application of the provisions in the preceding paragraph shall also be recognised in the other Contracting States.

Article Va

In matters relating to maintenance, the expression 'court' includes the Danish, Icelandic and Norwegian administrative authorities.

In civil and commercial matters, the expression 'court' includes the Finnish ulosotonhaltija/överexekutor.

Article Vb

In proceedings involving a dispute between the master and a member of the crew of a sea-going ship registered in Denmark, in Greece, in Ireland, in Iceland, in Norway, in Portugal or in Sweden concerning remuneration or other conditions of service, a court in a Contracting State shall establish whether the diplomatic or consular officer responsible for the ship has been notified of the dispute. It shall stay the proceedings so long as he has not been notified. It shall of its own motion decline jurisdiction if the officer, having been duly notified, has exercised the powers accorded to him in the matter by a consular convention, or in the absence of such a convention has, within the time allowed, raised any objection to the exercise of such jurisdiction.

Article VI

The Contracting States shall communicate to the Swiss Federal Council the text of any provisions of their laws which amend either those provisions of their laws mentioned in the Convention or the lists of courts specified in Section 2 of Title III.

PROTOCOL NO. 2
ON THE UNIFORM INTERPRETATION OF THE CONVENTION
Preamble

The High Contracting Parties,
Having regard to Article 65 of this Convention,
Considering the substantial link between this Convention and the Brussels Convention,
Considering that the Court of Justice of the European Communities by virtue of the Protocol of 3 June 1971 has jurisdiction to give rulings on the interpretation of the provisions of the Brussels Convention,

Being aware of the rulings delivered by the Court of Justice of the European Communities on the interpretation of the Brussels Convention up to the time of signature of this Convention,

Considering that the negotiations which led to the conclusion of the Convention were based on the Brussels Convention in the light of these rulings,

Desiring to prevent, in full deference to the independence of the courts, divergent interpretations and to arrive at as uniform an interpretation as possible of the provisions of the Convention, and of these provisions and those of the Brussels Convention which are substantially reproduced in this Convention,

Have agreed as follows:

Article 1

The courts of each Contracting State shall, when applying and interpreting the provisions of the Convention, pay due account to the principles laid down by any relevant decision delivered by courts of the other Contracting States concerning provisions of this Convention.

Article 2

1.   The Contracting Parties agree to set up a system of exchange of information concerning judgments delivered pursuant to this Convention as well as relevant judgments under the Brussels Convention. This system shall comprise:
— transmission to a central body by the competent authorities of judgments delivered by courts of last instance and the Court of Justice of the European Communities as well as judgments of particular importance which have become final and have been delivered pursuant to this Convention or the Brussels Convention,
— classification of these judgments by the central body including, as far as necessary, the drawing-up and publication of translations and abstracts,
— communication by the central body of the relevant documents to the competent national authorities of all signatories and acceding States to the Convention and to the Commission of the European Communities.

2.   The central body is the Registrar of the Court of Justice of the European Communities.

Article 3

1.   A Standing Committee shall be set up for the purposes of this Protocol.

2.   The Committee shall be composed of representatives appointed by each signatory and acceding State.

3.   The European Communities (Commission, Court of Justice and General Secretariat of the Council) and the European Free Trade Association may attend the meetings as observers.

Article 4

1.   At the request of a Contracting Party, the depositary of the Convention shall convene meetings of the Committee for the purpose of exchanging views on the functioning of the Convention and in particular on:

— the development of the case-law as communicated under the first paragraph first indent of Article 2,

— the application of Article 57 of the Convention.

2.   The Committee, in the light of these exchanges, may also examine the appropriateness of starting on particular topics a revision of the Convention and make recommendations.

PROTOCOL No. 3
ON THE APPLICATION OF ARTICLE 57

The High Contracting Parties have agreed as follows:

1.   For the purposes of the Convention, provisions which, in relation to particular matters, govern jurisdiction or the recognition or enforcement of judgments and which are, or will be, contained in acts of the institutions of the European Communities shall be treated in the same way as the conventions referred to in paragraph 1 of Article 57.

2.   If one Contracting State is of the opinion that a provision contained in an act of the institutions of the European Communities is incompatible with the Convention, the Contracting States shall promptly consider amending the Convention pursuant to Article 66, without prejudice to the procedure established by Protocol No. 2.

SELECTED
BIBLIOGRAPHY

AUSTRIA

1. *Austrian Civil Procedure: Basics and Trial Proceeding*

Ballon
Einführung in das österreichische Zivilprozeßrecht—Streitiges Verfahren, 7. Auflage, Graz 1997
Fasching
Lehrbuch des Österreichischen Zivilprozeßrechts, 2. Auflage, Wein 1990
Fasching
Kommentar zu den österreichischen Zivilprozeßgesetzen, 5 Bände, 1. Auflage, Wien 1959–1974
Rechberger, Simotta
Grundriß des österreichischen Zivilprozeßrechts (Erkenntnisverfahren), 4. Auflage, Wien 1994
Rechberger (Ed)
Kommentar zur Zivilprozeßordnung (JN and ZPO), Wien 1994
Stohanzl
Jurisdicktionsnorm und Zivilprozeßordnung, 14. Auflage, Wien 1990

2. *Austrian Execution Law*

Angst/Jakusch/Pimmer
Die Exekutionsordnung, 13. Auflage, Wien 1995

Heller, Berger, Stix
Kommentar zur Exekutionsordnung, 3 Bände, 4. Auflage, Wien 1969–1976
Holzhammer
Österreichisches Zwangsvollstreckungsrecht, 4. Auflage, Wien 1993
Rechberger, Oberhammer
Exekutionsrecht, Wien 1997
Schoibl
National report 'Enforcement in Austria', in Kaye ed, *Methods of Execution of Orders and Judgments in Europe*, Chichester 1996, 3 ff

3.   *(Austrian) Digest of International treaties*

Loewe
Zwischenstaatlicher Rechtsverkehr in Zivilrechtssachen, 1. Auflag, Wien 1984 mit ErgBand 1987

4.   *(Austrian selected) Introduction into the European Conventions Law*

Bajons/Mayr/Zeiler (Ed)
Die Übereinkommen von Brüssel und Lugano, Wien 1997 (incl for example SCHOIBL, Ausgewählte Zuständigkeitstatbestände in der Rechtsprechung des EuGH: Die gerichtlichen Zuständigkeiten am Erfüllungsort des Vertrages nach Art 5 Nr 1 und die Zuständigkeitsvereinbarung nach Art 17 des Brüsseler und des Luganer Übereinkommens, 61 ff)
Schoibl
Die inländische Niederlassung als Anknüpfungspunkt im osterreichischen internationalen Zivilprozeßrecht, in: Schuhmacher/Gruber Ed, Rechtsfragen der Zweigniederlassung, Wien 1993, 375 ff

BELGIUM

Born, H. and Fallon, M.
'Chronique de jurisprudence—Droit judicaire international (1978–1982)', *Journal des Tribunaux*, 1983, 212
Born, H. and Fallon, M.
'Chronique de jurisprudence—Droit judicaire international (1983–1986)', *Journal des Tribunaux*, 1987, 481
Born, H. and Fallon, M.
'Chronique de jurisprudence—Droit judicaire international (1986–1990)', *Journal des Tribunaux*, 1992, 401
Born, H.
'Le régime général des clauses attibutives de juridiction dans la Convention de Bruxelles', *Journal des Tribunaux*, 1995, 353

Caupain, M.
'Het toepassingsgebied van de Conventie van Brussel van 27 September 1968', *De gerechtsdeurwaarder*, 1991, 90

De Weerdt, I.
'Bevoegdheidsbeding in cognossement voor de Belgische rechter', *European Transport Law*, 1987, 317

Ekelmans, M.
'Note sur la litispendance internationale', *Revue de Droit Commercial Belge*, 1993, 1089

Ekelmans
'L'exclusion de l'arbitrage du champ d'application de la Convention de Bruxelles', *Journal des Tribunaux*, 1992, 495

Erauw, J.
'De verdragen van Brussel en Lugano uit mekaar houden voor internationale bevoegdheid en exequatur', *Revue de Droit Commercial Belge*, 1996, 772

Jenard, P.
'La Convention de Bruxelles et les Conventions d'adhésion', *Répertoire Notarial*, Tome XI, Livre VI, Droit Notarial

Jenard, P.
'Le cas de refus d'exécution le plus souvent retenu: l'article 27 alinéa 2', in *Les Conventions de Bruxelles et de La Haye en matière civile et commerciale*

De Leval, G. (ed.)
La Charte, Union Internationale des Huissiers, Looseleaf

Kohl, A.
'Les conditions de la reconnaissance d'une décisions intervenue contre un défendeur défaillant. Remarques au sujet de l'article 27, 2 de la Convention de Bruxelles du 27 Septembre 1968', *Actualités du Droit*, 1992, 819

Krings, E.
'Réflexion au sujet de la prorogation de compétence territoriale et due for contractuel', *Revue de droit international et de droit comparé*, 1978, 90

Laenens, J.
'Het internationaal privaatrechtelijk procesrecht en de bevoegdheidsclausules', *Tijdschrift voor Privaatrecht*, 1982, 215

Laenens, J.
'De doorwerking van het Europees Gemeenschapsrecht in het procesrecht. De civiele procesgang in Eurpees perspectief', *Rechtskundig Weekblad*, 1995–96, 1172

Lenaerts, K. and Verbruggen, M.
'Jurisprudentie van het Hof van Justitie van de Europese Gemeeschappen over het Verdrag van Brussel van 27 September 1968 betreffende de rechterlijke bevoegdheid en de tenuitvoerlegging van beslissingen in burgerlijke en handelszaken', *Revue de Droit Commercial Belge*, 1991, 760

Nelissen Grade, J.M., Verbist, J. & Raes, S.
'Belgium', *World Litigation Law and Practice* (Mytrick, R.E. (ed.), Transnational Juris Publishing, New York, 1989)

Pertegás Sender, M.
L'intérêt de l'enfant dans l'adoption internationale, RBDC/TBBR (Tijdschrift voor Burgerlijk Belgisch Recht) 1995, 278–283

Pertegás Sender, M.
Judgment commentary of E.C.J., 7 March 1995, *Fiona Shevill* (case C-68/93), *Col. J. Eur. L.* (Columbia Journal of European Law) 1995, 497–504

Pertegás Sender, M
Judgment commentary of E.C.J., 14 December 1995, *Peterbroeck v België* (case C-312/93), *Col. J. Eur. L.* 1995/96, 179–185

Das, H. and Pertegás Sender, M.
Het dossier 'Moreno en García': recht en diplomatie, *V.J.V.* (Vlaams Jurist Vandaag) 1996, 4–5

Pertegás Sender, M.
Judgment commentary of E.C.J., 14 March 1996, *Van der Linden* (case C-275/94), *R.E.D.I.* (Revista Española de Derecho Internacional) 1996, 342–345

Pertegás Sender, M.
Aanhangigheid, samenhang en voorlopige maatregelen, in: Van Houtte, H. en Pertegás Sender, M. (eds.), *Europese IPR-verdragen*, Leuven, Acco, 1997, 409 p., 115–137

Pertegás Sender, M.
Judgment commentary of Court of First Instance Gent, 10 January 1996, *T.B.H./R.D.C.* (Tijdschrift voor Belgisch Handelsrecht) 1997, 33–37

Pergegás Sender, M.
Mesures provisoires extra-territoriales et compétence international du juge belge, judgment commentary of Court of First Instance Hasselt, 20 September 1996, *T.B.H./R.D.C.* 1997, 323–325

Pertegás Sender, M.
De reikwijdte van de begrippen 'onderhoudsverplichting' en 'tot onderhoud gerechtigde' in het kader van het Europees Executieverdrag (EEX), *E.J.* 1997, 116–120

Pertegás Sender, M.
Judgment commentary of E.C.J., 9 January 1997, *P.W. Rutten v. Cross-Medical* (zaak C-383/95), *Col. J. Eur. L.* 1997, 292–298

Pertegás Sender, M.
De reikwijdte van de begrippen 'onderhoudsverplichting' en 'tot onderhoud gerechtidge' in het kader van het Europees Exeutieverdrag (EEX), *Echtscheidingsjournaal*, 1997, 116–120

Roland, R.
'La clause de juridiction du connaissement en droit belge', in *Liber Amicorum Lionel Tricot*, Deventer, Kluwer, 1988, 452

Taelman, P. and Fevery, D.
'La nécessité de procédures provisoires dans les litiges internationaux', *5th World Conference of Procedural Law – Transitional Aspects*, Taormina, 1995

Vandecasteele, A.
'La reconnaissance et l'exécution des mesures provisoires et conservatoires dans la Convention sur la compétence judiciaire et l'exécution des décisions en matière civil et commerciale du 27 Septembre 1968', *Journal des Tribunaux*, 1980, 737

Van Houtte, H.
'Het ogenblik van de betekening bij dagvaarding in het buitenland', *Revue de Droit Commercial Belge*, 1996, 814

Van Houtte, H.
'Wanneer verliest de Belgische rechter rechtsmacht over de beëindiging van een concessie-overeenkomst omdat de zaak bij een andere EEX-rechter aanhangig is?', *Revue de Droit Commercial Belge*, 1995, 420

Van Houtte, H.
'Belgium,' *Encyclopaedia of International Commercial Litigation* (Colman, A. (ed.) Graham & Trotman, London)

Van Houtte, H. and Pertegás Sender, M.
Europese ipr-verdragen, Leuven, Acco, 1997, 410 p.

Watté, N.
'La Convention de Bruxelles relative à la compétence judiciaire et à l'exécution des décisions: quelles version appliquer?', *Revue de Droit Commercial Belge*, 1996, 758

Watté, N. and Marquette, V.
'La Convention de Bruxelles et sa récente interprétation dans les matières commerciales', *Revue de Droit Commercial Belge*, 1996, 783

Wautelet, P.
'De patronaatsverklaring in het IPR', 1997 *Jura Falconis* 317–341

Wautelet, P.
'De verplichtingen van de koper', in *Het Weens Koopverdrag*, Van Houtte, H., Erauw, J. en Wautelet, P. (reds.), Antwerpen, Intersentia, 1997, 155–189

Wautelet, P.
'Juridische apsecten van export', 1997 *Economisch en Sociaal Tijdschrift*

De Wulf, H., en Wautelet, P.
'Internationale aspecten van faillissementen', in *De Nieuwe Faillissementswetgeving*, Dirix, E., Wymeersch, E. en Braeckmans, Y. (eds.), Kluwer, 1997

Wautelet, P.
Commentary on ECJ, 20 Feb. 1997, *Mainschiffahrts-Genossenschaft eG t. Les Gravières Rhénanes*, case C-106/95, *Columbia Journal of European Law*, 1997

Wautelet, P.
Commentary on Rb. Brussel, 10 September 1996, *Tijdschrift voor Belgisch Burgerlijk recht*, 1997

DENMARK

Schmidt
Kvalifikationsproblemet i den internationale privatret, Copenhagen 1954
'The Preliminary Question and the Question of Substitution in the conflict of Laws' in *Scandinavian Studies in Law* 1968, Stockholm 1968
International skilsmisse—og separationsret (doctoral thesis), Copenhagen 1972
Arveret, Copenhagen 1985 (together with three colleagues), Copenhagen 1985, 2nd ed. 1991

International formueret, Copenhagen 1987
'Commentary on the Judgments Convention' in *Kommenteret Retsplejelov*, 4th and 5th ed., Copenhagen 1989 and 1994
'The Incidental Question in Private International Law' in *Recueil des cours de l'Académie de Droit International*, vol. 233 (1992-II), Dordrecht 1993.
'Commentary on the Judgments Convention and the Lugano Convention' in *Karnovs Lovsamling*, 14th ed., Copenhagen 1996

ENGLAND AND WALES

Allwood
'Characteristic Performance and Labour Disputes under the Brussels Convention: Pandora's Box' (1987) 7 *Yearbook of European Law* 131
Austin
'The Infringement of Foreign Intellectual Property Rights' (1997) 113 *Law Quarterly Review* 321
Beaumont and Moir
'Brussels Convention II: A New Private Law Instrument in Family Matters for the European Union or the European Community?' (1995) *European Law Review* 268
Bell
'The Negative Declaration in Transnational Litigation' (1995) 111 *Law Quarterly Review* 674
Blackburn
Lis Alibi Pendens and *Forum Non Conveniens* in Collision Actions after the Civil Jurisdiction and Judgments Act 1982 (1988) *Lloyd's Maritime and Commercial Law Quarterly* 91
Borchers
'Comparing Personal Jurisdiction in the United States and the European Community: Lessons for American Reform' (1992) 40 *American Journal of Comparative Law* 121
Brice
'Maritime Claims: the European Judgments Convention' (1987) *Lloyd's Maritime and Commercial Law Quarterly* 281
Briggs
'The Unrestrained Reach of an Anti-Suit Injunction: A Pause for Thought' (1997) *Lloyd's Maritime and Commercial Law Quarterly* 90
Briggs and Rees
Norton Rose on Civil Jurisdiction and Judgments (1997)
Capper
'Worldwide Mareva Injunctions' (1991) 54 *Modern Law Review* 329
Carter
'Jurisdiction in Defamation Cases' (1992) *British Yearbook of International Law* 519

Cheshire and North
Private International Law, Chaps 10–16 (12th ed., 1992, Butterworths, London)

Collins
Civil Jurisdiction and Judgments Act 1982 (1983, Butterworths, London)
Essays in International Litigation and the Conflict of Laws (1996, Clarendon Press)
'Negative Declarations and the Brussels Convention' (1992) 109 *Law Quarterly Review* 545
'The Territorial Reach of Mareva Injunctions' (1989) 105 *Law Quarterly Review* 262

Dicey and Morris
The Conflict of Laws, Chaps 10–15 (12th ed., 1993, Sweet & Maxwell, London)

Dickinson
'Restitution and the Conflict of Laws' (1996) *Lloyd's Maritime and Commercial Law Quarterly* 556

Fawcett
'Trial in England or Abroad: The Underlying Policy Considerations' (1989) 9 *Oxford Journal of Legal Studies* 205

Guneysu
'The New European Bankruptcy Convention' (1991) 11 *Yearbook of European Law* 295

Harris
'Anti-Suit Injunctions—a home comfort?' (1997) *Lloyd's Maritime and Commercial Law Quarterly* 413
'Recognition of Foreign Judgments at Common Law—The Anti-Suit Injunction Link' (1997) 17 *Oxford Journal of Legal Studies* 477

Hartley
Civil Jurisdiction and Judgments (1982, Sweet & Maxwell, London)
'The Effects of the 1968 Brussels Judgments Convention on Admiralty Actions *In Rem*' (1989) 105 *Law Quarterly Review* 640
'Unnecessary Europeanisation under the Brussels Jurisdiction and Judgments Convention: the Case of the Dissatisfied Sub-Purchaser' (1993) *European Law Review* 506

Hill
The Law Relating to International Commercial Disputes (1994, Lloyd's of London Press Ltd.)
'Jurisdiction in Matters Relating to a Contract under the Brussels Convention' (1995) *International and Comparative Law Quarterly* 591

Hogan
'The Judgments Convention and *Mareva* Injunctions in the United Kingdom and Ireland' (1989) *European Law Review* 191
'Article 22 of the Brussels Convention and the Concept of "First Seisin"' (1992) *European Law Review* 555

'The Brussels Convention, *Forum Non Conveniens* and the Connecting Factors Problem' (1995) *European Law Review* 471

Hunter

'Reinsurance Litigation and the Civil Jurisdiction and Judgments Act 1982' (1987) *Journal of Business Law* 344

Jacob

Private International Litigation (1988, Financial Training Law and Tax)

Jung

'The Brussels and Lugano Conventions: The European Court's Jurisdiction; its Procedures and Methods' (1992) 11 *Civil Justice Quarterly* 38

Kaye

Development of the European Judgments Convention. A Personal Commentary (1998, Barry Rose Publishing, Chichester, England)

Civil Jurisdiction and Enforcement of Foreign Judgments (1987, Butterworths, London)

Private International Law of Tort and Product Liability (1991, Dartmouth, Aldershot)

The New Private International Law of Contract of the European Community under the Rome Contracts Convention (1993, Dartmouth, Aldershot, England)

International Contracts (1993, Barry Rose, Chichester)

An Explanatory Guide to the English Law of Torts (1996, Barry Rose, Chichester)

Damages for Personal Injuries: A European Perspective (1993, John Wiley & Sons Ltd, Chichester) Holding and Kaye, eds

Interpretation of Jurisdiction under the New Italian Private International Law Statute. Some Reflections and the English Experience, Chapter 3 in Salerno ed., 'Convenzioni internazionali e legge di riforma del diritto internazionale privato' (1997, Cedam, Italy)

Execution of Judgments in England and Wales, Chap. 4 in Kaye ed, 'Methods of Execution of Orders and Judgments in Europe' (1996, John Wiley & Sons Ltd, Chichester)

Place of Commission of International Torts, Chap. 8 in McLean ed., 'Compensation for Damage: An International Perspective' (1993, Dartmouth)

'The Geographical Scope of the Jurisdiction and Judgments Convention' (1987) 6 *Litigation Law Journal* 321

'Civil Claims in Criminal Proceedings in Courts of the Common Market: Risks to English Defendants' (1987) 7 *Litigation Law Journal* 13

'Transitional Scope of the Jurisdiction and Judgments Convention' (1988) 7 *Civil Justice Quarterly* 53

'Nationality and the European Judgments Convention' (1988) 37 *International and Comparative Law Quarterly* 268

'The Draft Domicile Bill' (1988) 18 *Family Law* 280

'Domicile: An Unsettled Question' (1988) 138 *New Law Journal* 773

'The Meaning of Domicile under United Kingdom Law for Purposes of the 1968 Brussels Convention' (1988) 35 *Netherlands International Law Review* 181

'No Security for Costs in Convention Enforcement Applications' (1989) *International Litigation and Arbitration* 4

'Extraterritorial *Mareva* Orders: Effects on Third Parties' (1990) 10 *Litigation Law Journal* 20

'*Mareva* Relief Over Actions Abroad' (1989) 133 *Solicitors' Journal* 865

'Powers of Disclosure of Foreign Assets in the English Courts' (1989) 139 *New Law Journal* 875

'Interlocutory Injunctions and Foreign Proceedings: Powers, Jurisdiction and Procedures of the English Courts' (1989) 86 *Law Society's Gazette* 27

'L'Exécution dans le Royaume Unie de Grande-Bretagne et d'Irlande des décisions rendues par les tribunaux belges en application de la Convention de Bruxelles de 1968 sur la compétence judiciaire et l'exécution des décisions en matière civile et commerciale' (1989) 108 *Journal des Tribunaux* 137

'Die Insolvenz des "International Tin Council" vor englischen Gerichten' (1989) 9 *Praxis des Internationalen Privat- und Verfahrensrechts* 179

'Der Beitritt des Vereingten Königreichs zum Brüsseler Übereinkommen von 1968 über die gerichtlichen Entscheidungen in Zivil- und Handelssachen' (1989) 9 *Praxis des Internationalen Privat- und Verfahrensrechts* 403

'International Contracts: Express Terms on Applicable Law, Jurisdiction and Arbitration' (1989) *Law for Business* 79

'Access to the Courts and Enforcement of Judgments in International Contracts' (1989) *Law for Business* 126

'The Role of the Courts in the Arbitration Process' (1989) *Law for Business* 327

'International Commercial Arbitration' (1989) *Law for Business* 368

'Jurisdiction in Shipowners' Liability Limitation Actions: *The Volvox Hollandia*' (1989) 10 *Business Law Review* 285

'Interim Jurisdiction under the European Judgments Convention' (1989) 8 *Litigation Law Journal* 267

'Jurisdiction of English Courts Based Upon Choice of English Law' (1989) 133 *Solicitors' Journal* 1537

'*Situs* of Debts and Jurisdiction to Make Orders of Garnishee' (1989) *Journal of Business Law* 449

'Property Restraint and Disclosure Orders in the English Courts: Extraterritorial Developments' (1989) 10 *The Company Lawyer* 227

'Greek Accession to the Judgments Convention: Transitional Effects in the UK' (1989) 9 *Litigation Law Journal* 47

'Examination of Judgment Debtors as to their Assets Abroad: Courts' Powers and Jurisdiction' (1989) *Lloyd's Maritime and Commercial Law Quarterly* 465

'Extraterritorial *Mareva* Orders and the Relevance of Enforceability' (1990) 9 *Civil Justice Quarterly* 12

'Jurisdiction in Shipowners' Liability Limitation Actions: *The Falstria*' (1990) 9 *Litigation Law Journal* 107

'International Trade Mark Infringement: Territorially Defined Torts and the Double Actionability Rule' (1990) 12 *European Intellectual Property Review* 28

'International Letter Box or Postal Jurisdiction—Not a Second Class Service' (1990) 9 *Civil Justice Quarterly* 330

'Business Insurance and Reinsurance under the European Judgments Convention' (1990) *Journal of Business Law* 517

'Service of Process on Agents Held Generally Invalid' (1990) *Business Law Review* 270

'Stay of Enforcement Proceedings under the European Judgments Convention: Factors Relevant to the Exercise of Discretion' (1991) *Journal of Business Law* 261

'Corporate Jurisdiction under the European Judgments Convention' (1991) 10 *Civil Justice Quarterly* 220

'The Judgments Convention and Arbitration: Mutual Spheres of Influence' (1991) 7 *Arbitration International* 289

'The Contracts (Applicable Law) Act 1990, Parts I and II' (1991) *Law for Business* 194 and 248

'The EEC Judgments Convention and the Outer World: Goodbye to *Forum Non Conveniens*?' (1992) *Journal of Business Law* 47

'International Jurisdiction over Companies. When is an Art Gallery Not an Art Gallery?' (1992) *International Journal of Cultural Property* 185

'Consensual Service of Process Allowed' (1992) *Business Law Review* 59

'The EEC and Arbitration: The Unsettled Wake of The Atlantic Emperor' (1993) 9 *Arbitration International* 27

'Colleges in Court' (1993) 137 *Solicitors' Journal* 816

'Forensic Submission as a Bar to Arbitration' (1993) 12 *Civil Justice Quarterly* 359

'Do Courts Possess a Jurisdictional Discretion in Intra-United Kingdom Cases?' (1994) *Personal Injury Law and Medical Review* 151

'Should there be a New International Jurisdiction Ground for Tourists?' (1994) *Personal Injury Law and Medical Review* 199

'Effect of the European Union's Rome Contracts Convention in the Light of the Previous English Law' (1994) *Trading Law* 385

'International Torts. The Party's Over' (1995) 2 *Personal Injury Law and Medical Review* 24

'The Date upon which an English Court Becomes Seised of Proceedings under the Brussels Convention' (1995) *Journal of Business Law* 217

'Security for Costs in International Cases' (1995) 2 *Personal Injury and Medical Law Review* 118

'A Further Limitation by the European Court upon the Scope of Application of the Brussels Convention' (1995) *Praxis des internationalen Privat- und Verfahrensrecht* 214

'Creation of an English Resulting Trust Held To Fall Outside Article 16(1) of the European Judgments Convention' (1995) *Praxis des internationalen Privat- und Verfahrensrecht* 286

'Recent Developments in the English Private International Law of Tort' (1995) *Praxis des internationalen Privat- und Verfahrensrecht* 406

'Intra-United Kingdom Jurisdiction. High Court Reverses Itself' (1996) *Personal Injury* 19

'Orders against Foreign EU Plaintiffs to Provide Security for Defendants' Costs: a Breach of European Law?' (1996) *Personal Injury* 221

'Security for Costs in International Cases: A Further Instalment' (1997) *Personal Injury* 75

Kaye and Prell

'Powers of English and German Courts to Freeze Parties' Assets by Way of Interim Relief: A Comparison' (1990) 7 *Trading Law* 130

Kennett

'*Forum Non Conveniens* in Europe' (1995) *Cambridge Law Journal* 552

'Place of Performance and Predictability' (1995) 15 Yearbook of European Law 193

Lasok and Stone

Conflict of Laws in the European Community (1987, Professional Books)

Layton

'The Interpretation of the Brussels Convention by the European Court and English Courts' (1992) 11 *Civil Justice Quarterly* 28

Layton & O'Malley

European Civil Practice (1989, Sweet & Maxwell, London)

Lipstein

'Enforcement of Judgments under the Jurisdiction and Judgments Convention: Safeguards' (1987) 36 *International and Comparative Law Quarterly* 873

Matthews

'Security for Costs and European Law' (1994) *Lloyd's Maritime and Commercial Law Quarterly* 454

McCaffery

'The Lugano and San Sebastian Conventions: General Effects' (1992) 11 *Civil Justice Quarterly* 12

Minor

'The Lugano Convention: Some Problems of Interpretation' (1990) *Common Market Law Review* 507

Morse

'Letters of Credit and the Rome Convention' (1994) *Lloyd's Maritime and Commercial Law Quarterly* 560

Peel

'*Forum Non Conveniens* and the Impecunious Plaintiff—Legal Aid and Conditional Fees' (1997) 113 *Law Quarterly Review* 43

Pieri

'The 1968 Brussels Convention: Four Years' Case Law of the European Court of Justice' (1987) *Common Market Law Review* 635

'The 1968 Brussels Convention: The Evolution of the Text and Case Law of the Court of Justice over the last Four Years' (1992) *Common Market Law Review* 537

Polak

'Articles of Association: Choice of forum, EEC Law, Jurisdiction, Shareholders' Title' (1993) *Common Market Law Review* 406

Reed and Kennedy
'International Torts and *Shevill*: the Ghost of Forum Shopping Yet to Come' (1996) *Lloyd's Maritime and Commercial Law Quarterly* 108

Rodger
'Article 17 of the Brussels Convention; Exclusivity is a Must?' (1995) 14 *Civil Justice Quarterly* 250

Rogers
'The Extra-Territorial Reach of the *Mareva* Injunction' (1991) *Lloyd's Maritime and Commercial Law Quarterly* 231

Rose
Restitution and the Conflict of Laws (1995, Gaunt & Sons)

Slater
'*Forum Non Conveniens*: A View from the Shop Floor' (1988) 104 *Law Quarterly Review* 554

Stern
'Judgments in Foreign Currencies: A Comparative Analysis' (1997) *Journal of Business Law* 266

St. J. Smart
'"Ordinarily Resident": Temporary Presence and Prolonged Absence' (1989) 38 *International and Comparative Law Quarterly* 175
'*Forum NonConveniens* in Bankruptcy Proceedings' (1989) *Journal of Business Law* 126
'Carrying on Business as a Basis of Recognition of Foreign Bankruptcies in English Private International Law' (1989) 9 *Oxford Journal of Legal Studies* 557
'Corporate Domicile and Multiple Incorporation in English Private International Law' (1990) *Journal of Business Law* 126
'Domicile of Choice and Multiple Residence' (1990) 10 *Oxford Journal of Legal Studies* 572
'Jurisdiction to Wind Up Companies Incorporated in Northern Ireland' (1996) 45 *International and Comparative Law Quarterly* 177

Stone
'The Lugano Convention on Civil Jurisdiction and Judgments' (1988) 8 *Yearbook of European Law* 105
'Civil Jurisdiction and Judgments—Recent Decisions' (1988) *Lloyd's Maritime and Commercial Law Quarterly* 383

Sturley
'Bill of Lading Choice of Forum Clauses: Comparisons between United States and English Law' (1992) *Lloyd's Maritime and Commercial Law Quarterly* 248

Tugendhat
'Media Law and the Brussels Convention' (1997) 113 *Law Quarterly Review* 360

FINLAND

Koulu, Risto
Täytäntöönpano Luganon ja Brysselin Sopimuksen Perusteella (Enforcement on the Basis of the Lugano and Brussels Conventions (1996, Lakimiesliiton Kustannus, Helsinki)
Moller, Gustaf
Luganokonventionen.- 'Fri rorlig for domar' (Freedom of Movement for Judgments). In Europisk ratt i utveckling. Festskrift utgiven I anledning av Juristklubben Codex' 50-ars jubileumm pp. 134–54 (1990, Helsingfors)
Parikka, Olavi
Luganon Sopimus ja Tuomioistuinten Toimivalta (The Lugano Convention and the Jurisdiction of Courts) pp. 808–17 (1993, Defensor Legis)

FRANCE

Ancel et Lequette
Grands arrêts de la jurisprudence française de droit international privé, Paris, Sirey
Baray
La plénitude de compétence du juge national en sa qualité de juge communautaire, Mélanges Boulouis, Paris, Dalloz, 1991
Batiffol et Lagarde
Droit international privé, Paris, Librairie Générale de Droit et de Jurisprudence (LGDJ)
Boulouis et Chevallier
Grands arrêts de la Cour de Justice des Communatés Européennes, Paris, Dalloz
Droz
Compétence judiciaire et effets des jugements dans le Marché Commun. Etude de la Convention de Bruxelles du 27 Septembre 1968, Paris, Dalloz, 1972
Gaudemet-Tallon
Les Conventions de Bruxelles et de Lugano, Paris, Librairie Générale de Droit et de Jurisprudence, 1993
Gothot et Holleaux
La Convention de Bruxelles du 27 Septembre 1968, Paris, Jupiter, 1985
Holleaux, Foyer et de Geouffre de La Pradelle
Droit international Privé, Paris, Masson
Loussouarn et Bourel
Droit international privé, Paris, Dalloz (précis)
Mayer
Droit international privé, Paris, Montchrestien
Mezger
Les grandes lignes de la Convention du 9 Octobre 1978 relative à l'adhésion

945

du Danemark, de l'Irlande et due Royaume-Uni à la Convention de Bruxelles, Travaux du Comité de droit international privé, 1980–1981, p. 15

Pluvette
La Convention de Bruxelles et les droits de la défense, Mélanges P. Bellet, 1991

Le Tallec
La Cour de cassation et le droit communautaire, Mélanges Boulouis, Paris, Dalloz, 1991

GERMANY

Commentaries—Monographs

Aull
Der Geltungsanspruch des EuGVÜ: 'Binnensachverhalte' und IZVR in der EU (1996)

Benecke
'Die teleologische Reduktion des räumlich-persönlichen Anwendungsbereiches' Art. 2 ff und Art 17 EuGVÜ, 1993

De Bra
Verbraucherschutz durch Gerichtsstandsregelungen im deutschen und europäischen Zivilprozessrecht (1992)

Gärtner
Probleme der Auslandsvollstreckung von Nichtgeldentscheidungen im Bereich der Europäischen Gemeinschaft (1991)

Geimer
in: *Zöller, Zivilprozessordnung* [sub: GVÜ] (20th ed., 1997)

Geimer/Schütze
Internationale Urteilsanerkennung Vol I/1 (1983)
Europäisches Zivilverfahrensrecht (1996)

Gottwald
in: *Münchener Kommentar Zivilprozessordnung* [sub: IZPR] Vol. 3 (1992)

Hausmann
in: *Wieczorek/Schütze, Zivilprozessordnung* (3rd ed., 1994)
Gerichtsstandsvereinbarungen nach dem EuGVÜ, in: *Reithmann/Martiny, Internationales Vertragsrecht* (5th ed., 1996, n. 2108, ss)

Huber
Die englische forum-non-conveniens-Doktrin und ihre Anwendung im Rahmen des EuGVÜ (1994)

Klinke
Brüsseler Übereinkommen und Übereinkommen von Lugano über die gerichtliche Zuständigkeit und die Vollstreckung gerichtlicher Entscheidungen in Zivil- und Handelssachen (2 Vols, 2nd ed., 1993)

Kropholler
Europäisches Zivilprozessrecht (5th ed., 1996)

Die Zuständigkeitsregeln des EuGVÜ, in: Handbuch des Internationalen Zivilverfahrensrechts Vol 1 Chapter III, 1982

Linke/Müller/Schlafen
in: *Bülow/Böckstiegel/Geimer/Schütze [ed], Internationaler Rechtsverkehr in Zivil- und Handelssachen*

Lohse
'Das Verhältnis von Vertrag und Delikt. Eine rechtsvergleichende Studie zur vertragsautonomen Auslegung' Art. 5 Nr. 1 und Art. 5 Nr. 3 GVÜ, 1991

Martiny
Anerkennung nach multilateralen Staatsverträgen: Handbuch des Internationalen Zivilverfahrensrechts Vol. 3, Pt. 2, Chap. II (1984)

Rauscher
'Verpflichtung und Erfüllungsort,' Art 5. Nr. 1 EuGVÜ, 1984

Rohner
Die örtliche und internationale Zuständigkeit kraft Sachzusammenhangs (1991)

Schlosser
'Bericht zu dem Übereinkommen vom 9.10.1978 über den Beitritt des Königreichs Dänemark, Irlands und des Vereinigten Königreichs großbritannien und Nordirland zum Übereinkommen, etc.,' ABI EG 1979, C 59/71 EuGVÜ (1996)

Trunk
Die Erweiterung des EuGVÜ-Systems am Vorabend des Europäischen Binnenmarktes (1990)

Volz
Harmonisierung des Rechts der individuellen Rechtswahl der Gerichtsstandsvereinbarung und der Schiedsvereinbarung im Europäischen Wirtschaftsraum (EWR) (1993)

Wolf
Vollstreckbarerklärung, in: Handbuch des Internationalen Zivilverfahrensrechts Vol. 3, Pt. 2, Chap. IV (1984)

Articles (since 1990)

Ackmann
'Ausländerarrest (s.917 Abs. 2 ZPO) bei Vollstreckung in einem EuGVÜ-Staat?,' IPRax (1991) 166

Albrecht
'Artikel 24 EuGVÜ und die Entwicklung des einstweiligen Rechtsschutzes in England seit 1988,' IPRax (1992) 184

Benicke
'Internationale Zuständigkeit deutscher Gerichte nach Art. 13, 14 EuGVÜ für Schadensersatzklagen geschädigter Anleger,' WM (1997) 945

Coester-Waltjen
'Sicherungsvollstreckung nach Art. 39 EuGVÜ in Irland,' IPRax (1990) 65
'Die Bedeutung des Art 6 Nr. 2 EuGVÜ,' IPRax (1992) 290

Dageförde
'Aufrechnung und Internationale Zuständigkeit,' RIW (1990) 873
de Lousanoff
'Die Anwendung des EuGVÜ in Verbrauchersachen mit Drittstaatenbezug,'
Gedächtnisschrift Arens (1993) 251
Ebert-Weidenfeller
'Nichtausschließliche Gerichtsstandsvereinbarung nach dem EuGVÜ,' RIW
(1992) 139
Endler
'Urlaubsfreuden und Art. 16 Nr. 1 EuGVÜ,' IPRax (1992) 212
Fuchs
'Erste schottische Urteile zum Erfüllungsort nach Art. 5 Nr. 1 EuGVÜ,' IPRax
(1991) 134
Geimer
'Ungeschriebene Anwendungsgrenzen des EuGVÜ: Müssen Berührungspunkte
zu mehreren Vertragsstaaten bestehen?,' IPRax (1991) 31
'Anerkennung und Vollstreckbarerklärung von ex parte- Unterhaltsentschei-
dungen aus EuGVÜ-Vertragsstaaten', IPRax (1992) 5
'Internationale Zuständigkeit und Gerichtsstand in Verbrauchersachen,' RIW
(1994) 59
Grunsky
'Voraussetzungen für die Anordnung von Maßnahmen des Beschwerdegerichts
nach Art. 38 EuGVÜ,' IPRax (1995) 218
Haas
'Der Ausschluß der Schiedsgerichtsbarkeit vom Anwendungsbereich des
EuGVÜ,' IPRax (1992) 292
'Beginn der Sicherungs(zwangs)vollstreckung nach Art. 39 Abs. 1 EuGVÜ,'
IPRax (1995) 223
Hanisch
'Internationale Arrestzuständigkeit und EuGVÜ,' IPRax (1991) 215
Heerstrassen
'Die künftige Rolle von Präjudizien des EuGH im Verfahren des Luganer
Übereinkommens,' RIW (1993) 179
Heß
'Gerichtsstandsvereinbarungen zwischen EuGVÜ und ZPO,' IPRax (1992)
358
'Amtshaftung als "Zivilsache" im Sinne von Art. 1 Abs. 1 EuGVÜ,' IPRax
(1994) 10
'Urteilsanerkennung, Inlandskonkurs und die Tücken der internationalen
Zustellung,' IPRax (1995) 16
von Hoffmann/Hau
'Deutscher Prozeßvergleich kein Anerkennungshindernis nach Art. 27 Nr. 3
EuGVÜ,' IPRax (1995) 217
Huber
'Verleumdungsklagen und Art. 5 Nr. 3 EuGVÜ vor englischen Gerichten,'
IPRax (1992) 263

'Forum non conveniens und EuGVÜ,' RIW (1993) 977

'Neues aus England zu Artt. 21, 22 EuGVÜ,' IPRax (1993) 114

Isenburg-Epple

'Grenzen des Ermessens in Art. 21 II des Europäischen Gerichtsstands- und Vollstreckungsübereinkommens vom 27.9.1968 (EuGVÜ),' IPRax (1992) 69

Jayme

'Grundfragen zum Anwendungsbereich des EuGVÜ—Zwei Vorlagen an den EuGH,' IPRax (1992) 357

'Ferienhausvermittlung und Verbraucherschutz: Zur einschränkenden Auslegung des Art. 16 Nr. 1 EuGVÜ,' IPRax (1993) 18

'Ein Klägergerichtsstand für den Verkäufer—Der EuGH verfehlt den Sinn des EuGVÜ,' IPRax (1995) 13

Jayme/Kohler

'Das internationale Privat- und Verfahrensrecht der EG,' IPRax (1989) 337; 1990, 353

Kaye

'A Further Limitation by the European Court Upon the Scope of Application of the Brussels Convention,' IPRax (1995) 214

'Creation of an English Resulting Trust of Immovables Held to Fall Outside Article 16(1) of the European Judgments Convention,' IPRax (1995) 286

Klima

'Anwendbarkeit des Art. 5 EuGVÜ auf Sachverhalte mit mehreren aufeinanderfolgenden Käufern,' RIW (1991) 415

Koch

'Internationale Prorogation im Statut einer Aktiengesellschaft,' IPRax (1993) 19

'Verbrauchergerichtsstand nach dem EuGVÜ und Vermögensgerichtsstand nach der ZPO für Termingeschäfte?,' IPRax (1995) 71

Kohler

'Die zweite Revision des Europäischen Gerichtsstands- und Vollstreckungsübereinkommens—Ein Überblick über dans EuGVÜ 1989,' EuZW (1991) 303

'Gerichtsstandsklauseln in fremdsprachigen AGB: Das Clair-obscur des Art. 17 EuGVÜ,' IPRax (1991) 229

Kubis

'Amtshaftung im GVÜ und ordre public,' ZEuP (1995) 846

Lindacher

'AGB—Verbandsklage im Reiseveranstaltergeschäft mit auslandsbelegenen Ferienhäusern und -wohnungen,' IPRax (1993) 228

Linke

'Aspekte des Beklagtenschutzes im Exequaturverfahren,' IPRax (1991) 92

'Zur Rechtzeitigkeit fiktiver Zustellungen im Sinne von Art. 27 Nr. 2 EuGVÜ,' IPRax (1993) 295

Lorenz

'Internationale Zuständigkeit für die Rückforderungsklage einer italienischen Bank nach fehlerhafter, Ausführung einer Giroüberweisung nach Deutschland,' IPRax (1993) 44

Mankowski
'Verlöbnisbruch, konkurrierende Deliktsansprüche und Rückforderung von Geschenken im Internationalen Privat- und Zivilprozessrecht,' IPRax (1997) 173

Mansel
'Streitverkündung und Interventionsklage im Europäischen internationalen Zivilprozessrecht' (EuGVÜ/Lugano-Übereinkommen), in: Jayme/Kommelhoff/Mangold (ed.): 'Europäischer Binnenmarkt: Internationales Privatrecht und Rechtsvergleichung' (1994)
'Vollstreckung eines französischen Garantieurteils bei gesellschaftsrechtlicher Rechtsnachfolge und andere vollstreckungsrechtliche Fragen des EuGVÜ,' IPRax (1995) 362

Milionis
'Praxis der Vollstreckung deutscher Titel in Griechenland nach dem EuGVÜ,' RIW (1991) 100

Niemeyer
'Die Vollstreckung deutscher Gerichtsentscheidungen in Spanien im Hinblick auf des EuGVÜ,' IPRax (1992) 265

Pfeiffer
'Zuständigkeitskonzentration im Auslandsmahnverfahren,' IPRax (1994) 421

Rauscher
'Der Arbeitnehmergerichtsstand im EuGVÜ', IPRax (1990) 65
'Gerichtsstandsbeeinflussende AGB im Geltungsbereich des EuGVÜ,' ZZP 104 (1991) 271
'Strikter Beklagtenschutz durch Art. 27 Nr. 2 EuGVÜ,' IPRax (1991) 155
'Zustellung durch Brief und Art. 27 EuGVÜ,' IPRax (1992) 71
'Prorogation und Vertragsgerichtsstand gegen Rechtsscheinhaftende,' IPRax (1992) 143
'Keine EuGVÜ-Anerkennung ohne ordnungsgemäße Zustellung,' IPRax (1993) 376
'Prozessualer Verbraucherschutz im EuGVÜ,' IPRax (1995) 289
'Grenzüberschreitende Ehrverletzung durch Presseartikel,' ZZP International (1996) 151

Rauscher/Gutknecht
'Teleologische Grenzen des Art. 21 EuGVÜ?,' IPRax (1993) 21

Reinmüller
'Zur Vollstreckung von Zustellungs- und Gerichtsvollzieherkosten im Rahmen des EuGVÜ,' IPRax (1990) 207

Roth
'Gerichtsstandsvereinbarung nach Art. 17 EuGVÜ und kartellrechtliches Derogationsverbot,' IPRax (1992) 67

Rüßmann
'Der Gerichtsstand des Erfüllungsortes nach Artikel 5 Nr. 1 EuGVÜ bei einer tonnage-to-be-nominated-charter,' IPRax (1993) 38
'Negative Feststellungsklage und Leistungsklage sowie der Zeitpunkt der endgültigen Rechtshängigkeit im Rahmen des EuGVÜ—Entscheidungs- und Klärungsbedarf durch den EuGH,' IPRax (1995) 76

Samtleben
'Europäische Gerichtsstandsvereinbarungen und Drittstaaten—viel Lärm um nichts?,' Zum räumlichen Anwendungsbereich des Art. 17 i EuGVÜ/LugÜ

Schack
'Rechtshängigkeit in England und Art. 21 EuGVÜ,' IPRax (1991) 270
'Die Versagung der deutschen internationalen Zuständigkeit wegen forum non conveniens und lis alibi pendens,' RabelsZ (1994) 40

Schlosser
'Sonderanknüpfungen von zwingendem Verbraucherschutzrecht und europäisches Prozessrecht,' Festschrift Steindorff (1990) 1379
'Gläubigeranfechtungsklage nach französischen Recht und Art. 16 EuGVÜ,' IPRax (1991) 29
'Das anfechtbar verschenkte Ferienhaus in der Provence und die internationale Zuständigkeit der Gerichte,' IPRax (1993) 17

Schmidt
'Anfechtungsklage des Konkursverwalters und Anwendbarkeit des EuGVÜ,' EuZW (1990) 219
'Kann Schweigen auf eine Gerichtsstandsklausel in AGB einen Gerichtsstand nach Art. 17 EuGVÜ/LuganoÜ begründen?,' RIW (1992) 173

Schumann
'Kein Arrestgrund der Auslandsvollstreckung im Bereich des EuGVÜ,' IPRax (1992) 302

Stadler
'Schuldnerschutz und Artt. 38, 39 EuGVÜ und seine Voraussetzungen,' IPRax (1995) 220
'Zeitpunkt der Vorlage der im Klauselerteilungsverfahren nach Art. 47 Nr. 1 EuGVÜ notwendigen Urkunden,' IPRax (1997) 171

Tepper
'Anwaltshaftung und EuGVÜ,' IPRax (1991) 98

Trunk
'EuGVÜ und Osteuropa,' IPRax (1991) 278

Ulmer
'Neue Tendenzen bei der Auslegung des Art 16 Nr. 1 EuGVÜ,' IPRax (1995) 72

Weigand
'Die internationale Schiedsgerichtsbarkeit und das EuGVÜ,' EuZW (1992) 529

Wolf
'Rechtswidrigkeit der Ausländersicherheit nach s.110 ZPO nach EG- und Verfassungsrecht,' RIW (1993) 797

Zimmermann
'Die Ausländersicherheit des s.110 ZPO auf dem Prüfstand des Europäischen Gemeinschaftsrechts,' RIW (1992) 707

GREECE

Alexandropoulou, E.
International Jurisdiction in Insurance Litigation according to the Brussels Convention, Scientific Yearbook Harm. 1982, 247
Protocol on Interpretation of the Brussels Convention of 27.9.1968/ 9.10.1978/25.10.1982: The Preliminary reference to the Court of the European Communities for Interpreation of the Convention, *Hell. Ep. Eur. D.* 1985, 357
Arvanitakis, P.
Determination of International Jurisdiction in Accumulation of Actions according to Internal Law and the Brussels Convention, Harm. 1992, 424
Gesiou-Faltsi, P.
Enforcement of Intercommunity Judgments according to the Brussels Convention of 1968/1978, *Hell. Ep. Eur. D.* 1982, 221
Enforcement according to the Community Brussels Convention of 1968/1978/ 1982, *Hell. Ep. Eur. D.* 1990, 613
Kaissis, A.
International Commercial Arbitration and the Brussels Convention, Thessaloniki 1995
Kerameus, K./Kremlis, G./Tagaras, Ch.
The Brussels Convention on Jurisdiction and the Enforcement of Judgments in Civil and Commercial Matters. Article-by-Article Commentary, Athens-Komotini 1989: Supplement 1989–1996
Kroustallakis, E.
The Brussels Convention (on International Jurisdiction and the Enforcement of Judgments in Civil and Commercial Cases) and the Hellenic Civil Procedural Law: Points of Contact and Points of Divergence, *Hell. Dik.* 1993, 469
Makridou, K.
Interpretation issues of the 'Tort' and 'Quasi-Tort' Venue of Art. 5(3) of Brussels Convention, Harm. 1990, 1169
Metallinos, S.
International jurisdiction of the Courts of the EEC Member States in Civil and Commercial Cases according to the Brussels Convention of 27.9.1968, D. 1977, 3
The Recognition of Judgments of the Courts of the EEC Member States in Civil and Commercial Cases according to the Brussels Convention 1968/1978, D. 1982, 715
Moustaira, E.
Forum Non Conveniens. Equity in the Frame of Legality, Athens-Komotini, 1995
The Doctrine of *Forum Non Conveniens* in England. Problems of Operation in view of the Brussels Convention 1968, in: Tribute to Elias Krispis, Athens-Komotini 1995, 255

Nikas, N.
The Litispendence Objection in Civil Trial, Thessaloniki 1991

ICELAND

Stefánsson, Ólafur and Stefánsson, Stefán Már
Luganosamningurinn um dómsvald og um fullnustu dóm í einkamálum, *Tímarit Lögfrœdinga* (1988) p. 201–3
Stefánsson, Stefán Már
Samræmd túlkun Luganosamningsins, *Tímarit Lögfrœdinga* (1993) p. 33–42

IRELAND

Byrne
The EEC Convention on Jurisdiction and Enforcement of Judgments (Round Hall Press, 1990)

ITALY

Attardi, A.
La nuova disciplina in tema di giurisdizione italiana e di riconoscimento delle sentenze straniere, Riv. dir. civ. 1995, I, 727
Attardi, A.
Litispendenza e oggetto del processo nella convenzione di Bruxelles, Giur. it. 1995, IV, 249
Balena, G.
I nuovi limiti della giurisdizione italiana (secondo la 1 31 maggio 1995 n. 218), Foro it. 1996, V, 209
Ballarino, T.
La prima sentenza della Corte di Lussemburgo sulla litispendenza, Foro pad. 1985, I. 146
Bariatti, S.
L'entrata in vigore della convenzione di Donostia – San Sebastian sulla giurisdizione e l'esecuzione delle sentenze, Riv. dir. internaz. privato e proc. 1992, 417
Bonnell, M.J.
La convenzione di Bruxelles del 1968 sulla competenza giurisdizionale e l'esecuzione delle sentenze – un modello da seguire nell'armonizzazione del diritto tra i sistemi di civil law e di common law, Riv. dir. comm. 1990, I, 737
Broggini, G.
Riconoscimento ed esecuzione delle sentenze civili straniere nel ius commune italiano, Riv. dir. internaz. priv. e proc. 1993, III, 833

Campeis, G., De Pauli, A.
Il processo civile italiano e lo straniero, Milano, 1996

Campeis, G., De Pauli, A.
La nozione di litispendenza 'europea', Nuova giur. civ. commentata 1989, I, 398

Consolo, C.
La tutela sommaria e la convenzione di Bruxelles: la 'circolazione' comunitaria dei provvedimenti cautelari e dei decreti ingiuntivi, Riv. dir. internaz. privator e proc. 1991, 593

Coscia, G.
Conflitti e contrasti di giudicati nella convenzione di Bruxelles del 27 settembre 1968, Riv. dir. internaz. priv. e proc. 1995, II, 265

Deli, M.B.
Gli usi del commercio internazionale nel nuovo testo dell'art, 17 della convenzione di Bruxelles del 1968, Riv. dir. internaz. privato e proc. 1989, 27

Gaja, G.
Sui rapporti fra la convenzione di Bruxelles e le altre norme concernenti la giurisdizione ed il riconoscimento di sentenze straniere, Riv. dir. internaz. privato e proc. 1991, 253

Giardina, A.
Proroga della giurisdizione ed usi del commercio internazionale, Jus 1990, 75

Leanza, U.
Interpretazioni giurisprudenziali della convenzione di Bruxelles e della convenzione di Lugano, Jus 1990, 77

Lizier Tessiore, M.E.
'Forum solutionis', convenzione di Bruxelles del 27 settembre 1968 e giurisprudenza italiana, Riv. trim. dir. proc. civ. 1980, 113

Lupoi, M.A.
La giurisdizione in materia di responsabilita' extracontrattuale nella convenzione di Bruxelles, Riv. trim. dir. proc. civ. 1992, 365

Luzzatto, R.
Giurisdizione e competenza nel sistema della convenzione di Bruxelles del 27 settembre 1968, Jus 1990, 9

Malatesta, A.L.
Litispendenza e riconoscibilita' di sentenze nella convenzione di Bruxelles del 1968, Riv. dir. internaz. priv. e proc. 1994, I, 511

Martino, R.
I limiti della giurisdizione italiana nei confronti dello straniero, Giust. civ. 1991, II, 88

Mengozzi, P.
L'interpretazione della convenzione di Bruxelles e i principi del diritto comunitario, Jus 1990, 91

Pau, G.
Oltre la convenzione di Bruxelles del 1968 sulla competenza giurisdizionale e l'esecuzione delle sentenze in materia civile e commerciale, Jus 1990, 111

Pocar, F.

Jurisdiction and the Enforcement of Judgements under the EC Convention of 1968, Rabels Zeitschrift, 1978, 429

Pocar, F.
La convenzione di Bruxelles sulla giurisdizione e l'esecuzione delle sentenze, Milano 1995

Silvestri, C.
Il 'forum contractus' e il contratto di agenzia, Foro it. 1992, I, 2738

Silvestri, C.
Sul concetto di litispendenza nella convenzione di Bruxelles, Foro it. 1994, I, 3193

Starace, V.
Le norme della convenzione giudiziaria di Bruxelles relative alla giurisdizione e la loro incidenza sulla riforma del processo civile italiano, Riv. dir. proc. 1985, 315

Vassalli Di Dachenhausen, T.
I rapporti della convenzione di Bruxelles con le altre convenzioni sulla competenza giurisdizionale e l'esecuzione delle sentenze in materia civile e commerciale, Jus 1990, 119

LUXEMBOURG

Le Cercle François Laurent/Wiwinius
Les Conventions de Bruxelles de 1968 et de Lugano de 1988 à travers la jurisprudence luxembourgeoise

Schockweiler
Les conflits de lois et les conflits de juridictions en droit international privé luxembourgeois

THE NETHERLANDS

Rene van Rooj & Maurice V. Polak
Private International Law in The Netherlands (T.M.C. Asser Instituut, The Hague and Kluwer Law and Taxation Publishers, Deventer-Antwerp-London-Frankfurt-Boston-New York, 1987)

Maurice V. Polak, Michiel J. de Rooj & Lilian F.A. Steffans
Supplement (T.M.C. Asser Instituut, The Hague and Kluwer Law International, The Hague-London-Boston, 1995)

NORWAY

Falkanger, Flock and Waaler
Tvangsfullbyrdelsesloven med kommentar (i.e. Commentaries to the Law on Enforcement), vol. I–II, 2nd edn, 1995

PORTUGAL

Marques dos Santos, Antonio
'Revisão e confirmaçã de sentenças estrangeiras no novo Código de Processo Civil de 1997 (Alterações ao regime anterior)' *in Aspectos do novo Processo Civil* (in course of publication), p. 105
Moura Ramos, Rui Manuel
'L'adhésion du Portugal aux conventions communautaires en matière de droit international privé', in *Das Relações Privadas Internacionais. Estudos de Direito Internacional Privado*, Coimbra, 1995, Coimbra Editora, p. 158
'La Convention de Bruxelles après la Convention d'Adhésion du Portugal et de l'Espagne', *Revue Hellénique de Droit International*, 1991, p. 165
'A Convenção de Bruxelas sobre competência judiciária e execução de decisõs: sua adequação à realidade juslaboral actual', *Revista de Direito e de Estudos Sociais*, v. 38 (1996), p. 3
'A Reforma do Direito Processual Civil Internacional', *Revista de Legislacão e de Jurisprudência*, Ano 130, p. 162
'Competência internacional em matéria contratual (Anotação ao Acordão do Tribunal da Relação de Lisboa de 5 de Dezembro de 1995)', *ibidem*, p. 174
Moura Vicente, Dário
'Da Aplicação no Tempo e no Espaço das Convençoes de Bruxelas de 1968 e de Lugano de 1988 (Anotação de Jurisprudência)', *Revista da Faculdade de Direito da Universidade de Lisboa*, 1994, p. 461
'A competência internacional no Código de Processo Civil Revisto: aspectos gerais', in *Aspectos do novo Processo Civil* (in course of publication), p. 105
Teixeira de Sousa, Miguel
'A Concessão de *Exequatur* a uma decisão estrangeira segundo a Convenção de Bruxelas', *Revista da Faculdade de Direito da Universidade de Lisboa*, 1994, p. 445
'Die neue internationale Zuständigkeitsregelung im portugiesischen Zivilprozeßgesetzbuch und die Brüsseler und Luganer Übereinkommen: einige vergleichende Bemerkungen, *IPRAX*, No 5 (1997), p. 352–360
'O novo regime do Direito português sobre a competência internacional legal, in *Estudos sobre o novo processo civil*, Les, Lisboa, 1997, p. 91
Teixeira de Sousa, Miguel and Moura Vicente, Dário
'Comentário à Convenção de Bruxelas de 27 de Setembro de 1968 relativa à competência judiciária e à execução de decisões em matéria civil e comercial e textos complementares', Lisboa, 1994, Editora Lex

SCOTLAND

Aird & Jameson
The Scots Dimension to Cross-Border Litigation (1996)
Anton
Private International Law (2nd ed., 1990)

Anton & Beaumont
Civil Jurisdiction in Scotland (2nd ed., 1995)
Stair
The Laws of Scotland, Stair Memorial Encyclopaedia (Vol. 4, where different parts of the Conventions are covered in the volume corresponding to the particular subject matter)

SPAIN

Abarca, P.
'Competencia judicial internacional en materia de difamación por artículos de prensa. A propósito de la sentencia del Tribunal de Justicia de 7 de marzo de 1995 (Fiona Shevill y otros c. Presse Alliance S.A.)', *Gaceta Jurídica de la CEE y de la competencia, Boletín*, 1996, May, no 113, pp. 5 ss
Alvarez Rubio, J.J.
Los foros de competencia judicial internacional en materia maritima (Estudio de las relaciones entre los diversos bloques normativos), San Sebastián, 1993
Alvarez Rubio, J.J.
'La regla de la especialidad en el art. 57 del Convenio de Bruselas de 1968, sobre embargo preventivo de buques (reflexiones en torno a la sentencia del TJCE de 6 diciembre 1994)', *Anuario de Derecho marítimo*, vol. XII
Alvarez Rodríguez, A.
'El lugar de situación de las sucursales, agencias o cualesquiera otros establecimientos como criterios determinantes de la competencia judicial internacional', *La Ley, Com. Eur.*, 1988, no 32, pp. 1 ss
Aragoneses Martinez, S.
'Diferencias y semejanzas del exequatur en la regulación del Convenio de Bruselas y la Ley de Enjuiciamiento civil, con especial referencia de la técnica del estudio de la astreinte', *RGLJ*, 1984, pp. 571 ss
Arenas, R.
'La litispendencia internacional. El art. 21 del Convenio de Bruselas de 1968 y el control de la competencia del Tribunal de origen (comentario a la STJCE de 27 de junio de 1991)', *Noticias CEE*, no 91/.92, agosto-septiembre 1992, pp. 103 ss
Arenas, R.
'Tratamiento jurisprudencial del ámbito de aplicación de los foros de protección en materia de contratos de consumidores del Convenio de Bruselas de 1968', *REDI*, 1996, 1, pp. 39 ss
Asín Cabrera, A.
'Interpretación del art. 21 del Convenio de Bruselas de 27 de septiembre de 1968. Noción de litispendencia', *Noticias CEE*, 1988, agosto/septiembre
Borrás, A.
'Competencia judical y ejecución de decisiones en la CEE', *Estudios de Derecho comunitario europeo*, Madrid, 1989, pp. 233–263

Borrás, A.
'Los convenios complementarios entre los Estados miembros de la CEE',
Noticias CEE, 1986, enero

Borrás, A.
'La competencia de los tribunales internos en materias de obligaciones contractuales (Comentario a la sentencia del TJCE de 15 de enero de 1987)',
Revista de Instituciones Europeas, 1987, 3, pp. 731–740

Borrás, A.
'Competencia judicial internacional y ejecución de resoluciones judiciales en materia civil y mercantil: del convenio de Bruselas de 27 de septiembre de 1968 al convenio de Lugano de 16 de septiembre de 1988', *Noticias CEE*, 1989, no 50, pp. 93–103

Borrás, A.
'La sentencia dictada en rebeldia: notificación y exequatur en el convenio de Bruselas', *Revista de Instituciones Europeas*, 1991.1, pp. 39–60

Borrás, A. (Ed)
La revision de los Convenios de Bruselas de 1968 y de Lugano de 1988 sobre competencia judicial y ejecución de sentencias: una reflexión preliminar española, Madrid, 1998.

Calvo Caravaca, A.L. and others
Comentario al Convenio de Bruselas relativo a la competencia judicial y a la ejecución de resoluciones en materia civil y mercantil, Madrid, 1994

Desantes, M.
La competencia judicial internacional en la Comunidad Europea, Barcelona, 1986

Droz, G.A.L.
'La Convention de San Sebastián alignant la Convention de Bruxelles sur la Convention de Lugano', *Revue critique de Droit international privé*, 1990, 1, pp. 1–21

Droz, G.A.L.
'Problèmes provoqués par l'imbrication des Conventions de Bruxelles (1978), de Lugano (1988), et de San Sebastiàn (1989), *Études de droit international en l'honneur de Pierre Lalive*, Bàle, 1993, pp. 21–30

Espinar, J.M.
'Competencia judicial y reconocimiento y ejecución de resoluciones judiciales en materia civil y mercantil en el àmbito de la Comunidad Europea', *Hacia un nuevo orden internacional y europeo. Estudios en homenaje al profesor Manuel Diez de Velasco*, Madrid, 1993, pp. 865–898

Estrada de Miguel, E.
'Competencia judicial internacional y reconocimiento y ejecución de decisiones judiciales extranjeras en la CE. Incidencia de su régimen en el Derecho español', *Liber amicorum Prof. Dr. D. José Perez Montero*, I, Oviedo, 1988

Fuentes Camacho, V.
Las medidas provisionales y cautelares en el espacio judicial europeo (Estudio del art. 24 del Convenio de Bruselas de 27 de septiembre de 1968, con especial referencia a la posición española), Madrid, 1996

Fuentes Camacho, V. – Nebot Lozano, J.M.
'Determinación de los documentos que, de conformidad con el Convenio de Bruselas de 27 de septiembre de 1968, deben acompañar a las solicitudes de ejecución de resoluciones extranjeras: algunas imprecisiones de su normativa reguladora', *La Ley (UE)*, 30 octubre 1997, pp. 1 ss

Gallego Caballero, J.
'Interpretación de los arts. 37 y 38 del Convenio relativo a la competencia judicial y a la ejecución de resoluciones judiciales en materia civil y mercantil de 27 de septiembre de 1968', *Noticias CEE*, 1992, October

Garcimartín, F.
El régimen de las medidas cautelares en el comercio internacional, Madrid, 1996

Garcimartín, F.
'The first application of the EEC Judgments Convention by the Spanish Tribunal Supremo', *IPRax*, 1993/6, pp. 426 ss

González Beilfuss, C.
Nulidad e infracción de patentes en la Comunidad Europea (Prologue, A. Borrás), Madrid, 1996

González Campos, J.D.
'Les liens entre la compétence judiciaire et la compétence legislative en Droit international privé', *Recueil des Cours*, vol. 156 (1977-III), pp. 222–376

González Campos, J.D.
'Las relaciones entre forum y ius en el Derecho internacional privado. Caracterización y dimensiones del problemas', *Anuario de Derecho internacional*, IV, 1977–1978, pp. 89–136

González Campos, J.D. – Fernandez Rozas, J.C.
Derecho internacional privado español. Textos y materiales, vol. I: Derecho judicial internacional, 2nd ed., Madrid, 1992

Guzmán Zapater, M.
'Cesión de crédito y noción de consumidor: segunda decisión del TJCE sobre la competencia judicial internacional en materia de contratos de consumo en el Convenio de Bruselas', *Revista juridica española La Ley*, 30 November 1993

Guzmán Zapater, M.
'La prorrogación de competencia en los contratos de venta concluídos por consumidores', *REDI*, 1987, 2

Iglesias, J.L. – Desantes, M.
'Extensión y límites de la jurisdicción española. Influencia del Convenio de Bruselas de 1968 en la LOPJ de 1985', *Las relaciones de vecindad*, Bilbao, 1987, pp. 453 ss

Iglesias, J.L. – Desantes, M.
'La quinta libertad comunitaria: competencia judicial, reconocimiento y ejecución de resoluciones judiciales en la Comunidad Europea', *Tratado de Derecho comunitario europea* (García de Enterría – González Campos – Muñoz Machado, dir.), volume III, Madrid, 1986, pp. 711 ss

Maseda, J.
'El art. 17, 5 del Convenio de Bruselas de 27 de septiembre de 1968: ¿pacto pro operario?' *La Ley (UE)*, 30 octubre 1997, pp. 5 ss
Miguel Zaragoza, J.
'El Convenio de adhesión de España y Portugal al Convenio de Bruselas de 1968, sobre competencia judicial y ejecución de sentencias', *Noticias CEE*, 1990, febrero
Palao Moreno, G.
'La aplicación de la regla *forum delicti commissi* (el art. 5, 3 del Convenio de Bruselas de 1968) en supuestos de difamación por medio de prensa), *Noticias de la Unión Europea*, no 141, 1996, pp. 75 ss
Quiñones Escamez, A.
El foro de la pluralidad de demandados en los litigios internacionales, Madrid, 1996
Rodríguez Benot, A.
Los acuerdos atributivos de competencia judicial internacional, Madrid, 1994
Rodríguez Benot, A.
'España en el espacio judicial europeo ¿primeros tropiezos jurisprudenciales?', *REDI*, 1994, 2, pp. 587 ss
Rodríguez Piñero, M.
'Competencia judicial y efectos de las decisiones judiciales en materia laboral en el Convenio de Bruselas de 27 de septiembre de 1968', *Relaciones laborales*, no 13, 1989, pp. 1 ss
Ruiz-Jarabo Colomer
'La aplicación en España del Convenio de Bruselas de 1968 y los criterios de competencia judicial internacional en materia civil', *Noticias CEE*, 1988, June
Zabalo Escudero, E.
'Aspectos jurídicos de la protección al consumidor contratante en el Derecho internacional privado', *REDI*, 1985, 1, pp. 109 ss

SWEDEN

Lennart Pålsson
Luganokonventionen. Stockholm, 1992
Bryssel- och Luganokonvenionerna. Stockholm, 1995
'Skiljeförfarande och Bryssel/Luganokonvenionerna' (Arbitration and the Brussels/Lugano Conventions), 1994 *Svensk Juristtidning* 1–22
'Säkerhetsåtgärder och andra interimistiska åtgärder i internationella tvister' (Provisional, including protective, measures in international disputes), 1996 *Svensk Juristtidning* 385–413
'*Lis Pendens* under the Brussels and Lugano Conventions', *Festskrift till Stig Strömholm* (Uppsala, 1997) 709–729
'The Unruly Horse of the Brussels and Lugano Conventions: The *Forum Solutionis*', *Festskrift til Ole Lando—Papers dedicated to Ole Lando* (Copenhagen, 1997) 259–282

SWITZERLAND

Bernet, M. and Ulmer, N.C.
'Recognition and Enforcement of Foreign Civil Judgments in Switzerland', 27 *The International Lawyer* 317–342 (1993)

Blessing, M.
'The New International Arbitration Law in Switzerland: A Significant Step towards Liberalism', 5 *Journal of International Arbitration*, Nr. 2, 9–88 (1988)

Bucher, A. and Tschanz, P.Y.
International Arbitration in Switzerland, Basle, Franfort-on-Main 1988

Butcher, A. and Tschanz, P.Y. (eds)
Private International Law. Basic Documents. Basle. Frankfort-on-Main 1996

Dessemontet, F. and Ansay, T. (eds)
Introduction to Swiss Law, 2d ed. Hague: Kluwer 1995

Karrer, P.A. and Arnold, K.W. and Patocchi, P.M.
Switzerland's Private International Law, 2d ed. Deventer and Zürich 1994

Samuel, A.
'The New Swiss Private International Law Act. 37 *International and Comparative Law Quarterly* 681–695 (1988)

Symeonides, S.C.
'The Swiss Conflicts Codification: An Introduction', In: 37 *American Journal of Comparative Law* 187–246 (1989)

Vogt, N.P.
'Jurisdiction of Swiss Courts in International Cases", 12 *Comparative Law Yearbook of International Business* 161–165 (1990)

ABBREVIATIONS

ENGLAND AND WALES

AC	Appeal Cases
All ER	All England Law Reports
BCLC	Butterworths Company Law Cases
CCR	County Court Rules
Ch	Chancery Division Law Reports
CMLR	Common Market Law Reports
ECR	European Court Reports
Fam	Family Division Law Reports
FLR	Family Law Reports
FSR	Fleet Street Reports
HL	House of Lords
I.L.Pr	International Litigation Procedure Law Reports
JCPC	Judicial Committee of the Privy Council
J	Mr/Mrs Justice
LCJ	Lord Chief Justice
LJ	Lord Justice
Lloyd's Rep.	Lloyd's Law Reports
MR	Master of the Rolls
P	Probate Law Reports
QB	Queen's Bench Division Law Reports
QC	Queen's Counsel
RPC	Restrictive Practices Court
RSC	Rules of the Supreme Court
SI	Statutory Instrument

Times   Times Newspaper Law Reports
WLR   Weekly Law Reports

FRANCE

D   Revue Dalloz
DMF   Droit Maritime Français
DP   Dalloz Périodique (previous name of the Revue Dalloz)
IR   Informations Rapides (a part of the Revue Dalloz)
JDI   Journal de Droit International
JCP   Juris Classeur Périodique, named also Semaine Juridique
Rev. Crit. DIP   Revue critique de droit international privé
SC   Sommaires Commentés (a part of the Revue Dalloz)

GERMANY

AG   Amtsgericht
AGBG   Gesetz zur Regelung des Rechts der Allgemeinen
            Geschäftsbedingungen
AVAG   Anerkennungs- und Vollstreckungsausführungsgesetz of 30
            May 1988 (BGBI II 121)
BAG   Bundesarbeitsgericht
BAGE   Entscheidungen des Bundersarbeitsgerichts (*reporter*)
BGB   Bürgerliches Gesetzbuch
BGBI   Bundesgesetzblatt
BGH   Bundesgerichtshof
BGHZ   Entscheidungen des Bundesgerichtshofts in Zivilsachen
            (*reporter*)
BSGE   Entscheidungen des Bundessozialgerichts (*reporter*)
CISG   United Nations Convention on the International Sale of
            Goods of 11 April 1980
EGBGB   Einführungsgesetz zum BGB
EKG   Einheitliches Gesetz über den internationalen Kauf
            beweglicher Sachen of 17 July 1973 (BGBI I 856)
EuZW   Europäische Zeitschrift für Wirtschaftsrecht (*journal*)
EWiR   Entscheidungen zum Wirtschaftsrecht (*journal*)
GWB   Gesetz gegen Wettbewerbsbeschränkungen
IPRax   Praxis des internationalen Privat- und Verfahrensrechts
            (*journal*)
KO   Konkursordnung
LAG   Landesarbeitsgericht
LG   Landgericht

LM	Lindenmaier-Möhring, Nachschlagewerk des Bundesgerichtshofs in Zivilsachen (*reporter*)
NJW	Neue Juristische Wochenschrift (*journal*)
NJW-RR	Neue Juristische Wochenschrift – Rechtsprechungsreport (*journal*)
OLG	Oberlandesgericht
ULIS	Hague Convention on the Unform Law of International Sales of 1 July 1964
UWG	Gesetz gegen den unlauteren Wettbewerb
WM	Wertpapier Mitteilungen (*journal*)
WuB	Wirtschafts- und Bankrecht (*journal*)
WZG	Warenzeichengesetz
ZIP	Zeitschrift für Wirtschaftsrecht (*journal*)
ZPO	Zivilprozessordnung
ZZP	Zeitschrift für Zivilprozess (*journal*)

SPAIN

AP	Audiencia Provincial
JPI	Juzgado de Primera Instancia
REDI	Revista Española de Derecho Internacional
RGD	Revista General de Derecho
RJC	Revista Juridica de Catalunya
TSJ	Tribunal Superior de Justicia
TS	Tribunal Supremo

SWEDEN

AD	Arbetsdomstolens domar
ILPr.	International Litigation Procedure
MD	Marknadsdomstolens avgöranden
ND	Nordiske domme i sjøfartsanliggender
NJA	Nytt juridiskt arkiv
RH	Rättsfall från hovrätterna